Microsoft® SharePoint® 2010

Administrator's Companion

Bill English
Brian Alderman
Mark Ferraz

PUBLISHED BY
Microsoft Press
A Division of Microsoft Corporation
One Microsoft Way
Redmond, Washington 98052-6399

Library of Congress Control Number: 2010933775

Printed and bound in the United States of America.

Microsoft Press books are available through booksellers and distributors worldwide. For further information about international editions, contact your local Microsoft Corporation office or contact Microsoft Press International directly at fax (425) 936-7329. Visit our Web site at www.microsoft.com/mspress. Send comments to mspinput@ microsoft.com.

Acquisitions Editor: Martin DelRe
Developmental Editor: Karen Szall
Project Editor: Karen Szall
Editorial Production: Custom Editorial Productions, Inc.
Technical Reviewer: Mitch Tulloch; Technical Review services provided by Con Group, Ltd.
Cover: Tom Draper Design

Body Part No. X17-09647

To the entire SharePoint Community—a group of outstanding, talented people from whom I've learned more than I ever thought possible.

—BILL ENGLISH

To my dad, Donald K. Alderman, who always inspired me with his motivation, dedication, and commitment to everything he did and everyone he met.

—BRIAN ALDERMAN

To my lovely wife, Megan, and my dearest daughter, Piper. You mean everything to me.

—MARK FERRAZ

Contents at a Glance

Contents

What do you think of this book? We want to hear from you!

Microsoft is interested in hearing your feedback so we can continually improve our
books and learning resources for you. To participate in a brief online survey, please visit:

microsoft.com/learning/booksurvey

Chapter 2   Understanding the Architecture of SharePoint 2010   57

PART III   BUILDING AND MANAGING A SHAREPOINT FARM

CHAPTER 10   Collaboration and Portals 473

CHAPTER 11   Search Server 2010 and FAST Search: Architecture and Administration 525

CHAPTER 16 Securing Information   779

PART V   ADVANCED TOPICS

CHAPTER 18 Aggregating External Data Sources   881

CHAPTER 22   Upgrading to SharePoint 2010   1035

What do you think of this book? We want to hear from you!

Microsoft is interested in hearing your feedback so we can continually improve our
books and learning resources for you. To participate in a brief online survey, please visit:

microsoft.com/learning/booksurvey

Acknowledgments

Bill English   Although there are three names on the cover of this book, there are many more who put time, blood, sweat, and effort into making this book a reality. To be sure, this book would not be in your hands if it wasn't for Karen Szall, editor at Microsoft Press.

How does one give ample credit to an editor who has shown significant patience, understanding, and professionalism in the face of difficulties? If I could, I'd instruct Microsoft to give Karen Szall a significant raise in pay with six months off in Maui and ask God to give her sainthood in the church. I honestly think that on this project, Karen endured more difficulties than all of my other editors combined and did so with grace, elegance, professionalism, and patience. She is a fantastic editor and an equally great person. My only hope is that she'll consent to work with me at some point in the future. Thanks, Karen, for keeping this book project going when it was stalled and understanding when difficulties arose. The entire SharePoint community is indebted to you.

I would be remiss if I didn't thank Mark Ferraz and Brian Alderman for being coauthors on this book with me. Mark is one of those guys who "gets it" about SharePoint. He consults full time on SharePoint in a Fortune 50 company and has the scars and experience to write great content. He's not really a guy who spends a lot of time building his "brand" in the SharePoint community, but he's rock solid on this product and is someone who everyone who reads this book should get to know. He's an enjoyable guy who is going to go places, I'm convinced. I've learned a great deal from Mark about SharePoint. Mark, thanks for writing great chapters and for helping us all understand this product better.

Brian Alderman comes from an educational background and did a great job writing some long chapters—the 100-page chapter on Central Administration is his. I admire his persistence in writing and sticking with something until it is done. He brought solid SQL knowledge to this book (something we missed in the last Administrator's Companion), and he helped us all better understand the relationship between SQL and SharePoint. Like Mark, Brian also doesn't do a lot in the SharePoint community, but he is also rock solid on this product and is a great guy to get to know. If you have a chance to take a SharePoint class through Mindsharp with Brian Alderman, I would highly advise that you do it. You won't be disappointed.

I also want to thank Penny Coventry, a great friend from Hinckley, UK, for writing the PowerShell chapters. I consider Penny the matriarch of SharePoint. Like me, she's been around since the 2001 days. She's quiet, unassuming, pleasant, and smart. Real smart. And her husband, Peter, is an Oracle developer. Yet, sitting at their dinner table, you'd never know it. There is no arrogance or pretense about them. Penny could easily be an MVP or an MCM, in my opinion. She knows this product very well from both the developer and administrator perspectives. Penny and I have written on several book projects now, and each one has been a huge privilege for me. Thanks, Penny!

I met Nikander and Margriet Bruggeman at a Microsoft meeting in Redmond a number of years ago. We have written several books together. Although I've not been able to get to know them as I would like, I know that they write great content, on time, in style, and with the book's elements highlighted. They are great authors who consult in the Netherlands and surrounding area in Europe. If you have a chance to work with them, please do so. You'll walk away a better person as a result.

Jason Gallicchio, Peter Abrue, and Roger Taylor worked together on the scaling out chapter when one of my original authors had to back out due to being over-committed. This was their first writing project, and while I think they found it challenging, I also think they used their real-world experience to help us understand how to scale out a farm. Peter and Roger built and maintain the entire Recovery.gov website in the Amazon cloud. They get four million unique hits each day at that site, and yet, running the entire farm in the cloud, they handle it with only four WFE servers. They know how to scale out a farm for a large deployment. Thanks, guys, for jumping in at the last minute and for getting a good chapter written for this book.

Daniel Webster is a lifelong friend of mine. I first met him back in the mid-90s at the old Valley Micro training center (it was sold in the late 90s). Daniel is a man of integrity, and it shows through in his insistence on getting the details right. Daniel was responsible for the search chapters, and he received some assistance from Suzanne George in pulling them together. I think they did the best that could have been done to get the chapters done within the page count that was handed to them. Frankly, Search and FAST could be the subject of an entire book as large as this one, so to condense such a large amount of information into two chapters is a real trick. I think they succeeded.

Suzanne George also took on the first chapter near the end of this project when another author backed out. Thanks, Suz, for taking on this chapter and getting it done so swiftly. I appreciate it. I also want to thank Brett Lonsdale for writing the Web Parts chapter. Brett, I know that writing isn't your first love, but I do want to thank you for doing it. I also want to thank Subramanian Sivaramakrishnan for writing the base content for the InfoPath chapter.

Mitch Tulloch did a great job in the technical editor role for this book. He added value by finding technical mistakes or not-well-stated concepts. Thanks, Mitch, for doing a great TE job. And Megan Smith-Creed provided a steady hand managing the many pieces while Julie Hotchkiss provided a clear and consistent copy edit.

Martin DelRe helped get this project rolling from a contract standpoint. I've worked with Martin on a number of projects, and I was very sad to see him move to another set of books that won't include SharePoint. I'll miss working with you, Martin. I wish you all the best in your future endeavors.

Others who added value to this book (though a couple may not know it because we researched topics and learned from their posts) include Ben Curry, Jie Li, John Holliday, Amanda Perran, Apran Shah, Dan Evers, Dan Herzog, Daniel Galant, Daniel Kogan, Zach Rosenfield, Kirk Stark, Dan Wesley, Luca Bandinelli, Frank Morales, Ram Gopinatham, Rick Taylor, and Todd Bleeker.

Back here in Minnesota, I'd like to thank my friends for sustaining me during some highly difficult times over the last 12 to 18 months: Dave and Meryl McGauvran, Mark Schneider, Jay and Dawn Herman, Bill and Ann Kinney, and Howard and Julie Tripp. I also want to thank my lovely wife, Kathy, for her continual support and my two children, David and Anna, for coming together to create a great family in which to live.

Most importantly, I want to thank my Lord and Savior, Jesus Christ, for your love and faithfulness. You have given me the talent and opportunity to write, and without you, I would be lost forever.

Brian Alderman   There are many people who supported me throughout this project that I want to thank. I want to begin by thanking Bill English for coauthoring the book, as well coordinating and managing the project with Microsoft Press. I also want to thank Mark Ferrarz for his contribution in authoring the book with us. I want to thank everyone at Microsoft Press that assisted in the project, including Karen Szall, Mitch Tulloch, Julie Hotchkiss, and Megan Smith-Creed. Thanks to Ben Curry for providing direction and assistance while writing the book. Thanks to my family and friends for their kind and encouraging words throughout the project.

Mark Ferraz   Involvement in a book project of this magnitude can be very rewarding, but also consuming at times. Accordingly, I'd like to thank the following people for their enduring support, friendship, and/or individual contributions. First I'd like to thank my wife, Megan, who was willing to put up with the late nights and weekend work associated with this project, shortly after the birth of our daughter, Piper. I could not have participated in this project without your willingness to take on the extra load that made my involvement possible. Coauthor

Bill English, without whom none of this would have been possible, thank you for your enduring patience and support. You are a mentor to me, and I am honored to have been able to work on this project with you. Coauthor Brian Alderman, thank you for working to ensure we closed any gaps in our collaborative work product. I'd like to thank all of the editors and technical reviewers from Microsoft Press. I'd also like to thank Karen Szall, our content development manager, for her diligence, brilliant coordinative capability, and for keeping us all in line and on time. I'd also like to thank Subramanian Sivaramakrishnan, Ankush Bhatia, Jeremy Liner, and Tejaswi Redkar for their content contributions and for being such a pleasure to work with. I respect and admire the skill and knowledge with which you perform your craft and feel fortunate to have been able to work with such knowledgeable experts in developing the content for this book. Lastly, I'd like to thank the SharePoint Teams and Microsoft for creating such a wonderful edition of the product with SharePoint 2010. You are all an amazing group of people doing fantastic work. Keep it coming.

Introduction

Welcome to *Microsoft SharePoint 2010 Administrator's Companion*! If you're reading this introduction, chances are good that you're interested in SharePoint 2010 administration. As you might suspect, this book is intended to be a reference on how to best deploy and manage this exciting product.

But despite the title, we have not assumed that only administrators will pick up this book and use it. You might be a project manager, an information management specialist, a network or SharePoint architect, or a power user who wants to learn more about SharePoint 2010 administration, design, and best practices. We have written this book with a wide variety of interested readers in mind:

- **Architects** will find good information in these pages about how to design a SharePoint implementation.

- **Power users** will benefit greatly from reading about site administration, the site templates that are available, and the Web Parts that ship with this product.

- **Content creators** will learn how to use document libraries to their full advantage.

- **Project managers** will find this a handy reference when working with SharePoint-oriented projects.

- **Information management specialists** will find ideas about implementation best practices when building taxonomies using content types.

- **Compliance specialists** can learn how SharePoint 2010 works with record and document management with a view to meeting compliance requirements.

As you can see, there is solid information in this book for a wide variety of professionals who will interface with SharePoint 2010.

How to Use This Book

This book contains not only great information about designing, deploying, and managing a SharePoint 2010 implementation; we've also included elements to help you understand the concepts and ideas better.

Look for book elements such as the following:

 Real World sidebar   Everyone can benefit from the experiences of others. Real World sidebars contain elaboration on a theme or background based on the experiences of others who used this product during the beta testing period.

Note   Notes include tips, alternative ways to perform a task, or additional information that needs to be highlighted.

Important   Boxes marked Important shouldn't be skipped. (That's why they're called Important.) Here you'll find security notes, cautions, and warnings to keep you and your network out of trouble.

More Info   Often there are excellent sources for additional information on key topics. We'll use these boxes to point you to recommended resources.

 Security Alert   Nothing is more important than security when it comes to a computer network. Security elements should be carefully noted and acted on.

Best Practices   Advice for best practices that we have gained through our own technical experience is presented in these elements..

 On the Companion Media   In some cases, we've been able to provide related material on the book's companion CD. These pointers let you know what is available.

System Requirements

The following are the minimum system requirements to run the companion CD provided with this book:

- Windows XP, Windows Vista, or Windows 7 operating system with the latest service pack installed and the latest updates installed from Microsoft Update Service
- CD-ROM drive
- Internet connection
- Display monitor capable of 1024 x 768 resolution
- Microsoft Mouse or compatible pointing device
- Adobe Reader for viewing the eBook (Adobe Reader is available as a download at *http://www.adobe.com*)

About the Companion Media

The companion CD contains the fully searchable electronic version of this book and additional materials you might find useful. Full documentation of the contents and structure of the companion media can be found in the Readme.txt file on the CD.

Support

Every effort has been made to ensure the accuracy of this book and companion content. As corrections or changes are collected, they will be added to a Microsoft Knowledge Base article accessible via the Microsoft Help and Support site. Microsoft Press provides support for books, including instructions for finding Knowledge Base articles, at the following website:

http://www.microsoft.com/learning/support/books/

If you have questions regarding the book that are not answered by visiting the site above or viewing a Knowledge Base article, send them to Microsoft Press via e-mail to mspinput@microsoft.com.

Please note that Microsoft software product support is not offered through these addresses.

We Want to Hear from You

We welcome your feedback about this book. Please share your comments and ideas via the following short survey:

http://www.microsoft.com/learning/booksurvey/

Your participation will help Microsoft Press create books that better meet your needs and your standards.

> **NOTE** We hope that you will give us detailed feedback via our survey. If you have questions about our publishing program, upcoming titles, or Microsoft Press in general, we encourage you to interact with us via Twitter at *http://twitter.com/MicrosoftPress*. For support issues, use only the e-mail address shown in the previous section.

## CHAPTER 1

Understanding the Basics of Collaboration in SharePoint 2010

In the past several years, a collaboration revolution has evolved. Now, traditional, single-purpose applications no longer satisfy users' hunger and drive to get more done. It was not so long ago that someone would write a document, send it by fax, e-mail, or postal service to colleagues, and then wait for their collaborative feedback to return. This process could take hours—or even days—before team members' changes could be incorporated in the original document to create a final version.

Today, managers in companies that are competing in the evolving global marketplace need to find ways to increase the efficiency of their workforce. Companies need their employees to be able to connect and work anywhere and anytime using a variety of devices to connect and complete their work.

SharePoint sites bring employees together to share information, data, and expertise by allowing interaction with others using standard Microsoft Office applications as well as standard Web browsers such as Internet Explorer or Firefox. The focus in this chapter is primarily on user collaboration through the Web browser and a general overview of collaboration in Microsoft SharePoint 2010.

SharePoint 2010 in Five Words

The SharePoint 2010 platform can be described in five essential words: collaboration, aggregation, organization, presentation, and publication. This brief overview, using those five words, describes what SharePoint is and what it does for your nontechnical users and decision makers.

- **Collaboration**   The basis of the SharePoint platform is collaboration. Emanating from the original Microsoft SharePoint Team Services (STS) that was provided free on the Microsoft Office 2000 Professional CD, STS was renamed Windows SharePoint Services (WSS) and formed the foundation for the Microsoft SharePoint Portal Server 2003 (SPS) and the Microsoft Office SharePoint Server 2007 (MOSS) platforms. It is now called Microsoft SharePoint Foundation Services (SFS). The core of this foundation remains a robust collaboration platform that supports workflows, security trimming, asynchronous interaction between team members, and other features that create an environment for collaboration. SFS is free and requires neither Client Access Licenses (CAL), a server license or, if utilized on the Internet, an Internet connector license.

- **Aggregation**   SharePoint 2010 allows you to aggregate information from a variety of dissimilar sources, such as databases, file servers, or websites. The aggregation technologies include, but are not limited to

  - Linking to the content

  - Indexing the content

  - Hosting the content

  - Really Simple Syndication (RSS) (if the content is published using RSS)

  - Business Connectivity Services (BCS) (if the content is in a database)

  The ability to aggregate content without necessarily hosting it is one of the strengths of SharePoint. A robust information management system must be able to aggregate information, especially if the aggregation of selected information is needed to combine that information into a collaborative effort.

- **Organization**   In nearly all scenarios, when data is aggregated, it also must be organized. Nearly all of us who have been in the information technology (IT) field for any length of time can think of file servers, databases, My Documents, and other repositories that have become little more than dumping grounds for all types of information. IT professionals (IT Pros) use phrases like "out of control," or "a total mess," or "nothing but rubbish" to describe repositories of information that lack organization. SharePoint 2010 provides a number of organization features, which include but are not limited to

  - Managed Metadata Service

- Content types
- Site columns
- Managed paths
- Summary Links Web Part
- Sites directory

Organizing information is an important task for any company that uses SharePoint. Simply moving information into SharePoint or indexing it won't give you the *findability* that you and your users will need. You must actively and consistently organize your information to make it useful.

- **Presentation**   After you have aggregated and organized your information, you'll need to present it in a pleasant and meaningful way. SharePoint Designer can help with the presentation layer. But so can the ability to present Business Intelligence (BI) information in a dashboard. Project data can be presented in meaningful ways using the project Web Parts in SharePoint 2010. All of the Enterprise Content Management (ECM) features, such as Document Management (DM), Records Management (RM), and Web Content Management (WCM), can be thought of as tools to accomplish aggregation, organization, and presentation.

- **Publication**   SharePoint makes it possible to publish information created and developed by a small group of team members for viewing by a wider audience. The Web Content Management is one of the most important tools available for publishing information, but you also have major/minor versioning capabilities in document libraries that allow documents to be published as they are developed.

Introducing SharePoint 2010 Capabilities

SharePoint 2010 builds on the value of SharePoint Server 2007 and provides a core team collaboration experience along with a strong, consistent, development platform that can be used to tailor the SharePoint experience to meet specific corporate and user needs. Microsoft SharePoint 2010 is focused on providing and satisfying business needs by

- Connecting and empowering people
- Cutting costs with a unified infrastructure
- Rapidly responding to business needs

The enhanced features provided in this release of SharePoint can be categorized into groups that help describe the various editions and features available. Table 1-1 describes these capabilities in detail.

TABLE 1-1 SharePoint 2010 Capabilities

CAPABILITY	DESCRIPTION
Sites	Engage employees, partners, and customers by utilizing Web-facing sites, workspaces to share information, data, and expertise. These sites can be located either inside or outside a firewall.
Communities	Utilize social networking concepts to connect people, engage employees, and streamline information organization.
Content	Provides quick, accurate, and secure access to information by driving compliance, reducing risk, and consolidating systems using content and role-driven rules during the creation, review, publication, and disposal of content.
Search	Find, explore, and connect to information across SharePoint lists, sites, external systems, and data sources such as file shares, websites, or line-of-business applications.
Insights	Enable users to improve business decisions by empowering decision makers, improving organizational effectiveness, and enabling efficiency by turning raw data into actionable conclusions that drive business results through the sharing of data-driven analysis.
Composites	Allow users to quickly create integrated, customized solutions that support power users and professional developers.

With the release of SharePoint 2010, as with previous releases, there are two basic platforms: SharePoint Foundation 2010 and SharePoint 2010. Table 1-2 describes the editions of SharePoint that are available.

TABLE 1-2 SharePoint 2010 Editions

EDITION	DESCRIPTION
INTRANET SCENARIOS	
Enterprise Client Access License (CAL)	Enables advanced scenarios for end users; provides full interoperability with external line-of-business applications, Web services, and Microsoft Office client applications.
Standard Client Access License (CAL)	Enables deployment of a business collaboration platform across all types of content, simplifying content management and business process across an organization.
INTERNET/EXTRANET	
SharePoint 2010 for Internet Sites, Enterprise	For organizations that want to create scalable customer-facing Internet websites or private secure extranet sites using the full Enterprise capabilities of SharePoint 2010.

EDITION	DESCRIPTION
SharePoint 2010 for Internet Sites, Standard	For small and mid-sized organizations that want to create public Internet sites or basic extranets using the Standard features of SharePoint 2010.
ENABLING TECHNOLOGIES	
SharePoint Designer 2010	A tool for advanced users and developers who want to create SharePoint solutions in an easy-to-use environment. No-code solutions can be created for many scenarios including collaborative sites, Web publishing, line-of-business data integration, business intelligence solutions, and more.
SharePoint Foundation 2010	For smaller organizations needing a solution for secure, Web-based collaboration to coordinate schedules, organize documents, and use team workspaces, blogs, wikis, and document libraries.

SharePoint Foundation Services provides a low-cost, entry-level solution for secure, Web-based collaboration. SharePoint Foundation 2010 allows collaboration among users to co-ordinate schedules, organize documents, and participate in discussion forums through team workspaces, blogs, or wikis. Because SharePoint Foundation is the underlying infrastructure for SharePoint Server, straightforward upgrade paths are possible as corporate needs require additional functionality and advanced content capabilities. Table 1-3 summarizes the capabilities for SharePoint Foundation 2010.

TABLE 1-3 SharePoint Foundation 2010 Capabilities

CAPABILITY	DESCRIPTION
Sites	Ribbon user interface, SharePoint Workspace, SharePoint Mobile, Office Client and Office Web Application Integration, and Standards Support
Communities	Blogs and Wikis
Content	Remote BLOB Storage, List Enhancements
Composites	Business Connectivity Services, External Lists, Workflow, SharePoint Designer, Visual Studio, API Enhancements, REST/ATOM/RSS support

For organizations that require scalable business platforms, SharePoint 2010 has been divided into two editions: Intranet and Internet/Extranet; each of these software editions has different fee structures based on the product purchased. Both editions share the capabilities with SharePoint Foundation and are listed in Table 1-3; they also have the additional capabilities listed in Table 1-4.

TABLE 1-4 SharePoint 2010 Capabilities

CAPABILITY	DESCRIPTION
Communities	Blogs and Wikis
	*Tagging, Tag Cloud, Ratings
	*Social Bookmarking, My Sites, Activity Feeds, Profiles and Expertise, and Organization Browser
Content	Remote BLOB Storage, List Enhancements
	*Enterprise Content Type, Metadata and Navigation, Document Sets, Multistage Disposition, Audio and Video Content Types
Insights	PerformancePoint Services, Excel Services, Chart Web Part, Video Services, Web Analytics, SQL Server Integration, Power Pivot
Search	Social Relevance, Phonetic Search, Navigation, FAST Integration, Enhanced Pipeline
Sites	Ribbon UI, SharePoint Workspace, SharePoint Mobile, Office Client and Office Web Application Integration, and Standards Support.
Composites	Business Connectivity Services, External Lists, Workflow, SharePoint Designer, Visual Studio, API Enhancements, REST/ATOM/RSS support.

Supported in SharePoint 2010 Server only.

This chapter explores the basic collaboration techniques that are available utilizing the Sites capabilities provided in SharePoint 2010.

Using SharePoint Sites and Templates

SharePoint 2010 comes with site templates to help you begin the journey into user collaboration. These templates provide a basic framework design for building SharePoint sites to meet an organization's needs and requirements. More often than not, these templates are used by organizations out of the box, with very few—if any—customizations. If you understand how to use the different templates that are available when designing and implementing a SharePoint installation, you can help ensure that both farm administrators and nontechnical users choose the correct site template to allow employees in your organization to collaborate effectively. SharePoint 2010 site templates can be categorized as follows.

- *Collaboration* sites allow users to quickly author and convey information (press releases, project information, events, announcements, and so on) through one or more

Web pages, blogs, or wikis. These sites contain document libraries, calendar items, tasks, and discussions.

- *Content* sites assist with the management of documents, using version and change controls.

- *Publishing* sites help SharePoint sites adhere to corporate workflow policies and procedures. For example, an extranet portal provides access to corporate content in a secure manner. Generally, extranet sites are exposed to the public Internet and require additional update processes and procedures.

- *Web database* sites are new in SharePoint 2010 and allow for advanced functionality and allow modifiable database templates that can be used or modified as necessary.

- *Search* site functionality has been revamped in SharePoint 2010, and it now provides a better overall user search experience, providing features such as phonetic name matching and query suggestions. These sites include pages for search results and advanced searches. The SharePoint Server 2007 search sites such as the Search Center have been deprecated.

SharePoint 2010 allows for the combination of one or more of these site types to provide the best possible user experience platform. Before identifying which primary site templates to use, you must first determine the primary purpose of the site. Table 1-5 identifies the templates available in SharePoint 2010 (items new to SharePoint 2010 are shown in *italics*).

TABLE 1-5 SharePoint 2010 Templates

SITE TYPE	SHAREPOINT 2010 SITE TEMPLATE
Collaboration	Document Workspace
	Group Work Site
	Issue Tracking
	Meeting Workspaces—Basic, Blank, Decision, Multipage, and Social Meeting
	Team
	Wiki
Content and data	Blog
	Document Center
	Document Workspace
	My Site Host
	Records Center
	Visio Process Repository
Publishing	*Enterprise Wiki*
	Publishing Portal

continued on the next page

SITE TYPE	SHAREPOINT 2010 SITE TEMPLATE
Web database	*Assets Web Database*
	Charitable Contributions Web Database
	Contacts Web Database
	Issues Web Database
	Projects Web Database
Search	*Basic Search Center*
	FAST Search Center
	Enterprise Search Center

The team collaboration site provides much of the functionality of the other sites.

Interacting with SharePoint Sites

The SharePoint 2010 user interface (UI) provides better user interaction and simplifies feature and content adjustments. The relocation of the Site Actions button to the upper left along with new action tabs simplify the ways a user can interact with the site. The new Ribbon bars are context- and security-sensitive, which means that they change depending on which user is logged in and what level of security role the user has.

The Ribbon displays possible actions that are available within the site. For example, a site administrator will see the Page tab, which allows modification to the page and the ability to add SharePoint Web parts, while a user who is not an administrator will not see this tab. Other features, such as the Quick Launch menu and site search text box function, remain similar in look to SharePoint Server 2007.

Site Creation in SharePoint 2010

Users designated as farm administrators within SharePoint 2010 can define and group sites, along with their respective subsites, using a common URL namespace. For example, a company could have a site URL of *http://contoso* and create multiple subsites URLs such as *http://contoso/operations/engineering*, *http://contoso/operations/IT*, or *http://contoso /operations/facilities*. No physical limit exists to the URL depth, and URLs can be adjusted to suit the needs of the users who use that site.

A top-level site, such as *http://contoso*, with its associated subsites, is referred to as a *site collection*. There are additional administrative settings that will apply to the entire collection of sites rather than any one individual site within the collection. For example, site quotas define the total amount of data that can be hosted within a site collection. Site quotas are applied at the site collection layer and cannot be broken down into quotas for each individual site. By contrast, user security applies specifically to an individual site, an individual Web Part, or a specific list item. Hence, different configurations apply at different levels within the

SharePoint platform, and your users will need to learn which settings apply at which levels in order to administer their site collections and sites properly.

When a top-level site is created, subsites are added to target collaboration flow and functionality. For example, consider a company intranet website where management wants to control access to change content. To do this, the top-level site might be configured as a publishing site to limit updates and require user workflows for publishing. However, the company's engineering department requires an intranet subsite for updating documentation, management of wikis, and project management functions. A new subsite might be created for this purpose so that access can be granted, as required, by the engineering department but still keeping those functions quarantined within a site. For more information, read the Real World sidebar, "Site Collection Creation with Multiple Databases," in Chapter 6, "Managing SharePoint 2010 Using Central Administration."

SharePoint 2010 enhances the administration-user interface by employing Silverlight to pop up new pages as needed, thereby retaining the users' context within the site. By clicking Site Settings in the upper-left corner of the SharePoint 2010 Central Administration application window, the Site Actions menu appears. New quick links as well as the traditional site settings provide easy access to most administrative functions, as illustrated in Figure 1-1.

FIGURE 1-1 Site Actions menu

> **NOTE** If you click the Site Actions button and the Site Actions menu does not appear, try adding the URL of the root site in the site collection to your trusted sites list in Internet Explorer.

The Site Settings link will take you to a page very similar to the SharePoint Server 2007 Site Settings menu. Although the page is formatted in a slightly different way, SharePoint 2010 navigation is similar enough to SharePoint Server 2007 to make navigation during the upgrade process easier for site and farm administrators. If Silverlight is installed, the new Silverlight administrative pages are accessible by clicking New Site in the Site Actions menu (refer back to Figure 1-1). This action opens the Create page shown in Figure 1-2. If Silverlight is not installed and you click New Site on the Site Actions menu, you will be taken directly to the New SharePoint Site page (Newsbweb.aspx).

From the Create page shown in Figure 1-2, choose the site template you want to use to create a new site. Then enter the site title and URL name and click the Create button. Because each site contains different lists and libraries, this chapter uses the Team Site template for demonstration purposes.

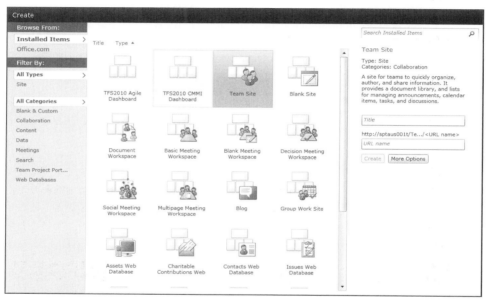

FIGURE 1-2 The Create page provides templates that you can select from to create a new site.

Editing Features in SharePoint 2010

SharePoint 2010 features a new and improved editing framework. With these enhancements, editing functionality becomes easier than it was in previous versions. One comment repeated over and over by power users when they start using SharePoint 2010 is "I didn't know SharePoint could do that!" SharePoint 2010 includes many common Microsoft Office functionalities, and as a result, users are more aware of the platform capabilities. Power users can modify and enhance the sites' content to provide collaboration and information to the user base. By default, the new Team Site home page has a Click To Edit feature, making content changes simple. These new editing features encourage data and information collaboration among users that is easy to create, find, and use. In addition, these features will encourage you to make SharePoint your principal choice for collaboration.

Rich Text Editing

The new Team Site home page contains a Click To Edit feature that makes content changes simple. Power users can easily upload images, create links, and add Web Parts with a click of the mouse. Users with design or higher access can click the Page tab on the Ribbon or choose Edit Page from the Site Actions menu. In SharePoint 2010, the Edit Page command opens the Wiki Page Home Page feature; it is enabled or disabled as requirements dictate. If the Wiki Page is disabled, the Team Site will display as the traditional SharePoint Server 2007 home page. To check if this feature is enabled or disabled, complete the following steps.

1. Click Site Actions and then select Site Settings.

2. Under the Site Actions group, click Manage Site Features.

3. Click Active or Deactivate, as shown in Figure 1-3.

FIGURE 1-3 Wiki Page settings

The SharePoint Ribbon

SharePoint 2010 uses a Ribbon similar to the Microsoft Office 2007 and Office 2010 Ribbon and, just like Office, items are logically grouped. Further, the SharePoint 2010 Ribbon can be customized as needed and retains the users' security context. Figure 1-4 contains an example of the Ribbon for the Team Site home page.

FIGURE 1-4 Team Site Edit Ribbon

As a page is edited, the Ribbon changes to make relevant operations available on the page or Web Part. For example, Figure 1-5 shows operations available for content editing on a page.

FIGURE 1-5 Team Site Edit Content Ribbon

SharePoint Dialog Boxes

New to SharePoint 2010 are the form dialog boxes, where functions such as creating a new item utilize forms that appear in the users' context window instead of redirecting the browser to a new page. To add a Web Part, users with proper permissions can click the Insert tab in the Action bar, select the Web Part button, choose the Web Part, and then click Add. During this process, the page context doesn't change. The ease with which power users can navigate and modify SharePoint sites should increase adoption and empower such users to do more with their sites. Further, the SharePoint 2010 wiki page allows users to insert Web Parts practically anywhere on the page.

Some of the most notable new Web Parts released with SharePoint 2010 are

- Silverlight viewer
- Media Web Part
- Chart Web Part
- HTML form Web Part
- iView Web Part
- Search Web Parts

One of the most frequently used Web Parts in SharePoint websites is the Content Editor Web Part. In SharePoint Server 2007, this Web Part allows users to enter information using a Microsoft Write experience. Using this Web Part, power users can type text inside the box and perform basic functions using—but not limited to—tables, fonts, and images. However, Microsoft Write is a very simple word-processing program, and administrators and users alike needed more features and capabilities than it could offer. Until SharePoint 2010 was introduced, however, the choices were either to teach HTML to the broad user base or have administrators or Web developers write code through the source editor.

SharePoint 2010 revamps and revitalizes the Content Editor Web Part so that it now resembles Microsoft Word more than Microsoft Write. No longer will users complain about broken URLs, tables not aligned when published, and so on. Business users will like this enhanced Web Part because it is so easy to use, styles can be applied to tags in Page Edit mode, and the user still has the ability to edit the HTML as necessary. Further, with the addition of the Ribbon, the Web Part easily converts to XHTML from the content editing Ribbon shown in Figure 1-5.

> **MORE INFO** You can learn more about Web Parts and how they are managed, inserted onto a page, and removed from a page by reading Chapter 19, "Web Parts and Their Functionality in SharePoint 2010.

Creating Rich Themes

As companies strive to brand themselves in an ever-changing marketplace, websites must quickly adapt. SharePoint 2010 has revised and enhanced the way in which power users and administrators create and apply themes to sites. One of the most important changes to site themes is the ability to inherit themes from the parent site. SharePoint 2010 makes theme changes significantly easier by providing three different methods for defining and changing themes.

- You can use Microsoft PowerPoint 2010, an application already known by most power users.
- You have access to enhanced Web-based site themes.
- You can create a CSS style sheet and attach to the master page.

Applying site themes assists content and Web managers in defining the content space by unifying the branding experience from other corporate media into the SharePoint website. Departments, divisions, and product lines can be defined using specific color palettes as needed.

Creating Themes Using the User Interface

You can create or change a basic color theme for a site directly through the UI for a site. Important feature enhancements to the Web interface include the ability to change the header and body font; the ability to change texts, accents, and hyperlinks; and a preview mode to view changes before they are applied to the site. To create or change a site, use the following steps.

1. Open the SharePoint site as a site administrator or Web designer.
2. Click Site Actions and then select Site Settings.
3. Under Look And Feel, choose Site Theme.
4. Click Select A Color to change a color of a specific element, or choose a theme from the list.
5. Click Preview to view the site changes before publishing.
6. Click Apply.

Creating Themes with Microsoft PowerPoint 2010

SharePoint 2010 no longer requires users to know and understand Cascading Style Sheets (CSS) to create a site theme. By utilizing a known application such as Microsoft PowerPoint 2010, power users can create and apply site themes quickly and easily. To change a website theme based on Microsoft PowerPoint 2010, follow these steps.

1. Open Microsoft PowerPoint 2010 and either create a new document or open an existing document. If you use an existing corporate PowerPoint document that already defines themes and colors for the enterprise, you might not need to perform steps 2 and 3.
2. Change the PowerPoint theme palette, if needed, by clicking the Design tab. Microsoft PowerPoint has many default themes available for you to use. Choosing a theme defines styles for the SharePoint site fonts, hyperlinks, and so on.

3. Choose a color palette for the site by clicking Colors. By default, there are many default color palettes available; choose one of the defaults or create a new color template. The colors chosen here define the site font colors for the SharePoint site.

4. Change the font styles as needed to further refine different text styles. Figure 1-6 shows a new Microsoft PowerPoint document with customized colors, fonts, and theme.

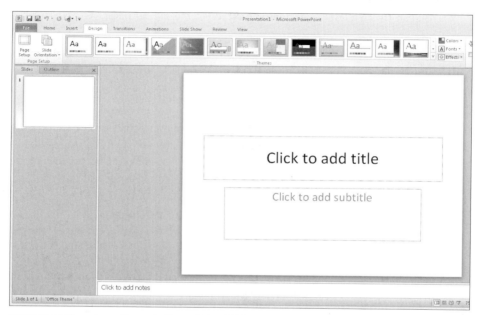

FIGURE 1-6 Changing a theme in PowerPoint 2010

5. Save the PowerPoint document as a Microsoft PowerPoint Theme (*.thmx).

6. Open your SharePoint 2010 top-level site, click Site Actions, and select Site Settings.

7. Under Galleries, click Themes.

8. Click Add New Item.

9. In the new window, browse to your file and keep / as the destination.

10. Click OK.

11. Open the SharePoint team site where you want to change the theme, click Site Actions, and then select Site Settings.

12. Under Look And Feel, choose Site Theme.

13. Select the newly uploaded theme and click OK.

After completing these steps, the SharePoint site will refresh to reflect the updated fonts, colors, and styles defined in the PowerPoint theme file. Additional customizations can be made, as necessary, by adjusting the theme file, via the user interface, or by creating customized style sheets.

Creating Themes Using Style Sheets

You may sometimes need to modify more than the colors and fonts of a website. You can create site themes using style sheets and then attach them to master pages through SharePoint Designer 2010. After you create a style sheet, you attach it to the master page by following these steps.

1. Copy your style sheet to the "14 hive" located by default at %ProgramFiles%\Common Files\Microsoft Shared\Web Server Extensions\14\Template\Layout\1033\Styles.

> **NOTE** The exact location of the CSS style sheet depends on the language pack installed as the default. In the URL in this step, 1033 has defined English as the language Locale ID.

2. Open the website in SharePoint Designer 2010, as shown in Figure 1-7.
3. Open the master page for your site (the default for a site is default.master).
4. Click Attach Style Sheet from the Ribbon.
5. Choose whether to apply to all pages or just the current master page and then click OK.

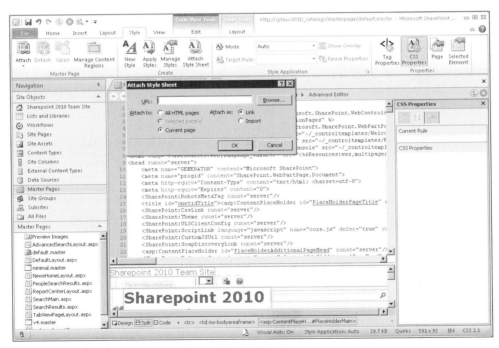

FIGURE 1-7 Changing a site theme in SharePoint 2010 Designer

Applying the Upgraded 2010 UI to All Sites

Because the UI has changed significantly in both SharePoint Foundation 2010 and SharePoint 2010, any customizations that rely on specific CSS classes and UI elements will work best for users in backward compatibility mode. When you initiate upgrades to either SharePoint Foundation 2010 or SharePoint 2010, the installer is able to choose either backward compatibility mode or the upgraded user interface mode. These modes may be toggled between backward compatibility and the new interface at the site collection level or site level.

- To preserve the look and feel of existing sites, choose the PSConfig or PSConfigUI.
- To preserve the look and feel of existing sites during an upgrade, you can attach the old content database to a new server farm using Stsadm.

You can use the Web interface to set all sites in a site collection to the upgraded UI (and prevent users from using the earlier interface). To do this, follow these steps.

1. Under Site Settings, click Site Collection Administration.
2. Click Visual Upgrade to display the page shown in Figure 1-8.

FIGURE 1-8 Apply Supported User Experience to all sites

3. Click Update All Sites to apply the new interface to all sites. Additionally, on this page, the site collection administrator can choose to prevent the upgrade of newly created sites in a site collection to the new experience. This is important if a SharePoint farm is unable to use the new look and feel for any reason.

Incorporating Rich Media Support

Rich media, a key component in the collaboration landscape, is another vehicle you can use to get targeted information to users. Training videos for employees, as opposed to on-site training sessions, are increasing in popularity as companies strive to reduce costs. Furthermore, in the "information now" age, users want information when they need it, where they need it, and within a few clicks of the mouse. A recent press release from Gartner, Inc., was titled "Gartner Predicts That by 2013, More Than 25 Percent of the Content That Workers

See in a Day Will Be Dominated by Pictures, Video or Audio" (at *http://www.gartner.com/it/page.jsp?id=834213*). Clearly there is a growing need for organizations to be able to store, find, and retrieve media in the same ways as documents. SharePoint 2010 is answering this challenge with rich media capabilities. SharePoint 2010 comes with

- The infrastructure to support storing and serving media using the asset library template
- Asset library support for RSS/podcasting while still supporting standard document library features
- The ability to play videos within SharePoint using the media Web Part or using remote locations
- Support for customized skins using Expression Blend 3
- Access to playback controls using the JavaScript object model

This evolution of rich media support allows SharePoint 2010 to seamlessly incorporate videos, audio, and pictures into the collaboration experience without extensive training or support. For example, the SharePoint Media Player can be included on any page with a few clicks of the mouse. To insert a Microsoft Silverlight Web part, complete the following steps.

1. Click Page in the Site Action toolbar.
2. Click Edit in the Ribbon.
3. Under the Editing Tools panel, click Insert.
4. Click Video And Audio.
5. Click inside the new Web Part to configure player settings. See Figure 1-9 for Silverlight Player options.

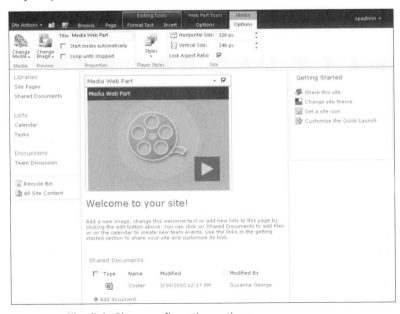

FIGURE 1-9 Silverlight Player configuration options

Working with Lists and Libraries

You add content to a SharePoint site using lists and libraries. Lists and their associated views provide a flexible mechanic for storing most kinds of information. Libraries, a special form of a list, usually store documents and their associated metadata. Lists and libraries provide users the ability to gain feedback instantly, get updates, and see historical information on data much more quickly and easily than using traditional methods of communication such as e-mail, network file shares, and so on.

SharePoint 2010, like previous versions, stores data in lists that are similar to Microsoft Excel spreadsheets. Much of the data consumed in SharePoint sites is located in lists, and each list item contains unique attributes. SharePoint 2010 offers standard templates to create lists as well as to provide the capability to create custom lists based on the structure and requirements of a user's application.

List Enhancements

SharePoint 2010 contains list enhancements to assist content administrators in gaining better control of their data. Configuration options and content control allow business users and content administrators to manage and ensure that fresh, relevant content to their users. Some of the list enhancements are

- New input form
- New list view
- Enhanced list lookup capabilities
- Referential integrity in the list—enforcing unique values
- Cascading deletes

List Input Form

One key to keeping data consistent in lists is the methodologies the users use to input data. If the user is required to upload data, remember links, and/or break information into separate pieces, each step paves the way to errors and input control issues. One change to lists that was frequently requested in the past has finally been added as an enhancement to SharePoint 2010: the ability to provide a single interface for adding list information, whether it is an image, document, link, or other textual information. Furthermore, the input screens, which were not always easy to use—especially for a beginner SharePoint user—have also been improved.

The new data entry forms for list items are much more user friendly. Gone are the difficult-to-edit HTML pages that defined user inputs; now an elegant pop-up form provides you with an easy method for user input. Figure 1-10 shows the new input form for SharePoint lists.

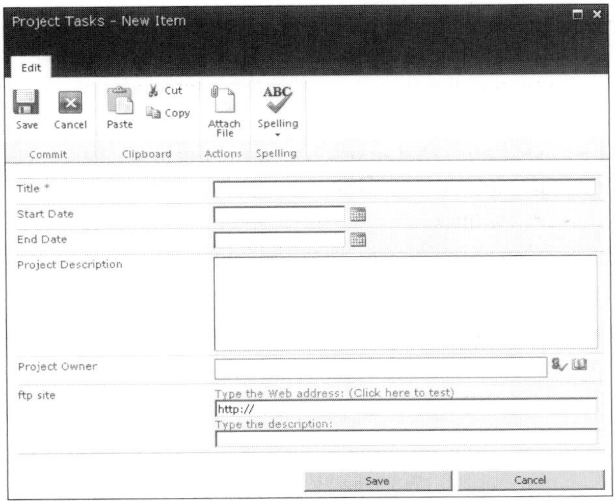

FIGURE 1-10 The new SharePoint 2010 list input form

The new Ribbon provides easy access to relevant information necessary for updating the list item. The Ribbon icons change depending on the context and the column type. For example, if you are working in a rich text field, you'll be presented with many familiar Microsoft Word functions, such as the Editing Tools tab on the Ribbon, shown in Figure 1-11.

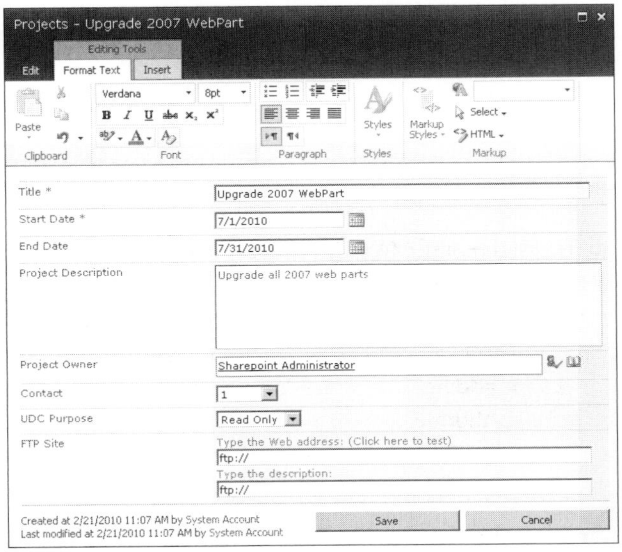

FIGURE 1-11 The Editing Tools tab on the Ribbon

Further, when you click the Insert tab under Editing Tools, the new forms that appear allow you to insert a table, picture, or link onto the page. You can also upload a picture directly into the rich text box to provide additional information as needed to describe the list item. The process of adding graphic elements to a page has been streamlined—no longer do you have to leave the Add or Edit form to first upload an image, then find the URL, and finally paste it in the box. Figure 1-12 shows the interface presented when an image is uploaded. Note that SharePoint will automatically upload the image into the list you specified.

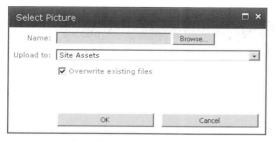

FIGURE 1-12 The Select Picture dialog box allows you to upload an image directly to the list you specify.

The seamless interface is continued, as shown in Figure 1-13, by prompting you for the title of the image and any other columns defined by the SharePoint library selected.

FIGURE 1-13 Set file properties for an uploaded image

After the file successfully uploads to the list, the List Edit page reloads and the Ribbon now contains a Picture Tools tab. This tab allows you to execute actions on the image, such as changing the picture, position, size, and URL information, as shown in Figure 1-14.

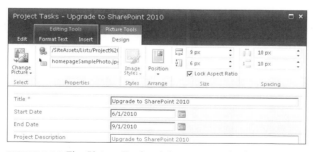

FIGURE 1-14 The Picture Tools tab lets you manipulate an image uploaded to a list.

Inserting a table is just as simple and also offers rich features you can use to customize the table. The methods are very similar to inserting a table in a Microsoft Word document, setting the rows and columns and selecting table styles and formatting elements. The Table Tools Layout tab on the Ribbon provides you with an array of table layout functions, shown in Figure 1-15.

FIGURE 1-15 The Table Tools Layout tab on the Ribbon

The Table Tools Design tab features the Ribbon shown in Figure 1-16.

FIGURE 1-16 The Table Tools Design tab on the Ribbon

The method for formatting URLs has been improved as well. When you insert a URL using the Ribbon, you can type a description, open the link into a new tab, and display an icon. Figure 1-17 shows the Link Tools tab on the Ribbon, with options for formatting hyperlinks.

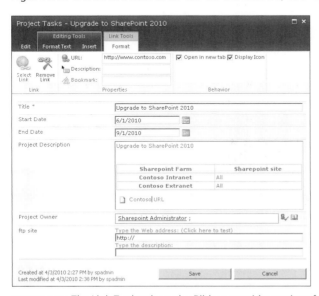

FIGURE 1-17 The Link Tools tab on the Ribbon provides options for formatting URLs as links on a page.

With SharePoint 2010, you have many options for entering information into lists, and with enhanced features such as the rich text box, you can clearly articulate the information requested by list content managers.

Another feature new to list form templates are the Add New and Edit forms. These forms are similar to each other, providing another consistent user interface. When you click Edit in the Ribbon, the Edit form opens and you can use it to perform data updates on the list item. When you edit an existing list item, you also can view more information about it to manage permissions, check version history (if available for the list), or delete the list item. The Edit form is shown in Figure 1-18.

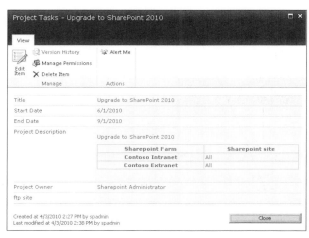

FIGURE 1-18 SharePoint 2010 Edit form

When you have updated the item, the list view will look like the screen shown in Figure 1-19. Notice that in the list view you see the full rich text of the list elements.

FIGURE 1-19 Rich text list view

The seamless data entry process provided in SharePoint 2010 will reduce data errors and frustration levels for all users. Now you can easily enter data in a format that suits your needs, and power users and content managers will have cleaner, more appropriate data with less expensive custom development efforts.

List Templates

When you create a new site, several lists are automatically available for use. The site developer should experiment with the different list types before determining which list template provides the best functionality and the features most needed. For example, the Team Site template will create Calendar, Tasks, and Status lists. Each of these lists will provide the user with different functionality.

As in previous versions of SharePoint, the custom list provides a good introduction to using and managing list data. When you create a custom list, it allows you to add views, columns, and items as needed, as shown in Figure 1-20.

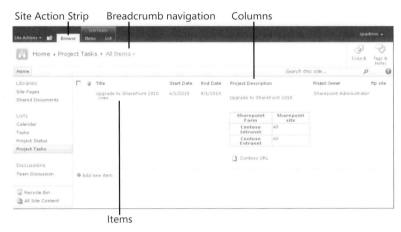

FIGURE 1-20 SharePoint site list view

- **Items**   Rows of individual data components.
- **Columns**   Define the types of data located in the row. Columns can be created to contain only certain information, such as e-mail addresses, URLs, and dates. Customized and lookup data types are also available. Columns such as Create/Modify Date and Create/Modified By are usually not shown by default; however, they are part of the list.
- **Site Action Strip**   Allows a user or content administrator to access and perform different functions on lists. You can find functions such as changing views, adding columns, and exporting data here.
- **Breadcrumb navigation**   As with previous version of SharePoint, breadcrumb navigation helps to define the user's location within the SharePoint Farm hierarchy. Having breadcrumb navigation available is important so users can quickly navigate within the various SharePoint sites. By default, breadcrumb navigation is replaced with the Ribbon as actions on content are available to the user.

The new Ribbon toolbars relocate common tasks and dynamically adjust based on your security role. The following images show what a content manager or administrator might see. Figure 1-21 shows the actions that can be completed on individual items in the list such as a document or list item.

FIGURE 1-21 Available actions on the Items tab

Figure 1-22 shows the actions that can be done on the list itself. These actions allow the administrator or power user to modify and create views, export list items to Excel or a document in other Office applications, and change list settings.

FIGURE 1-22 SharePoint 2010 Ribbon bars

Creating a List

The process of creating a list is very similar to creating a site. Several list templates are available; Figure 1-23 shows the available list templates using the new Silverlight menu controls. Each of the default templates shown in Figure 1-23 showcases different features that are available for use with list data.

FIGURE 1-23 SharePoint 2010 Create List types

To create a custom list, a content administrator can go to the SharePoint team site and follow these steps.

1. Click Site Actions and the select More Options to open a new window with all the SharePoint site templates available (Figure 1-23).

2. Click the List link.

3. Choose the list type you want to create.

4. Type the name for the list and then click Create.

After you have created a list, you will see the new, empty list appear along with the task Ribbon bars described in the previous section. Now you can add data, columns, and views to the list.

Managing List Columns

The power of lists resides in creating columns that will help to provide users with the metadata they want and need. As when designing a SQL database or other business application, it is important to understand the types of metadata users will require and how the data relates to other corporate information. For example, if a corporation wanted to upload all project files into a SharePoint document library, metadata would be required to link the files together. Thus, a column would need to be created that would hold the project name or identifying number so a user would be able to find all documents relating to a specific project. Other columns might be created that would link information such as clients and business groups. All SharePoint columns have a specific type and validation for associated data. Columns can be added to

- Show text and other basic information
- Provide predefined choices for the user for enhanced grouping or filtering
- Link to other site data
- Calculate values based on data in other columns

Figure 1-24 shows the list of standard column types available in SharePoint 2010.

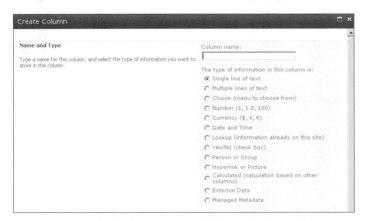

FIGURE 1-24 Standard column types available on the Create Column page

Creating, Editing, and Deleting Columns

You can insert columns to prompt a user to provide additional information for an item in the list. To add columns to a list, complete the following steps.

1. Open the list and click the List tab under List Tools.

2. Click the Create Column icon.

3. Type a short, descriptive name for the column.

4. Choose the column type for the information to be stored in the list.

5. Specify any additional settings as needed. The settings displayed are dependent on the column type and will dynamically change to reflect the column type you choose. You will find settings such as Required Information and Enforce Unique Values in this section.

> **NOTE** If you choose the Enforce Unique Values option, you will be asked to index the column. It is important to click OK so SharePoint will index the column to improve system performance. Further, if you are modifying an existing field to make it unique, SharePoint will validate the data and return an error if the data already in the column is not unique.

6. Add column validation as needed. You can specify a formula that will validate the data in this column when new items are saved to this list. The formula must return a true or false validation and cannot refer to other fields in the list. Example: If a column is named Length Of Project, a valid formula would be *[Length of Project] > 0*.

7. Type a description for the validation formula and an example of what is needed for the validation to pass. Example column description: *Please enter the number of days the project will last:* **40**.

8. Click OK to create the column.

When you have completed these steps, the list refreshes and returns the user context with the added column.

> **NOTE** If you plan to use column names in queries or through a Web service, SharePoint Application Programming Interface (API), or other method, columns names should not contain spaces for better behavior within queries and API calls. If the column is created as LengthofProject and then modified to show Length Of Project, it will be possible to reference the column through the various APIs as LengthofProject, yet have it display to users with the spaces included.

To see a list of columns created for a list, click List Settings in the Ribbon. All columns in the list display. If the column name is selected, you can modify the column settings as needed. Be careful when changing a column type, because SharePoint will warn you that data might be lost. For example, changing a rich text box to a single line of text will result in SharePoint dropping any data that is longer than the new type will support. The validation rules might need to be adjusted as well. SharePoint does not allow certain column types to be changed to other column types. If this is required, the columns must be deleted and re-created. Understanding the column data and its requirements avoids having to make column type changes to lists.

You can delete a column by clicking List Settings in the Ribbon, just as when you modify a column. When you select Delete, all the data in that column is deleted, and recovery is impossible using the SharePoint Recycle Bin.

> **IMPORTANT** Use caution when deleting a column, because data in a deleted column cannot be retrieved later.

Types of Columns

There are three common column types in SharePoint 2010: information, lookup, and calculated columns. New column types such as external data and managed metadata will be discussed in Chapter 14, "Administering Enterprise Content Management."

INFORMATION COLUMNS

The traditional information-gathering columns used in SharePoint, such as Single Line Of Text and Hyperlink Or Picture, allow the user to enter supporting information for the list item. For example, in a project list, supporting information could include a project description, the start and end dates of the project, and the project owner. Figure 1-25 shows an example of a new project list with these types of information columns.

FIGURE 1-25 List view of a project list with information columns added

LOOKUP COLUMNS

Lookup columns, enhanced to show additional column information from the referenced list, allow a user to link list data together. To create a lookup column in list view, complete the following steps.

1. Click List under the List Tools tab.
2. Click Create Column to display the Column page.

3. Type the column name.

4. Choose Lookup (Information Already On This Site).

5. Set the additional column settings for the column as shown in Figure 1-26.

    Notice the new options available in SharePoint 2010. Lookup columns are now able to show more than one column from the referenced list. To show additional column information from a lookup list, select the check box to Allow Multiple Values under the In This Column drop-down box. After you have selected the check box, columns will be created for each selected column metadata. This capability is important so the user can be presented with the necessary information with fewer clicks. In Figure 1-26, if a user needed the ability to view a contact's Mobile Number and Home Phone alongside the current list data, the Allow Multiple Values, Home Phone, and Mobile Number check boxes would all be selected.

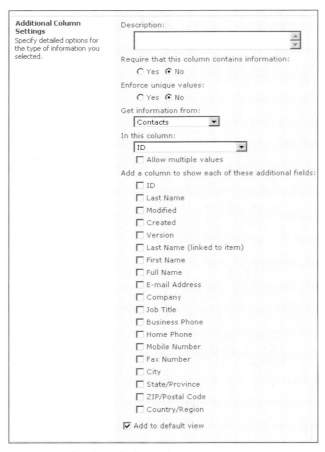

FIGURE 1-26 Creating a lookup column

6. Set the relationship by choosing whether to enforce relationship behavior when the list item is deleted. When an item in the target list is deleted, a *cascade* delete will delete all related items in this list. A *restricted* delete prevents deletion of a list item in the selected target list if one or more referenced items exists in the list. For example, a project list is created that details information about the projects in the engineering group. A secondary list, called Project Tasks, is also created, and it has a column lookup to the project list.

7. If the Enforce Relationship Behavior check box (shown in Figure 1-27) is selected and Restrict Delete is selected, the user cannot delete a project until all referenced Project Tasks have been deleted. If the Enforce Relationship Behavior option is selected and Cascade Delete is selected, as shown in Figure 1-27, all items in the Project Tasks will be deleted if the project list item is deleted.

FIGURE 1-27 Enforce Relationship Behavior option

8. With Referential Integrity selected, you will be prompted to index the column. Click OK.

9. Click OK to create the column.

Figure 1-28 shows the list with an added lookup column.

FIGURE 1-28 Default list view with added lookup column

The lookup column called Contact has a value of 1 in Figure 1-28, and the Contact:First Name column is also viewable in the list, thereby showing two columns from the referenced list for users. Since this lookup column was set to Cascade Delete when the column was created, this list entry will be deleted in the event that the user SharePointAdmin (the Contact:FirstName column entry) is deleted.

CALCULATED COLUMNS

Calculated columns bring content together from other columns in the list. In the section titled "Creating, Editing, and Deleting Columns" earlier in this chapter, you were asked to type the length of the project (see Figure 1-18). Since the project start and end dates are part of the list item metadata, the project length can be calculated by the system. A calculated column can be created by following these steps.

1.   Open the list and click List under the List Tools tab.

2.   Click Create Column to display the create Column page.

3.   Type the column name.

4.   Click Calculated Column.

5.   Create a formula based on existing columns, as shown in Figure 1-29.

6.   Click OK.

FIGURE 1-29 Adding a calculated column to a list

> **MORE INFO**   For additional information about how to use calculated values, navigate to *http://blogs.msdn.com/mcsnoiwb/archive/2008/05/04/sharepoint-formulas-in-calculated-columns.aspx.*

Indexing Columns

With SharePoint 2010, large lists are now a supported feature. SharePoint now enables sites to have virtually unlimited numbers of items in lists and libraries. However, the core of the SharePoint platform is Microsoft SQL Server, and performance is affected when large amounts of data are queried without the use of indexes. Therefore, it is important to index large lists to streamline overall performance.

When setting up indexes for large lists, consider the following points.

- Microsoft has increased the number of columns in a list index to 20 in SharePoint 2010.

- Each column index consumes resources in the database. Farm or content administrators should only add indexes to columns that will be actively used in views.

- Columns that have been set to allow multiple values cannot be indexed and will not be listed.

To add an index to a site, complete the following steps.

1. Click List under the List Tools tab and then select List Settings.

2. Click Indexed Columns.

3. When the current indexes on the list are shown, click Create A New Index.

4. Click the column that you want to use for the primary column in the index.

5. Select the secondary index column. If this field is left blank, the resulting index will be a single column index. If a second column is specified, the resulting index becomes a compound index in which only certain fields can participate.

6. Click OK.

Sorting and Filtering

Sorting and filtering list data, especially when there are a large number of items in a list, is beneficial not only for SharePoint performance as a whole, but also in assisting you in finding information quickly and easily in a list.

Lists in SharePoint 2010, like previous versions, allow users to sort and filter data using techniques generally found in other Microsoft Office applications. Each heading in the list view allows you to sort or filter the data based on your needs or requirements. For example, if you want to sort your tasks by date, a simple click on the Date column header to reformat the list data sorted by date. By clicking the Date column header again, the data in the column will be sorted in reverse date order, and you will see the list refreshed to show it in that order in the new list view. As shown in Figure 1-30, when the arrow in the header bar is pointing up, the list is sorted in ascending order; when the arrow in the header bar is pointing down, the list is sorted in descending order.

FIGURE 1-30 List sorting and filtering

Filtering, on the other hand, differs from sorting in that it allows you to view only the data in a list that meets specific criteria. Filtering lets you to sift through large amounts of data to find only the data you need, based on the information contained in a column you select. If you want to view all tasks due today, for example, click the arrow next to the Date Due column heading, and a drop-down list displays the available dates to use as a filter for the list. When you select today's date to use as a filter, only the tasks in the list due on that date will appear in the list view. You will see a funnel-shaped icon displayed in the column header when filtering is enabled.

IMPORTANT Not all columns support filtering. Notable columns are Multiple Lines Of Text and hyperlink.

List Views

Although user sorting and filtering are useful, an even more powerful feature is list views, in which you can use predefined sorting and filtering to determine what you see in the list—you do not need to resort or add a filter each time you view the list. List views allow users, content managers, and administrators to prefilter and/or sort lists to provide the user with only data relevant to the user. List views describe the data, columns, sorting of data, and the style used to present the data. Views, unlike traditional reports, are dynamic and refresh every time the page loads.

List views can be either public or private, meaning that the content manager or administrator can set up predefined views for all users to see, or a user can create a personal view that describes the list data in a way that suits his or her specific needs at the time. All of the sorting and filtering preferences can be saved for use later.

Farm and content administrators should consider the following points when working with list views.

- Only one indexed column can be used in a view filter. Even though filtering on different columns is possible, the first column in the view should be indexed to reduce the overall number of items returned.

- A view can encompass more than one search criteria; however, any view that uses an OR filter does not have any index benefits described here.

- Defining an item limit in the view does not provide the same results as a filtered view.

- You should always use a filter that will return no more items than needed. If a list has 10,000 items, for example, but 9500 of them are not needed daily, add a filter to the default view.

To create a list view, complete the following steps.

1. Click List under the List Tools tab and then select List Settings.
2. Click Create View.
3. Choose either a view format or the option to start from an existing view.
4. Type a view name.
5. Choose either a public or personal view.
6. Choose the columns and set the order in which the columns will be displayed.

7. Choose the sorting method needed—if none is chosen, the list will sort by ID.

8. Choose the columns to filter.

9. Choose whether to allow inline editing. If inline editing is enabled, each row will have an Edit button that enables edit features without requiring the user to leave the view. Inline editing is only available when the style is set to Default.

10. Choose whether to allow tabular view. These check boxes allow you to select multiple items in a view and perform bulk actions such as Delete.

11. Choose the columns to group by.

12. Choose totals, if needed.

13. Change the style for the view if needed.

14. Display all items with or without folders.

15. Choose an item limit to limit the amount of data that is returned to users of this view. You can either make this an absolute limit or allow users to view all the items in the list in batches of a specified size.

16. When a view has been enabled for mobile access, it is also possible to make the view the default view for users of mobile devices. This allows content views to be tailored for both the PC (which may have additional columns and/or graphics) and for mobile users, providing the latter with a simpler, lightweight view. When a mobile user views the list, she can click the key field (specified in the view in mobile settings) to view the entire content record.

17. Click OK.

When the view is created, the page is refreshed and the new view appears. To change the view back to the default, click the List tab in List Tools and click the arrow under Current View, as shown in Figure 1-31; then select Default from the drop-down list.

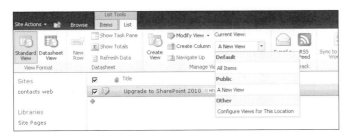

FIGURE 1-31 Changing the list view

To see the inline editing in action, select the check box to the left of the list item you want to edit. SharePoint highlights the row and the Ribbon changes to the Items action tab under List Tools, as shown in Figure 1-32. A new Edit button appears to the left of the first column. If you click the Edit button, you can list items within the view.

FIGURE 1-32 Edit list items within the view

To save the changes you make, click the blue Save icon. To cancel the edits you made, click the red X icon. To add new items using this view, click the green plus sign (+) icon found below the last item in the list.

Advanced List Concepts

Additional features in SharePoint 2010 lists allow for additional customization and administration of list data. By providing support for large lists, site columns, and advanced input forms, site administrators are able to control not only the data into the list, but server resources, global farm access to list data, and the methods users use to enter data into lists.

Large List Support

SharePoint has traditionally been able to support large lists; however, the challenge has always been to make the data in large lists available for retrieval and display in a timely and efficient manner. Although a user can create millions of items in a SharePoint list, the query operation slows as the size of the list grows. A new addition to SharePoint 2010 is large list support throttling. Throttling allows farm administrators to set manageable limits on the number of items queried from a SharePoint 2010 list. Using throttling, SharePoint 2010 encourages developers and farm administrators to control large list queries to improve the performance of a SharePoint farm.

Throttling thresholds are set on site collections. By default, standard users are throttled at 5000 items returned from a list, with a warning threshold at 3000 items. (See Table 1-6 for a list of items that would be throttled.) These values can be changed using Windows PowerShell commands. The throttling mechanic works as follows: If a user is pulling back a list with 4999 items, the query returns all of the data without error; however, if the user or query tries to retrieve 5001 items, an expensive query exception will be returned. The following parameters are set by default.

- Warning for user throttling at 3000 items
- Standard user throttling at 5000 items
- Super user throttling at 20,000 items

> **NOTE** Developers can request a throttle override from the Object Model by using *SPQuery.RequestThrottleOverride* and *SPSiteDataQuery.RequestThrottleOverride*, which will effectively cause SharePoint to ignore the throttling behavior.

TABLE 1-6 Items Throttled for a Standard User with Large List Support Throttling

NUMBER OF ITEMS RETURNED	QUERY RUN IN NORMAL LIST AS STANDARD USER
<5000 list items	Code and/or view query will run and return the required result.
>3000 list items	No exception is thrown and the code will run properly.
>5000 list items	An expensive query exception is thrown.
>5000 list items during time window OK for large queries	Query threshold is not applied, query runs even if the threshold has been exceeded.
Object Model Override = true and RequestThrottleOverride is overridden	Exception is thrown if list is throttled, and this property cannot be overridden by a normal user.

Using Central Administration, a farm administrator can configure a time frame in which these expensive queries can and cannot be run. Therefore, if a user wants to run a query with 5001 items at 5:30 P.M. and the time-frame limitation is between 8:00 A.M. and 5:00 P.M., the query would succeed. To see if a list is being throttled or within warning limits, go to List Settings and look at the bar that gives the number of items in the view/list.

To find out the current throttling limits, follow these steps.

1. Open a browser and go to the SharePoint Central Administration website.

2. Under Application Management, select Manage Web Application.

3. Select the Web application that you want to modify or view.

4. Click General Settings in the Ribbon and select Resource Throttling. Figure 1-33 shows the Central Administration Resource Throttling command on the General Settings menu.

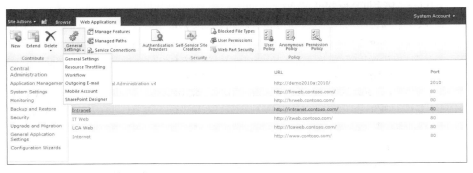

FIGURE 1-33 Resource Throttling

Figure 1-34, which displays list resource throttling parameters, is the first of several pages of information you will see with resource throttling settings. A farm administrator should be familiar with these settings before any changes are made to a SharePoint site. Also, it's important to test all new settings in a development environment before applying configuration changes in production.

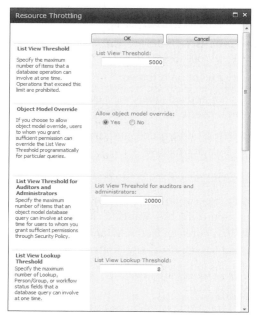

FIGURE 1-34 List Resource Throttling parameters

An Upgrade Warning: Setting Throttle Limits

When upgrading from SharePoint Server 2007 to SharePoint 2010, any list that contains a default view of more than the throttled limit (default: 5000) will not be immediately available until a new default view is created.

A farm administrator should become familiar with the Windows PowerShell commands, which will display and set the throttling limits. These commands are listed in Table 1-7, with examples.

TABLE 1-7 Windows PowerShell Commands for Displaying and Setting Throttling Limits

COMMAND DESCRIPTION	EXAMPLE COMMAND
Get max threshold values for Web application	$sitecol = Get-SPSite http://mysharepointserver:5000 $sitecol.WebApplication.MaxItemsPerThrottledOperationWarningLevel $sitecol.WebApplication.MaxItemsPerThrottledOperation $sitecol.WebApplication.MaxItemsPerThrottledOperationOverride $sitecol.WebApplication.AllowOMCodeOverrideThrottleSettings

COMMAND DESCRIPTION	EXAMPLE COMMAND
Get max threshold values for Web application— example usage	$sitecol = Get-SPSite http://mysharepointserver:5000 $sitecol.WebApplication.MaxItemsPerThrottledOperationWarningLevel = 2000 (set throttle warning to 2000 items – default 3000) $sitecol.WebApplication.MaxItemsPerThrottledOperation = 4000 (set throttle to 4000 – default 5000)
	$sitecol.WebApplication.MaxItemsPerThrottledOperationOverride = 30000 (set super user throttle to 30000 – default 20000) $sitecol.WebApplication.AllowOMCodeOverrideThrottleSettings = False (set code override for throttling to False – default True)
	Note: Values in this section are for example purposes and are not recommendations
Find large list throttle setting	$siteCollection.RootWeb.Lists["LargeListName"] (look for IsThrottled in results)

In summary, SharePoint 2010 large list support will support lists with

- Up to 50 million items—during read operations
- Configuration options for administrators per Web applications
- Privileged operational override support for users with site collection or list administration privileges
- Default query restrictions
- Throttling when a list reaches a predefined of items

Site Columns

In traditional database application development, calls are often necessary that refer to a set of table data multiple times during the application execution. By having a single authoritative source for data, applications can ensure consistency across all application modules. This is often true in SharePoint as well—to keep consistency across the SharePoint farm, a cross-site lookup column is required in some cases. Cross-site lookups cannot be done using a standard lookup column, however, so a site column should be used instead.

Site columns are defined at the site collection level and are accessible to all sites under the site collection. A few common examples of standard SharePoint site columns are FTP Site and Gender. The FTP Site column is a URL field in which a URL and description can be entered; a Gender column provides the user a choice of Male or Female. In both cases, there is no ambiguity about what the user will need to type across all SharePoint sites. The primary advantage of using a site column is its ability to provide a consistent user response for the column.

To link to an existing site column, complete the following steps.

1. Click List under the List Tools tab and then select List Settings.
2. Click Add From Existing Site Columns.
3. Select the site group All Groups.
4. Select the FTP Site column from Available Site Columns.
5. Click Add and then click OK.

Creating a Site Column

To create a new site column in SharePoint 2010 from the root of the site collection, complete the following steps.

1. Click Site Actions in the Ribbon and select Site Settings.
2. Click Site Columns under Galleries.
3. Click Create. You will see a new page that you use to create the column, setting the title, settings, and validation as necessary. When you have finished selecting the settings for the new site column, click OK.

> **NOTE**   If, as the site administrator, you plan on creating many new columns, you should consider creating a new Site Column Group.

Modifying a Site Column

To modify an existing site column in SharePoint 2010 from the root of the site collection, complete the following steps.

1. Click Site Actions in the Ribbon.
2. Click Site Columns under Galleries.
3. Click the site column you want to modify.

> **IMPORTANT**   As with lists, only certain changes to the list type are supported, and content might be lost when converting from one type to another, such as going from a multiple lines of text type to a single line of text.

4. Change or edit the group if needed.
5. Change settings as needed.
6. Set the Update All Columns Based Upon This Site Column option to Yes to update all of the site columns. This operation can take a while to run, and any customizations to child list settings might be lost.
7. Click OK.

Editing List Input Forms

As with most applications, managers often request at least one feature that generally requires costly customization. A software platform can provide a thousand features, but one department's managers will focus on a customization they think they must have but which is either not available or is cost prohibitive to provide.

Prior to SharePoint 2010, the process of customizing list input forms was a grueling, cumbersome task and required SharePoint Designer or a custom Web Part. SharePoint 2010 makes editing the input forms easier by utilizing the InfoPath platform. The Ribbon for the list includes a section called Customize List, shown in Figure 1-35.

FIGURE 1-35 List Ribbon

There are four icons in this section, which assist the content or developer in modifying the input forms. Table 1-8 lists these icons with descriptions of each.

TABLE 1-8 Icons for Modifying Input Forms

ICON	DESCRIPTION
Customize Form	The Customize Form icon allows a content administrator to use Microsoft InfoPath 2010 to create custom forms to add or edit items in the list.
	The Modify Form Web Parts icon allows a user to edit the default form Web Part and Web page using a Web browser interface.
	The Modify Form In SharePoint Designer icon quickly opens the form in SharePoint Designer 2010. You use SharePoint Designer to edit list settings, add or remove columns, and create new views, forms, workflows, and custom actions.
	The Create Quick Step icon allows you to create a custom Ribbon button to perform a custom action on a list. Creating a Quick Step will add a button to the Quick Steps group on the Items tab.

Modify Form Web Parts

You can make traditional Web Part changes to a new list form or edit the form within the Web browser. A content administrator can click the Modify Form Web Parts icon and select the appropriate form to edit. In the following example, the steps show you how to edit a new form and rearrange the Web Parts on the screen.

1. Click the Modify Form Web Parts icon and select Default New Form.

2. The Web Part property page opens, as shown in Figure 1-36, and you can use its options to make changes to the appearance, layout, and other advanced features. Under Advanced Features, a new option exists called Show Toolbar With Ribbon.

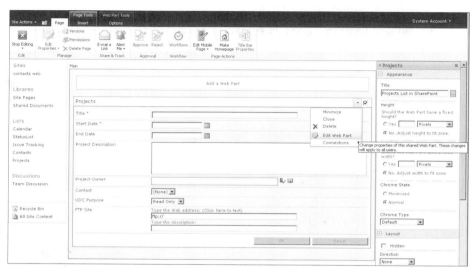

FIGURE 1-36 The Edit Web Parts property page

3. When you are finished making changes to the Web Part, click OK.

4. In the Ribbon, click Stop Editing.

You follow the same process to modify the Edit Page Web Part and the Default Display Web Part. For more information about managing Web Parts, see Chapter 19, "Web Parts and Their Functionality in SharePoint 2010."

Modify Form Using InfoPath 2010

Microsoft InfoPath 2010 can now be used to modify the list forms. Within a few minutes a new, customized form is created, which allows form content to be grouped logically depending on form requirements. In SharePoint Server 2007, InfoPath forms were cumbersome to create and maintain; however, with SharePoint 2010, modifying the look and feel of a form to comply with user requirements is easy. For example, generally when a start and end date is required on a form, it is easier for the user to fill out the form when the two date columns are side by side. The following process explains the steps you would use to move the End Date next to the Start Date in a list form.

1. Go to the SharePoint list and click the Customize Form button in the Ribbon.

2. Microsoft InfoPath 2010 will open to allow edits to the new form. Figure 1-37 shows a default list edit form. In the right pane you see the fields available to place on the list. Making edits in the form is as easy as creating a new row or column and dragging fields to the form with the mouse.

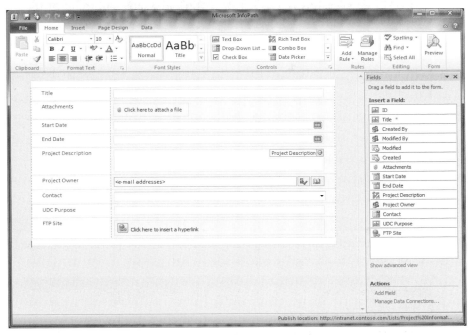

FIGURE 1-37 The default list edit form in InfoPath 2010

3. Make any additional changes to the page design by clicking the Page Design tab, as shown in Figure 1-38. You can modify the colors, fonts, and styles used in the page design as needed or required, similar to how you modify a spreadsheet in Excel.

4. When you have completed the changes you want to make, you should save the template and verify it for validity. To verify, click the File tab at the top of the page to open the Form Information panel. Click the Design Checker icon as shown in Figure 1-39 to verify the form contents and layout. After you run the Design Checker, control is returned to the form view (shown in Figure 1-37) and any errors are listed in the right pane. Fix the errors identified by the Design Checker, if there are any, and then return to the File tab to save and publish the form. If you are publishing more than one form type to a list or library, use Save As so the other forms are not overwritten.

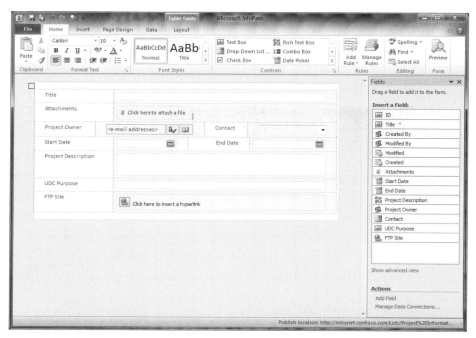

FIGURE 1-38 Changing the page design using the default list edit form in InfoPath 2010

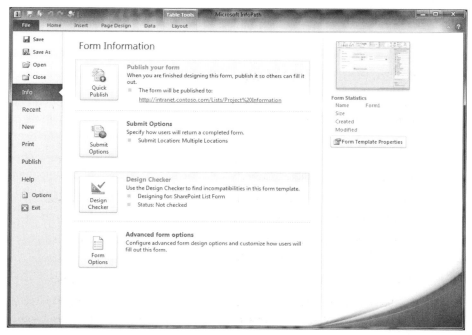

FIGURE 1-39 Design Form Page in InfoPath 2010

5. Publishing the form to SharePoint is as easy as clicking Publish Your Form. The SharePoint site is updated and all references to the Edit Form will now refer to the newly created list template. An example modification to the End Date field is shown in Figure 1-40. Notice that the Start Date and End Date fields are now located in this Project Information - New Item form.

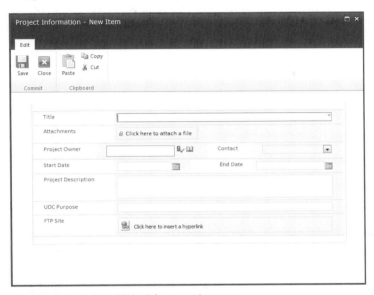

FIGURE 1-40 Newly published form results

State Service Error Message

If you see the error message when you try to publish a modified form, the SharePoint 2010 State Service is not created:

"The form cannot be rendered. This may be due to a misconfiguration of the Microsoft SharePoint Server State Service. For more information, contact your server administrator."

One possible cause for this error could be that the SharePoint 2010 farm was created manually without running the farm Configuration Wizard.

To configure the SharePoint 2010 State Service using Windows PowerShell commands, complete the following steps.

1. Open a browser and go to the SharePoint Central Administration website.

2. On the taskbar, click Start, select Administrative Tools, and then select Windows PowerShell Modules. This will start Windows PowerShell and load all associated SharePoint modules.

continued on the next page

3. In the Windows PowerShell window, create a service application by typing the following command.

```
$serviceApp = New-SPStateServiceApplication -Name "State Service"
```

4. Create a State Service database and associate it with a service application by typing the following command.

```
New-SPStateServiceDatabase -Name "StateServiceDatabase"
-ServiceApplication $serviceApp
```

5. Create a State Service Application Proxy and associate it with the service application by typing the following command.

```
New-SPStateServiceApplicationProxy -Name "State Service"
-ServiceApplication $serviceApp -DefaultProxyGroup
```

This will create the State Service service application, and InfoPath published forms should render properly. If you still see error messages when running custom forms, verify that the Web application is associated with the State Service service application.

Modify Form Using SharePoint Designer 2010

SharePoint Designer 2010 enables power users and developers to customize solutions—with little or no coding—that work for a variety of common scenarios ranging from collaborative sites and Web publishing to line-of-business integration, business intelligence, and human workflows. In this latest release, SharePoint Designer 2010 has been greatly enhanced and it is important to understand the changes in the new version. Features such as Contributor Settings, Database Interface Wizards, and Site Publish, Backup, and Restore no longer are available in SharePoint Designer 2010. For a full list of features that have been removed, refer to *http://technet.microsoft.com/en-us/library/cc179083.aspx*. Additionally, SharePoint Designer 2010 offers new features such as the ability to create Web Part Pages, master pages, lists, and workflows; setting permissions for individual users; and saving and deleting site templates, to name just a few.

In addition to the changes mentioned, you can extend the SharePoint 2010 Ribbon using standard development APIs to fulfill application and corporate requirements using SharePoint Designer 2010 or Microsoft Visual Studio 2010. You can customize both Ribbons and drop-down lists to display site lists, available Web Parts, workflows, or other information as needed.

As in other Microsoft Office 2010 products, Quick Steps can be created to execute a mini-workflow process. To create a Quick Step in the Ribbon that will update the full name of a contact if one hasn't been entered, complete the following steps.

1. Create a new contact list or open an existing contact list and click List under List Tools in the Ribbon.

2. In the Customize List section of the Ribbon, you will see icons that reflect the different actions available to customize the form. Refer to Table 1-7 for a description of the icons and their functions. To create a Quick Step, click the New Quick Step icon.

3. SharePoint Designer 2010 will automatically open and prompt you for the SharePoint site credentials. Enter an appropriate login and password.

4. SharePoint Designer will then ask if you want to start a new SharePoint workflow or an existing workflow on the Add A Button page, as shown in Figure 1-41.

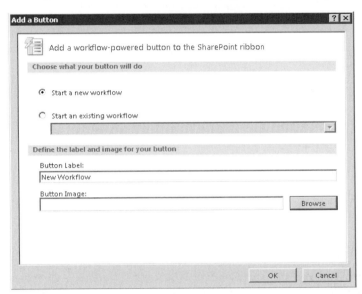

FIGURE 1-41 Using SharePoint Designer 2010 to add a new SharePoint workflow

5. Select the option to Start A New Workflow.

6. In the Button Label text box, type a label for the button you want to create.

7. Choose an image from the site. For example, you could use the Recycle Bin image at /_layouts/images/fgimg.png. You can click the Browse button to look for other images or type a path to the image you want to use directly in the Button Image text box.

> **NOTE** Be sure to enter the image URL as a reference to the SharePoint site, such as /images/imagefilename.png; do not hard code the URL prefix by using a URL such as *http://www.sharepointsite.com/images/imagefilename.png*. This will ensure that all users will have access to the image, no matter the site collection or URL by which the page is called.

8. Click OK.

9. The new Button Design page displays. The controls on this page will be similar to Microsoft Visual Studio Workflow. Using the workflow example as a guide, shown in Figure 1-42, create the workflow steps using the Condition, Action, and Step tabs in the Ribbon. This workflow will update the full name of a contact if one hasn't been entered on a list item.

> **MORE INFO** For more information on creating workflows in SharePoint Designer 2010, refer to *http://www.bing.com/videos/watch/video/getting-started-sharepoint-2010-creating-workflows-with-sharepoint-designer/10ts7flgd*.

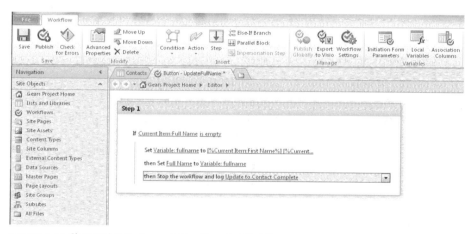

FIGURE 1-42 SharePoint Designer Add actions to Workflow

10. Save and publish the workflow as a new Quick Step. You will see the new Quick Step icon in your list when you click the List Tools – Items Tab. The new Quick Step icon will be located in the Quick Steps section of the Ribbon, as shown in Figure 1-43.

FIGURE 1-43 SharePoint Designer List with new Quick Step

11. To execute the new Quick Step, select the check boxes to the left of the list items you want to update and then click the new Quick Step icon. After the Quick Step has completed, a new field in the list will appear. In Figure 1-43, the new column name is called Button – UpdateFullName.

Microsoft Office Integration

SharePoint 2010 is more closely tied to the Microsoft Office application suite than previous versions. Along with the traditional Office integration features such as editing, check-out, and version control on Office documents, integration has been extended to include retrieving data from SharePoint lists and libraries. Integration to enterprise line-of-business (LOB) data is also available through the SharePoint Business Connectivity Services (BSC). More information on the BSC can be found in Chapter 18, "Aggregating External Data Sources."

SharePoint Workspace 2010

One of the more interesting Office integration components is the Microsoft SharePoint Workspace 2010, which allows you to take SharePoint sites offline but maintain edit capability. SharePoint Workspace 2010 is a more evolved form of the product called Microsoft Groove, which allowed users to synchronize data and files between different systems. Many of the features in the Groove application still remain; however, those features are now adapted to include the SharePoint 2010 framework. SharePoint Workspace 2010 is also included with Microsoft Office Ultimate 2010 and is a must have for any users who are mobile and out of the office on a regular basis.

When SharePoint Workspace 2010 has been installed on the client system, it can begin synchronizing to SharePoint 2010 sites. Depending on the size of the SharePoint sites that need to be synchronized, you should probably recommend to users that they connect their laptop or desktop computer to the corporate local area network (LAN) during the synchronizing process to ensure that all content is initially downloaded successfully. The user's computer must have adequate storage space, of course, to synchronize the SharePoint sites successfully.

The first time you execute the SharePoint Workspace 2010 application, you will need to create an account profile. When you complete the profile, the Launchbar is loaded (refer to Figure 1-45 for an idea of what the Launchbar looks like), and you will then need to attach to the SharePoint 2010 Server by completing the following steps.

1. Click New on the Home tab.

2. Type the SharePoint 2010 server name, such as **http://myservername**.

3. Click OK when asked if you want to synchronize the site.

4. Synchronizing will begin automatically, and when it has completed, you will see a notification page, similar to the one shown in Figure 1-44, that indicates the status of the synchronization process. You might find that there are some sites, lists, or libraries that are not supported yet.

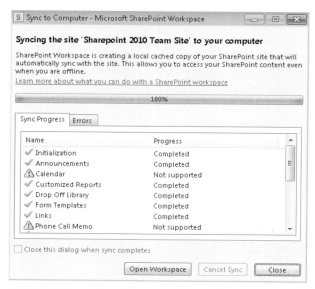

FIGURE 1-44 SharePoint Workspace synchronization notification page

5. At this point, SharePoint Workspace 2010 is now working online and will synchronize a single site at a time. If more than one site needs to be synchronized, the user must return to the initial SharePoint Workspace 2010 launch menu and create another link to a SharePoint site. The SharePoint Workspace Launchbar is shown in Figure 1-45. All sites that have been synchronized will be shown here.

When the site has finished synchronizing, there are a wide variety of actions you can perform on a site from within SharePoint Workspace 2010. For example, you can search items synchronized to the desktop from the Launchbar just as if you were accessing the SharePoint site in a browser. You can also set up alerts to notify a user of changes in the SharePoint site content.

FIGURE 1-45 The SharePoint Workspace Launchbar

To add a site contact, click the Add Contact button in the Ribbon; to delete a contact, highlight the contact in the main panel and press the Delete key on the keyboard.

To open or work on documents in a synchronized site, click the SharePoint site name from the Launchbar. The SharePoint site will open and provide access to the available lists, libraries, and other site content. Figure 1-54 is an example of a SharePoint team site synchronized to SharePoint Workspace 2010.

In Figure 1-46, content is available for the user to access either online or offline. This functionality allows a user to synchronize a SharePoint site to a laptop computer and access documents even when disconnected from the corporate network. Certain list types and pages are available only if the workspace is connected to the SharePoint site, however. These lists and pages are clearly identified in the workspace client. In Figure 1-46, the lists in the Available On Server column are only available when the user is connected to the corporate LAN.

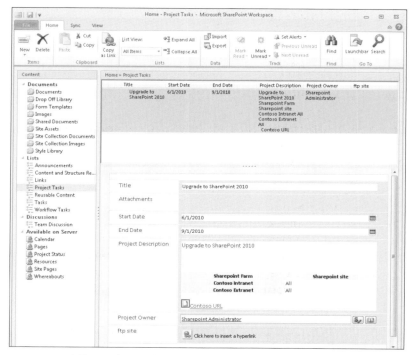

FIGURE 1-46 A SharePoint Workspace 2010 team site

The Project Tasks list in the example in Figure 1-46, however, is available offline and utilizes a customized InfoPath form for data entry. These forms are available offline, so users can enter data and synchronize it back to the server without error. Just as the SharePoint Ribbon changes based on field types, the Workspace client also changes. Some of the Ribbon items, such as workflow and custom Ribbon icons, are not available in the workspace; to use them, a user must connect to SharePoint Workspace 2010 using a Web browser.

In Figure 1-47, the Ribbon shows the actions you can take on a site that is synchronized through SharePoint Workspace 2010.

FIGURE 1-47 The SharePoint Workspace 2010 Ribbon

The Sync tab allows you to synchronize a site manually and provides you with the ability to redefine synchronization settings and check the status of the last synchronization operation. The View tab on the Ribbon is similar to the view settings in a Web browser—you can define and use different views on a list or library. In addition, you can use the View tab to open new workspace windows to view multiple sets of data at the same time, as shown in Figure 1-48.

FIGURE 1-48 SharePoint Workspace 2010 View Ribbon

In general, the new SharePoint Workspace 2010 is a valuable tool that has been added to the SharePoint suite of products to enable users to interact and collaborate when they are out of the office and unable to access a SharePoint site directly.

Microsoft Word 2010

One of the new features in Microsoft Office 2010 is a Share option that allows you to publish a document to a SharePoint site without manually uploading the file first. After you create a document in Microsoft Word 2010, for example, you can click the File tab and then select Share to open the page shown in Figure 1-49. Then click the Save To SharePoint option and select a SharePoint site location, and the document will be uploaded automatically to the SharePoint site.

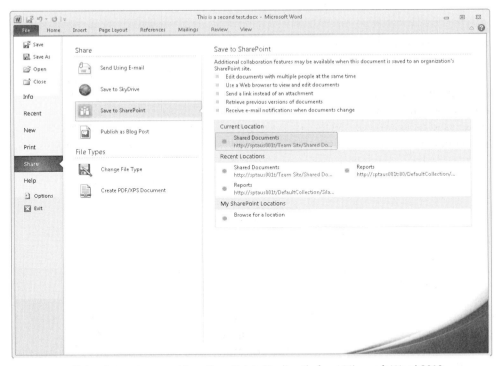

FIGURE 1-49 Uploading a document to a SharePoint site directly from Microsoft Word 2010

Also located under the File tab is the Info option, which displays SharePoint-related information about setting permissions, checking document properties, and version/check-out status. Figure 1-50 shows an example of the information that is displayed.

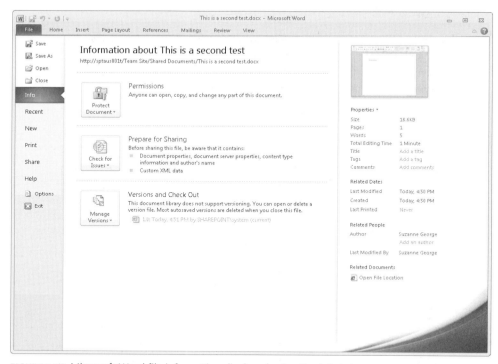

FIGURE 1-50 Microsoft Word file information displayed using the Info tab

Microsoft Word 2010 can also use SharePoint 2010 list data for mail merges and form information. The techniques for handling list data from SharePoint 2010 are similar for all Office products, such as Excel, and provide users with ubiquitous access to SharePoint information.

Support for Other Microsoft Office Products

With the release of SharePoint 2010 and Office 2010, the compatibility between applications is nearly seamless. Items such as the Ribbon allow a user to work, collaborate, and share information with colleagues, clients, and partners seamlessly and without concern for user locale, with only minimal training. Enhancements to products like Microsoft Excel 2010, for example, allow a user to process a very large list of line of business data from a remote system within seconds.

> **MORE INFO**   To see a list of features available in Microsoft Office 2010, go to
> *http://www.microsoft.com/office/2010/en/default.aspx.*

Microsoft Office 2010 and SharePoint 2010 allow users to work anywhere the need arises, collaborate better with SharePoint integration, and get work done faster than ever before.

Additional Information

This chapter has attempted to provide you with the basics of the collaboration and list functionality of SharePoint 2010. If you want to learn more, there are several resources available to administrators that provide in-depth information on how SharePoint 2010 works, including the following websites.

- SharePoint 2010 Technologies Page: *http://sharepoint2010.microsoft.com/Pages /default.aspx*

- System requirements and what's new in Microsoft SharePoint Foundation 2010: *http://technet.microsoft.com/en-us/sharepoint/ee263910.aspx#tab=1*

- System requirements and what's new in Microsoft SharePoint 2010 : *http://technet.microsoft.com/en-us/sharepoint/ee263917.aspx*

- Find a Microsoft partner to assist in a SharePoint Proof of Concept: *https://solutionfinder.microsoft.com*

Summary

SharePoint 2010 takes collaboration to a new level by offering organizations a mature, feature-rich platform to collaborate, manage information, and organize data in a smart, efficient manner. With the user interface and Office integration enhancements, SharePoint 2010 is setting the standard for collaboration systems. The remaining chapters in this book will help guide and advise you in making important administration decisions surrounding SharePoint 2010 to ensure a successful implementation and design for your unique enterprise or business.

In the next chapter, you'll turn your attention to the architecture of SharePoint 2010. Understanding how this product is built is essential for troubleshooting problems that arise, and you will learn about how SharePoint 2010 is built and how its components work together.

## CHAPTER 2

Understanding the Architecture of SharePoint 2010

As the Microsoft SharePoint product evolves, through each major version, the core concepts and design tenets employed by the team creating it have evolved along with it. The keystone that connects the design tenets with what you see in Microsoft SharePoint 2010 is the enterprise architecture.

The enterprise architecture is a plan for SharePoint 2010 that is far larger than any single product version. It consists of a vision for the future growth and development of the product, as well as a strategy for achieving that vision. It is also a long-term roadmap for the product, providing the extended course that the product team will travel over time. Beneath the surface of this product roadmap is the architecture for each release, which includes all of the details about how the product will be organized into logical components and how those components will work together. Although the roadmap directs the team towards a set of product capabilities, the design tenets provide a framework for decision making, and the underlying architecture describes the system in terms of services, components, and logic.

This chapter reviews the way SharePoint 2010 is built and provides a high-level description of its architecture. It explores the product's capabilities and the components that bring them to life. You will explore the building blocks that make up the application and the service components on which those capabilities are built. Finally, you will explore each of the components in detail, as well as learning how the application architecture connects with the system architecture that provides its foundation.

Enterprise Architecture

When the enterprise architecture plan for SharePoint 2010 was being developed, the following core concepts were central to the long-term vision for success. The team wanted a product architecture that would be

- Modular
- Extensible
- Scalable

Modular

The architecture of SharePoint 2010 is highly modular—that is, it is composed of separate parts—which represents a separation of concerns that improve the ability to maintain the product by enforcing logical boundaries between components. Central to a modular architecture is the concept that each modular component has minimal dependency on other components. This allows the larger application to be broken down into smaller component modules that, although they are not dependent on each other, come together to form the larger application.

Another feature of module architecture is the ability to reuse each module when needed as a building block for higher-level application elements. For example, the User Profile Service exists as a composition of various modular components. Each of those components potentially can be reused to create other services as well. Higher-level application components lay on top of the User Profile Service and its components.

Each separate encapsulated service within the system is connected through a set of common rules and standards known as a *provider framework*. This allows the underlying services to be exposed for presentation, management, and deployment processing. These services are the building blocks on top of which the application rendered in the browser becomes available.

Extensible

Extensibility is an architecture and design principal ensuring that an implementation takes future growth into consideration. Planning for future growth within the current architecture can minimize the effects of future changes. Extensibility provides integration capability that can be utilized in the implementation of future change or enhancement.

The architecture of SharePoint 2010 is highly extensible. In fact, many of the underlying components are built with an exposed application programming interface (API). As expected, these interfaces are available to third-party developers through the release of a software development kit (SDK). Furthermore, the product teams developing SharePoint also use this extensibility when developing many of the user-facing features of the product. Many included product features are delivered as SharePoint Features and Feature Elements, which represent extensions to the modular building blocks that form the base architecture of the system.

Scalable

One of the most important aspects of the overall system architecture for SharePoint 2010 is scalability. Microsoft wanted to be sure that the deployment of the software could be tailored to the specific anticipated needs of each individual implementation. SharePoint 2010 provides you with the ability to scale both out and up to meet the specific demands of your implementation. If you need more user interface capacity, you can add more Web front-end servers. If you need additional service capacity, you can add more application servers. If you need additional database capacity, you can add a database server. If you need to be able to handle more file caching or larger upload file sizes, you can add more system resources to existing servers. Whatever your particular needs, SharePoint 2010 allows you to design a topology that meets those needs with almost limitless flexibility.

Logical Architecture Components

The system architecture of SharePoint 2010 allows many of the application tier services to leverage the same underlying common services, such as storage and security. This allows for the uniform management of these services across the enterprise. Likewise, the presentation layer components share compatibility with the application tier services. This ensures that the entire service architecture is grouped logically both from the bottom up and from the top down.

From the bottom up, the architecture is organized into a set of independent services, whereas from the top down, the architecture is organized into a set of applications that use those services. The grouping of services into applications has simplified both the administration and the deployment of SharePoint 2010.

Service Architecture

With SharePoint Server 2007, Microsoft went to great lengths to move toward service-oriented architecture (SOA). Although the spirit of SOA was embodied within the product through the Shared Services Provider (SSP), having a single service application endpoint through which multiple services were exposed led to limitations. For example, most of the underlying interfaces for the SSP were not extensible by third parties, making it impossible to create your own services for use within the architecture. Other limitations, such as the inability to consume services including search and user profiles across the wide area network (WAN), also hampered the concept.

In SharePoint 2010, the service application architecture has been completely reorganized. The SSP concept has been abandoned in favor of a federated type of service application architecture that allows separate services to work together efficiently.

> **NOTE** *Federation* is the standardization of information systems and their means of interconnectivity, allowing user's data in one system to be transferred, and used by, another system.

The service architecture is based on two main components, the service application and the application proxy or connector. The service application is the manifestation of the actual service itself, which is reliant on a service instance running on an application server. The service is self-contained in that it includes both the functionality and the administrative interfaces for managing the service. The service is exposed to other applications using an endpoint that is made available through a service proxy. Each application connects as a client to the proxy, which in turn takes requests from the application and makes requests of the service on behalf of the application.

This architecture is incredibly flexible and extensible, allowing third parties to create service applications for use within the architecture, as well as providing for the consumption of those services across the entire enterprise. For example, this architecture could allow a single User Profile Service application that is consumed by multiple farms in different geographical locations.

Table 2-1 represents the service applications included with SharePoint 2010 by default. Additional service applications are present, but those listed in this table are the only ones that are configurable through the SharePoint Central Administration interface.

TABLE 2-1 SharePoint 2010 Service Applications

SERVICE APPLICATION	EXPLANATION
Access Database Services	Provides server-side processing and rendering of data stored in Microsoft Access databases.
Business Data Connectivity	Provides server-side access to line-of-business application data.
Excel Services	Provides server-side processing and rendering of data stored in Microsoft Excel spreadsheets.
Managed Metadata Service	Provides enterprise taxonomy, managed metadata storage, and content type syndication.
PerformancePoint Service Application	Provides Business Intelligence functionality previously provided as part of Microsoft PerformancePoint Server.
Search Service Application	Provides unified content crawling and indexing as well as federation.
Secure Store Service	Replaces the single sign-on (SSO) feature.
User Profile Service Application	Provides user profiles, user profile synchronization, My Site settings, and social tagging.
Visio Graphics Service	Enables dynamic viewing, refreshing, and sharing of data-driven Microsoft Visio 2010 diagrams.
Web Analytics Service Application	Provides Web analytics and usage analysis.
Word Automation Services	Provides server-side conversion of documents into formats that are supported by the Microsoft Word client application.

Figure 2-1 illustrates the larger logical component and application architecture of SharePoint 2010. In the following sections, you will review each of the logical components presented in the figure, to provide you with more detailed information about how the various service and components fit together to form the SharePoint product.

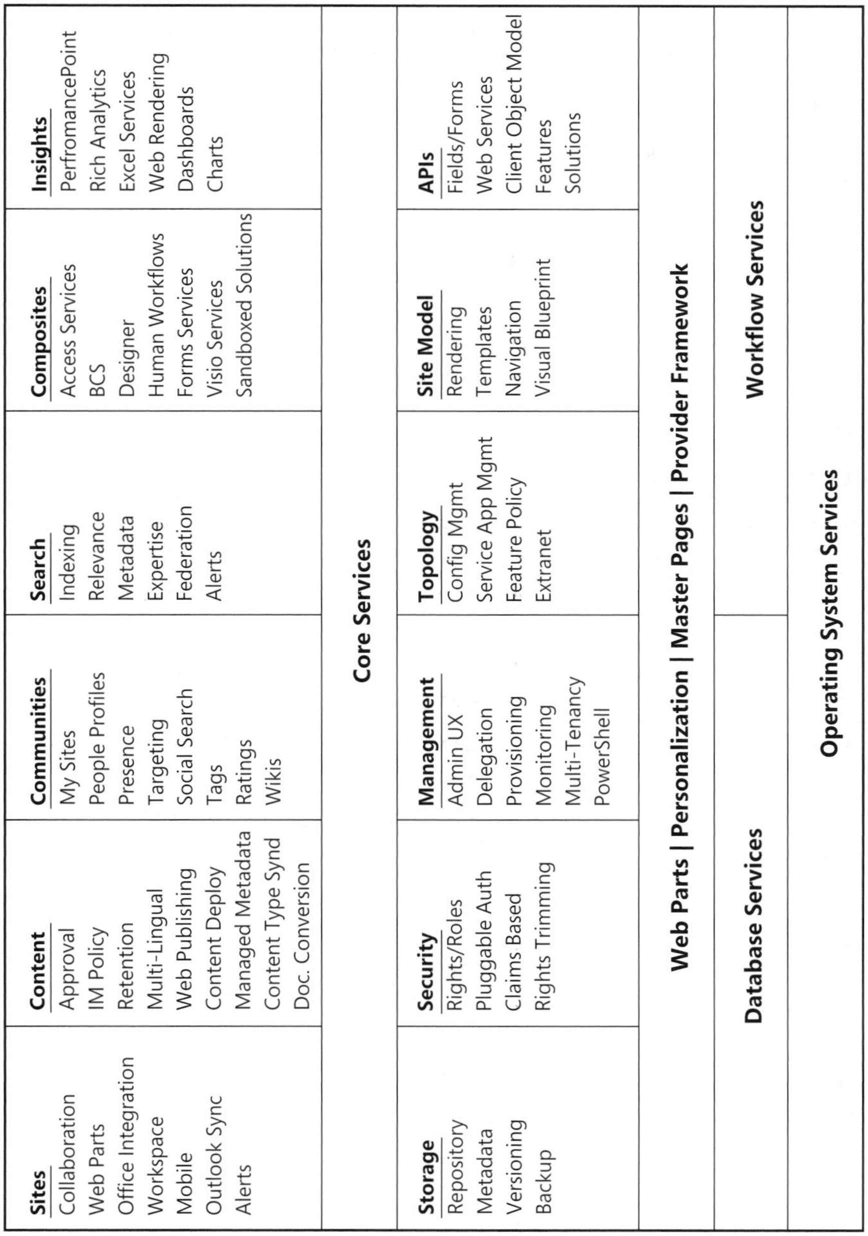

Sites	Content	Communities	Search	Composites	Insights
Collaboration	Approval	My Sites	Indexing	Access Services	PerfromancePoint
Web Parts	IM Policy	People Profiles	Relevance	BCS	Rich Analytics
Office Integration	Retention	Presence	Metadata	Designer	Excel Services
Workspace	Multi-Lingual	Targeting	Expertise	Human Workflows	Web Rendering
Mobile	Web Publishing	Social Search	Federation	Forms Services	Dashboards
Outlook Sync	Content Deploy	Tags	Alerts	Visio Services	Charts
Alerts	Managed Metadata	Ratings		Sandboxed Solutions	
	Content Type Synd	Wikis			
	Doc. Conversion				

Core Services

Storage	Security	Management	Topology	Site Model	APIs
Repository	Rights/Roles	Admin UX	Config Mgmt	Rendering	Fields/Forms
Metadata	Pluggable Auth	Delegation	Service App Mgmt	Templates	Web Services
Versioning	Claims Based	Provisioning	Feature Policy	Navigation	Client Object Model
Backup	Rights Trimming	Monitoring	Extranet	Visual Blueprint	Features
		Multi-Tenancy			Solutions
		PowerShell			

Web Parts | Personalization | Master Pages | Provider Framework   Workflow Services

Database Services   Operating System Services

FIGURE 2-1 The SharePoint 2010 logical architecture

Operating System Services

Windows Server 2008 provides the underlying architecture for the entire product. SharePoint 2010 requires the Windows Server 2008 64-bit edition and will not run on Windows Server 2003 32-bit or 64-bit editions.

The operating system provides access to storage, system level execution rights, and Internet Information Server 7.0 (IIS), on which the SharePoint service application and Web processes run. By separating the underlying operating system's logical architecture and management from the service architecture of SharePoint 2010, the application remains abstracted from the operating system, and therefore largely isolated. This helps separate the management of the operating system from the management of the application, and it follows good architecture practices. It also provides the application architecture more flexibility to run on future version of the operating system.

Database Services

SharePoint 2010 stores both configuration and content in Microsoft SQL Server databases and provides a common storage architecture across the entire system. This removes the incompatibility issues associated with multiple disparate database systems. Although you can enable external storage of binary large objects, this requires additional setup and configuration; the out-of-the-box product uses SQL Server for content storage. SharePoint 2010 can run on Microsoft SQL Server 2008 or Microsoft SQL Server 2005, although SQL Server 2008 is recommended because of new database mirroring and external storage capabilities.

Workflow Services

A hallmark capability of SharePoint 2010 is the workflow engine. Workflow services provide workflow capabilities exposed to end users in the system, as well as the ability for the system to execute tasks needed to facilitate administration of the system. Workflow services also facilitate the automation of the content life cycle for documents, including approval, publishing, and disposition. In SharePoint 2010, workflow services are provided by Windows Workflow Foundation (WF), which is part of the .NET Framework 3.5.

Supporting Services

The supporting services shown in Figure 2-1 include Web Parts, Personalization, Master Pages, and the Provider Framework. These services are provided by the .NET Framework and ASP.NET 3.5. These dependencies provide the underlying process architecture within which most of the SharePoint 2010 application services run.

ASP.NET 3.5

ASP.NET 3.5 is a Web application development framework that was first introduced by Microsoft in 2002. It allows developers to build highly dynamic websites, applications, and services. SharePoint 2010 has been built on top of the ASP.NET 3.5 Framework, and consequently uses the Framework as a provider of many core functionalities provided in the product. Rather than create a custom rendering engine, the team at Microsoft wanted to ensure that the page rendering and extensibility framework of ASP.NET 3.5 was employed within SharePoint 2010 both to enhance performance and as a way to provide third-party developers with a well-defined technology platform for integration and extensibility.

In addition to providing a native page rendering engine, which renders pages on behalf of SharePoint 2010, ASP.NET 3.5 provides code execution security features such as the Safe Mode Parser and Safe Controls List. The Safe Mode Parser ensures that only code that is authorized for execution will be run on the server side. This ensures that inline code included in content pages uploaded to a site will not be executed. Administrators can control the compilation of pages within the Web.config file and specify the scope through which application pages can be rendered. The Safe Controls List provides administrators the ability to specify which controls are safe for execution on the server. This is done by using the bin directory on the server for a given Web application.

Web Parts

The Web Part Framework used within SharePoint 2010 is inherited from ASP.NET 3.5. This provides additional flexibility for developers as well as a standard interface for the rendering of Web Parts within the system. Web Parts are modular, reusable, application server controls that can be added by end users at run time using the browser. Web Parts allow for end users to control the content, appearance, and behavior of the page. Web Parts can be dropped into a well-defined Web Part zone, which is a basically a designated place on the page within which Web Parts can be arranged and used. In specific circumstances, Web Parts also can be used within content areas on publishing pages. This capability is new in SharePoint 2010.

A Web Part consists of an assembly control that is installed on the server side and a Web Part Descriptor file. The assembly must be marked as a safe control for execution and must be stored either in the Global Assembly Cache (GAC) or in the Web application's bin directory. The assembly provides all of the functionality of the Web Part, such as the placement of content configured for a Web Part instance and what to do with the configuration settings specified. The Web Part Descriptor file is an XML file that provides the capability to export and reuse the configuration settings and content stored within a Web Part instance. Each Web Part used on a page is the application of the stored descriptor file being laid over the server-side assembly. Users cannot upload Web Parts directly to the server but can apply exported descriptor files through import to instantiate a new instance of a Web Part already installed on the server.

Personalization

SharePoint 2010 provides a rich set of features and functionalities for personalization. Users can personalize Web Part Pages and list views so that they see their personalized view of the content stored in a way that meets their own needs. The content is shown through what is called a *personal view* of the content, as opposed to the shared view that is available to other users. Administrators can specify if users should be allowed to create personal views of content within a given Web application, site collection, site, or list.

SharePoint 2010 adds new social features that enrich the personalized experience for end users, making it easier to establish their own personal identity with the organization as well as to connect with others. Additionally, users can target content to specific groups or users with audience targeting, making that content appear only to those users when viewed from the browser.

IMPORTANT Audience targeting is not meant to be used as a security measure. The content that is targeted is still present in the content page or Web Part Page, so it will be viewable to users who have access to those pages in edit mode.

Master Pages

Master pages are also derived from ASP.NET 3.5. Master pages provide a structured content presentation framework for all pages within a given site or site collection. Designers can define specific content areas within a master page for used by page authors. After they are defined, master pages are used in conjunction with layout pages. Layout pages provide an even more detailed definition of how content may be rendered on a page. Only the content areas defined on a master page can be used within a layout page at design time. Only the content areas and/or elements (such as Web Part zones) specified within the layout page can be used by the page author when creating or modifying the page.

Together master pages and layout pages provide a uniform way for designer to present a consistent look and feel through a site, maintaining that experience over time. Master pages and layout pages are stored at the root of each site collection. Publishing sites provide additional flexibility and functionality in both master pages and layout pages.

To learn more about publishing sites and their presentation elements, see Chapter 16, "Administering Web Content Management and Publishing."

Provider Framework

A provider framework is a set of rules and guidelines for communication between otherwise isolated system elements. Services are offered by providers using these rules and standards.

SharePoint 2010 uses services provided by the operation system, such as storage and security. SharePoint 2010 also uses services provided by IIS 7.0 and ASP.NET 3.5. You have seen how these services lay over one another to provide the set of unified services needed by

SharePoint 2010. But how does SharePoint consume these services, and how does IIS get what it needs from the operating system? Because these services are provided through a framework, they can leverage the well-defined standards and guidelines for communication. This makes it possible to integrate additional services and elements at a later time that can also leverage underlying services and provide services to application level components.

The .NET Framework provides the set of rules and guidelines used by SharePoint 2010 for communications between services and application elements. Based on a common language runtime (CLR), the .NET Framework provides a flexible development environment for creating new application components and allowing them to interface with other dependent services or objects. Combined with its enforcement of code security and trust, managed code, and runtime complication of code for different processor architectures, the .NET Framework offers a solid set of standards that can be used by developers and vendors alike for the creation of interoperable components that will fit into an integrated provider framework.

Core Services

Core services are services that are needed for SharePoint 2010 to function. The following sections provide additional detail about each of these services.

Storage

In SharePoint 2010, storage as a core service primarily involves the storage of information, with a secondary focus on the storage of the data that constitutes that information within the storage providers. Although information may be stored in various back-end systems, such as Microsoft SQL Server or Remote BLOB Storage (RBS), consider how the information is arranged within the application and made available for users. How is a document stored within the system? Where does it go? How is it tracked over time and made useful? How is it backed up and protected from loss? The main aspects of storage as a core service within SharePoint 2010 are

- Repository
- Metadata
- Versioning
- Backup

REPOSITORY

SharePoint 2010 presents an information architecture (IA) that allows for the storage of information at various levels. Two primary services provide for the storage of content within SharePoint 2010.

- Administration service
- Content service

The administration service is the service under which SharePoint Central Administration runs. The information stored by this service is mostly configuration information; however, other information such as diagnostic logging and health monitoring information are also stored by this service. Administrators access this service through SharePoint Central Administration and Stsadm.exe. The management of both the farm configuration database and the admin content database are performed primarily through this service.

The content service is the service under which user content is stored. When a new site collection, site, list, library, list item, or document is created, it is stored using the content service. The information within the content service is stored in a series of content databases. These databases are the primary storage unit for all content repositories in SharePoint 2010. The content service can run as one or many application pools. You can find more information about this process in the section titled "Application Pools" later in this chapter.

When implementing a SharePoint site, the site collection administrators and content owners can decide how to best arrange the repositories for information storage within the site. They can create a structure of sites, libraries, and folders for storing information within the system. After this structure of repositories is in place, list items and documents can be stored. When a user stores a document into the system, it is processed by the storage service provider and placed in the content database. In the case of RBS, the binary data may go to a file system, but with or without RBS, the item information, its metadata, and all associated system details are stored in the content database.

METADATA

Think of metadata as information about information. Metadata allows users to store additional information about an item stored within the system. This information could be used to classify data or simply add helpful details about the item. The careful application of metadata within a well-considered information architecture can result in increased information value that is generated because the item being stored is not very self-descriptive. Metadata allows users to describe the item in more detail, which greatly affects the value of the information value and the ability to search it.

In SharePoint 2010, the concept of metadata has been significantly expanded through the addition of the Managed Metadata Service and the associated field types. The Managed Metadata Service allows enterprise metadata structures to be defined and consumed from within multiple site collections. This means that metadata can be managed both inside and outside the site collection boundary, something not possible in prior versions.

For more information about the Managed Metadata Service, see Chapter 15, "Administering Enterprise Content Management."

VERSIONING

Versioning lets users track the storage history of an item or document. When enabled, versioning stores an additional referenced item in the storage system with every save operation. These items are linked together and presented as a single item to users. When users view the version history of an item or document, they can see what changes have occurred over time, when the changes were made, and who made them. A user can also revert a document to a prior version.

When used in conjunction with document check-in and check-out, versioning provides a robust way for multiple users to collaborate on a single document while preserving changes and avoiding save conflicts. Versioning can be configured to save only major versions, or it can be set to save both major and minor versions. When only major versions are stored, each saved copy of a document is available to all users with reader rights. When both major and minor versions are used, each save results in either a minor version or a major (published) version, depending on the selection option chosen at the time of the save.

While a document is in a minor version state (not published as a major version), it is considered a draft item; consequently, it can be viewed only by users with draft items visibility. When it is checked out, the document can be edited only by the user who checked it out. This ensures that no other user can make changes to the document while it is being edited by the user who checked it out.

Improvements included with Microsoft Word 2010 provide new capabilities to accommodate multiple users working together on a document simultaneously. Lists in SharePoint 2010 include new features that make it easier for list administrators to manage documents that are checked out to other users.

BACKUP

The information stored within SharePoint 2010 is stored in various places and brought together by the application for presentation to the user. SharePoint 2010 includes a robust set of options for backing up, restoring, and protecting this information from accidental deletion. SharePoint 2010 provides three primary facilities for keeping your information safe from loss.

- Farm backup
- Granular backup
- Recycle Bin

Farm backup provides a way for you to simply back up everything in the farm. This includes the farm configuration database, content databases, indexes, and configured Web applications. This provides an easy, integrated way to protect all of the information in the farm. Figure 2-2 shows a partial view of the components you can select when configuring a farm backup. You can schedule and monitor backup jobs, and you also can choose the number of process threads to use while performing backup and restore operations, as well specify a network file share for backup storage.

Select component to back up

Select the top-level component to back up. You can also click the name of a Web application to browse its contents.

Select	Component	Type	Description
☐	⊟ Farm	Farm	Content and configuration data for the entire server farm.
	SharePoint_Config	Configuration Database	Configuration data for the entire server farm.
☐	⊟ InfoPath Forms Services	Server Settings and Content	Administrator-approved content and settings for the server farm.
☐	Settings	Settings	Settings
☐	Data Connections	Data Connections	Administrator-approved data connection files.
☐	Form Templates	Form Templates	Administrator-approved form templates.
☐	⊞ Exempt User Agents	Exempt User Agents	The collection of user agents that receive InfoPath forms instead of Web pages.
☐	⊟ SharePoint Server State Service	State Service	Service for storage of temporary state information used by various SharePoint Server features.
	⊞ State Service	State Service Application	
☐	⊟ Microsoft SharePoint Foundation Web Application	Microsoft SharePoint Foundation Web Application	Collection of Web Applications
☐	⊟ SharePoint - 80	Web Application	Content and configuration data for this Web application.
☐	WSS_Content	Content Database	Content for the Web Application.
	[Timer Jobs Group]	Backup Group	Collection of components grouped together for backup and restore.
	⊟ WSS_Administration	Central Administration	Collection of Web Applications
	⊞ SharePoint Central Administration v4	Web Application	Content and configuration data for this Web application.

FIGURE 2-2 An example of the selection of components available when configuring a farm backup

Granular backup is new in SharePoint 2010, and it allows you to back up and restore information all the way down to the list level. You select a specific site collection to back up and have that backup saved to a network location. You can also export a site or list for import at a later time or in a different place. You can restore a site from unattached content databases, and you can monitor the progress of granular backup jobs and operations.

The Recycle Bin was introduced in SharePoint Server 2007 because users often delete information from lists and libraries only to realize later that they needed the information after all. The SharePoint Recycle Bin has two stages: The site level Recycle Bin is available to users of the site, and the site collection Recycle Bin is available only to site collection administrators. When users delete content from a list or library, the content is retained in the site level Recycle Bin for a number of days—the amount of time it is held is defined by the farm administrator. If a user decides he deleted the information by accident, he can restore that information by selecting it from the site Recycle Bin to restore it. Both lists and items can be restored from the site level Recycle Bin.

After the specified number of days for retention in the site level Recycle Bin pass, or if that content is deleted from the site level Recycle Bin by the user, the content is then stored in the site collection level Recycle Bin. The site collection level Recycle Bin is available only to site collection administrators, and it is limited to a percent of the live site quota for second-stage deleted items, as specified by the farm administrator. The two Recycle Bins provide a level of protection from accidental deletion of information by end users and thereby reduce the number of administrative backups that need to be performed for this purpose.

Security

Security services within SharePoint 2010 are multifaceted and full featured. These security services are explained in the following sections.

- Rights and roles
- Rights trimming
- Pluggable authentication
- Claims-based authentication

RIGHTS AND ROLES

Information access within SharePoint 2010 sites and lists is permitted through the application of rights and roles on either individual users or groups. To gain access to information within the system, an individual user or group must be added to a specific resource, such as a site, list, library, list item, or document. When adding the user or group, the administrator must select either individual rights for assignment or a role.

- Rights refer to individual permissions such as adding new content, viewing content, and removing or deleting content. Each of these operations would be associated with a specific right or permission within the system.

- Roles, or permissions levels, provide an array of specified rights that have been grouped together as a level. When granting permissions to a resource within the system, users can be added to an existing group or granted permissions directly through a permission level.

Additionally, groups may be associated with one or more permissions levels, thereby granting their members permissions to perform specific activities within the system. Groups, rights, and roles (permissions levels) provide a very granular way to control who can access specific resources and what they can do with those resources.

The application of security either can be inherited from the parent object/resource (this is called *security inheritance*) or defined individually for a specific object/resource. SharePoint 2010 includes new features that make it easier for site or list administrators to monitor and manage information within a container (site or list) that is individually secured.

RIGHTS TRIMMING

Rights trimming is based on the concept that users should only be able to see information they have access to. Because information access at the site collection level and below is only granted and never denied, rights trimming ensures that users are not able to see information for which they have not been granted access. This reduces or eliminates the occurrence of access denied errors and protects information from being disclosed simply by making the existence of such information known or by allowing unauthorized users to view its associated metadata.

PLUGGABLE AUTHENTICATION

With a pluggable authentication architecture, you can grant access to information within SharePoint 2010 through any authentication service. Whereas the default authentication provider for SharePoint 2010 is Windows Authentication, pluggable authentication allows you to use other single sign-on (SSO) providers that are already implemented within your organization as well as forms-based authentication or even your own custom provider.

CLAIMS-BASED AUTHENTICATION

Claims-based authentication is centered on the concept that applications can be identity aware. Claims-based authentication supports existing identity infrastructures such as Active Directory, Lightweight Directory Access Protocol (LDAP), Structured Query Language (SQL), Federation Gateways, or WebSSO. Claims-based authentication enables automatic, secure identity delegations in addition to providing a consistent API to develop SharePoint solutions. Claims-based authentication takes pluggable authentication to the next level—it allows individual claims about user attribute information to be validated and compared when providing access to specific information. It also extends authentication mechanisms to other systems and to Office client applications.

Management

SharePoint 2010 provides a variety of avenues for managing the system's configuration options and settings. The administration service is the primary gateway for interacting with the configuration database. Collectively, the management services in SharePoint 2010 provide ubiquitous access to settings and configuration using either the administrative user interface or Windows PowerShell 2.0. In the following sections, you will learn about the various elements of the management service in detail, including

- Administrative user experience
- Delegation
- Provisioning
- Monitoring
- Multi-tenancy
- Windows PowerShell

ADMINISTRATIVE USER EXPERIENCE

The administrative user experience in SharePoint 2010 has been significantly simplified in comparison to prior versions. The idea behind these changes is that systems administrators need access to more settings with less clutter. SharePoint Central Administration provides access to many of the settings and configuration areas need to set up and maintain the farm and Web applications. Table 2-2 lists the areas available within SharePoint Central Administration and includes a summary of the settings available within each.

TABLE 2-2 SharePoint Central Administration Areas

AREA	EXPLANATION
Application Management	Manage Web applications, content databases, service applications, and site collections
System Settings	Manage servers, services, farm features, alternate access mappings, and e-mail and text messaging options.
Monitoring	Review health problems and solutions, check timer job status, and view Web analytics reports.
Backup and Restore	Perform a farm backup, a site collection backup, or manage and monitor backup jobs.
Security	Manage the farm administrators group, service accounts, Web application policy, and information management policy.
Upgrade and Migration	Convert farm license type, enable enterprise features, enable features on existing sites, and check product, patch, upgrade, and database status.
General Application Settings	Manage external service connections, InfoPath form services, site directory, SharePoint Designer settings, search, and content deployment.
Configuration Wizards	Access configuration wizards such as the Farm Configuration Wizard.

DELEGATION

Delegated administrators are provided with contribute permissions to SharePoint Central Administration. The concept behind delegated administrators is that specific individuals will have access to a streamlined, trimmed-down version of Central Administration.

PROVISIONING

SharePoint 2010 includes the ability to provision new site collections, sites, lists, and pages automatically based on predefined templates. This allows for the consistent creation of new elements within the system. The definition of each underlying element is stored either on the file system, within the content database, or a combination of the two. For example, the base document library template is included on the system disk as part of the "14 hive," whereas a user-created library template will be based on that underlying definition but will be stored in the site templates gallery. When a new library is created based on the end user template, the underlying file system–based definition is created, and the overlay of the settings and content stored within the end user template is applied.

Although new site collections can be created using the SharePoint Central Administration website, SharePoint 2010 also allows users to self-provision new site collections.

MONITORING

SharePoint 2010 includes new monitoring capabilities for reviewing problems and solutions. A health analyzer feature lets you set defined rules that can be checked at specified intervals; you can even select to have problems repaired automatically. Additionally, monitoring provides the ability to manage and maintain time service jobs and definitions. Web analytics provide usage information for sites and content. Information management policy usage reports include details on the application of policy, and audit reports provide information on user access to information. Finally, diagnostic logging gives administrators the ability to collect information about warnings and errors that have occurred during process execution.

MULTI-TENANCY

SharePoint 2010 includes new capabilities for providing hosting services and delegated administrative access for customers. These features are expressed in the form of multi-tenancy within SharePoint 2010. Multi-tenancy is centered on the concept of the subscriber—the customer or tenant who owns or manages the site collections in the tenancy. Multi-tenancy also allows for data partitioned service applications to be associated with a subscriber. This lets multiple tenants share a single instance of a service application while keeping their data separate and secure.

Tenant administrators can manage the service application as though they were the only tenant using it, while other tenants do the same. Feature packs provide a way to group a set of features together and assign them to a subscriber. This ensures that the subscriber can use only those features that have been assigned. Feature packs also allow you to create different packaged offerings that can be made available to subscribers.

WINDOWS POWERSHELL

SharePoint 2010 includes the new SharePoint 2010 Management Shell, an enhanced Windows PowerShell prompt with access to more than 500 cmdlets that you can use to manage almost every aspect of your SharePoint 2010 implementation. By making the administrative interfaces available through Windows PowerShell, SharePoint 2010 becomes easier to implement and maintain through the use of scripts, a favorite tool among administrators.

Topology

The topology services provide administrators with the ability to manage SharePoint 2010 server farms, servers, and the overall physical deployment. There are many ways to arrange the service architecture and underlying hardware infrastructure to accomplish your implementation design goals. The topology services provide you with the flexibility to configure and reconfigure your servers and services without disturbing the underlying logical software architecture. SharePoint Central Administration includes settings pages that allow administrators to view and manage the list of servers that are members of the farm, as well as determine which services are running on each server. Although all of the services are installed on each

Web application server, only the appropriate services you need to fulfill a given server's role in the defined topology should be running.

Topology services allow for the seamless upgrade of software components on servers in the farm and also let you scale up or out as needed though the adjustment of server services or the addition of new servers to the farm. You can also configure multiple servers in each role to provide redundancy and fault tolerance, thereby allowing you to take individual servers offline for maintenance while minimizing the effect on users.

Site Model

The site model provided by SharePoint 2010 ensures the consistent provisioning of sites, lists, and pages in a clear way that can be leveraged by developers and administrators alike. The site model includes the container hierarchy of site collection, sites, and lists, as well as rendering, templates, navigation, and the presentation of page elements.

The container hierarchy within the site model provides a consistent structure for the creation and presentation of content. The top-level container in the site model is the site collection. Think of the site collection as a boundary for configuration and security management. Within the site collection boundary is an associated collection of sites (or Webs). These Webs are arranged in a hierarchy, and the top of the structure is the top-level site (TLS). Within each Web is a collection of lists. These lists are arranges as siblings, with the Web as the parent of each list. Within each list there is a hidden folder called the *root folder*. Users can create many folders in a traditional folder hierarchy within each list. Each folder can store multiple items. These items are siblings, and the parent of each item is the folder in which it is stored. Understanding this containment hierarchy gives developers and designers a clear picture they can use to make design and implementation decisions.

Templates provide a way for site administrators to save sites and lists for later use. The implementation of templates within SharePoint 2010 has changed slightly, compared to prior versions of the product. The .STP files have been replaced with .WSP files in the form of user solutions. Site and list templates can be used to create new sites and/or lists based on the template. Templates can include content, but item level security is not maintained, so you don't want to include content in a template if you have private content stored within the site.

Navigation is largely provided through ASP.NET 3.5, but it leverages the site model described previously in that it provides the left navigation, the quick launch, the top navigation, and the breadcrumb navigation.

APIs

SharePoint 2010 provides a standard application programming interface (API) to go along with its site model, service architecture, and provider framework. This API allows developers to create new list types, site definitions, and Web Parts that can be leveraged in the system as though they were native objects.

FIELDS AND FORMS

The entry of metadata information is made easier through forms and fields that are rendered for each list within the system. For example, when users upload new documents, they are presented with a form for the entry of information relating to each document. These forms are customizable within SharePoint Designer, or within Visual Studio in the case of a custom list definition. Each form consists of a series of fields (or field types). These fields provide the individual entry capability needed to capture information entered into the form. In addition to modifying the forms, developers can create their own custom field types that include special functionality or validation to ensure that the appropriate information is captured in the appropriate way.

WEB SERVICES

SharePoint 2010 includes a set of Web services that you can use to interact with the farm, sites, or lists. In the most common scenario, you would use these Web services within the context of a site to provide access to list data and the manipulation of site settings. These Web services can be found under the _vti_bin directory of a site. For a complete list of Web services available, consult the SharePoint Server SDK.

CLIENT OBJECT MODEL

A new feature in SharePoint 2010 is the client object model, which provides developers with a way to consume services from the server side while programming on the client site. This allows you to interact with list data dynamically using client site technologies such as JavaScript, AJAX, or Windows form applications that are running remotely. Operations are batched and sent to the client object model service when it is time for processing.

FEATURES AND SOLUTIONS

SharePoint 2010 includes a deployment framework that provides for the consistent deployment of capabilities across multiple Web front-end (WFE) servers. This deployment framework is made up of two primary elements: features and solutions.

SharePoint features are definitions files that describe implementable functionality, which can be instantiated at various levels within the system. Features exist as XML files within the file system of each WFE. For example, if a developer creates a new list definition and wants to make it available for creation within a site, that list definition can be delivered through a feature. When it is installed and deployed, the new feature appears within the Manage Site Features Settings page in the Site Settings area. This allows the site administrator to enable or disable this new functionality within her site.

So, how do these files get deployed to the file system of each WFE? Solution (.WSP) files provide a deployment framework for new files and features that need to be deployed to the content applications to make them available for use within the system. Solutions are stored within the farm solution store and deployed to content applications. After they are deployed, all of the included files are then copied to each WFE server and are appropriately registered. A solution file can include assemblies, resource files, images, pages, and a variety of well-defined XML files that are used for the creation of new objects within the system, such as sites and lists.

Capabilities

In the previous sections, you reviewed the logical component architecture on top of which SharePoint 2010 capabilities are built. In the following sections, you will review each of the capability areas provided by the system as defined by Microsoft for this release.

Think of capabilities as user-facing functionalities that provide direct business value. By empowering business users with these capabilities, SharePoint 2010 enables them to do more, faster, and with less effort. These capabilities also allow users to build their own tailored solutions using SharePoint 2010 that adhere to the defined business processes within their organization. These capability areas define SharePoint 2010 as a unique product in the marketplace and allow the expandability and flexibility needed to empower both customers and independent software vendor (ISV) partners to create their own unique solutions to line-of-business problems. Figure 2-3 shows each of the capability areas provided by SharePoint 2010. The following sections provide a review of these capabilities. Each area will be explored in more detail.

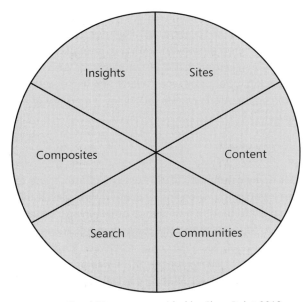

FIGURE 2-3 Capability areas provided by SharePoint 2010

Sites

SharePoint 2010 includes power collaboration capabilities. These capabilities are delivered in the form of site templates that are included with the product. By creating a Team Collaboration Site, small groups can work together on document deliverables and can track outstanding tasks, events, contacts, and other supporting list information.

Collaboration in SharePoint focuses on empowering users to take ownership of the site and its content, which will drive user adoption and self-support. A fluent user interface, with the familiar Microsoft Office Ribbon, delivers a contextual experience that lets users find the information they deem most relevant. Integration with the Office client applications improves productivity by allowing users to open, edit, and save documents to SharePoint using the applications most familiar to them.

Enhancements in the mobile experience give users the option of taking their work on the go. Improved mobile browser support allows users to access SharePoint data from most devices using the mobile browser interface. Microsoft Office Web Applications let users view Word, Microsoft PowerPoint, and Microsoft Excel documents on mobile devices. Microsoft Office Mobile 2010 and SharePoint Mobile Workspace 2010 provide Windows Phone users with a mobile rich client experience, allowing them to work directly on documents in real time or offline.

With Microsoft SharePoint Workspace 2010, users can synchronize their local offline enabled workspaces with both SharePoint and Microsoft Groove. Acting as a completely integrated offline client for SharePoint 2010, SharePoint Workspace gives users increased flexibility as they take work with them wherever they go. Microsoft Outlook Sync provides the ability to keep up to date with feeds, lists, and document libraries on mobile devices, using the familiar Outlook interface.

Finally, Web Parts provide a flexible way for users to tailor the experience within sites to meet their needs. By providing a wide array of out-of-the-box Web Parts for use within their sites, users can organize and present information the way they want it, based on their needs or the needs of their team. Personalization lets users tailor certain pages or Web Parts to meet specific needs, at the same time allowing other users who haven't personalized the page to see the shared view arranged by the editor. Alerts can be set on any item or list in the system to inform users of any changes made.

Content

The content capability within SharePoint 2010 provides many feature areas that are central to providing the management, publishing, retention, and disposition of content throughout the enterprise. Web publishing allows you to make information available to others in a structured way. Approval workflows provide a mechanism for automating the content approval and publishing process. Content deployment makes it easy to move content between staging and production of Internet-facing Web sites. Quick deploy allows for the on-demand deployment of specific content between sites. Multilingual capabilities provide an intelligent interface that detects a client user's language in addition to providing process automation for the translation of content between languages.

Managed metadata makes it easy to share common, well-understood field selection and taxonomical structures throughout your organization and across site collections. By scoping the metadata services at the site collection level as well as at the enterprise level, identified valuable structures can be promoted and can be easily made available across the enterprise. Furthermore, content type syndication makes the publishing of content types across multiple site collection possible. A new content type called *hub site collection* acts as a master copy for content types that are pushed down to subscribing site collections that leverage a common managed metadata service.

Document conversion lets users create content in familiar formats, such as Microsoft Word, and have that content converted into Web page content. This allows for an array of possible content source formats while ensuring that a common Web page content output is available for use within sites.

Communities

Communities provide the social networking backbone of SharePoint 2010. Central to the social capabilities is the concept of My Site, which provides each unique user with a home within the system. This gives users a place to bring together content from other sites, update profile information, join networks, and connect with other users based on interests or expertise. New activity feeds provide users a way to see what other users in their network are doing. Profiles let each user describe herself or himself. Profiles are synchronized with Active Directory, LDAP, or business data systems. When users have established an identity within the system, social search—or *people search* as it is commonly called—allows users to find one another quickly and easily.

User presence information allows users to contact one another instantly using Office Communicator through integration with Office Communication Server. Wikis and blogs provide familiar ways for groups and individuals alike to publish their thoughts, opinions, and knowledge in a quick, easy, and informal way. New social features such as tagging, notes, and ratings create a community context for content stored within the system. Users can tag content using tags stored within the managed metadata service, or they can create new tags on the fly. Notes can be added almost anywhere within the system and are brought together for a given user within her My Site.

Search

It's great to have all your information in a common system, but what good is it if you can't search for and find the information you need? SharePoint 2010 provides a comprehensive search capability, which includes a multitude of search experiences that are tailored to specific usages. From a simple list level search to a FAST enterprise search experience, SharePoint 2010 integrates the latest search technologies and makes them available in a unified way.

A robust indexing capability can be configured to search for content both inside and outside of the system. Bringing all of the content available within a common index delivers search query results quickly. Search results include relevance, best bets, and many other sophisticated search features you have come to expect.

Federation allows you to search multiple indexes in different physical locations in a unified fashion. By integrating with the back-end metadata capabilities within the system, the search feature becomes even more powerful, as users search for documents and content based on metadata fields and tags. Alerts keep users up to date on specific search queries as the results change over time, making it easy for users to keep up with content as it changes.

Composites

Business connectivity services provide a way for users to work with business data stored in other systems within SharePoint 2010. SharePoint 2010 expands on the connectivity capabilities of previous versions, allowing bidirectional interactions with business data as well as the ability to integrate with more third-party business systems. Access Services allow users to render and interact with data stored in Microsoft Access databases, and Visio Services provide a similar capability for data stored within Microsoft Visio files. SharePoint Designer provides a rich interface for creating publishing master pages, page layouts, human workflows, and customized pages.

Human workflows allow users to create workflows that are based on people processes and adapt those workflows to an ever-changing process as it evolves. Forms Services provide a robust way to render InfoPath forms within the Web interface, including the ability to leverage custom code and external data. Finally, Sandboxed Solutions let administrators upload and manage customization within their site collections. New isolation and throttling capabilities ensure that user customizations don't adversely affect other sites.

Insights

Microsoft PerformancePoint Server is now part of SharePoint 2010, enabling a whole host of new features for the analysis of business intelligence (BI) and decision information. Integrated rich analytics allow users to interact with BI data through client applications and the browser. Dashboards, key performance indicators (KPIs), and extensive charting capabilities complete the feature set in a powerful new way. As was the case in prior versions, Excel Services allows for Web rendering of Microsoft Excel data within the browser.

REAL WORLD   SharePoint 2010 and Middle Management

Throughout 2009 and into early 2010, most large enterprises did not view the demand for SharePoint 2010 very seriously because of the economic conditions looming over the global workforce. But the engineering workforce at one organization quickly identified the significant benefits that SharePoint 2010 offered compared to its previous version and lobbied their middle management, creating a business case for upgrading to SharePoint 2010. As a result, in the year 2010, SharePoint 2010 gathered enough attention to be on the CIO's top five most demanded projects list.

In this large organization, the demand for upgrading to SharePoint 2010 came from the bottom levels of the company and worked its way up. The engineers and architects created a high-value business case not only for upgrading their existing SharePoint service to SharePoint 2010 but also for deploying a new service to host business applications across the enterprise. Middle management offered significant resistance to adopting SharePoint 2010 because they were concerned that being an early adopter of a new product could pose significant risk to the existing service.

The consulting architect's recommendation was to create a quick pilot project for SharePoint 2010 that would incubate a number of key company-wide initiatives, not only proving the stability of SharePoint 2010, but also building organization capabilities around the new product. The pilot project would also help align central IT with various projects across the enterprise. This was a real opportunity for the IT department to jump ahead of business-specific project requirements and demands. Selecting the right product for a services deployment can make the difference between anticipating business needs and playing catch-up for years to come.

A similar demand arose from the engineering workforce in a financial institution when they realized that SharePoint 2010 would help them rationalize most of their business applications on a single platform with potentially less hardware than their existing SharePoint Server 2007 infrastructure. In this organization, middle management was agile and provided a bridge between technical and business groups across the enterprise. The proactive managers realized they would not be able to justify a new platform to upper management for an upgrade, however, because the company was experiencing extreme cost-cutting measures.

They thought creatively, and instead of focusing on one SharePoint 2010 project, they focused on creating a cross-organizational collaboration and business intelligence strategy by including all of their IT and business unit projects. The strategy was to leverage Microsoft's SharePoint Online service as the new platform instead of building everything themselves from scratch. The strategy demonstrated significant cost savings in terms of time to market and elasticity offered by the online platform in scaling up and down as per the demand. By moving to a cloud

SharePoint service, they would automatically benefit from SharePoint 2010 and be able to take advantage of future upgrade processes. Upper management was sold on the utility computing concept and quickly responded with funding for executing the collaboration and business intelligence projects across the enterprise, independent of the type of platform used. In this example, middle management executed the project on a short timeline because they were creative and proactive.

Both of these examples demonstrate the crucial role that middle management plays in driving IT service capabilities in any organization. Organizational culture plays an important role in determining how proactive middle management becomes. Organizational culture can be transformed from reactive to proactive by identifying key gaps in people, processes, and technology. In the first example, middle management was risk averse, and as a result became reactive to the needs of the business. In the second example, middle management identified and elected to take calculated risks, as long as the risks were managed. As a result, they were able to move several initiatives forward proactively.

As an architect, it is your responsibility to formulate your recommendations based on the best possible path for your customer. Likewise, it's equally important that you are willing to justify your position, even when your recommendations are not well received. In such cases, you should also try to explain clearly how your recommendation can transform IT capabilities into strategic assets rather than cost centers.

Every year Microsoft publishes a business value guide for IT and business professionals called "Microsoft in the Enterprise." This guide will help you align and analyze your IT capabilities with Microsoft products and services. Read the "Microsoft in the Enterprise" guide before you begin your project. You can find the 2009-2010 "Microsoft in the Enterprise" guide at *http://download.microsoft.com /download/B/8/8/B8804100-DA41-4771-BE70-FE878ED51AAB/2009-2010.MSFT-intheEnterprise.ResourceGuide.11.09.pdf.*

Deployment

SharePoint 2010 uses a traditional three-tier architecture based on the concept of server roles. These roles can be deployed on a single server or many servers. The three-tier roles are

- Web front-end server role
- Application server role
- Database server role

In a small farm deployment, server roles may be combined to deploy the entire application architecture on the minimum amount of resources from a hardware standpoint. For example, you can combine the Web server and application server roles on a single server or on multiple servers to achieve redundancy. Figure 2-4 illustrates the three-tier architecture employed by SharePoint 2010.

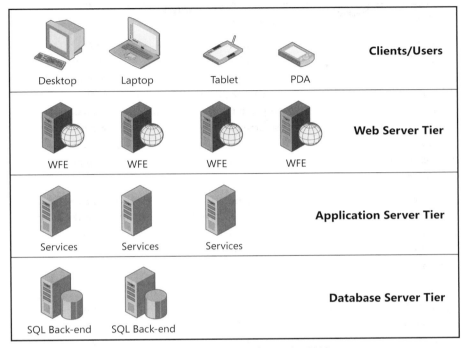

FIGURE 2-4 The tree-tier architecture employed by SharePoint 2010

Server Roles

The following sections provide additional details about each of the three server roles identified in the SharePoint 2010 architecture. This includes which functions each server role performs within the farm, as well as optional deployment alternatives to be considered when deploying each.

Web Server Role

Web front-end servers provide the user-facing access to the system. The Web Application Service runs on each Web front-end server in the farm. The Web server role provides the following capabilities.

- Hosts Web pages, Web services, and Web Parts that are necessary to process requests served by the farm.

- Directs requests to the appropriate application servers.
- This role is necessary for farms that include other SharePoint 2010 capabilities.
- In small farms, this role can be shared on a server with the query role.

Application Server Role

Application server roles are associated with services that can be deployed to a physical computer.

- Each service represents a separate application service that can potentially reside on a dedicated application server.
- You can group services with similar usage and performance characteristics on a server and scale them out onto multiple servers together. For example, you can combine client-related services into a service group.

BEST PRACTICE After deployment, look for services that consume a disproportionate amount of resources and consider placing these services on dedicated hardware.

Database Server Role

In a small-farm environment, all databases can be deployed to a single server. In larger environments, group databases by roles and deploy these to multiple database servers. The database server role provides the following capabilities.

- Stores content databases for content applications.
- Stores configuration data for the farm.
- Stores service application data.

BEST PRACTICE Consider using database mirroring or clustered database server environment for redundancy.

Deployment Topologies

SharePoint 2010 can be configured as a small, medium, or large farm deployment. Remember, the topology service provides you with an almost limitless amount of flexibility, so you can tailor the topology of your farm to meet your specific needs. It is also possible to configure farms that will experience a specific type of process load, such as a search or Excel Services, to optimize the topology for that load.

For example, if you wanted to have a medium farm that was optimized for search, you would separate the index server role from that of the query servers, perhaps even providing dedicated hardware for the query servers. In a large farm deployment, you may even consider designating a Web front-end server as a dedicated index target for use while crawling. If you are expecting to have a lot of users performing work with Excel Services, you might elect to have one or two dedicated Excel calculation servers to handle the load.

In the following sections, you will look at example deployment topologies for small, medium, and large deployment to illustrate how you might designate servers in each role and assign services.

Small Farm Deployment

When you are evaluating SharePoint 2010 or performing testing/development activities, a small farm deployment should be sufficient. In fact, you may elect to go with a single server farm configuration for development or configuration testing. Often a developer will elect to use a virtual machine for testing, because it's less expensive and can be brought up and down as needed. Alternatively, you could elect to deploy a two-tier farm, with all Web and service applications running on one server and a separate database server. For production purposes, a typical two-tier server farm that supports 10,000 to 20,000 users might appear as shown in Figure 2-5.

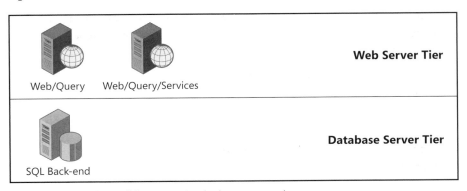

FIGURE 2-5 Example small farm two-tier deployment topology

In the case of an environment in which you anticipate moderate service usage, you might elect to deploy a three-tier farm, in which you separate the service applications from the Web/query servers. This provides redundancy from a Web front-end perspective while providing a dedicated hardware resource for service application execution. A typical three-tiered small farm deployment is shown in Figure 2-6.

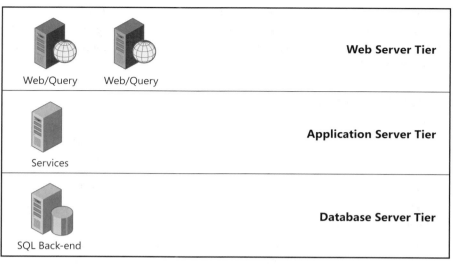

FIGURE 2-6 Example small farm three-tier deployment topology

If you were anticipating heavy search traffic and/or large search indexes with frequent crawls, you might elect to deploy a variation of the three-tier deployment topology that is optimized for search, as shown in Figure 2-7. By separating the search databases for all other databases, the farm optimized for search shown in the figure should be capable of handling search indexes with up to 10 million items.

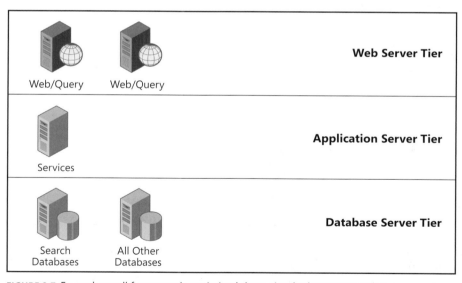

FIGURE 2-7 Example small farm search-optimized three-tier deployment topology

All of the small farm deployment topologies discussed here include one or more fault-tolerant servers. Remember, with these deployment topologies, it only takes a single hardware failure to bring down services in a non-fault-tolerant tier. This will affect your backup and restore planning in addition to your service level agreements. Although a small farm deployment is sufficient for smaller user bases, it may not be ideal for highly sensitive application needs that require uninterrupted service and fault tolerance. For these deployments, consider a medium farm deployment topology.

Medium Farm Deployment

When you need fault tolerance within your environment or find your small farm is inadequate for serving the needs of more business, it's time to consider a medium farm deployment. The advantage of a medium farm deployment is that it allows you to scale out servers and services based on their utilization and the anticipated amount of content hosted within the farm. By moving the index and query search roles to the application tier in conjunction with having dedicated database servers for search, the medium farm topology shown in Figure 2-8 is capable of handling search indexes with up to 40 million items.

The basic prerequisites for a medium farm include the presence of two dedicated Web front-end servers, which should not host any other service applications—they are dedicated to serving content applications. The second prerequisite for a medium farm is two combined search query and index servers, with at least one other application server for service applications. If you anticipate additional service application load, you can elect to scale out the application tier as needed, adding additional servers to handle specific service applications. Database redundancy is highly recommended for a medium farm deployment, and depending on your selection of hardware, you may want to add additional database servers or clusters as the volume of content grows. Figure 2-8 shows an example of a medium farm deployment.

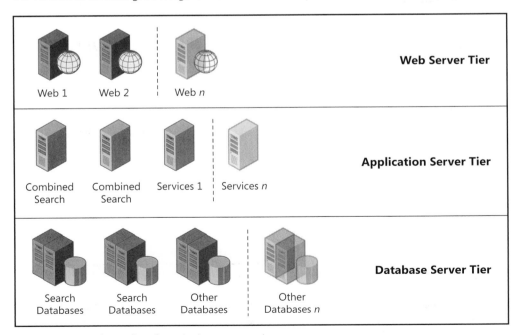

FIGURE 2-8 Example medium farm deployment topology

Large Farm Deployment

In the case of a large farm deployment, you should separate services and server roles so that you have dedicated processing power and redundancy where it is needed. This allows you to have servers that run or provide specific services according to the defined scale of the identified needs. For example, you can have a set of Web servers that are dedicated to service content applications, while another dedicated server handles the crawling of content applications (as an index target). You would separate the index and query roles and perhaps even provide multiple dedicated servers for each. You could have servers that are dedicated to running sandboxed code, Excel calculation services, or other specific service applications. Finally, you could have specific dedicated database servers or clusters for search, content, and service application databases. Figure 2-9 illustrates what a large farm deployment topology might look like.

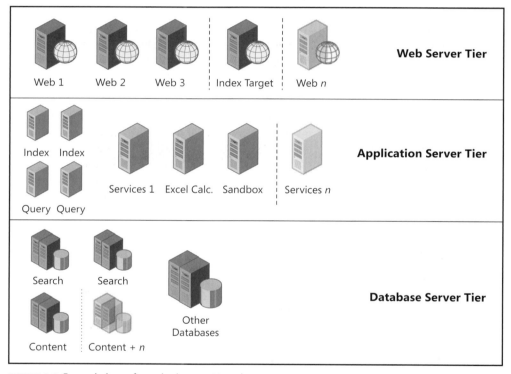

FIGURE 2-9 Example large farm deployment topology

Development and Testing Environments

One of the most often overlooked needs in today's SharePoint deployments is the need for both configuration/development and testing environments. Even if you think you can get by with a strictly out-of-the-box deployment, you will inevitably need a dedicated environment in which to create and automate your configuration. Likewise, you also will need an environment that is as close to production as possible for testing and validation of your design.

Even though you are not doing any custom development in your initial deployment, you will probably need to perform the automated configuration of new sites or services, at a minimum. Or, you may want to unit-test a new configuration for exploratory purposes. When you do want to run this kind of a test, what will you do? Will you be forced to put those activities on hold while you set up new environments?

> **BEST PRACTICES** You should have both a development/configuration environment and a dedicated testing environment.

Configuration/Development Environment

For each build you release to production, you will need an environment in which to flush out your design. Whether they are configurations you need to identify and test individually or development work you need to perform to implement your design, the right place to do these activities is your configuration/development environment. In most cases, this environment is a limited deployment, often consisting of only a single server.

Great! So, why can't you just test things in your testing environment? The answer is found in the type of testing you are doing. First, if you are doing development of any kind, you don't want to be doing it in your testing environment. You wouldn't want to install software and tools in the dedicated testing environment that wouldn't exist in production. Second, if you are trying something new in your design for the first time, you don't want to incur the contamination risk associated with doing it in your dedicated testing environment. If you find yourself needing to reproduce a defect spotted in production within your dedicated testing environment, you now have to deal with all of the other change you have introduced into that environment as a factor. This is not an ideal or efficient way of testing your deployment.

Dedicated Testing Environment

Ideally, you want your dedicated testing environment to look exactly like your production environment, although this may not be possible due to cost constraints. At a minimum, however, you should have each defined server role represented in your testing environment. For example, if you have dedicated index and query servers, make sure you have at least one of each in your testing environment. If you can't afford to implement your testing environment using hardware, do it with virtual machines. Although virtual machines are not truly representative of production, they are better than having no dedicated testing environment at all.

The purpose of the dedicated testing environment is to have a place to perform integration and functional testing of your design before it is implemented in production. Usually this means performing well-defined test cases, capturing and recording the results, remediating the problems, and analyzing the results in order to make a deployment decision. Additionally, this environment should sit between production deployments.

Unless you are readying a build for production deployment, you will need the testing environment ready to reproduce any defects identified within production. When you identify a potential fix for the defect, you would first unit-test that fix in your configuration/development environment, then move it to the dedicated test environment, and finally into production. The rigor involved in the movement of the build between each of these environments will vary based on your implementation of the system development life cycle (SDLC).

Example Deployment

Figure 2-10 shows an example deployment that includes a configuration/development environment as well as a dedicated testing environment.

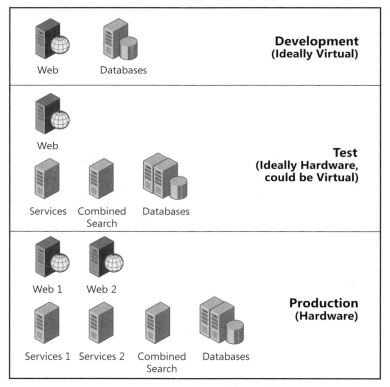

FIGURE 2-10 Example deployment including configuration/development and test environments

Application Pools

You need to understand how SharePoint 2010 interacts with Internet Information Server (IIS) through application pools. Central to understanding how this interaction works is an understanding of process threading and isolation. An application consists of one or more processes. It is easiest to think of a process as an executing program.

Each individual process provides the needed resources for running the program. These resources include the following.

- Virtual address space
- Executable code
- Open handles to system objects
- A security context
- A unique process identifier
- Environment variables
- A priority class
- Min/Max working set sizes
- Thread(s) of execution

When a new process starts, it is started on a single thread, the primary thread. After it is started, the process can create additional threads from any of its existing threads. Threads are the basic unit to which the operating system allocates processor time. A thread can execute any part of the process code and can be scheduled for execution by the process. Each thread created by a process shares its virtual address space and system resources. Furthermore, each thread maintains

- Exception handlers
- A scheduling priority
- Local storage
- A unique thread identifier
- Thread context

Understanding Application Pools

You can run IIS in worker process isolation mode, which allows you to separate different Web applications and virtual directories into process groups called *application pools*. When a Web directory or virtual directory is assigned to an application pool, that pool manages a worker process or set of worker processes within which the execution of the code associated with the application runs.

All of the applications within an application pool share the same worker process. Each worker process is executed under a separate instance of the worker process executable file, W3wp.exe. This ensures that each separate work process that is running provides an execution boundary, thereby providing a level of process isolation. This means that any execution problems encountered in one worker process will not affect other worker processes or the applications running in their application pools.

Application pools may serve many applications, but each application can be served by only one application pool. Each running application pool has individual settings related to its threading and the security identity under which its worker process will run. Because each application pool can run under a specified identity, process execution security is enhanced, thereby preventing unauthorized access to information being accessed by other application pools.

In summary, by running each application in its own application pool, you create a more isolated and secure process execution environment, and you insulate each application from potential execution errors experienced by another. The only by-product of process isolation that needs to be considered is that, by separating these processes, your service account configuration may become more complex; because each application is running in its own worker process, you may see an increased usage of system resources such as memory.

Default SharePoint 2010 Application Pools

When you configure SharePoint using the post-installation Farm Configuration Wizard, you will notice that the system comes preconfigured with five separate application pools. These pools provide process isolation for serving Web applications in addition to providing necessary service process execution pools. Table 2-3 includes the five application pools that are configured by the wizard, as well as the security context under which each pool runs.

TABLE 2-3 Default Application Pools

APPLICATION POOL	EXPLANATION	IDENTITY
SharePoint Central Administration v4	SharePoint Central Administration v4	Farm Administrator Account
SharePoint Web Services System	SharePoint Topology Service Application	Farm Administrator Account
SecurityTokenServiceApplicationPool	SharePoint Security Token Service Application	Farm Administrator Account
SharePoint Web Services Default	SharePoint Service Applications	Service Account
SharePoint – 80	Default preconfigured Content Application	Service Account

The SharePoint Central Administration v4 application pool provides the process execution under which the Administration service runs and also serves the SharePoint Central Administration website. The SharePoint Topology Service Application provides the topology service described in the section titled "Topology" earlier in this chapter. It facilitates changes to the farm and environment such as the addition or removal of server and services. The SharePoint Security Token Service Application services requests to issue, manage, and validate security tokens for Web applications. The SharePoint Web Services Default pool provides an execution process for all of the other configured services applications running on the farm. Lastly, the default preconfigured Content Application provides a process for the execution of the content service. It's important to note that additional content applications could share an application pool with each other, or ideally, from a security perspective, would each run under their own unique application pool with their own unique service account.

Summary

This chapter reviewed the architectural building blocks on which SharePoint 2010 is built. You learned about the enterprise architecture of SharePoint 2010 and explored its logical component architecture in detail. You reviewed the service architecture and the role of services within the logical architecture and the overall systems architecture. After discussing the underlying components, this chapter explained in detail each of the six capability areas included with the product.

By exploring the ways in which you can combine servers and services, you built a solid foundation to start working with sample deployment topologies. You reviewed small, medium, and large farm topologies and even discussed limited deployments for development and testing. Finally, you explored how SharePoint 2010 and IIS interact with one another through application pools. With an understanding of the basics of process threading and worker processes, you took a closer look at the default application pools that come with SharePoint 2010 and learned how to set up your application pools for optional security and process isolation.

PART II

Installation and Implementation

## CHAPTER 3

Optimizing SQL Server for a SharePoint 2010 Implementation

Microsoft SQL Server is the repository for all lists and libraries stored in Microsoft SharePoint 2010, as well as the location of most SharePoint 2010 configuration information. As the SharePoint administrator, you must understand how tightly integrated these two products are and how much SQL Server performance affects SharePoint's performance.

With more than 90 percent of your SharePoint information stored in SQL Server, you need to familiarize yourself with the SQL Server components that are used by SharePoint and how they affect SharePoint. In medium-size or larger organizations, you often have a separate database administrator (DBA) or even multiple DBAs who manage your SQL Server environments.

If you are fortunate enough to have dedicated DBAs, your ability to hold an intelligent conversation about SQL Server will benefit you when optimizing or troubleshooting problems with your SharePoint environment. The information in this chapter will be helpful in having that conversation with your DBAs, ensuring your SQL Server is running as efficiently as possible.

If you are the SharePoint administrator *and* the DBA for your company, this chapter will help you properly install, configure, and manage your SQL Server and SharePoint integration. Often the SharePoint administrator who is also the DBA doesn't receive proper SQL Server training, so it becomes more challenging for that person to recognize the degree of integration between SQL Server and SharePoint. Understanding the information in this chapter will help you ensure that SQL Server is providing optimal performance for your SharePoint farm.

About SQL Server

SQL Server is Microsoft's relational database product that provides a comprehensive, integrated data management and analysis software, enabling organizations to reliably and confidently manage their mission-critical applications like SharePoint. Over 90 percent of your SharePoint content and configuration information is actually stored in one of several SQL Server databases. The following information contains some of the most common SharePoint information that is physically stored in a SQL Server database.

- Lists
- Libraries
- Farm configuration information
- Central Administration information
- Service application information
- Search information
- Web application information
- Logging information
- Reporting Services
- Global content types
- Global metadata
- Information management policy information

Because SQL Server hosts so much of your SharePoint content, it must not be affected by any other applications that the SQL Server computer is hosting. Therefore, it is strongly recommended that you host your SharePoint 2010 farm on its own SQL Server installation.

SQL Server Versions

SharePoint 2010 supports two versions of SQL Server: 2005 and 2008 (including R2). Regardless of which SQL Server version you implement with SharePoint 2010, you must use the 64-bit edition of the SQL Server product. Within each version, Microsoft offers different product editions that you also must choose among when deciding which SQL Server database product to install to support your SharePoint 2010 farm.

This chapter discusses behavior with the implementation of SQL Server 2008 and SharePoint 2010 and suggests where to find information on SQL Server 2005 as necessary.

SQL Server 2008

SQL Server 2008 is the most current version of Microsoft's SQL Server product and is the recommended SQL Server version for use with SharePoint 2010. SQL Server 2008 includes several new features and enhancements that SharePoint 2010 can use to ultimately improve the performance, storage requirements, and security of your SharePoint 2010 content. Microsoft recommends that you use SQL Server 2008 because

- Significant enhancements ranging from data and backup compression to query performance and enhanced database mirroring are available without the need to modify your existing applications.

- It offers data encryption and database auditing capabilities within existing applications.

- Features like policy-based server management and new tools such as Performance Data Collection help you effectively manage the growth of your data.

- There have been many performance enhancements made throughout the technology stack, including enhancements within Analysis Services, Reporting Services, and Integration Services.

- New features such as query governor and data compression, along with general scalability enhancements, provide scalable solutions that are more reliable for very large enterprise systems.

MORE INFO   For additional information on the top new features available in SQL Server 2008, visit *http://www.microsoft.com/sqlserver/2008/en/us/whats-new.aspx.*

SQL Server 2005

SQL Server 2005 is also supported with SharePoint 2010, but you lose the previously listed enhancements included in SQL Server 2008. Microsoft's SQL Server 2005 64-bit edition will work sufficiently with SharePoint 2010 and still provide a robust, secure, and scalable SharePoint environment, but you will not be able to utilize the improvements listed in the SQL Server 2008 New Features Web page.

MORE INFO   For additional information about SQL Server 2005 features and functionality, please visit *http://www.microsoft.com/sqlserver/2005/en/us/top-30-features.aspx.*

SQL Server Instances

A SQL Server *instance* is simply a single installation of SQL Server on a server running a supported Windows Server operating system. A Windows server can host one or more installations of SQL Server, each one of which is considered an instance, and can be individually configured for instance-specific behavior. However, there is only one program group created that is used to manage the different instances on that server. For example, you will have only one SQL Server Management Studio interface. It is a best practice in medium-sized to large organizations for your SharePoint SQL Server instance to be the only installation of SQL Server on the server hosting that instance. This allows you to optimize the performance of SharePoint at the SQL Server instance level as well as the operating system level. These optimization options will be discussed later in this chapter.

> **NOTE** A Windows server can host up to as many as 50 SQL Server Enterprise Edition instances or 16 SQL Server Standard Edition instances on one server. Be careful about installing multiple SQL Server instances on one server and know how the hardware's capabilities can affect your SQL Server and SharePoint performance.

What is a SQL Server instance? A SQL Server instance is composed of three primary components.

- Relational database engine
- System databases
- User databases

The relational database engine is the software started using different Windows services that perform lookups, sorts, and other actions. These SQL services can be managed from within SQL Server or at the operating system level from within Windows Services, as well as by using the net command at the command line.

The system databases are the databases created during the installation, and they contain the metadata, or information about that particular SQL Server installation. They also contain SQL Server configuration information and all other information required by SQL Server to support the relational database engine.

The user databases are all other databases that are not system databases; user databases are created for storage of content in SQL Server. After you install SQL Server and during a complete installation of SharePoint 2010, two user databases are created initially—the configuration database (SharePoint_Config) and the Central Administration database (SharePoint_AdminContent). These two databases, along with all other databases that are created as you install service applications and create Web applications, are user databases.

Default SQL Server Instance

When you install SQL Server on a server, one installation can be designated as the default instance (but this is not required). It doesn't have a special network name; it is referenced by using the name of the computer. So in any client tools or programs, you can reference the default SQL Server instance simply by entering the name of the computer it is running on, like Server1 for the default SQL Server instance running on a Windows server called Server1. The names of the default instance services are MSSQLServer for the engine and SQLServerAgent for the SQL Server Agent. The default instance TCP/IP port is 1433. Often a Windows server hosting a single installation of SQL Server or one that has performed only the first installation of SQL Server utilizes this default instance.

Named SQL Server Instance

Every time you install SQL Server subsequently provides another instance of SQL Server, called a *named instance*. With named instances, you install another copy of the SQL Server Engine and the SQL Server Agent Services. For named instances, the names of the SQL services become MSSQL$*NameOfInstance* and SQLAgent$*NameOfInstance*. Using these named instance services, you can manage the various named instances separately from each other. You can specify different accounts to be used when starting the various services, allowing you to implement tighter security between the different instances of SQL Server.

Multiple SQL Server instances also give you the ability to have different SQL Server settings on each instance. One instance can use Windows Integrated security only, and another can used mixed security. You can also use these settings to control the location of your content databases for SharePoint 2010. During each SQL Server installation, a new set of registry keys is created and associated with the SQL Server and SQL Server Agent Services. This allows you to perform any registry customizations on one instance of SQL Server without affecting any other instance of SQL Server on the same Windows server.

Beginning in SQL Server 2005, Microsoft introduced a new service called the SQL Browser service. This service listens on UDP port 1434 and directs the connection to the proper dynamically chosen TCP/IP port for each named instance.

> **NOTE** Even if you have multiple named instances, you have only one SQL Server program group (per SQL Server version) and only one copy of the utility represented by each icon in the program group. You choose which instance you want to manage after accessing the utility.

How do you identify the named instances using a client, or during the installation of SharePoint 2010? The named instances are identified by the network name of the computer plus the instance name, similar to the following.

NameOfComputer\NameOfInstance

As an example, my SQL Server instance named SharePoint, running on a server named App01, becomes

App01\SharePoint

On completion of a successful installation, you will have your default instance of SQL Server, a named instance, named instances, or a combination of default and named instances. Regardless of the number of installations you have on that single computer, you treat all of them as if you had installed each of them on a separate computer, except that you use a single program group to manage the different instances. Furthermore, from within Microsoft SQL Server Management Studio, you need to register all subsequent installations of SQL Server after your first installation using the Register Server interface shown in Figure 3-1. This interface is accessed from within Management Studio by right-clicking an existing SQL Server instance and then clicking Register.

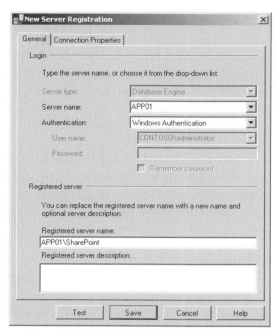

FIGURE 3-1 SQL Server 2008 Register Server interface

Types of Databases

Remember that there are two types of databases in SQL Server: system databases and user databases. SharePoint databases fall into the category of user databases from a SQL Server perspective. The SharePoint configuration database that contains all of the SharePoint configuration information is the most critical user database for SharePoint. If it becomes corrupt, it will prevent SharePoint from running correctly, even though the corrupted database will have minimal impact on the SQL Server instance.

SQL Server System Databases

Regardless of whether you perform a default instance or named instance installation of SQL Server, the results will always be the same—the following four system databases, shown in Figure 3-2, are created for you during the installation, and they can have a major impact on SQL Server and ultimately on SharePoint.

- Master
- Msdb
- Model
- Tempdb

FIGURE 3-2 SQL Server system databases

These four system databases work together in your SQL Server environment during the management and configuration of your SQL Server instance. These four system databases are created no matter what version of SQL Server you are using, and their reliability can directly affect SharePoint.

- **Master** The Master database contains all the required information that the database engine reads when it starts up. It includes SQL Server configuration information such as security settings, file locations, sort orders, and database locations. This database is essential to the success of the SQL Server instance functioning properly. If it is unavailable, the instance of SQL Server will not start, meaning your SharePoint content will be inaccessible.

- **Msdb** The Msdb database contains information used by the SQL Server Agent Service including scheduled SQL Server jobs, SQL Server operators, and SQL Server alerts, as well as information about the database maintenance plans. SQL Server jobs can be used to perform routine tasks like backing up your databases. Your operators are individuals who can be notified when a job completes successfully, fails, or both. The SQL Server alerts can be used to cause an automated action to occur, including backing up a SQL Server transaction log when it reaches a specified threshold.

    Database maintenance plans are generated using a wizard and allow you to create an entire plan for backing up, verifying integrity of your data, and generating logs on the backups that occur. This is a great tool for SharePoint administrators who may not be sufficiently familiar with SQL Server to schedule these events separately.

- **Model**   The third system database, called Model, is the "template" from which all user databases are created, including all of your SharePoint content databases. Modifications to this database can be helpful when you are adding new content databases to SharePoint and can help improve performance and minimize content database modifications. These options will be discussed later in this chapter in the section titled "Model Database Settings."

- **Tempdb**   Finally, the Tempdb database is the "work" area that the database engine uses to temporarily store data during some SQL operations. For instance, if you request data to be returned sorted by title or last name, the information is temporarily stored in the Tempdb database while the sort takes place. The results are returned to the end user from this temporary work storage. This database is similar to a cache in that every time you restart the MSSQLServer service, its contents are deleted and it begins empty.

Ensuring these four system databases are properly backed up is instrumental to a SharePoint farm recovery. In Chapter 17, "Data Protection, Recoverability, and Availability," you will find a thorough discussion about backing up and restoring your SharePoint information.

SharePoint User Databases

In addition to the SQL system databases, a typical SQL instance hosting a SharePoint farm will have at least three SQL Server user databases.

- Farm Configuration database
- Central Administration database
- Company Portal database

These three SQL Server user databases contain your SharePoint environment information regarding the installation, configuration, and content stored in SharePoint. In addition to these three databases, several more user databases are created as your farm grows or as you decide to take advantage of additional SharePoint functionality. For instance, if you choose to install SharePoint 2010 search functionality, three additional user databases are created: the Search Service Admin database, the Search Service Crawl database, and the Search Metadata database.

A number of different SharePoint databases are created when you choose to install the most common SharePoint service applications.

- **Usage and Health Data Collection Service Application**   This service collects and logs SharePoint health indicators and usage metrics for analysis and reporting purposes.

  - Logging database, which is the Microsoft SQL Server, MSDE, or WMSDE database that stores health monitoring and usage data temporarily and can be used for reporting and diagnostics.

- **Search Service Application**   This service provides search functionality.
  - Administration database, which replaces the Shared Services Provider database that was in Microsoft Office SharePoint Server 2007 and is instantiated once per Search application, aligning with the Administration Component. The Administration database hosts the Search application configuration and the access control list (ACL) for the content crawl.
  - Property database, which stores crawled properties associated with the crawled data and can include properties, history data, crawl queues, and so forth.
  - Crawl database, which hosts the crawled data and drives crawl. The Crawl database replaces the Search database in Microsoft Office SharePoint Server 2007.
- **User Profile Service Application**   This service includes user profiles and My Sites.
  - Profile database, which stores and manages user and associated information. It allows for a flexible schema that supports multiple data types, and it can be queried and updated.
  - Synchronization database, which stores configuration and staging data for synchronization of profile data from external sources such as Active Directory.
  - Social Tagging database, which stores social tagging records and their respective URLs, as well as notes created by users.
- **Web Analytics Service Application**   This service provides analytics that provide you with insights into your Web traffic, search, and SharePoint assets, enabling you to better understand your user and deployments.
  - Staging database, which stores unaggregated Fact Data, asset metadata, and queued batch data and provides short-term retention of this content.
  - Reporting database, which stores aggregated standard report tables, Fact Data aggregated by Site Group, date, and asset metadata, in addition to diagnostics information.
- **Managed Metadata Service Application**   This service publishes a term store, and optionally, a set of content types.
  - Term Store database, which is where your managed metadata is stored.
- **Secure Store Service Application**   This application replaces the single sign-on (SSO) service in previous versions of SharePoint.
  - Store database, which stores mapping of credentials such as account names and passwords.
- **Business Data Connectivity Service Application**   This service stores, secures, and administers external content types and related objects.
  - BDC_Service_DB database, which stores external content types and related objects.
- **State Service**   This application maintains temporary state information for InfoPath Forms Services.
  - State database, which stores temporary state information for InfoPath Forms Services.

In addition to your content databases and several service application databases, beginning in SharePoint 2010 you can now access any SharePoint content database, whether or not it is currently part of the farm. These types of databases, called *unattached content databases*, are used to recover items from lists or libraries that are no longer accessible from within SharePoint.

Ensuring that all of these SharePoint databases are properly backed up is instrumental to a multilevel SharePoint content recovery plan. Chapter 17 provides a thorough discussion on backing up and restoring your SharePoint information.

SQL Server Management Studio

SQL Server Management Studio is an integrated environment for accessing, configuring, managing, administering, and developing all components of SQL Server. SQL Server Management Studio combines the features of Enterprise Manager, Query Analyzer, and Analysis Manager, included in previous releases of SQL Server, into a single environment. Its intuitive interface, shown in Figure 3-3, allows you to complete administrative tasks using Object Explorer, which gives you the ability to connect to any server in the SQL Server family and graphically browse its contents.

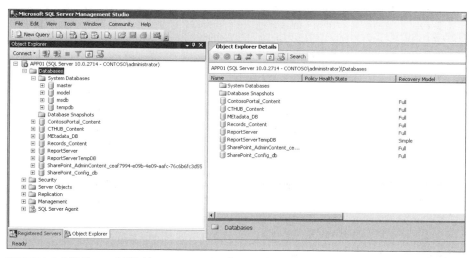

FIGURE 3-3 SQL Server 2008 Management Studio interface

Using Management Studio, you can connect to different SQL Server services that have been installed, all of which provide different functionality. These different SQL Server services include the following.

- Database Engine
- Analysis Services
- Reporting Services

- Integration Services

For instance, after connecting to the Database Engine service hosting your SharePoint content, you can manage the SQL Server system databases and your SharePoint user databases.

The properties of your SharePoint SQL Server instance can be viewed and configured in SQL Server Management Studio. The tool components of Management Studio include Registered Servers, Object Explorer, Solution Explorer, Template Explorer, the Object Explorer Details page, and the document window. To access a tool, click the View menu and then select the name of the tool you want to use.

System Stored Procedures and Transact-SQL (T-SQL)

Using scripts can provide a more efficient and optionally more automated way for you to perform SQL Server tasks. Transact-SQL statements, often called T-SQL statements, can be used to perform the same tasks you perform using SQL Server Studio Management. T-SQL statements provide a way for you to manage and access your SQL Server content, and most of the statements meet the ANSI-92 standards, providing an easy transition between SQL Server and other relational database products. You can write scripts using T-SQL statements as well as SQL Server system–stored procedures to manage your SharePoint SQL Server environment. System-stored procedures are pre-built T-SQL scripts provided by the installation of SQL Server and are helpful in managing your SharePoint instance or SharePoint user databases. Often the system-stored procedures and T-SQL statements are dynamic enough to allow you to provide parameters to specify what SQL Server object you want to run a command against.

There are two interfaces you can use to execute SQL Server stored procedures and the SQL Server Transact SQL statements: Query Analyzer and Sqlcmd.exe. Query Analyzer provides a graphical user interface for executing your statements or scripts. Alternatively, you can run Sqlcmd.exe from the command prompt, which also allows you to enter T-SQL statements or scripts.

There are two primary T-SQL options you may find helpful when managing your SharePoint SQL Server installation: the system-stored procedure sp_configure and the T-SQL statement ALTER DATABASE.

sp_configure Stored Procedure

The sp_configure stored procedure is used to manage SQL Server instance level settings. It can be used to modify installation level settings such as max server memory, min server memory, show advanced options, and user connections. Immediately after running the sp_configure command, you need to perform one of the two following steps.

- Issue the RECONFIGURE (or in some cases, RECONFIGURE WITH OVERRIDE) statement.

- Restart the instance of SQL Server.

Most instance level settings don't take effect until you perform one of the previous two actions to implement the new SQL instance level setting. Some instance level options are not available until you enable them, which you can do by issuing the sp_configure command with the show advanced options configuration option, as shown here.

```
sp_configure 'show advanced options', 1;
GO
RECONFIGURE;
```

> **MORE INFO** Additional information on the sp_configure system-stored procedure can be found in the SQL Server Books Online documentation.

ALTER DATABASE T-SQL Statement

The ALTER DATABASE statement is used to manage SQL Server database settings. This command can be used to modify your SharePoint user databases to modify settings such as size, maxsize, filegrowth, readonly, and moving files.

Most database settings take effect immediately or by taking the database offline and then bringing it back online. The following sample ALTER DATABASE statement connects to the Master database and then sets the Contosoportal database to read-only to prevent changes from being made to it.

```
USE master
GO

ALTER DATABASE contosoportal
SET read_only
GO
```

By becoming more familiar with the T-SQL syntax and the stored procedures available to modify your SharePoint SQL Server instance or SharePoint databases, you will be able to make timely changes more efficiently. Additional information on the ALTER DATABASE Transact-SQL statement can be found in the SQL Server Books Online documentation.

Windows PowerShell for SQL Server 2008

SQL Server 2008 introduced a set of Windows PowerShell SQL Server snap-ins that expose SQL Server functionality in Windows PowerShell. You can code Windows PowerShell scripts that work with all of your SQL Server objects. These scripts can be run in the Windows PowerShell environment, in SQL Server Management Studio, and as SQL Server Agent jobs.

The SQL Server 2008 Setup installs the following Windows PowerShell components when you choose either the client software or the Database Services nodes.

- Windows PowerShell 1.0, if Windows PowerShell is not already present on your computer
- The SQL Server snap-ins, .dll files that implement two types of Windows PowerShell support for SQL Server, SQL Server cmdlets, and a SQL Server provider
- The sqlps utility, which is used to run Windows PowerShell sessions that include the SQL Server snap-ins

SQL Server 2008 Management Studio supports starting Windows PowerShell sessions from the Object Explorer tree by right-clicking an object and then selecting Start PowerShell. Also, the SQL Server 2008 version of SQL Server Agent supports Windows PowerShell job steps. Be cautioned that each SQL Server Agent Windows PowerShell job step launches a sqlps process that consumes approximately 20 megabytes (MB) of memory. Running large numbers of these job steps concurrently can adversely affect performance.

If you want additional information on a specific SQL Server cmdlet, you can use one of the following Windows PowerShell commands.

- For example syntax on a specific cmdlet:

    ```
    get-help cmdletname -examples
    ```

- To obtain help on the parameters for a specific cmdlet:

    ```
    get-help cmdletname -parameters *
    ```

- For full details concerning a specific cmdlet:

    ```
    get-help cmdletname -full
    ```

These commands are not case sensitive. However, the spacing and the parameters have to be precise. For instance, the parameter *–full* cannot have a space between the – and *full*.

> **MORE INFO** Additional information on the available Windows PowerShell cmdlets for SQL Server can be found in the SQL Server 2008 Books Online documentation.

Installing and Configuring SQL Server 2008 for SharePoint 2010

The SQL Server 2008 instance hosting your SharePoint content can have a significant impact on SharePoint performance. It is highly recommended that each SharePoint farm have its own SQL Server instance and that this server is dedicated to hosting only SQL Server. This will allow for further optimizations, as discussed in the section titled "Optimizing SQL Server for SharePoint 2010" later in this chapter. It is important to understand what steps should be taken when installing and configuring SQL Server to achieve optimal SharePoint performance. Areas of concern regarding your SQL Server 2008 installation include

- SQL Server 2008 editions
- Hardware requirements
- Software requirements

SQL Server 2008 Editions

SQL Server 2005 and SQL Server 2008 are offered in several different editions, each of which includes different features, functionality, and limitations. To ensure that the level of availability, scalability, and fault tolerance of your SharePoint implementation meets the needs of your business, you must choose the appropriate edition of SQL Server to install for SharePoint. Table 3-1 lists some of the most common SQL Server 2008 editions and the features and limitations of each that you should consider when determining which edition of SQL Server to use to host your SharePoint content.

TABLE 3-1 SQL Server 2008 Edition Features and Limitations

EDITION	APPLICATION OR RECOMMENDED USAGE	CPU	MEMORY	DATABASE SIZE
Enterprise	Enterprise environments that need redundancy and built-in business intelligence	Operating system maximum	Operating system maximum	Unlimited
Standard	Shared data scenarios in departments and small to large businesses	4 CPU	Operating system maximum	Unlimited
Workgroup	Remote offices that need local instances of company data	2 CPU	4 GB	Unlimited
Developer	Full-featured edition for development and testing only	Operating system maximum	Operating system maximum	Unlimited
Express	Entry-level database ideal for learning and ISV redistribution	1 CPU	1 GB	4 GB
Compact	Embedded database for developing desktop and mobile applications	Operating system maximum	Operating system maximum	4 GB

Although there are several editions you could choose, the recommendation is to use the SQL Server 2008 Enterprise Edition for production because it provides the best option for high availability, scalability, fault tolerance, and support for business intelligence. Alternatively, if the Enterprise Edition is too costly or includes features and functionality that your organization won't need, you can use the SQL Server 2008 Standard Edition in production. These are the only two editions that should be used in any organization's SharePoint 2010 production environment.

In addition to the actual SQL Server 2008 installation, SharePoint 2010 requires the following SQL Server 2008 configuration.

- 64-bit only version of SQL Server 2008
- SQL Server 2008 Service Pack 1
- Cumulative update package 2 for SQL Server 2008 SP1

NOTE If you are using SQL Server 2005, it requires the 64-bit version with Service Pack 2 or later.

The SQL Server 2008 Developer Edition is free, but it cannot be used in a production environment. This edition provides all of the functionality of the Enterprise Edition, so you should use it during the development and test phase of SharePoint, and then it can be easily deployed to your SQL Server 2008 Enterprise or Standard production environment.

IMPORTANT The SQL Server Express Edition is the SQL Server edition installed if you choose to perform a basic SharePoint 2010 installation, but the Express edition of SQL Server 2008 will limit your SharePoint performance, scalability, and functionality, as shown in Table 3-1.

MORE INFO For additional information on all of these SQL Server 2008 editions, visit *http://msdn.microsoft.com/en-us/library/cc645993.aspx*. For information about the available SQL Server 2005 editions and their features and limitations, visit *http://www.microsoft.com/Sqlserver/2005/en/us/compare-features.aspx*.

SQL Server Hardware Requirements

Similar to installation of SharePoint 2010, SQL Server also has certain hardware requirements to ensure that it runs as optimally as possible. These SQL Server 2008 requirements are similar for both the Enterprise and Standard editions of your SQL Server instances that will be hosting your SharePoint content.

- CD or DVD drive for disc-based installations
- Memory
  - Minimum: 512 MB
  - Recommended: 2 gigabytes (GB) or more
  - Maximum: Operating system maximum
- Processor
  - Minimum: 1.4 GHz
  - Recommended: 2.0 GHz or faster

SQL Server is memory intensive, and adding more physical memory can greatly improve the performance of SQL Server. Use the following guidelines to determine how much memory to install to create an optimal SharePoint experience.

- 8 GB of RAM for
  - Less than 40 GB of content databases
  - Less than 15 content databases
  - Less than 800 users
  - Less than 175 concurrent connections
- 16 GB of RAM for
  - 40 to 60 GB of content databases
  - 15 to 25 content databases
  - 800 to 1200 users
  - 175 to 225 concurrent connections
- 32 GB of RAM for
  - More than 60 GB of content databases
  - More than 25 content databases
  - More than 1200 users
  - More than 225 concurrent connections

BEST PRACTICE SQL Server will run much more efficiently if there is a lot of available memory. Be sure to add as much memory as possible to your SharePoint SQL Server installation to optimize the SharePoint experience.

The disk space requirements vary, depending on the SQL Server features you choose to install and the actual system configuration. Table 3-2 lists the disk space requirements for the different SQL Server 2008 components.

TABLE 3-2 SQL Server 2008 Feature Disk Space Requirements

FEATURE	DISK SPACE REQUIREMENTS
Database Engine and data files, Replication, and Full-Text Search	280 MB
Analysis Services and data files	90 MB
Reporting Services and Report Manager	120 MB
Integration Services	120 MB
Client components	850 MB
SQL Server Books Online	240 MB

SQL Server Software Requirements

SQL Server 2008 also has software requirements that must be met for successful installation and to ensure that it runs efficiently and provides SharePoint optimal performance. The software required to install the Enterprise and Standard SQL Server editions falls into two categories—software installed prior to running the SQL Server setup and software installed during the SQL Server setup.

The software that is required prior to running SQL Server setup includes

- Windows Server 2008 operating system (Windows Server 2003 is supported but not recommended)
  - Windows Server 2008 with Service Pack 2 or later
  - Windows Server 2008 R2
- Windows Installer 4.5 or later
- Microsoft Internet Explorer 6 SP1 or later

The software that is installed during the SQL Server setup includes

- .NET Framework 3.5 SP1
- SQL Server Native Client
- SQL Server Setup support files

> **MORE INFO** For additional information on the SQL Server 2008 hardware and software requirements, visit *http://msdn.microsoft.com/en-us/library/ms143506.aspx#EEx64*. For information on the SQL Server 2005 hardware and software requirements, go to *http://technet.microsoft.com/en-us/library/ms143506(SQL.90).aspx*.

Optimizing SQL Server for SharePoint 2010

Adhering to the SQL Server requirements will improve your chances of a successful deployment of SharePoint. However, if you choose to adhere to the recommendations and not just the requirements, you can also improve the performance of SharePoint. Making changes within SQL Server can improve your SharePoint performance significantly.

After successfully installing a SQL Server instance to host your SharePoint content, you can make several configuration changes to optimize the SQL Server instance. These changes will ultimately improve performance for both SQL Server and SharePoint 2010. This section discusses the following types of changes in SQL Server.

- SQL Server memory settings
- Database file locations
- Model database default settings
- Database recovery model
- Tempdb fast drives and 10 percent size of total content database size

Each of these SQL Server settings can affect your SharePoint 2010 experience and make a positive impact on your users' SharePoint interaction.

SQL Server Memory Settings

SQL Server is a memory-intensive application, and by default it is selfish when it comes to memory utilization. In fact, SQL Server has two primary uses of memory: buffer cache (sometimes called *data cache*) and procedure cache.

Buffer cache holds data pages in memory so that frequently accessed data can be retrieved from it. Otherwise, you would have to retrieve the data pages from disk, slowing performance. Reading data pages from the cache optimizes performance by minimizing the number of required input/output (I/O) operations, which are inherently slower than retrieving data from memory.

Procedure cache holds the stored procedure and query execution plans to minimize the number of times the query plans have to be generated.

Both of these caches are important, but as you allocate more memory for SQL Server, most of it goes to the buffer cache, helping reduce the round trips to the disk for data.

To determine if you have the appropriate amount of random-access memory (RAM) allocated to your SQL Server instance, you can monitor the following two SQL Server performance counters.

- **SQL Server:Buffer Manager – Buffer Cache Hit Ratio**   Percentage of pages found in the DATA buffer without having to read from disk (good > 95%)
- **SQL Server:Cache Manager – Cache Hit Ratio**   Percentage of pages found in the PROCEDURE cache without having to read from disk (good > 85%).

By default, each SQL Server instance changes its memory requirements dynamically based on available system resources. This default setting can have a major impact on the operating system and on other applications, including other instances of SQL Server running on the same server. When SQL Server is using memory dynamically, it queries the system periodically to determine the amount of free physical memory and takes as much as needed to complete the task at hand. However, you can control how SQL Server uses memory after you install SQL Server by configuring two SQL Server server memory configuration options: min server memory and max server memory.

Default Memory Settings

The min server memory option is used to define how much memory to release back to the operating system when it is not being used. The SQL Server default setting for min server memory is 0 MB, which means it releases all requested memory back to the operating system if it is no longer needed. SQL Server does not immediately allocate the amount of memory specified in min server memory on startup. Use min server memory to guarantee a minimum amount of memory available to the buffer pool of an instance of SQL Server.

> **IMPORTANT**   When memory usage has reached this value due to client load, SQL Server cannot free memory from the allocated buffer pool until the value of min server memory is reduced.

The max server memory option is used to define the maximum amount of memory a specific SQL Server instance can access if needed. The default setting for max server memory is 2147483647 MB, which means it will request as much memory for the buffer pool as needed without regard to the performance of the server. Although allowing SQL Server to use memory dynamically is recommended, you should configure these memory options manually and restrict the amount of memory that SQL Server can access.

Before you set the amount of memory for SQL Server, you need to determine the appropriate memory setting. You do this by determining the total available physical memory and then subtracting the memory required for the operating system, any other instances of SQL Server, and other system uses, if the computer is not wholly dedicated to SQL Server.

There are two principal methods for setting the SQL Server memory options manually.

- Set the min server memory and max server memory options to the same value, which corresponds to a fixed amount of memory allocated to the SQL Server buffer pool after the value is reached.

- Set the min server memory and max server memory options to create a memory range. This is useful when system or database administrators configure an instance of SQL Server that is running in conjunction with other applications on the same computer like Exchange or any other line of business applications.

Running Multiple Instances of SQL Server

When running multiple instances of the SQL Server on one server, there are three approaches you can use to manage your physical memory.

- Use the max server memory option to control memory usage. Establish maximum settings for each instance, being careful to ensure that the total allowance is not more than the total physical memory on your server. Try to give each instance an amount of memory that is proportional to its expected workload or database size.

- Use the min server memory option to control memory usage. Establish minimum settings for each instance so that the sum of these minimums is 1 to 2 GB less than the total physical memory on your server. Again, try to establish these minimums proportionately to the expected load of the instance. Using this approach has the advantage of allowing instances that are running to use the remaining free memory if all of the instances are not running at the same time.

- Do nothing. This approach is not recommended, however, because the first instances presented with a workload will tend to allocate all the memory. Instances started later or that are idle may run with only a minimal amount of memory available. SQL Server makes no attempt to balance memory usage across instances.

NOTE You can change these settings without restarting the instances, so you can easily experiment to find the best settings for your usage pattern.

After you decide what the new min server memory and max server memory settings should be, you can use the Memory page of the SQL Server Instance properties as shown in Figure 3-4 to modify the default settings to reflect your calculated settings. These two options can also be configured using the sp_configure stored procedure, as described in the section titled "sp_configure Stored Procedure" earlier in this chapter.

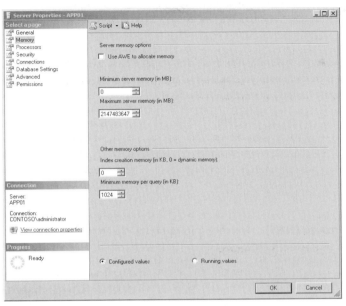

FIGURE 3-4 SQL Server default memory settings

Database Files and Their Location

The placement of your database files is critical to your SharePoint performance. When installing SQL Server, a default path is provided for your data and transaction log files. Usually, however, you will never want to use the default path. Instead, you should configure your SQL Server instance to modify the default database location, thereby improving performance. The types of files you will find here are introduced in this section.

Database Files

There are three types of files associated with a SQL Server database. Each database will have two of these files; the third file type is optional and may be used if you want to have multiple files associated with a single database. The three files associated with a database are

- **Primary data file**   The primary data file is the starting point of the database and points to the other files in the database. Every database has one primary data file. The recommended file name extension for primary data files is .mdf.

- **Transaction log files** Transaction log files hold all data modifications made to the primary data file and can be used to recover the database. You must have at least one log file for each database, although you can have more than one. The recommended file name extension for log files is .ldf.
- **Secondary data files** Secondary data files are optional, but they include all other data files associated with a database. The recommended file name extension for secondary data files is .ndf.

> **NOTE** SQL Server does not enforce the .mdf, .ndf, and .ldf file name extensions, but the consistency of these file extensions will help you, as well as anyone else who may work with this instance of SQL Server, easily identify the different kinds of files.

Storage Options

There are several options to consider when determining where your SQL Server files will be stored to provide optimal performance while balancing costs. The following storage options are the three most common.

- **Network Attached Storage (NAS)** Typically, this option has a high read and write I/O latency on a storage subsystem based on NAS or iSCSI technology. Not the most popular option, but it is available for your consideration.
- **Storage Area Network (SAN)** This allows you to spread I/O across every disk that is part of this storage option, but it can be adversely affected by read-intensive operations such as a full crawl. Generally, you want your SharePoint storage subsystem separate from all other applications and not have any shared storage, as you may have with a SAN because of the costs involved.
- **Direct Attached Storage (DAS)** DAS storage subsystems are cheaper, easier to maintain, and provide the SharePoint/SQL Administrator more control over virtual storage performance. It is a simple yet effective storage solution that is often less expensive than a SAN. You can also use expandable storage arrays that are basically "advanced" DAS systems. These systems function like a DAS, but they provide the added benefit of dual node (cluster) support.

Default Database Location

By default, your SharePoint database files are created on drive C of the SQL Server 2008 installation in the following directory.

C:\Program Files\Microsoft SQL Server\MSSQL10.MSSQLSERVER\MSSQL\DATA\

To improve performance and provide redundancy for your SharePoint content, you will want to place the database files elsewhere. You should place your data and transaction log files on a RAID 5 or RAID 10 array that will provide data redundancy so you will not lose any data if there is a disk failure. RAID arrays provide redundancy through data striping, mirroring, or a combination of both.

If a RAID array is not an option, you should at least separate your data files (.mdf) and transaction log files (.ldf) on different physical drives. By doing so, you will be able to recover the database if the hard drive containing the primary data file fails; you can do this by performing a transaction log restore. This configuration also increases I/O performance by reducing the large amount of read/write contention between the two file types. Data files are constantly written to and read from in an Online Transaction Processing (OLTP) environment, while transaction log files are typically only written to, and done so sequentially.

If you are unsure where your database files are located, you can access the properties of the database from within SQL Server Management Studio as shown in Figure 3-5, or you can enter the following T-SQL statements to retrieve the location and file names for the database named ContosoPortal_Content shown earlier in Figure 3-2.

```
USE ContosoPortal_Content
SELECT * FROM sysfiles
GO
```

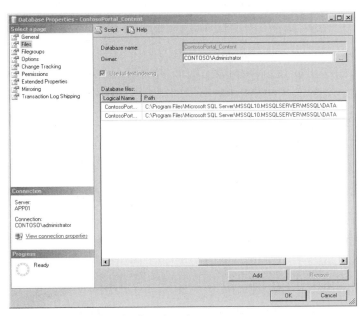

FIGURE 3-5 SQL Server database location

Modifying the Default Database Location

To make sure your databases are created on a RAID array or that the data files and transaction log files are located on different physical drives, you can modify the SQL Server Database Default Locations settings as shown in Figure 3-6.

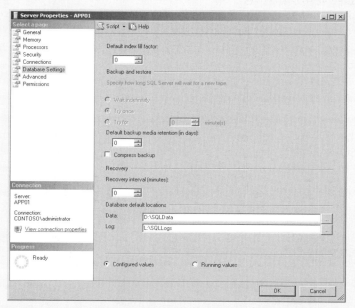

FIGURE 3-6 Modified Database Settings database default locations

IMPORTANT This setting does not affect existing databases—it affects only new databases created after the change to the Database Default Locations settings was made. To move existing databases, you have to detach, copy, and reattach the databases in SQL Server.

Model Database Settings

Every SharePoint database that you create inherits most of its database settings from the SQL Server system database called Model. After performing a default installation of SQL Server and then performing a default SharePoint installation, you may want to modify some of the Model database properties.

One of the first things you want to do after a successful installation of SharePoint 2010 is to access your SQL Server environment and make modifications to the Model database to help improve your SharePoint performance. Why is it important to do this after the installation of SharePoint? Although the two databases created during the installation—the configuration database and the Central Administration database—don't have to be very large, your content databases will probably need to be larger than the default settings on the Model database. Modifying the settings of the Model database will ensure that your content databases are created using optimal settings.

Model Database Default Settings

All new SharePoint databases will inherit most Model database properties. For instance, if you create a new database from within Central Administration, the new database will inherit the following properties from the Model database.

- Initial Size of primary data file
- Initial Size of transaction log
- Recovery model

However, some of these settings may not be adequate for the SharePoint databases that you will create. Figure 3-7 shows the default Files properties for the Model database.

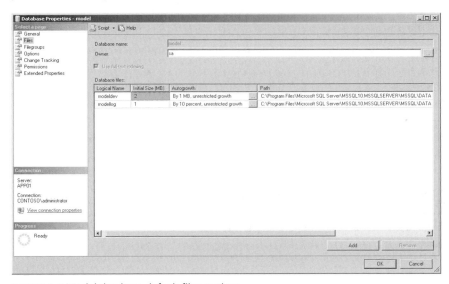

FIGURE 3-7 Model database default files settings

There are a few performance concerns with these Files settings. The Initial Size value is small; the Autogrowth value is small; and the Path of the files is pointing to the default directory on drive C.

Modifying the Model Database Settings

This section describes how to improve performance by modifying the Initial Size setting for your new SharePoint content databases by modifying the Initial Size value of the SQL Server Model database. However, this modification shouldn't be made without careful analysis and calculation.

INITIAL SIZE OF MODEL DATABASE

You may be wondering why it is important to consider the value of these settings before you create new databases. Because the Initial Size setting for new databases file is small and the Autogrowth option is enabled, whenever you try to add content to a database, SQL Server has to expand it using the incremental value in the Autogrowth setting. For instance, if you were to upload a 10 MB file into this database using the default Initial Size and Autogrowth settings, SQL Server would have to lock the database 8 to 10 times to grow the data file in 1-MB increments until there was enough room to accept the 10-MB file you wanted to upload. Furthermore, because the log file Initial Size is small and its Autogrowth setting is at 10 percent increments, this file would also have to grow to accept the file being uploaded. Also, each time these files are enlarged in 1-MB increments, it causes fragmentation of your hard drive. As you can imagine, this can have an enormous impact on your SharePoint performance.

This is why it is important that you carefully consider how much information will be contained within most of your SharePoint databases, as well as how much information will be added, modified, or deleted, before you modify the Initial Size setting in the Model database. After you make the change, all new databases created using the Model database will begin with that Initial Size value, which will eliminate—or at least reduce—the need for Autogrowth to occur. There is no magic number that is best for the Initial Size setting of the content databases; you must perform a careful analysis to make that determination yourself. However, the best practice is that the size of your content databases should not exceed 100 GB. This is a soft limit that will increase the chances of performing a recovery in less than four hours.

> **NOTE** Your database transaction log initial size is normally 25 percent of the size of the associated data file.

RECOVERY MODEL OF MODEL DATABASE

You can also modify the recovery model on the Model database, and its setting will be inherited by all newly created databases. This database setting is discussed in more detail later in this chapter, in the section titled "SharePoint Content Database Recovery Model," and you can modify this setting on the Database Properties page, as shown in Figure 3-8.

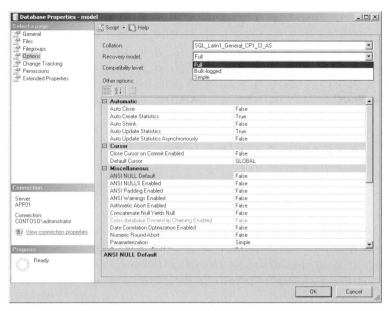

FIGURE 3-8 Model database recovery model settings

AUTOGROWTH SETTING OF MODEL DATABASE

Unlike the previous two settings, even if you configure the Model database with specific Autogrowth settings, they will not be applied when a new database is created through the Central Administration interface.

Is this a bad thing? Not necessarily. It's best to use the Autogrowth setting as more of an insurance policy on your databases. If the database does reach the maximum size, you want to make sure you have enough coverage; that is, you want to ensure it grows in larger increments rather than small increments (which can cause a negative performance impact on your server). Take the time to analyze and adjust the initial size of the Model database to reduce the likelihood of the Autogrowth occurring. However, if some massive entries are added to your SharePoint libraries, and this causes your content database to fill up, it won't prevent users from accessing the database—it will just slightly impact the performance while SharePoint performs the necessary Autogrowth.

Like the Initial Size settings of your Model database, the default Autogrowth settings are not optimal for a SharePoint farm. The default Autogrowth setting for data files is 1 MB, and the setting for your transaction log files is 10 percent. You should modify these SharePoint database settings immediately after you create a new database.

That is how modifying these settings differs from making changes to the Initial Size settings. You can't change the settings by increasing the values in the settings for the Model database; you need to change these settings after you create your SharePoint content databases. Speak to your DBA to confirm that the Autogrowth settings for your SharePoint databases have been increased to a more reasonable size—a value agreed on by everyone.

You also have a choice of having the Autogrowth occur using either a fixed incremental amount or a percentage of the existing size. You should use a fixed amount, like 1 GB, so if Autogrowth does occur, you will know how long the process will take. If you use a percentage, the Autogrowth time will vary depending on how large the file was originally.

When you configure your Autogrowth settings, you also have the opportunity to configure either unlimited file growth for the database files or to set a specific maximum file size. You should specify a maximum file size to prevent the entire drive that contains the database files from filling up. This is particularly important if the drives contain mission-critical data, because that data will not be accessible again until space is freed up on the drive.

Shrinking Your Content Databases

By default, SQL Server does not create an optimal configuration for your SharePoint integration. You must configure SQL Server to improve your SharePoint performance, by increasing the size of databases, adjusting database file location, and allowing for automatic growth of databases as needed.

Conversely, you also can configure your databases to automatically decrease in size by using the Auto Shrink option, as shown in Figure 3-9, or you can manually shrink them. This is done to free up space currently being used by your SharePoint databases. Although this option is available, you should use it sparingly. In fact, you should only shrink a database if you are confident that the database size won't have to be increased again to accommodate SharePoint content. Altering the size of a database is costly from a performance perspective, so you want to create an environment that avoids the need for a constant increase and decrease in the size of your databases.

> **NOTE** The SQL Server database Auto Shrink option should be used only in your SharePoint development environment, to assist in maintaining free space for your developers and minimize the size of the files they are working with during development.

The Auto Shrink operation causes fragmentation and is a resource-intensive operation that runs about every 30 minutes. It will perform a shrink only on databases that have more than 25 percent of free space in them.

> **IMPORTANT** Be extremely careful when shrinking databases so that you don't cause performance problems during the shrink operation or cause the database to have to grow back to a larger size using the Autogrowth settings.

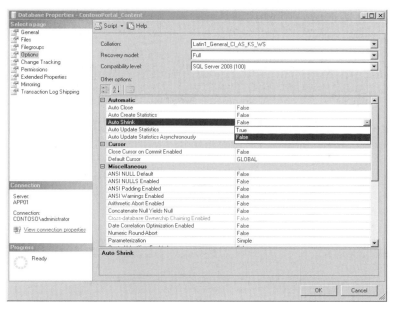

FIGURE 3-9 SQL Server Database Auto Shrink setting

The general recommendation is to perform a manual shrink on a database if more than 50 percent of the database size is free space and you need to recover that space. The manual shrink operation can be lengthy, so you should perform this operation during nonpeak hours. The following Transact-SQL command can be run from within Management Studio or from the command prompt using Sqlcmd.exe to manually shrink a database called UserDB to the amount of current data plus 10 percent.

```
DBCC SHRINKDATABASE (UserDB, 10);
GO
```

The following Transact-SQL command can be run from within Management Studio or from the command prompt using Sqlcmd.exe to manually shrink a database file called DataFile1 in the UserDB database to a total size of 7 MB.

```
USE UserDB;
GO
DBCC SHRINKFILE (DataFile1, 7);
GO
```

NOTE A database cannot be shrunk below its original file size or manually altered file size using the DBCC SHRINKDATABASE command. You can shrink the file that belongs to the database to a size smaller than the original or manually altered size by using the DBCC SHRINKFILE command.

Pre-Creating Your Content Databases

If your organization has a SQL DBA that manages all of your companies' databases, including your SharePoint databases, you have the option of asking your DBA to pre-create your content databases from within SQL Server. You can then point to these pre-created databases from SharePoint, SharePoint will recognize them, and the databases will become part of the farm.

The advantage of pre-creating databases is that all the Model database settings are inherited, including the Autogrowth setting that is not inherited when you create your content databases from within SharePoint. However, a disadvantage is that the default collation setting of the Model database is SQL_Latin1_General_CP1_CI_AS, which is not compatible with the required SharePoint database collation type. Therefore, your DBA will have to be sure that the pre-created content databases use the appropriate database collation type of Latin1_General_CI_AS_KS_WS, as shown in Figure 3-10.

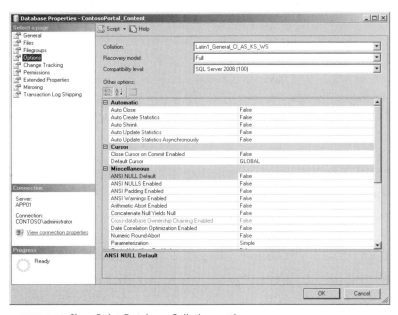

FIGURE 3-10 SharePoint Database Collation setting

> **BEST PRACTICE** During the installation of SQL Server that is dedicated to SharePoint, you can choose the SharePoint-required collation of Latin1_General_CI_AS_KS_WS. This will ensure it is used for all databases created in this instance of SQL Server, regardless of whether they are created from SharePoint or SQL Server.

The Latin1_General_CI_AS_KS_WS option translates to

- **CI**   Case Insensitive

- **AS**   Accent Sensitive

- **KS**   Kana Sensitive (Used to distinguish between two types of Japanese kana characters)

- **WS**   Width Sensitive

Whether you create your content databases from within SharePoint or let your SQL DBA create them, there are certain settings that you should check to make sure that your SharePoint databases are running as optimally as possible on your SQL Server. You should review your SharePoint SQL Server instance and each of your SharePoint content databases to ensure they meet the following criteria.

- SharePoint SQL Server Instance Settings

  - **Data Files Default Location**   Locate on a RAID array or a different drive than transaction log files; do not locate on the operating system drive

  - **Transaction Log Files Default location**   Locate on a RAID array or a different drive than data files; do not locate on the operating system drive

  - **Minimum Server Memory**   Calculation based on other applications, SQL Server instances, and the operating system requirements

  - **Maximum Server Memory**   Calculation based on other applications, SQL Server instances, and the operating system requirements

- SharePoint Database Settings

  - **Collation**   Must be Latin1_General_CI_AS_KS_WS

  - **Recovery Model**   Set to Full for content databases

  - **Transaction Log Files: Initial Size**   25 percent of combined data files' initial size

  - **Transaction Log Files: Autogrowth**   25–50 percent of the file's initial size

  - **Transaction Log File: Path**   Directory configured at the SQL Server instance

  - **Primary Data Files: Initial Size**   Calculated amount based on expected volume

  - **Primary Data Files: Autogrowth**   25–50 percent of the file's initial size

  - **Primary Data File: Path**   Directory configured at the SQL Server instance

  - **Secondary Data Files: Initial Size**   Calculated amount based on expected volume

  - **Secondary Data Files: Autogrowth**   25–50 percent of the file's initial size

Change the default path of your data and log files after you install SQL Server and before you start creating databases so that SharePoint will have fault tolerance and high availability. Check your available memory and determine what other applications, besides the operating system, will require physical memory, then calculate and set your minimum and maximum memory settings to avoid performance degradation of SharePoint and other applications running on that server.

Remember, the Autogrowth settings are a contingency for unexpected growth and should not be used as a day-to-day action. To avoid using Autogrowth except when absolutely necessary, analyze the amount of information you expect to be in your SharePoint databases and set their initial size to hold the anticipated amount of content. Use the full recovery model to provide the opportunity to recover information in the event of a hardware failure, as discussed in the next section.

Tempdb Database Settings

SharePoint performance can also be improved with a properly configured Tempdb database. The Tempdb database is the temporary work storage area that is used when sorting content, and its location and configuration can impact SQL Server performance—and ultimately SharePoint's performance. Similar to the Model database, the location, Initial Size, and Autogrowth settings for the Tempdb database can affect your overall SharePoint performance.

Make modifications to the Tempdb database similar to those suggested for the Model database. The Tempdb database is cleared out each time you stop and start your SQL Server instance, so if it isn't properly configured, it will experience the same growth issues as the Model database, causing performance issues for your users.

The following list contains recommendations for optimizing your Tempdb database in your production environment.

- Place the Tempdb database on the fastest I/O subsystem available. Use disk striping if there are many directly attached disks.
- Pre-allocate space for your Tempdb files by setting the Initial File size to a larger value so it can accommodate the typical workload in your environment.
- Create multiple data files to maximize disk bandwidth. This reduces Tempdb storage contention and yields better scalability.
  - Make each of these files the same size; this allows for optimal proportional-fill performance.
- Allow your Tempdb files to grow automatically as needed.
  - Set the file growth increment to a reasonable size to prevent the database files from growing in small increments. See Table 3-3 for suggested growth settings

TABLE 3-3 Suggested Tempdb File Growth Increments

TEMPDB FILE SIZE	FILE GROWTH INCREMENTAL VALUE
1–100 MB	10 MB
100–200 MB	20 MB
200 MB or more	10%

- Put the Tempdb database on disks other than those used by your content databases.
- Set the recovery model to simple, which is the default. This will automatically reclaim transaction log space and keep the space requirements to a minimum.

If you can separate only one database from the rest, make it your Tempdb, because SharePoint performs reads and writes to it constantly. Your SharePoint installation can't be faster than your Tempdb database. If possible, you should store the Tempdb database on a RAID 10 disk.

SharePoint Content Database Recovery Model

Every SharePoint database that you create inherits the recovery model of the SQL Server Model database for that instance of SQL Server. This recovery model determines how your transaction log information is managed after the information is written to your data files. There are three recovery models to choose from.

- **Full**   Retains all data in transaction log after writing it to the data file (the default).
- **Bulk-Logged**   Retains entries made in transaction log when bulk transactions occur.
- **Simple**   Purges all transactions from transaction log after writing them to data file.

The recovery model you choose for your SharePoint content databases will determine your recoverability options, and they also can affect the performance of SharePoint

What Is a Transaction Log?

A database transaction log is instrumental in maintaining data integrity within that database. The transaction log receives the following types of SQL Server actions, called *transactions*.

- New information added (Insert)
- Existing information changed (Update)
- Existing information deleted (Delete)

This means that if you add a document to a library (insert), modify a task in a list (update), or remove a document from a library (delete), the action is first written to the content database transaction log. After a short period of time (roughly 60 seconds), SQL Server runs a process called a *checkpoint*. This checkpoint reads the inserts, updates, and deletes stored in the transaction log and applies them to the data files for that database. After writing them to the data files, the simple recovery model removes those transactions from the transaction log file. Conversely, the full recovery model retains those transactions in the transaction log file

The recovery model setting will affect the recoverability of your data in the event of a disaster, but the setting also can have a negative affect on performance. The methods you use to back up your SharePoint content can have a major impact on recoverability and performance of SharePoint. In the following sections, you learn the advantages and disadvantages of using the full and simple recovery models for your SharePoint databases.

Full Recovery Model

The full recovery model is the default recovery model—unless you change it on the Model database—for your SharePoint content databases. This is the preferred recovery model because it means that after the information is written to the data files, you retain the information in the transaction log. This is helpful when you need to recover your SharePoint content if your data files become corrupt or are lost because of a hard drive failure. However, it only works if you are storing your transaction log files on separate physical drives.

Most production environments use the full recovery model because it provides you the opportunity to recover changes made to your SharePoint content if you lose your data files. You can recover lost data by performing a backup log action on the transaction log and then restoring this backup after you restore your SharePoint backups. For more information on the different backup types and how they are used to perform a disaster recovery, see Chapter 17.

A disadvantage of using the full recovery model is that when you perform a backup of your data using SharePoint, the information in the transaction log files never gets purged. The SQL Server transaction log files get purged only if you perform an actual SQL Server BACKUP LOG command. After performing a backup of the transaction log from within Management Studio or using the BACKUP LOG command, the information gets purged from the transaction log file, which reduces the size of the transaction log back to its initial file size. However, a backup performed from within SharePoint on one of its databases that is set to full recovery never performs an actual backup log action, which causes the transaction log files to grow to significantly.

The changes in the transaction log should be retained for recovery purposes until you perform another full database backup. To prevent the transaction logs from becoming too large, you can speak to your SQL Server DBA and ask her to schedule a backup of your transaction logs to separate media immediately after she performs a full database backup. Remember that the full database backup contains all the information in the transaction log, so you don't need the transaction log information anymore.

For instance, if you perform a full database backup every Sunday night and you are using the full recovery model, you can create a SQL Server job that runs after your successful full database backup to then back up the associated transaction log. However, you don't need this transaction log backup. You can simply delete the backup file that contains the transaction log backup.

You can avoid the large transaction log files using these two steps.

1. Back up the transaction logs using the BACKUP LOG command or from within Management Studio.

2. Delete the backup file created in step 1.

The following commands can be used to create a SQL server job that you can schedule to perform a full backup, a transaction log backup, and then delete the transaction log backup.

```
BACKUP DATABASE contosoportal TO DISK = 'C:\sqlbackups\fullbackup.bak'

BACKUP LOG contosoportal TO DISK = 'C:\sqlbackups\logbackup.bak'

DELETE 'C:\sqlbackups\logbackup.bak'
```

You perform the transaction log backup to purge the old transactions and prevent the transaction log files from becoming too large. Use the following steps to take advantage of the full recovery model while preventing the transaction log files from becoming too large.

1. Periodically perform a full database backup of your SharePoint database.

2. Immediately after a successful full database backup, back up the transaction log.

3. Delete the file created when you backed up the transaction log.

4. Optionally, schedule periodic backups of your transaction logs.

Using these steps will allow you to use the full recovery model that will be beneficial in a disaster recover scenario, at the same time preventing your SQL Server transaction logs from becoming too large.

Simple Recovery Model

The simple recovery model is used primarily in development environments, because the information is temporary or is being used for testing. When you use this recovery model, the information stored in the transaction log is purged after it is written to the data file.

The disadvantage of the simple recovery model is that it doesn't allow you to back up the transaction log. In the event that you have corrupt data files or you lose data during a hardware failure, you won't be able to recover the changes made since your last full or differential backup.

The advantage of the simple recovery model is that it never grows too large, because the transactions are purged as soon as they are successfully written to the data files. This prevents the need to create a job to back up the transaction log and delete the backup file created during the backup of the transaction log.

Although you might prefer using the simple recovery model in your development environment, it is a best practice to use the full recovery model in your production environments. This provides you the opportunity to recover all changes regardless of when the last backup was performed.

Discuss your options with your DBA to decide which recovery model is best for your specific situation and make sure that you have a proper recovery plan in place for your SharePoint implementation.

Verifying Data Integrity Using DBCC CHECKDB

The Transact-SQL programming language provides a number of Database Console Command (DBCC) statements that act as commands you can run to verify the integrity of your SQL Server. These DBCC statements can be grouped into the following categories.

- **Maintenance**   Maintenance tasks on databases, indexes, or filegroups
- **Miscellaneous**   Enable trace flags, remove DLLs from memory
- **Informational**   Gather and display various types of information
- **Validation**   Validate operations on databases, tables, and allocation of pages

The DBCC statements are designed to accept input parameters and return values and information. Some DBCC statements run on internal read-only databases to prevent blocking and concurrency problems while they execute. This is accomplished by creating internal snapshots of the database before running the command and dropping the internal database immediately after the command completes.

You should run the DBCC CHECKDB statement with REPAIR_REBUILD regularly on your SQL Server databases to verify the logical and physical integrity of all the objects in the specified database and perform some minor repairs to your database that will not result in any data loss. Here are a few of the operations the DBCC CHECKDB statement performs.

- Runs DBCC CHECKALLOC to check the consistency of the disk space allocation structures
- Runs DBCC CHECKTABLE to check the integrity of all pages on every table and view
- Validates the contents of the indexed views in the database

Optimizing Outside of SQL Server

If the server that is hosting SQL Server is dedicated to only SQL Server, there are some additional changes that can be made to help optimize SQL Server and improve the SharePoint experience for your end users. Some of these changes also can be applied to any volumes that are dedicated to SQL Server data.

Disk Storage Options

The location of your content is extremely important to recoverability, availability, and performance. The placement of your data files, log files, and even the Tempdb database can have a significant impact on SharePoint's performance and availability. For instance, you should store your databases on a RAID implementation; if that isn't possible, you should store your transaction log files (.ldf) and your data files (.mdf and .ndf) on separate physical drives for recoverability and better performance. Furthermore, these files should be on a separate drive from your operating system, which will help reduce contention.

Table 3-4 provides some recommended RAID implementations and I/O requests that should be targeted when you are planning your SharePoint and SQL Server integration.

TABLE 3-4 Database RAID Level and IOPS Recommendations

DATABASE TYPE	IOPS	RAID LEVEL
Content Database	.75 / GB	RAID 5 or 10
Transaction Log	2 / GB	RAID 10
Search Database	2 / GB	RAID 10
Tempdb	2 / GB	RAID 10

> **MORE INFO** There is an excellent best practices article written by Microsoft that goes into great depth regarding SharePoint storage. This paper can be viewed at *http://msdn.microsoft.com/en-us/library/dd758814.aspx.*

NTFS Allocation Unit Size

All file systems that Windows operating systems use to organize the hard disk are based on cluster (allocation unit) size. The cluster size is defined when you format your drive. The cluster size represents the smallest amount of disk space that can be allocated to hold a file. The smaller the cluster size, the more efficiently your disk stores information. However, when formatting the partition that will be storing your SQL Server data files, you should use a 64-kilobyte (KB) allocation unit size for your data, transaction logs, and Tempdb databases. SQL Server uses Extents to store data, which are groups of eight 8-KB pages that are physically contiguous to each other for a total of 64 KB. By doing this, it reduces the chances of I/Os that span multiple NTFS allocations, which could result in split or multiple I/Os required to retrieve your SQL data. Your performance improvement can be as much as 30 percent when using 64-KB allocation units.

> **IMPORTANT** Be aware that using allocation unit sizes greater than 4 KB results in the loss of the use of NTFS compression on the volume.

Run the chkdsk command to determine what your current allocation unit size is. For example, if you want to run this command on your root drive, you would type the following at the command prompt:

```
chkdsk   c:
```

It will take a few moments to run, but it will then return lines of information about your disk drive. One line of information is the allocation unit in bytes, as shown here.

```
4096 bytes in each allocation unit.
```

If you divide 4096 by 1024, you will see that your cluster size is 4 KB. Whatever number is returned in the chkdsk information as the allocation unit size, divide it by 1024 to determine the actual cluster size. To increase the cluster size, you can issue the following format command.

```
format E: /Q /FS:NTFS /A:64K /V:Data1
```

Following is an explanation of what each parameter used with the previous format command means.

- **E:**   Drive letter to format
- **/Q**   Quick format
- **/FS:NTFS**   File system (FAT or NTFS)
- **/A:64K**   Allocation unit size
- **/V:Data1**   Volume label

NTFS supports 512, 1024, 2048, 4096, 8192, 16-KB, 32-KB, and 64-KB allocation unit sizes. However, NTFS compression is not supported for allocation units above 4096.

> **IMPORTANT**   Issuing a format command erases all existing data and creates a data-free drive, as if you just purchased it. Be sure to copy all data to another drive before issuing the format command.

Monitoring SQL I/O with SQLIO.exe

SQLIO.exe is a tool provided by Microsoft that can be used to determine the I/O capacity of any storage configuration. You can use it to get an understanding of the performance behavior for your disk storage subsystem. Although it contains SQL in the file name, it is not limited to testing performance for SQL Server—it is more about measuring your disk storage I/O performance. There is a sample script file provided that you can modify to define the benchmark scenario you are testing. You must download SQLIO first, which you can do by visiting *http://go.microsoft.com/fwlink/?LinkId=115176*.

> **NOTE**   SQLIO is a free tool that is provided "as is," and there is no support offered for any problems encountered when using the tool.

You can use SQLIO to test a storage configuration, but when you do so, you need to test each volume individually and then add volumes until all volumes are tested together. This means that when testing a large number of volumes, there are several combinations. In these cases, focus on scalability as the number of volumes included in the test is increased (1, 2, 4, 8, and so on). Testing the volumes in this manner enables you to determine if there are any problems with a specific volume and if the expected cumulative throughput is reached with that particular storage configuration. SQLIO will return and summarize certain performance data during the test you run. When running the test, you can redirect the output to a text file to capture the performance information for later review.

> **MORE INFO**   For a complete set of the options available in SQLIO, see the Readme.txt file associated with the tool or run SQLIO.exe -?

These additional optimization options can be helpful when you want to really fine-tune your SharePoint SQL Server environment. If you are considering making these kinds of modifications, be sure to back up all your SQL Server content in case there is a problem.

> **MORE INFO**   For additional information on disk partition alignment, go to *http://msdn.microsoft.com/en-us/library/dd758814.aspx.*

Summary

This chapter provided information about the importance of SQL Server integration with SharePoint, because more than 90 percent of your SharePoint information is stored in SQL Server. Choosing the appropriate SQL Server edition and ensuring you have the proper hardware and software in place will ensure that SQL Server is running as optimally as possible, from the ground up. Post-installation changes that you make in SQL Server can have a major impact on your SharePoint performance. You should modify the minimum memory setting and maximum memory settings, along with the default location of your database and transaction log files on your SQL Server SharePoint instance, to improve the overall performance of SQL Server. In addition, you should modify the Model primary database file and transaction log files to reflect larger initial sizes and appropriate Autogrowth settings on all future SharePoint database files. Furthermore, the correct placement of the Tempdb database is instrumental to optimizing your SharePoint performance.

There are several databases for you to manage in SharePoint 2010, so becoming more familiar with SQL Server Studio Management, common administrative system stored procedures, Transact-SQL statements, and the Windows PowerShell cmdlets for SQL Server will help streamline the management of your SQL Server databases.

There are a lot of tools and a lot of SQL Server components involved in the management of SharePoint 2010, so take the time to learn how to use them, because they will be beneficial for the optimal performance of SharePoint.

CHAPTER 4

Installing SharePoint 2010

This chapter focuses on how to install Microsoft SharePoint 2010. It will help you prepare for the decisions that you have to make during the installation to ensure that you perform the installation appropriately. Similar to Microsoft Office SharePoint Services 2007, you can choose from two types of installations: you can install the SharePoint 2010 framework, which is now called Microsoft SharePoint Foundation 2010 (it was called Windows SharePoint Services in previous versions), or SharePoint 2010, which supports all intranet, extranet, and Web applications across an enterprise within one integrated platform. This chapter discusses both installation types and helps you become familiar with the nuances of each type when performing the installations.

This chapter also discusses some post-installation configurations for your farm. In addition, it explains the process for uninstalling SharePoint and provides information about some items that are not removed during the uninstall process.

Installing SharePoint 2010 is a fairly straightforward process, but the decisions you'll make during the installation are critical to your farm deployment. There's a lot for you to learn about the installation, and this chapter covers the following information about SharePoint 2010 installation components.

■ Introduction to SharePoint 2010 installation types

■ SharePoint 2010 prerequisites

■ Installing SharePoint 2010

■ Configuring SharePoint 2010

■ Removing a SharePoint 2010 installation

Introducing SharePoint 2010 Installation Types

Your first installation decision is selecting the appropriate SharePoint product for your implementation. After careful analysis, you can decide which edition will meet your organization's
needs. SharePoint 2010 is offered in two categories, with four editions within each of the
categories—a total of eight editions from which you can choose.

- Intranet (On Premise)
  - SharePoint Foundation 2010
  - SharePoint 2010 Editions
  - FAST Search Server 2010 for SharePoint
  - SharePoint Online
- Internet (Cloud)
  - SharePoint 2010 for Internet Sites, Standard Edition
  - SharePoint 2010 for Internet Sites, Enterprise Edition
  - FAST Search Server 2010 for Internet Business
  - SharePoint Online for Internet Services

> **BEST PRACTICES**   This chapter provides a brief overview of the two categories and the
> editions within each of them. After gathering, organizing, and analyzing your organiza-
> tion's requirements, you will be able to determine which editions fulfill your needs, and
> then you should perform in-depth research on the possible choices before deciding which
> one you will implement.

SharePoint Intranet Editions

There are four editions to choose from if you plan to implement SharePoint as an intranet, or
on premise, installation. These include

- SharePoint Foundation 2010
- SharePoint 2010
- FAST Search Server for SharePoint
- SharePoint 2010 Online

The following sections provide you with a brief overview of the features and advantages
of each of these editions to help you determine which one you should install for your internal
organization.

SharePoint Foundation 2010

In general, SharePoint Foundation 2010 is a good choice for smaller organizations or for department-level implementations, because it provides an inexpensive entry-level or pilot collaboration technology through a secure Web-based interface. This edition of SharePoint 2010 is free for you to download and install. You can use it to organize documents, organize schedules, and participate in discussions through blogs, wikis, workspaces, and document libraries using the underlying SharePoint infrastructure.

SharePoint 2010

SharePoint 2010 requires you to purchase and install the program, along with the appropriate client access licenses (CALs) that will be used by your internal organization. You can choose from two types of licensing options available for SharePoint 2010: Standard and Enterprise editions. The binaries that are installed are the same for both editions, but some features are disabled after you complete a Standard Edition installation. The same installation source files are used for both editions of SharePoint 2010, but the product key you enter during the installation determines if the installation will have a Standard or an Enterprise license. There is a price difference between the two editions, of course, so you should analyze what your requirements are before deciding which edition you need to purchase and install.

- **Standard Client Access Licensing** Organizations that want to deploy a business collaboration platform that can be used to manage multiple content types will find the Standard CAL option is the most cost-effective choice. With these licenses, you are able to use the core capabilities of SharePoint 2010 to manage your content and business processes, search and share information as well as users' expertise, and simplify how people work together across different organizations.

- **Enterprise Client Access Licensing** Organizations that want to take advantage of the advanced scenarios in SharePoint 2010 to allow end users to search, create, and work with data and documents in disparate sources using familiar and unified infra-structure, such as Microsoft Office and Internet Explorer, will choose the Enterprise CAL option. You can use the Enterprise CAL capabilities of SharePoint 2010 to integrate the program fully with external line-of-business (LOB) applications, Web services, and Microsoft Office client applications. This edition will promote better decision making by providing rich data visualization, dashboards, and advanced analytics along with more robust forms and workflow-based solutions.

The good news is that a Standard Edition of SharePoint 2010 can be upgraded easily to the Enterprise Edition in Central Administration without performing an additional installation. However, to change from an Enterprise Edition to a Standard Edition does require you to uninstall the Enterprise Edition and perform a new installation of the Standard Edition.

FAST Search Server for SharePoint

The FAST Search Server edition of SharePoint is an advanced version of SharePoint 2010, described in the previous section. It includes all of the functionality of SharePoint 2010 Enterprise Edition, with the addition of Microsoft FAST Search technology. The FAST Search features include contextual search (such as recognizing departments), more scalability of the search feature, and the ability to add metadata to unstructured content, making it easier to search.

SharePoint 2010 Online

This edition of SharePoint 2010 is a cloud version of the software that provides a hosted SharePoint solution for your organization, similar to the Microsoft Business Productivity Online Suite (BPOS). You can use this edition of SharePoint 2010 to provide your organization with the functionality of SharePoint without installing the product in-house. The SharePoint 2010 Online edition is available in two versions: Standard and Dedicated.

- **SharePoint Online Standard Version**   The Standard version is a shared version of SharePoint with multiple user bases, and it includes most of the functionality required to support a company intranet that is focused on communication and collaboration. The SharePoint Online version offers the following functionality.

  - Collaboration
  - Portals
  - Search
  - Content Management
  - Business Process and Forms

- **SharePoint Online Dedicated Version**   The Dedicated SharePoint Online version offers more functionality, including authentication methods and customizations, and it also requires separate installations on separate servers for each user base. A user base could be an entire company or simply a department, but each installation is handled independently.

SharePoint Internet Editions

There are also four editions to choose from if your organization wants to use an Internet, or cloud, implementation of SharePoint 2010. You would choose one of these editions if your organization will store SharePoint content that you want to make accessible by way of an extranet or the Internet.

SharePoint 2010 for Internet Sites, Standard Edition

This edition of SharePoint 2010 is for small to mid-size organizations that want to create public Internet sites or basic extranet sites using the standard features of SharePoint 2010. The functionality you have with SharePoint 2010 within your intranet can be made available on an extranet or a public-facing Internet implementation using this edition.

SharePoint 2010 for Internet Sites, Enterprise Edition

This edition is for larger organizations that want to create scalable customer-facing Internet websites or private, secure extranet sites using the Enterprise capabilities of SharePoint 2010. It is similar to the Internet Sites, Standard Edition, but more scalability and management functions are included in the Enterprise version of SharePoint 2010 for Internet Sites.

FAST Search Server 2010 for Internet Business

This edition of SharePoint 2010 adds the FAST Search engine to SharePoint 2010 for Internet Sites, Enterprise Edition. FAST Search for Internet Business provides public websites with flexible, search-driven capabilities including content integration and interaction management.

SharePoint Online for Internet Services

This edition is similar to the SharePoint 2010 Online edition, in that it provides a hosted SharePoint solution for your organization. However, it is anticipated that this edition will support more online capacity.

   This chapter will discuss several main points about installing SharePoint 2010 and will help you understand how SharePoint should be installed, regardless of what edition you are using. All of the following sections about the installation of SharePoint 2010 are relevant to any of the editions you choose to install.

SharePoint Server Roles

In planning the installation, you also need to consider the different servers that you need to have available to complete the installation of SharePoint 2010. In your deployment plan, you need to consider the number of Web front-end servers (WFEs) and application servers as well as their roles within the farm. There are four primary server roles required during a SharePoint installation.

- Web front-end server
- Application server
- Database server
- Active Directory server

The Web server role in SharePoint 2010 focuses on handling the requests of clients and rendering pages to them. The application role is optimized for processing requests in the background. SharePoint information is retrieved from the database server, and the Active Directory server provides user authentication.

> **BEST PRACTICES** Although it isn't required, best practice for optimal performance is to have these server roles reside on different computers. However, if your budget prohibits deploying different servers for each role, a single computer can host more than one of these roles.

Web Front-End Server

After a completing the SharePoint 2010 installation for the first time on a server, you have created your farm, and the server is performing both the Web front-end server role and the application server role. With the scalable architecture SharePoint 2010 provides, you should separate the roles so they reside on at least two different servers. You can have multiple WFEs hosting the Web applications that your users connect to, which will provide high availability and, if configured, load balancing.

Application Servers

Similar to SharePoint Server 2007, you can have multiple application servers managing and serving applications to the WFE servers. The architectural model of SharePoint 2010 offers great flexibility in terms of which servers provide which services. You can start by running several service applications on one server and expand the farm by spreading them across other servers.

For instance, a SharePoint 2010 server could run Excel Calculation Services without being accessed directly by clients. The same setup can be used for services such as Search or Profile Synchronization.

Database Server

The database server hosts the configuration, content, and service application databases for the SharePoint farm, but it can also host databases for other applications—although this is not recommended. Depending on the availability and your performance requirements, you may consider using a Microsoft SQL Server cluster. Alternatively, depending on the demand that SharePoint 2010 generates from the server, it can be beneficial to distribute databases across multiple SQL servers.

It is a good idea to establish strong communications with the SQL Server database administrators (DBAs) during the SharePoint 2010 planning process, to make it easier to exchange information about databases being created, database configuration, and backup and restore settings.

Active Directory

Active Directory is used by SharePoint 2010 for different purposes, each of which requires different preparation. First, SharePoint uses domain user accounts when running services. Second, domain user accounts are configured as identities for application pools in Internet Information Services (IIS).

User accounts from Active Directory can be imported into a SharePoint Profile database to enable enhanced social search capabilities. When user accounts are imported from Active Directory for use in user profiles, make sure that the metadata that describes the user is current. You can schedule changes to be imported in an incremental fashion. Additional information about users can be imported from other sources, such as a human resources (HR) system.

Preparing for SharePoint 2010 Installation

The following sections cover the requirements of a SharePoint installation as well as the tasks you must complete before performing the installation. You will discover that there are different ways to prepare the server for an installation of SharePoint 2010.

Specifically, the sections that follow will discuss the following SharePoint 2010 installation requirements.

- Hardware requirements
  - WFE/application server
  - Database server
- Software requirements
  - Operating system
  - Database server
  - WFE/application server
  - Client computers
- Active Directory accounts
- SharePoint 2010 preparation tool

You must make sure these required components are installed prior to performing your installation of SharePoint to ensure a successful installation and implementation of SharePoint 2010.

> **BEST PRACTICES** People often perform upgrades of existing operating systems and software applications. A best practice is to make sure that all components of your SharePoint farm are always fresh installs and not upgrades. Upgrades can bring problems from earlier installations and are normally not as reliable as a fresh installation. All of the required components for SharePoint 2010, including the operating system, SQL Server, IIS, Web front-end servers, and your client software, should be fresh installs to minimize integration problems.

Hardware Requirements

During the planning phase of your SharePoint 2010 deployment, you need to acquire the appropriate hardware to host your SharePoint implementation. There are two primary areas of concern when deciding what hardware to use that will support your SharePoint 2010 installation: the Web/application server and the database server. Choose these two components to provide optimal performance as well as reliability.

Web/Application Server

When choosing the servers that will perform the roles of Web front-end server or application server, make sure they meet the following hardware requirements.

- **Processor** 64-bit, 4 core, 2.5 gigahertz (GHz)
- **RAM** Minimum 4 gigabytes (GB); 8 GB recommended in production
- **Disk space** Minimum 80 GB

> **IMPORTANT** In a production environment, additional free space should equal at least two times the amount of RAM on the server to provide additional space for normal day-to-day operations and for memory dumps.

Database Server

The database server that is hosting your SharePoint SQL Server instance has the following minimum hardware requirements to ensure SharePoint is running efficiently.

- **Processors** 64-bit, dual processor, 3 GHz
- **RAM** Minimum 4 GB; 8 to 16 GB recommended in production

See Chapter 3, "Optimizing SQL Server for a SharePoint 2010 Implementation," for RAM recommendations for a SharePoint SQL Server production instance.

If you are deploying SharePoint FAST Search, the following hardware requirements should be met.

- Processor 64-bit, 4 CPU Cores, 2.0GHz; recommended 8 CPU cores
- RAM Minimum 4 gigabytes (GB); 16 GB recommended
- Disk Space 50 GB; 1 terabyte RAID5 across 6 spindles

Software Requirements

Prior to the installation of SharePoint 2010, you need to prepare the computer that is hosting SharePoint as well as any computers that will be accessing SharePoint. In the following sections, there are four primary areas of concern when you are preparing computers that will be used for the installation of SharePoint and those that will be accessing the SharePoint installation. These four areas include the operating system, the database server, the Web/application server, and client computers. By ensuring that these computers are properly configured before you begin, you will ensure a successful installation of SharePoint 2010 and provide both an optimal and reliable experience for your end users.

Operating System

As you saw in the hardware requirements, SharePoint 2010 will only run on 64-bit architecture, which means you have to install the appropriate 64-bit operating system on that hardware. SharePoint can run on either of the following 64-bit operating systems (with their required updates).

- 64-bit edition of Windows Server 2008 R2 Standard, Enterprise, or Datacenter editions and the WCF hotfix available at *http://go.microsoft.com/fwlink/?LinkID=166231*

- 64-bit edition of Windows Server 2008 Standard, Enterprise, or Datacenter editions with Service Pack 2 (SP2) and the WCF hotfix available at *http://go.microsoft.com/fwlink/?LinkID=160770*

> **NOTE** If you are running Windows Server 2008 with Service Pack 1 (SP1), the Microsoft SharePoint 2010 Products Preparation Tool will automatically install Windows Server 2008 SP2.

These operating systems must be running on any computer where you want to install SharePoint 2010, regardless of the role that server is going to perform in the farm.

Database Server

SharePoint requires SQL Server databases and prefers Windows Authentication. SharePoint is hardware agnostic, so the hardware configuration, physical location of the SQL server, and location of the databases (such as a Storage Area Network or SAN) are acceptable to SharePoint if SharePoint can communicate efficiently with its databases. SharePoint is unaware of any non-SharePoint databases on the SQL server. If you have multiple named instances of SQL, you will need to identify the instance you are using for SharePoint as part of identifying the SQL server during the installation and creation of several other SharePoint components.

The database server that is hosting your SharePoint SQL Server instance has the following minimum software requirements to ensure SharePoint 2010 will install and run correctly.

- Microsoft SQL Server 2008 R2

- 64-bit edition of Microsoft SQL Server 2008 with SP1 and cumulative update 2 for SQL Server 2008 SP1

- The 64-bit edition of Microsoft SQL Server 2005 with Service Pack 3 (SP3) and cumulative update 3 for SP3

Web/Application Server

If you have multiple WFEs, multiple application servers, or have chosen to separate your WFE role from your application server role, each of the servers will have additional software requirements. In addition to the operating system, the following software also must be installed on the computer before you can complete an installation of SharePoint 2010.

- Web Server (IIS) role (activated manually through Server Manager)
- Application Server role (activated manually through Server Manager)
- Microsoft .NET Framework version 3.5 SP1
- Microsoft Windows Identity Framework
- Microsoft Sync Framework Runtime v1.0 (x64)
- Microsoft Filter Pack 2.0
- Microsoft Chart Controls for the Microsoft .NET Framework 3.5
- SQL Server 2008 Native Client
- Microsoft SQL Server 2008 Analysis Services ADOMD.NET
- ADO.NET Data Services v1.5
- Windows PowerShell 2.0

> **NOTE** For Windows Server 2008 with SP2, the Microsoft SharePoint 2010 Products Preparation Tool cannot install Windows PowerShell 2.0 if Windows PowerShell 1.0 is already installed on the computer. Therefore, you must uninstall Windows PowerShell 1.0 before you run the Microsoft SharePoint 2010 Products Preparation Tool.

If you are deploying SharePoint FAST Search you should deploy it on 64-bit Windows Server 2008 SP2 or on 64-bit Windows Server 2008 R2.

There is also some additional software you can install to provide additional functionality in SharePoint 2010. Some of the most commonly installed optional software includes

- SQL Server Reporting Services Add-in for Microsoft SharePoint Technologies 2010
- Microsoft Speech Platform
- Speech recognition language for English
- Speech recognition language for Spanish
- Speech recognition language for German
- Speech recognition language for French
- Speech recognition language for Japanese
- Speech recognition language for Chinese

Client Computers

SharePoint 2010 supports several commonly used Web browsers. However, certain Web browsers may cause some SharePoint 2010 functionality to be downgraded, limited, or only available through alternative steps. In fact, there are some cases in which functionality is unavailable for noncritical administrative tasks.

As part of planning for your SharePoint deployment, review the Web browsers used in your organization to ensure that your end users experience optimal performance with SharePoint 2010. Web browser support in SharePoint 2010 is divided into two levels: level 1 and level 2. Although there is support for both levels of Web browsers, the administrative tasks for sites are optimized for level 1 Web browsers, and it is recommended you use level 1 Web browsers if possible.

LEVEL 1 WEB BROWSERS

Level 1 Web browsers take advantage of advanced features provided by ActiveX controls and also provide the most complete experience for the user. Level 1 Web browsers provide full functionality on all SharePoint sites, including your Central Administration website. Table 4-1 lists the operating systems and supported level 1 Web browsers for SharePoint 2010.

TABLE 4-1 Supported Level 1 Operating Systems and Web Browsers

OPERATING SYSTEM	WEB BROWSER
Windows XP, Windows Vista, Windows Server 2003, and Windows Server 2008	Internet Explorer 7, Internet Explorer 8 (32-bit), Mozilla Firefox 3.5
Windows 7 and Windows Server 2008 R2	Internet Explorer 8 (32-bit) and Mozilla Firefox 3.5

LEVEL 2 WEB BROWSERS

Level 2 Web browsers provide basic functionality so users can read and write in SharePoint 2010 sites and can perform basic site administration. However, because there are no ActiveX controls in level 2 Web browsers, and because there is different functionality in different browsers, those in level 2 may provide users with a different—and not necessarily optimal—experience compared to the experience level 1 browsers provide. Table 4-2 lists the operating systems and supported level 2 Web browsers for SharePoint 2010.

TABLE 4-2 Supported Level 2 Operating Systems and Web Browsers

OPERATING SYSTEM	WEB BROWSER
Apple MAC OS X Snow Leopard	Apple Safari 4.x and Mozilla Firefox 3.5
Windows XP, Windows Vista, Windows Server 2003, and Windows Server 2008	Internet Explorer 7 and Internet Explorer 8 (64-bit)
Windows 7 and Windows Server 2008 R2	Internet Explorer 8 (64-bit)
UNIX/Linux 8.1	Mozilla Firefox 3.5

If a browser is not listed in either Table 4-1 or Table 4-2, it is not supported in SharePoint 2010. For instance, Internet Explorer 6.*x*, Internet Explorer for Macintosh, and versions of third-party Web browsers that were released earlier than the Web browsers listed in Table 4-2 are not supported in SharePoint 2010.

Microsoft Office

SharePoint 2010 will again integrate tightly with Microsoft Office 2007 and Microsoft Office 2010. However, the Office 2010 integration will provide new functionality that won't be available in Office 2007. Some of the new features available when SharePoint 2010 and certain versions of Office 2010 are integrated include

- **Office Web Applications** Allows users will to read and write some Office files on a SharePoint 2010 server using only a Web browser.
- **Co-authoring** Allows simultaneous editing of the same document by multiple users.
- **Broadcast Slide Show** Allows you to broadcast completed slide shows to viewers who have only a Web browser.

Be sure to review the different Office editions and the features and functionality they include to ensure that they meet your SharePoint and Office integration needs.

Microsoft Silverlight

SharePoint 2010 includes an out-of-the-box Silverlight Web Part that allows for the easy insertion of rich media or rich applications directly into a SharePoint 2010 site. Silverlight is a cross-browser, cross-platform, and cross-device browser plug-in that helps you design, develop, and deliver applications and experiences on the Web. This optional component should be installed for an optimal user experience. SharePoint 2010 requires Silverlight version 3 or higher.

Active Directory

Planning is essential for every part of implementing SharePoint 2010, and a crucial part of preparing for the installation involves planning the various Active Directory accounts that will be needed during the installation and throughout your SharePoint implementation. SharePoint 2010 depends on Active Directory in several situations.

- SharePoint 2010 requires dedicated Active Directory user accounts to run services and act as application pool identities.

- When importing Active Directory user accounts, it is possible to restrict which accounts are imported, based on the values of specific attributes. Consider setting these values before running the first import job. A new option that is available lets you choose which organization units (OUs) to import from—even individual accounts from an OU can be selected.

- When configuring incoming e-mail, SharePoint is capable of creating contact objects automatically in Active Directory. The account that is configured as the application pool account for Central Administration needs create permissions in the dedicated OU.

Before creating your Active Directory accounts, you must plan for and create these dedicated accounts with the following considerations.

- Provide the minimal rights and permissions so they are available when needed, but do not provide more permissions than needed.

- New in SharePoint 2010 is the option to configure passwords to be changed automatically on a schedule you define.

IMPORTANT   It is strongly recommended that you use a dedicated account to log on and install SharePoint 2010. This account is often used as the identity of the Central Administration site application pool, but it is not necessary to do so. By design, the welcome menu displays System Account if that account is used to log on to any application pool or website. This means that you should not use your administrator account as an application pool identity or to install SharePoint 2010.

Table 4-3 provides a detailed list of the accounts Microsoft recommends for use to install and configure SharePoint 2010.

TABLE 4-3 SharePoint Installation and Configuration Accounts

ACCOUNT	PURPOSE	REQUIREMENTS
SQL Server services account	The SQL Server service account is used to run SQL Server. It is the service account for the following SQL Server services. ■ MSSQLSERVER ■ SQLSERVERAGENT If you do not use the default SQL Server instance, the services will be referenced as the following. ■ MSSQL$InstanceName ■ LSQLAgent$InstanceName	Use either a Local System account or a domain user account. If you plan to back up to or restore from an external resource, permissions to the external resource must be granted to the appropriate account. If you use a domain user account for the SQL Server service account, grant permissions to that domain user account. However, if you use the Network Service or the Local System account, grant permissions to the external resource to the machine account (domain_name\SQL_hostname$). Note: The instance name is arbitrary and was created when Microsoft SQL Server was installed.

Setup user account	The Setup user account is used to run the following.
	
	■ Setup
	
	■ SharePoint Products Configuration Wizard
		■ Domain user account
		
		■ Member of the Administrators group on each server on which Setup is run
		
		■ SQL Server login on the computer that runs SQL Server
		
		■ Member of the following SQL Server security roles
		
		   • **securityadmin** fixed server role
		
		   • **dbcreator** fixed server role
		
		If you run Windows PowerShell cmdlets that affect a database, this account must be a member of the **db_owner** fixed database role for the database.

ACCOUNT	PURPOSE	REQUIREMENTS
Server farm account or database access account	The server farm account is used to perform the following tasks. ■ Configure and manage the server farm. ■ Act as the application pool identity for the SharePoint Central Administration website. ■ Run the Microsoft SharePoint Foundation Workflow Timer Service.	■ Domain user account Additional permissions are automatically granted for the server farm account on Web servers and application servers that are joined to a server farm. The server farm account is automatically added as a SQL Server login on the computer that runs SQL Server. The account is added to the following SQL Server security roles. ■ **dbcreator** fixed server role ■ **securityadmin** fixed server role ■ **db_owner** fixed database role for all SharePoint databases in the server farm

SharePoint 2010 Preparation Tool

For the SharePoint Foundation or Server 2010 installation to complete successfully, the software listed in the section titled "Software Requirements" earlier in this chapter must be installed. You may be thinking that it is a lot of work to download and install each application individually. Great news! There is a SharePoint 2010 Prerequisite Installer that you can run to scan the server and check to see if the required software components and server roles are installed. If it discovers they are not present, the Prerequisite Installer will automatically install these components from their Internet location, or if you choose, from a local drive that contains the prerequisite software.

Local Prerequisite Command-Line Installation

You can install the SharePoint 2010 prerequisites using a command-line utility called Prerequisiteinstaller.exe. You can run this utility after you extract it from the respective SharePoint 2010 installation executable. For instance, if you are installing SharePoint Foundation 2010 that you downloaded to the directory C:\SharePointFoundationFiles, you would extract the installation files, including the Prerequisiteinstaller.exe application, using the following command.

```
c:\SharePointFoundationFiles\SharePoint.exe /extract:c:\SharePointFoundationFiles
```

As an alternative, if you are installing SharePoint 2010 that you downloaded to the directory C:\SharePointServerFiles, you would extract the installation files that include the Prerequisiteinstaller.exe application using the following command.

```
c:\SharePointServerFiles\OfficeServer.exe /extract:c:\SharePointServerFiles
```

Perform the following steps to complete a command-line installation of the required prerequisites.

1. Download the prerequisite software from *http://technet.microsoft.com/en-us/library /cc262485(office.14).aspx#section4/*.

2. Copy all the prerequisites to a folder such as C:\SharePoint2010\PrerequisiteFiles.

   Open Notepad.exe, copy the following content (without line breaks, and be sure to insert a space between the arguments), and save it to the same directory as the downloaded prerequisites. Name the file PrerequisiteInstaller.Arguments.txt.

   ```
   /Unattended:
   /W2K8SP2:PrerequisiteFiles\Windows6.0-KB948465-X64.exe
   /NETFX35SP1:PrerequisiteFiles\dotnetfx35.exe
   /PowerShell:PrerequisiteFiles\PowerShell_Setup_amd64.msi
   /WindowsInstaller:PrerequisiteFiles\Windows6.0-KB942288-v2-x64.msu
   /SQLNCli:PrerequisiteFiles\sqlncli.msi
   /ChartControl:PrerequisiteFiles\MSChart.exe
   /IDFX:PrerequisiteFiles\MicrosoftGenevaFramework.amd64.msi
   /Sync:PrerequisiteFiles\Synchronization.msi
   /FilterPack:PrerequisiteFiles\FilterPackx64.exe
   /ADOMD:PrerequisiteFiles\ADONETDataServices_v15_RuntimeOnly.exe
   ```

3. Double-click Prerequisiteinstaller.exe, located in the C:\SharePoint2010 folder.

4. After that file executes completely, all of the required prerequisites will be installed.

Internet Prerequisite Graphical User Interface Installation

You can also run the SharePoint 2010 prerequisite installer using a graphical user interface (GUI), which lets you automatically download and install prerequisite software from the Internet. To do this, either run Setup and select Install Software Prerequisites from the startup screen or double-click the extracted Prerequisiteinstaller.exe file.

USING THE PREREQUISITEINSTALLER.EXE GUI TO INSTALL PREREQUISITES

If you decide to use Prerequisiteinstaller.exe, complete the following steps.

1. Locate the file in the directory where you extracted it and double-click the Prerequisiteinstaller.exe file to open the Microsoft SharePoint 2010 Products Preparation Tool Welcome page, shown in Figure 4-1. Click Next.

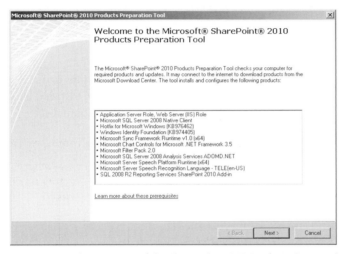

FIGURE 4-1 Welcome page of the SharePoint 2010 Products Preparation Tool

2. The License Terms for Software Products page shown in Figure 4-2 appears and requests that you agree to the licensing for each of the software components that will be installed by the Preparation Tool. Select the check box next to the option I Accept The Terms Of The License Agreement(s) to continue. Be sure to read the licensing agreement before choosing to agree to it and then click Next.

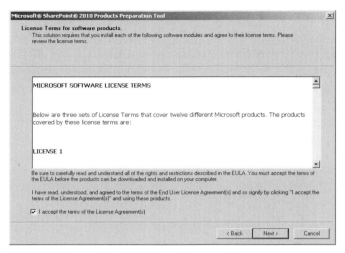

FIGURE 4-2 Preparation Tool License Agreements page

3. After clicking Next on the License Agreements page, the prerequisites begin to install, and the progress is displayed to show you the items that are being installed and how long the prerequisite installation has been running, as shown in Figure 4-3.

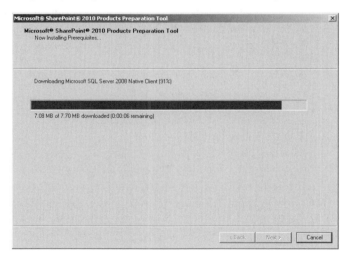

FIGURE 4-3 Prerequisites Installation Progress page

4. After all the prerequisites are installed, you see the final page, shown in Figure 4-4, that displays the products that were installed. If there were any errors during the installation, you will see them displayed on the Installation Complete page. If there aren't any errors that you need to resolve, or if you have documented the errors encountered during the installation and you are ready to exit the Preparation Tool, click Finish.

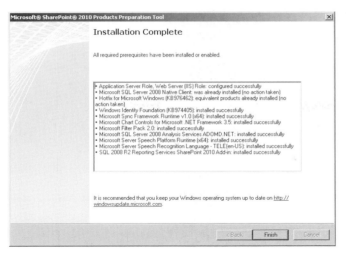

FIGURE 4-4 Prerequisites Installation Complete page

USING THE SETUP.EXE GUI TO INSTALL PREREQUISITES

If you decide to use Setup.exe from either the SharePoint Foundation 2010 or the SharePoint 2010 installation, locate the file in the directory where you extracted it and double-click the file to open the SharePoint installation startup screen. The startup screen for both editions of SharePoint contains the same three categories with the following seven self-explanatory options.

- Prepare
  - Review hardware and software requirements
  - Read the installation guide
  - Read the upgrade guide
- Install
  - Install software prerequisites
  - Install SharePoint Foundation (or Install SharePoint Server for SharePoint 2010 installation)
- Other Information
  - View Windows Update
  - Visit product website

Figure 4-5 shows the startup screen that displays when you double-click Setup.exe in the directory that contains the files you extracted for an installation of SharePoint Foundation 2010. Note that the second option in the Install category is Install SharePoint Foundation.

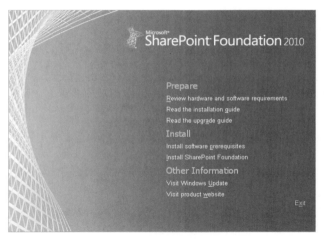

FIGURE 4-5 SharePoint Foundation 2010 Installation startup screen

If you are installing SharePoint 2010 Standard Edition or Enterprise Edition, double-click Setup.exe in the directory that contains the extracted SharePoint 2010 files to display a setup start screen similar to the one shown in Figure 4-5 for SharePoint Foundation 2010. However, this page, shown in Figure 4-6, displays SharePoint 2010 as the title, and it includes the option to Install SharePoint Server.

FIGURE 4-6 SharePoint 2010 Installation startup screen

NOTE You can also display this setup screen by double-clicking the Sharepoint.exe (or the file name specific to your installation type) file in the directory that contains the same SharePoint Server files that were extracted using the steps previously discussed in the section titled "Local Prerequisite Command-Line Installation" or by inserting the DVD that contains the SharePoint 2010 software.

Performing SharePoint 2010 Installations

After you install the prerequisites for SharePoint 2010, you are ready to perform the installation of SharePoint 2010. Remember that you can install either SharePoint Foundation 2010, or you can install SharePoint 2010 Standard Edition or Enterprise Editions; which edition you install is determined by the product key you supply during the installation.

Both SharePoint Foundation 2010 and SharePoint 2010 installations are performed in two phases. In the first phase, the binaries of the SharePoint installation are installed, and in the second phase, you actually create the SharePoint farm. Furthermore, each installation has other options that you need to be familiar with to ensure that your farm is built to handle the capacity you anticipate it will encounter.

SharePoint 2010 GUI Installations

You can perform two types of SharePoint 2010 installations: Standalone and Complete. Making the correct choice here has a major impact on the scalability of SharePoint 2010. The following sections discuss how to install the Standalone and Complete installation options of SharePoint 2010. It also guides you through the steps involved in both installations.

SharePoint 2010 Standalone Installation

The Standalone, or single server, installation option for SharePoint 2010 will create everything for you with minimal prompts during the installation, and it prevents you from adding other servers or building a farm. This installation type should only be used in the following situations.

- To evaluate SharePoint 2010 features and functionality
- To create a test environment
- To deploy a small number of websites with minimal administrative overhead

This installation type is not recommended for a production environment, and it has several limitations, including the following.

- It installs SQL Server Express 2008, which has several limitations including
  - 4 GB maximum database size
  - 1 GB memory supported

- Single processor support
- It installs Central Administration using default settings.
- It generates a random Central Administration port number.
- It creates the configuration database using a default database name of SharePoint_config_GUID (Globally Unique Identifier, that is randomly generated), and all commonly used service application databases.
- It creates a home site collection with the default database name.

PHASE ONE OF SHAREPOINT 2010 STANDALONE EDITION INSTALLATION

The following steps and illustrations guide you through the installation of SharePoint 2010 when you select the Standalone, or single server, edition.

1. Start the SharePoint 2010 installation using one of the methods discussed in the section titled "Local Prerequisite Command-Line Installation" earlier in this chapter, which will display the page shown in Figure 4-7.

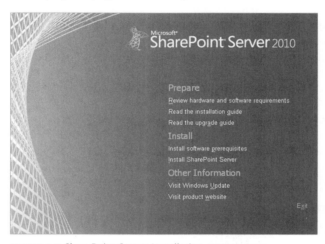

FIGURE 4-7 SharePoint Server Installation startup page

2. Under the Install category, click Install SharePoint Server, which momentarily presents the SharePoint file preparation page

3. Shortly after the file preparation page appears, you are prompted for the product key. The product key you enter here determines which functions will be enabled for you after the installation completes. An Enterprise level product key enables all functionality, whereas a Standard level product key installs the same functionality as the Enterprise but doesn't enable the functionality that is only available in the Enterprise edition. Enter the product key in the text box provided, as shown in Figure 4-8.

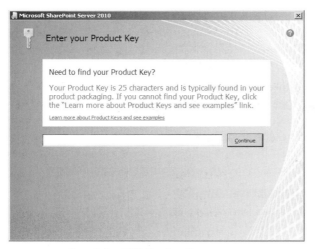

FIGURE 4-8 SharePoint 2010 Product Key page

4. The product key is validated, and if it is a valid product key, the Continue button becomes active, which allows you to continue to the license agreement page. You must select the check box to indicate that you accept the terms to make the Continue button on this page active; click the button to go to the next page of the installation.

5. The installation types shown in Figure 4-9 determine how much default configuration is performed for you during the installation. For this installation, click Standalone. Remember that means this is a single server installation and that the entire farm will reside on this one machine. Also remember there are several limitations in the Standalone installation, so be careful when making this choice.

FIGURE 4-9 SharePoint Server Installation Type page

6. After clicking the Standalone button, you will see the Installation Progress page for several minutes as the installation of SharePoint and SQL Server 2008 Express is performed for you.

When the installation is complete, the SharePoint product and SQL Server Express are installed, and phase one of the installation is complete. By default, the SharePoint Products Configuration Wizard opening page shown in Figure 4-10 has the option to begin the second stage of your SharePoint farm configuration. Phase two of the installation requires that you use the Active Directory SharePoint farm account that has the two required SQL Server privileges of dbcreator and securityadmin. These will be required for the account with which you are performing the installation in order for phase two to complete successfully.

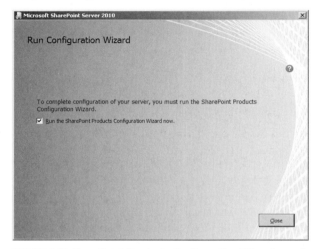

FIGURE 4-10 SharePoint Products Configuration Wizard opening page

In phase two of the Standalone installation, you will encounter major differences in the prompts that are presented to you and the farm configuration tasks that are performed, compared to a Complete installation. There are substantially more tasks completed for you during the farm configuration when you choose the Standalone option.

> **NOTE** You can clear the check box on the opening page of the wizard and instead begin the Configuration Wizard graphical interface at a later time by executing the Psconfigui.exe file located in the C:\Program Files\Common Files\Microsoft Shared\Web Server Extensions\14\BIN directory.

PHASE TWO OF SHAREPOINT 2010 STANDALONE EDITION INSTALLATION

In the second phase of a SharePoint 2010 Standalone installation, you are actually building and configuring your SharePoint farm using most of the default built-in options. Your configuration database, the Central Administration interface and its supporting database, and the service application are registered and started, and then their supporting databases are created. Finally, a default home site collection and its supporting database are created.

1. Click Close on the Run Configuration Wizard page of the SharePoint Products Configuration Wizard (Figure 4-10). You are presented with the Configuration Wizard Welcome page, shown in Figure 4-11.

FIGURE 4-11 SharePoint Products Configuration Wizard Welcome page

2. Click the Next button to begin building your SharePoint farm. The dialog box shown in Figure 4-12 appears, indicating that three services may have to be started or reset during the configuration.

> **IMPORTANT**   The notification that some services may need to be started or reset does not present issues if you are working with a new, dedicated Web server. However, if your server is currently serving other websites, restarting the Web services will disrupt services, which may be unacceptable during certain times. If this is the case, you'll need to perform this action during off hours. Also, it is highly recommended that you check network connectivity and DNS resolution from the server to the SQL Server prior to running the wizard.

FIGURE 4-12 SharePoint Products Configuration Wizard Restart Services dialog box

3. If you click No in the Restart Services dialog box, the Configuration Wizard ends and the farm is not built. If you click Yes, the farm build completes the 10 tasks required to build and configure your farm. You can monitor the progress of the farm build as shown in Figure 4-13.

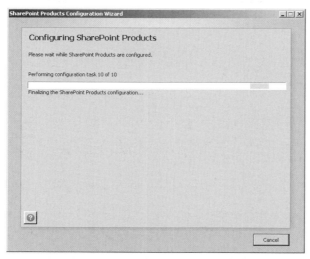

FIGURE 4-13 SharePoint Farm Configuration Progress page

NOTE If an error occurs during this section of the installation, you will see an error message that recommends that you view the operating system event log and a SharePoint specific setup log file. There will be a link to this file that you can view to help troubleshoot what caused the installation to fail.

4. When the Configuration Wizard completes successfully, you will see the Configuration Successful page, indicating the farm was successfully built. Click Finish.

During a Standalone installation, there are some additional configuration tasks that you need to perform. You will be prompted for information about how you want your first site collection built, and you will be asked to set the permission groups before your new site is created.

1. The first prompt asks you what site template you want to use for your first site collection, which by default is called Home. The default template is Team Site, but you can choose any of the available site templates contained within the four categories displayed in Figure 4-14.

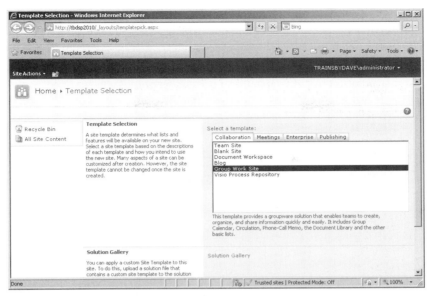

FIGURE 4-14 First Site Collection Template Selection page

2. The second prompt asks you what groups you want to use for your first Home site collection. The default group names are Home Visitors, Home Members, and Home Owners, as shown in Figure 4-15, but you can choose to create new permission groups by selecting the Create A New Group option and specifying the name of the new group.

FIGURE 4-15 Site Collection Permission Groups page

3. After you decide to use the default permission group names or specify new permission groups, click OK. The Processing page displays while your site collection and its associated permission groups are created.

4. When the new site collection has been successfully completed, you will see the new site displayed with the site template and permission groups you specified, as shown in Figure 4-16.

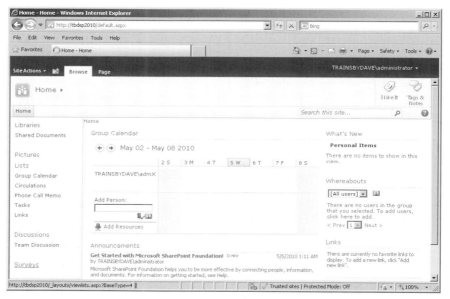

FIGURE 4-16 Top-level website interface

NOTE Remember that the last few steps are only performed during a Standalone SharePoint 2010 installation. The Configuration Wizard for a Complete installation is quite different; the steps involved in a Complete installation are explained in the section titled "SharePoint 2010 Complete Installation" later in this chapter.

Your Standalone farm has been created and you should verify it was successful by accessing Central Administration, shown in Figure 4-17. To do this, click Start, All Programs, Microsoft SharePoint 2010 Products, SharePoint 2010 Central Administration.

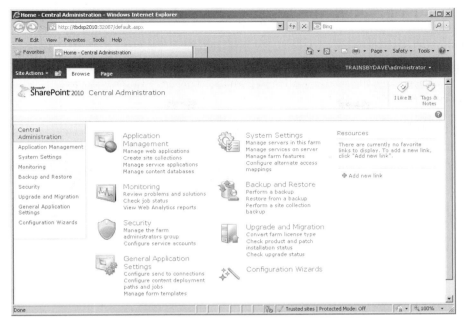

FIGURE 4-17 SharePoint 2010 Standalone installation Central Administration website

After you have completed a Standalone installation of SharePoint 2010, you can manage your SharePoint databases using SQL Server Management Studio. However, first you need to locate the SQL Server Management Studio application from the Microsoft website and download it. Then you must register your Standalone SharePoint SQL Server instance using *server-name*\SharePoint. For instance, if you ran a Standalone installation on Server1, you would have to register Standalone\SharePoint in SQL Server Management Studio to manage your SharePoint databases. In Figure 4-18, you can see the numerous databases that are automatically created for you during the Standalone installation. All of the databases shown, except the SQL Server system databases, are created for you during the Standalone installation.

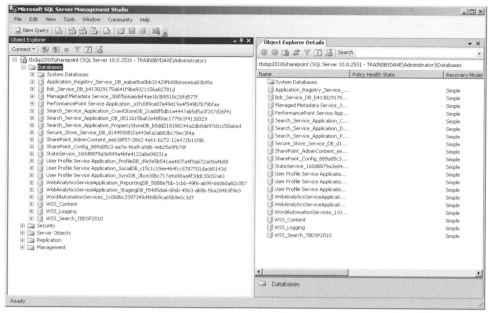

FIGURE 4-18 SharePoint 2010 Standalone installation databases

SharePoint Foundation 2010 Standalone Installation

The Standalone installation of SharePoint Foundation 2010 is quite similar to the same installation for SharePoint 2010 Standalone edition. The differences you will see during the installation itself are as follows.

- The installation pages will say SharePoint Foundation 2010 instead of SharePoint 2010 throughout phase one.
- You will choose Install SharePoint Foundation.
- You are not prompted for a product key (this version is free).
- This installation automatically creates a top-level website using the Team Site template.

After completing the installation, some of the most noticeable differences you will see include the following.

- There is no option to Convert Farm License Type in Central Administration.
- There are significantly fewer service applications available.

SharePoint 2010 Complete Installation

As you saw in the previous sections about SharePoint 2010 Standalone installation, there are several limitations when you choose the Standalone installation option. However, it does perform several additional tasks that aren't performed when you choose the Complete installation option. These additional tasks include installing SQL Server 2008 Express, creating several service applications, and creating your first site collection. None of these tasks occur automatically if you perform a Complete installation, so you must perform these tasks manually after the installation is finished.

PHASE ONE OF SHAREPOINT 2010 COMPLETE EDITION INSTALLATION

The following responses and figures are used to perform a Complete installation of SharePoint 2010. This is the preferred installation type and it is similar to the Standalone installation, but it provides much more scalability, performance, and reliability in your SharePoint 2010 server farm. However, the Complete installation does require you to have SQL Server already installed, which you will be asked to confirm during the Complete installation of SharePoint 2010.

Phase one of the SharePoint 2010 Complete installation is very similar to the first phase of the Standalone installation. In fact, the first five pages you see are exactly the same in both installations. However, when you choose Server Farm on the SharePoint 2010 installation type page shown in Figure 4-19, you will then see some additional pages in phase one that were not part of the Standalone installation.

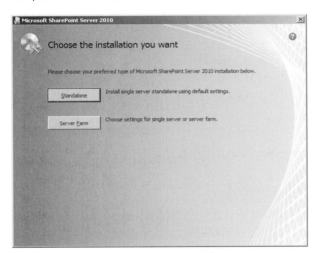

FIGURE 4-19 SharePoint Server Installation Type page

Click the Server Farm button to open the Server Type page shown in Figure 4-20. This page gives you two options: you can select a Complete installation (which is what you will select here), or there is another opportunity for you to choose the Stand-alone option, which performs the Standalone installation discussed in the section titled "SharePoint 2010 Stand-alone Installation" earlier in this chapter.

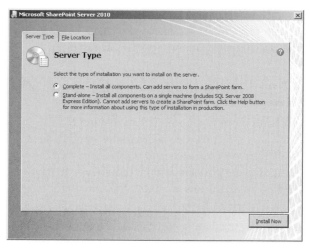

FIGURE 4-20 SharePoint Server Type page

Optionally, you can click the File Location tab to display the file location page shown in Figure 4-21. On that page, you can specify the location of the SharePoint 2010 product files as well as the directory that will contain the search index if the server where you are performing the installation is going to be used as a search server.

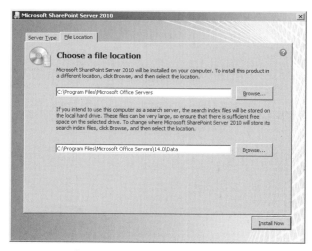

FIGURE 4-21 Choose the location of installed files on the File Location tab.

After clicking the Install Now button, you see the same two wizard pages that appeared during the Standalone installation indicating the progress and then completion of the installation. When the first phase of the installation is complete, the SharePoint 2010 product files have been successfully installed. By default, the SharePoint Products Configuration Wizard page provides you with the option to begin the second phase of the installation, your SharePoint Server farm configuration. Phase two of the installation requires that you use the

Active Directory SharePoint farm account that has the two required SQL Server privileges, dbcreator and securityadmin. You must have these privileges for the account you are using to perform the installation with in order for phase two to complete successfully.

> **NOTE** You can clear the check box on the opening page of the wizard and instead begin the Configuration Wizard graphical interface at a later time by executing the Psconfigui.exe file located in the C:\Program Files\Common Files\Microsoft Shared\Web Server Extensions\14\BIN directory.

PHASE TWO OF SHAREPOINT 2010 COMPLETE EDITION INSTALLATION

In the second phase of the SharePoint 2010 Complete installation, you are actually building and configuring your SharePoint farm using options that you specify throughout the wizard. In this phase, your SharePoint configuration database, Central Administration, and supporting database are created. Unlike the Standalone installation, there aren't any service applications created, registered, or started. Furthermore, no default home site collection is created. These additional farm options are created after the installation completes. They can be performed by running the Farm Configuration Wizard at the end of the installation or at a later time from within Central Administration, or you can configure each of these additional farm options manually.

You will notice several additional pages during this portion of the SharePoint 2010 Complete installation that you did not see in the Standalone installation.

1. Click Close on the Run Configuration Wizard page of the SharePoint Products Configuration Wizard or run Psconfigui.exe, and you are presented with the Configuration Wizard Welcome page shown in Figure 4-22.

FIGURE 4-22 Complete Installation Configuration Welcome page

2. Click Next on the Installation Configuration Welcome page to see the dialog box shown in Figure 4-23, which indicates that three services may have to be started or reset during the configuration.

> **IMPORTANT** The notification that some services may need to be started or reset does not present issues if you are working with a new, dedicated Web server. However, if your server is currently serving other websites, restarting the Web services will disrupt services, which may be unacceptable during certain times. If this is the case, you'll need to perform this action during off hours. Also, it is highly recommended that you check network connectivity and DNS resolution from the server to the SQL server prior to running the wizard.

FIGURE 4-23 Configuration Wizard Restart Services dialog box

3. If you choose to continue with the installation by clicking Yes, you will see the next page in the wizard, which determines if you are building a new farm or performing an installation on a server that will be joining an existing farm. Your response here affects what you see on the following pages. Select the option Create A New Server Farm on the page shown in Figure 4-24.

4. When building a new farm during a complete installation, you will see additional prompts that provide you with more control over the build and configuration of your SharePoint farm. As you can see in Figure 4-25, you can specify the name of the database server and optionally, the SQL Server instance name, if you don't want to use the default instance on that database server. This database server will host both the Central Administration database and the farm configuration database. You can modify the farm configuration database name, which by default is called SharePoint_Config.

To create the databases on this database server, you need to have the appropriate permissions in SQL Server and the appropriate firewall ports must be opened as discussed in the article located at *http://support.microsoft.com/kb/968872*. In the lower half of the page, you specify the account that has the required permissions to create the databases.

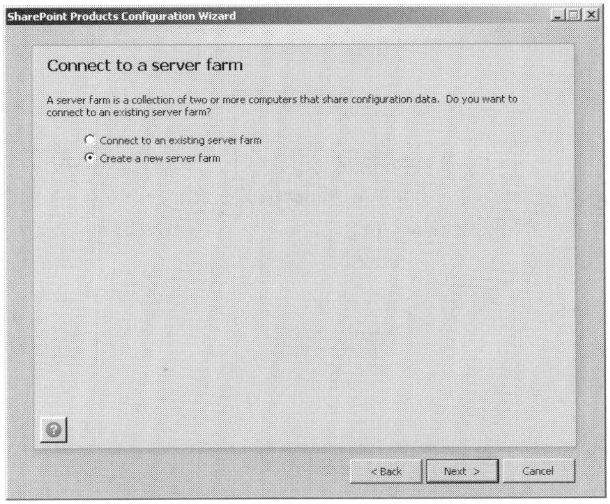

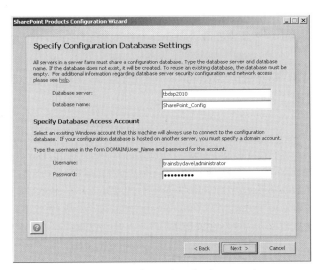

FIGURE 4-24 Building a new server farm

FIGURE 4-25 New farm configuration database settings

5. Next, you are asked for a passphrase, as shown in Figure 4-26. This passphrase is used to encrypt SharePoint configuration information and is also required when you add or remove servers from the farm.

> **IMPORTANT** This is a critical passphrase, and you should document and secure it for future farm configurations. This passphrase can be changed from within Central Administration, so as a reminder, you want to limit the number of users who have farm administration permissions and access to Central Administration.

FIGURE 4-26 Setting the farm security passphrase

The passphrase you specify must meet the Active Directory password requirements, which by default require that the passphrase contain a minimum of eight characters and at least three of the following four character groups.

- English uppercase characters (A through Z)
- English lowercase characters (a through z)
- Numerals (0 through 9)
- Nonalphabetic characters (such as $,%,#,!)

6. Unlike in the Standalone installation of SharePoint 2010, you can override the randomly generated Central Administration port number on the Configure SharePoint Central Administration Web Application page shown in Figure 4-27. The installation will still generate a port number for you, but in the Complete installation, you can select the Specify Port Number check box on the page and enter a port number of your choice.

> **BEST PRACTICES** When choosing a port number, choose one that you will easily remember in case you have to reinstall Central Administration; that way, you will be able to use the same port number. You can choose a port number between 1 and 65,535; however, you should choose a port number greater than 2048 to avoid any conflicts with default port numbers that Microsoft uses for specific communication purposes.

FIGURE 4-27 Configure SharePoint Central Administration Web Application page

7. You also can choose between NTLM and Kerberos as the authentication provider for user authentication when connecting to the farm. The recommended authentication provider is Kerberos, but be aware that there are some extra steps required to complete the configuration of Kerberos authentication. Choose NTLM during the installation—it is the default authentication provider—and if Kerberos is needed, you can configure it after the installation. This allows you to perform a simple installation of SharePoint 2010 and then configure the more advanced options after the installation has been completed successfully.

8. Make any modifications to the SharePoint Central Administration Web Application page and click Next to display the page shown in Figure 4-28, which is a summary of the responses you provided as you walked through the SharePoint Products Configuration Wizard. Review it carefully. If it is correct, click Next and the SharePoint farm and Central Administration configuration will be created using this information.

   If there is anything on this summary page that you want to revise, click the Back button the appropriate number of times to return you to the page that you want to modify and make the change. After doing so, click Next until you return to the summary page. Take one final look at the summary and click Next to complete the farm and Central Administration build.

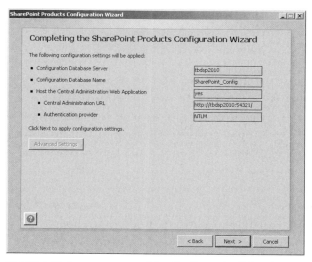

FIGURE 4-28 Summary page of the Configuration Wizard

9. While the farm is being built, you will see a progress page, shown in Figure 4-29, that provides information about what is taking place throughout the farm, so you can track the progress of the SharePoint farm and Central Administration build.

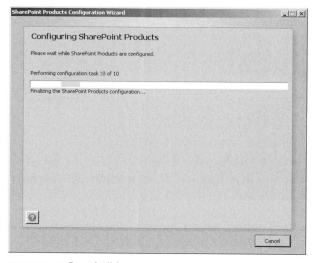

FIGURE 4-29 Farm build progress page

It is a good idea to monitor this progress page so that if an error does occur, you will know what step the build process was in when it failed, which will simplify the troubleshooting process. However, if the Configuration Wizard does fail, it will provide you information on why it failed as well as a link to a log file that will contain all the steps taken during the configuration process. More importantly, it will tell you what caused the Configuration Wizard to fail.

10. After the farm has been successfully built, you will see another summary page, shown in Figure 4-30. This page gives you the same information you saw in Figure 4-28, but in this case, it tells you that the information was used to successfully complete the farm build.

> **BEST PRACTICES** Make a screen shot of the page shown in Figure 4-30 and print and file it so that if someone inherits the SharePoint farm later on, they will know how the farm was initially built.

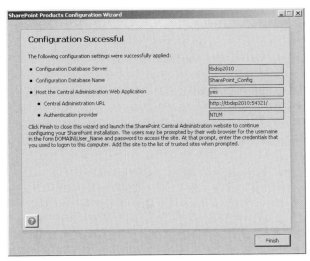

FIGURE 4-30 Configuration Successful page for the completed farm build

After the farm configuration completes successfully, SharePoint will automatically connect you to Central Administration and present the page shown in Figure 4-31.

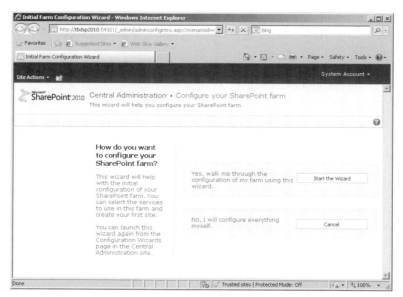

FIGURE 4-31 Configuring the new farm in SharePoint Central Administration

11. The Initial Farm Configuration Wizard start page that displays in Central Administration asks if you want to perform some additional tasks for your SharePoint farm. These include such tasks as creating, starting, and registering the most common SharePoint 2010 Service Applications and creating a top-level website. At this point, rather than running this configuration wizard, the recommendation is that you choose the option to configure everything yourself at a later time. You have more flexibility when creating and configuring the services individually rather than using the Farm Configuration Wizard. You can run the Farm Configuration Wizard from within Central Administration at a later time.

12. When you select the option to configure everything yourself later, the Help Make SharePoint Better page displays as shown in Figure 4-32. This page asks you to sign up for the customer experience improvement program that automatically uploads error reports to Microsoft. (If you do not want to participate in this program, you must choose the option No, I Don't Wish To Participate.) After clicking the OK button, you will be returned to the Configure Your SharePoint Farm page.

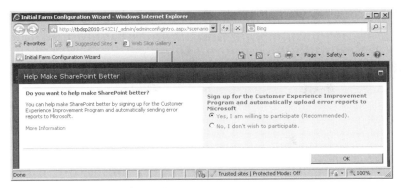

FIGURE 4-32 Help Make SharePoint Better page

13. If you choose not to run the SharePoint Farm Configuration Wizard but instead wait to configure everything individually as recommended, the installation of SharePoint and Central Administration is complete, and you will see the home page of Central Administration displayed as shown in Figure 4-33.

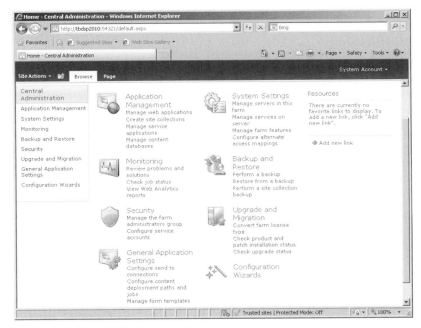

FIGURE 4-33 Central Administration home page

After installing a Complete edition of SharePoint 2010, if you use SQL Server Management Studio, you will see the two databases shown in Figure 4-34 that are automatically created for you during a Complete installation.

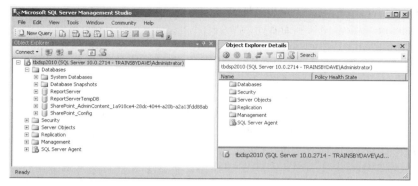

FIGURE 4-34 SharePoint 2010 Complete installation databases

NOTE These are the only databases created for you during a Complete installation if you do not run the Farm Configuration Wizard.

SharePoint Foundation 2010 Complete Installation

The SharePoint Foundation 2010 Complete installation is quite similar to the SharePoint 2010 Complete installation. The differences you will see during the installation are

- The screens will say SharePoint Foundation 2010 throughout phase one.
- You will choose Install SharePoint Foundation.
- You are not prompted for a product key (this version is free).

After completing the installation, some of the most noticeable differences you will see include

- There is no option to Convert Farm License Type in Central Administration.
- There is no option to View Web Analytics in Central Administration.
- There is no option to configure content deployment jobs and paths in Central Administration.
- Only two service applications can be configured using the Farm Configuration Wizard.
  - Business Data Connectivity
  - Usage and Health Data Collection

This is why you must decide if the Foundation edition of SharePoint 2010 will meet your organization's needs, or if you will need the Server edition of SharePoint 2010 for document organization.

Performing a Command-Line Installation of SharePoint

The previous sections in this chapter describe how to install SharePoint using the graphical user interface, which is a great way to learn and understand how SharePoint can be installed, but it isn't the most cost-effective way. So you should also be familiar with performing a farm installation using command-line utilities, and you should be able to create scripts that contain these commands. Scripts can be very helpful during a disaster recovery scenario or in a situation in which you want to have complete control of the configuration of the server when adding a server to a farm. It can save you a lot of time when your installation is fully automated.

All the steps you completed using the SharePoint Products Configuration Wizard can also be completed using Psconfig.exe from the command line. When the appropriate parameters are passed to the program, your farm can be built without any user intervention. This allows for a completely scripted installation of a farm; you can also fully automate the process of adding servers to your farm.

An automated installation can be broken up into three steps.

1. Install the prerequisite software on the server using Prerequisiteinstaller.exe.

2. Install SharePoint in the two phases discussed in this chapter.

   - Phase one: Install the SharePoint product and binaries using Setup.exe.

   - Phase two: Completing the actions included in the SharePoint Products Configuration Wizard using Psconfig.exe from the command line.

3. Run the Farm Configuration Wizard using Windows PowerShell cmdlets for SharePoint 2010.

Installing the Prerequisites

The section titled "Local Prerequisite Command-Line Installation" earlier in this chapter described how to run the Prerequisiteinstaller.exe to install the software that is required for a successful SharePoint installation. Review that section to install the prerequisites for a command-line installation of SharePoint 2010.

Installing the SharePoint Product Binaries

The Setup.exe command can be used to automate the installation of phase one of your SharePoint 2010 installation. The parameters for this command can be stored in an XML file, allowing you to run Setup.exe using the following syntax.

```
setup.exe /config C:\installPath\config.xml
```

Building the SharePoint Farm

Psconfig.exe is not new to SharePoint 2010, but it has been enhanced to provide additional functionality and can be used as a substitute for the SharePoint Products Configuration Wizard. Psconfig.exe provides you much more flexibility when building your farm, including the ability to specify the database name for your Central Administration database. Table 4-4 lists some of the most common parameters and features that can be used with Psconfig.exe interactively at the command prompt or within a script.

TABLE 4-4 Psconfig.exe Parameters

COMMAND	PARAMETERS	ACTION
Psconfig –cmd configdb –create –server <server> –database <database> –user <user> –password <password> –admincontentdatabase <database> –passphrase < passphrase>	–server = SQL Server –database = Name of configuration database –user = Database access account (Farm Admin) –password = Password for Farm Admin –admincontentdatabase = Name of content database for Central Administration website –passphrase = Farm passphrase	Configuration database is created with name specified on server specified. Content database for Central Administration is created with name specified. Passphrase is generated with phrase specified.
Psconfig –cmd helpcollections –installall		Installs the help collections
Psconfig –cmd services install	install	Installs services specified
Psconfig –cmd services provision	provision	Installs and provisions services
Psconfig –cmd installfeatures		Installs and activates all necessary features at the farm level
Psconfig –cmd adminvs –provision –port 11111 –windowsauthprovider onlyusentlm	–port = portnumber for Central Administration website –windowsauthprovider = authentication method	Creates and provisions the Central Administration website
Psconfig –cmd applicationcontent		Installs the Central Administration Web Application content files
Psconfig –cmd –installhealthrules		Creates a Health Rules list and adds Health Rules items

Installing and Provisioning the Service Applications

You can manage the service applications in SharePoint 2010 using either Psconfig.exe or using Windows PowerShell cmdlets. There are Windows PowerShell cmdlets specific to each service application. Table 4-5 lists just a few of the available cmdlets to manage your service applications from the command line or from within a script.

TABLE 4-5 Service Application Windows PowerShell cmdlets

SERVICE APPLICATION	WINDOWS POWERSHELL CMDLET
Access Services	New-SPAccessServiceApplication
State Service service application	New-SPStateServiceApplication
Performance Point service application	New-SPPerformancePointServiceApplication
Visio service application	New-SPVisioServiceApplication
User Profile service application	New-SPProfileServiceApplication

Each service application has different cmdlets and different configuration options. Be sure to review the Windows PowerShell syntax for each service application carefully to determine what options are available when creating your SharePoint 2010 service applications using Windows PowerShell. After writing your scripts, test them often to be sure they fully duplicate your current system so that you will have minimal work to do after running the scripts. It is also wise to document each script, and if there are multiple scripts, also document the order in which they should be run.

Configuring a SharePoint 2010 Installation

When you successfully complete the installation of any edition of SharePoint 2010, you will have a new program group on your Start menu called Microsoft SharePoint 2010 Products. The program group contains the three menu items shown in Figure 4-35. Use this group to manage and configure your SharePoint 2010 installations or in the event you need to rerun the Configuration Wizard.

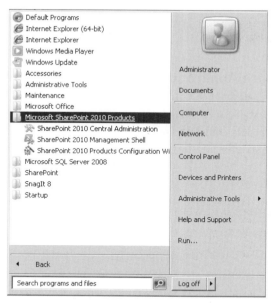

FIGURE 4-35 SharePoint 2010 program group on the Start menu

Running the Farm Configuration Wizard

If you decide later that you want to use the SharePoint 2010 Farm Configuration Wizard to install and configure your service applications, you can do so from within Central Administration. After you launch the wizard, you use the same interface that appears during the Complete installation, which is described step by step in the section titled "SharePoint 2010 Complete Installation" earlier in this chapter. However, in this case you will choose the first option on the wizard's opening page, Walk Me Through The Settings Using This Wizard. After you select this option, click Next to display the page shown in Figure 4-36. On this page, you specify the account that the services will use to operate.

> **BEST PRACTICES** Use an account other than the SharePoint farm account for improved security of your farm.

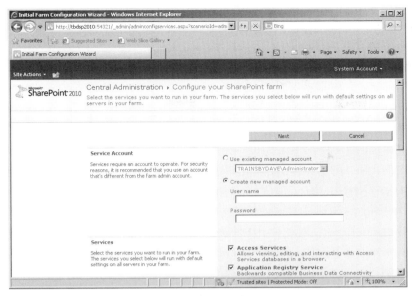

FIGURE 4-36 Configure your SharePoint farm services.

In addition to specifying the services account, there are 15 service applications, listed in Table 4-6, that you can choose from and specify that they be configured. By default, all of them are selected to be configured except the Lotus Notes Connector. However, you can clear any services you won't be using to improve the server's overall performance.

TABLE 4-6 Farm Configuration Wizard Service Applications

SERVICE APPLICATION	DESCRIPTION
Access Services	Allows viewing, editing, and interacting with Access Services databases in a browser
Application Registry Service	Provides backwards compatibility for Business Data Catalog API
Business Data Connectivity	Provides the ability to upload BDC models that describe your line of business interfaces
Excel Services	Allows viewing and interactivity with Excel files in a browser
Lotus Notes Connector	Search connector crawls data in a Lotus Notes server
Managed Metadata Services	Provides access to managed taxonomy hierarchies, keywords, and global content types
PerformancePoint Service Application	Supports monitoring and analysis of PerformancePoint Services such as storage and publication of dashboards

continued on the next page

SERVICE APPLICATION	DESCRIPTION
Search Service Application	Indexes content and responds to search queries
Secure Store Service	Stores data securely and associates it with a specific identity or groups of identities
State Service	Provides temporary storage of user session data
Usage and Health Data Collection	Collects farm-wide usage and health data and provides data reporting
User Profile Service Application	Provides support for My Sites, profile pages, social tagging, and other social computing
Visio Graphics Service	Enables viewing and refreshing of published Visio diagrams in Web browser
Web Analytics Service	Web Analytics Service Application
Word Automation Services	Provides framework for performing automated document conversions

After making the required changes, click Next to display a processing page that lets you track the progress as the services that were selected are configured.

> **NOTE** If there are problems with the configuration of any of the services, you can complete the remaining steps of the Farm Configuration Wizard and then resolve the issues with the services that couldn't be properly configured. Then you can rerun the Farm Configuration Wizard, choosing those previously troubled services. When you run the wizard subsequent times, you will only be able to access the check boxes of those services that aren't already configured.

After the services configuration completes, you are given the option to create a top-level site collection using the Create Site Collection interface shown in Figure 4-37. On this page, you can choose to skip or create the top-level site collection for the website. If you choose to create it, you need to provide the title, an optional description, and the website address or URL to access the site collection. Finally, you choose which site template you want to use to create the site collection from approximately 20 default site templates provided.

After the site collection for your top-level website is created, you will see a final Farm Configuration Wizard page, shown in Figure 4-38, that lists the services that were configured as well as the title and URL of your top-level website.

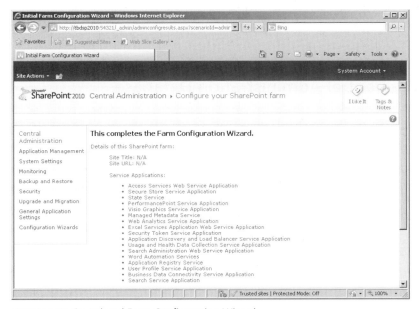

FIGURE 4-37 Creating a site collection for the top-level website

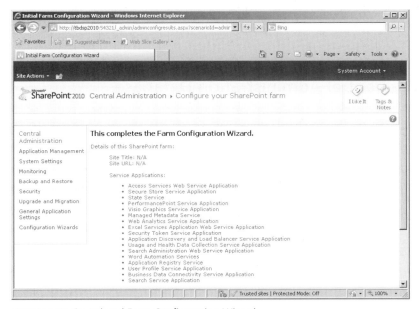

FIGURE 4-38 Completed Farm Configuration Wizard

After you run the Farm Configuration Wizard in SharePoint 2010, you can access SQL Server using Management Studio, and you will see the additional service application databases that were created by the Farm Configuration Wizard, as shown in the example in Figure 4-39.

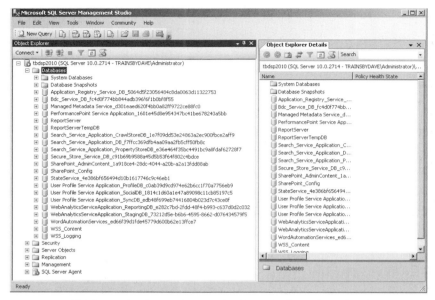

FIGURE 4-39 SQL Server databases after running Farm Configuration Wizard

Renaming the Central Administration Database

After the SharePoint configuration database, the Central Administration database is the second most important database that SharePoint uses, and unless you perform a command-line installation, it uses the default user name with a Globally Unique Identifier (GUID). This can make it challenging if you want to write scripts that reference the database using the default name. The following steps should be used with extreme caution, but if you follow them exactly, you can give the default Central Administration database a more user-friendly name.

1. Log on to your SQL Server with an account that has full access; ideally, you should use the same account that you used for your SharePoint installation.

2. Open the SQL Server Management Studio interface and locate the SQL Server instance that contains your Central Administration database. The database name will be something similar to SharePoint_AdminContent_<GUID>, as shown in Figure 4-40. Right-click the database name and choose the Rename command from the shortcut menu to enter edit mode. Then press Ctrl+C to copy the existing name of the database for later use. Click anywhere outside of the database name to exit edit mode.

IMPORTANT Be sure not to change the name at this point—it will be done at a later time.

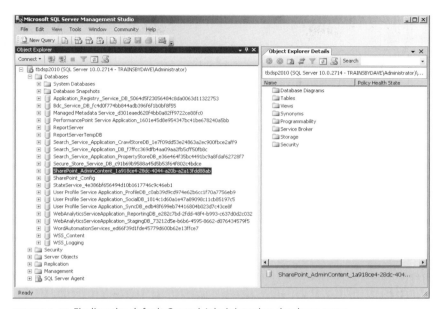

FIGURE 4-40 Finding the default Central Administration database name

3. While still in SQL Server Management Studio, back up the existing SharePoint_ AdminContent_*<GUID>* database by right-clicking the name of the database and then selecting the Tasks command. Select Back Up to open the Back Up Database dialog box. Use all of the default settings for the backup and then click OK.

4. When you have successfully backed up the database, restore the information from the backup that you just performed to a new database having a user-friendly database name such as CentralAdmin_Content_DB. Perform the restore by right-clicking the existing database name again and selecting the Tasks command from the shortcut menu. Select Restore and then Database to open the Restore Database dialog box shown in Figure 4-41. In the To Database section, type in the new database name and then click OK at the bottom of the dialog box.

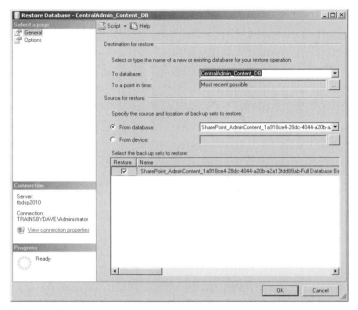

FIGURE 4-41 Restoring to a new database name

5. Open Central Administration. Under Application Management, click Manage Content Databases.

   a. Select the SharePoint Central Administration v4 Web application using the Web application drop-down list.

   b. Click the old database name, SharePoint_AdminContent_<*GUID*>.

   c. Use the Database status drop-down option to change the status from Ready to Offline.

   d. Do not select the option to remove the content database.

   e. Click OK.

   > **IMPORTANT** It is critical that you use the correct user name during this step or you will probably receive Access Denied error messages.

6. Log on to the server using the account that was used to provision the database. Usually this is the service user account that you configured SharePoint with when you provisioned the content databases during the installation of SharePoint 2010.

7. After opening the command prompt, perform the following steps.

   a. Type **cd C:\Program Files\Common Files\Microsoft Shared\Web server extensions\14\BIN** to change the directory to the SharePoint 2010 root so you can run the STSADM commands.

b. Delete the original Central Administration database, the one with the GUID that you copied earlier, using the following command (be sure to specify the UrlOfYourCentralAdministration and NamedInstanceOfYourSqlServer for your SharePoint installation names).

```
stsadm -o deletecontentdb -url http://UrlOfYourCentralAdministration:p
ortnumber -databasename SharePoint_AdminContent_<GUID> -databaseserver
NamedInstanceOfYourSqlServer or just the name of the SQL Server if there is no
instance name for the SQL Server.
```

c. Associate the newly created database with your Central Administration using the following STSADM command (again be sure to specify the UrlOfCentralYourAdministration and NamedInstanceOfYourSqlServer for your SharePoint installation names).

```
stsadm -o addcontentdb -url http:// UrlOfYourCentralAdministration:
portnumber -databasename SharePoint_AdminContent_DB -databaseserver
NamedInstanceOfYourSqlServer
```

8. Return to Central Administration. Under Application Management, click Manage Content Databases and refresh the page to verify that your Central Administration database reflects the new database name as shown in Figure 4-42.

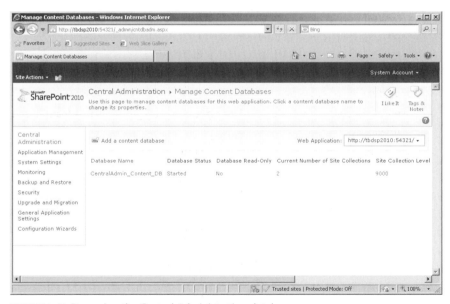

FIGURE 4-42 Renaming the Central Administration database

If you see a database with the new name, you can then be sure that the original Central Administration database is backed up, and you can delete it from SQL Server.

IMPORTANT If you attempt to delete the original SharePoint_AdminContent_<*GUID*> database and receive an error indicating there are existing connections to the database, you probably didn't disassociate the database from SharePoint. Repeat the process from the beginning.

Uninstalling SharePoint 2010

There may come a time where you need to remove SharePoint 2010 from a server to allow that server to be used by another application. Or you may upgrade your hardware in the future and want to repurpose the server for another role. The process of uninstalling SharePoint 2010 is the same for all editions of SharePoint 2010—the only difference is where you initiate the uninstall command that begins the removal of SharePoint 2010.

To uninstall SharePoint 2010, you run the Setup.exe program that you ran when you installed it. However, during the uninstall process, when the installation program does an inventory of the software that is on the server, it will not allow you to perform an installation but instead will request that you choose to repair or remove the installation.

NOTE Alternately, you can also remove SharePoint using the uninstall option within Add/Remove programs located in Control Panel of your operating system.

Follow these steps to uninstall SharePoint 2010 from your server using Setup.exe.

1. Locate the directory that contains the Setup.exe file for the edition of SharePoint 2010 that you are uninstalling. For instance, if you installed SharePoint 2010, then locate the Setup.exe file for SharePoint 2010. Alternatively, if you installed SharePoint Foundation 2010 and you want to remove it, then locate the Setup.exe file for SharePoint Foundation 2010.

2. Double-click the Setup.exe file to display the original installation startup screen. Choose Install SharePoint Server or Install SharePoint Foundation, depending on which Setup.exe file you ran. At this point, SharePoint takes inventory and discovers an installation of SharePoint already exists. Then you will see the Change Your Installation Of SharePoint 2010 page, as shown in Figure 4-43.

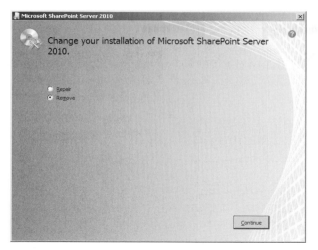

FIGURE 4-43 Change Your Installation Of SharePoint 2010 page

3. Select the Remove option and then click the Continue button. In the Verify Removal dialog box shown in Figure 4-44, you will be asked to confirm your selection to remove SharePoint from the server.

FIGURE 4-44 Verify Removal dialog box

4. If you click No in this dialog box, the removal of SharePoint 2010 is canceled. However, if you click Yes, the uninstall process continues. Another dialog box, shown in Figure 4-45, displays to warn you that if you continue with the uninstall process, you cannot undo it, and it might result in partial loss of functionality for sites that depend on that installation. It also warns you that if you installed the current SharePoint installation over a previous version of SharePoint, or if you Click Cancel after you click OK in the dialog box, you will have to run the SharePoint Products Configuration Wizard again to reconfigure your server farm. It again asks if you want to uninstall SharePoint 2010.

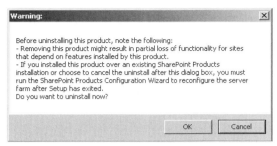

FIGURE 4-45 Uninstall Warning dialog box

5. When you confirm the uninstall, you will see the page shown in Figure 4-46 that shows the progress of the uninstall process. However, this page does not provide any really helpful information about what actions are being performed, or what percentage of the uninstall has been completed, or even the amount of time remaining before the uninstall completes.

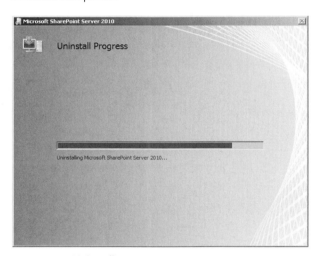

FIGURE 4-46 Uninstall Progress page

6. When the uninstall process is complete, you will see a final page that tells you that the uninstall has completed successfully, so you should now have a SharePoint-free server. However, after successfully performing an uninstall, note that the following SharePoint characteristics still exist on the server.

- C:\Program Files\Common Files\Microsoft Shared\Web Server Extensions\14
- Microsoft SharePoint Workspace Audit Service
- SQL databases including Configuration and Central Administration
- SharePoint Web Services Web Application in IIS 7.0
- SharePoint Web Services Application Pool in IIS 7.0

To reiterate once again the point about doing fresh installations of your software, these items all still existed on a server after performing a complete installation of SharePoint 2010 and then a removal of SharePoint. Always perform clean installations—this includes starting with a new operating system installation, not an upgraded operating system.

Summary

This chapter provided information about the different editions of SharePoint 2010 from which you can choose, and it also outlined the hardware and software prerequisites for SharePoint 2010. Similar to choosing the appropriate SQL Server edition, choosing the appropriate SharePoint 2010 edition has a significant impact on what your SharePoint 2010 implementation will be able to host. Upgrading, repairing, uninstalling, and reinstalling on the same machine is risky business, so it is recommended that you start with fresh installations of all the components that integrate with SharePoint 2010 to ensure that you have a solid installation with minimal chance of issues caused by corrupt software that was upgraded.

Responding to the requests throughout the wizards or writing your scripts to create the farm correctly for you can make a big difference in what you need to do at the post-installation configuration stage of a new installation. Use the step-by-step procedures in this chapter to ensure you have a properly configured farm.

Scripting your farm's installation and configuration can streamline your recovery process in a disaster recovery scenario. Although it may be challenging to write, test, and document the scripts, it is worthwhile to take the time to so, because the scripts will be invaluable if you have to rebuild your farm.

## CHAPTER 5

Using Windows PowerShell to Perform and Automate Farm Administrative Tasks

- Using Windows PowerShell: The Basics **195**
- Working with SharePoint 2010 Management Shell **210**
- Examples of SharePoint Administrative Tasks **234**

O ver the last couple of years, some SharePoint administrators have recognized the power of Windows PowerShell and have tried to use it, but with no built-in support, most administrators have found it too difficult. Microsoft SharePoint Foundation 2010 and Microsoft SharePoint 2010 now contain native support for Windows PowerShell with the SharePoint 2010 Management Shell. This chapter explores the SharePoint 2010 Management Shell and how to use Windows PowerShell to accomplish some basic administrative tasks. Chapter 12, "Using Windows PowerShell to Manage Search Services and FAST Search," builds on the information in this chapter, using search administrative tasks and scenarios.

There is an enormous amount of information available about Windows PowerShell on the Internet and published in books. The aim of this chapter is not to teach you Windows PowerShell, but to show you how to become familiar with the new Windows PowerShell cmdlets, pronounced *command-lets*, introduced in SharePoint 2010. However, for those who are relatively new to Windows PowerShell, this chapter begins by reviewing the basics.

Using Windows PowerShell: The Basics

Traditionally, administrating a server on which Microsoft products are installed has involved learning a number of administrator tools, such as graphical interfaces based on the Microsoft Management Console (MMC), known as *MMC snap-ins*; many command-line utilities; and perhaps a Windows Management Instrumentation (WMI) provider or Component Object Model (COM) objects that administrators can interface with using

VBScript. Until the release of SharePoint 2010, SharePoint Products and Technologies were no different than other Microsoft products in the number of available administrator tools. Administrators needed to rely on the Central Administration website, the SharePoint Products Configuration Wizard, and the command-line tools stsadm and psconfig. No one tool could do everything.

Each Microsoft product also had its own community, which created or extended the built-in tools to make an administrator's life easier. The tools an administrator needed were available, but they were scattered among many sources. This is all changing now that every administrative task can potentially be scripted or automated using Windows PowerShell.

The concept for Windows PowerShell is based on a study commissioned by Microsoft in the early 2000s. Originally based on the POSIX shell as specified in IEEE 1003.2 and influenced by Perl and UNIX shell, Windows PowerShell is a command shell and scripting language that is far more powerful than using the Windows command prompt (cmd.exe). Administrators love command-line tools because they can be batched together to automate repetitive tasks or to ensure that a set of tasks are completed again exactly as they were the last time they were executed. Windows PowerShell cmdlets offer administrators these same benefits. You can still use the traditional tools, but Windows PowerShell adds flexibility and breadth that the traditional tools do not provide.

> **NOTE** Community-led initiatives for previous versions of SharePoint include extensions to stsadm, published at *http://stsadm.codeplex.com/*; Windows PowerShell scripts for Windows SharePoint Services 3.0 and Microsoft Office SharePoint Server 2007 that can be found at *http://sharepointpsscripts.codeplex.com/*; and the CodePlex project "PowerShell SharePoint Provider" for Windows SharePoint Services 2.0 and Microsoft SharePoint Portal Server 2003, available at *http://www.codeplex.com/PSSharePoint*.

This section covers the following Windows PowerShell topics.

- What's new in the Windows PowerShell 2.0 release
- Architecture
- Installing Windows PowerShell
- Remote management

What's New in Windows PowerShell 2.0

Windows PowerShell 2.0 offers a number of new features and improvements from Windows PowerShell 1.0, including

- New cmdlets
- Remote Management and background jobs
- Windows PowerShell Integrated Scripting Environment (ISE)
- Windows PowerShell debugger

- Modules
- Advanced functions
- Transactions
- Steppable pipelines
- Events
- Script internationalization
- Online Help

As an IT professional, many of these new features will interest you. For example, you can remotely manage all the servers in your farm from your desktop, and when you become competent in Windows PowerShell, you will be able to create your own advanced functions using the Windows PowerShell scripting language that you can then use as cmdlets. In Windows PowerShell 1.0, the only way to do this was with a developer, using code and deploying files onto your farm.

> **MORE INFO** For more information about what's new in Windows PowerShell 2.0, see *http://technet.microsoft.com/en-us/library/dd378784.aspx* and *http://en.wikipedia.org/wiki /Windows_PowerShell*. Other resources can be found by using your favorite Internet search engine and entering the keywords What's New in Windows PowerShell 2.0 or the feature names listed previously.

Windows PowerShell Architecture

Why is Windows PowerShell so important? Windows PowerShell scripting language is object orientated, built on top of the .NET Framework—.NET Framework 3.5 for Windows Power-Shell 2.0—and based on the C# (pronounced C-sharp) programming language. This allows Windows PowerShell to access the underlying object models, to pass objects and their values (properties) from one Windows PowerShell command to another. This means you have almost the power of a developer without having to write, compile, and deploy code. The disadvantage is that it can be all too easy to cause havoc in your installation.

When the Microsoft product teams consider the tools they want to provide to administrators, they build them first on Windows PowerShell. Hence, with the installation of SharePoint 2010, a large number of administrative tasks can be completed natively with Windows PowerShell cmdlets, with no need to install software from community-led initiatives. If any additional cmdlets are required, you can create them using Windows PowerShell scripts and the Advanced Functions feature in Windows PowerShell 2.0, and developers within your organization can create new cmdlets. Using Windows PowerShell to help administer SharePoint is the way of the future, so it's important to start learning to use the built-in cmdlets as soon as possible.

At first, using Windows PowerShell may seem daunting, but if you have used the command prompt (cmd.exe) or have created batch files, you will soon be comfortable with the Windows PowerShell console. In fact, you can even use the Windows PowerShell console instead of the command prompt, because all the commands you currently use, such as dir, cd, and ping, work equally well in the Windows PowerShell console as they do in the command prompt. You may need to enclose command-line parameters in quotation marks to use the commands from within Windows PowerShell, but that is about the only modification you need to make. So there is no need to use two different windows to complete your administrative tasks.

NOTE By default, the command prompt has a black background, but this can be changed. Right-click the title bar and then select Properties. A Properties dialog box appears with four tabs: Options, Font, Layout, and Colors. You can change the font, background color, window size, and more. See the sidebar titled "Command-line Shortcuts" later in this chapter for more information about similarities between the two command-line interfaces.

There are two ways of using Windows PowerShell: either through a command-line interface, known as the Windows PowerShell console (powershell.exe), or through the Windows PowerShell Interactive Scripting Environment (ISE) graphical interface (Powershell_ise.exe). This chapter concentrates on using the Windows PowerShell console.

MORE INFO Following are some resources for more information on Windows PowerShell.

- *Windows PowerShell 2.0 Administrator's Pocket Consultant*, by William R. Stanek (Microsoft Press, 2009)

- "Scripting with Windows PowerShell" on the Microsoft TechNet Script Center at *http://technet.microsoft.com/en-us/scriptcenter/dd742419.aspx*.

- An aggregation of Windows PowerShell bloggers at *http://pipes.yahoo.com /powershell/englishbloggers*.

- A short introduction to Windows PowerShell in a free eBook at *http://blogs.msdn.com/mapo/archive/2007/07/17/windows-powershell-free-ebook-at-microsoft.aspx*.

- *Mastering PowerShell,* by Dr. Tobias Weltner, a free eBook at *http://blogs.msdn.com/powershell/archive/2009/07/17/free-powershell-v1-book-from-the-makers-of-powershell-plus.aspx*.

Command-line Shortcuts

All the same shortcuts that you use at the command prompt work in the Windows PowerShell console.

- To pause the display temporarily when a command is writing output, press Ctrl+S, and then press Ctrl+S to resume or press Ctrl+C to terminate execution.

- By default, up to 50 commands are stored in a buffer. You can move through the buffer by using the up arrow and down arrow keys to scroll through the commands so you can easily execute the next or a previous command.

- The buffered commands can be displayed from a pop-up window by pressing F7. Select the command you want to execute using the arrow keys, press Enter or F9, type the number of the command you want to execute, and then press Enter.

- The buffered commands can be displayed from the command line by typing the first few characters of the command you want and then pressing F8. The command-line interface searches though the history buffer for the first command that begins with the characters you typed.

- Using the auto completion capabilities of the Windows PowerShell command shell, you never need to type the complete name of a command. Type in the first few characters of the command you want and press Tab to cycle through all commands and available file names and folders in alphabetic order, or click Shift+Tab to cycle through the commands in reverse order.

- To copy and paste text, right-click the command-line interface title, click Mark, highlight the text you want to copy, and then right-click the window title again to copy the selected text automatically into the Clipboard.

- Commands are case insensitive and can be batched together and placed in a text file. By calling that file in the command-line window, the commands in the file are executed. These text files have an extension of .bat, .cmd, .vbs, or in the case of Windows PowerShell, .ps1. Commands in these files can be executed outside the command window by calling the file from the Run line or by double-clicking the file in Windows Explorer.

- Arguments can be sent to the command file being called. The arguments passed to your command file are stored in memory and accessed using variables. You can also create variables to store values needed as you complete a task. In Windows PowerShell, you reference variables by preceding the variable name by a dollar sign ($).

- Output from a command can be directed to a file named to the right of >. This will overwrite the file if it already exists. To redirect the output but append it to the file, use >>. Error messages that result from running a command can be redirected to a file named to the right of 2>, or they can be appended to a file by using 2>> or sent to the same destination as the standard output by using 2>&1.

- You can execute many commands on the same line. In Windows PowerShell, you separate commands using the semicolon character (;).

- Redirect the output of one command as input to another command by separating both command with a '|', known as a *pipe*. For example, dir | sort | more will display a sorted list of files in the current directory one page at a time. The pipe is the symbol located above the backslash on most keyboards.

- Aliases and shortcuts can be substituted for commonly used commands. For example, the ForEach-Object cmdlet can be replaced with ForEach or even with the percentage character, %. The question mark character, ?, can be used in place of Where or Where-Object. You can also use Get-Alias to return a list of aliases. Note that the use of aliases in scripts can make them difficult to understand.

Examples of these shortcuts can be found throughout this book.

Installing Windows PowerShell

Computers running Windows 7 or Windows 2008 R2 or later include Windows PowerShell 2.0 and Windows Remote Management (WinRM) 2.0. If you want to manage computers using earlier operating systems locally or remotely using Windows PowerShell, you will need to install both Windows PowerShell 2.0 and WinRM 2.0.

Installing Windows PowerShell 2.0 and WinRM 2.0

A copy of Windows PowerShell 2.0, together with WinRM 2.0, can be downloaded from *http://support.microsoft.com/default.aspx/kb/968929*. Ensure that you obtain the correct version; for example, if you install SharePoint on the 64-bit version of Windows Server 2008, you need to download and install the Windows 2008 x64 version of Windows PowerShell 2.0 and WinRM 2.0. After they are installed, you will find the executable for the Windows PowerShell ISE in the folder %SystemRoot%\System32\WindowsPowerShell\v1.0.

> **NOTE** If you going to be a heavy user of ISE, consider placing a shortcut for this program on your taskbar. On the Start menu, right-click Powershell_ise.exe and then select either Pin To Taskbar or Pin To Start Menu.

To use Windows PowerShell ISE on Windows 2008 R2, you need to add the Windows PowerShell ISE feature. This feature can be added using Windows PowerShell commands or the Server Manager. After you have installed SharePoint 2010 or SharePoint Foundation 2010, perform the following steps.

- Using Windows PowerShell, enter the following commands.

```
Import-Module Servermanager; Add-WindowsFeature "PowerShell-ISE"
```

- Using Server Manager, complete the following procedure.

    1. Start the Server Manager, click Features, and then select Add Features.

    2. In the middle pane of the Add Features Wizard, select the check box for Windows PowerShell Integrated Scripting Environment (ISE) as shown in Figure 5-1 and then click Next.

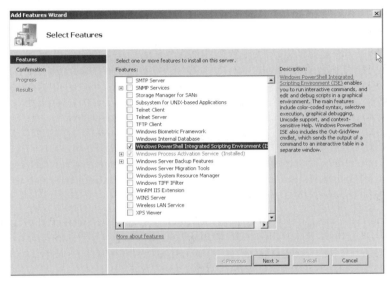

FIGURE 5-1 Install the Windows PowerShell Integrated Scripting Environment (ISE) feature

    3. On the Confirmation Installation Selection screen, click Install.

    4. On the Installation Results screen, click Close.

NOTE You may need to restart your server after the installation completes.

Working Within Your Execution Policy

Windows PowerShell is a powerful tool, and as with any other scripting language, it is all too easy to borrow someone else's code or download snippets from the Internet. Also, because the code files are just text files, it is easy for anyone to modify them and inject malicious code. Therefore, Windows PowerShell has a built-in security feature called *execution policy* that you can set on a per-user basis, and these settings are saved in the registry. To view your execution policy, type the following command in the Microsoft SharePoint 2010 Management Shell.

```
Get-ExecutionPolicy
```

If you are running the Management Shell on a SharePoint server, it is likely that the output from such a command is RemoteSigned, which means that you can run any commands inter-actively and you can use any scripts that are stored on the computer where you are logged in. However, if you want to run configuration files or scripts from remote sources, they need to be signed. You can change the execution policy if you start the Windows PowerShell console as an administrator and use the Set-ExecutionPolicy cmdlet, or you can change the registry key as follows.

```
HKLM\Software\Microsoft\PowerShell\1\ShellIds\Microsoft.PowerShell
```

 SECURITY ALERT The registry key is useful in conjunction with an Active Directory Group Policy. Manual modifications to the registry should be avoided, especially when Microsoft provides a cmdlet to configure Windows PowerShell execution policy.

To sign scripts, use the Set-AuthenticodeSignature cmdlet, which can be used to add an Authenticode signature to a Windows PowerShell script or other file.

In an organization that has multiple environments, such as development, system integra-tion, user acceptance test (UAT), pre-production, and production, consider the need to sign code on your production and UAT farms at minimum. You should also review the execution policy settings for these farms. You can set the execution policy in a Group Policy Object that targets either users or computers so that it cannot be overridden when someone logs on to your SharePoint servers.

MORE INFO For more information on Windows PowerShell execution policies and signing scripts, see the TechNet article "Heading Off Malicious Code" at *http://technet.microsoft.com/en-us/magazine/2008.01.powershell.aspx*, or type **Get-Help about_Execution_Policies** at a Windows PowerShell command-line interface. There is also a blog post that explains the process in detail. It is "ALLSigned: Signing Your PowerShell Scripts" and can be found at *http://sharepoint.microsoft.com/blogs/zach/Lists/Posts /Post.aspx?ID=53*.

NOTE If you are using Windows 7 as your desktop and you want to remotely manage Windows Server 2008 R2 for your SharePoint servers, you need the Remote Server Administration Tools (RSAT), which is required for the new Group Policy features and supports Windows PowerShell. RSAT is available from the Microsoft Download Center at *http://www.microsoft.com/downloads*. For more information, go to *http://technet.microsoft.com/en-us/library/dd367853.aspx* and *http://trycatch.be/blogs /roggenk/archive/2009/06/08/installing-windows-7-rsat-unattended.aspx*.

Managing Systems Remotely with WinRM

Windows PowerShell 2.0 introduces a new capability to manage your systems remotely from your desktop by using either WinRM or Internet Information Server (IIS). WinRM is often the mechanism used by administrators and the subject of this section. Remote Management involves not just the ability to run Windows PowerShell locally on your machine using the few commands that allow you to specify a computer name as an optional parameter; it also includes methods known as fan-in and fan-out remoting and background jobs.

- **Fan-in remoting** This allows many administrators to connect to an instance of Windows PowerShell running on the same remote servers—this is not supported out of the box in SharePoint 2010.

- **Fan-out remoting** This allows you to send a single Windows PowerShell command to run multiple remote instances of Windows PowerShell in parallel, and the results of those commands will be returned to your desktop. You would use this if you need to complete the same task on multiple servers. You no longer need to establish a Remote Desktop connection to each server in turn and then execute the commands locally on that server. You can create a set of Windows PowerShell commands and pass the server names to those commands, which then completes the same commands sequentially for each server whose name you provide.

- **Background jobs** Windows PowerShell 2.0 supports both local and remote background jobs. These are commands that execute asynchronously in the background with no interaction. When you execute a command in the background, the command prompt is returned immediately so that you can continue to execute other commands.

Configuring for WinRM

The WinRM Windows service must be started and configured for remoting on both your local computer and the server on which you want to remotely run commands. To find out if your server is running WinRM, type

```
Get-service winrm
```

To check if it is running on a remote server, type

```
Get-service winrm –computername $server_name
```

On your SharePoint server, this service should be running; however, if your local computer is running Windows 7 (or Windows Vista with Windows PowerShell 2.0 and WinRM 2.0 installed), you may need to start this service and enable remoting. You can do this by typing one command, Enable-PSRemoting, which executes two additional commands, Set-WSManQuickConfig and Start-Service WinRM.

> **IMPORTANT** If one of the network connection types is Public, the Set-WSManQuickConfig command will raise an Invalid Operation Exception. You will need to change the network connections to the network type of either Domain or Private to proceed.

The output to the Enable-PSRemoting command will look similar to the following example.

```
WinRM Quick Configuration
Running command "Set-WSManQuickConfig" to enable this machine for remote management
through WinRM service.
 This includes:
    1. Starting or restarting (if already started) the WinRM service
    2. Setting the WinRM service type to auto start
    3. Creating a listener to accept requests on any IP address
    4. Enabling firewall exception for WS-Management traffic (for http only).

Do you want to continue?
[Y] Yes  [A] Yes to All  [N] No  [L] No to All  [S] Suspend  [?] Help (default
is "Y"): y
WinRM has been updated to receive requests.
WinRM service type changed successfully.
WinRM service started.
Configured LocalAccountTokenFilterPolicy to grant administrative rights remotely to
local users.
WinRM has been updated for remote management.
Created a WinRM listener on HTTP://* to accept WS-Man requests to any IP on this
machine.
WinRM firewall exception enabled.
```

On a computer running a 64-bit version of Windows, you may see an additional confirmation message.

```
Are you sure you want to perform this action?
Performing operation "Registering session configuration" on Target "Session
configuration "Microsoft.PowerShell32" is not found. Running command
"Register-PSSessionConfiguration Microsoft.PowerShell32 -processorarchitecture x86
-force" to create "Microsoft.PowerShell32" session configuration. This will restart
WinRM service.".
[Y] Yes  [A] Yes to All  [N] No  [L] No to All  [S] Suspend  [?] Help (default is
"Y"):
```

To determine how WinRM is configured, the authentication method, and the port numbers it will access, use the following command.

```
winrm get winrm/config/service
```

This should result in an output similar to the following.

```
Service
    RootSDDL = O:NSG:BAD:P(A;;GA;;;BA)S:P(AU;FA;GA;;;WD)(AU;SA;GWGX;;;WD)
    MaxConcurrentOperations = 4294967295
    MaxConcurrentOperationsPerUser = 15
```

```
EnumerationTimeoutms = 60000
MaxConnections = 25
MaxPacketRetrievalTimeSeconds = 120
AllowUnencrypted = false
Auth
    Basic = false
    Kerberos = true
    Negotiate = true
    Certificate = false
    CredSSP = false
    CbtHardeningLevel = Relaxed
DefaultPorts
    HTTP = 5985
    HTTPS = 5986
IPv4Filter = *
IPv6Filter = *
EnableCompatibilityHttpListener = false
EnableCompatibilityHttpsListener = false
CertificateThumbprint
```

You can run winrm and winrm-related commands, such as the New-PSSession command, from either the Windows PowerShell console or the SharePoint 2010 Management Shell. However, these must be run as an administrator. To do this, right-click the Windows PowerShell console or the SharePoint 2010 Management Shell and then select Run As Administrator. You must be a member of the Administrators group on the remote machine or be able to provide administrator credentials to do this.

> **NOTE** When your local computer and the remote computer are in different non-trusted domains or in a workgroup, additional steps are required to configure remoting. The workgroup scenario is likely to occur when SharePoint Foundation is installed for external collaboration or in a small business environment rather than in a typical SharePoint Server installation. For information on how to configure remoting between two workgroup machines, see the blog post at *http://blogs.msdn.com/wmi/archive/2009/07/24 /powershell-remoting-between-two-workgroup-machines.aspx*.

Meeting Requirements for SharePoint PowerShell Remoting

To use WinRM to execute SharePoint PowerShell cmdlets on a remote machine, there are a number of additional requirements.

1. You must have access to a userid with the correct rights to execute those commands. These requirements are applicable whether you are remoting into a server or locally executing SharePoint cmdlets. The userid must meet the following criteria.

- Must be a member of the WSS_ADM_WGP local security group on the machine executing the commands.

- Must be a member of the SharePoint_Shell_Access SQL Server role on the configuration database.

- Must have access to the content database that you want to manipulate.

You can use the SPShellAdmin cmdlets to help you manage these requirements. When you run the Add-SPShellAdmin cmdlet to add a userid to the SharePoint_Shell_Admin role, you must be mapped to Security_Admin role on the SQL instance and the db_owner role to the relevant databases. You need to run the Add-SPShellAdmin cmdlet for each content database that you want the userid to access.

2. Designate one server in your farm as the server you will always use for remoting. On that server, increase the WinRM configuration option, MaxMemoryPerShellDB, to a large value, 512 or 1024. This configuration option limits the amount of memory a single remote process can use. Increasing the value will allow long-running commands to run without throwing OutOfMemory Exception errors. The command to display the values of the configuration options and sample output is shown here.

```
winrm get winrm/config/winrs

Winrs
    AllowRemoteShellAccess = true
    IdleTimeout = 180000
    MaxConcurrentUsers = 5
    MaxShellRunTime = 2147483647
    MaxProcessesPerShell = 15
    MaxMemoryPerShellMB = 150
    MaxShellsPerUser = 5
```

To modify the MaxMemoryPerShellDB setting, type the following Windows PowerShell command in the SharePoint 2010 Management Shell.

```
Set-Item WSMan:\localhost\Shell\MaxMemoryPerShellMB 1024
```

3. You must use Credential Security Provider (CredSSP) authentication. This authentication mechanism, introduced with Windows Vista, allows an application to delegate the credentials from one machine to another, a process called *double hopping*. This will enable you to provide the credentials that allow the SharePoint PowerShell cmdlets to talk to the Microsoft SQL Server that is hosting your SharePoint databases. If you do not use CredSSP and you try to remotely execute a SharePoint cmdlet, you are likely to receive a message that indicates the farm is unavailable. In the output from the Winrm get winrm/config/service command shown previously, notice that CredSSP is equal to False. There are several ways you can modify WinRM configuration options, including Group Policy, login scripts, and the command prompt. To enable CredSSP authentication though command-line interfaces, complete the following tasks.

a. On the computer from which you are remoting, such as your Windows 7 desktop, type the following command, where Web1 is the SharePoint server. Type **Y** when prompted to confirm that you want to enable CredSSP authentication.

```
Enable-WSManCredSSP -role client -DelegateComputer Web1
```

b. On the SharePoint server where you are remoting to, type

```
Enable-WSManCredSSP -role server
```

> **MORE INFO** For more information on multi-hop support in WinRM, see
> *http://msdn.microsoft.com/en-us/library/ee309365(VS.85).aspx.*

Using WinRM Remoting

The commands you need to start a remote session to remotely manage a SharePoint farm or one specific SharePoint server are similar to those in the following example.

```
$cred = Get-Credential contoso\spfarm
$sess = New-PSSession Web1 -Authentication CredSSP -Credential $cred
Invoke-Command -Session $sess -ScriptBlock `
    {ADD-PSSnapin Microsoft.SharePoint.PowerShell;}
```

> **SECURITY ALERT** You can limit the Windows PowerShell commands that a user can access during a remote session by using the *–ConfigurationName* parameter with the New-PSSession cmdlet or by using the Proxy cmdlet. For more information, see the blog post "Extending and/or Modifying Command with Proxies" at *http://blogs.msdn.com/powershell/archive/2009/01/04/extending-and-or-modifing-commands-with-proxies.aspx.*

When you enter the first command, a dialog box appears where you must type the password. This password and the user name are stored in the variable *$Cred*, which is used in the second command, New-PSSession, which establishes a persistent session with the remote server. Creating a persistent session is not necessary when using Windows PowerShell remoting, but if you do not establish a persistent connection, whenever you invoke a remote command that includes a SharePoint cmdlet, each Invoke-Command will also need to include the PSSnapin cmdlet. The third command, Invoke-Command PSSnapin, allows you to run SharePoint PowerShell cmdlets on the remote server.

Reference to the persistent session is stored in the variable *$sess*. You can direct any commands you want to that remote server by using this variable. In the following example, the cmdlet Get-SPServiceInstance is typed within the script block—the area between the curly brackets ({ }). The output from the Get-SPServiceInstance cmdlet returns the status of the services within a SharePoint farm.

```
Invoke-Command -Session $s -ScriptBlock {get-SPServiceInstance}
```

```
WARNING: column "PSComputerName" does not fit into the display and was removed.

TypeName                        Status    Id
--------                        ------    --
Business Data Connectivity      Online    3ad4d004-9ae3-4810-94bf-76cc43c9d507
Microsoft SharePoint Foundati... Online    81cc6474-fd6f-42ad-a932-25d67cff8cc1
Microsoft SharePoint Foundati... Disabled  cb3b976c-b451-4abe-b808-0c6d191ccd3d
Microsoft SharePoint Foundati... Online    5bac9c93-483a-4901-ae46-f6f7ae0a12a8
Central Administration          Online    0c24457f-b58e-4daa-895e-4acd35ef7543
Microsoft SharePoint Foundati... Online    155570fa-0d4c-495d-9f31-5250e83bdd75
Microsoft SharePoint Foundati... Disabled  c25ae170-c07d-48db-97b3-73b0d9b47e94
SharePoint Foundation Help Se... Online    8af8b8b1-92cb-48d2-8864-20a7e191d7c2
```

> **BEST PRACTICE**   You can type multiple commands in a script block, either on separate lines or on the same line separated by a semicolon (;). If only one command is entered in the script block, the semicolon is optional, but it is good practice to include it. You can also use local variables to generate a remote script block as in the following example.
>
> ```
> $url = "http://contoso.com"
> $myscript = "get-spsite $url"
> $sb = [scriptblock]::Create($myscript)
> Invoke-Command $sess -ScriptBlock $sb
> ```

You can use the Windows PowerShell Invoke-Command cmdlet to communicate with many sessions, either on the same server or on different servers, from your desktop. This cmdlet enables you to start multiple administrative tasks at the same time that are then run in parallel. However, if these tasks are long running, you will not get control back until the command on the remote machine finishes. This is known as *running the command interactively*. To run asynchronously as a background job so that the Windows PowerShell prompt returns immediately and you can enter other commands, append the *–AsJob* parameter to the Invoke-Command, or alternatively, use the Start-Job cmdlet. Using this technique can reduce the amount of time to complete your administrative tasks, compared to running them sequentially. An example of how this can save you a considerable amount of time is during the upgrade process, when each session runs a database-attach-upgrade, and the time taken to complete all database upgrades is limited only by the resources of your SQL Server.

If you have many short-running tasks to complete on a specific server and don't want to keep typing Invoke-Command, use one of the following approaches.

- You can enter an interactive session with that server by typing **Enter-PSSession $sess**. The command prompt will change from PS C:\Users*<userid>*, where *<userid>* is the name of the current user, to [*<remoteservername>*]: PS C:\Users*<remotecredentials>* \Documents, where *<remotecredentials>* is the userid you used for the CredSSP authentication. The command prompt reminds you that you are now submitting commands to the remote server. To return to interactive mode on your local computer, type **Exit-PSSession** or **exit**.

- Use the Import-PSSession remoting cmdlet, also known as *implicit remoting*, to bring commands from the remote session into the local Windows PowerShell session. An additional advantage of the Import-PSSession approach is that you can interact with your local file system and talk to SharePoint as if you were logged on locally to the SharePoint server. By default, the Import-PSSession cmdlet imports all commands except commands that have the same name as commands in your current session. You can also import a subset of commands and prefix them with a word you specify, so that it is obvious to you which commands are local and which are remote. In the following example, the word *Remote* is added as a prefix to all SPSite cmdlets.

```
Import-PSSession -session $sess -CommandName *-spsite -Prefix Remote

ModuleType  Name                    ExportedCommands
----------  ----                    ----------------
Script      tmp_1833f7bc-b269-4229... {Set-SPSite, Backup-SPSite, Get-SPSite,...
```

In this example, you can use all SPSite cmdlets as if they were local commands; for example, by typing **Get-RemoteSPSite** you can return all site collections that match the given criteria. These imported commands are stored in a temporary module that is deleted at the end of the session. To create a persistent module that you can use in future sessions, use the Export-PSSession cmdlet. The imported commands still run in the remote session from which they were imported and therefore may take longer to run than local commands.

When you have completed all of your tasks, you can delete the persistent connection between your local machine and the remote machine by typing **Remove-PSSession $sess**.

> **MORE INFO** For more information about Windows PowerShell remoting, see Chapter 4, "Using Sessions, Jobs, and Remoting" in the *Windows PowerShell 2.0, Administrator's Pocket Consultant,* by William Stanek (Microsoft Press, 2009), and the TechNet Magazine article "A Sneak Peek at Remote Management in Version 2.0" at *http://technet.microsoft.com /en-us/magazine/2008.08.windowspowershell.aspx*. Also take a look at the blog post "A Few Good WS-MAN (WinRM) Commands" at *http://blogs.technet.com/otto/archive/2007/02/09 /sample-vista-ws-man-winrm-commands.aspx*.

Working with the SharePoint 2010 Management Shell

To open the SharePoint 2010 Management Shell, click Start, and then select Programs, Microsoft SharePoint 2010 Products, and finally, SharePoint 2010 Management Shell, as shown in Figure 5-2.

FIGURE 5-2 Accessing the SharePoint 2010 Management Shell

The SharePoint 2010 Management Shell is a custom console; it is not the same console that opens if you open the default Windows PowerShell console, a shortcut to which is usually placed on the taskbar. A review of the properties of the SharePoint 2010 Management Shell shortcut exposes the command that is executed.

```
C:\Windows\System32\WindowsPowerShell\v1.0\PowerShell.exe  -NoExit  " &
    ' C:\Program Files\Common Files\Microsoft Shared\Web Server
    Extensions\14\CONFIG\POWERSHELL\Registration\\sharepoint.ps1 ' "
```

The shortcut points to the file Sharepoint.ps1. This is an example of a Windows PowerShell profile, which is identical to any other Windows PowerShell script file and is used to store frequently used elements that need to be automatically loaded at the start of a Windows PowerShell session. Hence, just like normal scripting files, profiles can contain functions, aliases, and variables, and they can load any Windows PowerShell extensions, snap-ins, or modules you might need. A Windows PowerShell snap-in (PSSnapin) is a .NET program that is compiled into DLL files and contains new cmdlets, functions, and/or providers. Windows PowerShell comes with a number of snap-ins, including Microsoft.PowerShell.Core, Microsoft.PowerShell.Host, and Microsoft.PowerShell.WSMan.Management, as well as modules such as

ActiveDirectory, FailoverClusters, and WebAdministration. As other products are installed on your computer, additional extensions will become available.

The main aim of the SharePoint profile file is to load the Windows PowerShell for SharePoint snap-in so you can then use the new cmdlets specific to SharePoint. The SharePoint profile file contains the following code, plus a signature.

```
$ver = $host | select version
if ($ver.Version.Major -gt 1)  {$Host.Runspace.ThreadOptions = "ReuseThread"}
Add-PsSnapin Microsoft.SharePoint.PowerShell
Set-location $home
```

This code obtains the version of Windows PowerShell, checks that it is greater than 1, and then if that is true, it sets the threading model so that the first thread will be reused, loads the SharePoint PowerShell snap-in, and then changes directory to the home folder, such as C:\users\<*userid*>, where *userid* is the person who is currently logged in. For more information on SharePoint, Windows PowerShell, and threading, see the sidebar titled "Memory Considerations When Using Windows PowerShell" later in this chapter.

The SharePoint PowerShell snap-in is not the only snap-in loaded into the SharePoint 2010 Management Shell. Therefore, not only can you use the SharePoint cmdlets, you also can use other cmdlets from the snap-ins that are loaded. To see all the snap-ins and the order in which they were loaded, type **Get-PSSnapin**. Your output should look similar to the following example.

```
Name        : Microsoft.PowerShell.Diagnostics
PSVersion   : 2.0
Description : This Windows PowerShell snap-in contains Windows Eventing and
              Performance Counter cmdlets.


Name        : Microsoft.WSMan.Management
PSVersion   : 2.0
Description : This Windows PowerShell snap-in contains cmdlets (such as
              Get-WSManInstance and Set-WSManInstance) that are used by the
              Windows PowerShell host to manage WSMan operations.


Name        : Microsoft.PowerShell.Core
PSVersion   : 2.0
Description : This Windows PowerShell snap-in contains cmdlets used to manage
              components of WindowsPowerShell.


Name        : Microsoft.PowerShell.Utility
PSVersion   : 2.0
Description : This Windows PowerShell snap-in contains utility Cmdlets used to
              manipulate data.
```

```
Name          : Microsoft.PowerShell.Host
PSVersion     : 2.0
Description   : This Windows PowerShell snap-in contains cmdlets (such as Start-
                Transcript and Stop-Transcript) that are provided for use with the
                Windows PowerShell console host.

Name          : Microsoft.PowerShell.Management
PSVersion     : 2.0
Description   : This Windows PowerShell snap-in contains management cmdlets used to
                manage Windows components.

Name          : Microsoft.PowerShell.Security
PSVersion     : 2.0
Description   : This Windows PowerShell snap-in contains cmdlets to manage Windows
                PowerShell security.

Name          : Microsoft.SharePoint.PowerShell
PSVersion     : 1.0
Description   : Register all administration Cmdlets for Microsoft SharePoint Server.
```

NOTE If you develop your own scripts that can be called from the command prompt or by double-clicking the file in Windows Explorer, and those scripts contain Windows PowerShell for SharePoint commands, make sure that you include the command to set the threading model and load the Windows PowerShell for SharePoint snap-in in your scripts. When calling a script from within a Windows PowerShell console, you can use the #requires tag at the top of your script.

 REAL WORLD **Customizing Your Console**

t is common practice to modify the profile file on the designated administrator machine. The profile could be altered so that it

- Contains all the snap-ins or modules used by all IT professionals in an organization or department.
- Tracks all Windows PowerShell commands executed.
- Changes the prompt to indicate the server name. In an organization with a multitude of servers, it is all too easy to start an administrative task on the wrong server, so anything that can help an administrator identify the server he is working on will be helpful, such as configuring the window title to list the name of the server.

An example of a custom profile could contain the following code.

```
<# ****************************************************************
 Copyright (c)2010, Contoso, All Rights Reserved
 ****************************************************************
Contoso PowerShell Profile - ContosoProfile.ps1
Author: Peter Connelly
Purpose: This profile sets the PowerShell window size, font and title
and loads the SharePoint snap-in
History: Version 1.0 01/02/2010 First version
#>
# Track all Windows PowerShell commands
$profilename = $MyInvocation.MyCommand.Name
$profilepath = $MyInvocation.MyCommand.Path
$transcriptFile = "C:\Contoso\Logs\Powershell_$profilename.log"
Start-Transcript $transcriptFile -append –force
Write-Output "Starting profile: $profilepath"


# Command from SharePoint Server 2010 profile file - SharePoint.ps1
$ver = $host | select version
if ($ver.Version.Major -gt 1)  {$Host.Runspace.ThreadOptions = "ReuseThread"}
Add-PsSnapin Microsoft.SharePoint.PowerShell
Set-location $home


# Check that this is a command-line interface and not the ISE
if ($host.name –eq "ConsoleHost")
{
  $width = 80
  $sizeWindow = new-object System.Management.Automation.Host.Size $width,40
  $sizeBuffer = new-object System.Management.Automation.Host.Size $width,9999
  <# Check to adhere to the following rules:
  The buffer width can't be resized to be narrower than the window's current
  width plus the window's width can't be resized to be wider than the
  buffer's current width. #>
  $S = $Host.UI.RawUI
  if ($s.WindowSize.width -gt $width)
  {
        $s.WindowSize = $sizeWindow
        $s.BufferSize = $sizeBuffer
  } else {
        $s.BufferSize = $sizeBuffer
        $s.WindowSize = $sizeWindow
  }
}
# Set foreground, background color and window title
$s.ForegroundColor = "Yellow";$s.BackgroundColor = "DarkBlue";
$s.WindowTitle = "$env:computername"
# ########################################################
# End of ContosoProfile.ps1
# ########################################################
```

> Because the profile script is automatically executed every time you run the SharePoint 2010 Management Shell, it should be signed. More information about customizing your console can be found at *http://technet.microsoft.com/en-us/library/ee156814.aspx*.

Understanding cmdlets

Window PowerShell cmdlets are utilities that are built on top of application interfaces, and in the case of SharePoint 2010, the SharePoint Object Module, and SharePoint Web Services, that allow administrators to complete a number of tasks.

In general, cmdlets use a verb-noun pair. The noun specifies the object you want information about or that you want to manipulate, and the verb states what you want to do with that object. The verbs and nouns are always separated by a hyphen with no spaces, and SharePoint cmdlet verbs have a prefix of SP. For example, if you want to get (the verb) information about all the content databases (noun) in your farm, you would use the following SharePoint cmdlet, which would give you the output shown.

```
PS C:\Users\Peter> Get-SPContentDatabase

Id                : a1d5c96c-a41a-43b3-bc5d-3f8a93b26046
Name              : WSS_Content_a2fde53006e04bf5aae434ffd3c8a19c
WebApplication    : SPWebApplication Name=SharePoint - 80
Server            : SQL
CurrentSiteCount  : 1

Id                : 363b11a3-6947-42f6-9df4-665eeff59c83
Name              : SPF_TeamsDB
WebApplication    : SPWebApplication Name=SPF_Teams
Server            : SQL
CurrentSiteCount  : 1
```

Windows PowerShell also provides a few cmdlets that help you to work with the other cmdlets. Two examples of these are Get-Command, which can be shorted to gcm, and Get-Help, which can be shorted to help. (Shortened names of cmdlets are called *aliases*.) Get-Command allows you to find cmdlets, and then Get-Help can provide you with basic information about a cmdlet after it is retrieved. (You'll see how to use the Get-Help cmdlet in the section titled "Getting Help" later in this chapter.) In the following example, the Get-Command finds all the cmdlets associated with SharePoint.

```
PS C:\Users\Peter>Get-Command -PSSnapin "Microsoft.SharePoint.PowerShell" |
>>sort noun, verb |Format-Wide -Column 3
>><ENTER>
```

The set of commands shown previously takes the output from the Get-Command cmdlet and pipes it to the sort cmdlet. The sort cmdlet sorts the data in noun-then-verb order so that all SharePoint cmdlets that manipulate the same object are listed together. The cmdlets that manipulate the same object are then sorted in verb order. To reduce the amount of scrolling necessary in the SharePoint 2010 Management Shell, the sorted data is piped to the format-wide cmdlet. Such a combination of Windows PowerShell cmdlets is quite common. The output from the command set would look similar to the following sample.

```
Start-SPAdminJob              Get-SPAlternateURL            New-SPAlternateURL
Remove-SPAlternateURL         Set-SPAlternateURL            Install-SPApplicationC...
Start-SPAssignment            Stop-SPAssignment             Get-SPAuthenticationPr...
New-SPAuthenticationPro...    Get-SPBackupHistory           Move-SPBlobStorageLoca...
Get-SPBrowserCustomerEx...    Set-SPBrowserCustomerEx...    Copy-SPBusinessDataCat...
.....(not all output shown)
Set-SPWebApplicationHtt...    Get-SPWebPartPack             Install-SPWebPartPack
Uninstall-SPWebPartPack       Get-SPWebTemplate             Install-SPWebTemplate
Set-SPWebTemplate             Uninstall-SPWebTemplate       Get-SPWorkflowConfig
Set-SPWorkflowConfig
```

Working with Objects

There are a considerable number of objects available in SharePoint, and as you might expect, there are more available in SharePoint Server than in SharePoint Foundation. By reading this book, you might have determined the relationship between these objects. For example, while a SharePoint farm can contain many Web applications, each SharePoint farm has one configuration database. Many of the SharePoint cmdlets use names that you can easily identify to determine which objects they will manipulate. To illustrate, the SPFarm cmdlets allow you to retrieve information about and back up or restore a SharePoint farm. For example, the SPFarmConfig cmdlet lets you retrieve and set properties for the farm.

However, there are a few cmdlet names that could confuse you. For example, the SPSite cmdlet allows you to manipulate site collections, and Chapter 2, "Understanding the Architecture of SharePoint 2010," explains that you can't create a site collection unless you have a Web application, which means using the SPWebApplication object. When a site collection is created, you choose a site template to create a site. In the SharePoint Object Model, this site is known as a *web* and not a site; hence, the object is named SPWeb. This can be quite confusing because the term "website" is often shortened to "site," and in the SharePoint Object Model, "site collection" is also shortened to "site." Because this terminology has been used through many versions of SharePoint and is used consistently by developers, it is easier for IT professionals to adopt this usage.

- A *web* is a website and can be manipulated using the SPWeb object.
- A *site collection* contains a collection of webs and can be manipulated using the SPSite object.

Figure 5-3 displays the most common objects and their relationships, but there are others, such as SPSiteCollection, which is a collection of SPSites.

The current selection of built-in cmdlets does not provide full coverage of all SharePoint objects, but you can write new cmdlets to manipulate these objects. To determine the objects associated with the SharePoint PowerShell cmdlets and the number of cmdlets per each object, use the commands in the following example, where a portion of the output is shown.

```
PS C:\Users\peter> Get-Command -PSSnapin "Microsoft.SharePoint.PowerShell" |
>>sort noun, verb | group-object -property noun
>><ENTER>

Count Name                        Group
----- ----                        -----
    1 SPAdminJob                  {Start-SPAdminJob}
    4 SPAlternateURL              {Get-SPAlternateURL, New-SPAlternateURL, Rem...
    1 SPApplicationContent        {Install-SPApplicationContent}
    2 SPAssignment                {Start-SPAssignment, Stop-SPAssignment}
...(not all output shown)
    6 SPWeb                       {Export-SPWeb, Get-SPWeb, Import-SPWeb, New-...
    4 SPWebApplication            {Get-SPWebApplication, New-SPWebApplication,...
    1 SPWebApplicationExtension   {New-SPWebApplicationExtension}
    2 SPWebApplicationHttpTh...   {Disable-SPWebApplicationHttpThrottling, Ena...
    2 SPWebApplicationHttpTh...   {Get-SPWebApplicationHttpThrottlingMonitor, ...
    3 SPWebPartPack               {Get-SPWebPartPack, Install-SPWebPartPack, U...
    4 SPWebTemplate               {Get-SPWebTemplate, Install-SPWebTemplate, S...
    2 SPWorkflowConfig            {Get-SPWorkflowConfig, Set-SPWorkflowConfig}
```

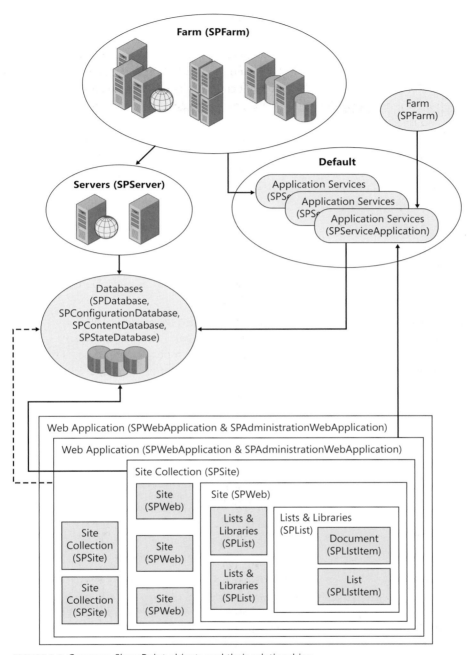

FIGURE 5-3 Common SharePoint objects and their relationships

Understanding Properties and Methods

Everything that SharePoint knows about an object is stored in data elements and values known as *properties*, which also describe the state of that object. For example, the SPContent-Database object contains all the information about the content databases within the farm.

Objects not only have properties, they also contain actions that determine how they can be manipulated. In object-oriented terminology, these actions, or different ways of acting on an object, are called *methods*. To determine the properties and methods for the SPSite object, use the cmdlets in the following example, where a portion of the output is shown.

```
PS C:\Users\peter> Get-SPSite | Get-Member


    TypeName: Microsoft.SharePoint.SPSite


Name                          MemberType  Definition
----                          ----------  ----------
AddWorkItem                   Method      System.Guid AddWorkItem(Sys...
BypassUseRemoteApis           Method      System.Void BypassUseRemote...
CheckForPermissions           Method      System.Void CheckForPermiss...
Close                         Method      System.Void Close()
ConfirmUsage                  Method      bool ConfirmUsage()
Delete                        Method      System.Void Delete(), Syste...
Dispose                       Method      System.Void Dispose()
...
ToString                      Method      string ToString()
UpdateValidationKey           Method      System.Void UpdateValidatio...
VisualUpgradeWebs             Method      System.Void VisualUpgradeWe...
AdministrationSiteType        Property    Microsoft.SharePoint.SPAdmi...
AllowDesigner                 Property    System.Boolean AllowDesigne...
AllowMasterPageEditing        Property    System.Boolean AllowMasterP...
....(not all output shown)
WarningNotificationSent       Property    System.Boolean WarningNotif...
WebApplication                Property    Microsoft.SharePoint.Admini...
WorkflowManager               Property    Microsoft.SharePoint.Workfl...
WriteLocked                   Property    System.Boolean WriteLocked ...
Zone                          Property    Microsoft.SharePoint.Admini...
```

> **BEST PRACTICE** Never miss an opportunity to pipe the Get-SP*<noun>* cmdlet to the Get-Member cmdlet. It is sometimes surprising what information an object is able to retrieve.

REAL WORLD **Performance Issues When Running Windows PowerShell Commands**

I f you want to find all the site collections in the farm, you can type **Get-SPSite**. However, the only output you will see is the URL of the site collections. For performance reasons, the Url property is the only property displayed by default. This is because site collections have many properties; if you display all of these properties for a large number of site collections, you will consume a large amount of memory, and the command will take a long time to run. Displaying just the Url property is almost instantaneous because it is cached. Therefore, you should refrain from running this command to display more than a few additional properties.

To display more than the default property, you can use the select Windows PowerShell cmdlet with the pipe (|) character. You also can use the wildcard character (*) with the select statement to list all the property values, as shown in the following example.

```
PS C:\Users\Peter> Get-SPSite "http://teams" | select *
```

```
ApplicationRightsMask          : FullMask
ID                             : cbf3290e-000e-4768-953c-99a983430283
SystemAccount                  : SHAREPOINT\system
Owner                          : CONTOSO\spadmin
SecondaryContact               : CONTOSO\peter
GlobalPermMask                 : FullMask
IISAllowsAnonymous             : False
Protocol                       : http:
HostHeaderIsSiteName           : False
HostName                       : teams
Port                           : 80
...(not all output shown)
AllowDesigner                  : True
AllowRevertFromTemplate        : False
AllowMasterPageEditing         : False
ShowURLStructure               : False
```

To get a list of all site collections in your farm, together with the name of the content database where they are stored (output that gives only the URL of the site collection and the content database name), you would use the commands as shown in the following example, which also shows the sample output.

```
PS C:\Users\peter> Get-SPSite | select url, contentdatabase

Url                          ContentDatabase
---                          ---------------
http://MySite                SPContentDatabase Name=Contoso_MySiteDB
http://MySite/personal/peter SPContentDatabase Name=Contoso_PersonalDB
http://MySite/personal/erin  SPContentDatabase Name=Contoso_PersonalDB
http://intranet.contoso.msft SPContentDatabase Name=Contoso_IntranetDB
http://teams                 SPContentDatabase Name=Contoso_TeamsDB
http://teams/sites/Finance   SPContentDatabase Name=Contoso_TeamsDB
```

Using Verbs

SharePoint uses common verbs that you have seen with other sets of cmdlets; there are also a number of new verbs added in SharePoint that you may not have seen. Again, you can find these by using the Get-Command cmdlet, as shown here.

```
PS C:\Users\Peter>Get-Command -PSSnapin "Microsoft.SharePoint.PowerShell" |
>>sort verb | group verb | sort count -descending
>><ENTER>

Count Name          Group
----- ----          -----
  139 Get           {Get-PluggableSecurityTrimmer, Get-SPAccessS...
  104 Set           {Set-SPAccessServiceApplication, Set-SPAlter...
   88 New           {New-SPAccessServiceApplication, New-SPAlter...
   77 Remove        {Remove-PluggableSecurityTrimmer, Remove-SPA...
   11 Update        {Update-SPFarmEncryptionKey, Update-SPInfoPa...
   10 Add           {Add-PluggableSecurityTrimmer, Add-SPClaimTy...
   10 Install       {Install-SPApplicationContent, Install-SPDat...
    8 Start         {Start-SPAdminJob, Start-SPAssignment, Start...
    8 Import        {Import-SPBusinessDataCatalogModel, Import-S...
    8 Export        {Export-SPBusinessDataCatalogModel, Export-S...
    8 Uninstall     {Uninstall-SPDataConnectionFile, Uninstall-S...
    7 Disable       {Disable-SPBusinessDataCatalogEntity, Disabl...
    6 Enable        {Enable-SPBusinessDataCatalogEntity, Enable-...
    6 Clear         {Clear-SPLogLevel, Clear-SPMetadataWebServic...
    5 Stop          {Stop-SPAssignment, Stop-SPEnterpriseSearchQ...
    4 Move          {Move-SPBlobStorageLocation, Move-SPProfileM...
    3 Initialize    {Initialize-SPContentDatabase, Initialize-SP...
    3 Upgrade       {Upgrade-SPContentDatabase, Upgrade-SPEnterp...
    3 Backup        {Backup-SPConfigurationDatabase, Backup-SPFa...
    3 Restore       {Restore-SPEnterpriseSearchServiceApplicatio...
    2 Resume        {Resume-SPEnterpriseSearchServiceApplication...
    2 Test          {Test-SPContentDatabase, Test-SPInfoPathForm...
    2 Suspend       {Suspend-SPEnterpriseSearchServiceApplicatio...
```

```
2 Revoke                  {Revoke-SPBusinessDataCatalogMetadataObject,...
2 Mount                   {Mount-SPContentDatabase, Mount-SPStateServi...
2 Grant                   {Grant-SPBusinessDataCatalogMetadataObject, ...
2 Dismount                {Dismount-SPContentDatabase, Dismount-SPStat...
1 Merge                   {Merge-SPLogFile}
1 Receive                 {Receive-SPSharedServiceApplicationInfo}
1 Disconnect              {Disconnect-SPConfigurationDatabase}
1 Unpublish               {Unpublish-SPServiceApplication}
1 Connect                 {Connect-SPConfigurationDatabase}
1 Rename                  {Rename-SPServer}
1 Restart                 {Restart-SPEnterpriseSearchQueryComponent}
1 Copy                    {Copy-SPBusinessDataCatalogAclToChildren}
1 Ping                    {Ping-SPEnterpriseSearchContentService}
1 Publish                 {Publish-SPServiceApplication}
```

As you can see, the most common SharePoint-related verbs are

- **Get**   Queries a specific object or a collection of object and retrieves information concerning that object. For example, you could use it to retrieve information on all service applications. Only Get commands return one or more objects; all other commands execute on one object at a time.

  ```
  Get-SPServiceApplication
  ```

- **Set**   Modifies specific settings of an object. For example, you could use it to set the site collection owner for a specific site collection.

  ```
  Set-SPSite http://teams –OwnerAlias contoso\peter
  ```

- **New**   Creates a new instance of an object, such as creating a new site collection.

  ```
  New-SPSite http://teams/sites/HR -OwnerAlias contoso\peter
   -Name "HR Team" -Template STS#0
  ```

- **Remove**   Removes (deletes) an instance of the object, such as a site collection and all its subsites. Because of the dangerous nature of this verb, you usually have to confirm this action by using the –*confirm* parameter. If this parameter is not present, you will see a message asking you to confirm the action, as shown here.

  ```
  PS C:\Users\Peter> Remove-SPSite http://teams/sites/HR
  Confirm
  Are you sure you want to perform this action?
  Performing operation "Remove-SPSite" on Target "http://teams/sites/Finance".
  [Y] Yes  [A] Yes to All  [N] No  [L] No to All  [S] Suspend  [?] Help
  (default is "Y"):y
  ```

Parameters are used throughout the examples shown here. These are the words prefixed with a hyphen (–). In the next section, you will look at the Get-Help cmdlet and learn how it can help you find out more about these parameters, including which parameters are available for use with different cmdlets.

Getting Help

Windows PowerShell contains an extensive built-in help system, and you can access it quickly by typing **help** at the command-line interface. This is an alias for the cmdlet Get-Help. You can even get help about Get-Help by typing **Get-Help Get-Help**. The output from such a command lists a description of the cmdlet, the syntax used by the cmdlet, parameter descriptions, examples, and other related notes. You also can use the Get-Help cmdlet to get help with the basic Windows PowerShell language. For example, you can use the following commands to get help about specific topics: Get-Help foreach, or Get-Help substring, or Get-Help variables.

> **NOTE** The best way to learn Windows PowerShell is to use its built-in help system. If you or your developers create new Windows PowerShell cmdlets, make sure you create your own help files. In addition to the built-in help, there are many resources on the Internet. For example, you can download a free Windows PowerShell Help 2.0 for either 32-bit or 64-bit from *http://www.primaltools.com/downloads/communitytools/*.

Help Files

Get-Help finds the information to display by using Extensible Markup Language (XML) files that are installed on the server. When you installed SharePoint, help files were installed along with the Windows PowerShell snap-in. These files can be found in %CommonProgramFiles% \Microsoft Shared\Web Server Extensions\14\CONFIG\PowerShell\Help or %CommonProgramFiles% \Microsoft Shared\Web Server Extensions\14\CONFIG\PowerShell\Help\<*locale*>, where *locale* defines the language of the computer, such as en-us. These files use the naming convention <*dll filename*>-help.xml, such as Microsoft.SharePoint.PowerShell.dll-help.xml, Microsoft.SharePont.Search.dll-help.xml, and Microsoft.Office.Access.Server.dll-help.xml. You can find which cmdlets use which XML help file by typing

```
PS C:\Users\Peter>Get-Command -PSSnapin "Microsoft.SharePoint.PowerShell" |
>>sort helpfile, name |
>>Format-Wide name -column 2 -groupby helpfile | more
>><ENTER>

    :

Get-SPExcelBlockedFileType          Get-SPExcelDataProvider
Remove-SPExcelDataProvider          Remove-SPExcelUserDefinedFunction
Set-SPExcelFileLocation


   HelpFile: C:\Program Files\Common Files\Microsoft Shared\Web Server Extensions
\14\CONFIG\PowerShell\Help\microsoft.office.access.server.dll-help.xml
```

```
Get-SPAccessServiceApplication      New-SPAccessServiceApplication
Set-SPAccessServiceApplication


   HelpFile: C:\Program Files\Common Files\Microsoft Shared\Web Server Extensions
\14\CONFIG\PowerShell\Help\Microsoft.Office.Excel.Server.MossHost.dll-help.xml


Get-SPExcelDataConnectionLibrary    Get-SPExcelFileLocation
Get-SPExcelServiceApplication       Get-SPExcelUserDefinedFunction
New-SPExcelBlockedFileType          New-SPExcelDataConnectionLibrary
New-SPExcelDataProvider             New-SPExcelFileLocation
New-SPExcelServiceApplication       New-SPExcelUserDefinedFunction
Remove-SPExcelBlockedFileType       Remove-SPExcelDataConnectionL...
Remove-SPExcelFileLocation          Set-SPExcelDataConnectionLibrary
Set-SPExcelDataProvider             Set-SPExcelServiceApplication
-- More -
```

> **MORE INFO**   You can find more information about the format of the cmdlet XML help
> files and how to make your own help files to complement new cmdlets you create at
> *http://blogs.msdn.com/powershell/archive/2006/09/14/Draft-Creating-Cmdlet-Help.aspx*
> and *http://blogs.msdn.com/powershell/archive/2008/12/24/powershell-v2-external-maml-
> help.aspx.*

ISE Help

In addition to the command-line help function, there is a graphical help file
(WindowsPowerShellHelp.chm) located at %SystemRoot%\Help\mui\<*LCID*> where *LCID* is the
locale identifier or language of your installation, such as 0409. You can access the graphical
help file when using the ISE by selecting the command you want help for and then pressing F1.
The chm file opens, and help is displayed for the command, as shown in Figure 5-4.

However, the chm file contains help only for the core Windows PowerShell cmdlets. If you
need SharePoint-specific help, you should use the SharePoint 2010 Management Shell and
the Get-Help cmdlet.

> **MORE INFO**   For more information on the Help feature in Windows PowerShell and how
> you can configure it to show help for aliases or how to disable local help and force ISE to
> get help directly from TechNet, see *http://blogs.microsoft.co.il/blogs/scriptfanatic
> /archive/2009/01/31/using-help-in-powershell-ise.aspx.* Microsoft recommends that you
> always check the online help to find the latest information and examples. The link to the
> online version can be found in the Related Links section when you use the Get-Help
> command.

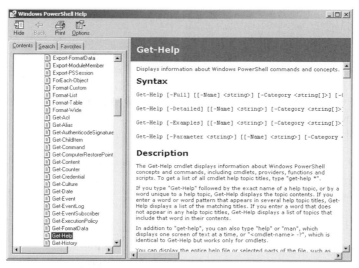

FIGURE 5-4 Windows PowerShell graphical help

Using Parameters

To find which parameters you can use with a cmdlet, type either **Get-Help <*cmdlet*>** or **Get-Command <*cmdlet*> -syntax**, where <*cmdlet*> is the name of the cmdlet you want parameter information about. For example, Get-Help New-SPSite or Get-Command New-SPSite –*syntax* will provide you with information about the parameters associated with New-SPSite. The Get-Help cmdlet also has several parameters associated with it, and depending on the amount of information you want, you can use them with the Get-Help command. If you know a cmdlet very well and do not want a descriptive explanation of what the cmdlet does, then you may simply want to see some examples of how to use the cmdlet, in which case you would type **Get-Help New-SPSite –examples**.

To learn about which parameters to use with a cmdlet, review the syntax section of the help results, as shown in the following output. Optional parameters are enclosed within square brackets ([ ]) and the values to be passed to the parameters are enclosed within angled brackets (<>). The following example shows the syntax section of the Get-SPSite cmdlet.

```
SYNTAX
    Get-SPSite [-AssignmentCollection <SPAssignmentCollection>]
    [-Confirm [<SwitchParameter>]] [-Filter <ScriptBlock>] [-Limit <String>]
    [-WebApplication <SPWebApplicationPipeBind>] [-WhatIf [<SwitchParameter>]]
    [<CommonParameters>]
```

```
Get-SPSite -Identity <SPSitePipeBind> [-AssignmentCollection
<SPAssignmentCollection>] [-Confirm [<SwitchParameter>]] [-Filter <ScriptBlock>]
[-Limit <String>] [-Regex <SwitchParameter>] [-WhatIf [<SwitchParameter>]]
[<CommonParameters>]

Get-SPSite -ContentDatabase <SPContentDatabasePipeBind> [-AssignmentCollection
<SPAssignmentCollection>] [-Confirm [<SwitchParameter>]] [-Filter <ScriptBlock>]
[-Limit <String>] [-WhatIf [<SwitchParameter>]] [<CommonParameters>]

Get-SPSite -SiteSubscription <SPSiteSubscriptionPipeBind> [-AssignmentCollection
<SPAssignmentCollection>] [-Confirm [<SwitchParameter>]] [-Filter <ScriptBlock>]
[-Limit <String>] [-WhatIf [<SwitchParameter>]] [<CommonParameters>]
```

Notice that there are four ways to use Get-SPSite, and each syntax has an
–AssignmentCollection parameter. The *–AssignmentCollection* parameter relates to an
important aspect of the built-in SharePoint cmdlet, which is examined in more detail in the
sidebar titled "Memory Considerations When Using Windows PowerShell," which appears
later in this chapter.

The first syntax example shown in the listing above has no mandatory parameter, so
the Get-SPSite cmdlet would have a scope of the farm or Web application. The other three
syntaxes have a mandatory parameter that defines the scope as site collection, content
database, or collection of site collections that subscribe to shared settings, features, and
services, as shown in the following code. As is the case with the other SPSite cmdlets, in a
large installation, this cmdlet could output a large amount of information, and the queries
to many content databases could severely affect the performance of the SharePoint servers.
Therefore, by default, the output reports only on the first 20 objects.

You can alter this output limit by using the *–limit* parameter, as shown in the following
example, which outputs all site collections that are stored in the Contoso_TeamsDB content
database.

```
Get-SPSite –ContentDatabase Contoso_TeamsDB –limit all
```

You can provide the values for these scope parameters, or in the case of the *–identity*
parameter, where the value is a URL, you can use the wildcard character (*). The default help
with no parameter provides a limited description of the command.

For more information, use the *–detailed* or the *–full* parameter. The *–full* parameter provides additional information about the parameters. For example, additional information about
the *–identity* parameter is shown on the following page.

```
PARAMETERS
    -Identity <SPSitePipeBind>
        Specifies the URL or GUID of the site collection to get.

        The type must be a valid URL, in the form http://server_name or http://
        server_name/sites/sitename, or a valid GUID (for example, 12345678-90ab
        -cdef-1234-567890bcdefgh).

        Required?                    true
        Position?                    1
        Default value
        Accept pipeline input?       True
        Accept wildcard characters?  false
```

If you look at the last five lines of the output, you see that it provides more information on how to use the *–identity* parameter. For example, the required value is equal to True, which indicates that the *–identity* parameter is a mandatory parameter for the Get-SPSite cmdlet. However, the position value is equal to 1, which means that if you place a URL of a site collection immediate after the Get-SPSite cmdlet, you do not have to use the *–identity* parameter because the URL will be read as the identity (URL) of a site collection, where all the property values for site collections that exist under the personal managed path are displayed, as shown in the following example.

```
Get-SPSite http://MySite/personal/* | Select *
```

Many of the parameters have a value enclosed in angle brackets, with the suffix PipeBind. This indicates that the parameter can accept an object variable of a specific type. For example, [–ContentDatabase <SPContentDatabasePipeBind>] means that the *–ContentDatabase* parameter can accept a SharePoint content database object, and this object can be passed to the ContentDatabase object either as a variable, or it can be piped in from the results of another cmdlet. When you pipe an object into a cmdlet, you do not need to type or use a variable. When you pipe an object from one cmdlet into another cmdlet, you do not have to specify the parameter, because Windows PowerShell checks the type of object and will match it to the correct parameter. The following example lists all site collections that are stored in any content databases that have the characters oso anywhere in their names.

```
Get-SPContentDatabase | where {$_.name -match "oso"} | Get-SPSite -Limit 50
```

Get-SPContentDatabase returns a collection of content databases, and then you need to check each content database to see if it matches our condition. The Where-object cmdlet, which has the aliases where or ?, acts like a loop, so it will check each content database object returned from the Get-SPContentDatabase cmdlet. The variable $_ represents one content database object, and .name is the content database property that needs to be matched for our query. The operator is *–match*.

Windows PowerShell has a number of operators, such as *–eq* (equal to), *–ne* (not equal to), *–lt* (less than), *–ge* (greater than or equal to), *–like* (matches a wildcard pattern), and *–notlike* (does not match a wildcard pattern). The *–like*, *–notlike*, *–match*, and *–notmatch* operators are used for pattern matching. The *–match* and *–notmatch* operators use regular expressions to determine whether a value does or does not contain a match for an expression.

> **MORE INFO** For more information on Windows PowerShell operators, see the section titled "Working with Expressions and Operators" in Chapter 5, "Navigating Core Windows PowerShell Structures," in *Windows PowerShell 2.0, Administrator's Pocket Consultant,* by William Stanek (Microsoft Press, 2009).

An alternative method to use instead of a WHERE statement is the *–filter* parameter, which uses the same syntax as the WHERE statement and can produce the same results. However, the *–filter* parameter executes on the server. Piping the results of the Get-SPContentDatabase cmdlet to the WHERE statement causes a SQL round trip to wherever the Windows Power-Shell client is running. Using the *–filter* parameter can result in a faster performance, allowing the command to leverage the filtering abilities of SQL instead of attempting a local search. However, when you use the *–filter* parameter, only the Owner, SecondaryOwner, and Lock-State properties can be accessed for SPSite cmdlets. A number of cmdlets have other parameters that allow you to filter the resulting output. For example, SPWeb provides parameters to filter output on the template or title of the site (web). Still, in many cases the *–filter* parameter can save you time—for example, finding all the blog sites in a farm of 4300 webs takes about 1.2 seconds with the *–filter* parameter, but it takes approximately 15 minutes if you use a WHERE statement. Following are several examples that use the *–filter* parameter.

- This example returns all site collections whose primary owner has the username peter.

  ```
  Get-SPSite -Filter {$_.Owner -eq "contoso\peter"}
  ```

- This example returns all websites in the *http://teams/sites/HR site* collection that were created using the Blank Meeting Workspace template.

  ```
  Get-SPSite http://teams/sites/HR | Get-SPWeb -Filter {$_.Template -eq "STS#03"}
  ```

> **NOTE** When you create a new site collection, if you do not specify a template or the template cannot be found, then you will need to create a website as the root of the site collection. You can do this by using the New-SPWeb command or by selecting the appropriate site template when you display the site collection for the first time in the browser.

To find details of the templates installed, together with the appropriate template ids, use the Get-SPWebTemplate cmdlet. A sample of the output of this command is shown here.

Name	Title	LocaleId	Custom
GLOBAL#0	Global template	1033	False
STS#0	Team Site	1033	False
STS#1	Blank Site	1033	False
STS#2	Document Workspace	1033	False
MPS#0	Basic Meeting Workspace	1033	False
MPS#1	Blank Meeting Workspace	1033	False
MPS#2	Decision Meeting Workspace	1033	False
MPS#3	Social Meeting Workspace	1033	False
MPS#4	Multipage Meeting Workspace	1033	False
CENTRALADMIN#0	Central Admin Site	1033	False
WIKI#0	Wiki Site	1033	False
BLOG#0	Blog	1033	False
SGS#0	Group Work Site	1033	False
TENANTADMIN#0	Tenant Admin Site	1033	False
ACCSRV#0	Access Services Site	1033	False
ACCSRV#1	Assets Web Database	1033	False
ACCSRV#3	Charitable Contributions Web Database	1033	False

On the Get-SPSite and Get-SPSiteAdministration, provide two other filters that use the SQL-driven filtering: the "Wildcard URLs" and regular expression (–*RegEx*) parameter, for example:

```
Get-SPSite http://intranet/sites/*
Get-SPSite "http://intranet/(sites|teams)/HR" -RegEx
```

Memory Considerations When Using Windows PowerShell

The default behavior of Windows PowerShell is that it runs a multithread environment and that each line, function, or script runs in its own thread ($host.Runspace.ThreadOptions == "Default"). This can cause memory leaks, but as you saw in the section titled "Working with the SharePoint 2010 Management Shell" earlier in this chapter, the SharePoint 2010 Management Shell runs each line, function, or script in the first thread ($host.Runspace.ThreadOptions ="ReuseThread"), which mitigates the problem—but memory leaks can still occur. Hence, the two SharePoint cmdlets that you should learn to use are the Start-SPAssignment and the Stop-SPAssignment. These relate to the –*SPAssignmentCollection* parameter that you may see used with a number of SharePoint cmdlets to return a "disposable object." In developer-speak, these are objects that implement the IDisposable Interface. If these objects are not disposed of correctly, they can cause memory leaks. In particular, this relates to the SPSite, SPWeb, and SPSiteAdministration objects. If you use cmdlets associated with these objects in one pipe and don't use variables to store the objects, the memory used is automatically disposed of at the end of a pipe. If you have a long pipe that obtains many objects, this can cause a shortage of memory on your SharePoint server, which then can have a noticeable effect on requests for pages from that server.

When you store any of the three objects in a variable, you then have to dispose of the memory assigned to that object. The following examples show the main methods of using these objects with variables and how to dispose of the memory.

- Use the simple method of using the SPAssignment cmdlets, in which all objects are kept in a global memory store that is released when the Stop-SPAssignment cmdlet is called.

```
Start-SPAssignment –Global
$sc = Get-SPSite http://intranet
$sc.Title
Stop-SPAssignment –Global
```

- Use the advanced method of using the SPAssignment cmdlet and tell it to track memory assigned to a specific variable. In the following example, the Start-SPAssignment cmdlet creates a named store that is pointed to by $o, and the variable $sc is associated with that named store and populated with information about the Internet site collection object. The Stop-SPAssignment cmdlet then releases the memory associated with the named store.

```
$o = Start-SPAssignment
$sc = $o | Get-SPSite http://intranet
Get-SPSite –Limit all
$sc.Title
$o | Stop-SPAssignment
```

- If you are used to developing on the SharePoint platform, then you can use a similar technique to that which you use in your code to overcome this issue. For example, use variables within one Windows PowerShell line and dispose of them at the end of that line.

```
$sc = New-SPSite("http://Intranet"); $sc.Title; $sc.Dispose()
```

This stores the site collection object in the variable $sc. The next command then prints out the title of the intranet site collection, and the last command releases the memory that stored the site collection object.

NOTE   This same command can be run safely using the following syntax.

```
New-SPSite(http://intranet) | Select Title
```

Be aware that the simple method of calling SPAssignment shown here also can cause memory problems. Any object you obtain between the Stop and Stop SPAssignment commands will be retained in the global assignment store and will not be released until the Stop-SPAssignment cmdlet is executed, whereas when you use the advanced method of calling SPAssignment, only the memory associated with variables you ask SPAssignment to track will be retained until the Stop-SPAssignment cmdlet is executed. Therefore, if you need to view large amount of information as you complete a task, and you do not want to starve the SharePoint server of memory, the advanced method of using SPAssigment is preferable. Use Get-Help About_SPAssignment to find more information.

cmdlets for SharePoint Foundation 2010

SharePoint Foundation 2010 contains over 240 SharePoint-related cmdlets. The exact number can be found by typing the following command.

```
@(Get-Command -PSSnapin "Microsoft.SharePoint.PowerShell").count
```

The most common objects that these cmdlets manipulate are the SPSite, SPServer, SPWeb, SPBusinessDataCatalogue, and SPConfigurationDatabase objects. Because Windows PowerShell is mainly an administrator's tool, and these are the components an administrator manages, this spread of cmdlet is not unexpected. These cmdlets also can be found in SharePoint 2010, which is built on top of SharePoint Foundation.

 ON THE COMPANION MEDIA The document "Microsoft SharePoint Foundation 2010 Cmdlet Reference" is included on this book's companion media. This document contains the output that you would see if you typed the following command in the SharePoint 2010 Management Shell.

```
PS C:\Users\Peter>Get-Command -PSSnapin Microsoft.SharePoint.PowerShell |
>>Sort Noun, Verb | Get-Help -detailed > CmdletHelp.txt
>><ENTER>
```

This command generates a list of cmdlet Help topics that is sorted by noun. This list contains the same Help for each cmdlet that you can view in the SharePoint 2010 Management Shell by typing the following command.

```
Get-Help <Cmdlet-Name> -detailed
```

The document contains help information that was current at the time that the document was produced. Microsoft recommends that you always check the online help to find the latest information and examples. You can find the link to the online version in the Related Links section when you use the Get-Help command.

cmdlets for SharePoint 2010

If you use the same Windows PowerShell command shown in the previous section to determine the number of cmdlets available in SharePoint 2010, you will find that there are more than 530 SharePoint-related cmdlets associated with SharePoint 2010. Specifically, that is the number of cmdlets associated with a full install of the Enterprise Edition of SharePoint 2010 without FAST Search installed. To identify the additional cmdlets that SharePoint provides, Windows PowerShell can help again. On a computer with both SharePoint Foundation and a version of SharePoint Server installed, type the following command, changing the name of the redirect file name to reflect the SharePoint installation.

```
PS C:\users\peter>Get-Command -PSSnapin "Microsoft.SharePoint.PowerShell" |
>> Sort noun, verb |group -Property noun -NoElement > cmdlet_sps.txt
>><Enter>
```

Copy the files to the same server and then type the following command.

```
PS C:\Users\Peter>Compare-Object -ReferenceObject $(Get-Content .\cmdlet_sps.txt) '
>>-DifferenceObject $(Get-Content .\cmdlet_spf.txt)
>><ENTER>
```

You will see output similar to the following example.

```
InputObject                             SideIndicator
-----------                             -------------
    8 SPContentDatabase                 =>
    3 PluggableSecurityTrimmer          <=
    3 SPAccessServiceApplica...         <=
    9 SPContentDatabase                 <=
    5 SPContentDeploymentJob            <=
    4 SPContentDeploymentPath           <=
    4 SPDataConnectionFile              <=
    1 SPDataConnectionFileDe...         <=
    2 SPEnterpriseSearchAdmi...         <=
    3 SPEnterpriseSearchLang...         <=
    4 SPEnterpriseSearchMeta...         <=
...
```

Only those objects that do *not* appear on both installations, and those for which the count of the number of cmdlets per object is different, will appear in this list. The SideIndicator column indicates from which file the object with its cmdlet count came.

In SharePoint 2010, the most common objects that are manipulated by cmdlets are similar to those in SharePoint Foundation. However, the main additional commands available in SharePoint 2010 are the 131 cmdlets that help you manage the search process. (There are only four cmdlets associated with searches for SharePoint Foundation). Type the following command to check this for yourself.

```
PS C:\Users\Peter>@(gcm -PSSnapin "Microsoft.SharePoint.PowerShell" |
>>where {$_.name -like "*search*"}).count
>><ENTER>
```

SharePoint 2010 contains more application services than SharePoint Foundation, such as Excel Services, InfoPath Services, Secure Storage, State Service, Microsoft Visio, and PerformancePoint. Therefore, on a SharePoint Server farm, there are more cmdlets that you can use to create, manipulate, and delete application service objects.

Performing Basic Administrative Tasks

There are two types of administrative tasks that are needed in a SharePoint installation: tasks that need to be completed once and from any server, such as creating a new Web application, configuring the primary owner of a site collection, or deleting a specific website; and tasks that need to be completed more than once on a specific server or on more than one server, such as starting a service on a server, adding or removing a server from the farm, or connecting the server to a specific configuration database. The majority of work you will need to complete as a SharePoint administrator is of the first type—it does not matter which server you are logged on to, because you can complete your work from any server.

Windows PowerShell makes it easier to complete both types of administrative tasks. You can loop around a large number of objects and incorporate the scripts into automated tasks so that administrative tasks can be completed in less time. Just because administrative tasks may be easy to complete using Windows PowerShell, however, you should not allow its use to circumvent the controls you may have in place. Some of these farm-wide tasks are very dangerous; they can affect the whole installation. In a production environment, such tasks should be under strict change management.

> **BEST PRACTICE** Many organizations allow administrative tasks to be completed only by using remote access to the production servers. Computer room access is strictly controlled, so interactive access at the server console is rarely allowed—usually only for hardware-related issues. In such environments, even remote access to the production servers is restricted to a small number of Administrative computers, which administrators have to connect to using a VPN or Remote Desktop. An Administrative computer should be configured to allow only certain users or IP addresses to instigate remote desktop sessions. If this is your scenario, remotely managing your SharePoint Installation using Windows PowerShell should also be restricted to that Administrative computer. Windows PowerShell has a number of built-in capabilities that can help you reduce the risk of tasks that affect the whole of a SharePoint installation; these were referred to in the section titled "Managing Systems Remotely with WinRM" earlier in this chapter.

Windows PowerShell provides a number of "voluntary" capabilities that could be classified as best practices. In the next sections, you will learn more about two of these, the *–whatif* parameter and transcripts.

Using the *–whatif* Parameter

Windows PowerShell is a powerful tool, and like any other scripting language, it is all too easy to borrow someone else's code or download snippets from the Internet. You might then execute them without knowing exactly what they do. Using signed scripts and the Windows PowerShell execution policy, as well as restricting who is allowed to load script files onto your SharePoint server, are ways that you can protect your resources.

Windows PowerShell provides a mechanism that allows you to try a command before you execute it—the *–whatif* parameter. Type the following command.

```
PS C:\Users\Peter> Get-SPSite http://teams/sites/* | Remove-SPSite –whatif
```

This command produces the following sample output that lists all site collections and the operation(s) that would be performed on these objects if you executed the command without the *–whatif* parameter.

```
What if: Performing operation "Remove-SPSite" on Target "http://teams/sites/Sales".
What if: Performing operation "Remove-SPSite" on Target "http://teams/sites/Blogs".
What if: Performing operation "Remove-SPSite" on Target "http://teams/sites/Finance".
What if: Performing operation "Remove-SPSite" on Target "http://teams/sites/Wikis".
What if: Performing operation "Remove-SPSite" on Target "http://teams/sites/HR".
```

Nothing has been deleted by trying the command with the *–whatif* parameter. The parameter tells the Remove-SPSite cmdlet to display the object that would be affected by the command without performing the command. In this example, it displays the objects that would be permanently deleted.

Generating Transcripts

A pair of Windows PowerShell cmdlets, Start-Transcripts and Stop-Transcripts, allows you to record all the commands that you type at the prompt, together with the output. All activity is recorded between the start and stop commands. If you do not type **stop**, the transcript is terminated when the console session is terminated. This could be very useful in your production environment, where the machine-wide profile contains the Start-Transcript cmdlet to record the Windows PowerShell activities of all users. The recording to the transcript file is complete when they exit the console.

> **IMPORTANT** Don't use a Windows PowerShell cmdlet or script for the first time in a production environment. Also, try to keep it simple—don't use or create aliases if scripts are going to be supported by administrators who are new to Windows PowerShell, and always use Windows PowerShell comments when you create or amend scripts.

Sometimes even experienced IT professionals can use the built-in cmdlets incorrectly with serious consequences, especially when cmdlets are used in combination with the pipe character. For example, if you type Get-SPSite | Remove-SPSite, all site collections in your farm will be permanently deleted. Everything—all the data in your lists and libraries, and all the content in your websites—would simply be gone. One likely result of this action is that all your help desk telephone lines would immediately ring. If one of the websites that disappeared was your main e-commerce Internet website, your company could quickly lose a great deal of money, and perhaps more importantly, the company could lose potential customers who might never return. To restore your farm, you would need your latest good backup tapes. The lesson of this example is simple: always use the *–whatif* parameter first!

Examples of SharePoint Administrative Tasks

Many administrative tasks must be completed on a daily basis, some are needed only occasionally, and then there are those few that are rarely required. Windows PowerShell can help with all of these types of tasks; in fact, you may discover that it is more critical to script a rarely executed task than one you perform every day. This may be because you need to execute that rare task quickly and correctly, because the ramifications of making even a small mistake while completing the task could be catastrophic. Throughout this book, you will see many examples of when and how to use Windows PowerShell. In the following sections, you explore a few examples that you may not have seen elsewhere.

> **SEE ALSO** There is a section of the Microsoft Script Center, *http://gallery.technet. microsoft.com/ScriptCenter/en-us*, that contains SharePoint-related scripts.

Deploying SharePoint 2010 with Windows PowerShell Scripts

During the lifetime of your SharePoint installation, there may be many tasks that you must complete (hopefully) only once, such as installing SharePoint and creating your farm. In large organizations with a variety of environments and many developers to support, however, you may find it prudent to develop scripts right from the outset that will build your SharePoint Web front-end (WFE) servers and your SharePoint applications servers, which host your applications services, such as InfoPath Services and search query and indexing services. In previous versions of SharePoint, you could complete such tasks using batch files and the SharePoint command-line tools psconfig and stsadm. You can still use these tools to automate the installation of your SharePoint 2010 and SharePoint Foundation 2010 servers. You will find more information about using these tools in Chapter 4, "Installing SharePoint 2010," so the details aren't repeated here. Microsoft has developed a script that is really the best practice for creating a SharePoint farm from scratch using Windows PowerShell. The order of these commands and parameters can be quite tricky, so Microsoft recommends that you use the Windows PowerShell module, SPModule, documented in the Microsoft's TechNet library article, "Install SharePoint Server 2010 by using Windows PowerShell", at *http://technet.microsoft.com/en-us /library/cc262839.aspx*.

> **MORE INFO** For information about SharePoint automation and the use of psconfig, stsadm, and Windows PowerShell, see *http://stsadm.blogspot.com/*.

When you work on a SharePoint installation, you will need to merge the logs. The Windows operating systems provide you with event logs to help you with your administrative tasks, and you can use the Windows PowerShell Get-Eventlog cmdlet to obtain detailed information from those logs. SharePoint also provides the Unified Logging Service (ULS). The ULS contains all application log events, and third-party logging software can be integrated into them as well. SharePoint 2010 includes several Windows PowerShell cmdlets for retrieving information and configuring the ULS. To find how ULS is configured on your farm, type the following command. (The sample output for this command is also shown here.)

```
Get-SPDiagnosticConfig
```

```
AllowLegacyTraceProviders                 : False
CustomerExperienceImprovementProgramEnabled : True
ErrorReportingEnabled                     : True
ErrorReportingAutomaticUploadEnabled      : True
DownloadErrorReportingUpdatesEnabled      : True
DaysToKeepLogs                            : 14
LogMaxDiskSpaceUsageEnabled               : True
LogDiskSpaceUsageGB                       : 3
LogLocation                               : %CommonProgramFiles%\Microsoft Sh
                                            ared\Web Server Extensions\14\LOG
                                            S\
LogCutInterval                            : 30
EventLogFloodProtectionEnabled            : True
EventLogFloodProtectionThreshold          : 5
EventLogFloodProtectionTriggerPeriod      : 2
EventLogFloodProtectionQuietPeriod        : 2
EventLogFloodProtectionNotifyInterval     : 5
ScriptErrorReportingEnabled               : True
ScriptErrorReportingRequireAuth           : True
ScriptErrorReportingDelay                 : 60
```

When diagnosing a problem, you can use cmdlets associated with the SPLogEvent object. You need machine administrator privileges to run these cmdlets, so you may need to start SharePoint 2010 Management Shell using Run As Administrator. Then you would use commands in steps similar to those shown in the following example.

1. Set up two variables to store the start day and the end date, for example.

```
$SDate = Get-Date -Day 13 -Month 04 -Year 2010
$EDate = Get-Date -Day 14 -Month 04 -Year 2010
```

Or the date could be today's date, but the event occurred approximately 15 minutes earlier than the current time. In this case, you set the variable to 20 minutes before the current time and 10 minutes before the current time.

```
$SDate = (Get-Date).AddMinutes(-20)
$EDate = (Get-Date).AddMinutes(-10)
```

2. Obtain a list of events between those two dates and times.

```
Get-SPLogEvent -StartDate $SDate -EndTime $Edate
```

If the *–EndTime* parameter is not provided, the event logs will be displayed up until the current date and time.

A tracking number, known as the Correlation ID, is associated with each request you make to SharePoint. This number is stored as a value in a property associated with the SPLogEvent object. SQL Profiler traces also show the Correlation IDs. This number is displayed on an Error page, as shown in Figure 5-5.

FIGURE 5-5 Error page showing the Correlation ID

In a large or heavily used SharePoint installation, many logs may be produced during the period when a problem occurs. You can use the Correlation ID to help troubleshoot errors by reducing the amount of log information that is returned to those entries that are associated with the incident. Again, set the *$sdate* and the *$edate* variables to reflect the time around the incident. For an incident that you can't reproduce and one of your users always can reproduce, you might tell the help desk to ask the user to take a screenshot of the error page so you can be sure to obtain the exact Correlation ID number. Then you can pipe the results of the command shown in step 2 to the Where-Object cmdlet, as shown in the following example.

```
PS C:\Users\Peter>Get-SPLogEvent -StartDate $SDate -EndTime $EDate |
  where {$_.Correlation -eq "68bc5cf4-5a8c-4517-a879-86e35e57c862"}
```

The output will display only event logs between the two dates that are related to the problem associated with that Correlation ID.

Managing SharePoint Services

After you have run the SharePoint 2010 Products Configuration Wizard to install SharePoint on your servers, you can use the SharePoint 2010 Central Administration website to launch the Farm Configuration Wizard. Although it will get you up and running very quickly, it might not configure your farm as you want; for example, the database names it creates will be in the format *name_GUID*, where *GUID* is a randomly generated, globally unique identifier. Also, the farm wizard uses the account entered as the Application Pool Identity for the default content Web application and starts the Web Analytics Service by default—both of which may not be desirable on a production farm.

Using the wizard may be sufficient if you want to create a quick prototype or perhaps if you are using SharePoint in a developer environment. However, if any of those environments are limited in their CPU power or in the amount of memory they have, the farm wizard may not be suitable either. For example, the Web Analytics Service uses a large amount of CPU, so your developers might be interested in stopping that service. There are other services that they might want to start and stop on a regular basis, especially if they are using their computers as their day-to-day desktop connections, where they read e-mails and complete documentations, as well as to run SharePoint for development or prototyping.

You can use tools such as the Central Administration website to manage the configuration; however, you may forget to execute all the tasks necessary to complete a configuration change. Instead, you can use Windows PowerShell scripts, which—after you have tested them to make sure that you have not forgotten any tasks—should make managing configuration changes more reliable and error free. You should store these scripts in a central location after they are developed, to make them convenient for fellow administrators to use and incorporate in their environments. Your developer may also thank you for developing these scripts. Such automated tasks might include the following items.

- To quickly delete a specific Web application, type

  ```
  Get-SPWebApplication http://teams | Remove-SPWebApplication -Confirm
  ```

- To remove the Web application, the IIS website, and all the associated databases, type

  ```
  Remove-SPWebApplication http://teams -Confirm -DeleteIISSite '
    -RemoveContentDatabases
  ```

If you do not run the Farm Configuration Wizard, you might find that you need a service that you originally thought you would not need. For example, if no application services are started, and then you try to use one of the SharePoint 2010 workflows, the Microsoft Visio diagram of the workflow progress will not be displayed. However, to solve this problem, you must do more than just create the Visio Application Service. There are other dependencies involved, one of which is the State Service Application. The state services can only be created in the Central Administration site, by using the farm wizard—something you will want to avoid as an administrator. To create the state service using Windows PowerShell, type the following commands.

```
PS: C:\Users\Peter>New-SPStateServiceDatabase -Name Contoso_StateService_DB |
>>New-SPStateServiceApplication -Name Contoso_StateService |
>>New-SPStateServiceApplicationProxy -Name Contoso_StateService_Proxy -Default
>><ENTER>
```

NOTE This command may not work in your environment if the associated service instance is not running. For a more comprehensive script, see "SP+PS 2010: PowerShell to Create a Service Application" at *http://sharepoint.microsoft.com/blogs/zach/Lists/Posts/Post.aspx?ID=50.*

Each service application is slightly different. For example, not all service applications require a database. Chapter 7 "Scaling Out a SharePoint Farm," contains more information about this. However, each service will require a service application proxy, which connects a Web application to the service application.

Using Windows PowerShell During the Upgrade Process

The following sections provide information about some Windows PowerShell commands you might find useful during an upgrade. The upgrade process is explained in more detail in Chapter 22, "Upgrading to SharePoint 2010."

Preparing for an Upgrade

After installing SharePoint 2010 and before upgrading, you can use the Test-SPContentDatabase cmdlet to check your SharePoint Server 2007 databases for current or potential issues, such as orphan data, missing site definitions, missing features, or missing assemblies. This cmdlet complements the pre-upgrade checker report mentioned in Chapter 22. Checking for these issues does not disrupt your SharePoint installation, and this cmdlet can also test the status of SharePoint 2010 databases, which can assist you in maintaining the continued health of your environment. The following example shows the command and its sample output.

```
Test-SPContentDatabase -name W_intranet -WebApplication http://www.contoso.msft
```

```
Category       : SiteOrphan
Error          : True
UpgradeBlocking : False
Message        : Database [W_intranet] contains a site (Id = [46ad6d70-9a5c-4d
                 e0-8daa-0f73f2466a6a], Url = [/]) whose id is already associa
                 ted with a different database (Id = [6987d2d8-6291-4ead-9eb0-
                 aefe7097a58e], name = [W_Intranet]) in the site map. Consider
                 deleting one of these sites which have conflicting ids.
Remedy         : The orphaned sites could cause upgrade failures. Try detach a
                 nd reattach the database which contains the orphaned sites. R
                 estart upgrade if necessary.

Category       : SiteOrphan
Error          : True
UpgradeBlocking : False
Message        : Database [W_intranet] contains a site (Id = [46ad6d70-9a5c-4d
                 e0-8daa-0f73f2466a6a], Url = [/]) whose url is already used b
                 y a different site, in database (Id = [6063e77c-991f-4c4b-b3a
                 c-68cb62e66502], name = [w_Internet]), in the same web applic
                 ation. Consider deleting one of the sites which have conflict
                 ing urls.
Remedy         : The orphaned sites could cause upgrade failures. Try detach a
                 nd reattach the database which contains the orphaned sites. R
                 estart upgrade if necessary.
```

Performing Post-Upgrade Tasks

The upgrade process is divided into two components, the content database upgrade and the visual upgrade. By separating these two components, your SharePoint team can decide to upgrade the Microsoft Office SharePoint Server 2007 Web application without users noticing the change, because their sites will maintain the old look and feel. Using the browser, they can preview what their site looks like with the new SharePoint 2010 look and feel and then decide when they permanently want to switch to the visual upgrade. After they make the switch, the browser will not allow them to switch back to the SharePoint Server 2007 look and feel.

The Set-SPWeb cmdlet does not have any parameter to help with this task; you will need to use the properties of the SPWeb object to complete this task. Type the following commands if you want to switch sites back to the old look and feel.

```
Start-SPAssignment –Global
$web = Get-SPWeb http://teams ;
$web.UIVersion = 3;
$web.UIVersionConfigurationEnabled = $true;
$web.Update();
Stop-SPAssignment
```

> **NOTE** Previously in this chapter, you created variables to store values and objects.
> Variable names are prefixed with the dollar sign, $. In the sample code shown here, you
> will see *$true* used. This, together with a number of other keywords that look like variables,
> is an example of a special variable. A special variable should be treated as a reserved
> word that you cannot use in your scripts to store values or object. The special variable
> *$true* represents the value True, *$false* represents False, *$null* represents null, and *$_* also
> has been used in this chapter and contains the current pipeline object. It is used in script
> blocks, filters, and the Where cmdlet.

After you run these commands, the website will revert to the SharePoint Server 2007 look
and feel. The Site Actions button will be in the upper-right corner, for example, instead of in
the upper-left corner. The Site Actions menu will have the Visual Upgrade option available,
although the Visual Upgrade option at the site collection level may not be enabled. To enable
the Visual Upgrade option at the site collection level, use the following commands.

```
$site = Get-SPSite http://teams
$site.UIVersionConfigurationEnabled = $true
```

When updating the properties of the SPSite object, there is no update method; the
changes to the SPSite properties take effect immediately. You could type the following line as
an alternative to the previous two lines of commands.

```
(Get-SPSite http://teams).UIVersionConfigurationEnabled = $false
```

To reset all "team" websites within a site collection back to the SharePoint Server 2007 look
and feel, use the following command.

```
PS C:\Users\zzspfarm> Get-SPsite http://teams |
>> Get-SPWeb –Filter {$_.Template -eq "STS#0}|
>> ForEach-Object {
>> $_.UIVersion =3;
>> $_.UIVersionConfigurationEnabled = $false;
>> $_.Update();
>> }
>><ENTER>
```

NOTE These commands also can be run on a site or site collection that has not been up-graded—that is, on a site that was created as a version 4 site, thereby making a SharePoint 2010 site look like a SharePoint 2007 site.

Summary

This chapter explains how you can become familiar with the new Windows PowerShell cmdlets introduced by SharePoint 2010. It explores the SharePoint 2010 Management Shell and how to accomplish some simple but powerful administrative tasks using one-line Windows PowerShell commands.

There are more than 500 SharePoint cmdlets. This chapter could not possibly explain each command; instead, its aim was to provide some general guidelines and good practices for us-ing SharePoint PowerShell in a production environment, such as the configuration and use of remote management, the voluntary use of transcripts, and the use of the *–whatif* parameter. You should not practice or try out Windows PowerShell commands for the first time on your production environment. Keep your scripts simple, use comments to document your scripts, and don't use or create aliases if the scripts are going to be supported by administrators who are unfamiliar with Windows PowerShell.

The chapter covered two important cmdlets, Start-SPAssignment and Stop-SPAssignment, in some detail. These cmdlets help with cmdlets that return disposable objects, such as SPSite, SPWeb, and SPSiteAdministration. Other SharePoint cmdlets were introduced to expand your knowledge of Windows PowerShell techniques. Chapter 12 builds on this chapter, using search scenarios. The next chapter continues the discussion of SharePoint 2010 farm manage-ment and specifically the Central Administration interface.

## CHAPTER 6

Managing SharePoint 2010 Using Central Administration

This chapter focuses on how to manage your Microsoft SharePoint 2010 farm and all of its components using Central Administration. You will learn about each of the Central Administration components to help you gain a better understanding of the different components that you can manage from within this interface. If you are familiar with Microsoft SharePoint Server 2007 Central Administration, you will see that you can perform most of the tasks you performed in SharePoint Server 2007—as well as some new tasks—in the SharePoint 2010 Central Administration interface. You will also quickly realize that the new look and feel introduced in SharePoint 2010 makes it easier to navigate and manage your farm.

Most all of your administrative tasks can be performed from within Central Administration, and becoming familiar with the available options within this interface will allow you to manage your SharePoint 2010 farm more efficiently. The new interface is better organized and customizable, which gives you the option of personalizing it as you like.

Introducing Central Administration

The Central Administration home page is the starting point for farm administrators after SharePoint 2010 is installed. The home page for Central Administration is only available as a Web page—it is not available as a Microsoft Management Console (MMC) snap-in. By default, the Central Administration site is configured and enabled only on the first SharePoint 2010 server in your farm. However, you can enable the Web page on additional servers if you wish. Each Central Administration site has its own Web application and its own application pool. With this default configuration, if any other configured websites or Web applications shut down or become corrupt, they will not affect the Web application hosting your Central Administration site.

There are two ways to access Central Administration.

- By using the default URL and port number configured during the installation.
- By using the Microsoft SharePoint 2010 Products program group, accessed through the following steps.
    a. On the Start menu, point to All Programs, select Microsoft SharePoint 2010, and then select Products.
    b. Select SharePoint 2010 Central Administration.

The home page of SharePoint 2010 no longer has the Operations and Application Management tabs that were present in SharePoint Server 2007. Instead, the features on the SharePoint 2010 Central Administration home page, shown in Figure 6-1, are grouped into the following eight major functional categories, which contain different farm configuration and management components.

- Application Management
- System Settings
- Monitoring
- Backup And Restore
- Security
- Upgrade And Migration
- General Application Settings
- Configuration Wizards

Each of the category headings can be accessed from the home page of Central Administration by clicking the icon next to the category, the title of the functional category, or title of the functional category on the left side of the page.

The home page also contains the Resources Web Part, which provides you with the ability to add new links to your Central Administration home page. To add a link, click Add New Link to display the dialog box shown in Figure 6-2. Enter the information requested in the dialog box and click Save. After you add a link, you will be able to access the site you specified from your Central Administration home page.

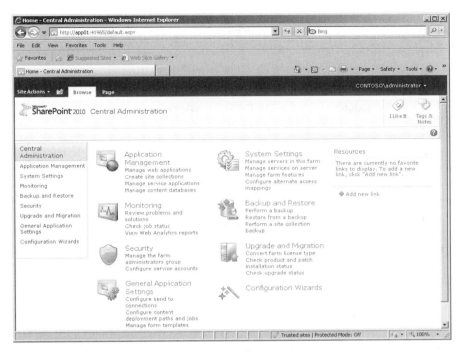

FIGURE 6-1 SharePoint 2010 Central Administration home page

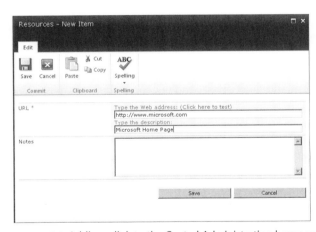

FIGURE 6-2 Adding a link to the Central Administration home page

The Resources Web Part is like most other lists, in that if you point to the Web Part and select the check box in the upper-right corner of the Web Part, the List and Items Ribbons will be displayed. Doing this allows you to make modifications to the list, such as adding columns, filtered views, or new items. You can also export and import to this list, which is important because it gives you the ability to build a set of links to support sites, third-party vendors, or My Sites that can be accessed directly from this Web Part.

The primary components of the Central Administration user interface (UI) haven't changed much from SharePoint Server 2007, so if you are familiar with that version of SharePoint, you will find many of the menus to be similar. However, there are some additional options and functionality available. One of the most obvious changes you will notice is how the introduction of the Ribbon interface simplifies the way you manage some of your SharePoint components from Central Administration, such as Web applications.

Web applications are still created and managed following the same general procedures as were used in SharePoint Server 2007, but you now manage the creation and configuration of the applications using a Ribbon interface on the Manage Web Applications page, as shown in Figure 6-3. The Ribbon makes it easier for you to view or change details about your Web application by clicking one of the supplied options on the Ribbon. This is an improvement from SharePoint Server 2007, in which many tasks required you to click different menus and often made it necessary to reselect the Web application each time. Now, you simply select the Web application you want to manage, and all configurable options for managing that Web application are easily accessible from the Ribbon interface.

FIGURE 6-3 The Web Applications Ribbon interface on the Manage Web Applications page

Navigating the Central Administration Home Page

The Central Administration home page is a SharePoint Foundation 2010 site; it has its own site settings and WSS "look and feel." You can add functionality to the page if you want, or you can even customize the page. Central Administration has four items located above the Central Administration title, which is also a hyperlink that will allow you to return to this main page from within the Central Administration site at any time. The following four actions, located on the upper left side of the screen shown in Figure 6-4, are available to you for navigation or customization of the Central Administration home page.

- Site Actions
- Breadcrumb navigation trail icon
- Browse (the default view)
- Page

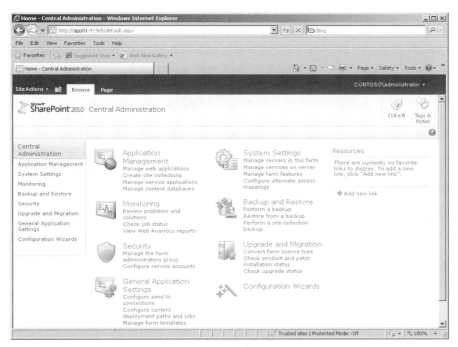

FIGURE 6-4 Central Administration home page actions for navigation and customization

Central Administration Site Actions Menu

Because the Central Administration is a SharePoint site, the Site Actions list, shown in Figure 6-5, is available. This option allows you to perform the same actions to your Central Administration site as you would any other SharePoint 2010 site.

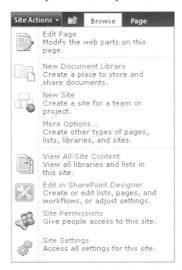

FIGURE 6-5 Central Administration Site Actions menu

This Site Action menu can be used to perform the following tasks for the Central Administration site.

- **Edit Page** Modify the Central Administration home page Web Parts.
- **New Document Library** Create a new document library to store shared documents.
- **New Site** Create a subsite within Central Administration.
- **More Options** Create all other SharePoint components, including pages and lists.
- **View All Site Content** View all lists and libraries within the Central Administration site.
- **Edit Site In SharePoint Designer** Make modifications to the Central Administration home page using SharePoint 2010 Designer.
- **Site Permissions** Manage permissions of the Central Administration site.
- **Site Settings** Access and manage all settings for the Central Administration site.

> **NOTE** You will find similar options on other sites throughout SharePoint when you click Site Actions.

Central Administration Breadcrumb Navigation Trail Icon

SharePoint 2010 introduces a new breadcrumb navigation trail icon, shown between the Site Actions and Browse options in Figure 6-6, that is available on all pages including the Central Administration home page. This icon allows you to easily determine where you are located within the Central Administration site and quickly navigate from a lower level component to a higher level component using the links available in the breadcrumb navigation trail.

FIGURE 6-6 Breadcrumb navigation trail icon

In most locations, the breadcrumb navigation trail also appears in the title bar area, as shown in Figure 6-7. This provides a quick overview that shows you where you are located without clicking the breadcrumb navigation trail icon. Note that links that appear dimmed in the title bar breadcrumb navigation trail are unavailable because they represent the current page.

FIGURE 6-7 Title bar breadcrumb navigation trail

Central Administration Browse Option

The Browse option on the Central Administration home page is the default view that is displayed when you first open SharePoint 2010 Central Administration. You can access the eight functional categories from this view using the Quick Launch bar on the left or from within the main section of the page.

If SharePoint detects a problem, this page may also present a SharePoint Health Analyzer information bar, which points to the Health Analyzer page that is discussed more fully in the section titled "Review Problems and Solutions" later in this chapter.

The SharePoint Health Analyzer bar shown in Figure 6-8 may appear in yellow or red on your screen. A yellow Health Analyzer Information bar indicates there were warnings discovered and reported. A red Health Analyzer information bar indicates there were errors discovered and reported. This analyzer bar will only display warnings or errors if the Health Analyzer discovers them as it performs the default health checks on your SharePoint farm.

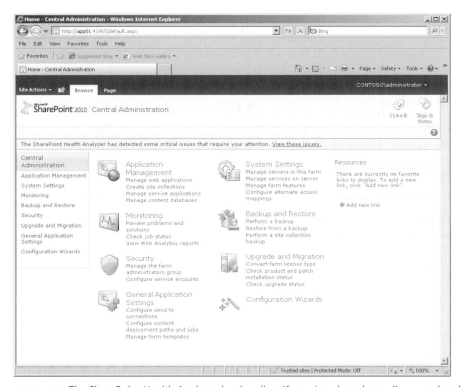

FIGURE 6-8 The SharePoint Health Analyzer bar is yellow if warnings have been discovered and reported.

To view the critical issues it is reporting to you, click the View These Issues link within the Health Analyzer information bar to display a Review Problems And Solutions report such as the one shown in Figure 6-9.

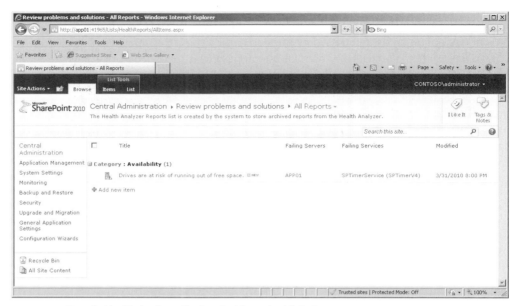

FIGURE 6-9 Sample Health Analyzer Review Problems And Solutions report

Central Administration Page Option

The Page option is used to modify your Central Administration home page. If you click this option, your Central Administration page will display as shown in Figure 6-10. The Ribbon available on this page allows you to customize the page. As you can see in the figure, the standard Ribbon that is displayed includes the following activated options.

- **Edit Page**
- **E-mail A Link**   Use this option to send an e-mail containing a link to this page.
- **Edit Mobile Page**   Use this option to configure which Web Parts are displayed and in what order.
- **Make Homepage (if it already is in Central Administration)**

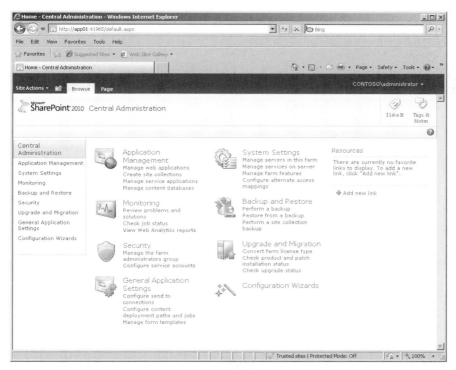

FIGURE 6-10 Page option on the Central Administration home page

By selecting the Edit Page option, you can customize the Central Administration home page. When the Central Administration home page is in edit mode, you can modify the two Web Part zones located on the page shown in Figure 6-11. One Web Part zone, labeled Right, is on the far right side of the page, and the second Web Part zone, called Left, is located on the bottom of the page. This can be helpful if you want to add more Web Parts to the home page for easier access and better management of your SharePoint implementation.

NOTE By default, the Administrator Tasks Web Part is not displayed on your SharePoint 2010 Central Administration home page. However, if you want to simulate the SharePoint Server 2007 environment, this Web Part is still available, and you can add it to one of the Web Part zones on the Central Administration home page by clicking Add A Web Part and selecting Administrator Tasks from the list of available Web Parts.

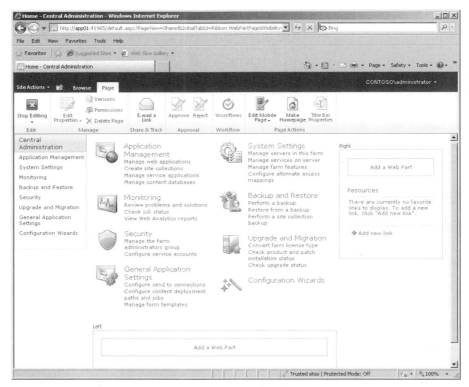

FIGURE 6-11 Central Administration home page in edit mode

Customizing your Central Administration home page will help you manage your farm more efficiently, with all of the critical information at your fingertips when you open Central Administration. However, having a thorough understanding of how to accomplish the various management tasks is what will ultimately keep your SharePoint farm running effectively and efficiently.

Performing Administrative Tasks Using Central Administration

There are several tasks that should be performed after a successful installation of SharePoint 2010 has been completed. Table 6-1 is not an all-inclusive list, but it includes the tasks you will most commonly perform in Central Administration to correctly complete your SharePoint farm configuration.

TABLE 6-1 Central Administration Post-Installation Farm Configurations

TASK NAME	DESCRIPTION
Configure the Central Administration application pool using a unique domain account	To avoid conflict and issues with site Web application pools, you should configure a unique windows account for the Central Administration application.
Configure service applications	You must configure each service application required for your farm before that service can be accessed by your Web applications.
Add servers to farm	By adding servers to the farm, you can provide redundancy.
Configure outgoing e-mail server	Required for users to receive alerts and notifications such as an invitation to a site.
Configure incoming e-mail server	Required if you want your lists to receive e-mail directly with their own e-mail address.
Add antivirus protection	Be sure to configure prior to documents being uploaded into SharePoint.

Application Management

Application Management is one of the functional categories on the Central Administration site in which you will spend a lot of time as a SharePoint 2010 farm administrator. As you can see in Figure 6-12, there are several configuration settings that can be made in this functional category that will help you manage your farm. You will manage your Web applications, site collections, service applications, and content databases from this page in the Central Administration website.

The creation and configuration of Web applications in SharePoint 2010 is very similar to how these same tasks were performed in SharePoint Server 2007, with a few enhancements. One of the improvements in SharePoint 2010 is the ability to create and manage Web applications that exist in Internet Information Services 7.0 (IIS 7). You can also use site management tools that enable you to configure and manage site collections, such as quota templates, and you can even configure auto site deletion rules.

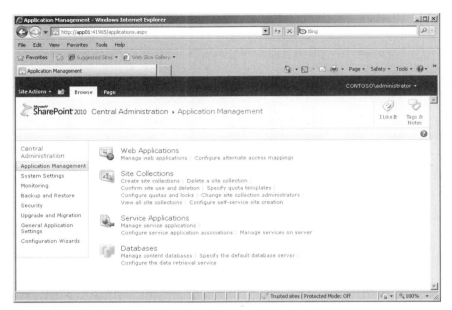

FIGURE 6-12 Application Management configuration options

Managing Web Applications

To host site collections and service applications, you need to have a hosting service to manage users' access. The hosting service for SharePoint 2010 is IIS 7. Although the term *Web application* has been used consistently in SharePoint over the years, you also may have heard these applications referred to using different terminology, such as websites or virtual servers.

IIS 7 is the application service that enables Microsoft Windows Server 2008 to host websites, SMTP (Simple Mail Transfer Protocol) servers, and FTP (File Transfer Protocol) sites and services, to name a few. The type of websites that IIS 7 can host depends on the software that is installed and configured within it. In the case of SharePoint 2010, you have installed the .NET Framework and the Windows Workflow Foundation, and with these two components, along with IIS, you have a feature-rich set of components that you can use to create your SharePoint 2010 Web applications.

Each Web application is accessed using one of the following three unique configurations.

- IP Address
- Port Number
- Host Header

After identifying what unique configuration you are going to use, you also need to identify an application pool, authentication method, database location, and optionally a mirrored database location. (You'll explore these in more detail shortly when you create a Web application.) After creating your Web application, you can do one of two things.

- Extend it to create a new site collection.
- Extend it to map to an existing site collection.

If you choose to extend the Web application and create a new site collection, you will also have to associate the top-level site with a site template such as a corporate portal or team site. Table 6-2 lists the default site template categories and site templates available within each category.

TABLE 6-2 Site Collection Template Choices

TEMPLATE TAB TITLE	TEMPLATE CHOICES
Collaboration	Team Site, Blank Site, Document Workspace, Blog, Group Work Site, Visio Process Repository
Meetings	Basic Meeting Workspace, Blank Meeting Workspace, Decision Meeting Workspace, Social Meeting Workspace, Multipage Meeting Workspace
Enterprise	Document Center, Records Center, Business Intelligence Center, Enterprise Search Center, My Site Host, Basic Search Center, Fast Search Center
Publishing	Publishing Portal, Enterprise Wiki
Custom	No templates are available by default, but other templates can be added.

When you create Web applications, it is important to decide if you want to associate each Web application with its own application pool in IIS. There are several reasons to consider this.

- Each application pool runs in its own memory space using a worker process, which means that if an application pool fails, it does not affect other Web applications using their own application pools. Web applications running in the same memory pool with other Web applications may be affected by any failure of other Web applications.
- The memory overhead of an application pool is 30 to 50 megabytes (MB) plus any memory for the applications running in the application pool process space. The various application demands can quickly drive the memory usage of an application pool to 800 MB or more. Multiple worker processes can be associated with a single application pool for resilience.

Not all SharePoint capabilities should be run from within one Web application. Although this is possible in certain situations, such as a limited, point-solution deployment, it is not advisable when SharePoint is deployed as an enterprise-wide service offering to an entire organization.

You can create a new Web application to run either homegrown code in an isolated memory space or in a unique security context, but another good reason to create multiple Web applications is that you can create a database for each one. This helps with database management size and in situations such as disaster recovery and Microsoft SQL Server maintenance jobs. So, if you need database isolation, then a new Web application is the cleanest way to accomplish this.

You might also need another Web application if you need a new root URL from which to build out a new set of managed paths and site collections. So, if you need URL independence, then a new Web application is the cleanest way to accomplish this.

Another reason to create a new Web application is to map a mission-critical process to a matrix of collaboration sites, document management efforts, and/or workflows. This means that isolating a mission-critical, complex process under a unique URL, security context, and database topology might be the right decision to make.

Finally, an important reason that new Web applications are created (as reported by IT administrators) is company politics. There might be no technical or information-organizational reason to create multiple Web applications, but because someone has the power and/or money to do so, she is able to get approval for her own Web application.

To review, it's never a good idea to have just one Web application to run all SharePoint capabilities, and the following are some of the most common reasons new Web applications get created.

- Run homegrown code in an isolated security context
- Provide unique security context
- Allow database independence
- Achieve URL independence
- Host mission-critical processes
- Company politics

Using the Web Application Ribbon

In SharePoint 2010, you manage Web applications by going to the Web Application page and using the Web Application Ribbon, as shown in Figure 6-13. The sections that follow will show how to create, delete, and configure Web applications using the options you can select on this Ribbon.

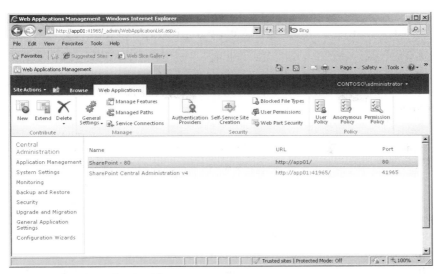

FIGURE 6-13 Web Application Management page

Creating a Web Application

To create a new Web application, select the New option on the left side of the Ribbon. This opens the Create New Web Application page shown in Figure 6-14.

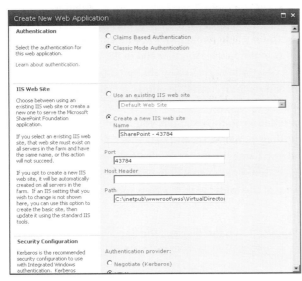

FIGURE 6-14 Create New Web Application page, Authentication and IIS Web Site sections

The first thing you must do when creating a new Web application is to select the authentication method. SharePoint 2010 introduces a new type of authentication called *claims-based authentication*, which can be used instead of the classic-mode authentication that is used in earlier versions of SharePoint.

The claims-based authentication model for SharePoint 2010 is built on the Windows Identity Foundation (WIF). Claims-based authentication in SharePoint 2010 enables authentication across Windows-based systems and systems that are not Windows-based by supporting delegation of user identity between applications. Using claims-based authentication, you can implement multiple forms of authentication on a single zone.

The other authentication option available on the Create New Web Application page, classic-mode authentication, refers to the Integrated Windows authentication model supported in previous versions of SharePoint, such as Windows SharePoint Services 3.0. In classic-mode authentication, no claims augmentation is performed, and there is no support provided for the new claims authentication features. Using classic-mode authentication allows you to implement all of the previously supported forms of authentication with a limit of one form of authentication for each zone.

When you create a Web application, it will automatically be allocated a random port number, a description field, and a folder location in the default local path. The default path is C:\Inetpub\wwwroot\wss\VirtualDirectories\portnumber. The application is not, by default, assigned a host header name. Therefore, you must specify in the Host Header text box on the Create New Web Application page shown in Figure 6-14 if you want to use a fully qualified domain name such as *http://portal.contoso.com* to access your Web application. You must ensure that this host header URL can be resolved by your users. Normally, this would be achieved by adding an entry into DNS pointing the URL to the Web server.

> **NOTE** Name your Web application descriptions and paths with a consistent logical naming convention to identify them easily in the folder structure and in IIS. For example, instead of using SharePoint (9845) as the description, use Corporate Portal (9845) and specify the same name for the path and the host header. In addition, name your databases the same way that you name your Web application names so that you have naming consistency across your implementation. In this example, you could name the first database Corporate_Portal_9845_1, then name the second database Corporate_Portal_9845_2, and so forth. You should also name the folder for the Web application files with the same name. Scroll to the end of the path name in the Path text box (refer to Figure 6-14) and replace the default name of the folder with the Web application name.

Scrolling down the Create New Web Application page displays the Security Configurations section as shown in Figure 6-15.

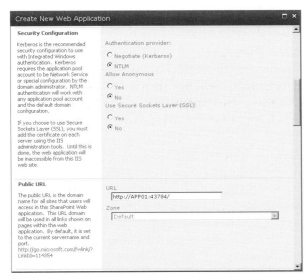

FIGURE 6-15 Creating New Web Application page, Security Configuration and Public URL sections

There are two authentication providers available for a Web application—Kerberos and NTLM. Web applications use these security mechanisms when they communicate with other servers and applications in the network, such as when they communicate with the Microsoft SQL server hosting the databases. By default, the authentication provider is set to NTLM for maximum compatibility with mixed domain models and user account permissions. Figure 6-15 shows the Security Configuration section on the Create New Web Application page. Web applications use these security mechanisms when they communicate with other servers and applications in the network, such as when they communicate with the Microsoft SQL server hosting the databases.

Kerberos is more secure than NTLM, but it requires a service principal name (SPN) for the domain account that SharePoint is using. This SPN must be added by a member of the domain administrators group, and it enables the SharePoint account to use Kerberos authentication.

When you choose NTLM, it does not matter what your domain account is, because the application pool will run as long as it has the required permissions to access the SQL server and the Web server. The required SQL permissions for a Web application account are as follows.

- Database Creator Role
- Security Administrator

Anonymous access can also be enabled on a Web application, which would enable users to gain access to the sites hosted on the Web application without authenticating. If you choose to do this, however, you also must enable anonymous access on the site itself—enabling it on the Web application only gets the users past IIS authentication. Enabling anonymous access is a useful configuration for any Internet-facing sites, such as a company website. For added security, you could also enable SSL certificates on the Web application. You can choose to use certificates from both your internal certificate authority and from an authorized certificate authority such as Verisign. However, you must install the SSL certificate on all servers where users are accessing your Web application or their access attempt will fail.

PUBLIC URL

The Public URL section of the Create New Web Application page (see Figure 6-15) lets you configure a public URL; that is, the default URL for users to access the sites hosted on this Web application. A public URL is used when configuring multiple front-end servers using the Windows Server 2008 network load-balancing service. The network load-balanced service enables administrators to create a cluster that will be shared by the network cards of all SharePoint servers configured in the load-balancing service configuration. However, in order for your users to connect to the cluster, you should also define a public URL in the Web application and in DNS so that the name resolutions match.

The load-balanced URL uses the default zone for user access, and this zone is matched to the URL mappings configured for the default zone in the Alternate Access Mappings Management page. Scrolling further down the Create New Web Application page displays the Application Pool section as shown in Figure 6-16.

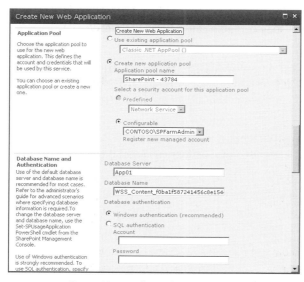

FIGURE 6-16 Create New Web Application page, Application Pool section

Application pools are used to configure the level of isolation between different Web applications and their hosted sites. Each application pool runs its own worker process. This means that an error in one worker process will not affect other worker processes hosting different application pools. From a planning point of view, it is not necessary to create a new application pool for every Web application, because Web applications can share application pools, and each new application pool can end up consuming up to 800 MB of physical memory very easily when users start connecting to websites hosted on the Web applications. However, if a site is critical to your business, you can create a separate application pool for the site so that there is less of a chance of that Web application being disrupted by an unstable Web application that resides in the same application pool.

Although some application pools are created during the installation, you should create at least one additional application pool to host the first Web application and its associated sites. When you create a new application pool, it is important to use a meaningful and descriptive name to make it easier to identify them in IIS. This is especially useful in a disaster recovery scenario when you might have multiple application pools and random port numbers.

There are two choices for selecting a security account that will be used by the application pool: predefined and configurable, as you can see in the Application Pool section of the Create New Web Application page shown in Figure 6-16. In most cases, you will want to select the configurable option, because it gives you the most flexibility for scaling out a server farm. Following are brief explanations of both application pool options.

- **Predefined** Provides built-in system accounts; local and network service.
- **Configurable** Allows you to define your own domain user account that will be used by the application pool to access the necessary services and servers, such as a SQL Server database. This account should be configured using the format *domain_name\ user_name*. It also requires the SQL Server database creator and security administrator server role.

NOTE You can create a new account by clicking the Register new managed account link.

Database Name and Authentication

By default, the database server name displayed in the Database Name And Authentication section of the Create New Web Application page is the SQL Server database configured in Central Administration—the one used when you first installed the product and configured your farm. However, it is possible to specify a different SQL Server instance for a new Web application.

When you configure the database account, it is also recommended that you use Windows authentication. For security purposes, your SQL Server database instance is set to accept only Windows authentication by default. However, the account must have database creator rights in SQL Server and must be configured using the format *domain_name\user_name*.

FAILOVER SERVER

New to SharePoint 2010 when creating a new Web application is the option to specify a failover server, as shown in Figure 6-17. This option allows you to host a mirrored copy of the content database for your Web application. Mirroring your content databases provides fault tolerance and can be helpful in a disaster recovery scenario. You can also use this option to provide a read-only environment for running reports, which will minimize database contention among your users.

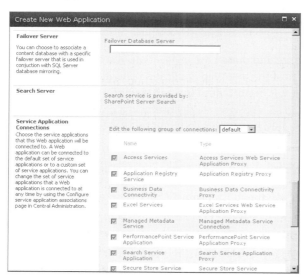

FIGURE 6-17 Create New Web Application page, Failover Server, Search Server, and Service Application Connections sections

SEARCH SERVER

To allow sites associated with your new Web application to be indexed using the Windows SharePoint Services Search service, you must have the service available on at least one server. If you have more than one server available, then you use the Search Server section to choose which server is responsible for indexing the content on the database using the SharePoint Services Search service. Associate the content database with a server that is running the Windows SharePoint Services Search service.

SERVICE APPLICATION CONNECTIONS

In the Service Application Connections section, select the service application connections that you want available to this new Web application by selecting either Default or Custom in the drop-down menu. You use the Custom option to select the specific service application connections that you want associated with this Web application. When you choose the Custom option, the check boxes for each service application are cleared and you then select the check boxes for the service applications that you want to associate with this Web application.

CUSTOMER EXPERIENCE IMPROVEMENT PROGRAM

The final configuration option is to decide whether you want to participate in Customer Experience Improvement Program, which gathers hardware information and data about how you are using SharePoint and periodically sends it to Microsoft. This information helps Microsoft identify which SharePoint features need improvement. If you choose the Yes option, you indicate that you are willing to participate in the program. The farm level setting for this same option must also be enabled to report this information to Microsoft.

Extending a Web Application

After creating a Web application, you have the option of extending the Web application, which allows you to expose the same content hosted in your initial Web application to a different group of users using a different URL or authentication method. You achieve this by specifying a different zone or entry method for the different group of users. A Web application that has been extended can use up to five different zones: Default, Intranet, Internet, Extranet, and Custom. This allows you to provide five different entry points to the same content using a different URL or authentication method.

If you choose to extend the Web application by selecting the Extend option on the Web Application Ribbon shown previously in Figure 6-13, the page shown in Figure 6-18 will be displayed. This option allows you to redirect requests made to that Web application to another already-provisioned site collection. This allows you to change the authentication mechanism on the extended Web application to another level of authentication, such as basic challenge response with an SSL certificate, to support external users connecting from the Internet. This method enables both Windows authenticated users and basic authenticated users to access the same site collection and content, but using unique URLs to access the site from internal and external networks.

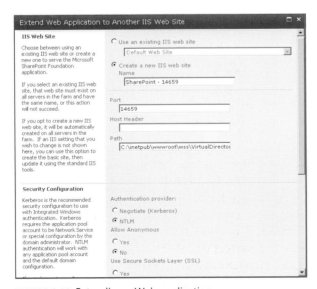

FIGURE 6-18 Extending a Web application

Deleting or Removing a Web Application

At some point, you might no longer need a particular Web application, or it might be replaced by another one, and you will need to remove the existing Web application. There are two options available for configuring a Web application to no longer be available: you can either remove it or delete it.

- **Remove SharePoint From IIS Web Site**   This action allows you to unextend the Web application and remove SharePoint Services from using the Web application in IIS. The Web application itself is not deleted and can still be used for reprovisioning a new site collection at any time.

- **Delete Web Application**   This option allows you to delete the Web application as well as the databases associated with the Web application. This completely removes all references to the Web application from your SharePoint farm, including all the content the Web application was hosting.

IMPORTANT   Back up the content databases before you delete a Web application in case you need to recover any data stored in the databases at a later time.

General Settings

The General Settings option on the Web Applications Ribbon lets you manage different aspects of the Web application. You will find the following six options on the drop-down list when you click the General Settings icon on the Ribbon. Each of these will be discussed in more detail in the following sections.

- General Settings
- Resource Throttling
- Workflow
- Outgoing E-mail
- Mobile Account
- SharePoint Designer

GENERAL SETTINGS

Table 6-3 provides a list of explanations of the different general settings you can configure for each Web application. These configurations are applicable to all site collections accessed by the Web application.

TABLE 6-3 Web Application General Settings

PROPERTY NAME	DESCRIPTION
Default Time Zone	All sites created on all Web applications take the time zone from the farm's global settings. With this setting, you can change the default time zone for all sites created on a specific Web application.
Default Quota Template	Allows you to create and assign a specific database quota limit on the total amount of content allowed to be stored for all site collections associated with a Web application. Multiple quota templates can be created and used by different Web applications.
Person Name Actions and Presence Settings	When users browse a site, they can see details of the online status of other users with instant messenger clients. If you prefer not to make this information available, you can disable the option. By default it is enabled for all Web applications.
Alerts	By default, alerts are enabled that allow users to create their own alerts on all sites they have access to on the specific Web application. You can also limit the number of alerts a user can set up. By default, this is set to 500 alerts per user.
RSS Settings	An RSS feed allows users to subscribe to lists and libraries in sites. To allow RSS feeds from lists and libraries, this option must be enabled. The default setting is enabled.
Blog API Settings	Enables you to turn off the Blog API, or alternatively, if you choose to keep it enabled, it can be set to allow user name and passwords to be sent via the Blog API.
Browser File Handling	Indicates whether security headers are included in documents displayed in Web browsers. If you select the Permissive setting, no headers are added. If you select the Strict setting, security headers are included in the documents and security is improved by disallowing automatic execution of Web content.
Web Page Security Validation	When a session has been established to the sites, the session will cease automatically if it has been idle for the specified amount of time, which by default is 30 minutes. If a user tries to access the page after it has been idle for the set amount of time, she will have to refresh the page or re-establish the connection.
Send User Name and Password in E-mail	Allows administrators to create or change a user's details in the site and have the new details e-mailed to the user. For additional security, you could choose to disable this functionality.
Master Page Settings for Application _Layouts Pages	Indicates whether the pages in the _Layouts folder are allowed to reference site master pages.

continued on the next page

PROPERTY NAME	DESCRIPTION
Recycle Bin	The Recycle Bin allows administrators in site and site collections to restore deleted items from lists and libraries. You can specify how long these items are stored in the Recycle Bin in their site and also how long the items remain in the site collection's Recycle Bin. The site collection Recycle Bin is a second-level Recycle Bin that captures all deleted content from site Recycle Bins.
Maximum Upload Size	Fixes the size of content that users can upload to a site in any single procedure. By default, this is 50 MB, and any file or group of files that a user tries to upload above this limit is rejected.

RESOURCE THROTTLING

SharePoint 2010 introduces the option to manage your SharePoint performance by specifying list view thresholds that control how much information can be involved in a database operation. These configuration settings will help optimize SharePoint by limiting the number of items that SharePoint handles during a single operation. Table 6-4 provides a list of settings and an explanation of these settings used to manage list resources.

TABLE 6-4 Web Application Resource Throttling Settings

PROPERTY NAME	DESCRIPTION
List View Threshold	Specifies maximum number of items a database operation can involve at one time. The default setting is 5000.
Object Model Override	The default setting is to allow individuals with sufficient permissions to override the list view threshold programmatically.
List View Threshold for Auditors and Administrators	Specifies maximum number of items a database operation can involve at one time for users who have been granted sufficient permissions. The default setting is 20000.
List View Lookup Threshold	Specifies the number of Lookup, Person/Group, or workflow status fields that a database query can involve in one operation. The default setting is 6.
Daily Time Window for Large Queries	Specifies the time when queries that exceed the thresholds can be executed. This setting usually designates hours outside of normal working hours. This is disabled by default.
List Unique Permissions Threshold	Specifies the maximum number of unique permissions a list can have at one time. The default setting is 50000.
Backward-Compatible Event Handlers	By default, event handlers are off, so users cannot use an event handler operation for a document library.

PROPERTY NAME	DESCRIPTION
HTTP Request Monitoring and Throttling	Controls whether the HTTP request throttling jobs are active or turned off. This option is enabled by default.
Change log	After 60 days, entries are deleted from the change log. You can change the length of time in days or set it to never delete entries.

WORKFLOW SETTINGS

The User-Defined Workflows option allows you to specify whether you want users to be able to deploy declarative workflows, such as those that are created using Microsoft SharePoint Designer 2010, on sites in this Web application. The default setting enables deployment of declarative workflows.

The Workflow Task Notifications specifies whether you allow either or both of the following kinds of nonauthenticated users to participate in workflows.

- Internal users who do not have access to the site
- External users who do not have access to internal network resources

Internal users receive an e-mail message that explains how to request access to the site (subject to administrator approval). External users receive an e-mail message that contains the attached document or list item for them to review or sign.

OUTGOING E-MAIL

All messages sent from SharePoint 2010, such as alerts, notifications, and site invitations, require an SMTP server to route the messages. This SMTP server can be any SMTP-compliant server, but you must be able to connect to it using port 25 from your SharePoint 2010 server. For example, you can use either the IP address, NetBIOS name, or the fully qualified domain name of your SMTP server, as long as all services necessary to locate the server are in place.

> **IMPORTANT** Firewalls between the Office SharePoint Server 2007 server and the mail server can cause outgoing mail to fail, so make sure that SMTP traffic is allowed.

When configuring your Web application's outgoing e-mail server settings, you can specify a different Outbound SMTP Server, From address, and Reply-to address for a specific Web application. For example, you could have e-mail sent to recipients from the address SPServer2010@constoso.com but then specify spsadmin@contoso.com as the reply address for the e-mail. The outgoing e-mail settings at this level override the settings configured at the farm level.

MOBILE ACCOUNT

A new feature in SharePoint 2010 allows administrators to configure a corporate Short Message Service (SMS) that can deliver alerts and notifications to users. This lets administrators receive system notification or health and monitoring alerts directly to their Windows mobile devices. You can also use a third-party SMS, and there is the option to specify a user name and password if required when the service is accessing the SMS provider.

SHAREPOINT DESIGNER

These are the same SharePoint Designer settings found under General Application Settings in Central Administration. They are used to specify whether SharePoint Designer is available for use within a Web application and if so what tasks can be performed using SharePoint Designer. There are four settings you can configure, as explained in the following list.

- **Allow SharePoint Designer To Be Used In This Web Application** Use this setting to specify whether users can edit sites using SharePoint Designer.

- **Allow Site Collection Administrators To Detach Pages From The SiteTemplate** Use this setting to specify whether to allow site administrators to detach pages from the original site definition using SharePoint Designer. Site collection administrators are always able to perform this operation.

- **Allow Site Collection Administrators To Customize Master Pages And Layout Pages** Use this setting to specify whether to allow site administrators to customize master pages and layout pages using SharePoint Designer. Site collection administrators are always able to perform this operation.

- **Allow Site Collection Administrators To See The URL Structure Of Their Web Site** Use this setting to specify whether to allow site administrators the ability to view and manage the URL structure of their website using SharePoint Designer. Site collection administrators are always able to perform this operation.

MANAGE FEATURES

There are also features that can be managed at the Web application level. This option allows you to activate or deactivate any of the default Web application features or any Web application custom features that have been installed. Similar to the farm level features, these features can be managed through Central Administration or from the command line using Windows PowerShell or STSADM.

MANAGED PATHS

Managed paths indicate which parts of the URL namespace is managed by each Web application in IIS. It also provides a way to define a taxonomy within the namespace by creating new site collections and associating them with specific namespaces, such as projects, as shown in Figure 6-19. There are two types of managed paths, explicit and wildcard. You use an explicit managed path to allow only a single site collection with a specific namespace, such as /ProjectA. You use a wildcard to create a category of site collections that includes the namespace in the URL and then all site collection names after it, such as /Projects/ProjectA.

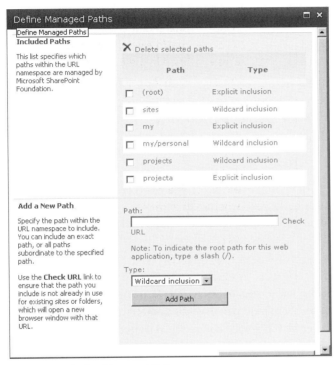

FIGURE 6-19 Define Managed Paths page

Service Connections

The Service Connections option on the Web Applications Ribbon allows you to view, and if you choose, to modify the service applications the Web application is associated with in SharePoint. The drop-down option shown in the text box at the top of Figure 6-20 allows you to change the setting from Default to Custom. When you select the Custom option, all service applications will be cleared, and you can choose which service applications you want associated with this Web application.

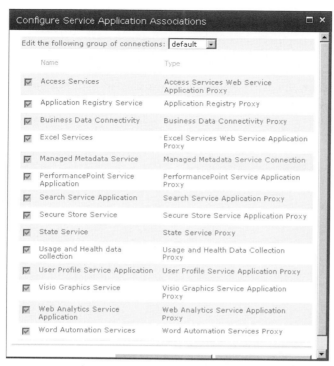

FIGURE 6-20 Configure Service Application Associations page

Authentication Providers

The role of the authentication provider is to define which type of authentication is aligned to a specific zone in a Web application. By default, all zones are created with Windows NTLM (NT LAN Manager), and it is recommended that you change this setting only after you have tested access to the content using NTLM. You can then change the Web application to support many different types of authentication depending on the access method. Available authentication options include the following.

- **Windows** Use the standard Windows authentication.

- **Forms** Create a forms authentication method; for example, you could create an authentication method using the SQL Server membership role provider to have user accounts stored in an SQL Server database to authenticate into sites hosted for external users.

- **Web Single Sign-On** Use for federated authentication mechanisms such as ADFS (Active Directory Federation Services). This option is useful for companies authenticating users between organizations.

- **Anonymous Access** Allows anonymous connections to the content through this zone.

- **NTLM Or Kerberos** Allows you to switch your authentication from the default NTLM to the preferred, faster, and more secure Kerberos. You can also enable Basic authentication if you want this zone to support basic authentication with Secure Sockets Layer (SSL).

The authentication provider is a way for SharePoint to provide an element of bridging capabilities. However, if you need more control of your authentication methods and more options such as security tokens or smart cards, then you will need a server, such as an Internet Security and Acceleration (ISA) server in front of SharePoint to manage the external connection. ISA server supports all of the authentication methods listed previously, plus many more methods for publishing and authentication.

Self-Service Site Creation

By default, users cannot create top-level sites or site collections. If the Self-Service Site Creation setting is enabled, it will permit users with self-service site creation permissions to create site collections under the /sites path or any path you specify within that Web application. After self-service site creation is enabled, a message displays in the announcements list of the root of the Web application informing users that self-service site creation has been turned on for that Web application. This announcement will contain a link to the page they can use to create additional site collections.

> **NOTE** If you want the site collections created in a path other than /sites, you have to create a wildcard inclusion managed path as discussed in the section titled "Managed Paths" earlier in this chapter.

If you decide to enable self-service site creation, be sure to consider the following issues.

- Generally you should require a secondary site collection administrator. Administrative alerts, such as those generated when quotas are exceeded or when checking for unused websites, will go to the secondary as well as the primary administrator.
- Define a storage quota and set it as the default quota for the Web application.
- Review the number of site collections allowed per content database. This setting combined with quotas will help you limit the size of your content databases.
- Enable unused website notifications so that sites that are no longer used can be identified.

Blocked File Types

All files that users try to upload into SharePoint 2010 with the file extensions contained in the list on the Blocked File Types page will be blocked automatically—they are prevented from being uploaded to the Web application. You can modify the list of blocked file extensions to add new extensions or remove any of the default extensions.

These blocked file types are not only enforced when uploading documents, they are also enforced on files that have file extension changes after they have been added to the list of blocked file types. For example, .exe documents are blocked. If you zip an .exe file, upload it with the .zip extension, and then try to unzip it in the document library, you'll find that the document will not extract because SharePoint blocks all files containing an .exe file extension—even if they are already in the library with a different extension.

However, if the user has wrapped the file in another file extension type that is allowed, the file can be uploaded, even though it can't be extracted. For example, if a user adds an .mp3 file to a .zip file, the .zip file is allowed—it is not blocked when it is uploaded so it is stored in SharePoint as a .zip file containing an .mp3 file. To prevent these sorts of files from being uploaded to a Web application, you can use a content filtering engine such as Microsoft Forefront that can detect blocked file types hidden in files with allowable extensions.

User Permissions

There are three different categories of permissions, each of which contains individual permissions that are applied by default to every new Web application. Every site collection and site created in that Web application will inherit these user permissions. The user permissions are used when you create or edit the permissions of a site group. You can remove any of the individual permissions by clearing the check box next to it, which will prevent that permission from being used in any site groups throughout the entire Web application. The following three categories of permissions can be configured.

- List permissions include the standard rights of a user for viewing, adding, or deleting a list item. The site groups you are in determine which list permission you get. A reader, for example, would have permission only to view items, whereas a contributor would also have permissions that would allow him to edit and delete items. When a user is added to a group with contributor permissions, the default Web application permissions for contributors would be applied.

- Site permissions deal with management rights in a site and include permissions such as creating new groups or applying them to a site. This is a good example of a case in which you might want to change the permissions for a Web application: You might not want any person in your Web application (including all of its sites) to have the ability to change the theme for a site, because that would change the standardized appearance. By removing the permission to apply a theme at the Web application level, you are able to prevent everyone—including your site administrator—from modifying the theme of the sites contained within the Web application.

- Personal permissions are permissions that allow a user to add Web Parts that are specific to them as an individual, such as Web Parts associated with users' My Sites. By removing permissions that allow individuals to add their own Web Parts, you could create a uniform look for all the pages and sites in the Web application, and users would be prevented from personalizing or changing the pages and sites with their own private content.

> **NOTE** When you remove user rights from a Web application, remember that the changes will also affect the administrators of the site collection. You cannot choose to have the user permissions affect only a select group of users in the Web application.

Web Part Security

A Web Part Page in SharePoint is a page on which you can add Web Parts into the Web Part zones that are located on the page. Most of the time, these Web Parts serve a single purpose, such as a document library or an announcements list. It is possible, however, to have Web Parts that connect to each other to help manipulate the data returned by one or several Web Parts viewed on the page. For instance, a user could select a customer name in one Web Part and then have only information about that customer displayed in the different Web Part. However, there is a performance increase on your Web servers when generating these types of views, so take that into consideration by planning and testing Web Part connections. By default, users are allowed to create Web Part connections on a page, and if you want to prevent them from doing so, you must select the option to prevent users from creating connections on the Web Part Security page.

> **NOTE** Remember that by preventing Web Part connections on the Web Part Security page, you will prevent all associated sites within the selected Web application from having connecting Web Parts.

The second option for security in Web Part Pages provides for accessing the Online Web Part Gallery. When a user wants to add a Web Part to a page, she is presented with a default gallery view. However, she can also use the advanced view to see all four of the available Web Part galleries if this option is enabled.

The Online Web Part Gallery includes Web Parts that provide MSN weather and stock news, among others. Keep in mind that the performance of the page will be affected when a user adds Web Parts, because the gallery must go to the online sites to retrieve the list of available Web Parts and then download the Web Part from the gallery to the user's computer. Furthermore, a Web Part can cause additional network traffic itself if it provides information that is constantly updated, such as a stock ticker. If you do not want your users to have access to these Web Parts, then you should select the option that prevents users from accessing the Online Web Part Gallery.

> **NOTE** If you want to use the Online Web Part Gallery but are unable to connect to the site, you might have to configure the outgoing proxy server settings. You can do this from within Central Administration by informing SharePoint which route to take when accessing the Internet for the gallery using something like Microsoft's ISA server.

The final option on the Web Part Security page allows you to manage whether contributors for the site are able to add or edit scriptable Web Parts on the pages contained within the Web application. The default setting is off for this option, but you can set it to allow users to add or edit scriptable Web Parts on the Web Part Pages in the Web application.

Policies for Web Applications

After you create a Web application and then extend the Web applications, as discussed in the section titled "Extending a Web Application" earlier in this chapter, URLs are created that are associated with a specific zone. There are five zone types in SharePoint 2010.

- Default
- Intranet
- Internet
- Extranet
- Custom

NOTE Zones in a Web application refer to the zones available in Internet Explorer that a user is using to access the site.

Using the User Policy option on the Web Application Ribbon, you can specify that a specific user or group of users that access SharePoint content from a specific Web application using a specific zone will have a custom set of rights applied. These rights will override the rights they would normally have if accessing the Web application from the default zone.

For example, a user accesses the internal SharePoint projects site using *http://portal.contoso.com* and he has full control access. However, when the user is outside the company, he accesses the same site using *http://internet.contoso.com*, and the Internet URL is an extended and mapped Web application in the Internet zone. When the user accesses the content from outside the office, using the Internet zone, then Internet policy—defined as deny access to everything except full read—applies, and he can only read content; he won't be able to add or change anything on the projects site.

There are four permission levels provided by default; however, you can create additional custom permission levels from within the Manage Permission Policy Levels dialog box. The four default permission levels are

- Full Control
- Full Read
- Deny Write
- Deny All

Use the following steps to configure a policy for users on a Web application.

1. Select the Web application for which you want to configure a new policy and click User Policy on the Ribbon.

2. Select Add User and then choose the zone that will be using the new policy from the drop-down menu. For users accessing the Web application using Windows authentication, you can select all zones. For remote users who will require read-only access, select the Internet zone.

3. Click Next.

4. Enter the user, group name, or e-mail address you want to apply the policy to. In this case, it would be Remote Users.

5. Select the specific permission you want to apply to the group that matches the zone type. For example, you could select Full Read access.

6. The final option is to have the user account masked as a system account. This means that all actions carried out by the user would be registered as a system account entry rather than the actual user account. Normally, you would not select this option.

7. Click Finish.

You can create as many policies as you need to control the level of access for many different groups of users accessing the Web application from multiple zones.

ANONYMOUS POLICY

The Anonymous Policy option on the Web Application Ribbon is used to set permission policies for anonymous user access for the different zones (Internet, Extranet, Intranet, Other), if your Web application is serving content in those different zones. The following list describes the available options for this policy.

- **None**   No policy is defined; this is the default option. No additional permission restrictions or additions are applied to a site's anonymous users.

- **Deny Write**   Anonymous users cannot write content, even if the site administrator specifically attempts to grant the anonymous user account that permission.

- **Deny All**   Anonymous users cannot have any access to content, even if the site administrator specifically attempts to grant the anonymous user account access to sites.

PERMISSION POLICY

The Permission Policy option on the Web Application Ribbon allows you to edit the specific permissions associated with one of the default permission levels or create a new permission policy level. Additionally, you can specify the particular permissions that are allowed or denied for site collections and sites throughout the Web application. The following permissions are available by default for this policy.

- Full Control
- Full Read
- Deny Write
- Deny All

You can create a new permission policy level by clicking the Add Permission Policy Level link and specifying a name for the new permission policy. You can also provide a description, as well as indicating whether site collection administrators and site collection auditors will have their normal permissions, which are Full Control and Full Read access respectively. Use the check boxes under the Grant and Deny options to specify the list, site, and person permissions that will be available when this policy is used. After creating a new permission policy level, you can create a user policy that uses the new permission policy.

Configuring Alternate Access Mappings

Alternate Access Mappings (AAM) are available to help SharePoint determine how to map a request that comes into a Web application to the correct URL and then serve the correct URL back to the client that requested the content. This very important role is useful for users who access their SharePoint Web applications from both internal and external locations because it ensures that the correct URL is served back to the user. This process makes sure that the links work as expected when users are navigating, browsing, and searching in SharePoint.

For example, if you have a Web application created with the URL *http://constosoportal.com*, this URL is the default Alternate Access Mapping entry because it was defined when the Web application was created.

However, when accessing it internally, you would prefer to have a more user-friendly name, such as *http://portal,* to provide a better user experience. You can do this easily by adding *http://portal* as an intranet AAM. After you do so, users who browse the portal using *http://portal* will see *http://contosoportal.com* displayed. Furthermore, all the URLs will follow the AAM mapping. For instance, if *http://contosoportal.com/hr* is a valid URL, then *http://portal/hr* would also be a valid URL when AAM is used.

Another example is when you have an external group of users who need to access SharePoint using https. You could extend and map a Web application to the portal Web application using *https://contosoportal.com.* You could then publish this URL to the outside using a reverse proxy product such as Microsoft's ISA Server, and when people connect to the content from the outside world, they will see the URLs returned as *https://,* not just *http://.*

Site Collections

The Site Collections section of the Application Management functional category gives the farm administrator the ability to manage all aspects of a site collection. You can remotely add new site collections to existing Web applications that have been provisioned with a site template, or you can configure a quota limit that applies to the content of all Web application site collections. This remote management facility provides administrators with an easy and centralized way to configure sites and site collections that exist on all available Web applications on the farm.

It is important to make sure you are making changes to the right Web application, however. For example, if you don't choose the correct Web application when you make changes, you could inadvertently specify a low quota limit to a Web application that hosts a site collection with content that already exceeds that quota limit, which could potentially prevent users from adding any new content to the document libraries and lists stored in that site collection. There are eight site collection management options that can be configured in Site Collections section of Application Management.

- Create Site Collections
- Delete A Site Collection
- Confirm Site Use And Deletion
- Specify Quota Templates
- Configure Quotas And Locks
- Change Site Collection Administrators
- View All Site Collections
- Configure Self-Service Site Creation

CREATE SITE COLLECTIONS

You can create new top-level site collections when you create your Web application or any time later using the Create Site Collections option in Application Management. You can create a top-level site collection using either the root URL of an unextended Web application or a managed path such as /sites or any other wildcard inclusion path you have created. See the discussion in the section titled "Managed Paths" earlier in this chapter that discusses configuring a managed path. When creating a new site collection, you will provide the following information.

- Title and description
- Website address using either the root of the Web application or a URL path
- A site template that will be used to create the new site collection
- A site collection administrator and a secondary administrator if required
- A quota limit template if required

> **NOTE** If you wanted to create a site hierarchy based on a managed path URL mapping called *projects*, you first need to create the new managed path called *projects* for the Web application. Then you can create each site collection using the projects URL path and add each new project as its own sub URL of the projects URL, such as *http://contosoportal /projects/ProjectA*.

Be sure to choose the correct Web application before creating the site collection so the collection is available in the correct Web application. Figure 6-21 shows the site collection called *Project A* being created in the wildcard inclusion managed path called *projects*.

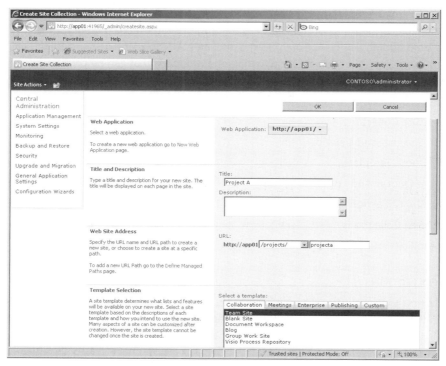

FIGURE 6-21 Creating a site collection using a wildcard inclusion managed path

DELETE A SITE COLLECTION

In the same way that you can create a top-level site collection, you also can delete a site collection from within the Site Collection category in Application Management. You begin doing so by selecting the site collection you want to delete from the drop-down menu on the Delete Site Collection page. After selecting Change Site Collection from the drop-down menu, you will see a list of site collections displayed for the Web application that you have most recently accessed. To display a list of site collections for a different Web application, use the Web Application drop-down menu located at the upper-right of the page to open the Select Site Collection page shown in Figure 6-22.

> **BEST PRACTICES** When you delete a site collection, all the content is deleted within it, including subsites, lists, and libraries. Therefore, you should perform a backup of the content database containing the site collection or export the site collection first, in case you need to recover the content at a later time.

FIGURE 6-22 Selecting a site collection to delete

After clicking OK on the Select Site Collection page, you will see the Delete Site Collection page displayed again with the entire path of the site collection shown along with a Delete button. Click Delete and then click OK on the confirmation dialog box to delete the selected site collection.

CONFIRM SITE USE AND DELETION

After enabling site use confirmations, SharePoint will e-mail all site collection owners of the specific Web application and ask for a confirmation that they are still using their site. There are two settings required to configure site use confirmation e-mails.

First you need to enable the option to send the notifications and set the time frame when you want the first notification to be sent. This time frame is calculated from the time the site was created or first accessed. By default, the first e-mail notification is sent out 90 days after the site is created or first accessed. Additionally, you can specify the time that the Web application is scanned to check for new site collections.

The second part of the configuration involves choosing if you want the site collection to be automatically deleted after a specified number of attempts to contact an administrator of the site collection and request that they confirm the site collection is still in use. If the site administrator does not confirm after the chosen amount of requests, the site collection and all its content will be deleted automatically. The default setting requires four notifications to the administrator before the site collection is automatically deleted. If all options are enabled with their default settings, then every 90 days a notification will be sent out to site collection owners, and if there is no replay from the administrator of a site after four contact attempts, then the site collection will be deleted.

> **IMPORTANT** If you are going to configure site collections to be deleted automatically, be sure to inform your site collection administrators of the consequences of not confirming site collection use from within the e-mail notifications they receive.

SPECIFY QUOTA TEMPLATES

Site quote templates are used to restrict the amount of content a site collection can contain. By default, there is one quota template defined for the user's personal sites (My Sites). This default quota setting is 100 MB of data for each user's My Site. Users are sent a warning e-mail when the site content reaches 80 MB. These settings can be modified to allow more or less content to be stored in My Sites.

Furthermore, you can create additional quotas that can be used for other site collections in your farm. The site quota templates that you create are available to all Web applications and all site collections.

SharePoint 2010 introduces a new performance feature that uses a point system to determine if specific user solutions are causing performance issues. You can choose to have the user solutions monitored using this point system, and if the solution exceeds the specified points, it will prevent that solution from running again. Points are accumulated using 14 pre-defined rules. When the recommended setting of 300 points is met, the solution that has exceeded the set amount of points will not run for the rest of that day, and the administrator will receive an e-mail informing them that the user solution has reached the threshold.

To create a new quota template, complete the fields shown in Figure 6-23 using the following steps.

1. Click Quota Templates.
2. Select Create A New Quota Template.
3. Select a template to start from; the default is New Blank Template.
4. Specify a name for your new quota template.
5. Specify a maximum storage limit for this quota template in megabytes (MB).
6. Specify a warning storage limit for this quota template in megabytes.
7. Optionally, specify the number of points that can be reached by user solutions.
8. Optionally, specify the number of points that must be reached to trigger an e-mail warning to be sent.

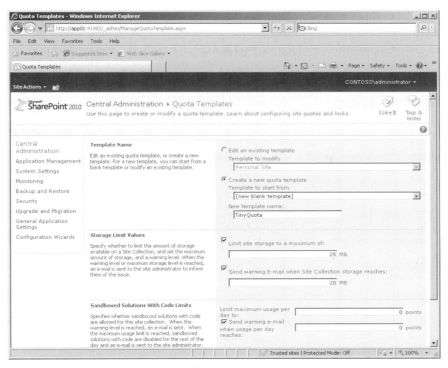

FIGURE 6-23 Creating a site quota template

CONFIGURE QUOTAS AND LOCKS

After you have created your quota templates, you can apply them to site collections. Alternatively, you can put a lock on a site collection to prevent certain uses of the site. You do this by selecting the site collection that you want to configure and then setting a lock or applying a quota template on the site collection.

Applying a Site Collection Lock   You can only lock an entire site collection; there is no option for choosing a site. There are four options when applying a lock to a site collection.

- **Not Locked**   This is the default option; it puts no restrictions on the site collection.
- **Adding Content Prevented**   This option prevents contributors from adding or uploading content into the site collection.
- **Read Only**   This option prevents users from deleting, modifying, and adding content to the site collection.
- **No Access**   This option prevents all users from accessing the site collection.

Setting a Site Quota You can also use the Configure Quotas And Locks interface to modify the site quota template or create a custom quota for the site collection. You do this by using the drop-down menu to choose one of the existing quota templates. You can override the available quota templates by specifying values in the Limit Site Storage To A Maximum Of and Send Warning E-mail When Site Storage reaches text boxes shown in Figure 6-24. Furthermore, you can modify the user solution resource quota for a specific site collection here as well. Notice that the defaults are 300 points maximum, with an e-mail notification generated at 100 points.

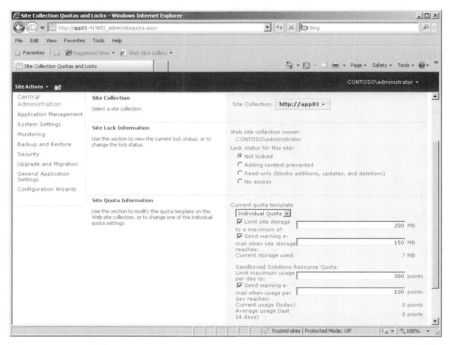

FIGURE 6-24 Site Collection Quota And Locks settings

CHANGE SITE COLLECTION ADMINISTRATORS

When you create a new site collection, you are prompted for a primary site collection administrator, and optionally, you can add a secondary site collection administrator. You can also change the primary and secondary administrator for the specified site collection.

> **NOTE** Although only two site collection administrators can be defined here, you can add more administrators using the People And Groups option at the site collection level.

VIEW ALL SITE COLLECTIONS

This option allows you to view a list of site collections per Web application. After accessing this page, confirm that the correct Web application is listed or choose the Web application you want from the drop-down menu to view the site collections associated with the Web application you have chosen.

CONFIGURE SELF-SERVICE SITE CREATION

This option was discussed in the section titled "Self-Service Site Creation" earlier in this chapter.

Service Applications

Service applications are new to SharePoint 2010 and replace the Shared Service Providers (SSPs) previously offered in SharePoint Server 2007. SSPs offered multiple services to all applications associated with the SSP, but they lacked the much-needed scalability and extensibility that service applications offer in SharePoint 2010.

A service application is a functional service of data or processing that, after it is configured, can be consumed by Web applications. All service applications are defined at the farm level, and some of these services can be consumed by other Web applications from other farms, which makes these service applications more scalable. Furthermore, some of the service applications can even store content in their own databases, creating a tighter integration between SharePoint and SQL Server.

After a service application is created, it can be consumed by any Web applications that require the resources or data provided by the service. If a particular service isn't configured correctly for all Web applications, you can create another instance of that service.

MANAGE SERVICE APPLICATIONS

When you click the Manage Service Applications link in the Application Management section of the Central Administration home page, you are presented with the Manage Service Applications interface shown in Figure 6-25, which contains a Ribbon interface for managing and configuring your service applications.

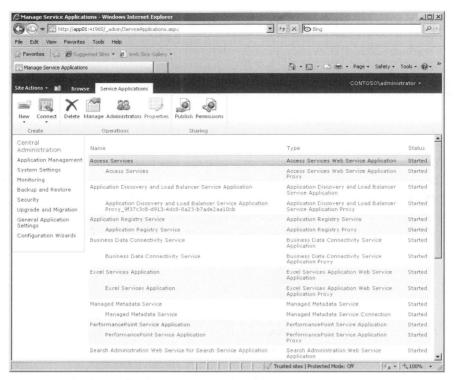

FIGURE 6-25 Service Application Management interface

Creating a New Service Application   From the Ribbon in the Manage Service Applications interface, click the arrow under the New button to display the different service applications that you can create for your farm. This option allows you to create and configure the first instance of the service application, or if necessary, you can create and configure multiple instances of a service application.

Connecting to a Service Application   From the Ribbon, click the arrow under the Connect button to display a list of service applications that you can connect to that are being hosted on another farm. To connect to an instance of a service application located on another farm, you need to specify either the address of the farm's discovery service or the address of the service application.

Deleting an Existing Service Application   You can also delete a service application from your farm configuration using the Ribbon in the Manage Service Applications interface. First click the row that contains the service application that you want to delete and then click the Delete icon on the Ribbon. This action presents a dialog box similar to the one shown in Figure 6-26, which requests that you select a check box indicating that you want to delete the data associated with the service application. The service application is deleted after you click the OK button.

FIGURE 6-26 Deleting a service application

Managing Your Service Applications You can use the Manage icon on the Ribbon to configure a service application running on your farm by first clicking the row that contains the service application that you want to manage and then clicking the Manage icon on the Ribbon. This action presents a page of configuration options that varies depending on the service application that you selected. After you configure the service application, click OK to save your changes.

> **NOTE** Alternatively, you can access the service application configuration options by double-clicking the name of the service application located in the list of service applications.

Identifying Administrators for Your Service Applications You can also configure who has permissions to manage each of your service applications in your farm from the Ribbon. To do this, click the row that contains the service application that you want assign permissions to and then click the Administrators icon on the Ribbon. This action presents a dialog box similar to the one shown in Figure 6-27, where you can add the accounts and identify the permission level for the accounts in the appropriate text boxes. When you finish, click the OK button and the permissions will be assigned to the user for that particular service application.

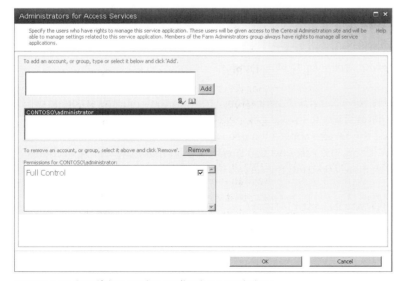

FIGURE 6-27 Specifying service application permissions

Configuring Properties of Your Service Applications Some service applications have properties that can be configured for them, like database name, failover server, and application pool configuration settings. You can configure the properties of a service application by first clicking the row that contains the service application you want to configure and then clicking the Properties icon on the Ribbon. Some of the common service applications that have configurable properties include the Business Data Connectivity, Manage Metadata Services, and PerformancePoint service applications.

Publishing a Service Application Some service applications can be configured to provide services to Web applications located in other farms. You access the settings to do so by clicking the Publishing icon on the Ribbon after clicking a row that contains a service application that is capable of providing its service to Web applications in other farms. The Publish Service Application page shown in Figure 6-28 contains the items you must configure to permit the service application to host Web applications from other farms.

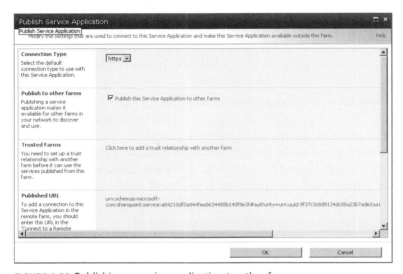

FIGURE 6-28 Publishing a service application to other farms

Configuring Permissions for a Service Application You can configure the accounts or principals that have the permissions to invoke the service application using the Ribbon. First click the row that contains the service application you want to configure and then click the Permissions icon on the Ribbon. The accounts you specify are normally the service accounts of the Web applications that are accessing the service application.

CONFIGURE SERVICE APPLICATION ASSOCIATIONS

When you click the Configure Service Application Associations link from Central Administration, you are presented with the Service Applications Associations interface shown in Figure 6-29, which allows you to associate the Web application or service application to an application proxy group.

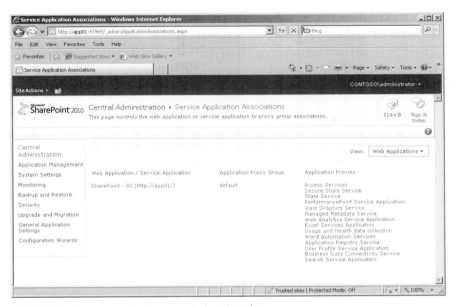

FIGURE 6-29 Service Application Associations interface

When you click the Web Application link on this page, you will see a list of associated service applications, and the service applications that are currently associated with the Web application link you clicked are checked. To modify a service application associated with the Web application, select Custom from the drop-down menu at the top of the page and select the service application check boxes for the service applications that you want to associate with the Web application.

The Application Proxy Group column indicates which application proxy group is associated with each of the Web applications listed in the Service Application Association interface.

Databases

When you create a Web application, you specify the database that will be associated with it. By default, there is only one database associated with a Web application, but each Web application is capable of having multiple databases associated with it.

MANAGE CONTENT DATABASES

You can use the Manage Content Databases interface to create, configure, and even delete the content databases associated with a Web application. The default settings for each content database has a maximum limit of 15,000 site collections, with a default warning limit of 9000 site collections. This warning limit notifies farm administrators when the database has exceeded 9000 site collections. However, these default settings can be modified to different settings as shown for the WSS_Content database in Figure 6-30. This modification allows you to control the size of your databases.

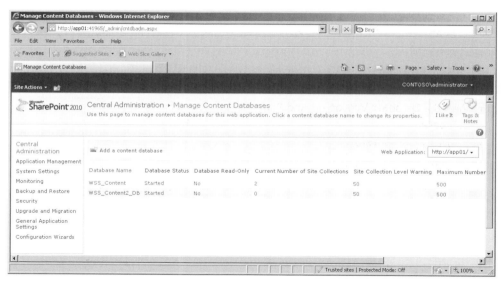

FIGURE 6-30 Manage Content Databases interface

This interface also indicates the number of site collections currently contained in each database, as well as the status of the database. By creating additional databases, you can control database growth by spreading the location of site collections across multiple databases. You could then limit the total number of site collections each database can hold to as little as one site collection per database.

 REAL WORLD **Site Collection Creation with Multiple Databases**

f a Web application has multiple databases and you create a new site collection, the database with the most available site collection capacity will receive the new site collection by default. For instance, if a database called *Wss_content1_db* has a maximum setting of 500 and currently contains 100 site collections, and another database called *Wss_content2_db* also has a maximum setting of 500 but currently contains only 50 site collections, when you create a new site collection, Wss_content2_db will receive the new site collection because it currently has fewer site collections. In fact, the next several site collections you create will also be stored in Wss_content2_db, until that database reaches the same number of site collections (100) as Wss_content1_db contains. However, if you want to control which database receives a newly created site collection, set all other databases for that Web application to Offline prior to creating the new site collection. This action will force the site collection into the only database with the database status of Ready. Remember to return the other databases to Ready after you create the new site collection so that when future site collections are created, they will be populated in the database with the most available site collection capacity.

You can add other databases by clicking the Add A Content Database link in the Manage Content Databases interface. Furthermore, you can configure your existing databases by clicking the name of the database, which allows you to perform the following actions.

- Change the database status between Ready and Offline; when the status is Offline, no new site collections can be added to the database.
- View the Database Versioning And Status section to check the status and version of the database.
- Specify a failover server.
- Modify the maximum number of site collections the database can contain.
- Modify the number of site collections the database can contain before administrators are warned.
- Specify which search server the database is associated with.
- Remove the content database from SQL Server.
- Specify which server will be running the timer jobs associated with the database.

SPECIFY THE DEFAULT DATABASE SERVER

The SQL server configured on the Default Database Server page indicates the default location where all new content databases will be created. If you move your SharePoint SQL Server instance to a new server, or if you create a named instance of SQL Server that is going to host all of your content databases, you can specify the new SQL Server instance on this screen. However, when you create a new Web application, you can still specify a database server other than the default server defined here.

CONFIGURE THE DATA RETRIEVAL SERVICE

When any connections are established to SharePoint 2010, they require the use of data services such as Simple Object Access Protocol (SOAP), Object Linking and Embedding, Database (OLEDB), Extensible Markup Language (XML), and Windows SharePoint Services to allow data consumers and data sources to communicate with each other. These services are Web services that return XML data from different data sources or manipulate data against those data sources. This Data Retrieval Service page is used to configure the communication and connectivity options associated with the data retrieval service.

System Settings

This functional category contains the following three core components that are used to manage different aspects of farm level settings.

- Server
- E-mail and Text Messages (SMS)
- Farm Management

The System Settings will be one of the first management pages that a farm administrator needs to visit when working in Central Administration, because it contains some of the core configuration requirements for the entire SharePoint farm.

Servers

In the Server category of system settings, you manage and configure your SharePoint farm servers and services, and you can obtain information about the SQL Server instance hosting your SharePoint content, including the name and version of the configuration database. You can also remove a server from the farm if a server is unusable for some reason.

SERVERS IN FARM

The Servers In Farm page, shown in Figure 6-31, lists all the servers that are participating in the farm. Servers are sorted by server name on this page. In the top section of this page, you can see the configuration database version that indicates which SharePoint version, service packs, and cumulative updates have been applied to the farm. This section also displays the name, and optionally the instance, of the SQL Server instance hosting your SharePoint farm's content, as well as the name of the farm configuration database.

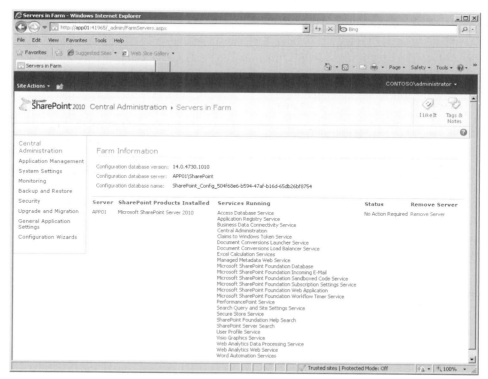

FIGURE 6-31 Servers In Farm page

The bottom section of this page list all the servers that are part of this farm, along with the specific SharePoint product running on each server, followed by a list of services each server is hosting. If there are any configuration issues, they will be listed in the Status column, which can help you identify what servers in the farm may not have the most current patches or service packs installed.

You can use the option to remove the server from the farm if you have a server that has become corrupted, and you have no chance to bring it back online as it is. To rebuild the server and join it back into the farm with the same name, you must first purge the entries from the configuration database for the old server using the Remove Server option on the Servers In Farm page.

MANAGE SERVICES ON SERVER

The list of services will only show you the services that have been started on the specific server. When you have many severs in the farm, the Services On Server page is the best place to go when you need to see which servers are running which service. Servers that are not running services but are configured as part of the farm as a service are also shown on the Services On Server page. For example, you would see the outgoing mail server for your SharePoint farm that resides on a server that is not actually part of the farm.

You can choose any server in the farm to view its services by selecting the server of choice from the Server drop-down menu at the upper left of the page. There are two views available to display the list of services: Configurable and All. To see just services that have configurable options, including the option to start and stop the service, you can use the default Configurable view. To see all services, including those that do not have configurable options, use the drop-down menu next to the Configurable view option to select All.

Some of the services listed on the Services On Server page shown in Figure 6-32 have links that indicate that additional configuration is necessary either before or after the service starts running. The hyperlink takes you to the services management page for that service so that you can perform the necessary configuration. For example, the SharePoint Server Search service allows you to access the Search Service Application to manage several configurable components of that service application.

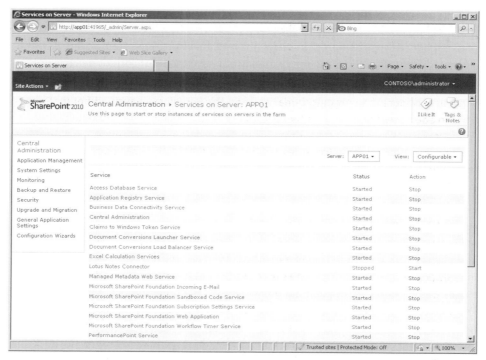

FIGURE 6-32 Services On Server page

E-Mail And Text Messages (SMS)

The E-Mail And Text Messages (SMS) section of SharePoint Central Administration provides the communication between SharePoint components and Microsoft Outlook using outgoing e-mail settings. Settings made in this section also allow e-mail messages to be received by SharePoint lists and libraries after you configure incoming e-mail settings. New to SharePoint 2010 is the ability to utilize SMS (Short Messaging Service) to deliver alerts and notifications to users, including health and monitoring information to your administrators.

CONFIGURE OUTGOING E-MAIL SETTINGS

For any messages to be sent from SharePoint 2010, such as alerts, notifications, and site invitations, you need to configure an SMTP (Simple Mail Transfer Protocol) server that will be responsible for routing the messages. This server can be any SMTP-compliant server that you can connect to using port 25 from the SharePoint 2010 server. The identification of this server can be specified as either the IP address, NetBIOS name, or a Fully Qualified Domain Name (FQDN) of the SMTP server. However, if you are using a NetBIOS name or an FQDN, a method of name resolution has to be available to locate the SMTP server.

When you configure the outgoing e-mail server settings, you can specify different From and Reply-to addresses for your e-mail messages. For instance, you could configure the From address that will display to mail recipients as SharePointAdmin@contoso.com, but then specify that users respond using the Reply-to address helpdesk@contoso.com. These settings are configured at the farm level and will be used by all Web applications unless they are over-ridden at the Web application level by specifying alternative values.

CONFIGURE INCOMING E-MAIL SETTINGS

SharePoint 2010 has the ability to allow e-mail messages to be routed directly to a list or library in a site so that the actual e-mail messages, along with any attachments, appear in the list or library. The principle behind this is very simple—you create a new list or library in a Team Site and enable it for e-mail. This creates a new contact in Active Directory using the SharePoint Directory Service, and people can send e-mail messages to the contact's mail address. When an e-mail message is sent to this address, it is routed to the configured drop folder on the SharePoint 2010 server. When it arrives in the drop folder, it will wait until the SPTimer service checks the folder and then routes the e-mail message to the list configured with that e-mail address.

Before configuring the incoming mail settings, you need an SMTP server available on the local SharePoint 2010 server to do mail routing. You add the SMTP service using the server manager to install the SMTP Server feature. For added security, you can add only the allowed mail servers in your organization to relay through this local SMTP server. This is accomplished using the properties of the SMTP service in IIS.

Generally speaking, you must complete the following tasks to configure the server side of incoming e-mail messages in SharePoint 2010.

1. Install the SMTP service using IIS.

2. In Active Directory, create an organizational unit (OU) in which the new distribution groups or contacts will be created.

3. In Central Administration, click Configure Incoming E-Mail Settings and specify the OU you just created in Active Directory settings for e-mail Web services.

NOTE   The name of the OU you create must be in the format of the full distinguished name, for example, OU=sharepointgroups,DC=contoso,DC=com.

Configuring Server Side Incoming E-Mail   To configure server side incoming e-mail, first click the Configure Incoming E-Mail Settings link and then complete the following steps.

1.   Select the Yes option to enable sites on this server to receive e-mail messages.
2.   Leave the default option of Automatic.

> **NOTE**   Use the Advanced setting if you need to specify a drop box other than that of the default SMTP service.

3.   Select the Yes option for the SharePoint Directory Management Service.

> **NOTE**   If you select the Use Remote option, you can specify another SharePoint server that is configured to manage the SharePoint Directory Management Service.

4.   Enter the full distinguished name of the OU where you want distributions lists to be created.
5.   Enter the name of the SMTP mail server.
6.   Select the permission options for the tasks that the users can perform.
7.   Specify the Incoming E-Mail Server Display Address.
8.   Specify the Safe E-Mail Server Settings.

Configuring List or Library Side E-Mail Settings   Now that you have configured the server side e-mail settings, you can now go to lists and libraries in SharePoint 2010 sites and configure them to receive e-mail as well as specify which e-mail address each list will used to receive e-mails. Use the following steps to configure these options.

1.   Navigate to a document library and select Library Settings on the Ribbon.
2.   In the Communications section, select E-Mail Settings to open the Change E-Mail Settings page.
3.   Configure any of the following options for incoming e-mail for that library.

   - **Incoming E-Mail**   Select Yes to enable e-mail on the library and specify the e-mail address.
   - **E-Mail Attachments**   Choose how you want to group the e-mail attachments that will be stored in the library. The default is for all attachments to be stored in the root folder.
   - **E-Mail Message**   Choose Yes to have the original e-mail message (.eml file) in the document library as an attachment.
   - **E-Mail Invitations**   Choose Yes if you want this library to receive and display meeting request e-mails.
   - **E-Mail Security**   Select the level of security on the document library to specify who can add items. By default, only those senders who have write access to the

library will be able to send e-mail items to the library; however, you can change this to allow all senders of mail to populate the library.

After completing the e-mail settings process, a contact is created in the specified OU in Active Directory using the directory service manager. If you want to add additional e-mail addresses to that contact to support external mail addresses, you can use the Active Directory Users And Computers tool to specify additional e-mail SMTP addresses.

CONFIGURE MOBILE ACCOUNT

A new feature in SharePoint 2010 allows administrators to configure a corporate SMS service that can deliver alerts and notifications to the users. This would allow administrators to receive system notification or health and monitoring alerts directly to their Windows Mobile device. SMS services can also be provided by third-party companies that may require user credentials when accessing the SMS provider. You can specify a user name and password if the service requires them.

Farm Management

You use this section of Central Administration to define farm level settings that control how the farm is accessed and what functionality is available at the farm level. This section also provides you with the opportunity to control how solutions are used in SharePoint 2010. Lastly, you can use settings in this section to configure what information is shared with Microsoft when errors are generated and how mobile alerts are received outside of the SharePoint farm.

CONFIGURE ALTERNATE ACCESS MAPPINGS

This topic was described in the section titled "Configuring Alternate Access Mappings" earlier in this chapter.

MANAGE FARM FEATURES

Features are a container of code that a developer can create and deploy to administrators, and then the administrators can decide which features to turn on or off depending on the requirements of the layer where they are. Features can be deployed to many of the layers in SharePoint depending on the particular functionality that the feature provides. Features are one of the few components that you will see throughout the SharePoint model. They appear at the farm level, Web application level, site collection level, and site level.

Features can also be deployed in a silent method so that they do not appear as features to be activated or deactivated, but rather, they can be deployed in a way chosen by the developers so that the code hides the feature activation option.

Features are also deployed when third-party products are installed, such as the Nintex workflow product, which has farm, site collection, and site level feature activation.

At the farm level, several out-of-the-box features are activated. However, if necessary, all of these out-of-the-box features can be deactivated. The following farm level features are available and activated by default.

- Connect to Office Ribbon Controls
- Access Services Farm Feature
- Data Connection Library
- Excel Services Farm Feature
- FAST Search for SharePoint Master Job Provisioning
- Global Web Parts
- Office.com Entry Points from SharePoint
- Office Synchronization for External Lists
- Social Tags and Note Board Ribbon Controls
- Spell Checking
- Visio Process Repository
- Visio Web Access

MANAGE FARM SOLUTIONS

Solutions are a way for developers to package all of the required components that are part of a custom solution (a custom Web Part, for example) and then pass the solution to the administrator so they can deploy and manage the farm solution.

There are two main elements involved in deploying a solution: adding the solution to the solution store and then deploying the solution from the solution store.

1. First you must add the solution to the solution store, which is a centralized collection point of all SharePoint solutions for the farm. Before a solution can be deployed, it must first be installed to the solution store using the following command.

    ```
    STSADM -o addsolution -filename
    ```

    or

    ```
    Add-SPSolution C:\solutionname.wsp
    ```

2. Next, deploy the solution from the solution store. You can do this using one of the following methods.

    - Using the graphical user interface, select Solution and then choose Deploy.
    - From the command line, enter the following command.

    ```
    STSADM -o deploysolution -name solutionname
    ```

    or

    ```
    Install-SPSolution -Identity solutionname.wsp -WebApplication URLofWebApplication
    ```

Farm solutions are an ideal way for administrators and developers to create, test, and deploy solutions without the developers needing access to the production servers. Developers create and test their solutions on their developer computers, and when they are ready to deploy them, they can package them into a .wsp file and pass the file to the administrator, who then adds the solution to the store and deploys it.

MANAGE USER SOLUTIONS

Site collections now have a Site Collection Solution Gallery that makes it possible for power users to upload their own solutions, bypassing the farm-managed solution approach. This can create potential performance or security issues for the administrator. Central Administration provides a way for administrators to manage user solutions by blocking specific code from running in site collections. Using the Manage User Solutions interface shown in Figure 6-33, the administrator can upload the same solution into the user solution management section and block it from running. Follow these steps to block a user solution.

1. Browse to the location of the solution.

2. Upload the solution.

3. Enter a reason that will be displayed to the user to explain why the solution is blocked.

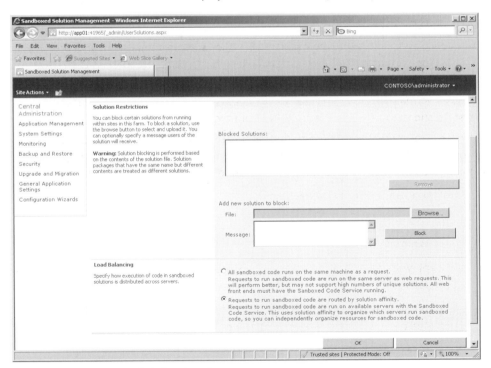

FIGURE 6-33 Manage User Solutions interface

Alternatively, you can choose to control how and where the user solution runs. You accomplish this by specifying that the solution can run if the code runs on the same computer as the request came from and that computer is running the User Code Service, or the solution can run if it uses solution affinity, which means that it will be organized and routed to available servers that are running the User Code Service.

CONFIGURE PRIVACY OPTIONS

You can configure the level at which Microsoft can collect information regarding the use and errors generated by your SharePoint 2010 servers, as shown in Figure 6-34. When errors are generated, the information about the error—plus information about your computer hardware—will be sent to Microsoft for analysis. The information collected is used to help improve SharePoint and is used to determine what will be included in patching and service packs.

It is also possible to provide online help in addition to the local help files by adding the ability to search both local and external help files hosted by Microsoft. This allows Microsoft to maintain a central online updated help system that provides users the most recent help-related content.

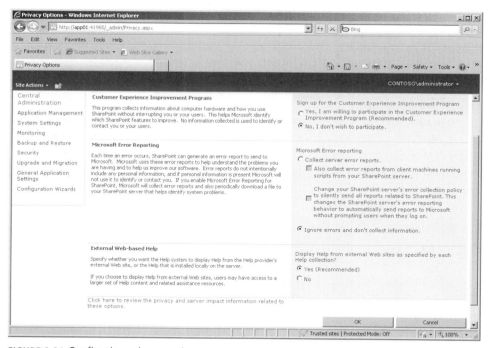

FIGURE 6-34 Configuring privacy options

CONFIGURE CROSS-FIREWALL ACCESS ZONES

The Configure Cross-Firewall Access Zone setting is specifically designed to help mobile users access SharePoint content from the outside world. To make sure that all mobile alerts and notifications are sent using the correctly published external URL, you can set the alternate access zone to be used from the Web application where the content is stored. If a link is included in a text message that you receive on your mobile device, the link will be accessible from that device. This provides similar functionality as Alternate Access Mappings does but in a way specific to mobile devices.

For example, if the users have content in the portal.contoso.com Web application site, but externally the zone that is published to the Internet is internet.contoso.com, then you must extend and map the Web application using the Internet zone for portal.contoso.com to specify that the Internet zone is the default for all mobile alerts and notifications for the portal.contoso.com Web application.

Monitoring

There have been significant improvements in how you can monitor your farm in SharePoint 2010. The Monitoring functional category provides a central location from which you can monitor a plethora of performance, logging, and reporting information about your farm. To help organize these features and make them easier to use, the Monitoring functional category has been divided into three main areas: Health Analyzer, Timer Jobs, and Reporting.

Health Analyzer

The Health Analyzer section of the Monitoring category in Central Administration gives you the opportunity to review and modify the predefined rules used to monitor your farm and review any problems that are reported. In addition to selecting how you want to review the problems, most of the problems reported provide an option to act on the reported problem in an attempt to resolve it.

REVIEW PROBLEMS AND SOLUTIONS

When a new service application, Web application, or even a new SQL Server database is created, SharePoint automatically creates the necessary monitoring definitions for the new item using out-of-the-box configuration. These default system-generated definitions are used to generate and report warnings and errors that you can view on the Review Problems And Solutions page shown in Figure 6-35.

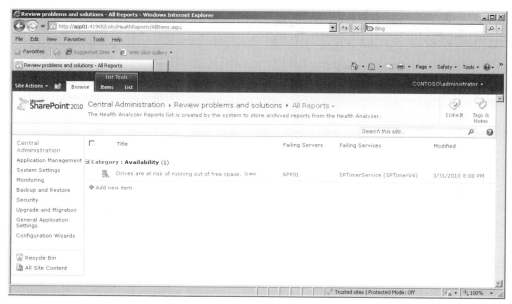

FIGURE 6-35 Review Problems And Solutions page

The page displays any problems that have been discovered in one of the following four categories.

- Configuration
- Security
- Performance
- Availability

Within each category, you see a list of reported problems (if there are any), and each problem in the lists is displayed as a hyperlink, which you can click to receive more detailed information about the problem, as shown in Figure 6-36.

One of the most helpful options provided in the details view is located within the Remedy section. It provides a link to a Microsoft Knowledge Base (KB) article about the problem and some possible steps to resolve the problem. This section and the Explanation section are the two areas that will help you understand and resolve the problem. After attempting to resolve the problem, you can click the Reanalyze Now icon in the Ribbon at the top of the page to determine if the problem has been resolved.

You can view general information about the rule of the reported problem by clicking the View link located in the Rule Settings section. This will display a page with details about the rule, as shown in Figure 6-37. These details can be used to determine the frequency with which the rule runs, to define an alert on the rule, or to run the rule immediately to determine if a problem currently exists instead of waiting until its next scheduled run.

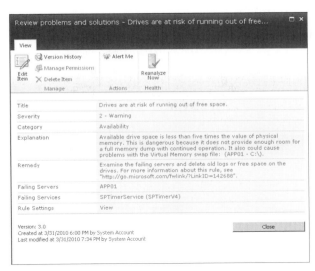

FIGURE 6-36 Details of a reported problem

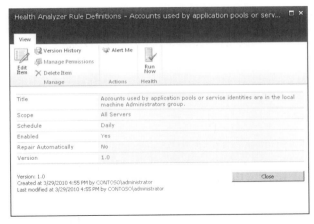

FIGURE 6-37 Rule details of reported problem

NOTE You can also access the page with details about a rule by clicking a rule displayed on the Health Analyzer Rule Definitions page, which is shown in Figure 6-38.

REVIEW RULE DEFINITIONS

The Health Analyzer Rule Definitions page shown in Figure 6-38 displays all the currently defined Health Analyzer rule definitions. This page provides you with information about each rule including schedule, whether the rule is enabled, and if it is configured to attempt to repair the reported problem automatically. Definitions are created automatically when the system detects a new service that has defined rule definitions associated with it. When the service is started, the definition rules will be added to the appropriate category.

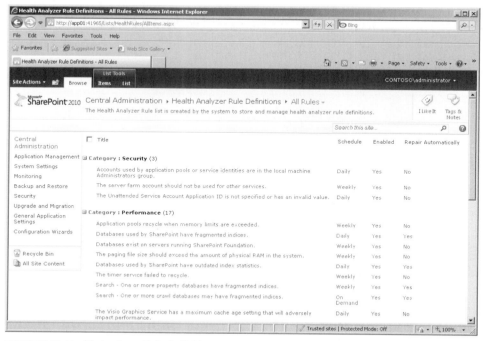

FIGURE 6-38 Health Analyzer Rule Definitions page

Click a rule on the Health Analyzer Rule Definitions page to display details about that rule, as shown in Figure 6-37. Then you can click the Edit Item icon in the Ribbon on the details page to display the rule definition, which you can then configure, or you can delete the rule.

Alternatively, you can access the page where you can configure or delete a rule by selecting the check box next to the rule on the Health Analyzer Rule Definitions page. This will display the Ribbon with the tools that allow you to manage the rule definition, as shown in Figure 6-39.

To modify the rule definition, click the Edit Item icon to display the Rule Definition Configuration page shown in Figure 6-40, which you can use to define the settings including schedule, scope, and automatic repair.

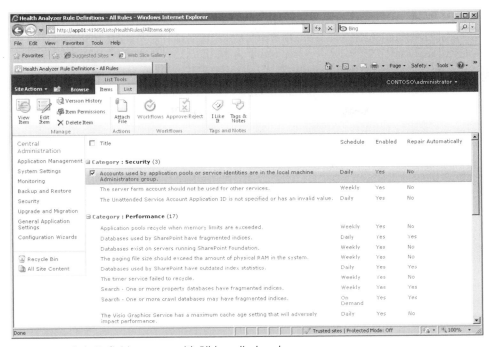

FIGURE 6-39 Rule Definitions page with Ribbon displayed

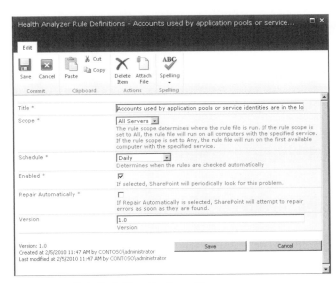

FIGURE 6-40 Rule Definition Configuration page

Timer Jobs

Timer jobs are created when service applications, Web applications, and other SharePoint components are created. When you create these components, a job is also created to perform a specific task at a specified frequency.

For example, when you create a new Web application, a disk quota warning job definition will be created that by default runs once a week. This timer job monitors quota limits to determine if either the warning or maximum thresholds have been attained. The job definition will trigger the necessary actions specified by the job.

REVIEW JOB DEFINITIONS

The Job Definitions page displays information about all the current definition jobs that are created. Each entry contains the following three columns, as shown in Figure 6-41.

- **Title** You may see duplicate titles that are associated with different components.
- **Web Application** Displays the name of the specific Web application the definition is running against.
- **Schedule** Shows the frequency of the timer job—how often it is scheduled to run.

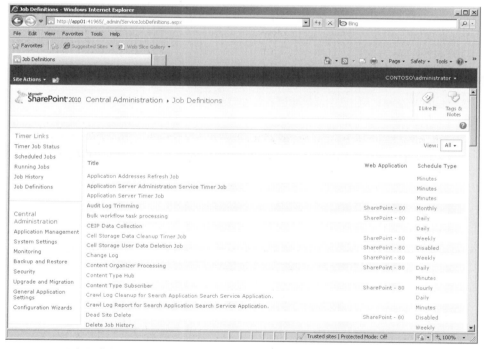

FIGURE 6-41 Job Definitions page

You will notice that some job definitions are listed only once. Normally, these job definitions are system jobs or farm level jobs, or they belong to a specific service application and there is only one occurrence of that application. Other jobs may be listed multiple times because each job is associated with a specific Web application; an example is the Disk Quota Warning job.

For additional information on a job definition listed on this page, click the title of the job, which is a hyperlink. This will display more details about the job, including a description, the application it is associated with, and the last time it ran. Additional options that can be configured are also available on this page and allow you to change the schedule, run the job immediately instead of waiting for the next scheduled time, or disable the job to prevent it from running. To select one of the following options, click the definition title.

- Change The Schedule
- Run The Job Now
- Disable The Job

IMPORTANT After you change the schedule, be sure to click OK to save your changes or the changes will not be applied.

Some job definitions are created only when a specific operation is being performed. For instance, if you are performing a backup, a job is created and will appear in this list. If a job created for a specific operation becomes corrupted, you can access it by clicking the hyperlink title for the job. Then click Delete to end the operation and remove the job from the list on the Job Definitions page.

NOTE You will get the Delete option only for jobs that were created to run in association with a specific operation. Jobs that are scheduled to run repeatedly have the Disable option instead of the Delete option.

CHECK JOB STATUS

The Timer Job Status page provides job status information in the following three categories.

- **Scheduled** Displays the next 10 jobs scheduled to run.
- **Running** Displays the jobs currently running.
- **History** Displays the history of the jobs that have run.

To see additional jobs within each category, you can click the hyperlink category title, or you can click the hyperlink button that displays the current number of items being displayed, which is located at the bottom of the category list, as shown in Figure 6-42.

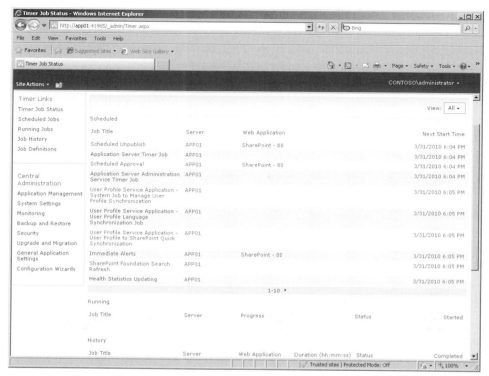

FIGURE 6-42 Timer Job Status page

Alternatively, you can filter the jobs displayed using the View drop-down menu at the upper right of the page, which allows you to reduce the number of jobs being displayed using one of the following five categories.

- All
- Service Applications
- Web Applications
- Server
- Job Definitions

Also, there are five links at the upper left of the page that you can use to display only the jobs that fall within one of the three categories previously introduced, go to the Job Definitions page, or refresh the current page using the Timer Job Status link.

Reporting

The Reporting section of the Monitoring category is used to manage two primary aspects of monitoring: logging and reporting. SharePoint 2010 provides significant improvements in both of these areas. You can use the settings provided to configure and view administrative and health reports that were generated based on logging settings you can also define here.

VIEW ADMINISTRATIVE REPORTS

The Administrative Reports page contains a document library that holds administrator reports that are generated by your logging configurations. The reports you will find in this library will depend on the services that are running and the configuration of the logging options, which are also located on the Administrative Reports page.

CONFIGURE DIAGNOSTIC LOGGING

You use the Diagnostic Logging page to configure the amount of diagnostic logging that will be captured using the Unified Logging Service (ULS). You can control the types of events, severity of events, repeating events, and log information including file location, size of logs, and how long to retain the logs. There are more than 20 different categories that you can choose to log information about, and each of them contains more granular options for specifying the types of events to log within the category, as shown in Figure 6-43.

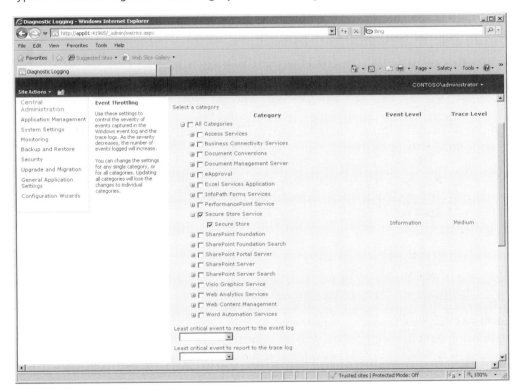

FIGURE 6-43 Diagnostic Logging Events page

Use the following steps to configure diagnostic logging.

1. Click Configure Diagnostic Logging under Reporting on the Monitoring page.

2. Select the main category of each event type you want to log.

3. Select either all or specific items within each category.

4. Select the least critical event level that you want to record in the event log.

5. Select the least critical event level that you want to report to the trace log.

Event Flood protection allows the ULS logging mechanism to identify repeating logging activities for the same event and suppress the event to prevent the log from filling up with the same alert that might be occurring every five seconds.

Your selection of events and the reporting levels have a direct impact on the size of your log files and the performance of your system. It is a best practice to store your log files on a separate disk, which can be specified in the Path option shown in Figure 6-44. You can also configure the length of time the files are retained as well as the amount of disk space in gigabytes (GB) that can be consumed by the log files.

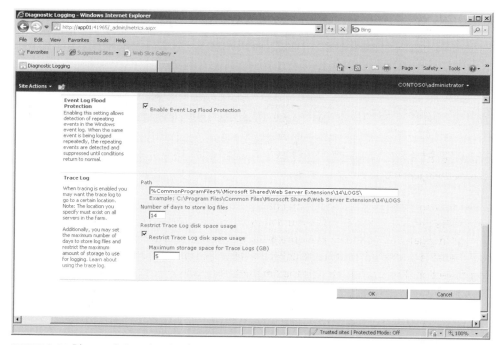

FIGURE 6-44 Diagnostic Logging Configuration page

CONFIGURE USAGE AND HEALTH DATA COLLECTION

You use usage logging to generate reports that show how your system is being used. After enabling usage logging, you specify which events you want logged, as shown in Figure 6-45.

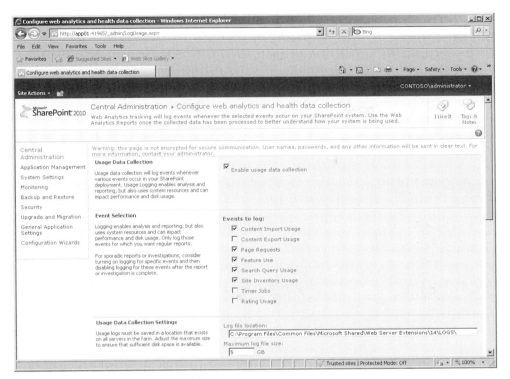

FIGURE 6-45 Configuring Usage Logging page

Similar to diagnostic logging, after you enable usage logging you can specify the location of the log files generated and the maximum amount of disk space that can be consumed by the logs in gigabytes, as shown in Figure 6-46. In addition to those settings, you can also choose to enable or disable health data collection as well as configure the schedule for health and log collection. The log collection is the timer job that runs to gather the information stored in the log files and then copy it into the SQL Server logging database. The SQL Server instance hosting the logging database and the name of the database are also displayed. The default database name is Wss_logging, and by default it contains the following information from all servers in the farm.

- ULS logs
- Event logs
- Select Performance Monitor counters
  - % Processor Time
  - Memory Available Megabytes
  - Avg. Disk Queue Length
  - Process Private Bytes (OWSTIMER and all instances of w3wp)
- Blocking SQL queries

- SQL DMV (Dynamic Management Views) queries
- Feature usage
- Information on search crawling and querying
- Inventory of all site collections
- Timer job usage

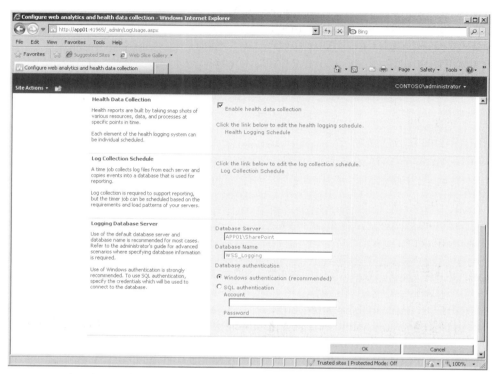

FIGURE 6-46 Logging configuration options

VIEW HEALTH REPORT

After enabling usage reporting and defining the schedule, and after the timer job has run to generate your logs, you can view two reports from the View Health Report page. You can select the type of report to display by clicking either Slowest Pages or Top Active Users, options available at the upper left of the page. Both reports allow you to filter the information that is presented by specifying options using the following drop-downs menus.

- **Server**   Display information from all servers or a specific one.
- **Web Application**   Display information from all Web applications or a specific one.
- **Show Items**   Specify the number of items to show on each page; options are 25 (default), 50, or 100.
- **Range**   Specify the time frame of the information to display; options are Last Day (default), Last Week, or Last Month.

After you select the options you want to see, click Go to view the report.

The column headings of each report can be used to sort the content based on that heading. For instance, if you want to view the Slowest Pages report by Average Duration beginning with the lowest average, you can click the Average Duration column heading to perform the sort. Clicking it a second time will sort it in the reverse order.

Slowest Pages Report   Using the filtering options you select, the Slowest Pages report provides information about each page that has been accessed and provides some access statistics. An example of a Slowest Pages report is shown in Figure 6-47. The Slowest Pages report contains the following columns of information about the pages, which all can be viewed using the horizontal scroll bar.

- URL of the page
- Average Duration (seconds)
- Minimum Duration (seconds)
- Maximum Duration (seconds)
- Average Database Queries (count)
- Minimum Database Queries (count)
- Maximum Database Queries (count)
- Number of Requests

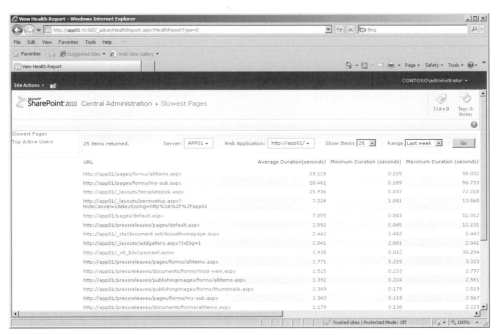

FIGURE 6-47 Sample Slowest Pages report

Top Active Users Report   Using the filtering options you select, the Top Active Users report, such as the one shown in Figure 6-48, provides the following information about the users accessing your farm.

- User
- Number of requests
- Last access time
- Percentage of successful requests

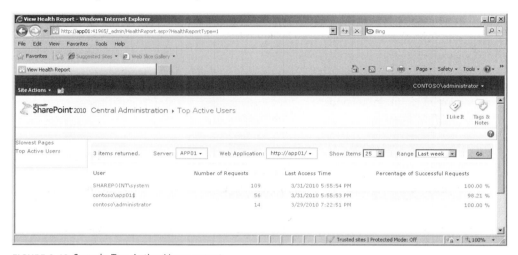

FIGURE 6-48 Sample Top Active Users report

Developer Dashboard

There is a developer dashboard that you can activate to display more detailed diagnostics concerning an activity, such as page load times, and can help you identify performance issues. You can enable the developer dashboard to constantly display detailed diagnostics, or you can choose to manage when this information is displayed by adding a developer dashboard button on your SharePoint interface. By default, the dashboard is disabled, but you can activate it using Windows PowerShell or STSADM by using the appropriate set of commands. The following sets of commands show you how to install the on-demand developer dashboard first using STSADM and then using Windows PowerShell.

STSADM

```
Stsadm -o getproperty -pn developer-dashboard
Stsadm -o setproperty -pn developer-dashboard -pv ondemand
```

Windows PowerShell

```
$wa = [microsoft.sharepoint.administration.spwebapplication]::lookup("$args")
$ws = $wa.webservice
$dd = $ws.developerdashboardsettings
$dd.displaylevel =
    [microsoft.sharepoint.administration.spdeveloperdashboardlevel]::OnDemand
$dd.update()
```

After executing these commands, you will see an icon next to the user name at the upper right of each page, as shown in Figure 6-49.

FIGURE 6-49 The developer dashboard icon appears next to the user name at the upper right of each page.

To display the additional diagnostic information all the time, you use the same commands, but instead of specifying ondemand as the developer dashboard type, you provide a command to create an on/off icon that enables and disables the dashboard as needed.

You use the icon to toggle between displaying and hiding additional detailed diagnostics. When you choose to display the dashboard, you will see information similar to what is shown in Figure 6-50.

FIGURE 6-50 Results from the developer dashboard

continued on the next page

But wait—it gets even better. If you click one of the options in the Database Queries section of the developer dashboard or click one of the items in the SPRequest Allocations, you will see even more information. For instance, if you click SELECT TOP(@NUMROWS) under Database Queries, you will see another page that contains the following three sections.

- Query Text
- Callstack
- IO Stats

You can use this additional information for in-depth troubleshooting or to analyze the performance of your system.

VIEW WEB ANALYTICS REPORTS

SharePoint 2010 introduces a service application that tracks Web application–level statistics that are stored in SQL Server so they can be easily accessed using different reports. Figure 6-51 is a summary report for a specific date range. This particular report contains five columns of information, but if you want to see a different type of report, click a report option on the left, where you can select from report layouts, including some that contain graphs.

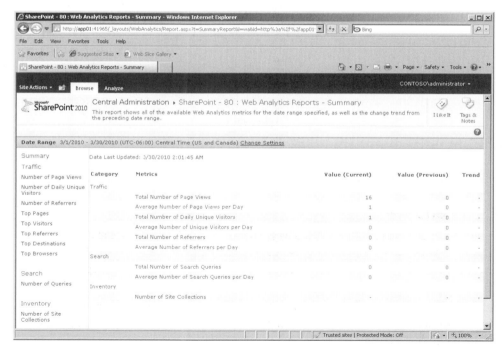

FIGURE 6-51 Web Analytics summary report

REVIEW INFORMATION MANAGEMENT POLICY USAGE REPORTS

The Information Management Policy Usage Reports page includes the settings shown in Figure 6-52. You can use the options on this page to set Information Management policies such as audit reporting and retention. When you enable these reports for a specific Web application, the reports will be generated in the location you specify, and there will be a separate file for each site collection. You can also specify a custom reporting template to be used when viewing the reports.

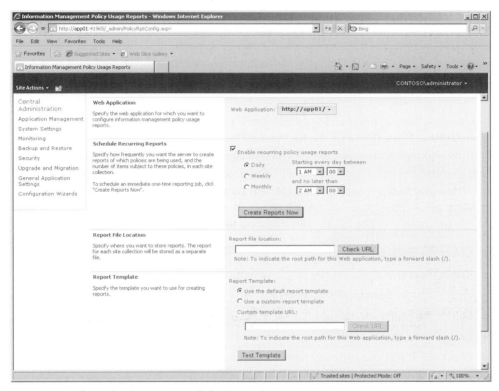

FIGURE 6-52 Information Management Policy Usage Reports page

Backup and Restore

Microsoft has made improvements in the ways SharePoint 2010 administrators can perform farm level backups as well as more granular backups of SharePoint information. SharePoint 2010 introduces the ability to perform site collection, site, library, and list backups, which could only be done using STSADM in previous versions of SharePoint.

See Chapter 17, "Data Protection, Recoverability, and Availability," for additional information regarding disaster recovery, including information about performing backups and restores of your SharePoint content.

Farm Backup and Restore

Similar to the Backup And Restore tools provided with SharePoint Server 2007, you can use Central Administration to perform both backups and restores. When you perform a backup, you can choose to store it on either a local or a network drive. However, if you grow beyond one server, your backups must be available to your SharePoint servers and your SQL servers, which means that you must use a network drive to perform restores on your servers.

> **BEST PRACTICES** Although it is not possible to perform a backup directly to an external tape device, when the backup is complete, you can move the backup files to a tape or other external device as a another step in the backup operation. It is a best practice to create a copy of the backup files using this technique whenever possible, because it adds a layer of protection by allowing you to store backups offsite.

To access the Backup And Restore utility, open a browser and go to the SharePoint Central Administration website, then click the Backup And Restore functional category. The backup and restore utilities are divided into two sections: Farm Backup and Restore And Granular Backup.

From the Farm Backup And Restore section, you can

- Start a new backup job
- Configure backup settings
- Check the backup job history
- Check the status of a currently running backup or restore job

From the Granular Backup section, you can

- Start a site collection backup
- Export a site or list
- Check the status of a currently running granular backup job

Backups can also be performed using Windows PowerShell or STSADM scripts, providing you the option of scheduling your backups.

PERFORM A BACKUP

After you click the Perform A Backup option under Farm Backup And Restore, a page similar the one shown in Figure 6-53 will be displayed, where you can choose what component you want to back up. You can back up the entire farm, just the farm configuration information, service applications, Web applications, or specific content databases. Similar to previous versions of the backup utility in SharePoint, you can select the entire farm or a single component to back up, but you cannot choose multiple components when performing a backup except to perform an entire farm backup.

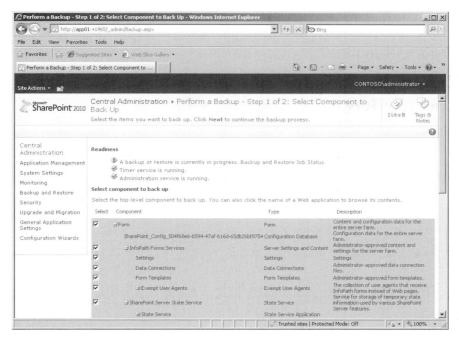

FIGURE 6-53 Selecting a component to back up

After specifying what components you want to back up, you can click the Next button to display the page shown in Figure 6-54, where you can configure the options for the backup. Use this page to specify the type of backup, the contents of the backup, and the location of the backup. If you decide you want to change which components will be backed up, you can click the Previous button located on the bottom of the page or select the appropriate option from the drop-down menu in the Backup Component section of the page to return to the previous page (shown in Figure 6-53).

The backup utility in Central Administration allows you to back up SharePoint Server at various levels, from a full SharePoint farm to a single list or library.

However, the backup utility has some limitations that you should note. For example, it has the following drawbacks.

- It does not allow backups to be scheduled.
- It does not allow backups directly to tape.
- It does not allow more than one SharePoint component to be backed up at the same time unless you back up the entire farm.

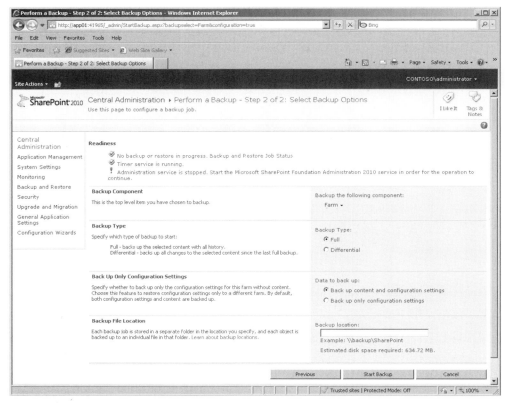

FIGURE 6-54 Backup operation configuration page.

RESTORE FROM A BACKUP

The Backup And Restore utility in Central Administration is also used to restore the backups of your SharePoint information, regardless of what tool you used to perform the backup. For example, if you run a Windows PowerShell script to perform your backups at regularly schedule intervals, you can restore one of those backups using this interface. You will need to know the name and location of the backup that you are restoring. You can enter the location of the backup file in the Backup Directory Location text box on the page shown in Figure 6-55. After specifying the backup location, you will see a list of the available backups in that directory. You can choose the backup that you want to restore and then click the Restore button to perform the restore.

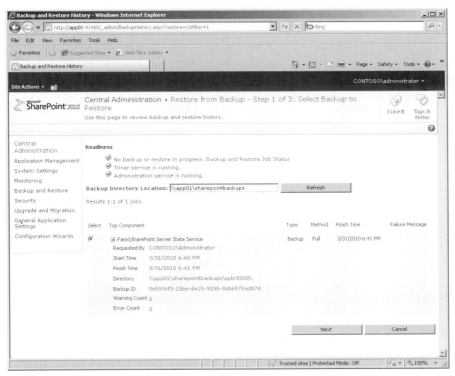

FIGURE 6-55 Selecting the backup you want to restore

The additional two steps in the backup and restore process (Select Component To Restore and Select Restore Options) and their configuration options are discussed in more detail in Chapter 17.

CONFIGURE BACKUP SETTINGS

The Configure Backup Settings page is used to define how the backup and restore operations will perform by default. If your backups run during evening hours, you can specify that additional threads be used during the backups, which should decrease the amount of time it takes to perform the backup operation. You can specify the number of threads for a restore operation. The number of threads can be set from 1 to 10; the default is 3.

If you have a default directory where all of your backups are stored, and you want this directory to be populated as the directory of choice when performing backups, you can set the default directory in the Backup File Location section of the Default Backup And Restore Settings page, as shown in Figure 6-56. This directory will also be populated automatically when you perform a restore operation using Central Administration.

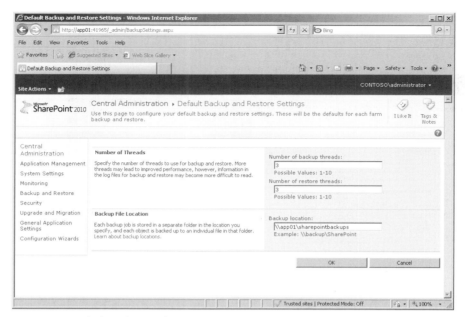

FIGURE 6-56 Default Backup And Restore Settings page

VIEW BACKUP AND RESTORE HISTORY

The options on the Backup And Restore History page allow you to view backup jobs that have already been performed that are located in the directory specified in the Backup Directory Location as shown in Figure 6-57. On this page, you can select a single backup to restore and then click the Begin Restore Process link to bring you to the second page of the Restore From Backup interface.

CHECK BACKUP AND RESTORE JOB STATUS

During a backup or restore operation, you can view its progress by clicking the Backup And Restore Job Status link to display information about the operation, as shown in Figure 6-58. This page automatically refreshes, or you can click the Refresh button to refresh it to provide current status information.

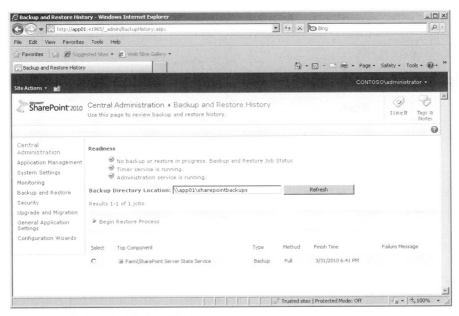

FIGURE 6-57 Backup And Restore History page

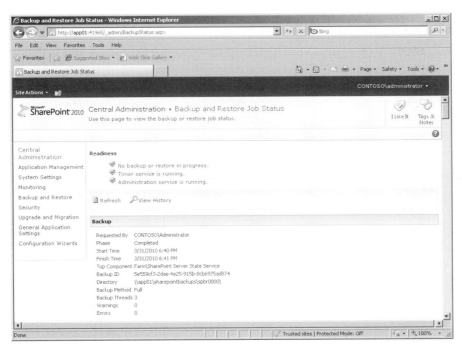

FIGURE 6-58 Backup And Restore Job Status page

Granular Backup

SharePoint 2010 provides a way for you to back up more granular items stored in SharePoint including site collections, sites, lists, and libraries. In previous versions you could only accomplish more granular backups using STSADM commands. Furthermore, you can now also recover data from a database that is no longer part of your SharePoint farm. For instance, if you were working on a project that had a site collection or site collections stored in one database that was not used to store any other site collections, and after the project was completed, the database was deleted, you could restore the database using a SQL Server restore so that you could again access the content in that database.

PERFORM A SITE COLLECTION BACKUP

Site collection backups allow you to use the Central Administration GUI to back up an entire site collection using the interface shown in Figure 6-59. You begin by locating the site collection that you want to back up in the Site Collection drop-down menu on this page. You then specify the name of the backup file and the location where you want to store it. If you choose the Overwrite Existing File check box, the backup overwrites a file that currently exists in that directory that has the same file name. Click Start Backup to back up the site collection to the file you specified.

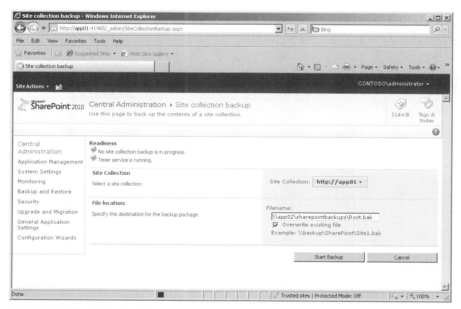

FIGURE 6-59 Site Collection Backup page

EXPORT A SITE OR LIST

The Site Or List Export interface lets you locate a list or library contained within a site and site collection and then export it to a specific directory in the specified file name. The file extension used when exporting content is .cmp, which you specify in the File Location area shown in Figure 6-60. Optionally, you can export the SharePoint security settings as well to keep the existing security configurations of the content intact. If you are using versioning on the library you are exporting, you can also choose what versions are exported using the Export Versions drop-down list. You can choose from the following version options when configuring your export.

- All Versions
- Last Major
- Current Version
- Last Major And Last Minor

IMPORTANT   Be very careful when selecting a version to use when exporting a library! The default for this setting is All Versions, which means that every version of every document in the document library will be exported. This can create a very large file, and it can impact the duration of the export process.

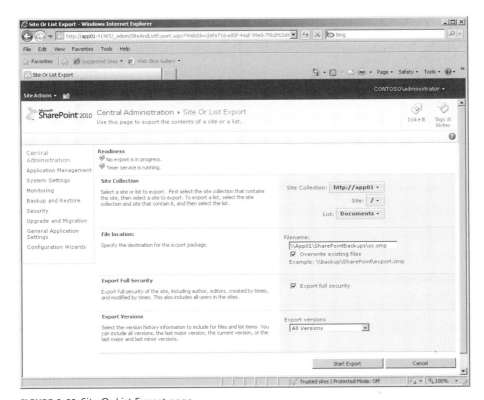

FIGURE 6-60 Site Or List Export page

RECOVER DATA FROM AN UNATTACHED CONTENT DATABASE

SharePoint 2010 introduces the capability to access databases that are available in SQL Server but aren't currently part of the farm's content databases. This eliminates the need to build a second farm to perform granular recoveries, which was the method recommended in SharePoint Server 2007 to recover data from an unattached database. Accessing unattached content databases directly in SharePoint allows you to restore site collections, sites, libraries, and lists from these SQL Server databases.

What does this mean? You can now access any restored SharePoint content database on any SQL server and use SharePoint to connect to it. Using the interface shown in Figure 6-61, you can browse the contents of the database, back up a site collection, or export a site or list to retrieve content from this database. After the backup or export completes, you can restore the content to the appropriate place in your existing SharePoint farm.

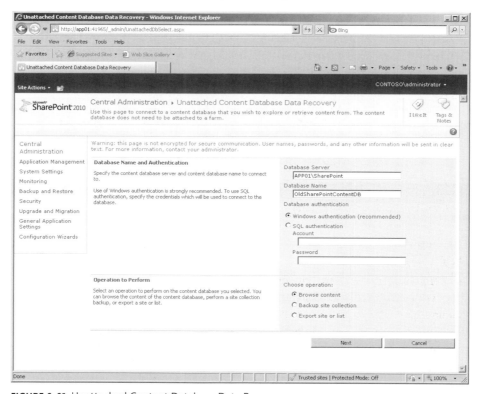

FIGURE 6-61 Unattached Content Database Data Recovery page

CHECK GRANULAR BACKUP JOB STATUS

The Granular Backup Job Status page (shown in Figure 6-62) allows you to view the status of site collection backups or site, list, or library export processes. The page is divided into two sections—one that displays the progress of a site collection backup and the other that displays the progress of an export operation. Each section on the page contains two categories of jobs—current and previous. This allows you to see information about jobs that have already completed as well as jobs that are currently in progress. You can use the Refresh link to refresh the data on the screen with current information.

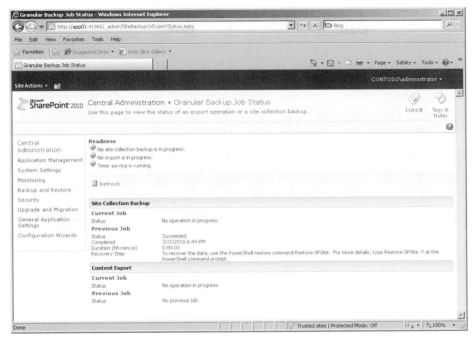

FIGURE 6-62 Granular Backup Job Status page

Security

SharePoint 2010 includes several security options that enable global configuration for better control of security. These options are accessed using the Security functional category in Central Administration. When you make changes to many of the options in this management section, they will have a global effect on all SharePoint 2010 servers in your farm, so it is important that you understand the available options. There are three general sections of security management in this category.

- Users
- General Security
- Information Policy

Users

This section provides configuration and management options for managing the farm administrators, Active Directory distribution groups, and user policies for Web applications.

MANAGE THE FARM ADMINISTRATORS GROUP

This setting allows you to add and remove users or groups as administrators in the SharePoint 2010 farm. You should always use an Active Directory security group so that you can easily swap out users in the group without affecting security in SharePoint.

Controlling the Number of Farm Administrators

By default, the BUILTIN\Administrators group has farm administration permissions. It is recommended that you add the Active Directory security group immediately after a successful installation of SharePoint and then remove the BUILTIN\Administrators group to prevent the members of this group from having full SharePoint administrator permissions. You want to be extremely selective about who becomes part of the Farm Administrators group, because they have the capability to perform any task at any level in the farm. There should only be a few select individuals who have these permissions.

Being an administrator in SharePoint 2010 does not give the user the right to create Web applications in IIS; that still requires local administrator rights on the server. Additionally, it does not give the user the right to manage databases in SQL Server. Additional permissions are required to perform SQL Server tasks such as backups, restores, and changes to database properties.

APPROVE OR REJECT DISTRIBUTION GROUPS

If you have chosen to enable incoming e-mail through the System Settings functional category, one of the options you have is to allow SharePoint groups to have e-mail addresses so that new distribution groups can be created in Active Directory. By default, when new distribution groups are created or deleted, these operations require farm administrator approval before the actual create or delete operation is performed in Active Directory.

SPECIFY WEB APPLICATION USER POLICY

This topic was discussed earlier in this chapter in the section titled "Policies for Web Applications."

General Security

There are several general security settings that are managed in the General Security section of Central Administration. Some of these security settings are farm level settings, and others are Web application settings. The following sections distinguish between these when discussing each of the General Security options.

CONFIGURE MANAGED ACCOUNTS

SharePoint 2010 introduces the concept of managed accounts, which are used to define an account in Active Directory and then configure it to automatically change the password. This enables SharePoint administrators to comply with strict Active Directory account policies in which service accounts need to have their passwords changed regularly to adhere to Active Directory policies. For this setting to work correctly, the Active Directory administrator must configure a Group Policy to enforce the password change policy.

This account management option allows SharePoint to update all the components that are using this service account with the new password change, which avoids disruption to any of the services using the Active Directory account, such as application pools.

You would use the interface shown in Figure 6-63 to specify the user name of the Active Directory account that will be registered as a managed account. You also use this page to specify when you want the password to be changed and if you want e-mail notifications sent before the password is changed.

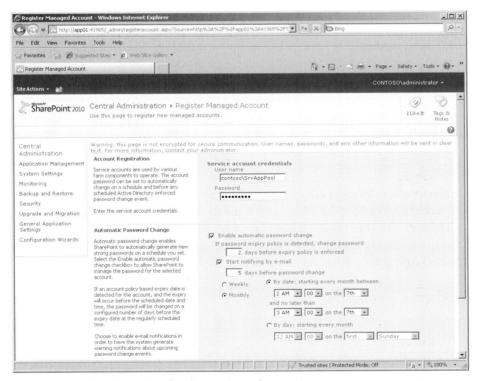

FIGURE 6-63 Registering and configuring a managed account

CONFIGURE SERVICE ACCOUNTS

This option allows you to manage service accounts that are being used by a SharePoint service, such as an application pool or service application. From the drop-down list on the Configure Service Accounts page, select the service you want to manage and then select the new account that you want it to use from the list of registered accounts. If your account is a new service account, then you can register it first from this page as a new SharePoint registered account.

CONFIGURE PASSWORD CHANGE SETTINGS

The Configure Password Change Settings option works in conjunction with the Configure Managed Accounts settings to automatically change passwords. To send notifications of the impending password changes, as well as to send error messages regarding the actual password change event, you must complete the fields in the Configure Password Change Settings interface. Specify the e-mail address where you want these notifications sent.

> **BEST PRACTICES** Use a farm administrators group e-mail address as the address to send these notifications so that all farm administrators know about the impending password change as well as any problems that might occur during the change event.

SPECIFY AUTHENTICATION PROVIDERS

This topic was discussed earlier in this chapter in the section titled "Authentication Providers."

MANAGE TRUSTS

Trusts are created when two farms are communicating with each other by allowing one of the farms to consume services from the other farm. This inter-farm configuration makes it easy for service applications to be shared between farms. When establishing the trust relationship between farms, the consuming farm must trust the root Certificate Authority (CA) for SSL on the farm that is hosting the shared service applications.

MANAGE ANTIVIRUS SETTINGS

Before you can manage antivirus settings, you must first install a SharePoint 2010–compatible antivirus product such as Microsoft Forefront. After you install the antivirus product, it will either update the page shown in Figure 6-64 for you, or you can open the page and modify the settings to determine how the antivirus software will manage SharePoint documents.

After the software is installed, you can use the Antivirus settings page to configure the level of scanning that you want to set. You can choose from the following four scanning options.

- Scan Documents On Upload
- Scan Documents On Download

- Allow Users To Download Infected Documents
- Attempt To Clean Infected Documents

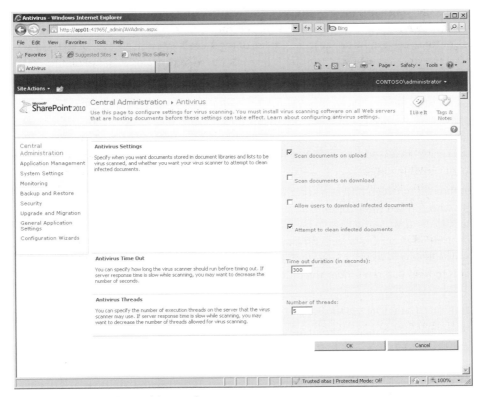

FIGURE 6-64 Configuring antivirus settings

You can also configure how long the virus scanner should run before it times out; the default is 5 minutes. Lastly, you can configure the number of threads that are used by the scanner. Both of these settings can impact the performance of both the scanner and the server hosting the antivirus software, so be sure to analyze the impact of any changes you make.

DEFINE BLOCKED FILE TYPES

This topic was discussed earlier in this chapter in the section titled "Blocked File Types."

MANAGE WEB PART SECURITY

This topic was discussed earlier in this chapter in the section titled "Web Part Security."

CONFIGURE SELF-SERVICES SITE CREATION

This topic was discussed earlier in this chapter in the section titled "Self-Service Site Creation."

Information Policy

There are two options available for defining general settings at the document level for utilization, access, and control in SharePoint 2010.

CONFIGURE INFORMATION RIGHTS MANAGEMENT

Security is always an important consideration for system administrators and management alike. Even though SharePoint 2010 has file security built into the document libraries, you still might require an additional layer of security. Information rights management (IRM) is built on top of a certificate-based infrastructure that allows users to restrict access to a document not just by name but also by their certificates. Information rights management requires both client- and server-based add-on software to work; there are also additional Client Access License (CAL) costs involved.

The difference between IRM and security is important to understand. Security focuses on regulating who can see what content. IRM targets what can be done with the content after it is accessed by the user. Some people have used the terms *security* and *privacy* to differentiate between the two concepts, with privacy describing the feature offered by IRM. Those who work extensively in the security field don't like the privacy term, but nevertheless, they are good terms to help you remember the difference between security and IRM.

CONFIGURE INFORMATION MANAGEMENT POLICY

Policies were introduced in SharePoint Server 2007, and except for a name change for one of the options (Expiration changed to Retention), they provide the same options at this level in SharePoint 2010. You can configure four farm level policies that are available for lists, libraries, and content types for use throughout the entire farm. Table 6-5 describes these default policies. By default, all policies are enabled and available throughout the farm, but all of them have the option of being decommissioned if you want to disable the functionality they provide.

TABLE 6-5 Information Management Policies

POLICY NAME	POLICY DESCRIPTION
Labels	Gives users the ability to view and add metadata labels in a document itself. These labels can be printed with the document and also can be searchable attributes.
Auditing	Allows list and libraries to audit the actions of users in the library such as modify or delete, download, and back up.
Retention	Provides a method for processing content that has been assigned an expiration setting, possibly through a workflow for archiving.
Barcodes	Allows unique barcodes to be inserted in documents that can then be printed with the document or searched.

Upgrade and Migration

The Upgrade And Migration option available in Central Administration is useful when performing upgrades, applying patches, and migrating content in SharePoint 2010. This functional category provides information about

- Upgrading from a lower-level SharePoint 2010 edition to a higher-level SharePoint 2010 edition (Standard Edition to Enterprise Edition)
- Upgrading from a previous version of SharePoint to a newer version of SharePoint (SharePoint Server 2007 to SharePoint 2010)
- Viewing the patch and service pack status of products in your SharePoint 2010
- Viewing the status of your SharePoint farm databases during an upgrade

Upgrade and Patch Management

This section is used to manage different aspects of upgrades, migrations, and deployment of service packs and patches as they become available for SharePoint 2010. There are six areas within this section that are used in most situations that involve adding new editions or new versions of SharePoint.

CONVERT FARM LICENSE TYPE

This option is used to upgrade from a lower-level edition of SharePoint to a higher-level edition. For instance, if you are running SharePoint 2010 Standard Edition and you realize your organization requires the functionality available in the Enterprise Edition, you can access this option to enter the Enterprise Edition product key. The product key you enter either during the installation of SharePoint or anytime afterwards using the Convert Farm License Type interface determines what functionality and features are available in your SharePoint installation.

When you install an edition of SharePoint initially, all of the software's features and functionality are installed, but the availability of some of the features is determined by the product key you originally entered. After you acquire an upgraded product key, you can enter the new product key and additional features can be enabled.

ENABLE ENTERPRISE FEATURES

After you enter a new product key for an upgrade, as described in the previous section, the Enable Enterprise Features interface allows you to enable the additional features and functionality available with the new product key. After you enable the Enterprise features, all newly created sites are able to access the Enterprise features and functionality.

ENABLE FEATURES ON EXISTING SITES

Even after you enter a new product key for an upgrade edition and then enable Enterprise Edition features, you still must enable the additional features and functionality on existing sites. The Enable Features On Existing Sites interface allows you to activate the new features on all existing sites in your farm.

CHECK PRODUCT AND PATCH INSTALLATION STATUS

This option allows you to view the effective version numbers of all products installed along with information about inconsistencies with any of the products on each server in your farm. Use this page during the patching process to determine if there are any servers missing a service pack or hotfix, or to determine if there were any problems during the patching process.

For example, if you have just added Service Pack 1 to your five SharePoint servers, and one server is not responding correctly to Reporting Service requests, you can view this page to determine if the troubled server has the same effective version of SharePoint as all the other servers. If you find that it doesn't, you will know what needs to be applied by checking the version to determine what it is missing. Then you can apply the missing fix to resolve the problem.

Also on the Check Product And Patch Installation Status page, you will notice some of the entries are highlighted. This indicates linked text that you can click to go directly to a relevant Knowledge Base (KB) article on the Microsoft website that will help you resolve the problem.

REVIEW DATABASE STATUS

You use this option to view the location of your databases and check the status of the databases that are being used throughout your entire farm. All content databases, service application databases, and even the configuration database are listed here. This page also shows you if there are any inconsistencies in the versions of the databases in your farm to assist in troubleshooting problems or issues you are trying to resolve.

You can click the name of one of your content databases to display the Manage Content Database Settings page, which allows you to modify the availability of the database, set the number of site collections allowed in the database, specify a failover server option, and even delete the database from SQL Server.

> **IMPORTANT** Be sure you have a backup of the database before you delete it, in case there is information in the database that someone needs to recover after the database has been deleted.

CHECK UPGRADE STATUS

You use the last option in the Upgrade And Migration area of Central Administration after performing an upgrade to verify the upgrade was successful or identify any errors that occurred during the upgrade process. This option not only shows if an upgrade fails, it also directs you to the SharePoint root directory, %CommonProgramFiles%\Microsoft Shared\ web server extensions\14\Logs, where you can find additional information about why it failed. There are two types of files generated in the Logs directory: an upgrade log (.log) and an upgrade error log file (.err). The upgrade error log file contains a consolidated version of any errors and warnings that occurred during the upgrade.

General Application Settings

General Application Settings provide you with the ability to manage settings for various applications that are available in SharePoint 2010. This functional category contains a lot of the items that don't fit particularly well under any of the other categories, so you will see that there are several different types of configurations you can perform with the settings in this category.

External Service Connections

This section allows you to configure Web application level Send To connectors and configure which Web applications can perform document conversions.

CONFIGURE SEND TO CONNECTIONS

This option is new to SharePoint 2010, and it allows farm administrators to create custom Send To connectors for each Web application that appears when a user chooses the Send To option for a document accessed from within that Web application. The configuration of a Web application Send To connection has two parts.

- Define the Send To location.
- Define the behavior that takes place when someone uses the Send To option.

To define the Send To location, you must enter a display name and the URL of the Send To location, as shown in Figure 6-65. This URL must contain a location of another document library.

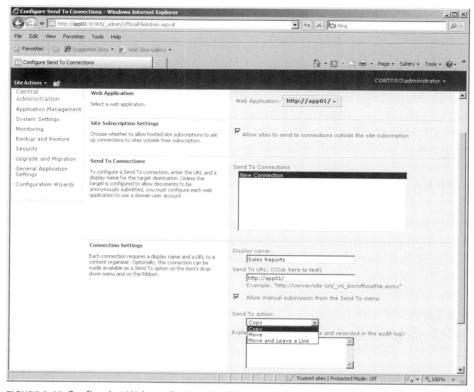

FIGURE 6-65 Configuring Web application Send To connections

If the Web application is configured to do so, the user can select the Send To locations using the drop-down menu available with the document or by clicking the document and then clicking the Send To icon on the Ribbon. After the user selects the Send To option for a document, the behavior you define for that Send To connection determines what happens to the original document. The following three options are available.

- Copy
- Move
- Move And Leave A link

The purpose of the Send To location has a great impact on what behavior will take place for the documents being sent to that location. For example, if the Send To action is being used to locate items in a central document repository, then you may want to move the document but leave a link to its new location.

CONFIGURE DOCUMENT CONVERSIONS

The document conversion feature is responsible for taking different types of files and converting them to HTML. This allows them to be uploaded to a defined pages library where the HTML version is needed. However, in order to configure this feature, the following two services first must be started on the Services On Server screen.

- Document Conversion Load Balancer Service
- Document Conversions Launcher Service

After these two required services are started, you can configure document conversion settings on the Configure Document Conversions page shown in Figure 6-66. To begin the configuration, you must first select the Web application to apply the conversion to and then enable the document conversion option by clicking the Enable Document Conversions For This Site option. Furthermore, you use the Load Balancer drop-down menu to specify the server responsible for performing the actual conversion. You then create a schedule defining how often you want the conversion process to run.

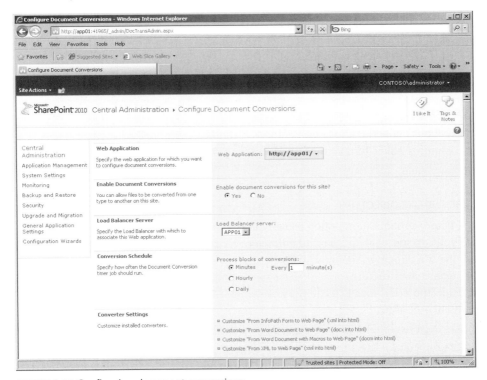

FIGURE 6-66 Configuring document conversions

InfoPath Forms Services

The forms services are used to configure, manage, and upload your forms into a central repository. The forms can then be consumed and used by users from within their sites. There are five management areas within forms services.

- Manage form templates
- Configure InfoPath forms services
- Upload form template
- Manage data connection files
- Configure InfoPath Forms Services Web Service Proxy

There are several form templates available out-of-the-box, but you may need to create and upload your own custom forms. After you have uploaded your forms, you can define the settings for the forms by configuring the forms services. At this point, you configure specific connection settings such as session state, post backs, and requiring SSL for basic authentication connections.

By default, forms service is not enabled to allow connections from Web services. If you want to allow this, access the Configure Forms Services Web Service Proxy interface and select the check box next to the Enable InfoPath Forms Services Web Service Proxy setting. Next, select the check box to Enable InfoPath Forms Services Web Service Proxy For User Forms.

Site Directory

The configurations defined in the Site Directory functional category allow you to determine where you want site collections created and whether or not you will scan for invalid site directory links.

CONFIGURE THE SITE DIRECTORY

The site directory configuration option allows you to specify a URL to the Site Directory page, and you can specify if you want to enforce new category site listings when a new site is created in the site directory. Site directories are used to create a taxonomy that provides an easy-to-navigate site structure for all sites created in the site hierarchy. As users create sites, they will be prompted to specify a category or several categories for new sites, such as operations, maintenance, or IT.

By default, users are not required to specify a category for new sites, however, which can make it more difficult for users to find sites using the site directory. By changing this setting to require a user to specify categories for all new sites, you can apply some measure of control for maintaining accurate listings.

SCAN SITE DIRECTORY LINKS

The other setting option available in the Site Directory functional category is the Site Directory Links Scan. This setting allows you to specify a site directory URL and then have it perform a lookup using a site's title and description against the sites listed in the site directory listing. If the scan finds any discrepancies, it will optionally change the title and description in the site directory to match the actual sites title and description. However, this operation does not fix broken links. Managing the sites listed in the site directory is a manual process.

SharePoint Designer

This topic was discussed earlier in this chapter in the section titled "SharePoint Designer."

Search

Search settings are used to manage Search service options. This is one entry point you can use to manage all of the Search service administrative settings as well as the performance impact the Search service has on your farm. Chapter 11, "Search Server 2010 and FAST Search: Architecture and Administration," provides additional information about managing Search service options.

FARM-WIDE SEARCH ADMINISTRATION

This option allows you to configure farm-wide search administration settings, including the following.

- **Farm-wide search settings**   Define the following three settings:
  - **Proxy Server**   Define proxy servers settings used when crawling external content.
  - **Time-out**   Specify the time the Search service will wait to connect to content sources while attempting to crawl content. By default, the settings are 60 seconds to establish the connection and 60 seconds for acknowledgment that the connection was established.
  - **Ignore SSL warnings**   Select the check box for this option if you trust the sites you are crawling even if the Search service encounters a site with a certificate that doesn't exactly match.
- **Access to Search service applications**   Provides lists of Search service applications with a link to the administrative tasks shown in Figure 6-67 that are associated with the search service application.

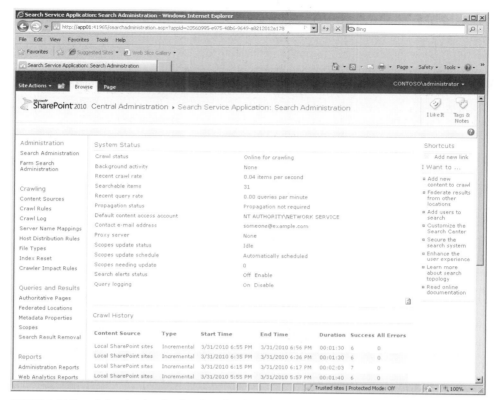

FIGURE 6-67 Search Service Application Search Administration page

CRAWLER IMPACT RULES

Use this option to define and manage crawler impact rules. Crawler impact rules are used to manage the performance of the crawler during the crawl. To create a new rule, click Crawler Impact Rules on the Search Administration page to open the Crawler Impact Rules page and then click Add Rule to complete the information shown in Figure 6-68. You can specify the URL of the site and the number of documents to crawl at one time. The more documents that are crawled simultaneously, the more the performance of the server will be impacted. The default is 8 documents, but you can decrease this setting to as low as 1 document or increase it to as high as 64 documents. Alternatively, you can specify that only one document gets crawled at a time and specify the number of seconds to wait between each document crawl.

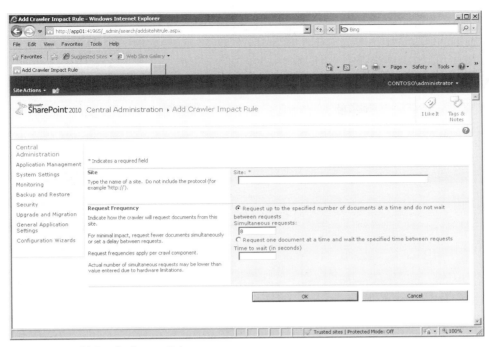

FIGURE 6-68 Add Crawler Impact Rule page

Content Deployment

In SharePoint 2010, content deployment is a feature of the Web Content Management (WCM) that allows multifarm topologies for deploying content from sites or site collections to remote sites or site collections. You could use the ability to transfer content in this way to create a staging environment in which you have an authoring environment that needs to go to an approval environment to be approved, and finally on to a production environment. You can use this flexibility of content deployment in both intranet environments and Internet-facing sites. Because you are deploying the content between site collections, this feature can be used between sites on the same server as well as sites on completely different farms. Multiple farms can have a configuration in which you have an Internet-facing Web site in one farm while another farm resides behind a firewall. You make changes to the Web site in the farm behind the firewall and then deploy those changes to the Internet-facing Web site at specified intervals.

CONFIGURE CONTENT DEPLOYMENT

Before you can create deployment paths and jobs, you must first enable the destination farm to accept incoming jobs, as shown in Figure 6-69. You can then specify which servers will be performing the import and export operations in the farm to allow deployment jobs to be sent and received by those servers in the farm. You can also enable encryption for improved security during the deployment of data, and you can specify the temporary storage location for files that are involved in the deployment process.

NOTE Make sure you have plenty of disk space on the temporary storage location folder, because some deployment jobs can be quite large if the source site contains a large amount of content in its lists and libraries.

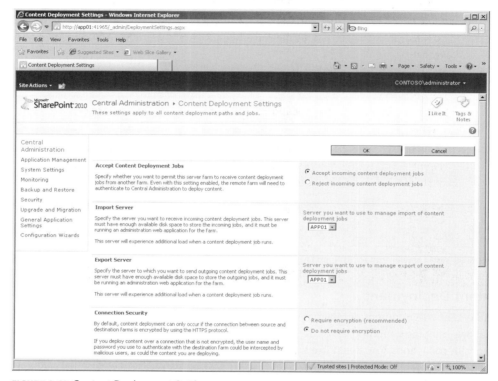

FIGURE 6-69 Content Deployment Settings page

CONFIGURE CONTENT DEPLOYMENT PATHS AND JOBS

In content deployment, you are restricted to deploying the content in one direction—it is not a two-way synchronization tool. To deploy content, you need to configure both a path and job. The path defines the source site or site collection as well as the destination site or site collection. The job defines the frequency with which the content is deployed. Furthermore, you can configure the deployment to affect only content that has changed since the last deployment, so you are not deploying content that has not changed. This reduces the amount of content being transferred.

Creating a Content Deployment Path   When a farm is enabled to accept incoming jobs, you can create the path between the sites and also the jobs that utilize those paths. A *path* in content deployment is a relationship between two specific site collections that must be configured; you also must designate the authentication method to use when a connection is established to complete the deployment. To create a content deployment path, complete the following steps using the Create Content Deployment Path page shown in Figure 6-70.

1. Enter a path name and description.

2. Select the source Web application and the associate site or site collection.

3. Specify the URL of the destination Central Administration website that will receive the incoming content. Ensure that the website has been enabled to receive incoming deployment jobs.

4. Specify the authentication method that should be used to establish the connection to the destination server.

5. Specify the destination Web application and the site or site collection that is receiving the content.

6. Indicate whether to deploy user names and security information along with the deployed content, such as the Access Control Lists (ACLs) and group membership for the content stored in the document libraries.

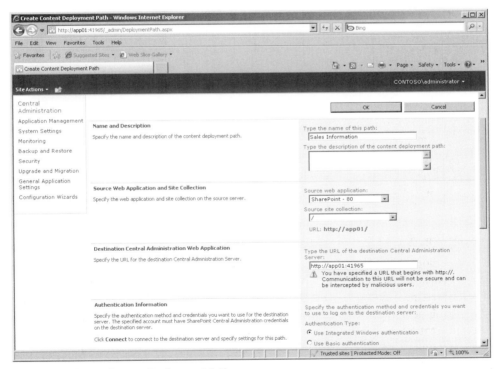

FIGURE 6-70 Create Content Deployment Path page

Creating a Content Deployment Job After you have defined a path, you can associate multiple jobs with the path to utilize the relationship between site collections. The jobs you create can be set up to deploy only certain sites in the site collection as well as to identify when the job is scheduled to run. To create a content deployment job, follow these steps using the Create Content Deployment Job page shown in Figure 6-71.

1. Enter a job name and description.

2. Select a path to use for the job. (You can only associate the job with one path.)

3. Specify whether or not you want to create and use SQL Server snapshots for the job.

4. Choose whether you want to deploy the entire site collection or subsites contained in site collection.

5. Create a schedule for the job that defines how frequently the deployment should occur.

6. Choose if you want to deploy all the content or just changes since the last time the job ran.

7. Define the settings for the e-mail notification process for job successes and failures.

You can also configure reports that will follow the progress of the jobs as they transfer between the site collections.

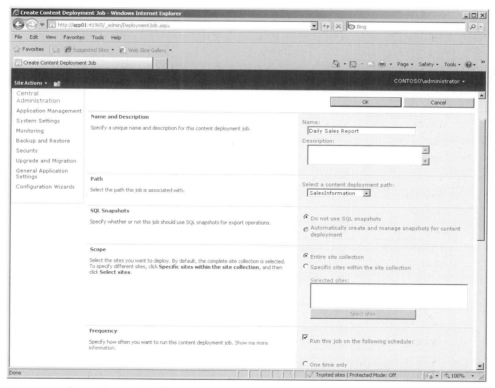

FIGURE 6-71 Create Content Deployment Job page

CHECK DEPLOYMENT OF SPECIFIC CONTENT

You use this option to check the deployment status for a particular object. Type the URL of the object in the URL box and then click Check Status to get details about the source and destination of the deployment process.

Configuration Wizards

By default, the Configuration Wizards functional category contains only one section, Farm Configuration, and one option within that section, the Launch The Farm Configuration Wizard link. Microsoft anticipates that additional wizards will be added to SharePoint Central Administration, either by Microsoft or other third-party vendors; when they are available, they can be stored in this functional category.

Launch the Farm Configuration Wizard

If you chose not to run the Farm Configuration Wizard during SharePoint installation, you can still run it at a later time by accessing it here, through Central Administration. You use this wizard to install and configure the numerous service applications available in SharePoint 2010.

After you launch the wizard, you will be prompted to specify if you want the wizard to walk you through the settings to install and configure the service applications, which is the default, or if you prefer to configure everything yourself. If you choose the option to configure the settings yourself, you will exit out of the wizard.

If you choose the option Walk Me Through The Wizard Settings, you will notice that any service applications that have already been configured are unavailable. However, if you have not installed any service applications before running the wizard, all of the available service applications will be selected to be installed and configured, except for the Lotus Notes Connector.

You can clear the check boxes associated with any service applications that you don't want the wizard to install and configure, then simply run the wizard again at a later date if you find that you require those services. After the wizard completes, it may prompt you to create a site collection for your intranet portal, and again you let the wizard create this site collection or choose not to do so and create your own at your convenience.

Summary

This chapter concentrated on the options available to you on the Central Administration home page, such as customizing the page and defining the services and roles that are provided by the servers in the farm topology. This chapter did not cover all of the sections of Central Administration, because other chapters in this book go into those topics in much more detail.

You looked at the configuration options for application management at both farm level and individual Web application level. Although not all the available options are required, many of them are enabled by default for all Web applications; it is a design decision to establish which services are required. The Web Application Ribbon in SharePoint 2010 also makes it very easy to configure multiple mechanisms of security and authentication that, combined with zone mapping for different user locations, provides a robust hosting and collaboration scenario.

You should now have an understanding of what you can manage through Central Administration, including the options available in SharePoint 2010 for configuring service applications, improved monitoring options, granular backup and restore options, upgrade and patch management, and SMS messaging.

Search was not addressed in the discussion of General Application Settings in this chapter because it is covered in detail in Chapters 11, 12, and 13.

One of the most important things to remember about configuring application settings such as managed paths and site quota templates in SharePoint 2010 is that a single change can have a cascading effect on many users and sites housed within a single Web application, so when you want to change settings, plan ahead and configure application settings at an early stage, before the site collections and sites are created.

Scaling Out a SharePoint Farm

This chapter focuses on Services Federation and scaling out your Microsoft SharePoint 2010 environment. As a SharePoint professional, you need to understand when and how to scale out your environment based on the unique needs that your organization faces day to day.

The chapter starts with a history of SharePoint farms and how they arrived where they are today. The rest of the chapter covers Services Federation and different aspects of scaling out servers. Services Federation focuses on the services themselves, whereas scaling out focuses on which servers host those services and the commensurate roles you will use to scale out your SharePoint environment as your environment grows and changes. These topics are presented in an order that is easy to follow for both the new and the seasoned SharePoint administrators. The new SharePoint administrator might do best by reading this chapter straight through, because each section forms a basis for the next section. After a brief look at the history of SharePoint farms, you'll learn about service applications, and then the chapter concludes with a discussion of how to add servers to your farm. Note that the examples for this chapter were created on the Amazon Cloud.

History of SharePoint Farms

In SharePoint Products and Technologies, the concept of shared services was first introduced in SharePoint Portal Server 2003. In that product, if you wanted to share My Sites or the search index between portals, you designated an existing portal as the Shared Services Portal. In most cases, you created a new portal to host those shared services, but you weren't required to do so. One shared services portal could have up to 99 child portals in that product. It was a "one size fits all" approach to shared services, but it also offered basic services that needed to be shared in multiportal environments.

In Microsoft SharePoint Server 2007, services were moved to a single Web application that you designated as the Shared Services Provider (SSP). The 2007 SSP allowed you to enable services and manage them from a central point within Central Administration. The SharePoint Server 2007 SSP provided the following services.

- Configuration profiles
- Audiences
- Excel Services
- Business Data Catalogs (BDC)
- Search services that could be shared between Web applications

You could create more than one SSP, but each Web application in the farm could be associated only with one SSP. If you did not need all the services or wanted to configure a Web application to utilize a specific service, however, you were not able to do this in SharePoint Server 2007.

These and other problems are corrected in SharePoint 2010. Microsoft restructured the entire service architecture, moving away from shared service providers (SSPs) and its all-or-nothing model to a more flexible and granular service application model. Each service can be enabled one or more times and can be associated (or grouped) in any way needed. This new model enables you to provision custom or third-party services integrated into business solutions and allows you to customize the services that are available extensively within designated Web applications. Figure 7-1 shows a comparison between the SSP architecture in SharePoint Server 2007 and the new service application architecture in SharePoint 2010.

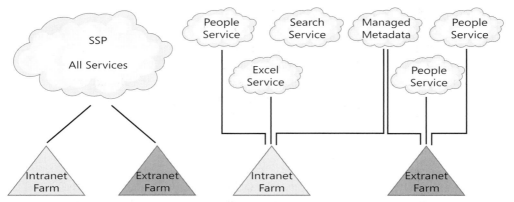

FIGURE 7-1 SSP architecture models in SharePoint Server 2007 (left) versus SharePoint 2010 (right)

The use of service applications, as shown in Figure 7-1, provides the new model adopted by Microsoft in SharePoint 2010 to replace the Shared Services Provider (SSP) model that was introduced in SharePoint Server 2007. This new service applications model is also incorporated into Microsoft SharePoint Foundation 2010.

Services Federation

In SharePoint 2010, you need to differentiate between services and a service application. A *service* is a component that provides an output that can be utilized by an application. A *service application* is an application that is built to utilize one or more services that exist in the environment. Services in SharePoint 2010 are the foundation for service applications. Some of these services are associated with service applications. You deploy your service applications by starting the associated services on the desired server, selecting those same services when running the initial Configuration Wizard, or by using Windows PowerShell. The number of services running varies depending on the business requirements of your environment.

Services that are commonly associated with a service application that can be consumed by Web applications are explained in Table 7-1 and Table 7-2.

TABLE 7-1 SharePoint 2010 Services

SERVICE APPLICATIONS	DESCRIPTION	STORES DATA?	CROSS FARM
Access Services	View, edit, and interact with Microsoft Access 2010 database in a browser.	Cache	No
Business Data Connectivity	Access line-of-business (LOB) data systems.	Database	Yes
Excel Services	Viewing and interact with Microsoft Excel files in a browser.	Cache	No
Managed Metadata Service	Access managed taxonomy hierarchies, keywords, and social tagging infrastructure as well as content type publishing across site collections.	Database	Yes
PerformancePoint	PerformancePoint Services enables users to create interactive dashboards that display key performance indicators (KPIs) and data visualizations in the form of scorecards, reports, and filters.	Database	No
PowerPoint	View, edit, and broadcast Microsoft PowerPoint presentations in a Web browser.	Cache	No
Search	Crawls content, produces index partitions, and serves search queries.	Database	Yes
Secure Store Service	Provides single sign-on authentication to access multiple applications or services.	Database	Yes
State Service	Provides temporary storage of user session data for SharePoint Server components.	Database	No
Usage and Health Data Collection	Collects farm-wide usage and health data and provides the ability to view various usage and health reports.	Database	No

SERVICE APPLICATIONS	DESCRIPTION	STORES DATA?	CROSS FARM
User Profile	Adds support for My Sites, Profiles pages, Social Tagging, and other social computing features.	Database	Yes
Visio Graphics Service	Allows viewing and refresh of published Microsoft Visio diagrams in a Web browser.	Blob Cache	No
Web Analytics	Provides Web Service interfaces.		Yes
Word Automation Services	Performs automated bulk document conversions.	Cache	No
SharePoint Foundation Subscription Setting Service	Tracks subscription IDs and settings for services that are deployed in partitioned mode. (Windows PowerShell only)	Database	No

The Microsoft Office Web applications are not cross-farm services. Microsoft Project Server 2010 stores data in a database. Table 7-2 provides details about these types of Web applications.

TABLE 7-2 Office Web Apps Services

OFFICE WEB APPS SERVICES	DESCRIPTION
<ul><li>Microsoft Word 2010 Viewing</li><li>Microsoft PowerPoint 2010</li><li>Excel Services in SharePoint 2010</li><li>Microsoft OneNote 2010</li></ul>	Office Web Apps is a new Web-based productivity offering from Microsoft Office 2010 suites. Office Web Apps services include companions to Microsoft Word 2010, Microsoft Excel 2010, Microsoft PowerPoint 2010, and Microsoft OneNote 2010. These Web-based applications are stand-alone applications focused on offering access to Word 2010, PowerPoint 2010, Excel 2010, and OneNote 2010 documents through any browser across multiple platforms. They provide lightweight creation and editing capabilities in standard formats, sharing and collaboration on those documents through the browser, and a variety of Web-enabled scenarios. Documents created using these Web applications are no different than documents created using the corresponding desktop applications. The associated services are used to prepare documents for viewing and editing in a Web browser.
Microsoft Project Server 2010	Hosts one or more Microsoft Project Web Access instances, exposes scheduling functionality and other middle-tier calculations on Microsoft Project data, and exposes Web services for interacting with Microsoft Project 2010 data.

Single and Cross-Farm Services

Some services can be shared across server farms, while other services can be shared only within a single farm. Services that support sharing across farms can be run in a central farm and consumed from farms in regional locations. In this example, the shared services farm is a services-only farm and sits in your Data Center. You have multiple regional locations with their own farms, and you now have child farms consuming services from a parent farm. Computing-intensive services, such as searching and indexing, can be configured in a central farm to minimize administration overhead and to scale out those services easily and efficiently as business requirements change. You can find more information on single and cross-farm services in the section titled "Planning Service Applications Architecture" later in this chapter. Table 7-3 provides a list of both single farm services and cross-farm services.

TABLE 7-3 Services Comparison of Single and Cross-Farm Services

SINGLE FARM SERVICES	CROSS-FARM SERVICES
Access Database Services	Business Data Connectivity
Excel Services	Managed Metadata Service
PerformancePoint	Search
PowerPoint	Secure Store Service
State Service	User Profile (People)
Usage and Health Data Collection	Web Analytics
Visio Graphics Service	
Word Automation Services	

Services Applications Logical Architecture

A service application provides a resource that can be shared across sites within a farm or, in some cases, across multiple farms. The architecture for service applications consists of the following components: Internet Information Services (IIS), Web applications, and application pools. Together they help make up the logical architecture.

Internet Information Services

All service applications in a farm reside within the same IIS website, SharePoint Web Services. Within this website, Service Applications are named utilizing a long GUID format. To see the individual Web service, you must look at the physical path of that service application or select the content view. The default path for all service applications is C:\Program Files\Microsoft Office Servers\14.0\Web Services, as illustrated in Figure 7-2.

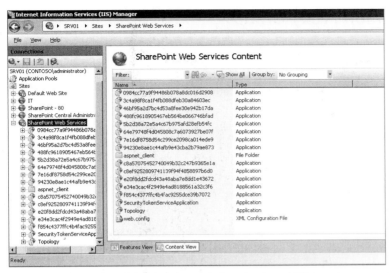

FIGURE 7-2 SharePoint IIS Web services website using long GUID naming convention

Web Applications

In SharePoint 2010, you can now configure Web applications to use only the services that are needed, rather than the entire set of services that are deployed. Just as you can now share across farms, you can also configure SharePoint 2010 to share service applications that can be shared across multiple Web applications. Web applications can also have multiple instances of the same service in a farm. You can simply create and deploy using unique names to the resulting service applications.

Application Pools

You can manipulate service applications within the application pool by deploying service applications to different application pools. This is done to achieve process isolation. Remember that each application pool has a worker process, and this is a one-to-one relation. So, more application pools equal more worker processes, which can have major performance impact on your servers. In some scenarios, the number of application pools versus server resources can present capacity planning decisions, depending on your company's business requirements. But this architecture does allow service applications to be isolated physically by creating separate instances of them and allowing them to be consumed within a separate application pool.

Service Application Proxy Groups

When you create a service application in SharePoint 2010, a service application connection is created. A connection is a virtual entity that connects Web applications to service applications. A connection is also referred to as an *application proxy*. A service application connection associates the service application to Web applications via membership in an application proxy group.

By default, a new service application connection is added to the farm's default proxy group of service application connections when you create the service application by using Central Administration. When you create a Web application, you can select the default proxy group, or you can create a custom proxy group of services. You can also add and remove service applications from the default proxy group at any time.

> **IMPORTANT** Custom proxy groups are not reusable across multiple Web applications. Each time you select the Custom option when creating a Web application, you are selecting services only for the Web application you are creating.

Some connections might include settings that can be modified. For example, assume you have a Web application called Finance, and it is connected to multiple instances of Excel Services service (default Excel Services and custom Finance Excel Services). You must indicate which of the connections is connected to the primary service application that hosts the Finance Excel Services, as Figure 7-3 illustrates.

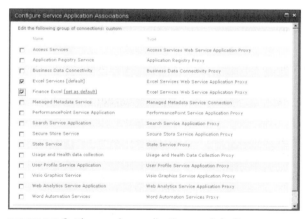

FIGURE 7-3 Setting service applications as default

> **IMPORTANT** To create a new service application group without using the Central Administration user interface (UI), you can use Windows PowerShell 2.0 commands; however, to add this group as a member of the Default service application connections group, you must use the *default* parameter.

Connections for services in the local farm are not created by the administrator, but these appear along with the list of service applications in Central Administration.

Publishing Service Applications

In SharePoint 2010, you now have the ability to extend a service application across farms; these service applications are called cross-farm services. Cross-farm services must be published first to the appropriate farm to be consumed by other farms.

Optimizing resources and reducing redundancy are two of the main reasons you would publish a service application. Another advantage is providing enterprise-wide services without installing a dedicated enterprise services farm. This was not the case in SharePoint Server 2007.

As mentioned earlier in the chapter, the following service applications are cross-farm services.

- Business Data Connectivity
- Managed Metadata
- People (User Profiles)
- Search
- Secure Store
- Web Analytics

For a farm to consume a service application that is published by another farm, the following three actions must be performed in the following order.

1. Administrators of both the publishing and consuming farms must exchange trust certificates.

   - An administrator of the consuming farm must provide two trust certificates to the publishing farm: a root certificate and a security token service (STS) certificate. An administrator of the publishing farm must provide a root certificate to the consuming farm.

   - To establish trust on the consuming farm, you must import the root certificate that was copied from the publisher farm and create a trusted root authority.

2. On the farm on which the application resides, an administrator must explicitly publish the service application.

3. An administrator must connect the consuming farm to the service application. You'll find step-by-step configuration instructions in the section titled "Configuring Service Applications" later in this chapter.

> **IMPORTANT** When working with trust certificates, you will need to use Windows PowerShell. These certificates are not available through the Certificate MMC.

Scaling Service Applications Architecture

Now that you know about the basic service applications components, you need to understand how they are applied to scaling out your SharePoint 2010 environment. SharePoint environments are broken down into tiers, with Web front-end servers constituting the Web tier, application servers included in the application tier, and database servers in the database tier.

Web Tier

All single farm and cross-farm services can reside on the Web tier, depending on the farm's topology. In small farms, it is likely that both the Web and application tiers will reside on the same servers.

Application Tier

This tier is where you'll host your service applications. SharePoint 2010 is structured so that users do not connect directly to an application in this middle tier. Instead, users always connect to servers in the Web tier, and then their calls are proxied to servers hosting the middle tier applications. In cases in which both tiers are located physically on the same servers, users still connect to the services in the Web tier and then are connected to the service applications. Figure 7-4 illustrates the client-related services for a single farm implementation.

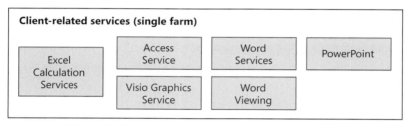

FIGURE 7-4 Client-related services

Figure 7-5 illustrates other services that can be installed in a single farm, but these are not services that your users will consume directly. These services support other applications that will produce information or a stable context in which information is better managed.

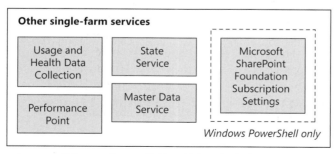

FIGURE 7-5 Other services available within a single farm

There are some services that can be consumed either within a farm or across a farm. For example, you can install the Managed Metadata Service (MMS) and utilize that within a single farm or utilize it across multiple farms. These services can also be consumed simultaneously within a farm and across farm boundaries. Figure 7-6 and 7-7 illustrates these services.

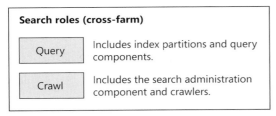

FIGURE 7-6 Cross-farm Search roles

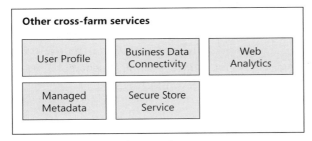

FIGURE 7-7 Other cross-farm services

Database Tier

The volume of content and business requirements for sizing will affect the number of content databases. Capacity planning for content databases is a core design function that you shouldn't ignore. SharePoint 2010 utilizes a plethora of databases for different tasks, and ensuring that your databases stay within the size needed for efficient backup and restore operations is an important aspect of your overall design considerations.

Figures 7-8, 7-9, and 7-10 help illustrate how important it is to plan correctly for the capacity your organization will require. You can see that you'll have a number of content databases to host content that users place in your SharePoint implementation, plus other databases that will support your service applications. Figure 7-8 illustrates the content databases in your farm, Figure 7-9 illustrates the possibility of having more than one index (note that each index has a separate property store for hosting the index's metadata), and Figure 7-10 illustrates other service databases that you will likely have in your deployment.

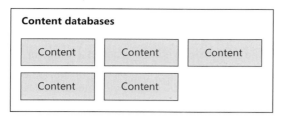

FIGURE 7-8 Content databases in SharePoint 2010

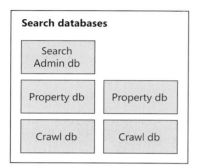

FIGURE 7-9 Search databases in SharePoint 2010

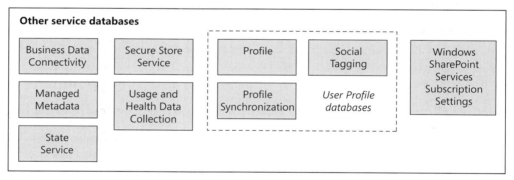

FIGURE 7-10 Other service databases in SharePoint 2010

Identifying a Logical Location of Services on Servers

Part of scaling out your farms is to know which services belong to which tier. When you have gained this understanding, you can combine that knowledge with demand estimates that you produce as part of your capacity planning activities. This information will help you know which servers you will need in your farm and which services will reside on which servers. In Figure 7-11, these services are recommended for hosting on your Web servers.

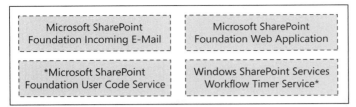

FIGURE 7-11 Web tier services in SharePoint 2010

NOTE Microsoft SharePoint Foundation User Code Service and Windows SharePoint Services Workflow Timer Service can also be deployed to application servers.

In larger environments, many SharePoint 2010 services and service applications will be hosted in the application tier on application servers dedicated to these purposes. In smaller environments, you'll find the Web front-end (WFE) servers playing a dual role of hosting application tier services on the same physical servers. Figure 7-12 illustrates the application tier services.

Access Database Services	Managed Metadata Web Service	Secure Store Service	Visio Graphics Service
Business Data Connectivity	Microsoft SharePoint Foundation Subscription Settings Service	SharePoint Server Search	Web Analytics Data Processing Service
Excel Calculation Services	PerformancePoint Service	User Profile Service	Web Analytics Web Service
Lotus Notes Connector	Search Query and Site Settings Service	User Profile Synchronization Service	Word Automation Services

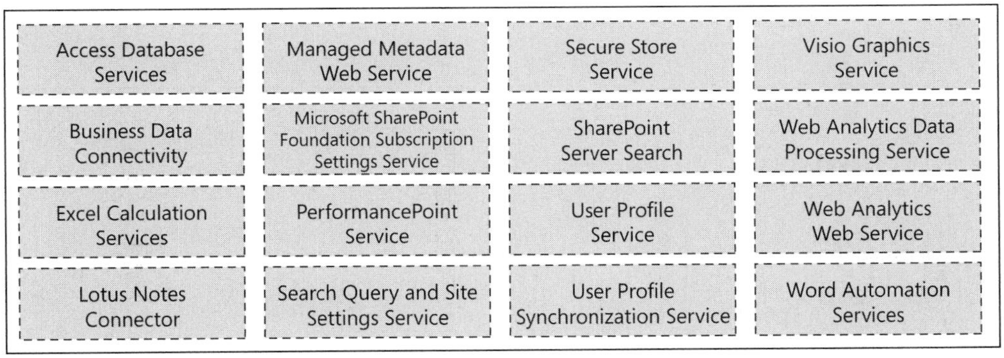

FIGURE 7-12 Application tier services

Planning Service Applications Architecture

The following list provides a short review of some of the terminology that is used in the discussion for scaling out service applications in SharePoint 2010 environments.

- **Service**   Actual program bits (binaries) deployed to servers in a farm to provide some type of functionality
- **Service machine instance**   Actual instance of the running service bits (binaries) running on an application server in the farm
- **Service application**   A specific configuration of the service in a farm

- **Service application proxy** A reference point to the service application that exists on the WFE
- **Service Consumer** A SharePoint 2010 feature that talks to the service application and provides the functionality to a user, such as a Web Part

Figure 7-13 illustrates a workflow process for service application architecture. Viewing this image from the bottom to the top, you move through a few layers to get to the services that an end user might be trying to consume. You can see that an end user can access a service consumer (a Web Part or a page). As you move upward, you see that a service consumer then communicates with a service application proxy. This proxy acts as the middle man and will continue relaying the request or communication to the service application. The service application then communicates with the service to perform the operation. Depending on the configuration and scaling of the farm, you could have multiple instances of Excel Services running on different application servers. This is where the physical instances of those services come in (service machine instances). There is redundancy within this because SharePoint 2010 has a built-in load-balance mechanism that will allow your requests to continue to be served even if an application server with that particular service is unavailable. In Figure 7-13, this redundancy is illustrated by the square around the four application servers and the two databases at the top of the figure.

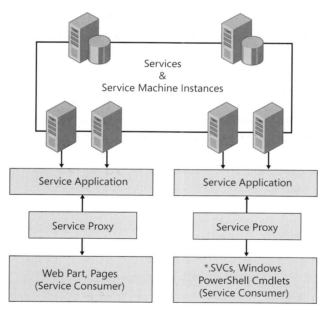

FIGURE 7-13 Service application architecture

You now have the ability to use the service applications individually as needed and to scale them in ways that help maximize your farm. When you are designing services architecture strategy for an organization, consider the ways in which you can configure the individual services to enhance your overall content sharing or isolation goals. Start thinking about grouping your services based on business requirements and compliances. The business requirements will change as the organization grows and you have to scale out your servers or redesign your farm into multiple farms.

> **NOTE** Planning for service application architecture is not necessary when you are using a limited deployment farm, but it is a good planning task to complete. Most limited deployment farms are proof of concept.

REAL WORLD   Planning a Service Application Architecture

When you plan your service application architecture, think about the following aspects of the architecture prior to configuring your service applications.

- **Richness**   The ability to deliver more features and allowing third parties to build their own "shared services"
- **Scalability**   The ability to handle larger loads, scale farms, and scale to the cloud
- **Flexibility**   The ability to be more malleable in terms of granularity

Another point of concern for administrators is performance. Understanding where your servers are in relation to the end users who are consuming those services is incredibly important. Services and the service applications associated with them can be hindered by not providing for proper performance. For instance, if you have the Search service on its own application server and it is indexing a few million documents, performance might be completely acceptable for users in the main office, but what about remote users or users in another office that may be in Europe or Asia? It is imperative that you understand how the architecture will affect performance throughout your system. You can also configure your service applications to either share resources across multiple Web applications or provide content and resource isolate. This granularity was something that was not possible in earlier versions of SharePoint.

> **NOTE** When planning your service architecture, be aware that that some of the service applications create their own databases when deployed, so additional SQL database planning and maintenance will be required.

Figure 7-14 provides a visual representation of how you could group service applications. Note that the default group is linked to multiple service applications and to two Web applications from which those services are being consumed. These service applications could be, for example, the Search service, the Metadata Manager service, or the People service. These service applications are also cross-farm services, so conceivably these Web applications could be sharing services coming from a completely different farm.

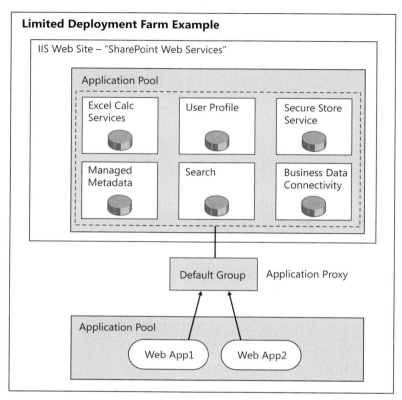

FIGURE 7-14 Shared service applications

Next, you can isolate a service application. This isolation can be due to regulatory or HIPPA compliances or some other internal business requirement. Service application isolation levels can be applied to any of the following.

- Application pool
- Web application
- Application proxy group

> **NOTE** If the service application is a cross-farm service, you could also isolate it by making it a separate farm. An example of this would be isolating the Search service on its own farm.

Figure 7-15 provides an example of an isolated service application. In this example, you can see that two Web applications are sharing services coming from the default proxy group. You also can see a third Web application that is isolated by itself, and you see the service applications that it uses—Search and Business Data Connectivity. You can imagine this as your human resources (HR) department using Search and a payroll or benefits database that contains confidential information. This information needs to be isolated and only consumed by HR, because it contains personally identifiable information (PII).

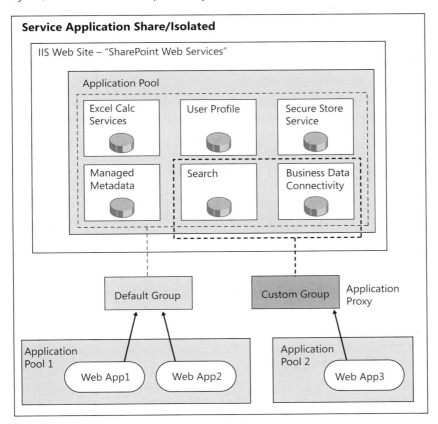

FIGURE 7-15 Shared and isolated service applications

Planning Topology Architecture

You can take the same approach to scaling out these service applications in multiple farms as you do for single farms. As user demand increases, you can scale up from a small to medium farm by adding more WFEs and applications servers, as well as additional service applications to the environment as needed.

Planning topology architecture has a few physical considerations that you need to address in order to plan how and what you will be scaling in your environments—your scaling will influence your physical topology. You should keep your host services physically close to your users and content and also keep your services close to your Active Directory to ensure better communication. Of course, your budget constraints also can affect how you plan your topology architecture.

In SharePoint 2010, when scaling out services within the same environment, you can add additional servers at each tier; when building out these application services, you always want to group similar services together. For example, a server can have just the search service on it or it might have only the cross-farm services on it. Finally, you scale SQL for your datacentric services or for business continuity requirements. As an example, you might decide to move your search databases to a server by themselves.

Some factors that might cause you to consider scaling out services include a company merger or acquisition, or your organization might have new and increasing search requirements. If you suddenly need to handle a much larger number of searches or have much many more documents to search, then scaling out by a couple of servers probably would not be able to handle the increase. When you face a major challenge like this, you need to look at splitting your services into another farm or multiple farms. You want to consider security boundaries, your usage/scaling loads, any political or company requirements, and you should also think about how you are going to apply patches, hotfixes, and updates to this new environment.

> **NOTE** The first service you should consider breaking into its own farm would be the Search service. This service is resource intensive, and in the section titled "Topologies for SharePoint 2010" later in this chapter, you will see that the larger farms are already moving you in this direction.

Figures 7-16 and 7-17 provide a high-level logical and physical view of cross-farm services. Figure 7-16 shows a logical view of cross-farm services. In this figure, you can see an example of three farms that represent Contoso's enterprise services farm, Contoso's EU farm, and Contoso's HR farm. The enterprise farm is currently publishing all enterprise class services that are consumable by the organization's other two farms. In addition, the EU farm is consuming all the publishing services, its own services, and the metadata service from the HR department's farm. Finally, the HR farm is consuming the publishing services and its own services. The key services for these farms to consume would be the Search service and the Secure Store service.

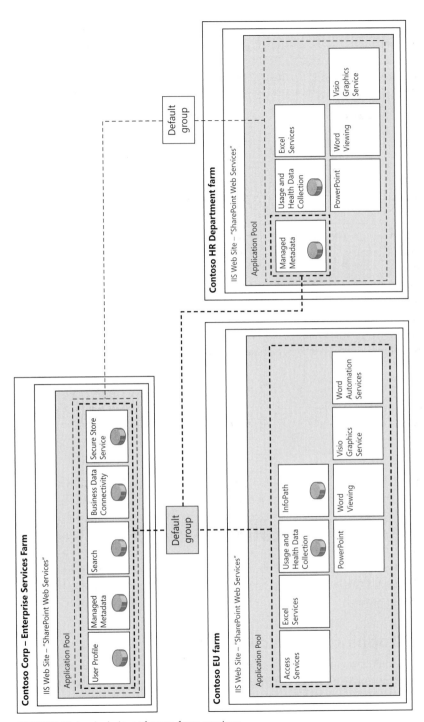

FIGURE 7-16 Logical view of cross-farm services

Figure 7-17 shows a physical view of another example of these same types of cross-farm services.

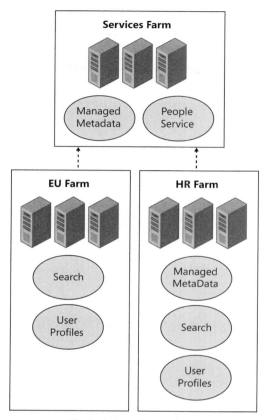

FIGURE 7-17 Physical view of cross-farm services

Configuring Service Applications

When you understand how you need to plan your service application architecture, you can then begin to configure it. Start the services you want and then deploy those services into service applications and groups.

Starting and Stopping a Service

Starting a service is the first step in the service application architectural process. If the service is not running, the service application will not know which server to send the request to.

1. Confirm that the user account performing this procedure is a member of the Farm Administrators SharePoint group.

2. Open a browser and go to the SharePoint Central Administration website.

3. Click System Settings, and then on the System Settings page, in the Servers section, click Manage Services On Server (Figure 7-18).

FIGURE 7-18 Services page

4. To change the server on which you want to start or stop the service, click Change Server on the Server drop-down menu and then click the server name that you want.

   By default, only configurable services are displayed. To view all services, on the View drop-down menu, click All.

5. To start or stop a service, click Start or Stop in the Action column of the relevant service.

6. Click OK to start or stop the service.

> **BEST PRACTICE** If a service application has a dependency on a service running on the server, you'll be able to install the service application without having an error message appear if the service is not started. Best practice is to ensure that the underlying services are started on the server before installing and configuring the service application.

Deploying Service Applications to an Existing Web Application

As an administrator to a SharePoint 2010 farm, you don't always get to start your farm from the beginning. Sometimes Web applications are already created, or new business processes change the default design. With this in mind, SharePoint 2010 allows you to deploy service applications to an existing Web application. To deploy service applications to an existing Web application, complete the following steps.

1. Open a browser and go to the SharePoint Central Administration website.

2. Under Application Management, click Manage Web Applications.

3. Click the Web application from the list of Web applications. The Web application will turn blue to indicate that it has been selected.

4. Select Service Connections from the Manage group of the Web Applications ribbon.

5. Select the service applications in the list that you want to deploy and then click OK to close.

Creating a Custom Application Proxy Group for a Web Application

In the event that the default proxy group does not meet your company's business requirements, you can create a custom application proxy group to satisfy your specific requirements. One example of this is could be exposing different user profile information on your extranet verses what is exposed on your intranet. To create a custom application proxy group through Central Administration, complete the following steps.

1. Open a browser and go to the SharePoint Central Administration website.

2. Click Application Management and then under Service Applications, click Configure Service Application Associations.

3. Select the Web application you want to modify.

4. Within the Web application, the Configure Service Application Associations screen shown in Figure 7-19 will have a new option: Edit The Following Group Of Connections.

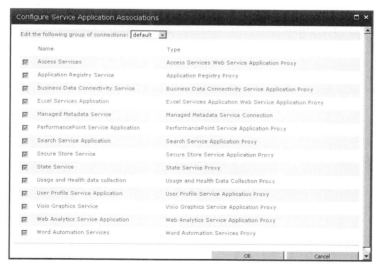

FIGURE 7-19 Configure Service Application Associations screen

5. Choose Custom from the drop-down list.

6. Select the appropriate service applications.

7. Click OK. The Web application now no longer uses the default group and has its own custom service application proxy group, as shown in Figure 7-20.

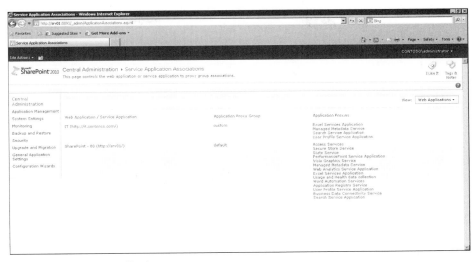

FIGURE 7-20 Custom application proxy group

NOTE To create a custom application proxy group with a custom name, you will need to use the Windows PowerShell command New-SPServiceApplicationProxyGroup.

Creating a New Instance of a Service Application

In SharePoint 2010, you have the option of creating multiple instances of the same service application. So, for example, you can configure your search service application multiple ways to resolve your company's different department requirements. To create a new instance of an Excel Services service application, complete the following steps.

1. Open a browser and go to the SharePoint Central Administration website.

2. Under Application Management, select Manage Service Applications.

3. Under Service Applications, select New from the Create group on the Service Applications Ribbon and choose a service application from the drop-down list, such as Excel Services Application, as shown in Figure 7-21.

FIGURE 7-21 Selecting a new instance of a service application

4. In this example, the Create New Excel Services Application screen will appear, as shown in Figure 7-22.

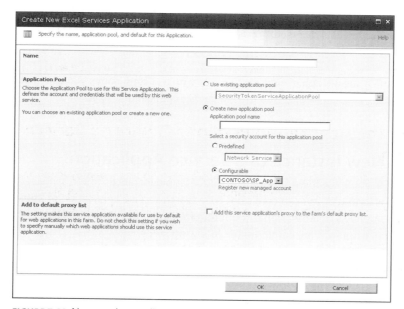

FIGURE 7-22 New service application instances of Excel Services

5. Choose a unique name for the service application.

6. Choose either to use an existing application pool or create a new application pool.

7. Select the security account for the application pool if you are creating a new application pool.

8. Choose whether to add to the default proxy list. Select the Add This Service Application's Proxy To The Farm's Default Proxy List check box if you are adding to the default proxy list.

9. Click OK to finish and the new instance is created, as shown in Figure 7-23.

FIGURE 7-23 Service applications list shows a new instance of Excel Services called IT Excel Services

Modifying the Application Pool of a Deployed Service Application

From time to time, you may need to change the application pool of a deployed service application. This could occur because of performance issues, or company protocol may dictate the change. To modify the application pool of a currently existing service application, complete the following steps.

1. Open IIS Manager. Browse to your server and open the Sites node.

2. Find and expand the SharePoint Web Services IIS website and select your service application, as shown in Figure 7-24.

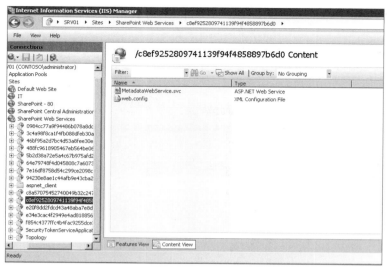

FIGURE 7-24 Selected service application in SharePoint Web Services website in IIS 7.0

3. On the right side of the screen, under Actions, select Basic Settings.

> **NOTE** Ensure that the Content view is selected, or Basic Settings will not appear.

4. An Edit Application dialog box will appear. Look for the Select button next to the application pool field, as shown in Figure 7-25. Click the Select button.

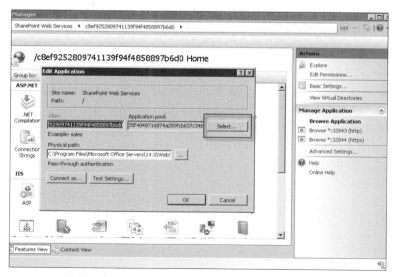

FIGURE 7-25 Select the application pool using the Edit Application dialog box.

5. Select your new application pool from the drop-down options. Click OK and then click OK again to exit the screen (Figure 7-26).

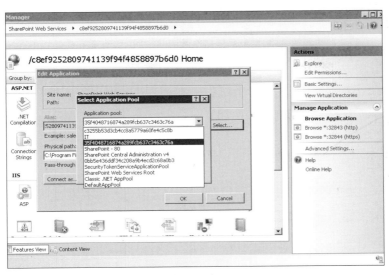

FIGURE 7-26 Selecting new application pool

Modifying the Service Applications in the Default Application Proxy Group

Although the default application proxy group is created automatically, if it does not fit the needs or requirements of your company, you can modify or add service applications to ensure that it does. To modify the service applications found in the default application proxy group, complete the following steps.

1. Open a browser and go to the SharePoint Central Administration website.

2. Click Application Management, and then under Service Applications, select Configure Service Application Associations.

3. Select the default Application Proxy Group, as shown in Figure 7-27.

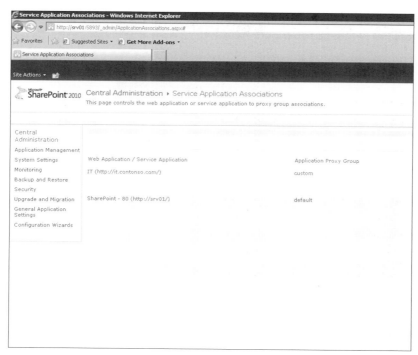

FIGURE 7-27 Select the default Application Proxy Group

4. In the Configure Service Application Associations screen, select or clear the appropriate service applications as shown in Figure 7-28.

FIGURE 7-28 Select or deselect service applications on the Configure Service Application Associations screen.

Publishing Service Applications

For a service application to be able to be consumed by a Web application, it must be published to the farm. To publish service applications, complete the following steps. These steps are only for publishing service applications that physically reside in the farm. (For information about remote farms, see the next section, titled "Publishing Service Applications to Remote Farms.")

1. Verify that the user account that is performing this procedure is a member of the Farm Administrators SharePoint group.

2. Open a browser and go to the SharePoint Central Administration website.

3. Under Application Management, click Manage Service Applications.

4. Select the row that contains the service application that you want to publish. Notice that after you select a service application, the commands on the Ribbon become available.

5. Click Publish on the Ribbon, as shown in Figure 7-29, to open the Publish Service Application screen.

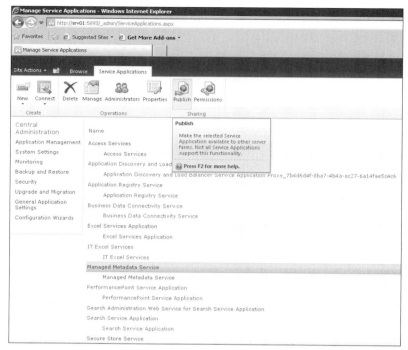

FIGURE 7-29 Publishing a service application

6. The Publish Service Application screen, shown in Figure 7-30, allows you to configure the service application as follows.

- Select the Connection Type that you want from the drop-down list.

- If you want the service application to be available to remote farms, select the check box for Publish This Service Application To Other Farms.

NOTE For more information about the option to publish a service application to other farms, read the section titled "Publishing Service Applications to Remote Farms" later in this chapter.

- Copy the published URL into Notepad or another text editor. You must provide this URL to remote farms to connect the remote farms to the published service application. The URL will be similar to this: *urn:schemas-microsoft-com:sharepoint:service:9c 1870b7ee97445888d9e846519cfa27#authority=urn:uuid:02a493b92a5547828e2138 6e28056cba&authority=https://ua_powershell:32844/Topology/topology.svc.*

- You can optionally provide descriptive text and a link to a Web page that will be visible to administrators of remote farms.

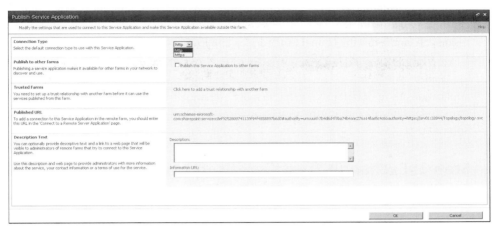

FIGURE 7-30 Configuring publishing service applications

7. After you have specified the publication options that you want, click OK to publish the service application.

If the service application that you are publishing is not a cross-farm service, your screen will not look like Figure 7-30; instead, it will look like Figure 7-31.

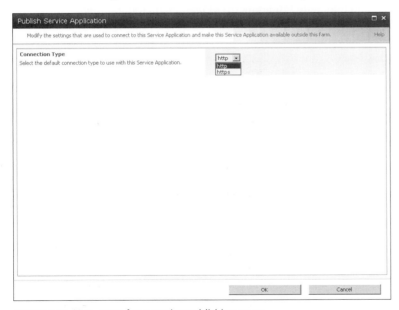

FIGURE 7-31 Non-cross-farm service publishing page

Publishing Service Applications to Remote Farms

To allow service applications to be consumed by remote farms, you must exchange trust certificates with the remote farm, explicitly publish the service application on the farm that it resides on, and explicitly connect the service application on the farm that is consuming it.

You use the SharePoint Central Administration website to publish a cross-farm service application. Publishing a cross-farm service entails the same three steps as publishing service applications to remote farms. First, you must exchange trust certificates with the remote farm, then explicitly publish the service applications, and finally, explicitly connect the service applications.

Step 1: Exchange Trust Certificates with the Remote Farm

In the first step of publishing service applications to remote farms, you export the root certificate from the consuming farm, export the STS certificate from the consuming farm, and export the root certificate from the publishing farm. Copy those certificates. Establish trust on the consuming farm and then import the certificates.

Exporting the Root Certificate from the Consuming Farm

To export the root certificate from the consuming farm, complete the following steps.

1. On a server that is running SharePoint 2010 on the consuming farm, verify that you meet the following minimum requirements of being a member of the SharePoint_Shell_Access role on the configuration database and a member of the WSS_ADMIN_WPG local group on the computer where SharePoint 2010 Products is installed (see Figure 7-32).

2. On the Start menu, click Administrative Tools.

3. Click SharePoint 2010 Management Shell.

4. At the Windows PowerShell command prompt (that is, PS C:\>), type each of the following commands, pressing Enter after each command. Replace <C:\ConsumingFarmRoot.cer> with the path of the root certificate, as illustrated in the example in Figure 7-33.

    ```
    $rootCert = (Get-SPCertificateAuthority).RootCertificate

    $rootCert.Export("Cert") | Set-Content <C:\ConsumingFarmRoot.cer> -Encoding byte
    ```

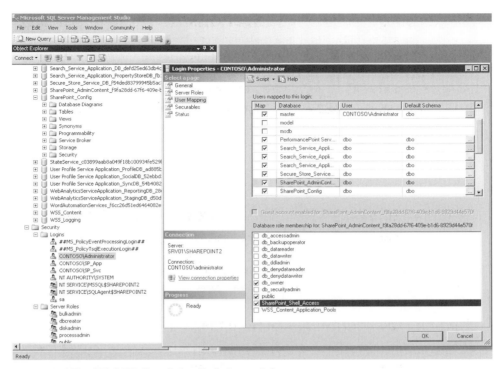

FIGURE 7-32 The SQL 2008 SharePoint_Shell_Access Role

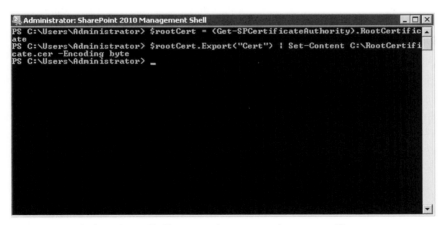

FIGURE 7-33 Windows PowerShell commands to export the root certificate

Exporting the STS Certificate from the Consuming Farm

To export the STS certificate from the consuming farm, go to the Windows PowerShell command prompt and type the following commands, pressing Enter after each command. Replace <C:\ConsumingFarmSTS.cer> with the path of the STS certificate, as illustrated in the example in Figure 7-34.

```
$stsCert = (Get-SPSecurityTokenServiceConfig).LocalLoginProvider.SigningCertificate

$stsCert.Export("Cert") | Set-Content <C:\ConsumingFarmSTS.cer> -Encoding byte
```

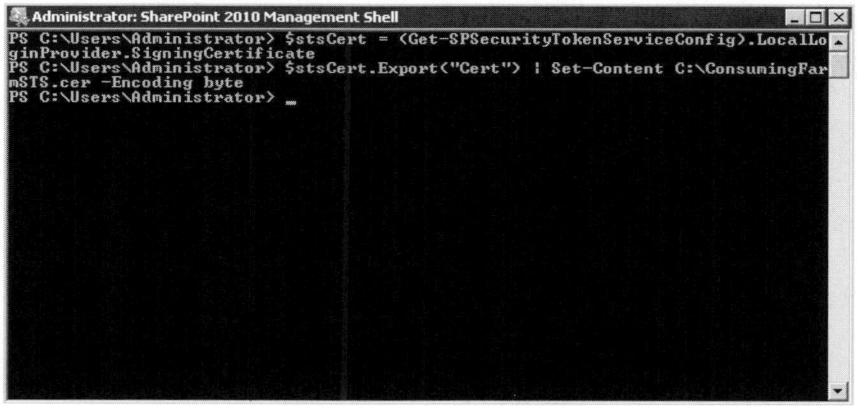

FIGURE 7-34 Windows PowerShell commands to export the STS certificate

Exporting the Root Certificate from the Publishing Farm

To export the root certificate from the publishing farm, complete the following steps.

1. On a server that is running SharePoint 2010 on the publishing farm, verify that you meet the following minimum requirements: You are a member of the SharePoint_Shell_Access role on the configuration database and a member of the WSS_ADMIN_WPG local group on the computer where SharePoint 2010 Products is installed.

2. On the Start menu, click Administrative Tools.

3. Click SharePoint 2010 Management Shell.

4. At the Windows PowerShell command prompt, type the following commands, pressing Enter after each command. Replace <C:\PublishingFarmRoot.cer> with the path of the root certificate, as illustrated in the example shown in Figure 7-35.

```
$rootCert = (Get-SPCertificateAuthority).RootCertificate

$rootCert.Export("Cert") | Set-Content <C:\PublishingFarmRoot.cer> -Encoding byte
```

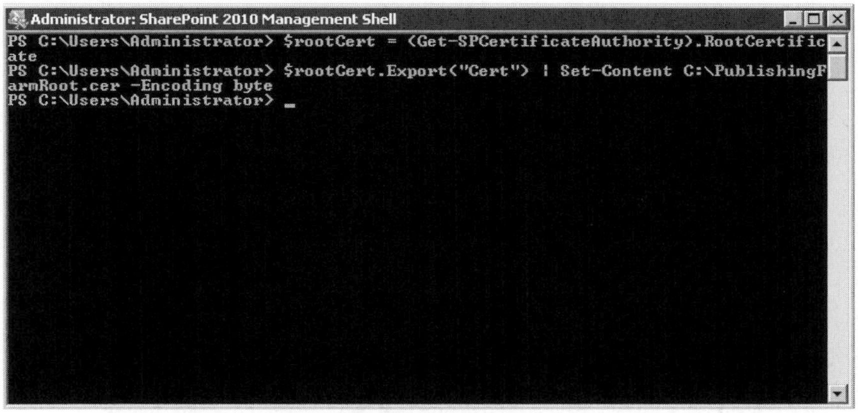

FIGURE 7-35 Windows PowerShell commands to export the publishing root certificate

Copying the Exported Certificates

Copy the root certificate and the STS certificate from the server in the consuming farm to the server in the publishing farm. Copy the root certificate from the server in the publishing farm to the server in the consuming farm.

Establishing Trust on the Consuming Farm

To establish trust on the consuming farm, you must import the root certificate that was copied from the publisher farm and create a trusted root authority.

Importing the Root Certificate and Creating a Trusted Root Authority on the Consuming Farm

To import the root certificate and create a trusted root authority on the consuming farm, go to the Windows PowerShell command prompt on a server in the consuming farm and type the following commands, pressing Enter after each command. Replace *<C:\PublishingFarmRoot.cer>* with the path of the root certificate that you copied to the consuming farm from the publishing farm and replace *<PublishingFarm>* with a unique name that identifies the publishing farm, as illustrated in the example in Figure 7-36. Each trusted root authority must have a unique name.

```
$trustCert = Get-PfxCertificate <C:\PublishingFarmRoot.cer>

New-SPTrustedRootAuthority <PublishingFarm> -Certificate $trustCert
```

FIGURE 7-36 Creating a root certificate on the consuming farm

Establishing Trust on the Publishing Farm

To establish trust on the publishing farm, you must import the root certificate that was copied from the consuming farm and create a trusted root authority. You must then import the STS certificate that was copied from the consuming farm and create a trusted service token issuer.

Importing the Root Certificate and Creating a Trusted Root Authority on the Publishing Farm

To import the root certificate and create a trusted root authority on the publishing farm, go to the Windows PowerShell command prompt on a server in the publishing farm and type the following commands, pressing Enter after each command. Replace *<C:\ConsumingFarmRoot.cer>* with the name and location of the root certificate that you copied to the publishing farm from the consuming farm and replace *<ConsumingFarm>* with a unique name that identifies the consuming farm, as illustrated in the example in Figure 7-37. Each trusted root authority must have a unique name.

```
$trustCert = Get-PfxCertificate <C:\ConsumingFarmRoot.cer>

New-SPTrustedRootAuthority <ConsumingFarm> -Certificate $trustCert
```

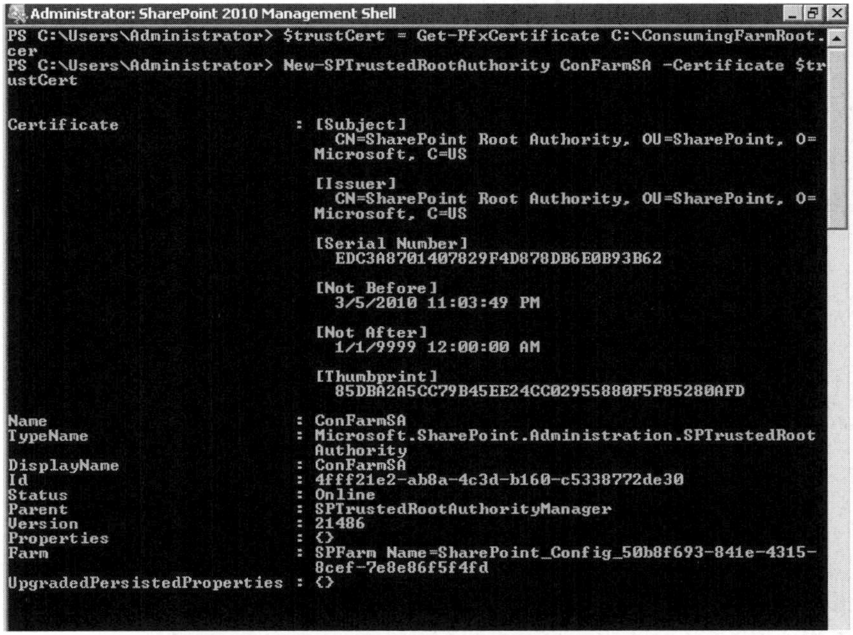

FIGURE 7-37 Creating the root certificate on the publishing farm

Importing the STS Certificate and Creating a Trusted Service Token Issuer on the Publishing Farm

To import the STS certificate and create a trusted service token issuer on the publishing farm, go to the Windows PowerShell command prompt on a server in the publishing farm and type the following commands, pressing Enter after each command. Replace *<C:\ConsumingFarmSTS.cer>* with the path of the STS certificate that you copied to the publishing farm from the consuming farm and replace *<ConsumingFarm>* with a unique name that identifies the consuming farm, as illustrated in the example in Figure 7-38. Each trusted service token issuer must have a unique name.

```
$stsCert = Get-PfxCertificate <c:\ConsumingFarmSTS.cer>

New-SPTrustedServiceTokenIssuer <ConsumingFarm> -Certificate $stsCert
```

FIGURE 7-38 Creating a trusted service token issuer

Setting Up and Enabling the Application Discovery And Load Balance Service Application

After creating the trusts and certificates, you need to activate the Application Discovery And Load Balance service application. This is also known as the Topology Service. This service provides other farms with the information needed so they can consume those cross-farm service applications.

1. First you must get the farm ID of the consuming farm. Use the following Windows PowerShell command to discover this, as shown in Figure 7-39.

```
(Get-SPFarm).Id
```

FIGURE 7-39 Windows PowerShell command to get the farm ID

2. After obtaining the farm ID of the consuming farm, go to the publishing farm and tell the service the ID of the farm so it can make it available to that farm. To do this, use the following Windows PowerShell commands (as shown in Figure 7-40).

```
$security = Get-SPTopologyServiceApplication | Get-SPServiceApplicationSecurity

$claimProvider = (Get-SPClaimProvider System).ClaimProvider

$principal = New-SPClaimsPrincipal -ClaimType   "http://schemas.microsoft.com/
sharepoint/2009/08/claims/farmid" -ClaimProvider $claimProvider -ClaimValue
<farmid from previous command>

Grant-SPObjectSecurity -Identity $security -Principal $principal -Rights "Full
Control"

Get-SPTopologyServiceApplication | Set-SPServiceApplicationSecurity
-ObjectSecurity $security
```

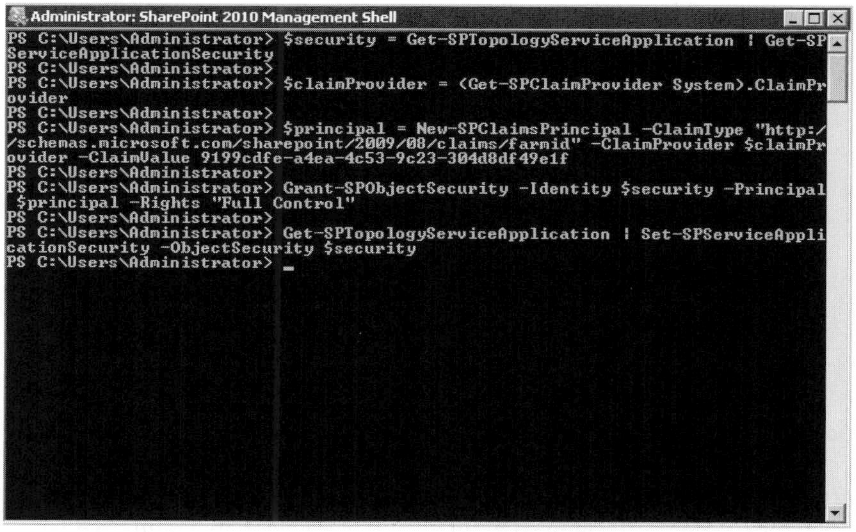

FIGURE 7-40 Enabling a farm to be seen with the Topology Service

Step 2: Explicitly Publish the Service Application

In step 1, you saw how to set up the exchange of trust certificates between the consuming and publishing farms. Now you must publish the service application that you want to have the consuming farm connect to in step 3. To publish the service application, follow these steps.

1. Verify that the user account that is performing this procedure is a member of the Farm Administrators SharePoint group.

2. Open a browser and go to the SharePoint Central Administration website.

3. Under Application Management, click Manage Service Applications.

4. Select the row that contains the service application that you want to publish. Notice that after you select a service application, the commands on the Ribbon become available.

5. Click Publish on the Ribbon to open the Publish Service Application screen.

6. The Publish Service Application dialog box allows you to configure the service application as follows.

   - Select the Connection Type that you want from the drop-down list.

   - Select the check box for Publish This Service Application To Other Farms to allow the service application to be consumed by other farms.

   - Under Trusted Farms, click the Click Here To Add A Trust Relationship With Another Farm link to edit or add certificates.

NOTE Step 1 in this section added the certificates through Windows PowerShell.

- Copy the published URL into Notepad or another text editor. You must provide this URL to remote farms to connect the remote farms to the published service application. The URL will be similar to this: *urn:schemas-microsoft-com:sharepoint:service:9c 1870b7ee97445888d9e846519cfa27#authority=urn:uuid:02a493b92a5547828e2138 6e28056cba&authority=https://ua_powershell:32844/Topology/topology.svc.*

- You can optionally provide descriptive text and a link to a Web page that will be visible to administrators of remote farms.

7. After you have specified the publication options that you want, click OK to publish the service application.

Step 3: Explicitly Connect the Service Application

After you have exchanged trust certificates with a publishing and consuming farm and explicitly published the service application, you must connect to the service application from the consuming farm to complete the process of publishing a service application to remote farms.

1. Verify that the user account that is performing this procedure is a member of the Farm Administrators SharePoint group.

2. Open a browser and go to the SharePoint Central Administration website.

3. Under Application Management, click Manage Service Applications.

4. Select the Connect option on the Ribbon and choose the service you want to connect to, as shown in Figure 7-41.

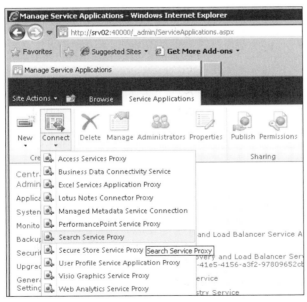

FIGURE 7-41 Connecting to a published service application

5. In the Connect To A Remote Service Application, enter the Farm or Service address URL and then click OK. The URL is found in the Published URL section when you publish the service application, as shown in Figure 7-42.

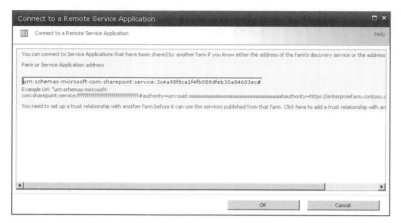

FIGURE 7-42 Adding a published service application URL to the consuming farm

6. As shown in Figure 7-43, you will see the service application and its availability.

FIGURE 7-43 Connected to a cross-farm service

7. Next, select the service application and click OK. If you do not want to add the default proxy list, clear the check box, as shown in Figure 7-44.

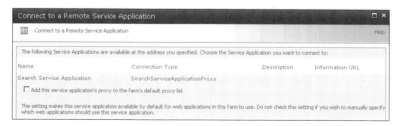

FIGURE 7-44 Selecting a cross-farm published service application

8. Next, create a unique name for your cross-farm service application and click OK.

9. A summary screen appears, telling you that you have successfully connected to a remote service application. Click OK. The service application will appear at the end of the list of service applications.

Topologies for SharePoint 2010

This section covers available topologies, Microsoft-approved assumptions, server roles, and a simplified scenario that provides you with an example of how you could scale out a farm.

SharePoint 2010 topologies can be broken into a limited deployment farm, small farm, medium farm, and large farm. These topologies allow SharePoint 2010 to be deployed on a single server or on many servers. SharePoint 2010 is designed to be scaled out using a three-tier system for its server roles, using server groups to build out your farm.

> **NOTE**   This section does not cover the large farm topology. A large farm is just a medium farm topology in which Search functionality is in a separate farm and the remaining servers are grouped by function.

Topologies and scaling are closely associated: you must understand your topology to be able to scale efficiently and accommodate different scenarios and organizational requirements. The following are some best practices to use when scaling out your farms.

- Limited deployments are up to 10,000 users (single box and 2 tier)
- Small farms
    - Assume 10,000 users per WFE.
    - Break out the application server due to moderate user usage.
    - Break out Search databases if optimizing for Search.
    - Search used for up to 10 million documents.
- Medium farms
    - Assume 10,000 users per WFE.
    - Break out application servers due to services using resources disproportionately. Examples might include Dedicated Excel Services or PowerPoint Services boxes.
    - Break out and combine query and crawl functions on a dedicated server and add a redundant query and crawl server.
    - Break out Search databases if optimizing for Search and add redundant SQL boxes for Search.
    - Search used for up to 40 million documents.
- Large farms
    - Search in its own farm.
    - Group servers by function.

Server Roles

As part of managing a server farm, you need to understand the basic roles that various servers perform in your farm. The following sections introduce you to the roles of the Web server, application servers, and database servers.

Web Server

A Web server is used to host Web pages, Web services, and Web Parts that are necessary to process requests served by the farm. A Web server directs requests to the appropriate application server. This is a necessary role for farms that include other SharePoint 2010 capabilities. In dedicated search service farms, this role is not necessary, because Web servers at remote farms contact query servers directly. In small farms, this role can be shared on a server with the query role.

When working with SharePoint, users connect only to the Web server—they do not connect directly to an application or database server. This is why the Web server is the most heavily utilized server in your farm. Client calls go in and out of the Web server, and that can represent a significant load during peak usage.

Application Server

Application server roles are associated with services that can be deployed to a physical computer. Each service represents a separate application service that can potentially reside on a dedicated application server. You can group services with similar usage and performance characteristics on a server, and you can scale out services onto multiple servers together. For example, client-related services can be combined into a service group. After deployment, look for services that consume a disproportionate amount of resources and consider placing these services on dedicated hardware when you decide to scale out your services and farms.

Database Server

In a small-farm environment, all databases can be deployed to a single server. In larger environments, group databases by roles and deploy these to multiple database servers. You might want to group and scale out Search and content databases to their own servers starting as early as the small farm, depending on usage requirements.

Scaling Out a Farm with Server Groups

The number of services and corresponding databases in SharePoint 2010 is greater than in the previous SharePoint Server 2007 releases. The recommendation for scaling out a farm is to group services or databases with similar performance characteristics onto dedicated servers and then scale out the servers as a group. This group is not enforced in the SharePoint Central Administration interface but instead is a logical group that you create on paper as you build out your farm.

For example, group all Search-related services onto one or two servers and then add servers to this group as needed to satisfy user demand for these services. In some cases, you might need to create a dedicated server group for a single service, such as Search or PerformancePoint services.

Combine service applications and related components (for example, databases) into several different logical groupings that can be used as a starting point; for scaling in large environments, the specific server group that evolves for a farm depends on the specific demands for each service.

> **NOTE** Remember that a server group is a planning concept—you will not find this term or concept in SharePoint Central Administration.

The remainder of this chapter introduces a scenario involving a company called Contoso Pharmaceutical, to provide you with an example of how the process of scaling out a farm can work. This company started out small, making only one product, then grew to a midsize company with several hundred products. The company's SharePoint farm also grew to accommodate Contoso Pharmaceutical's physical growth.

Contoso Pharmaceutical Small Farm Topologies

The IT department at Contoso Pharmaceutical installed a single farm SharePoint 2010 as a proof of concept. Most companies, when first deploying SharePoint 2010, take the single farm, single group approach. This is the default settings, and thus all the services are deployed in one default group. Even when using a small farm topology, however, the deployment has room to grow from a two-tier to a three-tier approach, as you can see in the following examples.

DESCRIPTION OF THE TWO-TIER APPROACH

When Contoso Pharmaceutical deployed SharePoint 2010 originally, all services were activated within the default group of services used for all Web applications in a farm. All sites had access to all of the service applications deployed in the farm. Contoso deployed a two-tier approach, with a Web tier and a database tier, as shown in Figure 7-45.

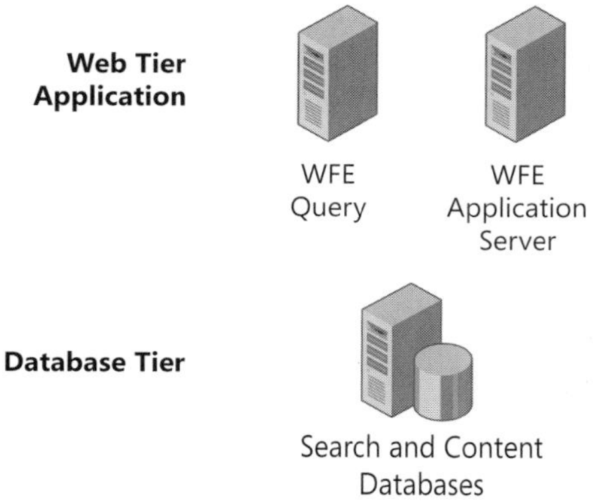

Web Tier
Application

WFE
Query

WFE
Application
Server

Database Tier

Search and Content
Databases

FIGURE 7-45 Two-tier small farm topology

Eventually, several department-wide collaborative initiatives created more of a demand for SharePoint 2010 within the corporate environment as well as more end-user adoption. These initiatives used services such as Excel Services, Access Services, and Search Services, which increased demand on the two-tier farm. As performance decreased due to this increase in usage, it was time to scale out this farm.

DESCRIPTION OF THE THREE-TIER APPROACH

Increased demand for application services and more end-user usage meant Contoso needed to separate the WFE and application server roles. In doing so, the farm was scaled out successfully to a three-tier configuration, with the query service remaining in the Web tier layer, but with a new dedicated application server providing services to all the departments within the enterprise. Figure 7-46 provides a view of this configuration with the newest server shown in the middle tier.

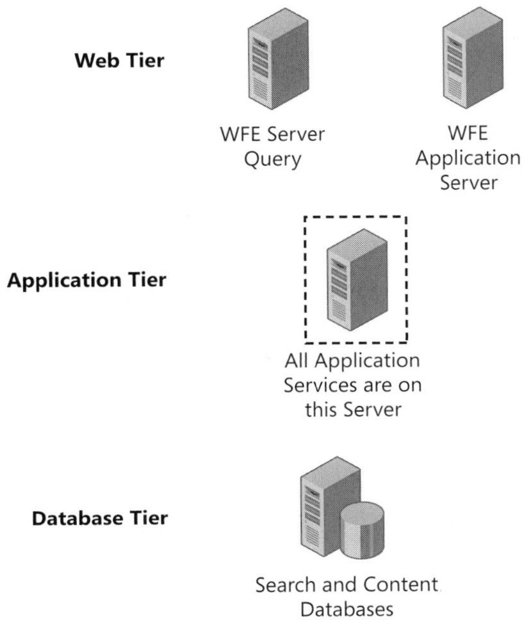

Web Tier

WFE Server
Query

WFE
Application
Server

Application Tier

All Application
Services are on
this Server

Database Tier

Search and Content
Databases

FIGURE 7-46 Three-tier small farm topology

Contoso took advantage of some key factors in moving into this new configuration. This provides the simplest architecture, with no server sharing roles. All the services on this farm are available to all Web applications, and this is the most efficient use of the farm's resources. Lastly, all of the service applications are managed centrally.

This environment does have a couple of disadvantages, however. It does not allow for the isolation of service data, and no departments or groups have been given permissions to manage their own isolated service applications.

RECOMMENDATIONS

This is the recommended configuration for most companies, at least initially. This configuration works well for hosting a large number of sites for a single company on the same farm and provides well for a limited number of intranet deployments and collaboration initiatives.

> **NOTE** Use this configuration if you want to optimize the resources required to run services within a farm or you want to share content and profile data across sites that otherwise require process isolation for performance or security reasons.

A small farm environment can consist of three servers: one Web front-end server, one Web front-end/application server, and one database server. Although this configuration is successful, it is also limited—it can handle up to 20,000 users. If your farm should have a mission critical application, you are faced with having no redundancy and additional points of failure in your design.

Points of failure include a single database server and a single server housing the service applications. This may be adequate to fulfill your business requirements, but if one of those boxes goes down, you will lose either your farm environment or that service application. If the service application is a cross-farm service being consumed by another farm, you now have a loss of functionality on not just one farm but on two farms.

Having one service application server is fine, depending on your usage demands, but if you have search requirements, you should think about scaling out that service to multiple servers to provide redundancy to your partitioned index and Search service. You already have redundancy with your query service because it is residing on your WFE.

This real world example would be suitable for a remote location using local services and consuming cross-farm services from a remote farm elsewhere.

Contoso Medium Farm Topology

Several years later, Contoso has become a midsize company with over 20,000 users and 30 terabytes of data in their SharePoint databases. The company's enterprise search requirements have increased, both in frequency of use by end users and in the size of the index. They are now handling more than 30 million documents.

DESCRIPTION

At this point, Contoso has optimized their farm to accommodate the large number of documents and the associated increased search and indexing requirements. Departments and divisions also have isolated service applications serving them.

Contoso can keep performance from declining by using dedicated application servers to handle query and crawling during searches. This approach is also useful because you can break off the index to have multiple fault-tolerant partitions. Departments can now isolate their service data, which will allow them to remain compliant with various regulations.

RECOMMENDATIONS

This configuration works well for companies that require services to be isolated, whether for security or performance reasons. It also allows those services to be consumed enterprise wide. This configuration is optimized with Search in mind, as Figure 7-47 shows.

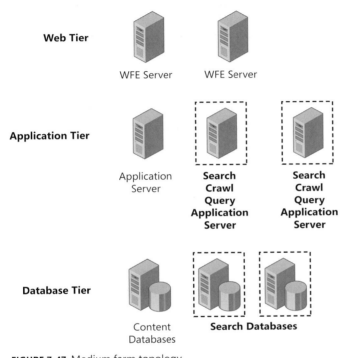

FIGURE 7-47 Medium farm topology

For an enterprise-level organization, a medium farm may not be big enough to handle the increased demands on SharePoint, and you might find that you need to scale out even more into a large-scale farm configuration.

The majority of production SharePoint environments will not reach this size, however. Recommended best practice is to continue grouping services and databases with similar performance characteristics onto dedicated servers and then scale out those servers into server groups. Figure 7-48 illustrates a practical example of this concept.

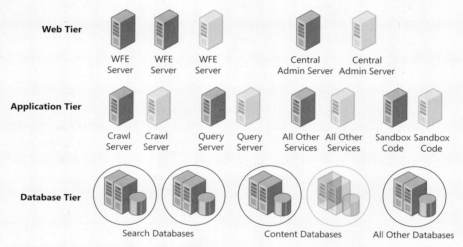

FIGURE 7-48 One example of a large farm topology

In this example, the Web tier consists of redundant WFE and Administration. The application tier breaks crawl and query into separate groups and also includes a sandbox code group. All other services are grouped together. Finally, on the database tier, search databases and content databases are clustered and grouped. All other databases are clustered on their own groups.

In this example, Search is included in the database tier; however, it is a recommended practice to break out Search at this level to its own farm. This recommended practice can be applied to all other cross-farm services. Scaling out a SharePoint 2010 environment is always dependent on the requirements and goals of your organization.

Summary

This chapter explained what service federation is and described the guidelines for scaling out your services. It also covered the components that make up a service application and discussed how to configure and modify those applications. The two service application models reviewed in this chapter were the single farm and cross-farm service applications, and guidelines were provided on when to scale out, when to isolate, and how to consume services.

You learned that you can modify service applications to make them completely isolated or shared by one or more Web applications. Some of these service applications can be cross-farm enabled or local only. The chapter explained that cross-farm services require a trust relationship established between a publishing farm and a consuming farm.

Service Application Architecture (SSA) in SharePoint 2010 has replaced the Shared Service Provider (SSP) architecture from SharePoint Server 2007. Because the "all or nothing" configuration model of SharePoint Server 2007 made it difficult to fine-tune the use of service applications associated with specific Web applications, Microsoft decided to take a more granular approach in SharePoint 2010 and now provides a flexible and scalable architecture that allows you to scale SharePoint environments to meet the requirements of your enterprise.

When scaling out, you learned what server roles (Web, application, and database) your farm can have and in what type of scenario you would scale out those services. You also learned that, when scaling out your service application architecture, you should scale out your Search service first and then scale out group services with the same functionality.

In the next chapter, you will learn about information management policies in SharePoint 2010.

Information Management Policies

This chapter discusses the use of information management policies as well as records management in Microsoft SharePoint 2010. It includes an introduction to information management policies, details about configuring information management policies at the farm level, and best practices for creating information management policies. Furthermore, this chapter discusses how to create a Records Center in SharePoint 2010 and how to utilize a new feature in SharePoint 2010 called In Place Records Management that allows you to declare a document as a record without having to send it to the Records Center.

Introducing Records Management and Information Management Policies

Organizations today are increasingly subject to state and federal regulations governing which electronic records they must retain, how long they should be retained, and how readily they should be made accessible to regulators. SharePoint users must be aware of the regulations that affect stored documents and should know how to use and apply the information management policies and records management features available for documents stored in SharePoint that have legal requirements. An example of two federal acts that apply to record keeping include

- **Health Insurance Portability and Accountability Act (HIPPA)**   Requires organizations that have access to personal health information to adopt security policies to safeguard the confidentiality of the data. Organizations must also monitor and control access to the data and maintain an audit trail available to regulators.

- **Sarbanes-Oxley Act (SOX)** Applies to publicly traded companies and requires that companies put in place extensive policies and procedures to control their financial information and to prevent fraud. It also requires that executives certify the validity of company financial statements and that independent auditors verify the financial controls put in place.

In addition to the rules and regulations that organizations must comply with for legal reasons, companies have found that defensive business practices also call for good data management to protect the company during litigation. Companies are often required to produce copies of documents and files deemed to be relevant to a lawsuit or prosecution. In some cases in which companies could not produce the requested documents, courts have ruled that documents that are not available are assumed to support the plaintiff's arguments. Organizations cannot afford to lose control of critical documents and e-mail messages.

What Is Records Management?

Records management enables a company to effectively manage a content item, or record, from inception to disposal in accordance with applicable laws, such as the federal regulations mentioned previously. A record is a physical or electronic document, an e-mail message, or some other form of digital information, such as an instant message transcript, that serves as evidence of an activity or transaction performed by the organization.

Records management is the process by which an organization defines what type of information it needs to classify as a record, how long it needs to retain the information, and how it will manage the information throughout its life cycle. Part of the challenge of records management is to identify and track information items that are legally or economically vital to the business. For example, an e-mail message that contains some reference to financial information about the company or about a client might well be considered a record. The other part of the challenge is to filter and purge items that do *not* need to be stored as records. As an example, an exchange of e-mail messages in which two employees of an organization decide where to have lunch might not be considered record material.

Although setting a policy that declares everything to be a record might seem to be a safe approach for an organization, this policy could be almost as harmful as not declaring any content item a record. For example, if a legal action requires that a company deliver the approximately one hundred e-mail records that pertain to a court case, and the best that the company's IT department can do is provide the 10,000 e-mail messages sent within a specific time frame, then the court may rule that delivering the relevant items buried within a mass of irrelevant data to be a form of obstruction. An additional benefit can be obtained from creating policies that determine what a company record is, rather than trying to store everything as a record—because records are stored based on content types, narrowing the definition of what constitutes a record can improve the ability of users to perform targeted searches that avoid returning irrelevant data.

A well-designed records management plan is essential for data retention policies to mesh with actual data management processes. For example, if a company's retention policy specifies that a document should be purged and destroyed after one year, then backups should be designed so that no backup more than a year old has a copy of the file on it. On the other hand, a retention policy that dictates that a document must be readily available for review for a period of three years requires that a live copy of any document be kept in a storage location from which it can be pulled without restoring it from backup. These types of organization-specific requirements dictate a need for every company to not only develop the appropriate policies but to implement and enforce those policies as well. There have been cases in which organizations have not followed their own policies and were required to retrieve specific data from archival backups and restore it onto their network, which is generally a very time-consuming and costly process.

A records management plan should contain the following elements.

- A compliance requirements document that defines the policies the organization must implement to ensure compliance with legal and regulatory requirements, along with the practices that employees must adhere to in accordance with the policies
- A chart that indicates who will be responsible for the different roles that must be filled in the records management process
- A file plan that identifies which types of information are considered records, where they are stored, the permissions and policies that govern them while they are active, and how and when to dispose of records

Compliance Requirements Document

The compliance requirements document explains the purpose of a compliance program and its benefits together with its essential components. It identifies the legal or business criteria to which the compliance plan must adhere and the metrics or other objective criteria that will be used to measure the effectiveness of the compliance plan. The compliance requirements document includes the formal policies that represent the organization's internal statement of the regulatory rules it must follow.

The compliance requirements document should also include specifications for ongoing training for employees at all levels and guidelines for the roles and involvement of senior management in the compliance process. Although it may not be practical for every organization, a formal compliance audit should also be carried out at regular intervals to ensure that the records management plan is meeting its objectives.

Records Management Roles

When developing the records management plan, it is important to consider who is responsible for the various roles that are involved in the creation and implementation of the plan. Since SharePoint 2010 is a content-rich application, some of these roles will include the SharePoint administrator, content managers, records managers, and compliance officers.

SharePoint Administrator

Administrators are responsible for the installation and configuration of the SharePoint 2010 servers that provide records management services to the enterprise. They create the Web applications and the Records Center site and configure the connection to the official file that lets users submit documents to the records center.

Compliance Officers

Compliance officers are usually associated with an organization's legal department and are often lawyers. They are responsible for understanding and interpreting the regulations and rules that the organization must follow. They develop the formal compliance policies that the company will implement and, as a result, they are the primary authors of the compliance requirements document and perform internal monitoring and auditing to ensure that the organization closely follows the records management plan.

Records Managers

Records managers are responsible for developing the file plan that applies the compliance requirements document to the different types of information items that the organization produces. The records managers may also be members of the organization's legal department or may be senior administrative staff members who have a thorough understanding of the organization's business practices and workflow. After the SharePoint administrators have created the Records Center site, records managers are in charge of configuring the document libraries and retention rules in the site. Records managers should be consulted at all points in the design of the records management system

Content Managers

Content managers work on the teams that create information items that will be designated as records. If necessary, the content managers configure team sites with the appropriate content types and workflows to facilitate the effective and efficient categorization of documents so that they can be routed to the appropriate location.

Information Workers

Information workers are the employees in an organization who create new documents and e-mail messages that need to be classified and routed to the records center for safeguarding. The goal of a reliable records management system should be to make it relatively easy for information workers to classify information accurately, or even automatically, as it is produced.

The File Plan

The file plan is a written document or set of documents that lists all of the types of information that an organization receives or produces and how each one should be classified and handled. Some information will be classified as a record when it is created, other information will be treated as a record only when it reaches a certain stage in its life cycle, and then there will be information that is either temporary or unimportant enough that it is not considered a type of record. The criteria used to classify a record will come from the organization's compliance requirements document produced by the compliance officer.

> **IMPORTANT** As part of your effort to train and educate your end users about how to use SharePoint Technologies, be sure to educate them about the file plan and any information management policies that apply to them. Users need to know when a document or record moves from being unofficial communication to being official communication, and they also need to know your company's policy to properly consume, store, and dispose of official records.

Although the details of what enters into the file plan will depend on the type of information that your organization is managing, there are usually some common elements in most plans. As shown in Table 8-1, these elements include a list of record types and the key information that must be associated with each type to ensure that it is filed properly. After an information item is classified as a record, it can be copied or moved into a SharePoint 2010 site based on the Records Center site template. This site serves as the storage area for both active and inactive documents that must be readily available as either an information resource for staff or as evidentiary material in litigation. Active documents are those that are still in use as part of a project or an ongoing e-mail discussion. These documents may continue to be updated over time, and new versions will be submitted to the repository as they are generated. The file plan will specify whether older versions of the same document are retained and for how long. Inactive documents are those that have reached their final version or have been submitted formally to an agency. Although employees will probably not generate any further versions of the document, the last version must be retained as an official record of the transaction.

TABLE 8-1 File Plan Elements

PLAN ELEMENT	PURPOSE
Record Type	The classification of the information item. Each record type corresponds to a set of typical documents or messages that need to be tracked and managed in the same way.
Required Fields	Any additional information that will be required when the document is submitted to the repository.
Retention	How long the document will be retained.
Disposal	How the document will be handled when it expires.
Audit	Whether access to the document will be tracked and logged along with the types of actions on the document that have to be logged.

It is important to distinguish between documents that are retained as records and those that are retained in an archive. Archived information is not classified as a record after the period for which it needs to be retained as a record has expired. At that point, the information is usually transferred to tape or printed out and placed in long-term storage with the expectation that it will be kept mainly for historical purposes. Archived data is generally not readily available for search and retrieval and it is not expected to be required for current research or legal discovery. But keep in mind that the legal discovery process can request any information deemed appropriate for the matter at hand, another reason to make sure expired data is properly archived.

In Table 8-2, you can see an example of a standard file plan filled out for several record types in an organization. As you can see, different document types have different record management requirements. For example, financial statements will be kept indefinitely in archival storage because of their historical value to the company, but e-mail correspondence is considered too voluminous and of too little value to archive in the long term.

TABLE 8-2 Sample File Plan

RECORD TYPE	FINANCIAL STATEMENTS	INVOICES	E-MAIL CORRESPONDENCE
Document ID	Finance-Doc-01	PO-Invoice_01	Email-Msg-01
Required Fields	Statement Date (date field)	Delivery Date (date field)	Subject (string property, single line of text)
Expiration	Retain for 7 years after Statement Date	Retain for 5 years after Delivery Date	Retain for 3 years from date created
Disposal	Archive and delete on expiration	Archive and delete on expiration	Delete on expiration
Audit	Audit View events only	None	None

Normally, your organization's legal department provides you with the storage and archive requirements for any documents in SharePoint that have legal requirements associated with them or that are considered important enough to require some form of records management.

What Are Information Management Policies?

Information management policies are sets of rules governing the automated management of documents, such as how long a file should be retained or which actions on the file should be audited. Each rule in a policy is called a *policy feature*. Policies in a records management system are configured by records managers to reflect the file plan requirements. The value of storing files in separate document libraries becomes obvious when you start designing the information management policies that you will apply to each library.

There are two recommended approaches for implementing policies in the repository: (1) create individual policies for each document library if the requirements are unique to the content in each library, or (2) create site collection policies to cover an entire set of record types and apply them to several document libraries as needed. You can either apply one policy for the entire document library, or if you configure the document library to allow multiple content types, then you can apply a separate policy to each content type. Figure 8-1 shows the four features available when defining an information management policy.

FIGURE 8-1 Information management policy features

After creating a policy, you implement it by associating it with a site collection, content type, list, or library. This association to a content type, list, or library can be accomplished using one of the three following methods.

- **Site Collection Policy**   Associate the policy features with a site collection policy and then associate that policy with a content type, list, or library.

- **Content Type Policy**   Associate a set of policy features directly with a content type and then use that content type in one or more lists or libraries.

- **List or Library Policy**   Associate a set of policy features directly with a list or library. However, you can only use this method when the library or list is not using more than one content type.

> **NOTE**   A policy feature might use one or more policy resources, which are programs that provide functionality to a policy feature. For example, a custom policy resource for the barcode policy feature could be used to generate a unique barcode value for a document.

Planning Document Policies

The use of policies can be simplified by planning how and where they will be used. This can be accomplished by first determining your organization-wide policy needs and then designing your site collection policies to meet those needs and distribute those policies for use as site collection policies for all relevant site collections. If any policy requires custom policy features or resources, those features and resources have to be installed and enabled on all server farms using that solution.

Policy Metadata

Policies often require the use of additional document properties or metadata. It is important to create consistent metadata properties that can be used throughout your entire farm. SharePoint 2010 introduces a service application called MMS (Managed Metadata Service) that is used to create enterprise-wide content types and metadata. This service application will host a Web application with a site collection that you can use to create your farm level content types and metadata properties, which eliminates the need to create them as a feature and deploy them to each site collection, as was the case in Microsoft SharePoint Server 2007. All Web applications that are associated with the Managed Metadata Service can consume any content type as well as metadata from the MMS service application.

For instance, when you configure the retention period of a document, you may need to use a SharePoint-provided date property or create a custom date property that will be used to determine when an action is performed on that document. For additional information on the MMS service application, see Chapter 14, "Administering Enterprise Content Management."

Implementing and Configuring Information Management Policies

You can control the use of the four information management policies—retention, auditing, barcodes, and labels—at the farm level using Central Administration. Any of these settings can be decommissioned at the SharePoint farm level using the interface shown in Figure 8-2. You access these settings using the Security category within Central Administration. If one of these settings has been decommissioned at the farm level, you will not be able to implement or configure that setting anywhere in the farm.

If you click any of the four policy features displayed here, you will have two options for configuring the feature:

- Available for use in new site and list polices
- Decommissioned: Unavailable to new site and list policies but still available in existing policies that use it

The barcodes policy feature has one additional configuration option that you can configure here. You can configure barcodes to include letters when SharePoint generates these barcodes. By default, the barcodes generated by SharePoint only contain numbers, but you can change this setting by clicking Barcodes and selecting the Letters (A-Z) And Numbers (0-9) option under Include The Following Characters In Barcodes, as shown in Figure 8-3.

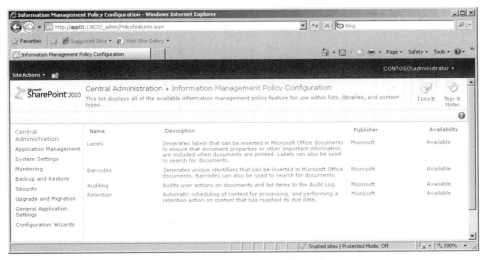

FIGURE 8-2 Farm level information management policy configuration

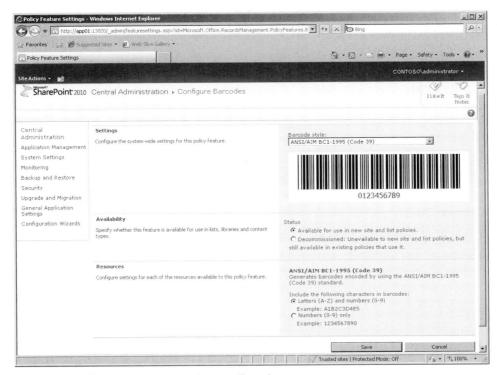

FIGURE 8-3 Configure barcodes to use letter and numbers

When you are ready to create an information management policy, the configuration is the same regardless of whether you are applying the policy to a content type, list, or library. You have to provide similar general information for each policy. This includes a name for the policy and an administrative description (Figure 8-4), which is seen by list managers when configuring information management policy. You must also supply a brief description that is displayed to the users when they access items that are associated with the information management policy. This can be used to notify them of any special processes as well as the settings of the policy.

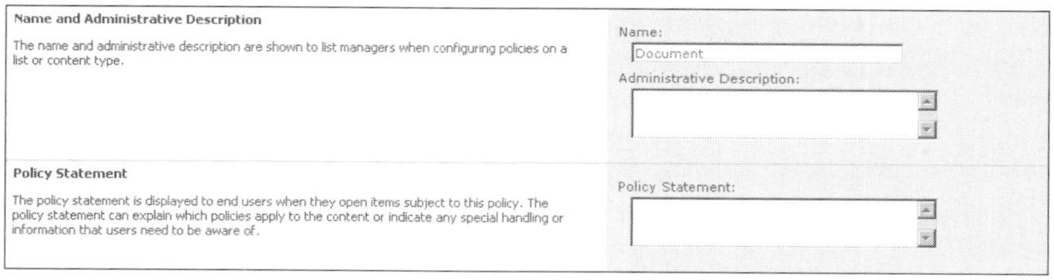

Name and Administrative Description
The name and administrative description are shown to list managers when configuring policies on a list or content type.

Name:
Document

Administrative Description:

Policy Statement
The policy statement is displayed to end users when they open items subject to this policy. The policy statement can explain which policies apply to the content or indicate any special handling or information that users need to be aware of.

Policy Statement:

FIGURE 8-4 Creating information management policy names and descriptions

Defining a Retention Policy

A retention policy allows you to specify how long a document will be retained and what will happen to the document throughout its life cycle. This is achieved by defining stages in its life cycle that occur sequentially. Additional stages can be added to the retention schedule in SharePoint, allowing you to manage entire life cycles from within SharePoint. After selecting the Enable Retention Policy Feature check box, you are required to click the Add A Retention Stage link to display the retention configuration options shown in Figure 8-5.

There are retention configuration options available for each stage of a document's life cycle, and you can use the retention configuration options to configure the following three properties.

- **Event** Specify the event that activates the stage based on a date property
- **Action** Specify the action that takes place during that stage
- **Recurrence** Optionally, force the action to occur repeatedly

The activation of an event is driven by a date property on the item or a custom event formula located on the server. You can use any of the SharePoint default date properties or a custom date property.

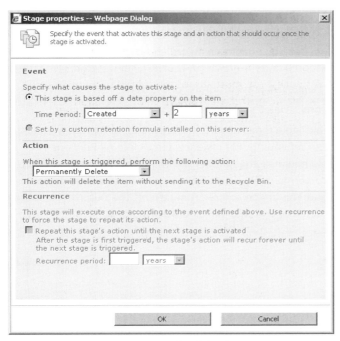

FIGURE 8-5 Retention Stage Properties dialog box

 REAL WORLD **Setting Expiration Dates**

In SharePoint 2010, you have the option to set an expiration time based on any date property available in the drop-down list shown in Figure 8-5, including when it was declared a record. You can specify values between 0 to 500 years, 0 to 6000 months, or 0 to 182,500 days from the date selected from the drop-down list. In reality, all three settings have the same maximum amount of time, so your choice of which to select is really based on how precise you want the date setting to be. Selecting days will give you a more precise setting than months, and months will be more precise than years. The precision of the retention period required by your organization should be determined by your legal team.

Next you choose one of the following actions to be performed during the stage of the retention policy you are configuring.

- **Move To Recycle Bin** Moves the item to the site collection recycle bin.
- **Permanently Delete** Deletes the item without sending it to the recycle bin.
- **Transfer To Another Location** Transfers the item to a Send To location that has been configured at the Web application level in Central Administration.

- **Start A Workflow**   Starts the specified workflow for this stage.
- **Skip To Next Stage**   Proceeds to the next retention stage without any modifications.
- **Declare A Record**   Declares the document as a record and begins a record retention policy stage if one exists.
- **Delete Previous Drafts**   Deletes all previous drafts of the item.
- **Delete All Previous Versions**   Deletes all previous versions of the document.

The Recurrence property is not available for all actions in the preceding list, but when it is available, it allows the action to occur repeatedly. For instance, the Delete All Previous Versions option can be repeated to help minimize the number of copies of a document that are retained. Conversely, if you chose to permanently delete a document, there will be no copies to delete again, so you can't configure this action as a recurring event. The Recurrence option is only available when you have selected one of the following three actions.

- Start A Workflow
- Delete Previous Drafts
- Delete All Previous Versions

 REAL WORLD   **Using Multiple Retention Stages**

I f you have a document that has legal requirements associated with it, you might be required to retain the final version of the document in the Records Center for three years and then archive it for four years, at which point you can permanently delete the document. This three-stage information management policy would look similar to the one shown in Figure 8-6 and outlined here.

Stage 1   One year after the date the document was created, it becomes a record, and delete all previous versions of the document are deleted.

Stage 2   Three years after a document was declared a record, it is archived to another location.

Stage 3   Seven years after it was declared a record, the document is permanently deleted.

FIGURE 8-6 An example of a three-stage document retention policy

Auditing

The auditing policy feature allows you to log events and operations performed on documents and list items. The auditing feature will track not only operations by users but also those of SharePoint itself and any custom code or Web services that access the document programmatically. Figure 8-7 shows the types of operations that can be audited.

FIGURE 8-7 Auditing options

To view the audit log, open the Site Settings of the repository site (or the root site in the site collection if the repository is a subsite). Under the Site Collection Administration section, click the Audit Log Reports link and it will take you to a page listing each of the audit reports produced. You can click the Run A Custom Report link to manually specify the parameters for a report, or you can click any of the predefined reports shown in Figure 8-8 to generate a Microsoft Excel–based report of the audit log data.

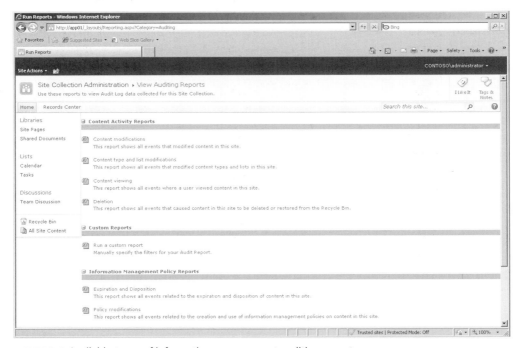

FIGURE 8-8 Available types of information management auditing reports

Barcodes

Document barcodes are another feature available in SharePoint that can help you mark and track both the physical and electronic versions of a document. A barcode provides a unique 10-digit identifier generated by SharePoint 2010 and rendered as an image. After the barcode is generated, you can view it by selecting View Properties from the document context menu. You can prompt users to insert the barcode into the document when they save or print the document, as shown in Figure 8-9. The barcode component that is shipped with SharePoint 2010 generates barcodes compatible with the "Code 39" barcode symbology (formally known as ANSI/AIM BC1-1995). SharePoint 2010 provides an extensible plug-in model for barcode components that can be used to add custom barcode generators.

FIGURE 8-9 Enabling barcodes

> **BEST PRACTICES** When using labels and barcodes, place them in either the header or footer of the document so that they appear on every page and don't overlay existing text.

Labeling

The labeling feature lets SharePoint 2010 automatically generate searchable text areas that are based on a formula that can include static text and document metadata. This lets you insert a line of text or an external value into the document as an image in much the same way that a label is affixed to a document for filing. For example, an organization might want to attach a label to a project document that includes the date it was created. You define the formula that will generate the label by using metadata-based identifiers such as Date Created in conjunction with descriptive text, and SharePoint creates the label for each document added to the document library.

To enable the label feature, check the Enable Labels option and enter a formula by combining text with valid column names inside curly brackets. In this example, the formula Date Created: {Date Created} will generate the Date Created: Date Created label, as shown in Figure 8-10, and the Date Created column will be time stamped with the system date when the document is created. Similar to barcodes, when you select the Prompt Users To Insert A Label Before Saving Or Printing option, users are given the option to insert the label into the document when they save or print the document. If the label is intended to become a permanent feature of the document, then use the Prevent Changes To The Labels After They Are Added option to keep the label from changing in the document. If the label is not inserted into the document, it will still be visible from the document's Properties window when a user selects View Properties from the document drop-down menu in the document library.

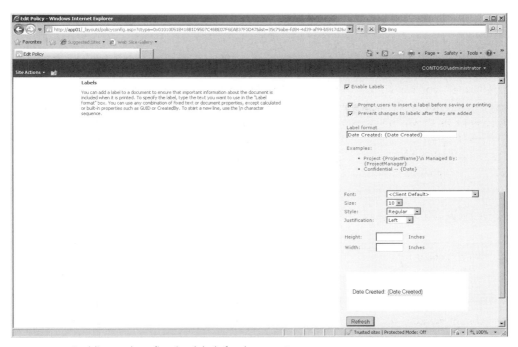

FIGURE 8-10 Enabling and configuring labels for documents

> **NOTE** Labels and barcodes are generated when the document is added to the document library. If the policies for labels and barcodes are applied to a document library with existing documents, they will not immediately display labels or barcodes, but when users make changes to the documents or to a document's properties, the changes will trigger SharePoint to generate labels and barcodes for the documents in that document library.

After you have configured your information management policies, it is important for you to review the usage of the information management policies that you defined, which can be achieved using the reporting capabilities provided by SharePoint 2010.

Generating Information Management Policy Usage Reports

To obtain information on which policies are being applied throughout your organization, you can configure information management policy usage reports to generate periodic reports on policy behavior. These reports are generated as XML files that will render as reports in Excel, or they can be opened in another application for further extraction and processing.

You configure policy usage reporting in Central Administration, as shown in Figure 8-11, which generates separate files for each site collection in the selected Web application. The reports will be generated and placed in a designated SharePoint 2010 site location such as a document library. Policy usage reports can also be generated using an alternate report template that must be available through a URL that you provide.

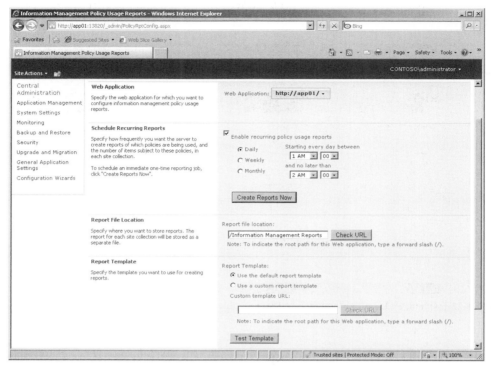

FIGURE 8-11 Configuring information management policy usage reporting

To configure information management policy usage reporting, complete the following steps.

1. Open a browser and go to the SharePoint Central Administration website.

2. Click Monitoring, and then under Reporting, click Review Information Management Policy Usage Reports.

3. If you want to generate scheduled reports, select the check box to enable recurring reports and specify the report schedule. You can also click Create Reports Now to generate a one-time report.

4. In the Report File Location text box, type the relative URL address for the document library where you want the reports to be placed. For example, if you want the reports to appear in a document library called Information Management Reports in a top-level site in the site collection, you would enter **/Information Management Reports** in the text box.

5. If you want to use a custom template, enter the URL address for the template in the Report Template box.

The default template used to store your information management reports displays the name of the report, which includes the date and time the report was generated. It also provides columns that list the site collection and the Web application of the report, as shown in Figure 8-12.

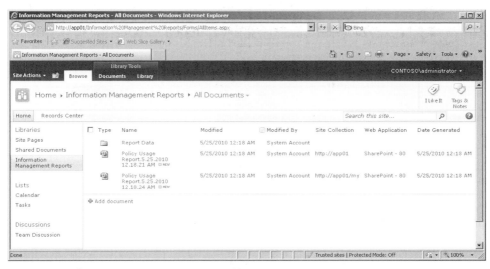

FIGURE 8-12 Information Management Reports library

Viewing Information Management Usage Reports

To view reports after they are generated, browse to the library location you provided and select the report you want to see. If you have Microsoft Excel installed, the report opens in Excel as shown in Figure 8-13; otherwise, it opens in the browser as a generic XML file.

Policy usage reports generally have the following tabs.

- **Introduction** Lists the site collection that the report is for and the date it was generated.
- **Report PivotTable** Provides a summary of the number of items in each site and lists which are subject to each policy.
- **Policies** Lists each policy by name.
- **Usage** Provides detailed data on the lists in each site as well as the number and percentage of items in each list.

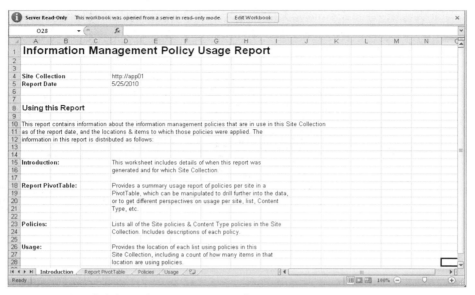

FIGURE 8-13 Sample information management policy usage report

Administrators and records managers might want to review how many policies are in place in a Web application and how many documents are affected by them. This information can help administrators identify which sites are using policies and which are not. It can also help compliance officers determine how effectively the compliance guidelines that have been formulated into the file plan are being implemented. For example, if a compliance officer notices that no policies are being applied to a particular document library in the repository, then it may turn out that data in that library is not being purged in a timely manner.

Viewing the Policies Report

The Policies report provides a list of policies defined in the report generated for the site collection within the Web application that you chose on the Information Management Reports page. The Policies page provides general information about the policies that have been configured. The general information about each policy is displayed using the columns shown in Figure 8-14.

Viewing the Policy Usage Report

The Policy Usage report provides a list of policies defined in the report generated for the site collection within the Web application that you chose on the Information Management Reports page. The Policies Usage page provides detailed information about the information management policies that have been configured along with the number of items that are using those policies. The detailed information about the policies is displayed using the columns shown in Figure 8-15.

All of these reports are helpful to the compliance manager and can be used to ensure that policies are applied at the proper locations throughout your SharePoint implementation.

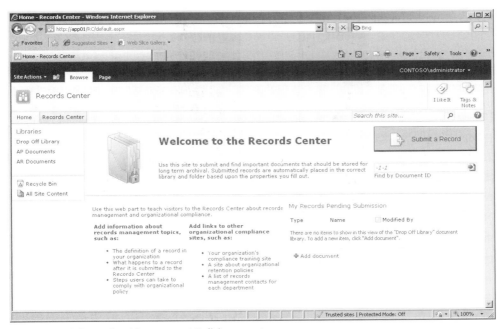

FIGURE 8-14 Information Management Policies report page

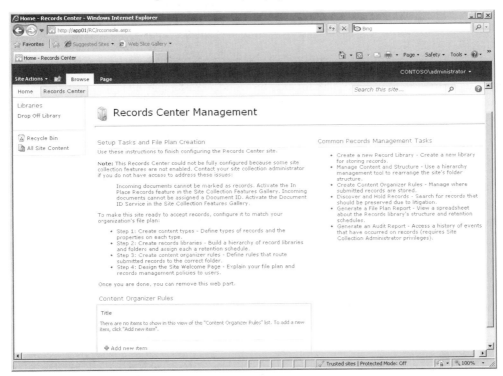

FIGURE 8-15 Information Management Policy Usage report page

Implementing and Configuring a Records Center

To configure a Records Center in SharePoint 2010, you begin by defining the content types that will be used to classify records throughout your enterprise. You then create a site based on the Records Center site template and configure the methods you will use to route documents to this site after they have been classified. Finally, you create information policies on the record libraries within the site to apply the rules dictated by the file plan. The following is a summary of the steps you should follow to implement a Records Center.

1. Create content types at the enterprise level using MMS.
2. Create a new Web application and use the Records Center template for site collection.
3. Create a records library in the Records Center for each content type.
4. Define required metadata on the document libraries or content types.
5. Define Information Management Policies to implement the File Plan rules.
6. Create content organizer rules to route documents to the correct records library.

Creating and Managing a Content Type

A content type is a reusable collection of settings that can be applied to a document to categorize its content. Content types are essential to the proper functioning of your Records Center because documents submitted to the Records Center are automatically organized by content type. To ensure that all records are routed correctly, it is important to configure your enterprise content types strategy before implementing your Records Center.

In a traditional file plan, record classifications are tracked by using identification keys or codes that organize the records files for easy browsing. For example, a file may be given a "Document ID" such as ACCT-DOC-001 that you would interpret as file number "1" of the "DOC" format in the "Accounting" division. These classification designators are often used to create a hierarchical structure of folders for organizing files. In SharePoint 2010, the recommended classification approach is to apply a specific content type to each document before it is submitted to the Records Center.

For every record type in your file plan, create a corresponding content type that users can apply to documents. Content types support inheritance, which allows you to base a new content type on an existing content type. In this way you can define a single content type with specific attributes and create a derived content type based on it. You can then add new attributes to the new content type to extend the definition. In some cases you may want to create several derived content types from the same parent type to distinguish different documents that otherwise have the same attributes. For example, the Financial Statement and Fiscal Report content types might be two subtypes of the parent type Finance Document, created to distinguish two specific types of documents in the same general category. Each type could then be routed into a different records library in the Records Center or they could be grouped together.

Inheritance for content types works only within site collections, not between them. You can create parent and child relationships between content types either within the same site or between a parent site and a child site. However, if you have several source sites that will submit documents to the Records Center, then you will need to re-create the content types in every site collection. A more efficient approach might be to create the content types using the Managed Metadata Service application service provided in SharePoint 2010. This service allows you to publish your content types to all site collections contained within any Web application consuming from the Managed Metadata Service. This ensures that the content types are uniform across the environment and are only deployed to the appropriate site collections.

For content to be correctly routed and stored in the Records Center, it is essential that users apply the appropriate content types to documents before they are submitted to the Records Center. If users upload existing documents to a document library, and the library is configured with multiple content types, then users will be prompted to select a content type for the document. Alternatively, users can create new content directly from content type templates by selecting the content type from the New menu in the document library. In both cases, the user must provide values for any required data fields associated with the content type. Content managers for each site collection should review documents periodically to ensure that they are being assigned the appropriate content types as defined in the file plan.

Creating the Records Center

The Records Center site is used in conjunction with content types in SharePoint 2010 to implement the file plan. The Records Center site template has been designed for use as the storage location for the "official" copies of all records in your organization. That does not mean that the file will be the only copy; there might also be other copies of a document in other sites, but the copy in the Records Center can be configured to prevent it from being changed.

> **BEST PRACTICES** You should create the Records Center on a separate Web application with the Records Center template selected as the root site collection to ensure that there is complete security separation between the center and any other sites. The security on the Records Center should be more restrictive than on other sites, set so that very few users have document edit privileges. Another advantage of using a separate Web application for the Records Center is that it will use a separate SQL Server database for all data stored in the application. This allows you to back up and restore the repository on a different schedule from other sites. Additionally, having the repository in a separate application makes it easy to set up indexing of content on a separate schedule.

The Records Center contains a number of specialized features that make it easy to use as a records management site. The Records Center contains the following Records Center–specific features.

- Content Organizer

- E-mail Integration with Content Organizer
- Hold and eDiscovery

Figure 8-16 shows a site created from the Records Center site template with two additional records libraries created and the site collection Document ID feature enabled. Records are added to the Record Center using the Submit A Record button on this page or using a farm-wide Send To Records Center option. By default, this page contains four Web Part zones, making this page easy to customize to provide additional information.

When a record is sent to the Records Center, it is placed in the Drop Off Library until the Content Organizer rules are assessed, at which point, if there is a destination available based on content type or metadata, it is sent to that records library. If there is not a Content Organizer rule for the document, it will remain in the Drop Off Library until a records manager determines where the record should be placed. The document can be routed to the correct location by locating the document in the Drop Off Library and then populating the properties required by a Content Organizer rule that will route it to the appropriate location.

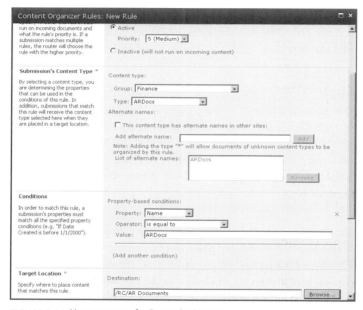

FIGURE 8-16 Home page of a Records Center

When users or workflows submit items to the Records Center, it is the job of the Web applications application pool to communicate and submit the record, rather than the user. There is a special group created in the Records Center site called Records Center Web Service Submitters, and this group allows you to define the various other application pool IDs to allow all of them to submit items using the Officialfile.asmx Web service.

After creating the Records Center site, you can access the configuration page shown in Figure 8-17 by clicking Site Actions and then selecting Manage Records Center. The Records

Center Management page outlines the tasks you should perform to complete the configuration of the Records Center. Notice that by default this page contains three Web parts that assist you in completing the configuration of your Records Center: Setup Tasks And File Plan Creation, Common Records Management Tasks, and Content Organizer Rules.

FIGURE 8-17 Records Center Management page

Setup Tasks And File Plan Creation

In the Setup Tasks And File Plan Creation section of the Records Center Management page shown in Figure 8-17, you will notice that the Records Center is not fully configured, and this section suggests you contact your site collection administrator and request activation of the In Place Records and the Document ID Service site collection features. Furthermore, there is a list of four steps you should take to complete the configuration of the Records Center, along with a brief description of each step. Upon completion and testing of these tasks, you can return to this page and remove this Web part.

Common Records Management Tasks

To the right of the Setup Tasks And File Plan Creation Web part, you will find another Web part that lists the common tasks that you can access from the Records Center Management page. Each task listed contains a hyperlink to the page that it references, providing you with easy access to those pages. Notice that this section provides other quick access points to create a new Content Organizer rule and to create a new records library. You will use some of these options more during the initial configuration of the Records Center; others you will not need to use until after you have completed the configuration of your Records Center.

Content Organizer Rules

The third section on this page provides another location for you to create new Content Organizer rules by clicking Add New Item. This displays a list of the Content Organizer rules that you have created, allowing you to quickly access the rules you have defined and, if necessary, make changes to those rules. Figure 8-18 contains a partial display of the Content Organizer Rules: New Rule configuration page you use to create new Content Organizer rules.

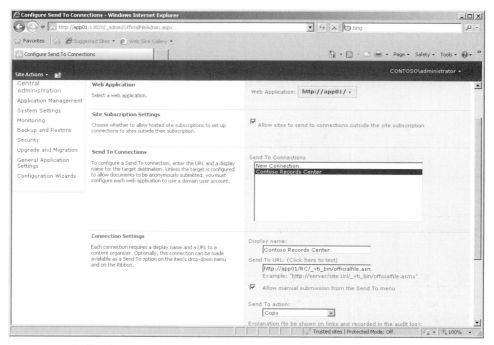

FIGURE 8-18 Configuring a new Content Organizer rule

This page allows you to provide a name for the rule and to set a priority for the rule of 1 to 9, with 1 the highest priority. This priority setting is used by the Records Center when a submitted record matches multiple rules. The router will choose the rule with the highest priority to determine where to route the record. After choosing the appropriate content type, all properties associated with that content type are available for defining the conditions that must be met for it to be routed to the specified target location. If there are multiple conditions defined in this rule, all conditions must be met for it to be routed to the destination library.

Figure 8-19 shows the Records Center Management page after activating the site collection features it suggested (shown in Figure 8-17), including the Document ID feature now shown. The Content Organizer Rules list now contains two rules.

FIGURE 8-19 Updated Records Center Management page

Creating Records Libraries

Record libraries serve as the storage locations for files in the Records Center. Each library can hold one type of file or many different types depending on how you want to group files for browsing and navigation. Files will be automatically routed into the records libraries based on the locations you configure in the Content Organizer list. In SharePoint 2010, you can create folders within records libraries, and they can be used as destination locations in the Content Organizer rules. Folders can be created automatically based on property values associated with the documents being routed, allowing the routing not to be based solely on content type as it was in SharePoint Server 2007.

When using the records library template to create a library in the Records Center, major versioning is automatically turned on for you. You can customize this after the library is created to remove the major versioning, or you can choose to enable major and minor versioning.

Defining Required Metadata

While planning what records libraries you need to create, consider what types of metadata you will want to track for the documents that are stored in each library. If there are columns of data already associated with the document in the source site, you will want to create the same columns on the destination records library in the Records Center. Otherwise, the metadata will be copied into the library but it will not be accessible through the website pages. You can also create additional columns in the records library to track metadata that is required by your file plan but was not present on the original document. For example, you may want to assign a tracking number to the file that is generated by an external document tracking system. The user would then be prompted for this number when she sends the document to the repository.

When a document is submitted to the Records Center, the Content Organizer rules are queried to determine which document library the file should be routed to, based on content type, document properties, and priority settings of the rules that are applicable to that document. That library is then queried to retrieve a list of columns that constitute the metadata that will be associated with the file. Existing document metadata that matches columns in the document library is automatically promoted and stored in the library columns. If there are metadata columns that are not already populated with data, then the user is presented with the Missing Properties page to provide the missing values. If the user fails to provide any required values or cancels the Missing Properties page, then the file is still copied to the Records Center, but it is placed in the Drop Off Library.

Applying Information Management Policies

Each of the records libraries will have information management policies applied to them to enforce the file plan distributed earlier. By default, each policy feature can have four configurable options; these options were discussed in the section titled "Implementing and Configuring Information Management Polices" earlier in this chapter. You can either apply one policy for the entire records library or, if you configure the records library to allow multiple content types, then you can apply a separate policy to each content type.

Creating Content Organizer Rules

At this point, you want to create the Content Organizer rules based on either content types or metadata to control where the document will reside in the Records Center. If you are specifying more than one property to determine where to route the document, all property values must be met to ensure proper routing. If you are using content types, you can define what library you want to receive the document. Regardless of what rules are used to route the document, all the records library information management policies are applied to the document after it is placed in the records library.

Creating a Farm Level Send To Option

The Send To function can be defined at two locations in the graphical user interface (GUI)—you can use either the advanced properties of a document library or the farm level configuration in SharePoint 2010 Central Administration.

The advantage of configuring Send To locations in Central Administration is that after you create them there, they are available to users in every site in a Web application in the farm, thus making it easy to deploy the central Records Center Send To location, regardless of where you use the Send To definitions. Another advantage of defining the Send To location in Central Administration is that you can now configure multiple Send To locations, which is useful in a company that has multiple Records Centers.

To configure the farm level Send To locations, go to SharePoint 2010 Central Administration, General Application Settings, External Service Connections, and select Configure Send To Connections to display the Configure Send To Connections page shown in Figure 8-20.

FIGURE 8-20 Creating a Send To Location in Central Administration

On the Configure Send To Connections page, choose the Web application where the Send To connection will reside and choose whether you want to allow sites within the Web application to be able to send items outside of the site.

When creating the connection, you must specify the URL of the Records Center with the addition of Officialfile.asmx. For example, if a Records Center is created in the RC subsite for the Web application called *http://App01/RC*, you would specify the following URL: *http://App01/RC/_vti_bin/officialfile.asmx*.

You also need to specify a user-friendly name in the name field; this is what users will see when they select the document in the library. Naming conventions are very important when creating multiple Send To locations that are available to users throughout the farm and when using the locally configured Send To locations.

You can also choose if you want to allow the manual use of Send To for the Records Center. You would leave this checked unless your approach for official files is to have the process automated by a workflow.

Finally, you choose what to do with the item being sent to the Records Center using one of the following three options:

- Copy
- Move
- Move And Leave A Link

After completing these options, click OK to create the Send To connection. You can visit this screen at any point to update or remove any configured Send To connections.

Placing a Hold on Records

One of the most important aspects of a records management system is how easily it allows records managers to identify and mark documents that are required for an investigation, audit, or in response to litigation that involves the organization. For example, a financial audit might require a company to produce all documents pertaining to the financial state of the organization for the past five fiscal years. If the policy applying to those documents had set them to expire and be deleted after five years, then it is possible that some of the required documents would be purged while the audit is occurring. This would hamper the audit and possibly result in fines and penalties for the organization.

The Records Center site contains a Holds option that is used to place policy locks on sets of documents in the Records Center, preventing them from expiring or being deleted while on hold. When an item is placed on hold, all automated expiration policies are suspended for that item and users are prevented from deleting the item. Creating a hold involves creating a new item in the Holds list, which can be completed by performing a search using the Search And Add To Hold page shown in Figure 8-21.

Alternatively, you can also locate the record in the Records Center, hover over the title of the document until you see an arrow, and then click Compliance Details to present the Compliance Details page shown in Figure 8-22. Click the Add/Remove From Hold link and specify the name of the hold. Conversely, you can use these same steps to remove the hold; instead of adding it to a hold, you can choose to remove it from a hold that was previously applied.

To view items that are on hold, you can access the Hold Reports under Holds And eDiscovery in the Site Settings section of the Records Center. This is also another place that you can place items on hold; simply click Holds and then add an item to the Holds list.

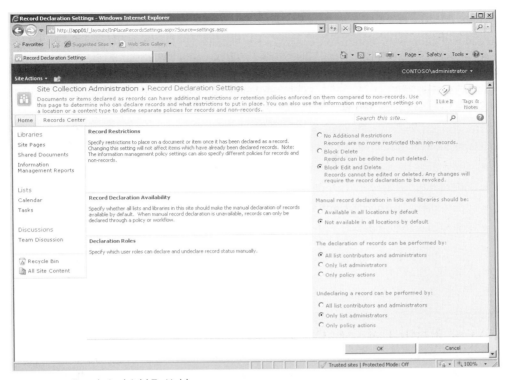

FIGURE 8-21 Search And Add To Hold page

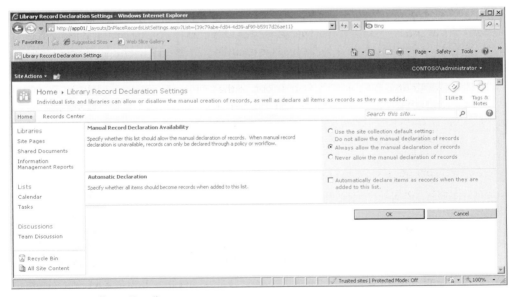

FIGURE 8-22 Compliance Details page

Generating a File Plan Report

You can also choose the option to Generate a File Plan Report from the Records Center Management interface, as shown in Figure 8-23. This option allows you to create an Excel file that outlines your file plan as currently configured in your Records Center. To create the file plan, you need to specify a location to store the plans. Each new report will be stored in this location separately, in the folder specified.

After you generate the file plan report, you can obtain detailed information on many aspects of the configured center file plan, such as

- Site details such as Declaration settings and number of items on hold
- Content types used in the policies
- Policy names associated with the content types
- Policy description details
- Description
- Versioning options
- Date the report was generated

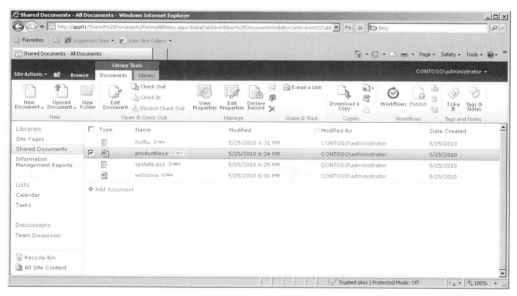

FIGURE 8-23 File Plan Report page

Notice there are two detail-specific tabs available to you that can provide you with specific information about retention policies and folder details.

The Retention Details tab contains columns based on how you have defined retention for the policy the report addresses. Figure 8-24 provides an example of how the retention details will appear with a single-stage retention policy defined.

FIGURE 8-24 File Plan Retention Details tab

The Folder Details tab contains information about the folder locations, paths, permissions, retention schedule, and content types, as shown in Figure 8-25.

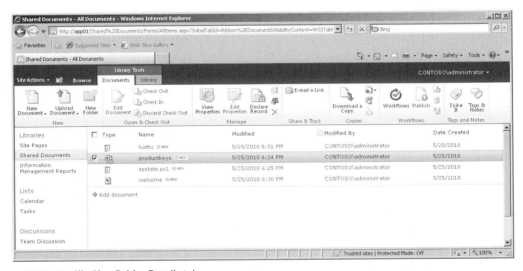

FIGURE 8-25 File Plan Folder Details tab

Generating an Audit Report

Audit reports allow you to examine specific areas of declared records activities. When you run a report, you must specify a location for each report generated; the location can be the same library for each report generated or a different one. After the audit report is generated, you can view information in four categories, each of which contains specific reports, as listed here.

- Content Activity Reports
  - Content modifications
  - Content type and list modifications
  - Content viewing
  - Deletion
- Custom Reports
  - Run A Custom Report   Allows you to specify the selection criteria, including date range, report restrictions, and events available from the Information Management Policies.
- Information Management Policy Reports
  - Expiration and disposition
  - Policy modifications
- Security and Site Settings Reports
  - Auditing settings
  - Security settings

As time passes and more information is generated, audit reports will provide vital information for compliance officers and auditors if this data is required as part of a litigation enquiry. Consider using custom reports for a more detailed picture of specific events, as shown in Figure 8-26. You can use this page to specify the location where the report will be created, what information will be contained within the report, the dates of activity that the report should contain, who can view the report, and the items that should be contained within the report.

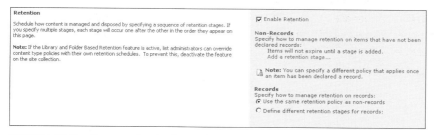

FIGURE 8-26 Creating a customized report

Implementing and Managing In Place Records

SharePoint 2010 introduces In Place Records Management, a feature that allows you to declare any document as a record—if it is located within a site collection that has this feature activated. This eliminates the need to have to send every document to the Records Center in order for them to be handled as a record.

After enabling this site collection feature, users can declare any document within the site collection as a record. These records now have policies and restrictions on them similar to those in the Records Center. The policies for these records can be added at either the content type or the document library containing the documents.

Implementing In Place Records at the Site Collection

To use In Place Records Management, you need to activate the In Place Records Management site collection feature. After doing so you can use the site collection record declaration settings shown in Figure 8-27 to control how the records are managed in the site collection. This page is divided into the following three sections.

- Record Restrictions
- Record Declaration Availability
- Declaration Roles

Within the Record Restrictions section, you can specify restrictions on how a document or item is handled after it has been declared a record. The three options available are No Addition Restrictions, which will allow the records to be handled in the same way as non-records; Block Delete, to prevent the deletion of the records; or Block Delete And Edit, to prevent both the deletion and editing of the records.

In the Record Declaration Availability section, you can specify whether all lists and libraries within the site collection can use manual declaration of records by default, or you can choose to not make the manual declaration the default behavior for all lists and libraries. When the second option is selected, you can only declare records using a policy or workflow.

Within the Declaration Roles section, you specify which user roles can declare or undeclare records manually. There are three options for the declaration and three options for the undeclaring of the records: All List Contributors And Administrators, Only List Administrators, or Only Policy Actions.

FIGURE 8-27 Site Collection Record Declaration Settings page

Configuring In Place Records in a List or Library

After implementing In Place Records at the site collection, you still have to manage which lists and libraries use the In Place Records feature. This is done by accessing the settings for the library or list, where you will now have a Record Declaration Settings option under Permissions And Management.

When you click this link, you will see the page shown in Figure 8-28. By default, the library inherits the manual record declaration settings from the site collection options. However, you can choose to override those settings and select either the Always Allow The Manual Declaration Of Records option or Never Allow The Manual Declaration Of Records option. Optionally, you can override the need to manually declare records in the list or library by selecting the Automatically Declare Items As Records When They Are Added To This List check box. After selecting this check box, the three options above the check box are no longer available as choices.

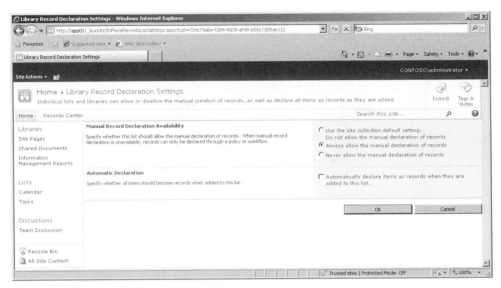

FIGURE 8-28 List or Library Record Declaration Settings page

Managing In Place Records in a List or Library

After you have enabled In Place Records for a list or library, you will are able to choose any item or document within that list or library and declare it as a record using one of two methods. You can use the Declare Record icon on the Ribbon as shown in Figure 8-29.

FIGURE 8-29 Documents Library with Declare Record option available on Ribbon

Another way you can declare a record on an existing document is to hover over the document name and click the drop-down arrow; then click Compliance Details to display the dialog box shown in Figure 8-30. You can then click the Declare As A Record link within the Record Status section of the screen.

FIGURE 8-30 Compliance Details dialog box

Regardless of the approach you take to implement an In Place record, there is an easy way you can look at a document library to determine if a document has been declared as a record. After declaring a document as a record, the icon displayed under the Type column within the library will have a little lock on the lower-right side of the icon, as shown with the Productkeys document in Figure 8-31.

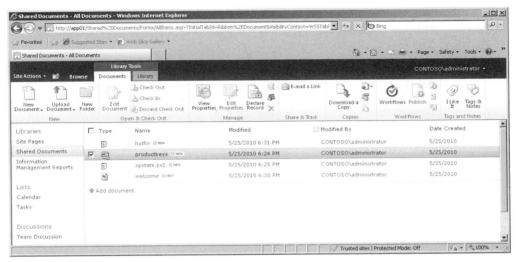

FIGURE 8-31 Declared record with Lock On File icon

With the appropriate permissions, you can also undeclare the record from within the Compliance Details dialog box by clicking the Undeclare Record link.

Managing Information Management Policies with In Place Records Activated

Earlier in this chapter you discovered how to enable and configure retention at a content type, list, and library. After activating the In Place Records site collection feature, you will have a different experience when enabling retention—you will see an additional option available that allows you to specify how you want the retention policy to behave for records and non-records, as shown in Figure 8-32.

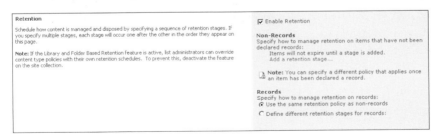

FIGURE 8-32 Enabling retention with the In Place Records feature activated

Summary

In this chapter, you examined information management policies and records management features in SharePoint 2010. The chapter began by discussing the concept of information management and records management from a high-level view to help you understand how critical information management is for organizations today that deal with large numbers of electronic documents. You reviewed the major elements of a document management plan, including defining the key roles in the organization, defining compliance requirements, and writing a file plan. You looked at the process of implementing the file plan in SharePoint 2010 using information management policies.

You were introduced to the different mechanisms for managing documents throughout their life cycles by implementing stages of retention. In addition to retention, this chapter discussed the use of barcodes, labels, and auditing. It also looked at the various reporting options available in SharePoint 2010 for viewing information management policy usage patterns.

The chapter also reviewed how to implement and configure a Records Center, which included the use of information management policies on the records libraries. You covered the important aspect of how to create and release holds in response to regulatory or legal needs. This chapter also discussed how to implement and configure new functionality in SharePoint 2010, the In Place Records Management feature, which is enabled and configured at the site collection level but can be managed at the list and library level. This new functionality eliminates the need for all records to be stored in a central repository by allowing users to declare any document as a record.

Organizing Information

This chapter outlines the *putability* side of a robust information architecture, which means that it focuses on how information goes into your SharePoint farm. It also outlines some of the latest research and thinking as it relates to the development of any information architecture. The technical administrator might find much of this nontechnical information boring or irrelevant—but nothing could be further from the truth. The most trouble that people will have with Microsoft SharePoint 2010 will not be with the technology itself, but instead will involve how to map the technology to the organization's business goals and ensure that the technology is not getting in the way of the organization functioning efficiently and effectively. Much of this discussion about information architecture directly impacts your deployment. Understanding the business layer better will help you be a better SharePoint administrator.

> **NOTE**   This chapter introduces a series of concepts that are presented in order to illustrate a larger argument. These concepts build on one another, so it is best to read this chapter as a single unit.

Developing an Information Architecture with SharePoint 2010

The development of an information architecture could consume several books by itself. Just Bing "information architecture" and you'll see a multitude of books, websites, and organizations that offer ideas and services on the organization of information. In the following sections, you'll take a brief look at the state of information organization in most organizations today and then delve into how to develop an information organization effort in your own organization.

Value of Information

What is the value of information in your organization? Because balance sheets for most companies don't track the soft costs of developing information, organizations often don't really know what their information is worth. If you were to ask most top-level managers how valuable information is to their organization, most would swiftly tell you that it is highly valuable. Yet it is often difficult to get those same individuals to agree to manage that information better. Managing information can form a competitive advantage.[1] In addition, the following statistics indicate that the need to manage information better is strong.

- Over 30 *billion* original documents are created and consumed each year.
- Cost of documents is estimated to be as much as 15 percent of annual revenues.
- 85 percent of documents are never retrieved.
- 50 percent of documents are duplicates of other documents in some way.
- 60 percent of stored documents are obsolete.
- For every $1 spent to create the document, $10 are spent to manage it.[2]

It's obvious that organizations are great at creating documents, but not so good at managing them. Most organizations have a strong tendency to commit more resources to create information and fewer resources to manage that information. As a result, operating knowledge is often undocumented, tacit knowledge is rarely documented, and knowledge is easily lost through transitions such as retirement or attrition. In most industries, it is becoming more important to retain key knowledge that can be taken by competitors, but most "how to" information is held in people's minds in an undocumented way.

So why do most companies not engage in a strong organization of their information? Frankly, excuses abound.

- "If we need it, we can usually find it. Just send an e-mail and someone will find it."
- "No one will ever sue us, and if we do get sued, we'll find what we need to defend ourselves."
- "We've got to pick our battles. If it costs $20 to file a document, $120 to find a misfiled document, and $220 to reproduce a lost document, then it's probably less expensive to find a misfiled document and reproduce a lost document than it is to ensure that every document is filed correctly."
- "Enterprise content management (ECM) is too expensive and there's little return on investment (ROI), so why invest in it?"

---

[1] Bill Gates, *Business @ the Speed of Thought* (New York: Grand Central Publishing, 1999).

[2] Roger Evernden and Elaine Evernden, *Information First* (Oxford, UK: Elsevier, 2003).

The reality is that you're already paying for a bad ECM through opportunity costs. A good ECM will lower your opportunity costs through better efficiencies. But in many organizations, you'll find these excuses proffered by those who don't see a need to invest in a better information organization effort. It will take time and persistent education to help those who hold these ideas recognize the need to invest in an information organization project.

In addition to the excuses about why better information management isn't worth the effort, sometimes companies aren't even using the resources they have very well. For example, in many organizations SharePoint is installed in such a way that it is working in conflict with other ECM systems. When asked how well SharePoint was working with other ECM systems, respondents to a recent survey[3] indicated that

- SharePoint is working in conflict with other ECM systems in their company. (29%)
- SharePoint is integrated with existing ECM suites. (16%)
- SharePoint is the only ECM suite used in their organization. (12%)
- SharePoint is used to "fill in some functions." (43%)
- The information technology (IT) department rolls out SharePoint with no input from record managers or ECM teams. (36%)
- They realize no one is in charge and that SharePoint and ECM are out of control. (14%)

SMS/text messages, blogs, wikis, and other Web 2.0 technologies are not part of the ECM solution in 75 percent of organizations. This represents a major risk to companies and prevents a large portion of collaborative activities from being managed properly. Compliance officers are wrestling with how to incorporate Web 2.0 technologies into their ECM compliance standards while ensuring that teams can collaborate effectively to achieve business goals.

What Is Putability?

Putability is the quality of putting content into an information management and retrieval system with the correct metadata. It is the degree to which you put quality information into your information management system and represents the first step in an overall information process. When it comes to developing an information process, you must pay attention to three essential parts, as shown in Figure 9-1. How information goes into any information retrieval system will directly impact how well it comes out.

FIGURE 9-1 Three essential parts to an information process

When it comes to putability, you must pay attention to two truths—ignore these at your own peril. First, what goes in must come out. This is the old "garbage in, garbage out" adage about computing that has been used since the 1960s, and it was originally developed to call attention to the fact that computers will unquestioningly process the most nonsensical

---

[3] AIIM, *Findability and Market IQ*, available at *http://www.aiim.org*.

of input data (garbage in) and produce equally nonsensical output (garbage out). It is amazing that otherwise very smart people will think they can load volumes of documents into SharePoint 2010 with little thought to organization and then expect to find individual documents quickly and easily. Chaos does not lead to organization, and organization is the foundation of findability.

The second truth associated with putability is that users will resist taking the time required to put quality information into the system. Managers seem to be especially resistant to having their information workers take time to properly tag their information as it goes into the system. It seems that the vast majority of information retrieval systems users mistakenly believe that as long as the information is indexed, they'll be able to find it. User resistance is one of the most difficult obstacles to overcome when implementing a robust information organization effort. When asked who is responsible for tagging information, a survey[4] elicited the following responses (multiple answers were allowed to this question, hence the total of more than 100 percent).

- Authors (40%)
- Records managers (29%)
- SMEs (25%)
- Anyone (23%)
- Don't know (12%)
- No one (16%)

This means that in many organizations, users simply don't know who is responsible for tagging information or are not directly assigned the tagging task to make that information more findable. In the absence of a governance rule that details who is responsible for tagging documents, the result is that anyone (and yet no one) will be able to apply metadata to a document. This is not a recipe for success.

What Is Findability?

Findability is the quality of being locatable or navigable.[5] It is the degree to which objects are easy to discover or locate. As with putability, there are some truths to which you should pay attention. First, you can't use what you can't find. So it really doesn't matter whether or not the information exists—if you can't find it, you can't use it. The corollary to this is that information that can't be found is pragmatically worthless. You might have spent millions to develop that information, but if you can't find it when you need it, it is worthless.

Second, information that is hard to find is hardly used. It stands to reason that users who won't take the time to put quality information into the system will also not take much time to find the information they need. Often, if users can't find information quickly and easily, they will simply e-mail someone who they think can find the information for them, or they may simply not include that information in their decision-making processes.

---

[4] AIIM, *Findability and Market IQ*, available at *http://www.aiim.org*.

[5] Peter Moreville, *Ambient Findability* (Sebastapol, CA: O'Reilly Media, 2002).

Of course, the more the information is *needed* by the user, the harder she will work to find it. But in the long run, users won't put out any more effort than they believe is minimally necessary to do their job.

> **NOTE** Out of the three parts to the information process, putability and findability are the most interwoven. The hosting of the information is merely the static retention of that information between the two major actions of putting information into the system and then pulling it back out. The main thing to remember is that the quality of information input into SharePoint 2010 directly impacts the output of information from SharePoint 2010.

Why are putability and findability important? Because you can do all of the following tasks correctly and still not succeed (from your user's viewpoint) with your SharePoint 2010 implementation.

- Capacity plan your servers correctly
- Scale out your farm correctly
- Implement all of the customizations correctly
- Implement a robust search and indexing solution
- Train your users correctly
- Write the business and technical requirements for your deployment
- Manage your servers so there are no errors or warnings in any of the event logs

The real success of any SharePoint implementation will be evaluated largely in terms of how well users can manage and find information using the features in SharePoint. Although the rest of the items listed previously are essential to a successful deployment, the support and furtherance of the *business goals* will be the final arbiter of whether or not the deployment is successful. In most environments, those business goals will be defined, in part, in information management terms.

How Well Is Findability Understood?

When respondents were asked the question "How well is findability understood in your organization?" in the Findability and Market IQ survey conducted by the Association for Information and Image Management (AIIM),[6] the following answers were given.

- It is well understood and addressed. (17%)
- It is vaguely understood. (31%)
- Not sure how search and findability are different. (30%)
- No clear understanding of findability at all. (22%)

This means that over half (52%) of the employees in organizations today that participated in the survey either don't know what findability is, or they are not able to differentiate find-

---

[6] AIIM, *Findability and Market IQ*, available at *http://www.aiim.org*.

ability from search technologies. Many believe that if they have a stand-alone search tool, then findability is being adequately addressed. Nothing could be further from the truth.

Search is too often viewed as an application-specific solution for findability. Search technologies focus on trying to ask the right question and on "matching" keyword queries with content under the assumption that if the right words are input as the query, the right content will be found. What you must understand is that findability is not a technology—it is a way of managing information that is embedded in the organization. Achieving success with the information process relies on well-defined patterns and practices that are consistently applied to the information. Although it is true that search technologies support efforts to find information, search can't fix the "garbage in, garbage out" problems present in most organizations today. The carelessness with which organizations manage information cannot be resolved by a technology.

The Paradox of Findability as a Corporate Strategy

When asked the degree to which findability is critical to their overall business goals and success, 62 percent of respondents indicated that it is imperative or significant. Only 5 percent felt it had minimal or no impact on business success. Yet 49 percent responded that even though findability is strategically essential, they have no formal plan or set of goals for findability in their organization. Of the other 51 percent who claimed to have a strategy, 26 percent reported that they used an ad hoc strategy—that is, they developed it only as needed—meaning that they had no strategy at all. Hence, 75 percent of organizations surveyed had no findability strategy, even though many believe it is strategically essential.

The Opportunity Cost of a Poor Information Process and Architecture

So, what are the opportunity costs of maintaining a poor information process and architecture? The information on cost studies is not robust, but the data available suggests that organizations are losing a lot of money on this problem. A good study[7] on the costs related to time spent searching for hard-to-find information suggests the following.

- Typical employees spend an average of 3.5 hours per week trying to find information but not finding it.

- These employees spend another 3.0 hours recreating information they know exists, but that they cannot find.

> **NOTE** An *opportunity cost* is the cost of passing up the next best choice when making a decision. For example, if an asset such as capital is used for one purpose, the opportunity cost is the value of the next best use of that asset. In this chapter, the opportunity cost is the value of work that is lost by the corporation because they choose to pay their workers to spend time working within a problematic information system instead of having their work focused on other potentially revenue-generating activities.

---

[7] Susan Feldman et al., *The Hidden Costs of Information Work* (IDC study, 2005).

This means that the average knowledge worker spends 6.5 hours per week searching for information, not finding it, and then recreating that information so that the worker can move forward in his or her job. At an average salary of $60,000 (US dollars) per year, this "lost" time equates to $9,750 per worker per year. In a company with 1000 employees, this equates to an annual opportunity cost of $9.7 million (US dollars). In addition, that company with 1000 employees will spend $5.7 million per year (US dollars) simply to have users reformat data as it moves between applications,[8] and they will spend another $3.3 million per year dealing with version control issues.[9]

 REAL WORLD **Organizing Information for a Call Center**

The reality is that if a company improves the organization and findability of its information, it will not see a real cost savings, because an opportunity cost is a *hidden* cost that is not easily measured. But a company should see improved productivity and improved revenue generation activities that will reveal themselves in other measurements that are (seemingly) disconnected from the cost of a project that improves information organization and management.

For example, at a call center providing telephone support for a company's products, the average call was consuming nearly five minutes. After an analysis was done to determine what activities were occurring during those five minutes, company executives learned that it took nearly two minutes for the employee accepting the inbound call to find all of the customer's contact and purchase information. After implementing an information organization project, a second analysis showed that employees were able to find the same information much more quickly—usually in less than 30 seconds—and this led to a significant decrease in the length of an average call. This meant that fewer people could work with the same number of calls, making each employee more productive. The opportunity costs were realized on the bottom line when the company came out with new products to support and they found that the call center didn't need to hire more individuals to work the phones because of the efficiency created by the successful information organization project.

So even though the increase in efficiency in handling inbound calls seemed disconnected from the information organization effort, in reality they were directly connected. The measurements of the information organization project's success had to be extrapolated from what appeared to be an unrelated cost savings from the call center's increased productivity.

[8] Ibid.

[9] Ibid.

So, what prevents workers from finding information? The AIIM survey[10] found the following reasons.

- Poor search functionality (71%)
- Inconsistency in how workers tag/describe data (59%)
- Lack of adequate tags/descriptors (55%)
- Information not available electronically (49%)
- Poor navigation (48%)
- Don't know where to look (48%)
- Constant information change (37%)
- Can't access the system that hosts the info (30%)
- Workers don't know what they are looking for (22%)
- Lack the skills to find the information (22%)

Note that the first three reasons users cite are really about the putability side of the information process. So if an organization inconsistently tags and describes information, then the users will experience a poor result set, which is described in this list as "poor search functionality."

A poor search functionality, from the viewpoint of the user, is really about a result set that is not helpful or is *irrelevant*. A relevant result set has content items that are useful and helpful to the user. In most cases, a poor result set that is blamed on a poor search technology is really just a mirror of a bad information architecture implementation. In other words, garbage was put into the system, and so the result set tends to be garbage, which results in the end user blaming the technology for a poor search functionality. However, if you have a strong information architecture coupled with users who work together to maintain a set of patterns and practices for how information is managed, then search results will likely be relevant to the user. Again, the real problem in the management of information does not have to do with technology, but rather with the people who interact with the information management and retrieval system—that is, with an organization's willingness to invest in the staff as well as the software so that, working together (people and software), they can establish a successful, usable information architecture.

_____

[10] AIIM, *Findability and Market IQ*, available at *http://www.aiim.org*.

Why Your Top-Level Executives Will Want a Robust Information Process and Architecture

There are not many things that get the attention of a chief executive officer (CEO) more swiftly than the ongoing threat (reality?) of legal action against your organization or the unintentional but preventable breach of customer and other confidential information.

In the US, thirty-five states have laws requiring that individuals be notified if their confidential or personal data is lost, stolen, or compromised. The Privacy Rights Clearinghouse has identified more than 215 million records of US residents that have been exposed through security breaches since 2005. A 2007 study by the Ponemon Institute found that the average cost of a data breach is $197 per record, which represents a 43 percent increase from 2005. They also found that the average total cost per reporting company was $6.3 million (US dollars). But the cost of lost business from the loss of goodwill and trust by customers increased as well, to an average of $4.1 million per company and $128 per compromised record. Lost business now accounts for 65 percent of data breach costs, compared to 56 percent in the 2006 study.

A 2009 CheckPoint Study found that the number one threat to a company's network security was employees who inadvertently exposed confidential information. Consider who manages the security of your SharePoint extranet sites. In the vast majority of cases, it is not the information technology team. Instead, it is the owner of the site—a nontechnical, often undertrained end user. When you implement an information architecture and process, you must consider the risk of inadequate training for your end users.

The other risk is legal action against your organization. As part of a litigation effort against your company, opposing counsel will ask the judge to allow them to "discover" information within your electronic systems to help them build their case against you. This process is called *e-discovery*. This process includes, but is not limited to, computer forensics, e-mail archiving, and online discovery of documents. If you have reasonable expectation to be involved in a case, then you have a duty to *preserve* evidence.

If you can't quickly produce documents and records, or if you don't have a well-defined set of policies that outline how information is to be managed in your organization, you're opening yourself up to serious legal exposure. You should, of course, consult with your legal team, but at minimum, your organization should undertake a litigation readiness review to ensure that if your company is involved in a legal action—even as a third party—you are able to find and produce records quickly and reliably.

SharePoint 2010, Putability, and Findability

There is a concept in marketing called the *long tail*[11] that was originally explained in the magazine *Wired*. The concept is rather simple, and when applied to a SharePoint implementation, it can help you understand why information that is held in SharePoint isn't necessarily more findable than information in a database or a file server.

In short, the concept is that, given the total number of items in a population set that *can* be found, the majority of those items will be seldom requested, while a minority of those items will be frequently requested. For example, most of your users are likely to visit your intranet portal, but only a minority of your users will visit any specific team site. But in most implementations, the number of team sites utilized will be far larger than the number of frequently accessed sites, like an intranet portal. The relationship is necessarily inverse and is illustrated in Figure 9-2.

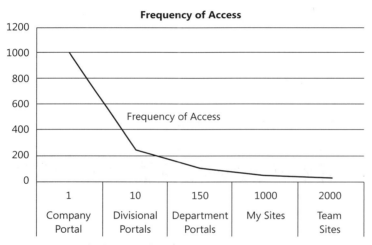

FIGURE 9-2 Sample "long tail" for a typical SharePoint 2010 implementation

When you realize that most of the sites, lists, and libraries that are created in a typical SharePoint 2010 implementation are seldom accessed by more than a handful of people, the planning issues for a SharePoint 2010 implementation take on important dynamics.

Although you will want to ensure that your heavily accessed portals are well planned, you should spend a similar amount of time ensuring that important information hosted in *infrequently* accessed team sites is just as accessible and findable.

The core of those planning issues should answer questions such as the following.

- How will users who frequently access team sites find those team sites?
- How will users who infrequently access team sites find those team sites?

---

[11] Chris Anderson, *The Long Tail* (New York: Hyperion Books, 2006).

- How will users who infrequently access team sites know what information is in those sites?

- How will users find documents corporate-wide when conducting an exhaustive search for a specific type of information?

- How will users find documents when looking for a sample of data that need not constitute an exhaustive search?

- Should you provide a federated navigation hierarchy for users to browse to find information? If so, how should you implement this?

These and other questions begin to get to the heart of findability within SharePoint 2010. Because most of what is created in SharePoint is in the long tail, most people who utilize SharePoint will not consume most of the information within the SharePoint 2010 implementation. Yet your implementation must make *all* of the information findable by a potentially large number of your users (assuming those users have permissions and a need to see the information).

Finding information merely by the document's content will not work in environments in which the data set is large. In most organizations, the use of words tends to be homogeneous, meaning that people in an organization tend to use a certain set of words repeatedly in their documents. For example, an accounting firm is likely to use a different set of words in its documents than a medical firm or a marketing firm, but within each of these companies, the employees will use the same words over and over again. When words are used in similar ways across multiple documents, those words lose their effectiveness at discriminating between documents. You enter a keyword in a query to discriminate between documents and find the specific one you want, but if the keyword you use is one that is used by all employees and appears frequently in many documents, it is really useless as a discriminatory tool.

Moreover, sometimes the same word can be used across multiple documents with very different meanings. For example, is it a horn (beep-beep), or a horn (a trumpet), or a horn (on an animal)? You might enter the keyword "horn" when you are looking for a document about a trumpet. But if you get a result set full of content items pointing to a car horn, then—even though the result set might be syntactically accurate—it will be irrelevant to you. What users want when they search for information is more than just a result set that matches their query—they want *meaning* within information. To the extent that the content items are meaningful to them (as well as useful and accessible), then they will view the result set as relevant.

Defining *meaning* in a query is best achieved through a complex query that not only requests documents with certain keywords but also specifies documents that have certain metadata characteristics. For example, you might be looking for the project budget for Customer A. You would normally expect that this document would contain the word "budget" along with the customer's name. However, it's also possible that the budget document doesn't contain the word "budget." So what are the possible ways to query and find this document?

In most environments, people will query only for keywords that they think (or hope) will exist in the document. In this example, you would normally query for the following words

- budget
- Customer A

If the document had metadata attached to it, you could further refine your query—if the metadata has been completed—by using the following criteria.

- Security level: "Confidential"
- Project name: "SharePoint 2010 Implementation for Customer A"
- Project lead: "Bill English"
- Project type: "Consulting"

You can see that by adding several metadata fields to the project budget document and then including those fields in your query (using the Advanced Query Web Part), you can be more confident of finding the document that you really need. More to the point, the better you can define the document that you're trying to find, the better you can inform the SharePoint 2010 search technologies of what you *mean* with your query. For example, if your company had completed 20 projects with Customer A, then merely querying for the words "budget" and "Customer A" would return at least 20 different results, 19 of which would likely not be relevant to your search. Moreover, depending on how information is managed, these two words could return hundreds of false positives, spurious results that lack relevancy to what you are looking for. But if you can enter the project name, the security level, and the current project lead (assuming that the project lead is different for different projects with this customer), then you help define what you *mean* by the keyword query of "budget" and "Customer A" with further, more discriminatory information.

For metadata to be helpful in finding information, the metadata must be

- discriminatory
- input accurately
- input consistently
- defined

Referring back to the discussion about the word "horn" and how it can have different meanings, the same principles hold true for metadata. For metadata to be discriminatory, the metadata words that are entered must have a specific meaning that is understood by all who use that metadata. In addition, those meanings must have discriminatory power between documents in either a stand-alone capacity or when used in conjunction with other metadata.

For example, assume you have three standard metadata fields that must be applied to each document, as follows.

- Security level
- Project name
- Department name

Each of these three metadata fields will have some discriminatory abilities when used by themselves. For example, assume you're looking for the budget file for Project A and the file's security level has been set to "confidential." If you enter the keyword "budget" and the security level "confidential," you'll get back results that include any budget for any project across all departments that has a security level of "confidential." So a single metadata field can have discriminatory abilities.

But you'll find that if you set up your metadata correctly, combining multiple metadata fields into the same query can return a much more relevant and concise result set. For example, if you enter the keyword "budget" and then enter "confidential" for the security level, "project A" for the project name, and "Information Technology" for the department name, you're assured that the results will only include those documents that have the word "budget" plus the three metadata values included in your query. That result set is likely to be much more focused and relevant because it is better defined.

For metadata to be meaningful, both the metadata field names and the range of potential values have to be defined and distributed. Hence, a glossary is needed to define the meaning of both the field names and the metadata values. And then the glossary needs to be distributed and utilized as a business tool.

Putability and the Managed Metadata Service

For all of the preceding reasons, the Managed Metadata Service (MMS) must be utilized if you want to significantly improve the findability of information in your environment. It is the only way you'll achieve consistent application of metadata to your data within SharePoint 2010. When your users consistently apply metadata to information, they will be able to find information more easily and quickly. The MMS is all about putability in your information architecture. (The Managed Metadata Service is covered in more detail in Chapter 14, "Administering Enterprise Content Management.")

Table 9-1 provides an outline of how content type syndication and the MMS achieve the metadata needs outlined to this point in this chapter.

TABLE 9-1 Alignment of the MMS with Metadata Criteria

METADATA CRITERIA	MANAGED METADATA SERVICE	NOTES
Discriminatory	X	■ Through the central management of content types, metadata fields can be controlled and applied.
		■ Closed choice fields can be promulgated across the enterprise, ensuring that metadata values selected have been vetted to make sure they are discriminatory.

continued on next page

METADATA CRITERIA	MANAGED METADATA SERVICE	NOTES
Input accurately	X	Closed choice fields can ensure that metadata is selected, rather than input, which will reduce or eliminate misspellings, undefined synonyms, or other extraneous data input.
Input consistently	X	By setting the metadata fields in the content types to require population, you can ensure that metadata is applied consistently.
Defined	X	Set the baseline for end-user education about metadata with the glossary that defines the metadata fields and possible values.

By the product team's own presentations, the MMS was built on four basic scenarios. The first scenario concerns consistency: Is the description of the data (the content type) the same across the enterprise? Do the metadata fields and the values input into those fields contain consistency in both structure and application? When you stop to think about it, content types and metadata are really about consistent governance, management, and standardization of information descriptors in the enterprise. In other words, if you develop content type "A" in site collection 1, is it the same construct as when it is used in site collection B? The MMS answers this question in the affirmative and yet provides localized extensibility for greater usability of the content type in specific scenarios.

> **NOTE** A *content type* is merely a data element plus metadata combined into a persistent structure that can be utilized throughout the SharePoint 2010 environment.

The second scenario is about identity: What is in the content type? Regarding the enterprise, does this content contain the same type of data and metadata? Understanding the construction of the content type helps you understand its focus, purpose, and meaning.

The third scenario involves location: Where is this content type and how can you use it? The MMS will allow you to pull down the content type from the hub and ensure that it is located in your site collection.

The fourth and last scenario is about life cycle: This scenario encompasses the creation, consumption, and disposition of the content type in the enterprise. More specifically, the content type can be mapped to a document's life cycle and then utilized across the enterprise in distinct ways using the information policies and workflow associations of the content type. So you can use workflows to move the document from one life-cycle stage to the next, ensuring that compliance is enforced, tracked, and audited.

Building an Information Architecture

The phrase "information architecture" was coined—or at least was brought to wide attention—by Richard Saul Wurman, a man trained as an architect who is also a skilled graphic designer and the author, editor, and/or publisher of numerous books that employ fine graphics in the presentation of information in a variety of fields. In the 1960s, early in his career as an architect, Wurman became interested in how buildings, transport, utilities, and people worked together and interacted with one another in urban environments. This spurred his interest in how information about urban environments could be gathered, organized, and presented meaningfully to assist architects, urban planners, utility and transport engineers, and especially people living in or visiting cities. The similarity of these interests to the concerns of the information profession is apparent. When a building architect designs a building that will serve the needs of its occupants, the architect must

- Ascertain the needs of those who will occupy the space and how they will use it
- Organize the needs into a coherent pattern that clarifies their nature and interactions
- Design a building that will—by means of its rooms, fixtures, machines, and layout—meet those needs

In short, Wurman developed the following characteristics for information architecture.

- The organization of the patterns inherent in data, making the complex clear
- The creation of the structure or paths to the information that allow others to find the knowledge[12]

Peter Moreville[13] and others expanded Wurman's thinking about information architecture to include the following elements.

- The combination of organization, labeling, and navigation schemes within an information system
- The structural design of an information space to facilitate task completion and intuitive access to content
- An emerging discipline and community of practice focused on bringing principles of design and architecture to the digital landscape[14]

Information architecture directly impacts the user's experience of how he consumes and manages information when working. Information architecture is not just an abstract, theoretical exercise. Jesse James Garrett developed the elements of the user experience within a website design context, connecting what is often seen as an unnecessary exercise to the day-to-day work of most users.[15] But his elements, shown in the following list, are easily transported to the use of information generally.

---

[12] *http://www.ischool.utexas.edu/~l38613dw/readings/InfoArchitecture.html*

[13] Peter Moreville, *Information Architecture for the World Wide Web* (Sebastapol, CA: O'Reilly Media, 2002).

[14] Peter Moreville, "Why IA Matters," a PowerPoint presentation available at *http://www.iainstitute.org/tools/.*

[15] Slide # 4 in Peter Moreville's PowerPoint presentation, "Why IA Matters," available at *http://www.iainstitute.org/tools/.*

- User needs and site design
- Functional and content requirements
- Interaction design and information architecture
- Interface and navigation design
- Visual design

Donna Mauer's ideas about the main elements of an information architecture incorporate business needs, user needs, and content design.[16] Where those three elements overlap is where you'll find your information architecture (Figure 9-3).

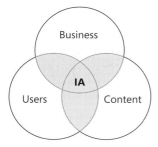

FIGURE 9-3 Mauer's three elements for an information architecture

To summarize this discussion, there is no clear consensus on what an information architecture is. Moreover, many confuse information architecture with the following.

- Interaction design
- Information design
- User-centered design
- User interface design
- Usability and usability engineering

Although all of these elements are components of an information architecture, they are really not the same as an information architecture. For example, the design of a user interface is merely the presentation layer of the information. Interface design doesn't describe how information is hosted and tagged. Hence, from the viewpoint of the authors, an information architecture (IA) is the art and science of structuring and organizing information *systems* that support business goals and objectives. The only thing you are doing when you construct an IA is specifying the *systems* that will hold the data that support the business. Within the IA, a content taxonomy (called an *operational taxonomy* in Figure 9-4) will provide the organization of the various types of content, relative to the business needs, user needs, technology support, and relationships between the various types of content.

---

[16] Donna Mauer, Information architecture PowerPoint presentation available at *http://www.iainstitute.org/tools/*.

Thus, you first need to understand what the business does and how the business really works before you can design an information architecture that will work successfully for that business. Without understanding what the business does—its core activities—it is difficult to know what systems (broadly speaking) will be needed to support the information the business will need to be successful. You may think that you should start by outlining all of the various types of information and work your way back to the systems. But this method can cause you to look at departmental or divisional information types as equivalent to enterprise-level information. If you first define the global systems based on the major activities of the company, it will help you organize the information within the systems based on how users interact with both the system and the information itself.

> **NOTE** In some organizations, the enumeration of systems alone is not sufficient because these organizations are highly process-based. Hence, these organizations would do well to include how the systems interact and how (generally speaking) information moves between systems as part of their overall IA.

Here is a suggested information architecture methodology that builds on these principles while emphasizing the business needs that form the foundation for the architecture when applied to an environment in which SharePoint 2010 is being implemented. Figure 9-4 illustrates this model.

Information Architecture Methodology

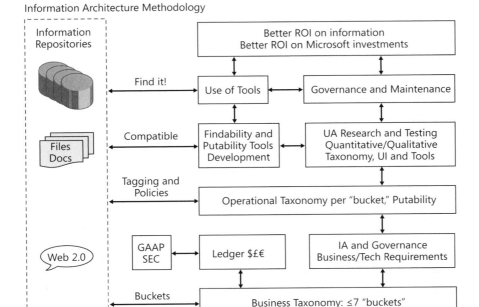

FIGURE 9-4 Information architecture model created for use with SharePoint 2010

The following sections discuss this taxonomy.

Business Taxonomy

The development of a business taxonomy is different than the development of a taxonomy for content. Recall that a taxonomy is nothing more than an organization of objects. When you talk about how a business is organized, you need to think in terms that are different from the company's organizational charts.

A business taxonomy can be thought of as containing seven or fewer "buckets." These buckets hold the organization's functions and values. Every organization has broad categories or buckets into which all of their activities fall. For example, every organization deals with money, so there will usually be one bucket called Money. Most organizations have customer service, which can form a second bucket. Some organizations have research and development departments, whereas others might not have in-house research capacity that forms a major part of their business.

Most software development companies would have—at a minimum—the following buckets: Money, Learning and Development, Production, Customer Service, and Sales and Marketing. Dividing the functions of a business like this can give you a handle on what parts of the business need their own operational taxonomy. Keep in mind that the business buckets do not necessarily represent the organizational chart.

Information Architecture, Governance, and Requirements

In this section, you will learn about how to plan and build an overall information architecture. It need not be detailed, and in most organizations, it will not be specific to divisions or departments unless those divisions require unique systems to host their unique information. For example, a research company such as 3M or Dow Chemical will have very different types of data among their various divisions, some of which is hosted by information-specific software programs. When this is the case, the IA will need to be built at the divisional as well as the enterprise levels.

Also, be aware that some IA will be process-based, such as when a system doesn't hold only static data, but instead hosts data and a process and moves that data through the process. Microsoft's Customer Relationship Management (CRM) program would be a good example. A lead is turned into an opportunity, which is turned into a quote, which is turned into an order, which is turned into an invoice. All the while, the data for the customer and opportunity are held in CRM and moved through the process. In addition, different types of data are added as the customer is moved through the process. Although SharePoint 2010 can be configured to be a process-based platform, it is configured out-of-the-box as a non-process-based platform.

So, your IA should include details about both types of data hosted in each system as well as specifics about any mission-critical processes and which systems will host those as well.

 REAL WORLD Information Architecture

Recently, a small company needed to develop its information architecture so that information could be more findable. This company provided critical information to its customers in the form of different product offerings. Even though the company had fewer than fifty employees, workers were having a hard time finding information related to the company's various product offerings, including which products customers had purchased, which information was embedded into which product, and how that information was vetted for quality control. The company believed this was mainly due to a lack of consistency in where information was held and how it was managed. No one had ever thought to organize their information and create governance on how information was to be managed.

It was fairly easy to develop an IA for this company. The company decided to hold all of its customer, partner, and vendor contact information and history in Microsoft's CRM (Customer Relationship Management) program. All of its collaboration information and document management efforts were to be accomplished in SharePoint. Exchange provided the company e-mail system and Live Meeting provided its conference platform. The business kept its accounting information in QuickBooks and outsourced payroll information. Information was secured using Active Directory, and employee information and corporate information were also hosted in SharePoint.

Although larger organizations might need to include 20, 50, or even 100 different systems to support all of their information, the process of forming the IA is really just a process of defining the systems involved in supporting, hosting, securing, and disseminating information. At the time of this writing, this small company was working to organize its content within these systems and to write policies and procedures to help everyone in the company find and manage information better. Recognizing that this represented culture change, the business gave employees one year to learn how to do this and to arrive at a decent information taxonomy that was part of its overall information architecture.

Whereas an IA is focused on systems, information architects organize content and design navigation systems to help people find and manage information better.

Governance

Governance is an inherent part of how the IA is constructed, because each system will require the development of engagement rules with that system. In short, governance includes the rules that determine how users interact with the systems and information and it also establishes who will enforce the rules—and make changes to the rules when needed. Without the second part—enforcement and management—governance is essentially useless. It is like a sporting event that has rules but no officials to enforce the rules.

> **BEST PRACTICES** Some organizations create long governance documents that are difficult to read. However, a best practice is to do the opposite and not place a rule in the governance document unless it adheres to the following guidelines.
>
> - Rule is clearly written.
> - Rule is concise.
> - Rule is enforceable.
> - Rule is communicated to users.

In a recent survey of 186 SharePoint deployments, fully two-thirds of the respondents were either unhappy or only partially happy with the state of their governance. The reasons for this were clustered around a lack of ability to enforce governance rules, lack of staffing to support the governance effort, and lack of upper management support for governance in general. These and other reasons continue to hamper SharePoint implementations as organizations grapple with the "people" side of their implementation. Understanding how information should be managed and how users should interact and utilize the features in SharePoint is essential to achieving a successful implementation.

> **MORE INFO** You can read about the survey of SharePoint deployments at *http://sharepoint.mindsharpblogs.com/Bill/archive/2010/03/06/SharePoint-Survey[coln]-How-Organizations-are-Staffing-Their-SharePoint-Teams.aspx*.

For example, in SharePoint 2010, you can turn on Self Service Site Creation (SSSC), which allows users to create new site collections without having to loop through the SharePoint farm administrators. Without some type of direction and education on how, when, and why to create new site collections, however, the ability of users to create site collections at will can lead to chaos in that part of your SharePoint 2010 deployment.

> **MORE INFO** You can download various sample governance plans from Microsoft's TechNet website at *http://technet.microsoft.com/en-us/office/sharepointserver/bb507202.aspx*.

Requirements

Every SharePoint 2010 deployment should be based on strong business requirements that both define the problem and outline the desired solution. Requirements are not something that you can just ignore and then expect to retrofit into the feature set of SharePoint 2010. They should be developed in a technology-agnostic environment and then turned into technical requirements before you select a software package to support those requirements.

It's pretty obvious that Microsoft has done a good job of building a software product whose features meet the needs of many businesses and their business problems; otherwise, SharePoint 2010 wouldn't be selling well and you wouldn't be reading this book. But it's also obvious that many companies implement SharePoint 2010 in an impulsive manner that doesn't account for the mapping of business requirements to the use of the technology.

Developing Business Requirements and Mapping Those Requirements to a Governance Plan

The first step in developing business requirements is to define the problem in business terms. Outlining its impact on the business is helpful to the quantification of the problem's severity. Following is an example of a problem definition.

Problem Statement: *When a document is being created by a team of users, they are complaining that they can't easily control which document is the latest and most up-to-date version.*

Problem Cause: *This problem can be created when documents are e-mailed to team members after being edited by one team member without knowledge that other team members are also editing the document at the same time.*

Problem Solution: *Users need a versioning control system that enforces a serial, not parallel, modification to documents by team members.*

Severity: *Users estimate they spend up to 3 hours per week just looking for the latest version of a document. At an annual average salary of $50,000 (US dollars), this equates to a loss of productivity worth $3750 per year per employee.*

You can see that this problem definition includes an outline of the business problem; it also identifies a business solution and provides information against which the problem's severity can be assessed. Turning the core business requirement into a technical requirement is the next step, as follows.

Technical Requirement: *(1) The system must support serial check-in, check-out, and versioning of documents; (2) The system must allow asynchronous, secured access to the document for editing; (3) The system must allow documents to be uploaded into the system from file servers and users' workstations; (4) The system must allow documents to be created from within the system itself.*

continued on next page

At this point, you have the technical requirements that support the versioning requirements. Notice that both the business and technical requirements are written in technology-agnostic language and you haven't backed your way into writing business requirements based on SharePoint 2010 features. So you can't assume at this point that SharePoint 2010 is the software package your organization will choose to use. However, when the technical requirements are completed, you then match those requirements to the feature set in SharePoint 2010 and, assuming there is a good match, you'll choose SharePoint to complete a Proof-of-Concept test. Assuming all goes well in the Proof-of-Concept test, you'll then choose to implement SharePoint 2010.

How would these requirements inform the governance document? The following sample wording could be used for the governance document.

Employees are required to utilize the Major/Minor Versioning features in a document library anytime a document is modified within SharePoint 2010.

To complete this discussion, users would need to be trained to use the Major/Minor Versioning of a document within a library as well as to know *the governance requirement that they must use this type of versioning*. That is, the users will be taught how to use versioning in SharePoint 2010, but they also must be reminded that the use of versioning is a requirement. Following is a sample text for a PowerPoint slide in the training presentation.

Slide Title: *Versioning in SharePoint 2010*

Slide Text:

Use the document library settings to turn on Major/Minor Versioning.

Check with the legal department on the number of versions to be retained for the type of documents you will host in the library.

NOTE: The use of Major/Minor Versioning is a requirement based on our company's business need and legal determinations.

By following this process, perhaps you can see how a business requirement can be turned into a technical requirement, which then informs the governance document, which then informs the training and education that you provide users learning to use the system. The combination of attention at these four levels will help ensure that SharePoint 2010 is utilized in the best possible way to support the goals of the business.

> **IMPORTANT** A common mistake committed when people write business and technical requirements is to take the feature set of SharePoint 2010 and downstep it into a specific organization's requirements. In other words, because the feature is available in the software product, you decided to build a business requirement and technical requirements that will require that feature. Don't do this—requirements are written to describe what is needed to solve a business problem, not to ensure a particular software product is selected for implementation.

Putability and Operational Taxonomies

In the following sections, you will learn how to create the taxonomy for each bucket in your business taxonomy. In most environments, you will not have any more than two to four metadata fields that you want attached to each document or record across the enterprise. But within each bucket, you'll have a more robust taxonomy that will be flexible and unique to that part of the business. For example, referring back to Figure 9-4, you'll notice that there is a place for the accounting, or the "Money" part of your business. Because this area of your business is already described and regulated by generally accepted accounting principles (GAAP), the U.S. Securities and Exchange Commission (SEC), and other regulations, a taxonomy already exists for this part of your business if you care to use it.

Don't re-invent the wheel when creating your taxonomy. Be sure to check out standard taxonomies that already exist for the different functions in your organization; you may find that you can use one or more of these with modifications. These standard taxonomies are a great place to start when planning your unique taxonomies.

Dublin Core

In its early days, the Dublin Core Metadata Initiative (DCMI) outlined a 15-element core set of metadata that they thought could be applied to any record or page anywhere in the world. These elements are outlined in RFC 5013, ANSI/NISO Standard Z39.85-2007, and ISO Standard 15836:2009. This standard of metadata is reflected in the Dublin Core content type that ships out-of-the-box with SharePoint 2010. If you need a place to start building your operational taxonomies, take a look at the Dublin Core. The following 15 elements make up the core set of metadata.

- Title
- Creator
- Subject
- Description
- Publisher
- Contributor

- Date
- Type
- Format
- Identifier
- Source
- Language
- Relation
- Coverage
- Rights

> **MORE INFO** You can learn more about the DCMI at *http://www.dublincore.org*.

Darwin Information Typing Architecture

The Darwin Information Typing Architecture (DITA) is an XML-based architecture for authoring, producing, and delivering information. To date, its main applications have been in technical publications with a focus on information interchange and reuse. DITA focuses on reuse with a *topic-based* core set of metadata. A common misconception is that DITA defines everything you could possibly want in content models. In reality, DITA defines only base models, and its developers expect that you will create your own topic types to meet your own information needs.

The DITA architecture defines four layers.

- *Delivery context*   The processing and delivery context
- *Typed topic structures*   The formal content structure
- *Common structures*   Metadata and table structures that can be shared with any topic
- *Shared structures*   Content models for structures that can be used in all documentation

> **MORE INFO** You can learn more about DITA at *http://dita.xml.org*.

Other Taxonomies

There are other types of base taxonomies that you might want to leverage, given the type of information that you're trying to organize. Following are some examples of existing taxonomies.

- *DocBook*   Popular content model for software documentation
- *SCORM*   An XML-based method of representing course structures

- **IPSV** Integrated Public Sector Vocabulary, an "encoding scheme" for populating subject elements of metadata, a standard developed in the United Kingdom
- **OpenDocument Format** An XML-based file format specification for Microsoft Office documents
- **XMP (Extensible Metadata Platform)** Adobe-led labeling technology that allows you to embed data about a file into the file itself
- **NewsML** A method designed to provide a media-type-independent, structural framework for multimedia news

There are also some predefined vocabularies that you might be able to leverage as you create your taxonomy.

- Gale Accounting Thesaurus (Gale Group, Inc.)
- European Education Thesaurus (Eurydice European Unit)
- ACM Computing Classification System (Association for Computing Machinery)
- *http://taxonomywarehouse.com*

Referring back to Figure 9-4, you'll see that the operational taxonomy layer is where you need to develop your tagging and putability policies. Based on the old "garbage in, garbage out" principle, you can understand that how information goes into SharePoint 2010 will directly impact how it comes back out. In this part of your information organization project for SharePoint, be sure that you take the time to understand not only the taxonomies and their values for the data you're describing, but also the policies that users must follow and the ways that the information repositories will accept the tagging of data.

Usability and Tool Development

Next, you need to develop the user interfaces and tools necessary for both putability and findability. An example of a findability tool would be a custom advanced Web Part that exposes key metadata for a multi-keyword query. An example of a putability tool would be a custom interface that allows a user to input metadata when a new document is first saved.

Content types can be viewed as putability tools, whereas search Web Parts would be considered findability tools. Table 9-2 offers some additional ideas on how SharePoint 2010 tools can be leveraged. This is not an exhaustive list.

TABLE 9-2 Putability and Findability Tools

TOOL/FEATURE	PUTABILITY	FINDABILITY	BOTH
Sites directory			X
Managed paths		X	
Content types	X		
My Site personalization		X	

continued on next page

TOOL/FEATURE	PUTABILITY	FINDABILITY	BOTH
Audiences		X	
Scopes		X	
Records center			X
Site columns			X
Folders		X	
Metadata Managed Service	X		
Search Web Parts		X	
Indexing		X	
Breadcrumb navigation		X	
URL and site design	X		

The tools that you utilize, whether out-of-the-box or customized, will depend on why you are implementing SharePoint 2010 in your organization, the type of data that will reside in SharePoint 2010, and the outcomes of your IOPS effort. Best practice is to utilize the tools and Web Parts that ship with SharePoint 2010 before writing any custom code. Moreover, if you can purchase third-party code instead of developing it yourself, that is also a smart choice.

Use of SharePoint and Maintenance

At this point, you're ready to roll out SharePoint 2010 and have your company's employees use the product. As part of your rollout plan, you'll want to ensure that employees have been trained well and that you're following regular procedures to enforce the governance plan. Also, be prepared to find that as your information grows, changes, and evolves, your IA and taxonomies will have to adjust as well. This is an ongoing, but not a constant, effort.

An Information Organization Project

This section outlines at a high level the steps necessary to complete an information organization project successfully. The first order of business will be overcoming resistance to the idea that your company's information really does need to be organized.

So, how do you get others in your company to accept the idea that they need to invest in an information architecture, and more specifically, in a project that leverages the information organization features in SharePoint 2010? This is never easy because the objections of decision makers are entrenched and familiar. Their objections usually center around difficult-to-justify costs and other excuses that there just isn't space to list here.

Overcoming these objections is not easy, and it will take some real work on your part. To engage in an Information Organization Project for SharePoint (IOPS), you'll need to understand that you're asking for change in how information is developed, managed, and disseminated. Such change is not a small thing. It is likely that there are many information kingdoms in your organization, with people who already take personal ownership of that information. That is not necessarily a bad situation, but it is something that must be recognized and leveraged as part of your IOPS effort.

There are (essentially) six phases to an IOPS. The following sections outline each phase and provide you with tools for achieving your goal of establishing a successful IOPS.

> **MORE INFO**   There are other paths that can be followed to help you with your SharePoint 2010 implementation. For example, BearingPoint has released its methodology on how to organize information, which is an open source standard for information management. You can learn more about this at *http://mike2.openmethodology.org/*. Moreover, the AIIM (Association for Information and Image Management, *http://www.aiim.org*) group has published several certifications that relate to SharePoint 2010 implementations. These are the Enterprise Content Management Specialist and Information Organization Specialist credentials. At the time of this writing, AIIM is introducing a SharePoint Specialist certification that bridges the gap between the SharePoint technology and their expertise in how to manage information. The phases presented in the following sections represent a suggested path on how to achieve a strong organization of information in SharePoint 2010. But this is only a suggested path. You might find that using the MIKE 2.0, AIIM, or another methodology will work better for your organization.

The information organization project introduced in the following sections is divided into six basic phases, as explained previously. The early phases are the most important, and each subsequent phase builds on the previous one. Moreover, the quality of success at each phase will directly impact the quality of success in the following phases.

Phase 0: Information Organization Assessment

In the first phase of the project, you'll want to gather information about its scope, including who the main stakeholders will be. You will also want to inform yourself about the environment in which you're working. Don't be fooled into thinking that you can bypass this stage because you are working on your own environment. Completing an information organization assessment questionnaire will enable you to collect what you need to know at the start of the project, to keep everyone involved informed of the project's progress, and to set proper expectations on how the IOPS will flow.

The questionnaire should cover the following topics.

- Definition of the documents that are in scope versus those that are out of scope
- Definition of the systems that are in scope versus those that are out of scope

- Definition of the processes and policies that are in scope versus those that are out of scope
- Statement of the technical environment that currently exists and what changes must be made to support the IOPS effort
- Definition of the problem that has given rise to the need for this project
- Definition of the desired outcome, which should be stated in measurable terms
- Discussion of the interview data that supports the project's effort
- Statement of the project's sponsor, project manager, and champion
- Outline of the communication plan for the project
- Outline of the project plan

As you can see in Figure 9-5, there is more to this phase than mere documentation of the problem, solution, and current environment. You also should document explicit business needs (not requirements), and you should conduct a cost of doing business analysis (CODB). Writing out the business needs is really how you'll define the findability problem in business terms. The persona interviews (explained later in this section) illustrate those needs in an easy-to-understand way, and the CODB quantifies the severity of the problem in opportunity costs.

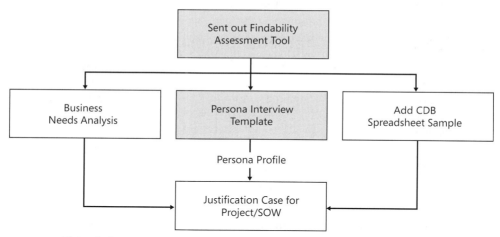

FIGURE 9-5 Phase 0 of an IOPS: Assessment

In this first phase, you also need to conduct a CODB analysis. This is different from a return on investment (ROI) analysis. In nearly all companies, the value of their information doesn't appear on the balance sheet, so it's nearly impossible to calculate a hard return on investment against the cost of an IOPS. However, you can more easily calculate savings based on increased efficiencies as a result of an IOPS. Those calculations need to be completed in Phase 0. Refer back to the section titled "The Opportunity Cost of a Poor Information Process and Architecture" earlier in this chapter for more information about performing a CODB analysis.

Do not overlook the persona interviews, because they form the basis of a CODB. Having a business analyst document current processes and the cost of those processes provides the foundation against which the savings calculation can be made. Persona interviews are conducted with real people whose stories and daily lives in the workplace are folded into a composite person with a fictitious name. When you have developed that persona, this fictitious person is used as an example of how the IOPS will improve that employee's life. It's usually best if three to five personas are developed, because different employee types will be affected in different ways.

You'll also need to do a findability study before you can create the statement of work (SOW). You'll need to gather both anecdotal and measured responses concerning how well employees are able to find the information they need and how easy that transaction is. Don't worry about measuring putability in this phase, since a poor findability solution will point out deficits in your putability processes.

When all of these activities are combined, you'll be able to describe the problem in real terms, quantify the opportunity costs in real dollars, express how the IOPS will improve efficiencies, and illustrate how the day-to-day work lives of employees will improve. All of this is included in a statement of work and is usually connected to a request for additional funding to complete the next four phases. At the end of Phase 0, you have outlined the costs, the staff, and the cycles necessary to complete the IOPS.

Phase 1: Business Requirements Development

In this phase, you'll focus on the development of the business requirements based on stakeholder interviews, the problem definitions from Phase 0, and a grassroots survey. You'll want to document the requirements and then hold a series of requirements workshops to check the requirements and ensure that everyone agrees on the definition of the problem as well as what is required in the solution.

This phase, illustrated in Figure 9-6, is an important step that involves much writing and consensus building, but it will not complete the groundwork for your IOPS. However, developing the business requirements in this phase is a necessary step to prepare for Phase 2, which involves turning these business requirements into technical requirements.

It could be argued that the business requirement effort should be moved back to Phase 0, and in some environments this will be the right way to conduct the IOPS. Placing the effort to develop business requirements in Phase 1, after the project has been approved and funded (which occurs after Phase 0), usually makes more sense, however, because of the cost and time consumption required to develop requirements. You would move the requirements development to Phase 0 if you were working with a customer who didn't need or want a cost justification for an IOPS, because they have already decided to get their information organized, and cost is a secondary consideration.

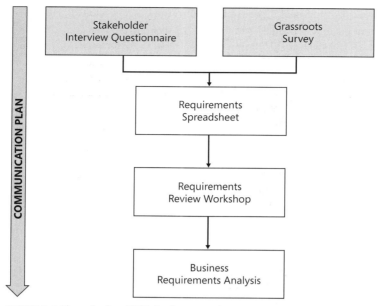

FIGURE 9-6 Phase 1 of an IOPS: Business requirements

Phase 2: Technical Requirements and Project Charter

In this phase, shown in Figure 9-7, you will focus on taking the business requirements and turning them into technical requirements. These technical requirements will connect your specific business requirements with the feature set available in SharePoint 2010. The technical requirements will also outline the current state of your organization's hardware and software and then describe any changes necessary to deploy SharePoint 2010 for your information organization project. Also as part of this phase, you'll need to document your current governance plan for SharePoint 2010 and then outline any modifications required as part of the SharePoint 2010 implementation.

The combination of the outputs from the first three phases will form the content and rationale for the project charter, which everyone involved should agree to before the project moves forward. Assume at this point that you have funding for the IOPS and the authority for those leading the project to make decisions, approve expenditures, and implement policy changes.

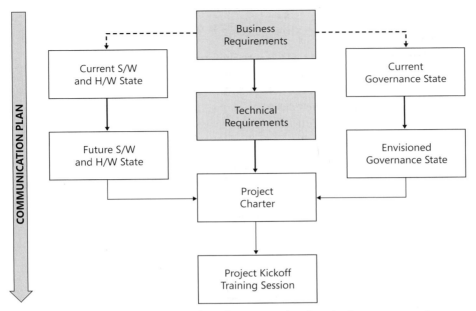

FIGURE 9-7 Phase 2 of an IOPS: Technical requirements and project charter

Phase 3: Audit and Analysis

Taking the output from Phase 2, you now need to inventory the documents and records that are in scope for the project and determine their security assignments. This should be an exhaustive inventory and will require third-party tools that can enumerate both the complete list of documents and well as their security descriptors.

This part of an IOPS can be rather difficult, because in the course of conducting the inventory, you want to discover old, outdated, or irrelevant data that can be discarded. You're working with a multitude of content owners to help them decide which documents they need to keep and which ones need to go. You're also uncovering security problems with documents and finding security processes and policies that will need to be updated to ensure the same problems don't occur again.

Using Search Technologies to Check Your Audits

One way to check your audit efforts is to index the content in question and then run queries against that index under different security contexts to see which documents appear in the result set. Recall that SharePoint 2010 search technologies index and honor the security descriptors on content that is crawled, so there can be times when you'll want to execute queries to see if the security is set properly.

For example, if Juan and Sue have access to a document and you're able to find that document using search technologies under your security context, then you can know that the security on that document is not set correctly. In one real-world example, a research company was implementing SharePoint 2010 search technologies for the first time, and after indexing its most critical, proprietary document, the company found that members of the IT staff were able to access those documents using the SharePoint 2010 Search feature. After looking at the security tab, the company was perplexed, because no one on the IT staff was listed as having permissions to those documents, either through inheritance or through group assignments. But when the company looked under the Advanced permissions, it was found that several global groups had been assigned pervasive, special permissions to nearly all of the documents and folders on the most "secured" file servers. The company immediately suspended its SharePoint 2010 implementation while it inserted a very fast NTFS audit project to ensure that all content was properly secured on its file servers before releasing the search technologies to users.

There will be times when executing a query against the index should produce zero (0) results. If structured correctly, the query can ensure that those documents in scope for the query are properly secured, meaning that they do not appear in the result set.

As part of Phase 3, you'll need to ensure that you have good communication with your users, because they will be guiding your decisions about which artifacts to keep and which to discard. It is not uncommon to encounter resistance at this phase from users who will claim that they don't have time to help with this decision-making process. At the beginning of the project, this resistance should be anticipated and addressed. Some ideas for managing this resistance include gaining authority to discard files that are more than a specified number of months or years old or to move documents that have not been included in the inventory into an unsupported file server that will be excluded from the project. Figure 9-8 illustrates the activities for this phase.

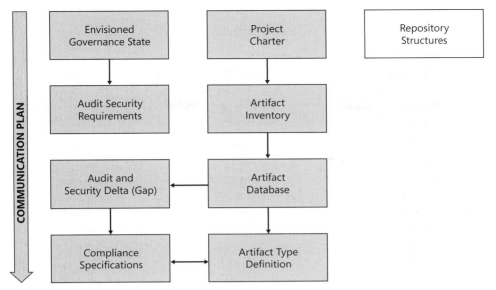

FIGURE 9-8 Phase 3 of an IOPS: Audit and analyze your documents

Phase 4: Development of Putability and Findability

In Phase 4, you develop the operational taxonomies, user interfaces, tagging policies, and educational materials that users will utilize in their ongoing management of information. This is a busy phase and involves high involvement for your end users. This highly visible phase must go well to ensure that your project is successful.

Refer back to the section titled "Building an Information Architecture" earlier in this chapter. In Phase 4, you will conduct nearly all of the tasks described in that section—the development of the business taxonomy can be conducted in parallel with Phases 0 through 3 in this larger methodology, but the rest of those activities will occur in the current phase. Refer to the detail provided in the previous discussion. Figure 9-9 illustrates the development of putability and findability in your information organization project. When you have planned the information architecture that will provide the structure for your project, it's time to move on to Phase 5, in which you will address the governance and maintenance of your information organization systems.

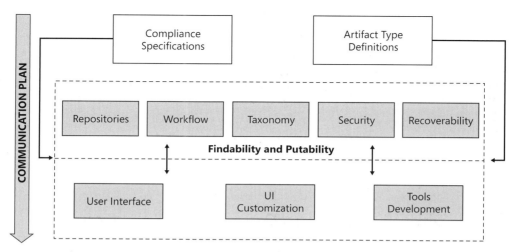

FIGURE 9-9 Phase 4 in the IOPS: Plan the information architecture

Phase 5: Governance and Maintenance

Phase 5 is an ongoing stage that supports and maintains not only the SharePoint 2010 implementation, but also the ongoing organization of information within the SharePoint implementation. Information will change over time, so your company may need to adjust the rules that guide how the information is organized and tagged. By regularly reviewing how information is managed, tagged, input, and found, you will help ensure that your efforts to organize information in SharePoint 2010 have not gone to waste.

Also, as your company matures in the area of managing information effectively, the governance rules that guide end users and the enforcement of those rules also will necessarily change. Ensure that you have a process for this change in place, and that there are identified personnel who are capable and authorized to make changes to the governance rules. Also make sure that these people can communicate those changes to your entire organization clearly and effectively.

Figure 9-10 illustrates this last phase, which is never really complete. By their nature, maintenance, review, assessment, and training are ongoing tasks that must continue indefinitely. As your organization changes and grows, you will need to make sure your information architecture can adapt. And as new employees join your company, you also need to be sure that they are trained properly in using the system you have in place. Orientation materials for new employees should cover your information architecture structure, its policies and procedures, and the rules of enforcement so that your organization doesn't experience incremental loss of use in information organization because of employees who don't understand how the system works.

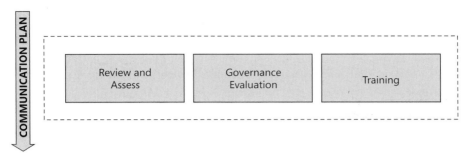

FIGURE 9-10 Phase 5 of an IOPS: Governance and maintenance

SharePoint 2010 Tools to Organize Information

SharePoint 2010 ships with a number of tools that can help you organize information. Table 9-3 outlines these tools and what they organize, but it is not intended to be an exhaustive list.

TABLE 9-3 Organizing Tools in SharePoint 2010

SHAREPOINT 2010 TOOL	INFORMATION ORGANIZED BY THE TOOL
Sites directory	Links to the root sites of site collections
Web applications	Root URLs and managed paths
Managed paths	Site collections that act as endpoints of the "path"
Site collections	One or more sites that host lists and libraries related to a common project or collaboration effort
Site	Lists and libraries
Lists and libraries	Documents and content items
Content types	Metadata that is related to a content element, such as a list item or document
Filtered views	List data based on preselected metadata, sorting, and/or grouping rules
Web Part zones	Web Parts and their display
Audiences	Reveals information based on audience membership
Records center	Official records that meet compliance requirements
MMS (Managed Metadata Service)	Tagging of information via content type syndication
RSS (Really Simple Syndication)	Information that is delivered via the RSS standard

When organizing information within SharePoint 2010, you'll need to understand that you have a group of embedded containers that ultimately hold the content. These containers can be organized in different ways, and that is why, referring back to Table 9-3, you'll find that some containers only organize other containers—they don't organize the information directly.

For example, Web applications host a root site collection plus managed paths. Managed paths host and organize site collections. Site collections host and organize sites and galleries. Sites host and organize Web Parts, but for our discussion, the focus is on lists and libraries. Lists and libraries host content items and site columns. Galleries—particularly the content type gallery—host content types, which are really predefined and reusable content items plus a defined set of site columns.

Hence, the URL organization, the managed path organization, and the way Web Parts are organized across sites within a site collection—all of these organizing tools affect how users navigate to and find information. Even though putability is focused on the granular level of tagging content items with metadata, the larger organization picture can also improve navigation to the content's hosting location if you pay attention to the various layers of container organization. Because this is more art than science, it is difficult to provide a model to show you exactly how to organize the various layers of SharePoint 2010 to make navigation work well. But if you pay attention to both the navigation and the search technologies as the two main ways users will find information within your SharePoint 2010 deployment, you will be able to organize the features of SharePoint 2010 to create an effective information architecture for your organization.

Summary

This chapter has discussed the value of information and why you need to consider putability as well as findability in information architecture and information organization projects. You've seen that there are significant opportunity costs associated with a poor information architecture and that SharePoint 2010 MMS aids in lowering those costs. The chapter outlined how to build an information architecture that is tailored to your business and discussed using basic, predefined taxonomies as a starting point rather than creating a completely new taxonomy. Finally, the chapter outlined briefly how an information organization project should proceed.

In the next chapter, you'll turn your attention to collaboration and how portals work in SharePoint 2010. Then the ensuing chapters will discuss the search and business intelligence technologies that support the concepts that have been presented in this chapter.

Collaboration and Portals

Throughout the lineage of Microsoft SharePoint products and technologies, there has always been one focal point: collaboration. Although the product suite has expanded with each major release, its roots as a collaboration tool remain evident and manifest themselves in the product's mature functionalities for streamlining collaborative work.

In simple terms, *collaboration* is the group activity through which people, usually from disparate locations or teams (or both), come together to work toward a common goal. The work product produced as a result of the collaborative activity is often a document deliverable, but this is not always the case. Sometimes the result of collaboration can be a successful event, meeting, or conference call.

Portal sites, on the other hand, are something altogether different. Rather than providing a place for people to work together to create a specific result, portal sites provide a grandstand from which to share the finished work product or key information with a large audience. This large audience might be the entire organization, or it might simply be a larger project team.

In some cases, the same small nuclear team will use a team collaboration site and a portal site. Although it may seem more convenient to do everything in a single site collection, the proper separation of the collaboration activity and the publishing activity is instrumental to the success of each, and failing to separate the two activities can potentially cause far-reaching capacity and content life-cycle implications.

People use the term *collaboration* to mean "working together toward a common goal." This is true in Microsoft SharePoint 2010 as well. For example, My Sites, a personal site that is provided by SharePoint as a dedicated repository for each individual user, works in conjunction with the User Profile Service to provide a holistic view of SharePoint user activities, site memberships, and organizational information.

Collaboration can take many forms. For example, when two people are talking on the telephone, they are collaborating in a synchronous fashion. When two people work together in a SharePoint team site, but do not work on the same document at the same time, they are collaborating in an asynchronous fashion.

SharePoint is an excellent platform for asynchronous collaboration. In most environments, asynchronous collaboration is more efficient than synchronous collaboration, because the parties involved need not coordinate their calendars and physical presence to participate.

SharePoint also provides the three basic collaboration paths: one to many, many to many, and many to one. For example, My Sites provides an individual with the opportunity to communicate and collaborate with the enterprise. This is a one to many collaboration path. Team sites provide team members with the ability to collaborate on documents and other types of information, which is a many to many collaboration path. Finally, portals provide an individual with a wealth of options from which to choose, so in effect portals offer a many to one collaboration path.

> **BEST PRACTICES** Turning off My Sites detracts from the full collaboration experience. Adopt an "embrace and train" mentality when it comes to the features of SharePoint—as long as those features support the business requirements for the installation of SharePoint within the organization.

In this chapter, you will explore the collaboration and portal capabilities provided within SharePoint 2010. Although publishing sites and Web Content Management (WCM) sites are covered in more detail in Chapter 15, "Administering Web Content Management and Publishing," in this chapter, you will learn about the capabilities provide by portal sites and how they can be used to compliment the collaborative activity. You will also review My Sites and the User Profile Service in detail to get an understanding of how these key elements of SharePoint 2010 work together with collaboration to provide a seamless end-user experience for both individuals and groups. In addition, you will learn about the social networking capabilities provided in SharePoint 2010, including social tagging, bookmarks, and notes.

Using Collaboration Sites

In a sense, team collaboration sites are the centerpiece of SharePoint, because the information that is published or archived originates from team collaboration sites. Since team collaboration means many different things to different people, SharePoint 2010 comes with a wide array of site templates as part of the base product. In the following section, you will review each of these site types and learn about when to use each.

It is a generally accepted best practice to segregate collaboration sites into a dedicated Web application that is set aside for this purpose. The reasoning behind this is simple. Collaboration is a highly active content manipulation activity—the content is not very static. Because the content is subject to so much change, the latest content must always be available for users, which requires a Web application that is properly tuned for threading and caching. Consider the contrast between this highly dynamic process and publishing and portals, in which the content is relatively static. In such circumstances, the use of caching and threading can result in fewer round trips between the Web front-end server (WFE) and the database server. This is good, because the content changes infrequently in a publishing or portal site, so you don't need or want every request to go all the way back to the database server.

> **IMPORTANT** This is really a factor for performance tuning, and although this chapter does not cover that topic in depth, it's important to mention it, because it affects how you plan the deployment of collaboration sites within your environment.

Because meeting workspaces often become integral to the collaboration activity, this chapter reviews the SharePoint 2010 capabilities in this area at a high level. You will find comprehensive information about what you need to know to understand, plan, and implement collaboration in your environment.

Collaboration Site Templates

Collaboration site templates are available under the Collaboration tab when you create a new site collection in SharePoint Central Administration, as shown in Figure 10-1.

FIGURE 10-1 The Collaboration tab in SharePoint Central Administration

Table 10-1 provides a brief explanation of each site template that is available in the Create Site Collection interface.

TABLE 10-1 Collaboration Site Template Types

TEMPLATE	USE
Team Site	A site for teams to quickly organize, author, and share information. This type of site provides a document library and lists for managing announcements, calendar items, tasks, and discussions. When used in conjunction with self-service site creation (SSSC), team sites provide end users with the ability to create collaboration sites that are self-organizing with a low transaction cost.
Blank Site	A blank site you can customize based on your requirements.
Document Workspace	A site for colleagues to work together on a document. It provides a document library for storing the primary document and supporting files, a tasks list for assigning to-do items, and a links list for resources related to the document.
Blog	A site for a person or team to post ideas, observations, and expertise that site visitors can comment on.
Group Work Site	This template provides a groupware solution that enables teams to create, organize, and share information quickly and easily. It includes Group Calendar, Circulation, Phone-Call Memo, a document library, and the other basic lists.
Visio Process Repository	A site for teams to quickly view, share, and store Visio process diagrams. It provides a versioned document library for storing process diagrams and lists for managing announcements, tasks, and review discussions.

Meetings Workspace Site Templates

Meeting workspace site templates are available under the Meetings tab when you create a new site collection in SharePoint Central Administration, as shown in Figure 10-2.

FIGURE 10-2 The Meetings tab in SharePoint Central Administration

Table 10-2 provides brief explanation of each site template that is available in the Create Site Collection interface.

TABLE 10-2 Meeting Workspace Site Template Types

TEMPLATE	USE
Basic Meeting Workspace	A site to plan, organize, and capture the results of a meeting. It provides lists for managing the agenda, meeting attendees, and documents.
Blank Meeting Workspace	A blank meeting site you can customize based on your requirements.
Decision Meeting Workspace	A site for meetings that track status or make decisions. It provides lists for creating tasks, storing documents, and recording decisions.
Social Meeting Workspace	A site to plan social occasions. It provides lists for tracking attendees, providing directions, and storing pictures of the event.
Multipage Meeting Workspace	A site to plan, organize, and capture the results of a meeting. It provides lists for managing the agenda and meeting attendees in addition to two blank pages you can customize based on your requirements.

Enabling Collaboration Features

Although the site types described in the prior section are created with some of the Team Collaboration features already enabled, these features can also be enabled within any SharePoint 2010 site collection. When activated, they will create a document library for Shared Documents, as well as Calendar and Tasks lists for the team. In addition, the collaborative list templates become available within the Create page, thereby allowing contributors to create new document libraries, task lists, and contact lists. These additional list types allow for a team or group to effectively leverage SharePoint 2010 as a collaboration solution.

Table 10-3 introduced the Team Collaboration features in detail as they are described within the feature management user interface.

TABLE 10-3 Team Collaboration Features

FEATURE	DESCRIPTION
Team Collaboration Lists	Provides team collaboration capabilities for a site by making standard lists, such as document libraries and issues, available
Group Work Lists	Provides calendars with added functionality for team and resource scheduling
Offline Synchronization for External Lists	Enables offline synchronization for external lists with Outlook and SharePoint Workspace

continued on the next page

FEATURE	DESCRIPTION
SharePoint Server Standard Site Collection features	Features such as user profiles and search, included in the SharePoint Server Standard License
SharePoint Server Standard Site features	Features such as user profiles and search, included in the SharePoint Server Standard License

To activate the collaboration features within an existing site collection, follow these steps.

1. From the top site within the site collection, use the Site Actions menu to select Site Settings.

2. Within Site Settings, select Site Collection Features, which can be found under the Site Collection Administration settings group.

3. Activate the SharePoint Server Standard Site Collection Features if it is not already activated.

4. Return to Site Settings.

5. Within Site Settings, select Manage Site Features, which can be found under the Site Actions settings group.

6. Activate the feature called SharePoint Server Standard Site Features if it is not already activated.

7. Activate the feature called Team Collaboration Lists if it is not already activated.

8. Optionally, activate the feature called Group Work Lists if it is not already activated.

9. Optionally, activate the Feature called Offline Synchronization For External Lists if it is not already activated.

A Note About Blank Sites

Blank sites are unique—they come without any features and functionality so you can enable the features you need for your specific requirements. Blank sites provide basic services from SharePoint Foundation 2010, as well as some of the collaboration features and capabilities listed in Table 10-3. However, if you don't need those features for your custom site implementation, you can simply deactivate them. Likewise, if you need some of the features that are not activated by default, simply activate them as needed.

Planning for Collaboration

Planning for collaboration sites involves forethought from an IT administrator's perspective. Because collaboration sites are usually managed and configured by the content owners themselves, it's sometime helpful to think of collaboration sites as a service offering. This is in alignment with the way Microsoft has deployed SharePoint as a service internally. By thinking in a service-centric way, you can align your SharePoint deployment with the diverse business needs of your users as well as take into account the infrastructure, support, performance, and capacity considerations. This section discusses the creation of a dedicated Web application for collaboration sites, the use of managed paths for further segregating and simplifying URLs for your users, and the process planning options for provisioning.

Web Applications

It is often a good idea to have a dedicated Web application or Web applications in the farm specifically for provisioning collaboration sites. This makes performance tuning and capacity planning much easier, because all of the site collections will be performing similar activities and the strain on the underlying software architecture is somewhat predictable. Although it's logical to assume that users will create workspace sites with collaboration sites, it's also possible that users will want to create workspaces as individual site collections as well. The guidance offered to users is to consider the purpose of a workspace before creating the workspace within an existing collaboration site. Does it really belong there? Is it related in any way to the purpose of the team or the common objective being pursued within the collaboration site collection? If not, it probably belongs in its own site collection. This ensures that the content life cycle of the workspace can be handled separately from that of the collaboration site, thereby allowing the workspace site to be deleted, either manually or automatically, far sooner than the collaboration site.

Consider creating two Web applications for collaboration: one for non-workspace collaboration site collections, and one for workspace site collections. This allows even further separation of these two similar but different site collection types. Further separating these site types allows you to use different default quota templates and automated deletion policies.

Figure 10-3 provides an example Web application allocation for a typical SharePoint 2010 farm, illustrating how separate Web applications for collaboration sites and workspace sites are created, and how those two Web applications fit into the larger picture of the entire implementation.

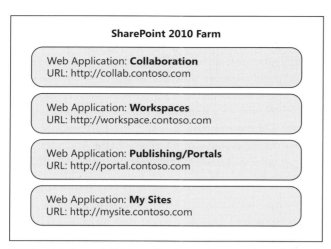

FIGURE 10-3 Example Web application architecture for collaboration Web applications

Managed Paths

Managed paths are a mechanism that allow for the definition of additional URL paths below Web applications. There are many reasons people decide to use additional managed paths. For example, although the default managed paths will work for most implementations, some people may find it useful to create additional paths for specific types of sites or organizational divisions. You may also want to be able to add a filter to your firewall or router to constrain a specific namespace to internal access only.

If you need to group sites by specific site type, you could use a managed path. An example of this would involve providing team collaboration sites for varying types of teams within your organization. In order to make the URL paths easier for users to understand, as well as to reduce the likelihood that multiple teams will request the same URL, you decide to create a managed path for departmental collaboration sites as well as a managed path for project sites. The managed paths would appear as

- Collaboration Web application
  - Departmental Sites—Managed Path "/dept"
  - Project Sites—Managed Path "/proj"

Some key concepts regarding Managed Paths include the following.

- Managed paths allow SharePoint to determine what portion of a given URL corresponds to the site collection URL.
- Managed paths can be defined per Web application.
- Managed paths can be explicit or wildcard.
  - Explicit managed paths allow a single site collection at the path URL.
  - Wildcard managed paths allow unlimited site collections to be created under the path URL.

To create additional managed paths for your collaboration Web application, perform the following steps.

1. Open a browser and go to the SharePoint Central Administration website.

2. Under Application Management, click Manage Web Applications.

3. Select the Web application for which you would like to add the new managed path.

4. After you select a Web application, click the Managed Paths menu item from the Manage group of the Web Applications Ribbon at the top of the screen, which will display a dialog box similar to the one shown in Figure 10-4.

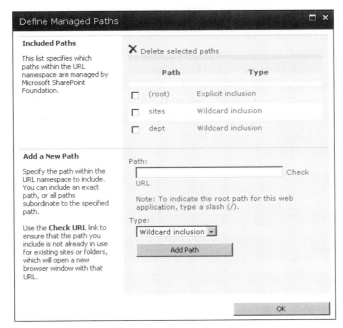

FIGURE 10-4 Adding a managed path for a Web application

5. In the Add a New Path section of the dialog box, enter the Path URL you want you add (e.g., dept) and click the Check URL link to verify that the path does not already exist or is not already taken by a site collection.

6. Select the type of path you want to add.

   ■ Wildcard Inclusion: Create many sites under this URL path.

   ■ Explicit Inclusion: Create a single site at this URL path.

7. Click Add Path to add the managed path, after which the path will appear in the provided list.

8. When you have finished, click OK to return to the Manage Web Applications page.

Provisioning

Provisioning is a very important consideration when it comes to planning for the deployment of collaboration sites. You need to consider how many site collections you might expect in specific time frames to determine which provisioning option suits your requirements best. There are three primary options for the provisioning of collaboration sites.

- Self-service site creation
- Request-based site creation
- Custom site provisioning application

SELF-SERVICE SITE CREATION

Self-service site creation is a built-in capability provided by SharePoint 2010. When enabled, users who have the Use Self-Service Site Creation permission are able to create sites in defined URL namespaces. This allows designated users to create site collections as needed but offers very little in the way of integrated guidance for when and how they should use specific types of sites and for what purpose. For this reason, you should be sure that associated user training activities coincide with enabling self-service site creation to ensure that users who have this capability are provisioning site collections in accordance with the way your organization has decided to leverage SharePoint.

To enable self-service site creation, perform the following steps.

1. Open a browser and go to the SharePoint Central Administration website.

2. Under Application Management, click Manage Web Applications.

3. Select the Web application for which you would like to enable self-service site creation.

4. After you select a Web application, click the Self-Service Site Creation menu item from the Security group of the Web Applications Ribbon at the top of the screen, which will display a dialog box similar to the one shown in Figure 10-5.

5. Select the On option to enable self-service site creation.

6. Optionally, select the Require Secondary Contact check box.

7. Click OK.

When you have enabled self-service site creation, an announcement will be added to the Announcements list on the home page of the top-level site within the Web application; it will provide a link to the site creation page, which can be found at _layouts/scsignup.aspx.

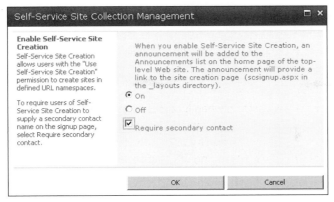

FIGURE 10-5 Enabling self-service site creation for a Web application

REQUEST-BASED SITE CREATION

Of course, if you want ultimate control over the site collections that are created, you can devise a request-based site creation process.

> **NOTE** The request-based site creation process is implemented completely outside of SharePoint.

Usually, request-based site creation entails establishing a well-documented process and evaluation criteria for the appropriateness of the request. When the request has been reviewed and approved, it can be sent to a designated administrator for fulfillment. Figure 10-6 illustrates this process.

There are advantages and disadvantages to this type of provisioning. The advantages include

- Complete control over which sites are created
- The ability to guide requestors appropriately based on their needs
- The ability to control site sprawl

Some disadvantages of this approach are

- Potential overburdening of the request evaluator as adoption increases
- Potential overburdening of IT support
- Possibly limiting technology adoption

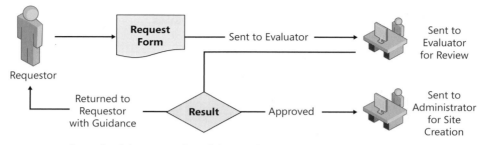

FIGURE 10-6 Example of the request-based site creation process

Remember, SharePoint is a user-centric technology, and although the request-based site creation approach has its administrative merits, you should implement it only after due consideration of the advantages and disadvantages of the technology.

Custom Site Provisioning Application

Often neither self-service site creation nor a request-based process will meet the requirements of an organization that wants to ensure that the requesting users' needs are matched with the best site type. If this is the case, one final option is a custom site provisioning application. This is not a book about custom development, but without going into the details about how to create such an application, it's worth mentioning that many organizations prefer this solution. The biggest reason for this is extensibility and customizability. Not only can a custom application provide users with more information to make better decisions about what site types best fit users' needs, it also can be enhanced to include information and guidance about how the organization wants to use SharePoint, include restrictions for use, and even implement custom feature-deployed organizationally specific solution components after site creation.

Integration with SharePoint Workspace 2010

Think of SharePoint Workspace 2010 as the Microsoft Office client for team collaboration in SharePoint 2010. Although Office Outlook continues to offer many enhanced features for synchronizing data and working offline with SharePoint list information and feeds, Microsoft SharePoint Workspace 2010 provides a complete rich experience for both online and offline use. With SharePoint Workspace 2010, you can have full fidelity access to a team collaboration site, including all the document libraries, lists, discussions, and documents. All of the information is presented in feed form, which allows you to view information that has changed since the last time you reviewed it. The best part is that SharePoint Workspace 2010 is included with Microsoft Office 2010 Professional Plus, making it a likely desktop application in the enterprise space and highly accessible to your users. Figure 10-7 shows SharePoint Workspace 2010 in action.

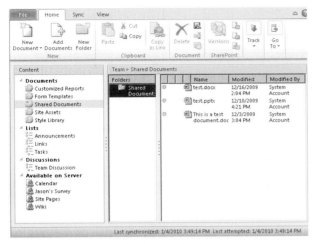

FIGURE 10-7 SharePoint Workspace 2010

After you have configured a workspace connection, as shown in Figure 10-7, you will be alerted when new unread data appears in that workspace. A sample alert is shown in Figure 10-8.

FIGURE 10-8 Alert notifying you of new unread information in a workspace

Choosing to Use Portal Sites

Chapter 15 covers Web Content Management (WCM) and publishing in depth, with a focus on publishing portals and Internet-facing websites. In the following sections, you will review portals as they are employed within an intranet/extranet environment. What is the difference? In terms of functionality, SharePoint 2010 provides the same site template and features for both. The difference is in how WCM sites are utilized as compared to a departmental or project portal, for example. Specifically, in the following sections you will learn about how portals are used internally as an accompaniment to collaboration sites. You will review some scenarios in which you might choose to use a publishing portal internally to complement collaboration, how to orchestrate the movement of content between collaboration sites and their associated portals sites, and what features are included within a publishing portal site.

Portal Site Scenarios

There are many possible scenarios in which you could elect to use a publishing portal site collection as part of a larger multiteam or multifaceted collaboration implementation. To understand why you would want to use a publishing portal, you first need to review and understand three primary capabilities offered by SharePoint 2010.

- **Collaboration**   Information you want to create and share among a team
- **Publishing**   Provides access to finished information you want to disseminate to others
- **Records Management**   Information you want to keep as evidence of your activities or for future purposes.

It's important to understand each of these capabilities and how they fit together in the design and implementation of an information management solution.

Collaboration

Of course, most of the heavy action occurs within the collaboration sites, where team members frequently create new information and work on collateral material together towards a common end goal. This activity might manifest itself in the form of tasks, calendar events, or—as is most common—documents. A hallmark of collaboration sites is the monumental mess that often occurs there as a result of collaboration activity. Everything needed by the team to be successful, from reference materials to the document deliverables themselves, resides in these sites. These sites also tend to have loose governance in that they are largely arranged and organized in real time by the team in a way that best meets the individual team's needs. It's a common misconception that collaboration sites should be heavily governed so that people external to the team would be able to easily locate and consume information. The reality is, in a proper implementation of the technology, these external people wouldn't have access to these sites in the first place, but would instead consume information from an associated portal site. Ideally, the only people who need access to a team collaboration site are the people on the defined team. Letting other sponsors or concerned parties into such sites tends to create more confusion than anything else, as those parties don't share the information context shared by the team itself. Consequently, these external viewers don't know which information is the latest and most relevant, and they can become confused and frustrated by all of the supporting material they must sift through to find whatever it is they are looking for. Allowing these external people into collaboration sites also can potentially stifle the collaboration activity, as the team members become all too aware that someone external to the team is looking over their shoulders, causing team members to become concerned about those people possibly making conclusions based on incomplete information.

Publishing

Publishing portal sites tend to be heavily governed, with a well-defined structure and information taxonomy. Because these sites have a highly controlled authorship and a wide viewing audience, this level of control is necessary to ensure that the information presented is easy to locate, meaningful, and ready for consumption. Often the small groups of people authoring content to these sites are designated team members or team leaders from the associated feeder collaboration sites, in addition to the communications people who ensure uniformity and consistency across the site.

Records Management

SharePoint 2010 provides a highly flexible set of features for managing the identification and archiving of record information. This information might be key document deliverables as moved through the content life cycle or other record information such as expenses, photographs, or communications between team members and external partners. Each organization defines and handles record information in accordance with its defined policies and procedures. In smaller collaboration implementations, the records management and archival functionality may or may not be used. As with most implementation decisions, an organization's specific requirements will determine whether this capability is ultimately needed.

Figure 10-9 illustrates how these three important capabilities included within SharePoint 2010 work together.

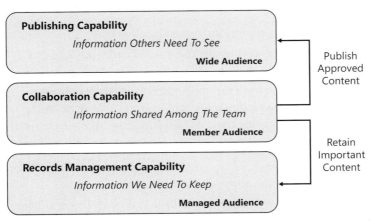

FIGURE 10-9 Publishing, collaboration, and records management work together to form a cohesive and complete information life cycle within an implementation.

Project Implementation Scenario

Consider that you have an implementation request for a large internal project. The project team consists of the following five well-defined teams, and each team has designated roles within the larger project.

- Design team
- Engineering team
- Communications team
- Testing team
- Implementation team

Each of these teams includes multiple team members. Assume for the purposes of this example that each team has 15 members. Also assume that there are external parties associated with the project, such as project sponsors, internal customers, and business representatives. As the project moves through its phases, more and more documentation deliverables will be created and published for these external parties to review. Additionally, these individual teams themselves will need a common area to exchange information that is relevant across the entire project, such as project level risks and issues, key milestone dates, and overall project status.

A common implementation mistake when working with these sorts of requirements is to attempt to satisfy them all within a single portal site collection. Although this might seem initially attractive because it implies simplification, the long-term effects can be potentially disastrous, especially in larger project scenarios. To understand why, let's review a few of the disadvantages associated with a single-site collection approach. This approach creates a single, super-massive site collection that

- Places lots of information that must be independently secured, requiring the breaking of security inheritance.
- Often results in inadvertent access to information owned by others.
- Creates potential capacity problems as content databases swell under the load of a super-massive site.
- Expands the failure footprint and effect of a technical problem within the site collection to all users of the project and their information.
- Makes it difficult to expose the appropriate information to other parties.

A preferred implementation approach would be to have separate team collaboration site collections for each of the five project subteams, with an overarching portal site collection for the published materials. The advantages of this approach include

- Each team collaboration site collection is administered by the content owners or their delegates.
- The portal site contains the information that is ready for consumption by third parties.
- Only the portal site is open to third parties.
- The portal site is accessible to all team members, allowing for information common to the entire project to be tracked cohesively.
- Subteam members do not have access to the in-progress information of other subteams, unless such access is needed and explicitly provided.

- Multiple site collections are far easier to manage from a capacity perspective.
- Information published to the portal can be processed through an approval workflow to ensure that it is ready for consumption by the larger group.

Figure 10-10 illustrates how this type of implementation can work.

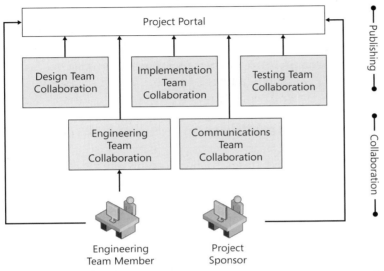

FIGURE 10-10 An example of how team collaboration sites and portals can work together to serve a larger project.

Publishing Portal Features

When a publishing site is created, you will notice that the site comes with additional functionality that doesn't exist within standard collaboration sites. Functionality for authoring and editing pages, managing content approval and deployment, as well as enhanced rich text editing functionality and style control, all become available. Additionally, libraries are created for managing pages, site assets, and site collection level styles and images. Table 10-4 describes these publishing features in detail as they are described within the Feature Management user interface.

TABLE 10-4 Publishing Features

FEATURE	DESCRIPTION
SharePoint Server Publishing Infrastructure	Provides centralized libraries, content types, master pages, and page layouts and enables page scheduling and other publishing functionality for a site collection.
SharePoint Server Publishing	Creates a Web page library as well as supporting libraries to create and publish pages based on page layouts.

You would not want to have these features enabled in team collaboration sites, because the additional functionality could potentially confuse users as well as hamper the collaboration process, which ideally would not employ the level of governance exposed by these additional features. Although these features can be enabled with any site collection, it's generally a good practice not to turn them on everywhere by default. This is why SharePoint 2010 doesn't enable them within all site types. In SharePoint Server 2007, there was a site template called a Collaboration Portal. This site type is noticeably absent from SharePoint 2010. This is an effort to guide customers into keeping collaboration and publishing separated. By doing so, each capability is optimized, performs better, and best complements the other.

To learn more about publishing sites and enabling the publishing features, see Chapter 15.

The Benefits of Enterprise Wikis

Enterprise Wikis combine all of the benefits of team collaboration sites with the ability to perform Web editing of pages directly. Enterprise Wikis also provide a host of new features, such as social tagging, ratings, and page layouts, features that are built on the publishing infrastructure in SharePoint 2010. Enterprise Wiki solutions offer a single platform for large-scale collaboration, content management, and increased productivity. By enabling Web editing capabilities, an Enterprise Wiki provides a flexible way for users to create content that takes advantage of the structure and security of SharePoint 2010. By providing editorial control, Enterprise Wikis allow administrators to control security permissions in such a way that only a subset of users can edit the wiki, while all users can view the wiki. Version control allows users to view previous versions of a wiki entry and see when and by whom changes were made. That way, if the changes made were incorrect or inappropriate, the entry can be rolled back to an earlier version.

The Enterprise Wiki feature in SharePoint 2010 provides a template that adds page rating, managed metadata, and customization capabilities. By using Microsoft SharePoint Designer 2010, a site designer can easily tailor the display of content by changing page layouts and can implement consistent branding by changing master pages. Unlike blogs, which are designed for more structured knowledge exchange and one-to-many communication, wikis enable a more collaborative experience by enabling entire groups of people to contribute knowledge. Users are able to update information as it changes with a wiki, whereas a blog provides a post-by-post state-in-time snapshot of a specific author's knowledge contribution.

Some general recommendations and limitations to keep in mind when implementing Enterprise Wikis in your environment include the following.

- Place high-traffic Enterprise Wikis in their own dedicated content database.
- An Enterprise Wiki cannot be migrated to the standard wiki without custom code.

MORE INFO Find out more about how to manage a wiki using SharePoint at *http://go.microsoft.com/fwlink/?LinkId=168889.*

Sharing Knowledge: The Social Experience

SharePoint 2010 provides significant improvements over prior versions of SharePoint in terms of social experience. New features such as blogs, wikis, team sites, social tagging, bookmarks, and notes provide a way for viewers and contributors alike to express themselves in a comfortable and natural way. This helps create a community aspect to content that lets users share their opinions on both content quality and relevancy. The following sections explore the social networking capabilities provided in SharePoint 2010.

The goal of social communities and the social experience is to provide a way for the organization to capture and collect informal knowledge. Social connections provide a way for users to associate with one another through enhanced profiles. Alerts and news feeds allow users to stay up to date. Expertise discovery allows users to find the people they need to connect with across the enterprise quickly and easily. SharePoint 2010 lets your users participate anywhere and work with peers online and offline, as well as collaborate on the go through the mobile user interface (UI).

Learn more about mobile access to SharePoint 2010 in Chapter 20, "Publishing SharePoint 2010 to Mobile Devices."

Social Features

To create a lively community experience and empower users to express themselves, qualify their areas of specialty, and find one another, SharePoint 2010 introduces a number of new social features. Some of these features will be familiar to those who have worked with SharePoint Server 2007, but they have been significantly updated to allow for a tight integration between features. The following social experience features are available in SharePoint 2010.

- My Sites
- Blogs and wikis
- Social tagging
- Expertise tagging
- Social search
- Bookmarks
- Ratings

My Sites

Think of My Sites as the central hub for information relating to each user's social experience in SharePoint 2010. The User Profile Service is where all of the user's information and attributes are defined, and the user's My Site is where the profile information is exposed. A My Site is represented through three primary tabs.

- My Newsfeed
- My Profile
- My Content

My Newsfeed is in essence the home page for your My Site, and it displays the activity feed for all users in your network. With My Newsfeed, you can actually see what your networks have been doing. My Profile displays your profile information. My Content is the entry page for the personal site where you can access your personal documents and pages and manage any content stored within the site.

The My Profile page has a new layout and includes the following tabs.

- **Overview**   Shows the activity feed in Published mode.
- **Organization**   Shows the new Silverlight-based organizational chart that allows you to navigate in the organizational structure.
- **Content**   Shows the latest content created by the user.
- **Tags And Notes**   Shows tags used and notes written by the user.
- **Colleagues**   Shows and manages the list of colleagues the user follows.
- **Memberships**   Shows and manages the list of site memberships.

The My Newsfeed and My Profile pages are available to all users and therefore are stored in the My Site Host site collection. My Content and any custom pages you create are stored in the individual user site collection. Figure 10-11 shows a My Site page.

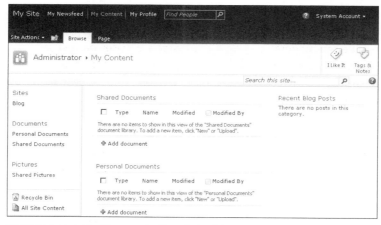

FIGURE 10-11 A My Site page in SharePoint 2010.

In addition to being able to update their activity feed, users can also post information on their Note Boards. A Note Board is similar to a public whiteboard, where users can post information that is captured historically and might be a bit lengthier than a status update. In effect, the Note Board is a micro-blogging utility. The Note Board is also available wherever social tagging is available, making it easy for users to add notes about sites, lists, or even items, as shown in Figure 10-12.

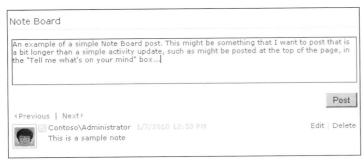

FIGURE 10-12 An example of a user's Note Board in action.

Blogs and Wikis

The concept of using wikis and blogs to communicate centers on providing increased freedom of discussion. Blogs and wikis enable any user to write Web pages and publish them for other users to see. SharePoint 2010 builds on the success of prior product versions while providing significant enhancements that make blogs and wikis more powerful for end users.

Blogs are essentially personal journals or commentaries created by individuals or teams for broad consumption. Communities use blogging to air their opinions or add to an existing body of material on a given subject area or specialty, but each individual blog entry remains static. Blog postings tend to be self-moderated. Blog sites provide a browser-based user interface for writing and publishing posts. Within SharePoint 2010, users can post to blogs using Windows Live Writer and Microsoft Word 2010.

A wiki is a website that enables users to add new content or edit existing content. As soon as you post a document entry on a wiki, all users are able to contribute to the entry by adding, editing, or amending the original document. Generally, these users do not have to ask permission, because everyone is empowered to contribute to the wiki. SharePoint 2010 provides a history of these changes, allowing the community to manage change and ensure the accuracy and relevance of the material.

This rapid development and revision of content in a shared, collaborative manner is what separates wikis from blogs—blog entries remain static, but wiki entries are dynamic and changing. After a user adds content to the wiki, that content becomes community content, and the entire community assumes ownership and responsibility. The wiki interface allows for users to edit wiki content directly within the browser, using a simple interface that gives any user the ability to contribute.

Social Tagging

SharePoint 2010 includes new features for collecting and managing social feedback. One of the key new features available is social tagging. Tagging and keywords leverage managed keywords and synonyms as well as provide the ability to manually enter new tags quickly and easily. Any list, item, or page can be tagged or notated. All of your tags and notes become available on your My Site. Keywords can be managed at the enterprise live through the Managed Metadata Service, which allows users to contribute to the enterprise tag continuum and gives administrators the ability to streamline and suggest keywords for tagging. You can even tag external sites by adding a link to your favorites or bookmarks toolbar. Figure 10-13 shows the tagging interface available to users on a list, page, or item.

Tags
Note Board
My Tags
blogs; SharePoint
Private: Do not show my tags on this item to others
Suggested Tags
blogs
SharePoint

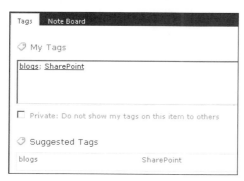

FIGURE 10-13 Users may add tags with keywords to any list, item, or page.

Because social tagging is managed as a taxonomy through the Managed Metadata Service, all of the same practices and principles that relate to taxonomy management apply. To learn more about managing enterprise taxonomies, see Chapter 9, "Organizing Information."

Expertise Tagging

Expertise tagging lets users define their skill set in a unique way that allows others within the organization to find a subject matter expert on a specific topic quickly and easily. Expertise tagging is related to a person and describes the person, such as what they do, which projects they work on, or what skills they have. SharePoint 2010 includes enhancements to what was previously known as the Knowledge Network. This feature is now called Outlook Social Connector, and it provides the ability to search e-mail messages for the identification of keywords and expertise automatically. Outlook Social Connector also allows users to view profile information about other users in their network, as well as keep contact records up to date. (You'll find more information in the section titled "Integrating with the Outlook Social Connector" later in this chapter.) Figure 10-14 shows the fields available for users to specify their expertise-related information.

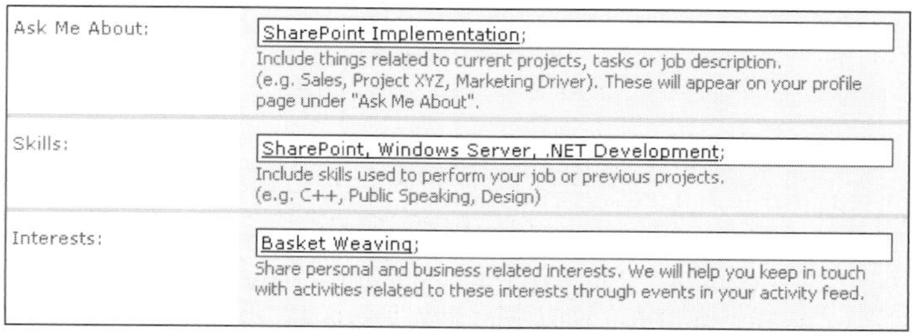

Ask Me About:
SharePoint Implementation;
Include things related to current projects, tasks or job description. (e.g. Sales, Project XYZ, Marketing Driver). These will appear on your profile page under "Ask Me About".
Skills:
SharePoint, Windows Server, .NET Development;
Include skills used to perform your job or previous projects. (e.g. C++, Public Speaking, Design)
Interests:
Basket Weaving;
Share personal and business related interests. We will help you keep in touch with activities related to these interests through events in your activity feed.

FIGURE 10-14 Expertise information from the Edit Profile page

Social Search

Social search, or people search as it is commonly called, has been vastly enhanced within SharePoint 2010. Since users can define expertise information both implicitly and explicitly, it's easy to search for someone who has knowledge on a specific topic. Users have the ability to specify expertise information within their My Site, and expertise information can also be gathered from e-mail messages. Users are also able to specify all of their profile properties from their My Profile page. When this information is stored and a crawl is performed, SharePoint 2010 produces the results in intuitive ways, either by performing a general people search, a search by name, or a search by expertise. Additionally, when users perform these kinds of searches, they can view the results with three Focus refinements—All, Name, and Expertise— which makes it easier for users to get the information they need from the results provided.

Figure 10-15 shows a people search in action. Notice the Focus refinements on the left.

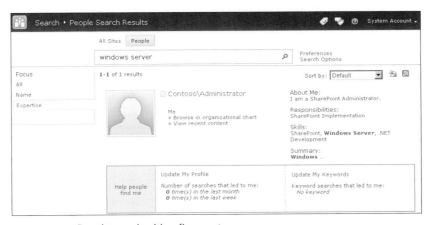

FIGURE 10-15 People search with refinements

Ratings

Ratings provide users with a way to rate the quality of content, which allows users to convey their general opinion of something without providing them with the ability to comment directly on the content. Ratings are available by default within Enterprise Wikis and publishing sites, but they must be enabled within collaboration sites. Ratings settings can be enabled at the list or library level.

Enabling ratings adds the ratings fields (average rating and number of ratings) to the content types currently within the list and to the default view. If you add new content types later and they don't already contain the ratings fields, you will need to add the ratings fields to them, either manually or by returning to the ratings settings page and updating the list. Disabling ratings removes the fields from the list (but not from the underlying content types) and from the default view.

To control whether a list provides ratings, perform the following steps.

1. From any document library, click the Library menu under Library Tools and then select Library Settings.

2. Click Ratings Settings on the Library Settings page.

3. Select Yes under Allow Items In This List To Be Rated? to enable ratings, or select No to disable ratings for the list, as shown in Figure 10-16.

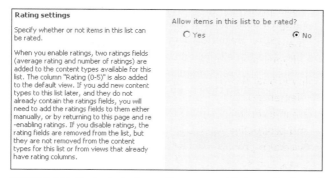

FIGURE 10-16 Control whether ratings are enabled on a list from the Library Settings page

Integrating with the Outlook Social Connector

The Outlook Social Connector is an integrated part of Microsoft Outlook 2010 when that application is purchased as part of Microsoft Office Home, Business, Professional Plus, and Pro editions. The Outlook Social Connector is a set of new features that help you keep track of your friends and colleagues while enabling you to expand your professional network. As you read your e-mail messages, glance down at the new People Pane to see the picture, name, and title of the sender. A rich, aggregated collection of information about the sender and recipients is included, along with the ability to add those people to your network with a single click.

Outlook Social Connector provides the following exciting and unique new features.

- **The People Pane**   Displays a name, picture, and title for your colleagues whenever reading a message from them.

- **Rich history**   Shows you a rich communications history for each person that sends you messages.

- **Activities**   Lets you download and see real-time activity for your colleagues.

- **Get Friendly**   Request someone as a colleague or friend with one click. Synchronize those colleagues with Outlook and keep them up to date as their information changes.

- **SharePoint 2010**   Connect to the new My Site social networking experience to see current activity feed information.

- **Extensible**   A public Software Development Kit (SDK) allows anyone to build a connection to business or consumer social networks.

Creating an Information Repository with the User Profile Service

This section covers the User Profile Service, which is an integral part of SharePoint 2010. The User Profile Service makes SharePoint 2010 a complete and effective collaboration tool by providing fundamental services such as user profile storage, social tagging, audiences, and My Sites. Although user profiles and related services were present as part of the Shared Services Provider in the previous version, SharePoint 2010 adds many new features such as social tagging, organizational profiles, user subtypes, and bi-directional profile synchronization.

Communities stand as a key capability in SharePoint 2010. The user profile server is the linchpin service that holds the various elements of communities together. The service stores information about all users of the system in a central location. This information is used by other services to provide an effective and productive collaboration environment. In addition to storing the user information, the service also provides a central repository for all social tags and notes, organization profiles, audiences, and synchronization information.

The term *user* within an IT environment is an identity that is associated with a certain role and permissions to perform some action in a system. This definition does not give much importance to the user itself but instead indicates what the user can do within the system. This approach is technology-centric, in which the emphasis is on systems and what the user can do within them. For a *collaboration tool* like SharePoint, this information is not sufficient, because the system should know *who* the user actually is, not just what the user's roles and permissions are. It should know the user not as an entity but as a *person*, a person who has a title, skills, interests, a personal site, photographs, and other unique characteristics.

The User Profile Service is based on an architecture that is person-centric. It focuses on the user as the key entity and includes all information that is stored in the system about the user. This architecture moves away from the technology-centric systems approach of an application. One of the main aspects of this person-centric approach is the social network. Within a social network, users who share common interests and skills or belong to the same business unit can now collaborate effectively with one another and share ideas.

Uses and Benefits of the User Profile Service

The User Profile Service in SharePoint 2010 provides the following benefits and uses for the enterprise.

User Profiles

One of the most important and fundamental uses of the User Profile Service, as the name suggests, is to store the user profiles—information about the users. The profile of a user can include a variety of information ranging from the user's personal contact information to organization-specific information such as the user's role or supervisor name.

The information stored in a user profile is highly customizable and can include new attributes that are specific to an organization. For example, a large organization might add an attribute called Organization Team that defines the team for which the user is a member. In addition to basic user information, SharePoint 2010 adds a new attribute called *social tags* that contain various tags (keywords) that can be added to a user's profile by other users. These tags can be used to find and track a user within an organization.

The information in a user profile can be pulled from external directory services, such as Microsoft Active Directory, Lightweight Directory Access Protocol (LDAP), and other Business Connectivity Services (BCS) connections. SharePoint 2010 can even pull user profile information from multiple data sources.

Organization Profiles

One of the new additions in SharePoint 2010 is a feature called Organization Profiles. An organization profile is very similar to a user profile, but the organization profile includes information about a team or a business unit within the organization. The organization profile behaves just like a user profile. It can have its own profile properties that describe the organization; it can be used in a people picker control, and so on. An organization profile can be planned in advance or created extemporaneously to bring together a group of people within an organization. The members of a profile can be categorized as leaders or members. Leaders are the members who control the profile and its memberships.

Profile Synchronization for User Profile Services

Most enterprises keep their user information in Active Directory or other directory stores. Information from these sources will need to be pulled into SharePoint for the creation of user profiles to allow users to find people by their expertise or other characteristics. This process of creation and synchronization of user, group, and organization profile information among the SharePoint profile store and other directory stores is performed by the Profile Synchronization Service. The Profile Synchronization Service can pull information from a variety of directory stores like Active Directory, LDAP, and other BCS models.

The Profile Synchronization Service in SharePoint 2010 provides a bi-directional synchronization between the SharePoint profile store and the enterprise directory store. Profiles from SharePoint can also be exported into the enterprise directory store. This bi-directional model is currently supported only for Active Directory and LDAP stores, however; it is not supported for the BCS service.

Another important feature of the Profile Synchronization Service is that it can synchronize data from multiple sources to bring information into a single user profile. You'll find more information in the section titled "Profile Synchronization" later in this chapter.

Audiences

SharePoint 2010 allows content and information on the system to be targeted to a specific set of users based on rules defined in the system. This specific set of users is known as an *audience* and can be complied using a variety of rules defined on the user properties, group memberships, organization reporting structure, and so on. The audiences that are created can be used in the people picker control and also to target Web Parts.

My Site Host

Within each SharePoint 2010 deployment, at least one site is dedicated for hosting My Sites. This dedicated site is called the My Site host. The My Sites for all of an organization's users are hosted under this site, and it serves many of the shared pages and features needed for interacting with profile information. The My Site host is also needed for the deployment of social features within SharePoint 2010.

If you used the Farm Configuration Wizard to set up your farm, you should already have a My Site host. If not, you can create from within SharePoint Central Administration, just as you would any other site collection. Be sure you use the My Site Host template.

My Site

A My Site is the personal site of a specific user within the enterprise. The site acts a repository for the user's documents, links, and other information. Each user's My Site also hosts the user's profile page, within which the user can edit his or her profile to identify interests, skills, colleagues, and so on. The My Site also hosts a My Content section, within which all personal content is stored; this section also includes a blog that lets the user share his or her views, ideas, and knowledge.

Social Tags and Notes

In its bid to be a complete collaboration and social networking product, SharePoint 2010 adds a new feature called Social Tags And Notes. This feature allows end users to tag various documents, Web pages, and items (including external pages) with keywords or tags. These tags can be used to describe the item or page and are useful later when searching for items. SharePoint 2010 also gives users the ability to add impromptu notes, items, pages, and even another user's profile. There is a built-in governance model through which an administrator can search, monitor, and delete tags that are not wanted.

User Profile Service Architecture

The underlying architecture of the User Profile Service supports and provides the services and features described in the section titled "Uses and Benefits of the User Profile Service" earlier in this chapter. The profile store is based on three back-end databases that store all user profiles and profile-related information. The three databases are the Sync database, the Social database, and the Profile database.

Figure 10-17 shows the User Profile Service architecture. The architecture also includes a caching element that helps maintain performance.

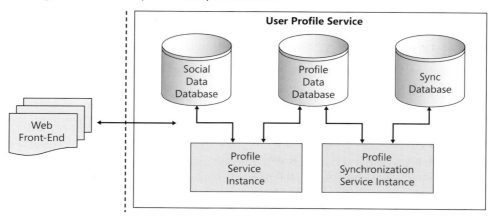

FIGURE 10-17 User Profile Service architecture

Web Front-End Servers

Though not directly part of the User Profile Service architecture, the Web front-end (WFE) servers request the information on behalf of the end-user client's browser. The WFE servers talk to applications servers, on which the User Profile Service is made available, which in turn communicates with the back-end database servers for profile information. The SQL databases provide information about colleagues, social tags, personalization sites, and so on. The User Profile Service on the application server provides the light user profile, which is stored in the mid-tier cache maintained by the application server. The WFE server has its own cache, known as the front-end cache, which is a light cache that stores the SQL connection string, the schema for the user profiles, and so on.

Application Servers

The application server hosts the User Profile Service and the User Profile Synchronization Service. Although the synchronization service is a separate service in SharePoint 2010 and is not part of the actual User Profile Service, they are covered together here for simplicity—and because they are dependent on one another. The User Profile Service is the service responsible for making the user profile features available to end users. This service hosts a mid-tier cache that holds the light user profile data, which includes information such as account names, e-mail addresses, and display names. The default size of the mid-tier cache is 256 megabytes (MB), and it is configurable based on business needs. Optimally, the cache is configured to cache the *most used* profile, as compared to the standard cache approach of storing the *last used* profile. By storing the most used data, the User Profile Service cache makes the information in a user profile that is most often visited or used more easily and quickly accessible.

The User Profile Synchronization Service is the service that pulls profile data from the external directory source into the SharePoint Profile store. Since the User Profile Service is a separate service in SharePoint 2010, the synchronization service needs to be set up separately after the profile service has been configured. The synchronization service has a one-to-one relation with a user profile service. Each user profile service can have only one synchronization service associated with it. The profile synchronization service also provides a feature to set up scheduled jobs that can run incremental profile imports.

Databases

The profile service in SharePoint 2010 utilizes three databases to store all profile data and related pieces of information. The following is a description of each of these databases.

- **User profile database**   The user profile database is used to store all the information present in a user's profile. The profile picture of the user is not saved in the profile database, but it is stored as part of the My Site content database. The profile database also stores the activity feed, a set of latest changes or activities related to the user across the system. These activities can range from a user adding a tag to a page to a user becoming a member of a group.

- **Social data database**   This is a new database that was added as part of SharePoint 2010 and supports the new social features of SharePoint 2010. The social data database is used to store tags, keywords, comments, bookmarks, and ratings that are related to various items present in the system. The database also stores other social data, such as term values for use on the news feed and the Tags And Notes page.

- **Sync database**   The synchronization database is used to store the staging sync data for Active Directory, LDAP, or other external directory stores that are providing data for the user's profile.

As part of the extended architecture, you will look at two related services that work in conjunction with the User Profile Service. These two services are the Search Service and the newly added Managed Metadata Service. The Search Service is used to index tags and make them available in search results as well as to provide the necessary security trimming. The Managed Metadata Service provides the metadata that is used for tagging various items within the system.

Setting Up and Configuring the User Profile Service

The User Profile Service is an independent service application that can be started and configured from SharePoint Central Administration. The management user interface provides a central location to monitor and maintain the User Profile Service application.

Make sure you have met the following prerequisites prior to starting the User Profile Service application from SharePoint Central Administration.

- There is an instance of the Managed Metadata Service.
- There is a managed path for My Sites such as /users.
- There is an application pool for My Sites.
- There is a My Sites host.

Starting the User Profile Service

To start the User Profile Service, complete the following steps.

1. Open a browser and go to the SharePoint Central Administration website.

2. Under Application Management, click Manage Service Applications.

3. Click the Service Applications tab at the top of the Application Management section to activate the Ribbon.

4. Click New in the Create group of the Ribbon and then click User Profile Service Application in the drop-down list, as shown in Figure 10-18.

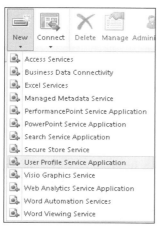

FIGURE 10-18 Create New User Profile Service Application

5. In the Create New User Profile Service Application dialog box shown in Figure 10-19, type a unique name in the Name text box. This is the name you want to assign to the User Profile Service application.

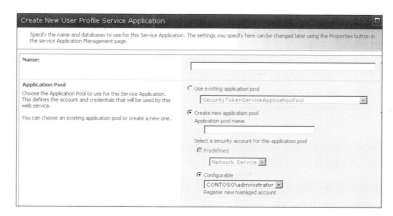

FIGURE 10-19 Create New User Profile Service Application dialog box

6. To assign an application pool to this application, either select Use Existing Application Pool or create a new application pool by following these steps.

   a. Select the Create A New Application Pool option.

   b. Type the name for the new application pool.

   c. Under Select A Security Account For This Application Pool, select Predefined to choose an existing predefined security account from the list, or select Configurable to choose an existing managed account. If you want to use a managed account that is not on the list, click the Register A New Managed Account link to register a new managed account.

7. The Profile Service application stores all the required information in three different databases. In the Profile Database section, enter the following information, as shown in Figure 10-20.

   ■ In the Database Server text box, type the name of the database server where the profile database will be located.

   ■ In the Database Name text box, type the name of the database where the profile information will be stored.

   ■ In the Database Authentication section, select Windows Authentication to use Integrated Windows Authentication to connect to the profile database, or select SQL Authentication to enter the network credentials that will be used to connect to the profile database.

   ■ In the Failover Server section, in the Failover Database Server text box, type the name of the database server to be used in conjunction with Microsoft SQL Server database mirroring.

FIGURE 10-20 Profile Database information

8. In the Synchronization Database section, enter the following information, as shown in Figure 10-21.

   ■ In the Database Server text box, type the name of the database server where the synchronization database will be located.

- In the Database Name text box, type the name of the database where the synchronization information for synchronizing user profiles with external databases will be stored.

- In the Database Authentication section, select Windows Authentication to use Integrated Windows Authentication to connect to the synchronization database, or select SQL Authentication to enter the network credentials that will be used to connect to the synchronization database.

- In the Failover Server section, in the Failover Database Server text box, type the name of the database server to be used in conjunction with Microsoft SQL Server database mirroring.

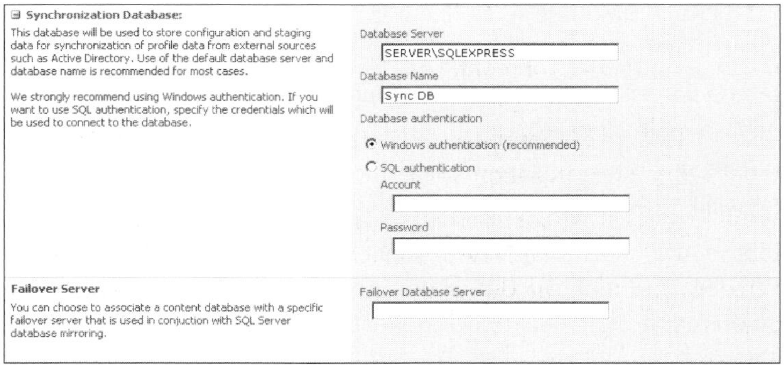

FIGURE 10-21 Synchronization Database information

9. In the Social Tagging Database section, enter the following information, as shown in Figure 10-22.

- In the Database Server text box, type the name of the database server where the social tagging database will be located.

- In the Database Name text box, type the name of the database where the social tagging information like tags and notes will be stored.

- In the Database Authentication section, select Windows Authentication to use Integrated Windows Authentication to connect to the social tagging database, or select SQL Authentication to enter the network credentials that will be used to connect to the social tagging database.

- In the Failover Server section, in the Failover Database Server text box, type the name of the database server to be used in conjunction with Microsoft SQL Server database mirroring.

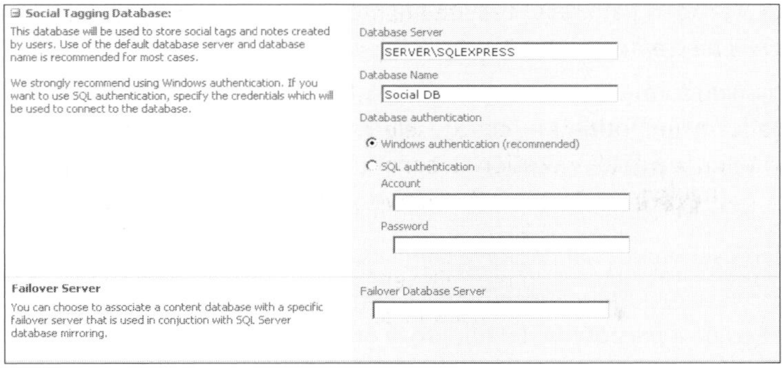

FIGURE 10-22 Social Tagging Database information

10. In the case of a multiserver environment, you can choose the application server on which you want to host the profile service. The Profile Synchronization Instance section lists all the servers added to the farm, and you can choose any server on which you want to run the Profile Synchronization Service.

11. The next couple of sections require information about the My Site application that will be associated with this User Profile Service application, as shown in Figure 10-23. In the My Site Host URL section, type the URL of the site collection where the My Site host has been provisioned.

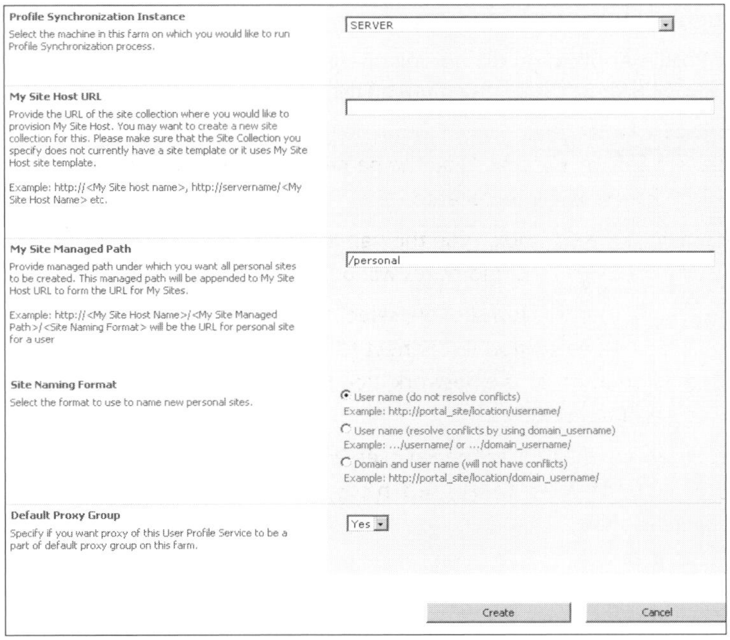

FIGURE 10-23 Create New Profile information

12. In the My Site Managed Path section, type the managed path where the individual My Site websites will be created.

13. Choose the naming format for naming new My Sites when they are created by selecting one of the following formats in the Site Naming Format section.

   - User name (do not resolve conflicts)
   - User name (resolve conflicts by using *domain_username*)
   - Domain and user name (will not have conflicts)

14. In the Default Proxy Group section, indicate whether you want the proxy of this User Profile Service to be a part of the default proxy group on this farm. Select Yes if you want to include the proxy and No otherwise.

15. Click Create to provision the new User Profile Service application.

Editing an Existing User Profile Service Application

To modify properties of an existing user profile application, perform the following steps.

1. Open a browser and go to the SharePoint Central Administration website.

2. Under Application Management, click Manage Service Applications.

3. Select the User Profile Service Application that you want to edit. When you make a selection, the row has a blue background of color and the Service Application tab Ribbon control on top of the page is enabled.

4. Click the Properties button under the Operations group.

5. The Edit User Profile Application dialog box opens. All edits that are required can be made in this dialog box, as shown in Figure 10-24.

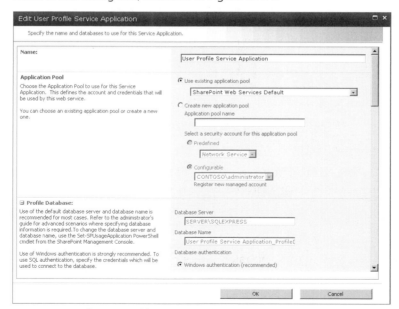

FIGURE 10-24 Edit User Profile Service Application dialog box

Delegating Administration of a User Profile Service Application

SharePoint 2010 allows farm administrators to delegate the administration activities of a service application to a service application administrator. A service application administrator can perform all administrative tasks related to the service application but cannot perform activities related to other service applications or change settings in Central Administration.

To delegate the administration role of the User Profile Service application, perform the following steps.

1. Open a browser and go to the SharePoint Central Administration website.
2. Under Application Management, click Manage Service Applications.
3. Select the User Profile Service Application you want to edit. When selected, the row has a blue background and the Service Application tab Ribbon control on top of the page is enabled.
4. Click the Administrators button under the Operations group.
5. In the Administrators For User Profile Service dialog box, type the user name in the people picker control, as shown in Figure 10-25, and then click Add.

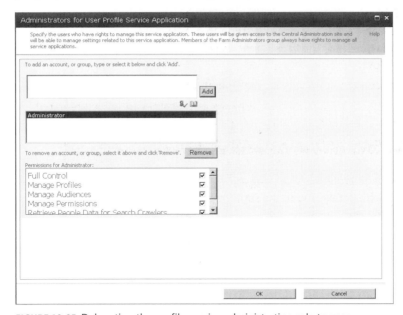

FIGURE 10-25 Delegating the profile service administration role to user

6. In the Permissions For Administrator section, select Full Control and click OK. This adds the specific user as the Administrator for the User Profile Service Application.
7. To remove a user from the Administrator role, select the user from the list and click Remove.

Creating User Sub-types

SharePoint 2010 introduces a new feature known as the user sub-type. A sub-type is a different type of user in SharePoint. For example, user types can be employees, contractors, interns, and so on. SharePoint 2010 allows these different types of users to coexist, and sub-types help to categorize users. Each of these user types can have a distinct set of profile properties. Use the following steps to create or remove a user sub-type.

1. Open a browser and go to the SharePoint Central Administration website.

2. Under Application Management, click Manage Service Applications.

3. Select the User Profile Service Application you want to edit.

4. Click the Manage button under the Operations group to open the Manage Profile Service page shown in Figure 10-26.

FIGURE 10-26 Creating user sub-types on the Manage Profile Service page

5. On the Manage Profile Service page, click Manage User Sub-types under the People section, which will take you to the settings page shown in Figure 10-27.

FIGURE 10-27 Create a new sub-type on the Manage User Sub-type settings page.

6. In the New Sub-types section, fill in the following information.

   ■ In the Display Name text box, type the name for the sub-type that you want to display to end users.

   ■ In the Name text box, type the internal name for the user sub-type.

7. Click Create and the new sub-type will be created.

8. To remove an existing sub-type, select the check box for the sub-type and click Remove.

Creating User Profile Properties

The user profile properties are basic building blocks for the profile service application. The properties are the attributes that help describe a user profile. Although the user profile properties concept was present in SharePoint Server 2007, there are certain changes in the current version that you will look at as you create a new profile property.

1. Open a browser and go to the SharePoint Central Administration website.

2. Under Application Management, click Manage Service Applications.

3. Select the User Profile Service Application you want to edit.

4. Click the Manage button under the Operations group.

5. On the Manage Profile Service page, click Manage User Properties under the People section.

6. On the Manage User Properties page, click New Property.

7. On the Add User Profile Property page shown in Figure 10-28, enter the following information in the Property Settings section.

FIGURE 10-28 Create a new user profile property on the Add User Profile Property settings page.

   ■ In the Name text box, type the internal name for the profile property.

   ■ In the Display Name text box, type the name for the profile property that you want to display to end users.

> **NOTE** One of the new features of SharePoint 2010 is built-in support for localization. The user can now add display values in different languages for each display field by clicking the Edit Language button.

- Choose the data type for this property from the Type drop-down list.

> **NOTE** Based on the type selected, additional fields might show up in this section. For example, for the data type string (Single Value), you can specify the maximum length of the property in the Length column, and you can also associate the property with a term set by selecting the check box for Configure A Term Set For This Property and then choosing the value from the drop-down list.

8. You can associate the property with any of the user sub-types by selecting the check box of the sub-type in the Sub-type Of Profile section.

9. Specify the description of the property in the Description text box in the User Description section, as shown in Figure 10-29. The description can be information about the property that will help users identify the property.

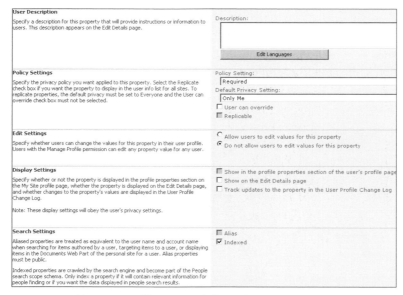

FIGURE 10-29 New user profile property information

10. You can specify the policies settings for the property in the Policy Settings section, as shown in Figure 10-28.

- Choose from the drop-down list whether the property is Optional, Required, or Disabled.
- For the Default Privacy setting, you can choose the users who can see this profile property.
- Select the User Can Override check box if you want the user to modify these settings.
- Select the Replicate check box if you want this property to display in the user info list for all sites.

11. In the Edit Settings section, you can choose whether the user can edit this property or not.

12. In the Display Settings section, you can choose how the user can view the property in the My Site Profile Property page or in the Edit Property page. You can also enable Track Updates To The Property to log changes in the user change log.

13. In the Search Settings section, you can specify whether the property is indexed or not. Indexing a property can make the property value return in search results. You can also enable a property to be aliased, which will make the property a suitable alias for the user in search.

14. In the Add New Mapping section, shown in Figure 10-30, you can map a user profile property to an attribute from an external data source. After a property has been mapped to an external attribute, the profile property will get a value from the attribute during synchronization. You can choose a Source Data Connection from the drop-down list, which contains all of the added external directory connections.

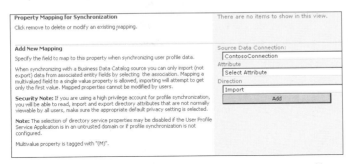

FIGURE 10-30 The Add New Mapping section for a new user profile property

15. Depending on the connection you select, the attributes field will be populated from that directory source. A new feature of SharePoint 2010 is that it enables profile properties to write back values to external directory sources (only for Active Directory and LDAP). You can choose whether the profile property value will be exported to the external data source or imported from the external data source by selecting the appropriate value from the Direction drop-down list.

16. When you are finished, click OK to create the new profile property.

Editing and Deleting Existing User Profile Properties

To edit or delete an existing User Profile Property, complete the following steps.

1. Open a browser and go to the SharePoint Central Administration website.

2. Under Application Management, click Manage Service Applications.

3. Select the User Profile Service Application you want to edit.

4. Click the Manage button under the Operations group.

5. On the Manage Profile Service page, click Manage User Properties under the People section.

6. On the Manage User Property page, select the property you want to edit and select Edit from the drop-down list. On the Edit User Profile Property page, shown in Figure 10-31, make the required edits and click OK.

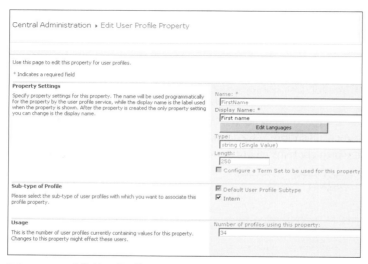

FIGURE 10-31 Edit User Profile Property page

7. To delete a profile property, select the property you want to delete on the Manage User Property page. From the drop-down list for the property, select Delete. Confirm the deletion on the dialog box and click OK.

Editing Profile Policies

SharePoint 2010 provides a centralized location for viewing and editing all policies for profile services. Through this centralized location, a user can see all the policies defined for the profile services in User Profile Properties, Colleagues, Memberships, and so on.

To edit a policy through this centralized location, complete the following steps.

1. Open a browser and go to the SharePoint Central Administration website.

2. Under Application Management, click Manage Service Applications.

3. Select the User Profile Service Application you want to edit.

4. Click the Manage button under the Operations group.

5. On the Manage Profile Service Page, click Manage Policies under the People section, which will bring you to a settings page, shown in Figure 10-32.

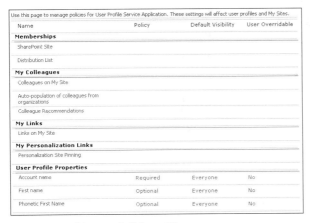

FIGURE 10-32 Manage Policies settings page

6. On the Manage Policies page, select the policy you want to edit. From the drop-down list for the property, select Edit, which opens the Edit Policy settings page, shown in Figure 10-33. On the Edit Policy page, make the required edits and click OK.

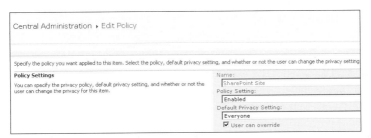

FIGURE 10-33 Edit Policy settings page

Creating and Configuring Audiences

Audiences were a feature of SharePoint Server 2007 that has been carried forward in SharePoint 2010 with few changes. The following steps provide a quick overview of how to create and configure a new audience in SharePoint 2010.

1. Open a browser and go to the SharePoint Central Administration website.

2. Under Application Management, click Manage Service Applications.

3. Select the User Profile Service Application you want to edit.

4. Click the Manage button under the Operations group.

5. On the Manage Profile Service Page, click Manage Audiences under the People section.

6. On the View Audience page, click the New Audience link.

7. On the Create Audience page, under the Properties section shown in Figure 10-34, specify the following information to create a new audience.

   - **Description**   Give a brief description about the audience.

   - **Owner**   Specify the owner of the audience.

   - **Include Users Who**   Each audience builds its members based on certain rules. Specify whether the users who become the members of this audience must satisfy all the rules defined or some of the rules defined.

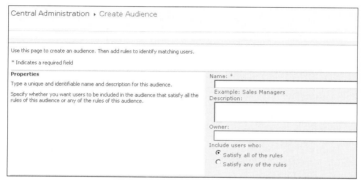

FIGURE 10-34 Create Audience page

8. Click OK to create the audience. When the audience has been created, the user is redirected to the Add Audience Rule page to add rules for the new audience. You can add a rule based either on the user or on some profile property.

9. In the Operand section on the Add Audience Rule page, choose whether the rule is based on a user or a profile property, as shown in Figure 10-35. If you choose to base the rule on a profile property, select the profile property you want to use from the drop-down list.

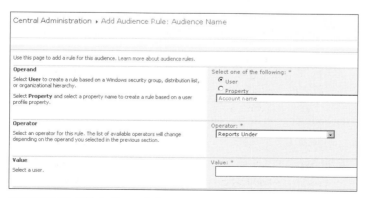

FIGURE 10-35 Add Audience Rule page

10. In the Operator section, select a valid operator from the list of available operators for the operand.

11. In the Value section, type the value in the text box and then click OK to add the rule to the audience.

12. When a rule has been created, the user is redirected to the View Audience Properties page, shown in Figure 10-36, which lets the user add new rules to the audience, view audience memberships, edit audience properties, or compile an audience.

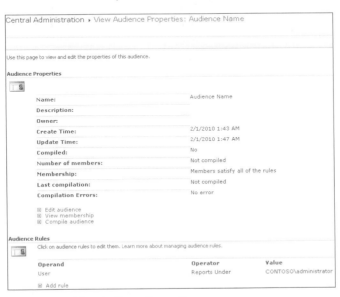

FIGURE 10-36 View Audience Properties page

Audience compilation is a process through which users are added as members of the audience based on the rules specified. After an audience is created, you must compile the audience at least once for it to add users as members of the audience. A scheduled job for audience compilation is generally preferred to add or update members of the audience.

Profile Synchronization

After you have created profile properties, user sub-types, and audiences, you need to configure the synchronization of the users and profile properties from a directory services source running within the enterprise. In the following sections, you will review how to configure synchronization connections, set up incremental scheduled jobs, and explore other synchronization features.

Before you proceed with the creation of a new synchronization connection, however, you need to start the User Profile Synchronization service on one of the servers in the farm and associate this service with the user profile application that would be using this synchronization service.

Starting User Profile Synchronization Service

To start the User Profile Synchronization Service, perform the following steps.

1. Open a browser and go to the SharePoint Central Administration website.

2. Under System Settings, click Manage Services On Server.

3. On the Services On Server page, select the server you want to start the synchronization service from the Servers drop-down list.

4. Click the Start link on the row corresponding to the User Profile Synchronization Service.

5. On the next page, select the user profile application to which you want to associate the service and click OK.

6. After the User Profile Service is started, navigate to Services.msc and ensure that the following services are running.

   - Forefront Identity Manager Synchronization Service
   - Forefront Identity Manager Service

7. Perform an iisrest command to restart IIS services and complete the provisioning on the User Profile Service.

Creating New Profile Synchronization Connection

To create a new profile synchronization connection, complete the following steps.

1. Open a browser and go to the SharePoint Central Administration website.

2. Under Application Management, click Manage Service Applications.

3. Select the User Profile Service Application you want to edit.

4. Click the Manage button under the Operations group.

5. Under Synchronization on the Manage Profile Service page, click Configure Synchronization Connections.

6. On the Synchronization Connections page, click Create New Connection.

7. On the Add New Synchronization Connection page shown in Figure 10-37, provide the following information to create a new synchronization connection.

   - **Connection Name** Type the name you want to give to this connection in this text box.

   - **Type** Select the kind of directory service you want to connect to for Synchronization in this text box.

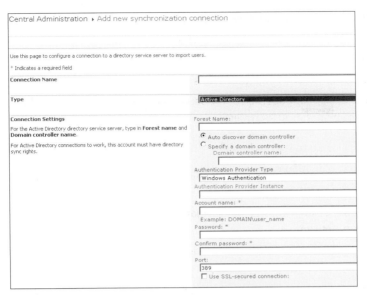

FIGURE 10-37 Add New Synchronization Connection page

8. In the Connection Settings section, provide the information required to make a connection for the synchronization process. The connection settings section changes based on the type of provider selected. For example, if you use Active Directory as your enterprise directory service, you will need to provide the following information.

- **Forest** Provide the name of the forest with which you want to synchronize data.

- **Domain Controller** You can provide a domain controller name in the text box if you have a preferred domain controller, or you can choose Auto Discover Domain Controller to let SharePoint discover one.

- **Authentication Provider** Choose the authentication provider you want to use for this connection. Because SharePoint 2010 allows claim-based and forms-based authentication, this information is required at the synchronization setup so that required user IDs can be pulled from the system for identification. For this example, use Windows Authentication.

- Provide the Username and Password that has the required permissions to fetch the user profile. For Active Directory, this account should have Replicate Directory Changes permissions to synchronize data.

- Select the Use SSL-Secured Connection check box if you want to use SSL.

- SharePoint 2010 has a new feature that allows multiple organizational units (OUs) to be used to pull information in a single connection. This can be achieved by clicking Populate Container and selecting the required OUs at the bottom of the Add New Synchronization Connection page.

9. Click OK to create the connection.

Editing Profile Synchronization Connection Filters

SharePoint 2010 lets you filter the data that is returned from the enterprise directory services. Although this feature was available in SharePoint Server 2007 as a text box in which you could type in the name of the required filter, SharePoint 2010 provides an Edit Connection Filters page through which you can create these filters.

To create a filter for a User Profile Synchronization connection, perform the following steps.

1. Open a browser and go to the SharePoint Central Administration website.
2. Under Application Management, click Manage Service Applications.
3. Select the User Profile Service Application you want to edit.
4. Click the Manage button under the Operations group.
5. On the Manage Profile Service page, click Configure Synchronization Connections under the Synchronization section.
6. On the Synchronizations Connections page, click the connection for which you want to configure the filter.
7. Select Edit Connection Filters from the drop-down list of the selected item.
8. On the Edit Connection Filters page, you can set up the filters on user attributes or group properties. Select the required filters in either of the sections and click Add.
9. Click OK.

Creating an Organization Profile

In this section you will look at how you can create a new organization profile. An organization profile is a new feature of SharePoint 2010 through which a group or team can have its own profile in the SharePoint system that has all the features of a user profile.

To create a new organization profile, perform the following steps.

1. Open a browser and go to the SharePoint Central Administration website.
2. Under Application Management, click Manage Service Applications.
3. Select the User Profile Service Application you want to edit.
4. Click the Manage button under the Operations group.
5. On the Manage Profile Service page, click Manage Organization Profiles under the Organizations section.
6. On the Manage Organization Profiles page, click the New Profile link.
7. On the Add Organization Profiles page, provide the following information to create a new organization profile, as shown in Figure 10-38.
   - **Name**   Type the name you want to give to the organization profile.
   - **About Us**   In this section, you can write a brief description about the profile.
   - **Organization's Former Names**   Add any former names by which the organization was called.

- **Team Site** Here you can provide the URL of the site (if there is one) for the organization or team for which you are creating this profile.
- **Parent** Type the name of the person or organization in the enterprise reporting hierarchy to which this new organization reports.
- **Organization Leader** In this section, you can provide the list of all users who act as leaders in this new organization.
- **Organization Members** In this section, you can add all the users who will be the members of this organization.

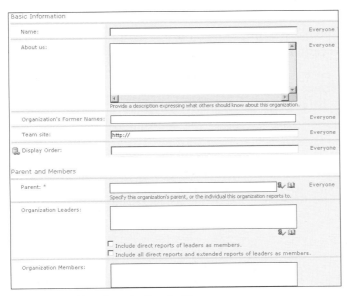

FIGURE 10-38 New Organization Profile page

8. Click Save And Close to add this new organization profile.

Setting Up My Sites

In the following sections, you will look at the steps that enable the My Site feature of the User Profile Service application. Setting up My Sites for users to use is a two-stage process. The first stage involves configuring the My Site settings; in the second stage, you grant permissions to allow users to use the My Site and social features.

Configuring the My Site Settings

To configure the My Site settings, complete the following steps.

1. Open a browser and go to the SharePoint Central Administration website.
2. Under Application Management, click Manage Service Applications.
3. Select the User Profile Service Application you want to edit.

4. Click the Manage button under the Operations group.

5. On the Manage Profile Service Page, click Setup My Sites under the My Site Settings section.

6. On the My Site Settings page, enter the following setup information, as shown in Figure 10-39.

   - **Preferred Search Center**   Specify the search center to which the user will be taken when she begins a search from the My Site Search page.

   - **My Site Host**   Specify the site under which the user's My Site will be created. All users who have My Site service provided by this user profile application will have their My Sites located under this site.

   - **Personal Site Location**   Specify a managed path under which the user's My Site will be created.

   - **Site Naming Format**   Choose one of the specified formats to determine how the users' My Sites will be named.

   - **Language Options**   Select this check box if you want the users to choose the language of their My Sites.

   - **Read Permission Level**   Specify the users or groups who will have read access to the user's My Sites.

   - **My Site E-mail Notifications**   Specify the sender's name for all My Site e-mail notifications.

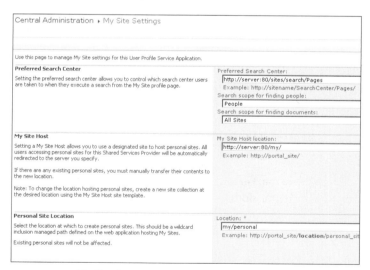

FIGURE 10-39 My Site Settings page

7. Click OK to complete the settings.

Configuring User Permissions

To configure user permissions for the My Sites feature, complete the following steps.

1. Open a browser and go to the SharePoint Central Administration website.

2. Under Application Management, click Manage Service Applications.

3. Select the User Profile Service Application you want to edit.

4. Click the Manage button under the Operations group.

5. On the Manage Profile Service page, click Manage User Permissions under the People section.

6. On the Permissions For User Profile Service Application dialog box, as shown in Figure 10-40, type the user names or groups to whom you want to grant permissions to use My Site and user social features.

FIGURE 10-40 Use the Permissions For User Profile Service Application dialog box to set permissions for My Site and social features.

7. Click Add and select Use Personal Features, Create Personal Sites, and Use Social Features to grant the required permissions.

8. Click OK.

Global deployment of My Sites is an important feature when your deployment spans several geographical regions and users in these regions collaborate with each other or move between regions. To explain the global deployment of My Sites, consider a scenario in which User1 has a My Site in Region1. Suppose all users in Region1 have their My Sites provided by UserProfileServiceApplication1. Now consider that User1 has access to a site that is in Region2, and User1 also has access to personal features of UserProfileServiceApplication2 that supports Region2. If User1 clicks on the My Site link on a site in Region2, he will be redirected to his My Site, which is hosted in the UserProfileServiceApplication2, and which is not the same as his original My Site located in UserProfileServiceApplication1. It would be better if User1 were directed to a single My Site regardless of within which region he clicks the link. To enable this, SharePoint 2010 has a feature known as Trusted My Site Host Locations, through which a User Profile Service Application can trust My Site hosts that are a part of a different User Profile Service Application, and can redirect users to their appropriate My Site host. To redirect users to their appropriate host, each trusted Host location has a target audience that determines the users for which My Sites are hosted in that particular host location. The My Site host of a User Profile Service Application is created at the time that User Profile Service Application is set up.

Setting up a global My Sites requires two main activities: (1) Creating audiences that consist of users whose My Sites will be hosted by the User Profile Service Application, and (2) Adding the trusted My Site Host links to each User Profile Service Application for the other My Site hosts.

The first step can be accomplished by using the Create Audience feature of the User Profile Service application. Each region must have an audience for itself and for all other regions that can host My Sites. During audience creation, you can apply rules to populate the audience with the appropriate users. For example, an audience called "Region1 My Site Users" can have a rule that defines that "All users whose Active Directory Location attribute is 'Region1' will get added to the audience." After you have created an audience, compile the audience and check that it is populated with the appropriate users.

The second step is adding My Site Host links to each user profile service application's trusted My Sites Hosts list and configuring the target audience based on the region that My Site host serves. This can be done through the Trusted Host Location page of the User Profile Service Application. For example, in this scenario you have two regions, Region1 and Region2. Region1's My Site host is *http://servername/MysiteRegion1* and its audience is called Region1 My Site Users. Similarly, Region2 has a My Site host called *http://servername/MysiteRegion2* and its audience is called Region2 My Site Users. So you will add two links each for the respective host locations to the trusted host locations page of each region's User Profile Service Application, and in the target audience, you will specify the correct audience for that host location.

You must complete both steps in each User Profile Service Application that is serving as part of the global My Sites deployment.

Summary

In this chapter you learned about the central role of collaboration and portals in SharePoint 2010. You reviewed the various templates available for site creation and how to enable specific features within sites. You explored site provisioning and how to decide which provisioning option works best for your implementation. You reviewed the integration with SharePoint Workspace 2010 and Outlook Social Connector. You discussed Enterprise Wikis, including how and when to employ them. You reviewed the new social features included with SharePoint 2010, including social tagging, search, expertise, notes, and others. You reviewed the new features included with My Sites and learned how they are central to the user experience provided in SharePoint 2010. Finally, you reviewed the User Profile Service in detail, learning how it works and how to set up and configure each of its service elements.

## CHAPTER 11

Search Server 2010 and FAST Search: Architecture and Administration

People are constantly seeking information, and the amount of information available is both exponentially increasing and overwhelming. As discussed in Chapter 9, "Organizing Information," findability methods include both navigation and search. Although planning and design are normally included in the navigation and site organizational design, planning is frequently overlooked in the implementation of search technologies. This chapter approaches the discussion of Microsoft SharePoint Search with a focus on planning and design considerations.

The chapter compares the various SharePoint Search family members and then discusses Microsoft SharePoint 2010 Search, followed by a description of the capabilities FAST Search for SharePoint adds. This information in this chapter is for farm level or application level search administrators and focuses on configuring the search topology and crawl processes. Configuring the query process falls more in the realm of customizing search results and will be covered in Chapter 13, "Customizing the Search Results and Search Center."

Introducing Enterprise Search

With the release of SharePoint 2010, Microsoft has significantly improved its enterprise search capabilities. The acquisition of FAST provided Microsoft with its flagship enterprise search product. An in-depth discussion of FAST is outside the scope of this book; however, the redesign of search in SharePoint 2010 has incorporated many of the features and functionalities of FAST technologies.

The goals for these enterprise search solutions are to

- Ensure that enterprise data from multiple systems can be indexed. This includes collaborative data stored in SharePoint sites, files in file shares, Web pages in other websites, third-party repositories, and other line-of-business systems such as CRM databases or ERP solutions.

- Ensure that content from multiple enterprise repositories systems can be queried both independently and from within the context of your business applications.

- Ensure that search results provide accurate ranking of the result set, if you expect users to adopt and use those search capabilities.

- Ensure that your enterprise search solution identifies people and expertise within your organization.

SharePoint 2010 provides an enterprise search platform for fulfilling these aims. As a brief overview, SharePoint 2010 includes a Connector Framework that enables the crawler to index files, metadata, and other types of data from various types of content sources. It also provides an indexing engine that stores the crawled data in an efficient manner in index files, and it provides query servers, query object models, and user interfaces for performing searches on the indexed data.

The suite of SharePoint 2010 technologies now includes five search products.

- Microsoft SharePoint Foundation 2010
- Microsoft Search Server 2010 Express
- Microsoft Search Server 2010
- Microsoft SharePoint 2010
- FAST Search Server 2010 for SharePoint

The first two have no additional licensing cost above that of the server operating system and IIS connectivity. Table 11-1 illustrates the high-level comparisons of the search features provided by each product.

TABLE 11-1 Comparing Features of the SharePoint 2010 Search Products

FEATURE	SHAREPOINT FOUNDATION 2010	SEARCH SERVER 2010 EXPRESS	SEARCH SERVER 2010	SHAREPOINT 2010	FAST SEARCH SERVER 2010 FOR SHAREPOINT
Basic site search	X	X	X	X	X
Best bets		X	X	X	X
Visual best bets					X
Similar results					X
Duplicate results					X
Search scopes		X	X	X	X
Search enhancement with user context					X
Crawled and managed properties		X	X	X	X
Query federation		X	X	X	X
Query suggestions		X	X	X	X
Sort results on managed properties or rank profiles					X
Relevancy tuning by document or site promotions		X	X	X	X
Shallow results refinement		X	X	X	X
Deep results refinement					X
Document Preview					X
Windows 7 Federation		X	X	X	X

continued on next page

FEATURE	SHAREPOINT FOUNDATION 2010	SEARCH SERVER 2010 EXPRESS	SEARCH SERVER 2010	SHAREPOINT 2010	FAST SEARCH SERVER 2010 FOR SHAREPOINT
People search				X	X
Social search				X	X
Taxonomy integration				X	X
Multi-tenant hosting				X	X
Rich Web indexing support					X

Although there are no hard-coded limits for the number of items that can be indexed by any of the products listed in Table 11-1, performance places some practical guidelines.

- SharePoint Foundation 2010 can index and search up to 10 million items per search server.

- Search Server 2010 Express can index and search up to 300,000 items if it is used with SQL Server Express, due to database size limitations. With SQL 2008, it can index 10 million items but is limited to a single index/query server role.

- A scaled-out Search Server 2010 farm or SharePoint 2010 farm can index and search up to 100 million items.

- A FAST Search Server 2010 for SharePoint installation can support extreme scale and can index and search over a billion items.

NOTE According to data on the Microsoft Enterprise Search blog site (*http://blogs.msdn.com/enterprisesearch*), the SearchBeta site was providing search for a corpus of approximately 72 million items with six query servers, two crawl servers, and six SQL servers.

Search Architecture

SharePoint Server 2007 defined two search roles, Query and Index. With the modularity of SharePoint 2010, these functions are defined as components, since any server could host multiple instances of each. Also, with the changes to the indexing process, the Index role has been renamed as the crawl component.

In SharePoint Server 2007, there were several bottlenecks in the search components. The most obvious was the single index server. However, even with multiple query components, the index was a single component and its size presented issues with replication, loading into memory, and traversing to retrieve results.

The design of search components in SharePoint 2010 included three goals addressed by scalability.

- Sub-second query latencies at large scale
- Fresher indexes
- Better resiliency and higher availability

These goals were accomplished by separating the system into components, some of which can be scaled out to remove bottlenecks or can be duplicated for resiliency. These components will be introduced as part of the discussion of search processes.

Search Tools

Before discussing the major functions of Search, you need to be familiar with three tools that are critical to both crawl and query processes. In addition, there are a couple of tools used only by the crawl process.

Language Detection

SharePoint 2010 language support for search includes 53 languages, which covers 97 percent of all people in the world.

Word Breakers

When the formatting is removed from crawled content and query strings, part of that formatting includes the spaces between words. A process is then required to break the string of characters into words before other processes can be applied to the words. Word breakers (or tokenizers) separate words into "tokens" when content is indexed and when queries are submitted. Word breakers, in general, separate words at spaces, punctuation, and special characters—except underscores. Word breakers are used during both indexing and querying.

This process is language dependent. SharePoint can recognize the language within the stream even if the language changes within a document. Along with language detection, word breakers have been greatly enhanced in this new product, especially in languages other than English. Particular attention has been focused on compound words, which are handled differently in different languages.

Custom Dictionaries

Custom dictionaries are still supported in SharePoint 2010. A custom dictionary file defines words or terms for the word breaker to consider as complete words. Custom dictionaries are not provided by default and are language specific, so you must create a separate custom dictionary for each language in which you need to modify the word breaker's behavior. The language-neutral word breaker does not use a custom dictionary. Thesaurus and Noise

Word files can be application specific, but custom dictionaries apply farm-wide to all search applications.

Custom dictionaries instruct the word breaker of their language that a particular combination of characters is a complete word that should not be broken up into separate tokens. Both indexing and querying processes will use existing custom dictionaries instructions that support the language and dialect of the word breaker being used. If a word exists in the custom dictionary, it is considered complete for indexing.

Terms that include special characters would be prime candidates for custom dictionaries. For instance, AT&T includes an ampersand that would be used by a word breaker to separate the term into two tokens, "AT" and "T," which are both noise (or stop) words and would be ignored in search queries. If the term "AT&T" were included in a custom dictionary for the appropriate language, then it would be treated as a unique word in both instances. You might also have hyphenated words that your organization's search system needs to treat as complete unique words; you would add such words to a custom dictionary.

Many industries have number sequences that need to be indexed. For instance, if you had a formula of numbers in the "725.5046.1.1" format, these numbers would be broken into tokens at the decimals. To index the complete sequence of numbers, you must add all instances of the numbers to custom dictionaries for each language in which they appear so that the entire number is treated as a unique token by the index and query processes.

Custom dictionaries can be created in Notepad but must be saved in Unicode format. The file naming convention must follow the *CustomNNNN*.lex format, where *NNNN* is the language hex code of the language.

Within the file, each entry must be on separate lines separated by a carriage return (CR) and line feed (LF). Other custom dictionary rules are

- Entries are not case sensitive.
- The pipe (|) character is not permitted.
- No spaces are permitted.
- The pound sign (#) character can be used anywhere in an entry except at the beginning.
- Any other alphanumeric characters, punctuation, symbols, and breaking characters are valid.
- The maximum length of an entry is 128 (Unicode) characters.

The custom dictionary files must be saved in the folder that contains the word breakers on all index and query servers in the farm. By default, this is the C:\Program Files\Microsoft Office Servers\14.0\bin folder.

You must restart the osearch14 service on all index and query servers in the farm after these custom dictionary files have been created or modified. Do not use the Services On Server page in Central Administration to stop and start the service. Either use the Services

MMC in Administrative Tools or type **net stop osearch14** or **net start osearch14** at the command line.

> **MORE INFO**   For a list of the supported language hex codes, see *http://technet.microsoft.com/en-us/library/cc263242.aspx*.

iFilters

iFilters tell the crawler how to "crack open" a file and to identify and index its contents. They are only used by the crawling process. Many iFilters have shipped with the new versions of SharePoint, including ascx, asm, asp, aspx, bat, c, cmd, cpp, css, cxx, dev, dic, doc, docm, docx, dot, eml, h, hhc, hht, hta, htm, html, htw, lnk, mht, mhtml, mpx, msg, odc, pot, pps, ppt, pptm, pptx, pub, stm, tif, trf, vsd, xlb, xlc, xls, xlsm, xlsx, xlt, and xml.

If you do not have an iFilter for a defined file type, the crawler gathers only the metadata for that document. You can add third-party iFilters or write your own. For example, if you need to index PDF files, then you can go to the Adobe website and download their iFilter for indexing PDF files. The download will give you the executable file and other files to successfully install the PDF iFilter.

Connectors

SharePoint 2010 indexing can use either the Connector Framework or the protocol handler API so your custom protocol handlers written for SharePoint Server 2007 will still work. The protocol handler API will not be supported in future products, however.

The SharePoint 2010 indexing connector has improved reliability and performance provided by higher fidelity conversation with SharePoint Web Service. It also reduces the load on the SharePoint sites with the addition of security-only crawls, improved batching of change log processing, and caching for common list item information. Improvements in telemetry and reporting provides views of security transactions processed in crawls and new crawl log functionality, such as filtering the crawl log by "top level errors."

The connector framework provides improvements over the protocol handler API.

- Attachments can now be crawled.
- Item-level security descriptors can now be retrieved for external data exposed by Business Connectivity Services.
- When crawling a Business Connectivity Services entity, additional entities can be crawled, maintaining the entity relationships.
- Time stamp–based incremental crawls are supported.
- Change log crawls that can remove items that have been deleted since the last crawl are supported.

Standard shared SharePoint 2010 indexing connectors that are also used by FAST Search for SharePoint include the following.

- **SharePoint content**   The crawler accesses data through the SharePoint Web service and uses Windows authentication (integrated) credentials. This connector supports full crawl using enumeration of content, but for incremental crawls it uses the change logs, including deleted items. It has built-in support for both NT and pluggable security trimming.

- **File shares**   The crawler accesses the file shares through their hierarchical structure with Windows authentication (integrated). ACLs are collected during crawl time and changes can be detected with time stamps or changes to the ACL.

- **Websites**   This protocol handler uses link traversal as the crawl method but does not provide a security trimmer. SharePoint sites can be configured to use this connector when they permit anonymous access, which reduces the overhead on both sides of the crawling effort. By default, if SharePoint sites are listed in a content source that uses this connector, the crawler will automatically switch to the SharePoint content connector.

- **People profiles**   People profiles are enumerated and crawled via the profile pages of the My Site host. Since the "Exposed" information selections are not truly NT ACLs, only information within a profile that is exposed to "Everyone" will be crawled.

- **Lotus Notes**   This connector used a protocol handler in Microsoft Office SharePoint Server 2007 but has been changed to use the Connector Framework in this version.

- **Exchange public folders**   Likewise, Exchange public folders were crawled with an HTTP protocol handler previously but now use the Connector Framework.

- **External systems**   Custom connectors are much easier to build in SharePoint Designer 2010 using the Connector Framework than with a protocol handler. These custom connectors can be built by creating external content types for the Business Data Connectivity Service or by using existing external content types.

> **NOTE**   Microsoft SharePoint 2010 Indexing Connector for Documentum can be downloaded from *http://www.microsoft.com/downloads/details.aspx?displaylang=en&FamilyID= 32d0980a-4b9a-4b0d-868e-9be9c0d75435*.

Search Components and Processes

The term *content source* refers to both the target servers that contain the content that needs to be indexed and the definitions of the start addresses, indexing schedules, and basic rules to instruct the crawler on how to crawl (index) the content. Crawl rules are used to further define how the content of specific URLs will be crawled, such as defining a different security context under which the crawler should crawl the content source instead of using the default crawling account.

Connectors contain the ability to connect to different content sources using different connection protocols, such as FTP, HTTP, or RPC. Protocol handlers used in SharePoint Server 2007 are still supported but are being replaced by the Connector Framework. Some connectors can be built in Microsoft SharePoint Designer without writing managed code.

There are really two parts to gathering the information from a content source. The first part is the enumeration of the content items that should be crawled. The connectors will connect to the content source and will walk the URL addresses of each content item, depositing each URL of each content item in the MSSCrawlQueue table. Although the basic search engine runs under Mssearcch.exe (O14Search), when a crawl is started, a new process under Msssearch.exe named Mssdmn.exe is spawned, and it is under this process that the content source is both enumerated and then crawled. After a sufficient number of URLs are placed in the MSSCrawlQueue, another Mssdmn.exe is spawned, and this process goes back to the content source connecting to each URL in batches (as determined by the crawler impact rules), opening each document at each URL in the current batch and then downloading first the metadata about the document and then the document's contents. Both of these data streams are run through several components in the process pipeline and then the content is placed in the full-text index while the metadata is placed in the SQL database property store.

When you start a new crawl of a content source, you'll notice that for a brief period of time, the status of the content source will appears as Starting. What this means is that if the Mssdmn.exe process (if it isn't already started) will be spawned, the connector is connecting to the content source to establish the connection through which the content will be indexed, and the URLs of each content item are being deposited into the MSSCrawlQueue. You'll see the status change to Crawling when the crawler is ready to open documents and download their content.

Increasing the number of start addresses within a single content source or increasing the number of content sources that are crawling multiple start addresses does not necessarily increase the number of Mssdmn.exe threads that are spawned.

In Search 2010, the number of crawl components across multiple servers can be increased as the workload increases, with automatic distribution of addresses, or if desired, specific addresses assigned to specific crawl components through Host Distribution Rules. The reduced workload provided by crawl partitioning speeds the crawling, which provides a faster refresh of indexes. In addition, the crawl component only builds and retains portions of the full text index until all designated query components obtain their copy. The crawl component never retains a full copy of the index.

The information used to track crawling now resides in tables of a separate Search_Service_Application database so that the crawling process does not impact other databases. This permits the crawling process to be stateless, since its status is stored in the SQL database, not in crawl logs on the crawl server. This permits the completion of a crawl by an alternate server if the first crawl component fails and is unable to complete the assigned tasks.

The indexing process extracts information from items retrieved by crawl components and places it in index format. This information includes full text index, metadata, URLs, and ACLs.

Query components accept requests from users for queries against the SharePoint indexes and return results in the requested XML format.

Index partitions are introduced by SharePoint 2010 as subsets of the overall index. With index partitions, no single query component searches the entire index. The workload is spread across multiple servers, reducing the query response time even though maintaining index partitions slightly increases the crawl effort. Multiple query components can host the same index partition, providing both reliability and throughput. Index partitions also can be supported by clusters of mirrored crawl components, providing resiliency in case of failures.

Index partitioning is based on a hash of the documentID assigned to each document. This basis permits indexes to remain roughly equivalent in size, which is essential to optimal response time. Query components can be identified as failover nodes that would host the same index as their partners, similar to a mirrored SQL database. A failover query component will receive queries only if the primary query component for an index partition fails.

Index propagation works much like it does in SharePoint Server 2007, including the crawl components pushing index files to the query components and waiting until they *all* successfully absorb the index before acknowledging that the documents are successfully crawled.

Indexes pushed to query components for a partitioned index are just the appropriate part of that index. The current propagation information is stored in the Search_Service_Application database in the MSSPropagationTasks table, and the MSSPropagationLog table keeps records of past events. The MSSPropagationTasks table is populated and depopulated by the crawl components, and the query components populate the MSSPropagationTaskCompletions table in response. The MSSPropagationErrors table will reflect any current deficiency, and the information there is entered every 10 minutes in a warning level event on the search admin component's server.

Indexes are absorbed by query components but aren't necessarily served in queries for a few seconds until the appropriate merges have occurred. Index propagation tasks that have stalled for at least five minutes because of a lack of success from a query component trigger a re-crawl of the contained data. Query components can be taken offline so they don't hold up the crawling process.

Query Federation is the formatting of queries in OpenSearch definition so that they may be processed by any OpenSearch query component, including SharePoint. In SharePoint 2010, the search object model and all query components are built around the OpenSearch model. Essentially, federated queries go to multiple query servers that respond individually, and the results are compiled to be presented in a Web Part.

Since no single query component holds the complete index, the Query Processor service must manage disbursing the queries and processing the multiple results lists returned. This is accomplished, using a round-robin load-balanced method, by one of the servers running the Search Query and Site Settings service (an Internet Information Services [IIS] service). By default, this service runs on each server that hosts a search query component. The service manages the query processing tasks, which include sending queries to one or more of the appropriate query components and building the consolidated results set to be returned to the Web front-end (WFE) server that constructed the query.

> **NOTE** At least one instance of the Search Query and Site Settings service must be running to serve queries. The service should be started on all servers that host query components that can be identified in the Search Application Topology section of the Search Service Administration page. It can be started from the Services On Server page in Central Administration or with the following Windows PowerShell cmdlet.

```
Start-SPEnterpriseSearchQueryAndSiteSettingsServiceInstance
```

Each query component responds to queries and sends the results from the index partition that it holds to the query processor from which it received the query. The query component is also responsible for the word breaking, noise word removal, and stemming (if stemming is enabled) for the search terms provided by the query processor. The multiple responses are combined to produce the results list. Since each partition contains only a portion of the complete index, the workload of compiling results lists is spread across multiple query components, producing a faster query response time. Each partition can also be mirrored on separate query components, providing increased performance or resiliency should a single instance of the partition fail.

The search information stored in SQL databases has also been spread across additional databases. Just as the full text index can now be partitioned, the metadata or property databases can be divided and placed on separate SQL servers for performance or can be mirrored for resiliency.

Finally, the search administration component synchronizes the crawling and query activities using information stored in the admin database. It is the admin component that assigns tasks to specific servers and reassigns them in case of a server failure. There can only be one search administration component per farm, and it resides on the server where the search service application was created.

A built-in load balancer distributes hosts from content sources across crawl databases unless overruled by a Host Distribution Rule. The crawl components then retrieve the content assigned to their crawl database when initiated by the admin component. A Host Distribution Rule can assign a specific host to a crawl database. This is particularly useful if a third-party connector is licensed per server or if crawling specific content requires additional crawl component resources.

Whereas SharePoint Server 2007 depended on SQL for cluster and mirror failover, SharePoint 2010 has native SQL mirror support and all databases can be mirrored.

Farm and Application Configuration

Defining, building, and maintaining an accurate and complete index is the cornerstone of accurate and complete search results.

This section covers the user interface (UI) management tools for administering the crawl process, including creating the Search application. The portions of search administration that manage and customize search results are covered in Chapter 13.

Search Support Staff

Most SharePoint farms and support teams are small and do not have the dedicated Search administrator that the product really requires and is designed to support. You will see in this chapter how search administration falls naturally into tasks that could be accomplished by separate teams.

In a larger environment or one in which the importance of search is acknowledged or is the pre-eminent purpose of the SharePoint farm, search administration would be accomplished by teams dedicated to

- Farm administration
- Search crawls
- Search queries (results)
- Custom search UI and use of search Web Parts
- Monitoring search performance and search activities

Farm-Wide Search Settings

Although most configurations are unique to the search service instance, the farm-wide settings are followed by all crawlers. Some settings that are identified as farm settings are just default settings that can be overwritten by local services settings. The settings page shown in Figure 11-1 can be accessed from the Central Administration page by clicking General Application Settings and then Farm Search Administration under the Search section.

FIGURE 11-1 Farm Search Administration page

The proxy settings are configured the same as for Internet Explorer, with the exception of an option that directs federated queries to use the same settings. The default connection timeouts of 60 seconds are for connections to content sources and for waiting for request acknowledgments. If the option Ignore SSL Warnings is selected, the browser will treat sites as legitimate even if their certificate name does not exactly match. If this setting is not selected, a site with a faulty SSL certificate will not be crawled.

All search service applications for the farm will be listed in the lower section of the page. The Search Administration page for the application can be accessed using the hyperlinked name. The link to Modify Topology opens the same page as the link provided on the Search Service Administration page. Because the topology is "per service," it will be discussed in the section titled "Managing the Search Service Topology" later in this chapter.

Managing Crawler Impact Rules

Crawler impact rules are an optional mechanism to control the rate at which the crawler indexes a source. These settings are also farm-wide configurations but are applied individually to each start address within a content source. The management page can be accessed from the Central Administration page by clicking General Application Settings and then Crawler Impact Rules, under the Search section. It can also be opened from Search Administration for any search service, but the configurations are always farm-wide. On the Crawler Impact Rules page, click Add Rule to open the Add Crawler Impact Rule page, shown in Figure 11-2, or select an existing rule to edit.

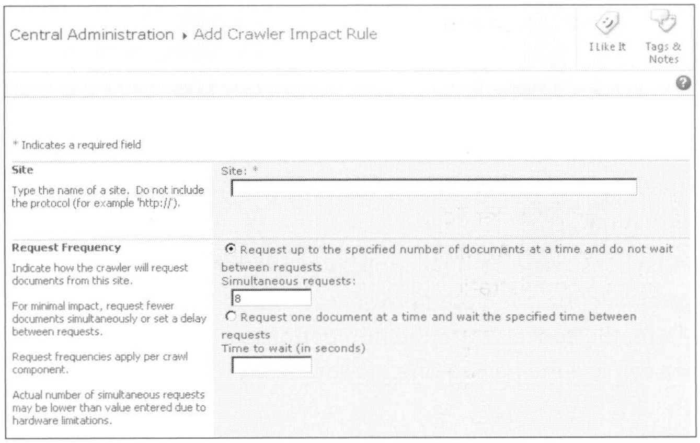

FIGURE 11-2 Add Crawler Impact Rule page

Valid crawl rules do not define the protocol (http://, https://, or file://) because the rule applies to all connectors. Following are some examples.

- Site name: **www**.contoso.com
- All inclusive: *****
- Domain: *****.contoso.com
- Machine name: **WFE01**

If you want to limit the number of simultaneous requests, you can change the default of 8 to 1, 2, 4, 16, 32, or 64. For example, if you set the default to 16, what you're really doing is instructing the crawler to grab the next 16 documents *for each start address* when the previous documents are done being processed by the indexer. So, if you have four start addresses, then the crawler will connect and download 64 documents (16 from each start address) simultaneously.

> **BEST PRACTICES**   Even though you can fill a content source with up to 50 start addresses, best practice is to keep that number much, much lower. The optimal number of start addresses will vary depending on your server resources available for indexing plus the available bandwidth between your indexing servers and the content sources. You can determine a level of optimization by using a combination of performance monitoring and the speed at which your indexes can be built.

You can also configure the crawler to request one document at a time and send the requests to the queue. There is a large difference between 1 simultaneous request and a 1-second delay. Rarely will you need to set the delay greater than 1 second.

> **NOTE**   Reducing the crawl rate can extend the crawl time so much that the crawl does not complete before it's time to start again.

Creating Search Applications

A single SharePoint 2010 farm can provide multiple instances of search services and applications. Because each of the services can crawl both SharePoint and other repositories and could be configured to federate queries to each other, you could design such a configuration for performance or to isolate information.

Because the search service can be consumed both by applications within the farm and from other farms, topology designs could include both farm search topology and enterprise search topology. Within a single farm, the concerns are the number of search services required; enterprise considerations can include having one or more SharePoint 2010 farms dedicated to search.

If you run the Farm Configuration Wizard after the SharePoint Configuration Wizard and do not clear the Search check box, a search service application is created called Search Service Application, along with the Search Service Application Proxy and the Search Administration Web Service, as shown in Figure 11-3.

FIGURE 11-3 Default search services shown on the Manage Service Applications page

To manually create a search service application, perform the following steps.

1. Open a browser and go to the SharePoint Central Administration website.

2. Under Application Management, click Manage Service Applications.

3. From the New menu, select Search Service Application, as shown in Figure 11-4, to open the Create New Search Service Application page.

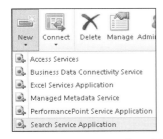

FIGURE 11-4 New menu from Manage Service Application page

4. In the Name section, type a unique name for the new search service application.

5. If you have not installed the FAST Search for SharePoint, you should only select None in the FAST Service Application section. If you have installed FAST, select which FAST role you want this search service application to provide.

6. In the Search Service Account section, expand the Search Service Account menu and then select the managed account that will run this search service application. This account must be a managed account, so only current managed accounts are listed.

NOTE All dialog boxes where managed accounts are required will provide a Register new managed account link to use should you need to designate an account as a managed account.

7. In the two Application Pool sections, you can select an existing application pool for the new search service application. To create a new application pool, click Create A New Application Pool and then complete the following steps.

   a. Enter a unique application pool name.

   b. Either use the Predefined built-in account security account or select Configurable to use an existing managed account. SharePoint application pools require a managed account, so only managed accounts are listed.

8. Click OK.

This process creates a new set of Search Administration Web Service, Search Service Application, and Search Service Application Proxy. This new search application will appear as an association option in the Service Connections configurations for each Web application in the farm.

Configuring the Search Application

The Ribbon of the Manage Service Applications page (refer back to Figure 11-3) presents several service configuration options for configuring search settings.

Publishing the Service

If you want other farms to consume services from the search service application, the service must be published. To publish the search service, follow these steps.

1. Highlight the service on the Manage Service Applications page (refer back to Figure 11-3) and click Publish on the activated Ribbon.

2. In the Publish Service Application dialog box, select http or https.

3. Select the Publish This Service Application To Other Farms check box. The URL of the service application appears in the Published URL section after it is published.

4. In the Description box, type a description that will display with the link to the published service application.

5. In the Information URL box, type a URL that provides Help information for this service application.

6. Click OK to publish the service application.

You need to establish a trust relationship between the farms to provide or consume services. This trust is based on certificates, not domain trusts. You also need to give the accounts or other principals that have access permission to invoke this service application. You add these in the dialog box that displays when you click the Permissions icon on the Ribbon. Permissions are given via claims from organizations, the local system, Active Directory, or Forms Authentication providers.

Delegating Administration

Members of the Farm Administrators group always have rights to manage all service applications. For the search applications, a team of search specialists generally administrate the Search configurations. Click the Administrators icon on the Ribbon (refer back to Figure 11-3) to specify the users to whom you will delegate the rights to manage this service application. These users will be given access to the Central Administration site but will only be able to manage settings related to this service application.

Modifying Properties

Click the Properties icon on the Ribbon to open a dialog box where you can configure the service account and the application pools used by search Web services.

Configuring Crawls

This chapter is concerned only with managing the search service topology and the crawl process. The areas of search management that focus on controlling or customizing queries and results are covered in Chapter 13.

The top portion of the Search Administration page is shown in Figure 11-5 and presents a dashboard of System Status information with links to configuration dialogue boxes for general search service configurations. On the left side of the page is a Quick Launch organized into three sections: Administration, Crawling, and Queries And Results. (The remaining portions of the page are discussed later in the sections titled "Reviewing and Troubleshooting Crawls" and "Managing the Search Service Topology.")

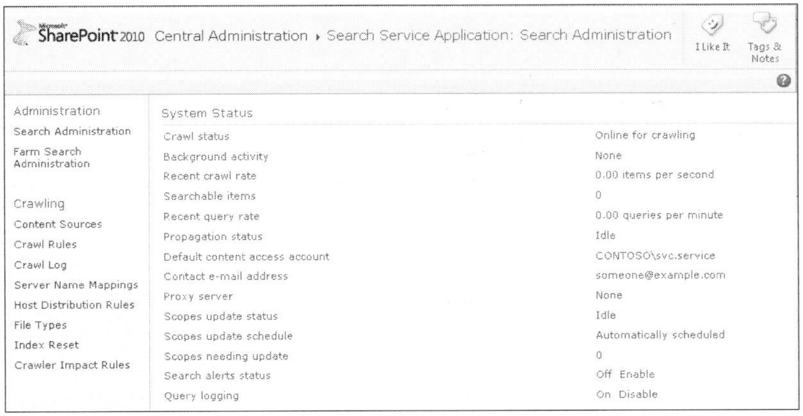

FIGURE 11-5 Top portion of Search Administration page

The top dashboard section presents information on the crawl and indexing processes as well as the recent query rate and scopes status. There are also six configuration links.

- The default content access account was entered when you ran the Farm Configuration Wizard and can be overridden here for this search service application's components.

- The Contact e-mail address is left behind by crawl components of this service. This should be a monitored e-mail address, in case the crawler is creating performance issues on remote sites.

- The Proxy server link opens the Farm Search Administration configuration and changes the farm-wide settings, although it does not indicate that it is not a local service setting.

- The scopes update schedule is a toggle between the automatic schedule of the timer job and manually triggered updates. If there are scopes to be updated, a link is presented to start the update process manually.

- Search alert status can be enabled/disabled here. Normally, it is automatically disabled during an index reset but must be manually enabled after the index is rebuilt.

- If you disable Query logging, no data will be available for query reports.

Creating and Managing Content Sources

The first step in setting up crawling is the creation of content sources. Click the Content Sources link in the Quick Launch (refer back to Figure 11-5) to open the Manage Content Sources page shown in Figure 11-6. This page continues the dashboard theme to give the status of each content source and crawl information that will be useful in scheduling crawls.

A content source is a collection of addresses that can be crawled with the same connector or protocol handler along with instructions about how deep to crawl from the start address, how often to crawl the collection, and at what priority.

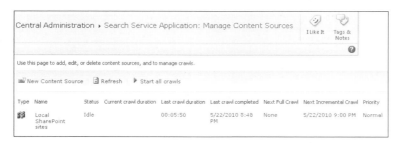

FIGURE 11-6 Manage Content Sources page

When creating a new content source, the name should be unique but meaningful to everyone managing the search service. The default content source types are

- SharePoint Sites
- Web Sites
- File Shares

- Exchange Public Folders
- Line Of Business Data
- Custom Repositories
- Lotus Notes (If the service is provisioned and started on the server.)

A start address cannot appear in more than one content source but does not have to start at the root of an application. A single content source can contain up to 50 start addresses and a search service application can have up to 50 content sources. Start address entries are not checked for accuracy during the creation of a content source. Start addresses should match the type of content source you are creating. For example, if you create a Web Sites content source, then be sure to not include start addresses that start with file:// or some other type of content that is not Web based.

The crawl settings configuration is dependent on the content source type selected and controls the depth of the crawl from the starting address. For a Web Site content source, this includes how deep to follow hops within the server and how far to follow hops to other servers. Unlimited in both scenarios would be to crawl the Internet, starting at the specified addresses.

You can create either Full Crawl or Incremental Crawl schedules or both. Crawl schedules are not required for content sources for which crawls will be managed manually. It is not necessary to schedule a full crawl, because starting an incremental crawl on a content source that has never been crawled will result in a full crawl.

The ability to choose Normal or High crawl priority for a content source is new in SharePoint 2010. Items placed in the crawl queue are always crawled in their order in the queue. Items from high priority content sources are always placed in the queue before those from normal priority content sources, without regard to when the crawls began on the content sources.

Finally, when creating a content source, you may choose to begin a full crawl as soon as the content source is created. Considering the resources consumed by full crawls, they are usually scheduled when resources are available.

By default, a Local SharePoint sites content source is always created for a search service, and all applications associated with the service are placed in that content source, as shown in Figure 11-7. Although this does ensure that all content will be crawled, it is seldom an optimum configuration because the crawls of content in different locations will generally need to be managed independently.

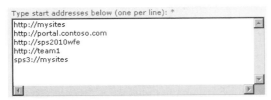

FIGURE 11-7 Start addresses for sample farm's Local SharePoint site content source

You can gain an understanding of the start addresses by examining the example shown in Figure 11-7. First, the address *sps3://mysites* is a special crawl of the user profiles using the profile pages of the My Site host. Profiles need to be crawled after they are imported and before audiences are compiled. Incremental crawls may not be required throughout the day at all, but certainly profile data needs to be crawled on a different schedule and priority than other content. Remember that profile data can be manually entered by users in addition to imported from databases.

Depending on how personal sites are used in your organization, the content of the *http://mysites* application will probably have a different schedule and priority than other content. The content of a portal can be more or less dynamic than that of a team collaborative site. The crawl scheduling for any content source must reflect two main considerations: how fast changes in the content source need to be reflected in your index and the rate at which changes occur at the content source. This is why, for example, you might crawl the company announcements folder every 4 hours but crawl *http://archive* only once every quarter.

So, crawl scheduling and priority are two reasons for creating a unique content source. Other reasons could include the need to define a scope based on a content source, unique crawl settings for depth and hops to off-site links, and crawl management.

 REAL WORLD   **Removing an Inadvertent Exposure**

In environments where security is important, occasionally content is sometimes inadvertently placed on websites with wider access than the material should be given. When this "spillage" material is removed, a full crawl must be run to prove that the material is not duplicated elsewhere and that the information is completely removed from the index. Dividing the content to be crawled into smaller content sources reduces the overhead of a full crawl.

Creating and Managing Crawl Rules

Crawl rules allow you to configure include/exclude rules, specific security contexts for crawling that are different from the default content access account, and the explicit path for the rule.

Crawl rules are global to the search service and are relative to the target address, not a content source. For example, you can have two content sources: one each for *http://SharePoint Server 2010/sites/IT* and *http://SharePoint Server 2010/sites/HR*. Both can be covered by one crawl rule with a path of *http://SharePoint Server 2010*. You can also specify a crawl rule for a subset of a content source, such as *http://SharePoint Server 2010/sites/HR /Records*, if *http://SharePoint Server 2010/* was the listing in the content source.

To manage existing crawl rules or create new ones, click the Crawl Rules link in the Quick Launch area (refer back to Figure 11-5), which opens the Manage Crawl Rules page shown in Figure 11-8.

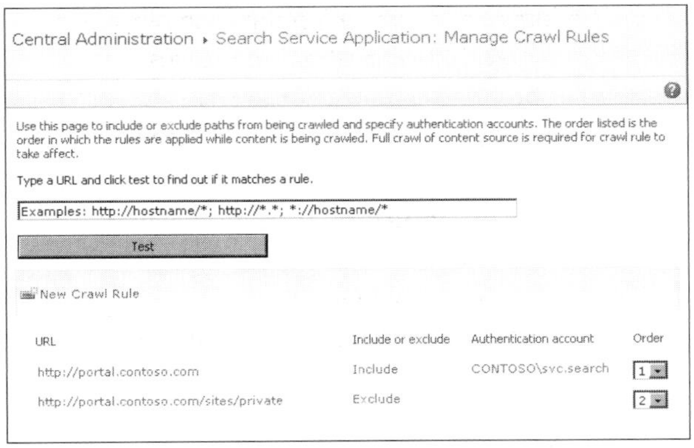

FIGURE 11-8 Manage Crawl Rules page

Crawl rules are applied in the order listed on the Manage Crawl Rules page. The Exclude rule overrides some content addressed by the Include rule that is applied first.

Often it is necessary for search administrators to omit only specific data that matches certain patterns from targets to either improve search results or to protect confidential data from being included. For example, typical items that should not be indexed are social security numbers, credit card information, or URLs with a specific parameter. Other types of information that is normally not crawled are Web pages outlining the site's privacy policies, acceptable use policies, or even the About Us pages.

Typically administrators create crawl rules that limit SharePoint crawlers from accessing specific links. Crawl rules require specification of each individual URL separately in the Exclude list via Central Administration. However, if you use a wildcard search such as \\servername\webfolder* you could keep the Exclude rule set small and prevent unwanted documents from being included in search results.

Starting in SharePoint 2010, crawl rules allow the user to match URLs using regular (regex) expressions. Now administrators can determine inclusion or exclusion based on regex expression syntax.

> **MORE INFO** More information about the regex expression syntax can be found at *http://www.regular-expressions.info/reference.html*. It is important to fully test all regex expressions.

Table 11-2 shows some examples of regex queries SharePoint 2010 supports.

TABLE 11-2 Regex Expression Examples

REGEX EXPRESSION	DESCRIPTION
fileshare\.*	Match all files under the filesystem share \\fileshare.
fileshare\((private)|(temp))\.*	Match all files under fileshare that are named either private or temp.
http://site/default.aspx[?]ssn=.	Match all links that have the parameter ssn= in the URL path.
http://site/default.aspx[?]var1=1&var2=.	Match all links that have a var1 specified and var2 matches anything.

Regex expressions enable crawl rules that require less administrative maintenance and provide a well-defined, dynamic set of rules that cover existing and future content. However, regular expressions cannot be used in the protocol component of the URL. Compare the following two regex URL expressions.

- *http://www.contoso.com/.** will match all URLs under contoso.com
- *.*/www.contoso.com/.** will match *http://.*//www.contoso.com/.** but this does not provide the intended results.

To create a new crawl rule from the Manage Crawl Rules page, perform the following steps.

1. Click the New Crawl Rule link, which opens the Add Crawl Rule page shown in Figure 11-9.

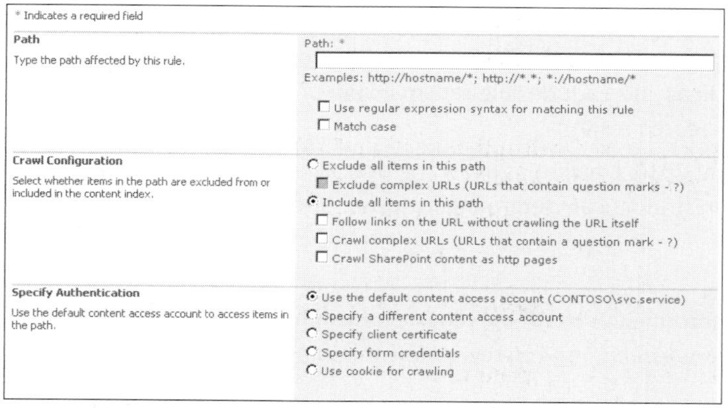

FIGURE 11-9 Add Crawl Rule page

2. Choose the path using regex expressions if needed. When you use regular expressions, you must select the Follow Regular Expression Syntax option. By default, the syntax of the regex expression and URL are case insensitive. If the target content is case sensitive, select the Match Case check box.

3. Choose whether to exclude or include items that match the pattern. If you select Include All Items In This Path, you also have the following options.

- **Follow Links On The URL Without Crawling The URL Itself**   This option is useful when the starting point of a crawl is a menu of links and you don't want the menu page in your index.

- **Crawl Complex URLs**   If you want to crawl content defined by a string after a '?', select this option. Complex URLs are common with SharePoint and also often point to information contained in databases. In many cases, it is useful to enter a global rule to capture all complex URLs: *http://*/** and check Crawl Complex URLs.

- **Crawl SharePoint Content As HTTP Pages**   The SharePoint connector includes security and versions. For anonymous, public-facing sites, the overhead of including this information is not necessary.

You can specify unique authentication using a crawl rule. In some instances, this is the only reason for the crawl rule, because it is the only way to override using the default content access account. Simply enter the user name and password to access the resource. You can also restrict Basic authentication. This account is not a managed account, so the password must be changed manually. This process should be documented in your search-and-indexing maintenance plan as well as in your disaster recovery plan. (For more information about disaster recovery, see Chapter 17, "Data Protection, Recoverability, and Availability.")

You can specify a client certificate for authentication, but the certificate must first exist in the index server's Personal Certificate Store for the local computer before it will show up in the selection list.

> **NOTE**   The crawler will be able to index Information Rights Management (IRM) files stored in SharePoint. However, to index IRM files in other storage, the certificate for the crawler account must have read permission on the files.

Crawl rules also support forms-based authentication (FBA) and cookie-based authentication unless the FBA has complex authentication pages that change content without refreshing the page or that require entries or selection based on content appearing on the page.

 REAL WORLD   **Using Crawl Rules to Keep an Index Clean**

One of the most frustrating aspects of building a usable index is ensuring that unnecessary or outdated content is not crawled by SharePoint. Taking the time to carve out portions of a website or file server to be indexed takes skill, testing, and patience.

What you want to do is to visit the content source and become familiar with it. Connect to the site or file share using the default content access account so that you can understand exactly what the crawler will see. Try to open a random set of files or Web pages to see if there are any security problems. Look at the site and

continued on next page

determine what information you don't want to appear in the index. Then note the paths and build your crawl rules accordingly.

Be sure to test your rules in a lab environment to ensure that your crawl rules are working correctly. Although most organizations will not take the time to ensure that their index is clean, experience has shown that those who take the time to build a targeted index to meet the needs of their users will have a better, more robust deployment.

Using Server Name Mappings

In scenarios in which content must be crawled using an address other than one of the Alternate Access Mapping URLs defined for user access to SharePoint content, you can create server name mappings to override how URLs are shown in search results and correct the name displayed to users. You can access the management page by clicking Server Name Mapping in the Crawling section of the Search Service management page of the Quick Launch navigation area (refer back to Figure 11-5). Click the New Mapping link to open the page to create the mapping. The configuration simply requires you to enter the address in the index to be replaced in search results and the address you want to use in the search results.

A server name mapping might be required when

- Content is crawled via HTTP but users will access it using HTTPS.

- It is necessary to crawl with Windows authentication when the user authentication method is not supported for the crawler, such as smart-card authentication.

- A file system is presented to users via WebDAV. The crawler must access via a file share to retrieve ACLs for security trimming search results.

- A file system is presented to users internally and you don't want the file server names exposed in the result set.

Controlling Host Distribution

In SharePoint Search 2010, the number of crawl components and crawl databases can be increased as the workload increases with automatic distribution of addresses, or if desired, specific addresses can be assigned to specific crawl databases using Host Distribution rules. You cannot even open the page to create a Host Distribution rule until more than one crawl database has been created. A rule can only be applied to a database that is associated with a crawl component. How to create and manage the search service topology is discussed in the section titled "Managing the Search Service Topology" later in this chapter. If a database is dedicated to accept Host Distribution rules assignments, it only accepts content assigned by rules and does not participate in automatic distribution of addresses.

The Host Distribution Rules management page is accessed from the Quick Launch menu of the Search Service Application Management page. Click the Add Distribution Rule link to display the Add Host Rule page shown in Figure 11-10 and then enter the host name without the protocol, select the appropriate database, and click OK. All content from that host will be placed in the database regardless of what protocol was used to crawl the content.

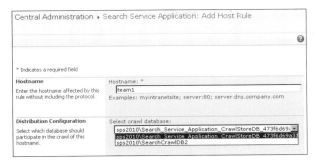

FIGURE 11-10 Add Host Rule page

The distribution of content across content databases can be viewed from the Auto Host Distribution page displayed in Figure 11-11. This page is accessed from the Host Name view of the Crawl Log management pages, which is discussed in the section titled "Reviewing and Troubleshooting Crawls" later in this chapter.

FIGURE 11-11 Auto Host Distribution page

Managing File Types

You can give each search service application a unique configuration that determines what type of files should be crawled. The list is controlled on the Manage File Types page accessed from the Quick Launch (refer back to Figure 11-5). Crawl components will only request the file types from content sources that appear on this page. Crawl rules can exclude file types included on this page from specific addresses, but they cannot include file types not listed on this page.

The page has a New File Type link that only requires entry of the file type extension. If there is no iFilter for the file type, then only the metadata (properties) for the files will be indexed. Unfortunately, SharePoint does not provide an interface to display which iFilters have been installed on your servers.

Add-on iFilters have their own installation processes that are generally individual to the product. SharePoint does not provide an installation tool for third-party iFilters. So, if you do need to crawl a new file type, be sure to

- Install the correct iFilter.
- Configure the Managed File Type for the new file.
- Install the graphic image for the file (usually available from the file type's manufacturer).
- Update the Docicon.xml file.

Resetting the Index

An index reset is probably the most drastic action that you can take on a search service application short of deleting the application itself. Resetting the crawled content erases all portions of the content index including the metadata databases, the index files on all query components, the crawl logs, and the crawl history. If you initiate a reset, no search results will be available until full crawls have been run on all content sources.

By default, search alerts are deactivated during the reset so that alerts subscribers do not have their inbox flooded with e-mails on every item matching their saved search alert. You will have to manually re-enable search alerts after the full crawls have been completed.

Managing Crawls

To manage crawls, you must understand the differences between full and incremental crawls. A full crawl will follow the instructions of the content source and the crawl rules to crawl the entire content source according to the content type, whether hierarchical, enumerated list, or link traversal. A full crawl will replace the current index for that content source and give you a new index. However, because some full crawls take many hours, the old index for that content source will remain on the index and query servers to meet query demand by your users and is only replaced after the full crawl has successfully completed. This means that, for a brief length of time, you'll have two full indexes of the same content source existing on your hard drives. Be sure you plan for enough disk space for committing full crawls.

What is crawled during an incremental crawl depends on the content type and how changes are detected for that content type. For a file system crawl or normal Web crawls, the date/time stamp is compared to a crawl history log. However, for SharePoint incremental crawls, the change logs maintained in the content databases are used. SharePoint 2010 now supports a very quick ACL-only crawl to update security information for index items. Most databases do not support incremental crawls. FAST technology supports change notifications from SQL databases that essentially "push" changes to the crawler, but the SharePoint 2010 Search feature does not.

The section titled "Configuring Crawls" earlier in this chapter described crawls in connection with creating content sources. In the following sections, you'll learn how to manage crawls from the Manage Content Sources page shown in Figure 11-12, which presents the tools for managing crawls.

FIGURE 11-12 Crawl management options from the Manage Content Sources page

Global Crawl Management

Crawls for all content sources can be managed globally with the toolbar option to Start All Crawls, which changes to Stop All Crawls and Pause All Crawls after crawls are started. The type of crawl initiated by the Start All Crawls option depends on several factors.

- It would follow the next crawl scheduled for each content source whether it is a full or incremental crawl.

- If a crawl has been paused, then that crawl will be resumed.

- If no crawl is scheduled and a full crawl has been completed, then an incremental crawl is started. However, remember that the first crawl of any content source is always a full crawl.

- If either type of crawl has been stopped, the next crawl will always be a full crawl. Therefore, careful consideration should be given to the impact of using the Stop All Crawls tool.

- The indexing process can always force a full crawl if it determines that enough errors exist in the index that an incremental crawl may not correct them.

> **IMPORTANT**   Although the crawl process is read-only and does not modify the files, it will change the last read date on some files, which can impact access auditing.

Content Source Crawl Management

The context menu of each content source presents crawl management tools. You can start both full and incremental crawls from the context menu. You can also use the menu to pause, resume, or stop an active crawl. Remember that any time a crawl is stopped or does not complete for any reason, the next crawl of that content source will be a full crawl, because the information in the crawl log and markers set on the change logs are considered inaccurate. When a crawl is paused, the instructions for the crawl and the information about the crawl are retained in memory on the host of the crawl component for use when the crawl is resumed.

User Crawl Management

SharePoint crawlers have always obeyed "Do Not Crawl" instructions embedded in Web content. SharePoint 2010 continues to offer content owners of lists, libraries, and sites the ability to add these instructions through the user interface and eliminate their content from search indexes. Site collection administrators can also flag site columns (metadata) to keep them from being crawled. Personally identifiable information (PII) is an example of information that should not be indexed on public sites. Be sure to have clear policies regarding what type of content should or should not appear in your index.

Scheduling Crawls

The management of crawl schedules is an ongoing process that may require daily monitoring and tweaking. The Manage Content Sources page presents information on the duration of the current and last crawl but does not indicate the type of crawl involved.

However, the Crawl History view of the crawl logs itemizes each crawl's start and end times with the calculated duration as well as the activity accomplished during the crawl. This information permits search administrators to adjust the crawl schedules as the corpus grows so that a crawl can complete successfully before the next crawl begins. Crawls must be scheduled as often as needed to meet the "freshness" requirements of your organization. You might need to adjust the topology of your search service to add resources to complete crawls often enough to meet these needs. When determining additional resources, consider the impact the additions will have on the WFEs being crawled and on the SQL servers hosting the content and search databases.

With the improvements in incremental crawl instructions, you may only schedule full crawls when required instead of on a regular basis. The crawl component can itself switch to a full crawl if

- A search application administrator stopped the previous crawl or the previous crawl did not complete for any reason.

- A content database was restored from backup without the appropriate switch on the STSADM –restore operation that allows the farm administrators to restore a content database without forcing a full crawl.

- A farm administrator has detached and reattached a content database.

- A full crawl of the content source has never been done.

- The change log does not contain entries for the addresses that are being crawled. Without entries in the change log for the items being crawled, incremental crawls cannot occur.

- Depending on the severity of the corruption, the index server might force a full crawl if corruption is detected in the index.

Finally, when is a full crawl required?

- When a search application administrator added a new managed property.

- To re-index ASPX pages on Windows SharePoint Services 3.0 or SharePoint Server 2007 sites.

> **IMPORTANT** Incremental crawls do not re-index views or home pages when content within the page has changed, such as the deletion of individual list items. This is because of the inability of the crawler to detect when ASPX pages on SharePoint sites have changed. You should periodically do full crawls of sites that contain ASPX files to ensure that these pages are re-indexed unless you have the site configured to not have ASPX pages crawled. This behavior is the same as in previous versions of SharePoint.

- To resolve consecutive incremental crawl failures. The index server has been reported to remove content that could not be accessed in 100 consecutive attempts.

- When crawl rules have been added, deleted, or modified.

- To repair a corrupted index.

- When the search services administrator has created one or more server name mappings.

- When the account assigned to the default content access account or crawl rule account has changed. This also automatically triggers a full crawl. Account password changes do not require or trigger a full crawl.

- When file types and/or iFilters have been installed and the new content needs to be indexed.

Reviewing and Troubleshooting Crawls

Troubleshooting crawls on content sources can be a frustrating and time-consuming task. This is why it is important to understand the crawl and indexing process and the associated tools that are used to reveal problems or errors at each stage of the crawl process. The following sections will discuss the crawl logs, then the crawl reports, then finish by discussing Diagnostic Logging.

The Search Administration page uses the Crawl History Web Part to present a summary of crawl activities, as shown in Figure 11-13. The hyperlinked content sources open the Edit Content Source page for that content source, and the hyperlinked numbers in the Success or All Errors columns open filtered views of the crawl log to display just those items.

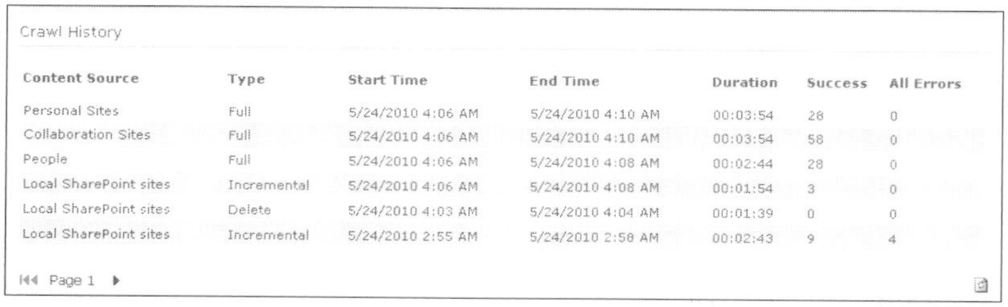

Content Source	Type	Start Time	End Time	Duration	Success	All Errors
Personal Sites	Full	5/24/2010 4:06 AM	5/24/2010 4:10 AM	00:03:54	28	0
Collaboration Sites	Full	5/24/2010 4:06 AM	5/24/2010 4:10 AM	00:03:54	58	0
People	Full	5/24/2010 4:06 AM	5/24/2010 4:08 AM	00:02:44	28	0
Local SharePoint sites	Incremental	5/24/2010 4:06 AM	5/24/2010 4:08 AM	00:01:54	3	0
Local SharePoint sites	Delete	5/24/2010 4:03 AM	5/24/2010 4:04 AM	00:01:39	0	0
Local SharePoint sites	Incremental	5/24/2010 2:55 AM	5/24/2010 2:58 AM	00:02:43	9	4

Crawl History

Page 1

FIGURE 11-13 Crawl History Web Part

> **NOTE** By default, the Web Part shows the last six crawls per page, but that number can be modified by editing the Web Part.

Using Crawl Logs

The crawl logs will be your tool for determining modifications needed for crawl settings including timeouts or crawler impact rules. They are also your primary troubleshooting tools for determining the cause of problems such as why the crawler is not accessing certain documents or certain sites. On the positive side, you can use the logs to see if an individual document has been crawled successfully, and if so—but the user is unable to find the document via a query—you'll be able to focus your troubleshooting efforts on helping the user refine their query. The crawl logs can be accessed from the Crawl Log link in the Crawling section of the Search Administration page or from the context menu for the content source on the Manage Content Sources page.

> **NOTE** Crawl logs may be your first indication of problems on your sites. If the crawler (which has Read permissions for everything) cannot access items, then users cannot access them either. Any URLs that exceed the protocol limitations may be exposed first in crawl log errors.

Each hyperlinked number on a crawl log page opens a filtered view of the log. So if you click a number on the page, notice that the log will have already filtered the view based on the status type, without regard to date or time. You can then apply other filters available from drop-down boxes.

The crawl logs have five different views that present different levels of information, filtering options, and drilldown capabilities. The default Content Source view, shown in Figure 11-14, presents summary counts of the five status types: Successes, Warnings, Errors, Top Level Errors, and Deletes.

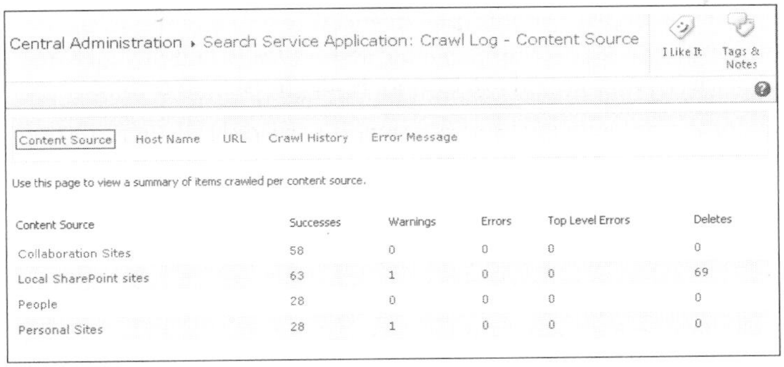

FIGURE 11-14 Crawl Log – Content Source view

After the crawl log is opened, other views can be selected from the toolbar. The Host Name view in Figure 11-15 presents a summary of items crawled per host as well as the same status type counts as the Content Source view, plus a total column. It provides a search box for locating specific URLs that is useful when crawling large numbers of URLs or finding errors for specific sites within a URL.

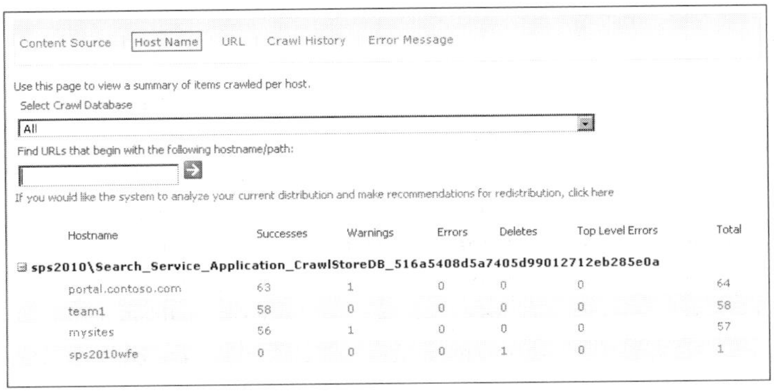

FIGURE 11-15 Crawl Log – Host Name view

The URL view shown in Figure 11-16 presents more information about the error, such as the error message, the content source, and the last time crawled. This list is normally extremely long, because it presents every action on every item. The advanced search filtering tool is useful for troubleshooting crawls and revealing user activities that create problems, such as uploading files with file names so long that the files cannot be opened or downloaded. It also reveals files that are too large for the default crawl settings. In this case, only the first portion of the file is indexed.

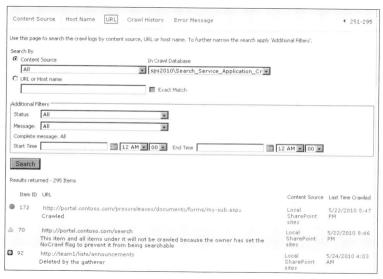

FIGURE 11-16 Crawl Log – URL view

The status message of each document appears below the URL, along with a symbol indicating whether the crawl was successful. Also notice that in the right-hand column of the table, the date and time of the message have been generated.

The status types are as follows.

- **Success** The crawler successfully connected to the content source, read the content item, and passed the content to the indexer.

- **Warning** The crawler connected to the content source and tried to crawl the content item, but could not for whatever reason.

- **Error** The crawler could not communicate with the content source.

- **Top Level Errors**   These are errors at the root of an application or site collection that would impact all content below. Top level errors can result in shorter logs, because identical errors for individual items in that container are not recorded.

- **Deletes**   Deleted by the gatherer. In Figure 11-16, the deletion was made because an application was moved from one content source to another.

The Crawl History view shown in Figure 11-17 gives information about specific crawls but does not provide any drilldown tools and only provides filtering on Content Source. This information is useful in adjusting crawl schedules and identifying the more dynamic content sources.

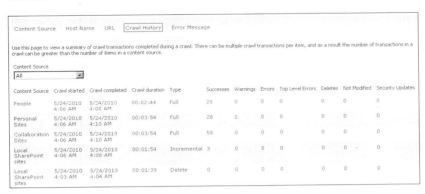

FIGURE 11-17 Crawl Log – Crawl History view

The Error Message view shown in Figure 11-18 aggregates all errors into a list of errors with a count of each. Clicking the hyperlinked number opens the URL view filtered to that particular error message. Other filters can then be applied to focus the presentation.

FIGURE 11-18 Crawl Log – Error Message view

Using Crawl Reports

SharePoint 2010 provides search administration reports enabled by default to help you to determine the health of your search service applications. All reports have filters to target the results. In the Reports section of the Search Administration page, the link to Administration Reports opens the Administrative Report Library, which contains a Search administration reports folder.

That folder contains basic search administration reports that show high-level monitoring data aggregated from all components for the selected search service application. There are two basic search administration reports for crawling.

- Crawl Rate Per Content Source, shown in Figure 11-19, which provides a view of recent crawl activity sorted by content source. The anchor crawl is the process in which anchor text from links between items is added to a full-text index catalog. It appears as a separate (virtual) content source.

- Crawl Rate Per Type shown in Figure 11-20 provides a view of recent crawl activity, sorted by items and actions for a given URL. These items and actions include modified items, deleted items, retries, errors, and others.

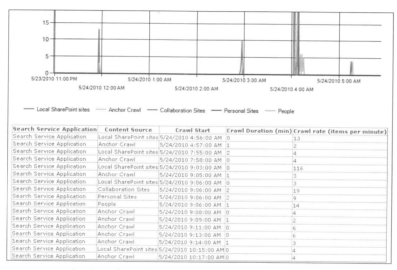

Search Service Application	Content Source	Crawl Start	Crawl Duration (min)	Crawl rate (items per minute)
Search Service Application	Local SharePoint sites	5/24/2010 4:56:00 AM	0	13
Search Service Application	Anchor Crawl	5/24/2010 4:57:00 AM	1	2
Search Service Application	Local SharePoint sites	5/24/2010 7:55:00 AM	2	4
Search Service Application	Anchor Crawl	5/24/2010 7:58:00 AM	0	4
Search Service Application	Local SharePoint sites	5/24/2010 9:03:00 AM	0	116
Search Service Application	Anchor Crawl	5/24/2010 9:05:00 AM	1	3
Search Service Application	Local SharePoint sites	5/24/2010 9:06:00 AM	0	3
Search Service Application	Collaboration Sites	5/24/2010 9:06:00 AM	2	19
Search Service Application	Personal Sites	5/24/2010 9:06:00 AM	2	9
Search Service Application	People	5/24/2010 9:06:00 AM	1	14
Search Service Application	Anchor Crawl	5/24/2010 9:08:00 AM	0	4
Search Service Application	Anchor Crawl	5/24/2010 9:09:00 AM	1	2
Search Service Application	Anchor Crawl	5/24/2010 9:11:00 AM	0	6
Search Service Application	Anchor Crawl	5/24/2010 9:13:00 AM	0	6
Search Service Application	Anchor Crawl	5/24/2010 9:14:00 AM	1	3
Search Service Application	Local SharePoint sites	5/24/2010 10:15:00 AM	0	4
Search Service Application	Anchor Crawl	5/24/2010 10:17:00 AM	0	4

FIGURE 11-19 Portion of Crawl Rate Per Content Source report

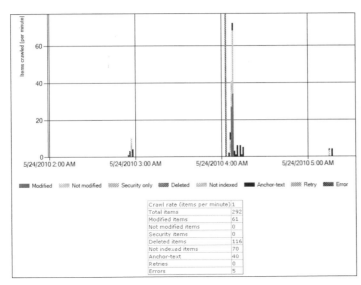

Crawl rate (items per minute)	1
Total items	292
Modified items	61
Not modified items	0
Security items	0
Deleted items	116
Not indexed items	70
Anchor-text	40
Retries	0
Errors	5

FIGURE 11-20 Portion of Crawl Rate Per Type report

In the advanced reports subfolder, there are three additional default reports. These reports show more in-depth monitoring data aggregated from all components for the selected search service application.

- **Crawl Processing Per Activity** This report provides a view of where crawl processing occurs in the pipeline, per minute. The timings per component are grouped by activity, such as filtering or word breaking.

- **Crawl Processing Per Component** This report provides a view of where crawl processing occurs in the pipeline, per minute. The timings are grouped by component, such as File Protocol Handler or Anchor Plug-in.

- **Crawl Queue** This report provides a view of the state of the crawl queue, displaying incoming links to process and outgoing transactions queued.

These five reports will help you determine when the search service topology needs modification. A SharePoint 2010 Products Management Pack is available for Microsoft System Center Operations Manager to provide more detailed performance monitoring.

Diagnostic Logging

Reports are derived from information first collected in logs, so for effective reporting you must configure the collection of data. To do this, open a Web browser, go to the Central Administration website, and open the Monitoring page. Under the Reporting heading, open the Configure Diagnostic Logging page and expand the Office Search Server. This page displays the current logging levels and provides settings to control the severity of events captured in the Windows event log and the trace logs. The number of events logged and the logging overhead will increase as the severity of the events decreases.

The following categories are available for SharePoint Server Search.

- Admin Audit
- Administration
- Advanced Tracing
- Anchor Plug-in
- Anchor Text Plug-in
- Anchor Text Plug-in Cache
- Anchor Text Plug-in Links
- Connector Framework
- Content Index Server
- Content Plugin
- File Protocol Handler
- Gatherer
- Gatherer Service Catalog
- HealthRule
- HTTP Protocol Handler
- Indexing
- Matrix Protocol Handler
- Notes Protocol Handler
- Plug-in
- Propagation Manager
- Query
- Query Processor
- Remote Exchange Store Protocol Handler
- Search service

Although you cannot configure categories individually within the page, you can select a collection of items to be configured alike at the same time and then click OK. You will then need to reopen the page to configure another selection of items differently.

For the event log, the reporting levels are

- None
- Critical
- Error
- Warning
- Information
- Verbose

For the trace logs, the event logging levels are

- None
- Unexpected
- Monitorable
- High
- Medium
- Verbose

Enabling Event Log Flood Protection suppresses logging of the same event repeatedly until the conditions return to normal.

On this page, you determine the location for the trace logs, the number of days to store them, and the amount of space reserved for them. Move them away from the operating system files, where filling the drive space could crash the system; it is preferable to have them on another spindle with no I/O conflict.

Logging normally would be set at a level that would expose abnormal activity and would increase when troubleshooting.

> **NOTE** The log file location is a farm-wide setting. The drive and full path must exist on all servers in the farm. This setting will not create the folder structure.

Managing the Search Service Topology

A single SharePoint 2010 farm can provide multiple instances of search service applications. Each service instance can support multiple component instances in a topology that can be designed for performance, for resiliency, or to isolate information.

The default topology of a new search service application will have a single instance of each component, all components on one application server, and all databases on one database server. The four components are as follows.

- Administration interface
- Crawl component (the crawler)
- Database set, broken into three databases: administration, crawl, and property
- Index partition

This topology can be changed using the Modify Topology link located on the Farm-Wide Search Administration page or from the Search Service Administration page. The SharePoint Search topology cannot be changed in stand-alone installations.

The Search Application Topology Web Part presents the initial topology in the lower portion of the Search Administration page, shown in Figure 11-21.

FIGURE 11-21 Search Application Topology Web Part with initial topology

The functions and interactivity of the components were discussed in the section titled "Search Components and Processes" earlier in this chapter. The following sections discuss why and how to modify the topology for both the crawl and query processes.

Scaling Considerations

The reason that the SharePoint 2010 product team broke out the search components was to provide robust scaling for the different aspects of the crawl and indexing process. Different implementations will find bottlenecks being created at different points in the overall indexing process, so by enabling the scaling of the different components, you can create a topology that fits your needs.

For example, if you need to reduce crawl times and increase index freshness, then consider performing the following actions.

- If the crawl component is overwhelmed, add more crawl component servers.
- If the crawl database is I/O bound on the SQL server, add crawl databases on same SQL server.
- If the SQL server bottleneck is memory or CPU, add SQL servers with additional crawl databases.

To reduce query latency, consider the following remedies.

- If full-text query latency is high, partition the index into smaller partitions. Each partition can contain ~10M items. You will generally need enough memory to fit 33 percent of the index in RAM to meet sub-second latency responses.
- If query latency is high because of the number of queries, add query components to mirror index partitions.
- If property query latency is high because the property database is I/O bound, add property databases to the same SQL server.
- If property query latency is high because of a memory or CPU bottleneck on SQL server, add property databases to additional SQL servers.

> **NOTE** You can use the SharePoint Backend Query Latency report provided by SharePoint 2010 to help determine where scaling out is needed to improve query latency.

To increase availability for query process, consider these suggestions.

- Deploy multiple query components with multiple index partitions.
- Deploy multiple mirrored query components and property store databases.
- Use clustered or mirrored database servers to host search databases.

To increase availability for crawling process, add crawl databases supported by multiple crawl components with redundant crawl servers. Normally, two crawl components can support a crawl database.

Modifying the Topology

To make any change to the topology, click the Modify button at the top of the page to open the topology management page partially shown in Figure 11-22. The view of components on this page can be organized by components or by server hosting the components. From the New menu, select the component that you want to create and add to the search application.

FIGURE 11-22 Manage Search Topology page menus

Changes to the topology are defined in the appropriate dialog boxes: New, Properties, or Delete. However, changes are not implemented until the Apply Topology Changes button is clicked. Clicking this button starts the SharePoint timer job, which accomplishes the actions required. You can make multiple changes to the search topology and then apply them all at once by clicking the Apply Topology Changes button. Because many changes can impact performance during their application, you might want to choose to define the changes in the management pages but use Windows PowerShell scripts to schedule their implementation.

To create a new component, click the New link in the upper-left corner of the page and select the appropriate component from the drop-down list. To edit the properties or delete a component, use the context menu of the component. There must be at least one instance of each component, so the Delete command will not be available in some instances. Also, for the query component, there is an extra menu item, Add Mirror, as shown in Figure 11-23.

FIGURE 11-23 Context menu for the query component

Crawl Databases

Crawl databases contain configurations and instructions required by the crawl component, tables used during crawls to queue items to be crawled, and log information used in crawl logs. Since a new crawl component must be associated with an existing or pending database, you should create the new database first.

The database can be hosted on a SQL server other than the default server. See the scaling considerations above to determine placement of the databases. Microsoft strongly recommends Windows authentication over the SQL authentication option. If you have mirrored SQL servers, you can associate the database with a failover database server. As discussed earlier, if you select the Dedicate This Crawl Store To Hosts As Specified In Host Distribution Rules option, the database will not participate in the automatic host distribution process. As long as there is more than one crawl database, any crawl database can be specified in a Host Distribution Rule.

> **NOTE** Crawl databases that have had crawl components associated with them cannot be deleted until the crawl components have been associated with another database.

Crawl Components

Use the New menu to create a new crawl component. The configuration is very simple. Crawl component names are zero-based and generated as they are built, not while they are pending. Select a member of the farm as the server to host this crawl component. Only servers with a complete installation will be listed. Select the Associated Crawl Database. If this database already has a crawl component associated with it, then you are adding a crawl component for resiliency. Since all of the crawl instructions including state are stored in a SQL database, one crawl component can easily pick up where another left off. If you are adding one or more crawl components to a new database, then you are spreading the crawl workload for performance.

Finally, you must specify the location on the server file system where the index files will be created and stored before they are propagated to the query servers. Unlike previous versions, the space requirements for this location are relatively small and constant, because the entire index is not stored on the crawl component server.

To redistribute existing content to the new database, you must use the Auto Host Distribution tool, which is available by clicking the If You Would Like The System To Analyze Your Current Distribution And Make Recommendations For Redistribution, Click Here link on the Host Name view of the crawl logs. The tool will give an estimate of the time required to redistribute the content. Crawls will be paused during this activity, and the redistribution status will be displayed on the Host Distribution Rules page. On the Search Administration dashboard, you will see that the crawl status is Paused For: Refactoring. Crawl activity will resume automatically after the content is redistributed.

If you remove the crawl components from a database and delete the database, the content will automatically be redistributed to other existing databases. Crawls will be paused during this activity as well.

Property Databases

New property databases are created to improve query performance. They can also be mirrored on SQL servers for resiliency. When creating a new property database, you not only get to select the SQL server instance, but you also can use your own naming convention or accept the recommended name. Again, either Windows or SQL authentication will work; Windows authentication is recommended. If you have SQL mirroring established, you may enter the name of the failover database server.

The name generated for the original property database for our demo farm was the name of the search service application appended with "PropertyStoreDB Appended With The Database GUID: Search_Service_Application_PropertyStoreDB_df97fb03501a4066a34f0ffffefbfc95." The generated name of the second database was SearchPropertyDB1. The naming convention for the Crawl Database followed a similar convention.

Index Partitions and Query Components

You can split the index into smaller partitions to speed up full-text queries. Each partition can contain approximately 10 million items, but you should plan on having enough memory to fit 33 percent of the index in RAM to meet sub-second latency responses. The index size and full-text queries must be monitored so that the topology design is kept current with the growth of search activities and performance standards.

To split the index, select Index Partition And Query Component from the New menu (though note that the dialog box that opens is titled Add Query Component). Select the farm member to host the index partition and query component and then select the existing property database with which this index will be associated. Then specify the location for the index file. Unlike the crawl component, the index component will store a complete copy of this partition of the index, so sufficient space must be reserved to handle the current partition and estimated growth.

Finally, there is a Set This Query Component As Failover Only option that is available even for the first query server associated with this index.

The command to add mirrors is tucked away in the context menu for the query component, as you saw in Figure 11-23. The property box for the new query component is the same as before, except the Associated Property Database is preconfigured and inactive. The failover option is still available. You would add mirrors for the index partitions to reduce query latency due to the number of queries. Note that the term "mirror" is used even though these are index files, not SQL databases.

FAST Search Server 2010 for SharePoint

FAST Search Server 2010 for SharePoint can bring Enterprise search capabilities into SharePoint with much of the ease of deployment, configuration, and management provided by SharePoint 2010. Like the first part of this chapter, the discussion of FAST Search Server 2010 will focus on the architecture and crawling improvements. Query and results improvements are covered in Chapter 13.

Introducing FAST Search Server 2010

FAST Search Server 2010 for SharePoint can be deployed across multiple servers to satisfy requirements for redundancy, performance, and capacity. Both SharePoint Search and FAST Search use the same crawling infrastructure, since SharePoint Search now incorporates the modularity of FAST Search. Adding more servers can be used to scale document volume, query volume, and processing power for content, query, and results. You can deploy, configure, and manage FAST Search through the user interface, Windows PowerShell cmdlets, XML configuration files, and command-line operations.

FAST Search Server 2010 for SharePoint uses SharePoint 2010 for query servers and crawling content, but adds additional servers in a FAST farm for processing content, producing index partitions, and processing queries. To save costs, a single FAST farm can be dedicated to search and shared across multiple SharePoint farms. As you might guess, a wide range of farm topologies are possible that can handle both simple and demanding requirements.

For larger environments, FAST Search Server 2010 for SharePoint uses rows and columns of servers to scale out to potentially unlimited content size and query volume, including built-in fault tolerance. To increase content processing capacity almost linearly, you add more columns of servers. To increase the query processing ability, you add more rows of servers. Fault tolerance is provided by deploying a minimum of two rows. The diagram in Figure 11-24 illustrates a configuration of FAST servers that can process approximately 100 million items.

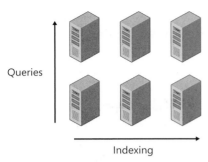

Queries

Indexing

FIGURE 11-24 FAST Search Server 2010 for SharePoint scaling diagram

The following is a list of some of the enhancements provided by FAST Search Server 2010 for SharePoint.

- Can search in any language
- Can detect 84 languages, although not all linguistic tools are provided for all languages
- Lemmatization (variations) improves recall (query for better includes good)
- Phrase search includes stop words (noise words), but keyword queries do not
- Only nouns and adjectives are expanded for precision (book > books not booked)
- Deeper refinements with exact counts of items including duplicates; retrieves metadata from entire results list, not just first 50 items
- Ability to sort results on any metadata
- Entity extraction

Architecturally, the FAST add-on products modify the content processing pipeline to be easily extensible with custom plug-ins. With SharePoint Search, you created a Search Service Application (SSA). With FAST Search for SharePoint, you will create two FAST Search Service Applications, the FAST Search Connector and the FAST Search Query.

These SSAs create the connections between the SharePoint Search components that crawl content and construct queries and the FAST Search components that process the content indexing and querying. These FAST SSAs essentially modify the processing "pipeline" to divert the indexing and querying processing from the SharePoint Search layer of the architecture to the more powerful FAST layer of servers.

This FAST Content Processing pipeline is constructed of a series of customizable plug-ins that can be managed with the user interface, cmdlets, or config files. In many stages of the pipeline, you will find plug-ins available to provide standard SharePoint or enhanced FAST capabilities. Out-of-box (OOB) plug-ins can be enabled or disabled as needed. The following plug-ins are enabled by default.

- Format conversion.
- Language detection and encoding for 84 languages.
- Lemmatizer: Linguistics normalization similar but superior to the stemming performed by SharePoint Search. Lemmatizing uses a dictionary to reduce words to their basic

form as in ate = eat. FAST Search Server for SharePoint 2010 performs linguistic processing for items returned by the crawl process before those items are indexed and for items in the query before the query is processed.

- Tokenizer: The word breakers for FAST are better than the SharePoint Search processes, particularly in non-English languages.

- Entity extraction: The entity extraction process detects various properties as known entities (such as names, locations, and dates) from the retrieved documents, and maps them as metadata into managed properties even if they are not natively defined as metadata within the documents. Users can now query these as properties or metadata, and they also can drill down or refine results based on these properties. You can create custom extractors using, for example, a dictionary (list) of product names, projects, or organizational units relevant to your organization.

- DateTimeNormalizer.

- Vectorizer: Creates a document signature that represents a document's content in a way that allows comparison between documents for similarity searching.

- WebAnalyzer: Anchor text and link cardinality analysis.

- PropertiesMapper: Maps metadata to crawled properties.

- PropertiesReporter: Reports detected properties or metadata.

Other optional plug-ins that are provided but are disabled by default include the following.

- XML Properties Mapper

- Offensive Content Filter

- Verbatim extractor loads dictionary for custom extraction like a list of product names, projects, or departments

- Field Collapsing

Architecture and Topology

FAST Search Server 2010 for SharePoint extends the three-tiered architecture of SharePoint Search 2010 into multitiered distributed farm architecture. The following sections describe the tiers and their components.

SharePoint WFE Servers

The standard SharePoint 2010 WFE servers will continue to provide the Query and Federation Object Model (OM), the Query Web service, and the Search Centers with the accompanying Web Parts customized to accept queries from and present results to users. The use of FAST Search should be transparent to users except for enhanced results.

Site collection administrators will be able to manage FAST Search functionality in Site Settings, just as they did for SharePoint Search. The number of WFEs will scale as required. You should consider using one or more WFEs dedicated as crawl targets if the crawls levels impact performance for users.

SharePoint Application Servers

The FAST Content SSA and Query SSA will be provided by SharePoint 2010 application servers in the parent farm. Depending on the workload, these servers may be able to provide other SharePoint services. These services can scale for performance and resiliency by adding query components to the Query SSA and crawl components to the Content SSA.

The Query SSA provides the connection to FAST query processing and both the query and the crawl components for people search. The Content SSA provides the connection to FAST crawl and index processing.

Both the parent SharePoint farm and remote SharePoint farms will interface with FAST using the SSAs on the parent farm. At this layer, FAST differs from SharePoint Search in that the SharePoint SSA provided both the crawl and query components, whereas FAST requires separate SSAs for each component.

FAST Application Servers

This layer provides the following components that can be hosted on one or more servers as required for performance and resiliency.

- Administration
- Content Distributor
- Item Processing
- Web Analyzer
- Indexing Dispatcher
- Indexer
- Query Matching
- Query Processing

Database Servers

SQL Server 2008 Enterprise servers will provide the following search databases in clusters and/or mirrored configurations.

- SharePoint Central and Site Administration
- Search Admin (FAST)
- Search Admin (Content and Query SSA including people search)
- Property (Query SSA people search)
- Search Crawl (Query SSA people search)

NOTE With FAST Search for SharePoint, the metadata is stored in optimized files on file system, not in SQL databases.

Scaling FAST Application Layer (Cluster)

All the FAST Search Server 2010 for SharePoint components can run on a single server. However, depending on how you scale out to run the components on one or more servers, the system can

- Index a larger number of items
- Handle more item updates
- Reduce indexing latency
- Respond to more queries per second

Figure 11-25 shows an example of a scaled-out cluster of components for the purpose of this discussion.

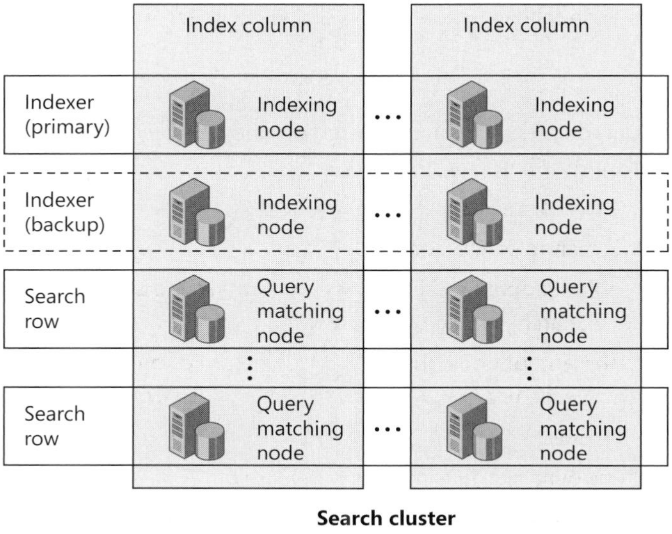

FIGURE 11-25 FAST Search components cluster

- **Index column** The complete searchable index can be split into multiple disjoint index columns (or partitions) when the complete index is too large to reside on one server. Queries will be evaluated against all index columns within the search cluster, and the results from each index column are merged into the final results list. Unlike SharePoint Search 2010, adding an index partition (column) here requires a complete re-indexing of all content, so accuracy in your original design is very important.

- **Search row** A search row contains set of search nodes (servers) hosting index partitions that together contain all items indexed within the search cluster. Adding search rows provides increased query performance and fault tolerance.

- **Primary and backup indexer rows** An index row provides an indexer for each partition. When you add a row of indexer nodes, they are configured as backup indexer nodes for fault tolerance. Both rows of indexers produce the same set of indexes, but only the primary indexer distributes the indexes to the query matching nodes.

Indexing Connectors

FAST Search Server 2010 for SharePoint uses the Connector Framework for indexing content, just as SharePoint 2010 does. In fact, most content sources can be crawled with the SharePoint 2010 connectors. However, FAST Search Server 2010 for SharePoint does offer three advanced SharePoint specific indexing connectors. The choice of indexing connector is influenced by the kind of content that you want to crawl, by the specific requirements of your organization, and (sometimes) just by an administrator's preference.

Even though these indexing connectors are known as the FAST Search connector, remember that it is a collection of connectors, not one separate indexing connector. As the FAST Search connector is associated with one or more content sources through the FAST Search Content SSA, the individual indexing connectors are used.

This FAST Search connector offers the following connectors with options for Web, database, and Lotus Notes content.

WEB CONTENT

- **SharePoint Sites**   Always use the SharePoint connector.
- **File shares**   Always use the File share connector.
- **Exchange**   Always use the Exchange connector.
- **People profiles**   Always use the People profiles connector. (Profiles are crawled through the FAST Search Query Search Service Application.)
- **Websites**   If you have a limited amount of websites without dynamic content, use the website indexing connector. However, use the FAST Search Web crawler when
  - You have many websites to crawl.
  - The website content contains dynamic data, including JavaScript.
  - The organization needs access to advanced Web crawling, configuration, and scheduling options.
  - You want to crawl RSS Web content.
  - The website content uses advanced logon options.

DATABASE CONTENT

Use the Business Data Catalog-based indexing connectors if

- The preferred configuration method is Microsoft SharePoint Designer 2010.
- You want to use time stamp–based change detection for incremental database crawls.
- The preferred management method is SharePoint 2010 Central Administration.
- You want to enable crawling based on the change log. This requires directly modifying the connector model file and creating a stored procedure in the database.

Use the FAST Search database connector when

- The preferred configuration method is using SQL queries.
- Advanced data joining operation options through SQL queries are required.
- You want to use advanced incremental update features. This connector uses checksum-based change detection for incremental crawls if there is no update information available. It also supports time stamp–based change detection and change detection based on update and delete flags.

LOTUS NOTES CONTENT

Use the Lotus Notes connector when

- The preferred management is Central Administration.

Use the FAST Search Lotus Notes connector when

- Full Lotus Notes security support is required, including support for Lotus Notes roles.
- You want to crawl Lotus Notes databases as attachments.

LINE-OF-BUSINESS DATA CONTENT

Use Business Data Catalog–based connectors when the data in your content source contains data in line-of-business applications and when you want to enable crawling based on the change log. This requires directly modifying the connector model file and creating a stored procedure in the database.

> **MORE INFO** Many new articles and documentation about FAST Search Server 2010 for SharePoint are being added to the Microsoft TechNet Library. These articles cover planning and architecture, deployment, operations, security, and troubleshooting, and there is also a technical reference guide for FAST Search Server 2010 for SharePoint Documents are available at *http://technet.microsoft.com/en-us/library/ff686963.aspx*. See this online resource for updated information.

Summary

This chapter covers the basic administration activities and methods for administrating Search in SharePoint 2010. Obviously, this topic could fill an entire book by itself, but the information in this chapter should give you a good start on your journey to becoming a great Search administrator. In the next chapter, you'll focus on the Windows PowerShell commands that are available to manage the Search and FAST technologies.

## CHAPTER 12

Using Windows PowerShell to Manage Search Services and FAST Search

This is the second chapter in this Administrator's Companion that deals solely with Windows PowerShell. Chapter 5, "Using Windows PowerShell to Perform and Automate Farm Administrative Tasks," provides you with the basis of working with Windows PowerShell and Microsoft SharePoint Products and Technologies (2010). This chapter covers more complex use of Windows PowerShell, specifically how to use it with search scenarios. This chapter should be read in conjunction with Chapter 11, "Search Server 2010 and FAST Search: Architecture and Administration."

 ON THE COMPANION MEDIA   The Windows PowerShell examples and source code presented in this chapter can be found on the companion media that accompanies this book.

Microsoft SharePoint 2010 provides both a basic search that you will find in Microsoft SharePoint Foundation 2010 and an enterprise search. Microsoft FAST Search Server 2010 for SharePoint provides additional functionality. This chapter covers both basic and enterprise search and then details FAST Search management and deployment.

NOTE   The scripts in this chapter use fictional URL Web names, such as, *http://intranet.contoso.msft* and *http://oldintranet.contoso.msft*. Use your own SharePoint website Web addresses when using these scripts.

Working with Basic Search

SharePoint Foundation 2010 provides a basic search that allows it to crawl only SharePoint sites in the same farm; that is, search cannot be configured to crawl external data sources. You cannot manually configure search crawling of a SharePoint Foundation farm, and search queries are scoped to a single site collection. However, SharePoint Foundation also includes the Help Search service, which can be managed. This service indexes the help system. The four search-related Windows PowerShell cmdlets in SharePoint Foundation (and in SharePoint Server) are

- Get-SPSearchService
- Get-SPSearchServiceInstance
- Set-SPSearchService
- Set-SPSearchServiceInstance

Whenever you are introduced to a new cmdlet, you can use the techniques explained in Chapter 5 to explore how to use them. For example, you can use the Get-Help cmdlet with the name of a specific cmdlet to get a description of the cmdlet, the syntax it uses, parameter descriptions, examples, and other information. The properties associated with the SharePoint Foundation Help Search service can be listed by piping into the select * command, as shown in the following example.

```
Get-SPSearchService | select *
```

Sample output generated by this command is shown here.

```
ServiceName                    : SPSearch4
PerformanceLevel               : PartlyReduced
TypeName                       : SharePoint Foundation Help Search
Required                       : True
AddStartAddressForNonNTZone    : False
MaxBackupDuration              : 2880
ProcessIdentity                : SPProcessIdentity
Instances                      : {, }
Applications                   : {}
JobDefinitions                 : {SharePoint Foundation Search Refresh}
RunningJobs                    : {}
JobHistoryEntries              : {, , , ...}
CanUpgrade                     : True
IsBackwardsCompatible          : True
NeedsUpgradeIncludeChildren    : False
NeedsUpgrade                   : False
UpgradeContext                 : Microsoft.SharePoint.Upgrade.SPUpgradeContext
Name                           : SPSearch4
DisplayName                    : SPSearch4
Id                             : 5f19c104-c5e6-4d06-9131-22b38afca689
```

```
Status                      : Online
Parent                      : SPFarm Name=SPF_Config
Version                     : 3081
Properties                  : {}
Farm                        : SPFarm Name=SPF_Config
UpgradedPersistedProperties : {}
```

By reviewing the properties, the relationship between the SPSearch4 service and other objects can be found. Therefore, one object can point to another object—for example, one of the properties of the Search service is JobDefinitions, which contains a list of any SharePoint timer jobs that are associated with this service. Again using techniques described in Chapter 5, you can get more information about the Foundation Help Search service timer jobs by using the following command.

```
(Get-SPSearchService).jobdefinitions | select *
```

Look at the sample output from this command shown here. There is only one timer job associated with this service, and by reviewing its properties, you can see that it is configured to run hourly to keep the help index synchronized with its content.

```
DisplayName           : SharePoint Foundation Search Refresh
Description           : Performs periodic synchronization functions for
                        the Microsoft SharePoint Foundation search service
                        .
Service               : SPSearchService Name=SPSearch4
WebApplication        :
Server                :
LockType              : None
Schedule              : hourly between 4 and 4
Title                 : SharePoint Services Search Refresh
LastRunTime           : 01/01/2010 16:04:00
Retry                 : False
IsDisabled            : False
VerboseTracingEnabled : False
HistoryEntries        : {, , , ...}
EnableBackup          : False
DiskSizeRequired      : 0
CanSelectForBackup    : False
CanRenameOnRestore    : False
CanSelectForRestore   : False
Name                  : SharePoint Foundation Search Refresh
TypeName              : Microsoft.SharePoint.Search.Administration.SPSear
                        chJobDefinition
Id                    : ced11b3b-470c-4d40-91a6-7f831dae8f79
Status                : Online
Parent                : SPSearchService Name=SPSearch4
```

continued on the next page

```
Version                   : 3115
Properties                : {}
Farm                      : SPFarm Name=SPF_Config
UpgradedPersistedProperties : {}
```

> **NOTE** The SharePoint Foundation Search Refresh timer job is the same as any other timer job and can be configured using the SPTimerJob cmdlet. For example, to schedule the timer job to run daily between specific times, type the following command.
>
> ```
> Set-SPTimerJob "SharePoint Foundation Search Refresh"
>     -Schedule "daily between 01:00:00 and 04:00:00"
> ```

By using similar commands, your familiarity with the objects that the SharePoint cmdlets expose will increase. Comparing information you can obtain using cmdlets to the experience of using the SharePoint 2010 Central Administration website can quickly make you familiar with the cmdlets. For example, to obtain more information about the Search service, type **Get-SPSearchServiceInstance | select ***. Sample output from this command is shown here and lists information such as the SQL Server where the search database is stored and the location of the index. Therefore, these properties are readily available within the Windows PowerShell environment to aid you in automating administrative tasks.

```
TypeName                    : SharePoint Foundation Help Search
SystemService               : False
DisplayName                 : Serve search queries over help content
Description                 : Serve search queries over help content
ManageLink                  : Microsoft.SharePoint.Administration.SPActionLink
ProvisionLink               : Microsoft.SharePoint.Administration.SPActionLink
UnprovisionLink             : Microsoft.SharePoint.Administration.SPActionLink
ProxyType                   : Default
WebProxy                    : System.Net.WebProxy
IndexLocation               : C:\Program Files\Common Files\Microsoft Shared\
                              Web Server Extensions\14\Data\Applications
SearchDatabase              : SPSearchDatabase Name=SPF_SearchService_WIN08R2
Server                      : SPServer Name=w08r2spf
Service                     : SPSearchService Name=SPSearch4
Instance                    :
Roles                       :
Hidden                      : False
CanUpgrade                  : True
IsBackwardsCompatible       : True
NeedsUpgradeIncludeChildren : False
NeedsUpgrade                : False
UpgradeContext              : Microsoft.SharePoint.Upgrade.SPUpgradeContext
```

```
Name                        :
Id                          : 8af8b8b1-92cb-48d2-8864-20a7e191d7c2
Status                      : Online
Parent                      : SPServer Name=w08r2spf
Version                     : 3067
Properties                  : {}
Farm                        : SPFarm Name=SPF_Config
UpgradedPersistedProperties : {}
```

This same information can be obtained using the SharePoint 2010 Central Administration website. Click Manage Services On Server and then click the SharePoint Foundation Help Search hyperlink, as shown in Figure 12-1.

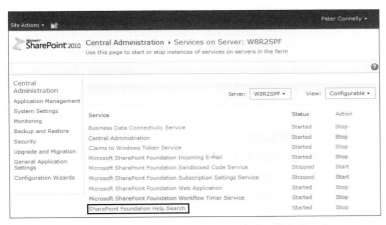

FIGURE 12-1 Services On Server: SharePoint Foundation Help Search

NOTE When you have to complete a task more than once, you should think about using Windows PowerShell to automate the task.

Using Enterprise Search

For small farms that are using SharePoint Server 2010, a fully functional enterprise search topology can be created by running the Farm Configuration Wizard; this can support an index of up to 10 million crawled documents. However, for large deployments, you must create your own search topology that suits your specific needs. You can create such a search topology using Windows PowerShell or the search administration pages contained within the SharePoint 2010 Central Administration website. SharePoint Server provides 126 Windows PowerShell cmdlets to create and manage enterprise search.

The search topology can consist of one or more Search Service Applications (SSA). Each SSA contains one or more query components and one or more crawl (content) components. Typically, the search administration component runs on the same server as the crawl components. Each crawl component is associated with one crawl database and crawls the content that is specified in that database. Query servers serve the results of queries to the Web servers and hold either the entire index or one or more index partitions of the index. Each index partition includes at least one query component, which services the results for its portion of the index.

Creating and Managing Search Application Topology

The SSA object is perhaps the most important object when managing your search topology. Type the command **Get-SPEnterpriseSearchServiceApplication | get-member** to see the number of properties and methods available for the SSA object. Without an SSA, you cannot create any other search-related objects. When you run the Farm Configuration Wizard, an SSA and its related SSA proxy are created and associated with the default service application proxy group. The SSA proxy connects Web applications to the SSA and the service application proxy group and groups together the service groups associated with a Web application.

Using the browser and the SharePoint 2010 Central Administration website, you can manage which service applications are associated with the proxy group by clicking Application Management in the navigation bar on the left side of the site. Then, in the Service Applications area of the page that opens, click Configure Service Application Associations.

To manage individual SSAs, click Manage Service Applications in the Service Applications area and then click the name of the SSA. For example, the SSA created by the Farm Configuration Wizard is named Search Service Application. The Search Administration page will be displayed when you click the name of the SSA, and at the bottom of the page, you will see details about the search application topology, as shown in Figure 12-2.

Several SharePoint Server cmdlets help you manage an SSA topology; the objects and associated cmdlets available are listed in Table 12-1. For more information about the cmdlets relevant to a specific object, use a command similar to the following one.

```
Get-Help *SPEnterpriseSearchServiceApplication
```

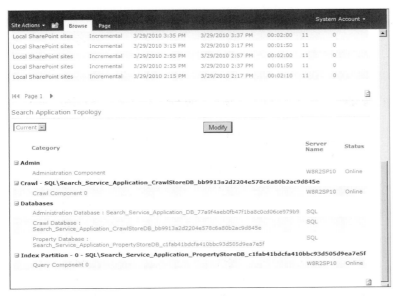

FIGURE 12-2 Search application topology details on the Search Administration page of the SharePoint Central Administration website

TABLE 12-1 SharePoint 2010 Enterprise Search Topology, Administrative, and Service Application Objects

OBJECT NAME	CMDLET COUNT	DESCRIPTION
Topology	2	Imports or exports a search topology using an XML file.
Administration Component	2	Used to retrieve and configure the administrative component of a Search Service Application.
Service Application	8	Used to retrieve, configure, create, delete, upgrade, restore, suspend, and resume a Search Service Application.
Service Application Proxy	4	Used to retrieve, configure, create and delete a Search Service Application proxy.

Creating an SSA topology in Windows PowerShell requires the use of several other enterprise search cmdlets, and they must be used in the correct order. Learning the proper order for the cmdlets and any other logic you need to create a robust set of commands comes with experience and testing. Do not expect to correctly create a Windows PowerShell sequence of command on your first attempt. However, if you make a process diagram, it will help you identify what actions you would complete if you were using the SharePoint 2010 Central Administration website, including what options you would check on the pages displayed and what information would be required. The sample process diagram shown in Figure 12-3 depicts the necessary components and the sequence of steps used in this section to create an SSA.

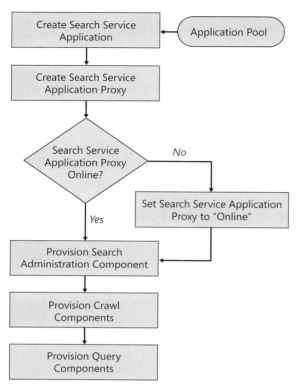

FIGURE 12-3 Components and steps needed to provision a Search Service Application (SSA)

NOTE When creating a large script for the first time, you will find it easier to use the Windows PowerShell Integrated Scripting Environment (ISE). Remember to add the relevant snap-ins.

To provision an SSA using Windows PowerShell, follow these steps.

1. Obtain a reference to the application object you intend to use or create a new application pool. In either case, save the reference to the application pool object in a variable so that you can easily reference it later in the command sequence. To list all application pools and then to save the reference to an existing application pool object, such as SearchAppPool, in the variable, type

```
$AppPool = Get-SPServiceApplicationPool SearchAppPool
```

Or to create a new application pool, type the following command on one line.

```
$AppPool = New-SPServiceApplicationPool -Name SearchAppPool
    -account Contoso\zzSPServices;
```

where SearchAppPool is the name of the new application pool, and Contoso\ zzSPServices is a registered managed account that will be used by the application pool. You can register an Active Directory userid as a SharePoint managed account by typing **$cred = Get-Credential contoso\zzSPServices**. You will be prompted for the password for the credentials and then you would type **New-SPManagedAccount –Credential $cred**.

2. Create an SSA. To complete this command, you must be an administrator on the local computer; therefore, make sure you start the SharePoint 2010 Management Shell as an administrator, and then type the following command on one line.

```
$SearchApp = New-SPEnterpriseSearchServiceApplication
    -Name ContosoSearchServiceApp -ApplicationPool $AppPool;
```

where ContosoSearchServiceApp is the name of the Search Service Application. If you need to create a FAST Search Server 2010 for SharePoint 2010 SSAs, then include the –*SearchApplicationType* parameter with a value of *ExtendedConnector*.

> **NOTE** A service application cannot be created unless an instance of the appropriate service is started on one of the servers in the farm. For the SSA, the SharePoint Server Search service, OSearch14, must be running on one of the servers in the farm. The SharePoint Server Search service is the process that will execute the SSA code. The Search service can run on multiple servers to share the load and provide resiliency. Use SharePoint 2010 Central Administration to check or start this service on the appropriate servers, or for a sample script, see "PowerShell to Create a Service Application" at *http://sharepoint.microsoft.com/blogs/zach/Lists/Posts/Post.aspx?ID=50.*

3. To check that the service application was correctly created, review the output when you type the following command.

```
$SearchApp
```

> **NOTE** The New-SPEnterpriseSearchServiceApplication cmdlet creates three databases: an Administration database, which will be named ContosoSearchServiceApp in this example; a database for the crawl store named ContosoSearchServiceApp_CrawlStore; and a database for the property store named ContosoSearchServiceApp_PropertyStore. To set a different database name, use the –*DatabaseName* parameter.

4. Create a Search Service Application proxy by typing the following command on one line.

```
$SearchAppProxy = New-SPEnterpriseSearchServiceApplicationProxy
    -Name ContosoSearchServiceApplicationProxy
    -SearchApplication $SearchApp;
```

> **NOTE** In a Web-hosted environment, use the –*partitioned* parameter with both the New-SPEnterpriseSearchServiceApplication and the New-SPSPEnterpriseSearchService-ApplicationProxy cmdlets.

5. Verify that the Search Service Application proxy is online; if it is not, change the status to online using the following command.

```
if ($searchappProxy.status -ne "Online") {
    $searchAppProxy.status = "Online";
    $searchAppProxy.Update();
}
```

6. Verify and, if necessary, add the Search Service Application proxy to the default proxy group using the following commands.

```
$pg = Get-SPServiceApplicationProxyGroup;
If ($pg.Proxies -notcontains $SsearchAppProxy) {
    Add-SPServiceApplicationProxyGroupMember $pg -Member $SearchAppProxy;
}
```

NOTE In Chapter 5, when the state service proxy was created, the parameter *–DefaultProxyGroup* was used to add the state service proxy to the default proxy group. Unfortunately, the cmdlet New-SPEnterpriseSearchServiceApplicationProxy does not have a similar parameter, hence the need for step 6.

Configuring the Search Administration Component

SharePoint Server provides two cmdlets, Get and Set, to manage the Search Administration component. Use the following two commands to configure the administration component for the search application referenced in the variable *$searchapp* to server SPS_APP1. If you are planning to host your crawl components on a different server, such as SPS_CWL1, then use that server name in the command.

```
$SearchInstance = Get-SPEnterpriseSearchServiceInstance SPS_APP1;

Set-SPEnterpriseSearchAdministrationComponent `
    –SearchApplication $searchapp –searchserviceinstance $SearchInstance;
```

NOTE In the previous example, the line continuation character (the back tick, also known as the backward apostrophe, `) was used to insert a line break. For long lines, using the line continuation character makes the script more readable, especially if you keep the length of the lines to the typical width of a screen. Then there is no need to use the scroll bar to review all the commands. You can also break a line using the pipe (|) character.

Provision Crawl Topology and Crawl Components

The next step in the process of creating a search application topology is to configure the crawl topology and components. SharePoint Server provides a number of cmdlets to help you create and manage the crawl-related objects listed in Table 12-2.

TABLE 12-2 SharePoint 2010 Enterprise Search Crawl Objects

OBJECT NAME	CMDLET COUNT	DESCRIPTION
Crawl Topology	4	Use to retrieve, set, create, or remove a crawl topology.
Crawl Database	4	Use to retrieve, modify, create, or remove a crawl database, which stores the crawl history data for a Search Service Application.
Crawl Component	3	Use to create, delete, or retrieve information about crawl components from a Search Service Application.
Crawl Content Source	4	Use to create, delete, retrieve, and configure content sources.
Crawl Custom Connector	3	Use to retrieve information and register or remove a protocol for custom crawling.
Crawl Extension	3	Use to retrieve, create, or delete extension rules.
Crawl Mapping	3	Use to retrieve, create, or delete crawl mappings.
Crawl Rule	4	Use to retrieve, set, create, or remove crawl rules.

By default, a Search Service Application created in Windows PowerShell has a crawl topology but is missing both crawl and query components. You can verify this by using either the SharePoint 2010 Central Administration website or by typing the following commands with the resultant sample output shown.

```
Get-SPEnterpriseSearchCrawlTopology -SearchApplication $searchapp
```

```
Id               : 00b976d0-c8f5-4ef6-9d95-a2605a5219d9
CrawlComponents  : {}
State            : Active
ActivationError  :


Get-SPEnterpriseSearchQueryTopology -SearchApplication $searchapp

Id               : 62247917-0a70-4119-9a5e-f4e4c7c3408b
IndexPartitions  : {70021b8f-f583-4b1c-a238-183afaefd5a3}
QueryComponents  : {}
State            : Active
ActivationError  :
```

There is also another issue: It is not possible to add a crawl and query component to the crawl and query topologies, because they are set as active and the state property is read-only and therefore they cannot be changed. This is true for any crawl or query topology, so when it is activated, if more crawl or query servers are added to the SharePoint farm, you will have to rebuild the appropriate topology—hence the need to script the search topology. If you attempted to add a crawl component to the pre-created crawl topology, you will see an error message similar to this one.

```
New-SPEnterpriseSearchCrawlComponent : Crawl topology is not inactive and cannot be
    changed.
At line:1 char:37
+ New-SPEnterpriseSearchCrawlComponent <<<<  -SearchApplication $searchapp
    -CrawlTopology
 $crawltop -CrawlDatabase $cs.name -SearchServiceInstance $searchinstance
    + CategoryInfo          : InvalidData: (Microsoft.Offic...hCrawlComponent:
    NewSearchCrawlComponent) [New-SPEnterpriseSearchCrawlComponent], InvalidOp
    erationException
    + FullyQualifiedErrorId : Microsoft.Office.Server.Search.Cmdlet.
 NewSearchCrawlComponent
```

> **NOTE** Read-only properties can be identified using the Get-Member cmdlet in conjunction with the object's Get- cmdlet, which in this case is Get-SPEnterprise-SearchCrawlTopology. This displays the properties and methods of the object. Property definitions that include *{get;}* are read-only, whereas read-write property definitions include *{get; set;}*. To alter read-only properties, review the methods available for the object and the parameters on the object's associated Set- cmdlet, if one is available.

The workaround for this problem involves creating new crawl and query topologies, which when created are set as inactive. This allows you to add components to the crawl and query topologies. To complete this task, you must include references to the following objects.

- **SSA object** Stored in variable *$searchapp*
- **Server on which the crawl components are to be installed** Stored in variable *$searchinstance*
- **Crawl topology** Stored in variable *$crawltop*
- **Crawl store database**

The variables *$searchapp* and *$searchinstance* were initialized and used during previous steps. Now you must create the crawl topology and obtain the reference to the crawl store. A Search Service Application can have one or more crawl store databases associated with it. References to these crawl stores are saved in the SSA property crawlstores. Therefore, you can obtain the reference to a crawl store database from the SSA variable *$searchapp*, which contains reference to at least one crawl store, ContosoSearchServiceApp_CrawlStore, the one that was created when the SSA was created. To provision a crawl component, use the following steps.

1. Create the crawl topology.

```
$crawltop = New-SPEnterpriseSearchCrawlTopology -SearchApplication $searchapp
```

2. Obtain a reference to the crawl store, ContosoSearchServiceApp_CrawlStore.

```
$cs = $searchapp.crawlstores | where {$_.name -match "Contoso"}
```

3. Create a new crawl component by typing the following command on one line. The sample output is shown below the command.

```
New-SPEnterpriseSearchCrawlComponent -SearchApplication $searchapp `
   -CrawlTopology $crawltop -CrawlDatabase $cs.name `
   -SearchServiceInstance $searchinstance;

Id              : 16e6b1e4-410f-4e94-a531-efc9dfc68a5a
ServerName      : SPS_APP1
IndexLocation   : C:\Program Files\Microsoft Office Servers\14.0\Data\Office Se
                  rver\Applications
CrawlDatabaseId : 23a83c6f-1ed3-4579-8e38-f311bbcbe4ea
State           : Uninitialized
DesiredState    : Uninitialized
```

4. When you have added all the crawl servers (components) to the crawl topology, set the new crawl topology as active by typing the following command.

```
Set-SPEnterpriseSearchCrawlTopology $crawltop -Active
```

REAL WORLD   Specifying an Index Location

When you create a new crawl component, additional parameters are available with the New-SPEnterpriseSearchCrawlComponent cmdlet to specify an index location. If you do not use this parameter, then the default location of the index will be %ProgramFiles%\Microsoft Office Servers\14.0\Data\Office Server\Applications. In a large implementation, you will probably not want to leave the index at this location or on the C drive. In this scenario, use the parameter shown in the following command.

```
New-SPEnterpriseSearchCrawlComponent cmdlet, -IndexLocation "D:\SPS\Indexes"
```

Provision Query Topology and Query Components

The next task in the process is to configure the query topology and components, which are created in a way similar to the crawl topology and components, except that a query component serves query results for a specific index partition and references the property store and not the crawl store. Hence the following directions include a step to reference the property store and an additional step to obtain a reference to an index partition.

> **IMPORTANT** The crawl topology needs to be active before the query topology and components can be created. The cmdlet Set-SPEnterpriseSearchCrawlTopology, used in the steps in the previous section, runs asynchronously, so you should use the command $ct.crawlcomponents to check that the crawl components are in a ready state before continuing with the following steps.

1. Create the new Query topology by typing the following command on one line.

    ```
    $querytop = New-SPEnterpriseSearchQueryTopology
       -SearchApplication $searchapp -Partitions 1;
    ```

2. Obtain a reference to the index partition.

    ```
    $indexpart1 = Get-SPEnterpriseSearchIndexPartition -QueryTopology $querytop;
    ```

3. Create a query component by typing the following command on one line. Set the variable *$searchinstance* to the name of the server that is the name of your query server. The sample output is shown following the command.

    ```
    New-SPEnterpriseSearchQueryComponent -IndexPartition $indexpart1 `
       -QueryTopology $querytop -SearchServiceInstance $searchinstance;
    ```

    ```
    WARNING: column "IndexLocation" does not fit into the display and was removed.

    Name                                         ServerName    Failover0 Sta
                                                               nly       te

    ----                                         ----------    --------- ---
    42592424-1915-4130-8d27-cf8d4cd2c5bb-query-0 SPS_APP1      False     Uni
    ```

4. Obtain a reference to the property store, ContosoSearchServiceApp_PropertyStore.

    ```
    $ps = $searchapp.PropertyStores | where {$_.name -match "Contoso"};
    ```

5. Associate the index partition to the property store.

    ```
    Set-SPEnterpriseSearchIndexPartition $indexpart1 -PropertyDatabase $ps;
    ```

6. When all the query servers (components) are associated with the query topology, set the query topology as active using the following command.

    ```
    Set-SPEnterpriseSearchQueryTopology -identity $querytop -Active;
    ```

```
Get-SPEnterpriseSearchCrawlTopology -SearchApplication $searchapp |
    where {$_.State -eq "Inactive"} |
    Remove-SPEnterpriseSearchCrawlTopology;

Get-SPEnterpriseSearchQueryTopology -SearchApplication $searchapp |
    where {$_.State -eq "Inactive"} |
Remove-SPEnterpriseSearchQueryTopology;
```

Administering Content Sources

There are four cmdlets you can use to manage content sources.

- Get-SPEnterpriseSearchCrawlContentSource

- Set-SPEnterpriseSearchCrawlContentSource

- New-SPEnterpriseSearchCrawlContentSource

- Remove-SPEnterpriseSearchCrawlContentSource

Just as with any other Windows PowerShell cmdlet, you can use Get-Help to learn more about them. For example, type **Get-Help net-spe*content*** to get more information about how to use New-SPEnterpriseSearchCrawlContentSource. Using wildcards reduces the amount of typing necessary.

To administer content sources, you first need to know which content sources are available. In Windows PowerShell, you can display a list of content sources and the status of the crawling for a specific Search Service Application with the following command (which is followed by an output example).

```
Get-SPEnterpriseSearchCrawlContentSource -SearchApplication $searchapp
```

Name	Id	Type	CrawlState	CrawlCompleted
Local SharePo...	2	SharePoint	Idle	05/01/2010 23:58:20
FilesShares	3	File	Idle	
Old Intranet	5	Web	CrawlStarting	

where the variable *$searchapp* contains a reference to a Search Service Application. This variable can be initialized by typing a command similar to

```
$searchapp = Get-SPEnterpriseSearchServiceApplication |
where {$_.name -eq "Search Service Application"};
```

To list all Search Service Applications, use the following command.

```
Get-SPEnterpriseSearchServiceApplication
```

The properties and methods that allow you to manipulate the collection of content sources can be found by piping the output of the Get-SPEnterpriseSearchCrawlContentSource into the Get-Member cmdlet.

Scheduling Content Sources

The content source object contains properties for both the full crawl and incremental crawl schedules: FullCrawlSchedule and IncrementalCrawlSchedule. These properties are references to a schedule object, which has its own properties and methods. You can schedule both the full and the incremental crawl for different types of periods. These are called *schedule types*, and they dictate the type of schedule object created and referenced by the FullCrawlSchedule and IncrementalCrawlSchedule properties. Following are the available schedule object types.

- **Daily** Use to specify the number of days between crawls.
- **Weekly** Use to specify the number of weeks between crawls.
- **Monthly** Use to specify the days of the month and months of the year when the crawl should occur.
- **MonthlyDayOf Week** Use to specify the days of the month, the weeks of the month, and the months of the year when the crawl should occur.

When full and incremental crawl schedules are defined, the schedule object type and the schedule details can be displayed as shown in the following examples and sample output. If a schedule is not defined, then the following commands will result in an error message, "You cannot call a method on a null-valued expression."

```
$csource = Get-SPEnterpriseSearchCrawlContentSource "Local SharePoint sites"
   -sea $searchapp;
$csource.FullCrawlSchedule.GetType();
```

```
IsPublic IsSerial Name                          BaseType
-------- -------- ----                          --------
True     False    MonthlyDateSchedule           Microsoft.Office....
```

```
$csource.FullCrawlSchedule;
```

```
DaysOfMonth     : Day2
MonthsOfYear    : January
BeginDay        : 30
BeginMonth      : 1
BeginYear       : 2010
StartHour       : 11
StartMinute     : 15
RepeatDuration  : 0
RepeatInterval  : 0
Description     : At 11:15 on day 2 of Jan, starting 30/01/2010
NextRunTime     : 02/01/2011 11:15:00
```

```
$csource.IncrementalCrawlSchedule.GetType();
```

```
IsPublic IsSerial Name                          BaseType
-------- -------- ----                          --------
True     False    DailySchedule                 Microsoft.Office....
```

```
$csource.IncrementalCrawlSchedule;
```

```
DaysInterval    : 1
BeginDay        : 29
BeginMonth      : 11
BeginYear       : 2009
StartHour       : 0
StartMinute     : 0
RepeatDuration  : 0
RepeatInterval  : 0
Description     : At 00:00 every day, starting 29/11/2009
NextRunTime     : 08/01/2010 00:00:00
```

By storing the schedule object in a variable, you can change many of the properties, as you have done for other object properties in previous examples; however, it is easier to use the Set-SPEnterpriseSearchCrawlContentSource cmdlet. The parameter –*ScheduleType* defines the type of crawl, which can be set as Full or Incremental. There are then a set of parameters to configure the schedules, summarized in Table 12-3.

TABLE 12-3 SharePoint 2010 Enterprise Search Full Crawl Schedule Parameters

PARAMETER NAME	NOTES
–*DailyCrawlSchedule,* –*WeeklyCrawlSchedule,* –*MonthlyCrawlSchedule*	Use to set the type of schedule. No value is necessary for these parameters; by specifying one of these parameters you set the schedule type.
–*CrawlScheduleDaysOfMonth*	Specifies the days on which to crawl when the –*MonthlyCrawlSchedule* parameter is used.
–*CrawlScheduleDaysOfWeek*	Specifies the days on which to crawl when the –*WeeklyCrawlSchedule* parameter is used.
–*CrawlScheduleMonthsOfYear*	Specifies the months on which to crawl when –*MonthlyCrawlSchedule* parameter is used. Valid values are 1 to 12.
–*CrawlScheduleRunEveryInterval*	The unit of the interval is dependent on the type of schedule. For example, if schedule type is daily and the value of this parameter is 6, then the schedule is run every 6 days.
–*CrawlScheduleRepeatDuration*	Use to specify the number of times to repeat the crawl schedule.

continued on the next page

PARAMETER NAME	NOTES
–*CrawlScheduleRepeatInterval*	Use to specify the number of minutes between each repeat interval.
–*CrawlScheduleStartDateTime*	Use to specify when the initial crawl should occur. This value cannot be set using the SharePoint 2010 Central Administration website. The default value is midnight on the current day

To schedule a full crawl at 11:15 on day 2 of every month, starting 09/04/2010 for the content source object reference to in the variable *$cscource*, use the following command.

```
Set-SPEnterpriseSearchCrawlContentSource $csource
-ScheduleType Full -MonthlyCrawlSchedule `
  -CrawlScheduleDaysOfMonth 2 -CrawlScheduleStartDateTime "09/04/2010 11:15";
```

To schedule a full crawl at 01:45 every day starting 08/07/2010 for the Local SharePoint Sites content source created in the Search Service Application referenced in the variable *$searchapp*, use the following command.

```
Set-SPEnterpriseSearchCrawlContentSource "Local SharePoint Sites" -sea $searchapp `
   -ScheduleType Full -DailyCrawlSchedule -CrawlScheduleStartDateTime
"08/07/2010 01:45";
```

Creating and Deleting Content Sources

Content sources contain data that refers to shared network folders, SharePoint sites, other websites, Exchange public folders, third-party applications, databases, and so on. These different types of content sources have different connection properties, and the SharePoint 2010 Central Administration Web pages prompt you appropriately for those properties. Each content source object represents one content source of particular content source type. To use Windows PowerShell to create a new content source object, you use just one cmdlet, New-SPEnterpriseSearchCrawlContentSource, no matter the type of content source object you want to create. Unlike the Central Administration Web pages, this cmdlet does not prompt for the relevant data; therefore, before you can successfully create content sources in Windows PowerShell, you need to be familiar with creating them in the browser.

The New-SPEnterpriseSearchCrawlContentSource –*Type* parameter specifies the indexing connector used to access data from the content source. The valid values for the –*Type* parameter are *web*, *SharePoint*, *custom*, *LotusNotes*, *File*, *Exchange*, *O12Business*, and *Business* (for the Business Connectivity Service) and are used to create the appropriate content source object. In this way, the content source object is similar to the schedule object described in the previous section—there are a number of types of content source objects, just as there are a number of types of schedule objects.

You cannot specify the crawl schedule for the new content source with New-SPEnterprise-SearchCrawlContentSource; therefore, you will need to configure it after the content source is created, using Set-SPEnterpriseSearchCrawlContentSource.

The three mandatory parameters for New-SPEnterpriseSearchCrawlContentSource are

- *–Type*
- *–Identity*, the name of the content source
- *–SearchApplication*

The following example and sample output show how to create a content source for a file share.

```
New-SPEnterpriseSearchCrawlContentSource "Contoso File Share" `
    -SearchApplication $searchapp -Type File `
    -StartAddresses file://win08r2/foldershare1, file://win08r2/foldershare2;
```

Name	Id	Type	CrawlState	CrawlCompleted
----	--	----	----------	--------------
Contoso File ...	3	File	Idle	

The following example and sample output show how to create a content source for a website.

```
New-SPEnterpriseSearchCrawlContentSource "Old Intranet" `
    -SearchApplication $searchapp -Type Web `
    -StartAddresses "http://oldintranet.contoso.msft/";
```

Name	Id	Type	CrawlState	CrawlCompleted
----	--	----	----------	--------------
Old Intranet	14	Web	Idle	

The following example and sample output removes the content source.

```
Remove-SPEnterpriseSearchCrawlContentSource "old intranet" `
    -SearchApplication $searchapp;
```

```
Confirm
Are you sure you want to perform this action?
Performing operation "Remove-SPEnterpriseSearchCrawlContentSource" on Target
"Old Intranet".
[Y] Yes  [A] Yes to All  [N] No  [L] No to All  [S] Suspend  [?] Help
(default is "Y"):
```

Starting and Stopping Content Source Crawling

You can obtain information about the status of crawling of content sources by using the properties CrawlState (alias for CrawlStatus), CrawlCompleted, and CrawlStarted. You can initiate crawling of content sources by using the methods StartFullCrawl and StartIncrementalCrawl. If you initiate an incremental crawl before you have run a full crawl, then the content source is fully crawled. There are also methods to pause, resume, and stop crawling.

Using the content source methods and properties, you can create several useful administrative scripts. The following script starts an incremental crawl for each content source that has a status of Idle that cycles through the collection of content sources associated with the Contoso Search Service Application.

```
$searchContoso = Get-SPEnterpriseSearchServiceApplication |
    where {$_.name -like 'cont*'};


$csources = $searchContoso | Get-SPEnterpriseSearchCrawlContentSource;


foreach ($csource in $csources) {
    if ($csource.CrawlStatus -eq "Idle") {
        Write-Host "Starting Incremental crawl for content source:" $csource.Name;
        $csource.StartIncrementalCrawl();
    } else {
        Write-Host "Incremental Crawl not started:" $csource.name " Status:" `
         $csource.CrawlState;
    }
}
```

In the next example, the script starts a full crawl for the content source associated with a specific Web application.

```
# Set variable to the save the name of the web application
$webapp = "http://intranet.contoso.msft"


# Get a list of Search Service Application proxies associated with the web application
$sp = (Get-SPWebApplication $webapp).ServiceApplicationProxyGroup.Proxies |
 where { $_.typename -like 'search*'};


# Get a list of content sources associated with the Search Service Applications
# that are set to crawl the web application. Wildcard comparison is included to
# check for any fully qualified domain name or any subsites or site collections
# that are specifically included in a content source.
$csources = foreach ($searcha in $sp) {
 Get-SPEnterpriseSearchServiceApplication |
 where { $_.name -eq $searcha.GetSearchApplicationName()} |
 Get-SPEnterpriseSearchCrawlContentSource |
 where {$_.StartAddresses -like $webapp + "*"};
}
```

```
# Start a full crawl for any content source whose status equal to idle
foreach ($csource in $csources) {
 $csource.StartFullCrawl() |
 where {$cs.CrawlStatus -eq "Idle"};
}
```

 REAL WORLD **Repeated Use of Commands**

I f you find that you are typing the same sets of commands again and again, you should enclose those commands in a function or store them in a file with the extension .ps1, known as a Windows PowerShell script. This allows you to reuse the set of commands without re-entering each command. For example, copy the set of commands shown in the previous example below the comment line in the following script. Because the function accepts the variable *$webapp* as its input parameter, delete the line that initializes the *$webapp* variable from the copied code.

```
Function Start-FullCrawlWebApp ([string]$webapp)
{

# Copy script below this line

} # End of Start-FullCrawlWebApp Function
```

Removing all comment lines (to save space here), your function should look similar to the following function.

```
Function Start-FullCrawlWebApp ([string]$webapp)
{

  # Copy script below this line
  $sp = (Get-SPWebApplication $webapp).ServiceApplicationProxyGroup.Proxies |
   where { $_.typename -like 'search*'};

  $csources = foreach ($searcha in $sp) {
   Get-SPEnterpriseSearchServiceApplication | `
   where { $_.name -eq $searcha.GetSearchApplicationName()} | `
   Get-SPEnterpriseSearchCrawlContentSource | `
    where {$_.StartAddresses -like $webapp + "*"};
  }

  foreach ($csource in $csources) {
    $csource.StartFullCrawl() | where {$cs.CrawlStatus -eq "Idle"};
  }
```

continued on the next page

The type [string] placed before the input variable *$webapp* ensures that the function receives the correct data. Prefixing an input variable with a type constraint is optional and will generate an error if the function is not used with the correct data.

To start a full crawl of the Web application *http://www.contoso.msft*, use the following command.

```
Start-FullCrawlWebApp -webapp http://www.contoso.msft
```

You can the place functions in Windows PowerShell script files, such as the Windows PowerShell profile as described in Chapter 5, so that they are always available whenever you start the SharePoint 2010 Management Shell.

> **MORE INFO** For more information about Windows PowerShell functions, see Chapter 6, "Mastering Aliases, Functions, and Objects," in *Windows PowerShell 2.0 Administrator's Pocket Consultant* (2009, Microsoft Press) by William R. Stanek, and the TechNet webcast "Functions, Filters and Efficiency in Windows PowerShell," by Don Jones.

Modifying Authoritative Pages and Search Metadata

Enterprise search in SharePoint Server is an enormous subject, and you will find more about the subject in the section titled "Deploying and Managing FAST Search with Windows PowerShell" later in this chapter. The following sections review two other search-related areas: authoritative pages and search metadata.

Configuring Authoritative Pages

For many years, people who work with electronic data have recognized that information workers spend a considerable amount of time searching for information to complete a task. And they spend that time not just using search engines, but also in a number of locations, such as file shares, intranet websites, customer records management systems, and so on. Although people do manage to find useful information, it may not be what they are originally looking for, and the time spent searching for information could be costing companies a great deal of money in wasted time. Implementing an enterprise search solution that indexes content and provides a suitable user interface can solve some of these productivity issues. An important part of the solution is to ensure that the search results are ranked according to relevancy and the user is provided with more than a simple search box to enter a query. This is where authoritative pages help, because they indicate links to content that are more important than others, and creating search metadata provides a filtering mechanism when searching for content.

The aim of authoritative pages is to categorize Web pages or sites into one of four authoritative levels. In the SharePoint 2010 Central Administration website, these levels are

- Most authoritative pages
- Second-level authoritative pages
- Third-level authoritative pages
- Sites to demote

You can use two sets of cmdlets in Windows PowerShell, as explained in Table 12-4, to complete similar tasks that rank Web pages or sites.

TABLE 12-4 SharePoint 2010 Enterprise Search Authoritative and Demoted Query Objects

OBJECT NAME	CMDLET COUNT	DESCRIPTION
Query Authority	4	Use to retrieve, set, create, and remove authoritative pages. The parameter –*Level* is used to assign an authoritative level, where values are 0, 1, or 2, and where pages with a value of 0 are the most valuable authoritative pages.
Query Demoted	3	Use to retrieve, create, and remove demoted site rules. A site that is added as a query-demoted site is de-emphasized in terms of relevancy. Therefore, pages from demoted sites will appear near the end of the search results.

The following examples and sample output show how to create, retrieve, amend, and delete authoritative pages.

```
# Assign www.contoso.msft as one of the most authoritative pages
New-SPEnterpriseSearchQueryAuthority -Url "http://www.contoso.msft" `
   -SearchApplication $searchapp -Level 0;
```

```
Url                              Level     Status
---                              -----     ------
http://www.contoso.msft/         0         StatusNotInitialized
```

```
# List all sites that are assigned an authoritative page level
Get-SPEnterpriseSearchQueryAuthority -SearchApplication $searchapp;
```

```
Url                              Level     Status
---                              -----     ------
http://intranet.contoso.msft/    0         StatusNotInitialized
http://www.contoso.msft/         0         StatusNotInitialized
```

```
# Change the authoritative page level to Second-level authoritative pages
Set-SPEnterpriseSearchQueryAuthority -Identity "http://intranet.contoso.msft" `
   -SearchApplication $searchapp -Level 1;


# Remove the assignment of an authoritative page level from a site
Remove-SPEnterpriseSearchQueryAuthority "http://www.contoso.msft" -sea $searchapp;
```

```
Confirm
Are you sure you want to perform this action?
Performing operation "Remove-SPEnterpriseSearchQueryAuthority" on Target
"http://www.contoso.msft/".
[Y] Yes  [A] Yes to All  [N] No  [L] No to All  [S] Suspend  [?] Help
(default is "Y"):
```

```
# Check that the authoritative page level for the site was removed.
Get-SPEnterpriseSearchQueryAuthority -SearchApplication $searchapp;
```

```
Url                                 Level      Status
---                                 -----      ------
http://intranet.contoso.msft/        1         StatusNotInitialized
```

The following example and sample output show how to create and retrieve information about demoted sites.

```
New-SPEnterpriseSearchQueryDemoted -Url "http://oldintranet.contoso.msft" `
   -SearchApplication $searchapp;
```

```
Url                                          CrawledDocumentCount
---                                          --------------------
http://oldintranet.contoso.msft/              4
```

Maintaining Metadata Categories and Properties

Enterprise search, as it indexes different content sources, discovers new properties, which are known as *crawled properties*, such as Author and Modified By. Properties are also known as *metadata*, and you can use the values of properties to limit the number of search results returned. However, the number of crawled properties can be enormous, and if each crawled property were exposed, it would result in a very busy and probably unusable search interface. SharePoint Server can be configured to identify those crawled properties that are important for the business needs, which in turn can be used in the search experience. This subset of crawled properties is referred to as *managed properties*. Metadata mapping is the process of mapping crawled properties to managed properties.

Crawled properties are grouped in metadata categories, based on the type of content source indexed. Therefore, categories help give meaning to the crawled properties, whose names are sometimes lengthy and obtuse, as well as aid in helping find the crawled property that you want to map to a managed property. In Windows PowerShell, a number of cmdlets are associated with objects to manage metadata crawled and managed properties, as shown in Table 12-5.

TABLE 12-5 SharePoint 2010 Enterprise Search Metadata Objects

OBJECT NAME	CMDLET COUNT	DESCRIPTION
Metadata Category	4	Use to retrieve, set, create, and remove crawled property categories.
Metadata Crawled Property	3	Use to retrieve, set, and create metadata crawled properties.
Metadata Managed Property	4	Use to retrieve, set, create, and remove metadata managed properties.
Metadata Mapping	4	Use to retrieve, set, create, and remove metadata managed property mappings.

Each Search Service Application maintains a list of crawled properties. The following example shows how to count the number of crawled properties maintained by the Search Service Application referenced by the variable *$seachapp*.

```
@(Get-SPEnterpriseSearchMetadataCrawledProperty –Search $searchapp).count
```

The following examples and sample output show the number of crawled properties by category and the number of crawled properties that are mapped to managed properties grouped by category.

```
Get-SPEnterpriseSearchMetadataCrawledProperty -SearchApplication $searchapp | `
    sort categoryname, name | group -property CategoryName;
```

```
Count Name                    Group
----- ----                    -----
   57 Basic                   {136, 77, 137, 78...}
    2 Business Data           {320, 321}
   14 Mail                    {122, 123, 124, 133...}
    3 Notes                   {322, 324, 323}
   22 Office                  {189, 186, 317, 182...}
   53 People                  {15, 16, 17, 18...}
  159 SharePoint              {201, 297, 295, 200...}
   51 Web                     {144, 113, 145, 114...}
```

```
Get-SPEnterpriseSearchMetadataCrawledProperty -SearchApplication $searchapp | `
    where {$_.isMappedToContents -eq $True} | sort categoryname, name | `
group -property CategoryName | sort count -Descending;
```

```
Count Name                    Group
----- ----                    -----
   67 SharePoint              {337, 291, 239, 238...}
   12 Web                     {113, 114, 115, 116...}
   10 Office                  {389, 388, 181, 177...}
    4 People                  {18, 20, 22, 48}
    3 Basic                   {137, 135, 101}
    1 Mail                    {125}
```

The following example and sample output shows the crawled properties "Manager" found in the "People" category.

```
$crawlprop = Get-SPEnterpriseSearchMetadataCrawledProperty `
  -SearchApplication $searchapp | `
  where {($_.categoryname -eq "People") -and ($_.name -like "*Manager*")};


$crawlprop;
```

```
Name                : urn:schemas-microsoft-com:sharepoint:portal:profile:Manage
                      r
CategoryName        : People
Propset             : 00110329-0000-0110-c000-000000111146
IsMappedToContents  : False
VariantType         : 31
```

The VariantType property indicates the data type of the crawled property. To map a crawled property to a managed property, both properties must be of the same data type. The New-SPEnterpriseSearchMetadataManagedProperty cmdlet uses the –*Type* parameter to specify the data type for managed property. Unfortunately, the values for –*Type* do not match the values for the VariantType property. The list of supported data types, with their associated VariantType values and –*Type* parameters, are shown in Table 12-6.

TABLE 12-6 Metadata Property Data Types

DATA TYPE	CRAWLED PROPERTY VARIANTTYPE	MANAGED PROPERTY –*TYPE* PARAMETER
Text	31	1
Integer	20	2
Decimal	5	3
Date and Time	64	4
Yes/No	11	5
Binary Data	65	6

Therefore, before you can automate the creation of a managed property from a crawled property, you need to create a script to translate values between the VariantType property and the –*Type* parameter. This can easily be achieved by using a hash table, also known as a dictionary, which allows you to store data in a key-value pair association, as shown in the following example.

```
$MetaDataTypes=@{31 =1;20=2;5=3;64=4;11=5;65=6}
```

Therefore, when you use $MetaDataTypes[$crawlprop.VariantType] where *$crawlprop. VariantType* has a value of 31, the output will be 1. This technique is used in the following example, which lists a function that, given a crawled property, will create a new managed property and map the crawled property to the managed property. The function accepts the following four input parameters.

- **$PropName**   The word or words that will uniquely identify the crawled property. Thus, you do not need to know the fully qualified name of a crawled property to use this function; you can simply enter part of the crawled property name.

- **$PropCat**   The category for the crawled property. The name of a crawled property can occur from different connectors. The category can be used to uniquely identify the crawled property.

- **$ManName**   The name for the new managed property.

- **$search**   The first few characters that will uniquely identify the name of the search application.

The function checks that only one crawled property exists and that the crawled property is not already mapped to an existing managed property before creating a managed property and creating the mapping.

```
Function Set-ManagedPropFromName
([string] $PropName, [string] $PropCat, [string] $ManName, [string] $search)
{
  # Create a hashtype to convert VariantType to -Type values for data types.
  # Supported data types:Text, Integer, Decimal, Date and Time, Yes/No, Binary Data
  $MetaDataTypes = @{31=1; 20=2; 5=3; 64=4; 11=5; 65=6}

  # Get Search Service Application object from value in input parameter $search
  $searchapp = Get-SPEnterpriseSearchServiceApplication | `
   where {$_.Name -like $search+"*"};

  # Get crawled property object that matches crawled category and crawled property
  # name provided from input parameters $PropCat and $PropName
  $crawledProp = Get-SPEnterpriseSearchMetadataCrawledProperty -Search $searchapp `
   -ErrorAction SilentlyContinue | `
   where {($_.CategoryName -eq $PropCat) -and ($_.Name -like "*"+$PropName+"*")};

  # If no crawled property identified or more than one crawled property identified
  # using name from input parameter $PropName, write error message
```

```
  If (@($crawledProp).count -ne 1)
  {
    Write-Host "Error: Crawled Property: $PropName had: " + `
     @($crawledProp).count + "occurrences.";
  } else {
    Write-Host "Crawled Property: $crawledProp found";

    # Check that property not already mapped to managed property
    If ($crawledProp.IsMappedToContents)
    {
        Write-Host "Error: Crawled Property property: $PropName already mapped.";
    } else {
      Write-Host "Check whether Managed Property already Exists";
      # Check whether Managed Property already exists.
      $ManProp = Get-SPEnterpriseSearchMetadataManagedProperty $ManName `
        -SearchApplication $searchapp -ErrorAction SilentlyContinue;

      If ($ManProp)
      {
        Write-Host "Error: Managed Property: $ManName already exists.";
      } else {
        Write-Host "Create Managed Property: $ManName"
        $ManProp = New-SPEnterpriseSearchMetadataManagedProperty $ManName `
        -SearchApplication $searchapp -Type $MetaDataTypes[$CrawledProp.VariantType] `
        -Description "$ManName : $PropCat" -Retrievable $True `
        -EnabledForScoping $True;

        Write-Host "Create Mapping";
        New-SPEnterpriseSearchMetadataMapping -CrawledProperty $crawledProp `
         -ManagedProperty $ManProp -SearchApplication $searchapp;
      }
    }
  }
} # End of Function Set-ManagedPropFromName
```

The following example and sample output shows how to use the Set-ManagedPropFrom-Name function defined previously to create a new manager property named ManagerAD and then map the Manager crawled property from the "People" category to the "ManagerAD" managed property:

```
Set-ManagedPropFromName -PropName "Manager" -PropCat "People" '
  -ManName "ManagerAD" -search "Search";
```

```
Crawled Property: 24 found
Check whether Managed Property already Exists
Create Managed Property: ManagerAD
Create Mapping

CrawledPropset            : 00110329-0000-0110-c000-000000111146
CrawledPropertyName       : urn:schemas-microsoft-com:sharepoint:portal:
                            profile:Manager
CrawledPropertyVariantType : 31
ManagedPid                : 407
```

Property mappings associated with a managed property must be deleted before the managed property is deleted. The following example finds the mapping associated with the ManagerAD managed property and removes the mapping before deleting the managed property.

```
get-SPEnterpriseSearchMetadataMapping -SearchApplication $searchapp `
    -ManagedProperty "ManagerAD" | Remove-SPEnterpriseSearchMetadataMapping
    -Confirm:$false;

Remove-SPEnterpriseSearchMetadataManagedProperty "ManagerAD" `
    -SearchApplication $searchapp -Confirm:$false;
```

BEST PRACTICES   Destructive cmdlets such as those with the verb Delete or Remove usually pause during execution to output a confirmation message, and they require user input to continue. This characteristic can be inconvenient when creating functions or scripts. When the *–Confirm* parameter is set to false, no such input is required. Keep in mind, however, that these destructive cmdlets were set up to require confirmation for a reason, and you must test your scripts thoroughly before using the technique involving the *–Confirm* parameter to override the need for user confirmation. You can also use the *–Confirm* parameter on many cmdlets to force confirmation of an action. To create scripts that support the *–Confirm* parameter, see "Supporting *–WhatIf*, *–Confirm*, *–Verbose*—in SCRIPTS!" at *http://blogs.msdn.com/powershell/archive/2007/02/25/supporting-whatif-confirm-verbose-in-scripts.aspx*.

Deploying and Managing FAST Search with Windows PowerShell

Microsoft acquired the Norwegian enterprise search company FAST Search & Transfer on April 25, 2008. This was the largest enterprise infrastructure acquisition ever made by Microsoft. The product acquired has now been released as part of the SharePoint 2010 product family. And just like any other technology, before you can start to automate administrative tasks, you need to understand the technology you are trying to automate. Because this section's topic is how to use Windows PowerShell with FAST Search Server 2010 for SharePoint, rather than an explanation of FAST Search Server 2010 for SharePoint, you need to read this section in conjunction with Chapter 11.

Briefly, when FAST Search Server for SharePoint is installed, it adds additional servers to your existing SharePoint Server topology, plus it installs software on servers that run Share-Point Server. FAST Search Server for SharePoint consists of the following three main parts.

- Servers that run FAST Search Server for SharePoint. This includes at least two servers. One is a server designated as a FAST Search Server (back-end), which runs services such as query matching, indexing, and document/item processing; the other is a server for monitoring FAST Search. One of the FAST back-end servers runs the administrative services. The admin server must be configured and running before you can add one or more non-admin servers to a multiple server deployment.

- FAST Query Search Service Application (SSA) installed on the SharePoint Server Web server to provide query Web Parts, integration capabilities, and query capabilities by using the query object model to talk to the FAST back-end for query matching and processing.

- FAST Content Search Service Application (SSA) installed on a SharePoint Server application server, where it replaces a portion of the crawler so that it can retrieve content that it then sends to the FAST back-end server for indexing.

There are several options that allow you to manage a FAST Search Server for SharePoint installation. These include

- **The SharePoint 2010 Central Administration website**   The administration pages can be found by navigating from Central Administration to Applications Management to Manage Service Applications, where you click the SSA you want to manage. You then can administer content sources and crawl rules as you do with SharePoint Server enterprise search. In the navigation area at left, you also can click FAST Search Admin-istration to administer the management of crawled and managed properties, property extraction, and spell checking. Not all server-related administrative tasks can be com-pleted using these Web pages, however.

- **FAST Search Windows PowerShell cmdlets**   These can be used for specific administrator tasks, including uploading a compiled dictionary to the resource store, creating a security user store, and mapping metadata to indexable fields. Just as there is a management shell for SharePoint Server, so there is a management shell for FAST Search for SharePoint.

- **SharePoint 2010 Management Shell**   Many of the cmdlets you've seen in this chapter and in Chapter 5 can be used to administer a SharePoint Server installation that has FAST Search Server for SharePoint installed. For example, you can use them to create Search Service Applications and content sources.

- **FAST Search administrative executable commands** These commands, such as nctrl, allow you to manage a FAST node.
- **The FAST Search Site Administration feature** This allows you to delegate management of FAST search keywords, user contexts, and site promotion and demotion to users who own the content. This is the easiest way to tune relevance.

> **IMPORTANT** Learning to use Windows PowerShell with FAST Search Server for SharePoint is more important than knowing how to use it to manage other aspects of SharePoint Server, because some administrative operations can only be performed by cmdlets or other command-line tools.

The following sections cover these topics related to FAST Search.
- Using the FAST Search Server 2010 for SharePoint Shell
- cmdlets for FAST Search Server for SharePoint 2010
- Adding FAST Search Server for SharePoint 2010 to a SharePoint 2010 Installation

 REAL WORLD Activating SharePoint Features

FAST Search Site Administration provides three links under Site Collection Administration on the Site Settings page. These links are FAST Search keywords, FAST Search site promotion and demotion, and FAST Search user context. For these links to be available, the Searchextensions feature must be enabled at the site collection level. Like many features scoped at the site collection or site (web) level, you might want to activate or deactivate the feature on many site collections or sites through your farm, depending on specific criteria. In a farm with many site collections or sites, it could take a considerable amount of time to complete this task using the browser. An alternative is to get a developer to create a small program that would automate the task, but another alternative provides an example of how Windows PowerShell can minimize the amount of time needed to complete such a task.

The SharePoint Server Enterprise Site Collection feature, also known as PremiumSite, is not visible through the browser. It is activated when the Searchextensions feature is activated; that is, Searchextensions is a hidden feature that cannot be activated from the Site Collection Administration Features page, but it can be activated using Windows PowerShell. Use the following script to activate the Searchextensions feature for all site collections within a Web application.

```
$SiteScope = Start-SPAssignment;
Foreach ($Site in ($SiteScope | Get-SPSite -webappl
   http://intranet.contoso.msft))
{
 if (!(Get-SPFeature searchextensions -site $Site.Url `
```

continued on the next page

```
     -ErrorAction SilentlyContinue;))
  {
    Write-Host "Enabling feature for site collection" $Site.Url;
    Enable-SPFeature "searchextensions" -Url $Site.Url;
  }
}
Stop-SPAssignment $SiteScope;
```

You can develop a similar script to deactivate the Searchextensions feature, and you can add other criteria to return only site collections within a specific Web application. When activating features scoped at the site (web) level, for example, you could filter the site returned to include only blog sites.

Using the FAST Search Server 2010 for SharePoint Shell

You can access the FAST Search Server 2010 for SharePoint shell by clicking Start, selecting Programs, and then selecting Microsoft FAST Search Server 2010 For SharePoint. Then select Microsoft FAST Search Server 2010 For SharePoint. A review of the properties of the shortcut exposes following the command.

```
C:\Windows\System32\WindowsPowerShell\v1.0\PowerShell.exe  -NoExit  " &
 ' C:\FASTSearch\\installer\scripts\shell\FastSearch.ps1 ' "
```

The Windows PowerShell profile file, FastSearch.ps1, contains the following code, plus a signature.

```
Add-PSSnapin AdminSnapIn
Add-PSSnapin Microsoft.FASTSearch.PowerShell

$FASTSEARCH = [environment]::GetEnvironmentVariable("FASTSEARCH","Machine")
$path = Join-Path -path $FASTSEARCH -childPath "bin"
$envpath = Join-Path -path $FASTSEARCH -childpath "etc"
Update-FormatData -AppendPath "$envpath\FASTSearch.Format.ps1xml"
cd $path
```

This profile file completes the following tasks.

- Adds two Windows PowerShell snap-ins so you have access to the new FAST Search Server for SharePoint cmdlets.

- Obtains the environment variable *%FASTSEARCH%* that contains the drive and folder where the FAST Search Server for SharePoint files were installed and stores the information in a variable, *$path*.

- Creates a variable, *$envpath*, to store the folder %FASTSEARCH%*foldername*. This variable is then used to reload the formatting data from the XML file FASTSearch.Format. ps1xml. The Format.ps1xml files in Windows PowerShell define the default display of objects in Windows PowerShell. To find out more about this file, type **Get-Help about_Format.ps1xml** in a Windows PowerShell console.

■ Change the current directory to %FASTSEARCH%\bin. This allows you to use the management shell to run FAST Search administration programs that live in the bin directory, such as psconfig and nctl, without specifying a path for them.

> **NOTE** The environment variable *%FASTSEARCH%* was created when FAST Search Server for SharePoint 2010 was installed, and by default the installation location is C:\FASTSEARCH. This folder and its subfolders contain a number of Windows PowerShell scripts that you can find by searching for .ps1, mostly in the %FASTSEARCH%\installer \scripts directory. You might consider adding this folder to the environment variable *%PATH%*, especially during the installation process. To have this directory added to the path variable every time you start the management shell, add the following lines to the profile file.
>
> ```
> $ScriptPath = Join-Path -Path $FASTSEARCH -ChildPath "installer\scripts";
> $env:path += "; $ScriptPath";
> ```

> **SECURITY ALERT** For some tasks, you will need to start the Microsoft FAST Search Server 2010 for SharePoint Shell as an administrator, such as when you complete the post-installation tasks. To do this, right-click Microsoft FAST Search Server 2010 For SharePoint and then select Run As Administrator.

When the FAST Search Server 2010 for SharePoint shell is started, you may receive an error message that says "FastSearch.ps1 cannot be loaded because the execution of scripts is disabled on this system," as shown in Figure 12-4.

FIGURE 12-4 Error message that you may see when opening the FAST Search 2010 for SharePoint shell

If this happens, complete the following procedure.

1. Close the management shell.
2. Right-click the Microsoft FAST Search Server 2010 For SharePoint shortcut and then click Run As Administrator. You will then see the error message "Cannot be loaded."
3. Type the following command and answer **Y** when prompted.

   ```
   Set-ExecutionPolicy RemoteSigned
   ```

You will see output similar to the following.

```
Execution Policy Change
The execution policy helps protect you from scripts that you do not trust.
Changing the execution policy might expose you to the security risks described
in the about_Execution_Policies help topic. Do you want to change the execution
policy?
[Y] Yes  [N] No  [S] Suspend  [?] Help (default is "Y"): Y
```

4. Close the management shell and then reopen it.

NOTE You must run the command Set-ExecutionPolicy as an administrator because it alters the registry key HKEY_LOCAL_MACHINE\SOFTWARE\Microsoft\PowerShell\1 \ShellIds\Microsoft.PowerShell. Execution policy settings are discussed in Chapter 5.

cmdlets for FAST Search Server 2010 for SharePoint

FAST Search Server 2010 for SharePoint shell enables access to eight administrative and over 70 FAST search–related cmdlets. You can see a list of these cmdlets by typing the following commands.

```
Get-Command -PSSnapin "AdminSnapIn";
@(Get-Command -PSSnapin "AdminSnapIn").count;
Get-Command -PSSnapin "Microsoft.FASTSearch.PowerShell";
@(Get-Command -PSSnapin "Microsoft.FASTSearch.PowerShell").count;
```

The following example and sample output shows the objects associated with the administrative and FAST Search Server for SharePoint cmdlets and the number of cmdlets per object that are available.

```
Get-Command -PSSnapin "AdminSnapin" | sort noun, verb | group noun
```

```
Count Name                        Group
----- ----                        -----
    1 CertificateHash             {Get-CertificateHash}
    1 CertificateHelper           {Get-CertificateHelper}
    1 FileHasAccess               {Get-FileHasAccess}
    1 FilesOnReboot               {Remove-FilesOnReboot}
    1 LsaPolicy                   {Set-LsaPolicy}
    2 Services                    {Remove-Services, Set-services}
    1 user                        {Set-user}
```

```
gcm -PSSnapin "Microsoft.FASTSearch.PowerShell" |
   sort noun, verb | group noun
```

```
Count  Name                    Group
-----  ----                    -----
    2  FASTSearchAdminDatabase  {Install-FASTSearchAdminDatabase, Uninstall-...
    1  FASTSearchConfiguration  {Set-FASTSearchConfiguration}
    4  FASTSearchContentColle...  {Clear-FASTSearchContentCollection, Get-FAST...
    1  FASTSearchDocumentProc...  {Get-FASTSearchDocumentProcessingPipeline}
    1  FASTSearchIPSec          {Set-FASTSearchIPSec}
    4  FASTSearchMetadataCate...  {Get-FASTSearchMetadataCategory, New-FASTSea...
    3  FASTSearchMetadataCraw...  {Get-FASTSearchMetadataCrawledProperty, New-...
    4  FASTSearchMetadataCraw...  {Get-FASTSearchMetadataCrawledPropertyMappin...
    4  FASTSearchMetadataFull...  {Get-FASTSearchMetadataFullTextIndex, New-FA...
    4  FASTSearchMetadataFull...  {Get-FASTSearchMetadataFullTextIndexMapping,...
    4  FASTSearchMetadataMana...  {Get-FASTSearchMetadataManagedProperty, New-...
    4  FASTSearchMetadataRank...  {Get-FASTSearchMetadataRankProfile, New-FAST...
....( not all output shown)
    1  FASTSearchSecurityWork...  {Get-FASTSearchSecurityWorkerNode}
    3  FASTSearchSecurityXMLA...  {Get-FASTSearchSecurityXMLAliaser, New-FASTS...
    3  FASTSearchSpelltuning    {Add-FASTSearchSpelltuning, Remove-FASTSearc...
    1  FASTSearchSpelltuningS...  {Get-FASTSearchSpelltuningStatus}
```

Many of these objects will look familiar to you, because they are similar to objects covered earlier in this chapter, in the section titled "Using Enterprise Search," but with the prefix FASTSearch in place of SPEnterpriseSearch. For example, the object FASTSearchMetadata-CrawledProperty looks similar to SPEnterpriseSearchMetadataCrawledProperty. This is because FAST Search Server for SharePoint shares many of the same functionalities as enterprise search in SharePoint Server. You can get more information about each cmdlet by using Get-Help and Get-Command. To obtain information on the properties and methods of each object, pipe the output from the cmdlet to select * or Get-Member, as previously used in this chapter and in Chapter 5.

> **MORE INFO** Microsoft has released substantial FAST planning and deployment documentation, as well as documentation on FAST cmdlets. You can download this documentation from the Microsoft download center at *http://www.microsoft.com/downloads* using the search keywords FAST 2010 PowerShell. The document "Optimize Search Relevance with Microsoft FAST Search Server 2010 for SharePoint" also contains examples of how to use cmdlets associated with the FASTSearchMetadataRankProfile and FASTSearchMetadataManagedProperty objects.

Adding FAST Search Server 2010 for SharePoint to a SharePoint 2010 Installation

After you have installed the FAST Search Server for SharePoint and completed the initial configuration, you must join the SharePoint 2010 installation with the FAST Search Server 2010 for SharePoint installation. The FAST Search servers are known as *back-end servers* because users do not connect directly to them. The SharePoint Web servers are the front-end servers. To join the Fast Search Server 2010 for SharePoint installation with your SharePoint 2010 installation, you must first complete a number of tasks. In the deployment documentation provided by Microsoft, you will find that several of these tasks use Windows PowerShell commands. Figure 12-5 shows the components that are created or configured to complete the joining of the two installations.

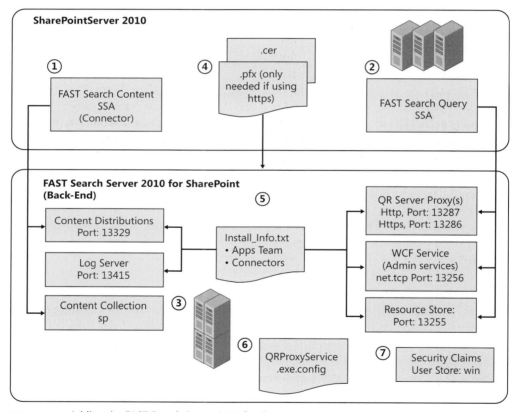

FIGURE 12-5 Adding the FAST Search Server 2010 for SharePoint as a back-end server for SharePoint 2010

The tasks you need to complete are listed here in the order that they are presented in the Microsoft deployment documentation. On the SharePoint Server installation, complete the following steps.

1. Create the content SSA.

2. Create the query SSA.

3. Enable queries from SharePoint Server to FAST Search and crawling content with the content SSA by creating certificates on the SharePoint Server installation and copying them to FAST Search.

On the FAST Search Server for SharePoint installation, complete the following steps.

1. Enable Click-Through Relevancy to ensure that click-through relevancy data is transferred from SharePoint Server to FAST.

2. Import the certificate to all FAST query back-end servers.

3. The default protocol to transfer query traffic is https. If you choose http, then you will need to amend the QRProxyService.exe.config file.

4. Create FAST Search Authorization (FSA) on all FAST query back-end servers.

In the deployment documentation, the two SSAs are created (steps 1 and 2 on the SharePoint Server installation) using the SharePoint 2010 Central Administration website; however, you can also accomplish these steps using Windows PowerShell. Earlier in this chapter, in the section titled "Using Enterprise Search," you learned how to create an SSA for enterprise search. To create the two FAST SSAs, you will use the same cmdlets, except here you configure them as the search application type ExtendedConnector. To complete the process, you need information from the file Install_Info.txt. This file was created on the FAST back-end server as part of the installation process, and it is stored in the %FASTSEARCH% directory. The content of a sample Install_Info.txt file is shown here.

```
===============================================================
FASTSearch: Installation Details
===============================================================


---------------------------------------------------------------
FAST Search Query Search Service Application configuration
---------------------------------------------------------------
Query Service Location HTTP (default):          http://W8R2BE01.contoso.msft:13287
Query Service Location HTTPS:                   https://W8R2BE01.contoso.msft:13286
Administration Service Location HTTP (default): http://W8R2BE01.contoso.msft:13257
Administration Service Location HTTPS:          https://W8R2BE01.contoso.msft:13258
Resource Store Location:                        http://W8R2BE01.contoso.msft:13255
Account for Administration Service:             contoso\zzFASTuser


---------------------------------------------------------------
FAST Search Content Search Service Application configuration
---------------------------------------------------------------
Content Distributors (for PowerShell SSA creation):  W8R2BE01.contoso.msft:13391
Content Distributors (for GUI SSA creation):         W8R2BE01.contoso.msft:13391
Default Content Collection Name:                     sp
```

```
-------------------------------------------------------------
Other services
-------------------------------------------------------------
Log Server:            W8R2BE01.contoso.msft:13415
SQL Server database:
jdbc:sqlserver://sql.contoso.msft;DatabaseName=FASTSearchAdminDB;integratedSecurity=true
```

> **IMPORTANT** If you are unsure about which protocol or port number to use during the installation process, refer to the file QRProxyService.exe.config, which is stored on every FAST back-end query server in the directory %FASTSEARCH%\bin. This is the configuration file for the query service, whereas the file Install_info.txt is for documentation purposes only and, over time, it may not be a true representation of the FAST installation.

Creating and Configuring the Content SSA

To create and configure the content SSA, open the SharePoint 2010 Management Shell and then follow these steps.

1. Check the status of the Windows Server service, SPAdminV4, which has a display name of SharePoint 2010 Administration. If the service is stopped, start it by typing the following command.

   ```
   Get-Service SPAdminV4 | Start-Service
   ```

2. Initialize variables to store the names of the application pool to be used for the SSA, the server name and port number for the content distributors, and the content collection.

   ```
   $AppPool = "FAST_Content_App_Pool"
   $ContDist = "FASTBE01.contoso.msft:13391"
   $contColl = "sp"
   ```

3. Create an SSA named FAST Search Content SSA by typing the following command.

   ```
   $ssa = New-SPEnterpriseSearchServiceApplication "FAST Search Content SSA" `
       -SearchApplicationType "ExtendedConnector" -DatabaseServer "sql.contoso.msft" `
       -DatabaseName "FASTConnectorDB" -ApplicationPool $AppPool
   ```

4. Configure the Search Administration component.

   ```
   $SearchInstance = Get-SPEnterpriseSearchServiceInstance SPS_APP1;

   Set-SPEnterpriseSearchAdministrationComponent `
       -SearchApplication $ssa -searchserviceinstance $SearchInstance;
   ```

5. Set the connection information to the FAST Search Server for SharePoint Installation.

   ```
   if (Get-SPEnterpriseSearchExtendedConnectorProperty -SearchApplication $ssa
   -id "ContentDistributors" -ErrorAction SilentlyContinue)
   ```

```
{
  # Property exists
  Set-SPEnterpriseSearchExtendedConnectorProperty -ID "ContentDistributors" `
-Value $contDist -SearchApplication $ssa;
} else
{
  # Property does not exist
  New-SPEnterpriseSearchExtendedConnectorProperty -Name "ContentDistributors" `
    -Value $contDist -SearchApplication $ssa;
}
```

```
Name                              Value
----                              -----
ContentDistributors               FASTBE01.contoso.msft:13391
```

6. Set the Content Collection information. Assuming this property does not exist, type the following command. A similar statement to the one shown previously also could be constructed.

```
New-SPEnterpriseSearchExtendedConnectorProperty -Name "ContentCollectionName" `
    -Value $contColl -SearchApplication $ssa;
```

```
Name                              Value
----                              -----
ContentCollectionName             sp
```

 REAL WORLD **Configuring Extended Properties**

The if-else script block in step 5 of the previous procedure is another example of a set of commands that you will use repeatedly, both in the next step when you create and configure the Query SSA and for other FAST service application properties, such as the configuration of User Context properties. This set of commands can be converted to a little helper function that you can use to set or configure any of the extended properties, whether for a FAST connector or a FAST query SSA property. The function takes advantage of the consistent naming convention of the cmdlets and uses a nice Windows PowerShell feature that allows you to build a string, which is the name of a cmdlet or function that you can then run by prefixing the string with the ampersand (&) character.

```
Function Set-FASTProp {
param ($SSA, [string] $Cmd, [string] $Prop, [string] $PropValue)
# Initialise $obj to Extended property object
$obj = "SPEnterpriseSearchExtended" + $cmd + "Property"
```

continued on the next page

```
$GetProp = &("Get-" + $obj) -Sea $ssa -id $Prop -ErrorAction SilentlyContinue

    if ($GetProp)
    {
      # Property exists
      &("Set-" + $obj) -SearchApplication $ssa -ID $Prop -Value $PropValue
    } else {
      # Property does not exist
      &("New-" + $obj) -SearchApplication $ssa -Name $Prop -Value $PropValue
    }
} # End of Function Set-FASTProp
```

With this function, you would then use the following command for step 6.

```
Set-FASTProp $ssa "Connector" "ContentCollectionName" $contColl
```

To configure the extended User Context property, type a command similar to the following.

```
Set-FASTProp $ssa "Query" "FASTSearchContextProperties" $UserProp
```

where the variable *$UserProp* contains a comma-separated string of user specific properties, such as "SPS-Location, SPS-Responsibility, SPS-School".

To list all the query Search Service Application properties, type the following command.

```
Get-SPEnterpriseSearchExtendedQueryProperty -SearchApplication $ssa
```

Creating and Configuring a Query SSA

To create and configure the query SSA, open the SharePoint 2010 Management Shell and use the following steps.

1. Initialize variables to store the names of the application pool to be used for the SSA, the server name and port number for the content distributors, and the content collection.

```
$AppPool = "FAST_Content_App_Pool"
$SrvName = "://FASTBE01.contoso.msft:"
$QueryLoc = "FASTSearchQueryServiceLocation"
$QueryLocV = "https" + $SrvName +"13286
$AdminLoc = "FASTSearchAdminServiceLocation"
$AdminLocV = "https" + $SrvName + "13258"
$AdminUser = "FASTSearchAdminServiceAuthenticationUser"
$AdminUserV = "Contoso\zzFASTuser"
$ResLoc = "FASTSearchResourceStoreLocation"
$ResSLoctV = "http" + $SrvName + "13255"
```

2. Create an SSA named FAST Search Query SSA and set the default search provider, by typing the following commands.

```
$ssa = New-SPEnterpriseSearchServiceApplication "FAST Search Query SSA" `
   -SearchApplicationType "Regular" -DatabaseServer "sql.contoso.msft" `
   -DatabaseName "FASTQueryDB" -ApplicationPool $AppPool;
Set-SPEnterpriseSearchServiceApplication $ssa -DefaultSearchProvider "FASTSearch"
```

3. Set the connection information to the FAST Search Server for SharePoint Installation using the Windows PowerShell function defined earlier.

```
Set-FASTProp $ssa "Query" $QueryLoc $QueryLocV
Set-FASTProp $ssa "Query" $AdminLoc $AdminLocV
Set-FASTProp $ssa "Query" $AdminUser $AdminUserV
Set-FASTProp $ssa "Query" $ResUser $ResUserV
```

4. To verify the property values for the query SSA, type the following command:

```
Get-SPEnterpriseSearchExtendedQueryProperty -SearchApplication "FAST Search Query SSA"
```

Summary

This chapter built on the information in Chapter 5. The aim of this chapter was not to detail each SharePoint Server or FAST Search Server search cmdlet, but to provide information about more complex uses of Windows PowerShell, specifically around search scenarios.

The chapter started by reviewing some of the techniques presented in Chapter 5, including the use of Get-Help Get-Command to learn about new or infrequently used commands and how to explore object properties and methods. Next you looked at the enterprise search cmdlets, creating objects such as Search Application Services (SSAs), and then you were introduced to the FAST Search Server for SharePoint cmdlets. Along the way, you created helper functions to minimize the amount of typing and testing needed to complete the process of creating scripts, and you learned a few more tricks, such as how to iterate through all the site collections in a Web application to activate a specific feature and how to create a command name in a string that can then be run.

CHAPTER 13

Customizing the Search Results and Search Center

Providing users with the ability to find the right content is traditionally a challenge for many IT organizations because data is typically spread from centrally managed file systems to financial and custom applications, to application portals such as SharePoint, and finally to end-user laptops. To solve this need for information, users began copying the same information wherever they needed it at the time, thus creating duplicate files across the enterprise and increasing the costs of the IT infrastructure. Traditional search applications either provided a complex user interface with fairly quick search results or easy-to-use search queries that returned the search results much more slowly.

Each of the search algorithms worked wonderfully until users wanted to switch from a complex to an easy query or vice versa. With Microsoft SharePoint 2010 Search and Microsoft SharePoint FAST Search, users are able to search for content with search experience much improved from traditional search applications and Microsoft SharePoint Server 2007 Search functionality. Microsoft says its goal is to help get the "right results on the first page," with content that can include not only SharePoint content, but also business data and people.

Benefits of the Search Features

SharePoint 2010 is able to search and index both structured and unstructured data while bringing together data spread across different applications and server environments. This requires the SharePoint Search Server, along with the content administrators, to import data into the SharePoint Search system, define categories that define the data, and expose those relationships to the user. SharePoint 2010 Search platforms provide the following features.

- Delivers similar content quickly to users through a single interface
- Provides a rich query language to support varying levels of customizations
- Promotes frequently visited pages or content higher in the search results
- Customizes search using built-in, customizable Web Parts
- Allows integration with external content providers

Providing users with these search functionalities is traditionally cumbersome and difficult to manage, but the SharePoint 2010 Search technology provides straightforward development and administration interfaces that include (but are not limited to) the following considerations.

- Manually adding or updating content to pages is expensive and it is difficult to meet expectations with content.
- Custom development is generally expensive and requires custom knowledge of search applications. By utilizing reusable business logic with user interface (UI) components and existing or new SharePoint infrastructure, IT organizations can leverage the same development and administrative staff for both functions.
- Because SharePoint Search is part of SharePoint 2010, you may see lower maintenance costs as a result of the framework that is very similar across all SharePoint applications.

All versions of SharePoint have benefited from the inclusion of the Microsoft FAST Search Server. Primarily, the new SharePoint version enhancements are centered on the user search experience and streamlined administration. Enterprises can now provide users with targeted, customizable, related information with an easy-to-use, conversational search experience. Furthermore, the search results provide key data that will direct the user to related information where more information on the search topic can be found. Finally, customizations to search parameters and targeted search phrases allow content managers to present targeted results, thereby directing users or customers to data using fewer searches and/or clicks of the mouse. This chapter will review these customizations and provide general guidance on their usage.

Introducing SharePoint Search

Providing users with relevant, useful information is a critical element in improving user efficiency in the workplace and on Internet-facing website applications. Search applications are one of the key ways companies can provide users with targeted information depending on their profile, previous search patterns, and peer rankings. SharePoint Search Server and SharePoint FAST Search Server 2010 have capabilities that enhance a user's search experience and can be customized to suit the needs of the Web application.

Traditional search engines provided static search results in a one-size-fits-all methodology. A user obtains the same set of results, without determination or discrimination of a user's needs or profile. For example, in a traditional search scenario, if a user searches for "gardening," he will get results that describe the definition of gardening, images relating to the topic, and many other gardening resources. However, a more relevant search experience might show gardening ideas, listing for local gardening clubs, and advice for gardening in his local climate zone. SharePoint 2010 is able to provide the enterprise with better, more relevant search experience by controlling the user experience, data input, and the ranking of searched content.

To get a better understanding of these concepts, it is important to compare how users perceive the data and how search applications interpret data. For example, in the gardening search described previously, a user might type **local gardening**, intending to find a local gardening club or organization, but all the search engine understands is "gardening" and so presents the results accordingly. To better comprehend the challenges surrounding search results, you must understand the underlying source data complexities. SharePoint data, from the search perspective, should be viewed from two perspectives: the input data and the data the search engine sees or understands. The input data, or the documents included in a SharePoint library or list, is defined by the document properties. These document properties help define what the searching user should come away with during a search operation, along with the complex data inside the document file itself. On the other hand, the search engine only understands data according to its ranking schema. The ranking schema includes a defined list of words, document properties, and ranking information; these are used for retrieval and ranking during the search process. To better illustrate this concept, Figure 13-1 shows source data from a Microsoft Word document with the ranking schema a search engine might have.

SharePoint Site Source Data

Welcome to your site!

Add a new image, change this welcome text or add new lists to this page by clicking the edit button above. You can click on Shared Documents to add files or on the calendar to create new team events. Use the links in the getting started section to share your site and customize its look.

SharePoint Search Engine Ranking Schema

Keywords	Keywords	Keywords	Document properties
welcome	image	by	Author: SharePoint Designer
to	change	clicking	Title: Welcome Page Text
your	this	the	Date: 5/1/2010
site	text	edit	Type: docx
add	or	button	Authority: 6
a	lists	above	Anchor: how-to documentation
new	page	you	

FIGURE 13-1 SharePoint 2010 ranking schema

Another challenge search engines face is determining the user intent. In the gardening example, the user typed **local gardening** in the search engine because he was looking for results on local gardening clubs; however, another user could type the same phrase when looking for local gardening climate zone information. In this case, the search engine needs more information to provide results that better suit each user's intent. A user searching for content may have to try a search several times before finding the appropriate results for the query.

If you want to customize the SharePoint Search experience, you need to understand the different aspects of search quality (relevance). One of the most often used components of search is the conversational user experience (ConversationUI). The conversational user interface consists of the elements that make up the search page itself—the search results, related search results, and visual best bets. Another aspect of search quality is the quality of the data collection itself. Simply put, search results are only as good as the data provided. If a user searches for gardening, but no documents relating to gardening exist, the search returns no results. Finally, the ranking and keyword management allows the content to be ranked according to predefined rules.

Table 13-1 shows the Search features available in SharePoint 2010.

TABLE 13-1 SharePoint 2010 Search Features

AREA	FEATURE
ConversationUI	Common UI framework, basic customized refiners, social definitions/social tag ranking, best bets
Ranking	Ranking improves with use
Customization	Basic ranking customization

Table 13-2 describes the features available with SharePoint FAST Server Search 2010.

TABLE 13-2 SharePoint 2010 FAST Search Features

AREA	FEATURE
ConversationUI	Deep, customizable refiners, document preview and thumbnails, visual and contextualized best bets
Ranking	Ranking improves with use
Customization	Extensive ranking schema management, keyword-based document boosts, sorting
Contextualization	Query-based, group-based

This chapter provides guidance and advice on customizing different aspects of SharePoint 2010 and SharePoint FAST Server Search 2010.

Improving the User Experience

SharePoint 2010 makes every effort to understand the intent of a query and to reduce the noise to the search engine. That is, to provide a better search experience for the user, SharePoint 2010 must parse and understand the search query and filter out information that isn't essential to a query's meaning.

Out of the box, SharePoint Search supports anti-phrasing. Anti-phrases refer to the parts of a query that do not contribute to its meaning. Words or phrases such as "How do I find" make sense to the user, but they do not provide added value to the search query. Filtering out words that aren't useful in the query is traditionally done by using noise word (stop-word) lists that remove the unnecessary words, such as "and," "the," and "I," from search queries. The use of stop-words can pose a problem because the words are always removed from queries. SharePoint resolves this issue by removing phrases using a more intelligent anti-phrasing process, so that a query such as "how do I do SharePoint" is transformed to "SharePoint." As a result, the search results are improved to include more SharePoint-related topics. Based on the search results that are then selected by the user, the search engine uses query recall to improve subsequent searches for the term "SharePoint."

Providing a good conversational user experience is one of the first—and more important—search criteria for delivering useful information to users. A conversational search experience allows a user to type search phrases and interact with the results as if she were talking to another person rather than to computer software. SharePoint 2010 out of the box provides a good starting point for queries and searching for the best qualified results. However, because the user can analyze and/or refine the resulting dataset, it is also important that the search system can adapt those results to improve search quality for future queries. These tasks help enterprises give users high quality and fast results, which in turn allow users to complete their tasks quickly and easily.

By default, the SharePoint 2010 FAST Search results page contains several elements that help satisfy these needs.

- **Input Search Box**   Allows the user to interact with the search engine
- **Visual Best Bets**   Presents customizable advertisements or suggested content based on the user's profile or search criteria
- **Document Preview**   Previews the document contents
- **Query Refiners**   Shows related results to the query
- **Similar Results**   Provides a new result set similar to a document or result item
- **Sort Options**   Enables sorting by custom metadata

Each of these functions is shown in Figure 13-2.

Input Search box　　Visual best bets　　Sort options

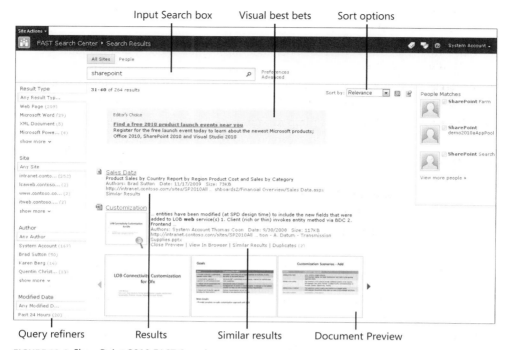

Query refiners　　　　Results　　　Similar results　　Document Preview

FIGURE 13-2 SharePoint 2010 FAST Search page

Contextual Promotions

Web applications such as SharePoint are able to provide information to a Web user based on their search actions, location, people, or relevant information. SharePoint Search takes these user-related objects and defines them as the "user context." For example, SharePoint Search is able to refine search results for a search query such as SharePoint Development to include results that could highlight SharePoint developers, provide a list of geo-located developers in the area, and determine related blogs or sites that focus on SharePoint development.

Contextual promotions allows the search engine to apply user contexts for best bets, visual best bets, and site promotions. These features allow users to see information that is most likely to be relevant, depending on the user's profile information, such as title, function, or department. As an example, a developer might be searching for specific, detailed information, whereas a sales manager might prefer to see a more high-level set of search results. Furthermore, with an increasingly global workforce, mobile and geographic location–based information must be considered as well.

The context information available from the user's profile and URL information allows enterprises to tap into search functionality and provide higher quality search results. Administrators and developers alike should be aware of the following context items available in the user context.

- **Location awareness**   Where is the user located: in the United States, Europe, or some other part of the world?

- **Device awareness**   Is the user on a mobile phone, a laptop, or at a computer in the corporate environment?

- **Referrer awareness**   How did this user get to this page: through a search engine like Bing, a social media site like Twitter, the current website, or a peer website?

- **Click patterns**   Analyze Web logs to determine how users generally navigate the site.

- **Time of day**   Do any search patterns exist relative to the time of day when different results are expected? Users executing a site search during business hours usually look for more business applications, whereas users performing the same search during off-hours could be looking for more home-use type products.

- **Personalize content**   Provide search result content to which the user relates.

In short, applying context depends on the intent of the user and what her predicted pattern might be. For global enterprises, when a user clicks on the corporate support pages, the landing page might include the local office address, a map with links to directions of the location, and key employee contact information. Each of these items can be based on the IP address in the user's context protocol. All browsers identify themselves with device-dependent content when accessing Web pages, which enables search applications to provide specific content as needed for a user and the user's device. It is also important to adapt rendering based on the user's device profile. For example, when building search pages for mobile phones, the element size should be adjusted so that it is smaller, to fit the devices' screen real estate. Furthermore, font choice and limited page content ensure a quick and positive user experience on a mobile device. A user accessing the same search site with a PC will expect a feature-rich content page and should receive as much related information as possible, based on the user's profile and context.

You can personalize the search results content using the SharePoint Server Search products. You can achieve these contextual promotions by optimizing the site layout and ranking features using keywords, promotions, and the users' context information.

Adding User Context Metadata

Metadata in SharePoint 2010 is important in returning quality user results to improve findability. Findability, as defined by Peter Moreville (2005), is a user's ability to identify and navigate the pages of a website to discover and retrieve relevant information resources. Metadata is used in SharePoint 2010 to categorize and rank information located in the SharePoint document store. To learn more about the topics of findability and putability, read Chapter 9, "Organizing Information."

The managed property administration is enhanced significantly to support the new search features. Each metadata property contains the ability to be a sort property, a query property, or a refiner property, and it can be mapped to either SharePoint document properties or external content for search queries. By defining query properties, end users can gain control of their refinement queries, sorting, and default language, as illustrated in Figure 13-3.

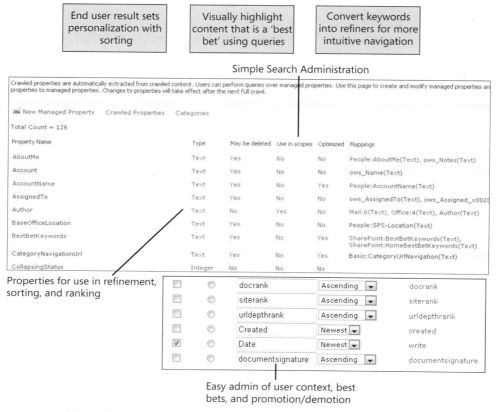

FIGURE 13-3 Managed properties

NOTE SharePoint 2010 is able to extract applied metadata, such as author information, from content created in Microsoft Office applications based on document properties. To view document properties on documents before they are uploaded to a SharePoint site, open Windows Explorer, right-click the document, and then select Properties from the shortcut menu to open the document's Properties dialog box. In the dialog box, click the Details tab to view information about the Author, Title, and other available document properties.

Filtering search information based on document metadata and managed properties allows the enterprise search application to retrieve user content information and provides specific filters to the search engine. Adding user context information to search keywords allows targeted search results to be displayed. After targeted results are created, they can be associated to best bets. A common example might be a geographic-based user context in which information is displayed depending on the region where the user is located.

Both SharePoint and FAST Search retrieve newly crawled properties that can then be used in managed properties. This activity presents two areas of concern. Previously, you could not determine from which documents the crawled properties were derived. SharePoint now has the capability to log the extraction from a specific document using a Windows PowerShell cmdlet.

The various metadata usage options each require an index, which impacts the storage (size) of the metadata database. Some of these options can be disabled in the UI, and others require the use of a Windows PowerShell cmdlet for configuration. Keep in mind that although disabling an option can reduce the database size, it obviously limits the use of the metadata in some functions and may break the Web Part currently configured for that usage. Also, since the search Web Parts are configured with XML files, they could be configured for functionality that is not available for some metadata. Be sure to document any nonstandard metadata usage configurations that you apply.

The managed properties currently being used by search can be retrieve with the cmdlet Get-SPEnterpriseSearchMetadataManagedProperty.

> **NOTE** The FullTextSQLQuery class doesn't return results if you use the = operator with a text-managed property and do not select the managed property's option, Reduce Storage Requirements For Text Properties By Using A Hash For Comparison. Therefore, you should select this option when the managed property is automatically generated by the crawling process.

To add a user geographical user context requires exposing the user property that is available and then configuring it for use by FAST user context. To expose the user property, follow these steps.

1. Open a browser and go to the SharePoint Central Administration website.
2. Click Application Management, and under Service Applications, click Manage Service Applications.
3. Click User Profile Service Application to select it and then click Manage in the Operations group on Service Applications Ribbon.
4. Under People, click Manage User Properties.
5. Edit an existing property or create a new property.
6. Fill in the appropriate values for the form depending on your needs and requirements.
7. Click OK. See Figure 13-4 for an example of the Edit User Profile Property page.

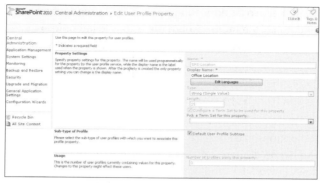

FIGURE 13-4 Edit User Profile Property page

To configure the property for use in FAST user context in search results, follow these steps.

1. Open a browser and go to the SharePoint Central Administration website.

2. At the root level of the SharePoint website, click Site Settings.

3. Click Fast Search User Context under Site Collection Administration to create or manage user contexts. The Add User Context page, as shown in Figure 13-5, creates a new user context.

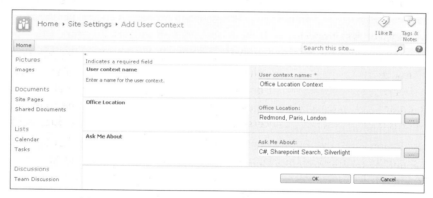

FIGURE 13-5 Add User Context page

4. Enter information as needed for the user context. Information entered here can be modified later in the Edit User Context page.

> **NOTE** Multiple items can be listed in the fields shown in Figure 13-5 if they are separated by commas. These items are interpreted by the system as OR clauses. In Figure 13-5, for example, the search server interprets Office Location as Redmond or Paris or London.

5. Click OK.

After the user context is defined, it can be applied to a best bet or a visual best bet, which narrows the scope of users to target information. If a user's profile context information Ask Me About column contains the data C#, a best bet appears in the search results, as shown in Figure 13-6.

FIGURE 13-6 User context search results

This out-of-the-box capability gives search applications more control over the content they provide to a user and helps to ensure that the user is presented with quality search results.

Using Managed Keywords

Managed keywords are the basis for creating best bets, visual best bets, and promotion. A keyword (also described as a *tag*) can be defined as a nonhierarchical term set called a keyword set. When keywords are added to a site or site collection, documents within that site prompt the user to enter a keyword that defines how the document appears in the search results. These keywords may be required as necessary when a user edits or uploads a document.

When using enterprise keywords (with SharePoint Server or SharePoint FAST Server), a user who is updating content in SharePoint can choose from either Enterprise Search terms or managed terms. This could be important if document content is needed to participate in SharePoint Server Search applications and/or SharePoint FAST Server Search applications. One of the primary differences between enterprise keywords and managed terms is that enterprise terms allow multiple values by default. Figure 13-7 shows how a user could apply enterprise search terms to a document.

FIGURE 13-7 Applying search terms to a document

When a user begins typing a value into the managed keyword field, a suggestion is provided from available search terms defined by the system. The managed term, as well as the term set, is displayed with the term's location in the hierarchy. Higher placement in the list indicates a larger search priority over lower items. If needed, the user can add a term set if permission is granted by the administrator. In Figure 13-7, the user is presented with two keywords, two users, and the option to create a new keyword.

Administrators should limit keywords to choices the user is likely to know or understand and should develop rules and/or roles for the addition of search terms. For example, if a user is creating a new engineering document for his product, he might need to include the names of the different consultants who also worked on the document so that other users in the department can find documents that were authored by a particular consultant. In this case, consultants are not employees of the company and cannot be assigned to people lookup columns, such as Responsible. Adding the consultant name to the keyword column links the document to the consultant when using the SharePoint search functions. If the consultant's name already exists in the list, it is shown as are the two names in Figure 13-7. However, if the consultant's name is misspelled in the keyword column, the user might add another keyword entry with the consultant's name spelled correctly. This can make the keyword lists long and provide confusing results if the data is not managed. For example, if there is a consultant named Sharjah, but the name is sometimes spelled Siharjah, then multiple entries exist for the same person. As with any data-based application, the better the data that is input to the system, the better the application results that will be returned.

To create a new managed keyword, follow these steps.

1. Click Site Settings from the Site Actions menu.

2. Click Fast Search Keywords under Site Collection Administration to display the Manage Keywords page, as shown in Figure 13-8.

FIGURE 13-8 Create Managed Keywords page

3. Click Add Keyword to display the Add Keyword page, shown in Figure 13-9.

FIGURE 13-9 Add Keyword page

4. In the Keyword Phrase box, type the search term.

5. Enter synonyms in the appropriate text box, if required. A two-way synonym tells the FAST Server to include results from the keyword when searches for the synonym are requested. You can use multiple synonyms if you separate them with semicolons.

> **NOTE** Synonyms are defined as terms that are similar to the keyword phrase. For example, if a company has a product line called chipset products with individual products called companyparta and companypartb, then a search administrator would type **COMPANYPARTA;COMPANYPARTB** as the synonym so that searches for parts will display related parts in the same product line.
>
> SharePoint FAST Search enables synonym and spelling variation expansion of queries or indexed documents. The query-side expansion adds synonyms or spelling variations to the query prior to the actual matching. The document-side expansion expands the document with synonyms in a separate part of the index. You can control the variation expansion one-way or two-way options from the page shown in Figure 13-9 in the same way as lemmatization at query time. (You can find more information about lemmatization in the section titled "Lemmatization" later in this chapter.) It is also possible to combine the two solutions.

6. Enter a keyword definition if needed.

7. Click OK.

After you create a managed keyword, you can apply best bets and visual best bets.

Adding Best Bets

Adding best bets to search results allows documents to be highlighted based on the search terms provided by the user. This feature ensures a higher quality search result because it targets individual search terms or user profile information. Best Bests can consist of one or more URLs or images. To create a best bet, complete the following steps.

1. Click Site Settings from the Site Actions menu.

2. Click Fast Search Keywords under Site Collection Administration, then hover over the number under Best Bets, and click Add Best Bet, as shown in Figure 13-10.

FIGURE 13-10 Adding a search best bet

3. Enter a title for the best bet.

4. Enter a URL for the page or document to be associated with this best bet.

5. If this keyword search specifically applies to only certain users, enter the user context information.

6. Enter the start and end date if required for publishing.

7. Click OK.

To see the search term in action, open the FAST Search site and type the term **SharePoint**, as shown in Figure 13-11. The document Office Customization is highlighted as a best bet for the term SharePoint.

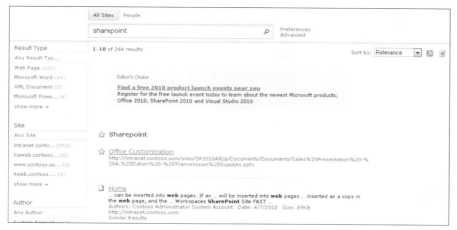

FIGURE 13-11 Best bet search results

Adding Visual Best Bets

Being able to show visual best bets when users are searching for a particular keyword is an important aspect of providing quality search results. Visual best bests can consist of one or more URLs or images. To create a visual best bet, use the following steps.

1. Click Site Settings from the Site Actions menu, click Fast Search Keywords under Site Collection Administration, and then hover over the number under Visual Best Bets.

2. Click Add Visual Best Bets, as shown in Figure 13-12.

FIGURE 13-12 Adding a visual best bet

3. Enter a title for the visual best bet.

4. Enter a URL for the visual best bet.

5. If this keyword search should apply to only certain users, enter the user context information.

6. Enter the start and end date if required for publishing.

7. Click OK.

If a user types **SharePoint** as a search term, as shown in Figure 13-13, an image is displayed at the top of the search results that shows information about SharePoint 2010 training.

FIGURE 13-13 Search results for a visual best bet

Advanced User Contexts

It is sometimes necessary to create more complex user contexts than a simple OR statement allows. SharePoint 2010 supports the creation of custom user contexts that allows for a context such as creating a location-based context as complex as "all Locations except Redmond and people with the user property Title having a value of Sales or with the user property Responsibility that includes SharePoint." Using Boolean notation, this context would be identified by the following statement.

```
(NOT(SPS-Location:Redmond)) AND (Title:"Sales" OR SPS-Responsibility:SharePoint)
```

If you create this example using the context process described in previous sections, you must create multiple contexts that are connected using keyword features and ultimately are subject to error.

SharePoint 2010 is capable of creating advanced user contexts using the Windows PowerShell interface.

> **IMPORTANT**   Before you attempt to use the following example, make sure that the correct server (named FAST in the example) is selected. The FAST cmdlets in Windows PowerShell are not available on the SharePoint hosts.

1. On the SharePoint farm, determine the Site-ID of the context/keyword to be defined. This Site-ID is used on the FAST Search nodes as a site collection feature.

   In a SharePoint 2010 Management Shell, run the following command:

   ```
   Get-SPSite -Identity "http://yoursite/"
   ```

2. On a FAST Search node, open the Management Shell and run the following commands.

   ```
   Add-PSSnapin Microsoft.FASTSearch.Powershell  # Register the FAST Search
   $ssg = Get-FASTSearchSearchSettingGroup -Name '<SiteID-GUID>' #Use site GUID from
       above
   $ctx = $ssg.Contexts.AddContext('newcontextname')  # Name given to the context
   $ae = $ctx.AddAndExpression()
   $or = $ae.AddOrExpression()
   $or.AddMatchExpression('Title', 'Sales')
   $or.AddMatchExpression('SPS-Responsibility', 'SharePoint')
   $not = $ae.AddNotExpression()
   $not.AddMatchExpression('SPS-Location', 'Redmond')
   ```

When these commands execute, a context with the name newcontextname is created and can be connected to a keyword feature like best bet or visual best bet using the administration user interface.

Using Language Detection

SharePoint 2010 automatically detects and understands 81 different languages, which allows language-specific content detection to occur during document and query processing. In cases in which document metadata defines the document language, this feature can be disabled. If a site administrator is asked to develop a multilingual SharePoint site, pages must include Web Parts that reflect language-specific search queries for data that does not belong to the page. For example, many enterprises have multilingual Internet-facing sites that redirect the user based on the default user browser language. In these cases, it is important to have central repositories for press releases, support documents, and so on.

SharePoint allows support for different pages and document translations based on either SharePoint site regional settings or individual sites. The FAST Search application is aware of these predefined settings and displays results accordingly. In SharePoint 2010, results are prioritized higher if they exist in the same language as the searcher.

Customizing the User Interface

In the past, users actively interacted with SharePoint search in two areas: constructing a query and viewing the search results. SharePoint 2010 has extended the Search user interface to make the process more interactive, particularly in the conversational aspects of both querying and refining search results. The Search user interface can be customized in the design of the Search Center, in the query Web Parts, and in the results pages.

Choosing and Customizing the Search Center

In your enterprise search design, you may choose to centralize all searches at a single location or to customize and control search with local Search Center sites. Although the search resources are provided at the application level, customizations of the user interface will be managed at the site collection level.

To permit delegation of site collection search configuration to search administrators who do not need site collection administrator rights to other content, you may use managed paths to create a Search Center site as a site collection root site with the appearance of a subsite in the URL.

SharePoint 2010 offers three Search Center site templates.

- **Enterprise Search Center**   This publishing site requires the Publishing Infrastructure feature to be activated for the site collection, but it does not require its parent to be a publishing site. This template was called Search Center With Tabs in the previous version.

- **Basic Search Center**   This template is appropriately named, because it offers only three basic search pages and is not designed to support multiple instances of the search pages.

- **FAST Search Center** This template is available even without FAST Search for SharePoint installed, but it requires a FAST Search server for functionality. It is a publishing site designed like the Enterprise Search Center except the pages use FAST Search Web Parts where appropriate.

SharePoint 2010 uses the Basic Search Center template to create the default Search Center site. In most scenarios, this Search Center site should be replaced with one created with either the Enterprise Search Center template or the FAST Search Center template to make customization easier.

Customizing the Enterprise Search Center

As a publishing site, the Enterprise Search Center presents three features that ease customization.

- All three search pages templates provided within the UI are page layout templates for the publishing process that are based on the Welcome page content type.
- All pages are stored in a publishing pages library with full publishing processes, approvals, and workflows available.
- The page layouts of the search and results pages contain a special field control that organizes links to other search pages within customizable tabs. Advanced Search pages do not have a Tabs field control. The Tabs field control uses link information stored in one of two link lists.
  - Tabs In Search Pages
  - Tabs In Search Results Pages

The three search pages of the Basic Search Center (default, advanced, and results) are Web Part Pages designed with Web Part placement like the publishing templates, but there is no provision for creating additional pages based on that design.

Creating New Search Pages

You can create a new search page from the Site Actions menu of any Enterprise Search Center page. Do not select New Page, as this does not create a publishing page with a page template choice option. To create a search page, follow these steps.

1. Select More Options from the Site Actions menu to open the Create page. Note that the presentation of this page varies greatly depending on whether or not you have Microsoft Silverlight installed.

2. Select Publishing Page and click Create to open the Create Page page shown in Figure 13-14.

3. Enter the appropriate information in the Title, Description, and URL Name text boxes.

4. Select the appropriate page template.

5. Click the Create button to create the new page and open it in edit page mode.

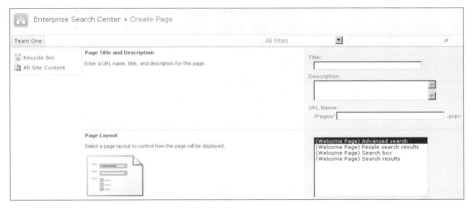

FIGURE 13-14 The Create Page page

> **NOTE** You will not always need a set of three pages for each customization. For instance, a single Search Box (query) page can contain multiple search boxes, each pointing to a unique search results page or People search results page. All search box Web Parts may not require a corresponding Advanced Search page.

Creating New Tabs

When a search page is in the edit page mode, the Tabs field control exposes links to management pages for adding new tab links or editing existing tab links, as shown in Figure 13-15. In this example, a custom tab has been added for a search page that returns results from the Clients database, and the tooltip is exposed.

FIGURE 13-15 Tabs field control

Clicking Edit Tabs opens the Tabs In Search Pages list page shown in Figure 13-16, from which the control builds the tabs. The results pages also have a tab control that uses another list, named Tabs In Search Results. Both these lists can also be accessed from View All Site Content.

FIGURE 13-16 Tabs In Search Pages list page

Clicking the Add New Item link or Add New Tab from the control on the page opens the dialog box shown in Figure 13-17.

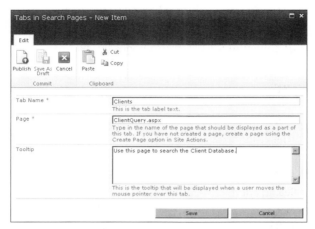

FIGURE 13-17 New Item dialog box for the Tabs In Search Pages list

The Tab Name field should indicate the purpose to users. The Page field can point to an existing or future custom page. The Tooltip field should expand to show the purpose of the search page.

After the custom set of search pages and tabs are created, the new query page can be accessed from its custom tab. The query Web Part can then point to the appropriate custom results page, and the Advanced query link can point to the appropriate custom advanced query page. When a user viewing a results page selects another results page tab, the query passed to the original page will be automatically passed to the results page opened by the new tab.

This combination of publishing page templates for creating custom search pages plus the controls that manage navigation tabs within the pages presents a Search Center site that can be quickly and easily customized to meet the search needs of your organization.

Configuring Custom Page Access

Although you have not yet learned about all of these, here are some of the ways that these custom pages can be accessed.

- Site collections can be configured to use a remote set of search pages.
- Scopes, both local and shared, can be configured for a specific results page.
- Query Web Parts at any location can be configured to use a specific results page in another location.
- More Results links on Federated Search Web Parts can point to custom results pages.
- Advanced Search links can point to custom advanced search pages.
- Links placed anywhere within your pages or link lists can point to custom query pages.

- Group Policy can be used to pre-populate Internet Explorer Favorites links to custom query pages.

- Internet Explorer and Windows Desktop Search can be configured to use custom query pages.

- Microsoft Office applications can be configured to use search pages by URL.

Customizing Search Pages

Other than the tab control, the basic three search pages are essentially the same in the Basic, Enterprise, and FAST Search Center sites. The customization of the pages involves the placement and customization of Web Parts.

Search results Web Parts in SharePoint 2010 are based on the Federation Object Model (FOM) and are used by both SharePoint Search and FAST Search. The Web Parts on a results page communicate with a shared query manager identified in the Web Parts as the Cross Web Part Query ID. This query manager receives the query passed to the page, gathers the requirements and query modifications from the results Web Parts, processes the query, and returns the results to the appropriate Web Parts. For new Web Parts to participate with existing Web Parts, the new Web Parts simply need to use the same query ID. Because the out-of-the-box Web Parts are no longer sealed, developers can extend their functionality instead of writing new ones from scratch.

Query Pages

The Welcome page of all Search Center sites is a basic query page named Default.aspx. Although this page seems rather simple, as shown in Figure 13-18, it supports a number of customization options.

FIGURE 13-18 Portion of the basic query page in edit mode

The page has two Web Part zones but only a single Search Box Web Part. You can choose to add other Web Parts, such as a content editor where instructions on how to search more effectively can be presented. Because Web Parts can be targeted by audience, you may add multiple instances of the same Search Box Web Part on the same page customized for different groups of users.

The Preferences link next to the Search Box allows you to apply the new "conversational" approach introduced in SharePoint 2010 Search; it opens the dialog box shown in Figure 13-19, where users can configure personal preferences for the configuration of the Web Part.

The user's first option regards the display of search suggestions as they type in query terms. These suggestions are retrieved from the history of successful queries. Users can also choose to override the default behavior of searching in the language of the browser and instead choose up to five languages to include in the search results. From that list, they can choose the default language, which is given a higher relevance ranking in the results list.

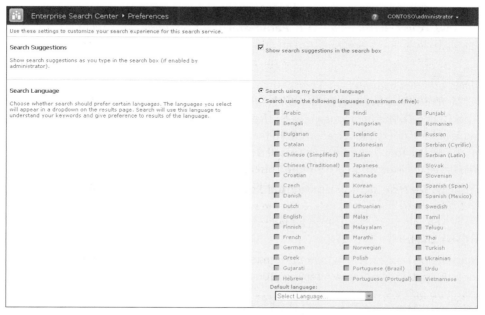

FIGURE 13-19 User Preferences dialog box for the Search Box Web Part

Search Box Web Part

The Search Box Web Part is used in both search and results pages and has the same functionality as the Search Box control on the master pages. To configure the properties of a Web Part on the Search page, perform the following steps.

1. From the Site Actions menu or the Page Ribbon of the page, select Edit Page.

2. In the Web Part zone, click the small down arrow for the Web Part to expose the context menu and then select Edit Web Part.

3. Expand the appropriate sections to configure properties as needed.

4. Click OK.

5. For publishing pages, you need to save, check in, and publish the page after making changes. For standard pages, the action is simply Stop Editing.

The Scopes Dropdown section of the Search Box Web Part is shown in Figure 13-20. The Dropdown mode options are the same as those of the Site Settings Search Settings page. The choices are as follow.

- **Do Not Show Scopes Dropdown, And Default To Target Results Page**   Does not display a scope drop-down list and sends the query to the results page with no scope selected. Normally, this will be a custom results page with Web Parts configured to use one or more scopes.

- **Show Scopes Dropdown**   Displays the scopes defined in the search drop-down display group and the contextual scopes in the scopes list.

- **Show, And Default To 'S' URL Parameter**   Displays the scopes defined in the search drop-down display group and the contextual scopes in the scopes list. The selected scope will be added to the query passed to the results page using the 's' parameter.

- **Show, And Default To Contextual Scope**   Displays the search drop-down list and automatically selects the This Site or This List scope as the default. Contextual scopes cannot be managed in the search drop-down list.

- **Show, Do Not Include Contextual Scopes**   Displays only the scopes in the search drop-down list that do not include This Site and This List contextual scopes.

- **Show, Do Not Include Contextual Scopes, And Default To 'S' URL Parameter**   Displays only the scopes defined in the search drop-down display group in the scopes list. The selected scope will be added to the query passed to the results page using the 's' parameter.

Normally, you do not need to enter text in the Dropdown Label box or modify the default automatic Fixed Dropdown Width setting (0).

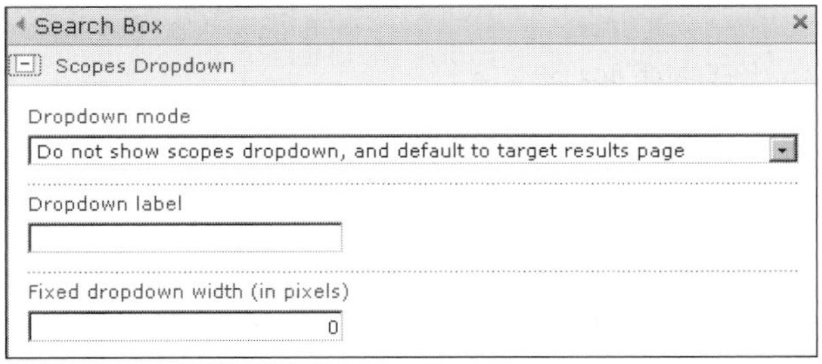

FIGURE 13-20 Scopes Dropdown section of the Search Box Web Part properties

The Query Text Box Label and Query Text Box Label Width text boxes are shown in Figure 13-21. Additional query terms can be added to the user-entered query; the Additional Query Description Label text box is usually empty. The text entered in this text box shown in Figure 13-21 limits the results to contracts. Any keyword query can be placed here, including scope definitions. Because these terms modify the query transparently to the user, appropriately labeling the query box will inform the user of its functionality. The prompt string will appear in the query box unless the focus is set there automatically or unless the cursor is placed there manually. The Append Additional Terms To Query check box is critical because the additional query terms entered in this section are not used unless it is selected.

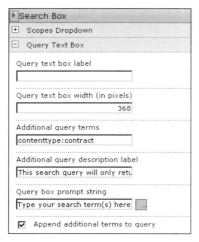

FIGURE 13-21 Query Text Box section of the Search Box Web Part properties

The search query box, shown in Figure 13-22, displays the configurations set in Figure 13-21.

FIGURE 13-22 Customized search query box

The Query Suggestions section, shown in Figure 13-23, controls the suggestions process, where the preferences page let users opt in or out. The Minimum Prefix Length setting determines how many characters a user must enter before suggestions are offered. The Suggestion Delay setting controls the response time, and the Number Of Suggestions To Display setting controls the maximum number of suggestions.

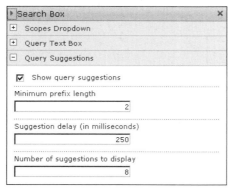

FIGURE 13-23 Query Suggestions section of the Search Box Web Part properties

The Miscellaneous section shown in Figure 13-24 is probably the most often used in customizing search. The first four entries control the Search button images.

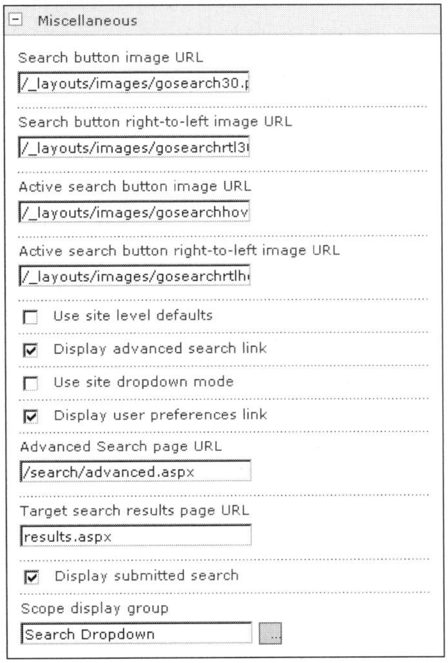

FIGURE 13-24 Miscellaneous section of Search box Web Part properties

Two switches, Use Site Level Defaults and Use Site Dropdown Mode, override the settings in the Scope Dropdown section. Use these options to establish centralized control of multiple search box Web Parts from the Search Settings of the site collection.

Below this, two switches control the advanced search and user preferences links at the end of the query box. You might choose not to offer an advanced search page for some searches, such as the People Query page in the Enterprise Search Center. Obviously, if you did not select the Show Query Suggestions check box in the previous section, you also might choose to remove the user preferences link. Remember that user preferences also control query languages.

In the Advanced Search Page URL box, you can direct the advanced search link to the appropriate custom page. This text box is active even if the Display Advanced Search Link check box is not selected. The URL entered will be a relative path for local pages.

The Target Search Results Page URL setting configures the target page for queries. Because the actual work of the search query is accomplished by the results page, you might configure custom query pages or custom query Web Parts where the only customization is the target results page.

The Display Submitted Search check box affects only Search Box Web Parts placed on a results page. By displaying the original query, these Web Parts permit the user to easily modify the query without retyping it. If you need to change the scope display group, you must type the name exactly as it appears in the site collection scope management page.

The Appearance, Layout, and Advanced sections are standard for SharePoint Web Parts. If you need to target to audiences, you can find the Audiences configuration in the Advanced section. By having multiple Search Box Web Parts targeted to different audiences on the same page, you can have a single query page customized to the user opening it.

Advanced Search Pages

The Advanced Search page contains the single Advanced Search Web Part shown in its default configuration in Figure 13-25.

FIGURE 13-25 Default advanced search Web Part

Although much of this Web Part can be customized easily in the property dialog box, three critical portions require modifying XML. The following information and illustrations will walk you through the properties to be modified as they appear. To edit the Advanced Search Web Part, first place the page in edit mode from either the Site Actions menu or the Page Ribbon. Then, to the upper right of the Web Part, choose Edit Web Part from the drop-down menu.

The first section of the Advanced Search Web Part is shown in Figure 13-26. These search box options enable the user to construct complex queries without knowing the appropriate query language structure. Each option includes a text label box and a selection to enable it.

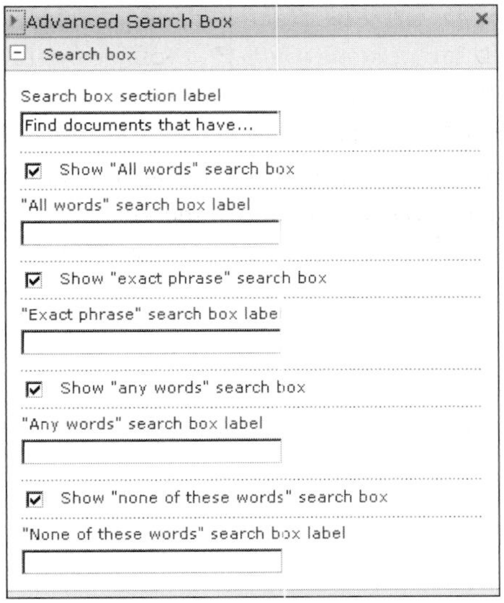

FIGURE 13-26 The Advanced Search Web Part properties Search Box section

The Scope section, displayed in Figure 13-27, presents a series of query filters with check boxes and label text boxes. Although the Display Group used by the scope picker is configured within this section, both the Language and Result Type pickers are controlled by an XML section that will be discussed later.

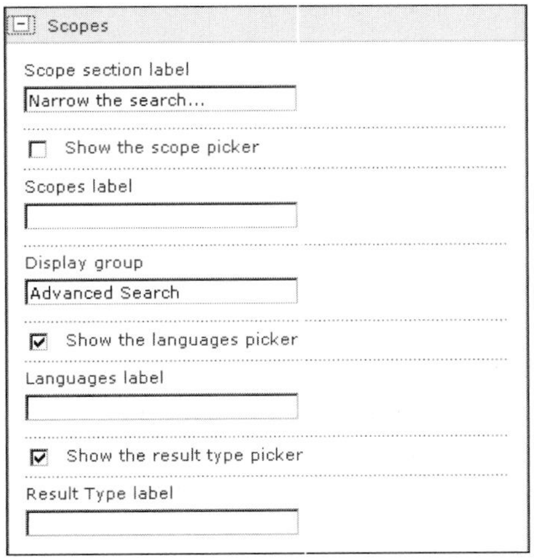

FIGURE 13-27 The Advanced Search Web Part properties Scopes section

The Properties section, shown in Figure 13-28, manages query filters that use managed properties. An XML string contained in the Properties text box controls the managed properties available for use here, as well as the languages exposed in the language picker and the file types defined in the result type picker.

To edit this code, place the cursor in the text box to expose the Builder text editor blue button to the right of the text box. Because the file is a single line in this editor, you may want to copy the entire text to your favorite XML editor, make changes, and paste the modified text back into the Builder for saving to the Web Part properties.

FIGURE 13-28 The Advanced Search Web Part Properties section

The first section of the XML defines the languages supported by search. For each language definition (LangDef), the display name is shown within quotation marks and the assigned language ID is also shown within quotation marks. You do not need to modify this portion. Following is just a small portion of the code as an example.

```
<root xmlns:xsi="http://www.w3.org/2001/XMLSchema-instance">
<LangDefs>
  <LangDef DisplayName="Simplified Chinese" LangID="zh-cn" />
  <LangDef DisplayName="Traditional Chinese" LangID="zh-tw" />
  <LangDef DisplayName="English" LangID="en" />
  <LangDef DisplayName="Finnish" LangID="fi" />
  <LangDef DisplayName="French" LangID="fr" />
  <LangDef DisplayName="German" LangID="de" />
  <LangDef DisplayName="Italian" LangID="it" />
  <LangDef DisplayName="Japanese" LangID="ja" />
  <LangDef DisplayName="Spanish" LangID="es" />
</LangDefs>
```

The next section specifies the languages by LangID to be displayed in the language picker, as shown in the following code sample. To change the languages displayed, simply add or remove lines from these default settings and save the code back to the Properties text box.

```
<Languages>
  <Language LangRef="en" />
  <Language LangRef="fr" />
  <Language LangRef="de" />
  <Language LangRef="ja" />
  <Language LangRef="zh-cn" />
  <Language LangRef="es" />
  <Language LangRef="zh-tw" />
</Languages>
```

The next portion is the Property Definition section, as shown in the following code block. These properties must be managed properties. Additional property entries must include the real managed property name, the data type, and the name to display in the Web Part.

```
<PropertyDefs>
  <PropertyDef Name="Path" DataType="text" DisplayName="URL" />
  <PropertyDef Name="Size" DataType="integer" DisplayName="Size (bytes)" />
  <PropertyDef Name="Write" DataType="datetime" DisplayName="Last Modified Date" />
  <PropertyDef Name="FileName" DataType="text" DisplayName="Name" />
  <PropertyDef Name="Description" DataType="text" DisplayName="Description" />
  <PropertyDef Name="Title" DataType="text" DisplayName="Title" />
  <PropertyDef Name="Author" DataType="text" DisplayName="Author" />
  <PropertyDef Name="DocSubject" DataType="text" DisplayName="Subject" />
  <PropertyDef Name="DocKeywords" DataType="text" DisplayName="Keywords" />
  <PropertyDef Name="DocComments" DataType="text" DisplayName="Comments" />
  <PropertyDef Name="CreatedBy" DataType="text" DisplayName="Created By" />
  <PropertyDef Name="ModifiedBy" DataType="text" DisplayName="Last Modified By" />
</PropertyDefs>
```

You can add managed properties to these definitions even if they have not been designated for use in a scope. After they are defined, these properties can then be used in the result types filter definitions as well as the managed properties filters.

```
<ResultType DisplayName="Word Documents" Name="worddocuments">
  <KeywordQuery>FileExtension="doc" OR FileExtension="docx" OR
FileExtension="dot" OR FileExtension="docm" OR
ileExtension="odt"</KeywordQuery>
  <PropertyRef Name="Author" />
  <PropertyRef Name="DocComments" />
  <PropertyRef Name="Description" />
  <PropertyRef Name="DocKeywords" />
  <PropertyRef Name="FileName" />
  <PropertyRef Name="Size" />
  <PropertyRef Name="DocSubject" />
  <PropertyRef Name="Path" />
  <PropertyRef Name="Write" />
  <PropertyRef Name="CreatedBy" />
  <PropertyRef Name="ModifiedBy" />
  <PropertyRef Name="Title" />
</ResultType>
```

There are result types for the following categories.

- Default
- Documents
- Microsoft Word Documents
- Microsoft Excel Documents
- Presentations

You can enter new managed properties as property definitions, and then create new result types or modify existing ones in this file. After you edit the string, save it back into the Property text box.

The Miscellaneous section contains a single setting for the target results URL, as shown in Figure 13-29. In particular, a custom Advanced Query Web Part might need to point to a custom results page where the presentation of the results Web Parts has been modified to meet business needs. This custom results page can also contain non-search Web Parts that connect to the search Web Parts.

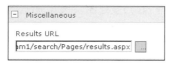

FIGURE 13-29 Advanced Search Web Part properties Miscellaneous section

A sample search query constructed by the advance search Web Part can be passed as the following.

```
ALL(searchterm) (DetectedLanguage="en") (IsDocument="True") Write>=02/01/2010
```

A knowledgeable user can enter the search in a basic query box as the following and achieve the same results.

```
searchterm DetectedLanguage="en" IsDocument="True" Write>=02/01/2010
```

However, most users will find the UI of the advanced search easier to use.

Customizing the Results Presentation

SharePoint 2010 provides the flexibility to control result page features such as document preview, sorting, and spell check. If a FAST Search capability is added to a mobile phone application, one or more features of the FAST functionality should be removed to ensure quick page download times. When a FAST Search site is created by default, the Results.aspx page has several different content areas that you can modify. Figure 13-30 shows the search results page and some of the major Web Parts.

FIGURE 13-30 Editing the search results page

The following sections describe each Web Part on the Results.aspx page and its function.

Refinement Panel

Previous versions of SharePoint did not support faceted search results. Faceted search results, also called refiners, provide users with alternative methods of exploring result data through the use of filtering. Using filters with different classifications across result sets of varying sizes while retaining counts of the documents found for each query provides users with detailed information, such as which documents are Microsoft Word documents in the result set or how many documents are written by a specific author. Faceted search results are located in the refinement panel.

When a user executes a search query, the refinement panel provides the user with relevant search categories (or metadata) for the first 50 items in the results list. These results are based on predefined search criteria. For example, if a user clicks the Microsoft Word hyperlink, all matching Word documents are shown in the search results. Several categories of refinement queries are provided by default: site-specific information, similar authors, company, and product category. All links under the Result Type heading allow the user to filter the result set to include only Microsoft Word documents, as an example. By default, SharePoint Server includes Result Type queries, as shown in Figure 13-31.

```
Result Type
Any Result Typ...
Web Page (209)
Microsoft Word (29)
XML Document (5)
Microsoft Powe... (4)
ZIP Archive (3)
Adobe PDF (3)
Visio (1)
show fewer ∧
```

FIGURE 13-31 Default Result Types

> **NOTE** Both SharePoint Search and SharePoint FAST Search include the refinement panel. However, the SharePoint Search refinement panel only reflects a count using the documents shown in the result set that has been security trimmed. To conserve resources, SharePoint Search security trims the results list as it is prepared for a view to be presented to the user. As a result, the count may change depending on sorting or filtering options. A user must view all items to get accurate counts. FAST for SharePoint Server security trims items as they are added to the results list and therefore provides accurate result counts.

You can apply refiners to a results page using the individual Web Parts on the search results page. You can also customize additional configurations through development tools, but the standard Web Parts and XML give you a great deal of capability without requiring code.

You can customize the refinement panel to reflect relevant data for the user. For an intranet site, you might want to use the full capabilities of the refinement panel; however, for an Internet-facing site, you might find that a limited subset is a better choice. In earlier versions, changing or creating result sets required a developer with knowledge of the SharePoint Server 2007 search engine. In SharePoint 2010, customizing search Web Parts can be done by a farm administrator.

To fully understand the options available in the refinement panel, open the search results page for edit and modify the Web Part. The Web Part properties look similar to those shown in Figure 13-32.

FIGURE 13-32 Refinement panel properties

IMPORTANT Each section in the property page contains distinct options available and you should change the options thoughtfully and with caution. This section doesn't cover all the options available in the search Web Parts. Be sure to test any changes in a development environment before changing them on a production server.

When the FAST Search site is created, the relevant data Web Part shows different sections that pertain to different filters that are available based on available metadata definitions. One such section is the Modified Date section, which a farm administrator could use, for example, to add a column that shows the past three months of data in addition to the defaults. SharePoint 2010 makes adding columns like this straightforward and editable with just a few steps.

To add a new relevant search query, open the Refinement section in the Refinement Panel as shown in Figure 13-33 and follow these steps.

1. By default, the Use Default Configuration check box is selected. Clear the check box to ensure that customizations are saved.

FIGURE 13-33 Refinement properties

2. Place your pointer in the Filter Category Definition text box to activate the Builder text editor blue button at the end of the text box. Click the button to open the editor. Copy and save the text in a text file. This text usually displays as one long line, so it is helpful to have line wrapping turned on in your text editor.

> **NOTE** It is best to open this file in Notepad; opening it in Microsoft Write or Microsoft Word could cause formatting issues.

3. The file is in XML format, and to add an entry to reflect the type of search condition being created, look for the following text.

```
<CustomFilter CustomValue="Past Month">
<OriginalValue>-30..</OriginalValue>        </CustomFilter>
```

4. Type the following text just after the text shown in step 3.

```
<CustomFilter CustomValue="Past Three Months">
<OriginalValue>-90..</OriginalValue>        </CustomFilter>
```

5. Look for the following line of text a few rows above the text you just added.

```
NumberOfFiltersToDisplay="6"
```

6. Add one to the number to reflect the new line you added into the XML.

```
NumberOfFiltersToDisplay="7"
```

7. Copy the code from the text file back into the Builder text editor from the Web Part. Figure 13-34 shows what the result might look like.

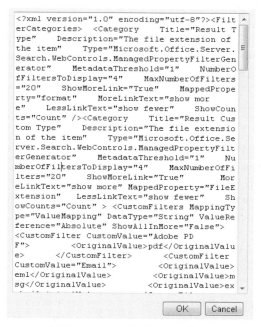

FIGURE 13-34 Refinement XML properties

8. Click OK, save the page, and check it in and publish it if required by the page library. Figure 13-35 shows the newly created Past Three Months relevant search.

FIGURE 13-35 Searching using the updated refinement XML properties

Alternatively, you also can add new relevant search categories. These search categories are tied to managed properties, so be sure to create the managed property first and run a full index before adding them using the previous procedure.

You can also find options under the refinement tab such as accuracy index, categories to display, and number of characters to display. The accuracy index allows the administrator to determine the number of results used to display the different relevancy searches. This is important if requirements exist that only show the top five or ten links and related search information on a mobile phone.

Search Core Results

Both SharePoint Search and SharePoint FAST Search use federated search Web Parts to display search results. Federated search Web Parts provide a method for retrieving search results from any OpenSearch 1.1 compliant search engine including SharePoint farms, an enterprise application, or other API accessible applications. Each product provides a unique Search Core Results Web Part and much of the customization for the search results is done in the properties of this Web Part. The figures show the properties from each product when necessary to reflect the different features. Figure 13-36 shows all the property sections available, but not all sections will be covered in this discussion. The following configuration items are necessary to achieve quality results for users.

- **Location**   The Location Properties section is expanded in Figure 13-36 and contains two crucial configurations. The Location drop-down list presents the Federated Locations defined at the search application level. SharePoint Search 2010 uses the Local Search Results as shown in Figure 13-36. FAST search uses the Local FAST Search Results. The Scope box provides the option to limit search results to one or more search scopes, which may be defined at the search application or local site collection level as defined by the search scope. You must type the exact scope name in the box because no drop-down list of possibilities is provided. The scope configuration option is normally used on custom search results pages or when using the Search Core Results Web Part to display fixed queries. To change or add a search scope, see Chapter 11, "Search Server 2010 and FAST Search: Architecture and Administration."

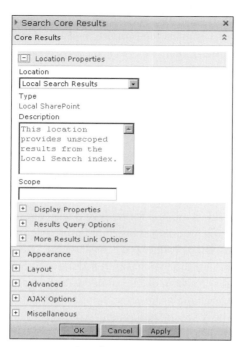

FIGURE 13-36 Search Core Results properties

- **Display Properties section** The FAST Search Web Part properties shown in Figure 13-37 include several configuration options in the Display section that are not available in SharePoint Search. There are check boxes to enable Similar Results, Document Preview for Microsoft PowerPoint, and Thumbnail Preview for Microsoft Word documents. The Maximum Number Of Document Previews And Thumbnails option controls the results displayed to users, whereas the Maximum Number Of Concurrent Requests For Document Previews And Thumbnails will impact the resources consumed by the display. The SharePoint Search 2010 Web Part (not shown) only has one configuration: Default Results Sorting, which has options for Relevance and Modified Date. Relevance is the default configuration. The rest of the configurations shown in Figure 13-37 are common to both Web Parts.

  The Fetched Properties and XSL Properties sections are discussed in the next section, "Customizing Search Results Metadata."

FIGURE 13-37 FAST Search Core Results Display Properties

- **Results Query Options section** The FAST Search Web Part properties shown in Figure 13-38 present configuration options for the Spellchecking feature, which is not available with SharePoint Search 2010. Enable Spellchecking options are Off, Suggest, and Rewrite. By default, spell checking is set to suggest the proper spelling for search terms. If the option is set to Rewrite, then the options are available for actions to perform if no results are returned.

  The remainder of the Results Query Options section is common to both search products. The default Query Language setting, Browser Locale, uses the language of the browser locale configuration unless overwritten by a user preference in the search box. Any language recognized by the search product may be selected from the drop-down list for this configuration.

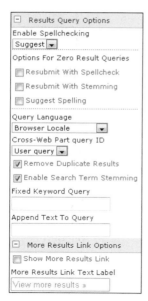

FIGURE 13-38 FAST Search Results Query properties

The Cross-Web Part Query ID options are User Query, Query 2, Query 3, Query 4, and Query 5. This ID is used by results Web Parts to identify the query manager that they share. Web Parts with the User Query option selected share the query sent to the results page. Those with Query IDs 2 through 5 share a Fixed Keyword Query and can be placed on any page where they process the query when the page loads.

Selecting the Remove Duplicate Results check box causes "duplicate" results to be merged. "Duplicate" in this case does not mean exact matches, because the SharePoint crawl component only indexes the first 16 megabytes (MB) of a file. If the content is the same in that first part of the file, even a variation in the file name does not disqualify a file from being considered a duplicate.

You can select Enable Search Term Stemming to link word forms to their base form. For example, variations of "run" include "running," "ran," and "runs." Stemmers are not available for all languages.

If Ignore Noise Words is enabled, any words listed in the noise word file for the query language are removed from queries. In SharePoint 2010, noise words are indexed and can be used for searches if this option is not selected.

The Fixed Keyword Query text box can specify that the query contain any search term, including filters such as managed properties and scopes. Do not enter anything in this box if using the User Query Cross-Web Part query ID as the entry will cause the Web Part to reject the user query. When placing multiple results Web Parts with Fixed Keyword Query entries, they must all use a unique Cross-Web Part query ID.

The value entered in the Append Text To Query text box differs from a value entered in the Fixed Keyword Query box in that it adds the terms and filters to the query entered by the user. This entry is transparent to the user as it is added on the results page and does not appear as part of the query.

- **More Results List Options section** This section is only useful if the Web Part is used to present fixed query results on a separate page, because the results page uses the Paging Web Part to expose the complete results. This option configures a link to a full results page to receive the query and present a full results list.

- **Appearance, Advanced, and AJAX Options sections** These sections are common to all Web Parts. If you need to target a Search Core Results Web Part to an audience, that option is in the Advanced section.

- **Miscellaneous Options section** Shown in Figure 13-39, this section contains some significant configurations for this Web Part. First, the default 1000 count for the Highest Result Page setting is the count for pages, not items in the result list. Given the default 10 results per page, 10,000 items in a result list is probably more than any user will examine even with the new Refinement Web Part filtering capability. Lowering this number when permissible will improve performance.

Discovered definitions appear in the lower portion of the Search Core Results Web Part as "What people are saying about <term>". These results are automatically extracted by the linguistic processing built into the indexing process. The process is seeking any phrase that infers a meaning. The smaller your index, the less likely you are to get a discovered definition.

If you clear the Show Search Results check box and configure the action links, you now have an Action Links Web Part. Enabling Show Action Links adds the action links options in the Location Properties section and removes the Query Language picker in the Results Query Options section.

When Show Messages is enabled, the Web Part displays error messages if an error occurs. This setting is useful when troubleshooting; otherwise, the Web Part does display when it has no results.

The Sample Data setting is present only for testing the XSL presentation, but the XSL Link setting permits centralizing style sheets to control the presentation of multiple Web Parts of the same type.

FIGURE 13-39 Miscellaneous properties section

MORE INFO To find out more about other search Web Parts, see *Microsoft SharePoint 2010 Administrator's Pocket Consultant* by Ben Curry (Microsoft Press, 2010), which will walk you through configuring search Web Parts step by step.

Customizing Search Results Metadata

It is often necessary to change or remove the metadata returned with search results. For example, an organization might want to change or remove the property Author and replace it with Department on their Internet-facing Search Center site. This could be especially important when information about individual corporate employees should not be searchable metadata.

NOTE In this example, you should assume that the metadata exists for Department and that a managed property has been created and associated with the metadata.

It is not necessary to delete or modify the managed property being displayed if all you need is to remove it or replace it with another managed property. To change the managed properties retrieved by the Core Results Web Part, use the following steps.

1. Open the search results page in edit mode.

2. Select Edit Web Part for the Search Core Results Web Part.

3. Expand the Display Properties section as shown in Figure 13-37 above.

4. Clear the Use Location Visualization check box so the Web Part will use your customizations instead of the configuration of the Federated Location Definition at the search application level.

5. Copy the entire XML string contained in the Fetched Properties text box into your favorite XML editor. This string defines much of the functionality of the Web Part. These managed properties are sent to the query manager as managed properties to

be retrieved for each search result in the result set. The Fetched Properties code in the Core Results and Search Action Links Web Parts is as follows.

```
<Columns>
    <Column Name="WorkId" />
    <Column Name="Rank" />
    <Column Name="Title" />
    <Column Name="Author" />
    <Column Name="Size" />
    <Column Name="Path" />
    <Column Name="Description" />
    <Column Name="Write" />
    <Column Name="SiteName" />
    <Column Name="CollapsingStatus" />
    <Column Name="HitHighlightedSummary" />
    <Column Name="HitHighlightedProperties" />
    <Column Name="ContentClass" />
    <Column Name="IsDocument" />
    <Column Name="PictureThumbnailURL" />
    <Column Name="PopularSocialTags" />
    <Column Name="PictureWidth" />
    <Column Name="PictureHeight" />
    <Column Name="DatePictureTaken" />
    <Column Name="ServerRedirectedURL" />
</Columns>
```

6. Locate the managed property and remove it from the string. In the example above, you will remove <Column Name="Author" />.

7. Add the managed property that will replace Author. For the example above, you would add <Column Name="Department" />.

8. Replace the default Fetched Properties code with your modified code.

9. After you add managed properties to this list, you must also modify the XSL to specify how the new property is to be displayed. There are two options for modifying the style sheet for the Web Part. In this section, you can click the XSL Editor button to expose the XSL code within the Web Part. You will probably find it easier to copy the code into your favorite editor for modification and then paste the modified code back into the editor to save it. In the Miscellaneous section, you can enter the URL for an external style sheet used by one or more Web Parts.

10. Test the new search criteria.

Improving Search Quality

If you use SharePoint 2010 as a business collaboration platform for the enterprise and Web to empower and connect people, high quality and structured taxonomies are essential. Although it is important to provide and control the end-user experience, it is also important to understand the underlying data and how results are displayed in the search results.

SharePoint 2010 provides capabilities that enable taxonomists, category managers, and administrators to create and manage terms and sets of terms across the enterprise. Using taxonomy to tag and classify information helps users find information quickly and easily, without regard to the physical location of the data.

Improving search quality through managed taxonomies is important to ensuring high-quality, low-cost search results. SharePoint 2010 components can be customized using the SharePoint search sites, which provide a significant time savings in critical knowledge-driven situations. This time savings can be seen by the user productivity improvements, reduction in IT costs, and an increase in organizational agility.

SharePoint 2010 contains many search improvements that provide administrators and content managers the ability to customize and refine search results, thereby adding value to the enterprise search applications.

Linguistics

Linguistic processing is one method Microsoft FAST Search Server uses to provide better search results. Linguistics uses languages structure and information so users can more easily find relevant data through search queries. Enterprises can, through the combined knowledge of linguistics fundamentals and understanding their business data, improve precision and recall of search results. Linguistics can be applied to SharePoint installations whether they are unilingual (single language) or multilingual (multiple languages). However, in multilingual installations, advanced tokenization algorithms are applied that understand language specific customizations or requirements. Additionally, documents are often written in different languages, and the crawl component must identify the language before linguistic processing can take place.

It is important to note that linguistics processing either alters the results by transforming the search query or enriches documents prior to indexing, which allows for grammatical forms and synonyms to be added to the index. This processing helps ensure, for example, that a user who is looking for the BAB stock price receives results from British Airways and not results relating to *baby*, *bad*, or other similar search terms. The choice of where to best integrate linguistic processing is usually defined by performance, practicality, and flexibility. By default, SharePoint 2010 provides good out-of-the-box support for linguistics.

Changes in SharePoint 2010 include multilingual tokenization (also referred to as word breaking), automatic language detection, improved compound term handling, and spelling variations, such as the ability to search for File_name.ext, for example, and also see results for Filename.ext and File name.ext.

> **MORE INFO** SharePoint Search uses the managed metadata term store to define translations as required. More information on this topic can be found in Chapter 14, "Administering Enterprise Content Management," and specifics regarding the importing of metadata can be found on the Microsoft TechNet website at *http://technet.microsoft.com/en-us/library/ee424396(office.14).aspx*.

Tokenization and Normalization

SharePoint 2010 is able to identify characters and symbols that separate words and are not relevant to the matching process. Configuration options such as which characters can be treated as the white space separator and split tokens are available as well, and there is an open tokenization framework for integration of customer specific tokenizers. Finally, a comprehensive Asian language-processing feature provides tokenization and language normalization as needed for languages such as Japanese and Chinese.

Spelling and Pronunciation

SharePoint Search detects names and phrases and automatically rewrites queries or provides search tips that are displayed to the end user. Custom phrase dictionaries may also be created, and phrasing can be combined with spell checking. SharePoint 2010 supports the following spelling searches.

- Simple spell check, which checks against language-specific dictionaries
- Phonetic spell check for phonetic similarities
- Advanced spell check against a custom list of words or phrases

Adding words to the default dictionary becomes important when enterprises want to tailor the dictionary to include product or industry-specific terminology. This functionality is shown in the example in Figure 13-40. The user typed the word "sharrepoint" and the SharePoint search engine asked the user, "Did you mean *sharepoint*?"

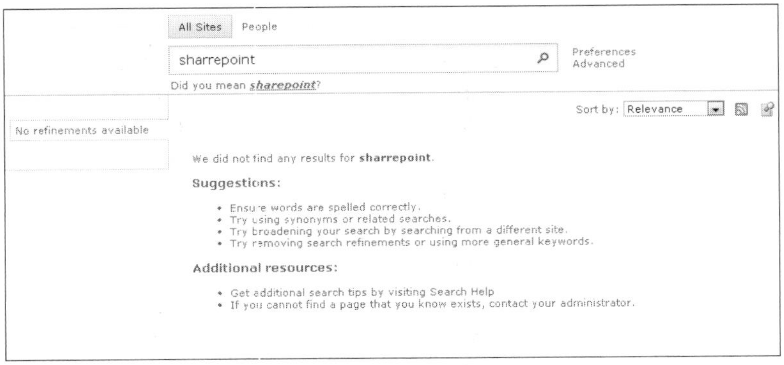

FIGURE 13-40 An example of the SharePoint spell check spell-tuning feature

SPELL-TUNING

SharePoint FAST Search supports a set of Windows PowerShell cmdlets that fine-tune the spell checking dictionaries against the content of the index. This spell-tuning process allows administrators to automatically update the spelling dictionaries and provides support for spell checking during the search process. When a user enters a search query, the spell checking process looks for misspelled query terms based on the spelling dictionary and suggests alternative spellings to end users through the "Did you mean" search feature, as shown in Figure 13-40. When spell-tuning is enabled, spell checking dictionaries are compared with the frequency of words in the index, thus ensuring that only suggestions relevant within the content that is indexed are provided. SharePoint FAST Search prioritizes term suggestions that occur more frequently in the content store. Table 13-3 shows the various cmdlets available for spell tuning.

TABLE 13-3 Windows PowerShell cmdlets for Spell-Tuning

WINDOWS POWERSHELL CMDLET	DESCRIPTION
Add-FASTSearchSpelltuning	Enable the spell-tuning processor to compare the spell checking dictionaries with the index.
Get-FASTSearchSpelltuningStatus	Retrieve the status of spell-tuning: active or inactive.
Reset-FASTSearchSpellChecking	Replace the "Did you mean" custom dictionaries with the default installation dictionaries.
Remove-FASTSearchSpellTuning	Disable spell-tuning and stop generation of new dictionaries. Disabling the spell-tuning feature restores the FAST Search engine to the default dictionaries provided by the original installation software.

Each of the commands in Table 13-3 should be run on the FAST Search engine server, because the Windows PowerShell cmdlets are not available on SharePoint application-only servers.

EXCLUDING WORDS FROM SPELL CHECK

Occasionally you will need to exclude a word from the spell checking feature, and as a result no alternative spellings will be shown with the "Did you mean" feature shown in Figure 13-40. For example, an administrator has a site that lists inventory by part numbers, such as PAR123, and the results page might include federated search data from Bing search. However, a competitor has a part number called PART123, and each time a user searches the site for PAR123, a suggestion is returned suggesting PART123. One method to resolve this issue is to add the term or phrase to the dictionary, and another is to exclude the term from the SharePoint spell checker.

You can exclude specific word suggestions from the search engine using Central Administration. To set the "Did you mean" feature to prevent a specific dictionary spelling suggestion, follow these steps.

1. Open a browser and go to the SharePoint Central Administration website.

2. Under Application Management, click Service Applications.

3. Click FAST Query SSA.

4. Click the FAST Search Administration link.

5. Click the Spell Checking Management link.

6. Click the Add Spell Checking Exception link.

7. Add the exception phrase, as shown in Figure 13-41.

FIGURE 13-41 FAST Query SSA Add Spell Checking Exception page

8. Click OK.

Lemmatization

SharePoint 2010 FAST Server contains the ability to perform an index and query expansion that allows the quick reference to words or phrases in a consistent way to provide a higher probability of returning high-value search results. *Lemmatization* is the process of mapping a word down to its base form or form variation, to improve the search recall. For example, "keyboard" is the base form or lemma value of "keyboarding," "keyboards," and so forth. Lemmatization can be added to the search feature using one of the following three methods.

- **Index expansion** As content is indexed, the lemma value (base search term) is stored in the index. This method provides quick search results but requires a larger index and utilizes additional disk storage.

- **Query expansion** As content is searched, the query searches for the lemma value and the opposite effect of index expansion occurs, in that it requires less physical disk storage, and search queries take longer for the website search applications. To perform search query lemmatization, the search query language must be known to decipher the base word or phrase.

- **Reduction** Expansion through reduction stores the reduced lemma value in the index; however, the original search term is reduced to the same value. This methodology is between other lemmatization types in terms of storage requirements, because it doesn't store more content than it needs.

The preferred approach currently is to perform lemmatization during the indexing process using either index expansion or reduction, because it is more difficult to control the search environment and language during the search query expansion process.

SharePoint 2010 handles lemmatization during indexing by expanding the given word into its base term and indexing the content. This provides high quality search results that are most likely to be relevant to the user. Lemmatization is applied to nouns, verbs, and adjectives, and it is independent of query language settings. Often, languages have complex inflections, phrases, and/or words that are similar in definition and are supported by the SharePoint FAST Search engine.

> **IMPORTANT** It is important to understand whether the specific content should be lemmatized, because it can affect performance and storage capacity. During planning and implementation of SharePoint FAST Search Server, take time to understand the data being ingested and indexed. As a general guideline, data that is small, highly structured, or requires exact text matching should not be lemmatized; data that is unstructured, feature rich, and contains many different large text-based documents will see a performance gain using lemmatization.

Entity Extraction

Enterprises consistently struggle with data located across multiple content sources and methodologies to bring the data together within a single search application. SharePoint 2010 provides an extensive entity extraction framework that detects names, locations, and other well-defined elements in local and remote content stores, such as a database. Several custom extractors are provided out of the box to extract specific data such as people's names, company names, and locations, and these can also be annotated to semantic structures in the text, such as paragraphs or sentences. This metadata search allows for faceted refinement, relevancy tuning, and targeted queries (such as searching only the author field).

Entity extraction automatically extracts defined metadata to create useful information based on unstructured data. Metadata extraction is available in both SharePoint Search and FAST Search products, whereas FAST Search also supports administration using the SharePoint Central Administration website as well as the concept of property extractors. Property extractors are used to define data that can be extracted for inclusion in managed properties but are not defined as properties within the document libraries. Examples of property extractors are

- Language-dependent entity extractors for people's names, company names, locations, and dates are defined by default.

- Language-independent entity extractors are available for price, measure, uppercase, acronym, e-mail, file name, ISBN, university, URL, newspaper (US), phone, zip code, ticker, date/time (ISO), and quotation.

- A noun phrase extraction document processor extracts phrases such as "competitive advantage," "project assessment," "value add," and so forth.

- Tools to create domain-specific entity extraction rules and dictionaries are provided and can be based on dictionary lookup, statistical, rules, or a combination of these.

Complete the following steps to improve the precision of the property extractors by editing the include lists and exclude lists.

> **NOTE** Excluded items are removed immediately, whereas included items take effect the next time the content is indexed.

1. Open a browser and go to the SharePoint Central Administration website.
2. Under Application Management, click Service Applications.
3. Select FAST Query SSA.
4. Select FAST Search Administration.
5. Select Manage Property Extraction to open the page shown in Figure 13-42.

FIGURE 13-42 Manage Property Extraction page

By defining items to be included or excluded using the method explained in the previous steps, the content processing pipeline adds or creates these metadata properties before the index processes content, creates normalization, and builds the final metadata. These properties can be used as part of refinement queries and relevance rankings.

Creating Search Rules

It is often necessary for search administrators to omit data that matches certain patterns from crawl files to either improve search results or omit confidential data located within a SharePoint site or federated search location. You can exclude content at varying levels within a SharePoint library or list. SharePoint document libraries and lists can be excluded as a whole, certain columns can be excluded, and/or columns can be excluded based on the security permissions of the user. For example, typical items that should not be included are SSN, credit card information, or URLs with a specific parameter.

Typically administrators create crawl rules that limit SharePoint crawlers from accessing specific links. Crawl rules require specification of each individual URL separately in the exclude list; you do this using the Central Administration website. However, you can use a wildcard search such as \\servername\webfolder* to keep the exclude rule set small and still prevent unwanted documents from being included in search results. You can use a wildcard search with a regular expression or regex to limit the number of search results given.

In both SharePoint FAST Search and SharePoint 2010 Search, crawl rules in SharePoint 2010 allow the user to match URLs using regular expressions. Now administrators can determine inclusion or exclusion based on regex syntax. Table 13-4 shows some examples of the regex queries SharePoint 2010 supports.

> **MORE INFO** You can find more about regex syntax at *http://www.regular-expressions.info /reference.html*. It is important to fully test all regex expressions using a tool such as Expresso, which can be found at *http://www.ultrapico.com/Expresso.htm*.

TABLE 13-4 Examples of Regex Queries

REGEX EXPRESSION	DESCRIPTION
\\fileshare\.*	Match all files under the filesystem share \\fileshare.
\\fileshare\((private)|(temp))\.*	Match all files under fileshare that are named either private or temp.
http://site/default.aspx[?]ssn=.*	Match all links that have the parameter ssn= in the URL path.
http://site/default.aspx[?] var1=1&var2=.*	Match all links that have a var1 specified and var2 matches anything.

Regex expressions enable crawl rules that require less administrative maintenance and a well-defined set of search rules. However, regular expressions cannot be used in the protocol component of the URL. Compare the following two regex URLs.

- *http://www.microsoft.com/.** matches all URLs under Microsoft.com, and
- *.*/www.microsoft.com/.** matches *http://.*://www.microsoft.com/.**, which does not provide the intended results.

To create a crawl rule that excludes files matching the URL parameter fileURL, complete the following steps.

1. Open a browser and go to the SharePoint Central Administration website.

2. Under Application Management, click Service Applications.

3. Click FAST Query SSA.

4. Click FAST Search Administration.

5. Click Crawl Rules to display a page similar to the one shown in Figure 13-43.

FIGURE 13-43 Add Crawl Rule page

6. Choose the path using regular expressions if needed. When regular expressions are used, you must select the Follow Regular Expression Syntax option. By default, the syntax of the regex expression and URL are not case sensitive. If you require case sensitivity, select the Match Case check box.

7. Choose whether to exclude or include items that match the pattern. In addition, select any check boxes as needed.

8. Specify authentication credentials as needed for the crawl rule.

9. Click OK.

Rank Profile

Because users create search queries with differing intents, SharePoint Search 2010 uses multiple relevance ranking modules. You can customize search result modules for a content search, a people search, and people search in conjunction with a content search. The ranking module used depends on the results Web Part that is used and the repository that is crawled.

SharePoint Search and FAST Search allow the creation of custom relevance ranking. Default modules provided as part of the search applications cannot be modified; however, custom modules can use the standard configuration to start and then you can customize them as necessary to meet the needs of an organization.

Both SharePoint FAST Search and SharePoint Search Server support two levels of rank profile customizations: customizations can be made with the user interface or by using the search queries sent by a Web Part or application. The SharePoint search index contains a rank profile that controls how ranking is calculated for items in a search query results list. Ranking a document within a result set is represented within the search application as an integer that represents the relevance of a particular item for a search query. This integer is defined as a combination of static rank and dynamic rank.

A static rank does not depend on the search query for its ranking information. A static rank is based on boost values that are stored in predefined managed properties. This static rank value is added to items at index time. Static rank boosting is efficient from a query performance point of view, because this boosting does not add any complexity to the query evaluation. Static rank points assigned to an indexed item are independent of the query/search words used. This means that static rank only indicates something about the general importance of a document due to predefined values assigned to metadata related to the item. It is not possible to modify a static score at query time. However, the ranking algorithm can be modified to collect static scores only from certain metadata.

Dynamic rank values depend on how well the search query matches an indexed item. An example of dynamic ranking would be the number of times a search term appears in a document relative to the number of words in the document. Another would be extra rank points assigned because the search term was in metadata or the file name or the document title instead of just in the document text.

A rank profile enables you to exert some control over the relative weight of each rank component for a search query. For example, is the content searched looking for the latest news? If so, the search results are defined by "freshness." In SharePoint FAST Search, the rank profile configuration defines relative weights for different components. You can define rank profiles as needed to support different user or application profiles. There is no limit to the number of rank profiles that you can create and apply during the search query at run time. Most frequently, default rank profiles are defined for a Search Center site that targets specific predefined user patterns. For example, you could define a Search Center site for sales representatives who need to see related Microsoft PowerPoint and other marketing material more often than engineering documents and set up rank profiles that would prioritize PowerPoint and documents containing project names ahead of Microsoft Word and Microsoft Excel files, even though an Excel document might have a higher match value to the search query.

You can also apply result sorting as a sort by parameter within the Search Center site to enable a user to find all of the Microsoft Word documents—and no other documents—relating to the search query, based on query search terms.

Finally, you can apply a rank profile based on the query used by the user. For example, if a user is looking for information about a product to give to a customer, a ranking can be applied that is based on the specific terms provided in the query.

After the rank is applied to an item, you can add boosts or attributes that influence the ranking algorithm and moves items in a result set up or down in relevancy. The following boosts are available.

- **Anchor text boost**   Defined as the weight an indexed item imposes over other documents in the collection.

- **Queries boost** Also known as click-through. The more a related item is clicked in result sets, the higher its rankings in the result set. A "30-day sliding window" is applied to click-throughs so that only more recent activities affect this boost.

- **Freshness boost** How recent is the creation date of a document—is the content "fresh"? A news application, for example, wants to boost this value to ensure the newest content is at the top of the list during search queries.

- **Managed property boost** Sets boost levels for managed properties or groups of managed properties.

- **Proximity boost** Defined by how closely related to the search query is the document; this is also referred to as URL proximity.

- **Context boost** How well does the document text or terms match the search criteria? For example, how well does text in the title column match the search query?

- **Quality boost** Set the boost depending on a managed property value such as a user rating, also referred to as user social tagging.

Changing these values can assist the user in quickly finding related information based on a search query. The following example shows how you can create a new rank profile with Windows PowerShell commands to use in the Search Center site. This custom rank profile ranks Microsoft PowerPoint documents higher in the search results.

To start, open the SharePoint 2010 Management Shell and then complete the following steps.

1. Get the current default rank profile for the Search Center site using the following command in Windows PowerShell.

```
$rp = Get-FASTSearchMetadataRankProfile –Name default
```

Figure 13-44 shows the results of this command as well as the options and values available for customization.

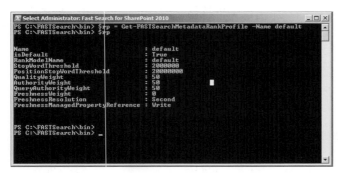

FIGURE 13-44 Windows PowerShell results for default rank profile

2. Copy the default template to a new variable for modification and assign a name for the rank profile using the following command.

```
$newrp = New- FASTSearchMetadataRankProfile –Name MSPPTBoost -Template $rp
```

3. Assign the managed property fileextension to a managed property variable for use in the boost command as follows.

```
$file = Get-FASTSearchMetadataManagedProperty -Name fileextension
```

4. Apply managed property boost to rank profile. Apply a lower number to increase the ranking. This command can also be used to update an existing managed property rank boost value.

```
$newrp.CreateManagedPropertyBoostComponent($file, "pptx,10")
```

5. Exit Windows PowerShell.

6. Open the FAST Search Center site results page in edit mode.

7. Edit the Search Action Links Web Part, which will open the Web Part properties shown in Figure 13-45.

8. Enabling a ranking profile makes it available as a sort option for users. Choose MSPPT-Boost to include in the Web Part sort options. You could also change the default sort order in the Display Properties Sorting Configuration options.

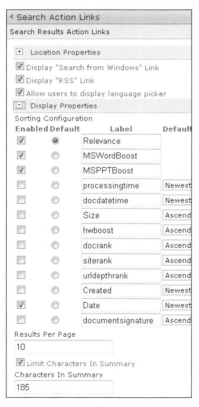

FIGURE 13-45 Search Action Links Web Part properties

9. Click OK to apply the changes you have made.

10. Save the changes to the Web page and exit Page Edit mode.

11. Choose the new custom rank sort from the Sort By drop-down list, as shown in Figure 13-46.

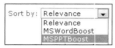

FIGURE 13-46 Selecting a boost rank profile from the Sort By drop-down list

12. The results are sorted giving PowerPoint documents a higher rank value, so these document types appear at the top of the search results. Notice in Figure 13-47 that the file XJ2000 Sales Presentation is ranked third in the first sort (at left), but using the custom ranking, it is ranked first in the results window (at right).

FIGURE 13-47 Search results with document boost

The ease and power with which farm administrators can control search results through rank profiles is apparent through this example; however, it is important to fully test any customizations to the rank profiles to ensure the results function as you intended.

XRANK

XRANK is a method in which dynamic filtering can occur during query execution using the XRANK operator, which is a part of the FAST Query Language (FQL). The method could be examining properties or text that is not part of the query string itself.

As a simple example, let's say your favorite U.S. presidents are Abraham Lincoln and George Washington. You want to elevate (boost) the ranking of any documents containing either of their names when someone searches for the term "president." In addition, you want any document that contains the names of *both* Lincoln and Washington to receive an extra boost. The XRANK statement would be as follows.

```
Xrank(Xrank(string("president"), person:string("Abraham Lincoln"), boost=5000),person:st
ring("George Washington"), boost=5000)
```

Dynamic ranking and weighting can also be generated automatically during query execution through applications and Web Parts. This "soft boosting" of specific data based on metadata properties allows applications to provide click-through applications that narrow search results. For example, you can develop an enterprise application requiring each product to be listed in detail with supporting documentation. You then create a metadata property that allows searching for all documents for a specified product. The application can call SharePoint search using XRANK parameters and apply the ranking properties accordingly.

```
xrank(xrank(and(\"product\"),filter(\"fileextension\":pptx)),string(\"{product_name}\",
mode=\"simpleany\"),boost=50000)
```

The query shown previously will find all documents with a type of product and a file extension of pptx. This will also boost all values with the specified *product_name,* a variable that is passed in through the application code. Negative boosting is also supported but cannot reduce the ranking value below 0.

The following list describes the general behavior of the default search rank profile.

- URLs clicked most often appear higher in the search results.
- Items containing the exact or similar query phrases are ranked higher.
- Search results in the same language as the query are ranked higher.
- Social tagging or ranking (1 to 5 stars) influences relevance ranking in SharePoint Search results but not in SharePoint FAST Search.
- User click-through activity within search results elevates the relevance of the document involved in future search results for a time period. This activity is stored in the search database for a specified time period and is transferred to the index, where it is used in ranking result sets. Since recent activities are more relevant than historical activities, a "sliding window" of 30 days limits the activities used in the ranking.

> **NOTE** SharePoint Server stores two types of information for use in the rank profile: "what people are clicking" and "what people are querying." This information is stored in the FAST database for a year, and the historical data is used to power query suggestions and relevance improvements. Query suggestions are based on the "what users queried for" history and use the full year of data stored in the database, whereas the relevance improvements are based on click-throughs and use only the last 30 days of FAST data.

Search Quality Summary

The biggest issue in customizing search results can be described as "precision versus recall." Higher precision returns the exact document found, based on the search query word or phrase; however, high recall does not exclude documents in the search results. By increasing the recall of the result set, precision is lost. Determining the balance between these elements is important to providing high-quality search results.

Improving Collection Quality

Even the best application and search engines are only as good as the data they crawl. If there is unnecessary or garbage data flowing into the system, no matter how beautiful or well-designed the search application is, it always returns less than favorable results. It is important to understand and ensure quality collection data to ensure users obtain quality search results.

The following tips aid in ensuring data is available for quick, efficient search queries.

- Encourage archiving of old or obsolete data.
- For large content stores, segregate premium or commonly accessed content on high-quality servers.
- For intranet sites, encourage social tagging to improve retrieval and document ranking.
- Encourage users to provide as much metadata as needed to ensure proper searching, such as author, dates, titles, and so forth.
- Encourage hierarchies for content to ensure a logical grouping of information.
- If multiple languages are supported, group by language and then subject.
- Avoid mixing multilingual metadata, text, and message files. This ensures quick, efficient searches through the indexes and provides better search results.
- Crawl the dynamic content stores more often to ensure fresh, relevant information.
- Don't index poor quality data. If a site collection doesn't have relevant data but contains too much garbage, exclude it from the search index.

Preventing Content Errors

Inevitably, you will encounter complaints or questions about search quality and query performance, and there are some general guidelines you can follow to assist in understanding, resolving, and preventing issues. The best method to prevent issues with customers is to listen to users and get feedback. Often users have suggestions to improve the efficiency of a search application. A user once asked why so many video search results are returned in his queries, and after investigating the problem, IT personnel found that the index server had indexed an unwanted network drive. The index store was reduced by 50 percent when the unwanted content was removed from the searched content, and as a result, the SharePoint Search application improved its performance dramatically. Not every user feedback received improves performance; however, by creating a simple feedback Web Part or discussion group, the gains achieved by keeping in close contact with users ensures that they feel the IT application team is listening and are more patient when other issues arise.

Another proactive step in ensuring search is performing efficiently is reviewing the site analytics reports. These reports contain information about popular queries and those queries that failed. To view the site analytics reports, open Site Settings and then click Site Web Analytics Reports under the Site Actions heading.

Other steps you can take include installing the Microsoft Operations Manager Extension for SharePoint 2010. More details on this subject can be found in other chapters in this book, but it is important to re-emphasize it here, because being aware of site performance is critical in ensuring a high-quality search application. Reviewing crawl log errors in Search Administration will identify content that the crawl components were unable to access. Using these tools, you can monitor items such as crawl events and address issues well before users complain that their data isn't returning in search results.

Looking at the best bets and visual best bets lists often provides a key into which crawl sources and/or indexes are most likely to be hit more frequently. Ensuring that these content sources are highly available prevents links or graphics from slowing down as content is accessed repeatedly.

Explore caching, too. For Internet-facing sites and global deployments, it is often helpful to activate caching either at the SharePoint Server level or using a service such as Akamai. This ensures content is pushed as close to the user as possible.

Finally, demote sites that either provide no value to search users or those that contain URL errors.

Diagnosing search issues follow the same general issue resolution guidelines most IT applications follow: identify the query in question, diagnose the issue, fix the problem, and deploy changes as necessary.

Diagnosing Content Issues

You may encounter some common recurring content search issues that are straightforward to diagnose. Table 13-5 provides some suggestions for resolving these types of search issues.

TABLE 13-5 Resolving Content Issues

ISSUE	SUGGESTIONS FOR RESOLUTION
My document is not in the index.	Check Search Administration in Central Administration to determine if the site and document crawled. Determine if the document can be retrieved via a URL. Determine if the document contains the query term.
My document is not in the top results.	Check boosts authorities. Demote poor quality sites. Use scopes to restrict search to the best data. Add best bets and/or keywords to promote the document. Customize ranking schema.
My results aren't fresh.	Crawl high value repositories more frequently. Migrate top tier data to SharePoint.
My document didn't crawl.	Add the site to the crawl rules. Add a contextual best bet or a visual best bet.
My document crawled but I can't retrieve it.	Ensure lemmatization is enabled and enable stemming. Check the spelling feature and ensure it is enabled. Use synonyms and acronyms. Create and/or index managed properties.
I can't find documents in other languages.	Show users how to use browser language settings. Use the language picker. Check the crawler language. Ensure keywords are managed for the appropriate languages.

Summary

In this chapter, you learned that the SharePoint 2010 Search feature provides a full user experience out of the box, and you can use it to make the most of enterprise content by promoting useful data through items such as best bets, ranking models, and query refinement. You also learned how FAST Search 2010 for SharePoint extended and enhanced the search capabilities of SharePoint 2010 Search.

Administering Enterprise Content Management

E nterprise Content Management (ECM) is a set of capabilities to facilitate the seamless management of the entire content life cycle for unstructured content in Microsoft SharePoint 2010. Both on its own and as a complement to the collaboration capability, ECM provides the larger unified platform within which key content processes occur. ECM is a capability within SharePoint that has been and continues to see significant investment and improvements from Microsoft. SharePoint 2010 provides many enhancements not available in prior versions, as well as a set of new feature areas for managing metadata across your enterprise and for managing digital assets. The core vision behind ECM in SharePoint 2010 is to provide a comprehensive content management solution that empowers *all* employees and drives compliance across *all* documents. By facilitating user participation with an easy-to-understand interface, ECM controls the risks associated with unstructured content, including social content, ultimately driving down management costs and the support burden, while also limiting corporate legal exposure.

This chapter explores the new capabilities provided in SharePoint 2010. It reviews many of the core concepts needed to leverage SharePoint 2010 as a service-oriented solution for document management, enterprise metadata management, records management, Web content management, and digital asset management. This chapter introduces the core concepts and functionality provided by ECM, and you will explore the implementation, setup, configuration, and management procedures needed to employ SharePoint 2010 as your complete ECM solution.

Document Management

The architectural elements that are central to SharePoint, such as document libraries, lists, and items, also provide the basis for many of the document management topics covered in this section. Document libraries were introduced in SharePoint 2003 and became an instant hit for users of the system. By providing an easy way to store and share documents, document libraries empower users by providing additional classification and organizational capabilities such as folders and library level metadata (columns). SharePoint Server 2007 introduced even more advanced capabilities such as versioning, document approval, integration with RMS, and a site level content type and site column capability that allowed site administrators to create implementation-specific schemas for the types of content that were to be stored within the system. These content types and their associated site columns can in turn be rolled down to libraries that employ the same parent content types, allowing for site collection–based metadata management that is completely integrated with the document storage capability.

SharePoint 2010 provides new features that extend those available in SharePoint Server 2007 by enabling the management of metadata across the entire enterprise. This includes the syndication of content types, the centralized management of site columns, and the keywords/values that fill them. The new service application architecture provides the ability for these ECM services to be data-isolated, shared, and subscribed to by Web applications or even site collections. The new architecture also allows services to be consumed across the wide area network (WAN) by remote SharePoint 2010 server farms.

SharePoint 2010 extends document management features in several areas, including the following.

- Open and save functionality
- Document sets
- Navigation
- Location-based metadata defaults
- Improved document center template

In the following sections, you will explore the basics of document management within SharePoint 2010, including a high-level overview of document libraries, key document management concepts, and the fundamental system elements used for document management. You will also review detailed procedures related to the configuration of document management within the system.

Document Libraries

Document libraries provide the basic building blocks for implementing document management within SharePoint. Document libraries are not the only place where documents can be stored (they can be added as attachments to other lists as well), but they are the designated document storage list type within the system. Within a document library, you can only store documents. Document libraries provide functional capabilities that are specifically designed for working with documents. Following are a few examples of this functionality.

- Check-in/check-out
- Versioning
- Approval
- Workflows
- Information management policies

Although many of these tools are also available with other list templates, the document library template provides access to them from the document management vector. For example, although all lists have workflow capabilities, document libraries come preconfigured with document-specific content types and workflows, ready for enhancing the document management user experience.

Creating a Document Library

To create a document library, visit the target site within which you want to create the library and perform the following steps.

1. From the Site Actions menu, select New Document Library, as shown in Figure 14-1.
2. Fill out the Name and Description for the new library.
3. In the Navigation section, choose the appropriate option if you want to have the new library available from the quick launch bar within the site.
4. In the Document Version History section, choose the appropriate option if you want to have a version created each time you edit a file in the new library.
5. Specify a document template for all new files created in the library under the Document Template section.
6. Click Create.

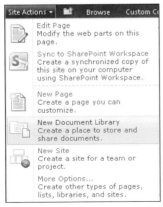

FIGURE 14-1 Select New Document Library from the Site Actions menu to create a new library.

After your new library is created, you will be forwarded to it. The library will appear as an empty list with a single link available that allows you to add a new document. At the top of the page, you will notice the new contextual Ribbon interface that is part of SharePoint 2010. The Ribbon will expose a Library Tools menu because you are in a document library. This menu will have two submenus.

- **Documents (menu)**   A menu for creating, deleting, uploading, and working with documents in the library.
- **Library (menu)**   A menu for working with the document library itself. This is where you will find the Library Settings button, along with access to library views and workflows.

Adding Documents to a Library

There are many ways to add documents to your new library. The following list provides a summary of the methods available for adding a document.

- Create a new document in the library via the New Document icon on the Ribbon.
- Upload a single document by clicking the Add New Document link within the library.
- Upload a single document by clicking the Upload Document icon on the Ribbon.
- Upload multiple documents by clicking the Upload Multiple Documents icon on the Ribbon, which opens the Upload Multiple Documents dialog box shown in Figure 14-2. This dialog box lets you either drag and drop files you want to upload or browse the file system for them.
- Save a document to the library directly from a Microsoft Office client application.

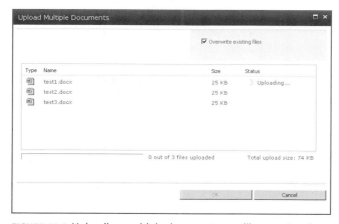

FIGURE 14-2 Uploading multiple documents to a library using the new drag and drop feature

Adjusting Document Library Settings

There are many tools you can use to manage documents within a document library. Many of these are provided as options that can be enabled or controlled through library settings. To view or change library settings, perform the following steps within the target document library.

1. On the Ribbon, select the Library menu under the Library Tools tab.

2. Click the Library Settings button. (You need Manage List permissions to access this button.)

3. From the Document Library Settings page, you can access the settings and options associated with each item, as listed in Table 14-1.

TABLE 14-1 Document Library Settings

SETTINGS	GROUP	DESCRIPTION
Title, description, and navigation settings	General Settings	Change the name and description, and specify if the library will be included in the Quick Launch.
Versioning settings	General Settings	Specify if content approval and check-out are required for the library and if a document version history is to be kept. Also included are granular options relating to version history and draft item security.
Advanced settings	General Settings	Allow management of content types, adjustment of the default document template, and adjustment of settings for opening documents. Set Custom Send To Destination, Folder options, Search visibility, and offline client availability. Specify if the library will be a Site Assets library, if items can be edited in Datasheet view, and if the library forms should be presented in a dialog box.
Validation settings	General Settings	Specify a formula for evaluation when new items are saved to the list as well as a message present to the user.
Column Default Value settings	General Settings	Specify a default value that is to be applied when new items are added in this location.
Ratings settings	General Settings	Specify if items in the list can be rated. This will create the ratings column for the list.
Audience Targeting settings	General Settings	Enable audience targeting for this list. This will create the targeting column for the list.

continued on the next page

SETTINGS	GROUP	DESCRIPTION
Metadata Navigation settings	General Settings	Select a list of available fields for use a navigation hierarchies within the list.
Per-location view settings	General Settings	Specify if this location inherits view settings from its parent, and if not, define the view settings for this location.
Form settings	General Settings	Specific to the use of InfoPath for the customization of the forms used by the list. Only available if supported.
Delete this document library option	Permissions And Management	Delete the document library and its contents, optionally sending them to the Recycle Bin if configured.
Save document library as a template option	Permissions And Management	Save the document library, and optionally its content, as a template. This template is saved to the site collection templates gallery and becomes available when creating a new library.
Permissions for this document library	Permissions And Management	Specify if the document library inherits its permissions from its parent, and if not, specify the permissions for this document library.
Manage files that have no checked-in version	Permissions And Management	Take ownership of files that are checked out to other users.
Workflow settings	Permissions And Management	Adjust list level workflow associations and settings.
Generate file plan report	Permissions And Management	Specify a location to which the file plan report is to be generated and run the report.
Information Management Policy settings	Permissions And Management	Specify library best retention schedules, the source of retention for the library (Content Types or Library and Folders), and source element–specific policies for retention.
RSS settings	Communications	Allow RSS for this list; specify the channel information, document options, columns, and item limit.

Versioning

Versioning is useful if you want to track the changes made to a document—at the document level—throughout the life cycle of the document. For example, if multiple people will be working on a document together, you may want each person to check in the document as a new version. In a file system environment, this usually means creating multiple copies of the same document and designating each as a version within the document name. This is difficult to manage and can be cumbersome. SharePoint 2010 allows you to specify if you want to keep only major versions or major and minor versions of a document.

If you choose to keep only major versions of a document, then every time a document is checked in, it will be a published version. If you decide to keep both major and minor versions of a document, SharePoint will provide an option during check-in that allows you to choose to check in the document as a major version (publish) or a minor version (draft).

When versioning is enabled for a document library, you can specify additional options such as the number of major versions to keep in the history and how many minor versions to keep for each major version, as shown in Figure 14-3. It's tempting to keep all prior versions of every document, but doing so can create additional unnecessary stored content, and this may violate potential compliance rules as well as impact library performance. Consider setting limits on these settings that will meet your requirements without making the limits so high that too many versions are saved.

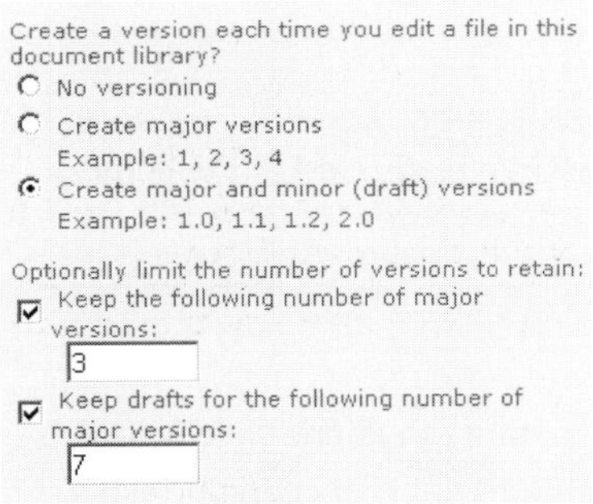

FIGURE 14-3 Adjusting versioning settings for a document library

When versioning is enabled, you can view prior versions of a document by accessing its version history. Version history is available from the Edit Control Block menu of an individual list item, or from that item's View Properties page.

Requiring Check-in/Check-out and Content Approval

By requiring document check-out before editing, you can ensure that multiple people do not attempt to upload different local copies of a document, thereby overwriting each other's changes. Check-in/check-out are particularly useful in conjunction with versioning. When you check in a document, you have the option of checking it in as a minor draft version or publishing it to the next major version.

Content approval ensures that any published major version of a document will remain in draft as pending approval until it has been reviewed and approved by a member of the Approvers group or an individual with approval permissions. This publishing workflow automation is built directly into the library by default and can be enabled from the Versioning Settings page, which can be found in Library Settings.

Draft Item Security

You may not want all readers within a library to see all documents that are stored in the library as drafts. Draft Item Security provides the ability to trim the listing of a document within the library based on the document's state in the publishing workflow. For example, if the document is in draft, you can set the library options so that only approvers and the author of the document have item visibility, or you can set the option so that all contributors within the library have draft item visibility. A third option lets you set the security level to allow all viewers the ability to see draft documents. Figure 14-4 shows the three options available for Draft Item Security within the Library Settings area.

Who should see draft items in this document library?
- Any user who can read items
- Only users who can edit items
- Only users who can approve items (and the author of the item)

FIGURE 14-4 Adjusting draft item security for a document library

NOTE Draft item security is not retroactive to documents that already exist in the library.

Information Management Policy

Information Management Policy (IM Policy) allows list administrators to define specific policies for content stored within the library. These policies ensure content adherence to corresponding compliance rules that have been defined for the library. An IM Policy optionally defines settings for the following items.

- **Retention** Schedule how content is managed and disposed by specifying a sequence of retention stages.

- **Auditing** Specify the events that should be audited for documents and items subject to this policy.

- **Barcodes** Assign a barcode to each document or item. Optionally, Microsoft Office applications can require users to insert these barcodes into documents.

- **Labels** Add a label to a document to ensure that important information about the document is included when it is printed.

Retention

Retention settings let you schedule how content is managed and disposed by configuring a sequence of retention stages. Each stage that is defined has an associated time period or retention formula that determines when a specific action occurs. The following actions are available for each stage.

- Move to Recycle Bin
- Permanently delete
- Transfer to another location
- Start a workflow
- Skip to next stage
- Declare record
- Delete previous drafts
- Delete all previous versions

Multiple stages can be defined for each policy, with each stage specifying a different time period. Each stage will occur only once unless Recurrence is enabled, after which that action will recur forever until the next stage is triggered. When records management is enabled within the site, separate retention schedules can be configured for record and non-record content. Figure 14-5 shows the setup options for each stage as they appear within the Stage Properties dialog box.

NOTE If the Library And Folder Based Retention feature is active, list administrators can override content type policies with their own retention schedules. To prevent this, deactivate the feature on the site collection.

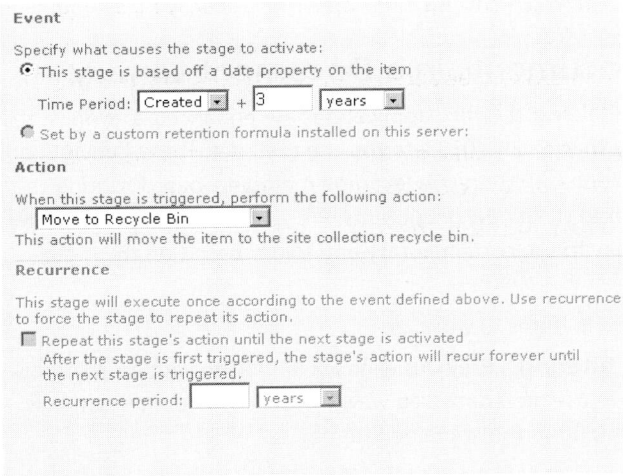

FIGURE 14-5 Creating a retention stage within an IM Policy

Auditing

Auditing specifies the events that should be audited for documents and items that are subject to the IM Policy. When the specified event occurs, an entry is written to the audit log for the site. This log can then be reviewed at a later time by administrators. IM Policies allow for the following audit events to be logged.

- Opening or downloading documents, viewing items in lists, or viewing item properties
- Editing items
- Checking out or checking in items
- Moving or copying items to another location in the site
- Deleting or restoring items

Barcodes

Barcodes are supported within SharePoint 2010 at the document level. By enabling barcodes with an IM Policy, users are able to associate a barcode with all documents subject to that policy. Optionally, you also may select to prompt users to insert a barcode before saving or printing a document.

Labels

Labels provide a way for you to ensure that important information about the document is included when it is printed. To specify a label, type the text you want to use in the Label Format box. You can use any combination of fixed text or document properties except calculated or built-in properties such as GUID or CreatedBy. To start a new line in the label format field, use the \n character sequence. You also have the ability to enforce font and style formatting for the label text as an option, as well as the ability to prevent changes to labels after they are added.

Opening and Saving Documents in a Document Library

The Open and Save functions within Microsoft Office applications are enhanced to work with SharePoint 2010 document libraries. SharePoint 2010 lets you use metadata-based navigation to find and open documents, in addition to letting you leverage metadata-based routing to automatically determine the location to store new documents. Predefined routing rules allow documents to be routed automatically to the correct library and folder based on the metadata profile for an item.

The two features that enable these features to work are

- **Metadata navigation and filtering**   Provides each list in the site with a settings page for configuring that list to use metadata tree view hierarchies and filter controls to improve navigation and filtering of the contained items.
- **Content Organizer**   Creates metadata-based rules that move content submitted to this site to the correct library or folder.

Both of these features, which are discussed in more detail in the following sections, are available at the site level, and the site administrator or site collection administrator can activate or deactivate them as needed from the Manage Site Features page, which you can open by selecting it from the Site Actions, Site Settings menu.

Metadata Navigation and Filtering

Metadata navigation and filtering features in SharePoint 2010 provide each list in the site with a settings page that allows you to configure a list to use metadata tree view hierarchies and set filter controls to improve navigation and filtering of the items contained in the list. Figure 14-6 shows an example of metadata navigation as it appears within a library after it has been configured.

FIGURE 14-6 Metadata navigation within a document library

To configure metadata-driven navigation for a document library, access the Metadata Navigation Settings page from the Library Settings page. This page allows you to change the settings for the following items associated with a list.

- Configure navigation hierarchies
- Configure key filters
- Configure automatic column indexing

The following sections describe each configuration option in detail and provide specific configuration instructions. When you have configured these settings appropriately for your document library, click OK to close the Metadata Navigation Settings page.

Configuring Navigation Hierarchies

Select from the list of available fields to use them as navigation hierarchies. Selected fields will appear under this list in the Site Hierarchy tree view. You can expand these fields and select one of their values to filter your current view to show only items matching that value.

Fields that are available for use as navigation hierarchies include columns that are one of the following types.

- Content type
- Single-value choice field
- Managed metadata field

Select the hierarchy fields that you want from the available fields and click Add.

Configuring Key Filters

Select from the list of available fields to use them as key filters. Selected fields will appear under this list in the Site Hierarchy tree view. You can use these fields to filter your current view to show only items matching a specific value.

Fields that are available for use as navigation hierarchies include columns that are one of the following types.

- Content type
- Choice field
- Managed
- Metadata field
- Person or group field
- Date and time field
- Number field

Select the key filter fields that you want from the available fields and click Add.

Configuring Automatic Column Indexing

You can use the Navigation Hierarchy and Key Filter columns to specify whether to automatically create indexes that will increase the performance of queries. This property is an option that allows you to specify if the indices should be automatically managed or not. You will see a link called Indexed Columns that lets you view the current list indexing configuration.

The Content Organizer

The Content Organizer feature, when enabled, allows you to create rules that facilitate the automatic organization of content based on a highly flexible set of criteria, including the evaluation of the content type, multiple property conditions, and a designated target location. When it is activated, the Content Organizer feature first creates a new library named Drop Off Library in the site. Files uploaded to this library are moved automatically to the correct library or folder according to rules created by the owner of the site. Additionally, options available within the Content Organizer configuration allow for the identification of documents being uploaded to a target library for processing.

Figure 14-7 shows the message presented by the Content Organizer when uploading content to the Drop Off Library, and Figure 14-8 shows the confirmation page that describes the final location where the uploaded document has been saved.

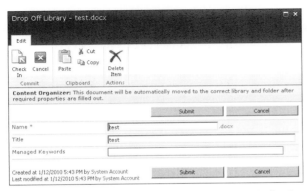

FIGURE 14-7 Notice the Content Organizer message indicating that the document will be moved to the correct library and folder after the required properties are filled out.

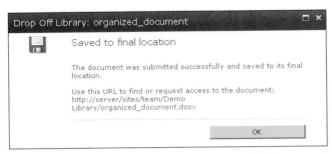

FIGURE 14-8 Confirmation window showing where the document has been stored

Because the Content Organizer is a new feature of SharePoint 2010 that has significant ramifications on how information is organized, it's important to understand when and where to use it from a design standpoint. There are times in both collaboration and publishing when you might elect to use this feature. For example, maybe you have a team drop-off library for reference material and you want to make a single person or a small group of people responsible for maintaining the storage of that information. Of course, within a records management paradigm, this feature is almost required to implement a standards-compliant file plan and records storage system. The important thing to keep in mind is that this feature, while flexible, also has the potential to become a problem if its use is not calculated and deliberate. Always tie the movement of content back to your business requirements and plan for the movement of content ahead of time. By doing so, you will be able to maximize the capability of this new feature without potentially creating an over-engineered problem.

Configuring the Content Organizer

To configure the Content Organizer, visit the target site, open the Site Actions menu, and select the Site Settings option. Note that this feature is enabled as a site feature, not a site collection feature. You may need to activate the Content Organizer feature to make it available. You can do this by selecting Manage Site Features under Site Actions, and then choosing the option to activate the Content Organizer feature. After you activate the Content Organizer, return to the Site Settings page. Click the Content Organizer Settings link, which is located in the Site Administration settings group. Table 14-2 provides a detailed list of the settings options available for the Content Organizer.

TABLE 14-2 Content Organizer Settings

SETTING	EXPLANATION
Redirect Users To The Drop Off Library	When this setting is enabled, users are redirected to the Drop Off Library when they try to upload content to libraries that have one or more Content Organizer rules pointing to them.
Sending To Another Site	When this setting is enabled, Content Organizer rules may specify another site that also has a Content Organizer as a target location.

SETTING	EXPLANATION
Folder Partitioning	When this setting is enabled, the organizer can automatically create subfolders when a target location has too many items. Required settings include the maximum number of items allowed within a single folder and a field formatting mask for created subfolders.
Duplicate Submissions	This settings dictates the method used when a file with the same name already exists in a target location. The options are to use SharePoint versioning if it is enabled, or to append unique characters to the end of the duplicate file names.
Preserving Context	When this setting is enabled, the Content Organizer will save the original audit log and properties in an audit entry on the submitted item.
Rule Managers	This setting specifies the user who manages the rules and can respond when incoming content doesn't match any of the provided rules. A rule manager must have the Manage Web Site permission to access the Content Organizer rules list from the site setting page. Enter users and/or groups using the provided contact picker. Options are provided for sending an e-mail message to rule managers when submissions do not match a rule or when content has been left in the Drop Off Library for a specified number of days.
Submission Points	This setting property provides the Web service URL for the Official File Web service as well as the e-mail address through which other sites or e-mail messaging software may send content to the site.

Setting Up Content Organizer Rules

To have the Content Organizer automate the movement of submitted content, you must provide it the following basic information in the form of rules.

- The type of content to organize
- The property conditions that must be met in order for the content to be organized
- The target location where content meeting the criteria should be sent

Content Organizer rules are managed in a special list that is accessible from the Site Settings page. This list helps you plan how content should be organized. Create rules that ensure that documents submitted are sent to the correct location and have the correct properties. As a site administrator, you may also set an alert on this list to be notified when any rules are created or modified.

Table 14-3 provides a detailed list of the settings that must be configured when adding or modifying a Content Organizer rule.

TABLE 14-3 Content Organizer Rule Configuration Settings

SETTING	EXPLANATION
Rule Name	Describe the conditions and actions of this rule. The rule name is used in reports about the content of this site, such as a library's File Plan Report.
Rule Status and Priority	Specify whether this rule should run on incoming documents and what the rule's priority is. If a submission matches multiple rules, the router will choose the rule with the higher priority. This setting may be set to Active or Inactive. If it is set to Active, you must specify a priority between 1 (highest) and 9 (lowest) for the rule. If it is set to Inactive, the rule will not run on incoming content.
Submission's Content Type	By selecting a content type, you are determining the properties that can be used in the conditions of this rule. In addition, submissions that match this rule will receive the content type selected here when they are placed in a target location. You also can specify alternate names that this content type may have in other sites. Adding the type "*" will allow documents of unknown content types to be organized by this rule.
Conditions	You may specify multiple conditions. To match this rule, a submission's properties must match all the specified property conditions (e.g., If Date Created Is Before 1/1/2000). Each condition requires a property, operator, and value.
Target Location	Specify where to place content that matches this rule. You can browse to select a location within the current site, or you may specify another site. When sending content to another site, the available sites are taken from the list of other sites with Content Organizers as defined by the system administrator. Select the Automatically Create A Folder For Each Unique Value Of A Property check box to force the organizer to group similar documents together. For instance, if you have a property that lists all the teams in your organization, you can force the Content Organizer to create a separate folder for each team.

Follow these steps to create a new rule for the Content Organizer.

1. Visit the target site, open the Site Actions menu, and select Site Settings.

2. Click the Content Organizer Rules link, which is located in the Site Administration settings group.

3. Open the List Tools menu from the Ribbon, select Items, and then select New Item.

4. Fill out the New Rule form with the appropriate values as defined in Table 14-3.

5. Click OK.

If submitted content does not meet the criteria of any of the provided rules, the settings may specify that the Content Organizer Rule Managers should be notified and asked to take action to determine the proper place for storing the content. Figure 14-9 shows the message a user uploading a document would receive if this occurs.

FIGURE 14-9 Confirmation showing that a document's location will change pending action from the administrator

Document Sets

SharePoint 2010 introduces the concept of document sets. Document sets enable you to use Microsoft Office 2010 to manage work products that span multiple documents. Document sets are special types of folders that are used to manage a single deliverable, or work product, that includes multiple documents. You can create document sets using the provided system templates, or you can customize these templates to create document sets specific to your organization or requirements. Versioning allows you to capture the state of the entire document set at various points throughout the content life cycle.

When activated, the document sets feature provides the content types required for creating and using document sets. The feature is available at the site collection level, and the site collection administrator can activate or deactivate it as needed from the Site Collection Features page, which you can open by selecting it from the Site Actions, Site Settings menu.

Because the document sets feature introduces a new content type, you can easily create new derived types based on the system-provided type. Each document set content type includes an additional document set–specific settings page. You can access this page by clicking on the document set content type from within the Site Content Types gallery, which can be found from the Site Settings page. On the Content Type Settings page, click the Document Set Settings link under Settings. Table 14-4 lists the configuration options available for each document set content type with a brief explanation of each option.

TABLE 14-4 Document Set Content Type Configuration Settings

SETTING	EXPLANATION
Allowed Content Types	Select from the list of available site content types to add them to the document set. Only content types specified will be allowed in the document set. To remove the document content type, you must first delete the Default Content item.
Default Content	If you want new document sets created from this content type to include specific items, upload them here and specify their content type. You may upload as many items as you need. You must specify the content type of each item. Think of this as a set of document templates that is included in the document set by default. There is also an option to add the name of the document set to each file name.
Shared Columns	Select which column values for the document set should be automatically synchronized to all documents contained in the set. You may specify the columns to be shared by selecting the check box next to the column name.
Welcome Page Columns	Select which columns to show on the Welcome page for the Document Set. Click each column you want to include from the available columns list and then click Add.
Welcome Page	You can customize the Welcome page used for this document set using either your browser to manipulate Web Parts on the Welcome page or SharePoint Designer to perform more advanced customizations. After completing your customizations, you can apply them to all child list and site content types using the Update List And Site Content Types option on this page.
Update List and Site Content Types	Specify whether all child site and list content types using this type should be updated with the settings on this page. This operation can take a long time, and any customizations made to these values on the child site and list content types will be lost. By default, this option is set to Yes. If you don't want to lose site and list level customizations already in place, you will need to change this option to No.

When you have configured a new document set content type, you can add it to a document library. To do so, visit the Library Settings page of the target library and click Advanced Settings. Select the option to enable the advanced management of content types and then click OK at the bottom of the page. When you are back on the Library Settings page, click the Add From Existing Site Content Types link in the Content Types section and select the new document set content type from the list.

When it is available within the library, you can create a new document set based on this content type. Simply visit the library by clicking the library's name in the breadcrumb navigation. Select the Documents menu under Library Tools in the Ribbon and then select the multiselect portion of the New button. Choose the new document set content from the provided menu. Fill out the provided form, including information for any required fields, and click OK. Figure 14-10 shows the Welcome page of a newly created document set.

FIGURE 14-10 The Welcome page of a newly created document set, with included content

Location-Based Metadata Default Values

SharePoint 2010 introduces the ability to specify default metadata values to be applied to items based on the location in which the item is stored. This simplifies the process of collecting valid metadata from end users. You can specify default column values for each content type or column binding at the root of the library, or alternately, you can specify default values for the root folder location itself. Additionally, you can specify default column values for each folder within the library. These default values are configured using the Change Default Column Values settings page, which can be accessed from the Library Settings page. As shown in Figure 14-11, the interface provided on this page is split into two sections. The left section is a tree view of the library's folder structure, where you can select the container for which default values are to be specified. The right section of the interface provides a listing of each available column, its type, and the specified default value for the selected container. Also provided is the source of the default value specified and which content types the column is used in. It is possible to specify different default values for the same column at each level of the container hierarchy.

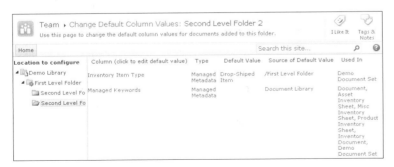

FIGURE 14-11 The Change Default Column Values settings page

It's important to have a plan when you enter this interface, and to keep track of what you are changing, because it's easy to think you are changing something at one level when the container selected on the left is actually on another level. If you don't specify a default value for a given level, the default value will be inherited from the parent, all the way back up to the document library itself.

Document Center Template

SharePoint 2010 updates the out-of-the-box template for a Document Center site. The new template is preconfigured to enable many of the new document management features covered in this section, including the new metadata-based navigation feature. Use a Document Center site to create, work on, and store documents. This site can become a collaborative repository for authoring documents within a team or a knowledge base for documents across multiple teams.

The Document Center site's Welcome page has been simplified to make it easier to use. It now includes the Upload A Document button, and the site's navigation is no longer shown in tree view. By default, the document library is configured to require check-out, and versioning is set to track both major and minor versions.

Enterprise Metadata Management

SharePoint 2010 includes new features that allow for the management of metadata across the entire enterprise. This new feature set represents a significant advancement in the way SharePoint can be employed as a content management solution. The ECM capability within SharePoint 2010 now exhibits a level of product and solution maturity previously available only in substantially more expensive point solutions. Enterprise Metadata Management in SharePoint 2010 ensures consistency, reliability, and ease of management. Additionally, it makes metadata available across any list type, rather than only within document libraries. Enterprise Metadata Management improves the user experience by reducing the effort for adding metadata and by demonstrating a clear return on the investment of that effort. The following new features have been added to enable Enterprise Metadata Management.

- Term store and term sets
- Shared content types
- Managed term fields

Before you dig into each of these features and capabilities, you need to understand how the Managed Metadata Service works within the service architecture. To use the Enterprise Managed Metadata features within SharePoint 2010, you first need to create a Managed Metadata Service application within SharePoint Central Administration. At least one such service must exist within the enterprise, and it must be published as a service application. Other sites may consume this service by way of a Managed Metadata Service Connection. If you used the post-setup Farm Configuration Wizard to set up and configure your services, one of each of the aforementioned service instances will already be present. If not, you will have to create, publish, and connect new instances of these services and configure any remote sites for consumption of these services if needed.

You can manage these services by clicking the Manage Service Applications link in the Application Management settings group on the front page of SharePoint Central Administration. Highlight the service you want to configure and then click the Properties button on the Ribbon. Table 14-5 shows the configuration properties available when configuring the Managed Metadata Service, and Table 14-6 lists the configuration properties available when configuring the Managed Metadata Connection Service.

TABLE 14-5 Managed Metadata Service Configuration Settings

SETTING	EXPLANATION
Name	Specify the name for this Managed Metadata Service.
Database And Database Server	Specify the database server and database name for this Managed Metadata Service, along with database connection authentication information.
Failover Server	Optionally, specify a database server that should be contacted as a failover instance for the database specified previously. You will need to configure database mirroring between the back-end SQL servers for this setting to function properly.
Application Pool	Choose the application pool to use for this service application. This defines the account and credentials that will be used by this Web service. You can choose an existing application pool or create a new one.
Content Type Hub	Enter the URL of the site collection (content type hub) from which this service application will consume content types. Each service only syndicates content types from one location.

TABLE 14-6 Managed Metadata Service Connection Configuration Settings

SETTING	EXPLANATION
This Service Application Is The Default Storage Location For Keywords	When enabled, this setting will use the connected instance of the Managed Metadata Service for storing keywords.
This Service Application Is The Default Storage Location For Column-Specific Term Sets	When enabled, this setting will use the connected instance of the Managed Metadata Service for storing column-specific term sets (managed metadata field term sets).

continued on the next page

SETTING	EXPLANATION
Consumes Content Types From The Content Type Gallery	When enabled, this service connection will consume content types from the content type hub specified for the connected Managed Metadata Service. This option is only available when a content type hub is specified for the connected Managed Metadata Service.
Push-Down Content Type Publishes Updates From The Content Type Gallery To Subsites And Lists Using The Content Type	When enabled, this setting will automate the process of updating site and list level content types using the updates published to a syndicated content type.

When these services have been set up and configured, you can start to take full advantage of the new Enterprise Metadata Management features provided by SharePoint 2010.

Content Types and Columns

The SharePoint 2010 content types feature provides a framework for the storage of content within a SharePoint site or list. This framework is expressed as a schema within which the designating features of a specific type of content are specified, such as the name and description of the content type. Additionally, each content type has an associated set of columns that are bound to that type, and consequently are bound to all content stored as a result of that type. For example, assume that you want to store documents related to inventory within your SharePoint site. To create a content type specific to inventory documents, you would derive the root document content type, which will come with its own predefined columns (Title, Author, CreatedBy, and so on). Now assume that you name your new content type Inventory Document. Then you will create or add new columns that are specific to the type of document content you want to store using the new content type. For example, you might want to include a column for inventory part number, so that users uploading documents of this type will have the option—or will be required—to enter a corresponding inventory part number. In this case, you would create the structure illustrated in Figure 14-12.

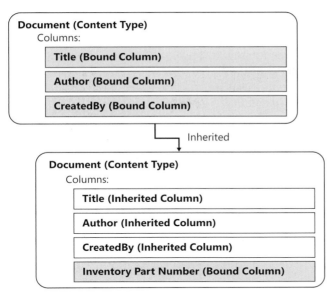

FIGURE 14-12 An example of an inherited content type structure; the shaded columns are bound and the other columns are inherited.

Content types are created and managed within the site content type gallery, and consequently they are available to all sites within the site collection that are located below the site in which the content type is defined. Columns may be defined at the list level (List Columns) or at the site level (Site Columns) and are often referred to as *fields*. When they are defined at the site level, columns are also available to all sites within the site collection that are located below the site in which the site column is defined. Because content types use inheritance, derived types by default contain all of the columns specified within parent types. Changes made to type definitions anywhere within the tree can be pushed down to the child types within the site and subsites as well as to any lists within those sites that leverage those content types.

In earlier versions of SharePoint, the content type and column architecture was limited by the fact that you could not share defined content types and columns between site collections. This meant that, in order to have the same types in multiple site collections, you had to create the content types and columns in each new site collection manually or resort to customization. SharePoint 2010 alleviates this limitation by providing the ability to define content types in a central location and have them automatically published to numerous site collections. The Managed Metadata Service provides a similar, yet even more flexible, capability for columns. It is more flexible because, in addition to syndication of columns, you can also define structured term sets, a kind of super selector field, for which the selection criteria and options are centrally managed and available anywhere the column is used.

Figure 14-13 shows an Inventory Document content type with a managed metadata column for the Inventory Part Number.

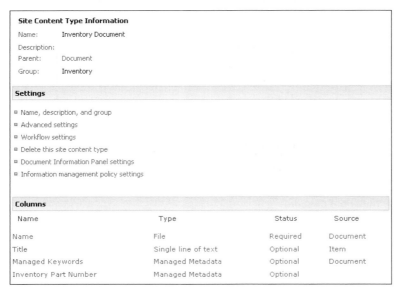

Site Content Type Information

Name: Inventory Document
Description:
Parent: Document
Group: Inventory

Settings

▫ Name, description, and group
▫ Advanced settings
▫ Workflow settings
▫ Delete this site content type
▫ Document Information Panel settings
▫ Information management policy settings

Columns

Name	Type	Status	Source
Name	File	Required	Document
Title	Single line of text	Optional	Item
Managed Keywords	Managed Metadata	Optional	Document
Inventory Part Number	Managed Metadata	Optional	

FIGURE 14-13 The new Inventory Document content type, as seen from the content type settings page

SharePoint 2010 provides new column types that you can use to define a content type. Figure 14-14 shows the Create New Column Settings page with a summary list of the out-of-the-box column types that are available.

Name and Type

Type a name for this column, and select the type of information you want to store in the column.

Column name:

My New Column

The type of information in this column is:

⦿ Single line of text
◯ Multiple lines of text
◯ Choice (menu to choose from)
◯ Number (1, 1.0, 100)
◯ Currency ($, ¥, €)
◯ Date and Time
◯ Lookup (information already on this site)
◯ Yes/No (check box)
◯ Person or Group
◯ Hyperlink or Picture
◯ Calculated (calculation based on other columns)
◯ Full HTML content with formatting and constraints for publishing
◯ Image with formatting and constraints for publishing
◯ Hyperlink with formatting and constraints for publishing
◯ Summary Links data
◯ Rich media data for publishing
◯ Managed Metadata

FIGURE 14-14 The Create New Column Settings page

Managed Metadata Fields

Managed Metadata fields are new in SharePoint 2010. These fields allow a user to select a value from Managed Metadata Service term store, which is described in more detail in the next section. Think of these fields as *super selector* fields. After you have configured these fields, you are presented with a taxonomical tree structure from which to choose a value, as shown in Figure 14-15. You can add or modify that structure if you have the appropriate permissions within the term store. Because these fields leverage the term store, and the term store is tightly scoped by level, Managed Metadata fields can provide a consistent metadata selection capability across sites collections, Web applications, and farms.

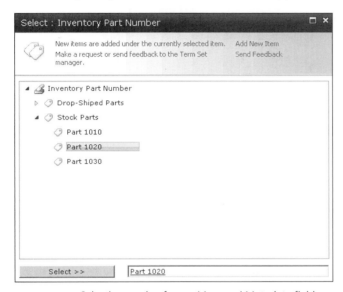

FIGURE 14-15 Selecting a value from a Managed Metadata field

Notice the Add New Item link at the top of the page, which can be used to contribute to the term set behind this field.

Managed Metadata fields can be added as columns to content types, lists, or document libraries. When adding a column, select the Managed Metadata type from the options list. You will then be able to select a term set from the term store or create a customized term set for the new column. A customized term set will be stored in the term store within the group created for the local site collection and can be promoted to the enterprise taxonomy at a later time by a term store manager, a group manager, or a contributor. Figures 14-16 and 14-17 show the options available for selecting or creating a term set when creating a new Managed Metadata field.

FIGURE 14-16 Select an existing term set from the term store for the new field.

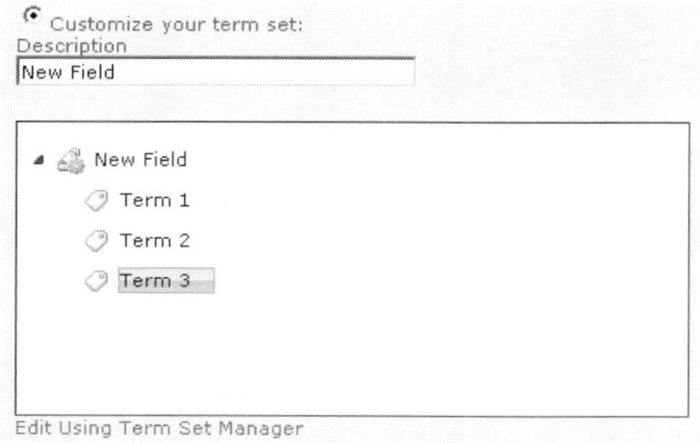

FIGURE 14-17 Create a customized term set for the new field.

Term Store and Term Sets

The Managed Metadata Service provides a managed term store that is used to store both keywords and term sets by default. It is possible to store keywords and term sets in different instances of the Managed Metadata Service, and it is also possible to create multiple instances of the Managed Metadata Service that serve site collection within a given Web application. The term store acts as a repository for terms to be used to tag items. You can combine terms to make term sets that then become available Managed Metadata fields. When creating or modifying a Managed Metadata field, you may select a term set from the term store or define a new custom term set on the fly. When it is defined, the new term set will be stored in the term store and will be available for management and/or use elsewhere within SharePoint. The use of a centralized term store enriches navigation, search, sort and filter, policy, and workflow functions. You can also track the usage of unmanaged terms to which you want to apply structure in the future.

Figure 14-18 shows the term store in action. The interface is divided into two sections. The left section provides a tree view of the term store, including groups, term sets, and individual terms as expressed in a Term hierarchy. Also on the left is a language selector, which enables the management of terms in multiple languages, and a search box for quickly finding a specific term set or term you want to manage.

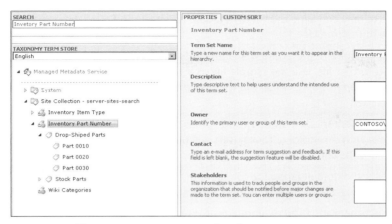

FIGURE 14-18 The term store management interface

Term Store Management, Groups, and Scoping

Term sets are managed within the context of a group. Groups are created within the term store. Term store administrators are permitted to create new groups at the enterprise level. These groups and their associated terms and term sets are available anywhere that service is consumed. The scope of term sets is tightly constrained—term sets created at the site collection level are managed at that level, through a group that is automatically generated for the site collection. Terms and term sets managed at the site collection level can be promoted to the enterprise level by using a copy or move operation. If a useful term set is created at the site collection level within a site and a term store administrator determines that the term set is useful and should be available enterprise-wide, she can move that term set to the enterprise taxonomy.

Although the Term Store Management tool is ubiquitous across the various levels at which it is accessible, users will only be able to see local and/or enterprise content for which they have access. Enterprise content that they don't have permission to access will be visible, but it will be noneditable.

The management hierarchy present in the term store is as follows:

- Managed Metadata Service (term store administrators)
    - Group (group managers and contributors)
        - Term Set (owner)

Site collection administrators are granted access to manage the group associated with the site collection by default, whereas farm administrators are not granted access to manage the Enterprise Term Store by default. When a term store is directly selected within the Term Store Manager interface, the configuration options shown in Table 14-7 are available.

TABLE 14-7 Term Store Configuration Settings

SETTING	EXPLANATION
Available Service Applications	A site may consume multiple metadata applications. Select the one to see in the tree view.
Sample Import	The SharePoint Metadata Manager can import a term set from a UTF-8 CSV format file. Use the sample file as a template for creating import files. Then import the file into the group that you want to create a new term set.
Term Store Administrators	You can enter user names, group names, or e-mail addresses. Separate them with semicolons. These users will be permitted to create new term set groups and assign users to the group manager role.
Default Language	Select the default language for all metadata in the system. All terms must have a label defined in their default language.
Working Languages	Select the translation of languages for terms in the term store. This will allow a term to have language-specific labels and translations.

Configuring Groups

Each group consists of its associated configuration options and a set of term sets. Groups can be created by a term store manager, or they can have been created automatically for a specific site collection. At the group level, it is possible to create new term sets or to import them from a CSV file. To manage the settings of a given group, select the group in the left pane. Table 14-8 provides a summary of the configuration properties that will become available in the right pane, and Figure 14-19 shows the Edit Control Block menu available for a group. To access this menu, select the group from the left pane and click the small arrow to the right of the group tree item, or you can right-click the group tree item to view the menu.

TABLE 14-8 Group Configuration Settings

SETTING	EXPLANATION
Group Name	Type a new name for this group as you want it to appear in the hierarchy.
Description	Type descriptive text to help users better organize and use term sets in this group.
Group Managers	Enter user names, group names, or e-mail addresses to grant group manager permissions. Separate multiple users with semicolons. These users will have contributor permissions and will also be able to add users to the contributor role.
Contributors	Enter user names, group names, or e-mail addresses. Separate them with semicolons. These users will have full permission to edit terms and term set hierarchies within this group.

FIGURE 14-19 The Group Edit Control Block menu

Configuring Term Sets and Terms

Each term set consists of its associated configuration options and a hierarchical set of terms. The terms are expressed in tree view, just as the user sees them when filling a field or tagging an item. To manage the settings of a given term set, select the term set in the left pane. Table 14-9 provides a summary of the configuration properties available in the right pane.

TABLE 14-9 Term Set Configuration Settings

SETTING	EXPLANATION
Term Set Name	Type a new name for this term set as you want it to appear in the hierarchy.
Description	Type descriptive text to help users understand the intended use of this term set.
Owner	Identify the primary user or group of this term set.
Contact	Type an e-mail address for term suggestion and feedback. If this field is left blank, the suggestion feature will be disabled.
Stakeholders	This information is used to track people and groups in the organization that should be notified before major changes are made to the term set. You can enter multiple users or groups.
Submission Policy	When a term set is closed, only metadata managers can add terms. When it is open, users can add terms from a tagging application. This option controls community involvement in the creation of new terms within the term set.
Available for Tagging	Select whether this term set is available to be used by end users for tagging. When the check box is cleared, this term set will not be visible to most users.
Custom Sort Order	A custom sort can be applied to child terms below this term set. Using a custom sort order will ensure that terms appear in a consistent order, regardless of the language or any changes in default labels. If you select to use a custom sort order, you will be provided with a list of the terms and given the ability to specify their sort order.

It is also possible to copy, reuse, move, or delete a term set. To do so, select the term set from the left pane and then click the small arrow to the right of the term set tree item, or you can right-click the term set tree item to view the menu shown in Figure 14-20. When you want to reuse a term set, you must select a destination for the term set. When you copy a term set, you are making a new term set that will include reused versions of the terms. The source terms will remain in the original term set. Moving and deleting a term set works as you would expect. Keep in mind that existing content will remain tagged, as it was before a deletion.

FIGURE 14-20 The Term Set Edit Control Block menu

Terms are configured in much the same way term sets are. Begin by selecting the term you want to configure from the left pane, and the configuration properties will appear in the right pane. Table 14-10 provides a summary of the configuration properties available in the right pane.

TABLE 14-10 Term Configuration Settings

SETTING	EXPLANATION
Term Name	This value is a display value and cannot be modified. To modify the name of the term itself, double-click the term name in the right pane and enter a new name.
Available For Tagging	Select whether this term set is available to be used by end users for tagging. When the check box is cleared, this term set will not be visible to most users.
Language	Select a language for the labels for the term you would like to edit. After you select a language, all of the labels you add for that language will be made available for editing.
Description	Descriptions will help users know when to use this term and allow them to disambiguate among similar terms.
Default Label	Enter one label as the default for this language.

SETTING	EXPLANATION
Other Labels	Enter synonyms and abbreviations for this term. You must enter a word or phrase per line, but you can enter as many other labels as needed.
Member Of	This table provides information such as a list of term sets where the term is being used, the parent term, the owner, and if the listed term is the source term.

It is also possible to copy, reuse, move, merge, or deprecate a term. To do so, select the term from the left pane and then click the small arrow to the right of the term tree item, or you can right-click the term tree item to view the menu shown in Figure 14-21. When you reuse a term, you select a destination for the term set. When you copy a term set, you are making a new term set that will include the properties and source of the original term. When you merge a term, you select another term with which to merge. Merging a term into another will collapse all of the synonyms and translations of the existing term into the selected term. Although content already tagged with the existing term will still be tagged as before, the merging of the term is irreversible. Deprecating a term will effectively disable it, making it unavailable for use by users but retaining it for use within the taxonomy. Moving and deleting a term set work as you would expect. Keep in mind that existing content will remain tagged as it was before the deletion.

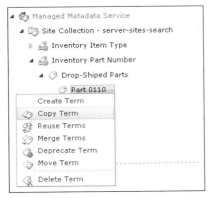

FIGURE 14-21 The Term Edit Control Block menu

Content Type Syndication

SharePoint 2010 includes a new feature called Content Type Syndication. As the name suggests, this feature provides you with the capability to publish content types from one designated site collection to other site collections, Web applications, or even farms. In prior versions of SharePoint, content types were limited to being configured within an individual site collection. To share content types consistently across multiple site collection, you often had to rely on custom code solutions or third-party tools. SharePoint 2010 allows you to share content types in much the same manner as enterprise metadata. When content types are published using Content Type Syndication, the back-end services ensure the following.

- Consistent application of metadata
- Consistent application of policy
- Consistent application of workflow associations

The following system and service elements are central to making Content Type Syndication work and must be configured prior to publishing content types.

- Content Type Syndication Hub
- Managed Metadata Service
- Managed Metadata Service Connection (Proxy)

Setting Up a Content Type Syndication Hub

Prior to configuring the service applications for syndication, you need to set up a special designated site where your source content types will be created and maintained. This will be a highly controlled site, and only people responsible for managing and maintaining these content types will have access. The hub can be based on any site template, but for the examples here, you will set it up within a team collaboration site, where the people managing these content types might want to collaborate with each other while they manage the content types.

Begin by creating a new site collection in SharePoint Central Administration. After you have created the new site, visit the site and activate the Content Type Syndication Hub site collection level feature. You can do this by clicking the Site Collection Features link in the Site Collection Administration settings group on the Site Settings page. Activating this feature will enable the functionality needed to publish, unpublish, and republish source content types.

Setting Up the Managed Metadata Service

With the Content Type Syndication Hub site in place, you now must configure the Managed Metadata Service to use this site as a designated content type hub. To do this, perform the following steps.

1. Open a browser and go to the SharePoint Central Administration website.
2. Under Application Settings, click Manage Service Applications.
3. Highlight the Managed Metadata Service instance you want to use to publish content types from the new hub site. To highlight, select the service in the table without clicking the service's name.
4. Click the Properties icon on the Ribbon.
5. Scroll down to the bottom of the Properties page to find the Content Type Hub property.
6. Enter the URL of the site collection you created for use as a content type hub.

7. Optionally, select the Report Syndication Import Errors From Site Collections Using This Service Application check box.

8. Click OK.

9. When you return to the Manage Service Applications page, select the Managed Metadata Service Connection and click Properties on the Ribbon.

10. Select the check box labeled Consumed Content Types From The Content Type Gallery At <http://UrlYouSpecified>.

11. Click OK.

After you have specified a content type hub for an instance of the Managed Metadata Service, you cannot change it or remove it. You may elect to disable the syndication of content types from that hub on the service connection side, but you would need to do so for every service connection in the enterprise that consumes content from the given service instance.

Publishing Content Types from the Hub

When you have established an active content type hub, you can begin to create content types for publishing. To do so, simply visit the site content type gallery, which can be found on the Site Settings page, and click Create to get started. When you have created your new content type and created or assigned the site columns, you are ready to set up the new content type for publishing. Figure 14-22 shows an example content type that has been created for publishing within the Content Type Syndication Hub site. Notice the new Region column, which is a managed metadata field.

FIGURE 14-22 Content type for syndication

After you have created the content type, click the Manage Publishing For This Content Type link, shown in the Settings in Figure 14-22. From the Content Type Publishing page, you can perform the actions described in Table 14-11.

TABLE 14-11 Content Type Publishing for This Content Type

ACTION	EXPLANATION
Publish	Make this content type available for download for all Web applications (and site collections) consuming content types from this location.
Unpublish	Make this content type unavailable for download for all Web applications (and site collections) consuming content types from this location. Any copies of this content type being used in other site collections will be unsealed and made into a local content type.
Republish	If you have made changes to this content type, the content type needs to be republished before the changes are available for download to all Web applications consuming content types from this location.

This page also provides publishing history information, including the date on which one or more service applications successfully published this content type. After you have selected the action you want to perform, click the OK button. Within a few minutes, the published content type should become available in site collections or Web applications that consume the associated Managed Metadata Service. The content is made available through the firing of a timer job that provides the back-end processing. If you want to check on the status of the job or run the job immediately, you can do so from the Monitoring area of SharePoint Central Administration. The job is named Content Type Subscriber, and it will be bound to the associated Web application that is consuming the service.

Configure Content Type Publishing in Subscribed Site Collections

How do you know if your site collection is receiving content types through syndication? There is a settings page available within Site Settings that allows you to review which services are publishing content types to your site collection. To access this page, click the Content Type Publishing link in the Site Collection Administration Settings group on the Site Settings page. The page provides the settings options and information described in Table 14-12.

TABLE 14-12 Content Type Publishing for a Site Collection

SETTING	EXPLANATION
Refresh All Published Content Types	The next time the Content Type Subscriber timer job runs, update all published content types. Select this check box and click OK.
Content Type Publishing Error Log	Contains errors that happened during content type syndication for this site. Click the link to view the log.
Hubs	Lists the service applications that are publishing content types to this site collection. To edit content types that have been published from these locations or to create and publish a new content type, select the hub URL. To view the subscribed content type on this site collection, select the content type name.

REAL WORLD   A Note on SharePoint Server 2007 Customizations

Many organizations quickly adopted SharePoint Server 2007 because they could see the strategic long-term benefits of the technology. In some cases, however, organizations determined that the functionality specific to Enterprise Content Management was insufficient for their detailed requirements. Then these organizations often opted to make significant customizations. The motives for these efforts varied. Some organizations needed tighter records management and improved automated movement of content that occurred behind the scenes; others needed a set of standardized content types and site columns across the entire enterprise.

As many of these organizations begin their efforts to upgrade to SharePoint 2010, there will be some big decisions to make about how to handle these customizations. Libraries that are riddled with event handlers, content types that are present in the file system hive, and customized retention and expiration workflows and field types abound. How do you correlate these existing customizations with the new features and functionality provided within SharePoint 2010? You have the following options when you want to upgrade to SharePoint 2010.

- Rebuild from scratch.
  - Create new sites.
  - Configure all of the features to meet your needs.
  - Migrate all of your content to the new sites.
- Go forward with your customizations.
  - Keep your existing customizations in place, where supported.
  - Use new features to meet new needs.
  - Upgrade your existing sites and keep your data in place.

- Remove customizations where there is feature overlap.
  - Use new features to meet the requirements met by existing customizations.
  - Remove customizations where you can, replacing them with the implementation of new features wherever possible.
  - Upgrade or migrate your existing sites based on the anticipated impact of the customization adjustments.

Some people assume that a major version upgrade means a hardware refresh and/ or a migration, and that's fine, because the tradeoffs described here will be easier if that's how the upgrade is handled. Of course, the word "migration" is used as if it's easy to accomplish, and it's not easy at all. Often you must purchase and use special tools to reclassify all of the information and preserve metadata during a migration.

If you are like most people who want to take advantage of the new features and management capabilities included in SharePoint 2010, but you have numerous overlapping customizations, you will need to either take those customizations forward or remove them where there is overlap.

When it's possible to remove customizations where there is overlap with new features, that is clearly the better option. Or course, you will need to define requirements for their removal, especially if you upgrade your sites in place. You may find that you need additional code or customizations to reclassify existing data or to back out the prior customizations and configure the new features. The key to success in this endeavor is to exercise good project management and requirements-gathering discipline. Clearly document what you have, what overlaps, and what you think you can safely remove. Design a plan for removing the prior customizations for sites that already exist while configuring the new features in their place. Where you must retain customizations that provide overlap in existing sites, and you still want to use the new features for newly created sites, you may have to update those customizations accordingly.

SharePoint Server 2007 marked a revolution in the world of collaboration and content management for mid-sized companies, as everyone did their best to move to a standardized platform that met most of their needs. In the process, however, it became one of the most overcustomized software packages in history. As you move forward into the world of SharePoint 2010, remember that, although the system provides ultimate flexibility, any customizations created will have to be maintained for years to come, especially during an upgrade.

Records Management

Records management was introduced with SharePoint Server 2007, with a special site template called the Records Center. The Records Center site provided a set of capabilities for managing, disposing, preserving, and holding records. Records Center sites were managed by a special group of people called *records managers*, whose responsibility it was to maintain the records stored in the site, as well as monitor and update the routing rules (file plan) to ensure that inbound records were stored in the correct place.

In SharePoint 2010, you can still manage records within a Records Center site, sometimes referred to as a *records archive*. You can also opt to manage records in place, alongside active documents where they are stored within the system. This is because many of the features previously provided as part of the Records Center site are now available as individual features that can be enabled within any site collection. This provides you with maximum flexibility when determining how best to manage declared records. For example, you could specify a different retention policy for documents declared as records, or you could have such documents moved to a records archive for storage and management. You could also opt for a mixture of in-place records management and archival records management, which involves holding a document in place as a record for a specific duration and then automatically moving it to a records archive for long-term storage and management.

The following sections examine the records management capabilities delivered with SharePoint 2010, including new features that enable you to perform records management in any site. You will also explore the administrative interfaces and configurable items of each feature and cover key concepts that Microsoft considered when developing the records management functionality in SharePoint 2010, including the topics in the following list.

- Records management and upfront preparation
- Records management features
- Improved Records Center site
- In-place records management
- eDiscovery and hold
- Retention and reporting
- Scalability

This section begins with a look at the need to perform upfront preparation before configuring records management.

Records Management and Upfront Preparation

In developing the new records management capabilities included with SharePoint 2010, the team at Microsoft defined three core design tenets for this release.

- Integrated governance
- Familiar and easy to use
- Flexible

Integrated governance translates into a records management experience that is tightly bound to the collaboration experience and that works on a variety of SharePoint objects. Microsoft wanted to create a system that was familiar and easy to use by finding a balance between feature richness and user freedom, and they wanted to find a solution that was extremely flexible and configurable to an organization's needs.

In keeping with these tenets, there are many ways to realize compliance goals, discoverability, and retention within SharePoint 2010. New features allow for the records management experience to be as absent or present as you deem necessary. You even have multiple options to control where you keep records and how they are processed.

The key to success with records management is to perform the upfront preparation needed to ensure you have everything required from a design standpoint. Records management starts with collaboration. If you don't think about how you want to handle record content from its inception, you will always find that you need to locate content that you cannot find, have inadvertently removed content that you needed to keep, or have retained content that you should have disposed of.

When deciding how to manage record content within SharePoint 2010, you have the following options.

- Manage records in a dedicated Records Center archive
- Manage records in place, wherever they are stored
- Use a hybrid approach of in-place and archival management

When determining which option is best for your purposes, you should evaluate the following considerations. It's important to think about each of these issues carefully to ensure that storing records alongside active documents will work in your environment.

- Sufficient governance in collaboration sites
- Regulatory requirements for compliance
- Backup schedule (of collaboration content databases)
- Collaboration site life cycle (and usage duration)
- Necessity of collaboration site users to have access to records
- Records manager scope of responsibility (records only, or active documents as well)

Records Management Features

Table 14-13 provides a summary of the features that are available for enabling records management functionality with sites. Note that not all of these features are used exclusively for records management, and many of them have already been covered in detail elsewhere. They are listed here because when these features are used together, they enable comprehensive records management capability within any site. You may choose to employ all of these features within a site, or you may want to use only the ones necessary to meet your requirements. When you create a Records Center site, all of these features will be activated by default.

TABLE 14-13 Records Management Features

FEATURE	LEVEL	EXPLANATION
Disposition Approval Workflow	Site Collection	Manages document expiration and retention by allowing participants to decide whether to retain or delete expired documents.
Document ID Service	Site Collection	Assigns IDs to documents in the site collection that can be used to retrieve items independent of their current location.
Document Sets	Site Collection	Provides the content types required for creating and using document sets. You create a document set when you want to manage multiple documents as a single work product.
In-Place Records Management	Site Collection	Enables the definition and declaration of records in place.
Library and Folder Based Retention	Site Collection	Allows list administrators to override content type retention schedules and set schedules on libraries and folders.
Content Organizer	Site	Creates metadata-based rules that move content submitted to this site to the correct library or folder.
E-mail Integration with Content Organizer	Site	Enable a site's Content Organizer to accept and organize e-mail messages. This feature should be used only in a highly managed store such as a Records Center.
Hold and eDiscovery	Site	Tracks external actions like litigations, investigations, or audits that require you to suspend the disposition of documents.
Metadata Navigation and Filtering	Site	Provides each list in the site with a settings page for configuring that list to use metadata tree view hierarchies and filter controls to improve navigation and filtering of the contained items.

Improved Records Center Site

The Records Center site template has been functionally improved and streamlined for a better user experience in SharePoint 2010. In addition to including all of the features described in the previous section, the Records Center now has a new clean look and layout. Central to the Welcome page, shown in Figure 14-23, is a very prominent Submit A Record button, which allows a user to upload a new record quickly and easily.

FIGURE 14-23 The Welcome page of the improved Records Center site

The site comes with two libraries. The first is the Drop Off Library, which is a special library created by the Content Organizer. (See the section titled "The Content Organizer" earlier in this chapter for details about the Drop Off Library.) The movement of content added to this library is controlled by the defined Content Organizer rules. These rules can specify content type and property conditions that must be met to have the content automatically organized.

The other library you will notice is the Record Library. You will upload finished documents to this library. Documents added to this library will automatically be declared as records. Additionally, you may use the metadata navigation feature to make this library easier to manage.

From the Site Actions menu of a Records Center site, you can access a special Manage Records Center menu item. The Manage Records Center page gives you one-click access to all of the activities you will need to set up your Records Center site for records management, as shown in Figure 14-24.

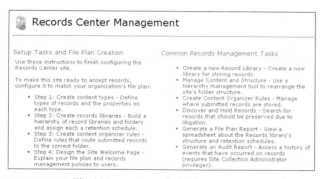

FIGURE 14-24 The Manage Records Center page

The new Records Center site simply brings together all of the features needed to perform records management in SharePoint 2010.

In-Place Records Management

The core concept behind in-place records management is the idea that you want to be able to declare record content within the same library where the content was created. This often means that record content will coexist alongside active content. Each organization is subject to its own unique set of regulatory requirements and usually has its own information retention policies. In-place records management provides a level of flexibility that enables organizations to implement and enforce those policies in a way that makes the process transparent for end users. Record content often is considered of value to an organization because it is evidentiary or substantiates business activities. It might also be information of value for protected reasons, such as in the case of proprietary information or industry secrets.

Integrated life-cycle features included with SharePoint 2010 allow records managers to schedule document archiving and to automate the process of moving documents between active document repositories and the records archive. This ability to move content automatically is provided by the Content Organizer. In conjunction with the Content Organizer, in-place records management provides an integrated way to control content by allowing users to declare that content in place, have that content disposed of in place, or move it to an archive at a specified time for further processing.

Site and List Level Declaration Settings

Documents or items declared as records can have additional restrictions or retention policies enforced on them compared to non-records. Use the Record Declaration Settings page to determine who can declare records and what restrictions to put in place. You access the Record Declaration Settings page by visiting the target site, clicking the Site Actions icon on the Ribbon, and then selecting Site Settings. Click the Records Declaration Settings link in the Site Collection Administration setting group. The page provides access to the settings described in Table 14-14.

TABLE 14-14 Settings Available on the Record Declaration Settings Page Within a Site

SETTING	EXPLANATION
Record Restrictions	Specify restrictions to place on a document or item when it has been declared as a record. Changing this setting will not affect items that have already been declared records. Note that the information management policy settings can also specify different policies for records and non-records. You may only select one of three options for this setting: select to have no additional restriction for record content, to only block the deletion of record content, or to block both the editing and deletion of record content.

continued on the next page

SETTING	EXPLANATION
Record Declaration Availability	Specify whether all lists and libraries in this site should make the manual declaration of records available by default. When manual record declaration is unavailable, records can only be declared through a policy or workflow.
Declaration Roles	Specify which user roles can declare and undeclare record status manually. Use this setting to specify if the declaration of records can be performed by all list contributors and administrators, only list administrators, or only policy actions. You also select the same specifications for the undeclaring of records.

You can also use the information management settings on a location or a content type to define separate policies for records and non-records. Within a given document library, you can specify the records declaration settings for that library. To access these settings, visit the target library and click Library Settings in the Library menu on the Ribbon. Then click the Record Declaration Setting link in the Permissions And Management Settings group. The page provides access to the settings described in Table 14-15.

TABLE 14-15 Settings Available on the Record Declaration Settings Page Within a List

SETTING	EXPLANATION
Manual Record Declaration Availability	Specify whether this list should allow the manual declaration of records. When manual record declaration is unavailable, records can only be declared through a policy or workflow. This setting allows you to use the site collection default setting, always allow manual declaration, or never allow manual declaration. Note that this setting is disabled if automatic declaration is enabled for the library.
Automatic Declaration	Specify whether all items should become records when added to this list. When enabled, items will be declared a record after the item is checked in the first time. When automatic declaration of items is enabled, check-in will also be required on this list before items can be edited.

Declare a Record Within a Library

To manually declare a record within a library, you must have manual record declaration enabled at the site collection or list library level. When it is enabled, these settings will make additional action buttons available on the Ribbon. When you click the file name of a document in a library to select it and the Documents menu appears on the Ribbon, you will see two new icons, Declare Record and Undeclare Record, as shown in Figure 14-25. You may use these icons to perform the actions each describes on the selected document or documents. You will be asked to confirm your selection by a prompt, after which the records are declared.

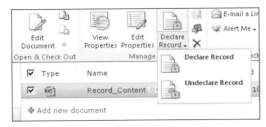

FIGURE 14-25 Declare a record in place within a document library.

After an item has been declared as a record, the Ribbon will be trimmed to exclude the menu items to delete or edit/delete an item.

Document Compliance Details

You may view the compliance details of any document within the system by opening the Edit Control Block menu of an item and selecting Compliance Details to open the dialog box shown in Figure 14-26. The resulting item compliance report includes information about the retention policy applied for the item, if it is exempt from the policy, the item's location in the library and its content type, and if the item is on hold or declared as a record. You may also generate an audit log report for this item to see what activity has occurred according to item's audit policy.

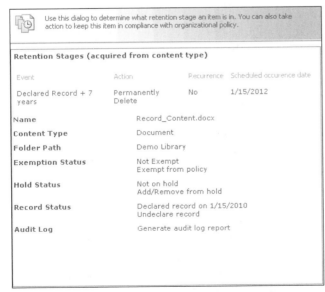

FIGURE 14-26 View the compliance details for a specific document.

eDiscovery and Hold

Holds are usually the result of litigations or investigations that require certain content to be held and produced, often by court order. SharePoint 2010 provides new enhancements that make it easier to manage holds and perform discovery efforts needed to identify content that must be placed on hold. The following sections review the basics of these features and how to configure each.

Configuring Holds

Holds are set up and managed through a special Holds list within each site collection. To get to this list, visit the target site, click the Site Actions icon on the Ribbon, and then select Site Settings. Click the Holds link under eDiscovery And Holds. Use the Holds list to track external actions like litigations, investigations, or audits that require you to suspend the disposition of items. Placing an item on one or more holds will preserve the item and suspend its disposition until the item is no longer managed by any holds. When you create a hold, you are required to enter a title for it. You also may enter a description for the hold and indicate who is managing the hold.

Placing a Hold on a Document

To place an individual document on hold, simply select the document from within the library. Access the document's Edit Control Block menu and select Compliance Details. In the Hold Status section, click the Add/Remove From Hold link. This will take you to the Item Hold Status page. On this page, you may add the item to a hold, remove the item from a hold, and optionally add comments. When you are done making your selections on the Item Hold Status page, click Save. You will then be returned to the document library, where you can view the individual compliance details of the item and will notice the updated hold status.

Performing eDiscovery

After you have defined a hold, you must locate all of the content for which the hold applies. To do so, you need to perform a discovery search and add all of the results to the hold. In SharePoint 2010, this process is called eDiscovery. To perform eDiscovery, you will need to access the Search And Add To Hold page. Visit the target site, click the Site Actions icon on the Ribbon, and then select Site Settings. Click the Discover And Hold Content link, which is located in the Hold And eDiscovery section. The Search And Add To Hold page provides the search options presented in Table 14-16.

TABLE 14-16 Search And Add To Hold Options

SETTING	EXPLANATION
Search Criteria	Specify the site that you want to search and the search terms related to the hold. You can specify complex searches using the keyword syntax. You also can preview the results before adding them to hold.
Local Hold Or Export	If your organization's policy allows this repository to store held content, you can keep the relevant content in place. Otherwise, documents can be copied to another repository. The destination location list is populated with all valid Document and Records Center locations as configured by the administrator.
Relevant Hold	Specify the hold to which the items should be subject. If the items will be kept in place, this list is populated based on the holds defined for this site and all parent sites. Otherwise, the list is populated with the valid holds for the destination location selected previously.

When you have selected these options, click Preview Results to view the content that will be placed on hold. If you are satisfied with the results, click Add Results To Hold at the bottom of the page. You will then receive a confirmation that the operation was scheduled, and you will receive an e-mail message notifying you when the items listed are added to the hold.

Viewing Hold Reports

After you have a hold configured and have added items to the hold, a report will be generated that includes information such as the items on hold and the search queries that have been performed for the hold. To view these reports, visit the target site, click the Site Actions icon on the Ribbon, and then select Site Settings. Click the Hold Reports link in the Hold And eDiscovery section. This will take you to the Holds Reports list, where the available reports will be grouped by hold.

Retention

SharePoint 2010 provides a robust set of features to define specific policies to manage information. (See the section titled "Information Management Policy" earlier in this chapter for more details about how to use these features.) This section will expand on the IM Policy discussion and explore features included with SharePoint 2010 that provide added flexibility while configuring the system for retention. For example, you cannot configure separate retention schedules for record and non-record content. Additionally, retention schedules can be multistaged with recurrence, providing you with the capability to define complex retention and expiration scenarios.

Library-Based Retention

You can use Information Management Policy to set up retention and expiration schedules by content type. Library-based retention policy allows you to set retention and expiration schedules either collectively for the entire library or by individual folder. A new File Plan Report gives you information about the containers in a site, enables you to manage containers, and explains how library-based retention and expiration is applied within the library.

To set up library-based retention, visit the library you want to configure, open the Library menu from the Ribbon, and select Library Settings. Click the Information Management Policy Settings link in the Permissions And Management section of the Library Settings page. By default, each library is set up to enforce the retention schedules set on its content types. To enable library-based retention, you will need to stop enforcing content type schedules and instead define a schedule for the library. To do this, click the Change Source link on the Information Management Policy Settings page and then select Library And Folders. It's important to remember that by using site content types to manage retention, you maintain consistency with the site's information policy. However, when you use library-based retention, the defined schedules will be enforced regardless of any schedule defined on the content types—content type schedules will be ignored when you select the library-based retention option.

After you have selected the Library And Folders option, a new Library Based Retention Schedule Settings area will appear. You may optionally enter a description for the new policy and set up one or many stages for the entire library, as shown in Figure 14-27.

FIGURE 14-27 Setting up a retention schedule for the entire library

When you have configured the policy for the base library, click OK. Then click the Change Source Or Configure The Library Schedule link to return to the Library Based Retention Schedule settings page. If you skip this step, any settings you specified for retention will not be saved.

To configure the retention for a specific folder within a library, click the folder within the Location To Configure tree view, which is located in the left pane on the Library Based Retention Schedule page. Each folder will provide options for inheriting the schedule from the parent library or folder, not expiring items, or defining its own retention schedule.

File Plan Report

After you have configured the retention schedule for the library and its folder, you should generate a file plan report for the library. You can do this by clicking the Generate File Plan Report for this library on the Folder Based Retention Schedule Settings page, or by clicking the Generate File Plan Report link on the Library Settings page. A file plan report is generated as a Microsoft Excel workbook and is broken down into three sections that are each represented as tabbed worksheet within the workbook.

The Summary worksheet includes information about the library such as the URL, folder count, item count, versioning settings, content approval settings, draft item security, and the source of the library's retention schedule. It also presents information about whether any record content exists within the library, as well as if any items are on hold. Lastly, it contains a table of content types bound to the library and their associated information management policies, if applied.

The Retention Details worksheet includes information about the retention schedule applied within the library as well as any information about folder-based retention, if configured.

The Folder Details worksheet presents a detailed table of information about each folder present in the library including the path, number of items, if the folder has unique permissions, the retention schedule, any content organizer rules that route content to the folder, and a list of available content types for the folder.

Figure 14-28 shows an example of the Summary worksheet in a file plan report.

Demo Library: File Plan Report

Site:	Team
URL:	http://server/sites/team/Demo Library/Forms/AllItems.aspx
Description:	Demo Library
Report Generated	2010-01-16T22:21:03
Created By:	System Account
Folder Count:	4
Item Count:	8
Versioning:	Create major and minor (draft) versions
Require Content Approval:	No
Draft Item Security:	Any user who can read items can see drafts
Source of retention schedules:	Library and folders
Has Records:	No
Has Items on Hold:	No

Content Type	Policy Name	Policy Description
Asset Inventory Sheet		
Demo Document Set		
Document		
Folder		
Inventory Document		
Misc Inventory Sheet		
Product Inventory Sheet		

FIGURE 14-28 The Summary section of a file plan report

Scalability

With the new features provided for records management in SharePoint 2010, you can scale records management to hundreds of millions of records across multiple site collections. This makes managing record content easier and more secure. The Content Organizer, with its ability to route content between site collections, allows you to move content in a more intelligent way to distribute the record load across multiple site collections. Content type syndication allows you to ensure that all of these site collections share the content types you specify.

Web Content Management

SharePoint 2010 includes new and improved features for Web content management that are designed to enhance both the authoring and publishing experience. Web content management and publishing are covered in detail in Chapter 15, "Administering Web Content Management and Publishing," but the following sections briefly highlight some of these enhancements and how they relate to content management in general. Specifically, you will learn about the enhanced functionality provided by SharePoint 2010 in the following areas.

- Accessibility and markup
- Content query
- Ratings
- Folders
- Page authoring
- Themes and branding

Refer to Chapter 15 for more information about these features.

Accessibility and Markup

The XHTML and cascading style sheet (CSS) have been simplified in SharePoint 2010 to reduce rendering time, and they are not WCAG 2.0 AA-compliant to meet accessibility requirements. Browser support for SharePoint 2010 has been expanded to include Firefox 3, Safari 3, and Microsoft Internet Explorer 8.

Content Query

Changes to the Content Query Web Part enable you to present cross-list views of content that are filtered on managed metadata fields. (Metadata fields are covered in more detail in the section titled "Managed Metadata Fields" earlier in this chapter.) Content authors have browser-based control over the fields/columns that appear in results presented by the Web Part, and page designers can create page layouts that contain cross-list views that respond to other content on the page. All of these features are available without the need to learn the complexities of XML or XSL.

Ratings

Ratings provide a new way for your users to express themselves by giving them the ability to rate content from any list or library. Use dynamic Web Parts that are based on the ratings metadata to filter, sort, and query content, which can add a whole new dynamic dimension to your content. See Chapter 10, "Collaboration and Portals," for more information about ratings and social computing.

Folders

Page libraries now support folders, providing greater scalability and making it easier to organize libraries that store large numbers of pages. Using the Content Organizer, you can create rules that allow for the automatic movement of content to a folder based on the supplied metadata.

Page Authoring

The new page authoring experience includes the addition of the familiar context-based Ribbon interface, making it easier access the controls you need without having to hunt between pages or menus to find the function you need. The Ribbon fully integrates the page authoring experience with the publishing approval workflow process and content deployment functions. A full-featured HTML editor provides a cross-browser rich-text editor for editing Web page content in Internet Explorer 8, Firefox 3, and Safari 3.

Themes and Branding

The entire themes engine has been rebuilt for SharePoint 2010 to provide a more powerful and flexible style-driven interface that is fully customizable from the browser. This allows site administrators and designers to manipulate the user experience from a Web-based user interface even if they have little or no CSS knowledge. The themes library comes filled with many out-of-the-box options so that you can quickly and easily customize a theme to meet your organization's specific design requirements.

Digital Asset Management

As the prevalence of rich media continues to grow, the information worker must store and access such content far more often. Whether the media files are images, video, or audio, there is a greater need than ever to store and manage this content in an intelligent way. In prior versions of SharePoint, you could store images easily enough, but audio and video made high demands on the architecture, and many organizations elected to block most common audio and video file types. Even if this were not the case, file upload limits often made it impractical to store such content within the system. SharePoint 2010 introduces new features and capabilities that have been designed and built specifically for storing, managing, using, and accessing rich media files.

A new Asset Library feature allows branded images, video, and other reusable content fragments from Microsoft Office applications to be quickly and easily stored and managed. Enterprise-managed metadata greatly enhances users' ability to find digital assets within these new libraries. Asset libraries are based on the standard SharePoint document library, so you get all the same metadata-driven navigation features in addition to new thumbnail-centric views, preview on hover, and video playback. The following sections cover the new and enhanced features available within SharePoint 2010 for digital asset management, including

- New content types
- Video streaming infrastructure
- User interface

New Content Types

New content types have been added to the system to support the storage and playback of audio and video assets. These new content types can be found in a new Digital Asset Content Types group within the Site Content Types gallery. Table 14-17 lists the new content types with explanations of what each type can do.

TABLE 14-17 New Digital Asset Content Types

CONTENT TYPE	EXPLANATION
Rich Media Asset	Upload an asset. This is the base content type for digital assets within the system. Each of the three following content types is derived from this content type. This content type includes fields for Preview, Thumbnail Preview, and Keywords.
Audio	Upload an audio file. Based on the Asset content type. Includes all of the fields from the Asset content type in addition to Author, Comments, Preview Image URL, Copyright, and Length (seconds).
Image	Upload an image. Based on the Asset content type. Includes all of the fields from the Asset content type in addition to Picture Size, Comments, Author, Date Picture Taken, and Copyright.
Video	Upload a video file. Based on the Asset content type. Includes all of the fields from the Asset content type in addition to Author, Comments, Preview Image URL, Copyright, Length (seconds), Frame Width, and Frame Length.

As always, you can create your own content types based on the supplied content types to meet your specific needs. For example, you can add new custom columns or field controls to a custom content type.

Video Streaming Infrastructure

SharePoint 2010 includes updates to the disk-cache management features that support the publication and streaming of digital video assets. These enhancements greatly reduce the performance strain on the Web front-end servers while streaming video, allowing you to store more video within SharePoint and making that video available immediately. See Chapter 15 for more information about setting up and configuring caching in your environment.

User Interface

Enhancements to the user interface enable the seamless playback of audio and video files in Web pages. A new multimedia player that is based on Microsoft Silverlight technology and an updated page model allow designers to apply skin to the player in order to provide a completely branded experience for the end user. The media player supports many popular video formats, including WMV and MP4. Because the new media player leverages Silverlight, as support for additional media formats and codecs become available, SharePoint will be able to take full advantage of those updates. The digital asset library provides a preview mode for audio and video files, and a new asset picker makes it quick and easy to find just the right rich media element for your purpose.

The asset library provides the following significant optimizations for digital assets.

- Thumbnail-centric view

- Metadata extraction for images

- RSS/podcasting support

- Hover preview with streaming

Figure 14-29 shows an asset library in action, with images and a hover preview.

FIGURE 14-29 An example of a digital asset library with images and a hover preview

Summary

SharePoint 2010 Enterprise Content Management features support multiple approaches to managing data, documents, Web, and digital content. A new capability for standardizing the way unstructured information is stored within the system allows you to mitigate risk and improve compliance. An easy-to-use interface with an intuitive design gives users incentives to capture metadata, making information more discoverable. New Web content management capabilities allow you to manage your Web sites and Web content more efficiently. In-place records management and the Content Organizer provide you with maximum flexibility to manage high-value record content. Finally, the architectural improvements relating to document storage and video streaming allow you to scale libraries to millions of documents and provide users with almost instant video response.

## CHAPTER 15

Administering Web Content Management and Publishing

Microsoft SharePoint 2010 provides a comprehensive set of features and functionalities for Web Content Management (WCM). WCM facilitates the creation and management of dynamic Web content, including HTML pages and their associated media files. Through WCM functionality, users can actively participate in content creation, control, editing, and essential Web maintenance functions. By contrast, Document Management (DM) is concerned with the management of physical and electronic documents within an environment. Records Management (RM) is concerned with the management of official records. WCM, DM, and RM are all subsets of the broader Enterprise Content Management (ECM) discussion.

Although the concepts involved in the management of Web content differ from those that govern the management of enterprise document content, many of the core principles and elements found within SharePoint 2010 remain consistent throughout both capabilities. The specific infrastructure, SharePoint features, and nomenclature used within this chapter refer collectively to Web Content Management and the activities associated with it as publishing.

The origins of the publishing capability can be traced back to Microsoft Content Management Server, which was folded into Microsoft Office SharePoint Server 2007 as the "publishing features." These features provided a flexible content authoring and management capability for the dissemination of information within an organization through a website. SharePoint 2010 includes many enhancements to these features, as well as additional capabilities, all of which are covered comprehensively in this chapter.

It is important to think of the WCM capability as a component of the larger unified platform that is SharePoint 2010. The publishing features made available through WCM support a wide range of deployment scenarios. From Enterprise Wikis and Internet-facing sites to divisional and corporate-wide intranet portals, WCM and the associated publishing features provide a consistent, controllable, and unified deployment experience for both users and administrators. WCM also provides the adjustable governance needed to ensure that company branding and compliance standards are met within highly controlled sites, while allowing sites that require less control, such as Enterprise Wikis, to be more unstructured. For community involvement and content creation, SharePoint 2010 introduces a robust set of tagging and rating capabilities that are sure to keep users engaged, even in sites where the publishing process is highly controlled.

Publishing sites and their features also provide a wide array of available functionalities for the creation and management of Web content. These features include a rich content authoring and page editing capability within the Web interface, as well as a robust and extensive authoring solution that offers the ability to author content from within the Microsoft Office 2010 System, including Microsoft Office Word 2010 and InfoPath 2010. The publishing framework provides the ability to easily manage site navigation and branding, enabling you to create a consistent content experience that is available cross-browser as well as from mobile devices.

This chapter provides details about the underlying publishing features and site types. Additionally, you will learn how users may author and create content using these features, and the specifics of deploying and administering publishing sites. The chapter also reviews how to set up content caching based on the identifiable requirements appropriate to your environment and use. Lastly, you will explore content deployment, how to set up and administer it, and when to use it.

Publishing Site Types and Features

The publishing capability within SharePoint 2010 consists of a series of SharePoint features and site templates that are selectable when you are creating a new site collection. Although publishing features can be activated within any site collection, some out-of-the-box site templates, such a Publishing Portal or Enterprise Wiki, come with publishing features already activated.

Publishing features provide the additional rich content authoring capabilities. It's important to remember that because publishing sites are built on top of the SharePoint 2010 Foundation framework, they will contain all of the base features and elements you could expect from any SharePoint site. These include lists, integrated workflow, alerts, integrated enterprise search, the Web Part framework, integrated security, audience targeting, and more.

Choosing the Right Site Type

SharePoint 2010 provides two primary site types that you can use to create a publishing site. On the Publishing tab, you will find the Publishing Portal and Enterprise Wiki site templates available when you create a new site collection in SharePoint Central Administration, as shown in Figure 15-1.

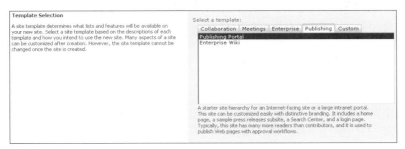

FIGURE 15-1 Select from the available templates under the Publishing tab when you create a new site collection.

Table 15-1 provides a brief explanation of each site template available within the Create Site Collection interface.

TABLE 15-1 Publishing Site Template Types

TEMPLATE	USE
Publishing Portal	A starter site hierarchy for an Internet-facing site or a large intranet portal. This site can be customized easily with distinctive branding. It includes a home page, a sample press releases subsite, a Search Center, and a login page. Typically, this site has many more readers than contributors, and it is used to publish Web pages with Approval workflows.
Enterprise Wiki	A site for publishing knowledge that you capture and want to share across the enterprise. It provides an easy content-editing experience in a single location that allows for co-authoring content, discussions, and project management.

In SharePoint Server 2007, an additional template type called Collaboration Portal was also available. The mixture of the terms *Collaboration* and *Portal* caused some confusion among customers, however. Most users ended up selecting this site type for all new sites, presuming that it provided all of the available features within the product. Although this was the case, the use of this template resulted in customers mixing publishing and collaboration activities, as well as excessive breaks in security inheritance and very large site collections that threatened capacity limitations. In SharePoint 2010, the distinction between collaboration and publishing is far better defined, with a single publishing site type available as a starter site type for both large Internet-facing sites and intranet portals. This was done to encourage customers to use the site types available on the Collaboration tab for collaboration, while reserving the enablement of the publishing features for sites in which that level of functionality and complexity is genuinely needed.

Enabling Publishing Features

Although the site types discussed in the previous section are created with the publishing features already enabled, these features can also be enabled within any SharePoint 2010 site collection. When activated, these features will create a document library and picture library for storing publishing assets. In addition, you will find options specific to the management of Web content available through the Site Actions menu and the Page Editor. These additional interface elements make it easy for content owners to manage changes with the page editing toolbar and the check out and content editor features.

Table 15-2 lists the publishing features with details about each as they are described within the Feature management user interface (UI).

TABLE 15-2 Publishing Features

FEATURE	DESCRIPTION
SharePoint Server Publishing Infrastructure	Provides centralized libraries, content types, master pages, and page layouts, and enables page scheduling and other publishing functionality for a site collection.
SharePoint Server Publishing	Creates a Web page library as well as supporting libraries to create and publish pages based on page layouts.

To activate the publishing features within an existing site collection, you will need to activate two separate and distinct features. The following steps outline the activation of these features.

1. From the top site within the site collection, use the Site Actions menu to select Site Settings.

2. Within Site Settings, select Site Collection Features, which can be found under the Site Collection Administration settings group.

3. Activate the feature called SharePoint Server Publishing Infrastructure.

4. Return to Site Settings.

5. Within Site Settings, select Manage Site Features, which can be found under the Site Actions settings group.

6. Activate the feature called SharePoint Server Publishing.

Publishing Workflows

Publishing workflows automate the process of sending a document or item to colleagues or managers for approval. The workflow makes this process more efficient because it provides a way to easily manage and track all of the tasks involved, as well as providing a record of the process after it is completed. The standard out-of-the-box workflow used for this purpose is the Approval workflow. The Approval workflow is associated with the root Document content type in each site collection and therefore is available automatically in document libraries. The default Approval workflow for document libraries is a serial workflow, within which tasks necessary for approval are assigned to participants one after another. In publishing sites, a version of the Approval workflow is associated by default with the included Pages library. Within this library, the workflow is used to manage the approval process for the publication of Web pages. You can always customize the existing Approval workflows, or alternately, you can create your own Approval workflow to meet the specific needs of your implementation. After you have created a workflow, you can then associate it with a list, library, or Content Type.

Defining the Business Process for Publishing

It is important to properly define your end-to-end business process for publishing before expecting content to be approved within your publishing site. First, capture your requirements for content approval. This can often be done on a single sheet of paper. You may find it helpful to illustrate your desired approval process flow and evaluate it with stakeholders prior to implementing it within the system. Remember, after content owners begin creating content for the site, they will need to publish it. If the approval process is not well understood and implemented properly, both users and approvers will become frustrated, and the overall adoption of the technology for that group of business users could be in jeopardy. As flexible as SharePoint 2010 is, with all of its features and functionality, there is no technology substitute for good project execution and communication.

When you have agreed on how to define the content approval process, it's time to implement it within SharePoint 2010. The out-of-the-box Approval workflow is often a good place to start. Review the settings available when you create a new Approval workflow association. Carefully write down each setting and note the settings needed to meet your specific requirements. If the out-of-the-box workflow will meet your needs, you can simply let users leverage it—it is available by default for all documents stored within the system. If you need to customize the workflow, which is most often the case, you will need to decide if you want to do this by modifying the existing workflow association on the root Document content type or by creating a new workflow association for a specific list or content type.

If there is no way to satisfy all of your requirements within the confines of the out-of-the-box Approval workflow, you will need to look at customizing the workflow to your specific needs. This can easily be done by using SharePoint Designer.

Designer has a host of new features in 2010 that make customizing and reusing custom Approval workflows quick and easy. You can modify the existing workflow by using the Copy And Modify command that is available when you right-click an existing workflow, or you may create a new workflow for content approval that meets your specific requirements. You can add or modify the rules processed within a workflow as well as the actions performed when the conditions of each rule are met. SharePoint Designer 2010 also provides a new import/export capability to Microsoft Office Visio, which allows you to take an existing workflow, export it to Visio, make your modifications within the familiar Visio interface, and then re-import those changes to either Designer or Visual Studio 2010. Figure 15-2 shows the menu options available as you work with site workflows in SharePoint Designer 2010. To access these menu options, open a site with SharePoint Designer 2010, and then select Workflows from the Site Objects menu at left.

FIGURE 15-2 SharePoint Designer has new features that allow you to import and export your content Approval workflow to Visio.

In addition, SharePoint Designer 2010 provides the ability to save a customized content Approval workflow as a Globally Reusable workflow, for use within any site in the site collection. You also can save a workflow as a template (.WSP file), after which you can import it into any site collection within your environment. This feature makes it possible for you to create or customize a content Approval workflow for your entire organization and then make that workflow portable, something you could not do in prior versions of the product.

After an Approval workflow is available, you may start it directly from a document or item in a list by clicking Workflows from the Edit Control Block menu and then clicking the name of the configured Approval workflow. Alternately, if the workflow is associated with a list and configured to automatically be part of the content approval process, a new instance of the workflow will be created when a user creates, changes, or publishes a document. When a new instance is created, the user will be required to fill out an initiation form, in which all of the details needed for workflow execution are captured. An example of what this initiation form might look like is shown in Figure 15-3. These details include the approvers, due dates, durations, and so on. When the workflow starts, a task will be assigned to the appropriate participants, and if enabled, e-mails will be sent out to each participant for whom a task is assigned. Participants may click the link provided in the e-mail to review the document, after which they may choose to approve, reject, or reassign their approval tasks. They may also elect to request a change to the document. When the workflow process is complete, the owner of the workflow is notified automatically. While the workflow is in progress, the workflow owner or participants may view the status of the workflow to see which participants have had tasks assigned to them and which tasks are still outstanding.

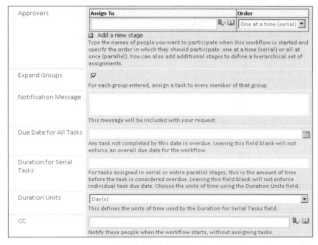

FIGURE 15-3 An example of the initiation form for an Approval workflow

It is also possible to manually start an Approval workflow directly on the list item by using the Edit Control Block menu on the item as shown in Figure 15-4. In addition, you may start an Approval workflow for a document that is stored in a SharePoint library directly from within the Microsoft Office Word 2010 interface. On the File menu, select Share, and any available workflows will be displayed in the lower-left part of the display, as shown in Figure 15-5.

> **NOTE** For e-mail alerts to work, you must have the server configured for alerts and you must have properly configured the outgoing mail settings.

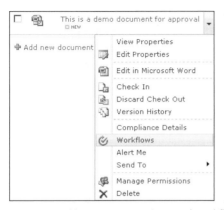

FIGURE 15-4 You can start an Approval workflow directly from the item menu within a list or library.

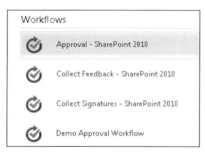

FIGURE 15-5 You can also start an Approval workflow directly from Microsoft Office Word 2010.

Branding

Branding is an important aspect of publishing sites because it allows the designer to create a tailored user experience for the presentation of content. A comprehensive review of the page model is discussed in the section titled "The SharePoint Page Model" later in this chapter. Although the topic of creating a custom Web experience through the modification of master pages, layout pages, and content pages is expansive and outside the scope of this chapter, it's important to touch on the flexibility available to you when creating a custom user experience for your publishing sites.

When a new out-of-the-box SharePoint 2010 site is created, users experience that site through the Web experience provided by the product by default. For example, when a team collaboration site is created, users are presented with an experience similar to what is shown in Figure 15-6.

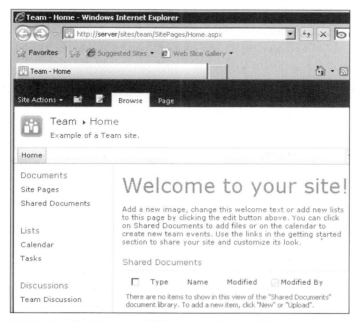

FIGURE 15-6 The SharePoint 2010 user experience within a newly created team site

Let's review the branding options available with SharePoint 2010 by breaking them down into four experience variants, as shown in Table 15-3.

TABLE 15-3 Branding and Customization Options Within SharePoint 2010

BRANDING	CUSTOMIZATION
Standard Page	This is the page as it comes with the site by default. It includes all of the navigation, search, and login elements expected as part of the standard product experience.
Standard Page with a Theme Applied	By selecting a theme for the site, you can customize the standard experience to include a different color scheme and presentation experience; however, the elements on the page will remain the same.
Secondary Master Page	By customizing the master page, you can add, remove, or rearrange the page elements presented on every page within a given site. For example, you could add a Web Part zone, move the search box, or implement a customized navigation.
Fully Customized User Experience	This approach is most often used to completely customize the Internet-facing user experience. This level of customization requires specific resources and planning in order to be successful, but it also offers the greatest flexibility from a visual presentation and design perspective.

Themes have been significantly improved in SharePoint 2010 to provide you with the flexibility required to completely control the color scheme of your site. You have the option to select a system-provided theme for use or as a basis for customizing that theme. When you select a theme, you can see a preview of the applied theme in addition to the specific colors included for each themed page element. If you customize a given theme, then that theme is shown as a custom theme. When you have selected your desired theme colors, you can preview the theme as it would be applied to your site within a new window by selecting Preview Theme from within the Site Theme settings page.

> **NOTE** You can access the Site Theme settings page from within Site Settings, under the Look And Feel settings group.

Using Variations

Content-centric sites revolve around the content itself, rather than the people creating that content, as in collaboration. Many organizations need to present that content to a wide range of audiences, including viewers with different browsers or who speak different languages. Internet-facing sites for larger organizations often face this challenge. In the same way that many of the world's largest consumer-focused companies provide various versions of their website for speakers of languages other than English or for specific national audiences, the publishing features in SharePoint 2010 allow administrators to define different versions of the same content for different user audiences. With Variations, SharePoint 2010 does most of the work needed to keep everything synchronized through special lists, libraries, and workflows. Some of the difficult work remains manual, however, such as the translation of content from one language to another.

Introduced as part of SharePoint Server 2007, many improvements have been made to Variations within SharePoint 2010. Reliability and server citizenship have been improved by moving operations to the timer service, and now those operations support pause and resume capabilities. You now have more control over the Create Hierarchies operation, and numerous user interface enhancements have been added. Variations within SharePoint 2010 also leverages the investments made in the new MUI (Multilanguage User Interface), which adjusts the user experience of the application based on the language of the user.

SharePoint 2010 Platform Enhancements

SharePoint 2010 offers many significant platform enhancements specific to the WCM features and capabilities. Table 15-4 includes a few of the main areas in which investments in the platform architecture have provided meaningful improvements for WCM. These enhancements are discussed in more detail throughout this chapter.

TABLE 15-4 Platform Enhancements Within SharePoint 2010 That Affect WCM

ENHANCEMENT	DESCRIPTION
Host-Header Site Collections	Although introduced within SharePoint Server 2007, support for Host-Header based site collections has improved substantially. These site collections can be created at a specific URL that is not part of the Web application's zones and/or managed path settings.
Streaming from the BLOB Cache	By allowing streaming from the Binary Large Object (BLOB) cache, SharePoint 2010 is better equipped to serve rich-media experiences including streaming video without placing undue load on database servers.
User Solutions	Because publishing sites often require customization, User Solutions will allow a wide array of customizations, including Web Parts, custom lists, and field controls, to be uploaded and deployed directly to a site collection.
MUI (Multilanguage User Interface)	Provides the ability to render an adjusted application experience based on the language of the user. This improves multilingual support from simple character sets to a complete UI experience.

NOTE To learn more about the platform enhancement provided with SharePoint 2010, visit *http://sharepoint.microsoft.com.*

Administering Publishing Sites

This section reviews the administration of publishing sites in more depth. Specifically, it covers the additional security elements that are included with the publishing features as well as some important best practices to keep in mind when you are securing your publishing sites. It also covers features that make it easy to manage your site structure and navigation, including how to reorganize your site to make things easier to find for viewers. You will learn about the concepts of Master and Layout Pages and explain how they fit into the larger page model. You will also review the different ways in which content owners can author and create the underlying content, and how to provide for the moment of content from feeder collaboration sites in which content is being created for dissemination through the publishing sites.

Security and Permissions

When you activate the publishing features within a site, you will notice that additional SharePoint security groups have been created that are specific to the publishing activities. SharePoint security groups are the mechanism for providing access to the site to identifiable users or groups. It is important that users only have access to the site through membership in the group or groups that best suit their level of participation in the publishing process. Each of these groups is associated with a permission level. Permission levels are the mechanism through which a user or group is granted the ability to perform specific tasks or actions within a site. These additional groups and permission levels are listed in Tables 15-5 and 15-6.

TABLE 15-5 Additional Security Groups Included When Publishing Features Are Activated

GROUP	DESCRIPTION
Approvers	Members of this group can edit and approve pages, list items, and documents.
Designers	Members of this group can edit lists, document libraries, and pages in the site. Designers can create master pages and page layouts in the Master Page Gallery and can change the behavior and appearance of each site in the site collection by using Master Pages and Cascading Style Sheets (CSS) files.
Hierarchy Managers	Members of this group can create sites, lists, list items, and documents.
Quick Deploy Users	Members of this group can schedule Quick Deploy jobs.
Restricted Readers	Members of this group can view pages and documents but cannot view historical versions or review user rights information.
Style Resource Readers	Members of this group are given Read permission to the Master Page gallery and Restricted Read permission to the Style Library. By default, all authenticated users are members of this group. To further secure this site, you can remove all authenticated users from this group or add users to this group.

TABLE 15-6 Additional Permission Levels Included When Publishing Features Are Activated

PERMISSION LEVEL	DESCRIPTION
Approve	Can edit and approve pages, list items, and documents.
Manage Hierarchy	Can create sites and edit pages, list items, and documents.
Restricted Read	Can view pages and documents but cannot view historical versions or user permissions. (This permission level replaces the default View Only permission level.)
Style Resource Readers	Members of this group are given Read permission to the Master Page gallery and the Restricted Read permission to the Style Library. By default, all authenticated users are members of this group. To further secure this site, you can remove all authenticated users from this group or add users to this group.

It is possible to create your own groups and/or permission levels if those provided for you are insufficient; however, this is discouraged unless absolutely necessary. If you determine that you need to change the default groups or permission levels, you should create a new group or level that is tailored to your specific needs rather than modifying those provided by the system. You also are discouraged from removing the default groups or levels provided, because this might produce access issues that can become difficult to diagnose without reviewing the default group and level settings in detail. You can always explore the specific permissions that are granted by a permission level by clicking on that level from within the Permission Levels settings page, which is located under Site Settings.

Site Structure and Navigation

Typically the structure of a publishing site collection is arranged in a content-centric fashion, where subsites provide a structure for navigation, and pages provide the content within those subsites. Rather than creating subsites for teams or groups of people, you might decide to create subsites based on a categorization or subclassification of content. For example, if your top site is your company's Internet-facing home page, you might have the content arranged by product area, corporate division, or continent. Of course, you have all of the features and capabilities available to you for managing content via content types and metadata as well.

Tradeoffs: Creating Pages vs. Subsites

Is it better to create pages within an existing site or to create a new subsite? The answer is, as is often the case in IT, it depends. Although it might seem as if pages and subsites produce a similar result, there are specific tradeoffs that you must consider when selecting one over another.

Pages

Pages are list items that are specifically designed for the presentation of Web content. Consider using pages whenever you want to post new content within an existing site structure. Even if you elect to create a new subsite, the content is still displayed on a page within that subsite, so in effect you use a page to display your content either way. In addition, pages inherit their look and feel from their associated page layout and master page. This is important, because the master page settings are controlled at the subsite level. So, if you want to easily create a page using a different master page, a subsite might be the better choice. Think of a page as a representation of information. That is, the page itself might present information that is different from other pages, but it doesn't represent a division of information.

Subsites

Think of a subsite as an information container. By itself, a subsite really does not directly display Web content to the user. It simply contains the pages that display Web content. Consider using a subsite when you need different security from that of the parent site, or when the information purpose is distinct and consequently requires a clear delineation from the parent site. For example, a company portal with an IT help desk uses the root portal site as the navigation pathway through which many divisions of information are reached—help desk information is only one type of information available within the portal. Additionally, the help desk information is managed by a specific team of people who are responsible for that information. Finally, you don't want help desk team members to change content within the root of the portal, because they are not responsible for that content. In this case, a new subsite for the help desk is the clear choice, because it will allow you to achieve a clear division of both information and security.

Summary

To summarize, the following considerations are an indicator that you might need a new subsite.

- The information has a different function from that of the information stored in the parent site.
- The information is not needed elsewhere within the site collection.
- The information has a different target audience than the parent site.
- The information requires different security from that of the parent site.
- The presentation of the information requires separate and unique settings.

If you find that the preceding criteria are not met, it is often both quicker and easier to simply use a page to display your additional content.

In the case of an Internet-facing site, your priority might be the user experience and how the presentation of content contributes to the needs of particular groups of users who may be looking for specific information about a product, for example. In the case of a divisional portal, on the other hand, your focus might be on the arrangement and categorization of content by department. What is most important is that you and your stakeholders put the necessary forethought into how you will be arranging content within the site, as well as how the content publishing and approval processes will work.

When you have determined how you will be organizing and arranging information within your site collection, it's time to create the site structure. This can be done using the standard Create Site functionality provided within the Site Actions menu, SharePoint Designer, or the Content And Structure function. The Content And Structure function, which is available by clicking Manage Content And Structure from the Site Actions menu, provides an easy way to manage the structure of your site collection within a familiar tree view/detail interface, while creating or removing any needed sites, lists, and pages along the way. Figure 15-7 shows an example of the Content And Structure window.

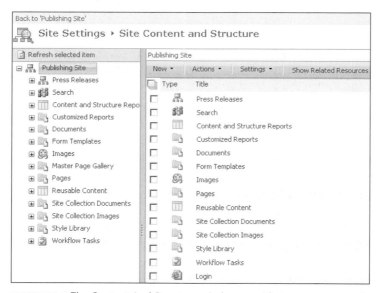

FIGURE 15-7 The Content And Structure window provides an easy way to view and modify the structure of your site collection.

In addition to the Content And Structure feature, there is a Navigation link located under Look And Feel, within Site Settings, that takes you to the Navigation Settings page. From here, you can control how navigation elements are displayed within the site. For example, you can elect to show subsites or pages within the Global And Current Navigation. You can also define sorting options as well as edit the Global And Current Navigation directly to add, hide, or delete specific items. There also is an option that allows you to make the Show Ribbon and Hide Ribbon commands available.

The SharePoint Page Model

The page model is a template-based page rendering system that provides for the presentation of content, which is manifested as individual page views. The content page itself, although addressable in the browser, contains only the user content entered in that page, not the entire user experience or even the layout of the content. The primary elements of the presentation layer are master pages, page layouts, field controls, and Web Parts. In the following sections, you review each of these elements in more detail, discuss their purpose, and provide examples of when you might use each to meet your requirements.

Master Pages

The master page is the base of the presentation layer, on which all other elements of the presentation are based. If the SharePoint presentation framework were the foundation of a building, think of the master page as the superstructure within which the floor layouts are created before the contents are placed on each floor. Master pages determine the placement of key page elements that will be present on every page. Examples of these elements include the search box, personalization links, login controls, logos, editing controls, CSS references, and server controls. In addition to these elements, a master page contains one or more content areas. Content areas are page real estate dedicated to the presentation of content. All SharePoint master pages must include the main content area, which is equivalent to the main body of a standard HTML page. Within this content area, the designers of page layouts have the flexibility of providing further definitions specific to the arrangement of content within the pages, based on that page layout.

Page Layouts

Page layouts are the middle of the presentation layer and provide the template for rendering content to the user. Every page layout must reference a master page for navigation and chrome. Within a page layout, a designer can define what content can be authored on a page. Field controls, Web Part zones, and Web Parts can be placed within content areas provided within the referenced master page and arranged according to the identified requirements for the presentation of content. Page content types form the foundation of the schema for content that will be presented within a page layout. Each content type defines the fields and/or field controls that are made available to the layout designer. You can define many page layouts for each content type.

Field Controls

Field controls are simple ASP.NET controls that you can create, and they are the smallest and most granular element in the presentation layer. Each field control is bound to fields in the page content type. Field controls provide designers with a fair amount of control over the content added by the author or content owner. For example, a Rich Text field can enforce specific styles or fonts. Field controls can also provide control of structure and branding through restrictions on authoring options. When the author is adding an image to the page, for example, a field control could determine whether he or she can use any image or only an image from a library within that site.

Web Parts

Web Parts are the most flexible presentation element available within the system. They provide a full gallery of controls for use within zones defined by Page Layout designer. This allows authors to control their selection and placement. Page Layout designer may also elect to place and configure a Web Part on the author's behalf by placing it in the Page Layout directly. Web Parts are covered in more detail in Chapter 19, "Web Parts and Their Functionality in SharePoint 2010."

SharePoint Designer Settings

SharePoint 2010 introduces additional functionality that gives administrators a modicum of control over the use of SharePoint Designer. In the past, it was difficult to restrict users from performing specific tasks with SharePoint Designer without restricting their ability to use it at all. SharePoint 2010 provides management of individual application capabilities both within the entire Web application as well as within each site collection. Web application level settings can be adjusted from within Central Administration by clicking Change SharePoint Designer Settings, which can be found under General Application Settings. Within an individual site collection, the settings are accessible from Site Settings, Site Collection Administration, SharePoint Designer Settings. Table 15-7 lists and describes each of the settings available. Each of the listed settings is available as a check box that is selected, or enabled, by default. As expected, disabling a setting or capability at the Web application level makes it unavailable for use or selection with individual site collections.

TABLE 15-7 SharePoint Designer Settings Control What Users Can and Cannot Do with the Tool

SETTING	DESCRIPTION
Enable SharePoint Designer	Specify whether to allow the editing of sites using SharePoint Designer.
Enable Detaching Pages from the Site Definition	Specify whether to allow detachment of pages from the original site definition using SharePoint Designer.
Enable Customizing Master Pages and Layout Pages	Specify whether to allow the customization of Master Pages and Layout Pages using SharePoint Designer.
Enable Managing of the Web Site URL Structure	Specify whether to allow management of the URL structure of sites using SharePoint Designer.

Although there can be a variety of reasons for creating a new publishing site, the fact remains that someone, somewhere, has to create content that will become available within that site for users to consume. Of course, there are multiple ways to create this content. In the case of a highly customized publishing site, such as an Internet-facing site, where most of the content is page content, the authoring would most likely occur in a staging site collection. However, if the publishing site is more of a portal site for a project or business unit, and most of the content is document content, it is common for this content to be created within team collaboration sites. The advantages of using a collaboration site for the creation of new document content are

- You can allow more people to contribute to the authoring process within a collaboration site, including people who are not designated to publish content to the publishing site.

- Collaboration tends to be a messy business, in which team members track documents, tasks, events, and reference materials, most of which should not be published to the publishing site.

- Content can easily be moved to the publishing site when it is ready to be approved for publishing.

Although there are multiple ways to move this content, the Document Send To feature within document libraries is the easiest method to implement and requires no customization. Introduced in SharePoint Server 2007, the Document Send To feature allows you to send library content to another SharePoint site library with only a few clicks. Figure 15-8 shows the Document Send To option as it is available on the Documents menu of a document library. To send content to another document library using this feature, the user must have write access to the destination document library. This makes it easy to restrict who can publish content to the publishing site collection. After the content is in the destination library, the publishing process workflows can begin, and the content approved and finally published for consumption by end users.

FIGURE 15-8 Use the Document Send To option to send a document to another SharePoint site library.

continued on the next page

If you have created a library in your collaboration site for the purpose of authoring content for a specific target library within the publishing site collection, you can set a Custom Send To Location for the originating library. Setting a Custom Send To Location makes the designated target location available from the Document Send To menu, thereby allowing authors to send content to the destination library without requiring them to enter the fully qualified destination address.

To set a Custom Send To Location within a library, perform the following steps.

1. Access Library Settings from within a document library.

2. Go to Advanced Settings and locate the Custom Send To Destination settings, as shown in Figure 15-9.

3. Enter a destination name under Custom Send To Destination. This is the name that will appear in the Documents menu for the library.

4. Enter the URL under Custom Send To Destination. This is the URL of the destination library to which content will be sent.

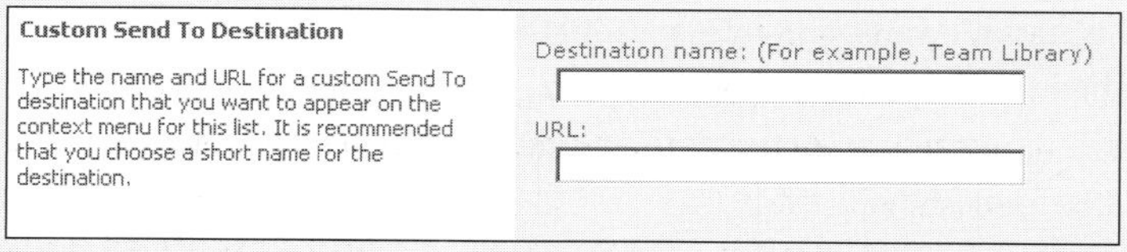

Custom Send To Destination

Type the name and URL for a custom Send To destination that you want to appear on the context menu for this list. It is recommended that you choose a short name for the destination.

Destination name: (For example, Team Library)

URL:

FIGURE 15-9 Set up a Custom Send To Destination to make it easier for users to send content to the destination library.

Control and Insight from Analytics

SharePoint 2010 includes new features that allow you to collect and report on a wide array of valuable metrics throughout the content improvement life cycle. The Analytics capability provides features for both Web Analytics and Social Computing. By collecting data about the usage of the site and the content, Analytics allows you to publish content, have that content be consumed by users, measure that consumption, and then analyze those activities in a meaningful way. Two types of data are collected: behavioral data and explicit data. Some examples of behavioral data include information about traffic, clicks, and search terms. Some examples of explicit data include information about ratings, social tagging, and notes.

Configuring Analytics

To configure Web Analytics at the farm level, perform the following steps.

1. Open a browser and go to the SharePoint Central Administration website.

2. Click the Monitoring link.

3. Select Configure Usage And Health Data Collection, which is located under Reporting Settings group.

4. To enable usage data collection, select the Enable Usage Data Collection check box, which is enabled by default.

5. Under Event Selection, you can specify the types of events for which you would like to collect data. Simply select the check boxes next to each type of data you want to see in the reports.

6. Under Usage Data Collection Settings, you can specify the Log file location and maximum log size.

7. To enable health data collection, select the Enable Health Data Collection check box.

8. Under Logging Database Server, you may specify the database server and database name, as well as the authentication settings, for the logging database.

9. When you are satisfied with your selections, click OK at the bottom of the page.

> **NOTE** There are also options to adjust the Health Logging and Log Collection Schedules. It is recommend that you complete your selection of settings on this page, click OK, and then return to the page in order to adjust these settings.

There are also configuration options for analytics at the site collection level. These options are available only to members of the Owners and Manage Hierarchy groups by default. The View Analytics permission protects analytics data and reports. Remember, analytics features can be enabled or disabled at the site collection level through feature activation and deactivation. Analytics configurations also can be adjusted using Windows PowerShell for highly specific setup options, such as for sites with heavy usage where log size considerations exist.

Analytics Reports

Analytics reports are available at both the site and site collection level. You can access these reports from Central Administration, under Monitoring, Reporting, and then View Web Analytic Reports. Table 15-8 provides a list of the reports available for reference. Viewers of the reports may filter data by date range or by URL, by way of the Analyze toolbar, which is available as part of the Report Viewer Ribbon. Viewers may also customize the UI of available reports using Microsoft Office Excel.

TABLE 15-8 List of Available Site and Site Collection Web Analytics Reports

REPORT	GROUP	LEVEL
Number of Page Views	Traffic	Site and Site Collection
Number of Daily Unique Visitors	Traffic	Site and Site Collection
Number of Referrers	Traffic	Site and Site Collection
Top Pages	Traffic	Site and Site Collection

continued on the next page

REPORT	GROUP	LEVEL
Top Visitors	Traffic	Site and Site Collection
Top Referrers	Traffic	Site and Site Collection
Top Destinations	Traffic	Site and Site Collection
Top Browsers	Traffic	Site and Site Collection
Number of Queries	Search	Site Collection
Top Queries	Search	Site Collection
Failed Queries	Search	Site Collection
Best Bet Queries	Search	Site Collection
Best Bet Suggestions	Search	Site Collection
Best Bet Suggestions Action History	Search	Site Collection
Search Keywords	Search	Site Collection
Storage Usage	Inventory	Site and Site Collection
Number of Sites	Inventory	Site and Site Collection
Number of Lists	Inventory	Site and Site Collection
Number of Libraries	Inventory	Site and Site Collection
Top Site Templates	Inventory	Site and Site Collection
Top Site Product Versions	Inventory	Site and Site Collection
Top Site Languages	Inventory	Site and Site Collection
Top List Templates	Inventory	Site and Site Collection
Top Library Templates	Inventory	Site and Site Collection

If the reports listed in Table 15-8 do not meet your specific requirements, you can create your own custom reports using custom code.

Authoring and Publishing Web Content

Now that you have your publishing site in place, along with a well-defined and implemented publishing content approval process, it's time to create some content. As you cover the material in this section, assume that the following prerequisites have been properly implemented and tested.

- A publishing site collection
- Security group membership and permissions levels
- Site structure and navigation
- Any needed additional master pages or needed modifications
- Any needed additional publishing pages content type or needed modifications
- Any needed additional page layouts or needed modifications
- Any needed additional field controls or needed modifications
- Any needed content Approval workflows or needed modifications
- Any needed additional Web Part configurations

Also assume that specific individuals or groups have been identified to participate in the defined content publishing process and are aware of their roles and responsibilities in that process.

There are many ways for authors to create the content that will become available through-out the site. The content may be created within the native SharePoint 2010 Web interface or, as discussed in the previous section, the content may be created in an associated collabora-tion site. The content also may be created within SharePoint Designer 2010 or as a document for conversion from Microsoft Office Word or InfoPath.

Web-based Content Authoring

SharePoint 2010 provides a high-fidelity, rich, Web-based content authoring experience. Information about the presentation elements is described in the previous section; here you will see how a designated content author and editor might work through the process of authoring and publishing a piece of content.

The creation of content from within the Web interface can be broken down into the following steps.

1. Create a new content page using the Create Page option from within the Site Actions menu.

2. Fill out the information required by the designer.

3. Add any rich media elements, such as pictures and/or video.

4. Submit the content for editor approval and publishing.

5. Review the content and take it live.

> **MORE INFO** You can find complete step-by-step instructions for this and other proce-
> dures in *Microsoft SharePoint 2010 Administrator's Pocket Consultant* by Ben Curry.

Smart Client Content Authoring

SharePoint 2010 allows authors to create content within rich client applications such as Microsoft Office Word or InfoPath and have that content automatically converted to page content with a publishing library. In this section, you review document conversion services and how to configure both your farm and your publishing site collection to leverage document conversion.

SharePoint 2010 includes the following document converters by default.

- Microsoft Office InfoPath Form to Web Page (.xml to .html)
- Microsoft Office Word Document to Web Page (.docx to .html)
- Microsoft Office Word Document with Macros to Web Page (.docm to .html)
- Extensible Markup Language (XML) to Web Page (.xml to .html)

Configuring Document Conversion Services

To configure a Web application for document conversion service, you will need to perform the following steps.

1. Open a browser and go to the SharePoint Central Administration website.

2. Click the System Settings link.

3. Select Manage Services On Server from the Servers Settings group.

4. Start the Document Conversions Load Balancer Service.

5. Start the Document Conversions Launcher Service.

6. On the Launcher Service Settings page, select the server, the load balancer server, and the port number, and then click OK.

7. Click the General Application Settings link on the left menu.

8. Click Configure Document Conversions, which is listed under the External Service Connections settings group.

9. On the Configure Document Conversions page (as shown in Figure 15-10), specify the Web application you want to configure, and select Yes to Enable Document Conversions, the Load Balance Server, and Conversion Schedule.

10. When you are satisfied with the settings, click OK.

NOTE You may also customize the Converter Settings for each of the available document converters from this page; however, doing so without clicking Apply or OK first may prevent the prior changes from taking effect.

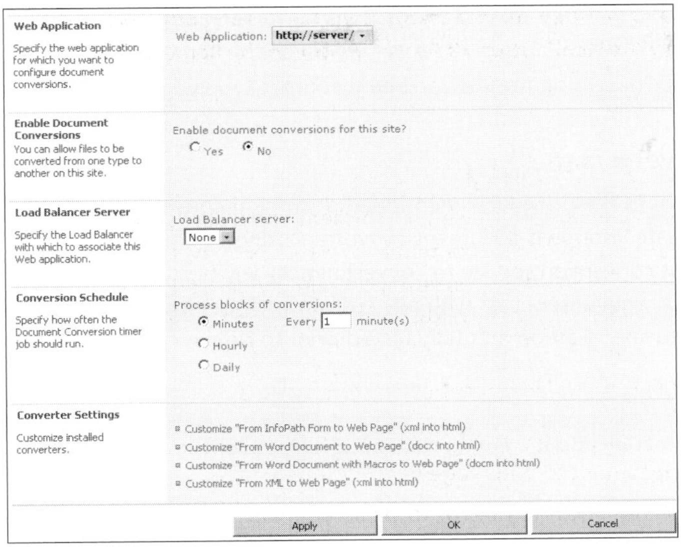

FIGURE 15-10 Configure Document Conversions within SharePoint Central Administration before attempting to use it within a publishing site collection.

After you have enabled Document Conversions for your Web application, you can upload documents for conversion to a document library within your publishing site. When a document of the appropriate type and with the proper extension is uploaded, you will see a new Convert Document option available in the Edit Control Block menu for that item, as shown in Figure 15-11.

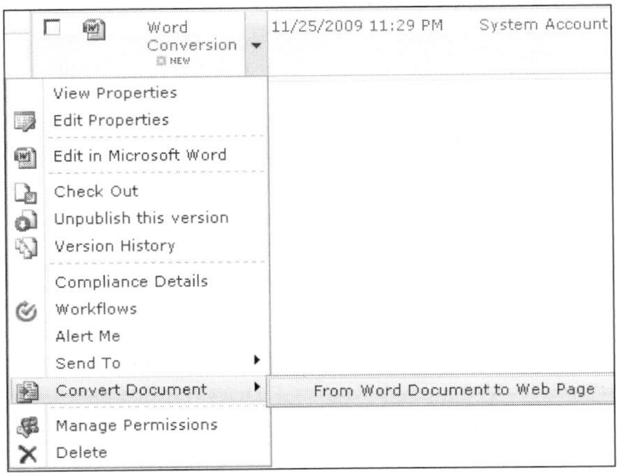

FIGURE 15-11 Select Convert Document from the Edit Control Block menu for the uploaded document.

When the document conversion service is available within a Web application, site administrators can configure how document conversion processing will be handled for individual content types. You can access these settings using the following steps.

1. Select Site Settings from the Site Actions menu.
2. Select Content Types from the Galleries settings group.
3. Select a document content type.
4. Click Manage Document Conversion for the document content type you selected.

Custom Document Converters

Although SharePoint 2010 provides the previously mentioned document converters by default, it is also possible to create your own document converters using custom code. This allows you to use the document conversion service to convert almost any type of document for publication, defined by your requirements. As with any custom code deployment, make sure your solution is designed to specification and fully tested prior to deployment into production.

> **MORE INFO** For more information about creating custom document converters, see the Microsoft SharePoint 2010 SDK.

Web Parts in Publishing Pages

Web Parts provide the content author a great deal of flexibility in the placement of content and settings used for content (you can find more about how Web Parts do this earlier in this chapter). In order to leverage Web Parts within a content page, the page layout must include a Web Part zone or zones. Table 15-9 lists the Web Parts that are available by default within a publishing site.

To add, remove, or modify Web Parts on a page, use the Edit Page function, which is in the Site Actions menu. After you have made your modifications, you will need to republish the page as well as get it approved, if required. Web Parts are covered in more detail in Chapter 19.

TABLE 15-9 Web Parts Available by Default Within a Publishing Site

WEB PART	GROUP	DESCRIPTION
Content Query	Content Rollup	Displays a dynamic view of content from your site.
Media Web Part	Media And Content	Use to embed media clips (video and audio) in a Web page.
InfoPath Form Web Part	Office Client Applications	Use this Web Part to display an InfoPath browser–enabled form.

WEB PART	GROUP	DESCRIPTION
Content Editor	Media And Content	Allows authors to enter rich text content.
Image Viewer	Media And Content	Displays a specified image.
Site Users	People	Use the Site Users Web Part to see a list of the site users and their online status.
Page Viewer	Media And Content	Displays another Web page on this Web page. The second Web page is presented in an IFrame.
Picture Library Slideshow Web Part	Content Rollup	Use to display a slideshow of images and photos from a picture library.
HTML Form Web Part	Content Rollup	Connects simple form controls to other Web Parts.
Relevant Documents	Documents	Displays documents that are relevant to the current user.
User Tasks	People	Displays tasks that are assigned to the current user.
XML Viewer	Content Rollup	Transforms XML data using XSL and shows the results.
Silverlight Web Part	Media And Content	Use to display a Silverlight application.
Summary Links	Navigation	Allows authors to create links that can be grouped and styled.
Table Of Contents	Navigation	Displays the navigation hierarchy of your site.
Web Analytics Web Part	Content Rollup	Displays the most viewed content, most popular search queries, or most popular clicked search results as reported by Web Analytics for the site or site collection.

Content Query Web Part

The Content Query Web Part is a very powerful Web Part that becomes available when the publishing features are activated. This Web Part allows you to define a query that will return specific types of information, to specify a scope of sites and subsites for that query, and to have the resulting information presented in a roll-up, a single view of information that is spread across multiple locations. Because content types provide the underlying schema of content pages within a publishing site, the Content Query Web Part gives page authors the ability to display information from specific content types and their descendants in a uniform way. For an example of this Web Part in action, simply click Edit Page on the Site Actions menu of the default home page of a new publishing portal site. In the top zone of that page, you will find a Content Query Web Part that is set up to display press releases.

Although specific configurations of the Web Part are outside the scope of this section, Microsoft has made additional improvements to the Content Query Web Part in SharePoint 2010. These improvements include a new capability called Content to Content Targeting, which allows authors to not only specify the content they want to display within the Web Part, but also allows them to filter the resulting content based on a field that is also present on that content page. The Web Part also supports data view mapping, which is the ability to specify specific fields for display in the Web Part, something that required complex XML editing in prior versions. Because SharePoint 2010 supports indexing on large lists, the performance issues associated with returning results from large lists using this Web Part have been modified. The Content Query Web Part also supports the managed metadata and taxonomy features provided in SharePoint 2010, which allow for queries that are filtered by managed terms.

Digital Media and Asset Libraries

More and more of the content viewed by information workers on a daily basis consists of pictures, video, or audio. SharePoint 2010 supports both media reuse and media publishing. Media reuse might include the management of highly governed media, such as in the case of brand management, or it also might include informal sharing and reuse of media between coworkers sharing screenshots or digital pictures. Media publishing includes scenarios such as streaming video delivery, online courseware, and the informal sharing and reuse of video assets. Investments in digital assent management within SharePoint 2010 have focused not only on the storage of media assets, but also on the use and/or reuse of that media within Web pages and Microsoft Office applications.

SharePoint 2010 includes an Asset Library template that is optimized for use with rich media. Additionally, SharePoint 2010 includes numerous infrastructure enhancements, such as streaming from the BLOB cache, that allow for the serving of media, while eliminating many of the performance bottlenecks that made serving such media a cause for concern in prior versions. SharePoint 2010 also includes rich media Web Parts and field controls, such as the SharePoint Media Player, that make adding and viewing media within a page quick and easy. Operations such as adding an image to a page, which was a multistep task in prior versions of SharePoint, now can be performed as a single step.

Asset Libraries

Asset libraries are new to SharePoint 2010, and they are optimized for digital assets such as images and video. Features of asset libraries include thumbnail-centric views, metadata extraction for images RSS and podcasting support, the ability to preview media on hover, and video playback preview. It's important to note that because an asset library is based on a document library, you still have access to the standard features you rely on for organizing information such as content types, workflows, and information management policies. Also available within asset libraries is the same metadata-driven navigation available within standard document libraries. Asset libraries also support the social features delivered with SharePoint 2010, such as rating, tagging, and notes.

Using Media from Within Microsoft Office Applications

Microsoft Office 2010 provides additional powerful features that make it easy to leverage digital assets stored within SharePoint 2010. It's now possible to look up digital media stored within a SharePoint asset library quickly and then, just as quickly, add that media to documents and presentations. The Office client applications fully support the ability to browse information using metadata and even include powerful lightweight media editing capabilities.

Rich Media Within Publishing Sites

It's easy to use media within a publishing site with SharePoint 2010. You can use the Media Web Part to add media to pages almost at will, and you also can leverage the Media Field Control for situations in which the publishing model, page layouts, and governance are tighter and more rigid. The Content Query Web Part also supports media in results, which adds a whole new dynamic level of rich media support within publishing sites with added capabilities to do media roll-ups. It's also easy to add media efficiently as you add content to a new page.

Reusable Content

The ability to reuse content is a feature that was introduced with SharePoint Server 2007. It allows for the storage and reuse of blocks of text or well-qualified HTML code within publishing sites. This is useful for smaller content elements that need to be placed on pages or within the layout design, because it allows those elements to be centrally managed and maintained. Reusable content is stored in the Reusable Content Library, which is located in the root of the site collection within sites on which the publishing features have been activated.

When adding content to the Reusable Content library, there is an option to have that content updated automatically. If the automatic update option is selected, anywhere you use the Reusable Content block within the site, it will be updated automatically when the source content is changed within the library. If the automatic update option is not selected, the content dropped on a page will be a copy of the content located within the library at the time it was added and will not be updated subsequently when changes are made to the content in the library.

The Reusable Content library also features a Show In drop-down option for each item that is added. When this option is selected, the added Reusable Content item will be made available in a drop-down menu during page editing. This makes it easier for page authors to leverage the content when creating or updating a page.

Configuring Content Caching

Caching is an ASP.Net technology that allows efficient delivery of content such as HTML pages, images, and media to a user's browser. Caching stores the requested content in server memory, which reduces the number of round trips required to generate the content from the database dynamically. SharePoint 2010 uses caching to improve the performance of publishing sites. In SharePoint 2010, you can configure at Web application, site collection, and page levels.

 REAL WORLD Considerations for Implementing Caching

The decision to implement caching requires proper planning within your implementation design, as well as a clear understanding of what the tradeoffs are associated with configuring caching at various levels. Caching ensures the fastest possible access to content that has already been accessed by other users. This has some disadvantages, however. For example, caching can be very memory intensive. Because many of the caching options covered in this section affect the serving of all content within a given Web application, it's important that you plan the implementation of Web applications within your environment accordingly. For example, consider having separate Web applications for collaboration and publishing. This allows you to configure the publishing Web application for caching, whereas you would only need to configure the collaboration Web application for minimal caching.

You need to use caching only when you have lots of users visiting sites where the content change frequency is low to moderate. An Internet-facing site would be an example of such a site. Because the content only changes every so often, caching allows that content to be stored on the Web front-end server for improved delivery performance. In the case of a team collaboration site, you would not want caching configured because the content change frequency is high, meaning most of the request traffic for the site is related to the modification of content within that site. In this case, configuring excessive caching would just consume additional system resources on the Web front end while providing little or no benefit.

In the following section, you will focus on how to plan for and use content caching to improve the performance of publishing sites.

Content Caching Overview

SharePoint 2010 provides three types of caches to improve the speed at which requested content loads in the browser: BLOB cache, page output cache, and object cache. Binary Large Object (BLOB) cache is used to cache binary files such as GIF, JPEG, and other similar formats on the Web front-end server. Page output cache is used to cache pages generated by SharePoint and is configured at the page, site, site collection, or Web application level. Object cache is configured at the site or site collection level to cache lists, libraries, site settings, and more. Object cache is stored in memory on the Web front-end server. Table 15-10 presents the different types of caching available, the content cached in each, and when to use them.

TABLE 15-10 Cache Types and Uses

CACHE TYPE	CONTENT CACHED	USE
BLOB cache	Binary files such as GIF, JPEG, AVI, MP3, and similar formats	For caching files at Web application level
Output cache	HTML content generated by SharePoint pages	For caching site pages at Web application, site collection, site, and page levels
Object cache	Web Parts, lists, libraries, site settings, and site content	For cross-list query caching and navigation caching

BLOB Cache

Files that hold images, audio, and video, as well as JavaScript and CSS files and more, are used in the rendering of Web pages and can be cached on the disk of the Web front-end servers using BLOB cache. BLOB cache is configured at the Web application level by way of the Web.config file, which is stored on each Web front-end server of the farm that is running the Web Application Service. This setting affects all site collections hosted within the Web application. BLOB cache reduces page load times by loading the binary files from the server's disk instead of loading them from the database; this also reduces the load on the database server. When a page is requested for the first time, the binary objects on that page are cached to the local server disk from the database server; subsequent page loads use the cached content, rather than requiring another round trip to the database server.

Planning for BLOB Cache

Because BLOB cache is disk-based caching, it must be configured on every Web front-end server in the farm. Plan ahead based on the following considerations when setting up BLOB cache within a SharePoint 2010 farm.

CHOOSING FILE TYPES TO BE CACHED

BLOB cache allows for multiple binary file types to be stored, and it is possible to configure specific files to be included in the cache. For instance, in the case of an Internet-facing portal site, read-only PDFs and .doc files can be cached so that their content is rendered quickly to a user's browser. In a highly collaborative site, media assets such as audio or video files can be cached; other project documents, including Word and Excel document files, can be excluded from caching. Consider the following scenarios when you are choosing which file types to cache.

- For a publishing site visited by anonymous users, enable caching for most of the file types rendered by the site.
- For a collaborative site, enable caching only on read-only media assets such as audio and video files.

Also be sure to consider that each Web application gets its own cache. If you have a site collection with a lot of read-only files, you may prefer to enable caching on all file types. If you have another site collection that is highly collaborative, however, you may prefer to cache the read-only media asset files but not other files. These two site collections have different caching needs, so it is better to move the site collection with lots of read-only content to a different Web application so that it can have its own cache settings to allow many files to be cached. This caching consideration further justifies the need to designate specific Web applications for specific types of sites and activities, such as one for Web application collaboration and one for publishing.

PLANNING FOR STORAGE

With BLOB caching, the cached files are stored on the local drive of the serving Web front-end server; therefore, it is important to choose a drive configuration that will ensure that there is adequate free space for the content to be cached. By default, the BLOB cache will be set up on the drive where SharePoint is installed, but consider the following options when you are choosing the right drive and configuration for the BLOB cache.

- Choose a physical drive that is not used by operating system for swap files or other processes; this will prevent conflicts with caching. Too many processes competing for disk access will affect performance adversely for the BLOB cache as well as for other processes.
- Choose a physical drive (not a partition) that is not being used for Unified Logging Service (ULS) logging. Storing BLOB cache and ULS logs on the same physical drive will affect performance.
- Choose a cache size that is 20 percent larger than the size of the content to be cached and ensure that the designated physical drive provides enough space for the cache.
- Allocate at least 10 gigabytes (GB) of space for caching. Lesser values will affect performance.
- In a load-balancing scenario, ensure that the configuration changes are made to the Web.config file on all Web front-end servers.

Configuring BLOB Cache

The following list describes the settings that you can configure for disk-based caching.

- **max-age** Specifies the maximum time in seconds that the client browser caches BLOBs that are downloaded to the client computer. If the downloaded items have not expired since the last download, the same items are not re-requested until the cache expires. By default, the *max-age* attribute is set to 86400 seconds (24 hours), but you can set it to a time period of zero or greater, up to 31536000 seconds (365 days).

- **Path** Specifies in the form of a regular expression which files are cached, based on the file name extension. By default, the following extensions are included: .gif, .jpg, .png, .css, and .js. If you have special file types that your Web pages reference, you must add those extensions to the cache.

- **changeCheckInterval** Specifies the time in seconds that the disk-based caching is updated on the Web server. By default, the *changeCheckInterval* attribute is set to 5 seconds. However, this value can be increased. The larger this value, the longer the time that content in the disk-based cache is not updated on the Web server.

- **Location** Specifies the location where the files are cached on the Web server. The value of this attribute must point to a valid drive letter and a valid directory or folder. The hard disk must also have sufficient free space to accommodate the specified cache size.

- **maxSize** Specifies the maximum size of the cache in gigabytes. After this value is reached, the cache is flushed until the size of the cache on disk is 20 percent less than the value specified in *maxSize* attribute. By default, the *maxSize* attribute is set to 10 GB. The minimum value allowed is 1 GB.

- **Enabled** Specifies whether disk-based caching is enabled or not. The *Enabled* attribute accepts any value that has a valid Boolean representative. The default value of this attribute is True.

- **policyCheckInterval** Specifies the time elapsed in seconds before disk-based cache settings are parsed again by the Web server. By default, the *policyCheckInterval* attribute is set to 60 seconds. However, you can set it to a larger value.

The following steps explain how to configure BLOB caching at Web application level by editing the Web.config file.

1. Click Start, point to Administrative Tools, and then select Internet Information Services (IIS) Manager.

2. In the Connections pane of the Internet Information Services (IIS) Manager, click the plus sign (+) next to the server name that contains the Web application and then click the plus sign next to Sites to view the Web application or applications that have been created.

3. Right-click the name of the Web application for which you want to configure the disk-based cache and then select Explore. Windows Explorer opens, with the directories for the selected Web application listed.

4. Right-click Web.config and then click Open With.

5. If the Windows dialog box appears, choose Select A Program From A List Of Installed Programs and then click OK.

6. In the Open With dialog box, click Notepad and then click OK.

7. In the Web.config Notepad file, find the following line.

```
<BlobCache location=""
path="\.(gif|jpg|jpeg|jpe|jfif|bmp|dib|tif|tiff|ico|png|wdp|hdp|css|js|asf|avi|flv
|m4v|mov|mp3|mp4|mpeg|mpg|rm|rmvb|wma|wmv)$" maxSize="10" enabled="false" />
```

8. In this line, change the *Location* attribute to specify a directory that has enough space to accommodate the cache size.

9. To add or remove file types from the list of file types to be cached, for the *Path* attribute, modify the regular expression to include or remove the appropriate file extension. If you add file extensions, make sure to separate each file type with a pipe (|), as shown in the code shown in step 7.

10. To change the size of the cache, type a new number for *maxSize*. The size is expressed in gigabytes, and 10 GB is the default.

11. To enable the BLOB cache, change the *Enabled* attribute from "false" to "true".

12. Save the Notepad file and then close it.

13. Recycle the Web application for the changes to take effect.

14. If you have multiple Web front-end servers in the farm, remember to execute steps 1 through 13 on each Web front-end server.

Bit Rate Throttling

Bit rate throttling is an IIS 7.0 extension that meters down the speed of data transfer between the server and the browser for media file types. The encoded bit rates of media file types such as Windows Media Video (WMV), MPEG-4 (MP4), and Adobe Flash Video are automatically detected, and the rate at which those files are delivered to the client over HTTP are controlled according to the bit rate throttling configuration.

When bit rate throttling is used, the media is delivered to the client at the highest possible rate for first few seconds and then throttles the transfer rate to a normal bit rate. This allows users to get started on the content they want to watch or hear right away. Bit rate throttling supports .asf, .avi, .flv, .m4v, .mov, .mp3, .mp4, .rm, .rmvb, .wma, and .wmv file types out of the box. This support can be extended to other media and file types as well.

SharePoint 2010 also introduces the Asset (Media) Library list type (see the section titled "Asset Libraries" earlier in this chapter for more information about this list type), and asset libraries are used for storing media file types. Configuring bit rate throttling on Web front-end servers of the farm that hosts media helps deliver asset media files effectively to end users.

> **MORE INFO** To learn more about setting bit rate throttling in IIS 7.0, visit *http://go.microsoft.com/fwlink/?LinkId=131775.*

Page Output Cache

Page output cache enables the caching of dynamic pages that are generated by SharePoint 2010, either by storing entire HTML or parts of the HTML content in the Web server's memory, which reduces the time needed to generate a page. If a SharePoint 2010 site is heavily used, caching its content even for a minute improves performance of the site. When a page is stored in the output cache, all subsequent requests are served from the cache without executing the code that created the page.

Page output cache can be configured at the Web application level using the Web.config files. At page, site, and site collection levels, the site collection administrator can use cache profiles to configure cache behavior. Let's explore how to set up page output caching.

Output Cache Considerations

Consider the following pros and cons of output caching before enabling it on a SharePoint 2010 site.

PROS OF USING OUTPUT CACHE

Output cache can provide the following benefits.

- After caching, each page and parts of a page receive faster response, which results in shorter latency for the user.
- The Web front-end server uses less central processing unit (CPU) time and energy to serve the same page after the initial rendering.
- The Web front-end server can handle more requests, due to the decrease in traffic enabled by output caching.
- For each page request for an output cached version of a page, the server does not have to
    - Make a round trip to the database to fetch the source code for the .aspx page and any user controls on the page.
    - Reload and re-render the controls.
    - Requery any data sources that the controls rely on for data.
- Each time a page is loaded from output cache, the load on the database server is reduced, which allows it to handle more requests.

CONS OF USING OUTPUT CACHE

Though output caching has many benefits, you should consider the following drawbacks to using output cache as well when planning to enable it.

- Output caching consumes additional memory on the Web front-end servers of the farm as the content is cached in memory. Ensure that each Web server on the farm has enough physical memory to handle the extra load.

- As the content is cached, if you have multiple Web front-end servers, users may see inconsistencies in the content they are served. This effect can be reduced by enabling sticky sessions, if they are supported, on the load balancer, which will ensure that a user will always be directed to the same front-end server during an active session.

- Enabling output caching for users with Read permissions will prevent them from seeing the latest content. This will not affect the user's ability to edit content.

- Caching can cause inaccurate search results to display to users. You should disable caching on the Search Results page and the search center site.

Output Cache Concepts

Before you learn about how to enable output cache, you should understand the following important aspects of output cache.

CACHE POLICIES

Cache policies help determine on what parameters the HTML content should be cached by the ASP.NET caching engine. SharePoint 2010 pages can be rendered in different versions based on parameters or users' rights. Cache policies help determine how each version of the cached page can be identified.

- **Vary by Param**   Allows you to vary the cached output depending on the GET query string or POST parameters.

- **Vary by Header**   Allows you to vary the cached output depending on the host header associated with the request.

- **Vary by Custom**   Allows you to vary the cached output depending on any custom string you define or by browser type.

- **Vary by User Rights**   Allows you to vary the cached output depending on the user's rights on the page. As SharePoint 2010 pages are security trimmed, this policy helps cache different versions of same page based on user's right.

CACHEABILITY

Cacheability determines the device on which the cache can be created. This parameter sets the value of the HTTP header Cache-Control. The following list explains the different cacheablity settings that are available.

- *NoCache*   Sets the Cache-Control: no-cache header. Without a field name, the directive applies to the entire request and a shared (proxy server) cache must force a successful revalidation with the origin Web server before satisfying the request. With a field name, the directive applies only to the named field; the rest of the response may be supplied from a shared cache.

- *Private*   Sets the Cache-Control: private header, which specifies that the caching should happen only on the client and not on shared caches.

- **Server** Specifies that the content is cached only on the origin server and not on the client.

- **ServerAndNoCache** Equivalent to a combination of the *Server* and *NoCache* settings; it indicates that the content can be cached only on the origin server and all others are explicitly denied cacheablity.

- **ServerAndPrivate** Indicates that the content can be cached on the originating server and on the client. The content cannot be cached on any other public servers (proxy servers).

- **Public** Indicates that the content can be cached on client and on any public caches, such as proxy servers.

CACHE PROFILES

SharePoint 2010 provides a fine-grained approach to caching with the help of cache profiles. Cache profiles allow the site collection administrators to define various values that can affect the caching mechanism of the site or page. The cache profiles have the following parameters that control caching.

- **Title** Sets the title of the cache profile.

- **Display Name** Sets the display name of the cache profile.

- **Display Description** Sets the description of the cache profile.

- **Perform ACL Check** Determines if all items in the cache are security trimmed.

- **Enabled** Determines if caching is enabled for a profile or not.

- **Duration** Specifies the amount of time (in seconds) to keep the content in cache.

- **Check for Changes** Specifies if a check should be made for content that has changed on the site and indicates that the cache should be cleared if the site content changes before the specified cache duration. Selecting this parameter will reduce the performance of caching.

- **Vary by Custom Parameter** Same as *Vary by Custom Parameter* cache policy.

- **Vary by Header** Same as *Vary by Header* cache policy.

- **Vary by Query String Parameters** Same as *Vary by Param* cache policy.

- **Vary by User Rights** Same as *Vary by User Rights* cache policy.

- **Cacheability** Defines the cacheablity parameter for the profile.

- **Safe for Authenticated Use** Determines if the profile can be used for authenticated users.

- **Allow Writers to View Cached Content** Determines if users with Edit permission can see the cached content.

SharePoint 2010 publishing sites have four predefined cache profiles that can be used for different scenarios. The following list shows the cache profiles available for a publishing site and explains the characteristics of each.

- **Disabled**   Caching is not enabled. This is the default cache profile.
- **Public Internet (Purely Anonymous)**   Caching profile for Internet publishing sites with anonymous access.
- **Extranet (Published Site)**   Caching profile for extranet publishing sites with authenticated user access.
- **Intranet (Collaboration Site)**   Caching profile for collaborative sites accessed within an intranet.

CREATING NEW CACHE PROFILES

SharePoint 2010 allows you to create new cache profiles that can be used within a site collection, site, or page. Use the following procedure to create a new cache profile.

> **IMPORTANT**   You should enable the Publishing Infrastructure site collection feature to enable output caching.

1. Navigate to the root website of the site collection. On the Site Actions menu, select Site Settings.
2. In the Site Collection Administration section, select Site Collection Cache Profiles.
3. Click Add New Item.
4. Enter all necessary data for the cache profile, as shown in Figure 15-12, and then click OK.

FIGURE 15-12 The Create Cache Profile page

Configuring Output Cache

Remember that the output cache can be configured at Web application, site collection, site, and page levels. The following sections deal with configuring output cache at these different levels.

CONFIGURING OUTPUT CACHE AT THE WEB APPLICATION LEVEL

At the Web application level, the configuration of output cache is done in the Web.config file. Follow these steps to perform the configuration.

> **IMPORTANT** You must have administrator privileges on the Web front-end server to edit the Web.config file. Make a backup of the Web.config file before you make any changes to it. Then if you make any mistakes when you are changing the output cache configuration, you will be able to restore the original file.

1. Click Start, point to Administrative Tools, and then select Internet Information Services (IIS) Manager.

2. In the Connections pane of the Internet Information Services (IIS) Manager, click the plus sign (+) next to the server name that contains the Web application and then click the plus sign next to Sites to view the Web application or applications that have been created.

3. Right-click the name of the Web application for which you want to configure the disk-based cache and then select Explore. Windows Explorer will open with the directories for the selected Web application listed.

4. Right-click Web.config and then select Open With.

5. If the Windows dialog box appears, choose Select A Program From A List Of Installed Programs and then click OK.

6. In the Open With dialog box, click Notepad and then click OK.

7. In the Web.config Notepad file, find the following line.

   ```
   <OutputCacheProfiles useCacheProfileOverrides="false" varyByHeader=""
   varyByParam="*"  varyByCustom="" varyByRights="true"
   cacheForEditRights="false" />
   ```

8. To enable the cache profile at the Web application level, change the *useCacheProfileOverrides* attribute from "false" to "true".

9. To override the *varyByHeader* attribute, type a custom parameter.

10. To override the *varyByParam* attribute, type a custom parameter.

11. To override the *varyByCustom* attribute, type a custom parameter.

12. To override the *varyByRights* attribute, change the value from "true" to "false". This will remove the requirement that users must have identical effective permissions on all securable objects to see the same cached page as any other user.

13. To override the *cacheForEditRights* attribute, change the *cacheForEditRights* attribute from "false" to "true". This will bypass the normal behavior in which people with Edit permission have their pages cached.

14. Save the Notepad file and then close it.

15. Recycle the Web application for the change to take effect.

16. If you have multiple Web front-end servers in the farm, remember to execute steps 1 through 15 on each Web front-end server.

CONFIGURING OUTPUT CACHE AT THE SITE COLLECTION LEVEL

The following steps explain the procedure to enable output cache at site collection level.

> **IMPORTANT** You must enable the Publishing Infrastructure site collection feature to enable output caching.

1. Navigate to the root website of the site collection. On the Site Actions menu, select Site Settings.

2. In the Site Collection Administration section, select Site Collection Output Cache. This will take you to the Site Collection Output Cache Settings page, as shown in Figure 15-13.

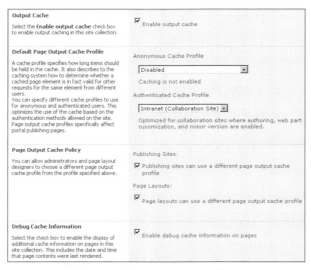

FIGURE 15-13 The Site Collection Output Cache Settings page

3. To enable output caching for this site collection, select Enable Output Cache.

4. Choose a cache profile for anonymous users from the Anonymous Cache Profile list. This profile will be applied when anonymous users access a site in this site collection.

5. Choose a cache profile for authenticated users from the Authenticated Cache Profile list. This profile will be applied when authenticated users access a site in this site collection.

6. Choose Page Output Cache Policy options.

   ■ If publishing sites can use a different output cache profile, select Publishing Sites Can Use A Different Page Output Cache Profile.

   ■ If page layouts can use a different output cache profile, select Page Layouts Can Use A Different Page Output Cache Profile.

7. If you want to display additional cache information on pages in this site collection, including the date and time that page contents were last rendered, select Enable Debug Cache Information On Pages.

8. Click OK.

CONFIGURING OUTPUT CACHE AT THE SITE LEVEL

The following steps will guide you to set up output caching at the site level.

> **IMPORTANT** You must enable the Publishing Infrastructure site collection feature to enable output caching.

1. Navigate to the root website of the site collection. On the Site Actions menu, select Site Settings.

2. In the Site Administration section, select Site Output Cache.

3. Choose one of the following Anonymous Cache Profile options:.

   ■ If you want to inherit a cache profile, click Inherit The Profile.

   ■ If you want to choose a cache profile from those currently available, select Select A Page Output Cache Profile.

4. If you want to apply these settings to all subsites of the root website, select Apply These Settings To All Sub-Sites.

5. Click OK.

CONFIGURING OUTPUT CACHE AT THE PAGE LEVEL

SharePoint 2010 allows you to enable caching at page level. This helps you optimize caching for the most-used pages of your site. Use the following steps to configure the authenticated and anonymous cache profiles that will be used in each page layout.

1. On the Site Actions menu, point to Site Settings.

2. Under Galleries, select Master Pages And Page Layouts.

3. On the Master Page Gallery page, point to the name of the page layout to which you want to apply a cache profile, click the arrow that appears, and then click Check Out.

4. Point to the page layout again, click the arrow that appears, and then click Edit Properties.

5. Do one or both of the following.

   - From the Authenticated Cache Profile drop-down list, select the authenticated cache profile that you want to apply to the page layout.

   - From the Anonymous Cache Profile drop-down list, select the anonymous cache profile that you want to apply to the page layout.

6. Click OK.

7. Point to the name of the page layout that you want to check in, click the arrow that appears, and then click Check In.

8. On the Check In page, select Major Version (Publish) and then click OK.

Object Cache

SharePoint 2010 allows caching of certain SharePoint content such as lists and libraries that are used in navigation or are accessed in cross-list queries. All field data for the entire page is cached, excluding any Web Parts. Object cache can be enabled at the site collection level and at the Web application level. You will explore the benefits of object caching and how to configure object caching.

Object Cache Considerations

The object cache can be optimized by performing various configurations as follows.

- **Size of the object cache**   Determines the amount of space allocated to object caching purposes. Allocating a considerable amount of space for the object cache improves the performance of the object caching, but larger object cache size affects memory usage on the Web front-end servers of the farm.

- **When to check for changes in cross-list query Web parts**   You can configure the cross-list queries to check the server for changes in data every time the queries run or at specific intervals. The amount of time specified for the intervals improves the performance of the caching.

- **Set a multiplier to use to retrieve more results than are requested**   The multiplier is used to ensure that all client requests are accommodated in a cross-list query and that a valid set of results is delivered.

Configuring Object Cache

You can configure object caching at Web application and site collection levels. The following sections deal with configuration of object caching.

CONFIGURING OBJECT CACHE AT THE WEB APPLICATION LEVEL

The following steps explain how to configure object caching at the Web level.

> **IMPORTANT**   You must have administrator privilege on the Web front-end server to edit the Web.config file. Make a backup of the Web.config file before you make any changes. Then if you make any mistakes when you are changing the object cache configuration, you will be able to restore the original file.

1. Click Start, point to Administrative Tools, and then select Internet Information Services (IIS) Manager.

2. In the Connections pane of the Internet Information Services (IIS) Manager, click the plus sign (+) next to the server name that contains the Web application and then click the plus sign next to Sites to view the Web application or applications that have been created.

3. Right-click the name of the Web application for which you want to configure the disk-based cache and then click Explore. Windows Explorer will open with the directories for the selected Web application listed.

4. Right-click Web.config and then select Open With.

5. If the Windows dialog box appears, choose Select A Program From A List Of Installed Programs and then click OK.

6. In the Open With dialog box, click Notepad and then click OK.

7. In the Web.config Notepad file, find the following line.

```
<ObjectCache maxSize="100" />
```

8. To change the size of the cache, type a new number for *maxSize*. The size is expressed in megabytes (MB), and 100 MB is the default.

9. Save the Notepad file and then close it.

10. Recycle the Web application or perform an IISRESET for the change to take effect.

11. If you have multiple Web front-end servers in the farm, remember to execute steps 1 through 10 on each Web front-end server.

CONFIGURING OBJECT CACHE AT THE SITE COLLECTION

To configure object cache at site collection level, you should enable the publishing infrastructure feature. The following steps explain the procedure for configuring object cache at the site collection level.

1. Navigate to the root website of the site collection. On the Site Actions menu, select Site Settings.

2. Under Site Collection Administration, select Site Collection Object Cache. This will take you to the Site Collection Object Cache settings page, as shown in Figure 15-14.

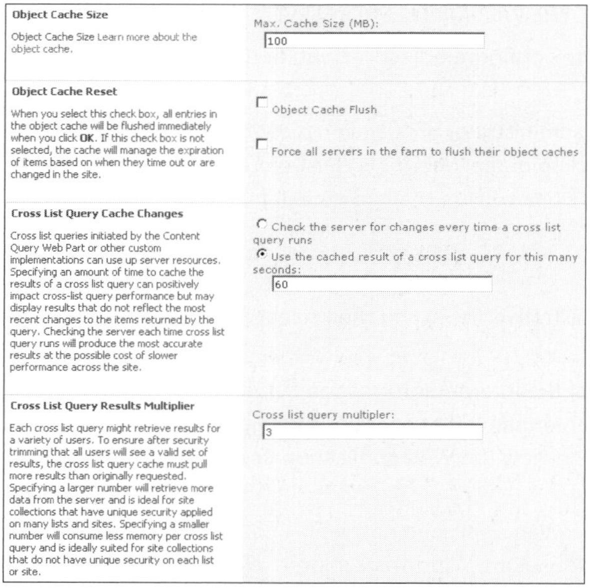

FIGURE 15-14 The Site Collection Output Cache Settings page

3. In the Object Cache Size section, type a value in the box to specify the amount of memory (in megabytes) that you want the object cache to use.

4. In the Cross List Query Cache Changes section, select one of the following options.

    ■ If your content changes frequently and you want to display the most accurate results possible, select Check The Server For Changes Every Time A Cross List Query Runs.

    ■ For site collections on which the improved performance you get from caching does not compromise the accuracy of the results, select Use The Cached Result Of A Cross List Query For This Many Seconds and specify the number of seconds before the check is performed.

5. In the Cross List Query Results Multiplier section, type a number from 1 through 10 to use as a results multiplier.

6. Click OK.

FLUSHING OBJECT CACHE

At times you might want to flush the contents in the object cache. The following procedure shows you how to do this.

1. Navigate to the root website of the site collection. On the Site Actions menu, select Site Settings.

2. Under Site Collection Administration, select Site Collection Object Cache.

3. In the Object Cache Reset section, do one or more of the following.

   - To force the current server to flush its object cache, select the Object Cache Flush check box.

   - To force all servers in the farm to flush their object caches, select the Force All Servers In The Farm To Flush Their Object Caches check box.

4. Click OK.

Managing Content Deployment

Content deployment is one of the main features of WCM. This feature allows you to copy content from a source site or site collection to a destination site or site collection. As an example, assume that you have an Internet-facing site with content that is authored, reviewed, and published by users on a company intranet. With SharePoint 2010, you can set up two farms to do this—one farm for the Internet and other for the intranet, with content deployment acting as the bridge between the farms.

Content deployment is capable of moving content pages and associated resources such as images, style sheets, and so forth—even Office documents and PDF files. Content deployment is also capable of moving security settings such as role definitions and users from source to destination. It is important to note that content deployment is not capable of moving assemblies, solutions, features, and other deployment components to the destination. There are various factors you must consider when implementing content deployment and planning how to configure content deployment in your environment.

Content Deployment Concepts

Content deployment in SharePoint 2010 is based on two important concepts—paths and jobs. Content deployment paths are used to link the source and the destination sites that are involved in the content deployment process. Content deployment jobs are based on a path and are responsible for extracting content from the source and copying it to the destination on a predefined schedule. You will learn more about content deployment paths, jobs, and other important aspects of content deployment in this section.

Content Deployment Paths

A content deployment path contains detailed information about the source site collection from which the content originates and the destination site collection where the content needs to be deployed. Each content deployment path contains the following pieces of information.

- Source site collection
- Destination site collection
- Authentication details that will grant the deployment job the necessary permissions on the destination site collection to deploy the content

- Information about whether the user names included in the content, such as author names, are to be deployed along with the content

- Information on how to deploy the permissions on the deployment location

Content Deployment Jobs

A content deployment job copies the content from the source location to the destination as defined in the content deployment path. A content deployment job definition contains the following information.

- Content deployment path
- Whether the job uses SQL snapshots
- Sites within the source site collection that need to be deployed
- Frequency at which the job needs to run
- Whether to deploy the entire content or just the changes made since the last deployment
- Whether to send e-mail notification upon job completion, and if so, the e-mail addresses to which the notification should be sent

There are three types of content deployment jobs types: Full, Incremental, and Quick Deploy. Full and incremental jobs are standard deployment job types that can be used while creating content deployment jobs, whereas Quick Deploy is a special job type that can be used by authors and editors to copy content on an ad hoc basis. An overview of these job types are as follows.

- **Full deployment job**   Copies all the contents from the source to destination, no matter what content was deployed during the last run of the job. A full deployment job will not remove content on the destination site collection even if the content is deleted from the source site collection. Use a full deployment job only if you know that no content will be deleted on the source site collection.

> **IMPORTANT**   A full deployment job should not be used as a primary or secondary backup solution.

- **Incremental deployment job**   Determines any changes, such as additions, deletions, and modifications to the source site collection, that have been made and then moves only those changes to the destination site collection. Incremental jobs perform a full deployment when run for the first time. After the first run, the incremental job keeps tabs on the changes made to the source site collection and copies only those changes to the destination site collection. You should use an incremental deployment job for most of your content deployment requirements.

- **Quick Deploy job**   A special type of job that allows the authors and editors to publish changes to the destination site collection immediately. Quick Deploy jobs are scheduled to run every 15 minutes. When a site collection is added to a content deployment path as a source site collection, the Quick Deploy job option is made available for use. The site collection must have publishing features enabled, and the user should be part of Quick Deploy users group in order to flag content for quick deployment. Farm administrators can run Quick Deploy jobs from Central Administration.

> **NOTE** Any type of site collection can be included in a content deployment path. Quick Deploy jobs will be made available only if the Publishing Infrastructure feature is enabled on the site collection.

Content Deployment Security

In a typical content deployment scenario, the destination will have a different security configuration than the source. It is also possible that the destination might have its own Active Directory against which the authentication is set up. Content Deployment allows you to copy some or all of the site level security settings from source to destination. The following are the security settings available as part of the content deployment job path.

- **All** Deploys all security-related settings from the source to destination. All is the default option. This includes permission levels, role definitions, groups, and user access to the content. This option is useful when the source and destination have the same security requirements. For example, if the authoring and staging farms have the same security settings guarding the content, you would choose the All security setting.

- **Role Definitions Only** Deploys only the role definitions and the access control lists that map the roles to the content. Users are not deployed as part of this option. You can choose this option if you want to maintain the same role definitions across source and destination, but have different users assigned to those roles.

- **None** Deploys no security information settings from source to destination. Use this option if you want to secure the content on the destination in a different manner than on the source. For example, if you are copying content from a internal staging farm to an external farm, the None option is best suited for the operation, because the external farm might have anonymous access enabled.

Content Deployment Considerations

The following are some important factors to consider when you are implementing content deployment.

Determine Whether to Use Content Deployment

The SharePoint 2010 publishing infrastructure provides in-place publishing, which allows authors and editors to create content and publish that content on the same site collection at a predetermined time using approval policies. The following factors will help you determine whether content deployment is required.

- **Farm topologies are completely different** In this scenario, the content authors and editors create content in an internal farm and publish it to a farm hosted for Internet or extranet users.
- **Farm has specific performance-tuning requirements** By separating the traffic generated by various types of users on different farms, it becomes easier to identify needed performance tuning adjustments.
- **Farm content is highly secured** If you do not want the authors to have access to publish content to the target farm, you can use content deployment to publish content from source to target farm.

Determine the Number of Farms

Typical content deployment requires two farms: a source farm where the content is authored and reviewed and a destination farm where the content is read. In some scenarios, you would need three server farms: a farm for content authoring, a staging farm, and a production farm. Using content deployment, it is also possible to move content from one site collection to another site collection within the same server farm.

Plan for Export and Import Servers

When you decide to use content deployment, you need to determine the servers that will be used for export and import purposes on the source and destination farms respectively, to reduce the impact to other services on both farms. The export and import servers should have the Central Administration service enabled.

Plan for Content Deployment Job Scheduling

Content deployment jobs can be scoped at the entire site collection or at the individual site level. Multiple job definitions can be associated with a single path. You have to decide whether one deployment job will deploy all of the content within a path, or if multiple jobs will be used for deployment of specific content within the path. If multiple jobs are used for the deployment of content within specific sites, you should arrange these jobs in such a way that the sites in the site collection hierarchy are deployed in top-down order. Processing should being with the root site in the collection, after which the next level of sites would be processed, and so on. You also must also plan the time at which the content deployment jobs will run. Pick a time during which there is minimal activity on the source farm and make sure that you do not schedule two content deployment jobs to run in parallel if they are pointing to the same path.

Plan for Large Jobs

A content deployment job copies all content from the source site collection as XML files and exports binary files into 10 MB CAB files. If there are files that are larger than 10 MB—video files, for example—then those files will be packaged into their own files, which will be larger than 10 MB. All these files are exported to the destination farm through HTTP post, and then they are extracted and updated into the destination site. You must make sure that both the source and the destination have enough storage capacity to handle the deployment job.

Plan for Change Log Settings

If you are planning to run content deployment jobs infrequently, ensure that the change log settings of the Web application are configured so that the change logs are kept long enough for the job run. By default, the change logs are kept for only 15 days, so if you are planning a job to run once every 20 days, then the change logs should be kept for at least 20 days so that the deployment job can pick up the changes for deployment.

Deploy to an Empty Site Collection for Initial Deployment

The destination site collection must be created without any site template; to do this, use the Select Template Later option. If the destination site collection has any content, the initial deployment will fail.

> **NOTE** The Blank Site template does not create an empty site collection, so do not use it for creating the destination site collection.

Configuring Content Deployment

This section explains the necessary configuration that you will need to perform to enable content deployment on a farm. The set of configurations vary based on the role played by the server farm.

- **Destination farm configuration** On the destination farm, configure content deployment settings to accept incoming deployment jobs.
- **Source farm configuration** On the source farm, define content deployment settings to specify the export server, path, and job.

Configure Content Deployment Settings

You must perform the following configuration on the destination farm first, because you cannot create a content deployment path without first configuring the destination farm to accept incoming deployment jobs. On the source farm, this configuration defines the export server and the temporary path to be used by the content deployment job.

1. Open a browser and go to the SharePoint Central Administration website; navigate to the General Application Settings page.

2. Under Content Deployment, click Configure Content Deployment. This opens the Configure Content Deployment page, as shown in Figure 15-15.

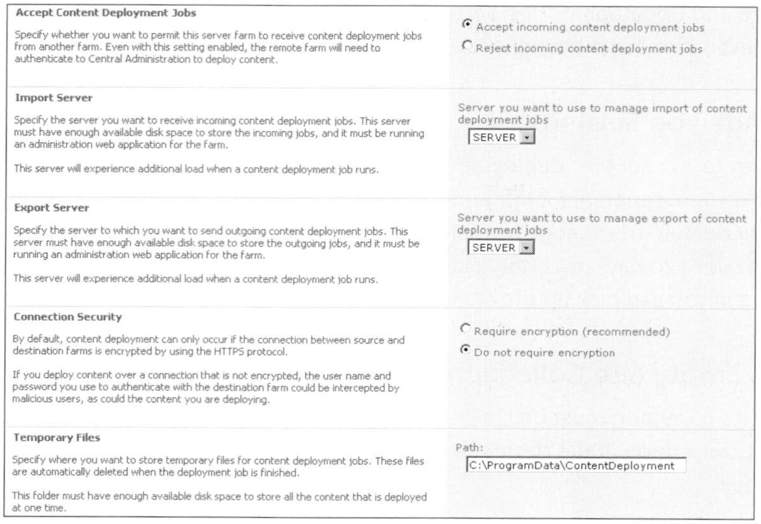

FIGURE 15-15 The Configure Content Deployment settings page

3. Select the Accept Incoming Content Deployment Jobs option in the Accept Content Deployment Jobs section of the page.

4. Select the Import Server, which will receive the content deployment job from the source. This selection is required on the destination farm.

5. Select the Export Server, which will send the content deployment job to the destination. This selection is required on the source farm.

6. In the Connection Security section of the page, select the Require Encryption option if you want to use SSL for transferring content; if a secure connection is not required, use the Do Not Require Encryption option.

7. In Temporary Files section of the page, specify the path to store the temporary files used by the content deployment jobs. Ensure that you select a drive that has enough free space for storing and extracting the CAB files used during content deployment.

8. In the Reporting section of the page, specify the number of reports to retain for each job.

9. Click OK to save your settings.

Create Content Deployment Path

When you create a content deployment path, you create a relationship between the source and destination site collections. The following steps explain the process of creating a content deployment path.

1. Open a browser and go to the SharePoint Central Administration website; navigate to the General Application Settings page.

2. Under Content Deployment, click Manage Content Deployment Paths And Jobs to open the Manage Content Deployment Paths And Jobs settings list, as shown in Figure 15-16.

FIGURE 15-16 The Manage Content Deployment Paths And Jobs settings list

3. Click the New Path link to open an entry page, as shown in Figure 15-17.

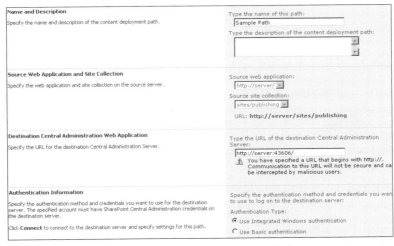

FIGURE 15-17 An entry page for creating a new content deployment path

4. Enter the name of the path in the Type Name Of This Path field.

5. Enter the description in Type The Description Of The Content Deployment Path field.

6. Choose the Source Web application in the Source Web Application And Site Collection section.

7. Choose the Source Site Collection in the Source Web Application And Site Collection section.

8. Enter the URL of the destination Central Administration Web application in the Type The URL Of The Destination Central Administration Server.

9. Select the Use Integrated Windows Authentication option as the Authentication Type if you want to use Windows Authentication for accessing the destination farm. Select Use Basic Authentication Option if the destination farm uses Basic Authentication.

10. Enter a User Name and Password.

11. Click Connect to validate your authentication details and to connect to the destination farm. If the authentication information is valid, you will see a Connection Successful message; otherwise, you will see an error message that provides reasons for the failure.

12. Select the destination Web application from the Destination Web Application drop-down list.

13. Select the destination site collection from the Destination Site Collection drop-down list.

14. If you want the user names to be deployed along with the content, select the Deploy User Names check box.

15. Select the security information to be deployed using the Security Information In The Content Deployment drop-down list. Choose All to deploy security roles, the access control list, and users to the destination farm; choose Role Definitions Only if you want deploy security roles and access control list to the destination farm; choose None to deploy no security information.

16. Click OK to create the content deployment path.

Create Content Deployment Job

The following steps explain how to create a content deployment job using the path you created earlier.

1. Open a browser and go to the SharePoint Central Administration website; navigate to the General Application Settings page.

2. Under Content Deployment, click Manage Content Deployment Paths And Jobs.

3. Click the New Job link to open an entry page, as shown in Figure 15-18.

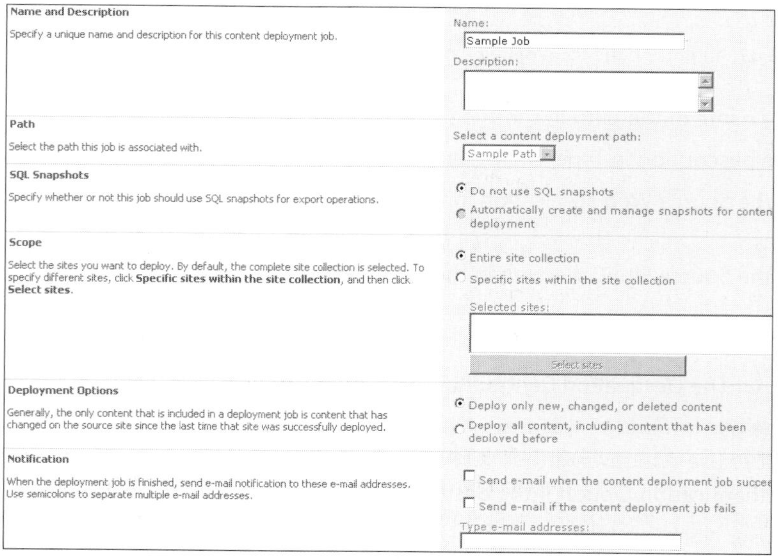

FIGURE 15-18 An entry page to create a new content deployment job

4. Enter the name of the job in the Name And Description section.

5. Enter a description of the job in the Name And Description section.

6. Select the path from the Select A Content Deployment Path drop-down list in the Path section.

7. Select the option to use SQL Snapshots for deployment by selecting the Automatically Create And Manage Snapshots For Content Deployment option in the SQL Snapshots section. If you decide not to use SQL Snapshots, select the Do Not Use SQL Snapshots option.

> **NOTE** New in SharePoint 2010, SQL Snapshots provide an improved method of moving content between farms and servers when compared to the standard XML file–based method. If you are running SQL Server 2008 Enterprise, you can take advantage of this new functionality.

8. If you want an entire site collection to be deployed by the job, then select the Entire Site Collection option in the Scope section. If you choose to deploy only parts of a site collection, select the Specific Sites Within Site Collection option and then click Select Sites.

9. In the Select Sites dialog box, choose whether or not you want to include subsites by clicking the drop-down menu next to the site name and then clicking the Select This Site (Contents Available At This Site Alone Deployed; Content From Subsites Are Not Deployed) option or the Select This Branch (Content From This Site And All Subsites Under This Site Are Deployed) option. Click OK.

10. Define the frequency of job execution by selecting the Run This Job On The Following Schedule check box.

11. Specify the frequency of execution by selecting one of the following options.

   - One Time Only Option And Select The Date And Time Of Execution, to run the job only once
   - Every Option And Select Frequency In Minutes, to run the job every 15, 30, or 45 minutes
   - Once An Hour Option And Specify At Minute, to run the job on an hourly basis
   - Once A Day Option And Specify At Time, to run the job on a daily basis
   - Once A Week Option And Specify Day And At Time, to run the job on a weekly basis
   - Once A Month Option And Specify Day And At Time, to run the job on a monthly basis

12. Select the Deploy Only New, Changed, Or Deleted Content option in the Deployment section of the page if you want to use incremental deployment. For full deployment, select the Deploy All Content, Including Content That Has Been Deployed Before option.

13. Select the Send E-mail When The Content Deployment Job Succeeds check box in the Notification section to send e-mails if the job succeeds. Select the Send E-Mail If The Content Deployment Job Fails check box to notify users if the content deployment jobs fails during execution. You also must specify a list of e-mail addresses for these notifications in the Type E-mail Addresses text box.

14. Click OK to save the content deployment job settings.

NOTE The SQL Snapshots option is disabled when using Microsoft SQL Server Express.

Configure a Quick Deploy Job

A Quick Deploy job is created as soon as the content deployment path is created. In this section, you will learn how to configure a Quick Deploy job.

1. Open a browser and go to the SharePoint Central Administration website; navigate to the General Application Settings page.

2. Under Content Deployment, click Manage Content Deployment Paths And Jobs.

3. Select the drop-down menu next to Quick Deploy Job For Path *path_name* and select the Quick Deploy Settings menu item to open a settings page, as shown in Figure 15-19.

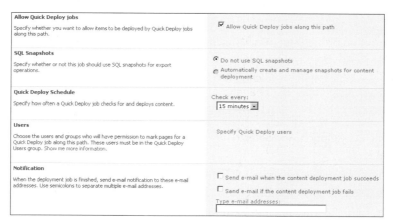

FIGURE 15-19 Adjust settings for the Quick Deploy job.

4. Select the Allow Quick Deploy Jobs Along This Path check box in the Allow Quick Deploy Job section to enable a quick deployment job. Note that the Quick Deploy Job will be disabled by default.

5. Select the Automatically Create And Manage Snapshots For Content Deployment option in the SQL Snapshots section to use SQL Snapshots for deployment. If you decide not use SQL Snapshots, select the Do Not Use SQL Snapshots option from the SQL Snapshots section. Do Not Use SQL Snapshots is the default option.

> **NOTE** New in SharePoint 2010, SQL Snapshots provide an improved method of moving content between farms and servers when compared to the standard XML file–based method. If you are running SQL Server 2008 Enterprise, you can take advantage of this new functionality.

6. Specify the schedule for deployment by selecting an interval in minutes from the Check Every drop-down list in the Quick Deploy Schedule section.

7. Specify users who can use a Quick Deploy job by clicking the Specify Quick Deploy Users link in the Users section. Clicking this link opens the Quick Deploy Users Group in the source site collection; you can add users to the group from this page.

> **NOTE** The Specify Quick Deploy users link will appear only if you are a member of the Site Collection Administrators group on the site collection associated with the Quick Deploy path.

8. Select the Send E-mail When The Content Deployment Job Succeeds check box in the Notification section to send e-mails if the job succeeds or the Send E-mail If The Content Deployment Job Fails check box to notify users if the content deployment job fails during execution. Specify the list of e-mail addresses for the notifications in the Type E-mail Addresses text box.

You can also run the Quick Deploy job from the Central Administration site using the following steps.

1. Open a browser and go to the SharePoint Central Administration website; navigate to the General Application Settings page.

2. Under Content Deployment, click Manage Content Deployment Paths And Jobs.

3. Select the drop-down menu next to Quick Deploy Job For Path *path_name* and select the Run Now menu item.

To view a history of Quick Deploy jobs, perform the following actions.

1. Open a browser and go to the SharePoint Central Administration website; navigate to the General Application Settings page.

2. Under Content Deployment, click Manage Content Deployment Paths And Jobs.

3. Select the drop-down menu next to Quick Deploy Job For Path *path_name* and select the View History menu item.

You can check the deployment status of a specific object by clicking the Check Deployment Of A Specific Object link in the Quick Links section of the Job History page. On the Content Deployment Object Status page, enter the URL of the object for which you want to check the deployment status and then click Check Status.

Summary

In this chapter, you explored many of the Web Content Management features and capabilities included with SharePoint 2010, showing how each capability is part of a larger unified platform for WCM, with added features for governance and community involvement.

You were introduced to the site types and the publishing features included as part of the WCM solution as well as publishing workflows and the importance of a well-defined content approval process. This chapter reviewed the mechanics of branding and touched briefly on each of the elements that make up the presentation layer. The chapter also reviewed some of the new platform enhancements included in SharePoint 2010 and Microsoft SharePoint Designer, and you examined the new Web Analytics features and how to leverage them to get the information you need to continuously improve your quality of content.

You learned about the high-fidelity content authoring options delivered in SharePoint 2010, including Web-based and smart client authoring options and also covered the additional rich-media capabilities and the Asset Library template.

The broad topics of content caching and content deployment were covered in significant detail, including when and how to use each type of caching and deployment, and you were presented with detailed configuration steps for configuration. The information provided in this chapter should provide you with a solid foundation for the successful implementation and use of SharePoint 2010's WCM capabilities in your deployment.

Securing Information

As Microsoft SharePoint Products and Technologies mature, more organizations are using SharePoint sites to upload sensitive information that needs to be properly secured. This phenomenon is predictable, since an increasing use of SharePoint for collaboration and information hosting activities would naturally lead users to upload information that needs to be secured. There is a perception among a sizable number of security professionals and information technology administrators that the SharePoint platform is not a secure platform. This generalization of the SharePoint platform is not warranted, as the information in this chapter will demonstrate.

Microsoft SharePoint 2010, when properly configured, offers tight security and can work well in rather demanding environments. But getting the product properly configured requires teamwork, training, and an understanding of how SharePoint security works. Depending on the level of security you want to achieve, both in terms of breadth and granularity, you might need to work with one or several layers of security available within the SharePoint platform. Understanding how all of SharePoint's security features work is the focus of this chapter. There is much to learn, so it's time to get started.

Introducing SharePoint Security

SharePoint security is managed at every level of the hierarchy. Conceptually, you can think of a SharePoint farm as consisting of a hierarchy of elements as shown in Figure 16-1. The important concept to understand here is that there are security settings at nearly every level and that these settings "pass through" or apply to the down-level containers, too.

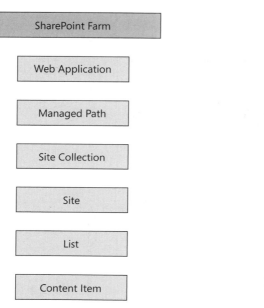

FIGURE 16-1 The hierarchy of elements in a SharePoint farm

When you take a long step back and look at how content is actually hosted in SharePoint, it is really accomplished within a series of nested containers: Content items are hosted in a list. Lists are hosted in sites. Sites are hosted in site collections. Site collections are hosted within managed paths (even the root site of a Web application is hosted in a hidden managed path called *root*), and managed paths are hosted in Web applications.

Granted, some content is hosted in publishing pages directly, so keep in mind that the previous paragraph's simple explanation is not making a sweeping statement without any exceptions in SharePoint. But it is fair to say that the majority of the content hosted in SharePoint in done so in lists. Document libraries, under the hood, are really just complex lists, with a customized view that exposes the documents instead of the list items to which the documents are attached.

The reason it is important to understand the structure—how SharePoint content storage is set up—is because different parts of SharePoint security are applied at different "layers." Some security is applied at the Web application layer, whereas other security is applied at the content item layer. Figure 16-2 offers an outline of how security is applied within SharePoint 2010.

> **NOTE** Site quotes, audiences, database status, and alternate access mappings are not security features in SharePoint 2010. Site quotes and database status instead are focused on setting capacity limits, alternate access mappings provide alternate URLs to the existing content, and audiences are really a view-crafting feature.

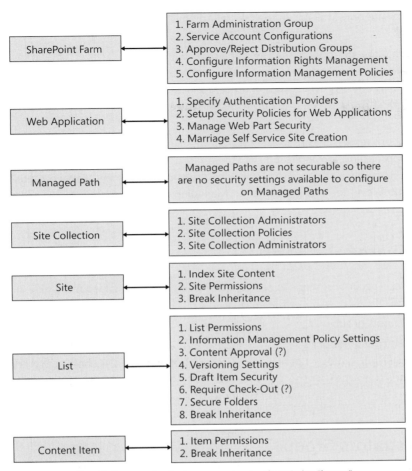

FIGURE 16-2 SharePoint security feature mapping to SharePoint "layers"

Security is commonly thought of as being applied to content, and although this is certainly true within SharePoint 2010, security is more than this. Security is about *access*—access to content, but also access to the containers that host the content. So it is reasonable to assume that by blocking access to a container at an upper layer, such as a Web application, you can effectively block access to an entire set of content without having to visit and configure each list in which the content resides.

The interplay of security settings at the different layers within SharePoint will force the information technology (IT) team and SharePoint users to communicate better about how security should be set. The product is designed to allow the management of security settings applied directly to content by nontechnical end users who are the owners of the content. IT personnel don't (at least not often) get involved in this process. However, there are some settings that are configured only by the IT administrators (or SharePoint farm administrations if you have a separate team managing your SharePoint deployment) through Central Administration, because they are only available in the Central Administration interface or through Windows PowerShell.

You might think that the appropriate manager of a particular SharePoint "layer" should be the individual who would make changes to the security settings for that layer. But since many of these security settings affect other settings in other layers, it is critical to maintain communication and coordination between those involved to ensure that SharePoint is secured correctly.

The following sections discuss these security settings and illustrate how the settings work. This is a pragmatic approach to the application of security for SharePoint, and after reading this chapter, you will have the confidence to properly secure your deployment. There is more information on the farm-level settings in Chapter 6, "Managing SharePoint 2010 Using Central Administration."

Securing a SharePoint Farm

There are five farm-level security settings to consider, and each one is explained more fully in the following sections.

- Farm administrators group
- Service account configurations
- Approve/reject distribution groups
- Configure information rights management
- Configure information management policies

Farm Administrators Group

Members of the farm administrators group have pervasive, complete access to all settings and content in the farm. Nearly all network operating systems and platforms have at least one account or group that has full and complete access to configuration settings and content. SharePoint is no different. Be careful about who you allow into this group, because they will have full access to all content hosted in the farm.

 SECURITY ALERT   Be sure that anyone who is placed in this group has undergone a security background check and has proven (as much as is reasonably possible) that he or she is a trustworthy individual. Remember, there are two elements from which developers can never protect their code: untrustworthy administrators and unwise administrators. Those who can't (or shouldn't) be trusted and those who make unwise decisions in their administration of an operating system or platform should not be entrusted with full administrative rights to SharePoint farms.

By default, the account under which SharePoint was installed, the BUILTIN\Administrators, and the application pool account for the Central Administration website are automatically members of the farm administrators group. You'll need to log in with one of these three accounts to add additional accounts to the farm administrators group.

BEST PRACTICES Be sure that whoever you add to this group has been fully trained to administer SharePoint 2010 properly and is knowledgeable about your organization's security policies.

Service Account Configurations

Service accounts are used to proxy user requests to the service and receive back the output from the service. For example, when a user makes a call for a document in a library, the call between the user and the Web front-end server (WFE) is made within the security context of the user. But when the WFE connects to the SQL database to retrieve the content, that call is made within the security context of the application pool account. By using this architecture, the user is unable to connect directly to the information stored in the SQL server, because those databases will not talk directly with the user's account—they will only talk with the application pool account.

Service accounts can be configured to secure transmissions between the WFE and service applications. Best practice would be to create a separate account for each service, thereby isolating the calls between the service applications and the WFE servers in unique security contexts.

Approving or Rejecting Distribution Groups

When a group in SharePoint is configured to receive e-mail messages, that configuration must be approved by a farm administrator before the group's e-mail functionality is enabled. This can be thought of as a security feature, because the farm administrator can decide which SharePoint groups should and should not receive e-mail messages. Because there is a chance that a group's e-mail alias will match another distribution group in your e-mail system, the SharePoint farm administrator should have a method available to check that the requested e-mail alias for a group does not conflict with existing aliases. You might see this happen, for example, when users from different sites use the default security groups for e-mail distribution lists. In addition, because e-mail messages can contain viruses, it is good for someone on the IT team to be involved in the approval of a distribution group.

BEST PRACTICES To ensure that you don't have conflicting group aliases in your e-mail–enabled groups, you should have a policy that requires all SharePoint groups to be explicitly created and uniquely named before they can have e-mail privileges enabled. In other words, default groups created by SharePoint should not be used as e-mail distribution groups.

Configuring Information Rights Management

Information rights management (IRM) is really about privacy, not security. But most people think of this feature as a security feature, so it is included in this section. The reason you should think of IRM as more about privacy than security is because IRM concerns itself with what a user can do with the information (or document) *after* the information has been accessed. For example, Joe might have full-control permissions to a document library, but after accessing the library and opening a document, Joe might not be able to print that document due to the IRM settings on the document.

SharePoint is agnostic about IRM settings. It preserves whatever settings are set on the document but doesn't really care if IRM settings exist or not. If you want to introduce IRM across a plethora of documents and other content items in your SharePoint farm, however, you'll need to configure IRM at the farm level.

> **MORE INFO** To learn how to configure IRM in SharePoint 2010, please consult Chapter 15, "Configuring Policies and Security," in *Microsoft SharePoint 2010 Administrator's Pocket Consultant* by Ben Curry (Microsoft Press, 2010).

Configuring Information Management Policies

Information management policies are designed to help you apply configurations to information uniformly. These policies are created first at the farm level, but they are applied at the content type or list level. If the policy contains configuration choices, those choices are selected and applied at the content type or list level as well. The four policies that ship with SharePoint 2010 include Labels, Barcodes, Auditing, and Retention. See Table 6-5 in Chapter 6 for a brief description of each policy.

Labels

Labels give you the ability to add metadata labels in a document. At the farm level, you can either enable or disable (decommission) this policy. Decommissioning the policy will remove it from availability throughout your farm; it is enabled by default. If you don't disable the Label policy at the outset of your deployment and users utilize this policy in some of their documents, when you decommission the policy, it will still be available in those documents that are currently utilizing it. However, it will not be available for new documents.

As a security measure, labels are indexed and can potentially cause sensitive information to appear in the results set if a document isn't properly secured. Although this is a potential problem for any document, labels might make this problem more sensitive if your information design is built around finding documents through keyword metadata.

Barcodes

For some reason, barcodes seem to be a point of confusion for a number of SharePoint administrators and users. The only thing barcodes do is allow you to track a physical document based on the barcode that is in it. This can be a security enhancement if you scan the document's barcode and associate that with a biometric identifier of the person who has control of the document. Barcodes can also allow you to track the location of the physical document in the workflow at any time.

Retention

Retention policies allow you to enforce end-of-use phases for documents and list items that are hosted in your SharePoint farm. At the farm level, you simply ensure that that policy is either enabled or disabled. But the policy itself is rich in configuration values and can make sure that you limit your exposure to liability if your organization is involved in a legal matter by ensuring that only up-to-date and official documents are available during the discovery process.

A thorough use of retention policies allows you to ensure that no old data exists in your SharePoint farm. One of the most common complaints about file servers is that they are hosting duplicative, outdated, and irrelevant content. Many administrators feel that well over 50 percent of the documents on their file servers could be classified in one or more of these three categories. Merely moving this content to SharePoint doesn't resolve this issue unless you do the following.

- Create disposition and end-of-life policies for the various types of documents and list items you will host in your SharePoint 2010 farm.

- Create content types for each of the various types of documents and list items and use the Microsoft Metadata Services Content Type Syndication feature to push out these content types to the site collections in your farm.

- As part of creating the content types, enforce retention policies for your content at the content type layer and ensure that the proper workflows are associated and in place in each site collection that will host each content type with a retention policy.

To be sure, it takes a lot of effort up front to comply with these suggestions by creating the proper content types, retention policies, and end-of-life policies for your documents. But the payoff later will be tremendous, both in terms of disposition compliance and in your ability to limit your organization's exposure to liability through the eDiscovery processes.

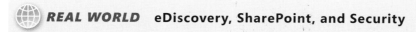

REAL WORLD   eDiscovery, SharePoint, and Security

A topic that is closely related to security is eDiscovery, which is any process in which electronic data is sought, located, secured, and searched with the intent of using it as evidence in a civil or criminal legal case. This includes, but is not limited to, computer forensics, e-mail archiving, online review, and proactive management. The emergent eDiscovery field augments legal, constitutional, political, security, and personal privacy issues.

eDiscovery was part of a formal amendment to the Federal Rules on Civil Procedure and was released on December 1, 2006. These rules complicate data storage and exposure to liability for every organization in the United States. The main point is that if you have a reasonable expectation that you will ever be involved in a legal dispute, even as a third party, you have a duty to preserve evidence that might be germane to that proceeding. This means that your IT and legal departments will need to work together more often and more closely.

The plain truth is that most companies are not ready for an eDiscovery process. For example, 57 percent of law firms surveyed said that their clients are not ready to find and produce information relevant to litigation, and 39 percent of in-house counsel reported that their companies are not prepared for eDiscovery.[1]

As part of your litigation readiness review, you should have your legal team specify which documents and records would be needed in an eDiscovery process and what the retention times should be for those records. Detailing this information is time consuming and can create an upfront cost, but the cost of *not* finding the right information or not finding all of the right information can cost your organization much more in a legal battle, both in terms of fines and in terms of a judgment. Utilizing the retention policies in SharePoint can lessen the administrative burden for ensuring that documents are both preserved for the right amount of time and purged after that time has expired.

[1] *Information Week*, September 23, 2008.

Securing a Web Application

This section introduces the security of a Web application and the planning issues that present themselves as part of this discussion. You will learn about three areas of security related to Web applications: zones, authentication providers, and Web application security policies.

Zones

In SharePoint 2010 nomenclature, a *zone* is essentially an inbound vector to the content in a database that is accessed through a Web application. Don't think of zones as any more complicated than this. SharePoint 2010 has five default inbound zones.

- Default
- Intranet
- Extranet
- Internet
- Custom

An authentication provider, an inbound URL (which can have alternate access mappings), and a Web application are associated with each zone, along with security settings that apply to anyone using the defined inbound vector to access content in SharePoint 2010.

When you create a new Web application, behind the scenes it is assigned to the Default zone with minimal security settings at this Web application layer. To change the security settings associated with the zone, you don't go to the zone directly because *there is no administrative interface for zone management*. Instead, you manage zones through the other feature interfaces, and when it is appropriate, the zone and security management settings will appear to apply security at the Web application layer.

Authentication Providers

In SharePoint 2010, you can specify the underlying authentication provider for a particular Web application's zone. This can be useful when using a Web application in a specific manner in which it makes sense to use an authentication provider other than Active Directory.

For example, if you want to expose a website in SharePoint to the Internet but quarantine the authentication of anyone using the site from Active Directory, you might decide to use forms-based authentication, which would allow users to create their own user name and password combination, stored in a SQL database, to support authentication only to that website.

The authentication providers that ship with SharePoint 2010 include

- Windows
- Forms
- Web single sign-on

Windows Authentication treats the user identity supplied by Microsoft Internet Information Services (IIS) as the authenticated user in an ASP.NET application. IIS provides a number of authentication mechanisms to verify user identity, including anonymous authentication, Windows-integrated (NTLM) authentication, Windows-integrated (Kerberos) authentication, Basic (base64 encoded) authentication, Digest authentication, and authentication based on client certificates.

Forms authentication enables you to authenticate the user name and password of your users using a login form that you create. Unauthenticated requests are redirected to a login page, where the user provides credentials and submits the form. If the application authenticates the request, the system issues a ticket that contains a key for re-establishing the identity for subsequent requests.

In the Web single sign-on (SSO) design, users authenticate only once to Active Directory to access multiple applications. Typically, you deploy this design when you want to provide customer access to one or more ADFS-secured applications over the Internet. With the Web SSO design, an organization that typically hosts a secured application in a perimeter network can maintain a separate store of customer accounts in the perimeter network, which makes it easier to isolate customer accounts and employee accounts.

Authentication providers are assigned at the Web application layer and associated with a zone. Each web application you create is automatically placed in the Default zone and permissions are wide open on that zone. For more information about zones and how they work in SharePoint 2010, see Chapter 6.

How Zones, Web Applications, and Security Work Together to Provide Secure Solutions

In this section, you'll see how zones, Web applications, and security options can be combined to provide a secure solution for a sample scenario: your company of 1000 SharePoint users is outsourcing the development work for your SharePoint 2010 farm to a Microsoft Certified Partner. Because of your company's security policy requirements, which forbid contractors from creating new site collections using self-service site creation, you need to provide secure access to your SharePoint farm to the contract developers while allowing the SSSC right for your employees—but not for your contractors.

Assume that the URL location in which the contractors are working is *http://portal*, because they are building out a new intranet portal for your company based on requirements that are not relevant to our example.

First, you'll need an existing Web application to work with. In this example, you have a new Web application called *portal* at *http://portal*. Now, assume that users in your organization connect to this portal through port 80 after having authenticated through Active Directory. The portal is published on your firewall and is available for SSL (443 Secure Sockets Layer) access as well for your users. But you also want to quarantine *http://portal* to prevent your consultants from using it, and instead create a different URL they can use to access the same content and customize it. In addition, you want to place additional security (restrictions) on what your users can do to *http://portal* after they have been authenticated.

The first step in accomplishing this scenario is to extend the portal Web application using a different URL. Open a browser and go to Central Administration, click the Application Management link, and then click the Manage Web Applications link. Then highlight the name of the portal Web application in the Web application list and click the Extend icon on the Ribbon (Figure 16-3).

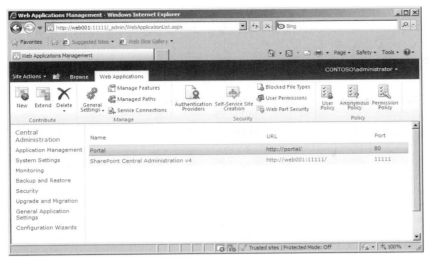

FIGURE 16-3 Highlight the Web application you want to extend and then click the Extend icon.

When you click the Extend icon, you are presented with a page that is similar to the New Web Application page, except that you won't be creating any databases. What you're doing is creating another IIS website that is provisioned by SharePoint 2010 with different configurations but is connected to the same set of databases as that of the Web application that was highlighted when you clicked the Extend icon. Another way to think about this is that you're creating a second inbound vector to those databases hosted by the original Web application.

Figure 16-4 shows the top part of a page that will configure the extended website. It can be a confusing page to work with if you don't fully understand what you're doing. For example, you might try to create a new website and then connect it to the Web application that you are trying to extend. You should understand that by the time you get to this page, you are already connected to the Web application that you want to extend, and you need to create a new website to make this happen.

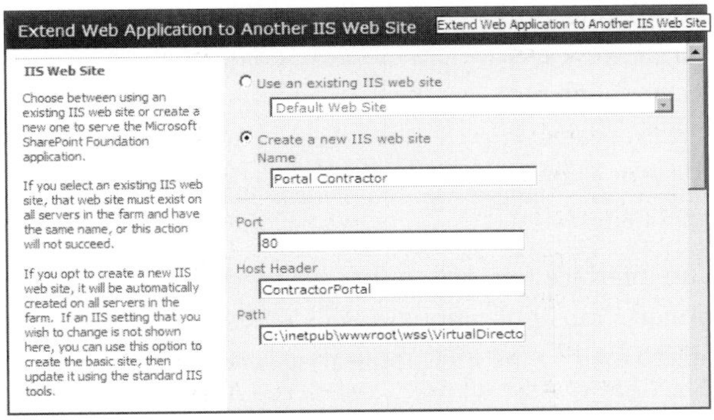

FIGURE 16-4 Creating a new IIS website to extend *http://portal*

When you create the new website that will extend an existing Web application, you will have a chance to select the authentication provider. You are not required to select the same authentication provider that was selected for the default Web application. In fact, selecting a different authentication provider for a different inbound vector is one of the main reasons that you extend a Web application (Figure 16-5).

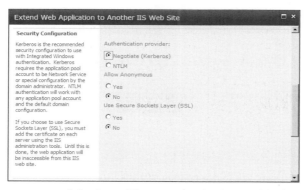

FIGURE 16-5 Selecting a different authentication provider for this extended Web application

Finally, at the bottom of this page, you'll be able to select the default URL and zone for this extended IIS website. Note that the default zone does not display, because that one is already taken by the original Web application. Among the four choices illustrated in Figure 16-6, Custom seems to be the correct choice, and is the one that should be selected.

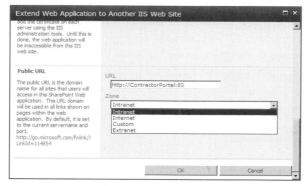

FIGURE 16-6 Viewing the remaining four zone choices plus the default public URL for this extended IIS website

You might think that there would be an interface to manage these extended Web applications, but there is not. You manage extended Web applications only when you are working with a Web application feature that needs to expose the IIS website that extended this Web application.

The one place in SharePoint Central Administration where you can see your Web applications and their extended IIS websites is the Alternate Access Mappings page, shown in Figure 16-7. However, you still need your documentation, because there is nothing in this view that indicates which URLs are extension websites and which are the root, default Web applications.

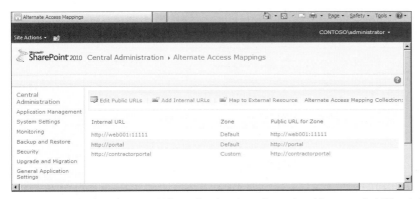

FIGURE 16-7 Viewing the root Web application, *http://portal*, and its extended IIS website, *http://contractorportal*, on the Alternate Access Mappings page

So in this scenario, now that you've extended the *http://portal* Web application and assigned it to the custom zone, it's time to secure that extended Web application. For purposes of this example, you'll focus on two of the three configuration options: permission policy and user policy; there is a brief explanation of the anonymous policy option.

You want to restrict what the contractors can do through their URL/zone assignments. The way to configure this is to create the permission policy that you will then assign to the Contractors user group. To create the permission policy, click the Permission Policy icon on the page for the Web application (the same page where you clicked the Extend icon earlier in this example).

When you click the Permission Policy icon, you are presented with the Manage Permission Policy Levels page, where you click the Add Permission Policy Level link to create a new permission policy. The Add Permission Policy Level page shown in Figure 16-8 appears, and you need to understand the options presented on this page.

The first thing you need to do is to give the new permission policy a name that is descriptive of what the policy will enforce. Second, you'll need to configure the site collection level permissions. Two types of permission are available, Administrator and Auditor. You can select both, either, or none of these options. Selecting the Administrator option gives the permission policy (and anyone assigned this policy) site collection administrator privileges in all of the site collections within this Web application, as long as the person uses the extended inbound vector that you are configuring. Site collection Auditor permission gives those individuals full read access to everything within the Web application, as long as they use the extended inbound vector that you are configuring to access the content. This is very useful for allowing auditors to review content without giving them modify capabilities and without having to visit each site collection within the Web application to assign audit level permissions.

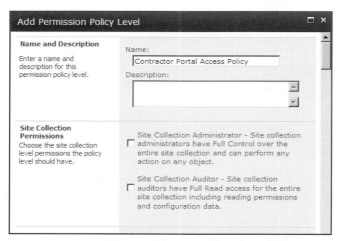

FIGURE 16-8 Add Permission Policy Level page

Scroll down this page to see that you have the opportunity to grant or deny permissions. If your compliance requirements include explicit deny permissions, this is place to configure and enforce them. The permissions listed on this page cannot be split up—this is as granular as they come in SharePoint 2010.

The permissions are separated into three groups: List, Site, and Personal. You can create any matrix of permissions for each policy permission level that you need. Be sure to document what you create, because there is no default reporting available in SharePoint 2010 for these permission policy levels. You can review what you've done in the user interface (UI), but if you are creating a plethora of these policies, it's important to document what you've done for faster reference. Also, be sure not to select both grant and deny permissions on the same or different permission policies that apply to the same groups. Doing so will negate the grant permissions.

In the sample scenario, you are going to deny self-service site creation (SSSC) permission to the Contract group because you don't want them to create new site collections within this Web application. Assuming that you have configured SSSC for your company users, this will ensure that employees can create new site collections but contractors cannot (Figure 16-9).

> **NOTE** You select the check boxes in the left column to grant selections and select check boxes in the right column to deny selections.

FIGURE 16-9 Denying the Contractor group SSSC permission

After saving this permission policy, Figure 16-10 illustrates that it will now be listed as an available permission policy to assign at the Web application layer.

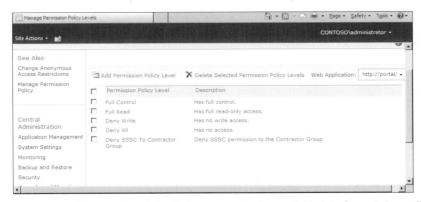

FIGURE 16-10 The new Permission Policy appears in the available list of permission policies for the *http://portal* Web application.

NOTE Permission policy levels are unique to each Web application. When you create a new permission policy level, it is assigned to the Web application that you are focused on. There is no UI to copy permission policies between Web applications, so in the absence of custom code, you must re-create permission policies for each Web application.

At this point in the scenario, you've done nothing to secure the extended Web application because you have not assigned a user policy to the extended zone using the newly config-ured Deny SSSC To Contractor Group permission policy. To do this, you set your focus on the *http://portal* Web application, click the User Policy button, and then select Add Users. The Add Users page with a zone selection drop-down list appears (Figure 16-11), and you'll use it to select the Custom zone. Note that only those zones that have existing websites will appear.

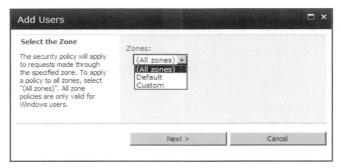

FIGURE 16-11 The Add Users page allows you to select the utilized zones where you want to apply the permission policy.

On the next page (Figure 16-12), you'll associate the permission level that you just created with the Contractor's Active Directory group, and this will complete the effort to apply a permission to a group of users who are instructed to use a different URL to access the portal content.

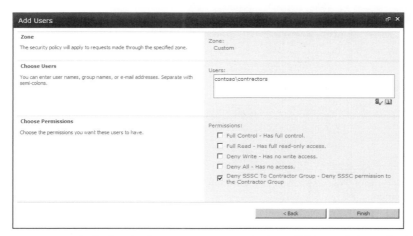

FIGURE 16-12 Assigning the Contractors group to the Deny SSSC permission policy level for the Custom zone

You might conclude that you are not yet finished, because there is nothing in the UI to enforce the instruction that contractors use their own URL to get the portal content—and you would be correct. To force contractors to use the contractor URL, you must create another permission policy level that denies all access to all content on the default zone for the URL *http://portal* and assign it to the Contractors group.

By doing this, when an individual who authenticates through Active Directory is identified as a member of the Contractors group, the only way that individual can access *http://portal* is to use the URL *http://contractorportal*, and her rights to SSSC will be denied.

Changing Authentication Providers for a Web Application

Technically speaking, you don't change authentication providers for a Web application—you change them for a Web application's zone. But after the authentication providers are made available, you can change them for a zone with a few simple clicks.

In Central Administration, click the Manage Web Applications link, select the Web application that you want to configure, and then click the Authentication Providers icon on the Ribbon. Note that the icons on the Ribbon will not be available until you select a Web application.

When you click the Authentication Providers icon, the Authentication Providers page displays and you will be able to see the utilized zones. Click the zone you want to configure. When you do this, the Edit Authentication page displays, as shown in Figure 16-13.

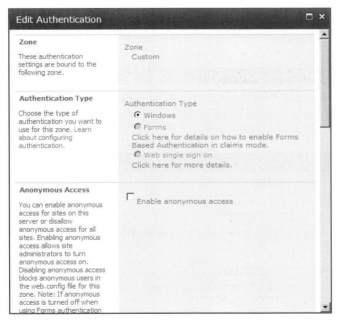

FIGURE 16-13 Edit Authentication page

On the Edit Authentication page, you can see which zone you are configuring, but you're not allowed to change zones from this page. You can select the authentication provider (called Authentication Type in the UI) you want to use. In this scenario, neither the enabled forms nor the Web single sign-on (SSO) options were selected, but if they had been, those two authentication providers would be available for selection.

For anonymous policy settings, click the Anonymous Policy icon on the Ribbon after selecting the Web application that you want to configure. Then you can set restrictions on anonymous access, including deny permission to write and deny permission "to all." The latter selection is a good way to ensure that you explicitly deny access to those authenticated as anonymous users for a particular zone (inbound vector). This is a positive way to make sure that anonymous users come into the site only from the vector you determine.

Managing Web Part Security

Even though you manage Web Part security through Central Administration, this security setting is applied at the Web application level. Web Part security at this level focuses on three aspects.

- Web Part connections
- Use of the online Web Part gallery
- Use of scriptable Web Parts

Each of these configurations is applied to a Web application so that you can allow, for example, Web Part connections within one Web application but deny them in another Web application. Figure 16-14 shows the page you use to set Web Part security within Central Administration.

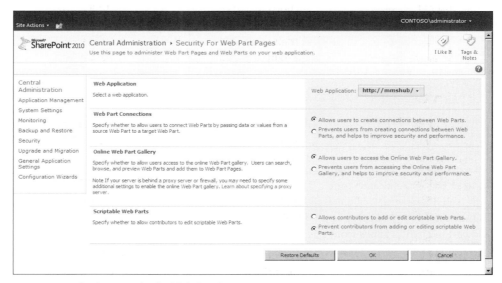

FIGURE 16-14 Setting security for Web Part Pages

You can either allow or deny connections between Web Parts. The security aspects of this decision derives from the fact that data can be passed between Web Parts, which can be used maliciously to download information from one Web Part to another. Because the connections operate within the security context of the application pool account for the Web application, some content can be presented to users who should not see it if the destination Web Part is not properly secured. Preventing Web Part connections helps eliminate this problem.

The online Web Part gallery is often turned off by SharePoint customers, even though it is turned on by default when you install SharePoint 2010. The reason many people turn off this feature is because they don't want users to install external Web Parts that have not been tested or approved in their environment. Best practice is to download the Web Parts you need from the online Web Part gallery and then turn off the feature and make the Web Parts you selected available from an internal Web Part gallery from which users can upload and install Web Parts in their sites.

Scriptable Web Parts allow a developer to write code that can run within the browser of the user visiting the website. Some code can cross-reference other content that is open within a tabbed browser; however, this can create a potential breach of security. Turning off this option will prevent scripts from running from within Web Parts and will improve the security of your deployment. This option is turned off by default and should be left that way unless you have a specific reason to enable scriptable Web Parts.

Self-Service Site Creation

Most people don't think of self-service site creation (SSSC) as a security feature because it is intended to offer users a way to create new site collections without having to loop through the IT department. Poorly named as the self-service "site" creation feature, it actually enables SharePoint users to create new site collections within a defined managed path and Web application. One of the hallmarks of a highly collaborative platform is that the collaboration spaces are easily created by the users at their initiation and the transaction cost is very low. Both of these elements are true for SharePoint 2010, but SSSC is turned off by default.

When to Enable Self-Service Site Creation

Why would you want to enable SSSC for a particular Web application and not for others? This is a design decision that should be based on your business requirements for your implementation of SharePoint 2010.

For example, does your company need a Web 2.0-type of implementation in which end users can create new collaboration spaces (without approval) for their own purposes? If so, then you'll need to implement SSSC.

In most designs, portions of the overall SharePoint 2010 implementation need to be highly managed and highly regulated. For example, an industry-specific process that moves documents through various sites as part of the implementation of that process within SharePoint will (in most scenarios anyway) require those

continued on the next page

site collections to be centrally managed by IT. But other portions of the overall implementation often ask for a "sandbox" or a "playground" in which end users can create and delete their own collaboration spaces as needed. SSSC was created specifically to fulfill this need.

SSSC should be viewed as an asset and a positive step toward the overall implementation of collaboration in SharePoint 2010. Certainly, not every implementation will require SSSC, but for those who need robust collaboration driven by end users, SSSC presents a good solution that your users will enjoy.

To enable SSSC, you need to work both within Central Administration and at the site collection level. First, within Central Administration, navigate to the Security page (Security.aspx) by clicking the Security link in the left pane. On the Security page, click the Configure Self-Service Site Creation link within the General Security Group.

Figure 16-15 illustrates the default screen that you will see. Note that this security setting is applied at the Web application layer, so the first step is to select the Web application in which you which to enable SSSC. The second step is to select the On option and then select the Require Secondary Contact check box. You'll select this option if you want to force end users to enter in another account—not their own—to be a site collection owner of the site collection they are creating using SSSC. In most instances, it is a best practice to select this option because this will create two accounts in which site collection ownership efforts can be exercised. This is especially helpful when one of the two accounts (users) is away, on assignment or on vacation, and owner level activities need to be executed within the site collection, such as adding a new site collection administrator.

FIGURE 16-15 Self-Service Site Collection Management page in Central Administration

After you have executed the proper configurations within Central Administration, you are ready to start letting your users create new site collections. This process is not as intuitive as it could be, so please remember the following information.

- You don't need to activate a feature at the site collection or site level to enable SSSC for your users.

- Unlike Microsoft SharePoint Server 2007, there is no corresponding configuration at the site collection level to enable SSSC.

- SSSC will be advertised in the root site collection of the Web application through an announcement in the Announcements Web Part, with a link to the site collection creation page (Figure 16-16).

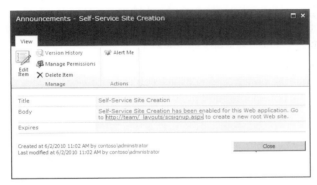

FIGURE 16-16 Self-Service Site Creation announcement

- Any site that does not have an Announcements Web Part already created will not display the SSSC link.

- For any Web application in which SSSC is enabled, you can use the following URL to create new site collections within that Web application.

```
http://<Name_of_Root_Site_Collection/_layouts/scsignup.aspx
```

What is helpful to understand is that even though there might not be a visual change for your end users when you enable SSSC for a given Web application, you can still provide the default URL directly to your users to give them the ability to create new site collections. Of course, you'll need to create the necessary managed paths within Central Administration.

NOTE One way to pass out the SSSC URL is to use a Links list and enter the URL as a new content item with a link name such as "Create A New Site" or something more appropriate for your environment and then publish this link on the home page of your root site collection for that Web application.

Securing Site Collections

The main security boundary in SharePoint 2010 is the site collection. Most of the configuration options for end users are scoped to this boundary as well. The following sections discuss what security options are available to be configured at the site collection layer as you work your way down the "stack" of layers in SharePoint 2010 (shown in Figure 16-2).

Custom Site Collection Policies

At the site collection layer, you can group different information policies together, which are then made available to list managers for use on content items within their lists. This can be useful if you have a large number of lists, each of which should be configured with the same information policy. You only have to create it once at the site collection level, and then you can apply it multiple times across multiple lists and libraries.

You can create as many site collection policies as you want—just be sure to give them descriptive names that indicate what the policy accomplishes. You can also export these policies from one site collection and import them into multiple site collections manually.

Auditing Activities in a Site Collection

Although some people will think that auditing should be included in a discussion on security, others will not, because it is merely a reporting tool that tells you what *has* happened in the site. Auditing cannot stop anyone from accessing anything to which they have permissions. Nevertheless, it is worth a brief discussion, because you can use auditing to help with compliance reports and to track chain of custody and chain of ownership for a legal dispute.

Auditing is turned on and reported at the site collection layer. The audit settings can be divided into several categories, as shown in Table 16-1.

TABLE 16-1 Audit Settings for a Site Collection

	DOCUMENTS AND LIST ITEMS	LISTS, LIBRARIES, AND SITES
Open	X	
Download	X	
Edit	X	X
Check-out/Check-in	X	
Move/Copy	X	
Delete/Restore	X	
Search		X

After you turn on auditing, especially if you are going to audit everything, be ready to see a long report, because nearly every click can be tracked in one way or another. To learn more about auditing, see Chapter 8, "Information Management Policies."

Security Trimming for Navigation

For sites that have the publishing features turned on, you have the option to turn off the security trimming of the navigation. The effect of this is that links in the navigation will appear even if the user does not have access to the sites where the links point. Security trimming for navigation is turned on by default, but in rare instances, you might want to turn it off, if for some reason it is imperative that your users see links to pages and sites to which they do not have permissions.

You can turn off this feature at the site collection level by clicking the Navigation Settings link, which will take you to the Navigation Settings page (Sitenavigationsettings.aspx).

Site Collection Administrators

It's important to distinguish between site collection administrators and site owners. The latter is a group given Full Control permissions through the local site, whereas the former is a role that has pervasive authority throughout the site collection. Those who have the site collection administrator role assigned to them have complete authority throughout the site collection. Breaking permission inheritance between sites or between a site and a list or library cannot keep out a site collection administrator.

A site collection administrator's ability to access any content in their site collection is a key reason that you'll need a number of site collections in which to host your collaboration. If you've been told that your organization can do most of their collaboration within a single site collection, don't believe it. At a minimum, each time you need a unique set of permissions at the site collection administrator layer, you'll need another site collection. Placing information in a site collection that the site collection's administrator should not see creates a security issue that can be resolved only by moving the content to another site collection or by removing those who should not see it from the site collection administrator's role.

Securing Sites

It is important for the end users in your organization to learn how to properly configure the security settings at the site level in your deployment. From a product design perspective, your nontechnical end users are the people who were meant to manage sites in SharePoint 2010. Because more and more security and site administration is being pushed to the desktop, it's important for your users to be trained well in how to administrate security at the site level.

The following sections discuss several security configurations that are applied at the site level.

Indexing Site and List Content

Security concerns itself with access to a resource. In SharePoint 2010, security can involve not only preventing access to a resource by a given set of users and/or group; it can also be used to create barriers that make finding the content more difficult. You will find that the Index Site and List Content configurations can be helpful in ensuring that a site and/or list content does not appear in the search results for SharePoint 2010.

To prevent a site from being indexed, navigate to the Site Settings link in your site and click the Search and Offline Availability link to open the Search And Offline Availability page (Srchvis.aspx). As you can see in Figure 16-17, you select the No option for the Allow This Site To Appear In Search Results configuration to ensure that the entire site's content is not indexed and will not appear in the search results.

> **IMPORTANT** Use this configuration option carefully, because if you choose not to index the content of a site, users won't be able to use the local Search feature to find local content.

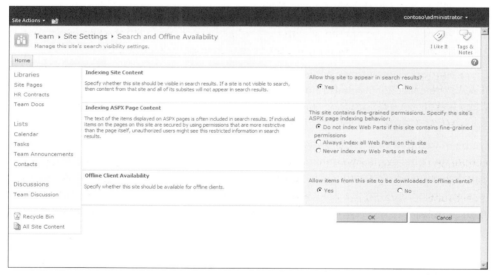

FIGURE 16-17 Search And Offline Availability page

At the list level, you can turn off indexing of individual lists by clicking the List Settings link and then clicking the Advanced Settings link. Among the various configuration options available is the setting to Allow Items From This List (Or Document Library) To Appear In Search Results. You can select either the Yes or No option (Yes is selected by default).

At both the list and the site levels (refer back to Figure 16-17), you will see the option to allow or deny Offline Client Availability. If you select the No option, the content of the site (or list) cannot be taken offline from the server. Because data breaches can occur when people unwittingly lose laptops or mobile devices while traveling or when they are otherwise not careful with information security when away from the office, disabling the offline capabilities of sensitive information provides another way to secure information in SharePoint 2010.

Site Permissions and Permission Inheritance

Site permissions and how permissions work in SharePoint 2010 are somewhat confusing topics, so the following sections simplify permissions for you, clearly illustrating what your users will need to know to successfully administer security in their sites. There are several parts to this discussion; first there is an overview of permission followed by a discussion of permission dependencies. Then you will learn about permission inheritance, followed by security groups, and then there is a discussion of using Active Directory groups in SharePoint.

Permission Overview

First, it is important to note that SharePoint only performs authorization of accounts to access resources. SharePoint does not perform authentication, which involves the creation of an access token that follows a user everywhere he goes on the network. This access token includes user's name, the groups to which he belongs, his SID, and all of the SIDs for the groups to which he belongs. SharePoint then uses this information, in concert with the SharePoint specific permissions, to authorize or deny the user's request for a given resource.

> **MORE INFO** To learn more about how Active Directory authentication works with access tokens, see the TechNet article titled "Access Control in Active Directory" at *http://technet.microsoft.com/en-us/library/cc785913(WS.10).aspx.*

In addition to any Active Directory permissions that might exist for a user, SharePoint has a base level of permissions that are unique to this product and that are assigned to users and group accounts. Before you examine how this all works, you first need to understand what the base permissions are in SharePoint 2010; these are presented for you in Table 16-2.

TABLE 16-2 SharePoint Base Permissions

PERMISSION TYPE	PERMISSION NAME	DESCRIPTION
List permissions	Manage Lists	Create and delete lists, add or remove columns in a list, and add or remove public views of a list
	Override Check-Out	Check in a document that is checked out to another user
	Add Items	Add items to lists and add documents to document libraries

continued on the next page

PERMISSION TYPE	PERMISSION NAME	DESCRIPTION
List permissions (continued)	Edit Items	Edit items in lists, edit documents in document libraries, and customize Web Part Pages in document libraries
	Delete Items	Delete items from a list and documents from a document library
	View Items	View items in lists and documents in document libraries
	Approve Items	Approve a minor version of a list item or document
	Open Items	View the source of documents with server-side file handlers
	View Versions	View past versions of a list item or document
	Delete Versions	Delete past versions of a list item or document
	Create Alerts	Create alerts
	View Application Pages	View forms, views, and application pages; enumerate lists
Site permissions	Manage Permissions	Create and change permission levels on the website and assign permissions to users and groups
	View Web Analytics Data	View reports on website usage
	Create Subsites	Create subsites such as team sites, Meeting Workspace sites, and Document Workspace sites
	Manage Web Site	Grant the ability to perform all administration tasks for the website as well as manage content
	Add And Customize Pages	Add, change, or delete HTML pages or Web Part Pages and edit the website using a Microsoft SharePoint Foundation–compatible editor
	Apply Themes And Borders	Apply a theme or borders to the entire website
	Apply Style Sheets	Apply a style sheet (.CSS file) to the website

PERMISSION TYPE	PERMISSION NAME	DESCRIPTION
	Create Groups	Create a group of users that can be used anywhere within the site collection
	Browse Directories	Enumerate files and folders in a Web site using SharePoint Designer and Web DAV interfaces
	Use Self-Service Site Creation	Create a website using self-service site creation
	View Pages	View pages in a website
	Enumerate Permissions	Enumerate permissions on the website, list, folder, document, or list item
	Browse User Information	View information about users of the website
	Manage Alerts	Manage alerts for all users of the website
	Use Remote Interfaces	Use SOAP, Web DAV, the Client Object Model, or SharePoint Designer interfaces to access the website
	Use Client Integration Features	Use features which launch client application; without this permission, users will have to work on documents locally and upload their changes
	Open	Allow users to open a website, list, or folder in order to access items inside that container
	Edit Personal User Information	Allow a user to change his or her own user information, such as adding a picture
Personal permissions	Manage Personal Views	Create, change, and delete personal views of lists
	Add/Remove Personal Web Parts	Add or remove personal Web Parts on a Web Part Page
	Update Personal Web Parts	Update Web Parts to display personalized information
	No Permissions Are Selected	Please select at least one permission

Note that these permissions cannot be broken down into more granular permissions. For example, the Add And Customize Pages site level permission includes the ability to add, delete, or change HTML pages or Web Part Pages and edit the website using a compatible SharePoint website editor. But you can't use this permission to assign someone the ability to add and change pages but not delete them. This permission can't be broken into smaller, more granular permission sets.

Now, some people might respond to this statement by saying that at the Web application layer, you can explicitly deny portions of this permission by employing the explicit Deny permission, and they would be correct. For example, you could explicitly Deny the Delete permission for a user or group of users, and then even though they might have that permission at the site collection or site level, the permission at the Web application layer would override the local permission and they would be unable to delete documents or list items.

But even at the Web application layer, you can't break down the permissions to their component parts. So the Add And Customize Pages site level permission cannot be broken down into Add, Delete, or Change permissions—it's all or nothing.

In SharePoint, these base permissions are grouped into *permission levels* that are then assigned to users and/or groups directly. Table 16-3 outlines which permissions are assigned to the more common permission levels that you'll discover in SharePoint.

TABLE 16-3 Permissions Level Assignments for the More Common Permission Levels in SharePoint 2010

PERMISSION TYPE	PERMISSION NAME	FULL CONTROL	DESIGN	CONTRIBUTE	READ	LIMITED ACCESS	APPROVE	MANAGE HIERARCHY	RESTRICTED READ	VIEW ONLY
List permissions	Manage Lists	✓	✓					✓		
	Override Check Out	✓	✓				✓	✓		
	Add Items	✓	✓	✓			✓	✓		
	Edit Items	✓	✓	✓			✓	✓		
	Delete Items	✓	✓	✓			✓	✓		
	View Items	✓	✓	✓	✓		✓	✓	✓	✓
	Approve Items	✓	✓				✓			
	Open Items	✓	✓	✓	✓		✓	✓	✓	

PERMISSION TYPE	PERMISSION NAME	FULL CONTROL	DESIGN	CONTRIBUTE	READ	LIMITED ACCESS	APPROVE	MANAGE HIERARCHY	RESTRICTED READ	VIEW ONLY
	View Versions	✓	✓	✓	✓		✓	✓		✓
	Delete Versions	✓	✓	✓			✓	✓		
	Create Alerts	✓	✓	✓	✓		✓	✓		✓
	View Application Pages	✓	✓	✓	✓	✓	✓	✓		✓
Site permissions	Manage Permissions	✓						✓		
	View Web Analytics Data	✓						✓		
	Create Subsites	✓						✓		
	Manage Web Site	✓						✓		
	Add And Customize Pages	✓	✓					✓		
	Apply Themes And Borders	✓	✓							
	Apply Style Sheets	✓	✓							
	Create Groups	✓								
	Browse Directories	✓	✓	✓			✓	✓		
	Use Self-Service Site Creation	✓		✓	✓		✓	✓		✓
	View Pages	✓	✓	✓	✓		✓	✓	✓	✓
	Enumerate Permissions	✓						✓		

continued on the next page

PERMISSION TYPE	PERMISSION NAME	FULL CONTROL	DESIGN	CONTRIBUTE	READ	LIMITED ACCESS	APPROVE	MANAGE HIERARCHY	RESTRICTED READ	VIEW ONLY
Site permissions (continued)	Browse User Information	✓	✓	✓	✓	✓	✓	✓		✓
	Manage Alerts	✓						✓		
	Use Remote Interfaces	✓	✓	✓	✓	✓	✓	✓		✓
	Use Client Integration Features	✓	✓		✓	✓	✓	✓		✓
	Open	✓	✓	✓	✓	✓	✓	✓	✓	✓
	Edit Personal User Information	✓	✓	✓			✓	✓		
Personal permissions	Manage Personal Views	✓	✓	✓			✓	✓		
	Add/Remove Personal Web Parts	✓	✓	✓			✓	✓		
	Update Personal Web Parts	✓	✓	✓			✓	✓		

Permission Dependencies

The assignment of some permissions requires the assignment of other permissions. In other words, there are some permission dependencies that need to be understood if users are to effectively manage permissions and security for their sites. What follows is an outline of the permission dependencies in SharePoint 2010.

The Open permission has no other dependencies. This permission is included in every permission level. If you give only this permission to a user account, that user (in theory) will be able to open a website, list, or library to access the items in that site or list. However, this permission only grants access to the containers. Without additional permissions on the items within the site or container, the user will be denied access to the site or container. The Open permission affects the behavior of documents that have server-side handlers, such as .xls files when Excel

Web Renderer is installed. Server-side handlers for a file type can be registered by adding a line to the Serverfiles.sml file in the SharePoint install location on the Web front-end server.

The View Pages permission, which grants the ability to view pages in a website, is dependent only on the Open permission. The combination of these two permissions will still not grant a user access to a site, because the permission to access content within the page or a list still has not been granted.

If you add the View Lists permission, which is dependent on the Open and View Pages permissions being granted, then the combination of these three permissions will grant a user access to a site, its pages, and its lists and the content items in the list. However, the combination of these three permissions is much less than is given in the View Only permission level. For example, if you combine these three permissions into a permission level that allows users to quite literally *view*—and only view—information, then they will be forced to view this information from the browser (since the ability to use remote interfaces such as SOAP or WebDav is not granted), and they will not be able to create alerts nor will they be able to view versions on the content items. If you have any application pages, under this permission set being discussed here, the user would not be able to view those pages. When viewing documents in a library, the user will see the documents and will be able to view and open them, but as you can see in Figure 16-18, the user will be able to perform limited actions on the document using the Ribbon after the document is selected. Those actions include

- E-mail a link to the document
- Download a copy of the document
- Use the Send To features
- View the document's properties
- Use the social tagging features

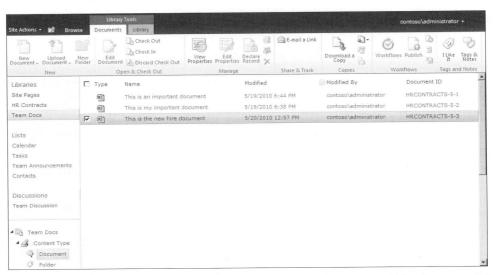

FIGURE 16-18 Viewing documents in a library with only the Open, View Pages, and View Items permissions

The View Application Pages permission is dependent only on the Open permissions, and it also requires a View Items permission before the user can access anything in a site or list. The View Application Pages is for form pages and *most* of the application pages. Specifically, it controls the application pages that inherit from the LayoutsPageBases class. This is the right that, for example, is removed from the Anonymous user when the lockdown feature in turned on, so that Anonymous users cannot open application pages. Other permission dependencies for SharePoint permissions are outlined in Table 16-4.

TABLE 16-4 Permission Dependencies

PERMISSION	DEPENDENCIES
Manage Lists	Open, View Items, and View Pages
Override Check Out	Open, View Items, and View Pages
Add Items	Open, View Items, and View Pages
Edit Items	Open, View Items, and View Pages
Delete Items	Open, View Items, and View Pages
View Items	Open and View Pages
Approve Items	Open, View Items, View Pages, and Edit Items
Open Items	Open, View Items, and View Pages
View Versions	Open, View Items, View Pages, and Open Items
Delete Versions	Open, View Items, View Pages, and View Versions
Create Alerts	Open, View Items, and View Pages
View Application Pages	Open and View Items
Manage Permissions	Open, View Items, View Pages, Open Items, View Versions, Browse Directories, Enumerate Permissions, and Browse User Information
View Web Analytics Data	Open and View Pages
Create Subsites	Open, View Pages, and Browse User Information
Manage Web Site	Open, View Items, View Pages, Add And Customize Pages, Browse Directories, Enumerate Permissions, and Browse User Information
Add And Customize Pages	Open, View items, View Pages, and Browse Directories
Apply Themes And Borders	Open and View Pages
Apply Style Sheets	Open and View Pages
Create Groups	Open, View Pages, and Browse User Information
Browse Directories	Open and View Pages

PERMISSION	DEPENDENCIES
Use Self-Service Site Creation	Open, View Pages, and Browse User Information
View Pages	Open
Enumerate Permissions	Open, View Pages, View Items, Open Items, View Versions, Browse Directories, and Browse User Information
Browse User Information	Open
Manage Alerts	Open, View Pages, View Items, and Create Alerts
Use Remote Interfaces	Open
Use Client Integration Features	Open and Use Remote Interfaces
Open	None
Edit Personal User Information	Open and Browse User Information
Manage Personal Views	Open, View Pages, and View Items
Add/Remove Personal Web Parts	Open, View Pages, View Items, and Update Personal Web Parts
Update Personal Web Parts	Open, View Pages, and View Items

For the most part, the permission dependencies are sparse, meaning that selecting one permission doesn't involve selection of a complex set of other permissions. This gives you and your site owners a great deal of flexibility in combining permissions into permission levels that are useful for a given situation. It also means that you can create permission levels that are more "lean" in what is granted to the user. You need not rely on the default permission levels if you want a more secure experience than what comes out of the box. Finally, security teams and compliance officers should be made aware of the robust and effective permissions that can be applied to accomplish a particular task in SharePoint and should have confidence that SharePoint is a secure system when configured properly.

> **IMPORTANT** There are two things that no software company—not Microsoft or Sun or Oracle or Novell or any other company—can guard against when it comes to security. No matter how well any software developers might write security features into their products, the reality is that they cannot—through technology alone—help you guard against an untrustworthy administrator and an unwise administrator. Those charged with securing information should be well trained, so that they can make good security decisions, and they should be trustworthy, so that you know they are not disseminating information to those who should not see it.

The default permission levels that are provided in SharePoint 2010 are there to enable people to be productive and to use the product's features as designed by the product team. The default groups are not there to ensure you have a highly secure experience. Instead, the groups represent the product team's assessment of general roles and responsibilities across a broad range of organizations, both in size and industry vertical. This is why, in many scenarios, you'll want to use the default groups when possible, but you should not be afraid to create new permission levels and assign them as needed to ensure that SharePoint is at the level of security needed for your environment.

Tips for Hardening a SharePoint Implementation

In most organizations, there is a healthy tension between allowing users to utilize a collaborative system like SharePoint and maintaining security at a level that meets organization and compliance requirements. Obviously, the more secure a resource is, the more effort required to access the resource. In a highly collaborative platform like SharePoint, users expect minimal effort to access the resources they need to do their jobs. So the art of hardening your SharePoint implementation involves balancing quick and painless access to resources with ensuring that the information in the farm is secured properly.

Here are some tips that you might consider when it comes to securing your SharePoint deployment.

- Recognize that not all of your SharePoint deployment will be secured at the same level or by the same people.

- Realize that some content in SharePoint will be highly secured and other content will be loosely secured.

- Since nontechnical end users are responsible for securing much of the information in SharePoint, ensure that they are well trained in how to secure their information, including the ability to create new permission levels and assign them appropriately.

Finally, if you need to provide minimum permissions to a site, take the time to look through the permission list and test a minimum set of permissions that are required to perform a particular task. For example, if browser access to content with view-only capabilities is sufficient, then you only need to grant Open, View Pages, and View Items permissions. The process of mapping minimum permission levels to user actions in SharePoint is something you and your users will learn over time and should be considered an iterative process.

Permission Level Inheritance

The site collection is the security boundary in SharePoint. Permissions within a site collection are inherited from the root site and, by default, all lists and pages inherit the same permission sets. Permissions can be broken at the site or list level so that unique permissions can be set at either level.

Note that for some templates, when the site is created, if a user chooses to use Unique Permissions, the creator is presented with a page (Figure 16-19) to create new security groups and populate them with user and/or group accounts. The Setup Groups For This Site page (Permsetup.aspx) allows you to create three new groups. But by default, the visitors group is configured to use the parent sites' Visitors group. The creator will need to select the Create A New Group option to completely sever inheritance from the parent site.

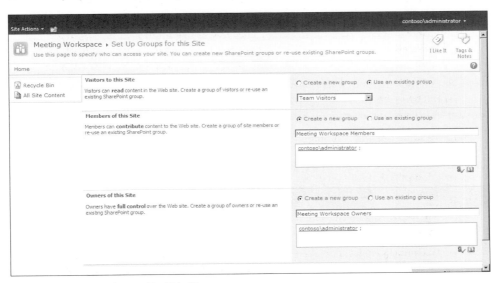

FIGURE 16-19 Set Up Groups For This Site page

The permission level inheritance is tied to user and group inheritance in SharePoint 2010. This is a change from SharePoint Server 2007, in which you could inherit or break inheritance for users and group and/or permission levels. When permission inheritance is broken, or if permissions are being assigned explicitly, as is the case for a root site of a site collection, then you'll see check boxes next to the security groups and users, but not next to the permission levels. Figure 16-20 illustrates explicit permissions for a workspace that is a subsite in a site collection. Note the check boxes next to the security groups and the reminder in the Ribbon that "This Web Site Has Unique Permissions."

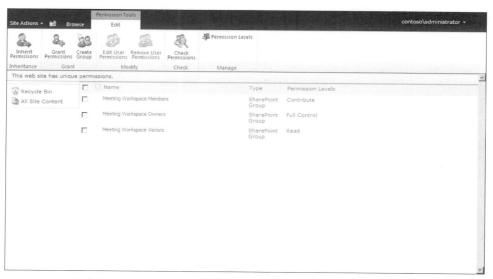

FIGURE 16-20 Explicit permissions where inheritance has been broken

Because this site is not inheriting permissions and it is a subsite in a site collection, there is an icon to Inherit Permissions in the Security Ribbon. If you click this icon and then follow the instructions on the page that displays, you can change the permissions of this site from explicitly set to inherited. Figure 16-21 illustrates this change.

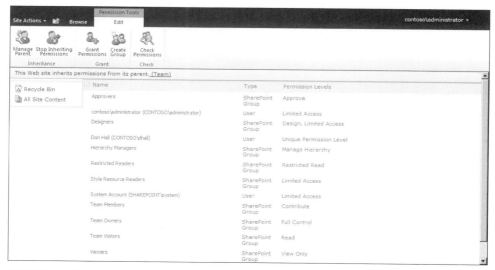

FIGURE 16-21 Site Permissions page with permission inherited

One of the more confusing aspects of inheritance is the inheritance of permission levels. On a subsite that has broken inheritance, you will see a Permissions Level icon in the Security Ribbon. When you select that icon, the Permissions Level page will display. Note that in Figure 16-22, you can see that you are inheriting permission levels, even though you have broken inheritance for the security groups. You might be tempted to look for a way to stop permission level inheritance, but you won't be able to do it through the user interface. However, permission level inheritance *can* be broken through the Object Model using custom code.

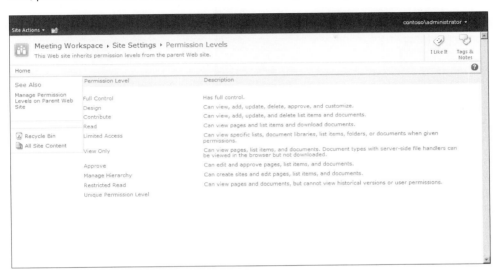

FIGURE 16-22 The Permissions Level page on a subsite that has broken inheritance

To break permissions between a site and a list, navigate to the list settings, click Permissions For This List, and then click the Stop Inheriting Permissions icon in the Security Ribbon. You can also use this same location to inherit permissions by clicking the Inherit Permissions icon in the Ribbon. These two icons—Stop Inheriting Permissions and Inherit Permissions—are context sensitive and will appear based on whether or not your site or list is inheriting permissions. For the root site in a site collection, that icon position will display a Grant Permissions icon, which you can use to grant permissions to a user or group.

Any time permissions are explicitly applied, you will see an icon labeled Check Permissions. Clicking this icon will present what is known as the "people picker" input box into which you will enter a user or group name and then click Check Now. SharePoint will show you, for the local site, all of the permissions for that user as well as how that user's permissions were obtained. Figure 16-23 illustrates the Check Permissions dialog box.

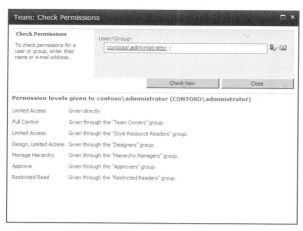

FIGURE 16-23 The Check Permissions dialog box opens when you click the Check Now button.

Groups

Groups are used to assign permission levels to multiple users or Active Directory groups in a single administrative action. SharePoint groups can be populated with other SharePoint groups, individual user accounts, and Active Directory groups. Different site templates (which are really nothing more than pre-built combinations of features) will have different default security groups. Table 16-5 lists the default groups that install with the more common site templates. Note that for most templates, you will find that only the site owners, site members, and site visitors groups will be created.

TABLE 16-5 Site Template and Default Group Matrix

GROUP NAME	PUBLISHING SITE	TEAM SITE	BLANK SITE	BLOG SITE	RECORDS CENTER	DOCUMENTS CENTER	ENTERPRISE WIKI	GROUP WORKSTIE	VISIO PROCESS REPOSITORY	BUSINESS INTELLIGENCE SITE
Approvers	✓									✓
Designers	✓									✓
Hierarchy Managers	✓									✓
Site Owners	✓	✓	✓	✓	✓	✓	✓	✓	✓	✓
Site Members	✓	✓	✓	✓	✓	✓	✓	✓	✓	✓
Site Visitors	✓	✓	✓	✓	✓	✓	✓	✓	✓	✓
Restricted Readers	✓									✓

GROUP NAME	PUBLISHING SITE	TEAM SITE	BLANK SITE	BLOG SITE	RECORDS CENTER	DOCUMENTS CENTER	ENTERPRISE WIKI	GROUP WORKSTIE	VISIO PROCESS REPOSITORY	BUSINESS INTELLIGENCE SITE
Style Resource Readers	✓									✓
Viewers		✓								✓
Contributors					✓					
Records Center Web Service Submitters For Records					✓					

The activation of some features will install additional security groups if they don't exist at the time the feature is activated. For example, a Team Site template, by default, has four groups (refer back to Table 16-5) instantiated when the site is created (assuming it is not inheriting permissions from a parent site). When the SharePoint Server Publishing Infrastructure feature is activated, these additional security groups are created. In fact, this feature essentially "installs" the following security groups (unless they already exist).

- Approvers
- Designers
- Hierarchy Managers
- Restricted Readers
- Style Resource Readers

What is interesting is that if you activate and then deactivate this feature, the security groups that were created through the feature activation process will persist past the deactivation process. SharePoint security is built in such a way that after a group is created, you must manually delete it to remove it from the site.

SharePoint groups can be populated with Active Directory users and security groups. You cannot populate SharePoint groups with other SharePoint groups or with Active Directory distribution groups. When a SharePoint group is populated with an Active Directory group, all of the nested Active Directory groups will also be granted permissions to SharePoint through the SharePoint group. The people picker in SharePoint does not enumerate nested groups for the site owner's consideration when adding an Active Directory group to a SharePoint group. This can represent a security danger because, by default, end users who are managing sites normally do not have access to Active Directory or a way to enumerate group memberships or a nested group chain in Active Directory. Best practice in this case is to purchase a third-party product that will plug into SharePoint and provide the additional security administration tools that end users need to effectively manage security for their sites.

Permission levels can be applied directly to Active Directory user or group accounts without first adding the users or groups to a SharePoint group. The base SharePoint permissions cannot be applied to either an Active Directory user or group or to a SharePoint group without first being grouped into a permission level. To assign a permission level directly to an Active Directory user or group, click the Site Actions menu and then click Site Permissions. Click the Grant Permissions icon in the Ribbon, select the Grant Users Permission Directly option (Figure 16-24), and then select the combination of permission levels you want to assign to this user and/or group.

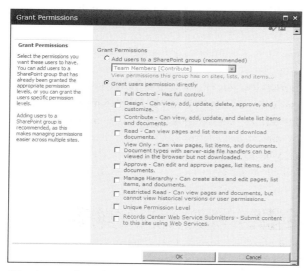

FIGURE 16-24 Grant Users Permission Directly page

To grant permissions to Active Directory users and/or groups within a SharePoint group, from the Site Permissions page, click the link of the group you want to populate and then use the people picker to find the users and/or groups you need to assign to the SharePoint group. When you have finished, those users and/or groups will have the SharePoint group's permissions to the site or list.

Using Active Directory Groups for SharePoint Security

It is common in IT teams to assume that SharePoint will be secured through the use of Active Directory security groups. Some people think that this method gives the IT department more control over who is being granted permissions in SharePoint as well as that it is easier to use an Active Directory group to assign permissions once instead of having the site owner assign the same permissions (potentially) multiple times through individual account permission assignments.

Except for those sites that have wide audiences, such as the intranet or a divisional portal, however, it is a best practice to allow site owners to populate their SharePoint groups with user accounts and not group accounts.

Securing Lists

Many of the same features for securing information at the site level apply to the list level, too. The following sections focus on those aspects of list security that are not redundant to managing security at the site level.

Although Information Management Policy Settings is a list-level security feature, there is an entire chapter on this topic, so you should refer to Chapter 8 for a review of this aspect of list security.

Content Approval

Content Approval is an advanced setting that prevents a new item in a list from appearing until the item has been approved by a user with approval rights. This setting must be enabled if you plan to use approval workflows that can be initiated with the publication of a minor version to a major version. Even in lists or libraries in which versioning is turned off, new items will still need to be approved before users with Read-Only permissions can view the content item. Figure 16-25 illustrates a document in a Pending state that has been uploaded to a library with Content Approval enabled.

FIGURE 16-25 Document in a pending state because the Content Approval feature is enabled

When the Content Approval feature is enabled, existing content items will be approved automatically. If Major/Minor versioning is also enabled, then the last major version will automatically be approved. Any existing documents that are checked out will automatically show as being Approved, but when they are checked in, they will go into a Pending state until the check-in action is approved.

The easiest way to approve a document is to click the drop-down arrow for the document and select the Approve/Reject menu item, then select the Approved option (Figure 16-26). Another way you can approve a document is to highlight it in the library and then click the Approve/Reject Ribbon icon in the Workflows section. If you need to see a list of all the documents or list items that need approval, click the Library tab in the Ribbon (for document libraries; for lists, click the List tab) and then, under Current View, select the drop-down arrow and select the Approve/Reject Items menu option. Figure 16-27 illustrates what the content approval list looks like when there are one or more items in the list.

> **IMPORTANT** Items that are in the Pending state can still be viewed by users who have permissions if they have the exact URL to the content item. The Content Approval feature, even though it is being discussed in this security chapter, is not a security feature by itself. Instead, like audiences, it is a view-crafting feature, but unlike audiences, it helps support approval workflows and the publishing of content items.

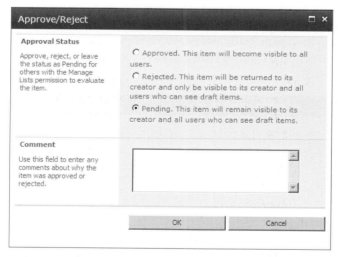

FIGURE 16-26 Approve/Reject page with comment input field

FIGURE 16-27 List of documents in a library in the Pending state

Versioning Settings

There are three types of version settings in SharePoint 2010: None, Major Only, and Major/Minor. When no versioning is selected, each time a content item is updated or uploaded into the list, it is immediately available for viewing by everyone who has at least View permissions to the list. Moreover, no version history is saved, so the only version of the content item is the current version. Because past versions are not saved, they cannot be retrieved.

Major Only versioning creates published versions each time a content item is updated or uploaded to a list or library. The main difference between no versioning and Major Only is that past versions of the content item are retained in their full-text form. But new versions are still immediately viewable and consumable by those with proper permissions.

Major/Minor versioning was first introduced in Microsoft SharePoint Portal Server 2001. It was taken out of Microsoft SharePoint 2003 and was put back into the SharePoint Server 2007 product; it has been retained in SharePoint 2010. Major/Minor versioning (M/M) allows for the development of a document or list item by a small team of content developers who then periodically publish updated versions of the document for a wider audience to consume. The versioning numbers will inform you which version of the document that you are working with. M/M versioning works with a two-numeral decimal system in which the number to the right of the decimal is the minor version and the number to the left of the decimal is the major version. For example, the version designation 0.2 means that you are on the second draft or minor version but have yet to publish a major version. The version designation 1.0 means that you have published your first major version of the document. The version designation 3.3 means that you have published three major versions, the third version is the current "public" version, and you are currently working on the third minor version, which you are using to create the fourth major version, which will be published for public consumption as 4.0.

Each time a document is published, the major versioning number will increment by one (1) and the minor version number will be reset to zero (0). Each time a minor version is checked in, the minor version number will increment by one (1), and the major version number will not increment or decrement.

The reason that M/M versioning can be viewed as a security feature is that currently published documents can continue to be viewed while updates to those documents are created in a secure, private way. You will want to use M/M versioning for documents that have public content that is updated periodically, such as a human resource policy manual, but for which you also want to hide the draft updates of those documents from public consumption.

Draft Item Security

Draft item security is only relevant when you have Major/Minor versioning enabled. Draft items are the same thing as minor versions and apply to all new documents created or uploaded into the library. Changing draft item security settings will not apply to those documents that already exist in the library.

The three settings for draft item security are

- Any User Who Can Read Items
- Only Users Who Can Read Items
- Only Users Who Can Approve Items (and the authors of those items)

The default setting is Any User Who Can Read Items, which represents a problem if you want to hide minor versions from those who would consume documents from the library with Read permissions. The entire point of Major/Minor versioning is to create publicly or widely consumed documents that can continue to be consumed from the same location in which they are also being updated. Leaving draft item security at the default setting makes the Major/Minor versioning feature somewhat useless. However, if the published document is consumed from another location, then those with Read permissions on the source location where the document is created and updated may be only those who can edit the document, too. In that scenario, the draft item security setting isn't that important, as long as the site owner controls who has Read permissions to the site and list.

Windows PowerShell Security

With STSADM and Windows PowerShell, all commands are run in the security context of the user executing the command. This means that any command can be run from any computer, but it also means that the user needs the proper permissions to run the Windows PowerShell commands. Hence, before you can create and run Windows PowerShell commands in SharePoint 2010, you must have the SharePoint_Shell_Access role on the configuration database (this is a SQL role), and you must be a member of the Windows group (on the computer you are using to execute the command) WSS_Services_Admin_WPG. To enable these permissions, use the Add-SPSShellAdmin cmdlet as shown here.

```
Add-SPSShellAdmin [-UserName] <String> [-AssignmentCollection <SPAssignmentCollection>]
[-Confirm [<SwitchParameter>]] [-database <SPDatabasePipeBind>] [-WhatIf
[<SwitchParameter.]]
```

> **MORE INFO** To learn more about how the parameters work for this cmdlet, see the Add-SPShellAdmin TechNet article at *http://technet.microsoft.com/en-us/library/ff607596.aspx*.

Because the command includes a database parameter, you'll need to give the user access to each database in which they should be allowed to run Windows PowerShell commands. By default, the Shell Admin role only gives the user access to the Configuration Database, so other database accesses must be granted manually. Keep in mind that additional permissions might be required for specific commands. For example, you might need Service Application permissions to run commands against a certain service application.

Service Application Permissions

When publishing applications between farms, you must set up permissions so that the consuming farm can consume the services of a published application in the publishing farm. The consuming farm will need permissions to the Application Discovery and Load Balancing Service Application on the publishing farm. After you set up the correct permissions, the consuming farm can be given permission to other service applications.

> **MORE INFO** The TechNet article titled "Set Permission to a Published Service Application" describes how to create service application permissions using both Windows PowerShell and the Central Administration interface. You can find this article online at *http://technet.microsoft.com/en-us/library/ff700210.aspx*.

Summary

In this chapter, you learned that permissions can be applied at various "layers" of SharePoint, including the farm, Web application, site collection, site, and list/library levels. This chapter presented a brief overview of how security works in SharePoint 2010 and offered several best practices regarding security. It also pointed you to online resources to help you configure Windows PowerShell security and service application permissions.

In the next chapter, you'll turn your attention to data protection and disaster recovery, topics that are of great interest to all SharePoint administrators.

## CHAPTER 17

Data Protection, Recoverability, and Availability

There are two primary components of disaster recovery: backup and restore procedures and redundancy. The backup and restore procedures combined with redundancy provide a foundation for disaster recovery, data protection, and business continuance for SharePoint 2010. Many organizations have backup and restore procedures but are unprepared to handle any type of disaster recovery that causes a disruption in business operations. All of the procedures you have in place for backup, restore, and continuity of operations should be thoroughly documented and assembled into a disaster recovery plan, and more importantly, these procedures should be consistently tested. Your disaster recovery plan should be considered one of the most important document sets in your organization's process library.

This chapter discusses six areas involved in keeping SharePoint running (or getting it running again quickly) through data protection, backup, and recovery operations.

- Disaster recovery and business continuity planning
- SharePoint 2010 disaster recovery tools
- Backing up SharePoint 2010 content
- Restoring SharePoint 2010 content
- High-availability options
- Ensuring a complete farm recovery

Introducing Disaster Recovery

What is disaster recovery planning? The National Association of State Chief Information Officers (NASCIO) describes it as follows.

> Disaster recovery and business continuity planning provides a framework of interim measures to recover IT services following an emergency or system disruption. Interim measures may include the relocation of IT systems and operations to an alternate site, the recovery of IT functions using alternate equipment, or execution of agreements with an outsourced entity.

This is an all-encompassing definition that succinctly outlines the steps necessary to resume Information Technology (IT) operations quickly after a catastrophic event.

Threats to the integrity of your data can be classified in three primary categories: natural, human-induced, and technological malfunctions. An example of a natural disaster is one caused by a fire, flood, earthquake, or tornado. A human-induced disaster is one caused by human error or intervention, which can be intentional or unintentional. Examples of human-induced disasters include viruses, accidental or malicious deletion or modification of information, or any other event that is directly related to human intervention and that causes an interruption of your technology infrastructure. A technological malfunction includes any software or hardware failure that is not a direct result of human error. You can probably guess that most disasters fall into either the human-induced or technological malfunction categories, and these are the main reasons you need a disaster recovery and business continuity plan.

 REAL WORLD   Ensure That It Works

It is common for an enterprise-level IT department to spend as much 25 percent of its budget on disaster recovery. Less than 50 percent of companies have a disaster recovery plan, however, and more than half of the ones that do have a plan don't conduct regular tests of its effectiveness. Honestly, a company may as well not have a disaster recovery plan if it isn't tested regularly. If a disaster occurs, you must be familiar with the steps necessary to perform an accurate and efficient recovery of each SharePoint component. Performing periodic tests of your disaster recovery plan will help you stay knowledgeable about what steps are necessary to recover from the different disaster types that can occur.

Every good SharePoint disaster recovery plan should include information about backup and restore procedures as well as redundancy, both of which will help achieve three primary disaster recovery goals: to minimize data loss, maintain data integrity, and minimize SharePoint downtime. Your backup strategy drives your restore strategy, which is what you will use to help recover your SharePoint content as efficiently as possible.

The Importance of Redundancy

A single word that summarizes the most effective solution for a SharePoint disaster recovery plan is *redundancy*. This means that you have multiple installations of all software and hardware that is utilized by SharePoint and the supporting components. Examples of multiple installations of software include

- SharePoint Web front-end (WFE) servers
- SharePoint application servers
- SharePoint Services
- SQL Server Instances
- SQL Server Database Mirroring
- Internet Information Services (IIS)
- Domain Name System (DNS)

Examples of multiple installations of hardware include

- Servers (Clustering)
- Hard drives (RAID implementations)
- Network routers and switches
- Network interface cards
- Extra power supply sources
- Extra cables

NOTE Although redundancy is used in almost all disaster recovery plans, there are some rare instances when it may not be part of the disaster recovery plan. For instance, nuclear power plants have a federal mandate to have a disaster recovery plan for operating entirely without computers.

The Role of Backups

Backups are copies of your SharePoint information that are used to replace lost or damaged information in the event of a disaster. This information includes SharePoint information stored in SQL Server databases as well as any other software that integrates with SharePoint containing information required for a successful recovery of SharePoint, such as IIS information, DNS information, Web application information, and search indexes stored on hard drives.

BEST PRACTICES   When considering the addition of third-party software, select software that doesn't require you to restore the basic functionality before you can restore any customizations to the software in the event of a disaster. The last thing you need during a disaster recovery effort is to discover that the third-party software you purchased was so deeply nested and integrated into the SharePoint platform that you couldn't restore basic functionality without restoring the third-party software. Be sure that you completely understand the backup and restore processes for all the third-party software in your environment.

The strength of your backup plan determines the steps you need to take to restore your SharePoint information during a disaster recovery, how quickly you can recover your farm, and whether there will be any loss of data.

Storing Backups

Often organizations keep a copy of backups locally to allow a speedy recovery of information after a disaster. However, the saying "location, location, location" is essential here! Remember that your three primary goals are to minimize data loss and downtime, as well as maintain data integrity. Keeping the backups in the same location as the "live" information you are using won't help in the event of a natural disaster. Therefore, you should keep another copy of the backups in a remote location. Depending on the type of natural disasters to which your area is prone, the remote location could be another area in the same building or a physical location far away from your main datacenter.

The type of media to which the information is backed up and the type of backups you use can have an impact on the amount of time it takes to recover your SharePoint information. For instance, backing up to a local network share will normally expedite both the backup and restore operations, compared to backing up or restoring from tape. However, you still may want to back up to tape (here is a good example of redundancy) so that you can ship the backup tapes to a remote location.

Types of SharePoint Backups

The types of backups you use also will affect the amount of time required to back up and restore SharePoint Information. SharePoint 2010 allows two types of backups: full and differential, both of which can be performed from within Central Administration, using Windows PowerShell, or using STSADM. Tools are discussed in the section titled "Using SharePoint 2010 Disaster Recovery Tools" later in this chapter.

You can perform a full or differential backup on the following components of SharePoint 2010.

- Entire farm
- Farm configuration information
- Service applications

- Web applications
- Content databases

A full backup contains all information within the specified SharePoint component, regardless of whether it has changed or not since the last full backup. It is a snapshot of the information within that SharePoint component. You always have to perform a full backup of the SharePoint component before performing a differential backup.

A differential backup only contains the information that has changed since the last full backup. This backup type can only be used after a full backup has been performed. A differential backup usually takes less time than a full backup, because you are only backing up the changes and not the data that hasn't changed. This reduces the amount of time that it takes to complete the backup. A differential backup can also be called a cumulative backup, because as time passes after the last full backup, more and more changes occur within SharePoint, which creates more information that needs to be backed up, which increases the backup time required.

> **BEST PRACTICES**   No matter what type of backup you perform, the backups should be performed after hours or during nonpeak hours to minimize contention between the information being accessed by the users and your backup jobs.

SharePoint 2010 introduces the ability to perform granular backups, which gives you the opportunity to create copies of site collections, sites, libraries, and lists contained in SharePoint. Granular backups do not provide the option of specifying a full or differential backup type, however; they will contain all the content, whether or not it has changed.

The method you use for your backups will determine if the backup process can be scheduled or if backups will have to be performed interactively. You may find this to be a determining factor when you are deciding which backup method to use. The section titled "Performing Backups and Restores" later in this chapter provides more information about scheduling backups.

Restores

The backups you perform regularly are created for use during the restore process. The restore process involves taking copies of the data that you have backed up and copying them to the original location to recover lost data. If there is existing data on the location, it will be overwritten during the restore process. If you lost the hard drive that contained the original information, you will copy the information from the backup to its original location on the new hard drive.

Restores also can be used to copy data to different locations if you want to share or create duplicate access points to your information. This can be helpful when sharing data between farms, or if you choose to move data from a test environment to a production environment.

SharePoint 2010 introduces the ability to perform granular restores at the site collection, site, library, and list levels. However, you cannot import data using Central Administration; this can only be done using the STSADM or Windows PowerShell command-line utilities. You can perform a second-stage Recycle Bin recovery from within Central Administration, and this provides an easy way for a site collection administrator to recover a deleted document quickly.

The restore process can be scheduled to occur at specified times, or it can be manually performed in real time, just like backups. Unlike backups, restores most often occur interactively—and they most often occur during a crisis, so it is imperative that you are completely familiar with the tools available to you for the restore process.

Your nongranular restores must occur in a specific order: the full database backup must be restored first; then you should restore your differential backups.

> **IMPORTANT** Analyze, define, and document your restore process. This will expedite the recovery of your SharePoint information and assist in achieving minimal data loss and maximum availability.

To summarize, designing a disaster recovery plan for your SharePoint information involves the use of redundancy of all SharePoint components including your data stored in your backups. The restore process is critical in disaster recovery because you are restoring the backups that contain a copy of your data, which again emphasizes the importance of redundancy in your disaster recovery plan.

Disaster Recovery Planning

Developing and implementing a SharePoint disaster recovery plan is not easy, because there are so many components integrated with SharePoint. A medium-scale or larger SharePoint Server installation has many infrastructure dependencies as well as core components like Web front-ends servers, search servers, and database servers. Nearly all of your SharePoint information is stored in SQL Server databases, but there are several other areas of concern when developing a disaster recovery plan for SharePoint. For instance, you have information stored in other applications, such as IIS and DNS, and even at the file system level. You also have to be concerned about hardware—hard drives, routers, switches, cables, and so on.

Disaster planning should also encompass the implementation of best practices to avoid or minimize the chance of a catastrophic event occurring in the first place. If you take the time to plan carefully, using a three-step process involving education, documentation, and preparation, you can build a comprehensive—and successful—disaster recovery plan that will benefit your organization in the short term and the long run.

Education

The education phase of disaster recovery planning involves the process of familiarizing yourself with all the integrated SharePoint components, so you know what you will need to do in the recovery process to minimize the disruption of your business infrastructure. Not all of the components you must be concerned with are contained within SharePoint, but because SharePoint is integrated so tightly with so many other applications, it is dependent on many of them to function.

Server Operating System

The most obvious component that SharePoint 2010 depends on is the Windows Server operating system. You should create a new operating system image of all non-database servers, and the image should contain all the service packs and patches that you have applied. You can use this image to quickly restore the operating system before SharePoint is reinstalled. However, be cautious; you should keep a different image for each farm server role, because changing the SID (Security Identifier) of a single image to create multiple SharePoint 2010 WFEs and application servers is not a recommended practice. Be sure to update your images every time you add a service pack or patch and when the SharePoint Root changes.

> **NOTE** The SharePoint Root is located at C:\Program Files\Common Files\Microsoft Shared\web server extensions\14\ and replaces the phrase 14 Hive.

You should create a network drive with all of your system images, installation sources, patches, and third-party software additions. Schedule backups for this drive at least once a week. This practice will allow you to rapidly restore the server while retaining your SharePoint 2010 farm consistency.

SQL Server

If you could back up only one server in your SharePoint 2010 farm, it would have to be your SQL Server. SQL Server contains more than 95 percent of your SharePoint information. SQL Server stores configuration information about your entire farm, the site collection content of your Web applications, your Web application settings, service application information, performance information, and several other important bits of SharePoint information.

If you aren't also the SQL Server database administrator (DBA), you should introduce yourself to the database administrator(s) who are managing the SQL Server instance or instances that are hosting your SharePoint content. Take the time to become familiar with their schedules, backup strategies, database failover options, and anything else they are willing to share with you about the SharePoint databases. You should also encourage them to collaborate with you in considering the SharePoint and SQL Server integration optimizations documented in Chapter 3, "Optimizing SQL Server for a SharePoint 2010 Implementation."

Internet Information Services

All SharePoint content is accessed through a Web service hosted by Internet Information Services (IIS). The configuration of your Web applications and application pools made from SharePoint are stored in the farm configuration database. However, any changes you make directly in the IIS Manager are not stored in the SharePoint farm configuration database; they are stored in an IIS configuration file. For instance, if you add an additional host header to a Web application using IIS Manager, it is not stored in the farm configuration database—it is stored in an IIS 7 configuration file.

The foundation of your Web application information stored in IIS is the configuration file. This is a repository for your IIS configuration information located in the directory C:\Windows\System32\inetsrv\config. This IIS configuration file is an XML file called Applicationhost.config, and you should update it only by using the IIS Manager application or the Appcmd.exe command-line tool. You should back up your IIS configuration file regularly so that you have an up-to-date version if you lose the IIS server hosting your SharePoint Web applications.

Third-Party Software

Most organizations have third-party solutions running on their SharePoint 2010 server farms. This might include backup software, Web parts, language packs, antivirus software, and custom code. Become familiar with this software and document how it is installed. Document any installation keys that are required and keep the installation media in a central location that is easily accessible during a recovery process. Be sure to reinstall any third-party Web Parts and custom code before redeploying your Web front-end (WFE) servers. Forgetting to do so on a load-balanced WFE will result in page errors and an inconsistent experience for the end user. As part of your disaster recovery planning, you should be cautious about installing products that extend the time required to recover your farm. Make third-party solutions dynamic enough to restore your farm with minimal delays.

Network Components

Since SharePoint 2010 hosts its content through a Web service and is network dependent, being familiar with all of the connection components is crucial to recovery or continuity of services. Be sure to include your network team in your disaster recovery planning process at an early stage to discuss and document all connecting pieces. The following list provides some examples of components you should discuss with your network team.

- **Switches** Redundancy, virtual LANS, Network Interface Card (NIC) teaming, port speed, duplex, dedicated backup LANs
- **Routers** Redundant paths, latency, hardware load balancing
- **Firewalls** Rules, redundancy, OS version
- **SAN (Storage Area Network)** Compatibility, capacity, speed, Host Bus Adapter
- **Cabling and electrical topology** Redundant cabling, processes for working in your raised floor, redundant power, uninterruptible power supplies, generators

Central Administration

With the exception of the SQL Server and the operating system, the server hosting the Central Administration Web application is the most important component in the recovery of a SharePoint installation. If you experience a complete loss of service, you will need to bring up the Central Administration server first and use it to re-establish connections to your SharePoint databases. You can use your Central Administration server Web application console to access the Backup And Restore user interface (UI), or optionally, use the STSADM or Windows PowerShell command-line tools. You can restore this server from a system image or by using the Windows Server Backup utility. After completing your restores, be sure to verify that your SharePoint installation–specific services are running using Central Administration.

Web Front-End Servers

In an out-of-the-box SharePoint 2010 implementation, Web front-end servers (WFEs) are stateless servers, meaning that they don't track client access, and any WFE can serve your SharePoint data. This eases restoration of a WFE by allowing you to install the application binaries and then connect to an existing SQL Server configuration database. The SQL Server configuration database populates any required information on the WFE to serve SharePoint content. The exception to this is when you are customizing Web application content. As an example, many WFEs will have branded images, custom pages, excluded managed paths, Web Parts, and specialized authentication mechanisms. All of these must be reinstalled after a WFE system rebuild, which reinforces the need to carefully document customized environments.

Search Server

If your indexes are not large, rebuilding the index after a system image restore is an efficient way to return current search and query functionality. Alternatively, you can reinstall SharePoint to an existing farm and enable it as a Search server in Central Administration. Conversely, if your index sizes are measured in gigabytes or terabytes, you will want to back up your indexes so they can be restored, providing a reasonably timed return to service. If you don't back up large content indexes, your search results can be incomplete for hours or even days, depending on the size of your content sources and the speed of your hardware.

MORE INFO A good source for more information about Search servers and indexing is the *Microsoft Office SharePoint Server 2007 Best Practices* (Microsoft Press, 2008).

Service Applications

You can use any of the SharePoint disaster backup tools to back up your service applications, or you can perform a full farm backup that includes all service applications. Don't forget that the flexibility of SharePoint 2010 allows for an easy reinstallation of your service applications should one of them fail. Also, if your organization relies heavily on a particular service application, you may benefit from having multiple instances of that service application hosted on your farm.

Documentation

Documentation ensures that you have identified and defined the remedies necessary to recover all components of your SharePoint farm. There are two categories of documentation: the SharePoint-dependent items and SharePoint component documentation. The SharePoint-dependent items you need to document include all dependent software, hardware, and network components supporting your SharePoint installation.

You also should document all SharePoint-specific components, including Central Administration settings, search and index settings, WFE, and service application settings. By documenting the SharePoint components and their dependencies, you will be able to recover your entire SharePoint farm or a subset of the farm. Organizations that document and prepare for disaster can swiftly react and stay operational after any type of catastrophe.

You should have detailed installation documentation that defines every setting and keystroke required to completely rebuild each server. Document every nuance of your servers, including items like WFE SharePoint Root customizations, and you won't have to worry about missed configuration options and forgotten software when rebuilding servers. Create a separate document for each server and include all relevant hardware information—the server name, BIOS and backplane versions, network interface cards, RAID controllers, and so on. Documenting your hardware configuration makes it easier to troubleshoot, download correct drivers, and effectively communicate with technical support in the event of failure.

You should also document all service packs, hotfixes, antivirus programs, and other software additions. When you have servers in a load-balanced cluster, it is very important that all machines have an identical configuration. If months have passed since a server build and you haven't documented additions, you will almost certainly forget a Web Part or similar piece of software when you have to restore the server. This sort of omission can create an inconsistent, negative user experience that can be very difficult to troubleshoot.

> **BEST PRACTICES**   Have your disaster recovery documents backed up to a source that is readily accessible and easily restored in the event of a disaster.

If you have your documentation stored only on your SharePoint site and SharePoint fails, you will not be able to use this documentation. Store hard copies of all of your disaster recovery documents onsite and offsite. In addition, versioning your server documentation can be an invaluable aid for rolling back changes when patches or third-party software affect usability and performance. You'll find more information in the section titled "Versioning" later in this chapter.

After you have thoroughly documented your farm installation, continually update your server documents. This creates a "living" document set that is always current, and it will be worth all the time it took to keep it current when you need the documents for restoring services. Create an appendix in your server documentation with version history and note the reason for changing your specific installation. If possible, verify any changes you make with your peers.

 ON THE COMPANION MEDIA Use the Disaster Recovery Template on the companion media as a guide to completing your organization's disaster recovery plan.

SharePoint-Dependent Documentation

This category should contain all of the information that you discovered during your meetings, lunches, and water-cooler conversations with network and SQL Server administrators and is specific to those components that are outside of SharePoint but are required for SharePoint to function. Have the administrators of your network and SQL Server create the documentation for items in this category to make sure it contains everything necessary to recover from a disaster.

OPERATING SYSTEM

Because there are several versions of operating systems in widespread use, you must document your specific installation, and keep the installation media easily available as well. Update your documentation whenever you apply service packs, patches, hotfixes, and any other changes or additions to the operating system to ensure that it is consistent on all servers in the farm.

SQL SERVER

Document the version of SQL Server you are using, along with the service packs, patches, hotfixes, and so on that have been applied to your SharePoint SQL Server instance or instances. Also, if you are performing SQL backups of your SharePoint databases, document the backup strategies and methods you are using, the backup schedule, and the location of backup copies, as well as any other information that will help you quickly recover your SharePoint databases.

INTERNET INFORMATION SERVICES

Document any modifications made to your Web applications through IIS Manager. Also document your backup schedule and the location of the IIS backups.

After talking to the administrators of these systems and becoming familiar with how they are integrated with SharePoint, you should identify any scheduled outages, such as maintenance windows, that you need to take into account during the planning stage for disaster recovery. Your disaster recovery plan will only be as good as the weakest link, so don't forget to involve the stakeholders early and convince your peers that a good disaster recovery plan is a solid investment.

SharePoint Component Documentation

This category of documentation contains the information specific to SharePoint, and it focuses on the different components within SharePoint. Your source for SharePoint component information should be your SharePoint farm administrators, who are the best people to write and maintain this critical documentation.

CENTRAL ADMINISTRATION

It is important to completely document the installation of all servers, but especially your Central Administration Web application server. This document should be secured and only be accessible to farm administrators. It should contain the following information.

- Farm account name and password
- Farm passphrase specified during initial creation of farm
- Port number of Central Administration
- SQL Server server name
- SQL instance name on SQL Server
- SQL Server account name and password
- Configuration database name
- Location of binaries (if not the default)

WEB FRONT-END

The following is a list of items that must be documented to successfully back up and restore a customized WFE.

- IIS Configuration
- Customized authentication software
- TCP ports on Web applications and extended Web applications
- IIS excluded managed paths and associated content
- Centrally located repository for IIS configuration backups
- SSL certificate backups

- IIS Logs at %SystemRoot%\system32\LogFiles\w3svc<IIS Virt Server ID>
- Web Parts installed into the Global Assembly Cache (GAC)
- Customized code located in the SharePoint Root

SEARCH SERVICE

Document your file index locations, the backup schedule for these indexes, and the location of these backups. Also be sure to include a list of the database names, the backup schedule for the search databases, the backup method, and the location of backup copies.

SERVICE APPLICATIONS

Document application service configuration information, associated Web application information, and database names, as well as the backup schedule, method, and location of the backups.

Preparation

Preparation involves testing the identified remedies that you established in the documentation process so that when a disaster occurs, you will know exactly what steps to take to recover from it—and you know how long it will take to accomplish the recovery.

Having a plan that won't work is of little use, so it makes sense to execute a simulation of your disaster recovery plan often, making sure to coordinate with your peers and stakeholders. Executing a disaster recovery plan on a production farm is generally a bad idea, but you can test the plan on secondary server farms and on system image restores in a development environment. If your organization has the resources to build a lab with a mock-up of your production environment, you can use it to test your disaster recovery plan. To minimize costs and overhead, a mock-up environment can be simulated using a virtual environment.

When you are testing your disaster recovery plan, try to test the plan with real-world scenarios involving Search server failures, SQL content database corruption, IIS corruption, network card failures, hard drive failures, and any other common issues you might face. This will provide you with valuable knowledge about how to bring back a failed SharePoint farm.

Many disaster recovery plans adequately cover all hardware, software, and system components, but leave out what may be the most important part of the equation—you and your associates. As an example, if the network administrator is on vacation when a disaster occurs, you may be able to quickly restore your SharePoint 2010 server farm, but it will be of little value if the network is still down. Make sure you and the other system administrators have a list of all administrators. This list should include shift schedules, home and cell phone numbers, vacation schedules and contact information, and any other relevant information you may need to round up the personnel you will need to implement your plan for restoration of service. Having this information available also will help make sure that you are meeting the defined service level agreements (SLAs) for your clients.

It is no accident that after major disasters large banks and brokerage firms do not lose data: their disaster recovery plans are well documented and carefully executed when needed. It is nearly impossible to execute a disaster recovery plan successfully if you do not know all of the dependencies in your environment, haven't accurately documented the steps required to perform disaster recovery at different levels, and haven't tested the success of your disaster recovery plan. Education, documentation, and preparation: remember that these are the three steps to creating a disaster recovery plan that will allow your organization to recover quickly and efficiently when calamity strikes.

But don't just file away that great plan you've created after you've finished testing it. You have to keep it current and viable. Perform tests monthly to remain familiar with exactly what has to be completed to recover any level of your SharePoint farm.

Using SharePoint 2010 Disaster Recovery Tools

SharePoint 2010 provides several tools to assist in backing up and restoring your SharePoint content, and you will use a combination of them for complete protection. Test each tool available to you within your environment and see what combination of tools works best with your disaster recovery plan.

This section discusses the following tools and provides information on how and when to use them.

- Versioning
- Two-stage Recycle Bin
- Central Administration
- Windows PowerShell
- STSADM
- SQL Server
- Read-only content databases
- Unattached content databases

Versioning

The most common method for restoring corrupted content is achieved with versioning functionality, which is available in all libraries in SharePoint 2010. This functionality is disabled by default, but after enabling it, you can restore a previous version of a document from within that library as shown in Figure 17-1. Versioning is your first line of defense against data corruption and user changes. Versioning can consume a lot of disk space, however, so be sure to take advantage of either automatic or manual version pruning, as discussed in Chapter 15, "Administering Web Content Management and Publishing."

Also be aware that if a user has the ability to modify a document, he can also delete it. Versioning does not protect content; it only preserves history by creating copies of content each time it is saved. If a document is deleted, it must be recovered from the Recycle Bin.

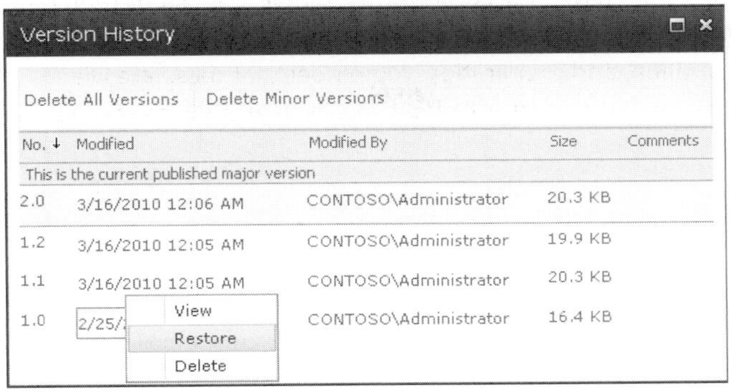

FIGURE 17-1 Restoring to a previous document using versioning

The Two-Stage Recycle Bin

For a user, the deletion of a document can be a disaster. Beginning with Windows SharePoint Services 3.0, Microsoft provided an out-of-the-box Recycle Bin solution that allowed users and administrators to recover deleted items, essentially eliminating the need for a third-party solution. The SharePoint Recycle Bin should be your first choice for restoring deleted files, and it is the easiest of the tools available for recovering content.

Microsoft SharePoint Foundation 2010 includes a two-stage, first-in/first-out Recycle Bin that allows for a second level of retention before content is permanently deleted from the system. By default, after a user deletes an item and then empties their user-level Recycle Bin, the items are retained in the second stage Recycle Bin for 30 days. Security trimming is used to provide each user with their own Recycle Bin view that displays the content that they have deleted from that site. A user can recover any of the following deleted items from the Recycle Bin.

- Documents
- List items
- Lists
- Document libraries

In addition to the end-user Recycle Bin, site collection administrators have access to a global view of the Recycle Bin (see Figure 17-2) that includes items deleted by all of the end users and allows the administrator to recover items that have been deleted by other users without affecting the value in the Modified By column. This is useful for those instances in which the original user is unavailable but content needs to be recovered. Also available to administrators is the second-stage Recycle Bin, where documents that have been deleted from the users' Recycle Bins are stored, so they still can be recovered by a site collection administrator.

FIGURE 17-2 A site collection administrator's second-stage Recycle Bin view

Administrators can access both Recycle Bin views by navigating to the Site Settings page for the top-level site in the site collection and then clicking the Recycle Bin link in the Site Collection Administration section. Only the second-stage Recycle Bin can be configured directly. The first stage can only be modified by the global Recycle Bin settings at the Web application level and can be configured within Central Administration. To do this, you would click Application Management, select Manage Web Applications, and then click the name of the Web application you want to modify. Finally, select General Settings from the drop-down menu accessible from the General Settings icon located on the Ribbon, as shown in Figure 17-3.

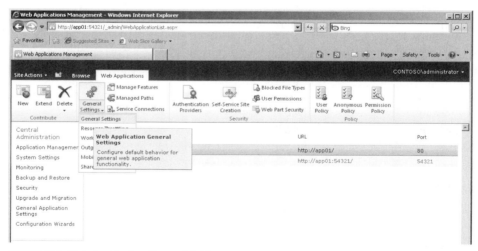

FIGURE 17-3 Web Application General Settings

By default, both the first and second stages of the user Recycle Bin retain deleted items for 30 days before automatically purging the items. Because this is a global setting, items do not expire to the second-stage bin; they are *expunged*. The only time an item enters the second stage is when a user or administrator empties the first stage. The second-stage limit is based on a ratio of the site collections storage quota rather than a set period of time. By default, the second stage of your Recycle Bin is limited to 50 percent of your site quota, but you should lower the value of this setting to fit your storage needs. You may think that raising this quota makes sense, but carefully consider before making the value higher, because incorrect stage configurations can waste large volumes of disk space. Figure 17-4 shows the settings you can modify for the second-stage Recycle Bin.

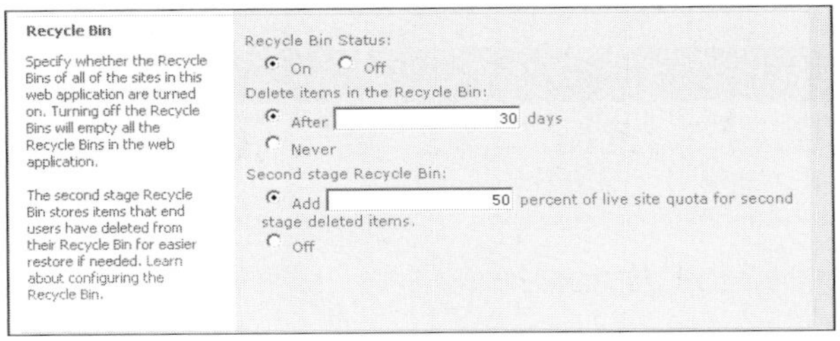

FIGURE 17-4 Second-stage Recycle Bin configuration options

The second-stage bin's capacity is in *addition* to the current site collection quota. Therefore, if you were planning for 100-gigabyte (GB) content databases using these default settings, they could reach 150 GB in size if you leave the default size of the second stage set at 50 percent (refer back to Figure 17-4). Also, if you do not enable Site Quotas, there is no limit on the Recycle Bin's second-stage storage capacity. If this is set in conjunction with clearing the time-based expiration setting, deleted items are retained indefinitely.

Keep in mind that your site collection administrators have the ability to permanently delete objects in site collections. With this in mind, be sure to choose site collection administrators for your critical sites carefully and provide all site collection administrators with adequate training.

If you encounter a shortage of disk space and need to recover some disk storage quickly, you can disable the second-stage Recycle Bin. This will cause all Recycle Bins to be emptied immediately and will release the disk space used by those Recycle Bins. The only way to recover any items that were in the Recycle Bin prior to disabling that functionality, however, is to perform a restore from a database backup or unattached content database.

Central Administration

The SharePoint 2010 Central Administration Backup And Restore interface shown in Figure 17-5 gives you the ability to perform several types of backups and restores, including

- Entire farm
- Farm configuration only
- Service applications

- Web applications
- Content databases
- Site collections
- Sites
- Lists and libraries

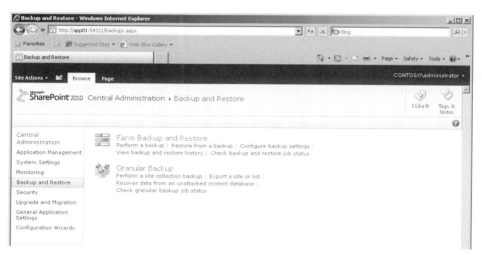

FIGURE 17-5 The Central Administration Backup And Restore interface

This additional functionality removes the burden from your SQL Server administrators and gives the SharePoint administrators more control over the backups of their SharePoint information from farm level down to list or library level. This is also the tool primarily used during the recovery of a database, whereas Windows PowerShell or STSADM are often used to backup SharePoint information because they can be scripted. This is because the Central Administration Backup And Restore interface is used during the recovery of a database, because this action often requires flexibility in performing the proper restore operations, depending on which restore operations need to be performed. Alternatively, Windows PowerShell commands or STSADM are often used to back up SharePoint information because they can be scripted and therefore scheduled to run at specified times.

You can also change the location of the file backups using the Backup And Restore user interface. However, if you need to change this location at a later time, be sure to leave your original backup location available for the length of time required to meet your SLAs. If you need to restore from a previously created backup source, change the location when viewing the Backup And Restore history.

Windows PowerShell

The SharePoint 2010 Management Shell provides you with a more flexible and dynamic way to perform backups and restores of your SharePoint information. Windows PowerShell also allows you to perform several types of backups and restores, including

- Entire farm
- Farm configuration only
- Service applications
- Web applications
- Content databases
- Site collections
- Sites
- Lists and libraries

SharePoint 2010 introduces its own set of Windows PowerShell snap-ins to extend the core functionality of Windows PowerShell by including SharePoint providers and SharePoint commands.

Information technology (IT) administrators are equipped with the tools necessary to have complete control and automation of system administration tasks, thereby increasing their productivity. The SharePoint 2010 Management Shell is a new command-line shell and task-based scripting technology that includes an intuitive scripting language specifically designed for IT administration. Windows PowerShell for SharePoint 2010 includes numerous system administration utilities with consistent syntax and naming conventions, as well as improved navigation of common management data such as the registry, certificate store, or Windows Management Instrumentation (WMI).

There are more than 300 Windows PowerShell for SharePoint cmdlets (pronounced "command-lets") available immediately when you install SharePoint 2010. The SharePoint 2010 Management Shell is the recommended command-line interface for SharePoint administration and is expected to replace STSADM.

The Windows PowerShell cmdlets also provide additional functionality not available in Central Administration such as backup file compression and SQL Snapshots, which provide the option to restore data to an earlier point in time.

Getting Help with Windows PowerShell SharePoint cmdlets

Because there are so many cmdlets to remember, you may need some help to keep track of what all of them can do for you. Use the following steps to create a text file that contains a list of the SharePoint-specific cmdlets.

1. Open the SharePoint 2010 Management Shell.

2. Type in the following command.

```
Get-command -noun sp* | out-file C:\SharePointCmdLets.txt
```

If you want additional information on a specific SharePoint cmdlet, you can use one of the following Windows PowerShell commands.

- For example syntax on a specific cmdlet:

    ```
    get-help cmdletname -examples
    ```

- For detailed information on a specific cmdlet:

    ```
    get-help cmdletname -detailed
    ```

- For technical information on a specific cmdlet:

    ```
    get-help cmdletname -full
    ```

These commands are not case sensitive. However, the spacing within the command and the parameters must be precise. For instance, you cannot type a space in the parameter *–full*. Make sure there is no space between *–* and *full*.

You'll find more information in Chapter 5, "Using Windows PowerShell to Perform and Automate Farm Administrative Tasks," and Chapter 12, "Using Windows PowerShell to Manage Search Services and FAST Search."

STSADM

The STSADM command-line utility also provides functionality to perform backups of the same components as Windows PowerShell does. If you are familiar with STSADM from SharePoint Server 2007, you can use STSADM commands until you become familiar with Windows PowerShell. You must be a member of the Administrators group on the local computer to execute the STSADM command, and you have to drill down into the SharePoint Root directory to execute the STSADM command. The SharePoint Root directory is located at C:\Program Files\Common Files\Microsoft Shared\Web Server Extensions\14\BIN.

> **NOTE** Alternatively, you can add the directory to the system environment variable path by following these steps.

1. Click Start, point to All Programs, select Control Panel, select System And Security, select System, and then click Advanced System Settings.

2. On the Advanced tab, click Environment Variables.

3. Under System Variables, select the variable Path and click Edit.

4. Add the following to the end of the Variable Value field.

```
;C:\Program Files\Common Files\Microsoft Shared\web server extensions\14\BIN
```

You must include the leading semicolon since the *Path* environment variable uses a semicolon as the delimiter between directories.

5. Click OK.

After accessing this directory or adding the directory to the *Path* system variable, you can issue STSADM backup commands to perform your backups and restores; you can also use STSADM to accomplish several other administrative tasks for SharePoint 2010. Generally, you can perform the same tasks using STSADM or Windows PowerShell cmdlets. However, Windows PowerShell cmdlets are more powerful and tend to be more efficient than STSADM commands.

You can use the STSADM command-line tool for a few other functions that are not available in Central Administration, including backup file compression and SQL Snapshots, which provide the option to restore data to an earlier point in time. Again, these functions are also available by using Windows PowerShell cmdlets.

> **BEST PRACTICES** Use either the Windows PowerShell or STSADM command-line utilities for backup and restore functions. These two options provide you with the ability to script your backups, and then you can schedule the scripts to run at specified times using Scheduled Tasks in Control Panel. This eliminates the need to interactively log into the graphical interface to perform your backups and restores.

SQL Server Backups

You can also have SharePoint information backed up by your SQL Server administrators or backup operators from within SQL Server. You may find this method useful if you have a SQL Server database administrator (DBA) who is responsible for all company content. Similar to performing SharePoint backups, SQL Server backups can be performed using a graphical user interface called SQL Server Management Studio, shown in Figure 17-6, or by using a Transact-SQL (T-SQL) BACKUP DATABASE command. T-SQL backups can be scripted and scheduled to run at specified times, similar to using Windows PowerShell and STSADM for backups.

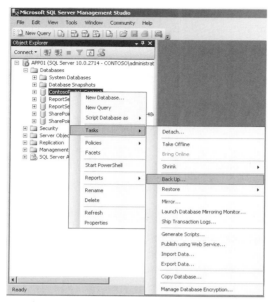

FIGURE 17-6 The SQL Server 2008 Studio Management backup interface

You have several different options available when backing up your SharePoint information from within SQL Server. Often only a SQL Server DBA will completely understand these options and can leverage them to streamline your SharePoint backups. Some of these SQL Server specific options include

- Create a copy of the database without affecting the scheduled database backup
- Set an expiration date for the backup
- Perform a transaction log backup
- Verify the integrity of the backup on completion
- Create a checksum on backed-up data to verify that data has not been tampered with after being backed up

Read-Only Content Databases

SharePoint 2010 introduces the capability of recognizing content databases that have been set to read-only in SQL Server. This can be helpful during a disaster recovery to prevent changes from being made to the content during the recovery. After changing a content database to read-only, all users (including SharePoint administrators) are prevented from making any changes to the information contained within the site collections stored in the read-only database.

> **IMPORTANT** This procedure is for content databases only and should not be set on the SharePoint configuration, Central Administration, or search databases.

The procedure to set the database to read-only can be performed using either SQL Server Management Studio or a T-SQL ALTER DATABASE statement. However, you must be a member of the SQL Server db_owner fixed database role for each database that you want to set to read-only.

The SQL Server read-only feature can be helpful in the following scenarios. (Each is discussed in further detail later in this chapter.)

- Disaster recovery
    - Mirrored databases
    - Log-shipping databases
- High availability
    - SharePoint patching
    - Mirrored databases

As you can see in Figure 17-7, even though the user is logged in as a SharePoint administrator, there are no commands available within Site Actions that allow the user to modify the site after the database is set to read-only. Also, the documents or list items contained within the content database cannot be modified.

FIGURE 17-7 SharePoint site actions when a database is set to read-only

Creating a Read-Only Farm for Disaster Recovery

SQL Server read-only content databases that allow you to create an entire read-only farm as part of your disaster recovery environment are something new to SharePoint 2010. The read-only farm also can be part of a highly available maintenance, patching, or upgrade environment by providing users access to the read-only content while the production farm is being updated. In a read-only farm, all your SQL Server content databases are set to read-only by your SQL DBA. All other databases including the configuration database, Central Administration content database, and search database, still have read/write access.

The following changes will be apparent to a user who accesses a read-only site.

- Most tasks that require writing to the content database are not available, because they are no longer available in the user interface, or because the user is no longer allowed to apply changes.
- All tasks that do not require writing to the content database are fully functional.
- Some tasks that do write to the content database appear to be available but will return errors when the user attempts to write to a read-only database.

Unattached Content Databases

SharePoint 2010 introduces the capability to access databases that are available in SQL Server but aren't currently part of the farm. This allows you to perform granular restores of SharePoint content using SharePoint. It eliminates the need to perform an alternate farm restore, which was required to perform granular recoveries in SharePoint Server 2007. Accessing unattached content databases will allow SharePoint administrators to connect to read-only content databases, restored SharePoint content databases, and content database snapshots. You are able to restore site collections, sites, libraries, and lists from these unattached content databases.

Using the interface shown in Figure 17-8, you can browse the contents of the database and retrieve any content you need to recover. After you export the content, simply import the content to the appropriate container within SharePoint.

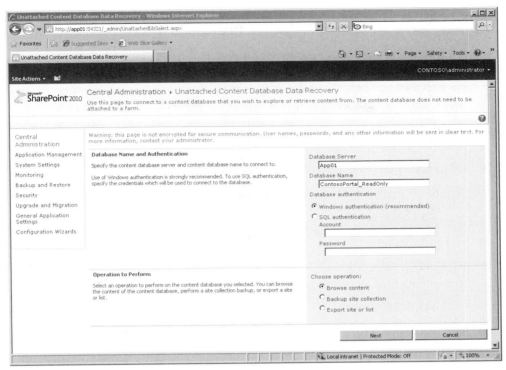

FIGURE 17-8 The Unattached Content Database Data Recovery interface

Performing Backups and Restores

In the following sections, you will learn how to perform backups and restores in SharePoint 2010 using Central Administration or the command-line tools; you will also learn how to back up and restore SharePoint 2010 using Windows PowerShell or STSADM. In addition, there is information about how to troubleshoot your backups and restores in the event you have problems with them. SharePoint 2010 includes the backup and restore options that were in previous versions and introduces several new options that allow you to perform SharePoint backups and restores at a more granular level. For more information, refer to the sections titled "The Role of Backups" and "Restores" earlier in this chapter. For information about the tools available, refer to the section titled "Using SharePoint 2010 Disaster Recovery Tools" earlier in this chapter.

Using Central Administration

The Central Administration user interface is the easiest way to perform a backup or restore operation. The backup and restore utilities are divided into two sections within the Backup and Restore interface: Farm Backup And Restore and Granular Backup. From the Farm Backup And Restore section, you can

- Start a new backup or restore job
- Configure backup settings
- View the backup or restore job history
- View the status of the backup or restore jobs currently running

New in SharePoint 2010, you can perform more granular backups at the site collection, site, list, and library level using Central Administration, from the Granular Backup section of the Backup And Restore interface. Use this interface to perform the following tasks.

- Start a site collection backup
- Export a site or list
- Recover data from an unattached content database
- Check the status of a currently running granular backup job

The Central Administration Backup And Restore utility does has some limitations that should be noted.

- It does not allow backups or restores to be scheduled.
- It does not allow more than one Web application or service application to be backed up at the same time without performing an entire farm backup.
- It does not allow you to make backups directly to tape.

IMPORTANT Restore operations can be performed only at the same level as the backup; as a result, the lowest level that you can restore with this tool is an individual list or library.

Although it is not possible to make a backup directly to an external tape device using this interface, you can move the backup files to tape or another external device as a separate step when the backup is complete. In fact, you should make a copy of the backup files using this technique whenever possible, because it adds another layer of protection by providing you with backup copies that can be stored offsite.

As with the Backup and Restore tools provided with Microsoft SharePoint Server 2007, you can back up to either a local or network drive using either Central Administration or the command-line tools. However, the location you specify for backups must be available to your WFEs and SQL servers, so often a network drive is required when the farm scales beyond a single server.

The backup process automatically creates subfolders in the specified location for each subsequent backup, with the exception of granular backups—no folder is created during a granular backup; instead, the backup file is created in the actual directory specified.

You can specify the location of the file backups when using the Backup And Restore user interface. However, if you need to change this location at a later time, be sure to leave your original backup location available for the length of time required to meet your SLAs. If you need to restore from a previously created backup source, change the location when viewing the Select Backup To Restore page.

If you are performing a backup to a file share, the following accounts require Change and Read share permissions on the target file share, and all NTFS security permissions are required, with the exception of Full Control.

- The account authenticated to Central Administration when using the UI
- The logged-on account when manually running Stsadm.exe
- The Run As account when scheduling scripted backups in Control Panel
- The Central Administration pool account in Internet Information Services
- The SQL Server account, if Local System is the SQL service account
- The SPTimer service account, if using the Central Administration UI (which is by default the same account used by the Central Administration App Pool)

Using Windows PowerShell

SharePoint 2010 introduces Windows PowerShell as the recommended command-line tool for managing your SharePoint farm backups and restores.

Your SharePoint 2010 disaster recovery plan will most likely include Windows PowerShell commands for scripting and automating your backup commands. For faster restore operations, you should also script your restore commands. Every backup and restore option available in the Central Administration Backup And Restore interface is also available using SharePoint 2010 Management Shell. In fact, the SharePoint 2010 Management Shell includes some options for backing up and restoring your SharePoint content that aren't available within Central Administration, including compression and the use of SQL snapshots discussed later in this chapter in the section titled "Site and Subsite Exports."

You can use Windows PowerShell for SharePoint 2010 to back up and restore SharePoint components manually or as part of a script that can be run at scheduled intervals. To use Windows PowerShell, you must be a member of the Administrators group on the computer that is running Microsoft SharePoint 2010 Central Administration.

If you do not use the *–Verbose* parameter with your backup commands, the Windows PowerShell command prompt window will not display any message—unless the operation fails. If the backup fails, you will receive a message similar to the one shown here.

```
Backup-SPFarm: The backup job failed. For more information, see the error log that
is located in the backup directory. At line: <line> char:<column>. + <cmdlet> <<<<
<location of error>
```

To assist in troubleshooting any SharePoint backup job that fails, generates errors, or generates warnings, review the Spbackup.log located in the Backup directory that you specified in the backup command. To troubleshoot any SharePoint restore job that fails, generates errors, or generates warnings, review the Sprestore.log located in the BackupShare folder from which you are restoring the backup.

When you perform SharePoint backup operations, a plain-text log file called Spbackup.log is created in the destination of your backups, as shown in Figure 17-9. You can view this log file to troubleshoot your backups.

Additionally, when you perform restore operations, a plain-text log file called Sprestore. log is created in the location of the backup you are restoring, and you can view it to troubleshoot your restore operations.

FIGURE 17-9 Sample Spbackup.log file

Similar to when you make a backup using Windows PowerShell, if you don't use the –*Verbose* parameter with your Windows PowerShell restore commands, the Windows PowerShell command prompt window will only display a message if the operation fails. If the restore operation fails, you will receive a message similar to the one shown here.

```
Restore-SPFarm: The job failed. At line: <line> char:<column>. + Restore-SPFarm <<<<
<Error Message>
```

Table 17-1 contains a list of the Windows PowerShell cmdlets and the associated SharePoint components that can be controlled using the corresponding cmdlet.

TABLE 17-1 Windows PowerShell Backup and Restore cmdlets

CMDLET	SHAREPOINT COMPONENT
Backup-SPFarm	Entire farm
	Service applications
	Web applications
	Content databases
Restore-SPFarm	Entire farm
	Farm configuration only
	Service applications
	Web applications
	Content databases
Backup-SPConfigurationDatabase	Farm configuration only
Backup-SPSite	Site collection
Restore-SPSite	Site collection
Export-SPWeb	Sites
	Subsites
	Libraries
	Lists
Import-SPWeb	Sites
	Subsites
	Libraries
	Lists

You can use the Windows PowerShell Backup and Restore cmdlets from within the SharePoint 2010 Management Shell or from within a script to perform a backup or restore operation. You use different cmdlets to perform backups and restores, depending on what level of a backup or restore you want. For instance, for a farm level backup, use the Backup-SPFarm cmdlet, but if you want to create a site collection backup, use the Backup-SPSite cmdlet. For a list of the backup and restore cmdlets, see Table 17-1.

Using the Backup-SPFarm and Restore-SPFarm cmdlets

The Backup-SPFarm and Restore-SPFarm cmdlets are used to perform backups and restores on the following SharePoint 2010 components.

- Entire farm
- Service applications
- Web applications
- Content databases

There are several parameters available when using the Backup-SPFarm and Restore-SPFarm cmdlets. These parameters and their uses are listed here.

- **–Directory <UNC path>** Specifies the (UNC) path of the backup folder. The UNC path should be created on a server in the same domain, with share and security permissions as previously defined. A unique directory beginning with SPBRnnnn will be created for each backup operation.

- **–ConfigurationOnly** Backs up site customizations only.

- **–ShowTree** Primarily used to identify single items that you want to back up, but this parameter is also useful for accessing a comprehensive view of your server farm. Be aware of the following indicators when viewing the results of the *–ShowTree* parameter.

  - Items between square brackets [ ] cannot be selected.
  - Items that have an asterisk * next to them are not selected to be backed up.

- **–Item** Indicates the name of the farm component, content database, service application, or Web application that you want to back up or restore. Type **Backup-SpFarm –ShowTree** to display a list of all farm components so that you can determine the exact name of the component. You can use the full farm path name as displayed from the *–ShowTree* option or just the name of the component if it is unique. Be sure to place double quotation marks around any items or paths that contain spaces.

- **–Percentage** Controls the granularity of on-screen feedback as the operation progresses. (If you are scheduling the script to run, this parameter will be of no value to you.) Supply a value between 1 and 100 to indicate at what percentage of the job you want the status information to appear. The default is 5, which means that an updated status display will appear as every 5 percent of the backup job completes.

- **–Force** Used to force the operation to complete.

> **NOTE** The Backup-SPFarm and Restore-SPFarm cmdlets also support all of the common parameters, such as *Verbose*, *Debug*, *ErrorWarning*, *ErrorAction*, and so on. To retrieve additional information on these common parameters, use the following command.

```
Get-help about_commonparameters
```

There are also some parameters that are specific to either the backup or restore cmdlets operations.

PARAMETERS SPECIFIC TO THE BACKUP-SPFARM CMDLET

The following parameters are specific to the Backup-SPFarm cmdlet.

- **–BackupMethod <Full | Differential>**   At least one full backup must first be performed before a differential backup can be performed on a new farm, database, Web application, or service application. Also, the most recent differential backup is required when restoring content.

- **–BackupThreads**   If you have a large implementation and require significant throughput on your backups, this option can increase the amount of processing time allocated to backups. Be careful; increasing this value on a production server can degrade the quality of service experienced by the end user. You can specify a value between 1 and 10, and the default is 1.

PARAMETERS SPECIFIC TO THE RESTORE-SPFARM CMDLET

The following parameters are specific to the Restore-SPFarm cmdlet.

- **–RestoreMethod <New | Overwrite>**   To restore to a different farm, such as a recovery farm, use the *New* parameter. To restore to the same farm, use the *Overwrite* parameter. If you use the *Overwrite* option, you will be prompted to confirm that you want to overwrite the existing data.

- **–RestoreThreads**   If you have a large implementation and require significant throughput on your backups, this option can increase the amount of processing time allocated to backups. Be careful; increasing this value on a production server can degrade the quality of service experienced by the end user. You can specify a value between 1 and 10, and the default is 1.

- **–BackupID**   This parameter is used to specify the globally unique identifier (GUID) of the backup that is to be restored. If you don't specify a *BackupID*, the most recent backup is restored. If you need to retrieve the *BackupID*, you can do so using the following command:

```
Get-SPBackupHistory -Directory <Backup folder> -ShowBackup [-Verbose]
```

You can view actual commands using Backup-SPFarm and Restore-SPFarm cmdlets in the section titled "Sample Windows PowerShell Backup and Restore Commands" later in this chapter.

Using the Backup-SPConfigurationDatabase cmdlet

SharePoint 2010 introduces the much-needed ability to back up and restore the farm configuration database. The configuration database backup operation creates a backup file containing the following farm configuration information extracted from the farm configuration database.

- Antivirus settings
- Information rights management (IRM)
- Outbound e-mail settings (only restored when performing an overwrite)
- Customizations deployed as solutions
- Diagnostic logging
- Workflow

This backup operation can be run regardless of whether or not the configuration database is currently attached to the farm. You can use this backup and restore process in the following scenarios.

- Move configurations from a test or development environment to a production environment.
- Move configurations from a stand-alone installation to a farm environment.
- Configure a farm to serve as part of a standby environment.

The following are some of the most common parameters used with Backup-SPConfigurationDatabase to back up your farm configuration

- **–Directory <UNC path>**   Specifies the (UNC) path of the destination backup folder. The UNC path should be created on a server in the same domain, with share and security permissions as previously defined.

- **–DatabaseCredentials**   Specifies the password for the administrator username for the SQL Server configuration database. This is only necessary if you are performing a backup of the database from an account that does not have the SQL Server db_backupoperator fixed database role.

- **–DatabaseName**   Specifies the administrator username for the SQL Server configuration database in the format of *domainname\username*.

- **–DatabaseServer**   Specifies the server where the SQL Server configuration database resides.

The following is an example of using Backup-SPConfigurationDatabase command.

```
Backup-SPConfigurationDatabase -Directory <Backup folder> -DatabaseServer <Database
server name> -DatabaseName <Database name> -DatabaseCredentials <PowerShell Credential
Object>
```

Using the Restore-SPFarm cmdlet to Restore Only Farm Configuration Information

In SharePoint 2010, you do not have to restore the configuration database, because you have the ability to restore the farm configuration directly. You can restore the farm configuration from a backup that used either the Backup Content And Configuration Settings option or the Backup Only Configuration Settings option.

To restore a farm configuration, use the Restore-SPFarm cmdlet in a command similar to the one shown here.

```
Restore-SPFarm –Directory <RestoreShare> –RestoreMethod Overwrite –ConfigurationOnly
```

You must use the –*ConfigurationOnly* parameter for this restore to complete successfully.

You can view actual commands using the Backup-SPConfigurationDatabase and Restore-SPFarm cmdlets in the section titled "Sample Windows PowerShell Backup and Restore Commands" later in this chapter.

Using the Backup-SPSite and Restore-SPSite cmdlets

SharePoint 2010 allows you to back up and restore site collection information using both Windows PowerShell and STSADM. Backing up a site collection using Windows PowerShell provides a method for automated scripting and scheduling capabilities.

The following are the parameters available for use with the Backup-SPSite cmdlet to perform a site collection backup.

- **–Identity**   A valid URL (including the http portion) of the site collection that you want to back up.

- **–Path**   A valid location and file name of the backup file that will contain the backed-up site collection.

- **–Force**   Indicates to overwrite an existing file if the file name associated with the *Path* parameter already exists.

- **–NoSiteLock**   Specifies that the site collection is not set to read-only during a site collection backup. Using this parameter can lead to possible data corruption during the backup process. Use the default behavior of the *Sitelock* option to avoid the chance of data corruption. If there aren't users accessing the site collection, you can safely specify this switch.

- **–UseSQLSnapshot**   Uses the content database snapshot when performing the backup.

In addition to these Backup-SPSite options, the Restore-SPSite cmdlet also has a set of parameters that you should be familiar with when restoring a site collection.

- **–GradualDelete**   Helps improve performance during the restore process if the site collection that you are restoring is 1 GB or larger. It will mark the site collection as deleted to prevent further access, and a SharePoint Timer job will gradually delete the data in the site collection instead of deleting the entire site collection at once; this way, it does not impact users accessing content in other site collections contained in the same database.

- **–DatabaseServer**   Specifies the server where the content database resides.
- **–DatabaseName**   Specifies the content database name. Use this parameter if you want to specify what content database you want the site collection restored in; otherwise, SharePoint will decide what content database it will be stored in.

To restore a site collection, use the Restore-SPSite cmdlet in a command similar to the one shown here.

```
Restore-SPSite -Identity <Site collection URL> -Path <Backup file>
```

You can view actual commands using the Backup-SPSite and Restore-SPSite cmdlets in the section titled "Sample Windows PowerShell Backup and Restore Commands" later in this chapter.

Using the Export-SPWeb cmdlet

SharePoint 2010 allows you to back up sites, subsites, libraries, and lists using both Windows PowerShell and STSADM command-line tools. Performing a granular backup of these components using Windows PowerShell provides a method for automated scripting and scheduling capabilities.

The following parameters are available with the Export-SPWeb cmdlet to perform these granular backups.

- **–Identity**   A valid URL (including the http portion) or GUID of the site, list, or library that you want to export. Alternatively, you can use the Get-SPWeb cmdlet and pass the ID to Import-SPWeb using the pipeline.
- **–Path**   A valid location and file name of the backup file that will contain the exported SharePoint component.
- **–Force**   Indicates to overwrite the existing export file if the file name associated with the *Path* parameter already exists.
- **–IncludeUserSecurity**   Retains the user security settings.
- **–ItemUrl**   Specifies the URL of the SharePoint component being exported.
- **–HaltOnWarning**   Stops the export process when a warning occurs.
- **–HaltOnFatalError**   Stops the export process when an error occurs.
- **–NoLogFile**   Prevents the generation of an export log file.
- **–IncludeVersions**   Indicates which type of file and list version history is included in the export operation. The version types include the following.
  - LastMajor of all files and list items (default)
  - CurrentVersion refers to the current version, either last major or minor

- LastMajorAndMinor refers to the last major and list minor version of files and list items
- All includes all versions of files and list items
  - **–NoFileCompression** Disables file compression of the export file. If this parameter is used during the export, it must also be used during the import.

You cannot use SQL Server or Data Protection Manager (DPM) to export a site, library, or list. If you receive any errors, you can review them in the Failure Message column of the Backup and Restore Job Status page in Central Administration. You can also find additional details in the *<file name>*.export.log file at the UNC path that you specified in the *Path* option of the Export-SPWeb command.

Using the Import-SPWeb cmdlet

Although you can use Central Administration, Windows PowerShell, or STSADM to execute an export command, you can also use Windows PowerShell or STSADM to import data. You can import a site, library, or list from a backup of the current farm, a different farm, or from a read-only database after it has been attached in SQL Server. Importing lists or libraries is one method you can use to restore, move, or copy items or documents from one farm to another. However, you cannot import a site, list, or library from one version of SharePoint to another. For instance, you could not import content that had been exported from SharePoint Server 2007 into SharePoint 2010.

The Import-SPWeb cmdlet uses most of the same parameters as the Export-SPWeb cmdlet, except that the *IncludeVersions* options are replaced with *UpdateVersions*, which offers the following three choices.

- **Append** Appends incoming content to existing content (default).
- **Overwrite** Overwrites existing content.
- **Ignore** Does not perform any action.

You can import a site, library, or list by using the Import-SPWeb cmdlet in a command similar to the one shown here.

```
Import-SPWeb –Identity <List or Library ID> –Path <Export filename>
```

You can view actual commands using the Export-SPWeb and Import-SPweb cmdlets in the next section, "Sample Windows PowerShell Backup and Restore Commands."

Sample Windows PowerShell Backup and Restore Commands

The following are examples of different Windows PowerShell commands you can use to back up and restore various components of your SharePoint environment.

 ON THE COMPANION MEDIA The following sample commands are also included on the companion media within the file SharePointPowerShellBackupandRestoreCmdlets.txt.

- The following Windows PowerShell commands can be used perform a complete farm backup followed by a restore.

```
Backup-SPFarm -Directory \\App01\SharePointBackups -BackupMethod Full

Restore-SPFarm -Directory \\App01\SharePointBackups -RestoreMethod New
```

- The following Windows PowerShell commands can be used to back up and restore a service application.

```
Backup-SPFarm -Directory \\App01\SharePointBackups -BackupMethod Full -Item "Excel
Services"

Restore-SPFarm -Directory \\App01\SharePointBackups -RestoreMethod New -Item
"Excel Services"
```

- The following Windows PowerShell commands can be used to back up and restore farm configuration information only.

```
Backup-SPConfigurationDatabase -Directory \\App01\SharePointBackups

Restore-SPFarm -Directory \\App01\SharePointBackups -RestoreMethod Overwrite
-ConfigurationOnly
```

- The following Windows PowerShell commands can be used to back up and restore your SharePoint content databases.

```
Backup-SPFarm -Directory \\App01\SharePointBackups -BackupMethod Full -Item
ContosoPortal

Restore-SPFarm -Directory \\App01\SharePointBackups -RestoreMethod New -Item
ContosoPortal
```

- The following Windows PowerShell commands can be used to back up and restore a site collection.

```
Backup-SPSite -Identity http://App01/Sites/ContosoPortal -Path \\App01\
SharePointBackups\PortalSiteCollection.bak -Force

Restore-SPSite -Identity http://App01/Sites/ContosoPortal -Path \\App01\
SharePointBackups\PortalSiteCollection.bak -Force
```

- The following Windows PowerShell commands can be used to export and import a subsite, list, or library.

```
Export-SPWeb -Identity http://App01/Sites/ContosoPortal/ -Path \\App01\
SharePointBackups\SharedDocuments.bak -Itemurl "Shared Documents" -Force

Import-SPWeb -Identity http://App01/Sites/ContosoPortal/ -Path \\App01\
SharePointBackups\SharedDocuments.bak -Force -IncludeUserSecurity
```

Using STSADM

SharePoint 2010 still supports the use of Stsadm.exe for managing your backups. Although the recommended command-line tool for managing your SharePoint farm backups and restores is now Windows PowerShell, STSADM has been enhanced to support all new backup and restore functionality supported in SharePoint 2010. Similar to Windows PowerShell, you can script and schedule STSADM commands to perform backups. Use STSADM commands until you have time to learn the Windows PowerShell commands for SharePoint that perform backup tasks. The backups that you perform using STSADM can be restored using Central Administration or Windows PowerShell.

Your SharePoint 2010 disaster recovery plan can include Windows PowerShell or STSADM commands that can be used to back up and restore your SharePoint content. All backup and restore options available in the Central Administration Backup And Restore interface are also available using STSADM. In fact, similar to Windows PowerShell, STSADM commands provide some additional functionality for performing backups and restores of SharePoint information that aren't available within Central Administration.

STSADM backups can be grouped into two categories: catastrophic backups and site collection backups. Catastrophic backups are identified by backup commands that include the *–BackupMethod* parameter and can be used to back up most everything in SharePoint, including the entire farm, Web applications, service applications, and your content databases. Site collection backups are backups that you perform for a specific site collection, indicated by specifying the *–Url* parameter when issuing the STSADM backup command.

The following is an example of a STSADM farm level backup in its simplest form.

```
stsadm.exe -o backup -directory \\backupservername\backups\ -backupmethod full
```

Catastrophic Backups

Backing up SharePoint information using STSADM provides a method for automated scripting and scheduling capabilities. It will also prevent SPTimer job errors and assure that your backups won't fail. The following are some of the most common parameters used with STSADM commands to perform catastrophic backups.

- **–Directory <UNC path>** The UNC path should be created on a server in the same domain, with share and security permissions as previously defined.
- **–BackupMethod <Full | Differential>** At least one full backup must be performed on a new farm or when adding a new Web or service application before you can make a differential backup. You must use the most recent differential backup when restoring content.
- **–Item** This parameter allows the backup of a single SharePoint component. You must enter information exactly as it exists or the backup will fail. The following is an example of how to use the *–Item* parameter if you want to back up a portal that is a Web application you want to back up.

  ```
  stsadm -o backup -directory \\backupservername\backups -backupmethod full  -item
  "Farm\Windows SharePoint Services Web Application\Portal"
  ```

- **–Percentage** The *–Percentage* parameter controls the granularity of on-screen feedback as the operation progresses. If you are scheduling the script to run, this is of no value.

- **–BackupThreads** If you have a large implementation and require significant throughput on your backups, this parameter can increase the amount of processing time allocated to backups. Be careful; increasing this value on a production server can degrade the quality of service experienced by the end user. By default the number of –BackupThreads is 1, the recommended number is 3, and the maximum number is 10.

- **–ShowTree** The *–ShowTree* parameter is primarily used to define single items that you want to back up, but it is also useful to access a comprehensive view of your server farm.

- **–ConfigurationOnly** This parameter will back up farm configuration information only.

- **–Quiet** Use this parameter to suppress output.

- **–Force** This parameter overwrites content at the destination if a file with the same name already exists.

Catastrophic Restores

You use restore commands to retrieve information from your backups that will replace the content databases that are currently in SQL Server.

You do not need to change anything in your backup procedure if you plan to do a restore, because by default the same source media is used during the restore operation that was used during the backup operation. The following parameters are used when restoring content to your farm.

- **–Directory <UNC path>** Specifies the directory that contains the backup data you want to restore.

- **–RestoreMethod <Overwrite | New>** Using overwrite restores content over existing data, and all the original content is lost. The *New* option allows you to restore information to a different location than where the backup was performed.

- **–BackupID <ID from backuphistory>** The ID information you need to use this parameter can be found with the following command.

```
stsadm.exe –o backuphistory –directory <UNC path> -backup
```

- **–Item** Restores a single SharePoint component.

- **–Percentage** Shows the granular process status of the restore procedure.

- **–RestoreThreads** If you have a large implementation and require significant throughput on your restores, this option can increase the amount of processing time allocated to the restore process.

- **–ShowTree** Shows the content that is available for restores.

- **–SuppressPrompt**   Uses the current user name and password for user name/password prompts.
- **–Username**   Specifies a user name for a Web application process account.
- **–Password**   Specifies a password for a Web application process account.
- **–NewDatabaseServer**   Specifies the name of a new database server to which you will restore your backup when you are restoring content from one database server to a different database server.
- **–Quiet**   Suppresses output.

Site Collection Backups

Backing up site collection information using STSADM provides a method for automated scripting and scheduling capabilities. The parameters are available when using Stsadm.exe for site collection backups.

- **–Url**   Specifies a valid URL (including the http portion) of the site collection that you want to back up.
- **–FileName**   Specifies a valid file name and the location of the backup file that will contain the backed-up site collection.
- **–OverWrite**   Indicates that the backup should overwrite the existing file if the file name already exists.
- **–NoSiteLock**   Specifies that the site collection lock is not set to read-only during a site collection backup. Using this parameter can lead to possible data corruption during the backup process.
- **–UseSQLSnapshot**   Uses the content database snapshot when performing the backup.

Site Collection Restores

Restoring site collections using STSADM provides a method for automated scripting and scheduling capabilities. The following parameters are available when using Stsadm.exe for site collection restores.

- **–Url**   Specifies a valid URL (including the http portion) of the site collection that you want to back up.
- **–FileName**   Specifies a valid file name for the backup file that will contain the backed-up site collection.
- **–OverWrite**   Indicates that the restore should overwrite the existing file if the file name already exists.
- **–HostHeaderWebApplicationURL**   Used when restoring a Web application.
- **–GradualDelete**   Marks the site collection as deleted to prevent further access while a SharePoint Timer job called Job-gradual-site-deletion deletes the data in the site collection gradually.

Site and Subsite Exports

Exporting sites and subsites using STSADM provides a method for automated scripting and scheduling capabilities. The following are the most common export parameters available when using Stsadm.exe to export sites or subsites.

- **–Url**   Specifies a valid URL (including the http portion) of the site that you want to export.
- **–FileName**   Specifies a valid file name for the backup file that will contain the exported site.
- **–OverWrite**   Indicates that the export should overwrite an existing export file if it already exists.
- **–IncludeUserSecurity**   Retains the user security settings.
- **–HaltOnWarning**   Stops the export process when a warning occurs.
- **–HaltOnFatalError**   Stops the export process when an error occurs.
- **–NoLogFile**   Prevents the generation of an export log file.
- **–Versions**   Indicates which type of file and list version history is included in the export operation. The version types include the following.
    - 1 = Last major version for files and list items (default)
    - 2 = Current version, either last major or minor
    - 3 = Last major and list minor version for files and list items
    - 4 = All versions for files and list items
- **–NoFileCompression**   Disables file compression of the export file.
- **–Quiet**   Suppresses the output of export progress.
- **–UseSQLSnapshot**   Use the content database snapshot when performing the export operation.

Site and Subsite Imports

Importing sites and subsites using STSADM provides a method for automated scripting and scheduling capabilities. The following are the parameters that are available when using Stsadm.exe for site collection imports.

- **–Url**   Specifies a valid URL (including the http portion) of the site that you want to import.
- **–FileName**   Specifies a valid file name of the backup file that contains the imported site.
- **–IncludeUserSecurity**   Retains the user security settings.
- **–HaltOnWarning**   Stops the export process when a warning occurs.

- **–HaltOnFatalError** Stops the export process when an error occurs.
- **–NoLogFile** Prevents the generation of an export log file.
- **–ActivateSolutions** Activates all solutions found during import.
- **–IncludeUserCustomActions** Allows the following options for how to handle custom actions found during import.
  - 1 = Ignore User Custom Actions
  - 2 = Include User Custom Actions
- **–Versions** Indicates which type of file and list version history is included in the export operation. The version types include the following.
  - 1 = Add new versions to the current file (default)
  - 2 = Overwrite the file and all its versions
  - 3 = Ignore the file if it exists on the destination
- **–NoFileCompression** Disables file compression of the export file.
- **–Quiet** Suppresses the output of export progress.

Sample STSADM Backup and Restore Commands

The following are examples of different STSADM commands you can use to back up and restore various components of your SharePoint environment.

 ON THE COMPANION MEDIA These commands are included on the companion media within the file SharePointStsadmBackupandRestoreCommands.txt.

- The following STSADM commands can be used to perform a full farm backup followed by a restore.

```
stsadm -o backup -url http://app01/ -directory \\app01\sharepointbackups
-BackupMethod Full -Quiet

stsadm -o restore -url http://app01/ -filename \\app01\sharepointbackups
-Overwrite
```

- The following STSADM commands can be used to back up and restore configuration information only.

```
stsadm -o backup -url http://app01 -directory \\app01\sharepointbackups
-configurationonly -quiet

stsadm -o restore -url http://app01 -filename \\app01\sharepointbackups
-configurationonly -quiet
```

- The following STSADM commands can be used to back up and restore a service application.

```
stsadm -o backup -directory \\app01\sharepointbackups -quiet -backupmethod full
-item "Excel Services"

stsadm -o restore -directory \\app01\sharepointbackups -item "Excel Services"
-quiet
```

- The following STSADM commands can be used to back up and restore a site collection.

```
stsadm -o backup -url http://app01/portalsitecollection -filename \\app01\
SharePointBackups\portalsitecollection.bak -overwrite

stsadm -o restore -url http://app01/portalsitecollection -filename \\app01\
SharePointBackups\portalsitecollection.bak -overwrite
```

- The following STSADM commands can be used to export and import a subsite, list, or library.

```
stsadm -o export -url http://app01/sites/contosoportal/Shared%20documents
-filename \\app01\sharepointbackups\SD.bak -quiet -overwrite

stsadm -o import -url http://app01/sites/contosoportal/Shared%20documents
-filename \\app01\sharepointbackups\SD.bak -quiet
```

Example of Performing a SharePoint 2010 Farm Backup and Restore

Typically, you will schedule your backups during off-peak hours using a script containing Windows PowerShell or STSADM commands. During a disaster recovery, you can use Central Administration to restore the backups that were generated by these scripts. This section demonstrates the use of Windows PowerShell to perform a farm backup, followed by an explanation of how to complete a Central Administration farm restore from the backup created using Windows PowerShell.

Performing a Farm-Level Backup Using Windows PowerShell

To begin, create a Windows PowerShell script .ps1 file containing the following command:

```
Backup-SPFarm -Directory \\App01\SharePointBackups -BackupMethod Full
```

This command is issued from the Central Administration server of your SharePoint farm, and it will perform a backup of all of your SharePoint information including all farm configuration information, databases, Web applications, and service applications. The *-Directory* parameter indicates that the network share called SharePointBackups on server App01 is where the folder should be created that will contain the files from this backup operation. The *-BackupMethod* parameter value *Full* indicates that you are backing up all SharePoint farm information.

When the command completes, you will see a directory located in the SharePointBackups directory with a name similar to spbr0000. The 0000 counter will increase in increments of 1 as you perform future backups.

Using Central Administration to Restore Your Windows PowerShell Backup

You can use Central Administration to restore the backup you created using Windows PowerShell by following these steps.

1. In Central Administration, in the Backup And Restore section of the Home page, click Restore From A Backup.

2. On the Restore From Backup – Step 1 Of 3: Select Backup To Restore page, select the backup job from the list of backups that contains the farm backup, as shown in Figure 17-10, and then click Next.

> **NOTE** If the correct backup job does not appear in the list, enter the UNC path of the correct backup folder in the Backup Directory Location text box and then click Refresh.

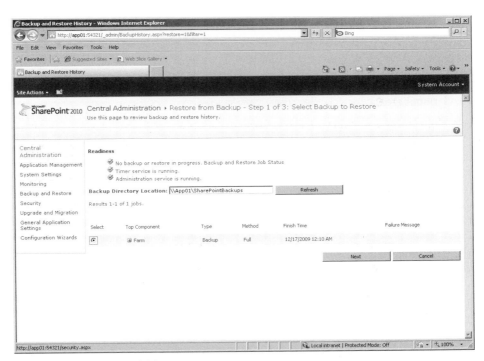

FIGURE 17-10 Backups available to restore

3. On the Restore From Backup – Step 2 Of 3: Select Component To Restore page, select the check box next to the top-level component that you want to restore, as shown in Figure 17-11, and then click Next.

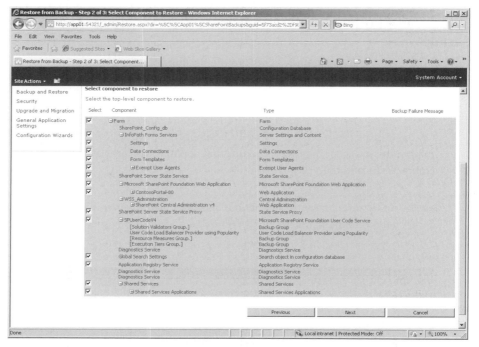

FIGURE 17-11 Farm components available to restore

4. On the Restore From Backup – Step 3 Of 3: Select Restore Options page, in the Restore Component section shown in Figure 17-12, ensure that Farm is the selection that appears in the Restore The Following Content list. In the Restore Only Configuration Settings section, ensure that the Restore Content And Configuration Settings option is selected. In the Restore Options section, select the Type Of Restore option. Use the Same Configuration option to restore the entire farm to the same server. Choose the New Configuration option to restore the entire farm during a disaster recovery or are migrating the farm to a different location. If you select the Same Configuration option, a dialog box will appear that asks you to confirm the operation. Click OK.

> **NOTE** If the Restore Only Configuration Settings section does not appear, the backup that you selected is a configuration-only backup. You must select another backup.

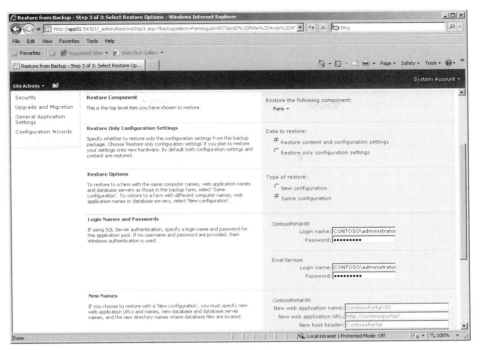

FIGURE 17-12 Selecting the type of restore to perform

5. Click Start Restore.

6. You can view the general status of all recovery jobs in the Status section at the top of the Backup And Restore Status page, as shown in Figure 17-13. You can also view the status for the current recovery job in the Restore section in the lower part of the page; the status displayed there automatically updates every 30 seconds. Alternatively, you can update the status details manually by clicking Refresh. If you receive any errors, you can review them in the Failure Message column of the Backup and Restore Job Status page. You can also find more details in the Sprestore.log file at the UNC path that you specified earlier in the Backup Directory Location text box.

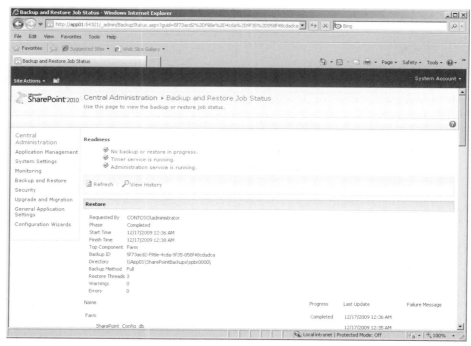

FIGURE 17-13 Restore job status

Using SQL Server for Backups and Restores

SharePoint information also can be backed up and restored by your SQL Server DBAs or by anyone who is a member of the SQL Server db_backupoperator fixed database role for that database. This method is often utilized when there is a SQL Server DBA who is responsible for all company data. SQL Server DBAs can perform backups and restores using SQL Server Management Studio or using the T-SQL BACKUP DATABASE and RESTORE DATABASE commands. A T-SQL backup also can be scripted and scheduled to run at specified times.

There are several additional options available when performing a backup from within SQL Server that often only a SQL Server DBA will completely understand; the DBA may be able to leverage these options to streamline the restore process, manage the backups, and ensure the integrity of the data. Some of these SQL Server specific options include

- Creating a copy of the database without affecting the scheduled database backup
- Setting an expiration date for the backup
- Performing a transaction log backup
- Verifying the integrity of the backup on completion
- Creating a checksum on backed-up data to verify that data was not tampered with

High-Availability Options in SharePoint 2010

SharePoint 2010 continues to support the high-availability options included in SharePoint Server 2007 and also introduces new options for increasing high availability of your SharePoint information. In the section titled "The Importance of Redundancy" earlier in this chapter, you learned how critical having multiple copies of important data can be in disaster planning, and as you create your backups, you are creating copies of your data. In this section, you will learn how SharePoint 2010 leverages redundancy to increase high availability by using some of the most popular underlying SQL Server technologies, including failover clustering, database mirroring, log shipping, and read-only databases. The following high-availability options are supported in SharePoint 2010.

- SQL database mirroring, both asynchronous and synchronous
- SQL Server log shipping
- Combined database mirroring and log shipping
- Read-only databases
- SQL Server failover clustering

The high-availability tools introduced in this chapter are specific to SQL Server 2008; a simple overview of them is provided here.

> **MORE INFO** For additional information about SQL Server high-availability options, you can refer to the SQL Server 2008 Books Online. If you are using SQL Server 2005, refer to the SQL Server 2005 Books Online for steps to configure the options for that version of SQL Server.

SQL Database Mirroring

SharePoint 2010 leverages SQL Server's high-availability technologies, such as database mirroring, to achieve high-availability architecture for SharePoint. In SharePoint 2010, you can specify a failover database for each content database using SharePoint Central Administration, Windows PowerShell, or STSADM.

Database mirroring maintains two copies of a single database that must reside on different SQL Server instances. Typically, these SQL instances reside on different computers. The SQL Server instance hosting the database that clients access is called the *principal server*. The second SQL Server instance, called the *mirror server*, contains a copy of the database on the principal server. The mirror server can be configured to act as a warm standby server and improve performance but not provide high availability, or it can provide high availability, but with a slight performance degradation. A mirroring session can only have one principal server and one mirror server. There are two types of mirrored sessions that can be configured; these are asynchronous and synchronous.

Asynchronous Database Mirroring

When SQL Server mirroring is configured in asynchronous mode, it is operating in high-performance mode. Under asynchronous operations, the transactions commit without waiting for the mirror server to write the log to disk, which improves performance. The mirror server tries to keep up with the log records sent by the principal server. However, the mirror database may experience some latency behind the principal database. When the principal server experiences a problem, the mirror server is only available as a warm standby database server, and there is a chance of some data loss because all transactions haven't been written to the mirror server in asynchronous mode.

Synchronous Database Mirroring

When SQL Server mirroring is configured in synchronous mode, it is operating in high-safety mode, which provides high availability. All the committed transactions from the principal database server are guaranteed to be written to disk on the mirror server. This process begins by performing an initial synchronization from the principal database to the mirror database. To ensure that the data on the two servers remains consistent, the active log from the principal database server is sent to the mirrored database server and applied to that server with minimal latency between the changes made on the principal database and mirrored database. This provides rapid failover without loss of data from committed transactions

The name of the database on both the mirror and principal server must be exactly the same for synchronous database mirroring to occur properly, and you must use Full Recovery mode on the databases.

To implement automatic failover, the session must have a third SQL server instance, the witness, which ideally resides on a third computer and simply monitors the principal server for connectivity. If the witness server discovers that the principal database server is unavailable for more than 15 seconds (by default), and there is still connectivity between the witness and mirror, then the mirror database server performs an automatic failover.

Mirroring has advantages over log shipping, since it is a function of the SQL Server engine and can provide synchronous replication. Database mirroring is more expensive and complex, since it requires three SQL Server instances when configured in synchronous mode.

SQL Server Transaction Log Shipping

SQL Server log shipping allows you to automatically send transaction log backups from a primary server database, often your production server, to one or more secondary database servers. These secondary servers can be used as hot standby servers as well as read-only content servers for generating reports. The primary server database transaction log backups are automatically shipped to each of your secondary database servers. Optionally, you can configure a third server, called a *monitor server*, that is responsible for monitoring the history and status of the backup and restore operations, and if configured to do so, will generate an alert if either of these operations fail.

Log shipping involves the following three jobs.

1. The primary server SQL Server agent backs up the transaction log of primary database.

2. The SQL Server Agent on the secondary SQL server initiates a copy of the primary server transaction log.

3. The Agent on the secondary server applies the copied transaction log to the associated secondary server database.

If you are log shipping to multiple standby servers from one primary server, steps 2 and 3 will be repeated multiple times. The schedule for this process will determine how current the secondary database server will be in the event that you lose your primary database server.

This technique is an advanced SharePoint 2010 configuration topic that is not within the scope of this book, but the following list is a good starting point to understand the basic elements of the procedure.

- Use the same domain and accounts for all like processes (farm, IIS Processes, SQL SA account).

- Use the same version (including updates) of SQL Server on both farms.

- Document content database to Web application mappings.

- Create the failover farm using a second SQL server (not just a second instance).

- Use identical, corresponding content database names when creating Web applications on the second farm.

- Configure a monitor server to track the details of the log shipping.

- Use full or bulk-logged recovery model of databases on primary server.

- Do not log ship Config or Central Administration databases.

- Ship logs to a second SQL Server and verify their integrity.

- Take the primary farm offline to test.

- Bring the failover farm content databases online.

- Bring the failover farm online.

- Browse using a different namespace, change the Domain Name System (DNS), or purchase third-party software that will handle the redirection to the new server.

- Use the same TCP port for both Central Administration Web applications for ease of configuration.

Transaction log shipping on a single LAN can work quite well to provide a failover farm in the event of a catastrophic hardware failure. The downside to transaction log shipping is the manual intervention required on the failover server, since the databases will be in recovery mode and must be brought online manually. Remember to change any settings in your DNS servers to publish the new farm's IP address, or simply educate your users about the second namespace in the event of a disaster on your primary server. Figure 17-14 is an example of log shipping configuration in which both farms are located at the same geographical location.

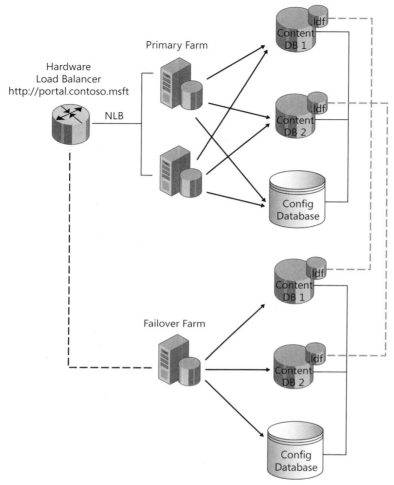

FIGURE 17-14 SQL Server transaction log shipping

Combining Database Mirroring and Log Shipping

Your principal database in a mirrored configuration can also act as the primary database in a log shipping configuration, or vice versa. This configuration allows you to use the database mirroring session running in either synchronous or asynchronous mode.

Although it is not required, you typically want to configure the mirrored session first, then your log shipping. Your mirrored principal database is configured as the log shipping primary database (becoming a principal/primary database), then one or more secondary server databases are configured. Furthermore, the mirror database is configured as a log shipping primary database (becoming a mirror/primary database).

For true high availability, your log shipping secondary databases should be on different servers than either the principal/primary server or the mirror/primary server.

IMPORTANT When using SQL Server transaction log shipping or database mirroring, it is important to remember that all errors, such as those caused by file corruption or incorrect data modifications, will be replicated from the primary farm to the failover farm.

SQL Snapshots

SharePoint 2010 allows full use of native SQL Server database snapshots. You can create, delete, and restore snapshots from within SQL Server or by using Windows PowerShell. After you create the snapshots, you can access them using STSADM or Windows PowerShell command-line tools.

SQL Server database snapshots are mechanisms that provide a read-only copy of your data that allows you to roll back to the data point in time when the snapshot was made, using an unattached content database or a content database snapshot. The SQL Server snapshot of the data made before it was modified stores the unmodified content in a snapshot database. You can then use that database to roll back to the unmodified data.

SQL Server Failover Clustering

SQL Server failover clustering provides high availability for SQL Server databases accessed by SharePoint 2010. Most medium- to large-scale SharePoint 2010 farms require a SQL Server cluster for fault tolerance. The basic two-server (often referred to as *nodes*) Active/Passive cluster configuration shown in Figure 17-15 provides fault tolerance, but it does not improve performance. This configuration is the easiest one to implement and provides high availability of your SQL Server databases.

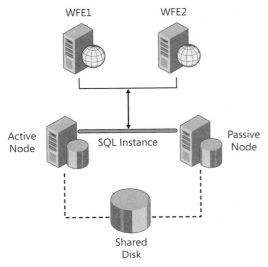

FIGURE 17-15 SQL Server clustering with SharePoint 2010

From within SharePoint, the failover cluster instance appears as a single computer, but it provides functionality that allows it to automatically roll over from the active server to the passive server if the active server becomes unavailable. This failover can take several seconds to several hours, depending on the size of your transaction logs. Frequently truncating your transaction logs increases SQL Server CPU and disk usage, and it also can reduce your chances of recovering SQL Server data after a hardware failure, but it does reduce the time required to failover to the passive node from the active node.

The failover cluster is a combination of one or more nodes and two or more shared disks. SharePoint 2010 references the cluster as a whole, providing a seamless automatic failover from the perspective of SharePoint, with little or no interruption or data loss.

Ensuring a Full Farm Recovery

As with SharePoint Server 2007, simply backing up your databases is not enough to allow you to recover from a failure of your entire SharePoint farm. SharePoint 2010 stores more configuration information in the content databases than Microsoft Office SharePoint Server 2007, but you still need to be concerned with the following non-SharePoint components to ensure a successful farm recovery.

- **SharePoint Root**   The \Program Files\Common Files\Microsoft Shared\Web server Extensions\14 folder often holds any customizations that your developers have made to your SharePoint implementation. These can include custom graphics, style sheets, and site definitions, to name a few possible modifications. It is important to back up the SharePoint Root on at least one of your Web front-end servers to ensure that these customizations can be recovered. Because the SharePoint Root should be identical on all Web front-end servers, it is not necessary to back up each one separately.

- **Inetpub folder**   This is another location that can be used to store customizations such as graphics and custom Web Parts. You also want to ensure that you have a copy of the Web.config file, because this contains any safe control entries required by custom or third-party Web Parts. Each Web application has a corresponding Inetpub folder on your Web front-end servers.

- **System Binaries**   In the event of server failure, you need to recover it to the state it was in before the failure. This can be done either by reinstalling all the system files, patches, service packs, and upgrades that were installed on the server, or by restoring your system files from backup. Often, backup utilities offer a disaster recovery option designed to recover your system to the exact state before the failure.

- **IIS Settings**   SharePoint relies on Web sites hosted by Microsoft Internet Information Server (IIS) to provide access to SharePoint information. It is therefore important that you have a backup of the IIS configurations for the SharePoint servers in the farm. You can do this by opening the IIS Management console from Administrative Tools on the Start menu, right-clicking the server object, selecting All Tasks, and then selecting the Backup/Restore Configuration option. Although SharePoint stores most IIS configuration information in the SharePoint Config_db, assigned IP addresses and host headers you add manually are backed up only with an IIS configuration backup. You can use the following commands to back up and restore your IIS 7 configuration information.

To back up the IIS configuration information, use the AppCmd.exe command found in %WinDir%\System32\Inetsrv as shown here.

```
appcmd.exe add backup "Your Backup Name"
```

To restore that backup, run the command shown here.

```
appcmd.exe restore backup "Your Backup Name"
```

- **SSL Certificates**   You should always keep a backup of your SSL certificates, including the private key. Although this can be retrieved from a system state operating system backup, you must restore the entire system state to access the certificate store that was backed up using Certificate Manager. A configuration backup should always include the use of a password so that the restore is portable and not restricted to the original Web server.

- **System State Data**   System state data includes the following items, which can be backed up by most disaster-recovery software as part of a normal system backup.

  - Start-up files
  - Registry
  - COM+ class registration database
  - IIS configuration (when running IIS)
  - Active Directory (domain controllers)
  - SYSVOL folder (domain controllers)
  - DNS (domain controllers)
  - Certificate store (certificate authority)

- **DNS Records**   Often when working with configuring access to SharePoint Web Sites, you need to add HOST (A) Records or CNAME (Alias) records in DNS. This application is also updated when performing a failover to other machines in your farm during a disaster. If your DNS server is hosted on a domain controller, the system state data will include the DNS information. If DNS is hosted on a member server or stand-alone server, however, you must back up the Zonename.dns file located at C:\Windows\System32\DNS.

Summary

This chapter provided you with the basic information you need to design and implement a SharePoint 2010 disaster recovery solution using redundancy and well-documented backup and restore procedures. Your SharePoint disaster recovery plan should achieve your goals to minimize data loss and minimize downtime. By using the disaster recovery tools contained within SharePoint and those outside of SharePoint, as well as performing consistent testing of your disaster recovery plan, you can efficiently achieve these two goals. Remember to take the time to determine which tools will provide you with the best solution for your disaster recovery plan by testing multiple methods of disaster recovery for your SharePoint installation and then making an informed decision about the best way to protect your SharePoint data.

Advanced Topics

Aggregating External Data Sources

Microsoft SharePoint Server 2007 introduced a number of new services and features that allowed business data to surface from back-end applications. With Microsoft SharePoint 2010, these features have been enhanced. Some of these features provide pre-built Web Parts, which display information from these external data sources on dashboards without the need for coding. Other features aggregate and transform data held in SharePoint before displaying the information to the user, and some are designed for connecting, mapping, and fetching data from external data sources. The services and features that fall into the first and last category, and which are described in this chapter, are the Microsoft Business Connectivity Services (BCS), originally called the Business Data Catalog. BCS is now available in the base product, Microsoft SharePoint Foundation 2010. Any version of SharePoint 2010 plus the BCS data definitions can be used to reveal external data in Microsoft Office 2010 applications, including Microsoft Outlook 2010, Microsoft Access 2010, Microsoft Workspace 2010, Microsoft Word 2010, Microsoft InfoPath 2010, and Microsoft Excel 2010.

This chapter attempts to describe some key elements of BCS from an administrator's perspective. You'll learn about BCS and how to use it. You'll look at the architecture of the BCS, including the security options. Then you'll take a look at managing the data connections and using the BCS features to build dashboards.

What Are the Business Connectivity Services?

The BCS is a SharePoint 2010 service application that bridges the gap between various applications that an organization uses for key business data from platforms like Siebel, CRM, and SAP to SharePoint sites, lists, search functions, and user profiles. The BCS application can take advantage of the shared services architecture (described in Chapter 7, "Scaling Out a SharePoint 2010 Farm"). A SharePoint 2010 farm can host of a number of BCS applications that can be configured independently by different sets of administrators. A specific BCS application can be shared across server farms, so that it can be managed centrally and consumed from different locations. The BCS application can also be partitioned for multi-tenancy, which is the term commonly used to describe the isolation of websites in a hosting environment. After a BCS application is created, its use can be divided into the following three areas.

- **Connectivity** This is the layer of BCS that connects to the external systems. This layer is referred to as Business Data Connectivity (BDC). (Note that this acronym was used in the previous version of SharePoint, where it represented the Business Data Catalog.) The connectivity layer uses the definitions in the Application Model, commonly known as the Model, or BDC Model, to connect to the external systems.

- **Presentation** External data can be presented in SharePoint by using External Lists, External Data Web Parts, External Data Columns, and External Data Search, as well as by using Microsoft SharePoint Designer 2010 to create a Data Form Web Part (DFWP) to display the data. External data can also be presented in Microsoft Office 2010 client applications.

- **Tools** Microsoft SharePoint Designer 2010 and Microsoft Visual Studio 2010 allow information workers, business analysts, and developers to define the Model and create dashboards and composite applications based on data from the external systems.

By using BCS, an organization can accomplish the following objectives.

- Reduce or eliminate the code required to access line-of-business (LOB) systems.

- Achieve deeper integration of data into places where a user works.

- Centralize deployment of data source definitions for use by both BCS and Office applications, such as Outlook 2010, Access 2010, and Workspace 2010.

- Reduce latency to access and manipulate data, because after a data source is defined in BCS, it will be immediately available on the Web applications associated with that particular BCS application.

- Centralize data security auditing and connections.

- Perform structured data searches.

SharePoint 2010 offers a number of new BCS features, including

- Data exposed as an external content type (ECT), which can be manipulated similar to other SharePoint objects, such as lists, Web Parts, and user profile properties

- External data accessed both online and offline by Office applications using the BCS data source definitions

- Additional connectivity options, such as Windows Communication Foundation (WCF) services, Microsoft .NET Framework connectivity assemblies, and custom data sources

- The introduction of a pluggable framework that developers can use to create new BCS connectors to access and manipulate external data sources

- Support for batch and bulk operations in a single call, thereby reducing the number of round trips to the back-end systems

- Reading binary large object (BLOBs), which is particularly useful for streaming data, such as video, from external systems

- Improvements in the packaging and deployment of BCS solutions that can be used immediately by SharePoint sites and proactively distributed and deployed (the push model) to the clients or users using the Visual Studio Click Once deployment method

- Enhancements with the application programming interface (API)

NOTE One feature often cited as new for BCS in SharePoint 2010 is the ability to write-back to external systems. You could create SharePoint Server 2007 BDC data source definitions that allowed you to update or inset data into the external data sources; however, none of the out-of-the-box Web Parts exposed this feature. You needed a developer to create a custom Web Part to match the data source definition. Now in SharePoint 2010, as the external data is exposed as a SharePoint (external) list, you can use the same familiar methods of manipulating the data as you would when data is stored in a traditional SharePoint list—you do not need a developer to create an interface.

Using the Business Data Connectivity Service Application and Model

The BCS is a service application, just like Form Services, Access Services, and Excel Services, and you can create a new BCS application just like other service applications, using one of the following methods.

- **Farm Configuration Wizard**   When you use the Farm Configuration Wizard to create all service applications and the BCS application is created at that time, the name of the database is Bdc_Service_DB_<*GUID*>, where *GUID* is a randomly generated number. This database is the location for the external content type (ECT) repository or metadata store.

- **Manage Service Applications Web page**   You can create the BCS application yourself and choose your own database name by using the SharePoint 2010 Central Administration website and selecting New in the Create group on the Service Application tab on the Ribbon.

- **Windows PowerShell** You can also create a BCS application using the cmdlet New-SPBusinessDataCatalogServiceApplication.

After the BCS application is created, the next step is to define the external systems and data that can be used on your site and on your dashboards. You may need the following two types of information to present information from your external systems.

- The base metadata for the data stored in the external system
- Localized names, properties, permissions, and custom environment settings

A single XML file, known as the BDC Model, can describe both sets of information; however, you can separate these two sets of data into the BDC Model file for the base metadata and a resource file for the localized names, properties, permissions, and custom environment settings.

The external data declared in the BDC Model details the data connection, data formats, and methods, such as create, read item, read list, update, and delete for the external system. Administrators use the BDC Model to register the external system in a SQL Server database. Thereafter, SharePoint 2010 uses the declared APIs to access data from the external systems.

After the BDC Model is imported into SharePoint 2010, the external data is made available to any Web applications associated that BCS application. Figure 18-1 shows the high-level interaction between the external data, ECT repository, features, and applications.

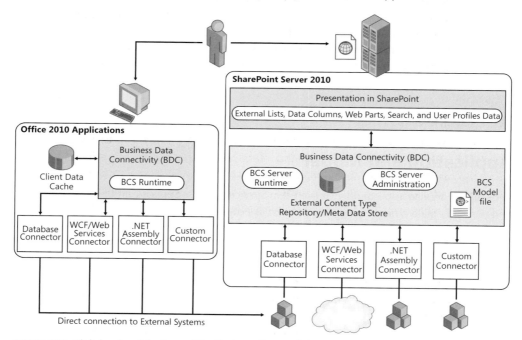

FIGURE 18-1 High-level architecture of the Business Connectivity Service

Although this book is focused on administrator tasks, it is important that you understand the administrator tasks in relationship to the other tasks that need to be completed for a successful solution based on the BCS. The next few sections cover the following BCS topics.

- Business Data Connectivity (BDC) layer
- External content types
- BDC Models and resource files

Business Data Connectivity Layer

The BCS data connectivity layer, or the BDC, uses connectors to access the external systems. The built-in connectors allow you to connect to databases, cloud-based services, Windows Communication Foundation (WCF) endpoints, Web services, the .NET assembly that gathers data from multiple sources, and custom external systems that have nonstatic interfaces that change dynamically. An improvement in this version of SharePoint is the introduction of batch and bulk operation for retrieving external data. When multiple documents are retrieved, it is also possible to retrieve the documents in chunks, which reduces the number of round trips to retrieve the data.

The BCS database, known as the external content type (ECT) repository or metadata store, stores and secures ECT and related objects defined in the Model. It does not contain external data; it only contains information about the external system. All the BCS database SQL Server tables associated with the BCS are prefixed with the two characters AR, which stand for Application Registry, the initial name for the BCS. The metadata store is accessed by the BDC administration and runtime interfaces, which are discussed in more detail in the following sections.

BDC Administration

This interface creates, reads, updates, and deletes objects within the metadata store. All of the SharePoint 2010 built-in features will use this interface. For example, the BCS administration Web pages use this interface to import the Model, as does the external data picker in any of the external data Web Parts. The BDC caches all the ECT information, so most of the time a call to the administration interface will result in manipulating objects from the cache instead of making round trips to the ECT repository. Caching objects provides faster access to the ECT. If the BDC sees a change to an object, it clears and then loads the cache.

> **NOTE** A timer runs once every minute on each server to look for any changes to the metadata objects. If the logic within the timer job sees a change, it clears the cache and then reloads it. Therefore, after you change metadata, you must wait up to a minute for changes to propagate to all the servers in the farm. The changes take effect immediately on the computer on which you make them.

BDC Runtime

The BDC runtime abstracts the interface between the application solutions and the external systems into the BDC object model. The runtime calls the administration interfaces to find the location and format of the data so that it can call the appropriate connector, which in turn gets the external data. This process causes network traffic between the Web front ends and the servers that host the BCS application. Examples of the built-in features that use the BDC runtime are External Lists, External Data Web Parts, the Retrieve Data link, and the Refresh icon in the External Data Column of a list or library.

BDC is now available on Office 2010 client applications as well as SharePoint 2010. The Office 2010 client applications include BCS rich client extensions that provide user interface elements and a symmetrical BDC runtime to the BDC runtime that runs on the server. The BDC runtime provides an intuitive, "stereotypical," consistent object model, independent of the external system; therefore, developers need to understand only the BDC object model to extract data from the external systems whether they are developing code for the client or the server.

The BDC runtime consists of an infrastructure component to provide runtime connection management and shared security services to the external systems. Access to the external systems is the responsibility of the BDC connectors. The BDC runtime, whether it is on the client or SharePoint 2010, uses the same connectors, and therefore, the client does not need to connect back to SharePoint to access the external data.

The Office 2010 clients have a SQL Compact Edition client database installed that caches external data and allows access for both online (connected) and offline (disconnected or cached connection mode). If amendments are made while the client is offline, they are stored in the client data cache and committed to the external system when the client is next online.

> **NOTE**   The SQL Server CE database also contains a transient, in-memory optimized copy of the BCD Model.

External Content Types

External content types (ECTs) are a new concept in SharePoint 2010 and are the building blocks of BCS, similar to the entity object in SharePoint Server 2007. External content types refer to external data objects and defines the fields, methods, and the behavior of the data in SharePoint and Office client applications. Both read and write capability is included, along with batch and bulk operation support. ECTs are defined in the BDC Model. The data objects defined by the ECTs can be displayed on SharePoint 2010 sites using Web Parts, External Columns in lists and libraries and in External Lists, or in Office 2010 applications where ECTs are the framework for creating Office Business Applications or OBAs.

BDC Models and Resource Files

External content types are metadata objects defined in the BDC Model XML file, which usually use the extension *.bdcm*. Resource information can be included in the BDC Model file or in a separate resource XML file, which usually has an extension of *.bdcr*. The creation of the base metadata information and the resource information is an important activity. You can create the base metadata information using the External Content Type Designer in SharePoint Designer 2010, Visual Studio 2010, an XML editor, Notepad, or third-party tools such as bdcmetaman from Lightning Tools. You can create or configure resource information after the BDC Model data is imported; for example, you can use the Central Administration website pages to configure permissions. You can use Visual Studio 2010 to create a separate file. After you complete the configuration of the external system, you can export the Model data and the resource data into separate files using the Central Administration website.

> **NOTE** You can only use SharePoint Designer 2010 to create a model XML file for SQL Server databases, Web and WCF services, and .NET connectivity assemblies. For other types of external systems, you must edit the Model XML file in Visual Studio 2010, an XML editor, or a third-party tool.

The BDC Model is usually created by a business analyst, a developer, or database administrator (DBA). Among them, they have the knowledge of the external system or database as well as how the data will be used. They do not need to be able to write code, although to import the BDC Model into a BCS application, they must have Edit permissions at the BCS level, which are usually assigned to service application administrators of the BCS application.

One purpose of the Model is to describe how the BDC runtime will obtain the data from the external system—that is, it describes the interface. Another purpose of the Model is to add meaning to the interface and data. It describes what can be done with the interface and the relationship between the different types of data. For example, using BCS, you can create, read, update, delete, and query (CRUDQ) external data in SharePoint and Office client applications, if the external system supports the operations and is modeled appropriately in the BDC service.

> **NOTE** Not all Office client applications can write to the external system, even though the external system supports the operations and they are correctly modeled in the BCS. For example, in Word 2010, BCS exposes read-only data in content controls that map to External Data Columns in a SharePoint document library, and you can import a BDS Model into Access 2010 to create read-only tables.

The BDC Model contains a hierarchy of XML elements, each containing text or other elements that specify the external system settings and structure. The Model must conform to the standards for well-formed XML, so all element names are case sensitive. The Model must also conform to the schema described in the file Bdcmetadata.xsd. When you have a separate resource file, the schema definition file is BDCMetadataResource.xsd. Both files are stored in the TEMPLATE\XML SharePoint installation root folder, which by default is C:\Program Files\Common Files\Microsoft Shared\Web Server Extensions\14. The Model looks similar to Figure 18-2, which illustrates the main metadata object definitions.

FIGURE 18-2 A sample BDC Model file

> **MORE INFO** To get started with the BCS, you can find sample model files at
> *http://msdn.microsoft.com/en-us/library/ee559369(office.14).aspx.*

The metadata object hierarchy can be seen by reviewing the XML tags of the Model file, which defines the data structures, such as Model, LobSystem, LobSystemInstance, Entity (which represents an external content type), Method, Parameter, and TypeDescriptor objects, where Lob is the acronym for line of business, which is another term for external system. Using these data structures, the Model file describes the external system, such as the server name, connection string, and authentication method. Following is a list of the main metadata XML tags. (For a list of all metadata objects, refer to *http://msdn.microsoft.com/en-us/library /ee559369.aspx.*)

- **LobSystem**   This object represents the external system and is the root note of the Model file.

- **LOBSystemInstance**   This object provides authentication and the connection string information.

- **Entity**   This is the key object of the metadata and refers to the ECT. An ECT relates to information from the external system, such as the author, a customer, a sales order, or a product. An entity belongs to a single LOB system and must have a unique name. Entities contain identifiers, methods, filters, and actions. Each entity should define two properties: an identifier (which, in database terms, is the primary key) and a default column. An identifier is used to uniquely identify a particular instance of an entity. In SQL terms, this is the column designated as the primary key. Each entity also consists of a number of child XML element tags. Following is a description of the key components of or related to entities.

  - **Methods**   These are operations related to an ECT, such as Create, Read Item, Update, Delete, and Read List. If the data source is a database, the method is a stored procedure or a SQL statement; if the data source is a Web service, the method is a Web method. The metadata must detail everything that SharePoint 2010 needs to know to call that method and, therefore it can be likened to interface descriptions. For each ECT, there should be a method defined as a *Finder* method, which will return one or more instances of an entity, such as Read List, or a *SpecificFinder* method, Read Item, which will return a specific instance of an entity.

  - **Filters**   These components limit the number of entities returned from a method.

  - **Actions**   These can provide a link to the external system and can be used to provide write-back scenarios—for example, sending an e-mail, opening a Microsoft Office InfoPath form that writes back to the LOB application using a writable Web service, or opening a new browser window pointing to the external system's website. Actions are associated with an ECT, and therefore, wherever the ECT is displayed, the action link will be visible if an action is defined.

  - **Associations**   These components link related entities within an external system. For example, if there are two ECTs named Authors and Books, you should create an association to link authors to the books they have written. This enables you to use Web Part connections to create dashboards with related information.

  - **Access Control List**   Defines permissions for the Model objects.

The good news is that SharePoint Designer can create the Model files with the correct XML tags when SharePoint Designer is used to create an ECT. You import the Model file into the BCS metadata store by clicking the Save icon. If a developer creates a model file or a third-party tool, or you need to transfer a model file for a development environment to the production environment, then the Model file can be imported into SharePoint 2010 using the Central Administration website. Refer to the section titled "Managing Data Connections" later in this chapter for more information on how to do this.

Understanding the BCS Security Options

The following sections introduce the security options that are available when you use the BCS—authentication, authorization, and access control. Authentication is the process of verifying that a user is who he or she claims to be; authorization is the process of finding out whether the user, once authenticated, is permitted to access the data; and access control is managing access to the business data exposed using the BCS.

There are two scenarios to consider with BCS: The first is the SharePoint 2010 use of BCS, exposing information on Web pages; the second is the use of BCS in the Office client applications. Figure 18-3 shows the three major components, the Office client, SharePoint 2010, and external data sources.

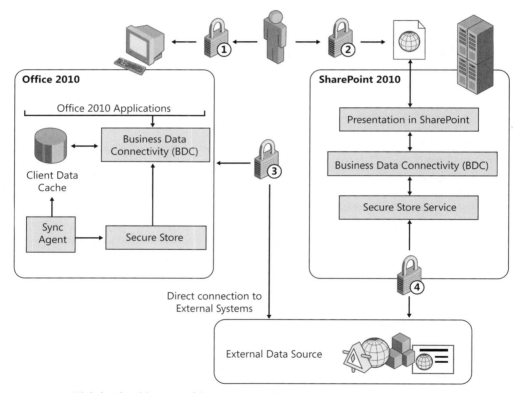

FIGURE 18-3 High-level architecture of the Business Connectivity Service

Each lock in Figure 18-3 identifies a form of authentication as follows.

- **Lock 1** Logging on to your computer using your Windows credentials.
- **Lock 2** The authentication by Internet Information Services (IIS) on the SharePoint 2010 Web front-end (WFE) server. In many SharePoint implementations, if your SharePoint site is classified in the browser's intranet zone and uses integrated authentication, you are not prompted for credentials. In such a configuration, your

Windows credentials are used to authenticate you. When the SharePoint site is configured for forms-based authentication (FBA), IIS will prompt for your credentials.

- **Lock 3** The additional authentication required when an Office application such as Outlook 2010 is configured to display contact information from a Customer Relationship Management (CRM) or Enterprise Resource Planning (ERP) system.

- **Lock 4** Authentication from SharePoint 2010 to the external data sources via integrated authentication using Kerberos to flow the credentials across multiple systems, Secure Store Services (SSS), Security Assertion Markup Language (SAML) claims, or token-based authentication.

Locks 3 and 4 represent the additional security requirements that an external data source may impose. This is a very common scenario for business data, because of the administrative implications of aggregating data from external data sources when building dashboards in SharePoint 2010, which makes lock 4 of particular interest.

To understand the BCS SharePoint 2010 security options, it is important to understand the roles of the application pool and the search content access accounts. The following list summarizes main points to keep in mind about the BCS.

- When the business data is exposed through the BCS on a Web page, the BDC runtime runs within an IIS worker process (W3wp.exe), and therefore it is using the IIS application pool credentials for that worker process.

- When the BCS is used for crawling, it runs in the filter daemon process (Msadmn.exe), and therefore it is using the search content source account. Unlike the NTFS file system, which consistently uses the same protocol for authentication and authorization, business applications will either use Windows authentication or a proprietary method of authentication and authorization. Hence, when the BDC indexes the business application, it cannot acquire security information from the back end. Therefore, if a business application is crawled, result sets from a keyword search will not take into account any access control configured at the source.

The following sections explain the BCS security options when data is exposed using the BCS interfaces.

Authentication Modes

The following are the two authentication modes in BCS.

- **Trusted subsystem** The SharePoint 2010 WFE servers control authentication and authorization and retrieve data from the external system using a fixed identity. SharePoint 2010 primarily supports the trusted system model for access services and resources. In the trusted system model, a system account is used to access services and resources on behalf of all authenticated users so that administrators do not have to specify access for each user. The fixed identity is the application pool ID or a group ID retrieved from the SSS database. If the external system is configured to use identify federation authentication, the user's identity is passed to the Secure Token Service (STS) to obtain the user's token or claim.

- **Impersonation and delegation** In this authentication model, the external system delegates authentication to the WFEs, and the application pool ID impersonates the user. The application pool ID then connects to the external system on the user's behalf by using Kerberos or SSS, or by passing the user's name as a parameter. Use this model if you want application-level authorization of the business data.

 SECURITY ALERT In any system in which credentials are sent between servers, an attacker can possibly compromise the security solution. Ensure that you secure your infrastructure appropriately—for example, by using Kerberos, Secure Sockets Layer (SSL), or Internet Protocol Security (IPSec).

The BCS authentication mechanism uses either credentials, in the form of a user name and password, or claims-based authentication in the following modes.

- **PassThrough** The user's authentication information is passed by the BDC runtime through to the back-end system. This mode will always incur a double hop unless SharePoint 2010 and the external system are installed on the same computer, which usually only occurs in a development, prototyping, or demonstration environment. In most installations, Kerberos is needed to use this method with Windows authentication; otherwise, a login failed message is displayed. In the Central Administration website and in SharePoint Designer 2010, this mode is called User's Identity.

- **RevertToSelf** If a user logs on with Windows authentication, the BDC runtime will use the application pool ID to impersonate that particular user. RevertToSelf authentication allows SharePoint 2010 to revert back to the IIS application pool ID before requesting data from the external system. In External Lists, this means the application pool for the content page; for timed workflows, it means the process that runs the workflow; and so on. The application pool of a SharePoint farm is a highly privileged account, and Microsoft does not recommend using RevertToSelf authentication in a production environment. If you used RevertToSelf in SharePoint Server 2007, then during the upgrade process, you should review the use of this authentication mode. In the Central Administration website and in SharePoint Designer 2010, this mode is called BDC Identity. See the sidebar titled "Security Alert: RevertToSelf Models" later in this chapter for more important information about using this authentication method.

- **1818Credentials** The user's identity is matched in SSS to the external system and retrieves the individual or group credentials that should be used to access the external system. These credentials are passed to the BDC runtime and are used to access the external system. If the data source is a database, SharePoint 2010 authenticates by using Windows or database (custom) identities from the SSS. If the data source is a Web service, non-Windows (custom) identities from the SSS are used for basic or digest authentication, depending on the configuration of the Web service. To use this mode in the Central Administration website or in SharePoint Designer 2010, use either Impersonate Windows Identity or Impersonate Custom Identity.

REAL WORLD BCS Authentication and Identity Delegation

M any Web 2.0 applications such as Windows Live ID, Yahoo! BBAuth, Google Account Authentication API, and Netflix with OAuth use Identity Delegation. You can use these Web 2.0 applications as BCS external systems. The Model for solutions based on data from these Web 2.0 applications cannot be created using SharePoint Designer but will need to be created by a developer using Visual Studio.

Security Alert: RevertToSelf Models

A ny person who can create or edit RevertToSelf models can make themselves administrators of SharePoint. In SharePoint Server 2007, this was not a big security issue, because you could only upload the Model file using the Central Administration website, and most people who could access SharePoint Central Administration to complete this task were SharePoint farm administrators anyway. Now that more people can upload model files using SharePoint Designer, however, this is more of a security risk. Therefore, RevertToSelf authentication is disabled by default in SharePoint 2010. When a user tries to import or change the authentication mode to RevertToSelf, an error message displays. The error message that displays when using SharePoint Designer is shown in Figure 18-4.

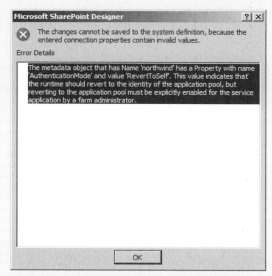

FIGURE 18-4 RevertToSelf import error dialog box.

continued on the next page

Microsoft recommends strict limits on the use of RevertToSelf authentication mode. If you use it at all in a production environment, make sure that ALL of the following conditions are true.

- You are using SharePoint Foundation 2010, because it does not support the SSS application.
- You do not have resources to create a custom SSS.
- You trust all of the people who use SharePoint Designer as completely as if they were SharePoint administrators.
- The application pool account is locked down so that the attach surface exposed to a malicious user of SharePoint Designer is limited.

RevertToSelf can be turned on by code or by using Windows PowerShell as shown in the following example, where the variable *BCSName* is the name of your BCS application.

```
$bcs = Get-SPServiceApplication | where {$_.displayname -eq $BCSname};
$bcs.RevertToSelfAllowed = $True;
```

The RevertToSelf property only affects the importing of new models or modifying an existing model to using this authentication mode.

Authorization

There are two methods of controlling user access to data managed by the BCS.

- Back-end authorization, if the business application can perform per-user authorization
- Middle-tier authorization, which provides central security and auditing abilities using the BCS permission settings and SharePoint list/library security configuration options

After the Model file is imported into the BCS, you can manage permissions centrally using the BCS administration Web page to define permissions on objects in the metadata store for a specific BCS application, or at the BDC Model, external system level, or ECT level. These objects you can secure using the Central Administration website or through the use of Windows PowerShell, are referred to as "individually securable metadata objects." You cannot define permissions at the item level in an External List. However, if you add an External Data Column to a list or library, a copy of the data is placed in that list or library, and therefore you can exploit the item-level security available in those lists and libraries.

In the BDC Model, if an ECT contains an Audit property set to True, an entry is written to the audit log every time one of the ECT's methods is executed. If an External Data Column is added to a list or library, then the ECT method used to copy the external data to the list or library will result in an entry in the audit log, and thereafter, when the list or library is accessed, no entry is created in the audit log—only the default auditing features in SharePoint 2010 are available.

Each object has an access control list (ACL) that specifies which user, group, or claim has which rights on the object. Objects that are not individually securable metadata objects inherit the ACL from their immediate parent and are referred to as "access-controlled metadata objects." Depending on the object for which the user or group is being granted permissions, the permission level specifies the actions that the user or group can take on that object. All permissions on objects in the BCS can be set using the following values: Edit, Execute, Selectable In Clients, and Set Permissions, as shown in Table 18-1.

TABLE 18-1 Business Connectivity Service Permissions

PERMISSION	APPLIES TO	DESCRIPTION
Edit	Access-controlled metadata objects	User with this permission can perform the following actions: ■ Update ■ Delete ■ Create child object ■ Add property ■ Remove property ■ Clear property ■ Add localized display name ■ Remove localized display name ■ Clear localized display name Give Edit rights to administrators and users who use SharePoint Designer.
Set Permissions	Individually securable metadata objects	User with this permission can manage BCS permissions on the object. This permission is usually only given to BCS service application administrators.
Execute	ECT, Method Instance	User with this permission can execute operations via various runtime API calls; that is, they can view the data of an ECT returned from a finder method. In most scenarios, you would assign this right to all users who have access to SharePoint.
Selectable In Clients	ECT	User with this permission can use the external data picker to configure Web Parts and lists and create External Lists. This permission should be available to administrators and users who design solutions using the browser or SharePoint Designer.

Managing Data Connections

The BCS allows you to connect your external systems to Web applications without writing any code. To manage the BCS data connections to the external systems, you need to perform the following administrator tasks.

- Configure page creation (SharePoint 2010).

- Set access permissions, auditing, and authentication settings. (Security was detailed in the section titled "Understanding the BCS Security Options" earlier in this chapter.)

- Configure Single Store Service if any of the BDC model imported into the metadata store plan to use this authentication mechanism.

- Import the BDC model that contains the metadata information.

- Deploy custom business data solutions such as dashboards if any have been created.

You will use the Service Application Information page, shown in Figure 18-5, to view, add, modify, and delete BDC models, external systems, and ECTs, as well as to configure permissions. In SharePoint 2010, there is an additional group on the Ribbon to manage ECT profile pages. The Service Application Information page displays information from the metadata store in three different views: BDC Models, ECT, and external systems.

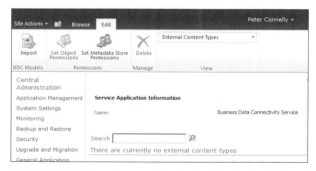

FIGURE 18-5 Business Connectivity Service Application Information page

Setting BCS Permissions

As described in the "Understanding the BCS Security Options" section earlier in this chapter, you can set permissions on the following objects.

- The metadata store
- Model
- External system
- ECT

Setting permission on the repository should be one of the first tasks you complete after you have created a BCS application. Use the following steps to complete this task.

1. Open a browser and go to the SharePoint Central Administration website.

2. Under Application Management, click Manage Service Applications.

3. On the Service Applications page, click the name of the Business Data Connectivity Service for which you want to manage permissions.

4. On the Service Application Information page, click Set Metadata Store Permissions on the Edit tab of the Ribbon.

5. On the Set Metadata Store Permissions page, shown in Figure 18-6, enter the appropriate users or groups and assign the appropriate permissions. Permissions set at this level can be copied to any Model, external system, or ECT imported into this specific BCS.

6. Click OK.

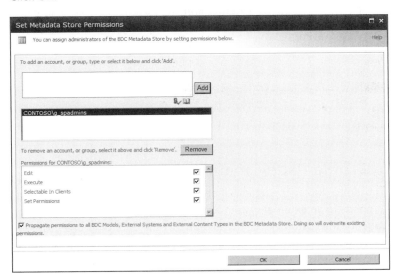

FIGURE 18-6 Add Users/Groups on the Set Metadata Store Permissions page

To set permissions on one or more models, external systems, or ECTs, complete the following steps.

1.   On the Service Application Information page, in the View group on the Edit tab, select BDC Models, External Systems, or External Content Types from the drop-down menu, as shown in Figure 18-7.

FIGURE 18-7 View BDC Models, External Systems, or External Content Types

The page displays only objects of the type you have chosen.

2.   Select the objects you want to modify and then click Set Object Permissions in the Permissions group on the Edit tab.

3.   On the Set Object Permissions page, enter the appropriate users or groups and assign the appropriate permissions.

Configuring Profile Page Creation

The profile page is used to display the details of an instance of an ECT. For example, when you create an ECT that points to an external system where all your customer details are stored, then the profile page for the customers' ECT would display the details for one customer. You do not create a profile page for each customer—instead, when you pass a customer ID to the profile page, it pulls the customer details from the external system and displays information about the customer, such as name, address, country, telephone number, and any other properties or fields that are defined in the BDC Model. In SharePoint Foundation, you must build these profile pages yourself and place controls or Web Parts to display the data. In SharePoint 2010, you can create profile pages with one click of a button using the Central Administration website or SharePoint Designer.

ECT profile page configuration can be different for each BCS application in your SharePoint farm. Prior to configuring the profile page location for your BCS application, you need to create a site that will host the profile pages and set the permissions so all users who have access to the data from the external system can also access this site. The Read-only permission right is usually sufficient for such users.

When you use SharePoint Designer to create profile pages, then you must map to users who access the data from the external system so that, at a minimum, they have the Design permission level, which contains the Add and Customize Pages permission right.

IMPORTANT If you create a new Web application to host the profile site, ensure that the Web application is associated with all BCS applications that will create profiles on that Web application.

After you have set permissions on the repository, you should then configure Profile page creation. Use the following steps to complete this task.

1. Open a browser and go to the SharePoint Central Administration website.

2. Under Application Management, click Manage Service Applications.

3. On the Service Applications page, click the name of the Business Data Connectivity Service that you want to configure.

4. Click Configure in the Profile Pages group on the Edit tab to display the Configure External Content Type Profile Page Host dialog box, as shown in Figure 18-8.

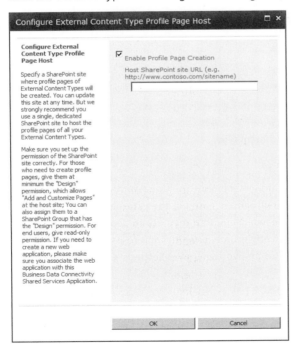

FIGURE 18-8 Configuring External Content Type Profile Page Host

5. Select Enable Profile Page Creation and type the URL of the site where the profile page will be hosted.

6. Click OK.

Creating BDC Models

You can create the BDC Model using SharePoint Designer 2010, Visual Studio 2010, or an XML editor. The most easy and effective way of creating a model is to use SharePoint Designer 2010. However, SharePoint Designer only creates BDC Models for WCF/Web Services, SQL Server, or .NET assemblies. Use the following steps to create a BDC Model for an SQL Server database.

1. Open SharePoint Designer 2010 and then open a SharePoint site where you want to create your dashboard.

2. In the left navigation pane, click External Content Types to open the External Content Types pane that lists the ECT created on this site, as shown in Figure 18-9.

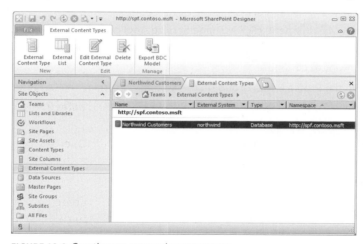

FIGURE 18-9 Creating an external content type

> **NOTE**   After you have created and tested your BDC Model and you are creating it in a development or prototyping environment, you use the External Content Types pane to export the BDC Model to a file, which you can then use to deploy the BDC Model in your SharePoint 2010 production environment. If you want to use the BDC Model in an Office 2010 application, make sure that you select the Settings: Client option when you export the BDC model.

3. In the New group on the Ribbon, click External Content Type. The summary view of the ECT is displayed, as shown in Figure 18-10.

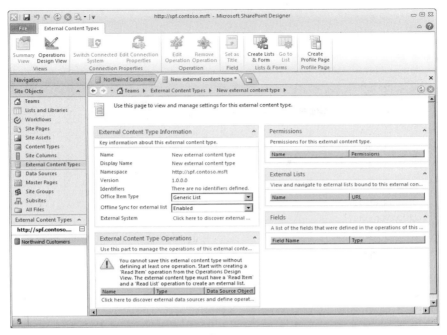

FIGURE 18-10 Summary view of an external content type

4. Click New External Content Type to the right of Display Name and enter the name of the ECT.

5. Click the Click Here To Discover External Data Sources And Define Operations link to the right of External System to display the operations design view of the ECT.

6. Click Add Connection.

7. In the External Data Source Type Selection dialog box, select the appropriate data source type, such as SQL Server, and then click OK to display the source type connection dialog box.

8. Enter the connection details and then click OK. For example, for a SQL Server source type, enter the database server name, the database name, and the authentication type: User's Identity, Impersonated Windows Identity, and Custom Identity. For the two impersonated identities, you will need to supply the secure store application ID.

9. In the Data Source Explorer, expand the database node by clicking the plus sign (+) to the right of the database name and then expand Tables.

10. Right-click the table you want to create a BDC Model for and then click the operation for the methods you want to create, as shown in Figure 18-11. Depending on the operations exposed by the external system, you can add the operations Create, Read Item, Update, Delete, and Read List.

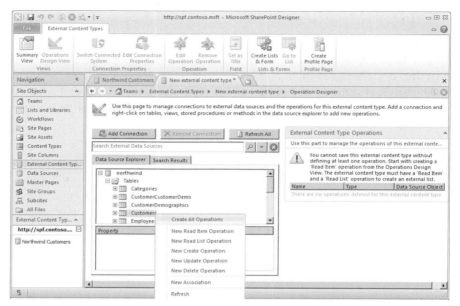

FIGURE 18-11 Creating an ECT operation

11. The Operation Properties dialog box opens. Use this dialog box to specify parameters for the operations and then click Next.

12. Select the field that you want to use as an Identifier and those fields you want to display in the external data picker when adding an External Data Column to a list or library or when configuring the external data Web Parts.

13. Click Next to display the Filter Parameters Configuration page and then click Add Filter Parameter. Always add a filter of type limit with a value of less than 2000 to prevent poor performance. If your business requires more than 2000 rows of data to be returned, then you will need to increase the throttle value of the BCS. See the section titled "Using External System Throttling" later in this chapter to learn more about throttling.

14. Click Finish and then Save. This will create and import the Model to the BCS service application that the SharePoint site is associated with.

> **NOTE** SharePoint Designer does not have support for creating resources; you will need to use an XML editor or Visual Studio 2010 to create a BDC project and add a new BCS resource item. Alternatively, if you have configured these properties after you have imported the Model, you can export the resource file separately using the Central Administration website.

Importing BDC Models

Remember that the key to a successful solution based on the BCS is the information defined in the BDC Model, which you import into a BCS database also known as the metadata store. The data then becomes available to all the Web applications that the BCS service is associated with. In the previous section, the BDC Model was created and imported into the metadata store in one activity. In a production environment, this may not be allowed. To import a BDC Model using the Central Administration website, use the following steps.

> **NOTE** When Visual Studio is used to create a BDC Model and optionally a resource file, they are commonly included in a solution package (.wsp). Solutions can be uploaded at the SharePoint farm level using the stsadm –o addsolution command or by using the Add-SPSolution Windows PowerShell cmdlet. After they are uploaded, solutions can be managed using the Manage Farm Solutions page on the Central Administration website.

1. Open a browser and go to the SharePoint Central Administration website.

2. Under Application Management, click Manage Service Applications.

3. On the Service Applications page, click the name of the Business Data Connectivity Service where you want to import the Model file to display the BCS Application Information page shown in Figure 18-5. On the BCS Application Information page, you can manage permissions, export the BDC Model, or delete the BDC Model.

4. Click Import on the Edit tab of the Ribbon to display the Import BDC Model page shown in Figure 18-12.

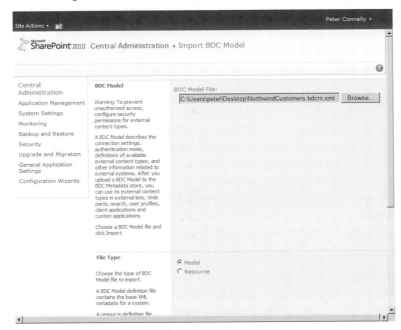

FIGURE 18-12 Import BDC Model page

5. In the BDC Model section, either click the Browse button to navigate to the Model file or type the location of the Model file in the text box.

6. If you are importing a resource file, select the resources defined in your model file in the Advanced Settings section.

 SECURITY ALERT When you choose to import permissions that are defined in your BDC model and an entry for a ECT already exists in the ACL, its value is overwritten with the permission information from the imported file.

7. Click Import to display the Importing Web page. The import process parses the file and validates it. If errors are found during the import process, the Web page will display additional information. Information can be found in the Windows event logs and the SharePoint 2010 log file located at %ProgramFiles%\Common Files\Microsoft Shared\ web server extensions\14\LOGS, where the relevant messages will be in the Business Data category. You might have to pass this information back to the developer or designer of the Model. The software development kit (SDK) contains more information on troubleshooting metadata exceptions and interpreting the log files.

A successful import will result in the message "Application definition was successfully imported." The import process can identify any deficits that the ADF has, in which case you will see the message "Application definition was successfully imported" message together with any warnings issued, similar to the Web page shown in Figure 18-13. The BDC Model file is validated with appropriate warnings displayed.

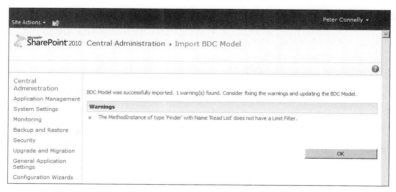

FIGURE 18-13 BDC Model imported successfully with warnings

8. Click OK to display the Service Application Information page.

After you have imported a BDC Model, SharePoint 2010 separates the external system and the ECT information. You should view these and give appropriate access rights according to your requirements, especially if you have chosen to copy all permissions to descendants at the metadata store level. You should then create a profile page for the ECT.

If you have errors in your BDC Model and need to make amendments, before you re-import the BDC Model, change the version number within the BDC Model or delete the external system.

Creating a Profile Page

After you create the BDC Model, you then need to create a profile page for each ECT, which you can use to view an instance of an ECT. On SharePoint 2010, it is easy to create a profile page using either SharePoint Designer or the Central Administration website. The following procedure explains how you can create an external data action named View Profile that will be added to any instance of an ECT pointing to the profile page. This external action is the default action for the ECT, so when users click any external data item, they will be redirected to the profile page.

To create or update a profile page, follow these steps.

1. Open a browser and go to the SharePoint Central Administration website.

2. Under Application Management, click Manage Service Applications.

3. On the Service Applications page, click the name of the Business Data Connectivity Service where the ECT is defined to display the BCS Application Information page shown earlier in Figure 18-5.

4. On the Service Application Information page, in the View group on the Edit tab, select External Content Types from the drop-down menu, as shown earlier in Figure 18-7.

5. Select the ECT for which you want to create a profile page, and in the Profile Page group on the Edit tab, click Create/Upgrade.

6. You will see a dialog box with information concerning the create/upgrade profile page process. Click OK.

7. The Profile Page Creation Succeeded dialog box appears, as shown in Figure 18-14. Click OK.

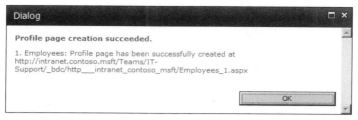

FIGURE 18-14 Profile Page Creation Succeeded page

The External Content Types view of the Service Application Information page refreshes and the link to the newly created profile page is listed in the Default Action column of the ECT, as shown in Figure 18-15.

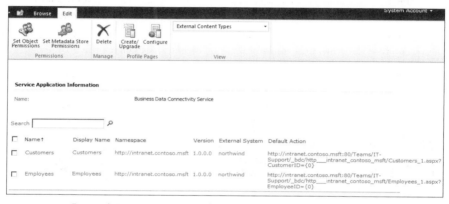

FIGURE 18-15 External Content Types with Default Action column

IMPORTANT   If a profile page already exists, clicking the Create/Upgrade icon will re-create the profile page, overwriting the previous one, unless you have changed the site that is hosting the profile pages. Any customizations you made to the previous profile page will be lost. If you created your own custom external action and defined it as the default action, then the profile page created by this procedure will become the default action.

IMPORTANT   When a SharePoint 2010 site is an upgraded SharePoint Server 2007 site that includes BCS data, profile pages, and actions, then the first time you complete the preceding procedure, you will create a new profile page. The previous profile page will not be overwritten, and the action for that profile page will be renamed to View Profile (SharePoint Server 2007).

NOTE   To create a profile page for SharePoint Foundation, you will need SharePoint Designer or a developer to create the external action using the procedure outlined in the next section.

Creating External Data Actions

Actions provide a link to the external data source. Actions are URLs that are usually defined in the BDC Model on an ECT basis. You can add more actions, modify existing actions, or delete existing actions after you have imported the BDC Model, and you can do this without having to delete the application and re-import the BDC Model. To add actions, follow these steps.

1. Open a browser and go to the SharePoint Central Administration website.

2. Under Application Management, click Manage Service Applications.

3. On the Service Applications page, click the name of the Business Data Connectivity Service where the ECT is defined to display the BCS Application Information page that was shown earlier in Figure 18-5.

4. On the Service Application Information page, in the View group on the Edit tab, select External Content Types from the drop-down menu, as shown earlier in Figure 18-7.

5. From the drop-down menu for the ECT for which you want to add a new action, click Add Action.

6. On the Add Action Web page shown in Figure 18-16, type a name for the action, type the URL, specify whether to launch the action in a new browser window or not (default), add parameters to the URL if required, and add the icon to display next to the action. You can choose from the Delete, Edit, or New actions, or you can choose your own image.

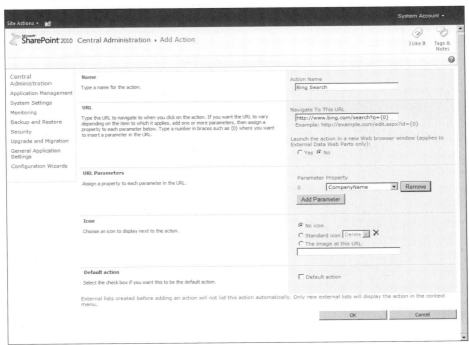

FIGURE 18-16 Add Action page

7. Click OK.

> **NOTE** New actions added to an ECT are not available on existing External Lists created from that ECT. Only new External Lists created from the ECT will display the action.

Wherever an instance of an ECT is displayed, the actions will be visible and presented as a drop-down list, as shown in Figure 18-17.

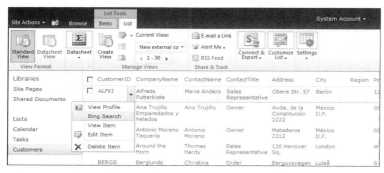

FIGURE 18-17 External data actions

When the View Profile action is selected, the profile page is displayed, as shown in Figure 18-18. The profile page generated by SharePoint Designer and the Central Administration website consists of two Web Parts: the Business Data Item Builder Web Part, which has a Web Part connection to the Business Data Details Web Part. These Web Parts and other Business Data Web Parts are described in Chapter 19, "Web Parts and Their Functionality in SharePoint 2010."

FIGURE 18-18 A populated ECT profile page of a customer instance

Although actions are limited to a URL, you can open a client application from a URL. Two ways you can do this are by writing a Web Part that opens the client application or by writing an Internet Explorer pluggable protocol handler.

Modifying BDC Objects

After the BDC Model is imported, you can change the following values, using the Central Administration website.

To modify one of the objects—BDC Models, external systems, or ECTs—follow these steps.

1. Open a browser and go to the SharePoint Central Administration website.

2. Under Application Management, click Manage Service Applications.

3. In the View group on the Edit tab of the Service Application Information page, select BDC Models, External Systems, or External Content Types, as shown in Figure 18-19.

4. From the drop-down menu, select the view options. For example, if you have chosen to display all external systems, then you can view all ECTs associated with those external systems, and then you can choose to view a specific ECT or add an action to an ECT, as shown in Figure 18-19.

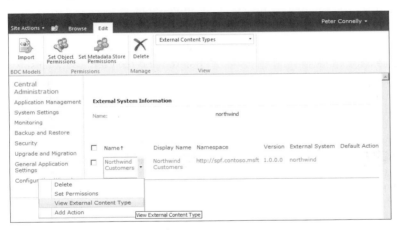

FIGURE 18-19 Viewing an external content type

For database and Web Services external systems, you can modify the property settings by selecting settings from the drop-down menu. For database external systems, the property settings you can modify include authentication mode, server name, database name, and secure store target application ID, as shown in Figure 18-20.

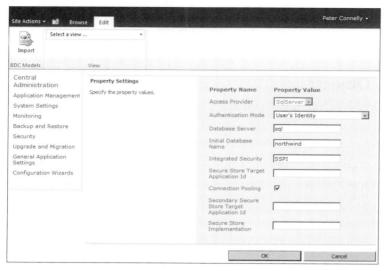

FIGURE 18-20 Modifying database property settings

For a Web service, you can modify the authentication mode, Web service URL, Web service proxy timeout, and SSS information.

To delete one or more BDC Model, external system, or ECT, complete the following steps.

1. Open a browser and go to the SharePoint Central Administration website.

2. Under Application Management, click Manage Service Applications.

3. In the View group on the Edit tab of the Service Application Information page, select BDC Models, External Systems, or External Content Types, as shown earlier in Figure 18-7.

4. Select the check box for each model, external system, or ECT you want to delete and then in the BDC Models group on the Edit tab of the Ribbon, click Delete.

5. When you are presented with an informational message dialog box warning you that this operation cannot be undone, click OK.

IMPORTANT When you delete a BDC Model, all external content types and external data sources that are contained in the Model and that are not also contained in another model are deleted along with the BDC Model.

Using External System Throttling

BCS throttling is enabled by default to prevent Denial of Service attacks. You are most likely to see the effect of this feature if you created no limit filter on the BDC Model and the attempt by the BCS runtime to retrieve data from the external system is taking too long. Each

BCS application can have a number of throttle configurations, and each configuration can be tuned to a throttle type and/or scope. Following are the five throttle types.

- **None**   No throttle type specified
- **Items**   The number of ECT instances returned, such as the number of customers or employees
- **Size**   The amount of data retrieved by the BDC runtime in bytes
- **Connections**   The number of open connections to a database, Web service, or .NET assembly
- **Timeout**   The time until an open connection is terminated, in milliseconds

The throttle scopes refer to the external system connection type, where the Global scope includes all connector types, such as database, Web service, WCF, and .NET Assembly connectors, except for custom connectors. The other scopes are Database, WebService, WCF, and Custom. Not all combinations of throttle types and scopes exist when a BCS application is first created. The rules that exist are

- Global scope, Throttle type Connections
- Database scope, Throttle type Items, and Timeout
- WebService scope, Throttle type Size
- WCF scope, Throttle type Size, and Timeout

You can retrieve and amend the throttling rules by using the Business Data Windows PowerShell cmdlets, as shown in the following examples, where the variable *BCSName* is the name of your BCS application.

```
$bcsproxy = Get-SPServiceApplicationProxy | where {$_.displayname -eq $BCSname};
```

To display the throttling configuration for a BCS application you would use the following SharePoint cmdlet, where the output is shown.

```
Get-SPBusinessDataCatalogThrottleConfig -ServiceApplication $bcsproxy `
    -Scope Global -ThrottleType Connections;
```

```
Scope        : Global
ThrottleType : Connections
Enforced     : True
Default      : 200
Max          : 500
```

The output displays five properties. The three properties that you can amend are

- Enforced, which defines if the rule is enabled
- Default, which effects External Lists and custom Web Parts, although custom Web Parts can override this value and therefore can present more data than External Lists

- Max, which is the limit used when custom Web Parts override the value in the Default property

To disable a throttling rule, use the following command.

```
Get-SPBusinessDataCatalogThrottleConfig –ServiceApplication $bcsproxy `
   –Scope Global –ThrottleType Connections | Set-SPBusinessDataCatalogThrottleConfig `
   –Enforced:$False;
```

To modify a throttle rule, use the following command.

```
$dbrule = Get-SPBusinessDataCatalogThrottleConfig –ServiceApplication $bcsproxy `
   –Scope Database –ThrottleType Items;
$dbrule | Set-SPBusinessDataCatalogThrottleConfig –Maximum 2000000 –Default 5000;
```

For more information on Windows PowerShell and SharePoint 2010 see Chapter 5, "Using Windows PowerShell to Perform and Automate Farm Administrative Tasks," and Chapter 12, "Using Windows PowerShell to Manage Search Services and FAST Search."

Building Composite Solutions

Now that you have configured the BCS application, created and imported BDC Models, and created actions, building composite solutions and aggregating data from external systems on dashboards is a relatively easy process, if you understand your business data and the data users need to see. You can use the browser or SharePoint Designer, or you can use External Lists and External Data Columns, or if you have SharePoint 2010, you can use the External Data Web Parts. You can then exploit the default behavior of Web Parts, lists, and libraries, such as defining an audience, targeting, filtering, and using Web Part connections.

External Lists

You create External Lists using the browser, SharePoint Designer, Windows PowerShell, or code. When you have created these lists, you will find that they have similar functionally to other SharePoint lists you are familiar with; however, you cannot associate RSS feeds to External Lists. There is also no datasheet view, nor can you bind workflows to the data, because the data is not in SharePoint, so you can't trigger workflows on data changes. However, using SharePoint Designer, you can create a site, list, or reusable workflow that accesses one or more External Lists.

To create an External List using the browser, complete the following tasks.

1. Open the site where you want to create the External List.
2. Click Site Actions and then select More Options.
3. On the Create page, click External List.

> **NOTE** If you have a large number of list types, you will find the External List option if you filter by List and Data categories.

4. On the New page, enter the name and description of the list and then select whether you want to create a link to this list in the Quick Launch bar. To the right of the External Content Type text box, click the Select External Content Type icon, as shown in Figure 18-21.

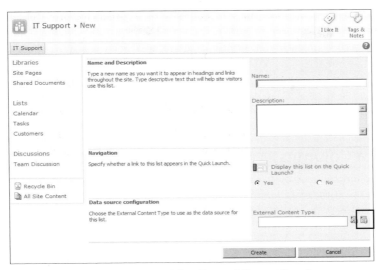

FIGURE 18-21 New External List – Select External Content Type icon

5. The External Content Type Picker dialog box appears, as shown in Figure 18-22. Select the ECT, which defines the external system that you want to display in your External List, and then click OK.

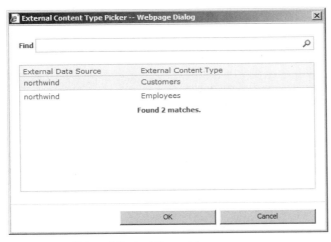

FIGURE 18-22 External Content Type picker

6. On the New page, click Create.

Business Data Web Parts

SharePoint 2010 ships with seven generic external data Web Parts, six of which are functionally the same as they were for the Business Data Web Parts in SharePoint Server 2007. The seventh is a new Web Part—the Chart Web Part. These Web Parts can be used to display any ECT from the BCS without writing any code. After they are configured, they will automatically be named after the entity data they are displaying. The Web Parts that display data from the LOB systems query the metadata cached on each Web front-end server, and then the instance data is retrieved from the data source.

To use the Business Data Web Parts on a site, you must activate the SharePoint Server Enterprise Site Collection features at the site collection level. Web Parts are described in more detail in Chapter 19.

External Data Columns

An External Data Column allows you to add data from an ECT to a standard SharePoint list. In SharePoint Server 2007, these were referred to as Business Data columns. If an External Data Column is added to a document library, then they can be made available as content controls in Word 2010.

To add a business data column to a list, complete the following tasks.

1. Navigate to the list or library where you want to add the column.

2. To display the Ribbon, click List within List Tools and then click Create Column in the Manage Views group to display the Create Column dialog box.

3. In the Name And Type section, enter a column name and select the External Data type. This column type can hold any ECT. The dialog box redisplays, and you will now see Check and Select ECT icons in the Additional Column Settings section.

4. Click the Select External Content Type icon to display the External Content Type Picker dialog box, as shown in Figure 18-23. Choose the appropriate ECT and click OK. The dialog box closes, and you will see that the Additional Column Settings section contains a list of properties associated with this entity, as shown in Figure 18-23.

5. From the Select The Field To Be Shown On This Column drop-down list, select a field and then click any related data you want to display. For example, you might choose to display a customer's name with the customer's business address and phone number. You can select the Add To All Content Types option and the Add To Default View option to add the column and additional fields to the default view.

6. Click OK.

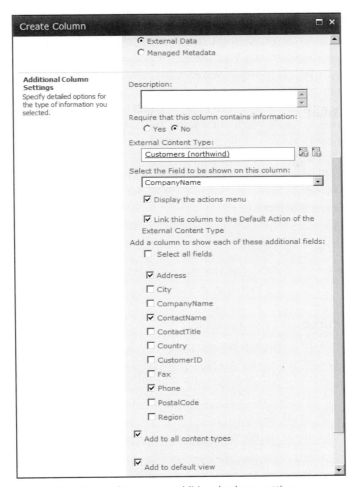

FIGURE 18-23 External Data type additional column settings

Now when you add a new list item, you can use the External Data Select icon to display the Choose External Data dialog box. Up to this point, SharePoint 2010 used the BDC administrator object model to retrieve the information from the cached metadata held in the Web front-end server. When the list is displayed, the BDC runtime object model connects to the external data source, and it copies the data into the list, unlike the external data Web Parts, which contain only a link to the external data. To update the data in the list, you can click the Refresh icon to the right of the External Data Column name. A Web page is displayed that warns you that this operation could take a long time. If you click Yes, the data source is contacted to return the necessary data. By copying the business data in the list, the business data within the list has inherited all list type operations, such as view and filter.

External Data Search

The BCS comes with search indexing connectors that enable SharePoint 2010 to index and provide full-text searches of the external systems. In fact, SharePoint Server search uses BCS search indexing connectors to index Exchange public folders, Lotus Notes, and Documentuum, among others. In SharePoint 2010, the BCS search improvements include the indexing of BLOBs, so that users can now search for attachments; it also now supports incremental crawls and item level security. However, importing a BDC Model that defines an ECT does not make the external data automatically available within Search. The metadata must have defined an *IDEnumerator* method, which is used in conjunction with the *SpecificFinder* method to return data from the data source. Then you must configure Enterprise Search to search the business data. The following sections explain how you configure Enterprise Search to search the business data, a process that consists of three steps.

1. Add a content source.
2. Map crawled properties.
3. Optionally, create a search scope, customized search pages, custom search queries, or all three.

Adding a Content Source

To include the content from a data source in the Enterprise Search, you must create content sources. For each content source, you have the choice of creating a content source for all the data defined in the BDC, for each LOB system, or for a combination of LOB systems. To create a content source for business data, complete the following steps.

1. Open a browser and go to the SharePoint Central Administration website.
2. Under Application Management, click Manage Service Applications.
3. On the Service Applications page, click the name of Search Service Application (SSA) that you want to index the external system.
4. On the Search Administration page, under Crawling, click Content Sources in the left navigation pane to display the Manage Content Sources page.
5. Click New Content Source, type a name, and then in the Content Source Type section, click Line Of Business Data. The Add Content Source page refreshes and a drop-down list is populated with BCS applications and a list of all external systems for the selected BCS application is displayed, similar to the list shown in Figure 18-24.

   You can set the crawl schedules for the incremental and full crawls at content source creation time or later. Incremental crawls are only possible if a *LastModifiedDate* property is one of the return fields in a *SpecificFinder* method for an entity. Similarly, you can start a full crawl immediately. See Chapter 11, "Search Server 2010 and FAST Search: Architecture and Administration," for more information on the Search Settings options.

6. Click OK, and then if you haven't already done so, complete a full crawl.

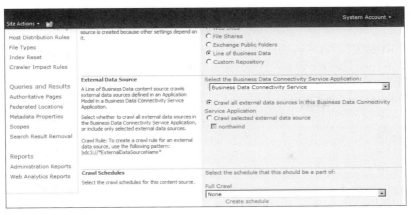

FIGURE 18-24 Adding a line-of-business (LOB) content source

 SECURITY ALERT   Ensure that the identity used to index the external system has the necessary permissions.

Mapping Crawled Properties

In SharePoint 2010, the Enterprise Search feature is able to discover new properties, known as "crawled properties." To make a crawled property available to a user, you need to make sure it is included in the search index and mapped to a metadata property as detailed in the following steps.

1. Wait for a full crawl to complete on the new content source, and then on the Search Administration page, under Queries and Results, click Metadata Properties.

2. Click Crawled Properties and then click Categories to display the Categories page. If this is the first time you have crawled a business data content source, the Number Of Properties column for the Business Data category should not be zero if the crawl process was successful, your BDC Model was correctly defined, and the search index identity had the correct permissions.

3. Click the Business Data link in the Category Name column to display the Crawled Properties – Business Data page.

    For each ECT that has an *IDEnumerator* method, there will be at least one property name for each *TypeDescriptor* defined in the *SpecificFinder* method. Any property that has a Yes in the Mapped To Content column is already included in the search index. The default configuration, which you can amend, is to include only text properties in the search index.

4. To include a property in the search index—for example, one of the non-text properties—click the property name in the Property Name column. In the Mappings To Managed Properties section of the Edit Crawled Property page, select the Include Values For This Property In The Search Index option and then click OK.

5. To map a crawled property, you can choose an existing managed property or create a new one. It is likely you will choose to create a new managed property as follows.

   a. In the left navigation pane, click Metadata Properties, and then on the Metadata Property Mappings page, click New Managed Property. The New Managed Property Web page is displayed.

   b. In the Name And Type section, enter a name in the Property Name text box and select a type of information for the property.

   c. In the Mappings To Crawled Properties section, click Add Mapping. The Crawled Property Selection dialog is displayed.

   d. In the Select A Category drop-down list, select Business Data. This dialog box will show only properties that are of the specified type and included in the index. If the number of properties available is greater than the dialog box can display, you will see a yellow arrow icon, which you can use to scroll through the properties, or alternatively, you can use the Find feature.

   e. Select the required property and then click OK. The dialog box closes, and the crawled property appears in the text box.

   f. Select the Allow This Property To Be Used In Scopes option to make the property available for use in defining search scopes.

   g. Click OK, and repeat this procedure for each crawled property you need to map to a metadata property.

6. In the left navigation pane, click Content Sources. For the appropriate content source you created, select Start Full Crawl from the drop-down list.

After you have completed steps 1 and 2, you should be able to find data from the external data sources. The search results page provides links to the entity's profile page.

Customizing the End-User Experience

If you want users to limit the search for keywords to a specific business data source, you can create a search scope with a rule that specifies the content source you created. You could also create a new tab in the Search Center to display the search results associated with this content source, as described in Chapter 13, "Customizing the Search Results and Search Center."

External Data and User Profiles

By default, SharePoint 2010 can import a list of domain users from the Active Directory Domain Services (AD DS), a Lightweight Directory Access Protocol (LDAP) server, IBM Tivoli Directory Server (ITDS), Novell eDirectory, Sun Java System Directory Server, or external systems. To add a user profile import based on the data from external systems, complete the following process. You can find more information about user profiles in Chapter 10, "Collaboration and Portals."

The use of the data from external systems with user profiles is a two-step process.

1. Import data from the external system into the profile database using the ECT defined in the BDC Model.

2. Map the profile properties to the external data.

To import data from an external system into the profile database, follow these steps.

1. Open a browser and go to the SharePoint Central Administration website.

2. Under Application Management, click Manage Service Applications.

3. On the Service Applications page, click the name of the User Profile service application where you want to import the external system data.

4. Under Synchronization on the Modify Profile Service page, click Configure Synchronization Connections to display the Synchronization Connections page and then click Create New Connection.

5. On the Add New Synchronization Connection page, enter a name for the connection and select Business Data Connectivity from the Type drop-down list. The page refreshes and you will see ECT Select and Check icons in the Connections Settings section, as shown in Figure 18-25.

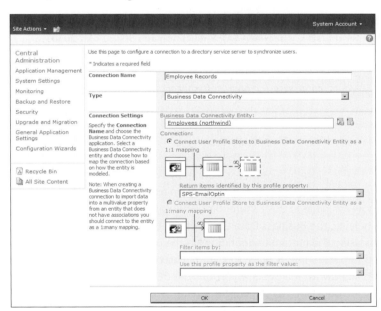

FIGURE 18-25 User Profile Import – Create a New Connection page

6. Click the Select icon to display the External Content Type Picker dialog box (as shown in Figure 18-22). Choose the appropriate external data source and click OK to close the dialog box.

7. Choose either the 1:1 mapping or 1:many mapping connection type.

Use the mapping connection type to map external data source information specific to one user, such as when a SAP system contains a user's personal details. If your data source returns one row of personal data per user, then use the 1:1 mapping connection. In this situation, you would select the user profile property, such as the AccountName from the Return Items Identified By This Profile Property drop-down list. In the metadata, this information has to map to an Identifier property for the external content type, with a matching *SpecificFinder* method. Both the user profile property and the identity type must match—for example, they both must be text; one cannot be defined as an integer and the other as a text string. If your data source contains more than one row per user, then use the 1:many mapping connection. From the Filter Items By drop-down list, select the property in the entity that identifies the rows in the data source for a user, and then in the second drop-down list, which is labeled Use This Profile Property As The Filter Value, select the profile property whose value can be used as the filter value.

NOTE Microsoft has jointly developed a solution built on top of BCS that will allow interoperability between SAP application and SharePoint 2010 called Duet Enterprise for Microsoft SharePoint and SAP. You can find more information about this solution at *http://blogs.msdn.com/bcs/archive /2009/11/24/duet-enterprise-for-microsoft-sharepoint-and-sap.aspx*.

Summary

In this chapter, you have explored the Business Connectivity Service (BCS) application, previously known in SharePoint Server 2007 Enterprise Edition as the Business Data Catalog. The BCS application is now available in both SharePoint Foundation 2010 and SharePoint 2010. The BCS connectivity layer, the Business Data Connectivity (BDC), uses connectors to access the external systems using the metadata definitions in the BDC Model. After the external system's metadata is imported into a BCS application, you can use the external data in the SharePoint sites associated with the BCS application. The BCS provides a number of mechanisms for presenting the data, such as the Business Data Web Parts, External Data Columns, Search, user profiles and—new in SharePoint 2010—External Lists. This reduces the need to write custom code to retrieve data from external systems and provides standard methods for integrating external data with data held within SharePoint sites, lists, and libraries, thereby allowing for the creation of dashboards that can aggregate data from a number of external systems as well as with data stored in SharePoint.

## CHAPTER 19

Web Parts and Their Functionality in SharePoint 2010

Introducing Web Parts

Web Parts are components that offer reusable functionality when added to a Web Part Page. An example is a Web Part that provides the current weather forecast for your region. Because every user is not from the same region, you can add a weather Web Part to different pages and offer the same functionality on each page, yet users would be able to customize the functionality on each page, too. For example, users could customize the weather forecast by setting their own postal codes using the Web Part properties; then each user would see the weather forecast for his or her own region. In Microsoft SharePoint Server 2007, you added Web Parts to Web Part zones. In Microsoft SharePoint 2010, you add them directly to a region on the page, as you can see in the "Managing Web Parts" section of this chapter. The important thing to remember is that you write Web Parts just once—and then you can reuse them any number of times.

Web Parts continue the ongoing effort by Microsoft to provide users with an easy way to build plug-and-play websites.

Before You Begin Developing Web Parts

Most developers know that you can access data quickly with very little code. However, if you are creating a fully functional Web Part that offers filtering, sorting, categorization, conditional formatting, and numeric formatting options, you can find yourself authoring a Web Part that takes months or years to finish. Then you have to maintain it and support it. And what happens if the developer who authored the Web Part leaves the company? All this effort and expense might not be necessary, however.

SharePoint 2010 offers a vast range of different types of Web Parts. Whether you want to aggregate content from other sites, display list content, or display a Silverlight component or line-of-business data, it is likely you could find a Web Part that provides that functionality out of the box. Indeed, there are so many Web Parts in SharePoint 2010 that it would be time consuming to learn about all of them. Unfortunately, companies often make the mistake of spending time and money developing custom Web Parts when the Web Part they need is already available with SharePoint, simply because they didn't take the time to research the Web Parts that ship with SharePoint. Because a lot of SharePoint functionality is expressed through Web Parts, it stands to reason that the product team provides a catalog of available Web Parts that offer specific functionality that you can add to a Web Part Page or wiki site.

Out-of-the-box Web Parts also offer a consistent "look and feel," which means that once a user has grasped the concept of one Web Part, it is easy to grasp the concept of another. This consistency extends to other features of Web Parts; for example, each Web Part offers the same context menu and shares many of the same properties, such as those found in the Appearance, Layout, and Advanced sections of all Web Parts. Even when you author your own custom Web Part, you inherit these properties. You can set these properties by clicking the drop-down arrow on the Web Part itself and then choosing either the Modify Shared Web Part or Modify My Web Part option, depending on your permissions to the site.

Managing Web Parts

In SharePoint 2010, you now insert and manage Web Parts using the Ribbon. Just like in previous versions of SharePoint, you initially put the page into Edit mode by choosing Site Actions and then Edit Page at the upper-left corner of the page. Then under the Editing Tools tab, select the Insert tab. When you are in Edit mode, the Ribbon appears as shown in Figure 19-1.

> **NOTE** In some templates, such as the Collaboration Portal template, you will not immediately see an Editing Tools tab. However, if you click a spot on the page that accepts Web Parts, the Editing Tools tab will appear and you'll be able to add Web Parts to the regions on the page that will accept them.

FIGURE 19-1 The Ribbon provides the features that allow you to insert Web Parts

Adding Web Parts

In SharePoint Server 2007, you insert Web Parts into a Web Part zone. The Web Part zones are predefined by the site definitions default.aspx. Although new Web Part zones can be added to the page using SharePoint Designer 2007, if you reset the page to the site definition, you lose your Web Part zone. This difficulty has been addressed in SharePoint 2010 so that now sites and Web Part Pages contain one big content zone. Within the content zone, you can insert text, images, reusable content, video and audio, and Web Parts. Your pages will flow better and you will have more control over the look and feel. Figure 19-2 shows content and a Web Part being inserted.

> **NOTE** You may see different categories of Web Parts, depending on the Features that you have enabled within your Site Collection.

FIGURE 19-2 The choice of Web Parts categorized by type in SharePoint 2010

The list of Web Parts is categorized by type, allowing you to navigate to the Web Part you want more easily. An About The Web Part section also describes the functionality of each Web Part and provides you with the option to select the section of the page in which the Web Part will be added.

To add a Web Part to a page, you must place your cursor in the target zone or region and then click the Add button in the lower-right corner of the screen. This loads the Web Part onto the page. After it is on the page, you can move the Web Part between zones or regions using a drag-and-drop method, but you cannot use this method to add the Web Part to the page initially.

Editing Web Parts

After you have added the Web Part to the content area, point to the Web Part to display a shortcut menu, shown in Figure 19-3. The shortcut menu provides you with the options to minimize, close, delete, edit the Web Part, connect it to another Web Part, or export it.

Depending on the Web Part and your permissions, you may not see all of these options. Third-party Web Parts may also offer additional choices. Users are often confused about the difference between closing and deleting a Web Part, because they both remove the Web Part from the page. Closing a Web Part maintains the properties that you set even though the Web Part is not visible, and you can retrieve it again using the Insert Web Part option without the need to reconfigure it. Deleting a Web Part removes the Web Part permanently. To move Web Parts, you can simply drag them using the mouse within or across content areas.

FIGURE 19-3 The Web Parts shortcut menu

 REAL WORLD **Removing a Broken Web Part**

t is quite common for a user to add a Web Part to a page and then find that the page produces errors. This can occur for several reasons, especially if the Web Part is a custom component. You can remove a Web Part from a page even if you cannot navigate to it, however. Use the site URL but add *?contents=1* to the end of the URL in the address bar. The Web Part Page Maintenance page appears. Use this interface to remove the problematic Web Part, as shown in Figure 19-4.

FIGURE 19-4 You display the Web Part Maintenance page by using a URL parameter.

The log files that you can find in the SharePoint Root folder under Logs provide useful information about any Web Part errors that have occurred. ULSViewer is a useful tool you can use to see live information written to the log files if you are looking for an error in the log files that may occur from a custom Web Part. You can download ULS Viewer from *http://code.msdn.microsoft.com/ULSViewer*.

Quite often Web Parts are the reason SharePoint pages to load slowly. Slow load times can be caused by poor configuration, such as attempting to roll up too much information in the Content Query Web Part, or by poor development by third-party companies. You can turn on the Developer Dashboard to help you find out which Web Part is causing this behavior by providing you with the following information.

- A breakdown of the request/response cycle with timings for each operation
- A breakdown of the response times for each database query that the Rendering process triggers
- A breakdown of the load times for each Web Part on the page

There are typically two ways to modify Web Part properties. You can either select Edit Web Part from the shortcut menu or click Open The Tool Pane, which is displayed in the majority of the available Web Parts.

After you have the tool pane open, you will notice that the properties are categorized. The categories, which are Appearance, Layout, and Advanced, will display for all Web Parts as long as you have permission to modify them. As well as these three categories, you will also usually see other categories of properties that are specific to the selected Web Part. In Figure 19-5, you can see Appearance, Layout, and Advanced as well as Query and Presentation categories, which are specific to the Content Query Tool Part.

> **NOTE** The Content Query Web Part is only available to add to a Web Part Page if you have activated the Publishing Feature. Publishing must be turned on for the site collections and for the site in which you are adding the Content Query Web Part.

FIGURE 19-5 The Content Query Tool Part providing options for Query and Presentation categories

Appearance

The Appearance category contains the following properties.

- **Title** Allows the user to change the title of the Web Part to a more suitable title. For example, if you are using the Content Query Web Part to roll up tasks for a user who is logged on, you might want to provide a title such as My Tasks instead of Content Query Web Part.

- **Height & Width**   The default Height and Width settings allow the Web Part to expand to fit the content within the boundaries of the content area. You can also set a fixed value for Height and Width.
- **Chrome State**   The Web Part chrome describes the border, menu, and title of the Web Part. This can be minimized or normal.
- **Chrome Type**   The Chrome Type setting allows you to choose between variations in how the Web Part is displayed, such as Title Only or Title And Border.

Layout

The Layout category provides the following properties.

- **Hidden**   The Hidden attribute allows the Web Part to be hidden within the zone. This is useful for Web Parts such as filter Web Parts that have a purpose on the page but do not need to be seen unless the page is in Edit mode.
- **Direction**   The Direction property allows the text within the Web Part to be justified to the left or to the right.
- **Zone**   The Zone properties allow you to change which Web Part zone the Web Part is to be in, and which order from top to bottom. This can also be changed by dragging and dropping the Web Part.

Advanced

The Advanced category is only displayed for users with Full Control on the site. The category contains the following properties.

- **Allow Options**   Use these to select what users without Full Control of the page are allowed to change, such as the Allow Minimize option. You can also select whether the user is allowed to close the page. This means that the site administrator can enforce rules such as ensuring that the Web Part is never deleted.
- **Export Mode**   You can decorate each property within the Web Parts tool pane with an attribute within the tool parts code that specifies the sensitivity of the property. For example, consider a password property within a Web Part. When exporting that Web Part, you would not want the password to be exported. As the site administrator, you can control whether properties decorated with sensitivity attributes should or should not be exported.
- **Title URL**   In some Web Parts, the title of the Web Part is a hyperlink. An example of this is a List View Web Part. By clicking the List View Web Part's title, you will navigate to the Lists default view. The URL for the hyperlinked title can be changed using this property.
- **Description**   Provides a description of the Web Part, which is displayed when the Web Part is being inserted.

- **Icon Image URL**   You can set the Category and Title URLs to allow a user to click the link, which can take them to a custom description page or external URL.

- **Import Error Message**   Import error messages are often vague. However, you can customize the error message to provide more information, such as how to obtain support from your company if the Web Part cannot be added.

- **Target Audiences**   Every Web Part can be targeted to a specific audience, which allows different Web Parts to be displayed depending on the profile setting for the user who is currently logged on.

- **Help URL**   Administrators can also add a help URL to describe to users how to use the Web Part.

Connecting Web Parts

Web Parts can be connected to each other for many reasons, such as providing a filter value to a consuming Web Part. For example, you might have the current user filter a Web Part passing through the current user name to a List View Web Part such as Tasks. You can connect the current user Web Part to the Task List View Web Part and then map the user name to the Assigned To column. You can also connect Web Parts to display content in alternative ways, such as displaying line-of-business data from Business Connectivity Services to the Chart Web Part.

Figure 19-6 shows an example in which the Current User Filter Web Part is connected to the Documents List View Web Part showing Documents that are modified or checked out to the current user.

FIGURE 19-6 Connecting filter Web Parts in SharePoint 2010

Exploring New and Improved Out-of-the-Box Web Parts

The Web Parts available out of the box with SharePoint 2010 have been organized into several categories. You can enable and disable many of these categories or Web Parts using features at the site collection level. For example, if you enable the SharePoint Server Publishing Infrastructure, you will add a total of six Web Parts to your site to support the publishing activities such as the Content Query Web Part.

In this section, you'll use the Team Site template with publishing turned on as the basis for the discussion of available Web Parts. Other templates will alter some of your content, but not substantially. The categories in which Web Parts are groups in the Team Site template are as follows.

- Lists And Libraries
- Business Data
- Content Rollup
- Document Sets (Requires the Document Sets feature to be activated at Site Collection Level)
- Filters
- Forms
- Media And Content
- Outlook Web App
- Search
- Social Collaboration
- Miscellaneous

It isn't possible to cover every Web Part in depth in the following sections, however. Some will be mentioned briefly and a few will be discussed in depth.

Lists And Libraries Web Parts

The Web Parts that ship with SharePoint in this category include those that have been available since Microsoft SharePoint Portal Server 2003: Announcements, Shared Documents, Tasks, Discussions, and Calendar.

One new Web Part that warrants note is the Drop Off Library. This document library is provisioned to look at the properties of a document as the document is uploaded into the library. Then, based on the rules that the library owner configures for the properties of the documents that are uploaded into the library, the document is automatically moved to another library. You can think of this library as a way to move documents to their proper hosting location automatically, based on their metadata assignments.

Displaying Content with Web Parts

SharePoint is full of content stored in lists and libraries. The content includes list items, documents, and images. The Content category provides you with Web Parts that display content in different ways. There are rollup Web Parts that aggregate content from lists or libraries in subsites along with Web Parts that display the content of a specific list or library.

Every document library and list Web Part within SharePoint can also be presented as a Web Part on the page, using a Web Part known as a List View Web Part. Some of the lists within a site would be useful if they were displayed on the home page of the site as well as by navigating to the list by using the Quick Launch. As an example, you could display the Announcements list on the home page of a team site so that members of that site see the announcements as soon as they navigate to the page.

SharePoint 2010 improves on the performance and user interface of the List View Web Part. The performance has been improved by providing AJAX options and therefore allowing the data to refresh automatically rather than by page refresh. Cache options have also been improved for the Web Part. Both of these options help improve page load times within your SharePoint environment. The new AJAX options can be seen in the tool pane when you edit a Web Part (see Figure 19-7).

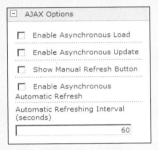

FIGURE 19-7 The AJAX options that are available in almost every SharePoint 2010 Web Part allow pages to refresh more quickly and reduce the number of round trips of .aspx pages.

The user interface of the List View Web Part, shown in Figure 19-8, provides better toolbar options, which can be turned on or off in the tool pane by turning the toolbar option on or off. It also displays the document icon, alternate row colors, and an Add New Item link at the bottom of the list items, which provides a quick way to add content.

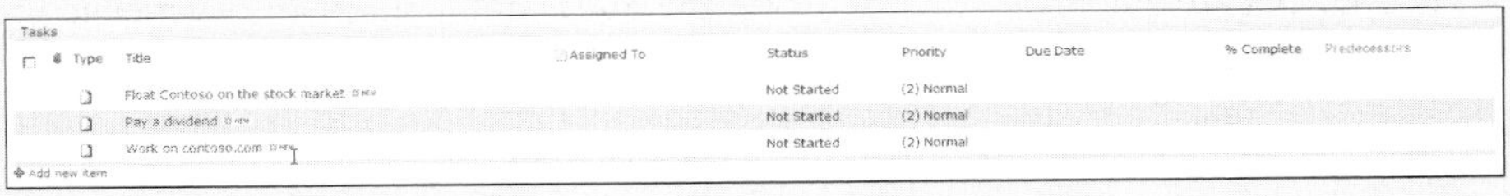

Tasks								
	Type	Title	Assigned To	Status	Priority	Due Date	% Complete	Predecessors
		Float Contoso on the stock market		Not Started	(2) Normal			
		Pay a dividend		Not Started	(2) Normal			
		Work on contoso.com		Not Started	(2) Normal			
Add new item								

FIGURE 19-8 List View Web Part and its improved user interface

Because site collections can become large in terms of the amount of data they host, it is sometimes helpful to roll up certain types of data into a single view. Don't expect site members to visit each site they belong to on a daily basis to check for new assigned tasks, documents, or announcements. The Content Rollup Web Part addresses this problem. It aggregates information (list items) from lists on multiple sites of the site collection and adds them to one Web Part. This one Web Part allows you to navigate to access your content.

Business Data Web Parts

The Business Data Web Parts in SharePoint 2010 are somewhat similar to what is available with SharePoint Server 2007. The purpose of the Business Data Web Parts is to present line-of-business data on Web Parts Pages. Each of the Web Parts can be connected to other business data Web Parts to provide the ability to drill down through data, such as to select a customer and then see the order history for that customer. The Web Parts can be used throughout SharePoint on Web Part Pages, team sites, dashboard sites, and workspaces. They can provide flexibility for the information worker to customize or personalize some aspects of the Web Part.

Figure 19-9 shows the Insert Web Part option, used to add a new Web Part on the page, displaying the choice of Web Parts in the Business Data category.

FIGURE 19-9 Business Connectivity Services Web Parts available using the Insert Web Part option

Business Data Actions

The Business Data Actions Web Part provides users with a list of actions that they can perform on a row of data from an external content type.

> **NOTE** What was called an Entity in SharePoint Server 2007 is now called an external content type in SharePoint 2010. It is effectively a dataset that contains an enumerator, methods, filters, and actions that can be used on a result set such as a table or stored procedure.

An *action* can be almost any URL that accepts parameters. The actions provide endless functionality to information workers who want to do more with the business data than just present it in a list or library. For example, think about what an end user needs to do with customer information. If the end user is a sales representative, he might want to search for customer information in an Internet search engine, look the customer up in a customer relationship management (CRM) system, or even send an e-mail to that customer.

The custom actions are created at the time of authoring the external content type using Visual Studio, SharePoint Designer, or a third-party tool. The following is an example of what a custom action looks like.

http://www.bing.com?searchparameter={0}

The {0} is a placeholder for one of the column values for a specific row. For example, if you click the custom action on Sven Freitag, the action would be a URL that looks like the following.

http://www.bing.com?searchparameter=Sven%20Freitag

The Business Data Actions Web Part is not the only place where these actions can be run; they can also be run from the title property in the Business Data List Web Part.

Business Data Catalog Filter

This Web Part is very useful within dashboard pages where your line-of-business data can involve data stored within a back-end system such as an Oracle database, but you also have related data stored in SharePoint lists and libraries. For example, your customer information might come from the CRM application by way of Business Connectivity Services (BCS), but your proposals for each customer are stored within a SharePoint document library.

Therefore, to link this information together, you can configure the Business Data Catalog Filter Web Part to provide you with a choice of rows whereby you can select a customer. A Web Part connection can then be sent to the List View Web Part to allow the filtering of documents. Therefore, if you want to see all documents related to Sven Freitag, you would select Sven Freitag from the Business Data Catalog Filter Web Part.

Business Data Item

The Business Data Item Web Part displays one row of data from an external content type in a columnar format. This Web Part is used out of the box on the profile page that is generated when the external content type is created. The Business Data Item Web Part contributes to a well-laid-out dashboard page. Quite often your tables will contain too many columns to display all of them on the screen using the Business Data List Web Part. For example, a table containing customer information could have the following columns.

- Customer ID
- Company Name
- Address
- Address2
- City
- State
- ZIP

- Country
- Telephone
- Fax
- Website

Displaying all of that information in a horizontal table layout would take up too much room on the page. Instead, you might decide to show only the company name, city, and state columns. This would take up less room but still allow you to drill down if required. In other words, you link the Business Data List Web Part to the Business Data Item Web Part that shows all of the columns. Because the Business Data Column Web Part is displayed in columnar format, the width of the page doesn't matter. To show detailed information, you simply need to click the name of one of your customers.

Although the Business Connectivity Services Web Parts still play a big role in BCS, the external list is a preferred method of displaying line-of-business data from an external content type because it also provides create, read, update, and delete (CRUD) capabilities. The external list can also be added to a SharePoint page just like a List View Web Part. They might not look very impressive initially, but when they are added to a Web Part Page, the additional columns, formatting, grouping, and so forth can be set in SharePoint Designer 2010 just like with any List View Web Part or Data View Web Part. An external list is shown in Figure 19-10.

	ProductID	ProductName	SupplierID	CategoryID	QuantityPerUnit	UnitPrice	UnitsInStock	UnitsOnOrder	ReorderLevel
	1	Chai	1	1	10 boxes x 20 bags	18.0000	39	0	10
	2	Chang	1	1	24 - 12 oz bottles	19.0000	17	40	25
	3	Aniseed Syrup	1	2	12 - 550 ml bottles	10.0000	13	70	25
	4	Chef Anton's Cajun Seasoning	2	2	48 - 6 oz jars	22.0000	53	0	0
☑	5	Chef Anton's Gumbo Mix	2	2	36 boxes	21.3500	0	0	0
	6	Grandma's Boysenberry Spread	3	2	12 - 8 oz jars	25.0000	120	0	25
	7	Uncle Bob's Organic Dried Pears	3	7	12 - 1 lb pkgs.	30.0000	15	0	10
	8	Northwoods Cranberry Sauce	3	2	12 - 12 oz jars	40.0000	6	0	0
	9	Mishi Kobe Niku	4	6	18 - 500 g pkgs.	97.0000	29	0	0
	10	Ikura	4	8	12 - 200 ml jars	31.0000	31	0	0
	11	Queso Cabrales	5	4	1 kg pkg.	21.0000	22	30	30

FIGURE 19-10 An external list displaying data

Status Indicator

SharePoint Server 2007 saw the introduction of a Key Performance Indicator (KPI) Web Part that has now been replaced with the Status Indicator Web Part. PerformancePoint Services in Microsoft SharePoint 2010 provides a far better KPI view than that of the previous KPI Web Part.

Status indicators are configured via a status list Web Part that can be created within any site to show the status of SharePoint list values, a Microsoft Excel workbook, Microsoft SQL Server Analysis Services, or Fixed Values. Goals can be set for each cell or row, or the data can be entered manually, depending on your source. The Status Indicator Web Part is then configured to point at your status indicator list and then displays the KPIs as required. The Status Indicator Web Part can also be connected to the Status Indicator Details Web Part to allow a user to drill down to see details. The Status Indicator Web Part is shown in Figure 19-11.

FIGURE 19-11 The Status Indicator Web Part preconfigured to display a key performance indicator

Content Rollup Web Parts

Content Rollup Web Parts focus on aggregating and displaying data from other sources. For example, the RSS Viewer Web Part lets you display either external feeds or feeds provided from SharePoint lists. The RSS Viewer Web Part is actually based on the Data View Web Part; it receives the same type of AJAX page refreshes as well as the ability to apply the same conditional formatting/filtering/sorting options that you would receive using SharePoint Designer 2010 on the Data View Web Part. Figure 19-12 is an example of a style-configured RSS Viewer Web Part.

FIGURE 19-12 The RSS Viewer aggregating content from a popular SharePoint blog site

Another example is the Sites In Category Web Part, which display links to other SharePoint sites that are listed with a certain category definition. The Summary Links Web Part is still available in SharePoint 2010, and it allows site members to group and style links to any URL-addressable location. This gives them a way to build out a customized navigation from the site that fits their explicit needs without the assistance of a developer.

For site collections that contain a number of subsites and libraries, there is the Table Of Contents Web Part, which will expose the hierarchy of a site collection in a navigable view.

> **MORE INFO** To learn more about the RSS standard, visit *http://www.rssboard.org /rss-specification*.

The Content Query Web Part (CQWP) is a rollup Web Part that lets you aggregate SharePoint list items, including documents from document libraries from anywhere within the site collection. Consider that in every subsite you have a tasks list with tasks assigned to you. The Content Query Web Part can be configured to roll up the task lists to one Web Part in a central location. The Web Part can also be used to provide navigation to content pages or even as an RSS viewer. Figure 19-13 illustrates a task list being rolled up throughout a site collection.

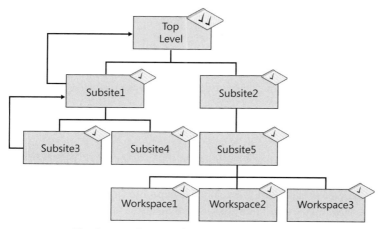

FIGURE 19-13 The Content Query Web Part can aggregate data throughout a site collection.

The tool pane for the Content Query Web Part provides both a Query category and a Presentation category. Within the Query category, you specify locations from which you want to aggregate data. You then specify the type of content that you want to aggregate by choosing the list type and/or the content type. If you have created a custom content type that inherits from a parent, you can select the check box to include Child Content Types. Another nice feature available with the Content Query Web Part is the ability to target the rolled-up content for a specific audience—the user who is logged on. Audience Targeting needs to be enabled at the list level, and each list item needs to be targeted for the CQWP to filter the results. Figure 19-14 displays the query properties.

Within the Presentation category, properties exist that allow you to change the look and feel of the results. You can change sorting, grouping, and styles. If you are handy with XSL, you can create your own styles and store the XSL file in the style gallery at the top-level site. The Presentation category gives you the ability to display content in whatever way you like. For example, you can choose to display Calendar List items in a calendar view. One of the new features of the Content Query Web Part is the ability to add multiple columns instead of just the title. The same result can be achieved in SharePoint Server 2007, but it requires a lot of work, including the modification of XSL and XML files and the knowledge of the programmatic column names. Media Links can also be displayed and streamed through the Content Query Web Part, allowing you to display and run movie files from within the Web Part.

FIGURE 19-14 The Content Query Web Part query properties

Document Sets Web Parts

This is a new category with two new Web Parts that were added because of the new functionality of document sets in SharePoint 2010. To see this category you will need to enable the Document Set Feature. Essentially, a set of documents can be treated as a single entity for purposes of metadata and workflows—something that wasn't available in SharePoint Server 2007.

The two Web Parts in this category are the Document Set Contents and the Document Set Properties. The contents Web Part displays the contents of the document set, whereas the properties Web Part displays the properties of the document set.

Filter Web Parts

As the category name implies, these Web Parts filter data for easier viewing. For example, the Current User Web Part allows you to filter data based on who is viewing the page. This is different from audiences, which are built by filtering user profile data, SharePoint groups, or Active Directory groups. Instead, Filter Web Parts give you the ability to filter based on the security settings for the user so that only those items to which the user has permission will display.

The Filter Web Parts in SharePoint 2010 provide filtering options for other Web Parts using Web Part connections. Web Parts that can be filtered include List View Web Parts, Data View Web Parts, Business Data Web Parts, Content Query Web Parts, and also third-party Web Parts that consume the same connection type such as the Lightning Conductor Web Part from Lightning Tools. Figure 19-15 displays the Filter Web Parts available.

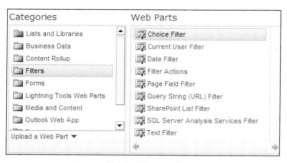

FIGURE 19-15 The available Filter Web Parts

The available sections are

- **Choice Filter**   Enter choices using the tool pane such as Departments (sales, marketing, IT, and so on). Users can then select one of the options, which will filter the results in the consuming Web Part.

- **Current User Filter**   Obtains the current user name for the user who is logged on. This can then be connected to a consuming Web Part to filter the results, such as a Task List View Web Part. Connecting to columns such as Assigned To or Created By creates useful filtering scenarios so that only content intended for the user who is logged on is displayed.

- **Date Filter**   The Date Filter Web Part filter provides a date or date range to a consuming Web Part so that filtering on columns such as Due By will limit the results returned.

- **Filter Actions**   The Filter Actions Web Part is used when two or more Filter Web Parts are placed on a page, allowing you to combine the results of two or more filters.

- **Page Field Filter**   Pages within SharePoint are made up of properties such as Title. The Page Filter Web Part can take the property from the page and use it to filter the contents of another Web Part. This is especially useful when it is used with Content

Pages. For example, if the page is called Sales, it can filter results of all other Web Parts using the value Sales.

- **Query String (URL) Filter**   A page URL can contain a query string such as *http://contoso.com/pages/default.aspx?Department=sales*. The Query String (URL) Filter Web Part can then obtain the query paramater and pass it to consuming Web Parts for filtering purposes.

- **SharePoint List Filter Web Part**   The SharePoint List Filter Web Part can filter other Web Parts using a SharePoint list as the source of the filter. Figure 19-16 displays the tool pane of this Web Part, showing how the List, View, and Field Web Parts are selected as the sources of the filter.

- **SQL Server Analysis Services Filter**   Filters the contents of Web Parts using a list of values from SQL Server Analysis Services cubes. This is useful when building business intelligent dashboards.

- **Text Filter**   This Web Part offers a text box that allows users to enter any value, which will act as a filter value on consuming Web Parts.

FIGURE 19-16 Configuring the SharePoint List Filter Web Part

Forms Web Parts

This new category contains two new Web Parts. The first is the HTML Viewer Web Part, which allows you to build controls that connect to other Web Parts. This Web Part is not helpful unless it is connected to other Web Parts that contain data.

The HTML Form Web Part lets you provide custom HTML and Javascript to create a form that resides on a Web Part Page. The HTML Form Web Part is very useful as a filter Web Part when connected to other Web Parts such as a List View Web Part or even external lists. The following sample code creates a drop-down list from which users can select a department and send the selected department to a connected Web Part for filtering. For example, if your documents have a column called Department, by connecting the Web Parts, your users would be able to choose a department to filter by using the Forms Web Part.

```
<B>My Custom HTML Form Web Part</B><br/>
Select a department
<select>
 <option value="Sales">Sales Department</option>
 <option value="Marketing">Marketing Department</option>
 <option value="IT">IT Department</option>
 <option value="Accounts">Accounts Department </option>
</select>
<input type="button" value="Go"
onclick="javascript:_SFSUBMIT_"/>
</div>
```

The result of this code is shown in Figure 19-17.

FIGURE 19-17 The result when the HTML Form Web Part is configured using custom HTML code

The second Forms Web Part available is the InfoPath Form Web Part, which allows browser-enabled InfoPath forms to be displayed within the Web Part. The forms retain their functionality when displayed in this Web Part.

Media And Content Web Parts

This category contains the Content Editor Web Part, which allows site members to add and display content in nearly any manner they prefer. The Content Editor Web Part (CEWP) is not a new Web Part. It has been around since Microsoft SharePoint 2003 and is one of the most useful Web Parts available, especially to developers. The CEWP can be used to display the inbox from Outlook Web Access (which incidentially is far more powerful than the Inbox Web Part), override styles from the style sheets, hide Quick Launches, and run custom JavaScript or JQuery. If you need to get some client-side code onto a Web Part Page, the Content Editor Web Part is the tool you need to do it.

The Page Viewer Web Part displays other Web pages in an iFrame, which is useful if you want to display Web pages from dissimilar websites in a single view.

The Picture Library Slideshow Web Part provides you with an easy way to browse images that are stored within a picture library. Your images can be displayed in a random or sequential order, which you can set using the tool pane. The option only allows you to aggregate from one library at a time, although the Content Query Web Part can be used for the same purpose. Figure 19-18 displays a Picture Library Slideshow Web Part used to display a complex diagram image from a picture library.

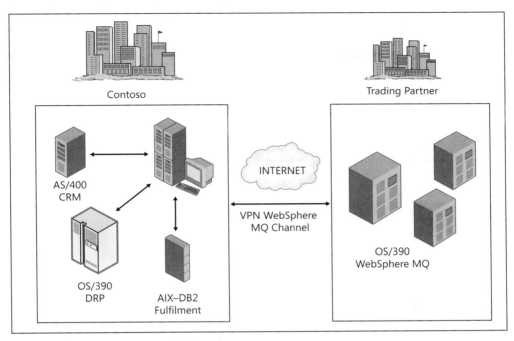

FIGURE 19-18 The Picture Library Slideshow in use

SharePoint Server 2007 shipped with a This Week In Pictures Web Part. The Picture Library Slide Slideshow Part provides better slideshow controls and displays images automatically without having to refresh the page.

Outlook Web App Web Parts

This category contains the Web Parts that allow you to have Outlook Web Access (OWA) functionality for your e-mail inbox on a SharePoint page. These Web Parts are basic in nature and do not replace the advanced functionality of OWA.

> **NOTE** If you need OWA functionality in a SharePoint site, consider using the Page Viewer Web Part to display the OWA page in an iFrame.

Navigation Category Web Parts

Another way to classify the Web Parts that aid in findability is to group them by Navigation or Search. Navigation is the act of clicking a series of links to arrive at the location that contains the data or documents you're trying to find. Search is the act of entering a keyword query that will return a result set of content items with links to the data or documents. The Navigation category isn't displayed in the Team Site template, so this sidebar will help you understand the group of Navigation Web Parts.

The majority of the Web Parts within the Navigation category are carried over from the previous version of SharePoint, including the Categories, Sites In Categories, Site Aggregator, Summary Links, and Table Of Contents Web Parts. In an earlier version of SharePoint, there was a Site Directory Web Site that provided the ability to link to subsites, workspaces, lists, or any other links to aid navigation. Each listing (link to a site) could be categorized using the following Web Parts.

- **Categories**   Creates categories of links within the Site Directory to organize content. This Web Part has been improved by introducing AJAX functionality.
- **Sites In Categories**   Provides sites from the Site Directory within a specific category.
- **Summary Links**   Used commonly in the Sites Directory. The Summary Links Web Part allows you to categorize and style any link marked as approved.
- **Table Of Contents**   Provides a table of contents of your sites. This Web Part contains three categories of properties in the tool pane: Content, Presentation, and Organization. The Content section lets you select a starting site for the table of contents. Presentation allows you to style and change display properties of the table of contents, and the Organization section provides the ability to change the sorting and grouping options.

Search Web Parts

The SharePoint 2010 Search Results page is made up of many Web Parts that can be configured to provide you with a customized search experience. The Web Parts discussed in this section can be used to configure your search results page.

Advanced Search Box

The Advanced Search Box, shown in Figure 19-19, provides users with the ability to search using more than just a text box containing keywords. You can enter multiple search criteria using the Advanced Search Box Web Part.

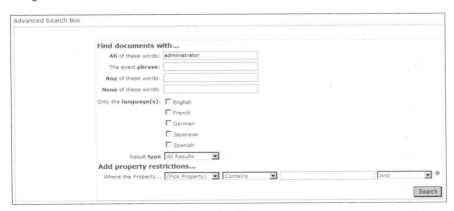

FIGURE 19-19 The Advanced Search Box Web Part

Dual Chinese Search

The Dual Chinese Search Web Part allows users to select from either traditional or simplified Chinese when entering search criteria. This Web Part can also be configured to obtain this value from the browser.

Federated Results

The Federated Results Web Part displays Search results in a structured XML view, which can be styled using out-of-the-box or custom XSLT. The location of the search results is set using the options available on the tool pane, which include the following.

- Internet Search Results
- Internet Search Suggestions
- Local Search Results
- Local People Search Results
- Local FAST Search Results

The tool pane shown Figure 19-20 displays the location property of the Federated Results Web Part commonly used on Search result pages.

FIGURE 19-20 The Federated Search Result Web Part tool pane showing the location property

Refinement Panel

The Refinement Panel Web Part enables searchers to minimize large results by refinement of the results by type, site, author, or modified date. Using the tool pane for this Web Part, you can modify the accuracy index by choosing the top number of results to analyze in order to refine them.

Search Core Results

The Search Core Results Web Part displays the results of your search. This Web Part includes a number of settings you can apply, including location, description, and scope within the location properties, along with results sorting, number of characters to display in the summary of each returned item, and the number of characters in each URL. Developers can customize the XSLT of the Web Part to display the results in an alternate way.

Related Queries

The Related Queries Web Part will display any related queries to the performed search.

Search Action Links

The Search Action Links Web Part displays actions that the user might want to perform on the returned results. The following actions can be displayed or hidden using the tool pane.

- Relevance View
- Modified Date View
- Search from Windows
- Alert Me
- RSS Link

Search Best Bets

Using the Search Best Bets Web Part, administrators or content authors can create keywords within SharePoint from the Site Settings page. These keywords can be associated with a returned result and marked as the best bet result for that particular search term.

Search Paging

The Search Paging Web Part provides users with navigation between the result sets, which by default will show 50 returned items at a time.

Search Statistics

The Search Statistics Web Part displays the speed of a search. Other statistics can be shown, such as the number of results shown on a page, total number of results, search response time, and latency traces. The Search Statistics tool pane is shown in Figure 19-21.

FIGURE 19-21 The Search Statistics Tool Pane displaying the statistic options available

Top Federated Results

The Top Federated Results Web Part shows and highlights the top items (you specify the number) returned from a specified location.

Social Collaboration Web Parts

With the advent of social computing and collaboration comes the introduction of social collaboration Web Parts. There are six Web Parts in this category. The one that you are likely to use most often is the Tag Cloud Web Part.

Tagging, introduced in SharePoint 2010, is an easy and natural way to provide navigation to content. If the User Profile service and My Sites service is enabled, users can tag documents, list items, lists, pages, sites, and external content. Each tagged item can be selected to display within the Tag Cloud Web Part. For example, when uploading a document to a SharePoint

2010 document library, users can enter their own metadata, which tags the document, as shown in Figure 19-22. The Tag option is displayed on the Ribbon that is displayed at the upper right of every page, allowing you to tag the document and choose when the tag will display.

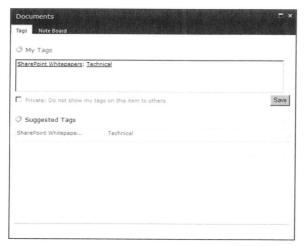

FIGURE 19-22 Entering tags for use with the Tab Cloud Web Part

To tag external content , click the Tagging icon at the upper right of your page. You will see a link that says Right-Click Or Drag And Drop This Link To Your Browser's Favorites Or Bookmarks Toolbar To Tag External Sites. If you click the Tagging icon when browsing external sites, the Tagging interface shown in Figure 19-23 will open, allowing you to tag non-SharePoint websites and pages.

The tagging information is stored within your SharePoint user profile, which you can visit and manage by clicking the Welcome link and then selecting User Profile. When users have been tagging content, it is useful to display the results within the Tag Cloud Web Part, as shown in Figure 19-23.

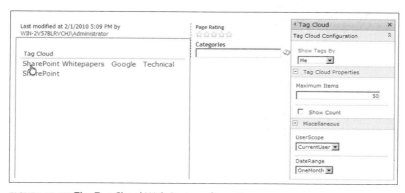

FIGURE 19-23 The Tag Cloud Web Part configuration

Other Web Parts

This section discusses a few other Web Parts that do not appear in the Team Site template.

The Data View Web Part

The Data View Web Part (DVWP) is often overlooked because it requires Microsoft SharePoint Designer to configure it. The DVWP can display data within a grid from many different types of data sources such as lists, libraries, XML files, SOAP Services, REST Services, direct database connections, or linked sources. When you have completed the configuration of the data source, you can manipulate the grid view from within SharePoint Designer. This used to be somewhat confusing in Microsoft SharePoint Designer 2007, but in Microsoft SharePoint Designer 2010, everything is laid out using the Ribbon instead of tabbed dialog boxes, which makes the manipulation more straightforward.

As shown in Figure 19-24, the Ribbon contains options that allow you to configure filters, sort and group columns, provide parameters (useful when connecting to chart Web Parts), insert formulas, set up pagination options, and add or remove columns.

> **NOTE** By adding columns to the grid, you can insert formulas or calculations in your data.

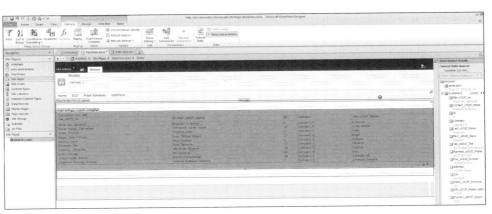

FIGURE 19-24 The Data View Web Part in SharePoint Designer 2010

The Data View Web Part also provides conditional formatting. Conditional formatting within the Data View Web Part is very useful for hiding or formatting content based on a specific condition. In Figure 19-25, a column was inserted to display three traffic light images (Red, Amber, and Green). Two of the images are configured to hide, depending on the Hide When condition, to provide basic key performance indicator functionality. Figure 19-25 displays conditional formatting configured to display a KPI image based on a condition.

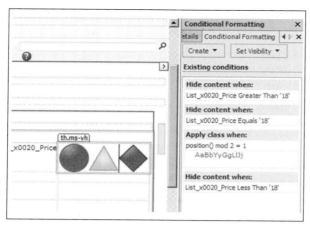

FIGURE 19-25 Configuring conditional formating using SharePoint Designer 2010 on the Data View Web Part

When the page is saved using SharePoint Designer, it can be viewed in the browser and tested. In Figure 19-26, you can see the traffic light indicators displayed in the last column; which indicator is displayed depends on a specific condition: the price of the product. This same functionality can be used on any data source with the Data View Web Part.

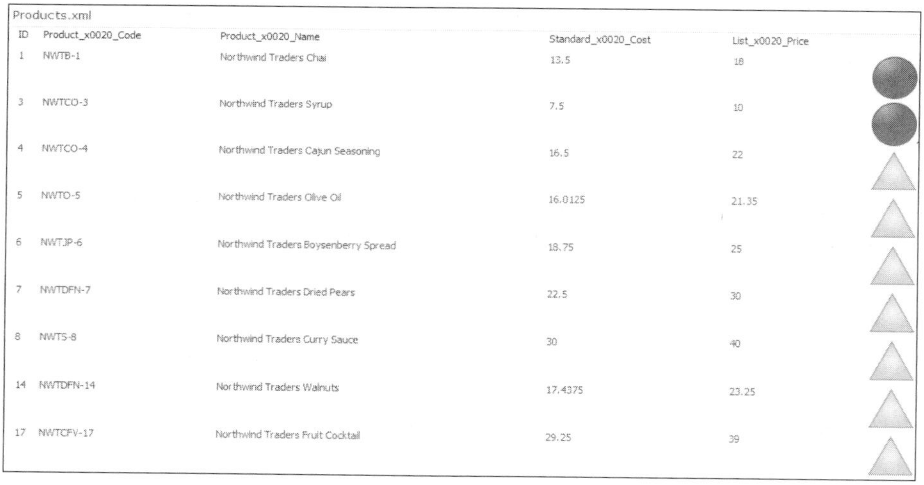

Products.xml

ID	Product_x0020_Code	Product_x0020_Name	Standard_x0020_Cost	List_x0020_Price	
1	NWTB-1	Northwind Traders Chai	13.5	18	●
3	NWTCO-3	Northwind Traders Syrup	7.5	10	●
4	NWTCO-4	Northwind Traders Cajun Seasoning	16.5	22	▲
5	NWTO-5	Northwind Traders Olive Oil	16.0125	21.35	▲
6	NWTJP-6	Northwind Traders Boysenberry Spread	18.75	25	▲
7	NWTDFN-7	Northwind Traders Dried Pears	22.5	30	▲
8	NWTS-8	Northwind Traders Curry Sauce	30	40	▲
14	NWTDFN-14	Northwind Traders Walnuts	17.4375	23.25	▲
17	NWTCFV-17	Northwind Traders Fruit Cocktail	29.25	39	▲

FIGURE 19-26 The KPIs that display using SharePoint Designer and conditional formatting

The Data View Web Part not only allows you to view data; for some data sources, you can configure it to allow create, read, update, and delete (CRUD) functionality. Consider carefully before enabling the CRUD functionality on a data source, however, since your underlying data source might contain referential integrity rules or validation rules that the DVWP will not be aware of. This can result in an error being displayed if a user attempts to insert an inapropriate value.

The Linked Sources option of the Data View Web Part is especially useful. Linked Data Sources allow you to merge two lists, and the lists do not need to be of the same type. Or, it can provide a one-to-many type relationship based on a column name and type in common. You can use this capability to merge two or more task lists together, acting as a rollup Web Part, or to provide documents related to each task if they have a field in common.

The Data View Web Part has been improved to offer AJAX functionality, better caching, and support for additional data sources including Representational State Transfer (REST) services.

PerformancePoint Services in SharePoint 2010 Web Parts

Microsoft PerformancePoint Services 2007 is a stand-alone product that sits alongside SharePoint Server 2007 to provide business intelligence dashboards through Web Parts that provide score cards, key performance indicators, trends, and charts. SharePoint 2010 Enterprise Edition incorporates PerformancePoint as a service in the same way it does with Excel Services and Form Services. There is a site collection–scoped feature used to enable the PerformancePoint options, and a site-scoped feature that requires enabling to make the PerformancePoint Web Parts available. Administrators can manage data connections within a data connections library that provides connection capabilities to Analysis Services, SQL Server, SharePoint lists, and Excel Services.

SharePoint 2010 provides you with a PerformancePoint Dashboard Designer that allows you to create and manage dashboards such as reports, strategic maps, analytics, scorecards, and filters. The Web Parts discussed in this section can be added to SharePoint pages and consume or provide Web Part connections to other SharePoint Web Parts.

Reports

The Reports Web Part allows you to display analytic charts, grids, SQL Server Reporting Services Reports, Excel Services reports, and the strategy map.

Scorecard

The Scorecard Web Part provides view functionality for the scorecard. Without the Scorecard Web Part, the user is not able to render the KPIs in the dashboard. Scorecards may be linked to other Web Parts, such as filters and reports, to create an interactive dashboard experience. Users can use the Scorecard Web Part to do the following.

- Locate and add a Scorecard View Web Part to a dashboard.
- Add KPIs—new and existing—to a scorecard.
- Enter an advanced scorecard design surface to define relationships between KPIs and objectives as well as edit KPI and objective properties.
- Build a new scorecard, launching the scorecard design surface.

Filter

The PerformancePoint Filter Web Part enables users to filter the results of other SharePoint Web Parts and PerformancePoint Web Parts via Web Part connections. When you connect the Web Parts, you can select or provide a filter value that will cause the consuming PerformancePoint Web Parts to receive a value they can use to filter the results.

StackSelector

Dashboards can become very busy Web Part Pages. PerformancePoint now provides the ability to create layers of Web Parts—known as *stacks*—within a page. The StackSelector Web Part allows you to then choose the stack you want to display by selecting it from a drop-down list.

Web Analytics

A new Web Part in SharePoint 2010 is the Web Analytics Web Part. This Web Part provides useful information on the page such as

- Frequency of visits
- Popularity
- Popularity rank-trend
- Filtering options for title and department

The Web Part can be scoped to the current site collection, the current site only, or the current site and all subsites. You can use item limits and specify a period to control the volume of content that is displayed. Figure 19-27 shows the tool pane of the Web Analytics Web Part and how it can be configured.

FIGURE 19-27 Configuring the Web Analytics Web Part

Office Client Web Parts

Microsoft Office 2010 plays a much bigger part in SharePoint 2010 than it did in the previous versions of SharePoint. The Excel Web Access Web Part was available in SharePoint Server 2007, but you will see other new Office Client Web Parts in SharePoint 2010, such as the Info-Path Form Web Part.

Excel Web Access

Excel Services was introduced in SharePoint Server 2007 and provides you with the ability to show named ranges or objects from an Excel workbook within SharePoint using Excel Services. The Excel client is not required to display and interact with the workbook. Excel Services provides an Excel Web Access Web Part that can be used to display one of these objects, such as a chart from a workbook or table, to render it within the Web Part. You can use the Filter Web Parts to dynamically switch content within the Web Part based on end-user choice. Excel Web Access Web Parts provide business intelligence to dashboards or Web Part Pages throughout SharePoint.

InfoPath Form

Microsoft InfoPath 2010 is a product you use to create electronic forms that are either completed using the InfoPath client or InfoPath Form Services, which ships with the Enterprise Edition of SharePoint 2010. After you have designed an InfoPath 2010 form, you can publish it to an InfoPath Form Services library (basically, a document library) that will allow forms to be completed and stored within the library while promoting fields from the form as columns. This powerful feature allows users to sort, group, create workflows, and view completed forms from within SharePoint. The InfoPath Form Web Part allows a specified form that has been published to a form library to be displayed within a SharePoint Web Part Page so that users can easily create InfoPath 2010 content and submit it to the library without leaving the SharePoint 2010 environment.

WSRP Viewer

The WSRP Viewer Web Part provides you with the ability to display portlets, which are pluggable user interface software components that are managed and displayed in a Web portal. Portlets can be Java-based or Web Sphere–based. This can be a very powerful tool if your company has not fully integrated SharePoint and has a mixture of technologies in place for its portals. By using the WSRP Viewer, you can display content within SharePoint 2010 from these other technologies.

Silverlight Web Part

Saving the best until last! Microsoft Silverlight Web Parts have been scarce in earlier versions of SharePoint. And, although you could get them to run, it meant making a lot of changes to the Web.config file to allow them to run. Microsoft now supports Silverlight in SharePoint 2010 and has also provided a Silverlight Web Part for your convenience. Developers can create Silverlight applications using Microsoft Visual Studio and other Microsoft products, such as Microsoft Expression Blend, to create great-looking, media-rich applications.

When you add a Silverlight Web Part, you will be prompted for the URL to the XAP file. After you enter the URL, your Silverlight application will execute within a SharePoint page. Figure 19-28 shows an example of a SharePoint Silverlight Web Part.

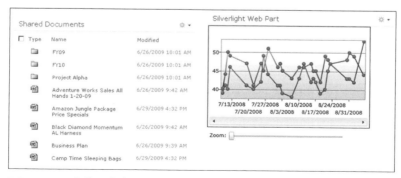

FIGURE 19-28 A SharePoint cocument library connected to a Silverlight application

Summary

This chapter introduced you to managing Web Parts within SharePoint 2010 and explained some of the changes that have occurred between versions that affect how you add Web Parts, connect them, and set properties. You should always consider using existing out-of-the-box Web Parts that can provide you with the functionality you need before making the decision to develop your own custom Web Parts. You explored many of the out-of-the-box Web Parts available in SharePoint 2010, including those in the Search, Content Rollup, and Business Connectivity Services categories, and learned about how to use List View Web Parts and Data View Web Parts, among many others.

Publishing SharePoint 2010 to Mobile Devices

With the advent of mobile devices came a mini information revolution, as everyone grabbed smart phones and proceeded to attempt to connect to everything from favorite websites to line-of-business applications. It wasn't long before people demanded mobile access to their SharePoint data as well. With more and more organizations building their information storage, collaboration, and publishing infrastructures on the SharePoint platform, it only makes sense that more and more users want to be able to get to that data, from wherever, whenever, securely. The market share of smart phones rises steadily, and better and faster data services are widely available, which has led to more mobile applications and the need for additional secure access to data for those applications.

Compounding this rapid mobile data expansion is the variety of scenarios within which a user needs secure mobile access to company information. The days when mobile devices were expensive and provided to users by an organization's information technology (IT) department are long gone. Today, users needing secure mobile access to information could have company-provided devices, or they may have purchased their own devices and want to use them to connect to company systems.

Microsoft recognized these changing market dynamics and has made significant investments in mobile device software, technologies, and the secure access mechanisms needed to glue them together. Investments with multiple original equipment manufacturer (OEM) partners have brought about the concept of the *converged device*. The focus has been on end-user experience and the leveraging of these devices as a platform for applications and services.

This chapter explores the ways you as an implementer and administrator can make data stored within Microsoft SharePoint 2010 available to users in a variety of mobile device access scenarios. Beginning with an understanding of the options available for mobile access, this chapter also reviews the detailed configuration steps needed to implement each within SharePoint. You will learn about enhancements delivered with SharePoint 2010, such as SMS Alerts, and features provided within SharePoint 2010 and Microsoft Office Mobile 2010, such as Microsoft SharePoint Workspace Mobile 2010, mobile search, mobile views and document viewers, and mobile Web Parts.

Introducing SharePoint Mobile in 2010

Microsoft SharePoint 2010, Microsoft Office Mobile 2010, and Mobile Document Viewers provide many enhancements that are the result of substantial Microsoft investment in mobile data access capabilities. The new SharePoint Workspace Mobile 2010 provides the capability to connect to SharePoint sites in a secure manner from Windows Mobile devices, includes a simple but effective interface for working with SharePoint data, and also provides for offline access to that data. Microsoft Office Web Applications provide the ability to view documents while on the go from almost any third-party mobile device, and mobile search allows users to find the information they need quickly and easily. Lastly, mobile views, which offer trimmed-down versions of SharePoint sites designed for mobile devices browsers, allow for access to list data and Web Parts in a familiar manner. In the following sections, you will explore each of these capabilities in more detail.

> **NOTE** Products built on Microsoft SharePoint Foundation contain mobile document viewers and hosting pages.

Microsoft Office Mobile 2010

Microsoft Office Mobile 2010 allows users to view and edit Microsoft Office Word, Microsoft Office Excel, and Microsoft Office PowerPoint documents using mobile devices. Users can edit documents sent as e-mail attachments or retrieved directly from a SharePoint site via SharePoint Workspace Mobile 2010. With a recognizable look and feel, Office Mobile 2010 provides a familiar user experience for mobile users. Whether you are simply reviewing documents while on the go, or you need to make edits, take notes, or modify a presentation, you can do it all from the comfort of your Windows Phone with Office Mobile 2010. The mobile applications included in Office Mobile 2010, as shown in Figure 20-1, are

- Office Word Mobile 2010
- Office Excel Mobile 2010
- Office PowerPoint Mobile 2010

- Office OneNote Mobile 2010
- SharePoint Workspace Mobile 2010

FIGURE 20-1 Office Mobile 2010

SharePoint Workspace Mobile 2010

SharePoint Workspace Mobile 2010 is new in Office Mobile 2010 and is available for devices running Windows Mobile 6.5 and later. By providing a familiar user experience for working with SharePoint data as well as offline access capabilities, SharePoint Workspace Mobile 2010 is a powerful new tool for increasing the mobility of users. The main features of SharePoint Workspace Mobile 2010 are

- Familiar interface for working with SharePoint lists and document libraries
- Offline access for SharePoint data synchronized with the device
- Ability to directly edit Office documents (Word, Excel, PowerPoint, and OneNote)

Figure 20-2 shows an example of the SharePoint Workspace Mobile 2010 experience.

FIGURE 20-2 SharePoint Workspace Mobile 2010

🌐 *REAL WORLD* Using Mobile Access Abroad or at Home

Mobile devices are being purchased more and more by consumers who use them for a combination of business and personal activities. With the increased availability of mobile devices that can make phone calls, access the Internet, take photographs, read e-mail, compose documents, and play music and video games, the world becomes just a little smaller, and people become less and less reliant on the bulk of a desktop or even a laptop computer.

SharePoint 2010 provides mobile device access options from almost any phone or device and a rich user experience from Windows Phone devices. With Microsoft Office Mobile SharePoint Workspace 2010 installed, people can collaborate on SharePoint data and documents from anywhere, at any time. For example, if you get an alert on your phone from your publishing site, with SharePoint Workspace Mobile 2010 you can respond to the request for publishing of new content immediately. Not only can you participate in the workflow, but you can also verify the document or task from your device. Why is this all important? Why do people care about working on their phones if they can just log in from their computers and do everything they need to from there?

Imagine for a moment that you are in Moscow. As the lead engineer for your project, you and a few others from your company have been discussing the advantages of using your widget with your Russian counterparts, and you have been working with them to implement the project within their systems. It's the end of a long day, with meeting after meeting. Your laptop battery is dead, it's 6:00 P.M., and you're hungry. Now, you're riding on the Metro back to your hotel, and your phone vibrates in your pocket. It's an e-mail from your boss back in Houston, Texas, where it's 9:00 A.M.

The e-mail is brief and vague, and almost before you've finished reading it, you receive several additional messages from the team's SharePoint site. You have to build a presentation for a big meeting tomorrow, and you also need to review some requests to change the documentation for your last big project. You sigh as you realize the day is not over yet, and you make your way to a nearby restaurant. When you get to the restaurant, however, you realize there are no power outlets for your laptop, and no Internet connection. You smile and order anyway, pointing to the picture of the food you want to eat. Everything you need to access is right there in your pocket, and you simply load the SharePoint 2010 mobile application on your phone, completing most of your work before you even finish your meal.

If you can't relate to this scenario, imagine instead that you have just arrived home when you receive an alert on your phone that a spreadsheet has been updated with the latest totals for a shipment you were working on. Your laptop is still plugged in to its docking station back at the office, a full 45 minutes away. Last month, you would have needed to pack up your laptop, bring it home, and log onto your SharePoint site to review the updates online. Now you simply load the SharePoint 2010 mobile application on your phone and view the alert before your garage door has finished closing.

Then you can open the spreadsheet and review the information that was updated, noticing immediately that the numbers are not correct. After checking out the document and making the minor updates, you check in the document again and create a new task for your coworker to verify the numbers you've edited. Then, stuffing the phone into your pocket, you walk through the door to your family, just in time for dinner. They won't have to wait for you today, and you have just saved yourself the hassle of having to catch up in the morning.

Microsoft Office Web Applications

Microsoft Office Web Applications provide the user the ability to work with Microsoft Office Word, Excel, PowerPoint, and OneNote documents online from personal computers, mobile devices, and the Web. Office Web Applications are available to customers using products built on Microsoft SharePoint Foundation 2010. When Office Web Applications are installed, documents stored in SharePoint libraries can be opened in the Web browser directly. In addition, the PowerPoint Web application enables the PowerPoint Broadcast Slide Show features, which allows you to broadcast a PowerPoint slideshow to users who can access the broadcast in a Web browser. Users of Window Mobile phone devices can leverage Microsoft Office Mobile 2010 as a preferred method for working with Office documents. Users of other devices, of which there are many, also can leverage mobile document viewers as a quick and easy way to access certain Microsoft Office documents from within the SharePoint 2010 mobile interface or from an SMS alert link. The Microsoft Office document types supported by mobile document viewers are

- Microsoft Office Word
- Microsoft Office Excel
- Microsoft Office PowerPoint
- Microsoft Office OneNote

The Word Mobile Viewer includes many exciting new features, including

- Page content rendering (text and image view)
- User interface (UI) with toolbar and menu areas
- Page navigation
- Page thumbnails
- Document property
- Find

The Excel Mobile Viewer includes many exciting new features, including

- Spreadsheet rendering
- UI with toolbar and menu areas
- Sheet navigation
- Show chart/illustration images
- Named item view
- Document property
- Find

The PowerPoint Mobile Viewer includes many exciting new features, including

- Slide content rendering (outline and slide view)
- UI with toolbar and dialog boxes
- PowerPoint Broadcast
- Slide navigation
- Slide thumbnails
- Document property
- Find

The mobile viewers included with Office Web Applications support the file formats listed in Table 20-1.

TABLE 20-1 Supported File Types

MOBILE VIEWER	SUPPORTED FORMATS
Word Mobile Viewer	.doc, .docx, .dot, .dotx, .docm, .dotm
Excel Mobile Viewer	.xlsx, .xlsm, .xlsb
PowerPoint Mobile Viewer	.ppt, .pptx

To use Office Web Applications and mobile document viewers within your deployment, you first must perform the following activities.

- Install Office Web Applications
- Activate the Office Web Applications services
- Activate the Office Web Applications features

Installing Office Web Applications

Follow these steps to set up Microsoft Office Web Applications for use. You must go through these same steps on each Web front-end (WFE) server in the farm. Be sure to complete these steps before continuing to the next section in this chapter.

1. Copy the Web Application Companions (WAC) Server Setup file to a local drive on the server.
2. Run the WAC Server Setup file.
3. Enter the product key code for your SharePoint installation.
4. Select a file location for the search index files. These files can be large, so make sure you select a drive with adequate disk space.
5. Monitor the installation process to completion.
6. Run the SharePoint Products Configuration Wizard.
7. When you have completed all the steps to configure the installation using the wizard, close the window.

Checking the Status of Office Web Application Services

After you have installed the software and run the SharePoint Products Configuration Wizard, you need to activate the services on each server. If you just ran the SharePoint Products Configuration Wizard for the first time, the services might already be deployed and activated. You can also set up these services through the Farm Configuration Wizard. If you ran the Farm Configuration Wizard prior to the installation of Office Web Applications, you should check the status of these services manually, and if needed, activate them manually or via Windows PowerShell. To determine if the services are running, perform the following steps.

1. Open a browser and go to the SharePoint Central Administration website.

2. Click the Manage Services On Server link located under the System Settings action group.

3. Check the status of each of the following services.

   - Excel Calculation Services
   - PowerPoint Service
   - Word Viewing Service

Activating Services and Creating Application Proxies

If any of the Office Web Application services are not running, start them and create a service application proxy for each. You can do this within the SharePoint Central Administration interface or by using Windows PowerShell. To start the services and create proxies manually, perform the following steps.

1. Open a browser and go to the SharePoint Central Administration website.

2. Click the Manage Services On Server link located under the System Settings action group.

3. If the Excel Calculation Services service is not already started, click Start and then follow the prompts for setting up this service.

4. If the PowerPoint Service is not already started, click Start.

5. If the Word Viewing Service is not already started, click Start.

6. Click the Central Administration link on the left menu to return to the main page.

7. Click the Manage Service Applications link, which is located under the Application Management action group.

8. If the Excel Services application does not already exist in the list, click New from the action menu and select Excel Services Application. Name the application Excel Services, use the SharePoint Web Services Default application pool, and click OK.

9. If the PowerPoint Service application does not already exist in the list, click New from the action menu and select PowerPoint Service application. Name the application PowerPoint Service, use the SharePoint Web Services Default application pool, and click OK.

10. If the Word Viewing Service application does not already exist in the list, click New from the action menu and select Word Viewing Service application. Name the application Word Viewing Service, use the SharePoint Web Services Default application pool, and click OK.

You can also set up the service instances using Windows PowerShell. To do so, run the following script after customizing it to meet the needs of your environment.

```
$serversToActivate = @("contosoapp1","contosoapp2")
$svcInstanceNames = @("Word Viewing Service", "PowerPoint Service",
"Excel Calculation Services")
foreach ($server in $serversToActivate) {
foreach ($svcInstance in $svcInstanceNames){
    $svcID = $(Get-SPServiceInstance | where
        {$_.TypeName -match $svcInstance} | where
        {$_.Server -match "SPServer Name="+$server}).ID
    Start-SPServiceInstance -Identity $svceID
}
}
```

You can also set up the service application proxies using Windows PowerShell. To do so, run the following script.

```
$appPool = Get-SPIisWebServiceApplicationPool -Identity "SharePoint Web Services Default"
New-SPWordViewingServiceApplication -Name "WdView" -ApplicationPool $appPool |
New-SPWordViewingServiceApplicationProxy -Name "WdProxy"
New-SPPowerPointServiceApplication -Name "PPT" -ApplicationPool $appPool |
New-SPPowerPointServiceApplicationProxy -Name "PPTProxy"
New-SPExcelServiceApplication -Name "Excel" -ApplicationPool $appPool
```

Activating Site Collection Features

After the service application proxies are set up, you will need to activate the Office Web Applications features in any existing site collections where you want to enable these capabilities. This is only necessary for existing site collections, because new site collections will already have these features in place. First, review how you would enable the Office Web Application features within an existing site collection.

1. From the top site within the site collection, use the Site Actions menu to select Site Settings.

2. Within Site Settings, select Site Collection Features, which can be found under the Site Collection Administration Settings group.

3. Activate the feature called Office Web Apps.

> **NOTE** There are two additional features, Office Mobile Web View feature and PowerPoint Viewing For Office Mobile, that enable you to view Word and PowerPoint documents from Windows Mobile and Windows Phone devices. These features will not be active on new sites by default, but you can activate them at the site collection level when needed.

You can also activate site collection features using Windows PowerShell. To activate the Office Web Applications feature for all existing site collections, run the following script. Note that you may get an error regarding the PowerPoint Broadcast site collection when you run this script if you used the Farm Configuration Wizard to set up Office Web Applications.

```
$webAppsFeatureId = $(Get-SPFeature -limit all | where {$_.displayname -eq
"OfficeWebApps"}).Id Get-SPSite -limit ALL |foreach{ Enable-SPFeature
$webAppsFeatureId -url $_.URL }
```

It's important to mention that when the feature is activated, libraries will be configured by default to open relevant documents using Office Web Applications instead of the Office client application. You can override this functionality at the site collection and document library levels. To disable the setting for all site collections and revert back to client applications, run the following script.

```
$webAppsFeatureId = $(Get-SPFeature -limit all | where {$_.displayname
              -eq "OpenInClient"}).Id
Get-SPSite -limit ALL |foreach{
              Enable-SPFeature $webAppsFeatureId -url $_.URL }
```

To disable the setting for all document libraries within a given site, run the following script after customizing it to meet the needs of your environment.

```
Get-SPWeb -site http://webappsites/site1 |% {}{$_.Lists}{$_.Update()} |%
{$_.DefaultItemOpen = $false}
```

You can also disable the new default open behavior within a single document library using the Advanced Settings interface in Library Settings, as shown below in Figure 20-3.

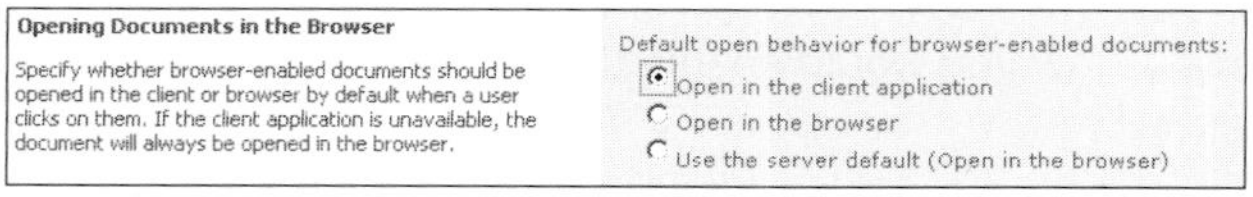

FIGURE 20-3 Change the default open behavior for an individual document library.

Controlling Service-Specific Settings

It is possible to control granular service options for each of the Office Web Applications services. Each service provides a specific set of switches and toggles that can be manipulated to control the behavior of the service. To access these settings, open a browser and go to the Central Administration website and then click Manage Service Applications, highlight the appropriate service application, and click the Properties icon on the Ribbon. The following options are available for each service.

EXCEL SERVICES

- **Global Settings** Define load balancing, memory, and throttling thresholds. Set the unattended service account and data connection time-outs.

- **Trusted File Locations**   Define places from which spreadsheets can be loaded.
- **Trusted Data Providers**   Add or remove data providers that can be used when refreshing data connections.
- **Trusted Data Connection Libraries**   Define a SharePoint Document Library from which data connections can be loaded.
- **User Defined Function Assemblies**   Register managed code assemblies that can be used by spreadsheets.

The detailed configuration options and settings for Excel Services are described in more detail in Chapter 21, "Business Intelligence, Reporting Services, and PerformancePoint Services."

POWERPOINT SERVICE

- **Supported File Formats**   Specify which presentation types users will be able to view using this PowerPoint Service Application. If a file format is not selected, users of this service will receive an error message when attempting to view a file of that format in the Web browser.
- **Broadcast Site**   Users can connect to a broadcast site from at least Microsoft PowerPoint 2010 and broadcast a slideshow to remote attendees who can watch it in a Web browser. This setting shows a site URL only if a default broadcast site was created during service creation.
- **PowerPoint 97–2003 Presentation Scanning**   To provide added security when loading PowerPoint 97 to PowerPoint 2003 presentations, the PowerPoint Service Application performs extra checks before those documents are opened. These checks have an impact on overall server performance. Only disable this setting if you trust *all* documents loaded by this instance of the service.

WORD VIEWING SERVICE

- **Supported File Formats: Viewing**   Specify which document types users will be able to view using this Word Viewing Service Application. If a file format is not selected, users of this service will receive an error when attempting to view that file type in the Web browser.
- **Embedded Font Support**   To preserve visual fidelity across different machines, a user may choose to embed a font within the document. Use this setting to determine whether or not embedded fonts are used when viewing documents.
- **Word 97–2003 Document Scanning**   To provide added security when loading Word 97 to Word 2003 documents, the Word Viewing Service Application performs extra checks before those documents are opened. These checks have an impact on overall server performance. Only disable this setting if you trust *all* documents loaded by this instance of the service.

- **Recycle Threshold**   Specify the number of Word documents that a process should be allowed to render before the process is recycled. Changes to this setting require an IISReset to take effect.

- **Total Active Processes**   Specify the number of worker processes dedicated to viewing Word documents. This value must be less than the WCF connection limit for this machine. Changes to this setting require an IISReset to take effect.

PowerPoint Broadcast Slide Show Setup

The PowerPoint Broadcast Slide Show feature enables presenters to broadcast a Microsoft Office PowerPoint 2010 slideshow to users who access the broadcast using a Web browser. If you installed Office Web Applications prior to running the Farm Configuration Wizard, the wizard will create a broadcast site for you at *http://<defaultwebapp>/sites/broadcast/*. If this site already exists, you need to visit the site and ensure that any users who want to give broadcasts are members of the Broadcast Presenters group, and that all users who will be viewing broadcasts are members of the Broadcast Attendees group.

If you are running a farm on which you installed Office Web Applications after running the Farm Configuration Wizard, or you find that the broadcast site doesn't exist, you need to set up, create, and configure the site collection. Before doing so, you must perform all of the service and service application proxy setup described in the section titled "Activating Services and Creating Application Proxies" earlier in this chapter. After you have completed those steps, perform the following steps to create the PowerPoint Broadcast site collection.

1. Open a browser and go to the SharePoint Central Administration website.
2. Under the Application Management Settings, click Create Site Collections.
3. Enter a Title (such as PowerPoint Broadcast Site).
4. Enter a Description (such as A Site For Performing Slideshow Broadcasts).
5. Specify a URL (such as *http://<servername>/sites/broadcast/*).
6. In the Template Selection area, click the Enterprise tab and select PowerPoint Broadcast Site.
7. Specify a Primary and Secondary site collection administrator.
8. Optionally, specify a Quota Template.
9. Click OK.

After you have created the site collection, make sure that any users who want to give broadcasts are members of the Broadcast Presenters group and that all users who will be viewing broadcasts are members of the Broadcast Attendees group.

STARTING A BROADCAST

To start a broadcast, open PowerPoint 2010, navigate to the Slide Show tab, and click Broadcast Site Show. Then select the Broadcast site created in the prior step and click Create Broadcast. The default service setting is for Microsoft's public Broadcast service, which requires that the recipient of the broadcast have a Windows Live ID. To use the site collection created in your farm, click Change Broadcast Service, add a new service, and enter the URL of the site such as *http://<servername>/sites/broadcast/*. You will then receive a temporary link that you can share with others. If they have access to the site, they can use that link to see a synchronized view of your slideshow while you present it.

USING GROUP POLICY TO ADJUST BROADCAST SERVICE SETTINGS

If you want all of your users to have the broadcast site available from within PowerPoint without needing to know that site URL or having to add the site manually, you can specify and propagate this setting using Group Policy. Before doing so, you need to download the Office 2010 Administrative Template files. When you have downloaded those files, create a Central Store for ADMX files on your primary domain controller and copy the ADMX and ADML files included in the Office 2010 Administrative Template files to that folder. This must be done prior to attempting to edit the policy settings within the Group Policy Editor.

> **MORE INFO**   To learn how to set up a Central Store for ADMX files, see
> *http://technet.microsoft.com/en-us/library/cc748955(WS.10).aspx.*

To modify the policy settings for the Broadcast Services, perform the following steps.

1. On the primary domain controller, open Group Policy Management from Administrative Tools.
2. Create or select the policy object you want to edit.
3. Right-click the policy object and select Edit.
4. Navigate to User Configuration, Policies, Administrative Templates, Microsoft PowerPoint 2010, Broadcast folder.
5. Enable the Disable Default Service setting.
6. Navigate to the Broadcast Services subfolder.
7. Double-click Configure Broadcast Service 1.
8. Enable Configure Broadcast Service 1 and fill out all the required information as shown in Figure 20-4, including the URL for the broadcast site in your farm.
9. Click OK.
10. Type the following command at the command prompt of your client computer and then press Enter.

    Gpupdate /force
11. Close and reopen PowerPoint.
12. Go to the Slide Show menu and select Broadcast Slide Show.
13. You should now see the service you specified in the GPO as the default service for use in broadcasting the slideshow.

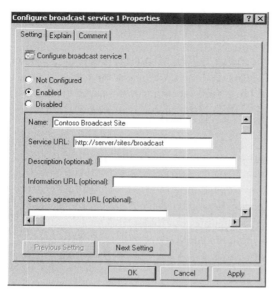

FIGURE 20-4 Configure broadcast service 1 GPO settings

Mobile Search

Mobile search in SharePoint 2010 does not require any special configuration. The features included provide for both content and people search. Full support of search scopes is provided as shown in Figure 20-5, along with the new capability to add filters and scopes. Finally, mobile search works with business data as well.

FIGURE 20-5 Mobile search

Mobile Views

Mobile views were first introduced in Microsoft Office SharePoint Server 2007. A *mobile view* provides access to a SharePoint site in a trimmed-down version for presentation in mobile device browsers, where load times for the full version would be slower and screen real estate is at a premium. In SharePoint 2010, mobile views have been substantially improved so that they provide almost full fidelity access to SharePoint content. Lists, images, and even Web Parts are now displayed in simplified, concise, and familiar form using mobile views. Furthermore, the mobile view for individual pages is directly editable within publishing sites. Document libraries include filters, a details view, and the ability to open documents directly with Office Mobile Web Applications if they are installed and configured.

In SharePoint 2010, the system automatically detects the browser type and redirects to the mobile view. To manually reach a mobile view of a page, list, or library, simply add **?mobile=1** at the end of the page URL, such as *http://<servername>/sites/site1/default.aspx?mobile=1,* and you will be redirected to the mobile view. SMS alerts or e-mail sent to a user's mobile device include a link that can be accessed directly using a mobile browser.

Supported Web Parts, Pages, Lists, Libraries, and Columns

In this section, you will review the supported Web Parts, lists, and columns that are presented within mobile views.

The following Web Parts are supported within mobile views.

- WSS Web Parts
  - List View
  - Image View
- SharePoint 2010 Web Parts
  - RSS Viewers
  - Colleague Tracker
  - Interest Tracker
  - Sharing Center
  - Recent Activities
  - Ask Me About
  - Business Data Item View

Not all lists, pages, and libraries are supported within mobile views. Table 20-2 includes those that are supported in mobile views and their associated view styles. Table 20-3 includes support details for list columns within mobile views. Also new to mobile views is the ability to view all site content within a given site, which includes information about lists, libraries, and subsites.

TABLE 20-2 Support Lists, Pages, and Libraries Supported and Their Associated Styles

LISTS/PAGES/LIBRARIES	VIEW STYLE
List (CustomList)	List mobile view (default style)
Announcement	List mobile view
Calendar	Calendar mobile view
Contact	Contact mobile view
Task	List mobile view
Document Library	Doc Lib mobile view
Picture Library	Picture Lib mobile view
Link	List mobile view
Virtual List	Virtual List mobile view
Web Part Page	Web Part mobile view
Wiki Page	Wiki mobile view
Blog	Blog mobile view

TABLE 20-3 Lists, Pages, and Libraries Supported by Mobile Views and Their Associated Styles

COLUMN NAME	SUPPORT
Single line of text	Yes, Edit and View
Multiple lines of text	Yes, View only
Choice	Yes
Number	Yes
Currency	Yes
Date and Time	Yes
Lookup	Yes
Yes/No	Yes
Person or Group	Yes, but does not support multipicker
Hyperlink or Picture	Yes
Calculated	Yes
Rating (0–5)	Yes, View only
Audience Targeting	Yes

List Settings for Mobile Views

Mobile views can be enabled or disabled for a given SharePoint list view. To make a view a mobile view, perform the following steps. Remember that these settings apply only to public views.

1. From any list or library, select the Library menu under Library Tools.

2. Click the Modify View button, which is directly to the left of the Current View field label.

3. Within the View Settings page, scroll down to the Mobile section, as shown in Figure 20-6.

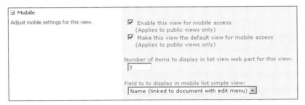

FIGURE 20-6 Mobile view settings for a given list view

4. Select from the options provided if you want this view to be enabled for mobile access and if it should be the default view for mobile access.

5. Select the number of items to display in the list Web Part for this mobile view.

6. Select the field to display in the mobile list view.

Previewing Mobile Access Device Options

There are many choices available within the marketplace today for mobile devices. From Windows Mobile– and Windows Phone–based devices to iPhone-, Blackberry-, Google-, and Symbian-based devices, SharePoint 2010 provides an avenue for mobile data access. This section reviews these choices at a high level, provides information on access methods from each, and discusses overall support for SharePoint mobile access.

Windows Phone

Windows Phone is the evolution of Window Mobile. Windows Phone provides a more efficient and unified user experience, with additional optimization for mobile access, as well as additional productivity tools. Windows Phone also provides the richest end-user experience for mobile data access to SharePoint. Included in the options available to Windows Mobile phone users is the new Microsoft Office Mobile 2010, which includes mobile-rich clients for Office Word, Excel, and PowerPoint. Also included in Microsoft Office Mobile 2010 is SharePoint Workspace Mobile 2010, which provides a simplified and familiar interface for working with SharePoint lists and documents and also gives access to synchronized data offline. Of course, like most devices, Windows Mobile phone devices can leverage mobile viewers, as provided by Office Web Applications.

Other Devices

As the smart phone market continues to grow, the number of options available for device owners is rapidly increasing. From Blackberry and iPhone to Google and Nokia, there is something for everyone in the marketplace. The main point to keep in mind, however, is that no matter what device a user chooses, if it offers a compatible Web browsing experience, the device should be able to take advantage of mobile access to SharePoint data. Of course, the users might not have access to the new Microsoft Office Mobile 2010 with many of these devices, but they will have access to sites, lists, and views with mobile pages, as well as the ability to view Office documents through mobile viewers as provided by Office Web Applications.

Setting Up SMS Alerts

Short Message Service (SMS) Alerts are similar to e-mail alerts in SharePoint 2010. When the option for SMS Alerts is configured at the farm or Web application level, users can select to receive SMS Alerts. When a user wants to be made aware of changes on a list, library, or item, the user selects Alert Me from the Library submenu of the Library Tools menu. After completing the required information, the user selects Text Message (SMS) as the delivery method for the alerts, as shown in Figure 20-7, and then specifies a telephone number to use for sending alerts. A user can optionally choose to have the URL of the site associated with the change included in the message.

If the user entered a telephone number while using this feature in a prior session, the system will remember that number for future use. Notice that the user can select either E-mail or Text Message as the form of delivery for alerts, not both. Users must create two separate alerts to receive both e-mail and SMS alerts.

FIGURE 20-7 Selecting the delivery method for alerts

The benefit of SMS Alerts is that the user doesn't need access to e-mail in order to receive up-to-the-minute notifications of changes within SharePoint. This can be beneficial if the user does not have access to e-mail while out of the office, especially if the user is not using a company-provided smart phone or other e-mail–enabled device. The other benefit is that the SMS feature arguably delivers messages faster than e-mail, but this varies based on the e-mail delivery mechanism in place. For example, if the e-mail–to–device delivery system is a push system, the difference in delivery time is negligible. Simply put, SMS is fast, assuming the providers' systems are not bogged down by heavy traffic. To configure SMS Alerts, you need to specify a mobile account within SharePoint Central Administration. You can identify a mobile account to use for the entire farm or for a specific Web application; however, only one mobile account may be configured within a farm. The decision to specify a mobile account for the entire farm or for a particular Web application will depend largely on the scale of your implementation and the specific requirements. For most small- and medium-sized implementations, specifying a mobile account at the farm makes things easier, because it enables the user alert option farm-wide and requires no additional configuration.

To specify a mobile account, you need to have procured a compatible online SMS service, which is offered by an Office 2010 Mobile Service provider. These providers expose the ability to send SMS messages online. After you configure the SMS service, the server communicates directly with the provider's Web service, which send the SMS messages to user devices. Selecting and signing up for one of these services is part of the mobile account configuration process, which is explained in the sections titled "Configuring a Mobile Account at the Farm Level" and "Configuring a Mobile Account at the Web Application Level" later in this chapter. Finally, if the user elects to have a URL included in the SMS Alert, and you want the user to be able to use that URL to access information in SharePoint 2010, you need to ensure that the information is externally available in a secure fashion. Secure mobile access scenarios will be covered in more detail in the section titled "Exploring Mobile Access Scenarios" later in this chapter.

Mobile Account Prerequisites

To configure a mobile account within SharePoint 2010, you need to meet the following prerequisites.

- You must be a member of the Farm Administrators group.
- The Simple Mail Transfer Protocol (SMTP) service must be installed and configured.
- A Secure Sockets Layer (SSL) connection must be used between the SharePoint server and the provider.
- The farm must be able to communicate to the selected service provider's service.

Configuring a Mobile Account at the Farm Level

To configure a mobile account at the farm level and enable SMS Alerts for the entire organization, perform the following steps.

1. Open a browser and go to the SharePoint Central Administration website.
2. Click Systems Settings on the left menu.
3. Click Configure Mobile Account, which is in the E-mail And Text Messaging (SMS) settings group.
4. In the Text Message (SMS) Service Settings section, click the Microsoft Office Online link to access a list of service providers.
5. On the Find An Office 2010 Mobile Server Provider page, choose your wireless service provider's country or region and then choose your wireless service provider.

After making this selection, you are directed to a third-party website through which you may apply for the SMS service. When you receive the required information from the provider, you can return to the Mobile Accounts Settings page to enter the information.

6. Enter the URL of the SMS service in The URL Of The Text Message (SMS) Service text box and click Test Service to confirm that the URL is correct and the server can successfully communicate with the service.

7. Enter the user name and password information assigned to you by the third-party SMS service provider in the User Name and Password text boxes and then click OK.

After you have configured the mobile account, users will be able to subscribe to alerts.

Configuring a Mobile Account at the Web Application Level

To configure a mobile account at the Web application level and enable SMS Alerts for users within that Web application, perform the following steps.

1. Open a browser and go to the SharePoint Central Administration website.

2. Click Application Management on the left menu.

3. Click the Manage Web Applications link, then expand General Settings, and click Mobile Account.

4. On the Web Application Text Message (SMS) Service Settings page, in the Web Application section, select the Web application for which you want to configure a mobile account.

5. On the Mobile Accounts Settings page, in the Text Message (SMS) Service Settings section, click the Here link to access a list of service providers.

6. On the Find An Office 2010 Mobile Server Provider page, choose your wireless service provider's country or region and then choose your wireless service provider.

7. After making this selection, you are directed to a website through which you can apply for the SMS service. When you receive the required information from the provider, return to the Mobile Accounts Settings page and enter the information.

8. Enter the URL of the SMS service in The URL Of The Text Message (SMS) Service text box and then click Test Service to confirm that the URL is correct and the server can successfully communicate with the service.

9. Enter the provided user name and password information, as received from the SMS service provided, in the User Name and Password text boxes and then click OK.

When you have configured the mobile account, users will be able to subscribe to alerts within the Web application selected.

Configuring a Mobile Account Using Windows PowerShell

To configure a mobile account at the Web application level using Windows PowerShell and enable SMS Alerts for users within that Web application, perform the following steps.

1. Open the SharePoint Management Console.

2. In the command window, run the following command after customizing it to meet the needs of your environment.

```
get-spwebapplication -identity<http://localhost> | set-spmobilemessagingaccount
-identity sms[-serviceurl<http://localhost/abc.asmx>]
```

After you have configured the mobile account, users will be able to subscribe to alerts within the Web application selected.

Exploring Mobile Access Scenarios

When and how users will access information on mobile devices will differ based on your specific implementation, the level of participation of users involved with the data, and the security requirements for accessing the data. This section explores three primary access scenarios to illustrate when you might consider using each. These scenarios are

- Anonymous users connecting through mobile browsers
- Authenticated users connecting to internal resources from mobile devices across a firewall
- Authenticated users connecting to internal resources from mobile devices through a secure access gateway

Anonymous Mobile Browser Access

Although this type of access is usually associated with publishing sites, and even more specifically with Internet-facing sites, anonymous mobile browser access is still a common access scenario worth covering. In this scenario, the user with the mobile device connects from the Internet while the Web front-end (WFE) server might be located in the perimeter networks. The firewall configuration for this scenario can be similar to a configuration for granting access to authenticated users.

Keep in mind the following main points about this configuration.

- The user is connecting from the public network (Internet).
- The user is connecting to a SharePoint site that is already addressable publicly.
- The user is connecting anonymously, so no authentication considerations exist.

Authenticated Cross-Firewall Access

Cross-firewall access refers to a scenario by which SharePoint sites are published externally. In this case, the user is connecting from the Internet with anonymous access and can also connect as an authenticated user with contributor access to data within SharePoint sites. The user might be connecting using a mobile browser, or they might be using a mobile access client such as Office SharePoint Workspace Mobile 2010. There are a variety of firewall options for this type of setup, the most secure of which is a back-to-back firewall configuration in which the serving WFE is located in the perimeter network. This might not always be possible, however, and many organizations have already invested in their infrastructure for serving traffic to Internet requestors. Consider the following points when configuring cross-firewall mobile access.

- The user is connecting from the public network (Internet).
- The user is connecting to a SharePoint site that may or may not be publicly addressable.
- The server may be located behind one or more firewalls.
- The user will be authenticated, perhaps even as a contributor.
- SSL is recommended to ensure the security of authentication information.

Authenticated Secure Gateway Access

In this final scenario for mobile access, assume that there is a server or device acting as a reverse proxy, which is handling requests on behalf of users in a secure manner. This server or device might be handling the authentication of users as well as encrypting user connections. This server or device might be the lone firewall, or it might be a secondary firewall solution, the latter of which is far more secure. The section titled "Setting Up UAG for SharePoint" later in this chapter explains how to configure Microsoft Forefront Unified Access Gateway (UAG). When implementing this scenario, keep the following considerations in mind.

- The user is connecting from the public network (Internet).
- The user will be authenticated, perhaps even as a contributor.
- The user is connecting to a SharePoint site that may or may not be publicly addressable, through the secure access gateway.
- The secure access gateway may be located behind one or more firewalls.
- SSL is recommended to ensure the security of authentication information.
- SSL encryption may be handled by the secure access gateway solution.

Examining Common Firewall Configurations

To facilitate secure external access for mobile devices, you can employ a variety of different firewall configurations. Many organizations have already implemented security and firewall solutions that facilitate the separation of their internal and perimeter networks from the public Internet. Usually, you will find that you can leverage existing implementations when providing mobile access. However, depending on the existing setup, in some cases additional security concerns may lead you to re-evaluate your current solutions, after which you may find that additional firewall devices or network segmentations are necessary. This section reviews the following three example configurations, which are considered typical.

- The Internet Edge Firewall Solution
- The Multi-homed Firewall Solution
- The Back-to-Back Firewall Solution

Many mobile devices also offer one more possibility—the ability to connect to internal network resources using a secure Virtual Private Network (VPN) connection. Although this might seem like a quick and easy way to deploy access for mobile devices, this option opens up a myriad of issues that could cause additional security concerns. For example, when a device has access to a network through a VPN, it is likely to have an internal network address and possibly have access to additional network resources (depending on the configuration) in addition to the intended SharePoint sites. Security breaches such as these pose potential problems when mobile devices with access through a VPN are procured and operated directly by the end user, because the vulnerability of the internal network increases through the use of unauthorized software or the introduction of a virus or malware. Remote access through a VPN also does not satisfy the requirements of the three access scenarios described in the previous sections. Specifically, remote VPN access cannot facilitate anonymous access to sites. In addition, VPN access for mobile devices can prove significantly slower than the firewall solutions described previously, because most VPN solutions employ to encryption and compression methods that add processing time.

Edge Firewall

Figure 20-8 illustrates an example of an edge firewall configuration. Notice that there is only a single firewall device standing between the Internet and the internal network. Also notice that both the SQL back-end server and the WFE servers are on the same network—the internal network. Of course, this increases the security risks associated with this configuration for two reasons: (1) There is a single point of failure with only one firewall; and (2) should the WFE become compromised, it can allow access to the entire internal network. For these reasons, you should consider this configuration only as a last resort—even though it is currently the most common configuration found in small to mid-sized enterprises.

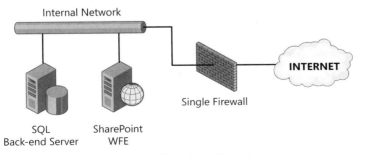

FIGURE 20-8 Example of an edge firewall configuration

Multi-homed Firewall

Figure 20-9 illustrates an example of a multi-homed firewall configuration. Notice that there is only a single firewall device standing between the internal and public networks in this configuration, as in the edge firewall configuration. What differentiates the multi-homed firewall configuration from the edge firewall configuration is the addition of the perimeter network. The perimeter network may or may not share a physical network segment with the internal network, but at the very least, it must be on its own logical network or VLAN.

The diagram in Figure 20-9 shows that the SQL back-end and WFE servers are on the same network, although this does not necessarily need to be the case. Traffic from the WFE can be routed to the SQL back-end server by way of the firewall device as well, although this does require additional configuration.

The multi-homed configuration shares a limitation with the edge firewall configuration—here again there is a single point of failure because there is only one firewall device. However, the multi-homed configuration is more secure than the edge firewall configuration in the way that traffic is routed to the SharePoint servers from the Internet. Since the internal and perimeter networks remain separate, even if only logically, a compromised WFE server would not have unlimited access to internal network resources. For these reasons, this configuration is preferable to that of the edge firewall, but it is still not quite as secure as the back-to-back firewall configuration, which is described in the next section. The multi-homed configuration is common in mid-sized enterprises, where resource constraints often limit the complexity and cost of firewall implementations.

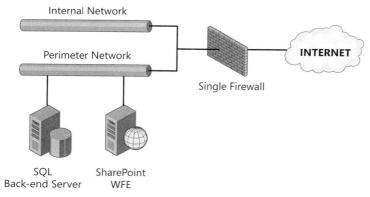

FIGURE 20-9 Example of a multi-homed firewall configuration

Back-to-Back Firewall

Figure 20-10 illustrates an example of a back-to-back firewall configuration. Notice that there are two firewall devices standing between the internal and public networks. What differentiates the back-to-back firewall configuration from that of the edge and multi-homed firewall configurations is the additional separation of the internal and perimeter networks. The perimeter network is completely separate from the internal network, with all traffic from the Internet restricted to servers located on the perimeter network.

In this configuration, the firewall rules on the primary or external firewall are less restrictive, to allow traffic from the Internet to reach the WFE servers. The firewall rules on the secondary or internal firewall are far more stringent, which greatly restricts traffic from the servers located on the perimeter network. The diagram in Figure 20-10 shows the separate SQL back-end and WFE servers networks, with the traffic coming from the WFE allowed to pass through the secondary firewall.

The key to the security of this configuration lies in the fact that the secondary firewall allows this traffic to pass only if it originates on the perimeter network servers. Additionally, the address and server name information are completely concealed from the public network, making it impossible to directly address any resources located on the internal network from the Internet. This firewall configuration is considered the most secure of the three configurations presented here, because it adequately segments and controls the traffic between all three networks and reduces the exposure to a single point of failure. This configuration is often found in larger organizations and is particularly common in SharePoint implementations where extranet access or Internet-facing sites are present.

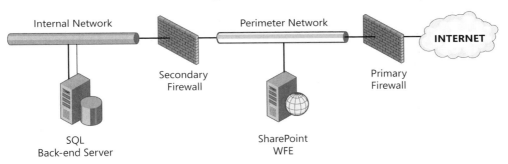

FIGURE 20-10 Example of a back-to-back firewall configuration

Secure Access Gateway Configuration

Microsoft Forefront Unified Access Gateway (UAG) incorporates many of the features previously found in Microsoft Internet, Security, and Acceleration (ISA) server. For the purposes of this section, you will review the implementation of UAG as a complement to the previously described firewall configurations, because UAG can be used as a stand-alone gateway with the edge firewall solution, as an addition to a multi-homed firewall configuration, or as a back-end firewall.

The main difference between implementing these three firewall configurations with or without UAG is the location of the SharePoint servers when authenticated access is provided to external users. By implementing UAG as a secure access gateway solution, SharePoint servers can be located entirely on the internal network, which is arguably the most secure place for them. This location may be where the servers were initially implemented, as is often the case for a collaboration-centric implementation. Figure 20-11 illustrates this configuration variation, showing the SharePoint servers located on the internal network. Of course, locating the SharePoint servers on the internal network will not work if your requirements include extranet access for users who will not be authenticated by the UAG gateway, or anonymous access for users of Internet-facing sites. In these cases, the servers should be located in the perimeter network, even if the UAG gateway remains present to provide secure access to a subset of authenticated users.

In the case of an implementation in which a UAG gateway is added to an existing multi-homed or back-to-back firewall configuration, you could add the UAG server to complement the configuration, with the intent to eventually move the SharePoint servers from the perimeter network to the internet network if external access requirements allow the change.

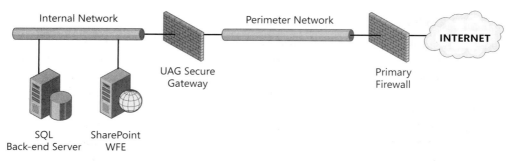

FIGURE 20-11 An example of a secure access gateway firewall configuration

The next section details the step-by-step configuration you will need for a UAG solution that will allow authenticated access on mobile devices. You will examine how the configuration should be set up on the UAG server and the configuration required on the SharePoint farm. As is the case in prior versions of ISA server, it is still possible to use UAG as a traditional firewall stand-in for one of the configurations discussed by creating a simple Web Listener and Firewall Policy Publishing Rule for such access. This section does not review this traditional option because it does not differ significantly conceptually from that of a traditional third-party hardware-based reverse proxy/firewall solution. The focus of the next section is instead on the new secure access gateway setup provided by Microsoft Forefront UAG server.

Setting Up UAG for SharePoint

Forefront Unified Access Gateway is the next generation edge access server from Microsoft. This section explores how to set up Unified Access Gateway to access SharePoint sites using mobile devices. You will need to complete these major steps to set up UAG for SharePoint.

- Set up SharePoint Alternate Access Mapping (AAM) for Cross Firewall Access.
- Create an application portal trunk in UAG.
- Set up the SharePoint application in UAG under the UAG trunk.

To access SharePoint sites from mobile devices, the SharePoint devices have to be accessed and the SharePoint Web application must be exposed to the mobile network. The first step is to set up SharePoint Alternate Access Mapping (AAM) for the Web application that is going to be exposed for mobile access. The AAM allows mapping of the internal SharePoint sites to an URL accessible from outside. The external URL is configured as one of the applications in the UAG's portal trunk.

Important Considerations

Before you delve into the necessary configurations to publish SharePoint sites using Unified Access Gateway, consider the following important aspects of SharePoint and UAG.

Alternate Access Mappings

Alternate Access Mappings or AAMs provide a mechanism for directing Web requests to the correct Web applications. More importantly, AAMs provide users accessing the Web application from the defined mapping with a consistent users' experience by mapping all of the URLs that would normally appear to have the address of the default Web application URL to the external URL. AAM is a cornerstone in exposing internal SharePoint 2010 sites to Internet and extranet zones. For example, the internal team sites portal for a company that is accessed using *http://teamsites/* can be accessed from the Internet using *http://teamsites.contoso.com*. You do this by configuring an AAM and specifying an Internet Zone URL for the Web application.

Public Host Names

Public host names are the means by which each Web application is identified when published through the UAG and accessed remotely. The public host names assigned to the Web applications must share the UAG trunk's parent domain name. Table 20-4 shows examples of valid and invalid public host names.

TABLE 20-4 Valid and Invalid Public Host Names

UAG TRUNK PUBLIC HOST NAME	TRUNK'S PARENT HOST NAME	VALID SHAREPOINT PUBLIC HOST NAME	INVALID SHAREPOINT PUBLIC HOST NAME
access.contoso.com	contoso.com	teams.contoso.com	teams.com
		public.contoso.com	public.example.com

Setting Up SharePoint for Cross-Firewall Access

Alternate Access Mapping allows you to expose your SharePoint Web applications to different zones, including an extranet, the Internet, and so on. To expose the SharePoint sites to mobile devices, you must create an AAM that points to the Internet zone for your Web application. The following steps explain how to create the AAM for a mobile access scenario.

1. Open the Central Administration site.

2. Select Configure Alternate Access Mappings in the System Settings section.

3. Click Show All for Alternate Access Mapping Collection and then click Change Alternate Access Mapping Collection. In the dialog box, select the Web application you want to configure for mobile access.

4. Click the Edit Public URLs link.

5. Enter the URL (as shown in Figure 20-12) that you want to use for mobile access in the Internet zone.

6. Click Save to save your configurations.

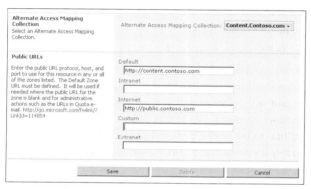

FIGURE 20-12 Alternate Access Mapping for Internet and mobile access

IMPORTANT   The cross-firewall configuration is ideal if you are planning to use Windows authentication for Internet access to your SharePoint sites. If you are planning to use a different authentication provider, you must extend the Web application with the URL you want to use for the Internet Zone, and then configure the authentication provider.

Now you have configured the SharePoint Web application for cross-firewall access. Next you need to set up the UAG configuration that will enable access to this Web application from Internet and mobile devices using the access gateway portal.

When to Extend and When to Use AAMs

Some people are confused about when to use Alternate Access Mappings and when to extend a Web application to a zone. You might ask: Why do I have to extend my Web application to another zone when I want to have IIS respond to a new host header? Why can't I simply add a URL for the existing Web application zone?

The answer may be slightly counterintuitive, but it's relatively easy to understand.

When you create a Web application in SharePoint, the default Web application URL specified is the only URL host header for which the corresponding Internet Information Services (IIS) website will respond. If you need the SharePoint WFEs and IIS to respond to a different URL host header, you must extend the Web application to a different zone.

If you simply need to have the URL links served by the Web application appear to be different from the default URL host header, such as is the case with a secure access gateway, you can accomplish this by simply adding a Public URL using AAM.

This might be difficult to comprehend initially, because when you want to have the website respond to an additional host header in IIS, you simply add that host header to the website, and it is there immediately. Logically the AAM interface looks and feels a lot like this familiar IIS process, but deceivingly, it's not the same process, because an Alternate Access Mapping is just that—a mapping, not an actual served URL.

Another difference is that an extended Web application allows for different authentication mechanisms and the serving of the same content across these authentication mechanisms, in addition to being on different request URLs. In the case of a secure access gateway, or any other reverse proxy type configuration, the AAM is the perfect choice, because it maps the user surfaced links and URLs in such a way that the requests are routed to the proxy or gateway device, rather than the WFEs. Then the proxy or gateway device sends that traffic to the WFEs by way of the default URL Web application. AAMs make this type of off-boxed/proxy configuration possible.

However, if you need to create a simple firewall rule for external access to SharePoint data, and the user requests will be processed directly by the WFEs, an extended Web application provides you with both the mapping and the additional host header response capabilities along with other benefits, such as the authentication options.

Creating Application Portal Trunk in UAG

The steps involved in creating the application portal trunk are as follows.

NOTE The Forefront UAG team was finalizing the 2010 release when these procedures were developed, so you might see some minor variations. Check Technet for any updates at *http://technet.microsoft.com/en-us/library/ff84041.aspx.*

1. Launch the Unified Access Gateway Management console.

2. Expand the Forefront Access Gateway node.

3. Right-click the HTTP Connections node and select New Trunk from the shortcut menu to open the New Trunk Wizard.

4. Click Next on the Welcome page of the wizard.

5. Select the Portal Trunk option and click Next to create a portal trunk, which in turn can publish SharePoint sites.

6. In the Setting The Trunk dialog box, specify the following details and click Next.

   ▪ Trunk Name

   ▪ Public host name

   ▪ External Web Site IP address, HTTP port, and HTTPS port

7. On the Step 4 – Authentication dialog box shown in Figure 20-13, specify the authentication server by clicking Add and then selecting the authentication server listed.

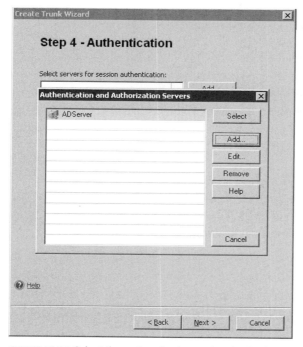

FIGURE 20-13 Select the authentication and authorization server for a portal trunk.

MORE INFO   Refer to the Unified Access Gateway documentation at *http://technet.microsoft.com/en-us/library/ff358694.aspx* to learn how to set up the authentication and authorization server.

8. Click Select to confirm the selection and then click Next.

9. On the Step 5 – Endpoint Security dialog box shown in Figure 20-14, select the Use Forefront UAG Access Policies option and click Next.

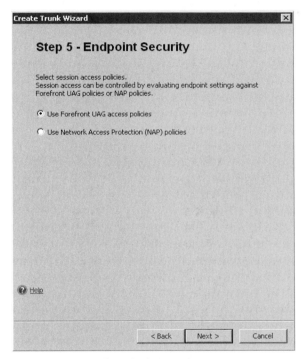

FIGURE 20-14 Specify Endpoint Security.

10. On the Step 6 – Endpoint Policies dialog box shown in Figure 20-15, accept the default Endpoint Policies and click Next.

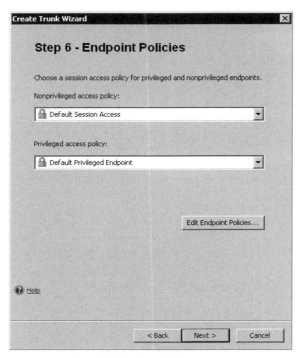

FIGURE 20-15 Specify Endpoint Policies.

11. On the Completing The Create Trunk Wizard page, review your selections and then click Finish to create the portal trunk. This portal trunk can be used for creating application portals for SharePoint sites behind the firewall.

Publishing SharePoint Through a Portal Trunk in UAG

After you have set up the portal trunk in the UAG, you can publish various applications through this portal trunk. The following sections explore how to publish SharePoint sites using a portal trunk and then enable access to mobile and handheld devices.

Adding a SharePoint Site as an Application to a Portal Trunk

To add a SharePoint site as an application to the portal trunk, complete the following steps.

1. Launch the Unified Access Gateway.

2. Expand the HTTP Connections node.

3. Select the portal trunk you created earlier.

4. In the Applications section shown in Figure 20-16, click Add to publish a SharePoint site in UAG using the Add Application Wizard.

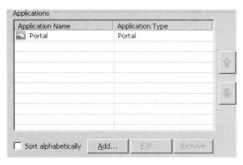

FIGURE 20-16 Click Add to publish a SharePoint site as an application to a portal trunk.

5. Click Next on the Welcome page of the Add Application Wizard.

6. On the Step 1 – Selection Application page shown in Figure 20-17, select the Web option, select the Microsoft SharePoint 2010 application template from the drop-down list, and then click Next.

FIGURE 20-17 Select the Microsoft SharePoint 2010 template.

7. On the Step 2 – Application Setup page shown in Figure 20-18, provide a name for your SharePoint application by typing a value in the Application Name text box and clicking Next.

FIGURE 20-18 Specify an application name.

8. On the Step 3 – Endpoint Security page, select the following values and then click Next.

   a. For Access Policy, select Default Web Application Access.

    b. For Upload Policy, select Microsoft SharePoint 14 Upload.

    c. For Download Policy, select Microsoft SharePoint 14 Download.

    d. For Restricted Zone Policy, select Default Web Application Restricted Zone Access.

9. On the Step 4 – Deploying An Application page shown in Figure 20-19, select one of the following and then click Next.

■ Select Configure An Application Server to publish a load-balanced SharePoint farm.

■ Select Configure A Farm Of Application Servers to let UAG load-balance your SharePoint farm.

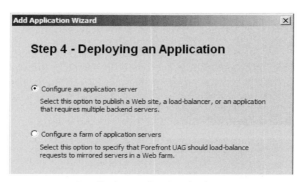

FIGURE 20-19 Specify the application deployment.

10. On the Step 5 – Web Servers page shown in Figure 20-20, capture the following details.

    a. Select the IP/Host option.

    b. In the Addresses section, double-click the list and then enter the IP address associated with the public host name of SharePoint Web application to be published.

    c. In the Paths section, add additional site collections that you would like to publish apart from the root site collection (/) by double-clicking the list and adding the paths.

    d. Select the HTTP port option and specify the port used by your Web application. In case of an SSL-enabled Web application, use the HTTPS port option and specify the port.

    e. Specify the Public Host Name assigned in Internet zone AAM of the Web application.

    f. Click Next.

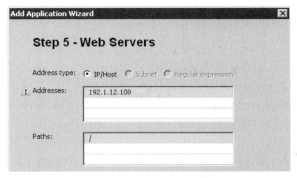

FIGURE 20-20 Define the Web server associated with the SharePoint Web application.

11. On the Step 6 – Authentication page, perform the following actions.

   a. Select the Use Single Sign-On To Send Credentials To Published Applications check box for the portal trunk to send the user's logon credentials to the SharePoint site.

   b. In the Select Authentication Servers section, select the authentication server for the SharePoint Web application by clicking Add, and then in the Authentication and Authorization dialog box, select the server and click Select.

   c. Select the Both option for the portal trunk to use both 401 request and the HTML form mechanism to submit the logon credentials.

   d. Click Next.

> **MORE INFO** Refer to the Unified Access Gateway documentation at *http://technet.microsoft.com/en-us/library/ff358694.aspx* to learn how to set up the authentication and the authorization server.

12. On the Step 7 – Portal Link page, specify the following details.

   a. Select Add A Portal And Toolbar Link to include the SharePoint site as a link in the UAG portal website.

   b. Type the Portal Name for the SharePoint site.

   c. Optionally, enter the Folder in which the SharePoint portal link should be displayed.

   d. Enter the Application URL for the SharePoint site.

   e. Enter the Mobile URL for the SharePoint site. This URL will be used by mobile devices to access the SharePoint site.

   f. Enter the Icon URL to be shown along with the SharePoint site link.

   g. Optionally, enter a Short Description for the SharePoint site.

   h. Optionally, enter a Description for the SharePoint site.

    i. Select the Open In A New Window check box to have the SharePoint site launch into its own window when user clicks the link.

    j. Click Next.

13. On the Step 8 – Authorization page, select the Authorize All Users check box to allow all authenticated users to access the site.

14. On the Completing The Add Application Wizard page, click Finish to create the SharePoint site link in the portal trunk.

Enabling Mobile Access for a SharePoint Link in a Portal Trunk

To enable the application portal to work on handheld devices and mobile browsers, perform the following configurations.

1. Launch the Unified Access Gateway.

2. Expand the HTTP Connections node.

3. Select the portal trunk you created earlier.

4. In the Applications section, select the application you created for SharePoint and click Edit.

5. In the Application Properties dialog box, navigate to the Portal Link tab.

6. In the Application Supported On section, select the Handheld Device and Mobile Internet Browser check boxes.

7. Click OK to complete the configuration.

Summary

SharePoint 2010 provides many new features that make the mobile data access experience richer for users, in addition to providing more mobile data access options. These new features and options allow users to have a more complete SharePoint experience, no matter where they are or what type of device they are using. This chapter reviewed the many options available to both administrators and users for leveraging mobile devices with SharePoint 2010. In particular, it covered the new Microsoft Office Mobile 2010, Office Web Applications, and mobile pages and mobile views. In addition, it described the device options for mobile devices at a high level, and it explained the compatible mobile data access options. The chapter also reviewed SMS Alerts in detail and provided a step-by-step guide for configuring alerts. The chapter introduced several mobile access scenarios and introduced the common firewall configuration options that are available. Finally, this chapter explored the concept of a secure access gateway using Microsoft Forefront UAG and provided a step-by-step configuration example to show you how to set up a secure access gateway for accessing SharePoint 2010 data.

## CHAPTER 21

Business Intelligence, Reporting Services, and PerformancePoint Services

According to recent studies, fewer than 20 percent of all employees within a company have access to the data and tools that they require to make effective decisions in their everyday work. According to Gartner research, this disturbing fact incited many CIOs to make business intelligence (BI) strategies their #1 priority in 2009. The expectation is that implementation and execution of business intelligence strategies will remain a top priority at least for the next few years. Therefore, business intelligence is an important part of Microsoft SharePoint 2010, and Microsoft's goal is simple: it must help companies take business intelligence to the masses.

Decision Making and BI

After answering the essential question of why business intelligence is important, it is equally important to talk about what business intelligence is: It is the process by which you gain insight into a business by collecting data in a way that makes it easy for end users to understand and analyze the data to support business decision making. Because of this, business intelligence solutions are also known as *decision support systems* (DSS). The basic premise of a business intelligence solution is that something has to be measurable for it to be manageable.

Typically, business intelligence technologies include historical and current views of business operations, and they may also include predictive views. Common traits of a business intelligence solution are that they provide analysis, data mining, business performance management, and benchmarking capabilities. Visualization is an important part of human cognitive processes, and pictorial representations have proven to be more effective as a way to capture some types of information compared to sometimes lengthy verbal descriptions. Therefore, visualizing data using forms such as charts, graphs, scorecards, decomposition trees, and performance maps is usually an important part of any business intelligence solution.

Traditional business intelligence solutions consist of collecting and analyzing data. Most new business intelligence initiatives also focus on the collaborative decision making that happens after collecting and analyzing data. These tasks are well-suited to SharePoint 2010, which allows you to

- Connect people to data.
- Connect people to each other.
- Cut costs with a unification infrastructure.
- Respond rapidly to business needs.

This new brand of business intelligence solutions is also known as *collaborative decision making* (CDM), in which social software is combined with business intelligence platform capabilities.

A typical business intelligence solution has to deal with several issues in sequence, and Microsoft fortunately offers a large suite of products that can help you handle these issues. First of all, you will probably need to collect data from different locations. Both Microsoft SQL Server Integration Services and Microsoft BizTalk Server can help you to achieve that. Then you will need to store the data somewhere, and SQL Server is a logical choice for this task, especially if you are planning to use other Microsoft products to implement a business intelligence solution. You can store data in a relational data model, but if you need to perform advanced analysis on the data, you can leverage Microsoft SQL Server Analysis Services to build OLAP cubes. If you need to present and interact with data and collaborate on decision making after that, you can use a combination of products available, including SharePoint, Microsoft Business Connectivity Services, Microsoft PowerPivot, Microsoft Excel Services, Microsoft Visio Services, Microsoft SharePoint Search, FAST Search, SQL Server Reporting Services (SSRS), and Microsoft PerformancePoint Services. Finally, most business intelligence solutions allow end users to export data to other formats to allow them to further manipulate the information in a specialized client tool such as Microsoft Excel, arguably one of the most popular analysis and planning tools around the world.

This chapter focuses on two products that are keystones in SharePoint-based business intelligence solutions: Microsoft SQL Server Reporting Services 2008 and Microsoft PerformancePoint Services 2010. Both are powerful products that can provide a major boost for your business intelligence solution.

Establishing a Common Language

Before you begin to use SQL Server Reporting Services 2008 and PerformancePoint Services 2010, it's useful to get familiar with a set of terms and concepts explained in this section. When working with business intelligence solutions, you will encounter these terms and concepts quite often. At the bottom level is the concept of key performance indicators (KPIs). The term *key performance indicator* was first used in 1961 by D. Ronald Daniel and Jack F. Rockart of McKinsey & Company. The term expresses how an organization defines and measures progress towards its goal. KPIs are also known as *key success indicators* (KSIs).

Applying KPIs to Goals

To establish KPIs, a business needs to analyze its mission, identify all stakeholders, and define goals. Then you can establish KPIs to measure progress towards those goals. Stakeholders must agree to every KPI before you begin to apply them. KPIs can be applied to any quantifiable measurement, such as

- Sales numbers
- Profit numbers
- Percentage of happy employees
- Student graduation rates in a school
- Number of points scored by a football team

Subjective goals often can be lofty, such as aspiring to be the greatest car business in history who sells the greatest cars ever created, but they can also be difficult—or sometimes even impossible—to quantify. Therefore, you should avoid subjective goals when defining KPIs.

KPIs should reflect the main goals of a business and should be considered long-term assets. As long-term assets, you will want to change the definition of an existing KPI or way it is measured very rarely. If you break this rule, you will probably end up losing valuable historical information. The goals of KPIs typically change as external factors cause business goals to change or as a business gets close to achieving a particular goal, but the key performance indicators should remain constant.

KPIs can be scoped to multiple levels, from the entire organization, to a department or a single person, as long as they express a key goal within the scope. Every KPI has an actual, which is a number that expresses the actual situation, and it also has a target, which expresses the desired situation or goal. Depending on the way you define a KPI, a low number for a target can be a good or a bad thing. Most KPIs also contain a trend indicator (usually a color or some type of icon) that provides a visual indication of whether you are getting closer or farther away from your goal. For instance, the trend indicator might display a green light if the actual reaches or surpasses the target, or it might display a red light if the actual drops below a certain threshold. Some KPIs also have a weight, a concept that is useful if you want to calculate an overall score across multiple KPIs that expresses how well the business is doing.

Creating Scorecards with KPIs

Business scorecards contain one or more KPIs and provide fast and better insight into the health of a company, department, or activities of a person. Most often, a business scorecard contains a small selection of essential KPIs that are the focus point of the scope on which they operate. Business scorecards are usually—but certainly don't have to be—targeted towards decision makers within a company.

Business scorecards and KPIs are not meant to be static overviews of data. Usually a business intelligence solution brings new functionality to the table by making it easy to add interactivity to KPIs and business scorecards in the form of drilling (e.g., Why is the New York office doing so great? Which of their products sold well?) and filtering capabilities (e.g., Show me the figures for the last quarter.).

A business scorecard is a derivative of a balanced scorecard, a concept introduced by Kaplan and Norton in 1992. Traditionally, the business scorecard contains overviews of financial data. A balanced scorecard is based on the premise that financial data is very important, but not more important than other business perspectives. A true balanced scorecard always provides insight in four equally important perspectives.

- **Financial** This perspective provides insight into financial matters, such as the financial goals of the company. Regardless of the presence or absence of business intelligence initiatives, usually companies have a solid grip on this perspective (otherwise a company will not survive very long).

- **Customer** This perspective provides insight into customer satisfaction. This perspective primarily serves as an indicator of future company performance. If most of your customers are unhappy, they will eventually find another company that meets their needs, which doesn't bode well for the future of a company.

- **Internal** This perspective provides insight in internal business processes. Metrics about internal business processes allow managers to know how well the company is running. For example, a manager might be interested to learn how the company is dealing with customer complaints.

- **Learning and growth** This perspective provides insight in knowledge development within the company. This relates to topics such as employee training, having access to knowledge repositories, and corporate cultural attitudes related to individual and corporate self-improvement. As an interesting side note, there has been some research indicating that 80 percent of the most successful companies excel in this area.

A balanced view of all these perspectives ensures excellent insight into organizational performance. The major difference between a balanced scorecard and a business scorecard is that the latter can be as unbalanced as you want it to be. It is perfectly acceptable if a business scorecard contains just one or a few KPIs, and therefore, it is easier to create this type of scorecard.

A final comment about scorecards: If a business scorecard contains only KPIs that express essential information about the highest abstraction level of a company—its vision—it is sometimes called an *enterprise scorecard*.

Table 21-1 provides an overview of the different types of scorecards mentioned in this chapter.

TABLE 21-1 Scorecard Overview

SCORECARD TYPE	DESCRIPTION
Business scorecard	Contains one or more KPIs that express a particular focus point for a company. A business scorecard is a derivative of a balanced scorecard.
Scorecard	Usually used as a synonym for business scorecard.
Balanced scorecard	Provides insight in four equally important perspectives: ■ Financial ■ Customer ■ Internal ■ Learning and growth
Enterprise scorecard	A business scorecard that only contains KPIs that express the vision of a company.

Understanding Dashboards

Scorecards are typically displayed in a dashboard. A dashboard is a user interface that, not unlike automobile dashboards, presents information in a way that is easy to understand. A dashboard might contain multiple scorecards, independent KPIs that are not part of any scorecard, standard reports (reports that don't contain KPIs), and other nonbusiness intelligence functionality (such as a discussion board). Dashboards are normally a part of a portal, and a portal may contain one or more dashboards.

Every business intelligence solution needs data with which to operate. This data will be coming from a simple data repository, such as an application database, a data mart that contains all data about a specific business area, or a data warehouse that contains all data about the entire business. Data consists of measures (also known as *facts*). A measure contains the information that the end user wants to see. A good example of a measure is the number of sales.

A dimension expresses how end users want to analyze data. Location is a very popular choice for many companies to use as a dimension; it enables you to ask questions such as how many sales are coming from the Seattle headquarters, for example. Many dimensions are hierarchical in nature. If you are interested in locations, a hierarchy consisting of continent > country > province > city might be a logical one. The term *level* refers to the position within a hierarchical dimension. If the end user starts analyzing data by looking at the data for a country, a country is a first-level dimension. If the end user then drills down to a specific province, a province is a second-level dimension, and so on.

Figure 21-1 summarizes the most common hierarchical structure of such a business intelligence solution. Remember that a portal can contain multiple dashboards, and a dashboard can contain multiple scorecards, KPIs, standard reports, and other non-BI functionality. It would be a rare thing if all business information is stored in the portal itself, so normally a business intelligence solution will retrieve its information from elsewhere—from another data repository, data mart, and/or data warehouse.

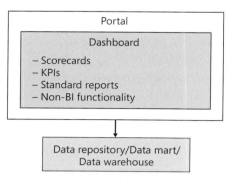

FIGURE 21-1 Hierarchical structure of a business intelligence solution

SQL Server Reporting Services 2008

In a typical business intelligence solution, you need all sorts of reports. PerformancePoint Services (see the section titled "PerformancePoint Services 2010" later in this chapter) excels in the creation of KPIs and scorecards. If you need other type of reports (tabular, interactive, visual, or freeform), you'll need SQL Server Reporting Services. SQL Server Reporting Services is a server-based report generation platform that provides the means to create, deploy, and manage reports, and it is a reporting platform that integrates well with SharePoint. The integration of SQL Server Reporting Services with SharePoint includes the following features.

- SharePoint lists are used to store report server content.
- Reporting Services adds application pages to SharePoint that allow you to manage SQL Server Reporting Services by using a SharePoint interface.

In addition to offering ready-to-use reports, SQL Server Reporting Services 2008 allows end users to create specific reports that are based on predefined models. It also allows you to export reports manually to other formats such as Excel. SQL Server Reporting Services 2008 is released as a part of SQL Server Express, Workgroup, Standard, and Enterprise editions, so you don't need to purchase a separate license to start using it.

What's New in SQL Server Reporting Services 2008

SQL Server Reporting Services 2008 has introduced a significant amount of new features in the following key areas.

- Report authoring
- Report processing and rendering
- Architecture and tool changes
- Report programmability

> **NOTE** There have also been interesting innovations regarding report programmability, such as the ability to preprocess report definitions and support for data-driven subscriptions and job management for situations in which SQL Server Reporting Services 2008 is deployed in SharePoint integrated mode. However, these innovations aren't discussed here because they are outside the scope of this chapter. For more information, please visit *http://www.microsoft.com/sqlserver/2008/en/us/reporting.aspx*.

Report Authoring

SQL Server Reporting Services 2008 has always enabled you to create reports that consume data coming from many types of data sources. Newly added in SQL Server Reporting Services 2008 is the ability for reports to consume data from Teradata databases (databases that use Teradata relational database software and are specifically designed for data warehousing). There have been vast additions to the collection of data visualization features in the form of a new chart data region that can include bar/column cylinders, pyramids, funnels, polars, radars, stocks, candlesticks, range bars, smooth areas, smooth lines, stepped lines, box plot charts, Pareto charts, and histograms. An example of a funnel chart created with SQL Server Reporting Services 2008 is shown in Figure 21-2.

FIGURE 21-2 Example of a funnel chart

Also, there is a new gauge data region that displays one or more gauges (such as a ther-mometer gauge). An example of a gauge data region is shown in Figure 21-3.

FIGURE 21-3 Example of a gauge data region

The tablix data region is a major enhancement that improves report flexibility; it replaces the old table, matrix, and list data regions. A tablix data region is a flexible grid layout that supports multiple row and column groups and allows the display of subtotals, totals, and grand totals. A cell within a tablix data region can contain any other report item, such as another data region. This allows you to combine table, matrix, and list structures and cre-ate complex reports that integrate traits of various report types. An example of a tablix data region is shown in Figure 21-4.

FIGURE 21-4 Example of a tablix data region

Another long-awaited feature is added support for text and HTML. In SQL Server Report-ing Services 2008, the text box report item allows you to apply various style elements, and you now can import basic HTML from a field in your application database for safe display in the report.

There have also been improvements in the Report Designer, a tool that integrates with Visual Studio.NET, but because that is a developer-oriented topic, it won't be discussed in this chapter. You can visit *http://www.microsoft.com/sqlserver/2008/en/us/reporting.aspx* for more information. SQL Server Reporting Services 2008 includes another tool that is used to create reports, a tool that will be used primarily by end users. It is called Report Builder 2.0, and it contains new features like enhanced data layout, visualization, text formatting, and on-demand rendering in an Office-like authoring environment.

Finally, new report elements have been added that provide more control over the way page headers, footers, sections, margins, columns, column spacing, and pagination are handled and rendered.

Report Processing and Rendering

Report processing and rendering have undergone some important changes too. Most importantly, SQL Server Reporting Services 2008 now allows you to export a report to a Microsoft Word document (Word 2000 or later), which is possible through the addition of a Word rendering extension. It also includes enhancements for the already existing Microsoft Excel rendering extension in the form of support for rendering subreports and nested data regions. The CSV data-rendering extension is improved by removing layout information from the output. This is a step forward, because data-only content is much easier for other applications to process. The rendering model now supports on-demand report processing that renders each page of a report as you view it. With this feature, support for viewing large amounts of data in SQL Server Reporting Services 2008 reports has improved dramatically and also provides an improved first-page response time.

Architecture and Tool Changes

The SQL Server Reporting Services 2008 architecture has been redesigned thoroughly, which has made it more scalable and easier to manage. The most significant change is that in SQL Server Reporting Services 2008, it is possible to run the report server as a true middle-tier application that doesn't have to be hosted on a Web front-end server; you can host it on a dedicated application server. In the section titled "Understanding the Architecture of SQL Server Reporting Services 2008" later in this chapter, you can take a close look at the architecture of SQL Server Reporting Services 2008 in SharePoint integrated mode.

The tools that you need to manage SQL Server Reporting Services 2008 in SharePoint integrated mode have undergone changes so that their functionality no longer overlaps. The set of tools itself hasn't changed and consists of the following items.

- **Reporting Services Configuration**   Used to configure and manage a report server installation. Use this tool to set service accounts, create or manage report server databases, configure URLs, set the unattended execution account, configure report server e-mail settings, and manage encryption keys, if you choose to use them.

- **SQL Server Management Studio**   Used to manage database server properties, create shared schedules, configure role definitions and view permission levels, and manage scheduled jobs that are currently in progress on the report server. The most important thing this tool doesn't do is manage permissions, because all content management needs to be done through the normal SharePoint interface.

- **Reporting Services Add-in for SharePoint**   Used to specify all sorts of settings such as integrating new report servers with SharePoint, specifying the authentication mode used by the SharePoint site or farm, specifying report processing time-outs, enabling logging, and enabling customized report building using the Report Builder tool.

Ultimately, the biggest enhancement to the Reporting Services toolset has been the addition of support for SharePoint 2010. The next section, "Understanding the Architecture of SQL Server Reporting Services 2008," discusses the architecture of SQL Server Reporting Services 2008 in more detail.

Understanding the Architecture of SQL Server Reporting Services 2008

SQL Server Reporting Services 2008 comes in various modes:

- **Native mode**   Report server runs as a stand-alone application server.
- **SharePoint Integrated mode**   Report server runs within a SharePoint farm and end users access reports via a SharePoint front-end.
- **Native mode with SharePoint Web Parts**   You can use two special Web Parts in a SharePoint site to view reports that are stored and processed on a report server that runs in native mode.

Since this book is about SharePoint, this section concentrates on discussing the architecture of SQL Server Reporting Services 2008 when installed in SharePoint integrated mode. For more information about the other two modes, refer to *http://msdn.microsoft.com/en-us /library/bb326345.aspx*.

For a thorough understanding of the architecture, it is useful to start with an explanation of the concepts of reports, data sources, and report models.

The SQL Server Reporting Services 2008 world revolves around reports that are defined in an XML dialect called Report Definition Language (RDL). RDL files contain a mixture of markup and data queries in SQL that are rendered to a variety of formats by SQL Server Reporting Services 2008, most notably HTML but also formats like Excel, PDF, CSV, XML, TIFF, HTML Web archive, and Word. In case a specific scenario requires more output formats, you need to either buy or develop custom report generators. The following code listing displays a part of an RDL file.

```xml
<?xml version="1.0" encoding="utf-8"?>
  <Report xmlns:rd="http://schemas.microsoft.com/SQLServer/reporting/reportdesigner"
  xmlns:cl="http://schemas.microsoft.com/sqlserver/reporting/2010/01/componentdefinition"
  xmlns="http://schemas.microsoft.com/sqlserver/reporting/2010/01/reportdefinition">
  <AutoRefresh>0</AutoRefresh>
  <DataSources>
    <DataSource Name="DataSource1">
      <ConnectionProperties>
        <DataProvider>SQL</DataProvider>
        <ConnectString>
          Data Source=sharepoint2010;Initial Catalog=AdventureWorks
        </ConnectString>
        <IntegratedSecurity>true</IntegratedSecurity>
      </ConnectionProperties>
      <rd:SecurityType>Integrated</rd:SecurityType>
      <rd:DataSourceID>c24ffda1-b9f1-45d6-9a53-47fcf5404110</rd:DataSourceID>
    </DataSource>
  </DataSources>
  <DataSets>
    <DataSet Name="DataSet1">
```

```
<Query>
  <DataSourceName>DataSource1</DataSourceName>
  <CommandText>
    SELECT ProductID, Name, ProductNumber FROM Production.Product
  </CommandText>
  <rd:UseGenericDesigner>true</rd:UseGenericDesigner>
</Query>
<Fields>
  <Field Name="ProductID">
    <DataField>ProductID</DataField>
    <rd:TypeName>System.Int32</rd:TypeName>
  </Field>
  <Field Name="Name">
    <DataField>Name</DataField>
    <rd:TypeName>System.String</rd:TypeName>
  </Field>
  <!-- The rest of the XML file is omitted for clarity reasons. -->
```

In SharePoint, RDL files are stored in report libraries. In itself an RDL file is useless, because it doesn't contain information about specific data sources. Therefore, every RDL file needs to be connected to a report data source (RSDS) file. RSDS files are also known as *data source definition files*. Such files contain information about the data source type (such as Oracle or SQL Server) and specific information about the data source, such as a connection string. In SharePoint, RSDS files are stored in data connection libraries. You can edit them by opening the Item Action menu of an RSDS file and then choose Edit Data Source Definition. Figure 21-5 shows a sample RSDS file that is opened in SharePoint.

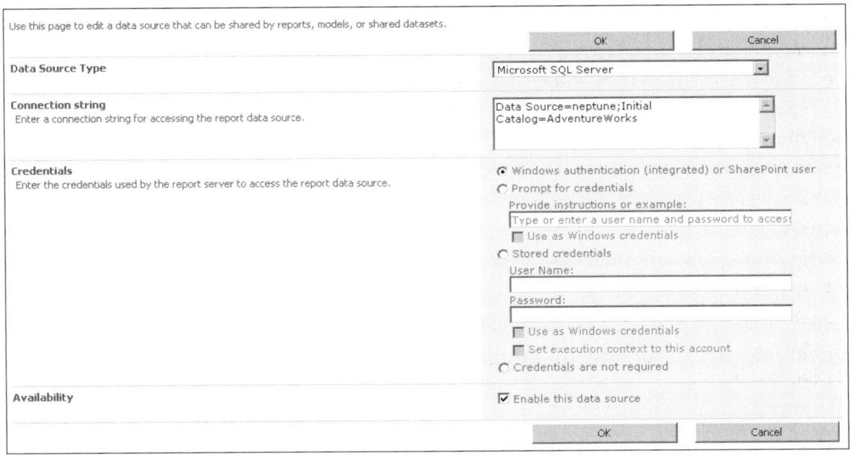

FIGURE 21-5 Edit data source definition of a sample RSDS file

Finally, you can have SQL Server Reporting Services 2008 report models that are also stored in SharePoint report libraries. Models are defined using an XML language called Semantic Model Definition Language (SMDL), and the file extension for report model files is .smdl. Like reports, report models (also known as *report schemas*) are linked to data sources, and they contain entities that represent database tables. The SharePoint action menu contains an extra option called Load In Report Builder that causes the Report Builder tool to load. The Report Builder (see Figure 21-6) is a ClickOnce application, so if it hasn't been installed already, it will do so immediately. The Report Builder leverages report models to allow end users to create and save their own reports based on these predefined models by choosing relevant fields from the predefined scheme and using them to generate customized reports.

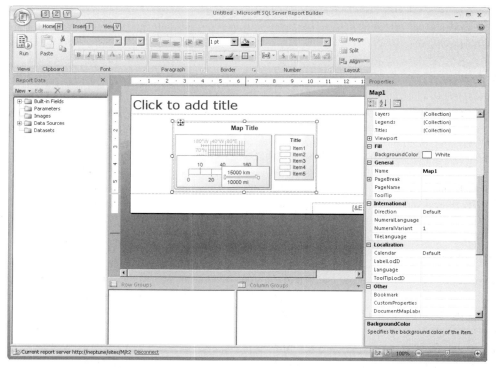

FIGURE 21-6 Report Builder

A high-level overview of this architecture looks like Figure 21-7.

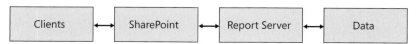

FIGURE 21-7 High-level overview of SQL Server Reporting Services 2008 in SharePoint integrated mode architecture

Clients Tier

You can use a multitude of clients to interact with the report server. If you are only consuming reports stored in SharePoint, all you will ever need to use is a browser. Developers will use the Report Designer extensively; this tool integrates with Visual Studio.NET and allows developers to create report server reports and deploy them to SharePoint. End users who want to create their own reports will use the Report Builder, which provides on-demand report creation in an Office-like authoring environment. Compared to the Report Designer, Report Builder is a simplified tool that does not offer all the features that Report Designer does, but it provides end users with an easy-to-use option to customize reports.

Alternatively, you can build or buy custom rich clients or custom ASP.NET pages that interact with SQL Server Reporting Services 2008 in the exact way that suits your company. Rich clients can optionally leverage the ReportViewer Windows Forms control; ASP.NET pages can use the equivalent ASP.NET ReportViewer Web control. Both controls can render reports obtained from the report server. The ReportViewer Windows Forms control renders reports on the client side.

SharePoint Tier

The SharePoint part of the architecture overview consists of SharePoint itself, complemented by the Reporting Services add-in. The Reporting Services add-in needs to be installed on every SharePoint Web front-end server and contains a report viewer Web Part, reporting pages that can be used to manage the report server, and a proxy that is able to communicate with the report server. In addition, the SharePoint tier will also contain all the reports, data sources, and report models.

Report Server Tier

The next part of the SQL Server Reporting Services 2008 architecture is the report server itself. Since the SQL Server Reporting Services 2008 release, the report server runs as a stand-alone true middle-tier application that doesn't have to be hosted on a Web server. The report server accomplishes this feat by integrating more closely with the operating system itself by using HTTP.SYS directly. HTTP.SYS (or the HTTP protocol stack) is an HTTP listener that is implemented as a kernel-mode device driver, a core component of the Windows operating system. SQL Server Reporting Services 2008 also reuses SQL Server's networking stack, SQL Server internal components, the SQL operating system, SQL Common Language Runtime (CLR), and SQL Network interface. This allows SQL Server Reporting Services 2008 to provide native support for ASP.NET, among other things.

The dependency SQL Server Reporting Services 2008 had on Internet Information Services (IIS) had several drawbacks, including the following.

- The complexity of managing IIS led to increased support costs.

- Other applications hosted on IIS were able to impact SQL Server Reporting Services 2008.

- There were many settings in IIS that could impact SQL Server Reporting Services 2008.

- The requirement of installing SQL Server Reporting Services 2008 on a Web front-end server sometimes completely blocked the deployment of SQL Server Reporting Services 2008 in the enterprise.

Most common IIS settings, as well as the NTLM, Kerberos, Negotiate, Basic, and Custom security modes and SSL certificates, are supported in the new architecture. Note that IIS settings that were not supported are now not allowed at all. This holds true for the following settings.

- Anonymous authentication

- Digest authentication

- Client certificates

IMPORTANT The lack of support for client certificates also means that smart card authentication is not supported for SharePoint/Report Server scenarios in any way—not in the Report Server application tier, and not in the SharePoint 2010 WFE.

SQL Server Reporting Services 2008 (sitting directly on top of HTTP.SYS) and IIS (which also leverages HTTP.SYS) can coexist on the same server. This doesn't result in any conflicts, except for the scenario in which the server consists of the combination Windows XP 32 bit/IIS 5.1. Companies that have developer machines that match this configuration should keep this in mind. In all other scenarios, SQL Server Reporting Services 2008 and IIS can share a single port, and both SQL Server Reporting Services 2008 and IIS make URL reservations in HTTP.SYS.

You can use wildcard characters in URL reservations, but you should note that IIS only makes weak wildcard reservations. A weak wildcard reservation uses the wildcard character * to indicate that the reservation catches all requests not handled by others. SQL Server Reporting Services 2008 uses strong wildcard reservations by default. A strong wildcard reservation uses the wildcard character + to indicate that the reservation catches all requests. As a result, URLs that *can* be handled by SQL Server Reporting Services 2008 *will* be handled by SQL Server Reporting Services 2008, because they take precedence over IIS virtual directories.

All URL reservations are stored in HTTP.SYS and they must be reserved prior to being used. After adding a URL reservation, HTTP.SYS will start to accept requests for this URL. SQL Server Reporting Services 2008 stores copies of its URL reservations in the RSReportServer.config file, and it tries to register all URLs listed there at run time. This means, essentially, that SQL Server Reporting Services 2008 uses a simplified version of IIS virtual directories. In IIS, a virtual directory handles HTTP requests and can have many settings. In SQL Server Reporting Services

2008, a virtual directory is able to handle HTTP requests just as well, but from the viewpoint of SQL Server Reporting Services 2008, the virtual directory is nothing more than a name.

Because SQL Server Reporting Services 2008 doesn't use and depend on IIS, it needs to be able to handle authentication requests itself. Because of this, SQL Server Reporting Services 2008 contains a new authentication subsystem that supports both Windows-based authentication and custom authentication.

MEMORY MANAGEMENT

Memory management has improved quite a bit in SQL Server Reporting Services 2008. The report server now contains an infrastructure for process memory monitoring that is dynamic and self-managing: it reduces throughput in memory pressure situations. Also, report processing uses a file system cache to adapt to memory pressure. To make it easier to monitor SQL Server Reporting Services 2008, it is now also possible to receive memory events from the server, and administrators are allowed to set minimum (the amount that is minimally claimed by the report server) and maximum (a threshold that the report server will never exceed) targets. This is a huge advantage over previous releases, in which the report server took all available memory.

You also can adjust the settings for the application domain recycling behavior using the RSReportServer.config file. This configuration file can be found at the following location.

%ProgramFiles%Microsoft SQL Server \MSRS10_50.MSSQLSERVER\Reporting Services\ ReportServer

The following code listing contains the configuration settings for the application domain recycling behavior.

```
<Service>
  <RecycleTime>720</RecycleTime>
  <MaxAppDomainUnloadTime>30</MaxAppDomainUnloadTime>
<!-- The rest of the XML file is omitted for clarity reasons. -->
</Service>
```

The RecycleTime element specifies how often the application domain is recycled. The default value is 720 minutes. The MaxAppDomainUnloadTime specifies the wait time in minutes during which an application domain is allowed to shut down during a recycle operation. The default value is 30 minutes.

LOG FILES

As a consequence of not using IIS anymore, SQL Server Reporting Services 2008 can't rely on the IIS logging mechanism, so it has its own trace log file, called the Report Server HTTP Log. You can find all of the SQL Server Reporting Services 2008 trace information about the RS service and background processing in this log file. The actual name of the Report Server HTTP Log is ReportServerService_HTTP_<*timestamp*>.log; it is a file located in the

LogFiles folder beneath the [SQL Server instance]\Reporting Services folder. This file stores all records for all HTTP requests and responses handled by SQL Server Reporting Services 2008 (except for request overflows and time-outs, because these types of requests don't reach the report server). You need to enable this logging mechanism explicitly by modifying the ReportServerService.exe configuration file, which is located in the bin folder of the Reporting Services installation folder. This configuration file also allows you to specify a different file-naming convention. The ReportServerService configuration file is a normal ASCII text file and can be opened in Microsoft Notepad or any other text editor. Its format resembles the IIS W3C extended log file. If you need more information about the Report Server HTTP log, refer to *http://msdn.microsoft.com/en-us/library/bb630443.aspx.*

The other report server log files are

- **Report Server Execution Log**   Includes information about reports that are executed by SQL Server Reporting Services 2008. This log file allows you to find out how often reports are requested and how much time is spent processing reports.

- **Report Server Service Trace Log**   Contains information about SQL Server Reporting Services 2008 operations and is ideal for debugging applications running within SQL Server Reporting Services 2008 or investigating specific problems in SQL Server Reporting Services 2008. This file is located in the LogFiles folder of Reporting Services and is named ReportServerService_<*timestamp*>.log.

- **Windows Application Log**   Contains event messages. Use this log to find out about events occurring on the local report server installation.

- **Windows Performance Logs**   Contain a set of custom Reporting Services performance objects that can be used to monitor SQL Server Reporting Services 2008 performance. Use this log to create performance logs; you can identify which performance counters to collect.

- **Setup log files**   Contain setup messages including warnings and other data for troubleshooting. These files are created during the setup of SQL Server Reporting Services 2008 and are located in a log folder at %ProgramFiles%\Microsoft SQL Server\100\Setup Bootstrap\Log\. The name of the log folder has the following format: YYYYMMDD_hhmmss. When Setup runs in unattended mode, log files are created at %Temp%\sqlsetup*.log.

MORE INFO   You can find more information about each of these logs on the MSDN SQL Server Developer Center at *http://msdn.microsoft.com/en-us/library/ms157403.aspx.*

Data Tier

The data section in the architectural overview consists of multiple data repositories that SQL Server Reporting Services 2008 needs to function in SharePoint integrated mode, including the following.

- **Report catalog**   The report catalog consists of two separate databases, the ReportServer database (RSDB) and the ReportServerTempDB database (RSTempDB). The ReportServer database contains all kinds of metadata required by SQL Server Reporting Services 2008, such as execution log files. The ReportServerTempDB database stores temporary snapshots while reports are running.

- **Report data**   This is the data coming from various data sources used in the reports themselves.

- **Report server configuration files and registry**   SQL Server Reporting Services 2008 stores configuration information in both the registry and in configuration files that are stored on the file system. The modification of configuration files might be required in more advanced scenarios. The MSDN article "Configuration Files (Reporting Services)," which can be found at *http://technet.microsoft.com/en-us/library/ms155866. aspx*, contains more information about SQL Server Reporting Services 2008 configuration files.

- **SharePoint configuration database**   This database is where the configuration information for the entire SharePoint farm is stored.

- **SharePoint content database**   This database is where SQL Server Reporting Services 2008 reports are stored in SharePoint integrated mode.

Detailed Architectural Overview and Common Scenarios

Figure 21-8 provides a detailed architectural overview of the report server in SharePoint integrated mode.

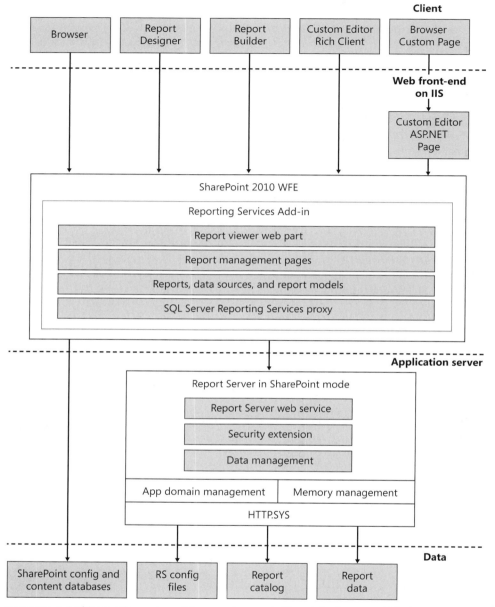

FIGURE 21-8 Architectural overview of the report server in SharePoint Integrated Mode

This means that a single server deployment of SQL Server Reporting Services 2008 contains a SharePoint installation (including the Reporting Services Add-in), the report server itself, and a database server holding SharePoint configuration and content databases as well as the report catalog. The data that SQL Server Reporting Services 2008 will report about is typically stored in other places. This is shown in Figure 21-9.

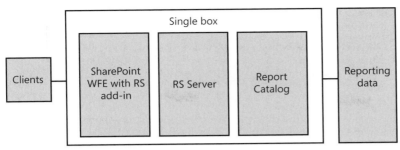

FIGURE 21-9 A single-server deployment of SQL Server Reporting Services 2008

In a scaled-out deployment of SQL Server Reporting Services 2008, you will find multiple clients connecting to a SharePoint farm. A load balancer divides traffic across multiple SharePoint Web front-end servers. All front-end servers in the SharePoint farm must have the Reporting Services Add-in installed. Requests are passed on (also divided by a load balancer) to a report server farm consisting of multiple report servers and a single report catalog. In this scenario, it is also true that the data SQL Server Reporting Services 2008 reports about is typically stored outside of the SharePoint and report server farms. Figure 21-10 shows an overview of a typical SQL Server Reporting Services 2008 scaled-out deployment.

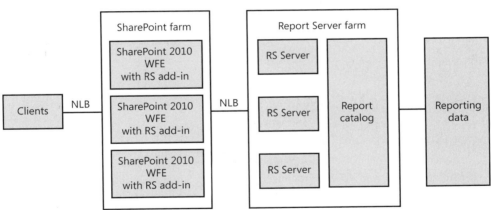

FIGURE 21-10 A scaled-out deployment of SQL Server Reporting Services 2008

Installing and Configuring SQL Server Reporting Services 2008

The installation and configuration of Reporting Services 2008 in SharePoint Integrated mode can be accomplished by creating a new reporting database that runs in SharePoint Integrated mode. The following steps must be followed to install Reporting Services in SharePoint Integrated mode.

1. Install a SharePoint 2010 instance.

2. Install SQL Server 2008 R2 Reporting Services. SQL Server Reporting Server 2008 R2 can be installed with the installation of SQL Server 2008 R2, as a SQL server component, or as a stand-alone component.

3. Configure Reporting Services using the Reporting Services Configuration Manager. (This step will be discussed in more detail later in this section.)

4. Download and install the SQL Server 2008 R2 Reporting Services Add-in for SharePoint 2010, which can be found at *http://www.microsoft.com/downloads /details.aspx?FamilyID=16bb10f9-3acc-4551-bacc-bdd266da1d45&displaylang=en*. This add-in needs to be installed on a single WFE (even when your farm has more) and is necessary for the integration with SharePoint 2010. After installing the add-in and configuring Reporting Services, you will be able to publish Reporting Services content to a SharePoint site. This add-in contains the following items.

- Report Viewer Web Part
- Web application pages
- Multizone support
- SharePoint list support

> **NOTE** You can use SharePoint lists as the data source for building reports with the Report Builder.

- Ribbon user experience

Configuring Reporting Services

After you install Reporting Services, you must configure Reporting Services, which you can do using the following procedure.

1. Launch the Reporting Services Configuration Manager by selecting Configuration Tools from the SQL Server 2008 R2 menu. The Reporting Services Configuration Connection dialog box that opens is shown in Figure 21-11.

FIGURE 21-11 Reporting Services Configuration Connection dialog box

2. Specify the correct name in the Server Name text box and click Connect. The Reporting Services Configuration Manager opens, as shown in Figure 21-12.

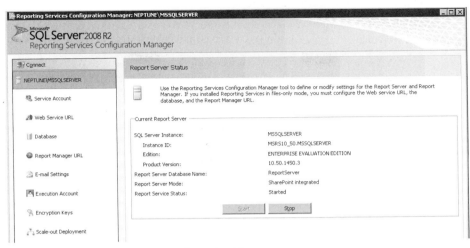

FIGURE 21-12 Reporting Services Configuration Manager

3. Click the Database tab, shown in Figure 21-13, to reveal the Report Server Databases screen.

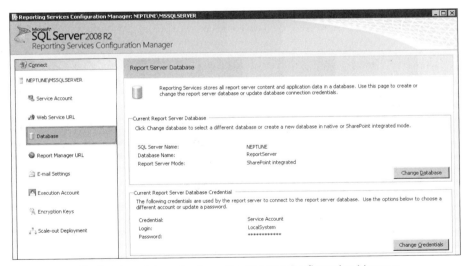

FIGURE 21-13 The Database tab on the Reporting Services Configuration Manager

4. Click Change Database to create a new database in SharePoint Integrated mode. This opens the Report Server Database Configuration Wizard, as shown in Figure 21-14.

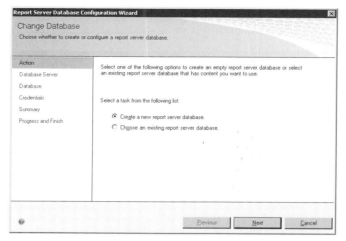

FIGURE 21-14 Report Server Database Configuration Wizard

5. Select the Create A New Report Server Database option and click Next. The next step of the wizard is the Database Server step, as shown in Figure 21-15.

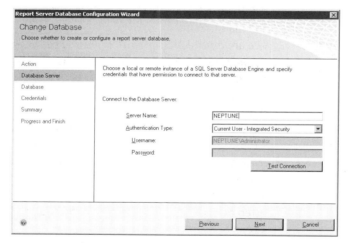

FIGURE 21-15 The Database Server tab on the Report Server Database Configuration Wizard

6. Make sure that the name in the Server Name text box is correct and select the correct entry from the Authentication Type drop-down list. There are two options here, Current User – Integrated Security or SQL Server Account. In the latter case, you must provide a valid user name and password. Click Test Connection to test the connection to the database server. Click Next if the connection succeeds; this will take you to the Database step in the wizard, as shown in Figure 21-16. If the connection test is unsuccessful, you'll need to troubleshoot connectivity to the server.

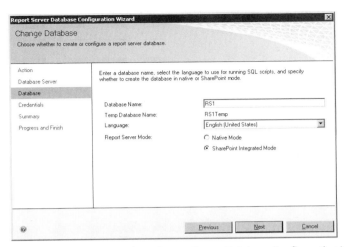

FIGURE 21-16 Database tab on Report Server Database Configuration Wizard

7. Specify the correct name in the Database Name text box and select an option in the Language drop-down list for the language you want to use for running SQL scripts. Make sure you select the SharePoint Integrated Mode option and click Next.

8. The next step is to specify the credentials that the report server will use to connect to the report server database. There are three authentication types you can choose from: Windows Credentials, SQL Server Credentials, or Service Credentials, as shown in Figure 21-17. If you have a least-privileged domain user account that has permission to log on to the computer and has access to the database, you should choose Windows Credentials. If you don't have that, you can choose Service Credentials to connect using the Report Server account itself. This way, the server connects using integrated security so credentials are not encrypted or stored, although the Report Server account typically doesn't qualify as a least-privileged account. Finally, you can opt to use SQL Server Credentials, in which case a connection is made using a SQL Server login account. This last option is ideal in situations where Report Server is located on a server in a different, non-trusted domain or on a server that is located behind a firewall. Make a selection and click Next.

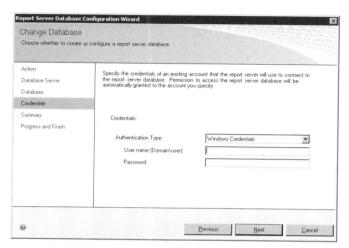

FIGURE 21-17 Credentials tab on Report Server Database Configuration Wizard

9. The wizard presents an overview of the configuration and the status of the configuration, as shown in Figure 21-18. When the status bar indicates that the configuration is complete, click Finish.

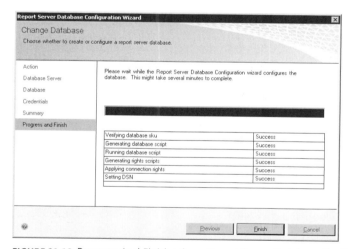

FIGURE 21-18 Progress And Finish tab on Report Server Database Configuration Wizard

Configuring Report Server Integration with SharePoint Central Administration

After running the Reporting Services Configuration Manager, the next step is to configure the report server integration in SharePoint Central Administration, using the following procedure.

1. Launch the SharePoint 2010 Central Administration website.

2. Click the General Application Settings tab. There should be a Reporting Services section available. (If you don't see it, you have not yet successfully installed the Reporting Services Add-in.) The Reporting Services section contains the following links, which you can see in Figure 21-19.

- Reporting Services Integration
- Add A Report Server To The Integration
- Set Server Defaults

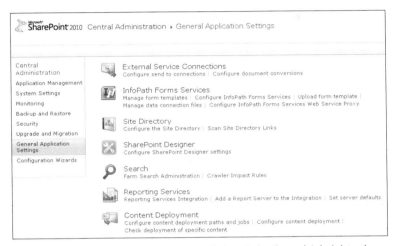

FIGURE 21-19 Reporting Services section of SharePoint Central Administration

3. Click the Reporting Services Integration link. This opens the Reporting Services Integration page, as shown in Figure 21-20.

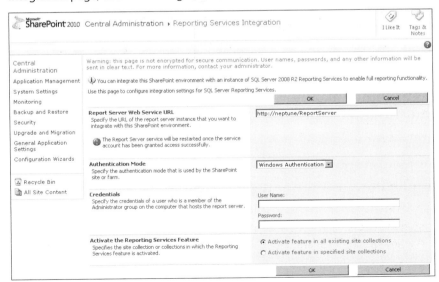

FIGURE 21-20 Reporting Services Integration page

4. In the Report Server Web Service URL section, specify the report server Web service that you want to use with SharePoint. This URL can be found in the Reporting Services Configuration Manager at the Web Service URL tab.

5. In the Authentication Mode section, select either Windows Authentication or Trusted Account as the authentication mode of choice. If you choose Trusted Account mode, SharePoint sends an additional header with a security token representing the identity of the SharePoint user that is currently interacting with Reporting Services application pages to the report server. SharePoint sends this request under the identity of the trusted account. The report server then impersonates the SharePoint user and checks if this user is allowed to access a report server item or perform a report server operation. In other words, the trusted account itself doesn't need to have access to any report items and operations. On the other hand, if you choose Windows Authentication, you must also enable Kerberos. In that case, any SharePoint calls made to the report server are sent under the Windows identity of the current SharePoint user. This account must have permission to access the report server as well as report items and operations. If a SharePoint Web application is configured for Forms authentication, the Authentication Mode setting is ignored and the request header will always contain a security token for the impersonated account of the SharePoint user.

6. In the Credentials section, specify the user credentials that are used to connect with the report server.

7. In the Activate The Reporting Services Feature section, specify the site collection or site collections in which the Reporting Services feature is activated.

8. Click OK. The next page contains the results of integrating Reporting Services with SharePoint, as shown in Figure 21-21. The number of entries may differ if the account you are adding already has access to the SharePoint farm or already is a member of the WSS_WPG group.

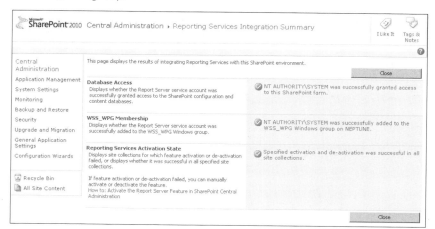

FIGURE 21-21 Reporting Services Integration Summary page

9. Click Close.

10. Click the Add A Report Server To The Integration link. This opens the Reporting Services Integration page, which you can see in Figure 21-22.

FIGURE 21-22 Integrate a report server.

11. In the Report Server section, specify the server name of the report server.

12. Click OK. A Web Page dialog box opens, where you must specify the credentials for retrieving the Reporting Services service accounts.

13. Click OK.

14. Click the Set Server Defaults link. This opens the Reporting Services Server Defaults page, as shown in Figure 21-23.

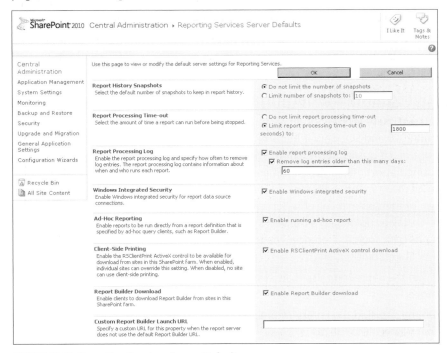

FIGURE 21-23 Reporting Services Server Defaults page

- In the Report History Snapshots section, you can specify the number of default snapshots. This will be the number of copies of report history that will be retained.

- In the Report Processing Time-out section, specify the number of seconds a report can run before it times out.

- In the Report Processing Log section, you can enable the report processing log and specify how often to remove old log files. The log files are stored in the \Microsoft SQL Server\MSSQL.n\ReportServer\Log folder. Each time the service is restarted, a new log file is created.

- In the Windows Integrated Security section, you can enable Windows integrated security for report data source connections. If you choose to do so, Reporting Services uses Windows integrated authentication mode to access data sources.

- In the Add-Hoc Reporting section, you can enable the creation of customized reports using Report Builder.

- In the Client-Side Printing section, you can enable the download of the RSClientPrint ActiveX control, which contains printing options to print reports that are available in SharePoint.

- In the Report Builder Download section, you can enable the download of Report Builder so that users can download Report Builder to make customized reports.

- In the Custom Report Builder Launch URL section, you can specify a custom URL for the launch of Report Builder. If you specify a custom URL, the default Report Builder URL will not be used to launch Report Builder.

15. Click OK.

The report server is now installed and configured in SharePoint Integrated mode.

Deploying and Managing Reports

Unfortunately, there is not enough room in this chapter to discuss all the topics related to SharePoint 2010 and SQL Server Reporting Services 2008 integration. At the time of writing, there is not much quality information available about this topic. However, the MSDN article "Configuring Reporting Services for SharePoint 2010 Integration" does contain a very nice overview of recommendations for Service Account configuration. This section provides a discussion of the deployment of reports from an existing to a new SharePoint environment, which is as easy as uploading a report to a list in a new SharePoint environment and then updating its data source reference. The following procedure explains how to deploy a report to another SharePoint server.

1. Go to the SharePoint site that contains the report and the data source that you want to move.

2. On the site, find the library where you report files are stored and select the report file that you want to move.

3. In the Copies group, select Download A Copy.

4. Repeat steps 2 and 3 for the report data source file.

5. Go to the SharePoint site where you want to place your report.

6. Upload the report in the destination library.

7. Upload the report data source file in the destination library.

8. Change the data source that is specified in the report.

9. Go to the library where the report is located, click the action menu, and select Manage Data Sources, as shown in Figure 21-24.

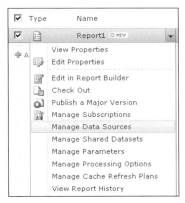

FIGURE 21-24 Select Manage Data Sources.

10. Click the name of the data source. This opens a page where you can specify the connection type and the data source link, as shown in Figure 21-25. Here you can edit the data source link. Click OK when you are finished.

FIGURE 21-25 Specify the data source link.

11. To edit the data source definition, go to the library where the report data source file is located and click the action menu of the report data source file you want to edit. Select Edit Data Source Definition.

12. This opens a page that allows you to specify the connection string you want to use, as well as the credentials used to access the data source. Click OK when you've finished selecting the appropriate options.

PerformancePoint Services 2010

PerformancePoint 2007 has undergone a major change in the 2010 release of SharePoint. It used to be a separate product that required a separate license; now it has become an integral part of SharePoint 2010 called PerformancePoint Services 2010. It is no longer possible to purchase PerformancePoint Services as a stand-alone product. This integration helps companies that want a pervasive business intelligence solution that incorporates the tools they use everyday at a relatively low cost. PerformancePoint Services 2010 is a SharePoint shared service, eliminating the need to purchase specialized applications

Although the pricing and licensing model has changed radically, the focus of PerformancePoint Services 2010 hasn't changed much. It still provides tools that scrutinize your company's data to

- Monitor the health of your company.
- Analyze company data at a detailed level.
- Plan for the future.

What's New in PerformancePoint Services 2010

The biggest change of all has been discussed already: PerformancePoint Services 2010 has become an integral part of SharePoint and is no longer available as a separate product. In terms of the functionality, the main investments that have been made in PerformancePoint Services 2010 took place in the following areas: scalability, security, and monitoring and analysis capabilities.

The scalability part of the new enhancements is realized because PerformancePoint Services 2010 is built on top of the scalable SharePoint framework (see Chapter 2, "Understanding the Architecture of SharePoint 2010," for more information). PerformancePoint Services 2010 has become more scalable because it is able to leverage the SharePoint shared services framework, which handles tasks such as load balancing, credential management, caching, and settings storage. Also, because PerformancePoint Services 2010 is implemented as a shared service, it can be hosted on a dedicated application server. As a result, the SharePoint Web front-end server is no longer overburdened by the load caused by PerformancePoint Services 2010, which increases overall performance. Being able to build on the SharePoint shared service framework brings lots of advantages to PerformancePoint Services 2010, such as

- Uniformity in the way all shared services (such as PerformancePoint Services 2010) are administered via SharePoint Central Administration or via Windows PowerShell scripts. This is also known as *syndication*.
- Because it is a shared service, PerformancePoint Services 2010 can be reused within multiple SharePoint farms or within multiple SharePoint site collections within a single SharePoint farm.
- The SharePoint shared service model offers load-balancing capabilities between multiple instances of a PerformancePoint Services service.

- PerformancePoint Services 2010 benefits from SharePoint's backup and recovery capabilities, which allows restores of a complete site collection, a single site, or list content to a previous version or point in time.

- PerformancePoint Services 2010 benefits from SharePoint's improved logging and auditing features.

The security-related functionality enhancements have been considerable. The following list provides an overview of the highlights in this area.

- The SharePoint authentication provider is now responsible for authenticating users.

- The old PerformancePoint Server roles and permissions model have been replaced by the SharePoint security model that allows you to set fine-grained permissions on dashboard content.

- Web front-end servers and application servers hosting PerformancePoint Services 2010 support claims-based authentication for content access. Claims-based authentication is based on the industry standards WS-Federation, WS-Trust, and Security Assertion Markup Language (SAML). This allows you to integrate PerformancePoint Services 2010 with any authentication mechanism.

- PerformancePoint Services 2010 leverages the SharePoint Secure Store Service (which used to be called the Single Sign-On Service) for data source access. The Secure Store Service stores a mapping between SharePoint user accounts and Active Directory user accounts. PerformancePoint Services 2010 uses a token received from the Secure Store Service to retrieve the Active Directory user credentials to access data sources, which resolves the double-hop problem in three-server deployments (wherein Windows credentials expire after a single connection).

- PerformancePoint Services 2010 uses Shared Identity impersonation for data source access instead of using the relatively high privileged application pool identity. The SharePoint Secure Services manages the storage of these shared identities, and they are defined during the provisioning of the PerformancePoint Services 2010 shared service or afterward by an administrator. PerformancePoint Services 2010 impersonates the SharePoint Identity as soon as it tries to access a data source. Farm installations require the use of shared identities, but single-server deployments still allow the use of built-in accounts for data source communication.

- PerformancePoint Services 2010 introduces the concept of trusted locations. Trusted locations restrict the use of PerformancePoint Services 2010 content types to specific sites so that only a specific group of users is able to access PerformancePoint Services 2010 content.

There have also been quite a few enhancements to the monitoring and analysis capabilities of PerformancePoint Services 2010; it now includes new report types, better filtering and navigation capabilities, and improved integration with SharePoint. The following list provides an overview of the highlights in this area.

- It is now possible to use SharePoint site templates for dashboard design. This allows you to change the appearance of PerformancePoint Services 2010 in sites, document libraries, or lists.

- PerformancePoint Services 2010 offers seamless integration into SharePoint because dashboard elements are now available as SharePoint Web Parts. PerformancePoint Services 2010 also leverages SharePoint lists to store content, and it is implemented as a SharePoint shared service.

- PerformancePoint Services 2010 integrates with Microsoft Office 2010 applications such as Microsoft Visio 2010, Microsoft Excel 2010, and Microsoft Project Server 2010.

- PerformancePoint Services 2010 supports multiple browsers such as Internet Explorer 8, Firefox 3.0, and Safari 3.0.

- PerformancePoint Services 2010 offers new SharePoint content types that can be used to customize dashboard interaction without a single line of code.

- PerformancePoint Services 2010 includes multiple dashboard element enhancements.
  - Filters are now compatible with SharePoint filters and can be reused across dashboards.
  - KPIs can now use calculated metrics, can easily show variance, and can have multiple "actual" values.
  - Scorecards have better support for navigating dimension hierarchies, and you can connect them to filter-enabled Web Parts on the same dashboard page using the SharePoint Connected Web Part framework. This makes it easier to display context-specific content on the dashboard page.
  - KPIs can now be placed on columns and automatically display cube-defined default formatting.
  - Scorecards allow time intelligence formula editing and improved value and status filtering. Filtering also supports non-numeric values and empty rows and columns.

- Reports have been improved in several ways.
  - Reports now include analytic pie chart views.
  - There is a new built-in report type called KPI Details.

- Support for Office Web Components (OWC) in reports is deprecated. Because of this, Spreadsheet, PivotTable, PivotChart, and Trend Analysis Chart report views are no longer available. Except for the Trend Analysis Chart report view, all types of report views can be recreated with Excel Services reports.

Understanding the Architecture of PerformancePoint Services 2010

PerformancePoint Services 2010 can be accessed by multiple clients and relies heavily on the SharePoint 2010 infrastructure. The diagram shown in Figure 21-26 provides a detailed overview of the architecture of PerformancePoint Services 2010.

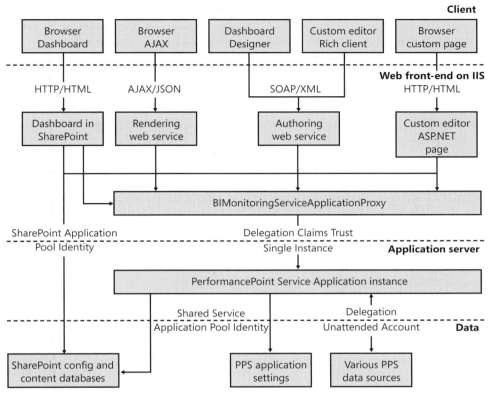

FIGURE 21-26 Architecture overview of PerformancePoint Services 2010

As the diagram shows, it's possible to use multiple clients to interact with PerformancePoint Services 2010. First, you can use the browser to open a dashboard in SharePoint. Such a dashboard could contain multiple reports, scorecards, Web pages, and Web Parts. Alternatively, you can use the browser to open a report viewer that uses AJAX to communicate with PerformancePoint Services 2010. You could also use the browser to navigate to any custom ASP.NET pages that your company has built or bought that interact with PerformancePoint Services 2010. It is also possible to use or create rich clients that interact with PerformancePoint Services 2010 directly. The most notable examples of such rich clients are Excel and ProClarity Analytics (a tool created by a company recently acquired by Microsoft). Both tools allow end users to work with data without restrictions, which allows them to analyze data in the way they prefer. Excel is particularly good for working with grid data, and ProClarity Analytics is excellent for data visualization. Finally, you can use Dashboard Designer, a ClickOnce application specifically built for creating dashboards, scorecards, and KPIs.

Although the AJAX-enabled report viewer talks to the rendering Web service (PPSRenderingService.json) and the Dashboard Designer, and (optional) custom-rich clients talk to the Authoring Web service (PPSAuthoringService.asmx), those services mainly act as pass-through services. Eventually all clients talk to a proxy (the BIMonitoringServiceApplicationProxy) that communicates to the PerformancePoint Services 2010 shared service, which is a PerformancePoint Services Windows Communication Foundation (WCF) interface called BIMonitoringService.svc. The PerformancePoint Services SharePoint service is responsible for processing complex PerformancePoint Services tasks while it leverages existing general services of the shared services framework, such as credential management, load balancing, and settings storage. Finally, the PerformancePoint Service Application retrieves SharePoint configuration and content information, reads PerformancePoint Service Application settings, and consults other data sources that PerformancePoint Services 2010 reports about.

Installing and Configuring PerformancePoint Services 2010

PerformancePoint Services 2010 is installed with SharePoint 2010, but the PerformancePoint Service Application is not created automatically. The PerformancePoint Service Application will also create a service application proxy. This proxy facilitates Web service calls between the Web front-end server and the application server using the Windows Communication Framework.

Creating a PerformancePoint Service Application

It is possible to create a new PerformancePoint Service Application using the SharePoint Central Administration website. The following procedure shows how to do this.

1. Open a browser and go to the SharePoint 2010 Central Administration website.

2. In the Application Management section, select Manage Service Applications.

3. From the New menu, select PerformancePoint Service Application, as you can see in Figure 21-27.

FIGURE 21-27 Create a new PerformancePoint Service Application.

4. A page opens where you can specify settings for the PerformancePoint Service Application, as shown in Figure 21-28.

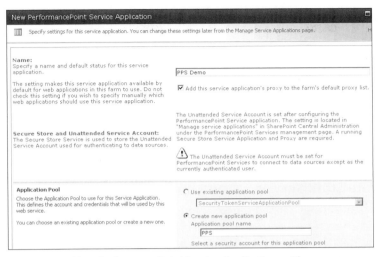

FIGURE 21-28 New PerformancePoint Service Application settings page

5. Specify a name for the PerformancePoint Service Application. For PerformancePoint Service Applications, this name must be unique. The PerformancePoint Service Application will also have a service application's identity—a GUID—to distinguish the service application from other service applications.

6. Select the Add This Service Application's Proxy To The Farm's Default Proxy List check box. With this setting, you specify that the service application instance is added to the farm's list of default service applications.

7. You can use an existing application pool or to create a new application pool; creating a new application pool that runs under a domain account is recommended. Making use of the predefined option imposes a security risk because these accounts have too many privileges.

8. Click Create.

9. The next page shows a summary of the additional configuration steps, as you can see in Figure 21-29. The additional steps are

   - Define An Unattended Service Account
   - Enable The Performancepoint Web Application And Site Collection Features
   - Configure trusted locations

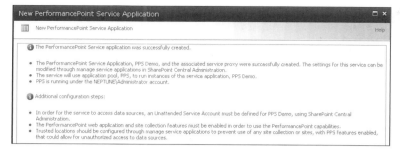

FIGURE 21-29 New PerformancePoint Service Application summary page

10. Click OK.

Creating a Secure Store Service

The next step is to create an unattended service account to connect to data sources. To do this, you first must create a secure store service. The unattended service account cannot use the application pool identity to connect to data sources. The unattended account must be a domain account, and the password of this account is stored in the secure store. The following procedure shows how to create a new secure store service.

1. Launch the SharePoint 2010 Central Administration website.

2. In the Application Management section, select Manage Service Applications.

3. From the New menu, select Secure Store Service, as shown in Figure 21-30.

FIGURE 21-30 Create a new Secure Store Service

4. Specify a name for the Secure Store Service Application in the Service Application Name text box, as shown in Figure 21-31.

FIGURE 21-31 New Secure Store Service

5. Specify a name for a new application pool, as shown in Figure 21-32, and click OK. The secure store service will be added automatically to the default proxy group.

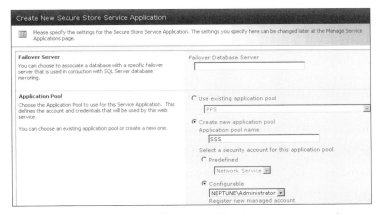

FIGURE 21-32 Create a new application pool for the secure store service

At this point, the PerformancePoint Service and the secure store service are created and started.

6. Launch the SharePoint 2010 Central Administration website.

7. In the System Settings section, select Manage Services On Server. This page should look like Figure 21-33.

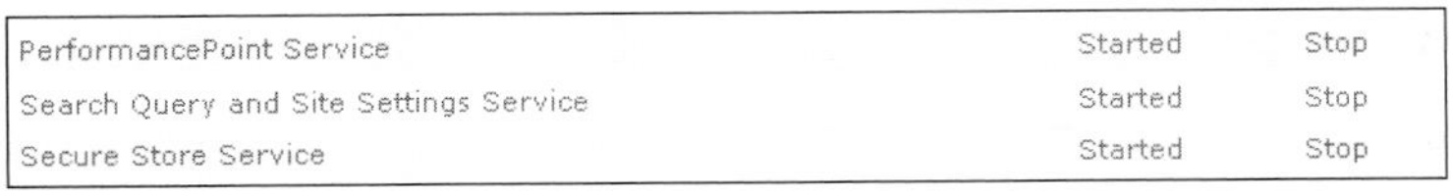

PerformancePoint Service	Started	Stop
Search Query and Site Settings Service	Started	Stop
Secure Store Service	Started	Stop

FIGURE 21-33 Start the PerformancePoint Service

Defining an Unattended Service Account

There is a difference between a service application and a service application instance. If you want to use a different set of settings, you have to make another service application. The next thing to do is to define an unattended service account, and the following procedure shows how to do this.

1. Launch the SharePoint 2010 Central Administration website.

2. In the Application Management section, select Manage Service Applications.

3. Click the Secure Store Service link, or alternatively, select the secure store service you created and click Manage in the Operations group. Both options allow you to manage the properties of this secure store service. You will see an error (shown in Figure 21-34) indicating that there is no Secure Store Application key.

FIGURE 21-34 Error message indicating that there are no keys in the secure store service

4. Select Generate New Key in the Key Management group.

5. Specify a pass phrase and confirm it, as shown in Figure 21-35. This pass phrase is the only way to get the encrypted data. Make sure to save the pass phrase, because if you want to refresh the key, you will need to have it.

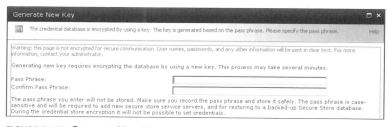

FIGURE 21-35 Generate New Key page

This pass phrase must contain at least 8 characters; these characters must include at least three of the following four groups:

- Uppercase characters A through Z

- Lowercase characters a through z

- Numerals 0 through 9

- Nonalphabetic characters such as !, $, /, ?, %

6. When you have finished specifying a pass phrase, click OK.

7. The error message will be replaced by a new message, shown here.

```
There are no Secure Store Target Applications in this Secure Store Service
Application. You can create a new Target Application from the Manage Target
Applications group in the Edit ribbon group.
```

Adding a PerformancePoint Service Application

The next step is to add the PerformancePoint Service Application to the Secure Store Service Application. The following procedure shows how to do this.

1. Launch the SharePoint 2010 Central Administration website.

2. In the Application Management section, select Manage Service Applications.

3. Select the PerformancePoint Service link, or alternatively, select the PerformancePoint Service you created and click Manage in the Operations group. Both options allow you to manage the properties of this PerformancePoint Service.

4. Click PerformancePoint Service Application Settings, as shown in Figure 21-36. The next page shows that the name of the Secure Store Service Application has been detected. This page contains all the configuration settings for the PerformancePoint Service Application. In PerformancePoint 2007, this configuration information was stored in the Web.config file.

FIGURE 21-36 Manage PerformancePoint Services page

5. Specify the user name you want to use for the unattended service account for authenticating with data sources, as shown in Figure 21-37. The credentials will be added to the target application. Make sure you use an account with the least privileges possible. Best practice is to avoid using an existing user account and to create a new account specifically for the PerformancePoint Service Application.

FIGURE 21-37 PerformancePoint Service Application settings page

6. Click OK.

Defining SharePoint Locations as Trusted Data Source Locations

The next procedure shows how to define SharePoint locations as trusted data source locations.

1. Click Trusted Data Source Locations as shown in Figure 21-36 previously. You can choose to trust the data source in all SharePoint locations or only in specific locations. If you choose the latter and click Apply, a new link becomes available: Add Trusted Data Source Location. If you click this link, an Edit Trusted Data Source Location page opens, as shown in Figure 21-38.

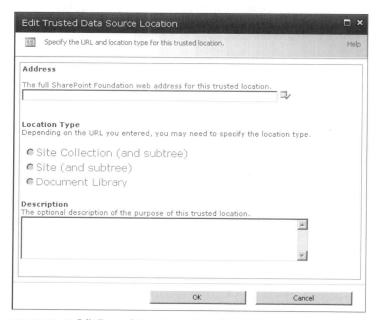

FIGURE 21-38 Edit Trusted Data Source Location page

2. On this page, you can specify the location type. The options available are a SharePoint site collection (and subtree), a SharePoint site (and subtree), or a library to store data sources. If you are finished, click OK.

Now you have added a Trusted Data Source location.

Defining SharePoint Locations as Trusted Content Locations

The next procedure shows you how to define SharePoint locations as trusted content locations.

1. Click Trusted Content Locations as shown in Figure 21-36 previously. You can choose to trust content such as dashboards and scorecards in all SharePoint locations or only in specific locations.

2. If you choose to trust only specific locations and click Apply, a new link becomes available: Add Trusted Content Location. Click this link to open the Edit Trusted Content Location page. This page looks the same as the Edit Trusted Data Source Location page you saw previously in Figure 21-38.

NOTE If you create a new Web application and you want to make use of PerformancePoint Services, make sure you choose Classic Mode Authentication (shown in Figure 21-39); otherwise, PerformancePoint Services will not work.

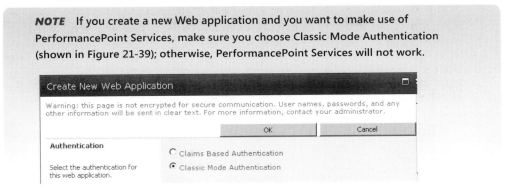

FIGURE 21-39 Create New Web Application page

After configuring the PerformancePoint Service Application, you can go to your SharePoint site and open the Dashboard Designer. There is nothing new here; the Dashboard Designer in SharePoint 2010 is the same one that was used in SharePoint Server 2007.

Upgrading PerformancePoint Server 2007

This section discusses how to import data from PerformancePoint Server 2007 into SharePoint 2010.

First, it's important to know that you don't have to use a Business Intelligence Center site as the destination site when upgrading PerformancePoint Server 2007 to SharePoint 2010. You can migrate PerformancePoint data to any site created with any site template, as long as the appropriate content types are associated to the destination lists and document libraries in that site. The following list provides an overview of these content types.

- PerformancePoint KPI
- PerformancePoint scorecard
- PerformancePoint indicator
- PerformancePoint report
- PerformancePoint filter
- PerformancePoint dashboard

When you have taken care of choosing destination lists and document libraries, migrating data with the PerformancePoint Services 2010 content migration tool will work.

Furthermore, you will find that there are no longer any site number restrictions. You can move content to any number of sites in the same or different Web applications. Using the PerformancePoint Services 2010 content migration tool, you can point at source content you want to migrate and then select to which lists or document libraries you want to migrate this content.

This also means you can move data that is from multiple PerformancePoint Server 2007 installations. Run the PerformancePoint Services 2010 content migration tool for every installation and the tool will retrieve content from the source PerformancePoint Server 2007 application database to a SharePoint 2010 destination list or document library.

The PerformancePoint Services 2010 content migration tool doesn't recreate existing PerformancePoint Server 2007 site structures, so you need to make sure that you set up a new site structure (it doesn't have to match the old site structure) in SharePoint 2010 before you start migrating content.

PerformancePoint Server 2007 roles and permissions do not exist in SharePoint 2010, but the PerformancePoint Services 2010 content migration tool will create equivalent sets of permissions in SharePoint 2010. Please note that the PerformancePoint Services 2010 content migration tool doesn't use predefined SharePoint 2010 roles because the permission sets associated to these roles may have been altered during the course of its existence. Windows group memberships are not migrated to a new server. This means that users that existed in the local administrators group on a PerformancePoint 2007 server will not be added automatically to the local administrators group on the PerformancePoint 2010 server.

Before migrating content, you need to ensure two other things. First, you need to make sure that you're migrating content to a destination location that is set up to be a trusted location. You can do that using the SharePoint 2010 Central Administration website. Second, you need to configure an unattended service account for PerformancePoint Services 2010. Both the configuration of trusted locations and unattended service accounts are discussed in the section titled "Installing and Configuring PerformancePoint Services 2010" earlier in this chapter.

During content migration, you should understand that there is an important distinction between dashboard definitions and exported dashboards. Both are migrated to the new environment, but there is a problem with exported dashboards. The actual .aspx files that make up the exported dashboard have references to the old PerformancePoint 2007 server that will immediately (if the new server can't access the old one) or eventually (if the old server ceases to exist) become broken references when you migrate them. Therefore, you should open the dashboard definition and export it again so that those .aspx files will be recreated with re-established links that point to the new location.

When migrating content, you also may need to update data source references after migrating to a new location. For instance, the old environment may have referred to an instance of Analysis Services 2005, and now you want to use an instance of Analysis Services 2008. It's also possible that the unattended service account that you are using in the new environment won't have access to the various data sources you are using.

The following procedure shows you how to migrate PerformancePoint Server 2007 content to a PerformancePoint Services 2010 location.

1. Launch SharePoint 2010 Central Administration website.

2. In the Application Management section, select Manage Service Applications.

3. Click the PerformancePoint Service link for the service you've created, or alternatively, select the PerformancePoint Service you've created and click Manage in the Operations group. Both options allow you to manage the properties of this PerformancePoint Service.

4. Click the Import PerformancePoint Server 2007 Content link shown in Figure 21-40.

FIGURE 21-40 Manage PerformancePoint Services page

This opens the Import PerformancePoint Server 2007 Content Wizard, which helps you to upgrade PerformancePoint Server 2007 content to PerformancePoint Services 2010.

Please note that the following items will not be migrated to the new environment.

- Spreadsheets
- Trend analysis charts
- Pivot tables
- Pivot charts

The reason that these items won't be migrated is simple: They are not supported in PerformancePoint Services 2010 because their functionality overlaps with other Microsoft technology. You will need to recreate these types of items completely.

After you have chosen which items you want to migrate, the wizard checks the security configuration in the Web.config file of PerformancePoint Server 2007. It uses this information and applies it to all data sources that are being moved. Possible security configurations are as follows.

- A single shared user account is used to access all data sources.
- A single shared user account is used to access all data sources and its user name is stored in the Web.config file.
- The user's own account is used to access all data sources.

In the next step, you need to log on to a PerformancePoint Server 2007 instance, which requires you to specify a server name and appropriate credentials. Please note that the information you provide here is not going to be used again and isn't stored anywhere. It is only used once to log on to the SQL Server that houses the PerformancePoint Server 2007 application database (also known as the PerformancePoint Server 2007 content database).

Then the wizard asks you to select a PerformancePoint 2007 content database. If you want to move multiple installations of PerformancePoint 2007, you must run this wizard multiple times.

On the next page of the wizard, you enter the site collection, site, and name of the list where you want to move the content. You need to do the same thing for the data source and point it to a destination document library. It is a best practice to always use an empty list or document library as the destination. Otherwise, if there are list items in an existing list that have the same name as PerformancePoint content, content will be upgraded erroneously. To prevent loss of data, it is best to always use an empty list or document library.

The final page of the wizard shows the status of the import and what kind of content, such as scorecards or dashboards, is being moved. If all goes well, you will see a reassuring list of green check marks on the status page.

Migrating Content to Another SharePoint 2010 Location

This section explains how to move content from one SharePoint 2010 site into a set of lists or document libraries located in another SharePoint 2010 site. This is a very common scenario that you will encounter, for instance, when you are moving data from a test server to a production server.

Before you start moving content, you need to complete a small checklist of tasks.

- Make sure you have set up and configured a PerformancePoint Service Application that will be used by the destination Web application.
- Recreate the current site and list structure in the destination Web application.
- Think about a security structure and implement it.

The first point in the checklist is self-evident; without a destination Web application that is connected to a PerformancePoint Service Application, migration won't work. The second point is that the PerformancePoint Services 2010 content migration tool doesn't recreate existing site structures (this is identical to migrations from PerformancePoint Server 2007 instances). You need to recreate the exact same site structure in the destination Web application. Failing to do so results in broken PerformancePoint references. Lastly, you need to implement a security structure, because existing permissions from a SharePoint 2010 source will not be migrated to a SharePoint 2010 destination. Instead, the existing destination security structure will be used.

You use the PerformancePoint Dashboard Designer to migrate content from a SharePoint 2010 source to a SharePoint 2010 location. PerformancePoint Dashboard Designer is a ClickOnce application that needs to be downloaded and installed once from a Business

Intelligence Center. You can do this by creating a new site collection using the Business Intelligence Center template. After you have created the BI center, you need to click the Start Using PerformancePoint Services link and click the Run Dashboard Designer button, which starts the download and installation of the client (note that a client requires .NET Framework 3.5 SP1). The rest of the chapter assumes you have already installed PerformancePoint Dashboard Designer. The following procedure explains how to migrate content from a SharePoint 2010 source to a SharePoint 2010 location.

1. Launch the PerformancePoint Dashboard Designer by clicking Start, selecting All Programs, and then selecting SharePoint. Select PerformancePoint Dashboard Designer.

2. Load an existing dashboard.

3. Click the Office button and then select the Save Workspace As option to save the existing dashboard as a Dashboard Designer Workspace.

4. Point the Dashboard Designer to the destination location. You can do this by choosing Designer Options, which can be opened by clicking the Office button, choosing the Server tab, and specifying a new location.

5. Click Import Items, which is located at the upper right on the Ribbon.

6. Browse to the previously created Dashboard Designer Workspace.

7. Select the items you want to copy to the destination location.

This action will cause the Import Items To SharePoint Wizard to start copying PerformancePoint content to the new location. The final screen in the wizard displays a summary that allows you to open the migration log files if you want to see more details.

There are a couple of issues you need to be aware of when it comes to moving PerformancePoint 2010 content. The first one is that when you select an object in Dashboard Designer, it loads all of the dependencies of that object. For example, opening a dashboard definition in SharePoint Designer will cause all of its dependencies to be loaded. This means that you should always choose objects that are high in the hierarchy when moving content (a top-down approach) to save time.

Dashboard Designer allows you to skip existing data sources during content migration. Typically, you will migrate them once, update data source references in the destination location (which is often needed in a new environment), and after that leave them as they are. This way, you will have to update those references only once.

You might wonder if you can use existing SharePoint site migration and backup and restore capabilities with PerformancePoint content. That is not a good idea—you should always use Dashboard Designer to migrate that content, because PerformancePoint keeps all of its site collection references between the objects as part of the objects themselves. Dashboard Designer ensures those references will also be updated, whereas SharePoint migration tooling just migrates the content and leaves those references as is. However, you can use the SharePoint backup and restore tools as long as you restore content to the same site structure. In that case, the references don't need to be updated.

Summary

In this chapter, you learned what business intelligence is all about and why it is important. This chapter discussed two keystone technologies involved with implementing business intelligence solutions: SQL Server Reporting Services 2008 and PerformancePoint Services 2010. The chapter then explained what SQL Server Reporting Services 2008 is and reviewed the new features that this release contains. You looked at the architecture of SQL Server Reporting Services 2008 and learned how to install it in SharePoint integrated mode. The final point in the chapter's discussion of SQL Server Reporting Services 2008 explained how to deploy and manage reports. Then the chapter introduced PerformancePoint Services 2010 and covered its new features, followed by a discussion of its architecture. You learned how to install and configure PerformancePoint Services 2010, and then you learned how to upgrade from PerformancePoint Server 2007 and how to migrate PerformancePoint Services 2010 content to another SharePoint 2010 location.

Upgrading to SharePoint 2010

This chapter primarily focuses on how to upgrade from Microsoft SharePoint Server 2007 to Microsoft SharePoint 2010. It will help you understand what an upgrade is, explain how to prepare for an upgrade, differentiate between the types of upgrades, perform the type of upgrade you have chosen to perform, and complete post-upgrade configuration. The information in this chapter also can help you prepare for the decisions that you have to make during an upgrade to ensure that the upgrade is completed successfully.

Upgrading to SharePoint 2010 can be challenging, and it requires a lot of thought and planning, so you want to be sure you are well prepared to upgrade your farm. There are several items to consider when you decide to perform an upgrade, and this chapter will help you make the correct decisions by discussing the following SharePoint 2010 upgrade topics.

■ What an upgrade is, and if and when you should perform an upgrade

■ The differences among the available types of SharePoint 2010 upgrades

■ Preparing for an upgrade to SharePoint 2010

■ Performing an actual upgrade to SharePoint 2010

■ Tasks to perform after a successful upgrade to SharePoint 2010

Introduction to SharePoint 2010 Upgrades

You must plan an upgrade carefully in advance, and everyone involved with managing SharePoint must agree on the best approach for your organization when deciding whether you should perform an in-place upgrade to SharePoint 2010 or a migration upgrade to SharePoint 2010. An in-place upgrade involves upgrading your current SharePoint configuration from its existing implementation to SharePoint 2010. Alternatively, a database attach upgrade, or what this chapter will refer to as a migration upgrade, involves creating a new SharePoint 2010 farm and then migrating your current databases to the new farm.

You are probably familiar with recommendations that you should not perform an in-place upgrade to more recent software, because you potentially can bring residual issues or challenges from the previous version into the new version. SharePoint is no different than any other type of software with respect to these sorts of considerations, and it is highly recommended that you perform a migration upgrade by installing SharePoint 2010 and then migrating your SharePoint content and configuration settings from your existing version to avoid problems that can be caused during an in-place upgrade or anytime after the in-place upgrade.

Because SharePoint is often an enterprise-wide solution, you have to be careful when performing an upgrade to avoid or minimize any interruption of service. Most SharePoint enterprise interruptions are caused by upgrades from previous versions or to a more robust version (for example, upgrading from SharePoint Foundation 2010 to SharePoint 2010). Most versions of SharePoint are significantly different from their predecessors, which can cause system administrators many days and nights of frustration because of the differences and customizations between the old and the new versions, or more likely because of a lack of planning for and understanding of the upgrade process. This chapter will not only address the mechanics of an upgrade but also the pros and cons of each of the two major upgrade processes introduced.

Philosophy

For those of you who are familiar with the upgrade process from Microsoft SharePoint 2003 to Microsoft SharePoint Server 2007, there is some good news. The upgrade process was redesigned with the administrator in mind. Administrators were extremely frustrated with upgrade issues in the 2003 to 2007 paths, because they experienced poor performance as well as a lack of documentation and appropriate tools to use during an upgrade.

SharePoint 2010 makes great strides in improving the upgrade process in all of these areas. In order to enhance the upgrade process, the following requirements had to be met and actions had to be taken:

- Early detection of upgrade issues
  - Provide administrators with correct tools to perform the upgrade
  - Inform administrators about critical issues prior to performing the upgrade
- Feedback to administrator during upgrade

- Incur no data loss

- Keep content and current settings intact

- Decrease the amount of downtime required by implementing processes that mitigate unnecessary downtime

- Eliminate fatal errors and continue on when possible

- Be reentrant; prevent catastrophic failures that necessitate complete restoration

How It Works

If you have a good understanding of what comprises an upgrade, it will be easier for you to understand how an upgrade works. In simple language, an upgrade is an ordered sequence of steps. Each step completes an action. For an upgrade to finish successfully, each sequential step must finish completely and successfully.

There are two major phases in an upgrade: the first phase occurs while running PSConfig.exe, and the second phase occurs in a timer job. The reason the second phase occurs in a timer job is because administrators often perform upgrades using Remote Desktop/Terminal Server (RDP) connections, and during the upgrade, the remote connection to the server is lost.

Figure 22-1 is a high-level overview of the upgrade process. In the second phase, certain steps are highlighted to illustrate that certain service applications and content databases are upgraded during the upgrade process in timer jobs that do not affect the rest of the upgrade.

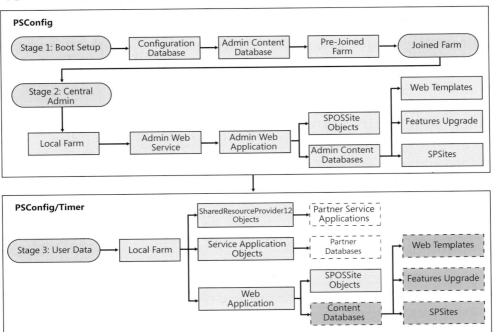

FIGURE 22-1 The two-phase upgrade process

The upgrade process consists of a sequential series of steps that are linked together and have the following characteristics.

- Each sequence of steps acts on certain objects dictated by the tasks the steps perform.

- Each sequence of steps is one of the three stages of the update.

- Each task can also include a series of steps.

- Each successful update in the series updates the object schema.

- If a task fails, the process continues on with the next step in the upgrade until all steps have been completed. If the upgrade needs to be restarted, it will resume from where it last failed, avoiding the need to start the upgrade from the beginning again.

SharePoint 2010 Upgrade Types

Having a thorough understanding of what upgrade options are available can influence how you ultimately install SharePoint 2010. There are several factors that you need to take into consideration before deciding on how to get to SharePoint 2010.

- Current hardware architecture (32-bit or 64-bit)

- Current operating system hosting your current SharePoint and Microsoft SQL Server software

- Current edition and version of SharePoint

- Current edition and version of SQL Server

> **IMPORTANT** To perform an upgrade to SharePoint 2010, you must have SharePoint Server 2007 with Service Pack 2 (SP2) installed.

SharePoint 2010 Upgrade Scenarios

After determining what your current hardware and software SharePoint Server 2007 environment is, you next need to determine the type of upgrade you can use to upgrade to SharePoint 2010. There are two primary upgrade scenarios: an in-place upgrade and a database attach upgrade. However, there are also two variations of these primary upgrade approaches.

- Hybrid approach 1: read-only databases

- Hybrid approach 2: detach databases

Table 22-1 contains compares these four different upgrade options.

> **NOTE** The gradual upgrade, in which you run two sets of SharePoint binaries installed side by side, is no longer supported for SharePoint 2010.

TABLE 22-1 SharePoint 2010 Upgrade Options

UPGRADE TYPE	PROS	CONS
In-place upgrade You have the ability to install SharePoint 2010 on the same hardware as the current version of SharePoint. You can also upgrade the content and settings in the server farm as part of a single process.	Farm-wide settings are preserved and upgraded. Customizations are available in the environment after the upgrade, although manual steps may be required to upgrade or rework them.	Servers and farms are offline while the upgrade is in progress. The upgrade proceeds continuously. Consequently, you must allocate enough time for all content to be upgraded in sequence.
Database attach upgrade You can upgrade the content for the environment on a separate farm. The result is that you do not upgrade any of the services or farm settings. You can upgrade the databases in any order and upgrade several databases at the same time.	You can upgrade multiple content databases at the same time, which results in faster upgrade times overall than an in-place upgrade. You can use a database attach upgrade to combine multiple farms into one farm.	The server and farm settings are not upgraded. You must manually transfer settings that you want to preserve from the old farm to the new farm. Any customizations must also be transferred to the new farm manually. Any missing customizations may cause unintended losses of functionality or user experience issues. Copying databases over a network takes time and bandwidth. You must plan for that. You need direct access to the database servers.
Hybrid approach 1: Read-only databases You can continue to provide read-only access to content during the upgrade process. For this approach, you set the databases to read-only while the upgrade is in progress on another farm.	The existing farm can continue to host non-upgraded sites (in read-only mode) while you upgrade the content. As a result, there is minimal downtime for users. You can upgrade multiple content databases at the same time, which results in faster upgrade times overall than an in-place upgrade. You can upgrade hardware in addition to software.	The server and farm settings are not upgraded. You must manually transfer settings that you want to preserve from the old farm to the new farm. Any customizations must also be transferred and upgraded manually. Any missing customizations may cause unintended losses of functionality or user experience issues. Copying databases over a network takes time and bandwidth. You must plan for that. You need direct access to the database servers.

continued on the next page

UPGRADE TYPE	PROS	CONS
Hybrid approach 2: Detach databases You can take advantage of an in-place upgrade's ability to upgrade content and settings while adding the speed of a database attach upgrade. For this approach, you use an in-place upgrade to upgrade the farm and settings and to detach and upgrade multiple databases in parallel (on the same farm or a separate farm).	Farm-wide settings can be preserved and upgraded. Customizations are available in the environment after the upgrade, although manual steps may be required to upgrade or rework them. You can upgrade multiple content databases at the same time, which results in faster upgrade times overall than an in-place upgrade.	Copying databases over a network takes time and bandwidth. You must plan for that. You need direct access to the database servers.

IMPORTANT When using an in-place upgrade approach, you are performing an actual upgrade of your existing environment to SharePoint 2010. Conversely, performing a database attach upgrade is more of a migration upgrade and is considered a safer upgrade option.

Special Cases

In addition to the previously discussed common SharePoint 2010 upgrade approaches, there are five special case upgrades that you can choose to perform as well. These special case upgrades listed in Table 22-2 are helpful if you determine that none of the four common upgrade approaches will work or will be an efficient approach for your organization's upgrade to SharePoint 2010.

TABLE 22-2 SharePoint 2010 Special Case Upgrades

SPECIAL CASE TYPE	UPGRADE APPROACH
Upgrading from a 32-bit to a 64-bit edition of SQL Server	If you need to upgrade from a 32-bit to a 64-bit edition of SQL Server, you should perform that upgrade before you upgrade to SharePoint 2010 to ensure the best performance benefits. Ensure that you perform only one upgrade at a time to avoid upgrade failure. For more information, see "Migrate an Existing Server Farm to a 64-Bit Environment (Office SharePoint Server 2007)" located at *http://technet.microsoft.com/en-us/library/dd622865.aspx*.

SPECIAL CASE TYPE	UPGRADE APPROACH
Upgrading from a 32-bit to a 64-bit edition of SQL Server *(continued)*	The following are two options for upgrading from a 32-bit to a 64-bit edition of SQL Server. ■ You can back up all the databases for the farm, perform the upgrade, and then restore the databases. (This option is supported and recommended because you will have a full backup, and after you restore the databases, you do not have to change anything within SharePoint 2010). ■ You can move the SQL Server databases that you want to upgrade to a different 64-bit edition of SQL Server. You must add the different 64-bit edition and then run a command to the computers running SharePoint 2010 to point them to the new 64-bit edition of SQL Server. (This option is supported but not recommended because it requires more work in SharePoint 2010 when, for example, the databases change location).*
Upgrading from a 32-bit operating system to a 64-bit operating system	If you are using a 32-bit operating system, you must migrate to a 64-bit operating system before you upgrade. For more information, see "Migrate an Existing Server Farm to a 64-Bit Environment (Office SharePoint Server 2007)" located at *http://technet.microsoft.com/en-us/library/dd622865.aspx.*
Upgrading from Microsoft SharePoint Portal Server 2003	Upgrade to Office SharePoint Server 2007 and then upgrade to SharePoint 2010. For more information about how to migrate from SharePoint Portal Server 2003 to Office SharePoint Server 2007, see the Migration and Upgrade Resource Center for Office SharePoint Server 2007 at *http://go.microsoft.com/fwlink/?LinkID=104403.*
Upgrading from Windows SharePoint Services 3.0	Use the database attach upgrade method to upgrade the content databases from Windows SharePoint Services 3.0 to SharePoint 2010. This process upgrades the data in the content databases but does not transfer any farm settings.
User-Copy-Only	This method is used when you want to retain all of your current information in SharePoint Server 2007, but you want to implement a new information architecture (IA). You build your new SharePoint 2010 farm and then export the content out of the SharePoint Server 2007 farm and import it into the SharePoint 2010 farm in the new IA design.

If you upgrade a SQL Server version—for example, from SQL Server 2005 SP2 to SQL Server 2008—you can perform this upgrade before, during, or after you upgrade from a 32-bit to a 64-bit edition of SQL Server.

As you can see, there are several types of upgrades you can perform and several items you must consider before beginning an upgrade to SharePoint 2010. It is important to take the time to familiarize yourself with all components of your existing SharePoint implementation to ensure you have a successful upgrade to SharePoint 2010.

SharePoint 2010 Upgrade Paths

Now that you are familiar with the upgrade types, you need to also become familiar with the upgrade paths available when upgrading to SharePoint 2010. Understanding the supported upgrade paths will help you make a well-informed decision on how to perform the upgrade to SharePoint 2010. You'll first need to determine if an upgrade to SharePoint 2010 from your current implementation is even possible.

Supported Upgraded Topologies

The first thing you need to do is analyze and document your current SharePoint configuration and all of its supporting components to determine if it will be possible for you to perform an upgrade to SharePoint 2010. There are several considerations that you must be familiar with when determining if you are going to upgrade to SharePoint 2010.

When you upgrade to SharePoint 2010, you must upgrade to the same kind of installation. For instance, you can only upgrade your current stand-alone SharePoint installation to a SharePoint 2010 stand-alone installation, or upgrade your current server farm to a SharePoint 2010 server farm. During an upgrade, you cannot upgrade from a stand-alone installation to a farm installation or vice versa using an in-place upgrade. However, that doesn't mean you are committed to staying with the current type of installation; it just means you must change the size and scale of a server farm to suit your requirements either before or after you upgrade to SharePoint 2010. Alternatively, if you perform a database attach upgrade, you are able to attach your databases to a different installation type.

This means that migrating from a stand-alone server to a SharePoint 2010 farm configuration is a two-step upgrade. In step 1, you will create a new farm using your current version of SharePoint and move the databases from the stand-alone server to your newly created farm. Step 2 is then to perform the upgrade of your current version server farm to a SharePoint 2010 farm.

> **MORE INFO** For additional information on the upgrade path when performing a migration upgrade from a stand-alone server to a SharePoint 2010 farm configuration, visit the website at *http://technet.microsoft.com/en-us/library/cc262325.aspx*.

You also must follow this two-step upgrade if your current version of SharePoint is running on 32-bit hardware. In this case, you cannot perform an in-place upgrade to SharePoint 2010. You must perform a migration upgrade by first obtaining 64-bit hardware and then installing SharePoint 2010; the final step in a migration upgrade is migrating your content from SharePoint Server 2007 to your new SharePoint 2010 farm.

> **MORE INFO**   For additional information on the upgrade path for migrating an existing server farm to a 64-bit environment, visit the website at *http://technet.microsoft.com/en-us /library/dd622865.aspx.*

Upgrade Restrictions

Most Microsoft Office SharePoint Server 2007 installations can be upgraded to SharePoint 2010, but there are some restrictions. Table 22-3 lists the SharePoint Server 2007 and SharePoint 2010 server editions that can be upgraded to specific SharePoint 2010 editions using an in-place upgrade, and it lists those in-place upgrades that are not supported.

TABLE 22-3 SharePoint In-Place Upgrades to SharePoint 2010

CURRENT EDITION	NEW EDITION (SUPPORTED IN-PLACE UPGRADE)
Office SharePoint Server 2007 with SP2, Standard Edition	SharePoint 2010, Standard Edition
SharePoint 2010, Standard Edition	SharePoint 2010, Enterprise Edition
Office SharePoint Server 2007 with SP2, Enterprise Edition	SharePoint 2010, Enterprise Edition
Office SharePoint Server 2007 with SP2, Trial Edition	SharePoint 2010, Trial Edition
SharePoint 2010, Trial Edition	SharePoint 2010, full product

The in-place upgrades listed in Table 22-3 are the simplest forms of upgrades that you will encounter when performing most upgrades to SharePoint 2010. However, there are cross-product upgrade scenarios that you may also encounter, and you should be familiar with these in case you have to perform some of the less common types of upgrades. Table 22-4 lists both the supported and unsupported SharePoint upgrade options that you also could encounter.

TABLE 22-4 Cross-Product In-Place Upgrades to SharePoint 2010

CURRENT EDITION	NEW EDITION (SUPPORTED)
Windows SharePoint Services (WSS) 3.0 with SP2	SharePoint Foundation 2010
Microsoft SharePoint Foundation 2010	SharePoint 2010
Microsoft Search Server 2008	SharePoint 2010 or Microsoft Search Server 2010
Microsoft Forms Server 2007	SharePoint 2010
Microsoft PerformancePoint Server 2007	SharePoint 2010
Microsoft Project Server 2007 with WSS 3.0 with SP2, or SharePoint Server 2007 with SP2	SharePoint 2010 Enterprise Edition plus Microsoft Project 2010

As you can see, there are several options to choose from when deciding whether you will need to use a two-step approach for an upgrade, or whether the upgrade you are considering is simple enough to perform in one step to move from your current version of SharePoint to SharePoint 2010.

Remember: It is strongly recommended that you perform a migration upgrade of your existing content to a new farm rather than upgrading your current farm because of the possible residual negative effects.

Preparing to Upgrade to SharePoint 2010

After taking the time to become familiar with upgrade paths and types available to you and making a decision to upgrade to SharePoint 2010, you are ready to prepare for the upgrade. The amount of preparation that you perform will have a great impact on the success of the upgrade. In the following sections, you will learn what you need to do to prepare for an upgrade to SharePoint 2010 to minimize or eliminate any potential issues during the upgrade process. To help you prepare for the installation, you should understand the following topics.

- Best practices for upgrading to SharePoint 2010
- How to run and test a full backup of your SQL Server information
- How run the pre-upgrade checker tool

Ten Best Practices for Upgrading to SharePoint 2010

If you are performing an upgrade from SharePoint Server 2007 to SharePoint 2010, Microsoft has identified 10 best practices that you should follow to help streamline the upgrade and minimize any problems during the upgrade.

- Install Service Pack 2 on your current SharePoint Server 2007 servers before upgrading. This applies to all upgrade types. If you add the October 2009 SharePoint Server 2007 cumulative update as well, it enhances the pre-upgrade checker tool used during the upgrade process.

- Ensure that the existing SharePoint Server 2007 environment is functioning properly and remove all unnecessary or unused components from your existing implementation.

- Migrate existing SharePoint Server 2007 servers to 64-bit before performing an in-place upgrade to SharePoint 2010.

- Run the pre-upgrade checker to help identify potential upgrade problems.

- Perform a trial upgrade on a test farm that mirrors your production farm. This will provide you with the following benefits.

  - You will become familiar with upgrade user interface.

  - You can determine which upgrade approach will work best for your environment.

  - You can test the new look and feel of the upgraded farm.

  - You can determine customizations that you must complete.

  - You can determine the amount of time necessary to perform the upgrade.

  - You will know what you need to plan for during the upgrade, such as resource availability.

- Plan for the hardware capacity you will require for SharePoint 2010, including enough disk space, processor capacity, and memory.

- Perform a full backup of your entire farm and all supporting components, such as Internet Information Services (IIS) and 12 hive.

- If performing a database attach upgrade, set existing databases to read-only. This is optional, but it allows your users to continue to access your SharePoint content without being able to modify it.

- Avoid adding servers to the new farm during the upgrade. If additional servers are required, add them before you perform the upgrade or after the upgrade, but not during the upgrade.

- After the upgrade finishes, review the upgrade logs and the Upgrade Status page to discover any upgrade issues.

The upcoming sections of this chapter provide additional information about some of these best practices, but this is a good starting place to verify you have performed the proper tasks prior to performing the upgrade process. Using this list will help you to take the steps required to recover from an unsuccessful upgrade or to ensure that your successful upgrade includes everything from your previous installation of SharePoint.

Backing Up and Testing Your SharePoint Farm

A critical aspect of performing any type of upgrade is to be able to roll back to the current environment if there are problems with the upgrade. With most of your SharePoint content stored in SQL Server, it is imperative that your SharePoint databases are backed up prior to performing an upgrade. By doing so, in the event the upgrade fails and you need to roll back to your current environment, you will have a copy of the information as it was prior to beginning the upgrade.

 REAL WORLD **The Importance of Testing the Rollback Strategy**

It is extremely important that you test your rollback strategy prior to performing an upgrade. In my experience, the backups have failed during the recovery process on several occasions. If this happens, it can leave your organization in turmoil. So it is important to not only back up all the SharePoint databases prior to performing an upgrade, but also always test your recovery to ensure that after you restore database backups, the farm is still operational.

Backing Up Your Current SharePoint Farm

Backups of SharePoint data are often performed by your SQL Server database administrator (DBA). However, some SharePoint administrators are also the SQL DBAs for their SharePoint implementation. It is important that you know what should be backed up prior to performing an upgrade. The following databases should be backed up (if they exist).

- Farm configuration database
- Central Administration database
- Search database
- WSS help search database
- Shared Service Provider (SSP) database
- SSP search database
- Single sign-on (SSO) database
- My Sites database
- All content databases

For more information about backing up your SharePoint farm databases, see Chapter 17, "Data Protection, Recoverability, and Availability."

BEST PRACTICE You should also back up all SharePoint customizations including site definitions, Web Parts, new features, and all other files that you would need in case you have to roll back to the previous version's environment.

Testing Your SharePoint Farm Backups

Backing up your SharePoint farm content is just one step in preparing for your SharePoint farm upgrade. However, what if the upgrade fails and you need to roll back to your previous SharePoint environment—but the backup media is corrupt? Or the restore operations of the backups are successful, but you are unable to access your sites because DNS entries or Alternate Access Mappings are missing? What if the host headers you added to your Web applications are lost during the upgrade and you haven't backed up the IIS 6.0 metabase?

The best way to ensure that you have successfully backed up everything that you need to roll back to your previous SharePoint is to test the rollback process. You should perform this test prior to starting the upgrade so you can discover any problems before they occur in your production environment.

It is highly recommended that you duplicate your production environment in a nonproduction environment that includes a Web server computer and SQL Server. Use this environment to restore your backups, and after the backups are restored successfully, install all of your farm customizations (such as site definitions, Web Parts, and new features), and then verify that the restored farm is fully functional. After a successful restore and a complete test in a nonproduction environment, you will have proven that if the upgrade process fails, you will be able to roll back to your current environment with no loss of data or functionality.

Running the Pre-Upgrade Checker Tool

If you have made the decision to perform an in-place upgrade instead of a migration upgrade to SharePoint 2010, you want to take every precaution to ensure that the servers on which you will be performing the upgrades meet the requirements of SharePoint 2010. The steps you take to ensure your servers are ready for an upgrade will eliminate or reduce the likelihood that the upgrade will fail and require a rollback, as discussed in the section titled "Backing Up and Testing Your SharePoint Farm" earlier in this chapter.

The best way to check your existing SharePoint servers is to run the pre-upgrade checker tool provided by Microsoft. This tool is free, and it will report on the status of your environment and SharePoint sites before you upgrade to SharePoint 2010. You can acquire this tool by installing Service Pack 2 of SharePoint Server 2007. Alternatively, an updated version of the pre-upgrade checker is also available when you install the October 2009 cumulative update for SharePoint Server 2007. You can find this and other SharePoint Server 2007 cumulative updates at *http://technet.microsoft.com/en-us/office/sharepointserver/bb735839.aspx*.

> **IMPORTANT** The pre-upgrade checker tool does not prepare the environment for an upgrade; it is used to help the administrator prepare for the upgrade by informing them of what to be aware of before performing an upgrade to SharePoint 2010.

The pre-upgrade checker tool extends the functionality of the Stsadm.exe command line tool by performing a check on your existing SharePoint implementation to determine if it is appropriately configured and to report other information that will help you prepare for the SharePoint 2010 upgrade. During the evaluation of your current SharePoint farm, the pre-upgrade checker evaluates and returns the following information.

- A list of all servers and components in the farm, and whether the servers meet the requirements for upgrading, which include 64-bit hardware and the Windows Server 2008 operating system
- The alternate access mapping URLs currently being used in the farm
- A list of all site definitions, site templates, features, and language packs that are installed in the farm
- Whether all customizations in the farm are supported (such as database schema modifications)
- Whether there are any database or site orphans in the farm
- Whether there are missing or invalid configuration settings in the farm (such as a missing Web.config file, invalid host names, or invalid service accounts)
- Whether the SQL databases meet the requirements for an upgrade—for example, checking for databases set to read/write and any databases and site collections currently stored in Windows Internal Database larger than 4 gigabytes (GB)

The SharePoint servers that you will be upgrading to SharePoint 2010—or that you will perform a migration upgrade on —must meet the minimum requirements discussed in Chapter 4, "Installing SharePoint 2010."

To run the pre-upgrade checker tool, open a command prompt as an administrator, change to the %CommonProgramFiles%\Microsoft Shared\Web Server Extensions\12\BIN directory, and type the following command.

```
stsadm -o preupgradecheck
```

In addition to the results within the command prompt window, another window is displayed, as shown in Figure 22-2, that contains a report from the command within a Web browser window.

If you have not installed Service Pack 2 or the October cumulative update on every server in the farm, you may receive errors concerning the SPTimerV3 service, and you also may see logon errors when you try to restart the service manually. If this occurs and you have successfully installed Service Pack 2, you will need to run the update KB971620 to fix the product license state from the evaluation/trial to fully licensed implementation. After you install this update, you should run the pre-upgrade checker tool again.

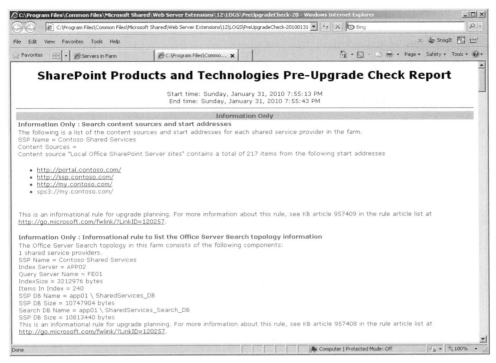

FIGURE 22-2 Pre-upgrade check Web page report

> **NOTE** It isn't uncommon to run the pre-upgrade checker multiple times. For example, if you ran it to perform the initial evaluation of your server farm but cannot perform the upgrade for a few weeks, you should rerun the tool again just prior to the actual upgrade to check for any last-minute issues that may have appeared since the first time you ran the tool.

The pre-upgrade checker tool checks both the local server and your farm-level settings. The information returned by this tool can be used to determine how you will proceed. The results of the pre-upgrade checker will allow you make the following determinations.

- The type of upgrade to perform, in-place or database attached upgrade
- The upgrade site collections that contain customized sites
- Customizations that may have to be reapplied or redone after the upgrade completes

After you run the pre-upgrade checker, the report it generates will automatically be displayed in your default browser. If you want to view this report at a later time, you can do so by opening it from its location, which is as follows.

%CommonProgramFiles%\Microsoft Shared\Web Server Extensions\12\LOGS

The reports are named using the format PreUpgradeCheck_*YYYYMMDD-HHMMSS-SSS-random_number*.htm, with the following file naming conventions.

- *YYYYMMDD* is the date. *YYYY* = 4-digit year; *MM* = 2-digit month; *DD* = 2-digit day.

- *HHMMSS-SSS* is the time. *HH* = 24-hour clock; *MM* = minutes; *SS* = seconds; *SSS* = milliseconds.

- *random_number* is used to differentiate among simultaneous runs of the tool.

NOTE In addition to the .htm version of the report, there also are .txt and .xml versions of the report located in the same directory, as shown in Figure 22-3.

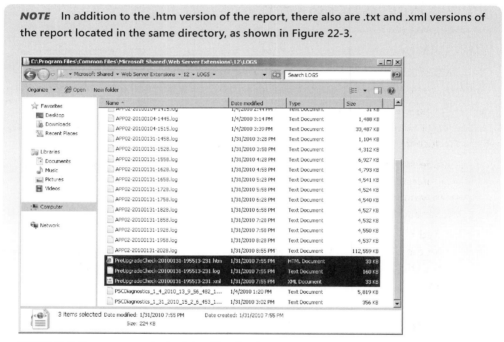

FIGURE 22-3 The pre-upgrade check log files directory

These reports are useful in helping you determine if there will be any issues during the upgrade to SharePoint 2010. The logs contain the following information.

- The checks that were performed

- The issues discovered by the checks

- Suggestions on how to resolve the issues or a link to a Knowledge Base article to help resolve the issues

After resolving all issues reported during the pre-upgrade check, you are ready to upgrade to SharePoint 2010 using one of the several ways introduced in earlier sections in this chapter.

Your next step in the upgrade process is to perform the actual upgrade to SharePoint 2010. However, you should first make sure that all the servers in the new farm meet the hardware and software requirements discussed in Chapter 4 of this book.

SharePoint 2010 Upgrade Considerations

During the actual upgrade, there are several items you need to consider to ensure an efficient, timely, and smooth upgrade for your end users. These considerations affect how you will perform the upgrade and the appearance of the new farm after you complete the SharePoint 2010 upgrade steps.

Upgrade Process Considerations

While performing the SharePoint 2010 upgrade, there are two considerations you will want to be aware of during the upgrade.

- You want to minimize the downtime of your SharePoint farm.
- You want to minimize the impact on your users after the upgrade is completed.

Microsoft has provided some upgrade options to assist you in both of these challenges after deciding to upgrade to SharePoint 2010. There are two options you can choose from to help you reduce the amount of time it takes to upgrade the farm.

- Upgrade multiple databases at one time. Use the detach databases hybrid approach for upgrading to upgrade multiple databases at a time. Be aware, however, that you may notice an impact on performance if you run multiple database upgrades simultaneously.
- Use read-only databases during the upgrade process. Use a database attach upgrade and set the current SharePoint Server 2007 databases to read-only so users still have access to their content but cannot make any changes to that SharePoint Server 2007 content.

Upgrading the SharePoint User Interface

SharePoint 2010 includes a new feature that allows the server administrator or site owner to determine when and if the new look for SharePoint 2010 is implemented for a particular site collection. The server administrators can choose to adopt the new look and feel for all sites during upgrade, let site owners make the choice after upgrade, or keep the old look and feel for all sites; this last choice is the default.

If the upgrade is performed using an in-place upgrade, the server administrator lets the site owners decide after the site is upgraded if they want to change to the new 2010 SharePoint appearance by providing a preview option for the site user interface. The user can choose between the SharePoint Server 2007 user interface and the new SharePoint 2010 interface.

Upgrading Features

In SharePoint Foundation 2010, every feature has a version number specified in the corresponding Feature.xml file. These feature versions are now tracked in the SharePoint content database according to scope, which can be a server farm, a Web application, a site collection, or a website. When a feature is activated at a specified scope, an associated instance is created with the current version of the feature. When a new version of the feature is deployed, SharePoint Foundation detects the new version by comparing the instance version numbers specified in the Feature.xml file.

When you perform a feature upgrade, the feature instances that need to be upgraded are upgraded according to the upgrade actions specified in the new Feature.xml file. This file contains a section that is used to specify the upgrade actions required to upgrade a particular feature instance to the most current version.

Features are upgraded in the following order: server farm level, Web application level, site collection, and then specific websites. Website feature instances are upgraded from the top-level or root site and progress down through the child sites. If an error occurs during the feature upgrade, the upgrade stops for the specified feature instance and records the error in an Upgrade.log file. However, the upgrade continues to run on the other feature instances.

NOTE Feature upgrades can only be performed using farm administrator credentials.

Five Steps to a Successful Upgrade to SharePoint 2010

Regardless of the upgrade type you decide to perform, you should perform the following five general steps sequentially during an upgrade.

1. Run prerequisite installer on ALL servers in your server farm.

2. Install SharePoint 2010 on ALL servers in your server farm using Setup.exe.

3. Install any required language packs for SharePoint 2010 (optional).

4. Run the SharePoint Products Configuration Wizard to create your SharePoint 2010 Central Administration website.

5. Run the configuration wizard on the remaining servers in the farm in any order.

IMPORTANT In a multiple server farm, it is extremely important to run the prerequisite installer and SharePoint 2010 Setup.exe on ALL servers in the farm before running the SharePoint Products Configuration Wizard on any server in the farm! That is, you must complete steps 1 and 2 on all servers in the farm before you complete step 4 on any server in the farm.

Performing a Database Attach Upgrade

The database attach upgrade (migration upgrade) approach is the preferred upgrade method. This approach is useful because you can continue to use your current SharePoint farm, which minimizes downtime during the upgrade, and it is also helpful when you need to move to new hardware. When you perform a database attach, you perform a migration upgrade of your content to an entirely new farm, but you do not migrate the SharePoint Server 2007 configuration settings, which reduces the possibility of bringing along any problems from your SharePoint Server 2007 server farm. This approach contains two stages.

- First, you prepare the new farm environment for the upgrade to SharePoint 2010.
- Second, you attach your current databases to your new farm environment to complete the upgrade process.

All of the required steps to complete this process are in the next two sections. It is important that you follow these steps to ensure a successful upgrade. As explained in the section titled "Preparing to Upgrade to SharePoint 2010" earlier in this chapter, you should have already practiced performing this upgrade—including testing the completed upgrade—to make sure you won't encounter any unexpected problems.

Preparing the New Farm Environment for the Upgrade

In the first stage of this upgrade type, you create the new SharePoint 2010 farm environment. In this stage you are going to take several steps to create an environment that will allow your current farm to be "moved" to the new SharePoint 2010 farm environment. Before you begin this stage, you must ensure that everything that was discussed in Chapter 4 has already been completed.

During this first stage of the database attach upgrade, you will perform two primary tasks.

- Create and configure the new SharePoint 2010 environment.
- Verify the new SharePoint 2010 environment.

Creating and Configuring the New SharePoint 2010 Environment

In this first set of tasks, you take the same steps you would to prepare for an installation of SharePoint 2010, and you complete the installation of SharePoint 2010 to create your new farm environment. This stage of the upgrade requires you to complete the following three steps.

1. Install SharePoint 2010.
2. Re-create your Web applications, reapply configuration settings, and copy over all customizations.
3. Manually transfer the customizations into your new SharePoint 2010 farm.

After completing these three steps, you are ready to verify that the new configuration contains all of the required configurations, Web applications, and customizations. However, to ensure that everything is created and configured correctly, be sure to refer to the following step-by-step procedures as a guideline for performing this first set of tasks for this upgrade approach.

INSTALLING SHAREPOINT 2010

In this first step, you must complete an installation of SharePoint 2010 on all servers in the farm. Remember to follow these steps when installing SharePoint 2010 on your new farm servers.

1. Ensure you meet the hardware and software requirements for SharePoint 2010 as listed in Chapter 4.
2. Complete the installation using the steps listed in Chapter 4.
3. Verify the installation of SharePoint 2010 completed successfully and accurately as described in Chapter 4.

You should perform these three steps on each server that you are planning on using in your new SharePoint 2010 farm.

DUPLICATING YOUR WEB APPLICATIONS AND FARM CONFIGURATIONS

In the next step of stage 1 of the update, you recreate your existing environment within your new environment, so that when you move your content to the new environment, all the current behavior is available on your server farm. Use the following guidelines to ensure you duplicate your current environment in your new environment.

1. Create a Web application for each application in your SharePoint Server 2007 environment. Use the same default URL as your existing Web applications.
2. Manually apply all of the following configuration settings.
   - Alternate Access Mappings
   - Farm-level security and permission settings
   - Incoming e-mail settings
   - Outgoing e-mail settings
   - Managed paths, including /sites
   - Quota templates
   - Service settings, including Search settings

> **IMPORTANT** Your services settings must be created on your new farm before you upgrade the data using the database attach upgrade approach.

3. If you are upgrading My Sites and User Profiles, you must ensure that the following steps have been completed prior to the upgrade.
   - Create a new Web application for My Sites.

- Enable the Metadata Service Application.
- Enable the User Profile Service Application.
- Create a proxy for the User Profile Service Application.
- Associate the new proxy with the default proxy group.

MANUALLY TRANSFERING ALL FARM CUSTOMIZATIONS

You will also want to manually copy the customizations you have in your current environment, including those that are required for your sites to function properly. These customizations include

- Language packs
- Custom site definitions
- Custom style sheets, including cascading style sheets
- Custom Web Parts and Web services
- Custom features and solutions
- Settings modified in the Web.config file
- Form templates (XSN files) and data connection files (UDCX files) for InfoPath

> **IMPORTANT** You must export these files from your current environment and import them into the SharePoint 2010 environment using Stsadm.exe commands.

Verifying the New SharePoint 2010 Environment

After you have created and configured your new environment, you should perform tests to make sure it contains everything required before you upgrade your data. This verification process involves the following two steps that you complete in your new SharePoint 2010 farm.

1. Test your Web applications.
   a. Create a new Web application.
   b. Restore the copy of the content database associated with the Web application.
   c. Run the Windows PowerShell Test-SPContentDatabase cmdlet to verify all customizations exist in new environment.

> **NOTE** You can use this cmdlet against the original content database, but that database should not be in use when you run the cmdlet.

2. Run the Stsadmenumallwebs command in your SharePoint Server 2007 environment to obtain a list of templates associated with each site and verify that they are installed in

your SharePoint 2010 environment. The syntax for running this command is similar to the following.

```
stsadm -o enumallwebs-databasename<databasename>[-databaseserver<database server
name>]
```

> **NOTE** The output from this command is not very user friendly; however, you can import it into Microsoft Word or Microsoft Excel and format it so that it makes more sense.

Attaching Your Existing Content Databases to Your New SharePoint 2010 Farm

In the second stage of a database attach upgrade, you attach the content databases from your existing farm to the new SharePoint 2010 farm environment. This stage has three primary steps you will follow for each content database that you are attaching to your new farm's SQL Server instance.

1. Verify that you have appropriate permissions to perform SQL tasks.
2. Associate the restored databases with the Web applications in the new farm.
3. Verify that the database attach upgrade completed successfully.

Verifying That You Have the Required SQL Server Permissions

The first action that you want to take in this stage determines if you have the required permissions to perform SQL Server backups on your existing SharePoint SQL Server instance. Furthermore, you want to determine that you also have the required permissions to restore the SQL databases on the new farm's SQL Server instance. The SQL Server permissions required to perform the backup operation on your current farm are specific to the database. That means for each content database that you are going to back up, you need to be a member of the following fixed database roles.

- db_owner
- db_backupoperator

In preparation for the SQL Server restore operations, you must be a member of the local Administrators group, and you also must be a member of specific roles in order to successfully complete a SQL Server restore operation. However, on the restore operation, the required permissions aren't just at a database level; they are also at the SQL Server level. You need the following permissions on the SharePoint 2010 SQL Server instance.

- The dbcreator fixed server role
- The db_owner fixed database role

The steps for backing up and restoring your databases will vary depending on the version of SQL Server you are running. Remember that SharePoint Server 2007 supports integration with Microsoft SQL Server 2000, SQL Server 2005, and SQL Server 2008. However, SharePoint 2010 only supports integration with SQL Server 2005 and SQL Server 2008. For the steps required to perform a database backup operation or a database restore operation, visit the Microsoft website and locate SQL Server Books Online to find the manual for your specific SQL Server version. Documentation for SQL Server products is available for download on any computer from SQL Server Books Online.

Associating the Existing Content Databases with Their New Web Applications

After you have completed the backup and restore process, you can associate the databases with the new Web applications that you created in the SharePoint 2010 farm. To perform this process correctly, follow these three steps in the order shown.

1. Execute a Windows PowerShell cmdlet called Test-SPContentDatabase.
2. Execute a Stsadm.exe –o command called addcontentdb.
3. Verify the upgrade for first database of each Web application.

WINDOWS POWERSHELL TEST-SPCONTENTDATABASE CMDLET

The Windows PowerShell Test-SPContentDatabase cmdlet checks the Web application to verify that all the required customizations for that database are installed. This command does not make any changes to the database; it just creates a report from it by entering the cmdlet in the following format.

```
Test-SPContentDatabase  –Name<databasename>-WebApplication<URLofNewWebApp>
[-ServerInstance<ServerInstanceName>][-DatabaseCredentials<Domain\username>]
```

After the command completes, it will return information about potential issues such as

- Missing files
- Missing site definitions

- Missing features
- Missing assemblies

The results from this command will also give you helpful information regarding possible fixes for the identified problems and whether or not they will prevent the upgrade from completing successfully.

This may be an iterative process, where you run the command, resolve the identified issues, and run the command again to identify any new issues. Run this command as many times as necessary to get a clean report, or one that you are confident will allow you to complete the upgrade process.

STSADM –O ADDCONTENTDB COMMAND

After resolving any potential issues identified by the Test-SPContentDatabase cmdlet, you are ready to associate the database to the Web application. Take the following items into consideration when adding your content databases.

- The first content database that you add must contain the root site for the Web application.

> **NOTE** If you are unsure what content database contains the root site, you can locate the top-level site collection for the Web application in Central Administration, and when you click the top-level site link, it will specify what database it resides in.

- Do not create any site collections on the Web application until all content databases have been restored.
- Any remaining content databases can be added in any order.
- You cannot add the same content database more than once to a farm, even if you want to add it in different Web applications.
- You cannot add the same site collection more than once to a farm, even you want to add it in different Web applications, because each site collection has a globally unique identifier (GUID) stored in the configuration database.

> **NOTE** If you need a duplicate copy of a site collection in your farm, you can restore the database to an alternate farm. You can then back up the site collection from that database and restore it in your new farm, and at that time it will create a unique site collection and GUID.

The command and required parameters you use to add a content database to your new SharePoint 2010 SQL Server instance are as follows.

```
stsadm -o addcontentdb -url<URLofWebApp> -databasename<databasename>
```

This command has some optional parameters, which are listed with a brief description of each in Table 22-5.

TABLE 22-5 Optional Parameters for addcontentdb

PARAMETER	DESCRIPTION
−databaseserver	If not provided, the default server is used.
−databaseuser	If not using Windows authentication, you must specify the SQL authenticated account and the −databasepassword parameter.
−databasepassword	If not using Windows authentication, you must specify SQL authenticated account and the −databaseuser parameter.
−forcedeleteupgradelock	Removes the upgrade lock on the database.
−preserveolduserexperience	When set to true, the default maintains the previous SharePoint versions interface. When set to false, sites reflect the new interface in SharePoint 2010.
−sitewarning	Number of site collections allowed in content database before generating a warning in the Windows event log.
−sitemax	Maximum number of site collections allowed in the content database.
−assignnewdatabaseid	Assigns new database ID to database. Useful for making copies of a database and assigning it to the same farm.
−clearchangelog	Clears the change log. Useful for oversized change logs, restoring a database to a previous point in time, and causing the content to be recrawled.

Verifying That the Upgrade Operation Was Successful

The last step in the database attach upgrade approach is to perform a verification to make sure that the databases were attached successfully and the Web applications are running correctly. You can accomplish this verification by viewing the Upgrade Status page, as shown in Figure 22-4, which is located in Central Administration.

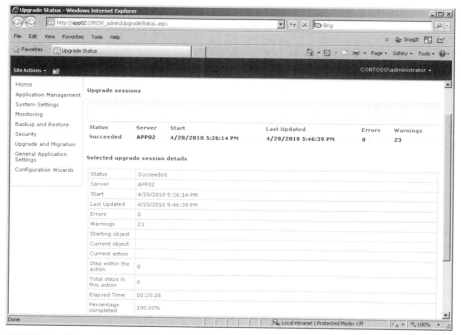

FIGURE 22-4 Central Administration Upgrade Status page

In addition to the Upgrade Status page in Central Administration, there are two types of files generated in the %CommonProgramFiles%\Microsoft Shared\Web Server Extensions\14\ LOGS directory: an upgrade log (.log) and upgrade error log file (.err), as shown in Figure 22-5. The upgrade error log file contains a consolidated version of any errors and warnings that occurred during the upgrade.

The logs are named using the format Upgrade-*YYYYMMDD-HHMMSS-SSS-random-number*.log, with the following file naming conventions.

- *YYYYMMDD* is the date. *YYYY*=4-digit year; *MM*=2-digit month; *DD*=2-digit day.

- *HHMMSS-SSS* is the time. *HH*= 24-hour clock; *MM*=minutes; *SS*=seconds; *SSS*=milliseconds.

The previous procedure is the preferred method of upgrading to SharePoint 2010, because it provides the flexibility to move to different hardware, it prevents configuration problems from moving from the old to the new environment, and it allows users access to your current SharePoint environment while the upgrade is taking place. However, it may not be the easiest option for upgrading to SharePoint 2010, as you will see in the next section, with a discussion of how to perform an in-place upgrade.

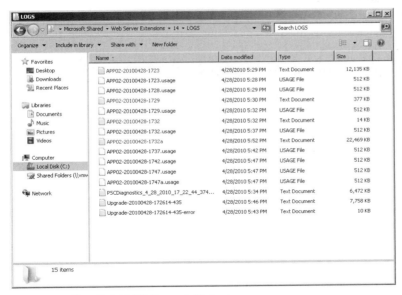

FIGURE 22-5 SharePoint 2010 Upgrade Status logs

Performing an In-Place Upgrade

An in-place upgrade is an easier upgrade from SharePoint Server 2007 to SharePoint 2010, because the farm configuration data and the content in the existing farm are all upgraded at one time on your existing hardware, and in a fixed order. This upgrade process does not allow your users to access SharePoint during the upgrade process, however. In fact, when you start the in-place upgrade process, Setup takes the Web server offline, making the websites unavailable until the upgrade is finished, when it brings them back online. After you begin an in-place upgrade, you cannot roll back to your previous SharePoint version or even pause the upgrade process.

> **NOTE** Prior to performing an in-place upgrade, you can disconnect all the users from your server farm by stopping the World Wide Web Publishing Service (W3SVC) on all of your Web front-end (WFE) servers.

Similar to the database attach upgrade process, the in-place upgrade process uses the following five sequential steps in a two-phase approach to ensure a successful upgrade to SharePoint 2010. However, the major difference is that instead of performing these five steps in your new farm, you will run them on the servers in your existing farm.

1. Run the prerequisite installer on ALL servers in your server farm.

2. Install SharePoint 2010 on ALL servers in your server farm using Setup.exe. Run it on the server hosting Central Administration first, and then on all other servers in any order.

3. Install any required language packs for SharePoint 2010 (optional).

4. Run the SharePoint Products Configuration Wizard on your SharePoint 2010 Central Administration website, which upgrades this server, the configuration database, the services, and the content databases sequentially.

    This process then creates a timer job that upgrades each site collection, and after each site collection has been upgraded, the upgrade is complete on this server.

5. Run the configuration wizard on the remaining servers in the farm in any order.

> **BEST PRACTICE** Remember to test your upgrade approach in a nonproduction environment to identify any issues with the upgrade prior to performing the upgrade in production.

You will use the same Setup.exe program to upgrade to SharePoint 2010 as you did when you performed an installation of SharePoint 2010, as discussed in Chapter 4; however, you will see some different options during the upgrade that weren't shown during the installation.

Installing the In-Place Upgrade

You are ready to perform an in-place upgrade to SharePoint 2010 after installing your prerequisites. To perform an in-place upgrade to SharePoint 2010, complete the following steps.

1. Start the SharePoint 2010 installation by clicking Setup.exe for SharePoint 2010, which will display the SharePoint installation screen shown in Figure 22-6.

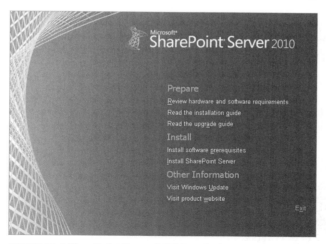

FIGURE 22-6 SharePoint Server 2010 installation screen

2. Under the Install category, click Install SharePoint Server, which opens the SharePoint file preparation screen shown in Figure 22-7.

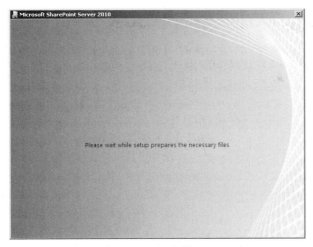

FIGURE 22-7 SharePoint Server 2010 file preparation screen

3. Shortly after the file preparation screen appears, as shown in Figure 22-8, you will see the Enter Your Product Key screen, where you are prompted to enter the product key. The product key you enter here determines which functions will be enabled after the installation completes. An Enterprise-level product key enables all functionality, whereas a Standard-level product key installs the same functionality as the Enterprise-level product key but does not enable the functions that are only available in the Enterprise Edition.

FIGURE 22-8 SharePoint Server 2010 Product Key screen

4. After you enter the product key, it is validated. If it is a valid product key, the Continue button becomes active, which allows you to continue on to the license agreement page shown in Figure 22-9. You must select the check box that indicates that you accept the terms in order to be able to click the Continue button and move on to the next screen of the installation.

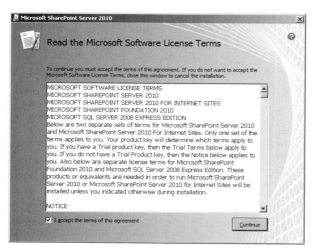

FIGURE 22-9 Microsoft Software License Terms screen

You will then see the Upgrade Earlier Versions screen shown in Figure 22-10, which explains that Setup has detected an earlier version of SharePoint on the server, so an upgrade to SharePoint 2010 will be performed. The information on the Upgrade Earlier Versions screen also notes that this portion of the upgrade installation will only upgrade the farm configuration database and the Central Administration database; all other databases will be upgraded later in the upgrade process.

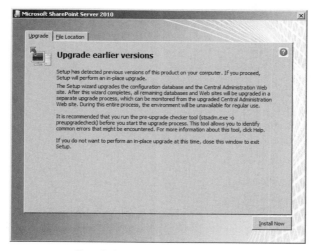

FIGURE 22-10 SharePoint Server 2010 Upgrade Earlier Versions screen

5. Optionally, you can click the File Location tab to display the file location screen shown in Figure 22-11 and then specify the location of the SharePoint 2010 product files as well as the directory that will contain the search index, if the server where you are performing the upgrade is going to be used as a search server.

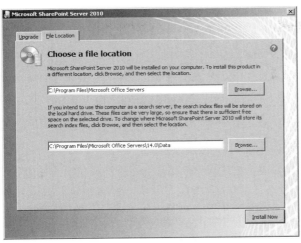

FIGURE 22-11 SharePoint Server 2010 file location screen

6. Click the Install Now button. You will see the installation progress screen shown in Figure 22-12 for several minutes as the upgrade to SharePoint 2010 is performed for you.

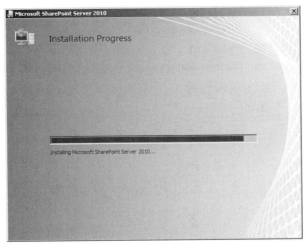

FIGURE 22-12 SharePoint Server 2010 Installation Progress screen

When the installation is complete, the SharePoint product binaries are installed, completing stage 1 of the upgrade. By default, the SharePoint Products Configuration Wizard opening page shown in Figure 22-13 provides you with the option to begin the second stage of your SharePoint farm upgrade configuration.

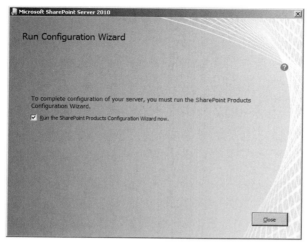

FIGURE 22-13 SharePoint Products Configuration Wizard opening page

Configuring the In-Place Upgrade

After performing the in-place upgrade, you can begin the configuration. In this phase, you will see major differences in the prompts that are presented to you and what configuration tasks are performed when compared to an installation. You will find that you perform substantially fewer tasks during an upgrade than during a complete installation.

NOTE You can choose to clear the Run The SharePoint Products Configuration Wizard Now check box on this page and begin the Configuration Wizard graphical interface at a later time. You can start the Configuration Wizard by executing the Psconfigui.exe file located in the C:\Program Files\Common Files\Microsoft Shared\Web Server Extensions\14\ BIN directory.

1. Click Close on the Run Configuration Wizard page of the SharePoint Products Configuration Wizard (or when you run Psconfigui.exe). You are presented with the Configuration Wizard Upgrade Welcome page, shown in Figure 22-14.

FIGURE 22-14 SharePoint Upgrade Welcome page

2. Click Next on the Configuration Upgrade Welcome page, and you will see the page shown in Figure 22-15, indicating that the installation may require the restart of these three services: Internet Information Services, SharePoint Administration Service V4, and SharePoint Timer Service V4. This should not present issues for your SharePoint users, because the in-place upgrade already requires that no SharePoint users be connected during the upgrade process. However, if your server is currently serving other websites, then restarting the Web services will disrupt services, which may be unacceptable during certain time periods. If this is the case, you'll need to perform this upgrade during off-hours.

FIGURE 22-15 Configuration Wizard Service Restart page

3. A new option during the installation of SharePoint 2010 is the request for a passphrase, as shown in Figure 22-16. This passphrase is used to encrypt SharePoint configuration information and is also required when adding or removing servers from the farm. This is a critical password and should be documented and secured for future farm configurations. This password can be changed using Windows PowerShell, so as a reminder, you want to limit the number of users who have farm administration permissions. Enter the passphrase and confirm it by entering it a second time. Then click Next.

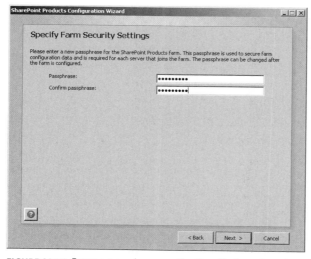

FIGURE 22-16 Enter a passphrase on the Specify Farm Security Settings page.

4. You will see the Visual Upgrade options page, as shown in Figure 22-17. This allows you to choose whether the site owners, site collection administrators, or farm administrators can change to the new SharePoint 2010 interface at a later date. This reduces the anxiety of your SharePoint users about having to adapt to a new environment overnight. This default setting gives site owners and administrators more control over the look and feel of the sites by providing more of a gradual upgrade approach to SharePoint 2010.

> **IMPORTANT**   New sites that are created after an upgrade has completed will automatically use the new SharePoint 2010 interface. Only sites that existed prior to the upgrade will have the option to upgrade the user interface at a later date.

Alternatively, the administrator can choose to upgrade to the new user interface immediately after the upgrade to SharePoint 2010 completes. Furthermore, if the administrator decides to perform the user interface upgrade during the upgrade process, she can also choose to retain any custom pages that have been deployed or remove custom pages by resetting them back to their original templates.

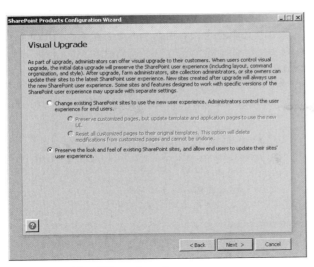

FIGURE 22-17 Visual Upgrade options page

5. Click Next. The last screen of the SharePoint Products Configuration Wizard, shown in Figure 22-18, presents you with summary information about the associated SharePoint SQL database server and the name of the SharePoint configuration database that is going to be upgraded to SharePoint 2010.

NOTE After you run the SharePoint Products Configuration Wizard, SharePoint Server 2007 will no longer be available. You cannot pause or roll back this upgrade process. Always be sure you back up your environment before you perform an upgrade to SharePoint 2010.

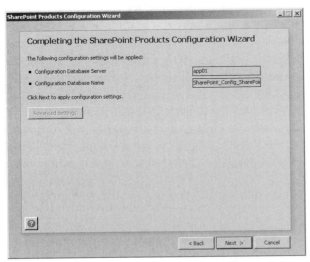

FIGURE 22-18 Completing the SharePoint Products Configuration Wizard

6. Click Next on the Completing the Upgrade Configuration Wizard page. You then will see an informational message displayed, as shown in Figure 22-19. This message reminds you that each server in the farm has to run the same SharePoint products and patches before you perform the upgrade to SharePoint 2010. It also reminds you to run both Setup.exe and the SharePoint Products Configuration Wizard on each server in your farm to complete the farm upgrade.

> **IMPORTANT** Setup.exe has to be run on all farm servers prior to running the SharePoint Products And Technologies Configuration Wizard on the server hosting Central Administration. This is not obvious from the information given in the dialog box shown in Figure 22-19. Only click OK in this dialog box if you have run Setup.exe on all servers in the farm, or if you are running a single-server farm. To refresh your memory on the process, review the steps in the section titled "Five Steps to a Successful Upgrade to SharePoint 2010" earlier in this chapter.

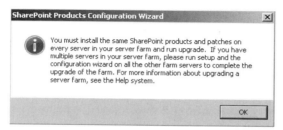

FIGURE 22-19 SharePoint Products Configuration Wizard Upgrade reminder message

During the upgrade process, a page similar to the one shown in Figure 22-20 will display to provide you with information on the progress of the upgrade. Ten tasks are performed during the upgrade process, and this screen keeps you abreast of the status of these tasks.

7. After the 10 tasks have been completed, you will see a message that tells you the farm configuration has been successfully updated, as shown in Figure 22-21. However, the server farm upgrade has not finished. The SharePoint Products Configuration Wizard actually creates a timer job that continues to perform the upgrade of your content and service databases and site. This upgrade process is performed on each individual content database and site collections sequentially, causing it to take more time to complete. Click Finish and then the Upgrade Status page from within Central Administration will display, providing you with information about the upgrade. This page automatically refreshes every 60 seconds to keep you current on the progress of the upgrade.

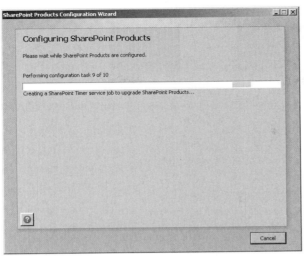

FIGURE 22-20 The SharePoint Products Configuration Wizard upgrade progress interface

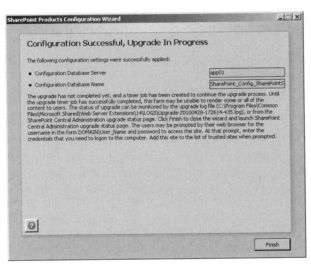

FIGURE 22-21 Successful Configuration screen

NOTE If you want to view the Upgrade Status page after closing it, you can open the page from the home page of Central Administration by clicking Check Upgrade Status. For more detailed information, you can view the upgrade logs located in C:\Program Files\ Common Files\Microsoft Shared\Web Server Extensions\14\LOGS. The title of the log file will begin with Upgrade and it will have a timestamp naming convention, as described in the section titled "Verifying That the Upgrade Operation Was Successful" earlier in the chapter.

Performing a Hybrid Upgrade Approach

A hybrid approach combines an in-place upgrade with the process of detaching and attaching databases to allow you to upgrade multiple databases at the same time—and possibly even on separate hardware—while still preserving some settings. You use this approach to simultaneously upgrade multiple content databases, thereby completing the upgrade more quickly than a standard in-place upgrade. These hybrid upgrades use the following upgrade techniques.

- Detach and upgrade multiple databases in parallel.
- Perform an in-place upgrade on your farm and settings.

Hybrid Approach 1: Read-Only Databases

When you choose to use a read-only databases hybrid upgrade approach, your users will continue to have access to their SharePoint content, but they will be unable to make changes to the content during the upgrade. This approach minimizes the perceived downtime while you are upgrading to a new farm. This approach also allows you to move to different hardware and to perform multiple content database upgrades in parallel.

The hybrid upgrade does require you to manually transfer settings and customizations to the new farm, however. It also can make your content outdated if the upgrade takes too long. The size of your content databases will have a major impact on how long the upgrade process will take for each database.

Hybrid Approach 2: Detach Databases

When you perform an upgrade using a detach databases hybrid approach, you detach your databases during the upgrade. This approach performs an in-place upgrade using the same general five-step process described in the section titled "Five Steps to a Successful Upgrade to SharePoint 2010" earlier in this chapter, but in addition, you perform the following two steps in SQL Server.

- Detach your content databases prior to running Setup.exe.
- Attach your content databases after running the SharePoint Products Configuration Wizard.

This approach allows you to perform an in-place upgrade of your farm settings as well as all customizations. However, because you are detaching the databases, you are able to upgrade multiple databases at one time. In this approach, be aware that you must not allow users to access SharePoint content during the upgrade. The size of your content databases will have a major impact on how long the upgrade process will take for each database.

Both of these hybrid approaches have some advantages and disadvantages, but they do provide you with an opportunity to expand on the two primary upgrade options available. The upgrade approach you choose will depend on what your upgrade requirements are and whether or not your current farm meets the minimum hardware and software requirements.

Upgrading from SharePoint Portal Server 2003

You may need to upgrade a Microsoft SharePoint Portal Server 2003 environment to SharePoint 2010. Although there is not a direct path to complete this upgrade, it can be done using a two-stage process.

- First, you must upgrade SharePoint Portal Server 2003 to SharePoint Server 2007.
- Then, you can upgrade SharePoint Server 2007 to SharePoint 2010.

This is a great time to utilize the option of upgrading to SharePoint 2010 using the user-copy-only method and restructuring your SharePoint farm by exporting the information out of SharePoint 2003 and importing it into a newly designed SharePoint 2010 farm.

This process will require more planning and effort to ensure that you have a successful and safe upgrade. Most SharePoint 2003 environments probably aren't installed on the required hardware or software that SharePoint 2010 requires. This often means that you have to build a new farm with SharePoint 2010 that meets the hardware and software requirements.

The following steps would be required to upgrade from SharePoint Portal Server 2003 to SharePoint 2010.

1. Prepare for the upgrade from SharePoint 2003 to SharePoint 2010.

   a. Prepare your SharePoint 2003 farm by running the pre-upgrade checker tool and documenting all of the discovered customizations.

   b. Build a temporary SharePoint Server 2007 farm.

   c. Build and configure your full SharePoint 2010 farm.

2. Upgrade SharePoint 2003 to SharePoint Server 2007.

   a. Detach the SharePoint 2003 content databases from the farm and take the farm offline.

   NOTE Alternatively, you can leave the databases attached but make a copy of the them so that you can quickly roll back to the original farm if necessary.

   b. Attach the SharePoint 2003 content databases to the SharePoint Server 2007 farm and upgrade them.

   c. Verify that the SharePoint 2003 content databases have been correctly upgraded and that the SharePoint Server 2007 farm is functioning properly. Be sure everything is working correctly here before upgrading to SharePoint 2010!

3. Upgrade SharePoint Server 2007 to SharePoint 2010.

   a. Detach the SharePoint Server 2007 content databases from the farm.

   b. Attach the SharePoint Server 2007 content databases to the SharePoint 2010 farm and upgrade them. (To expedite the upgrade, perform multiple database upgrades in parallel.)

   c. Verify that the SharePoint Server 2007 content databases have been correctly upgraded and that the SharePoint 2010 farm is functioning properly.

These several upgrade scenarios should encompass most upgrades to SharePoint 2010 that you will encounter. Only you can decide which one will work best for your organization. However, the preferred method is to perform a database attach upgrade.

Performing Post-Upgrade Configurations

Even though you have taken the correct steps for a successful upgrade to SharePoint 2010, there are still some additional tasks you must perform to complete the SharePoint 2010 upgrade. Specifically, service applications have now replaced the SharePoint Server 2007 Shared Service Provider.

Shared Service Provider Upgrade

Shared Service Providers (SSP) have been replaced by service applications, and there are several of them to be configured in SharePoint 2010. Review Chapter 7, "Scaling Out a SharePoint Farm," for more information on service applications. This section does not discuss the configuration details of each available service application; however, depending on the type of upgrade you performed, there are a few service applications that you will want to address shortly after a successful upgrade to SharePoint 2010. This will ensure that they continue to provide the services they were providing in SharePoint Server 2007.

Taxonomy Data and Photo Store for Profile Services

After performing an upgrade to SharePoint 2010, you should run two Windows Power-Shell cmdlets to upgrade your taxonomy information. In SharePoint Server 2007, your farm taxonomy information was stored in the SSP database as part of the Profile Services information. However, in SharePoint 2010, the taxonomy information is now stored in the managed metadata database. To utilize this data, you have to create a service application for the Managed Metadata Service. After creating this service application, you need to open Windows PowerShell and execute the following Windows PowerShell cmdlet to update the profile and taxonomy information and move that information into the Metadata database.

```
PS C:\>Move-SPProfileManagedMetadataProperty
-ProfileServiceApplicationProxy<SPServiceApplicationProxyPipeBind> -Identity <string>
```

> **NOTE** To upgrade and use the SharePoint Server 2007 taxonomy data, the User Profiles Service proxy and Managed Metadata Service proxy must be in the same proxy group.

You must copy any photos that were stored as profile pictures, normally in the Share Pictures library of My Site, to the User Photos library on the My Site host. You can accomplish this step by executing the following Windows PowerShell cmdlet.

```
Update-SPProfilePhotoStore -MySiteHostLocation<MySiteHostURL>
```

Upgraded InfoPath Form Templates

During a database attach upgrade, your InfoPath form templates were exported from your old environment and imported in your new environment when you created it. After your upgrade, you should now update the links used in those upgraded form templates to point to the correct URLs. To do this, use the following Windows PowerShell cmdlet.

```
Update-SPInfoPathAdminFileURL -find <URLToReplace> -replace <NewURL>
```

Security Configurations

After completing a database attach upgrade, all farm administrators have full administrative permissions to all service applications. If you want to restrict the amount of access to the service applications, you should check the configuration of each service application and make the required permission change.

You also need to migrate users and permissions from SharePoint Server 2007 to SharePoint 2010 using the following Windows PowerShell cmdlets.

```
$w = Get-SPWebApplicationhttp://<ServerName>/
$w.MigrateUsers(True)
```

Summary

This chapter provided information about the different ways you can upgrade to SharePoint 2010, with information about how an upgrade is similar to an installation insofar as the servers have to meet the hardware and software prerequisites for SharePoint 2010.

You learned that performing a database attach upgrade provides you much more flexibility during the upgrade process. This flexibility includes the ability to minimize downtime by continuing to provide access to the SharePoint Server 2007 content during the upgrade, moving your server farm to new hardware, and reducing the chance of upgrading bad configuration settings. It also is generally faster than other upgrades, because you can upgrade multiple databases simultaneously. However, this process requires more planning and more configuration than an in-place upgrade.

This chapter also explained that performing an in-place upgrade can be advantageous because it maintains all of your farm and configuration settings. However, it does require you to disable user access during the upgrade process, and it can take longer than other upgrades because each content database is upgraded serially and can't be upgraded in parallel unless you use one of the hybrid approaches. The in-place upgrade is initiated using Setup.exe and has screens similar to the installation wizard, which may make it easier for you to perform the upgrade.

Regardless of which upgrade type you choose, however, this chapter made it clear that you should perform practice upgrades in a nonproduction environment as many times as necessary until you can perform an upgrade without any issues identified.

You also learned that one of the biggest post-upgrade tasks you have is the configuration of the powerful service applications. Be sure to verify the outcome of your upgrade prior to allowing your users to access it.

Creating and Managing Workflows

The success of an enterprise is largely determined by the effectiveness of its business processes. Automating business processes enables the organization to be more productive. One of the core elements of any information architecture is workflows. Workflows act as the glue that connects users and information. Computers are designed to complete processes as fast as possible, but those processes must wait for people to complete forms, make decisions, or share information about decisions external to the system—all of which does nothing to maximize the effective use of technology. Microsoft SharePoint 2010 includes a robust workflow platform that can be used to automate processes in an integrated way that allows them to occur seamlessly within the information architecture.

Workflows were introduced in Microsoft Office SharePoint Server 2007 and were primarily used to collect and review feedback on content, perform content approvals, and collect signatures, as well as perform other similar activities. SharePoint Server 2007 workflows were based on the Windows Workflow Foundation included with the .NET 3.0 Framework. Workflows in SharePoint 2010 are much improved and are based on the Windows Workflow Foundation (WF) included with the .NET 3.5 Framework.

Workflows in SharePoint 2010 can be classified as either human workflows or system workflows. Human workflows are designed for integrating people's actions with the system. For example, the approval of a document would be considered a human workflow. System workflows are designed for moving data within sites or applications, such as publishing content from a collaboration site to a public Internet-facing site.

Understanding Human Workflows

Human workflows in SharePoint 2010 are used for defining how people work and collaborate. These workflows apply business logic to the SharePoint content and execute business rules either on demand or automatically. For example, document approval and feedback, collaborative reviews and discussions, gathering signatures on documents, and translation of content into specific languages are some of the human workflows available in SharePoint 2010.

SharePoint 2010 acts as a platform to host workflows. This enables an organization to implement various custom workflows that cater to their business requirements. These workflows can tie together various business processes that span all of an organization's departments on a single collaboration platform.

For example, assume an organization has a defined process for recruitment officers of the Human Resources (HR) department to submit a list of resumes along with an initial assessment of each candidate's competencies to each business unit's interview panel. The interview panel then conducts the interviews and submits their assessments on technical competency with a review status of *selected* or *rejected*. If the candidate is selected, the business unit's hiring manager must conduct a second interview and inform the HR department about whether the candidate will be recruited. The HR department then negotiates the compensation and other related details with the candidate and completes the recruitment process. As you can see, this is a multidepartment/multistage, people-intensive business process. SharePoint 2010 can be used for implementing this business process through custom workflows with the help of either InfoPath forms or ASP.Net, which will act as the interface to capture the data involved in the process.

Understanding System Workflows

System workflows in SharePoint 2010 are used primarily for automating processes that interact with the content and data stored in SharePoint. These workflows, when triggered by users, will move data in and out of SharePoint. For instance, your organization might want to create workflows that move documents from collaboration sites to the record center when the document's expiration date is reached. The end users are not involved in the process of moving the document or even in triggering the workflow. The workflow in this case is based on the state of the document. System workflows can be created to interact with external systems and collect data, which can be imported into SharePoint 2010.

Another instance in which you can use system workflows is to send periodic reports on data stored in SharePoint, such as consolidated expense reports on a monthly basis, or the number of help desk tickets closed by service level on a weekly basis. For all these scenarios, workflows can be created and activated on the sites needed. The end user can associate these workflows to a site or library as needed and define the schedule (such as monthly or weekly) or state (document is published, expired, etc.) on which the workflows should run. SharePoint 2010 Web Analytics and Usage reports are system workflows that send periodic site usage and analytical reports to selected participants.

> **NOTE** Timer jobs can be used for some of these activities, but timer jobs can be activated and managed only by SharePoint 2010 farm administrators. End users cannot control the execution of the timer jobs. The choice between using a timer job and using system workflows should be based on end user's control over the process in terms of schedule and other possible factors. If the end users do not need to control the process, then choose timer jobs; otherwise, choose system workflows.

Workflows in SharePoint 2010

SharePoint 2010 is a rich workflow platform that provides a wide range of predefined work-flows and a rich set of workflow modeling and development tools. In the following sections, you explore the concepts of SharePoint workflows, improvements provided in SharePoint 2010, and the set of workflows available by default in SharePoint 2010.

Any SharePoint workflow has defined stages for information processing, along with unique forms for the collection of data. Typically, a workflow has the following stages: association, initiation, and a set of tasks. At each stage, a form is used to collect information from the end users. In addition, after a workflow is created, it can be modified—a fourth stage.

Workflow Stages and Forms

The business logic of a workflow is implemented through a set of tasks and their associated business rules. In addition to these tasks, each workflow has an association, initiation, and modification stage.

- **Association** When an administrator associates a workflow template with a document library, list, or site, he or she might be able to set options that will apply to every workflow instance created using this association. An ASP.Net or InfoPath form that is associated with the workflow is used to collect the needed association data from the administrator.

- **Initiation** The initiator of a workflow might be allowed to specify options when the workflow instance is started. For example, in the approval workflow scenario, the initiator is allowed to specify different stages in approval and the list of workflow participants in each stage, as well as define how much time each participant has to complete his or her task. An initiation form is associated with the workflow for the initiator to specify the initiation data. The initiation data is available for workflow developers and modelers to use during the execution business logic.

- **Task Forms**   A workflow instance interacts with the participants through defined workflow tasks. The running workflow instance must display a form to the participants for them to complete their task. The task form collects the data from the participant. For example, in the approval workflow scenario, data collected might include whether the document is approved or rejected, along with comments. Depending on the complexity of the workflow, a number of task forms can signify different stages of the workflow.

- **Modification**   The creator of a workflow can allow it to be modified while it is running. For example, a workflow might allow the addition of new participants while running, or it might allow an extension of the due date for completing tasks. If this option is used, the workflow must display a form that captures a participant's changes.

SharePoint 2010 Workflow Types by Packaging and Deployment

Workflows in SharePoint 2010 can be classified as declarative or compiled, based on how they are created, packaged, and deployed.

- **Declarative workflows**   You create declarative workflows using Microsoft SharePoint Designer 2010 and deploy them using Extensible Object Markup Language (XOML) files. Declarative workflows are created using rules, actions, and a set of parameters without writing any code. These rules, actions, and parameters are captured in the XOML file and are compiled at run time from the content database of the Web application.

- **Compiled workflows**   Compiled workflows are also created with a set of rules and actions in the form of steps and parameters, but they are compiled into an assembly and deployed into the Global Assembly Cache (GAC). Developers create compiled workflows in Microsoft Visual Studio 2010, and these workflows are packaged into features and solution packages (WSP). Compiled workflows allow the developer to write code to perform actions that are not available in Visual Studio 2010 workflow project templates.

SharePoint 2010 Workflow Types by Associations

SharePoint Server 2007 allowed workflows to be associated with items on a list or library, whereas SharePoint 2010 adds the capability to associate a workflow with a site as well. With this improvement, SharePoint 2010 has three types of workflows by association.

- **List workflows** This type of workflow is associated with a list or library and is initiated using an item or document in that list. An example would be the Translation Management workflow, which is associated with the translation library by default.
- **Content type workflows** Content type workflows are associated with content types and are available to all lists or libraries within which those content types are used. Workflows can also be associated with a list content type. An example would be the Collect Feedback and Content Approval workflows, which are associated with the Document content type.
- **Site workflows** Site level workflows are new in SharePoint 2010. Site workflows are associated with a site and are independent of any item or document. In SharePoint 2010, Web Analytics workflows are site workflows and are used to send usage analysis reports to participants. Custom site workflows can be created using Visual Studio 2010 and SharePoint Designer 2010.

SharePoint 2010 Workflow Improvements

SharePoint 2010 provides many improvements to the workflow platform when compared with prior versions of the product. You have already been introduced to site workflows, which were not provided in SharePoint Server 2007. Improvements have been made to the authoring tools as well, making SharePoint 2010 a powerful workflow hosting platform. You will learn more about specific improvements made to the workflow platform within SharePoint 2010 in the following sections.

Workflow Modeling Tool Improvements

SharePoint 2010 workflows can be created using Visual Studio 2010, SharePoint Designer 2010, and Microsoft Visio 2010. Visual Studio 2010 has improved workflow project templates and workflow activities. Visual Studio 2010 also allows the developer to create and deploy SharePoint solution package (WSPs), making it easier to develop, deploy, and debug workflows.

SharePoint Designer 2010 provides a streamlined user interface for developing workflows. SharePoint Designer 2010 also allows you to edit out-of-the-box workflows to meet your specific business requirements. In SharePoint Designer 2007, you could use only ASP.Net for creating workflow forms, whereas in SharePoint Designer 2010, you can create InfoPath-based forms. Note that to use this functionality you must have InfoPath 2010 installed on the same computer where SharePoint Designer is installed. SharePoint Designer 2010 includes a task process designer that lets you define different outcomes for the activities in the workflow.

Also, business processes designed in Visio 2010 can be imported into SharePoint Designer 2010 for deployment. Visio 2010 supports Business Process Modeling Notations (BPMN), which makes it easy for end users to create complex business processes that can be deployed as workflows in SharePoint 2010 using SharePoint Designer 2010.

Site Workflows

In prior versions of SharePoint, you could only associate a workflow with a list item for execution. In SharePoint 2010, workflows can be associated with a site, which gives information workers the flexibility to create workflows that are not dependent on changes to list items. Site workflows have to be started from the Site Actions menu of a site. Site workflows should be started manually or through the SharePoint API.

Reusable Declarative Workflows

Reusable declarative workflows are created using SharePoint Designer 2010. These workflows are created once and can be associated with multiple lists in the same site as well as lists in other site collections.

Impersonation in Declarative Workflows

SharePoint 2010 allows information workers to create portions of a workflow that can impersonate the workflow author's permissions instead of those of the logged-on user. This allows the workflow to perform actions that cannot be executed with the permissions of the user who is logged on.

Timer-Based Execution

In prior versions of SharePoint, the entire workflow was executed on the Web front-end server by the Internet Information Services (IIS) worker process even if workflow activities did not involve any user interactions. In SharePoint 2010, the workflow execution is performed by the Timer service if

- The workflow activity does not involve any user inputs.
- The workflow is continued from a delay timer.
- The workflow is triggered by an external event.

Workflow List Events

SharePoint 2010 provides an option for developers to perform the initiation and completion of workflows through events. The four SharePoint workflow list level events are Starting, Started, Completed and Postponed. These events can be handled like other list events, using an event receiver and project templates that are available in Visual Studio 2010. These events are available only for the workflows associated with lists; they will not work for site workflows.

Pluggable Workflow Service

In prior versions, workflows enabled users to participate in business processes that were automated within SharePoint, but it was difficult to tie the workflow execution back to external systems. This problem has been addressed in SharePoint 2010 with the help of a Pluggable

Workflow Service that provides interfaces through which SharePoint workflows can interact with external systems and vice versa.

The Pluggable Workflow Service interface is exposed through the CallExternalMethod and HandleExternalEvent methods. CallExternalMethod allows a workflow to interact with external systems using asynchronous messages. HandleExternalEvent allows the external systems to trigger an event on the workflows and in turn allows the workflow to respond to the event from the external system. The Pluggable Workflow Service is adopted into the SharePoint workflow platform from Window Workflow Foundation, which is provided as part of the .NET 3.5 Framework.

Improved Compliance Capabilities

SharePoint 2010 allows farm administrators to configure Web applications to enable or disable user-created workflows. This capability provides a control to the farm administrators to isolate Web applications where such workflows are not allowed; it also prevents end users from creating such workflows. For example, you can prevent end users from creating workflows on record center Web applications.

Farm administrators can also control how to handle task notifications to workflow participants who do not have access to the content on which the workflow is executing. This setting allows different configurations for internal and external users. This configuration option (to give workflow access to those who do not have access to the content) is available at the Web application as well.

Predefined Workflows of SharePoint 2010

In the following sections, you will see the list of workflows available within SharePoint 2010 and review when to use them. SharePoint 2010 includes the following predefined workflow templates, which address common business scenarios.

- Collect Feedback
- Approval
- Disposition Approval
- Collect Signatures
- Three-state
- Translation Management

You can customize all of these workflows based on your specific requirements. For example, you can modify the Approval workflow so that it provides a multistage approval process with a different kind of task allocation for each stage. Moreover, SharePoint 2010 allows you to copy these predefined workflows and customize them using SharePoint Designer 2010.

Collect Feedback Workflow

The Collect Feedback workflow routes a document or item to a group of people for feedback. Reviewers provide the feedback, which is then compiled and sent to the workflow initiator. By default, the Collect Feedback workflow is associated with the Document content type, and therefore it is automatically available in document libraries. You can use this workflow to request feedback on the documents from a group of reviewers and then use the information gleaned from the workflow to update the document with the suggested changes. This workflow is highly effective when collaboratively developing document content.

Approval Workflow

The Approval workflow routes a document or item to a group of people for approval. By default, the Approval workflow is associated with the Document content type, and therefore it is automatically available in document libraries. A version of the Approval workflow is also associated by default with the Pages library of a publishing site and can be used to manage the approval process for the publication of Web content.

The Approval workflow provides a staged approval model (that is, the first set of approvers can undergo the review and approval process, then the next set of approvers, and so on). Each stage or approval set can also have its own behavior. For example, members of the first group of approvers can do their review in serial approval order (one after the other), while members of the second group can do their review in parallel (reviewers can provide feedback in any order), and so on.

An Approval workflow is useful in many common business approval scenarios, including expense report approval, interview candidate selection processes, and contract approval.

Disposition Approval Workflow

The Disposition Approval workflow manages document expiration by letting participants decide whether to keep or delete expired-documents. The Disposition Approval workflow is used in record management scenarios and hence available only in a Records Center site. Disposition approval workflows can be associated with content types by configuring Information Management Policy settings. You can use the Disposition Approval workflow in your record center sites for records that need special attention at the time of expiration.

Collect Signatures Workflow

The Collect Signatures workflow routes a document that was created within an Office application to a group of people to collect their digital signatures. This workflow must be started within Microsoft Office 2007 or 2010 applications such as Microsoft Word. Participants must complete their signature tasks by adding their digital signatures to the documents in the relevant client program. By default, the Collect Signatures workflow is associated with the Document content type and therefore is automatically available in document libraries. However, the Collect Signatures workflow appears only if the document stored contains one or more Microsoft Office signature lines.

Three-state Workflow

The Three-state workflow is designed to track the status of a list item through three states (phases). It can be used to manage business processes that require organizations to track a high volume of issues or items, such as customer support issues, sales leads, or project tasks.

The Three-state workflow is so named because it tracks the status of an issue or item through three different states, and through the two transitions between the states. For example, when a workflow is initiated on an issue in an Issues list, SharePoint 2010 creates a task for the assigned user. When the user completes the task, the workflow changes from its initial state (Active) to its middle state (Resolved) and creates a new task for the assigned user. When the user completes that task, the workflow changes from its middle state (Resolved) to its final state (Closed) and creates a final task for the user to whom the workflow is assigned at that time. Note that this workflow is only supported on lists, not document libraries.

> **NOTE** The Three-state workflow is the only workflow available in SharePoint Foundation 2010.

Translation Management

The Translation Management workflow manages manual document translation by creating copies of the document to be translated and by assigning translation tasks to translators. This workflow is available only for Translation Management libraries and is used with site variations.

Workflow Modeling and Development Tools

A workflow consists of two parts: a set of actions that encapsulate the business process and a set of forms that interact with the user for collecting inputs. Thus, workflow development revolves around these two activities: the creation of the business rules and the creation of forms for interaction. SharePoint 2010 workflows can be developed using the following tools.

- **Visio 2010** Used to create business processes with Business Process Modeling Notations (BPMN), which can be imported into SharePoint Designer for deployment. This tool is aimed at the business process engineer or consultant whose primary focus is designing business processes for the organization.

- **SharePoint Designer 2010** Used for modeling new workflows or modifying predefined workflows using rules and action steps. This tool is aimed at the information worker.

- **Visual Studio 2010** Used for creating reusable workflows within Workflow Foundation's Workflow Designer. This tool is aimed at the developer who possesses the requisite knowledge needed in both the .NET framework and the SharePoint API.

Table 23-1 provides a summary of these tools, with the intended audiences of each.

TABLE 23-1 Workflow Modeling Tool and Target Audience

WORKFLOW MODELLING TOOL	FEATURE	AUDIENCE
Visio 2010	<ul><li>Flowchart-based design using BPMN</li><li>Business user–friendly prototyping</li></ul>	Business users
SharePoint Designer 2010	<ul><li>Rules-based design</li><li>Rich human workflows</li><li>No-code reusability</li><li>Modify predefined workflows</li><li>Site collection level deployment</li></ul>	Information workers
Visual Studio 2010	<ul><li>Graphical design</li><li>Build custom activities</li><li>Develop pluggable services for interaction with external systems</li><li>Modify SharePoint Designer and predefined workflows</li><li>Farm deployment</li></ul>	Developers

In addition to these tools, ASP.Net and InfoPath are also used to design forms that are part of SharePoint 2010 workflows. As explained in the section titled "Workflow Stages and Forms" earlier in this chapter, there are four stages in the life cycle of a workflow: association, initiation, tasks, and modification. A separate form is required at each stage to collect input from the user. After you have created these forms, you can associate them with the appropriate workflow stage.

Microsoft Visio 2010

Microsoft Visio 2010 is a popular modeling tool used to create business process blueprints. With Visio 2010, business users can define their own workflow layouts before exporting them to SharePoint Designer 2010 for association with a list or site. This lets business users use a familiar graphical tool to define the steps in the workflow themselves, instead of having to communicate their needs to designers or developers. The resulting Visio workflow can be used as the initial building block for the workflow's implementation.

Visio 2010 includes a new template called Microsoft SharePoint Workflow, which has a set of activity and conditional shapes that are dedicated to SharePoint Workflow design, as shown in Figure 23-1.

FIGURE 23-1 SharePoint Workflow Conditions and Actions in Visio 2010

The workflows designed in Visio 2010 cannot be used directly in SharePoint 2010, however. You must import a Visio workflow into SharePoint Designer 2010 and then deploy it into SharePoint 2010. Also, the Visio workflow activities do not support any shape data. For example, you can drag and drop an e-mail activity into your workflow, but you cannot specify values for To, CC, Subject, or mail content. This data must be specified within SharePoint Designer before you deploy the workflow in to SharePoint 2010. See Figure 23-2 for a sample Visio workflow diagram.

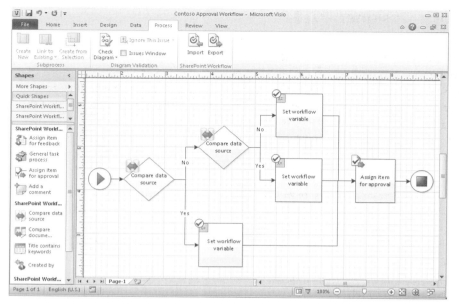

FIGURE 23-2 A SharePoint workflow in Visio 2010

Visio 2010 also provides a design checker for SharePoint workflows. You should use the design checker to ensure that the workflow can be deployed in SharePoint 2010. After checking the diagram for any errors, it can be exported into SharePoint Designer 2010 for further processing.

When you export the Visio diagram, the export process creates a file with the .vwi extension, which is nothing more than a compressed archive file that contains the following.

- **[Content_types.xml]**   Contains the file extension and mime type of each type of file included in the VWI file

- **Workflow.vdx**   The Visio definition file that has the diagram layouts and file properties

- **Workflow.xoml**   Contains the workflow actions that are to be deployed in SharePoint 2010

- **Workflow.xoml.rules**   Contains the workflow rules that are to be deployed in SharePoint 2010.

As explained earlier, Visio workflows have to be deployed into SharePoint 2010 with the help of SharePoint Designer 2010. This gives the business users the freedom to define workflows that can later be deployed into SharePoint using SharePoint Designer. This approach takes the burden away from the developers and information workers, because the core of the workflow is already in place in the form the Visio diagrams.

SharePoint Designer 2010

Microsoft SharePoint Designer 2010 is an application that is available as a free download; it was developed for the information workers' community. Microsoft SharePoint Designer 2010 enables information workers to add application logic (implemented as a workflow) to SharePoint sites. If a developer creates a workflow using Visual Studio, that workflow must be deployed on a server running SharePoint 2010 like any other feature. This means that the SharePoint administrator has to make sure the code is stable and not malicious, so that the SharePoint platform is not destabilized by the code. The ability to create straightforward workflows that are tied to documents and list items is very useful to users.

SharePoint Designer workflows offer an attractive alternative to code-based workflows built using Visual Studio 2010, as you have control over the list of activities that users can implement while building these workflows. Moreover, it is also possible to for you to determine if a Web application or site collection should allow SharePoint Designer workflows at all. This level of governance with respect to the ability of end users to define their own logic makes SharePoint Designer a stable modeling tool for workflows.

One more important aspect of SharePoint Designer–based workflows is that these workflows are declarative workflows and not compiled workflows. These workflows are based on simple rules and are compiled from the content database every time the workflow is associated with a list, library, or site. The use of rules in creating the workflows makes it easier for the information worker to create workflows. It is also easy for them to explain these workflows to business users in plain terms.

Improvements in SharePoint Designer 2010

SharePoint Designer 2010 has many improvements over its predecessor; some of the key improvements are listed here.

- SharePoint Designer 2010 can be used for creating reusable workflows, which can be used in different lists within the same site.
- SharePoint Designer 2010 can package the workflows into SharePoint solution package (WSP).
- SharePoint Designer 2010 can be used for creating workflows with both serial and parallel activities.
- SharePoint Designer can import SharePoint workflows created in Visio 2010 using Business Process Modeling Notations (BPMN) and deploy these workflows into SharePoint 2010. This feature makes it easier for the business users to create workflows, which can be enhanced and deployed to SharePoint 2010.
- SharePoint Designer can use InfoPath 2010 Forms for creating association, initiation, modification, and task forms. SharePoint Designer 2007 allowed only ASP.Net forms for these purposes.

Creating and Deploying Workflows in SharePoint Designer 2010

You will briefly explore how to create workflows in SharePoint Designer 2010 and see how to deploy these workflows into SharePoint 2010. You will also see how to import a Visio-based workflow into SharePoint Designer, where it can be enhanced with shape data and then deployed into SharePoint 2010.

To begin, explore the process of creating and publishing declarative workflows using SharePoint Designer 2010.

1. Launch SharePoint Designer 2010 and open a site.

2. You can create a new workflow or edit an existing workflow using one of the following three options.

   ■ From the New group on the Site tab of the Ribbon, select List Workflow or Reusable Workflow.

   ■ Select the File tab and then select Add Item. Choose to add a List Workflow, Reusable Workflow, Site Workflow, or Import Visio Workflow.

   ■ Select Workflows under Site Objects in the Navigation pane. Then select List Workflow, Reusable Workflow, or Site Workflow from the New Group on the Workflows tab. Alternatively, you can click Edit Workflow after selecting Globally Reusable Workflow or Reusable Workflow.

3. Based on the workflow type you select, specify the workflow association information, which includes Name, Description, and List (for a List workflow) or Content Type (for a Reusable workflow).

4. You can add a set of Conditions And Actions that represents your business process.

5. For each task added to the workflow, you can define task properties, including whether a change request is allowed, whether the user can reassign the task, whether overdue mails have to be sent, and so on. See Figure 23-3 for a sample Process Properties dialog box.

6. After you complete your workflow design, you can check to find if the workflow has any errors by selecting the Check For Errors menu item on the Save Ribbon. If any errors are detected, fix the errors by taking the necessary corrective action.

7. You can publish the workflow to SharePoint 2010 site by selecting the Publish menu item on the Save Ribbon.

This process will make your workflow available on the SharePoint 2010. The workflow will be associated with a container (list or site) or as a site-wide reusable workflow.

> **NOTE** SharePoint Designer 2010 cannot be used for creating workflows that can be used across the farm. SharePoint Designer 2010 reusable workflows can be imported into Visual Studio 2010 and then published as a farm-wide workflow template.

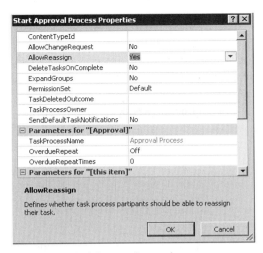

FIGURE 23-3 Task Process Properties

Importing Workflows from Visio 2010

As explained earlier, you can model the workflows in Visio 2010 and then import them into SharePoint Designer 2010. Imported workflows can be further developed by providing action-able data for the shapes added in Visio 2010. To import a Visio-based workflow in SharePoint Designer 2010, perform the following steps.

1. Open the site in SharePoint Designer.

2. Select Workflows from the Site Objects Panel.

3. Select the Import From Visio from Manage group on the Workflows tab.

4. In the Import Workflow From Visio Drawing dialog box, click Browse and select the exported Visio SharePoint workflow diagram (VWI file).

5. Click Next.

6. Select the type of workflow to import by selecting either List Workflow or Reusable Workflow.

7. Based on the workflow type you select, perform one of the following actions (see Figure 23-4).

   - If you select List Workflow, choose the list to which this workflow must be associated from the Specify The SharePoint List This Workflow Will Be Attached To drop-down list.

   - If you select Reusable Workflow, choose content to which this workflow must be associated from the Run On Items Of This Content Types, Or Any Child Content Types drop-down list.

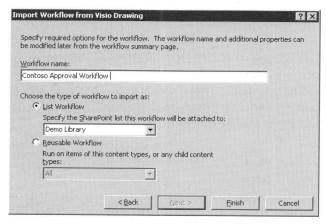

FIGURE 23-4 Import a workflow from a Visio drawing

8. Click Finish to import the workflow into SharePoint Designer. See Figure 23-5 for a
   sample Visio SharePoint workflow diagram imported into SharePoint Designer.

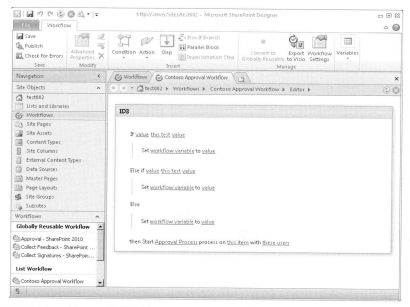

FIGURE 23-5 Imported Visio SharePoint workflow diagram without any data

9. Now you can define values for the conditions and actions that are part of the imported
   workflow. After defining data for the shapes, you can verify and publish the workflow.

Visual Studio 2010

Visual Studio 2010 is a development tool for developing various types of applications and services. It provides development project types for different SharePoint customizations and project templates for SharePoint 2010 workflows. Visual Studio 2010 uses the Windows Workflows Foundation (WF) designer to define a workflow's activities, the order in which to execute them, and the conditions in which to perform them. In the following sections, you explore some of the important aspects of workflow development within Visual Studio 2010.

Visual Studio Workflow Project Types

A developer can create sequential or state machine workflows in Visual Studio 2010. Alternatively, it is possible to import a SharePoint Designer–based reusable workflow to create a workflow solution. Visual Studio 2010 provides a project template, shown in Figure 23-6, for all of these types of workflow development activities.

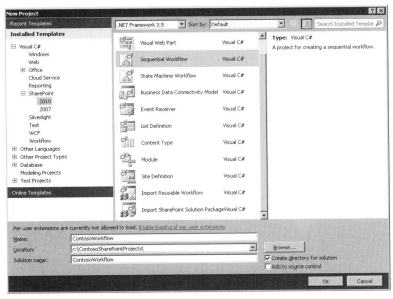

FIGURE 23-6 SharePoint 2010 project templates in Visual Studio 2010

The figure contains the following list of SharePoint 2010 project templates available in Visual Studio 2010 (some of which are not workflow oriented and are not a focus of this chapter).

- **Sequential Workflow**   In a sequential workflow project, the activities happen in a specific sequence from start to finish. You can branch these activities with the help of conditions. This type of workflow is ideal for creating approval or feedback collection scenarios, where activities happen in sequence: first there is a request for feedback or approval, then the feedback or approval is sent, and so forth.

- **State Machine Workflow** A state machine workflow represents a set of states, transitions, and actions. The steps in a state machine workflow execute asynchronously, and they are triggered by actions and states. One state is assigned as the start state, and then, based on an event, a transition is made to another state. The state machine can have a final state that determines the end of the workflow.

- **Import Reusable Workflow** This project type is used for importing a SharePoint Designer 2010–based reusable workflow for further development, by adding code or activities that are not supported by SharePoint Designer.

Standard Workflow Activities in Visual Studio

The activities available for use while developing a workflow appear in the Toolbox on the left side of the screen, as shown in Figure 23-7. A developer can drag these activities onto the design surface to define the steps in a workflow. The properties of each activity can then be set in the Properties window that appears in the lower-right corner. The Base Activity Library of Windows Workflow Foundation provides a group of fundamental activities, and SharePoint 2010 also provides a set of activities designed expressly for creating workflows.

FIGURE 23-7 Visual Studio 2010 standard workflow activities

The following workflow activities are commonly used when designing SharePoint 2010 workflows.

- **OnWorkflowActivated** Provides a standard starting point for a workflow. This activity can accept information supplied by a SharePoint administrator by using the Association form when the workflow is associated with a document library, list, content type, or site. It can also accept information supplied by the Initiation form when the workflow is started. Every workflow must begin with this activity.

- **CreateTask** Creates a task assigned to a particular user in a task list. This activity also has a SendEmailNotification property that, when set to True, automatically sends an e-mail message to the person for whom this task was created.

- **OnTaskChanged** Accepts information from the Task Completion form, which can be used in the rules and other actions in the workflow.

- **CompleteTask** Marks a task as completed.

- **DeleteTask** Removes a task from a task list.

- **OnWorkflowModified** Accepts information from the Modification form, which can then be used to change how this instance of the workflow behaves. If the workflow's creator chooses not to include any instances of this activity in the workflow, that workflow cannot be modified while it is running. This activity is responsible for reassigning a task to another use, adding more participants to a running workflow, and so on.

- **SendEmail** Sends an e-mail message to a specified person or group of people.

- **LogToHistoryList** Writes information about the workflow's execution to a history list. The information in this list is used to let users see where a workflow is in its execution, look at the workflow's history after it is completed, and more. To allow this kind of monitoring, the workflow's author must write information to a history list at appropriate points in the workflow's execution. Because it provides its own mechanism for tracking workflows, SharePoint 2010 doesn't support the Windows Workflow Foundation's standard tracking service.

Creating Workflows in Visual Studio

The creation of a simple workflow in Visual Studio 2010 begins with choosing the template—a sequential or state machine workflow. (Figure 23-8 shows an example of a workflow created using the Sequence template.) After selecting the appropriate template, you specify a site that will be used for deploying, debugging, and testing the workflow during development. You then specify the workflow association type as either a Site or List workflow. Finally, you specify the workflow history and the task list to use for testing the workflow. At this point, the graphical workflow designer is displayed; this is where you define the workflow logic.

A simple workflow in Visual Studio 2010 begins with an OnWorkflowActivated activity and then uses a CreateTask activity to assign a task to participants in the workflow. The standard WhileActivity can be used to wait until the users complete the tasks and provide necessary data through the task form, which is shown as part of task activity. An OnTaskChanged activity executes within the WhileActivity, extracting whatever information the user has entered on that form. Based on the information collected, the workflow can use the CodeActivity activity to perform any complex logic and update data on the item or document with which this workflow is associated.

SharePoint 2010 provides all activities that are available in Visual Studio 2010 under SharePoint Workflow. These activities are designed to perform typical activities that a user would perform in the SharePoint 2010 environment. The business logic a workflow implements is determined by the developer of the workflow. In fact, a developer authoring a workflow is free to create and use custom activities and is not restricted to activities provided by SharePoint 2010 or Windows Workflow Foundation.

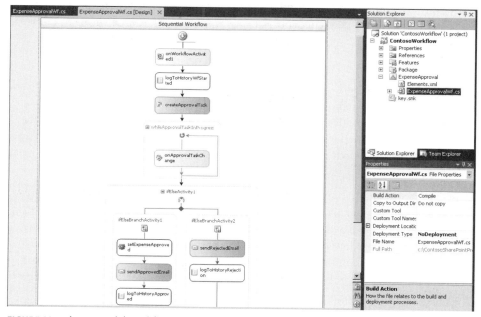

FIGURE 23-8 A sequential workflow in Visual Studio 2010

Apart from designing the workflow's logic, the workflow developer is also responsible for creating the forms that will interact with the users. There are four types of forms a workflow developer can create: Association, Initiation, Task, and Modification forms. As the workflow develops, you must do some work to pass information between the workflow and its .ASPX or InfoPath forms. The Microsoft.Windows.SharePoint.Workflow namespace exposes an object model for developers. By using the types in this namespace, the creator of a workflow can pass information from a form to the workflow and vice versa.

After the workflow and its forms have been created, you use a SharePoint Feature to package the workflow for deployment. An Element.xml file, part of the feature definition, is used for binding the forms with the workflow. When the feature definition is created, this feature, along with other features, pages, and so on, are packaged into a solution (WSP) for deployment. Visual Studio 2010 project templates are capable of creating the solution packages.

As the workflow developer, you can debug the workflows in Visual Studio 2010 simply by pressing the F5 key, which deploys the workflow, activates the workflow on the chosen site, and associates the workflow to the list or site chosen earlier. The developer can complete the necessary workflow tasks and see that the control comes back to the Workflow Designer for the next task on the workflow. This way you can validate that each activity on the workflow is executing as expected and yields the correct results. After validation, the developer delivers the solution package to be used on a SharePoint 2010 farm.

A SharePoint farm administrator must then install and deploy the solution to all Web applications where the workflow is to be used. The site collection administrators can activate the workflow feature on their site collection. The new workflow will now be visible to the site administrators as a workflow template that can be associated with a document library, list, content type, or site.

Workflow Modeling Tools Comparison

Use Table 23-2 to help you determine which workflow development tool is best for creating your workflows.

TABLE 23-2 Workflow Modeling Tools Comparison

FUNCTIONALITY	SHAREPOINT DESIGNER 2010	VISUAL STUDIO 2010
Can be scoped to a site collection	Yes	Yes
Workflows are accessible in client applications (other than the browser)	Yes	Yes
Can use ASP.Net forms as workflow's forms	Yes	Yes
Can use InfoPath forms as workflow's forms	Yes	Yes
One-click publishing available for workflows	Yes	Yes
Can be used for modifying predefined workflows	Yes	Yes
Can be used to create workflows with serial activities	Yes	Yes
Can be used to create workflows with parallel activities	Yes	Yes

continued on the next page

FUNCTIONALITY	SHAREPOINT DESIGNER 2010	VISUAL STUDIO 2010
Can be used to create sequential workflows	Yes	Yes
Workflows can be created using only actions that are approved by SharePoint administrators	Yes	No
Can use Visio 2010 to create workflow logic	Yes	No
Workflows can be deployed remotely from workflow authoring environment	Yes	No
Can be used to create state machine workflows	No	Yes
Need to write code	No	Yes
Additional activities (other than the ones provided by SharePoint 2010) can be used in creating workflows	No	Yes
Workflow can be modified while it is running	No	Yes
Can be used to create workflow that is made available across the farm	No	Yes
Can be used to create custom workflow activities	No	Yes
Can be used to create workflows that interact with external systems	No	Yes

Planning for Workflow Deployment

Using workflows in SharePoint 2010 to automate business processes is a significant decision. There are some important considerations that administrators should be aware of to ensure the efficient implementation of these workflows. Some of the factors to be aware of include security issues, information disclosure, and the elevation of privileges. After effective planning, you can perform necessary configurations for workflow deployment and eventually activate workflows for the users of your farm or site.

Identify Roles Involved

As an administrator, you should be aware of various different roles involved in creating, deploying, and running workflows. In the following sections, you explore these roles and their associated responsibilities. Understanding these roles and how they impact workflow development will help you plan and mitigate any issues that can occur during the development life cycle or workflow execution.

Architects

Architects are responsible for identifying the appropriate business processes to be developed as workflows, based on the value created by the workflow to the organization. They are also responsible for selecting the workflow development tools, workflow development language, and the best practices that align with the enterprise architecture. Architects provide oversight of the various systems involved and how they will be integrated to automate the business processes of the organization. Architects ensure smooth transition of business strategies to vision scope to logical architecture to physical architecture to operational systems.

Workflow Developers

Developers are responsible for developing workflow templates, forms, and the assembly that contains the business logic used during workflow execution. This assembly is called a workflow schedule and is created using Visual Studio 2010. Developers are also responsible for packaging the workflow forms and assembly into a workflow feature and then into a solution package, which will be deployed to a SharePoint farm. Workflow developers are responsible for any issues that are encountered while executing custom workflows deployed in the SharePoint environment.

Information Workers

Information workers are responsible for modeling workflows using SharePoint Designer 2010. Information workers use the administrator-approved list of workflow activities to model their workflows and associate the workflows to a list, library, or a site. They can also create reusable workflows for a site collection. Information workers can create workflow steps that execute with the same permission as they have at the site level.

Farm Administrators

Farm administrators are typically part of the IT operations team. They are responsible for the Central Administration settings that will impact workflow development, deployment, and execution. Accordingly, they have the following responsibilities.

- **Manage Central Administration workflow settings** Farm administrators can control general workflow settings, such as task alert results and external participant settings, within the SharePoint Central Administration website.

- **Deploy Workflow Solution Package and features**   Farm administrators can install solutions that contain workflow features and deploy workflow features to Web applications. Optionally, they also can activate those features on a site collection, making them available for association.

Site Collection Administrators

Site collection administrators are responsible for controlling the workflows that can be used within their sites. All custom and predefined workflows are deployed as features. By deactivating these features, the site collection administrator can prevent these workflows from being used within their site collection.

List Administrators

List administrators are groups or individuals with Manage List or Web Designer permissions. They can add specific workflows to a list and control their execution at the list level. Their responsibilities include

- **Adding a workflow**   List administrators associate (add) a workflow template to a list or content type, according to the business needs of the list or content type. This association makes the workflow template available to end users, who can then select default values and settings.
- **Removing a workflow**   List administrators can remove a workflow association from a list or content type, or they can prevent new instances from running.
- **Terminating a workflow**   If a workflow instance fails with an error or does not start, the list administrators can stop a running workflow instance by using the Terminate This Workflow link on the Workflow Status page. The Workflow Status page is visible to all participants of a workflow, but the link required to terminate a workflow link is reserved for list administrators.

Site Users

Site users are primarily participants of the workflows and are responsible for completing various tasks assigned to them by the workflow instance. They can also delegate the workflow tasks to other participants if the workflow provides such a feature.

Security Considerations

As an administrator, the security of your environment is one of your primary responsibilities. Implementing workflows in your SharePoint environment requires proper planning, and you should be aware of potential issues that can be caused by the workflows.

Workflows Run as Administrators

The most important security concept to be aware of is that workflows run as part of the system account in SharePoint 2010, through the identity provided within the application pool settings on the server computer. This means that within SharePoint 2010, workflows have administrative permissions. On the server, workflows have the same permissions as the application pool, which frequently has administrator permissions. These permissions enable workflows to perform actions that ordinary users cannot perform, such as routing a document to a specific location (for example, a records center) or adding a user account to the system.

 SECURITY ALERT You cannot restrict the administrative privileges given to workflows. It is up to the workflow code to detect user actions, and based on those actions, continue or roll back changes, or impersonate a user to mimic that user's permissions.

As an administrator of your SharePoint environment, you must understand the actions that the workflow will perform so that you can assess the possible risks associated with the elevation of permissions and help the developer mitigate any security concerns.

Impersonation in Declarative Workflows

Declarative workflows created using SharePoint Designer 2010 allow the information worker to configure the workflow steps (part of the workflow) to run using their permission. In SharePoint 2010, declarative workflows always run in the user context of the workflow initiator unless an impersonation step is encountered. If an impersonation step is encountered, the declarative workflow is run in the context of the workflow author. This feature is very useful for workflow authors, because it allows for the creation of workflows that perform activities that cannot be performed by a participant but are necessary for the workflow to complete.

Through a safe and scoped form of privilege elevation, site actions can be automated through workflow. This reduces the burden on the SharePoint site administrator. Automation of a high-security process using workflows is useful in publishing and approval scenarios in which specific actions are enabled to impersonate someone other than the workflow's initiator. The following are some of the scenarios where an impersonation step can be used.

- **Publish to a secure list** A workflow author can create a workflow that would allow a contributor to publish the content he or she is authoring to a secure library to which the contributor does not have access.

- **Granting permissions to users** As a site administrator, you would like to allow business users to grant permissions to lists on your site. So you want to create a workflow in which a request is raised by a user who seeks access to a secured list. An approver user in the site can approve the request and the workflow will grant the requester access to the site. The approver user need not have list administration privileges to perform this action.

The following is the list of activities that can impersonate the workflow author:

- Set Content Approval Status (as Owner)
- Create List Item (as Owner)
- Update List Item (as Owner)
- Delete List Item (as Owner)
- Add/Remove/Set/Inherit List Item Permissions (as Owner)

Knowing that the information worker can create impersonation steps will help you assess any security threats that could be posed by such workflows.

Permissions to Start Workflow

List administrators can restrict the permission level that is required to start a workflow during the association process. Administrators can select either of two permission levels to start a specific workflow association: Edit Item or Manage List.

The default setting for associating a workflow allows users with Edit Item permissions to start a workflow manually. This means that any authenticated SharePoint 2010 user on the list who has Edit Item permissions can start an instance of the workflow association. If the administrator selects the option to require a user to have Manage Lists permissions to start the when the workflow is created, only list administrators can start an instance of this association.

Because workflows are designed to be used by standard contributors, most workflows do not require the restriction to Manage List permissions. However, administrators can use this setting for workflows such as a document disposal workflow and other cases in which the administrator wants only certain people to execute the disposal actions.

 SECURITY ALERT   By default, user-defined workflows are enabled for all sites on the Web application. When user-defined workflows are enabled, users can define workflows in a workflow editor such as the SharePoint Designer 2010. Users who define these workflows must have Manage List permissions on the site to which they are deploying the workflow. The information worker can create workflows with the impersonation step. So, if you think that these declarative workflows are a threat to your site, you can prevent user-defined workflows on your Web applications until the threat is identified and removed.

Information Disclosure

Workflows that execute on your site can disclose information through tasks allocated to the users, through workflow tasks, or through task notifications to users who would not otherwise have access to this information. Some of these information disclosures can be prevented by configuration settings.

Task Notifications to Users Without Access

When a user starts a workflow, he or she can assign people to participate in the workflow. But in some cases, some of the participants may not have access to the list or site where the workflow is started. As the workflow executes, tasks are created for these participants and task notifications are sent so that they can act on the tasks. The task notifications can contain a link to the task, document, or list item, in addition to any message provided by the workflow imitator, thus leading to information disclosure. Also, these participants could be internal or external users (employees of your partner companies, for example).

SharePoint 2010 allows you to control whether such notifications can be sent and also whether they can be sent to both internal and external users.

Workflow Tasks and Workflow History

Tasks created as part of workflow execution are created in a standard task list on the site. Anyone with contribute permission to the task list can view all tasks on this list; this means that users might see links to documents to which they do not have access. Apart from tasks, a workflow also leaves a trail of actions performed during workflow execution to a workflow history list. Any user with view permission can see data captured in the workflow history list.

Securing tasks and workflow history items can be done in several ways. One way is for an administrator to set list level permissions. If disclosure should be private—that is, not publicly available but available to a specific group of people—then an administrator can create a new task or history list and set permissions for the list that are targeted to that group. If administrators do not want anyone to see history events on a workflow status page, they can remove view permissions to the workflow history list from which the status page pulls its information. Users who do not have permissions to view the history list itself, or any item on the list, will receive an Access Denied error when they open any status page that pulls data from that history list.

As an extreme case, an administrator can request that workflow authors set permissions for the tasks or workflow history items so that only users who are participating in the workflow can see these tasks. The CreateTask activity has a SpecialPermissions property that gives only specified permissions to access the newly created task. The LogToHistoryList activity does not have such a property, so to set per-item permissions on history list items, developers must use the object model (OM) in SharePoint 2010.

IMPORTANT Using item level permissions can impact the performance of your SharePoint site. Use this capability with caution.

Tampering with Tasks and Workflow History Items

Any contributor can modify tasks or history items if there are no restrictions on those lists. This means that malicious users can modify task descriptions to give participants incorrect instructions or to order participants to click malicious links. To change the perceived results of a process, malicious users also can add false or inaccurate history events or can modify history events to make them false or inaccurate.

Task and history lists behave as normal lists in a site. By default, there are no restrictions on either task lists or history lists. To avoid spoofing and tampering attacks, administrators must determine the vulnerabilities that exist within their site and either restrict access to columns in a list (for example, make vulnerable columns such as task descriptions read-only so that only the workflow can set them on item creation), set special permissions on the list, or set item level permissions on the list items.

IMPORTANT Do not use a workflow history list as an auditing tool for workflows. Plan to use the SharePoint Audit Log capability for auditing workflows and their actions. See the following sidebar titled "Real World: Workflow History Lists vs. Event Audit Trails" for more information.

 REAL WORLD   Workflow History Lists vs. Event Audit Trails

A key benefit of workflows is the ability to track execution data to provide a view into the progress of the workflow. The workflow history list is a repository for this data, where a workflow status page can search for data related to a workflow instance and make this information available to users. Users can see all items to which they have access in the history list.

However, because the workflow history list tracks information, users might assume that it can be used as an audit trail of events. This is not the case, because a workflow history list is not a security feature. History lists are standard SharePoint lists that are used for storing events and are visible to any user. These lists have no special permissions associated with them. By default, users can modify and add events if they have Edit and Add permissions within the history list. To audit events, use SharePoint's Audit Log feature. Only administrators can access this log, and the log does not require additional work to protect it from tampering attacks.

Setting Up Workflow Configurations

Various factors must be considered to enable workflows within SharePoint, as you know. In the following sections, you learn how to employ specific configuration settings to control your SharePoint 2010 environment for workflow deployment.

Web Application Configurations

At the Web application level, you can control two important settings: one that enables user-defined workflows and one that provides task notifications for unauthorized users.

Enabling or Disabling User-Defined Workflows

You can specify whether you want users to be able to deploy declarative workflows, such as those that are created by using Microsoft SharePoint Designer 2010, on sites in a particular Web application. The default setting enables deployment of declarative workflows. When this setting is enabled, users who have been granted Design permission level on the site at minimum can create and deploy workflows using the Workflow Editor in Microsoft SharePoint Designer 2010. To adjust this setting, perform the following steps.

1. Open a browser and go to the SharePoint Central Administration website.

2. Under Application Management, click Manage Web Applications.

3. On the Web Applications Management page, click the Web application that you want to configure.

4. In the Manage group of the Web Applications tab of the Ribbon, click General Settings and then select Workflow from the list that appears.

5. In the Workflow Settings dialog box (Figure 23-9), in the User-Defined Workflows section, perform one of the following steps.

   - To enable declarative workflows for sites in this Web application, click Yes. This is the default option.

   - To disable declarative workflows for this Web application, click No.

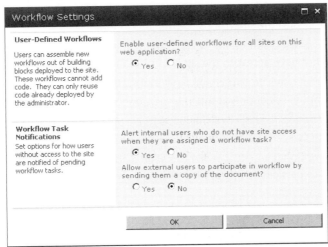

FIGURE 23-9 Use the options in the Web Application Workflow Settings dialog box to enable or disable user-defined workflows.

6. Click OK to close the Workflow Settings dialog box.

Configuring Task Notification for Unauthorized Users

You can allow either or both of the following kinds of unauthorized users to participate in workflows: internal users who do not have access to the site and external users who do not have access to internal network resources. For internal users, an e-mail message that explains how to request access to the site (subject to administrator approval) is sent to users. For external users, an e-mail message that includes an attached document or list item for the participant to review or sign is sent to users.

> **NOTE** When you enable access to the external users to receive the documents, the workflow might expose sensitive information to the external users.

To configure this setting, perform the following steps.

1. Open a browser and go to the SharePoint Central Administration website.
2. Under Application Management, click Manage Web Applications.
3. In the Name column on the Web Applications Management page, click the Web application that you want to configure.
4. On the Manage group of the Web Applications tab of the Ribbon, click General Settings and then select Workflow in the list that appears.
5. In the Workflow Task Notifications section of the Workflow Settings dialog box (refer back to Figure 23-9), perform the following steps.
   a. In the Alert Internal Users Who Do Not Have Site Access When They Are Assigned A Workflow Task option, select one of the following options.
      - **Yes**—Use this option to send to send an e-mail message to internal users who do not have access to the site. This is the default option.
      - **No**—Use this option if you do not want to send an e-mail message to internal users who do not have access to the site.
   b. In the Allow External Users To Participate In Workflow By Sending Them A Copy Of The Document option, select one of the following options.
      - **Yes**—Use this option to allow external users to participate in a workflow by sending them a copy of the document.
      - **No**—Use this option if you do not want to send a copy of the document to external users to participate in workflow. This is the default option.
6. Click OK to close the Workflow Settings dialog box.

Preserving Workflow History

A workflow is made up of a sequence of events such as workflow initiation, task creation, and task completion. When you add a workflow, you specify a task and history list that workflow instances of that workflow association will use to track the events for the workflow. The workflow history contains key information about each event including date, status, participant, and description.

SharePoint 2010 runs a daily Workflow Auto Cleanup job to remove workflow instances and related task entries 60 days after a workflow is completed or canceled. You can disable the Workflow Auto Cleanup job if you want to keep workflow data available longer. However, as with any SharePoint list, site performance may be affected as your workflow history and task lists grow in size. If you are concerned about the size of these lists, you can enable the Workflow Auto Cleanup job. As an alternative, you can create a separate history and task list for each workflow association.

To adjust the Workflow Auto Cleanup job and its settings, perform the following steps.

1. Open a browser and go to the SharePoint Central Administration website.

2. On the Quick Launch, click Monitoring.

3. In the Timer Jobs section of the Monitoring page, click Review Job Definitions.

4. In the Title column of the Job Definitions page, click the Workflow Auto Cleanup link that is associated with the Web application for which you want to disable automatic workflow cleanup.

5. On the Edit Timer Job page, perform one of the following steps.

    ■ Click Disable to disable the Workflow Auto Cleanup job.

    ■ Click Enable to enable the Workflow Auto Cleanup job.

Deploying Workflows

After you prepare a workflow for use in SharePoint 2010, deployment of the workflow varies depending on whether it is a predefined workflow, a SharePoint Designer workflow, or a Visual Studio custom workflow. The following sections provide a high-level overview of the procedures required for deploying each type of workflow.

Deploying Predefined Workflows

Predefined workflows are already installed on the SharePoint farm when you install SharePoint 2010. The deployment of predefined workflows is focused on activating the workflow features and associating the workflow with lists and libraries. The following procedures must be carried out to deploy a predefined workflow.

1. Activate the workflow features pertaining to predefined workflows.

2. Associate the workflow with list, library, content type, or site.

3. Start and verify the workflow.

Deploying Declarative Workflows

Declarative workflows are created by end users using SharePoint Designer 2010, and they are associated with a list, library, content type, or site by SharePoint Designer tool itself. The following procedures are associated with deploying a declarative workflow.

1. Create and deploy declarative workflow using SharePoint Designer.
2. Start and verify the deployed workflow.

Deploying Custom Workflows

Custom workflows created using Microsoft Visual Studio 2010 are created as features and packaged into solution files. The deployment of a custom workflow starts with solution installation, feature activation, and finally association. The following procedure allows you to deploy a custom workflow.

1. Create the custom workflow in Visual Studio 2010. Package it as a feature, which is then packaged as a solution file.
2. Install and deploy the solution into SharePoint farm.
3. Activate the workflow feature at site collection level.
4. Associate the workflow with a list, library, content type, or site.
5. Start and verify the workflow.

Activating a Workflow

You must activate both predefined and custom workflows before they can be used. Use the following procedure to determine whether the workflow that you want to use is active, and then activate the workflow as necessary.

1. On the top level of the site collection, on the Site Actions menu, click Site Settings.
2. In the Site Collection Administration section on the Site Settings page, click Site Collection Features.
3. On the Features page, click Activate next to the workflow feature that you want to activate. The Status column displays Active to indicate that the feature is now active. See Figure 23-10 for a list of site collection features.

> **NOTE** In SharePoint Foundation 2010, there is only one predefined workflow—the Three-state Workflow—and it is active by default.

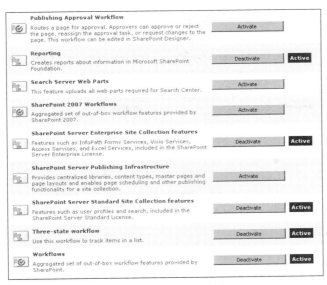

FIGURE 23-10 List workflow site collection features

Adding a Workflow Association

This procedure is applicable for both predefined and custom workflows. When you add a workflow association, you assign a task list and history list to use with the selected workflow. You can use the default task list, select another existing task list, or create a new one. As SharePoint lists grow, site performance might be adversely affected. If your SharePoint environment will have many workflows, consider creating a separate task list and history list for each workflow to avoid potential performance problems. The workflow can be associated with a list or a library, content type, and site.

Associating a Workflow with a List or Library

Use the following steps to associate a workflow with a list or document library. Note that some workflows, such as the Three-state workflow, require you to create a column in your list in which the workflow can display status. For example, before you add the Three-state workflow to a list, you first should create a column of the Choice type and assign three choices to the column, signifying the start, middle, and end state of the Three-state workflow.

1. Browse to the list or library to which you want to add a workflow.

2. Perform one of the following steps.

   - For a list, on the List Tools tab, click List.

   - In the Settings group, click Workflow Settings and then click Add A Workflow.

   - For a library, on the Library Tools tab, click Library.

   - In the Settings group, click Workflow Settings and then click Add A Workflow.

3. In the Workflow section of the Add A Workflow page shown in Figure 23-11, select the workflow template that you want to associate with this list or library.

4. In the Name section, type the name that you want to use to identify this workflow to users of this list or library.

5. In the Task List section, specify a task list to use with this workflow.

6. In the History List section, select a history list to use with this workflow.

7. In the Start Options section, select from the following options.

   ■ To allow the users to start the workflow manually, select the Allow The Workflow To Be Manually Started By An Authenticated User With Participant Permission check box.

   ■ If you want only list administrators to start the workflow, select the Require Manage Lists Permissions To Start The Workflow check box.

   ■ In many scenarios, you'll see a check box selection that appears dimmed for the option Start This Workflow To Approve Publishing Of A Major Version Of An Item. This option will become available when you have enabled content approval, selected major/minor versioning in the library settings, and you have selected an Approval workflow.

   ■ To allow the workflow to be started when a new item or document is created, select the Start This Workflow When A New Item Is Created check box.

   ■ To allow the workflow to be started when a new item or document is updated, select the Start This Workflow When An Item Is Changed check box.

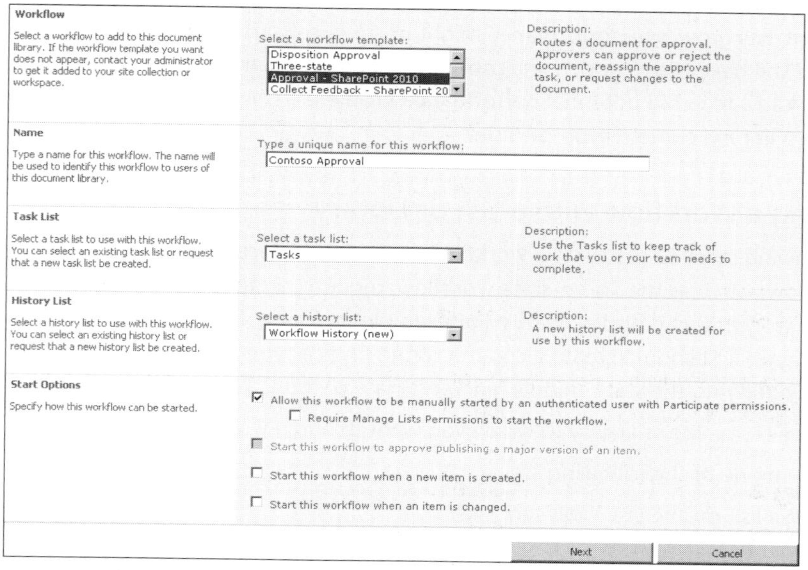

FIGURE 23-11 Library or List Workflow Association page

8. If the workflow that you selected has additional configuration options, click Next and customize the settings that are on the next page in order to complete the creation of your workflow. For purposes of illustration, the Three-state workflow is being used here to complete this section.

> **NOTE** If you select the Disposition Approval workflow, there is only an OK or Cancel button at the bottom of the page. Selecting the other workflows, such as Three-state or Collect Signatures, will result in a Next or Cancel button combination at the bottom of the page, indicating that you must provide additional information on the following screen to fully configure the workflow.

9. On the next page, shown in Figure 23-12, you can select the various states of the workflow and the associated tasks that will be assigned at each stage. You can also specify e-mail settings at each stage so that through the combination of task assignment and auto-generated e-mail messages, you can ensure those involved in the workflow are kept fully informed (and tasked!) as the documents move through the workflow.

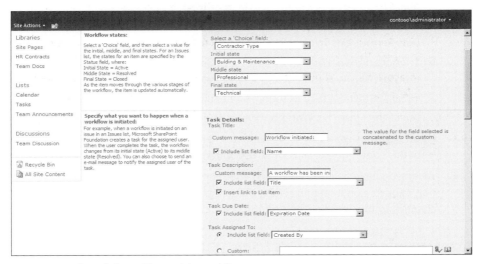

FIGURE 23-12 Completing a Three-state workflow

10. When you have finished specifying your configuration options, click OK to apply your changes to the workflow association.

Associating a Workflow with a Site Content Type

Use the following steps to associate a workflow with a site content type.

1. On the home page for the site, select Site Settings from the Site Actions menu.

2. In the Galleries section of the Site Settings page, click Site Content Types.

3. In the Site Content Type column on the Site Content Types page, click the content type to which you want to add a workflow association.

4. On the page for the content type you selected, in the Settings section, click Workflow Settings.

5. On the Workflow Settings page, click Add A Workflow.

6. In the Workflow section of the Add A Workflow page shown, select the workflow that you want to add.

7. In the Name section, type the name that you want to use to identify this workflow to site users.

8. In the Task List section, specify a task list to use with this workflow.

9. In the History List section, select a history list to use with this workflow. The history list displays all events that occur during each instance of the workflow.

10. In the Start Options section, specify the following:

   ■ To allow the users to start the workflow manually, select the Allow The Workflow To Be Manually Started By An Authenticated User With Participant Permission check box.

   ■ If you want only list administrators to start the workflow, select the Require Manage Lists Permissions To Start The Workflow check box.

   ■ To allow the workflow to be started when a new item or document is created, select the Start This Workflow When A New Item Is Created check box.

   ■ To allow the workflow to be started when a new item or document is updated, select the Start This Workflow When An Item Is Changed check box.

11. If you want this workflow to be applied to all of the content types that are inheriting from this content type, select the Yes option.

12. When you have finished specifying your configuration options (including options that might be on a second screen that are not illustrated here), click OK to apply your changes to the workflow association.

Associating a Workflow with a Site

Use the following steps to associate a workflow with a site.

1. Browse to the site from which you want to add a workflow association.

2. On the Site Actions menu, click Site Settings.

3. In the Site Administration section of the Site Settings page, click Workflow Settings.

4. On the Workflow Settings page, click Add A Workflow.

5. In the Workflow section of the Add Workflow page shown in Figure 23-13, select the workflow template that you want to associate with this site.

6. In the Name section, type the name that you want to use to identify this workflow to site users.

7. In the Task List section, specify a task list to use with this workflow.

8. In the History List section, select a history list to use with this workflow.

9. In the Start Options section, specify whether the workflow can be manually started by an authenticated user who has Participate Permissions and whether Manage Permissions are also required to start the workflow.

> **NOTE** You can only start site workflows manually.

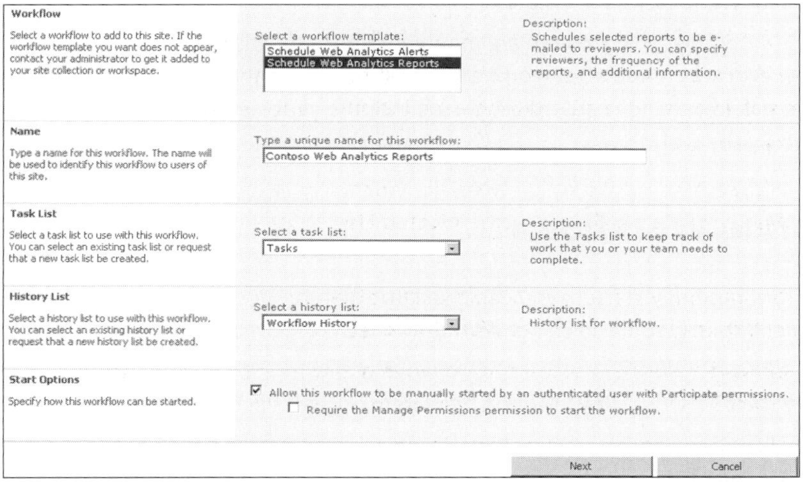

FIGURE 23-13 Add a workflow to a site

10. When you have finished specifying your configuration options, click OK to apply your changes to the workflow association.

> **NOTE** If your permissions are explicitly set on the site, list, or library in question, then instead of seeing the option Allow This Workflow To Be Manually Started By A User With Participate Permissions, you will see the option Allow This Workflow To Be Manually Started By A User With Edit Item Permissions. This occurs on all lists and libraries after you have visited the Site Workflows list and you are a site owner or you have the Edit Item permissions applied to your account at the site level.

Starting and Verifying the Workflow

This procedure is applicable for predefined, declarative and custom workflows. After you activate a workflow and add it to a list, library, content type, or site, an authenticated user can run the workflow on an item in the list or a document in the library, or in the case of a site workflow, on a site. When you add the workflow, specify whether you want the workflow to run automatically or manually. If the workflow is configured to start automatically, the default settings are always used when the workflow begins. If the workflow is configured to start manually, the user can modify the default settings, such as specifying workflow participants and a due date. The workflow runs on items in the list or documents in the library with which the workflow is associated.

As the workflow is executing, ensure that all relevant tasks are being created and are assigned to the correct participants. Ensure that the correct updates are made when the users complete the tasks assigned to them. Check that task notification e-mail messages are being sent to the users as the tasks are assigned.

If you have workflows that execute an impersonation step, ensure that the permissions before workflow executions and after workflow executions are in the intended state and that no unwanted permission changes are made. Ensure that the expected permissions are supposed to be granted by the workflow.

Monitoring Workflows

After a workflow has been started, you can check the general workflow status in the associated list or document library. You also can check the workflow reports, which contain the details on the start time and duration of the workflows. You can troubleshoot the errors that occur during workflow execution. Let us explore here how you can monitor the workflows in detail.

Workflow Status

You can check the workflow status of list or library workflows and site workflows using the following procedures.

Workflow Status for List or Library Workflows

Use these steps to check detailed workflow status for items in a list or library.

1. Browse to the list or document library that contains the workflow for which you want to check the status.

2. In the row of the item for which you want to check the status, click the link in the workflow status column.

3. On the Workflow Status page (Figure 23-14), view the following information about the workflow.

   - Name of the person who initiated the workflow
   - Date and time the workflow was started
   - Date and time the workflow was last run or resumed
   - Name and link to the document or item involved in the workflow

- Current status of the workflow

- Visio diagram type visualization of the workflow, if it is a SharePoint Designer workflow and workflow visualization was published with the workflow

- List of tasks assigned to workflow participants

- Lists of all events that have occurred in the history of this instance of the workflow thus far (for example, workflow initiation, task creation, task completion)

- Links to modify, cancel, and terminate the workflow that may appear, depending on the type of workflow you are viewing

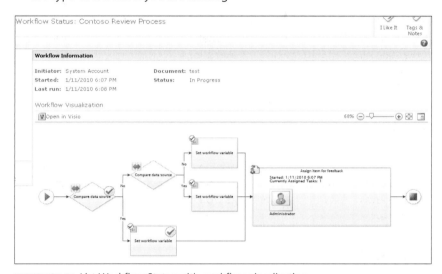

FIGURE 23-14 List Workflow Status with workflow visualization

Workflow Status for Site Workflows

Use these steps to check detailed workflow status for site workflows:

1. Browse to the site for which you want to check workflow status.

2. On the Site Actions menu, click Site Settings and then click Workflows.

3. On the Workflows Settings page (Figure 23-15), perform one of the following procedures.

   - To view the status of workflows that are running, click the name of the workflow in the My Running Workflows section.

   - To view the status of workflows that have completed, click the name of the workflow in the My Completed Workflows section.

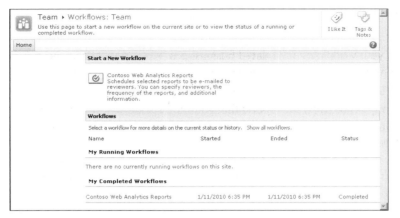

FIGURE 23-15 Site Workflows Settings page

4. On the Workflow Status page (Figure 23-16), view the following information about the workflow.

   ■ Name of the person who initiated the workflow

   ■ Date and time the workflow was started

   ■ Date and time the workflow was last run or resumed

   ■ Current status of the workflow

   ■ List of tasks assigned to workflow participants

   ■ List of all events that have occurred in the history of this instance of the workflow thus far (for example, workflow initiation, task creation, task completion) in the Workflow History section

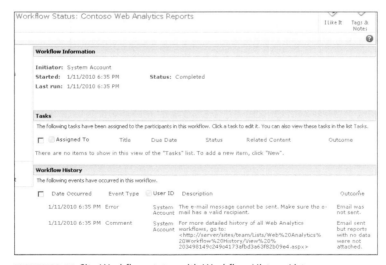

FIGURE 23-16 Site Workflow status with Workflow History List

Workflow Reports

SharePoint 2010 provides individual and aggregate workflow reports to enable you to assess the efficiency of your workflows and related business processes. You can use these reports to locate problems with processes or to determine whether a group or individual is meeting performance targets for a particular business process.

There are two types of workflow reports that you can use. The first one is a workflow usage page at site collection level, which will display all workflows available within your site, the number of workflows that are active, and number of times each workflow has been associated. SharePoint 2010 also provides a detailed activity level report that is made available through a Microsoft Excel report. There are two Excel reports: an Activity Duration report and a Cancellation and Error report.

Viewing Site Collection Workflow Usage Summary

You can display a list of available workflows for the site collection, their usage summary (active or inactive), how many times these workflows have been associated, and how many instances of each active workflow are currently running. To view the site collection workflow usage summary, perform the following steps.

1. Verify that you are a member of the site collection administrators group on the site collection that you are configuring.

2. Browse to the top-level site of the site collection in which you want to view workflow reports.

3. On the Site Actions menu, click Site Settings.

4. In the Site Administration section of the Site Settings page, click Workflows to display the Site Collection Workflows report (Figure 23-17).

FIGURE 23-17 Site Workflow usage report

Viewing Workflow Performance Analysis Reports

SharePoint 2010 provides two predefined Excel reports that provide aggregate analysis of workflow history for each workflow instance: the Activity Duration report and the Cancellation and Error report. The Activity Duration report provides data about how long each activity within a workflow takes to complete, as well as how long it takes for all tasks in the workflow to complete. The Cancellation And Error report shows the workflows that have been cancelled or that have encountered errors before completion. Each of these reports is provided as an Excel formatted file.

> ***NOTE*** **If you are using custom workflows, the appropriate parameters must be specified in the workflow template to generate the data for these reports.**

1. Verify that you have Edit Item permissions to view individual workflow reports.
2. Browse to the list or document library that contains the workflow for which you want to view reports.
3. Point to the item or document that is involved in the workflow, click the arrow that appears, and then click Workflows.
4. In the Running Workflows section of the Workflows page, click the name of the workflow for which you want status. If no workflows are listed in this section, no workflows are currently running on the selected item.
5. In the Workflows History section of the Workflow Status page, click View Workflow Reports link.
6. On the View Workflow Reports page, locate the workflow association for which you want to view the reports, and perform one of the following steps.
   - To view information about how long it is taking for each activity within a workflow to be completed and how long it takes each instance of the workflow to be completed, click Activity Duration Report. See Figure 23-18 for a sample Activity Duration report.

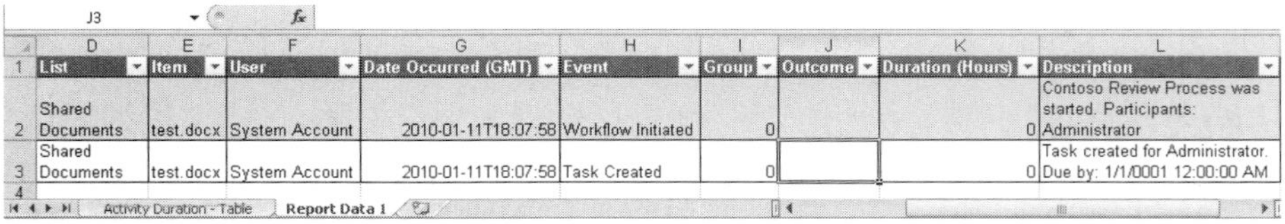

List	Item	User	Date Occurred (GMT)	Event	Group	Outcome	Duration (Hours)	Description
Shared Documents	test.docx	System Account	2010-01-11T18:07:58	Workflow Initiated	0		0	Contoso Review Process was started. Participants: Administrator
Shared Documents	test.docx	System Account	2010-01-11T18:07:58	Task Created	0		0	Task created for Administrator. Due by: 1/1/0001 12:00:00 AM

FIGURE 23-18 An Activity Duration report

   - To view information about which workflows were canceled or encountered errors before completion, click Cancellation & Error Report. See Figure 23-19 for a sample Cancellation & Error report.

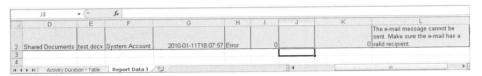

FIGURE 23-19 A Cancellation & Error report

7. In the File Location section, click Browse, specify the location to which you want to save the report, and then click OK.

Troubleshooting Workflow Issues

Workflows are affected by problems in the user environment—especially problems with the state of list items that a workflow operates on and the server settings that govern workflows. When a problem is detected, workflows fail. The most common reasons for workflow failure include a defect in the workflow design, network issues, or restricted user permissions. Because workflow operation depends on of all these factors and the complexity with which workflows are built, troubleshooting workflows can be challenging.

Detecting Workflow Errors

A workflow can fail for many reasons. For example, a workflow may be designed to create a new item in a library, but the library might have been deleted. Or failure might occur because user permissions have changed since the workflow was started. This prevents the workflow from completing the intended activity. When a workflow does not complete successfully, its final status appears in the column with that workflow's name, in the list with which the workflow is associated.

Typically, this column displays In Progress when the workflow is executing, and it displays Completed when the workflow finishes successfully. If the workflow fails, the final status messages that you might see in this column are as follow: Error Occurred, Stopped, Failed On Start (Retrying), or Failed On Start. Based on the type of workflow, the troubleshooting mechanism you will use also differs.

Resolving Workflow Errors

When the final status of a workflow is Error Occurred, Stopped, Failed On Start (Retrying), or Failed On Start, the first step in troubleshooting the workflow is to determine the cause of the error. The troubleshooting method that you use depends on the type of workflow in which the error occurred. Different methods are required for a SharePoint 2010 predefined workflow, a SharePoint Designer 2010 workflow, or a Visual Studio 2010 custom workflow.

Predefined Workflows

Issues with predefined workflows can be resolved by investigating the workflow history list. The workflow history displays the current state and all the previous states for a running workflow. When an error occurs in a workflow, the last event in the workflow history list is titled Error. The list provides information about when the error occurred, but the list typically does not provide a description of the problem—to avoid revealing sensitive information that could lead to a security issue. The most common errors are caused by connectivity problems, incorrect e-mail settings, or restricted user permissions. In case the workflow history lacks the information you need to resolve the problem, you can use Visual Studio to debug the predefined workflows.

> **IMPORTANT** Debug the workflows only in the development or staging SharePoint 2010 environment. Debugging workflows in a production environment can cause disruptions to the end users working on the environment.

SharePoint Designer 2010 Workflows

For Microsoft SharePoint Designer workflows, when you create the workflow, you can add actions that write to the history list at any point in the workflow. This information helps you determine the last successful step that the workflow completed before the error occurred and also the step in which the error occurred.

Visual Studio 2010 Custom Workflows

If a custom workflow is well written, you can use the workflow history to track the status of the workflow and why it failed. Ensure that you communicate the logging requirements to the workflow developers so that they use the LogToWorkflowHistory activity to write all necessary information to the workflow history. You can also rely on the Unified Logging Service (ULS) logs to track failures during workflows.

If you could not use either the workflow history list or the ULS logs to determine the root cause of failure, you have to seek the help of developers to debug the workflow in Visual Studio 2010. You have to simulate your production-use development environment to debug the workflow. When you determine the cause of the failure, if it was due to configuration related issues, you can correct the problem by making necessary configuration changes in your environment. If the cause was related to defects in code, you have to follow the development life cycle to fix, stabilize, and finally deploy the workflow into production.

Summary

In this chapter you have seen how workflows can be leveraged to automate business processes and how SharePoint 2010 provides a robust workflow hosting platform. You have explored the different types of workflows provided by SharePoint 2010. You have also reviewed the tools that are available for creating workflows, including Visio 2010, SharePoint Designer 2010, and Visual Studio 2010. This chapter described how you can use these tools to create workflows for use within SharePoint 2010.

As an administrator, you should be aware of various factors and considerations regarding the development and deployment of workflows within your environment. You have also explored various configurations that will help you prepare your environment as well as the processes required for deploying workflows. You have reviewed detailed step-by-step procedures for performing many of these tasks within SharePoint 2010. Finally, you examined how to monitor workflow and troubleshoot common workflow-related errors.

Index

Symbols and Numbers

B

T